FEDERAL WEALTH TRANSFER TAXATION

Fourth Edition

By

Jeffrey N. Pennell
Richard H. Clark Professor of Law
Emory University

AMERICAN CASEBOOK SERIES®

THOMSON

WEST

Mat #40117401

West Group has created this publication to provide you with accurate and authoritative information concerning the subject matter covered. However, this publication was not necessarily prepared by persons licensed to practice law in a particular jurisdiction. West Group is not engaged in rendering legal or other professional advice, and this publication is not a substitute for the advice of an attorney. If you require legal or other expert advice, you should seek the services of a competent attorney or other professional.

American Casebook Series and West Group are trademarks registered in the U.S. Patent and Trademark Office.

COPYRIGHT © 1996 WEST PUBLISHING CO.
COPYRIGHT © 2003 By WEST GROUP
        610 Opperman Drive
        P.O. Box 64526
        St. Paul, MN 55164–0526
        1–800–328–9352

ISBN 0–314–14453–6

 *TEXT IS PRINTED ON 10% POST CONSUMER RECYCLED PAPER*

Summary of Contents

Table of Contents

Preface

Professors Kahn and Waggoner at the University of Michigan School of Law prepared the first two editions of this casebook. The third edition was an update by Professors Pennell and Kahn. Because Professors Kahn and Waggoner no longer teach the course matter, Professor Pennell brought the text up to date to reflect the 2001 legislative shenanigans and other important substantive changes. This text reflects developments through 2002.

Users of prior editions may recall that the organization of the book was not close to the order in which various wealth transfer tax provisions appear in the Code. That well considered structure was a bit unusual to some users and has been modified in this edition, which presents a more traditional structure for studying the estate, gift, and generation-skipping transfer taxes. It is not a total slave to the order in which Congress organized the inclusion, deduction, and computation provisions of the Code, but it does combine materials in a manner that better corresponds with the Code. Notwithstanding that reorganization, the core of the book remains the original insightful work of Professors Kahn and Waggoner. Any new or lingering errors are Pennell's responsibility alone.

Omitted from this edition are the prior materials on the income taxation of estates and trusts, beneficiaries and grantors, which now is available to interested users on the internet at TWEN online. Seek http://lawschool.westlaw.com or Professor Pennell for information on how to access those chapters.

This text does not attempt to integrate an in-depth study of property law, nor of estate planning, because most law schools offer separate instruction on wills, trusts, future interests, and estate planning. There are occasional textual sketches of the way property law deals with the type of transaction under consideration, and snippets of the estate planning implications of various aspects of the wealth transfer taxes. These sketches provide an immediate relevance to the subject at hand, and some cases involve tax consequences that depend upon the property law characterization of a transaction, but otherwise these diversions merely provide the reader with a more broad perspective.

In addition, many questions have been rephrased in a manner such that any reader may divine the proper result (sometimes by reading the material that immediately follows). This is primarily meant to assist readers who do not have the luxury of studying with a professor in a structured law school course. It also reflects an attitude that "hiding the ball" with unanswered (or unanswerable) questions is not very appropriate in a subject as complex as this. The wealth transfer taxes — particularly the estate and gift taxes — are not well organized or integrated, and there are few major theoretical threads that tie the course together. The collateral effect of these changes is not to discourage class attendance. Rather, instructors are freed from having to provide so much basic course information and can use valuable class time to add meaning and dimension to the study, in a way that cannot be provided in any reasonably sized book.

Unlike some more traditional law school casebooks, it is expected that these various changes will provide value to readers who cannot take a law school course (or to those who do but who may need a resource for use after the course is over), perhaps as an alternative or an addition to a soup-to-nuts treatise. Using cases and rulings provides a framework in which to understand legal principles revealed in textual discussions in a way that a bare treatise may not. As a special note to students: various questions and note materials cite authority of some sort, in many cases with a brief statement of the holding. It is not anticipated that you will study authorities that are not reproduced in the casebook. They are included merely to direct you to authority on (or analogous to) the issues raised, and assist those users engaged in self study or research. Those consumers should note that tables at the end of the book have been expanded to make the text a more useful reference tool than traditional casebooks designed exclusively for classroom use.

Ultimately, I hope that this book, tailored specifically for students of all varieties, provides a useful pedagogy and organization of topics and components, one that is intuitive and therefore beneficial, no matter how readers are required to approach the study of our wealth transfer taxes. Please correspond with me about the book, and the study of this important element in the wealth transmission process.

I welcome your questions, comments, suggestions, corrections, and constructive criticism.

Jeffrey N. Pennell

FEDERAL WEALTH TRANSFER TAXATION

Fourth Edition

Chapter 1

INTRODUCTION

Federal law taxes the donative transfer of wealth. There are four separate federal tax systems, any one or more of which might be implicated by a particular donative transfer or set of donative transfers — the federal income tax, estate tax, gift tax, and generation-skipping transfer tax. Each of these federal taxes may have state counterparts, but this book does not cover state tax law. State taxes are normally of lesser importance in estate planning practice, and most state laws are patterned substantially after their federal tax counterparts. For example, all states now impose a so-called "sponge" or "pick-up" estate tax that is based on the federal estate tax gross estate and a state death tax credit that was phased out by legislation adopted in 2001 — §2011 was repealed effective in 2005. As of 2002 the "pick-up" tax was the only death tax imposed in 60% of the states.[1] The state law posture is expected to change as states replace the lost revenue provided by the state death tax credit, either by restoring prior estate or inheritance taxes or by reforming their pick up tax to refer to the amount that was imposed prior to repeal of §2011.

The federal income tax covers many items, of which the income taxation of donative transfers or of their post-transfer income stream is only a small part. The federal estate, gift, and generation-skipping transfer taxes, on the other hand, focus exclusively on donative transfers. Together, they constitute the federal system of taxing donative transfers. The material in this book is organized principally around the federal transfer tax system. References to relevant income tax aspects of particular transfers are provided as appropriate.

---

1.   Only Ohio and Oklahoma impose additional estate taxes in excess of the §2011 credit amount. This may change as the §2011 credit is phased out, with ultimate repeal in 2005. Another 14 states impose an inheritance tax that is separate from and in addition to their §2011 tax. See note 5.

Prior to 1976, the estate and the gift tax statutes operated independently. Each tax had its own structure, tax rates, exemptions, and other rules. Testamentary transfers were taxed separately from inter vivos gifts. In 1976, Congress "unified" this dual transfer tax system by adopting a single transfer tax base, subjecting that base to a comprehensive rate schedule, and reducing the tax produced by that schedule by a "unified credit." Nevertheless, even with these changes, the system is still structured as a dual transfer tax system and, for several important reasons, favors inter vivos gifts over transfers at death.[2] That preference is undergoing a change as the unified credit increases for estate tax but not for gift tax purposes, all as the law phases into an enacted repeal of the estate and generation-skipping transfer taxes slated to become effective in 2010 but *not* repeal the gift tax. We will learn more about these oddities in place, later in this study. The generation-skipping transfer tax is separate from the estate and gift taxes.[3]

The unified credit, granted by §§2010(a) and 2505(a), is coordinated in a manner that allows any individual to transfer up to a designated amount free from estate or gift taxation. Although these Code provisions appear to grant an exemption for both tax purposes, we will come to learn that they permit only a single, aggregate, tax-free transfer for the two taxes combined.

PART A. HISTORY AND OVERVIEW OF THE FEDERAL TRANSFER TAX SYSTEM

1.   *The Federal Estate Tax.* First adopted in 1916, the federal estate tax is a tax on the transfer of property at death. To prevent avoidance of the tax by transfers during life, it also reaches some inter vivos transfers that are substitutes for testamentary transfers. The tax is usually based on the date of death value of the transferred property, and the tax rates are graduated.

The 1916 federal estate tax was not the first federal excise on donative transfers of family property. There were scattered earlier periods when federal taxes were levied on the *receipt* of property, not on its transfer. In the nature of inheritance taxes, these taxes were imposed on the beneficiary, not on the transferor.

---

2. This favor is mirrored at the state level. Only Connecticut, Louisiana, North Carolina, and Tennessee impose a gift tax at all.

3. Although it is slated for repeal in 2005, federal law grants the same form of state GST credit that prompted every state to enact a state pick-up estate tax. Alabama, Arizona, California, Colorado, Florida, Hawaii, Illinois, Indiana, Iowa, Kansas, Maryland, Massachusetts, Michigan, Missouri, Montana, Nebraska, Nevada, New York, North Carolina, Ohio, Rhode Island, South Carolina, Tennessee, Texas, Virginia, and Washington have adopted a generation-skipping transfer pick-up tax, recognizing that doing so costs their citizens absolutely nothing because it merely diverts to the state money otherwise destined for the federal government.

One obvious way of taxing the beneficiary is to include gifts, bequests, and inheritances in taxable income. Although the federal income tax of 1894 took this approach, this form of taxation was invalidated after only a year. It, along with the income tax as a whole, fell when the Supreme Court in Pollock v. Farmer's Loan & Trust Co., 158 U.S. 601 (1895), held the income tax unconstitutional. The Sixteenth Amendment became effective in 1913, which enabled Congress to reinstate the income tax. In doing so, Congress chose to exclude gifts, bequests, and inheritances from taxable income.[4]

A more common method of taxing the beneficiary is through a pure inheritance tax (sometimes also called a legacy tax or a succession tax). Because inheritance tax rates are progressive for each beneficiary, such a tax usually yields lower revenues than an estate tax for a decedent who divides his or her estate among several beneficiaries rather than giving it to only one. Inheritance taxes are still in force in only 14 states.[5] Federal inheritance taxes were in force for a grand total of only 17 years.[6]

Under Article I, §§2 and 9, of the United States Constitution, Congress may not impose an unapportioned direct tax on property, but it may impose an indirect tax on the transfer of property. The constitutionality of the current federal estate tax was upheld in New York Trust Co. v. Eisner, 256 U.S. 345 (1921), as a tax on the transfer of property, not on its ownership. The Court held that the estate tax was an indirect tax that need not be apportioned. The Court in *New York Trust* relied extensively on Knowlton v. Moore, 178 U.S. 41 (1900), a prior case in which the Court had reached the same conclusion with respect to the federal inheritance tax of 1898. Using the same grounds, the Court in Bromley v. McCaughn, 280 U.S. 124 (1929), upheld the federal gift tax. For additional discussion of the constitutionality of federal estate and gift taxes, see Lowndes, Kramer & McCord., ESTATE AND GIFT TAXES ch. 3 and §22.3 (3d ed. 1974). The

---

4. Section 102, which has a common counterpart under the income tax of the various states. One reform proposal is to simply repeal the wealth transfer taxes and the exclusion, making wealth acquired by onerous activity or beneficence equally taxable as income.

5. Connecticut (phase in effective after 2004), Indiana, Iowa, Kansas, Kentucky, Louisiana, Maryland, Nebraska, New Hampshire, New Jersey, North Carolina, Pennsylvania, South Dakota (repealed with respect to intangibles and nonresidents), and Tennessee have state inheritance taxes.

6. From 1797 to 1802, from 1862 to 1870, and from 1898 to 1902. Inter vivos gifts were made liable to the federal tax in 1864. An unsuccessful effort was made by the Senate Finance Committee in 1918 to switch from an estate tax back to a federal inheritance tax. See S. Rep. No. 617, 65th Cong., 3d Sess. 15 (1918), in 1939-1 C.B. (pt. 2) 127. Another unsuccessful effort was made in 1935, this time by the House Ways and Means Committee, which sought to add a federal inheritance tax and a federal tax on the donee of inter vivos gifts in addition to the federal estate and gift taxes. H.R. Rep. No. 1681, 74th Cong., 1st Sess. 8-12 (1935), in 1939-1 C.B. (pt. 2) 642, 648-651. For a more detailed review of these early federal taxes, see West, THE INHERITANCE TAX 87-96 (2d ed. 1908); Schultz, THE TAXATION OF INHERITANCE 150-156 (1926).

related question of whether Congress may retroactively alter the tax laws and affect transactions already completed or may tax decedents already deceased is considered later in this book.

The federal estate tax can be divided into four steps:

(1) compute the value of the property includible in the decedent's "gross estate";

(2) compute the "taxable estate" by deducting from the gross estate the value of the deductions that are allowable in determining the decedent's "taxable estate";

(3) compute the "tentative estate tax" by applying the estate tax rates (set by §2001) to the sum of the decedent's "adjusted taxable gifts" (post-1976 taxable gifts not included in the gross estate) and the decedent's taxable estate; and

(4) compute the net estate tax that must be paid by subtracting from the tentative estate tax both (i) the amount of gift taxes that would have been payable on post-1976 gifts if current tax rates were applicable when the gifts were made, and (ii) the allowable credits.

Thus:

	Gross Estate
−	Deductions
=	Taxable Estate
+	Adjusted Taxable Gifts
=	Tentative Estate Tax Base
×	§2001 Estate Tax Rate Schedule
=	Tentative Estate Tax
−	Gift Taxes on Post-1976 Gifts
−	Credits
=	Net Estate Tax

In determining the value of the decedent's gross estate, note that the gross estate is not limited to property owned by the decedent at death. Certain property transferred inter vivos is includible, as is property over which the decedent held a general power of appointment.

The allowable deductions, which are subtracted from the gross estate to determine the taxable estate, are the marital deduction, the charitable deduction, the deduction for funeral and administration expenses, a deduction for state death taxes (added in 2001, effective after 2004), a deduction for certain qualified family owned business interests (repealed in 2001, effective after 2003), the deduction for certain losses incurred during the administration of the estate, and the deduction for most bona fide debts and claims against the decedent's estate.

Determining the tentative estate tax is complicated by the unified estate and gift tax regime. Under that regime, the unified rate schedule is applied to the sum of the decedent's taxable estate plus the aggregate amount of taxable gifts made by the decedent after 1976 that are not already included in the gross estate. From this amount is subtracted the aggregate amount of gift taxes that would be payable under current gift tax rates with respect to all gifts made by the decedent after 1976.[7] Although not described in the Code as a credit, this gift tax offset works in a similar fashion to a credit in determining the net estate tax.

In effect, the decedent's total inter vivos and testamentary transfers are treated as if they were all made at death. Nevertheless, the system includes in the decedent's gross estate certain property transferred during life. The sole reason for this is that property brought back into the gross estate is includible at its estate tax value while the aggregation of inter vivos gifts is based on the value of the donated property at the time of the gift. Thus, post-gift fluctuations in value are taken into account in determining the tax base if the transferred property is included in the gross estate. The net effect is that, except for the different value that may be utilized in determining the tax base (and for a "tax exclusive" system of taxing gifts, discussed later), the cost of transferring property essentially is the same under the progressive rate structure whether the decedent's donative transfers occurred during life or at death or were split between inter vivos and testamentary transfers.

The net estate tax payable is determined by applying a number of credits against the tentative estate tax. These credits are the credit for state death taxes (for decedents who die before 2005; thereafter this credit is a deduction), the credit for foreign death taxes, the credit for federal estate taxes paid on certain prior transfers and, if any property was given away prior to 1977 but included in the decedent's gross estate, a special credit for gift taxes paid on those pre-unification gifts. Most importantly, the §2010 unified credit is applied to offset the tax on the taxpayer's aggregate donative transfers, whether transferred during life or at death. Although the unified credit is applied against any gift tax otherwise payable on gifts made after 1976, the amount of unified credit allowable against the estate tax is not reduced by the amount of unified credit previously used by the decedent against the gift tax. Notwithstanding the appearance of granting this credit twice, we will see in Chapter 14 that this technique does not constitute a double allowance of the credit (because of the inclusion of gifts in the estate tax base). Can you explain the tax-equity reason why Congress adopted this credit approach rather than merely increasing the exemption (which functions as a deduction) that was granted prior to 1977? The answer lies in

---

7. In other words, instead of using the transfer tax rates applicable when a post-1976 gift was made, the deduction or offset for gift taxes on such transfers is computed by applying the transfer tax rates that are applicable when the decedent died. If the tax rate schedule at the decedent's death is the same as the rates that were applicable when the gift was made, the amount of the deduction will equal the amount of gift tax that was actually paid (or payable) when the gift was made.

the progressive rates historically applied to the transfer taxes. It is possible to create an exemption and tax rate schedule that accomplish the same tax consequence to all taxpayers that a credit provides, but it is more complex.

2.   *The Federal Gift Tax.*   A federal gift tax was enacted in 1924, approximately eight years after adoption of the present estate tax. As originally enacted, the gift tax was largely ineffective because it was computed on an annual basis, without regard to gifts made in prior years. As a result, each year a donor began giving anew at the bottom brackets in the progressive tax system. The original tax was repealed in 1926 but, as revived in 1932, has remained in effect as an impost computed on a cumulative basis: The tax rates now applicable to a gift are determined by reference to the total amount of prior taxable gifts made by the donor, rather than by reference only to taxable gifts made in a particular year.

The gift tax is designed to complement both the income and estate taxes by taxing transfers that may reduce either or both of the donor's taxable estate or future taxable income. Adoption of the unified rate schedule in 1976 reduced — but did not eliminate — the estate tax savings of making gifts inter vivos. Although the gift tax supplements both the income and estate taxes, the three taxes overlap to some extent and the treatment accorded a transaction is not necessarily consistent — there is no *pari materia* — among the three systems. Thus, a donor must resolve three separate questions: (1) whether the transfer is a taxable gift; (2) whether the transferred property will be included in the donor's gross estate at death, notwithstanding the inter vivos transfer; and (3) whether the transfer constitutes a taxable exchange or a prohibited assignment of income that is subject to income tax. A related question arises if the transfer is made in trust: (4) whether the post-transfer income from the transferred property will be taxable to the grantor instead of to the trust or its beneficiaries.

Property transferred by a donor can be subjected to gift taxation and also included in the donor's gross estate at death, and post-transfer income from the property may (but need not) be taxable to the donor. For example, an irrevocable transfer with a retained life estate is a taxable gift of the remainder interest, notwithstanding that the transferred property is included in the donor's gross estate, and the retained income will be taxed as the donor's income notwithstanding that it may be accumulated and not distributed to the donor. Any punitive aspect of imposing both gift and estate taxes on a single transaction is usually removed by the fact that the gift tax already paid is effectively applied against the gross estate tax. Including transferred property in the decedent's gross estate is not, however, the same as including a gift in the donor's estate tax base. Property included in the gross estate is valued on the applicable estate tax valuation date. A gift included in the tax base under the unified rate procedure is valued at the date the gift was made. Most donors regard this as a sufficient reason in itself for making gifts during life that are not includible at death because they anticipate that the property will appreciate in value, making the gift tax value lower than the estate tax value.

As we will see in Chapter 14, there are other tax advantages to making inter vivos gifts. As we also will see, however, if the applicable exclusion amount rises and the highest marginal tax rate declines, both as Congress enacted in 2001, there will be a time when the wealth transfer tax is a flat tax and the shift of future appreciation will then be irrelevant. Try an easy example to persuade yourself of this reality: your client has an asset worth $100x today that will double in value prior to death. The tax rate is a flat 45%, meaning that a transfer at today's value will generate $45x of tax and leave $55x, which will double in value prior to death, leaving $110x. If the client instead holds onto the $100x and it doubles in value prior to death, the $200x then taxed at 45% will produce $90x of tax and again leave $110x when the dust settles. Shifting the appreciating asset by gift garners no advantage *unless* the client can pay the $45x of tax with other assets that would not grow in value, in which case the client can shift the appreciation on the dollars that otherwise would have been used to pay the gift tax, and avoid estate tax on that element of appreciation.

The gift tax is applied on a calendar year basis. The first step in determining a donor's gift tax consequences for a calendar year is to identify the transfers or other transactions that the donor made during that year that constitute "gifts" for gift tax purposes, and to determine the value of those gifts. A taxpayer's transfer of cash without consideration to a child as a birthday present almost certainly constitutes a gift, and there are many less obvious circumstances in which gift tax consequences can arise. Even the determination of the amount of a gift can be more complex than merely ascertaining the value of the property.

The second step is to ascertain whether any amount of the gifts made by the donor during the calendar year is excludable. Section 2503(b) provides that an inflation indexed "de minimis" amount of gifts made by a donor during a calendar year to each separate donee is excluded from the donor's taxable gifts, but only gifts that do not constitute "future interests" can qualify for this exclusion. Thus, a donor could make gifts of this amount (it was $3,000 for decades, then $10,000, which grew to $11,000 in 2002 under an index for inflation, and may grow larger) to each of literally dozens of the donor's intended beneficiaries every year without incurring any gift tax. Indeed, the donor may not be required even to file a gift tax return. This exclusion commonly is referred to as the gift tax annual exclusion.

From the amount of taxable gifts made during a calendar year (after reflecting all exclusions), the third step is to subtract any allowable charitable or marital deduction to compute the amount of taxable gifts, to which the gift tax rate schedule is then applied in the final step. To determine the appropriate rate of tax, however, it is necessary to aggregate current taxable gifts with all taxable gifts made by the donor in previous taxable periods. The greater the amount of prior gifts, the greater the rate of tax on gifts made during the current year. Gifts made before and after 1976 are subject to this aggregation for gift tax purposes, and the rate schedule applied is the same rate schedule that is employed for estate tax purposes. As with the estate tax computation, the tax imposed on the aggregate amount is then reduced by the gift tax payable at current rates on the prior gifts in the tax base, leaving only the incremental tax on the current gifts to be paid or applied against the donor's unified credit.

A special provision permits spouses to divide equally between them all gifts made by either to third parties; the "split-gift" portion allotted to each spouse is treated as if it were actually donated by that spouse and is subjected to tax notwithstanding which spouse was the actual donor. Thus, if a donor made a gift of $24,000 to X and if the donor's spouse consented to split-gift treatment, then the donor is treated as having made a gift of $12,000 to X, of which the annual exclusion amount may be excluded, and the consenting spouse is treated as having made a gift of $12,000 to X, of which another annual exclusion amount may be nontaxable. Once a portion of a gift is allocated to a spouse by virtue of this election, that portion of the gift is treated for all gift tax purposes as having been made by that spouse and all exclusions, deductions, and future tax computations are applied accordingly. The gift-splitting election is available anew for each calendar year.

Although the 1976 changes removed some of the tax incentives for making inter vivos rather than testamentary transfers, several advantages remain, including the benefits derived from gift splitting. Other perceived tax benefits from making gifts are: the annual exclusion, an aspect known as the "tax exclusive" computation of the gift tax, avoidance of transfer tax on any post-transfer appreciation in value, a significant difference in how value is determined, and a shift of the income tax burden on any income generated by the transferred property. Some of these are transitory, as we will see in Chapter 4.

3. *The Federal Generation-Skipping Transfer Tax.* The generation-skipping transfer tax was first adopted in 1976 and was completely restated in 1986. The tax is imposed on transfers under a trust or equivalent arrangement (such as a life estate) that shift enjoyment to persons who are more than one generation below the transferor (such as to grandchildren or more remote beneficiaries). In general, the tax applies to any distribution to such a "skip person" or upon the termination of all intervening interests in nonskip persons (for example, termination of a child's life estate). Unlike the estate and gift taxes, which are imposed today under ostensibly progressive rates, the generation-skipping transfer tax is a flat excise computed at the highest marginal rate under the unified tax structure, making it the most expensive of the transfer taxes in most cases. Certain exclusions are available (such as a rough equivalent to the gift tax annual exclusion), and an exemption is available, although its application is not as straightforward as is a deduction or the unified credit. That exemption began at $1 million (indexed for inflation — it was $1.12 million in 2003), and after 2003 it is equal to the estate tax applicable exclusion amount.

In general, the tax applies to generation-skipping transfers made after September 25, 1985, although post-'85 transfers from trusts that were irrevocable on that date may be exempt.

4.   *Proposals for Transfer Tax Revision.*   For many years, proposals have been advanced to revise or even repeal the federal wealth transfer tax laws. Three major institutional studies have been made of the transfer tax system, complete with recommendations for change. The first was a five-year study undertaken by the American Law Institute in the 1960s. See American Law Institute, Federal Estate and Gift Taxation: Recommendations of the American Law Institute and Reporters' Studies (1969) (hereafter cited as ALI Recommendations). The Treasury Department of the Johnson Administration in the late 1960s also produced a study. See U.S. Treasury Department, 91st Cong., 1st Sess., Tax Reform Studies and Proposals (Committee Print 1969) (hereafter cited as Treasury Department Studies and Proposals). The third study was produced by the American Bankers Association and presented in 1973 in hearings before the House Ways and Means Committee. See American Bankers Association Discussion Draft of Transfer Tax Statute and Explanatory Comments, in Hearings on General Tax Reform before the House Committee on Ways and Means, 93d Cong., 1st Sess. pt. 9 (1973) (hereafter cited as American Bankers Association Discussion Draft). TRA 1976, ERTA 1981, and TRA 1986 all made substantial changes in the wealth transfer tax laws inspired in part by these three studies, but many recommendations have not been adopted.

Rather than consider any of these remaining reform proposals, in 2001 Congress enacted legislation that entirely repeals the estate and generation-skipping transfer taxes, effective in 2010. There is a "sunset" provision that brings both taxes back into full force in 2011, however, and the gift tax is not repealed at all. As a result of these changes, until or unless a future Congress makes the repeal permanent or eliminates the repeal entirely nothing notable has occurred, including all the needed reforms recommended by the institutional studies (of which none favored repeal of the basic wealth transfer tax system). For proposals for more radical change, all of which suggest that the tax be imposed on the transferee rather than on the transferor but none advocating total abandonment either, see Halbach, *An Accessions Tax*, 23 REAL PROP. PROB. & TR. J. 211 (1988); McNulty, *A Transfer Tax Alternative: Inclusion Under the Income Tax*, 2 TAX NOTES at 24–27 (1976); Commission to Revise the Tax Structure, Reforming the Federal Tax Structure 18 (Fund for Public Policy Research, 1973). See also Simons, PERSONAL INCOME TAXATION ch. 6 (1938).

PART B.   PURPOSES OF TRANSFER TAXATION

Congress' purpose in enacting the estate tax in 1916 and the gift tax in 1932 was to raise revenue. See H.R. Rep. No. 922, 64th Cong., 1st Sess. 1-5 (1916), in 1939-1 C.B. (pt. 2) 22–25; H.R. Rep. No. 708, 72d Cong., 1st Sess. 1-8 (1932), in 1939-1 C.B. (pt. 2) 457–462. Today, the revenue raised by the transfer tax system is quite small in comparison with the federal government's total receipts — hovering around 1%. It is generally agreed that the revenue-raising function of the transfer tax system is not paramount; a very small rate hike under the income tax could easily replace all revenue lost by repeal of these taxes. So why should the system be retained? One overriding purpose of the system is to reduce large concentrations of family wealth. Congress pointed to this purpose in enacting large increases in amounts exempt from transfer taxation in 1981. Senate Report No. 144, 97th Cong., 1st Sess. 124 (1981), stated:

Historically, one of the principal reasons for estate and gift taxes was to break up large concentrations of wealth. Generally, small- and moderate-sized estates have been exempt from the estate and gift taxes. . . .

With the existing level of unified credit (which permits cumulative tax-free transfers of $175,625), the estate tax is imposed on estates of a relatively small size, including those containing family farms or closely held businesses. Imposing the tax on these smaller, illiquid estates often results in forced sales of family enterprises.

The committee believes that the unified credit should be increased to offset the effects of inflation and to provide estate and gift tax relief to smaller estates, especially those which consist of family businesses.

There is no empirical data to support the oft heard complaint that the wealth transfer tax causes the demise or forced sale of family farms and closely held businesses. Nevertheless, the unified credit has been increased to exempt over 99% of all decedent estates ($1 million in 2001, slated to rise to $3.5 million in 2009). At these levels the tax does little to impact any but the most massive fortunes and the history of large family fortunes probably would tell us that the federal estate tax is not needed to fragment most large wealth holdings: inheritance and improvidence, ineptitude, and mere fickle fortune take a far greater toll on most dynastic wealth over several generations. In a sense, the tax may only accelerate what is inevitable in those situations anyway.

A third reason, expounded by Graetz, *To Praise the Estate Tax, Not to Bury It*, 93 YALE L.J. 259 (1983), is that wealth transfer taxes add a measure of progressivity to the present tax system with a lesser impact on capital formation than an additional income tax. Under this reasoning, wealth transfer taxes catch income or wealth that slipped through the income tax net and do so at a more convenient time to pay.

Several relatively recent events suggest two additional reasons to have a wealth transfer tax. The generation-skipping transfer tax is grounded on the premise that wealth should be taxed at each generation. This premise implicitly underlies the accessions tax models as well, because they presume that the receipt of wealth is an entitlement that ought to be taxed, just as income is. The other reason, which was brought into focus by the collapse of Eastern European communism, is based on the fact that people in capitalist societies are able to amass wealth for transmission to the natural objects of their bounty because the government, the economy, and society as a whole make it possible. The theory is that, in the whole process of accumulation and transfer, our system of government and society is a silent partner that is entitled to its share of the wealth of those citizens who benefit from the opportunities they are afforded. The wealth transfer tax is the most convenient way — it comes at a relatively easy time — to pay back the contributions that the government, the economy, and society made to the decedent's accumulation of wealth. On the other hand, to the extent that the decedent's wealth was the residue of previously taxed income, one might question whether it is gouging for the government (and society) to take out an additional slice at the decedent's death. Your view may vary based on whether you ever expect to inherit from that 1% of the decedent population.

The Canadians tax appreciation in assets at death in lieu of a wealth transfer tax. Is that a more palatable form of extracting a share of the decedent's gains than an estate tax? Would an increased income tax be a better solution, or is a tax on wealth — in whatever form imposed — appropriate for other, perhaps more political or emotional, reasons? Would a change to some other system yield disadvantages that would outweigh any perceived advantages, and does the cost of making a change argue in favor of the status quo?

PART C.   PROFESSIONAL RESPONSIBILITY

Two opinions of the American Bar Association Standing Committee on Ethics and Professional Responsibility and one appellate court opinion on liability for malpractice are reproduced in this part. The specter of ethical or malpractice violations is substantial in the estate planning context. Particularly troublesome are the myriad conflict of interest situations in which an attorney may be mired and the possibility for liability being premised thereon. See generally Pennell, *Professional Responsibility: Reforms Are Needed to Accommodate Estate Planning and Family Counselling*, 25 U. MIAMI INST. EST. PLAN. 18-1 (1991).

Circular 230 is the government's collection of rules found in various regulations that relate to practice before the Internal Revenue Service; it is the government's ethics rules for tax practitioners, with which all individuals who practice before the IRS must comply. These rules are in addition to the rules of ethics imposed by their professions. The following statement appears in a release containing proposed amendments to Circular 230, published in the Federal Register on October 8, 1992:

In 1985, the American Bar Association ("ABA"), in Formal Opinion 85-352, adopted a standard requiring that a return position be supported by a "realistic possibility of success if litigated." This standard replaced . . . the less stringent "reasonable basis" standard of ABA Formal Opinion 314 (1965). In 1986, . . . Treasury issued a proposed amendment to Circular 230 that generally would have prohibited a practitioner from advising or preparing a return position unless the practitioner determined that the position would not subject the taxpayer to the substantial understatement penalty. . . .

In 1987, the ABA and American Institute of Certified Public Accountants ("AICPA") responded to the proposed amendments by submitting proposals to the Service recommending that a realistic possibility standard for return preparation be incorporated in Circular 230. In 1988, the AICPA amended its Statements on Responsibilities in Tax Practice to replace its "reasonable support" standard with a "realistic possibility" standard that is similar, but not identical, to the standard for lawyers under ABA Formal Opinion 85-352.

In 1989, Congress revised the penalties for income tax return preparers in §6694 of the Internal Revenue Code to generally reflect the revised ABA and AICPA return preparation standards. See H. Rep. No. 247, 101st Cong., 1st Sess. 1396 (1989) ("The committee has adopted this new standard because it generally reflects the professional conduct standards applicable to lawyers and to certified public accountants"). Final regulations under §6694 were issued by Treasury on December 30, 1991.

In light of these developments, Treasury is withdrawing the 1986 proposed amendments to Circular 230 and is proposing a standard of conduct under §10.34(a) that more closely reflects the realistic possibility standards adopted by professional organizations and the preparer penalty provisions of §6694 of the Code and regulations thereunder. Because Circular 230's role in regulating practitioner conduct differs from the role played by the ABA and AICPA guidelines and Internal Revenue Code penalties, the proposed amendments provide that a practitioner may be disciplined under Circular 230 only if a failure to comply with the realistic possibility standard is willful, reckless, or a result of gross incompetence. A pattern of conduct is a factor that will be taken into account in determining whether a practitioner acted recklessly or through gross incompetence. A practitioner will not be considered to have acted willfully, recklessly, or through gross incompetence with respect to a return position if there was reasonable cause for the position and the practitioner acted in good faith. . . .

Under the new return preparer standard of conduct in §10.34(a)(1), a practitioner may not advise a client to take a position on a return, or prepare the portion of a return on which a position is taken, unless (i) the practitioner determines that there is a realistic possibility of the position being sustained on its merits (the "realistic possibility standard"), or (ii) the position is not frivolous and the practitioner advises the client to adequately disclose the position. In addition, a practitioner may not sign a return as a preparer if the practitioner determines that the return contains a position that does not satisfy the realistic possibility standard, unless the position is not frivolous and is adequately disclosed to the Service. Section 10.34(a)(4) defines "realistic possibility" and "frivolous" for purposes of this section.

Proposed §10.34(a)(2) generally requires a practitioner to advise a client of penalties reasonably likely to apply to a return position, of any opportunity to avoid the penalties by disclosure, and of the requirements for adequate disclosure. Proposed §10.34(a)(3) generally permits a practitioner to rely without verification on information furnished by the client. However, the practitioner may not ignore the implications of the information and must make reasonable inquiries if the information appears incorrect, inconsistent or incomplete.

§10.34 Standards for advising with respect to tax return positions and for preparing or signing returns.

(a) *Standard of conduct—*(1) *Realistic possibility standard.* A practitioner may not sign a return as a preparer if the practitioner determines that the return contains a position that does not satisfy the realistic possibility standard, unless the position is not frivolous and is adequately disclosed to the Service. A practitioner may not advise a client to take a position on a return, or prepare the portion of a return on which a position is taken, unless—

(i) The practitioner determines that there is a realistic possibility of the position being sustained on its merits (the "realistic possibility standard"); or

(ii) The position is not frivolous and the practitioner advises the client to adequately disclose the position.

(2) *Advising clients on potential penalties.* A practitioner advising a client to take a position on a return, or preparing or signing a return as a preparer, must inform the client of the penalties reasonably likely to apply to the client with respect to the position, of the opportunity to avoid any such penalty by disclosure, if relevant, and of the requirements for adequate disclosure.

(3) *Relying on information furnished by clients.* A practitioner advising a client to take a position on a return, or preparing or signing a return as a preparer, generally may rely in good faith without verification upon information furnished by the client. However, the practitioner may not ignore the implications of information furnished to, or actually known by, the practitioner, and must make reasonable inquiries if the information as furnished appears to be incorrect, inconsistent, or incomplete.

(4) *Definitions.* For purposes of this section:

(i) *Realistic possibility.* A position is considered to have a realistic possibility of being sustained on its merits if a reasonable and well-informed analysis by a person knowledgeable in the tax law would lead such a person to conclude that the position has approximately a one in three, or greater, likelihood of being sustained on its merits. The authorities described in [Treas. Reg.] §1.6662-4(d)(3)(iii) of the substantial understatement penalty regulations may be taken into account for purposes of this analysis. The possibility that a position will not be challenged by the Service (e.g., because the taxpayer's return may not be audited or because the issue may not be raised on audit) may not be taken into account.

(ii) *Frivolous.* A position is frivolous if it is patently improper.

(b) *Standard of discipline.* As provided in §10.52, only violations of this section that are willful, reckless, or a result of gross incompetence will subject a practitioner to suspension or disbarment from practice before the Service.

Formal Opinion 85-352
Tax Return Advice; Reconsideration of
Formal Opinion 314, July 7, 1985

A lawyer may advise reporting a position on a tax return so long as the lawyer believes in good faith that the position is warranted in existing law or can be supported by a good faith argument for an extension, modification or reversal of existing law and there is some realistic possibility of success if the matter is litigated.

The Committee has been requested by the Section of Taxation of the American Bar Association to reconsider the "reasonable basis" standard in the Committee's Formal Opinion 314 governing the position a lawyer may advise a client to take on a tax return.

Opinion 314 (April 27, 1965) was issued in response to a number of specific inquiries regarding the ethical relationship between the Internal Revenue Service and lawyers practicing before it. The opinion formulated general principles governing this relationship, including the following:

> [A] lawyer who is asked to advise his client in the course of the preparation of the client's tax returns may freely urge the statement of positions most favorable to the client just as long as there is a *reasonable basis* for this position. (Emphasis supplied).

The Committee is informed that the standard of "reasonable basis" has been construed by many lawyers to support the use of any colorable claim on a tax return to justify exploitation of the lottery of the tax return audit selection process.[8] This view is not universally held, and the Committee does not believe that the reasonable basis standard, properly interpreted and applied, permits this construction.

However, the Committee is persuaded that as a result of serious controversy over this standard and its persistent criticism by distinguished members of the tax bar, IRS officials and members of Congress, sufficient doubt has been created regarding the validity of the standard so as to erode its effectiveness as an ethical guideline. For this reason, the Committee has concluded that it should be restated. Another reason for restating the standard is that, since publication of Opinion 314, the ABA has adopted in succession the Model Code of Professional Responsibility (1969, revised 1980) and the Model Rules of Professional Conduct (1983). Both the Model Code and the Model Rules directly address the duty of a lawyer in presenting or arguing positions for a client in language that does not refer to "reasonable basis." It is therefore

---

8. [Most citations and footnotes in original sources have been omitted. Those retained have been renumbered. — Ed.] This criticism has been expressed by the Section of Taxation and also by the U.S. Department of the Treasury and some legal writers. See, e.g., Robert H. Mundheim, Speech as General Counsel to Treasury Department, reprinted in *How To Prepare and Defend Tax Shelter Opinions: Risks and Realities for Lawyers and Accountants* (Law and Business, Inc. 1981); Rowen, *When May a Lawyer Advise a Client That He May Take a Position on a Tax Return?* 29 TAX LAWYER 237 (1976).

appropriate to conform the standard of Opinion 314 to the language of the new rules.

This opinion reconsiders and revises only that part of Opinion 314 that relates to the lawyer's duty in advising a client of positions that can be taken on a tax return. It does not deal with a lawyer's opinion on tax shelter investment offerings, which is specifically addressed by this Committee's Formal Opinion 346 (Revised), and which involves very different considerations, including third party reliance.

The ethical standards governing the conduct of a lawyer in advising a client on positions that can be taken in a tax return are no different from those governing a lawyer's conduct in advising or taking positions for a client in other civil matters. Although the Model Rules distinguish between the roles of advisor and advocate,[9] both roles are involved here, and the ethical standards applicable to them provide relevant guidance. In many cases a lawyer must realistically anticipate that the filing of the tax return may be the first step in a process that may result in an adversary relationship between the client and the IRS. This normally occurs in situations when a lawyer advises an aggressive position on a tax return, not when the position taken is a safe or conservative one that is unlikely to be challenged by the IRS.

Rule 3.1 of the Model Rules, which is in essence a restatement of DR 7-102(A)(2) of the Model Code,[10] states in pertinent part:

> A lawyer shall not bring or defend a proceeding, or assert or controvert an issue therein, unless there is a basis for doing so that is not frivolous, which includes a good faith argument for an extension, modification or reversal of existing law.

Rule 1.2(d), which applies to representation generally, states:

> A lawyer shall not counsel a client to engage, or assist a client, in conduct that the lawyer knows is criminal or fraudulent, but a lawyer may discuss the legal consequences of any proposed course of conduct with a client

---

9. See, for example, Model Rules 2.1 and 3.1.
10. DR 7-102(A)(2) states:

In his representation of a client, a lawyer shall not:

(2) Knowingly advance a claim or defense that is unwarranted under existing law, except that he may advance such claim or defense if it can be supported by good faith argument for an extension, modification or reversal of existing law.

and may counsel or assist a client to make a good faith effort to determine the validity, scope, meaning or application of the law.

On the basis of these rules and analogous provisions of the Model Code, a lawyer, in representing a client in the course of the preparation of the client's tax return, may advise the statement of positions most favorable to the client if the lawyer has a good faith belief that those positions are warranted in existing law or can be supported by a good faith argument for an extension, modification or reversal of existing law. A lawyer can have a good faith belief in this context even if the lawyer believes the client's position probably will not prevail.[11] However, good faith requires that there be some realistic possibility of success if the matter is litigated.

This formulation of the lawyer's duty in the situation addressed by this opinion is consistent with the basic duty of the lawyer to a client, recognized in ethical standards since the ABA Canons of Professional Ethics, and in the opinions of this Committee: zealously and loyally to represent the interests of the client within the bounds of the law.

Thus, where a lawyer has a good faith belief in the validity of a position in accordance with the standard stated above that a particular transaction does not result in taxable income or that certain expenditures are properly deductible as expenses, the lawyer has no duty to require as a condition of his or her continued representation that riders be attached to the client's tax return explaining the circumstances surrounding the transaction or the expenditures.

In the role of advisor, the lawyer should counsel the client as to whether the position is likely to be sustained by a court if challenged by the IRS, as well as of the potential penalty consequences to the client if the position is taken on the tax return without disclosure. Section [6662(d)] of the Internal Revenue Code imposes a penalty for substantial understatement of tax liability which can be avoided if the facts are adequately disclosed or if there is or was substantial authority for the position taken by the taxpayer. Competent representation of the client would require the lawyer to advise the client fully as to whether there is or was substantial authority for the position taken in the tax return. If the lawyer is unable to conclude that the position is supported by substantial authority, the lawyer should advise the client of the penalty the client may suffer and of the opportunity to avoid such penalty by adequately disclosing the facts in the return or in a

---

11. Comment to Rule 3.11; see also Model Code EC 7-4.

statement attached to the return. If after receiving such advice the client decides to risk the penalty by making no disclosure and to take the position initially advised by the lawyer in accordance with the standard stated above, the lawyer has met his or her ethical responsibility with respect to the advice.

In all cases, however, with regard both to the preparation of returns and negotiating administrative settlements, the lawyer is under a duty not to mislead the Internal Revenue Service deliberately, either by misstatements or by silence or by permitting the client to mislead. Rules 4.1 and 8.4(c); DRs 1-102(A)(4), 7-102(A)(3) and (5).

In summary, a lawyer may advise reporting a position on a return even where the lawyer believes the position probably will not prevail, there is no "substantial authority" in support of the position, and there will be no disclosure of the position in the return. However, the position to be asserted must be one which the lawyer in good faith believes is warranted in existing law or can be supported by a good faith argument for an extension, modification or reversal of existing law. This requires that there is some realistic possibility of success if the matter is litigated. In addition, in his role as advisor, the lawyer should refer to potential penalties and other legal consequences should the client take the position advised.

It was in a Report of the Special Task Force on Formal Opinion 85-352 of the ABA that the one-in-three likelihood of success standard was suggested and, although that position is not stated in the Formal Opinion, its incorporation in Circular 230 causes it to be the standard. The Task Force also stated that "[a] position to be asserted in the return in the expectation that something could be obtained by way of concession in the bargaining process of settlement negotiations would not be the new standard, unless accompanied by a realistic possibility of success, if litigated."

Does the fact that Code §6694, dealing with return preparer penalties, only relates to income tax returns bear in any way on the ethical obligations of tax practitioners in other areas of the tax law? For example, in the course of representing a client, what are your ethical obligations to the client and to the government if you learn that taxable gifts were made in prior years but never reported? Would your answer change if you learned this information only after the client had died, or only after you had assisted in preparing the client's estate tax return?

5. *Other Responsibilities.* Formal Opinion 210 and Horne v. Peckham, both reproduced below, deal with other responsibilities owed by lawyers toward clients. Formal Opinion 210 holds that it is permissible for lawyers to advise their former will clients of any changes of fact or law that might defeat the client's testamentary purpose as expressed in the will, and suggests that there "might even" be a duty to do so. No subsequent authority has yet established that such a duty exists, but it is not much of a stretch to conclude that a client who regularly receives newsletters or other communications from an attorney as part of a client-retention or marketing plan reasonably relied on the attorney to advise the client about changes in the law that make the client's plan no longer appropriate or effective. ABA Standing Committee on Ethics and Professional Responsibility Informal Opinion 1356 (1975) held that such contact is not a prohibited form of solicitation and limited case law states that the attorney has no duty to keep clients informed about changes in the law. Stangland v. Brock, 747 P.2d 464 (Wash. 1987). Quaere, however, how long this insulation from liability will last. This is a topic of special importance to estate planners in view of the vast number and significance of changes in the federal wealth transfer tax system that have been wrought in recent years.

Formal Opinion 210
March 15, 1941

An attorney may properly advise a client for whom he has drawn a will of the advisability of reexamining the will periodically and may from time to time send notices to the client advising him of changes in law or fact which may defeat the client's testamentary purpose, unless the attorney has reason to believe that he has been supplanted by another attorney.

A member calls attention to the effect on testamentary dispositions of subsequent changes in general economic conditions, of changes in the attitude or death of named fiduciaries in a will, of the removal of the testator to a different jurisdiction where different laws of descent may prevail, of changes in financial conditions, family relationship and kindred matters, and then inquires whether it is proper for the lawyer who drew the will to call attention of the testator from time to time to the importance of going over his will. . . .

The inquiry presents the question as to whether such action on the part of a lawyer is solicitation of legal employment and so to be condemned.

Many events transpire between the date of making the will and the death of the testator. The legal significance of such occurrences are often of serious consequence, of which the testator may not be aware, and so the importance of calling the attention of the testator thereto is manifest.

It is our opinion that where the lawyer has no reason to believe that he has been supplanted by another lawyer, it is not only his right, but it might even be his duty to advise his client of any change of fact or law which might defeat the client's testamentary purpose as expressed in the will.

Periodic notices might be sent to the client for whom a lawyer has drawn a will, suggesting that it might be wise for the client to reexamine his will to determine whether or not there has been any change in his situation requiring a modification of his will.

Horne v. Peckham discusses the extent of lawyers' liability for malpractice if a client's sought-for tax objectives have not been achieved. The objective of the client in *Horne* was to shift the income tax consequences of an item of property to lower-bracket taxpayers, which failed because the arrangement established by the client's lawyer ran afoul of the so-called grantor trust rules found in §§671-678.

Horne v. Peckham
97 Cal. App. 3d 404 (1979)

PARAS, Acting Presiding Justice. Defendant, an attorney, appeals from a judgment entered after a jury awarded damages of $64,983.31 against him for legal malpractice in connection with the drafting of a "Clifford Trust" for plaintiffs Roy C. Horne (Horne) and Doris G. Horne, husband and wife. He contends that the judgment should be reversed or in the alternative that another attorney, Thomas J. McIntosh, upon whom he relied for advice, should indemnify him.

In 1960, Horne obtained a patent for processing low grade wood into defect-free material known as "Perfect Plank Plus." In 1962, he founded a business called "Perfect Plank," and in 1967 began to produce the patented product. The business was incorporated in 1965, with the Hornes as sole shareholders. Horne anticipated that production of the product might generate substantial income, so he became interested when he read in a newsletter of the tax advantages of a so-called "Clifford Trust." On July 18, 1967, on the recommendation of Herbert McClanahan, his accountant, he went to defendant and asked him to prepare such a trust, Horne's three sons to be its beneficiaries.

Defendant testified he told Horne ". . . that I had no knowledge of tax matters. I had no expertise in tax matters; that if somebody else could figure out what needed to be done, I could draft the documents." He said that McClanahan had provided him with ". . . a couple of pages of translucencies . . . governing Clifford Trusts," and he also consulted the two-volume annual set of American Jurisprudence on federal taxation, which included a discussion on Clifford Trusts; he otherwise relied on McClanahan's judgment.

The original plan was to put the patent, which had 10 more years of life, into the trust. However, on October 11, 1967, Horne told defendant he no longer desired this and asked ". . . if it wouldn't be just as good to put in a [non-exclusive] [l]icense . . ." of the patent rights. Horne testified that he preferred not to put the patent itself into the trust, because the substantial royalties from it would result in more money than should properly be given to his sons.

Defendant testified he told Horne that ". . . I didn't know whether . . . [a license] would be just as good or not, but that we were having a high-priced tax expert come up here — like the following day — who was undoubtedly going to charge plenty of money for the consultation, and that we should ask him on that point." The tax expert to whom defendant referred was McIntosh, an attorney from Albany, California, who had been recommended by McClanahan as an expert in deferred compensation and profit-sharing plans. Such plans for Horne's company were to be discussed at a meeting with McIntosh arranged by McClanahan and scheduled for the next day, October 12. Unknown to defendant, McIntosh had been licensed to practice law less than a year, although he was also a certified public accountant and had worked for two and one-half or three years as a tax accountant.

The meeting of October 12 was attended by Horne, his wife, one son, McClanahan, defendant, and McIntosh. Defendant testified that he asked McIntosh whether it would be just as effective to transfer a license agreement into the contemplated trust as the patent itself, and received an affirmative answer. He further testified that Horne had been talking of a nonexclusive license during the meeting, thus McIntosh should have been aware that such a license was contemplated. However, defendant also testified that no one told McIntosh that the contemplated license would have a five year duration.

Horne testified that he thought the subject of license versus patent arose at that meeting, but he had no independent recollection of it. McIntosh testified that even though at his deposition he thought he recalled such a discussion, he did not recall it at trial.

Sometime after the meeting, defendant drafted the final documents and sent them to McClanahan for approval. He had no further discussions or correspondence with McIntosh. The documents were signed in November 1967, although dated February 1, 1967, the date production of the product began. The first document was an irrevocable trust agreement between the Hornes as trustors and McClanahan, defendant, and one Bill Ryan as trustees for the Horne's three sons, to terminate in twelve years (1979). The second was a license agreement between Horne and Perfect Plank, granting the corporation a license to produce the patented product for two years with an option to renew for an additional three years, in return for royalty payments determined by production; inter alia, the agreement stated "This license is not exclusive. Licensor retains the right to issue other licenses of the same patent to any other parties whatsoever." The third document was an assignment to the trustees by Horne of Horne's rights under the license agreement thus furnishing the trust with a corpus.

The license royalties were paid into the trust until 1970 when the Internal Revenue Service (I.R.S.) audited Horne's tax returns. Horne was notified of the audit by mail sometime prior to March 18, 1970, and knew within a few days thereafter of a challenge to the favorable tax aspect of the trust. In August 1970, the I.R.S. assessed a deficiency on the ground that the trust did not transfer tax liability for the licensor's income to the beneficiaries. Horne hired McIntosh to contest the assessment.

After losing at the first administrative level, Horne conceded his tax liability rather than contest it further. On May 12, 1972, he sued defendant for damages for malpractice. On June 18, 1973, defendant filed a cross-complaint for indemnity against McIntosh and his law partnership. After a jury trial, judgment was entered against defendant on the complaint, and in favor of McIntosh on the cross-complaint.

I. Defendant's first argument on appeal is that "It is not legal malpractice (negligence) on the part of an attorney general practitioner to draw documents without doing research on a point of law on which there is no appellate decision or statute in point."

The argument has two parts: first, that the trust documents were in fact valid as a tax shelter; second, that even if invalid, their invalidity is so debatable that he should not be liable for making an error regarding a matter about which reasonable attorneys can disagree. He is wrong on both points. The documents are invalid for their intended purpose, and the invalidity is rather obvious. To demonstrate this, one need go no further than the original *Clifford* case, from which the name "Clifford Trust" is derived, and the legislation it brought about.

In Helvering v. Clifford, 309 U.S. 331 (1940), the United States Supreme Court held that notwithstanding "niceties of the law of trusts or conveyances, or the legal paraphernalia which inventive genius may construct as a refuge from surtaxes," id. at 334, the grantor of a trust may be taxed as owner, depending on "an analysis of the terms of the trust and all the circumstances attendant on its creation and operation." Id. at 335. . . .

Following the *Clifford* decision, the I.R.S. adopted regulations to implement it, and these formed the basis for sections 671–678 of the Internal Revenue Code . . . . Directly applicable to the present case is §675 . . . .

If the *Clifford* decision and §675 were to be deemed insufficient authority, Commissioner v. Sunnen, 333 U.S. 591 (1948), cited by defendant himself, provides (and provided in 1967) further authority to establish the trust's invalidity as a Clifford Trust. . . .

In light of the foregoing, it is apparent that there is no merit to defendant's contention that there was "no appellate decision or statute in point." Internal Revenue Code §675 and the *Sunnen* case were very much in point.

II. Defendant's second contention is that "An attorney in general practice does not have a duty to refer his client to a 'specialist' or to recommend the 'assistance of a specialist' or be guilty of malpractice."

The court gave a jury instruction which states:

> It is the duty of an attorney who is a general practitioner to refer his client to a specialist or recommend the assistance of a specialist if under the circumstances a reasonably careful and skillful practitioner would do so.
>
> If he fails to perform that duty and undertakes to perform professional services without the aid of a specialist, it is his further duty to have the knowledge and skill ordinarily possessed, and exercise the care and skill ordinarily used by specialists in good standing in the same or similar locality and under the same circumstances.
>
> A failure to perform any such duty is negligence.

This instruction is based upon California's Book of Approved Jury Instructions (BAJI), Instruction No. 6.04, which is found in that work's section on medical malpractice. Its applicability to legal malpractice presents an issue of first impression. Defendant points out that legal specialties were not officially recognized in California until 1973, and therefore contends that he could not have had a duty in 1967 to refer his client to a specialist or to meet the standard of care of a specialist.

We cannot accept this contention. A California survey in 1968 revealed that two-thirds of the attorneys in the state at that time limited their practice to a very few areas, frequently to one only. 44

Cal. St. B.J. 140 (1969). Thus, in the words of a leading treatise, the recent debate over official recognition of specialists must be considered "academic," for "[t]he reality is that many attorneys have become specialists." Mallen and Levitt, Legal Malpractice §114 at 172 (1977). Moreover, "[i]n those jurisdictions which recognize specialties or permit the attorney to make such a designation, taxation is one of the areas of law most commonly acknowledged." Id. §268 at 368. Taxation also was one of the three specialties initially recognized in California. (See 51 Cal. St. B.J. 549, 555 (1976)).

Defendant himself recognized the existence of tax specialists in 1967 when he advised Horne in 1967 that he was not a tax expert, and that such experts existed. Of course, the fact that the specialty exists does not mean that every tax case must be referred to a specialist. Many tax matters are so generally known that they can well be handled by general practitioners. (See Bucquet v. Livingston, 57 Cal. App. 3d 914 (1976).) But defendant himself acknowledged his need for expert assistance throughout his testimony, insisting he had no opinion of his own as to the tax consequences of the trust. Under the circumstances he cannot argue persuasively that it was error for the court to give the above quoted instruction.

III. Defendant's next contention is that the question of law involved here was one upon which reasonable doubt may be entertained by well-informed lawyers, and therefore he should not be found liable for committing error. He relies upon Lucas v. Hamm, 364 P.2d 685 (1961), which held (as restated in Smith v. Lewis, 530 P.2d 589, 596 (1975)), that "the rule against perpetuities poses such complex and difficult problems for the draftsman that even careful and competent attorneys occasionally fall prey to its traps."

But Lucas v. Hamm did not condone failure to do research, and Smith v. Lewis makes it clear than an attorney's obligation is not satisfied by simply determining that the law on a particular subject is doubtful or debatable: "[E]ven with respect to an unsettled area of the law, . . . an attorney assumes an obligation to his client to undertake reasonable research in an effort to ascertain relevant legal principles and to make an informed decision as to a course of conduct based upon an intelligent assessment of the problem." Id. at 595. In other words, an attorney has a duty to avoid involving his client in murky areas of the law if research reveals alternative courses of conduct. At least he should inform his client of uncertainties and let the client make the decision.

In any event, as stated above, there was nothing sufficiently doubtful or difficult about the invalidity of the trust documents in this case to permit invocation of Lucas v. Hamm as controlling precedent. . . .

The judgment is affirmed.

EVANS and REYNOSO, JJ., concur.

Consider the following kinds of inquiries raised by a case such as *Horne.*

(a)   Do you think there is any doubt that attorney Peckham committed negligence when he failed to discover that attorney McIntosh, the so-called "tax expert," was a rookie tax lawyer?

(b)   What do you think are the ethics of the attorney back-dating the trust documents in *Horne* to "the date production of the product began" rather than the date of execution some nine months later? Would attorney Peckham have any other liability to consider as well?

(c)   If referral to a specialist is necessary to avoid malpractice, why do you think it so seldom is done in the legal profession? What types of issues, both ethical and practical, would you want to address in pursuing referrals to more expert colleagues, and what issues must the attorney accepting the referral consider?

(d)   Do you know when the statute of limitation begins to run on legal malpractice in the estate planning arena? What kind of malpractice insurance should you obtain in light thereof?

PART D.   ADMINISTRATION OF THE TAX LAWS

6.   *Sources of Tax Law.*   The most important source of tax law is the Internal Revenue Code. The legislative history of a statutory provision (the committee hearings and reports, the record of the debates, and the various changes made in a bill during the legislative process before it became a statute) may be helpful in construing the Code's provisions. Of the several sources of legislative history, the most frequently useful are the committee reports, which are also the most readily accessible (often reproduced in volume 3 of the Cumulative Bulletin, which is a government publication discussed below, for the year in which major tax legislation is enacted). The reason the House Ways and Means Committee and the Senate Finance Committee reports of a revenue bill are so useful is because they contain a technical analysis of each provision of the bill and, generally, the avowed reason for its enactment. These reports often are used, sometimes verbatim, in drafting the regulations, which is the second most important source of guidance in the interpretation of tax legislation.

Regulations that interpret the Internal Revenue Code are promulgated by the Treasury Department pursuant to §7805, which authorizes the Secretary of the Treasury to promulgate regulations, or pursuant to various Code provisions that compel the Secretary to promulgate regulations (typically on topics Congress just did not want to address). Compare, e.g., §§2701(e)(6) and 2703(a)(3) and (b)(4). A regulation is entitled to great weight and should be held invalid by a court only if there is no statutory language to support the regulatory construction, the regulation is inconsistent with the statutory language, or the regulation constitutes an unreasonable construction. As a rule of thumb, which (like virtually all generalizations) is subject to exceptions, if a statute may be construed reasonably to have one of several meanings, the courts typically will treat a regulation's selection of one of those meanings as conclusive. In Commissioner v. South Texas Lumber Co., 333 U.S. 496, 501 (1948), the Court stated: "This Court has many times declared that Treasury regulations must be sustained unless unreasonable and plainly inconsistent with the revenue statutes and that they constitute contemporaneous constructions by those charged with administration of these statutes which should not be overruled except for weighty reasons." On occasion the government takes a position that is contrary to a regulation that favors the taxpayer, but it has been singularly unsuccessful on those occasions. See, e.g., Estate of Graham v. Commissioner, 46 T.C. 415, 424–425 (1966).

Regulations are numbered according to the type of tax to which they relate and the section of the Code they construe. Each regulation has a prefix number that indicates the tax area involved. For example, the prefix "1" designates an income tax regulation; the prefix "20." designates an estate tax regulation; the prefix "25." designates a gift tax regulation; and the prefix "26." designates a generation-skipping transfer tax regulation. The number following the decimal point is the same as that of the Code section the regulation construes. Thus, Treas. Reg. §25.2701-1 is a gift tax valuation regulation under §2701, and Treas. Reg. §20.2041-2 is an estate tax regulation construing §2041 of the Code. There are three regulations construing §2041, and they are differentiated by the suffix "-1," "-2," and "-3," respectively.

An additional interpretative guide is the published rulings promulgated by the Commissioner of Internal Revenue. It generally is assumed that the government is obliged to adhere to its published rulings and taxpayers may rely on statements of position that are made in them, if the facts and circumstances in another case are substantially similar to those in the Ruling. This is not entirely correct, as there is case law to the effect that the government may deviate from a published ruling, and may do so even retroactively.[12] Given that reality it should come as no surprise that courts are not ever bound by published rulings and often give little weight to

---

12.   See Dickman v. Commissioner, 465 U.S. 330 (1984); Dixon v. United States, 381 U.S. 68, 72-75 (1965); Automobile Club of Michigan v. Commissioner, 353 U.S. 180, 183-184 (1957). But see Rauenhorst v. Commissioner, 119 T.C. 157 (2002).

them[13] Indeed, in some circumstances it is obvious that the government promulgated a published ruling in anticipation of a case it knew it was going to litigate, then cited its own ruling as support for its position. In such cases, the courts correctly note that the ruling is no better — really no different — from a position stated on brief. In the proper application of the ruling process, the principal function of rulings is to advise the public (and the government's agents) of the government's position on an issue when the ruling was promulgated, so that a taxpayer who asserts a contrary position is on notice that the government may litigate. On occasion the government proposes a litigation position in a published ruling that has no support in the law, and the government never subsequently litigates that issue. The government's apparent purpose for issuing such rulings is to chill taxpayer conduct that it finds objectionable but not unlawful. A good example of this is Rev. Rul. 79-353.

For many years, most published rulings were designated as "Revenue Rulings" (Rev. Rul.). The government also publishes "Notices," which are indistinguishable from Revenue Rulings except for their different designation. Another type of ruling is called a "Revenue Procedure" (Rev. Proc.), but a smaller number of those are issued each year. The government also promulgates "information releases" (IR), formerly called "technical information releases" (TIR), which are simpler and briefer than most Revenue Rulings, and cover a variety of administrative matters in the form of Announcements and Technical Directives. All of these pronouncements are published first in a weekly document called the Internal Revenue Bulletin (I.R.B.), which are accumulated twice a year and published in a volume called the Cumulative Bulletin (C.B.). The citation to each ruling indicates the year in which it was promulgated. Thus, "Rev. Rul. 79-353" was Revenue Ruling number 353, promulgated in 1979. The number 353 does not, however, reflect the order of promulgation of the ruling; it only serves to distinguish it from other rulings promulgated in that year. In addition to designating the ruling, the citation also indicates where the ruling is located. The citation Rev. Rul. 79-353, 1979-2 C.B. 325, tells us that the ruling can be found on page 325 of the second volume of the 1979 Cumulative Bulletin. Rulings issued before the appropriate cumulative bulletin volume is published are cited to the weekly Internal Revenue Bulletin in which the ruling appears. For example, Rev. Rul. 73-399, 1973-39 I.R.B. 8, appeared at page 8 of the Internal Revenue Bulletin issued for the thirty-ninth week of 1973. Today the I.R.B. page number will become the C.B. page number, so if you knew that Rev. Rul. 2002-20 was issued in the 10th week of the year, which falls in the first half of the year, the I.R.B. cite will become a 2002-1 C.B. cite at the same page. To minimize the size of this casebook, citations

---

13. Note, however, that in Gino v. Commissioner, 538 F.2d 833, 835 (9th Cir. 1976), the court indicated that it would give some added weight to an established Revenue Ruling. But see Estate of Lang v. Commissioner, 613 F.2d 770, 776 (9th Cir. 1980).

to Revenue Rulings do not refer to the Cumulative Bulletin or Internal Revenue Bulletin in which the ruling is located. A table of contents in each Cumulative Bulletin makes it easy to find any ruling quickly if the number and year are known.

In addition to published rulings, the Commissioner also announces whether the government agrees with (acquiesces or "acq.") or will continue to challenge (nonacquiesces or "nonacq.") certain adverse decisions of the Tax Court. These acquiescences and nonacquiescences are published in the first few pages of the Internal Revenue Bulletins and ultimately in the Cumulative Bulletins.

Taxpayers won the right under the Freedom of Information Act also to have access to private rulings issued by the government to its own personnel or to taxpayers who sought advice on a particular transaction or issue. Before embarking on a transaction or before filing a return in connection therewith, a taxpayer or a District Director or Appeals Office Chief who wishes to know the government's position may request the National Office of the Internal Revenue Service to rule on an issue. The government's answer comes back in the form of a Private Letter Ruling addressed to the taxpayer or a Technical Advice Memorandum that goes to the government employee who requested it. These are not reviewed by others in the National Office before promulgation and therefore are not authority for anyone else to rely on or even to cite.[14] See §6110(j)(3). Only the taxpayer who requested a Private Letter Ruling may rely on the position stated and then only if the National Office does not retract the ruling first, only if the taxpayer accurately stated all of the relevant facts in the ruling request, and only if the law does not change after the ruling was given.

The government has shown a disconcerting tendency since the mid-1980s to issue revenue rulings only on mundane or noncontroversial issues and use the nonprecedential form of private rulings and technical memoranda to "test the water" with positions on more difficult or sensitive issues (although, in all fairness, of the over 100 rulings sometimes promulgated in any week, most are of no significance to any other taxpayer; unfortunately, there are enough gems included each week that knowledgeable practitioners read these religiously). These rulings are identifiable by a unique seven or nine-digit number reflecting the year and week of issuance, and a unique three-digit identifier. For example, Technical Advice Memorandum 9205001 was the first ruling issued in the fifth week of 1992, and Private Letter Ruling 200224007 was the seventh ruling issued in the 24th week of 2002. Rulings are requested by sending a letter to the Commissioner, according to

---

14. Despite the statutory declaration that private rulings are not to be used or cited as precedent, taxpayers do cite them; and courts (including the Supreme Court) have referred to them as evidence of the position that the government held during the period of time when the ruling was in effect. See, e.g., Rowan Companies., Inc. v. United States, 452 U.S. 247, 260 n.17 (1981).

People do cite them even though they're not precedential

procedures established by the government. Private Letter Rulings are referred to in this book as "PLRs" and Technical Advice Memoranda are referred to as "TAMs."

The first Revenue Procedure promulgated each year contains updated information regarding procedures for issuance of rulings, determination letters, and information letters, and for entering into closing agreements. The second Revenue Procedure promulgated each year contains updated information regarding procedures for issuance of technical advice memoranda to District Directors and Appeals Office Chiefs. The third Revenue Procedure promulgated each year contains updated information regarding subjects or issues upon which advance rulings, determination letters, and memoranda will not be issued. A similar list in the international arena is found in the seventh Revenue Procedure each year. Each year's promulgation supersedes the prior year's counterpart. Subjects upon which rulings will be issued in the income, gift, estate, and generation-skipping tax arenas include both prospective and completed transactions, if the request is made before a return is filed, and may include estate tax guidance even if the tax liability relates to the estate of a living person.

No rulings will issue on the computation of taxes, on actuarial factors for valuation purposes, or on the factual issues that are determinative for estate tax purposes. Similarly, rulings will not issue with respect to hypothetical cases, as contrasted to transactions already entered into, or as to transactions that the taxpayer represents will take place. See 3 Nossaman & Wyatt, TRUST ADMINISTRATION AND TAXATION 53A.03 (2002 rev. ed.). Pending the adoption of regulations that may affect a particular issue, a ruling will not be promulgated if the issue cannot readily be resolved until those regulations are issued, unless the issue arises under the 1986 or subsequent legislation. A taxpayer seeking a determination letter or a letter ruling must pay the government a fee, the schedules for which are set forth in the first Revenue Procedure for the year. With respect to technical advice, taxpayers may request that an issue be referred for technical advice, and there is a procedure to appeal a District Director's decision not to respect a request for such guidance.

Some PLRs and TAMs are of sufficient interest that they are studied further by the National Office and eventually serve as the basis of a published Revenue Ruling. On very rare occasions, courts refer to these rulings as evidence of an interpretative position held by the government during a certain period of time, but otherwise these are of no value other than to give taxpayers an idea of where the government's "head is at." See note 14 at page 28.

Court decisions construing a statutory provision are also important tax sources. Tax litigation is tried either in the United States Tax Court (originally called the Board of Tax Appeals), the United States Court of Claims, or the appropriate United States District Court. The taxpayer may choose the court in which to litigate. If the Tax Court is the forum chosen, the taxpayer need not pay the deficiency unless and until the case ultimately is lost. The taxpayer need only file a petition with the Tax Court for redetermination of the asserted deficiency and either the taxpayer or the government may appeal an adverse decision to the appropriate United States Court of Appeals and may appeal from an adverse decision by that court by seeking certiorari to the United States Supreme Court. A taxpayer who does not wish to litigate in the Tax Court must pay the asserted deficiency to the government and then file a claim for refund. After this claim is denied by the government (or after six months has expired from the date the claim was filed), the taxpayer may sue for a refund in either the appropriate United States District Court or the United States Court of Federal Claims, again as the taxpayer elects. An appeal may be taken to the appropriate court of appeals from an adverse district court judgment or to the Federal Circuit Court of Appeals from the Court of Federal Claims, and certiorari to the Supreme Court may be sought from any court of appeals decision. In addition to a difference in the level of expertise of the various courts among which the taxpayer may select, other deciding factors in the decision of how to challenge a deficiency are the nature of any precedent that binds a given court and whether the taxpayer wishes to stop the accumulation of interest by paying the deficiency and collecting interest from the government if the taxpayer wins.

The United States Tax Court Rules of Practice and Procedure 142(a)(1) (Interim Rule) provides:

The burden of proof shall be upon the petitioner, except as otherwise provided by statute or determined by the Court; and except that, in respect of any new matter, increases in deficiency, and affirmative defenses, pleaded in the answer, it shall be upon the respondent [the Commissioner]. . . .

In Welch v. Helvering, 290 U.S. 111, 115 (1933) (Cardozo, J.), the Court said: "The Commissioner['s] . . . ruling has the support of a presumption of correctness, and the petitioner has the burden of proving it to be wrong." But in Weimerskirch v. Commissioner, 596 F.2d 358, 360 (9th Cir. 1979), the court said: "[B]efore the Commissioner can rely on this presumption of correctness, the Commissioner must offer some substantive evidence [supporting his deficiency determination]." In addition, Congress altered the §7491 burden of proof rule in 1997, which effectively shifted the burden of persuasion. The government must produce some reasonable determination upon which an asserted deficiency relies, which the taxpayer must rebut with evidence that is credible enough that a reasonable person *could* believe it (*not* the more rigorous "more likely true than not" standard of prior law), which then shifts the burden to produce evidence back to the government for rebuttal. The burden of persuasion is on the government, however, in the sense that a 50-50 equipoise of evidence results in a taxpayer victory. Thus, the taxpayer still carries the burden of production—most notably of documents and proof of valuation. But once the taxpayer has met its obligation to produce credible evidence to support its position, the government then must counter with evidence of its own or risk losing the case under the burden of persuasion.

Reflecting the modesty of this change is Tax Court Interim Rule 142, which describes the shift in the burden of going forward with the proof once the taxpayer has provided credible evidence to support the taxpayer's position. However, with respect to §7477 Tax Court declaratory judgments regarding valuation, the taxpayer continues to bear the burden of production and of persuasion. It also is well to remember than none of these changes is relevant unless: the taxpayer has met a significant administrative proceeding requirement of producing all information reasonably requested by the government in discovery, the case has gone to court, and the taxpayer falls under a $7 million net worth threshold. This net worth threshold does not apply to estates (*or* to revocable inter vivos trusts that make a §645 election, but only during the period of that election).

PART E.   EFFECT OF STATE LAW

Although federal law imposes wealth transfer taxes on the transfer of interests in property, property interests with minor exceptions (such as United States Savings Bonds and patents) are creatures of state, not federal, law. Therefore, the existence of characteristics specified in federal laws must be determined under state law.

In certain cases, the applicability of state law is clear because the tax statute expressly refers to state law — as, for example, in §2053(a), which provides for deductions from the gross estate of certain debts of the decedent and expenses of the estate "allowable by the laws of the jurisdiction . . . under which the estate is being administered."

In other instances, federal law appears to displace state law by providing a uniform federal definition for a term that also is defined by state law — as, for example, §§2041(b) and 2514(c), defining a "general power of appointment," or §§2518(b) and 2046, defining "disclaimers." Even in these instances, however, state law may determine the presence or absence of elements contained in the federal definition.

Frequently federal law is silent on the relevance of state law. In these cases, the tax administrator, taxpayers' representatives, and the federal courts have looked to state law to determine the existence of requisite characteristics simply because there is no other governing law. See Gallagher v. Smith, 223 F.2d 218 (3d Cir. 1955).

Once the question of state law has been identified, it becomes necessary to examine the statutes and the cases of the governing jurisdiction. In the absence of an applicable case or statute, federal courts will attempt to determine what the highest state court would decide, using the doctrines of Erie Railroad v. Tompkins, 304 U.S. 64 (1938), and Klaxon Co. v. Stentor Electric Manufacturing Co., 313 U.S. 487 (1941). Occasionally, in an estate tax case, the estate or its beneficiaries adjudicate a state law question in a state court prior to the final federal determination. Prior to the Supreme Court's *Bosch* decision below, the general rule was that an adjudication on the merits by the state court was binding for federal estate tax purposes if the state court proceeding was free of "collusion." Blair v. Commissioner, 300 U.S. 5 (1937); Freuler v. Helvering, 291 U.S. 35 (1934). *Bosch* changed all that.

Commissioner v. Estate of Bosch
387 U.S. 456 (1967)

Mr. Justice CLARK delivered the opinion of the court.

These two federal estate tax cases present a common issue for our determination. Whether a federal court or agency in a federal estate tax controversy is conclusively bound by a state trial court adjudication of property rights or characterization of property interests when the United States is not made a party to such proceeding.

In No. 673, Commissioner of Internal Revenue v. Estate of Bosch, 363 F.2d 1009, the Court of Appeals for the Second Circuit held that since the state trial court had "authoritatively determined" the rights of the parties, it was not required to delve into the correctness of that state court decree. In No. 240, Second National Bank of New Haven, Executor v. United States, 351 F.2d 489, another panel of the same Circuit held that the "decrees of the Connecticut Probate Court . . . under no circumstances can be construed as binding" on a federal court in subsequent litigation involving federal revenue laws. Whether these cases conflict in principle or not, which is disputed here, there does exist a widespread conflict among the circuits[15] over the question and we granted certiorari to resolve it. We hold that where the federal estate tax liability turns upon the character of a property interest held and transferred by the decedent under state law, federal authorities are not bound by the determination made of such property interest by a state trial court.

(A) NO. 673, COMMISSIONER V. ESTATE OF BOSCH. In 1930, decedent, a resident of New York created a revocable trust which,

---

15.   Illustrative of the conflict among the circuits are: Gallagher v. Smith, 223 F.2d 218 (3d Cir. 1955); Estate of Faulkerson v. United States, 301 F.2d 231 (7th Cir. 1962); Estate of Pierpont v. Commissioner, 336 F.2d 277 (4th Cir. 1964).

as amended in 1931, provided that the income from the corpus was to be paid to his wife during her lifetime. The instrument also gave her a general power of appointment, in default of which it provided that half of the corpus was to go to his heirs and the remaining half was to go to those of his wife. In 1951 the wife executed an instrument purporting to release the general power of appointment and convert it into a special power. Upon decedent's death in 1957, respondent, in paying federal estate taxes, claimed a marital deduction for the value of the widow's trust. The Commissioner determined, however, that the trust corpus did not qualify for the deduction under §2056(b)(5) and levied a deficiency. Respondent then filed a petition for redetermination in the Tax Court. The ultimate outcome of the controversy hinged on whether the release executed by Mrs. Bosch in 1951 was invalid — as she claimed it to be — in which case . . . the trust would therefore qualify for the marital deduction. While the Tax Court proceeding was pending, the respondent filed a petition in the Supreme Court of New York for settlement of the trustee's account; it also sought a determination as to the validity of the release under state law. The Tax Court, with the Commissioner's consent, abstained from making its decision pending the outcome of the state court action. The state court found the release to be a nullity; the Tax Court then accepted the state court judgment as being an "authoritative exposition of New York law and adjudication of the property rights involved," 43 T.C. 120, 124, and permitted the deduction. On appeal, a divided Court of Appeals affirmed. It held that "[t]he issue is . . . not whether the federal court is 'bound by' the decision of the state tribunal, but whether or not a state tribunal has authoritatively determined the rights under state law of a party to the federal action." 363 F.2d at 1013. The court concluded that the "New York judgment, rendered by a court which had jurisdiction over parties and subject matter, authoritatively settled the rights of the parties, not only for New York, but also for purposes of the application to those rights of the relevant provisions of federal tax law." Id. at 1014. It declared that since the state court had held the wife to have a general power of appointment under its law, the corpus of the trust qualified for the marital deduction. We do not agree and reverse.

(B) NO. 240, SECOND NATIONAL BANK OF NEW HAVEN V. UNITED STATES. [Because No. 240 presented essentially the same legal question, its facts are omitted.] The problem of what effect must be given a state trial court decree where the matter decided there is determinative of federal estate tax consequences has long burdened the Bar and the courts. This Court has not addressed itself to the problem for nearly a third of a century. In Freuler v. Helvering,

291 U.S. 35 (1934), this Court, declining to find collusion between the parties on the record as presented there, held that a prior in personam judgment in the state court to which the United States was not made a party, "[o]bviously . . . had not the effect of res judicata, and could not furnish the basis for invocation of the full faith and credit clause. . . ." Id. at 43. In *Freuler's* wake, at least three positions have emerged among the circuits. The first of these holds that ". . . if the question at issue is fairly presented to the state court for its independent decision and is so decided by the court the resulting judgment if binding upon the parties under the state law is conclusive as to their property rights in the federal tax case. . . ." Gallagher v. Smith, 223 F.2d 218, 225 (3d Cir. 1955).

The opposite view is expressed in Faulkerson's Estate v. United States, 301 F.2d 231 (7th Cir. 1962). This view seems to approach that of Erie R. Co. v. Tompkins, 304 U.S. 64 (1938), in that the federal court will consider itself bound by the state court decree only after independent examination of the state law as determined by the highest court of the State. The government urges that an intermediate position be adopted; it suggests that a state trial court adjudication is binding in such cases only when the judgment is the result of an adversary proceeding in the state court. Estate of Pierpont v. Commissioner, 336 F.2d 277 (4th cir. 1964). Also see the dissent of Friendly, J., in *Bosch*, No. 673.

We look at the problem differently. First, the Commissioner was not made a party to either of the state proceedings here and neither had the effect of res judicata; nor did the principle of collateral estoppel apply. It can hardly be denied that both state proceedings were brought for the purpose of directly affecting federal estate tax liability. Next, it must be remembered that it was a federal taxing statute that the Congress enacted and upon which we are here passing. Therefore, in construing it, we must look to the legislative history surrounding it. We find that the report of the Senate Finance Committee recommending enactment of the marital deduction used very guarded language in referring to the very question involved here. It said that "proper regard," not finality, "should be given to interpretations of the will" by state courts and then only when entered by a court "in a bona fide adversary proceeding." S. Rep. No. 1013, Pt. 2, 80th Cong., 2d Sess. 4 (1948). We cannot say that the authors of this directive intended that the decrees of state trial courts were to be conclusive and binding on the computation of the federal estate tax as levied by the Congress. If the Congress had intended state trial court determinations to have that effect on the federal actions, it certainly would have said so — which it did not do. On the contrary, we believe it intended the marital deduction to be strictly construed and applied. Not only did it indicate that only "proper regard" was to be accorded state decrees but it placed specific limitations on the allowance of the deduction as set out in §§2056(b), (c), and (d). These restrictive limitations clearly indicate the great care that Congress exercised in the drawing of the Act and indicate also a definite concern with the elimination of loopholes and escape hatches that might jeopardize the federal revenue. This also is in keeping with the long-established policy of the Congress, as expressed in the Rules of Decision Act, 28 U.S.C. §1652. There it is provided that in the absence of federal requirements such as the Constitution or Acts of Congress, the "laws of the several states . . . shall be regarded as rules of decision in civil actions in the courts of the United States, in cases where they apply." This Court has held that judicial decisions are "laws of the . . . state" within the section. Moreover, even in diversity cases this Court has further held that while the decrees of "lower state courts" should be "attributed some weight . . . the decision [is] not controlling . . ." where the highest court of the State has not spoken on the point. And in West v. A.T. & T. Co., 311 U.S. 223 (1940), this Court further held that "an intermediate appellate state court . . . is a datum for ascertaining state law which is not to be disregarded by a federal court *unless it is convinced by other persuasive data that the highest court of the state would decide otherwise.*" Id. at 237 (emphasis supplied). Thus, under some conditions, federal authority may not be bound even by an intermediate state appellate court ruling. It follows here then, that when the application of a federal statute is involved, the decision of a state trial court as to an underlying issue of state law should a fortiori not be controlling. This is but an application of the rule of Erie R. Co. v. Tompkins, where state law as announced by the highest court of the State is to be followed. This is not a diversity case but the same principle may be applied for the same reasons, viz., the underlying substantive rule involved is based on state law and the State's highest court is the best authority on its own law. If there be no decision by that court then federal authorities must apply what they find to be the state law after giving "proper regard" to relevant rulings of other courts of the State. In this respect, it may be said to be, in effect, sitting as a state court.

We believe that this would avoid much of the uncertainty that would result from the "non-adversary" approach and at the same time would be fair to the taxpayer and protect the federal revenue as well.

The judgment in No. 240 is therefore affirmed while that in No. 673 is reversed and remanded for further proceedings not inconsistent with this opinion.

It is so ordered.

[The dissenting opinions of Mr. Justice DOUGLAS, Mr. Justice HARLAN, and Mr. Justice FORTAS are omitted.]

Bosch is not limited to marital deduction issues. Although the majority opinion in *Bosch* relied on the legislative history of the marital deduction in reaching its decision, the *Bosch* rule has been applied by lower federal courts to other tax matters. See Verbit, *State Court Decisions in Federal Transfer Tax Litigation:* Bosch *Revisited*, 23 REAL PROP., PROB. & TRUST J. 407 (1988); Wolfman, Bosch, *Its Implications and Aftermath: The Effect of State Court Adjudications on Federal Tax Litigation*, 3 U. MIAMI INST. EST. PLAN. Ch. 2 (1969). In United States v. White, 853 F.2d 107 (2d Cir. 1988), the court relied on *Bosch* for the proposition that the government is not bound by a state court decree approving expenses of administering a decedent's estate for purposes of deducting those expenses from the decedent's gross estate under §2053.

7.   *Government's Interpretation of* Bosch. In Rev. Rul. 69-285, the government interpreted the *Bosch* decision as follows:

A state court decree is considered to be conclusive in the determination of the Federal tax liability of an estate only to the extent that it determines property rights, and if the issuing court is the highest court in the state.

Is this what *Bosch* held? See if you can determine from what part of the *Bosch* opinion the government derived the requirement that a decision of the highest court of the state is controlling only if the decision "determines property rights."

In Warner v. Trust Co. Bank, 296 S.E.2d 353 (Ga. 1962), the Supreme Court of Georgia construed an ambiguous trust document created by the decedent's predeceased wife as not conferring an inter vivos general power of appointment on the decedent.[16] In TAM 8346008, the government ruled

---

16.   RESTATEMENT (THIRD) — PROPERTY (Wills and Other Donative Transfers) §11.3 (Tent. Draft No. 1, approved by the American Law Institute on May 16, 1995), provides a list of constructional preferences for resolving ambiguities in wills and other donative documents. One of those preferences is for "the construction that gives more favorable tax consequences than other plausible constructions." See also Putnam v. Putnam, 316 N.E.2d 729, 737 (Mass. 1974), in which the court said that "[i]t would be a rare case in which a conflict of terms or an ambiguity in a will should be resolved by attributing to the testator

that it was not bound by and need not give any weight to *Warner*. The reason given was that *Warner* did not determine property rights because, as the decedent was dead, the question of the extent of the decedent's power during life was moot. In ruling that *Warner* was not controlling for federal estate tax purposes, the government explained its interpretation of *Bosch* more fully:

[Under *Bosch*, the state decision must "determine property rights"] because the Court specifically said the question before it was "whether a federal court or agency in a federal estate tax controversy is conclusively bound by a state trial court's *adjudication of property rights or characterization of property interests*" (emphasis added). The Court's drafting of the issue in this fashion clearly indicated to the Service the Court's acceptance of the federal court's position "that state judgments must deal with property rights and have some effect under state law before they are binding on subsequent tax litigation." *Lanigan v. Commissioner*, 45 T.C. 247 (1965). See also Stansbury v. United States, 82-1 U.S. Tax Cas. (CCH) ¶13,469 (N.D. Ill. 1982), where the court similarly interpreted *Bosch*.

The estate tax case at issue in this TAM was not the *Warner* case itself, but a substantially similar case. The government had previously ruled that *Warner* was not controlling for federal estate tax purposes in the *Warner* case itself. See TAM 8339004.

8.   *Reformation and Modifications of Donative Documents by State Courts.* It is a well-established principle of state law, recognized by numerous state supreme court decisions, that inter vivos trusts (and other documents effecting gratuitous inter vivos transfers) can be reformed on a proper showing that the terms of the transfer were the product of mistake, including a mistake regarding the tax consequences of the transfer. See 4 Palmer, THE LAW OF RESTITUTION ch. 18 (esp. §§18.6, 18.7) (1978).

Both the RESTATEMENT (SECOND) OF PROPERTY (Donative Transfers) §34.7 and Comment *d* (1992) and the RESTATEMENT (THIRD) — PROPERTY (Wills and Other Donative Transfers) §12.1 (Tent. Draft No. 1, approved by the American Law Institute on May 16, 1995) extend the reformation

---

an intention which as a practical matter is likely to benefit the taxing authorities and no one else." Similarly, in Estate of Branigan, 609 A.2d 431, 437 (N.J. 1992), the court said that "the doctrine of probable intent reasonably assumes, in its several possible applications, a widely-accepted intent on the part of most testators to save taxes. The basic principle underlying the doctrine of probable intent is that it is reasonable to impute to the decedent a general intent that reflects 'impulses . . . common to human nature.'" Authority authorizing reformation for tax minimization purposes is compiled in 1 Casner & Pennell, ESTATE PLANNING §4.1.1 n.5.1 (2002).

remedy to wills. The RESTATEMENT (THIRD) §12.2 adds a provision authorizing state courts to modify donative documents if they fail to achieve the donor's tax objectives, but only on a showing of a "reasonable prospect that the proposed modification will be effective for federal tax purposes." Id. §12.2 Comment d.

9.   *Action Before the Fact.* Unlike most state court determinations, which occur after a taxable event, the following Ruling illustrates how a taxpayer may effect a change that will bind future tax consequences. Consider whether any tax consequences flow from the taxpayer's action.

Revenue Ruling 73-142

Advice has been requested whether the value of certain property transferred in trust by the grantor-decedent is includible in his gross estate under §2036 or §2038 of the Internal Revenue Code of 1954, under the circumstances described below.

The decedent made substantial gifts of property in trust for the benefit of his wife and children. Under the terms of the trust instrument, the decedent reserved the unrestricted power to remove or discharge the trustee at any time and appoint a new trustee, with no express limitation on so appointing himself. The trustee was given unrestricted power to withhold distribution of income or principal and to apportion between income and principal notwithstanding any rules of law to the contrary. In 1965, in a non-adversary action in which the decedent was petitioner, a lower state court construed the trust instrument to mean that the decedent had reserved the right to remove and appoint a trustee only once; that this power did not include the right to appoint himself; and that once having exercised that power, decedent would have exhausted his reserved powers. The decedent, subsequent to the decree, did remove the original trustee and appoint another (not himself) so that under the interpretation of the court he no longer had such a right as of the date of his death in 1970. It appears that the decree is contrary to the decisions of the highest court of the state.

In light of the holding in Commissioner v. Estate of Bosch, 387 U.S. 456 (1967), the specific question asked is the effect to be given the above-mentioned court decree in determining the estate tax consequences of the trust. . . .

If the decedent reserved the unrestricted power to remove or discharge a trustee at any time and appoint himself as trustee, the decedent is considered as having the powers of the trustee. Treas. Reg. §§20.2036-1(b)(3), 20.2038-1(a)(3).

In *Bosch* the Supreme Court of the United States held that where the Federal estate tax liability turns upon the character of a property interest held and transferred under state law, federal authorities are not bound by a determination made of such property interest by a state trial court. Recognizing that state law as announced by the highest court of the state is to be followed, the Court held that, where there is no decision by the highest court, the federal court must apply what it finds state law to be, after giving proper regard to decisions of other courts of the state.

A close reading of the *Bosch* decision discloses that it does not in any way indicate that a lower court decree that is inconsistent with the ruling by the state's highest court on the particular issue is void as between the parties to the action. The problem involved in *Bosch* concerns the effect to be given such lower court decree where the same issue is critical in the determination of a Federal tax question. The Court concluded that "federal authorities are not bound" by a determination of a property interest by a state trial court. This does not mean that the parties to the state court action are not bound by the decree.

In this case the lower court had jurisdiction over the parties and over the subject matter of the proceeding. Thus, the time for appeal having elapsed, its judgment is final and conclusive as to those parties, regardless of how erroneous the court's application of the state law may have been. Consequently, after the time for appeal had expired, the grantor-decedent did not have the power to appoint himself as successor trustee. The aforesaid rights and powers which would otherwise have brought the value of the trust corpus within the provisions of sections 2036 and 2038 of the Code were thus effectively cut off before his death.

Unlike the situation in *Bosch*, the decree in this case was handed down before the time of the event giving rise to the tax (that is, the date of the grantor's death). Thus, while the decree would not be binding on the government as to questions relating to the grantor's power to appoint himself as trustee prior to the date of the decree, it is controlling after such date since the decree, in and of itself, effectively extinguished the power. In other words, while there may have been a question whether the grantor had such power prior to the decree, there is no question that he did not have the power thereafter.

Accordingly, it is held that the value of the property transferred to the inter vivos trust is not includible in the grantor-decedent's gross estate under §2036 or §2038 of the Code.

Chapter 2

PROPERTY OWNED AT DEATH AND VALUATION PRINCIPLES

PART A.   INCLUSION IN THE GROSS ESTATE

Code Reference: *Estate Tax: §2033*

1.   *Probate Estate.*   A decedent's probate estate consists of property owned *at death*. Probate property is subject to the decedent's debts (including taxes), funeral expenses, and expenses of administering the estate, to various local law family allowances, and possibly to dower or the forced share of a surviving spouse. The balance (residue) passes to the decedent's testamentary devisees or intestate heirs.

From inception of the federal estate tax in 1916, a decedent's probate estate has been the core item in the gross estate. The provision requiring inclusion of the probate estate (now §2033) has undergone little change since 1916.[1]

---

1.   The original version was narrower than the present §2033, limiting inclusion to "all property, real or personal, tangible or intangible, wherever situated," but only to the extent the decedent's interest was (1) subject to the payment of debts and administration expenses and (2) to distribution as part of the decedent's estate. Revenue Act of 1916, 39 Stat. 756, 777. The two limitations were deleted in 1926, essentially bringing §2033 to its current form and increasing the "certainty . . . that the gross estate shall include the entire interest of the decedent at the time of his death in all the property." H.R. Rep. No. 1, 69th Cong., 1st Sess. 15 (1925), in 1939-1 C.B. (pt. 2) 315, 325.

This expansion of §2033 was important because, in several states, real property owned by a decedent at death was not subject to payment of administration expenses. Crooks v. Harrelson, 282 U.S. 55 (1930), ultimately held that real property in those states was not included in the gross estate under the original version of §2033.

Section 2033 was amended in 1962 to delete the then-existing exclusion of real property situated outside the United States. This deletion was precipitated by adoption of the §2014 credit against the estate tax for foreign death taxes. Because the credit diminished the potential for double taxation of property subject to foreign death taxes, the

Household Goods and Clothing. The Internal Revenue Service's Audit Technique Handbook for Estate Tax Examiners ¶(11)00 states that examiners should expect to see household goods reported on almost every estate tax return. On valuation, the Handbook provides:

There are numerous techniques which are useful in determining whether household goods are properly reflected in the estate tax return. . . . :

(a)   examiner's knowledge of decedent's social standing in the community;

(b)   inspection of the residence and its furnishings, if still intact and undistributed;

(c)   submitted appraisals;

(d)   personal property tax assessment sheets in States having a personal property tax;

(e)   inspection of insurance policies covering household goods, including endorsements for valuable items (this may give an indication of total value);

(f)   canceled checks made in payment of household furnishings (this technique may be employed in cases where inspection of canceled checks for several years is being made in connection with some other issue in the return, as, for example, the amount of adjusted taxable gifts. These records may also disclose insurance policies for tangible personal property not listed on the household goods policy);

(g)   if household furnishings have been sold, a complete listing with sale prices will usually be obtainable;

(h)   decedent's home and furnishings may have been described and photographed in a . . . magazine or . . . local newspaper;

(i)   decedent's will may mention specific items of household goods, such as antique furniture, objects of art, silverware, etc.;

(j)   probate court files may disclose a complete list of household goods;

(k)   the decedent's forms 1040 may disclose gifts to charity of valuable personal property, such as antique furniture, indicating the type of assets which the decedent should have owned at death;

---

exclusion was eliminated because it had encouraged investment in real estate located in countries that imposed lower death taxes than the United States. See S. Rep. No. 1881, 87th Cong., 2d Sess. 117 (1962), in 1962-3 C.B. (pt. 3) 707, 823.

(l)   the beneficiaries of the decedent's estate may have taken substantial charitable deductions for the contribution to charity of decedent's personal effects, even though those items were returned at nominal estate tax values. In such situations, appropriate adjustments should be made . . . .

With respect to clothing, the Handbook takes a more lenient approach:

(1)   The clothing which the decedent owned at death usually does not have a "fair market value" of any particular significance. You should not be overly concerned if such utilitarian personal effects are returned at very nominal values or, indeed, if they are not separately mentioned at all on Schedule F. There is little to be gained by inquiring into such items; on the contrary, needless antagonism may be generated by such personal probes.

(2)   There are exceptions, of course. For example, . . . [u]nreported items may be disclosed by inspection of the homeowner's insurance policies for a specific endorsement, and inspection of the cancelled checks for payments relating to purchases, repairs or storage. In any event, . . . the examiner must exercise judgment and maintain a sense of propriety. . . .

    Property Owned, But Not Beneficially.   Section 2033 includes in the gross estate property *beneficially* owned by the decedent at death. Treas. Reg. §20.2033-1(a). Ordinarily property that is titled in the decedent's name is owned beneficially, but the title is not conclusive. Sometimes a decedent may hold title to property but not be its beneficial owner. A trustee, for example, holds legal but not beneficial title to trust property; consequently, trust property normally is not §2033 includible in a trustee's gross estate. Similarly, a purchase-money resulting trust arises by operation of law if a person purchases property with someone else's money. If it can be shown that the payment was not a loan to the purchaser, was not made in discharge of a debt owed to the purchaser, and was not a gift to the purchaser, then a resulting trust may exist in favor of the person who supplied the money for the purchase. See RESTATEMENT (SECOND) OF TRUSTS §§440-460 (1959). Property titled in the decedent's name is not includible in the decedent's gross estate to the extent state law recognizes such a resulting trust against the decedent. Rev. Rul. 78-214.

    Effect of "Tax-Exempt" Status on Inclusion.   Certain properties, or their income streams, are "tax-exempt." The income tax-exempt status of such items does not immunize them from inclusion in a decedent's gross estate because, as stated in Treas. Reg. §20.2033-1(a), the estate tax "is an excise tax on the transfer of property at death and is not a tax on the property transferred." United States v. Wells Fargo Bank, 485 U.S. 351

(1988) ("project notes" were not exempt from wealth transfer tax notwithstanding language of a statute stating that they "shall be exempt from all taxation now or hereafter imposed by the United States"); United States Trust Co. v. Helvering, 307 U.S. 57 (1939) (war risk life insurance); Greiner v. Lewellyn, 258 U.S. 384 (1922) (municipal bonds); Rev. Rul. 81-63 (state public housing agency bonds); Rev. Rul. 60-70 (certain lump sum payments under the Railroad Retirement Act of 1937); Rev. Rul. 55-622 (life insurance payable under the World War Veterans Act of 1924 and various similar Acts).

Illustration. *D* died, survived by *B*, who died six weeks later, before *D*'s will was offered for probate. *D*'s will bequeathed $100,000 to *B* and further provided that, if *B* predeceased *D*, the $100,000 bequest should go to *X*. Is there any reason to suggest that the $100,000 bequest should not be includible in *B*'s gross estate under §2033? See Price v. United States, 610 F.2d 383 (5th Cir. 1980), *aff'g per curiam* 470 F. Supp. 136 (N.D. Tex. 1979). *B*'s personal representative might prevent inclusion by filing a "qualified disclaimer" pursuant to §§2046 and 2518. In some but not all states a personal representative is authorized to disclaim bequests on behalf of a decedent. Compare Estate of Hoenig v. Commissioner, 66 T.C. 471 (1976), *acq.*, and Estate of Dreyer v. Commissioner, 68 T.C. 275 (1977), *acq.*, with Detroit Bank & Trust Co. v. United States, 80-2 U.S. Tax Cas. (CCH) ¶13,382 (E.D. Mich. 1980) (all three decisions were rendered under pre-1982 law), and see the 1990 version of Uniform Probate Code §2-801(a). Added in 1981 to eliminate a requirement that a disclaimer had to be valid under state law to be effective for estate and gift tax purposes, §2518(c)(3) (which applies to the estate tax under §2046) is satisfied if a timely "written transfer of the transferor's entire interest in the property" is made to a person who would have received the property if a qualified disclaimer had been made. This amendment to §2518 may make it easier for *B*'s personal representative to avoid inclusion of *D*'s bequest in *B*'s gross estate. Otherwise, we will see in Chapter 13 that the §2013 previously taxed property credit will mitigate the double tax consequences of inclusion in *D*'s estate followed almost immediately by inclusion in *B*'s estate.

2.   *Property Interests Expiring at Death.* Property interests that expire because the decedent dies are not includible in the gross estate under §2033. As the Commissioner ruled in Rev. Rul. 75-145, "[s]ection 2033 does not embrace interests held by the decedent during his life but which terminate on his death. . . . The decedent must at the time of his death possess rights that he can transmit to a survivor." Consider how the principle of Rev. Rul. 75-145 applies in the following examples, in which *D*'s mother, *M*, a widow, bequeathed the residue of her estate in trust. The full value of this trust property was included in *M*'s gross estate under §2033. *D*, her only child, was 58 years old when *M* died. *D* received the income from *M*'s trust for life and at *D*'s death the trust property was delivered to *D*'s then living children in equal shares.

(a) The income paid to *D* increased *D*'s includible net worth when *D* died, but none of the trust corpus divided among *D*'s surviving children is includible in *D*'s gross estate. How would this result differ if *D* had died with no living children? Consider what else D owned in this trust.

(b) *D* had three children, *A*, *B*, and *C*, all of whom were living at *M*'s death. *A*, however, predeceased *D*; *B* and *C* survived *D*. No part of the value of any portion of the trust is includible in *A*'s gross estate, because of the condition of survivorship that made *A*'s interest contingent. See Commissioner v. Rosser, 64 F.2d 631 (3d Cir. 1933); Estate of Field v. Commissioner, 22 B.T.A. 915 (1931).

(c) Assume that, instead of a life estate of the "normal" variety (measured by the life of the income beneficiary), *D* had a life estate per autre vie, to receive the income from *M*'s trust for the life of *X*; at *X*'s death the trust principle is to be delivered to *D*'s children in equal shares. How would you value the interest includible in *D*'s estate if *X* (age 50) was still living?

(d) What if *D* was to receive the income from *M*'s trust for *D*'s life and at *D*'s death the trust property is to be delivered to *A* if then living, otherwise to *B*. When *B* died, *D* (age 70) and *A* (age 42) were still living. The value of *B*'s interest in the trust is includible in *B*'s gross estate; what is that interest and how would you *value* it? Consider the deferred payment of estate tax permitted by §6163; why is this provision necessary? More importantly, consider the significance of the drafting of these interests and whether a good planner would have done this differently.

In Rev. Rul. 76-472, the government gave the following guidance on the inclusion and valuation of contingent future interests in the owner's gross estate:

> In general, future interests in property that a decedent owns at death are taxed just as possessory interests. Thus, the value of a vested remainder interest is includible in the value of a remainderman's gross estate under §2033 of the Code even though the remainderman dies before obtaining possession of the property. See Frazer v. Commissioner, 6 T.C. 1255 (1946), *aff'd*, 162 F.2d 167 (3d Cir. 1947); Utley v. United States, 290 F.2d 188 (9th Cir. 1961). If the decedent's vested remainder interest is to take effect upon the termination of the life estate of another, the present value of the decedent's interest is ordinarily ascertainable by use of the actuarial formula set forth in . . . the regulations. However, if the amount of decedent's interest is subject to possible future diminution by reason of the occurrence or nonoccurrence of a contingency, the valuation of such interest does not always lend itself to mere mechanical application of actuarial formulas. See Rev. Rul. 61-88, 1961-1 C.B. 417.

In the instant case the decedent's remainder interest is subject to being diminished by either the birth or adoption of children by *M* [age 53]. To properly reflect either one of these possible contingencies, the remainder interest should be valued in accordance with the general rules for the valuation of property set forth in Treas. Reg. §20.2031-1(b). See Rev. Rul. 67-370, 1967-2 C.B. 324; Rev. Rul. 61-88, 1961-1 C.B. 417.

In making the valuation, the actuarial value of the decedent's remainder interest, ascertained by the formula set forth in . . . the regulations, should be the starting point. Consideration should then be given to all known facts and circumstances that might tend to decrease such value, with due regard for (1) the certainty that a woman who has reached the age of 53 years will not bear children is far greater than that which attends most other human affairs and (2) the unlikelihood that a woman of that age will adopt a child.

Debts Owed to a Decedent.   Debts owed to a decedent are probate assets. Consider the result, however, if the debt is forgiven or canceled at death. For example, assume that *Y* purchased property from *D*, giving *D* an unsecured $10,000 promissory note. At *D*'s death two years later, *Y* owed *D* the full $10,000 plus unpaid interest of $1,200. *D*'s will forgave *Y*'s debt (principal and interest), which was thereby canceled. Were the estate tax consequences the same as in the following case?[2] If not, how do these situations differ? Cf. Estate of Buckwalter v. Commissioner, 46 T.C. 805 (1966).

Estate of Moss v. Commissioner
74 T.C. 1239 (1980), *acq. in result only*

[The Commissioner determined a deficiency in the taxpayer's (petitioner) estate tax on the ground that promissory notes (self-canceling installment notes — SCINs) held by the decedent prior to death but that were extinguished by their own terms on the decedent's death before full payment were includible in the decedent's gross estate.]

---

2.   For income tax purposes, TAM 9240003 stated that *Y* does not have discharge of indebtedness income under §61(a)(12) because *D*'s cancellation qualified for the gift exception. In Frane v. Commissioner, 998 F.2d 567 (8th Cir. 1993), the decedent held an installment note at death on which he had reported income on the installment method. Because the terms of the installment note cancelled it on the decedent's death, the court held that any income that had been deferred by the installment method (in that case it was capital gain being reported in installments as the notes were paid) was taxable under §§453B and 691(a)(5) in the estate's first income tax year.

Because the cancellation of *Y*'s debt was testamentary (as contrasted to a self-executing cancellation), any unrecognized income will be included in the gross income of *D*'s estate.

IRWIN, J. We must first decide whether the promissory notes which were extinguished upon decedent's death are includible in his gross estate.

. . .

Section 2033 . . . provides that "the value of the gross estate shall include the value of all property to the extent of the interest therein of the decedent at the time of his death." There is no requirement under §2033 that the property interest be subject to the payment of charges against the estate and expenses of administration or that the interest be subject to distribution as a part of the estate. Therefore, although the facts in *Austin* [*v. Commissioner*, 26 B.T.A. 1216 (1932)] may be indistinguishable, it is no longer authority for the proposition for which petitioner cites it. There is language in the decision, however, which although dicta supports petitioner's position; the Board stated that "the situation here is somewhat like that of an interest or estate limited for the life of the decedent."

In *Estate of Buckwalter v. Commissioner*, 46 T.C. 805 (1966), decedent's son was indebted to a bank on a 20-year note due in 1971 bearing 4.5% interest. Decedent proposed that he and his son enter into an arrangement whereby decedent would pay off the unamortized principal of his son's note on December 31, 1954. The son would pay him the identical monthly amounts which would have been due the bank, except that interest would be computed at 2.5% so that the entire loan would be repaid in 1968 rather than in 1971. The son was instructed to keep the transaction secret, the payments were to be a "matter of honor" and the decedent stated that it was [his] intention not to show "in any way that [the son was] in any way indebted to me, otherwise [decedent] would be required to pay in Penna. a personal property tax each year." Decedent recognized that he probably would not be alive at the end of the amortization period, and stated that his son was to be entirely free of any obligation to his estate. He added a long postscript to the letter setting forth a summary schedule of 30-day payments, showing components of interest and principal in each such payment in December of each year as well as "balance of amortized principal" until final payment in 1968. He also stated that his son might "cut away" the schedule and "destroy the rest of the letter after all details are consummated."

In a second letter to his son about a week later, after the proposal had been accepted, decedent stated that he was sending his son a schedule for payments and credits for the period January 1, 1955, to May 23, 1962, and that for the period thereafter he had "a schedule made up to show complete amortization of an honor loan," which he intended to seal and enclose in his lock box with a legend on the envelope in his son's handwriting reading "Personal Property of Abraham L. Buckwalter, Jr." In a single sentence, decedent informed his son that he could "consider the proposition on my part as a form of annuity at 2 and ½%."

We held that decedent had an interest in a debt owed to him by his son at the time of his death and that the unpaid principal was includable in his gross estate under §2033. The taxpayer there argued that in substance, decedent merely had purchased an annuity from his son which terminated with his death, and therefore, nothing should be included in his gross estate. We disagreed with the contention that the substance of the transaction was an annuity and held that decedent had an interest in the loan at the time of his death.

Respondent contends that decedent, in this case, simply chose to pass the funeral home business to his employees under the guise of the notes which were canceled upon death rather than through his will as he had planned prior to 1972 and, therefore, this case is no different than the situation in *Buckwalter*.

Petitioner argues that the case at bar is factually distinguishable. We agree. In *Buckwalter*, the decedent retained control of the entire debt until his death. The son was not relieved of the debt until he removed the evidence of the loan after the decedent's death. Therefore, at any time prior to his death, decedent could have revoked his decision to cancel the debt at his death and required the son to be obligated to his estate. The decedent sought to achieve the same result as a bequest in a will by keeping the details of the loan contained in a sealed envelope in his own lock box and permitting the son to cancel the debt at his death.

This is not the case here. The parties have stipulated that decedent's sale of stock for which the notes were issued was a bona fide sale for adequate and full consideration. The cancellation provision was part of the bargained for consideration provided by decedent for the purchase price of the stock. As such, it was an integral provision of the note. We do not have a situation, therefore, where the payee provided in his will or endorses or attaches a statement to a note stating that the payor is to be given a gift by the cancellation of his obligation on the payee's death.

We believe there are significant differences between the situation in which a note contains a cancellation provision as part of the terms agreed upon for its issue and where a debt is canceled in a will. The most significant difference for purposes of the estate tax is, as petitioner points out, that a person can unilaterally revoke a will during his lifetime and, therefore, direct the transfer of his property, at his death. All interest that decedent had in the notes lapsed at his death.

. . .

We agree, therefore, with the statement in *Austin* that the situation here is analogous to that of an annuity or an interest or estate limited for decedent's life. Since there is not [sic] interest remaining in decedent at his death, we hold that the notes are not includable in his gross estate.

Valuing a Self-Canceling Feature. An issue of some challenge is how the proper premium for a self-canceling feature should be determined. Consider that a self-canceling installment note may be viewed as a normal installment note with an added premium to cover the contingency of the holder's death before full payment. That premium essentially finances private, decreasing-term life insurance that pays when the holder dies; in effect, proceeds equal to the outstanding installments are received and then used immediately by the debtor to pay those outstanding installments. Under such an analogy, the taxable event occurs as of (or perhaps immediately after) the holder's death. For estate tax purposes, the holder's estate has a wash because the estate's right to a deemed payment of the outstanding installments is includible in the gross estate, but that amount is offset by a §2053 deduction for the holder's obligation to pay the insurance proceeds to the debtor. If the premium charged for the self-canceling feature was determined properly, it should constitute full and adequate consideration for the obligation and should support the estate tax deduction. How would you ascertain the amount of the proper premium?

After-Acquired Property. *A*'s will bequeathed $50,000 to "*B* or *B*'s estate." *B* died testate in July, leaving the residue of *B*'s estate to *X*. *A* died two months after *B*. Although local law varies on these points, assume that *A*'s bequest became part of *B*'s probate estate and that it passed to *X* under *B*'s residuary provision. For a discussion of such matters from a property law standpoint, see generally Browder, *Trusts and the Doctrine of Estates*, 72 MICH. L. REV. 1509, 1520-1522 (1974).

The $50,000 subject of the bequest was includible in *A*'s gross estate. The question whether it also is includible in *B*'s gross estate is partially addressed by Rev. Rul. 65-217, below. Consider again the §2013 previously taxed property credit if it is includible.

Revenue Ruling 65-217

Advice has been requested whether Federal . . . estate taxes are imposed (1) upon bonuses awarded under a corporation's bonus plan to a decedent employed before his death but paid thereafter, and (2) upon bonuses awarded after his death.

The employer corporation established a bonus plan to provide incentive and awards to employees who contribute to the success of the corporation. The decedent was an employee of the corporation at the time of his death. Control of the plan is vested in a Bonus and Salary Committee. An employee is eligible for consideration for a bonus if at the end of the year he is receiving a salary at or above the monthly rate as the Committee from year to year determines. Under the terms of the plan, if the amount of the award exceeds $1,000, such award is paid in installments as it is "earned out" by the beneficiary by continuing service with the corporation. A beneficiary whose employment is terminated by dismissal for cause or who voluntarily terminates his employment loses his right to "earn out" the bonus awards unless the Committee decides otherwise. In case of death of a beneficiary during his "earning out" period, his unpaid and undelivered awards are paid and delivered to his legal representative at such times and in such manner as if the beneficiary were living.

The decedent was eligible for bonus awards and, at the time of his death, had been awarded bonuses which were unpaid. Six months after his death, an award was also made for services rendered during the year of his death, such award being payable in installments. . . .

[S]ection 2033 of the Code provides that "the value of the gross estate shall include the value of all property to the extent of the interest therein of the decedent at the time of his death."

. . . In the instant case, the beneficiary had a conditional right to "earn out" the bonuses which had been awarded before death. Death converted the conditional right into an unconditional right to the unpaid portion of such bonuses. Under §2033 of the Code, such unconditional right is property. Consequently, the value of such property is included in the decedent's gross estate under §2033 of the Code.

However, the bonus awarded subsequent to the decedent's death was subject to the control of the Committee which had the absolute discretion to determine who should participate in the awards and the amount of the award each individual should receive. The decedent had no legal right to an award until such action was taken by the Committee.

The bonus awarded subsequent to the death of the decedent is not property in which the decedent had an interest at the time of his death. Consequently, the value of such bonus is not includible in his gross estate under §2033 of the Code. . . .

[The Service also determined that the bonuses awarded to the decedent before his death but payable thereafter, and the bonuses awarded after his death, were "income in respect of a decedent" under §691 and therefore subject to income tax.]

Social Security and Similar Governmental Death Benefits. The Social Security Act provides for a lump sum payment, not to exceed $255, to the surviving spouse of an insured person. In Rev. Rul. 67-277, the government ruled that the value of these death benefits is not included in the insured person's gross estate. The government stated:

Examination of the nature of the payments under that section of the Social Security Act discloses that the decedent had no control over the designation of the beneficiary or the amount of the payment since these are fixed by statute. Furthermore, the decedent had no property interest in the "Federal Old Age and Survivors Insurance Trust Fund" from which the payment is made.

In view of the foregoing, it is held that the lump-sum death payment received by the widow or widower of the deceased . . . does not constitute property of the decedent at the time of his death within the meaning of §2033 of the Internal Revenue Code. Accordingly, the lump-sum death payment to the widow or widower is not includible in the decedent's gross estate for Federal estate tax purposes. Compare Rev. Rul. 66-234, 1966-2 C.B. 436.

Similar rulings include Rev. Rul. 56-637 (worker's compensation awards payable on death to beneficiaries of a deceased employee designated by statute were not includible in the employee's gross estate); Rev. Rul. 69-8 (wrongful death recoveries under the Federal Death on the High Seas Act were not includible in the decedent's gross estate); Rev. Rul. 76-102 (an annuity payable to an employee's surviving spouse under the Federal Coal Mine Health and Safety Act of 1969 was not includible in the employee's gross estate); Rev. Rul. 76-501 (an annuity payable to the decedent's surviving spouse from the Federal Republic of Germany under that nation's Law on Indemnification for National Socialist Injustices was not includible in the decedent's gross estate); Rev. Rul. 79-397 (a death benefit payable under the Public Safety Officers' Benefit Act to the survivor of an officer who died in the line of duty was not includible in the decedent's gross estate); Rev. Rul. 81-182 (the value of monthly benefits payable to a decedent's spouse under the Social Security Act was not includible in the decedent's gross estate). But compare Rev. Rul. 75-505 (half the value of a survivorship annuity payable on the death of a retired state court judge to the decedent's surviving spouse under the Judicial Retirement System of Texas was included in the decedent's gross estate under §2039; the other half of the benefits was not includible because it was attributable to the surviving spouse's own community property interest).

Rev. Rul. 60-70 took the position that death benefits payable under the Railroad Retirement Act of 1937 to beneficiaries designated in the statute are not includible in the employee's gross estate "for the reason that the decedent had no control over the designation of the beneficiary or the amount of such payment, since these are fixed by statute and since the decedent had no property interest in the fund from which such annuity or other payment is made." The Railroad Retirement Act further provides for a lump-sum payment to be paid under certain circumstances to persons designated by the employee. The government's position was that the value of payments made under this latter provision *are* includible in the employee's gross estate under §2033.

Naked Death Benefits.   In Estate of Bogley v. United States, 514 F.2d 1027 (Cl. Ct. 1975), the board of directors of two corporations in which the decedent was a principal shareholder, officer, and director approved on the same date in 1955 nearly identical documents (one a "resolution," the other a "motion") that provided in part that:

in consideration of past services and services to be rendered by [the decedent and other named officers], the Corporation is authorized upon the death of any of these officers to pay their estate or named beneficiary [an amount equal to] the total compensation received by the officer for the past two years prior to his death.

During his life the decedent never designated a beneficiary, and upon his death in 1967 the payments were made to his estate. After an extensive review of the principles of contract law, the court held that the value of these payments was not includible in the decedent's gross estate:

[A]ll we have here in the corporate motion and resolutions were expressions of intention or policy and not offers to [the decedent]. . . . The word "authorized" is a word of permission and not one of obligation in private contracts. . . . It is clear that there was no acceptance by [the decedent] of any offer by [the two corporations] because said corporations made no offers to him. . . . For the foregoing reason, . . . the corporations were not contractually bound to make the described payments.

The board of directors of a third corporation in which the decedent was a principal shareholder, officer, and director passed in 1958 a resolution that provided in part that:

in the event of death of any of the present officers [naming the decedent and others] the surviving widow or estate is to receive [an amount equal to] two years' salary based on amount being paid at time of death. . . . [Such payments] to be covered in part by an insurance policy . . . and expense of same to be borne by the Corporation.

A second resolution was passed by the board about a month later, which in part stated:

Whereas, a question has arisen with respect to the intention of [the previous] resolution . . . pertaining to the payment of two years' salary to the widow or estate of certain of the officers . . . and whereas it is desirable to clarify the fact that such resolution was intended to impose a contractual obligation on the corporation; now, therefore, be it resolved, that [the payments are] in recognition of the past services theretofore rendered to this Corporation by the several said officers, and in consideration of the future services to be rendered by each of them.

The court held that these resolutions constituted offers to the decedent, which he accepted. The resulting contract effected an indirect inter vivos transfer to the decedent's wife, not a testamentary transfer to her. The value of the death benefit therefore was not includible in the decedent's gross estate under §2033.[3]

The inclusion of employee death benefits will be considered in more detail in Chapter 9, when we study §2039. The includibility of employee death benefits, however, is not exclusively governed by §2039, a point that is underscored by *Bogley*. The type of death benefit at issue in *Bogley* often is called a naked death benefit because it is not joined with pension or retirement benefits, and §2039 is not applicable to naked death benefits. In cases in which §2039 or the other "string" provisions (§§2035 through 2038) are not applicable the government has frequently attempted to use §2033 to include the value of such benefits in the employee's gross estate. *Bogley* and other decisions have rejected this approach. Estate of Porter v. Commissioner, 442 F.2d 915 (1st Cir. 1971); Estate of Tully v. United States, reproduced at page 301; Kramer v. United States, reproduced at page 539. In *Tully*, for example, the court said: "[The Commissioner] would use §2033 as a 'catch all.' The simple answer to this is that §2033 is not a 'catch all,' . . . but applies to situations where decedent kept so much control over an item of property that in substance he still owns the

---

3.   The court further held, however, that the value of the death benefit *was* includible in the decedent's gross estate *under §2037*. We will study §2037 in Chapter 5.

property." Instead of urging the application of §2033, the government can rely on other provisions to capture naked death benefits.

Estate of DiMarco v. Commissioner, 87 T.C. 653 (1986), reproduced at page 857, involved a "death benefit only" plan in which a survivors income benefit was payable by the decedent's employer (IBM Corp.) to a beneficiary that the employer designated and over which the decedent had no control. Presumably because the decedent lacked control over the plan at death, the government argued that the decedent made a gift of that benefit during life, but that the gift was not taxable until the decedent died. The court rejected this contention, for reasons that are discussed in the opinion in *Levin* reproduced below. But the court also stated that "we question whether decedent ever owned a property interest" because "decedent never acquired fixed and enforceable property rights in the survivors income benefit that he was capable of transferring . . . ." Accordingly, the taxpayer avoided all wealth transfer taxation on that benefit. How does the following case differ?

Estate of Levin v. Commissioner
90 T.C. 723 (1988)

JACOBS, Judge. Respondent determined a deficiency . . . premised on the theory that Stanton A. Levin (the decedent) made an inter vivos transfer or gift to his spouse of a post-mortem annuity payable by Marstan Industries, Inc. (Marstan), a corporation which he controlled, under its Officers' Surviving Spouse Plan (the Plan). After concessions, the issues for decision are (1) whether the commuted value of said annuity is includible in the decedent's gross estate pursuant to either §2035 or §2038, or alternatively, (2) whether said annuity constituted an inter vivos gift by the decedent to his spouse subject to gift taxation under §2511. . . .

On November 5, 1980, Marstan's Directors adopted a Plan, effective October 1, 1980, which provided for the payment of an annuity to the surviving spouses of the officers of Marstan who died while in the employ of Marstan and who met certain eligibility requirements. . . .

In order for the post-mortem annuity to be considered the decedent's property, Marstan must have been contractually obligated to make the annuity payments. In our opinion, Marstan offered the decedent and other qualified corporate officers a surviving spouse's annuity if they remained in the employ of Marstan. The decedent's continued employment constituted his acceptance of the Company's offer and served as the consideration for the benefits to be paid under the Plan. In essence, the surviving spouse's annuity constituted deferred compensation payable upon the death of the qualified corporate officer. Thus, the surviving spouse's annuity was property procured as a result of the decedent's rendering services to Marstan.

Petitioner contends, however, that because the Plan was revocable, it did not amount to a binding contract but was at most a "mere expectancy" that the decedent's spouse would receive a future benefit. We disagree.

Under Pennsylvania law, Marstan's obligation under the Plan, unless terminated by the Board of Directors, was fixed and could be enforced by the decedent's widow at the time of death.

It was highly unlikely that Marstan's obligation under the Plan would be terminated unless the decedent consented to such termination. The decedent owned over 80% of Marstan's voting stock, and in reality the Plan could not be terminated without his approval. . . . Thus, the decedent had more than a "mere expectancy" that his spouse would receive a lifetime annuity.

In addition, it was highly unlikely that the decedent would consent to a termination of the Plan. The Plan was obviously instituted to benefit the decedent, who was the controlling shareholder of Marstan. The Plan was not offered to all employees of Marstan. It was tailored to fit the decedent's particular situation, and at the Plan's inception, he was the only person qualified to receive a benefit under the Plan.

In conclusion, we believe that Marstan was contractually obligated to pay the post-mortem annuity benefits to the decedent's widow, since the annuity was procured by consideration furnished by the decedent. Therefore, for purposes of §2038, the annuity is property in which the decedent transferred an interest during his lifetime to his spouse.

The fact that the right to receive the post-mortem benefits was contingent (from the decedent's widow's viewpoint), in our opinion, is not relevant. Additionally, we deem not relevant the fact that the decedent could not have received any of such payments. The decedent's previous and continued employment with the Company was the source of the post-mortem payments to the widow, and the transfer of such payments was the potentially taxable event.

Having determined that the decedent transferred a property interest in the annuity to his spouse, we now must determine whether the decedent retained the power to alter, amend, revoke, or terminate such transfer. Although the Plan could not be amended or terminated by the decedent in his individual capacity, he was able to do so as a member of the Board of Directors in conjunction with the other members. Decedent's ability to amend or revoke the Plan in conjunction with other Marstan board members is a sufficient "power," to compel inclusion of the value of the post-mortem annuity in the decedent's estate.

Petitioner places great emphasis on the occasions that the other board members acted in contradiction of the decedent's wishes. However, it is the existence of the right to amend or terminate the Plan, rather than the likelihood of its exercise, that is the controlling factor. Moreover, in this case, we believe the ability of the other board members to go against decedent's wishes is largely illusory.

Petitioner cites Estate of DiMarco v. Commissioner, 87 T.C. 653 (1986), to support its position. In *DiMarco* we held that the decedent did not make a taxable gift of a survivor's income benefit pursuant to a plan established and maintained by his employer (IBM) within the meaning of §2503. The facts in this case are clearly distinguishable from those in *DiMarco*. In *DiMarco* the decedent was not a controlling shareholder of IBM nor was he an officer or director thereof. Unlike the decedent herein, the decedent in *DiMarco* was not able to alter, amend, revoke or terminate the IBM plan by which the widow received a survivor's income benefit. In contrast, the decedent herein, by virtue of his control of Marstan, was able to structure and amend the plan to suit his needs. Thus, our holding herein that the commuted value of the post-mortem annuity payable to Mrs. Levin is includible in the gross estate of the decedent pursuant to §2038(a)(1) is not contrary to the holding in *DiMarco*.

A second basis for respondent's determination of the deficiencies is his contention that the annuity constitutes an inter vivos gift from the decedent to Mrs. Levin such that either an estate tax should be imposed pursuant to §2035(a) or a gift tax should be imposed pursuant to §2511. However, neither of these sections applies in the absence of a completed inter vivos gift, whether direct or indirect, from the decedent to Mrs. Levin.[4]

---

4.   Respondent also relies on Rev. Rul. 81-31, 1981-1 C.B. 475, for imposition of the gift tax and argues here that we should adopt its reasoning and holding. As we previously stated in Estate of DiMarco v. Commissioner, 87 T.C. 653, 661 n.8 (1986):

> To the extent that this ruling can be read as holding either that a transfer of property can become complete for gift tax purposes by reason of the death of the donor, or that it is permissible to treat a completed transfer of property as an open transaction and to value the transferred property and impose the gift tax at some time other than when the completed transfer occurs, we regard the ruling as being inconsistent with the gift tax statute and the regulations.

[Rev. Rul. 81-31 was retracted by the government in Rev. Rul. 92-68, 1992-2 C.B. 257. —ED.]

It has long been recognized that a transfer of property is not complete for purposes of the gift tax provisions, and is therefore not subject to gift tax, if the donor retains control over the disposition of the property. Here, the decedent retained control over his wife's right to the post-mortem annuity because he could defeat the transfer by terminating his employment with Marstan prior to his death, by divorcing his spouse or by agreeing to terminate the Plan. Because the decedent retained such control over the property transferred, in our opinion no gift occurred.

If an employee held a large percentage of a corporate employer's stock at death (as was the case in *Levin*), the question whether a death benefit payable by that corporate employer is includible in the decedent's gross estate is only significant if that obligation is not subtracted from the value of the stock, which is required to avoid double estate taxation of that death benefit.

In thinking about assets that expire with a taxpayer's death, consider an irrevocable inter vivos trust created by *D*, who provided that the trust income was to be paid to *D* for life, remainder to *X*. We have §2036 because §2033 does not require the value of the trust to be included in *D*'s gross estate. See Chapter 5. Now, consider the right result if that trust had provided that the income was payable to *A* for the life of *D*, remainder to *X*. Should §2033 or any other provision require the value of the trust to be included in *D*'s gross estate at death? We will study §2037, also in Chapter 5, to see the circumstances in which the trust might be includible in *D*'s gross estate.

Finally, imagine that *D* purchased real property and, although the purchase price was provided entirely by *D* individually, placed the title in the names of *D* and *A* as joint tenants with the right of survivorship. We will learn in Chapter 7 that §2040 is needed because §2033 does not mandate inclusion of the value of the real property in *D*'s gross estate if *D* dies before *A*. Nor would §2033 require inclusion in the estate of *A* if the order of deaths were reversed. It is not too early to ask yourself the question whether anything *should* be includible in *A*'s gross estate if *A* dies first.

3.   *Ownership in Substance.* Does §2033 apply to property a decedent arguably "owns in substance" at death, or is §2033 limited to formal or technical ownership of property? Although the question has not been definitively answered, the Commissioner has never successfully used §2033 to include property that was not owned by the decedent in the technical or formal sense at death. This largely explains the unusual position the government tried to sustain in *DiMarco*, and why it was necessary to proceed under other provisions of the Code in *Levin*. Together with the naked death benefit cases that also exemplify this point, these decisions illustrate one particularly tortured issue upon which the jurisprudence still is not particularly consistent or gratifying. See also the Commissioner's own statement in Rev. Rul. 75-145, in which the government held that, under §2033, "the decedent must at the time of his death possess rights that he can transmit to a survivor." Only property or interests in property owned in the technical or formal sense meets this criterion. Pointing in the other direction are suggestions that §2033 may reach more than just property owned in the technical or formal sense. What parameters would define an expansive application of §2033?

In Helvering v. Safe Deposit & Trust Co., 316 U.S. 56 (1942), the Supreme Court held that property over which the decedent held a general testamentary power of appointment was not includible in his gross estate under §2033. In a footnote, however, the Court added:

In declining to pass upon [whether §2033 reaches economic interests that are equivalent to ownership], we do not reject the principle we have often recognized that the realities of the taxpayer's economic interest, rather than the niceties of the conveyancer's art, should determine the power to tax. See Curry v. McCandless, 307 U.S. 357, 371, and cases there cited. Nor do we deny the relevance of this principle as a guide to statutory interpretation where, unlike here, the language of a statute and its statutory history do not afford more specific indications of legislative intent. Helvering v. Clifford, 309 U.S. 331.

4.   *Dower, Curtesy, and Like Interests.*   What is now §2034 was enacted in the Revenue Act of 1918. H.R. Rep. No. 767, 65th Cong., 2d Sess. 21 (1918), in 1939-1 C.B. (pt. 2) 86, 101, which accompanied its enactment, explained:

It was the intention of the framers of the original [1916] Act that dower, curtesy, and estates created in lieu of dower or curtesy should be included in the gross estate, and your committee believes that the Treasury Department has correctly ruled in requiring them to be so included. Since a dispute has arisen with reference to this question, your committee deems it advisable to provide specifically that these estates shall be included in the gross estate.

You may want to study §2034 if your state is one of the few that still recognize dower or curtesy interests.

5.   *Cemetery Plots.*   Treas. Reg. §20.2033-1(b) indicates that the value of the part of a cemetery lot owned by a decedent that is designed for interment of the decedent and members of the decedent's family is not included in the decedent's gross estate. The rationale for this exclusion is found in the fundamental concept of the wealth transfer tax that makes it constitutional — it is an important (and easily remembered) critical element of this tax. Forgotten what it is? Refresh your recollection at page 3. Would this rationale suggest exclusion of the value of any other property owned by a decedent at death? In this connection, compare Treas. Reg. §20.2053-2. Must the value (and how would you determine that?) of the decedent's body be included in the gross estate? See Note, *The Sale of Human Body Parts*, 72 MICH. L. REV. 1182, 1262-1263 (1974).

not includible in decedent's Gross Estate

6.   *Wrongful Death Recoveries.*   Before promulgating Rev. Rul. 75-127, below, the government claimed that wrongful death recoveries by a decedent's estate were includible in the decedent's gross estate. As you read, think about what might have accounted for the government's about-face.

Revenue Ruling 75-127

Advice has been requested whether the values of proceeds received in settlement of claims under wrongful death statutes in the two situations described below, are includible in the gross estates of the decedents under §2033 or, alternatively, under §2041 of the Internal Revenue Code of 1954.

Situation 1. A Connecticut decedent died as a result of a collision between the automobile in which he was a passenger and a train. The accident occurred in Connecticut. A settlement was reached by the executor of the decedent's estate and the negligent railroad company in satisfaction of claims for damages arising by reason of the wrongful act that caused the decedent's death. The amount paid in settlement consisted solely of the settlement proceeds for the decedent's wrongful death. Nothing was included for the pain and suffering or medical expenses of the decedent. Under the terms of his will, the decedent bequeathed his entire estate to his surviving wife and two children.

Situation 2. Same facts as above, only the decedent was a resident of the State of Iowa and the accident occurred in Iowa.

At common law, no recovery was available for damages resulting from a wrongful act after the death of the injured party. Any cause of action for personal injury abated at the death of the injured party. To abrogate this rule, the various states have enacted what are commonly called "wrongful death acts." Generally, these acts take one of two forms: "death acts" or "survival acts." "Death acts" include the type discussed in Rev. Rul. 54-19, 1954-1 C.B. 179 (involving New Jersey law) where the statute creates a new cause of action, after the death of the injured party, for the benefit of certain beneficiaries. Under a "survival act," the cause of action for personal injury resulting in death survives the victim's death and passes to his personal representative to be pursued as an asset of the probate estate.

The States of Connecticut and Iowa have enacted "survival acts." Conn. Gen. Stat. Ann. §52-555 (Supp. 1974) and Iowa Code Ann. §611.20 (1950) both provide that a cause of action for injuries resulting in death survives the victim's death and may be brought by his representative. Additionally, under Conn. Gen. Stat. Ann. §45-280 (Supp. 1974) and Iowa Code Ann. §633.336 (Supp. 1974) any recovered proceeds are subject to debts of the decedent's estate and are disposed of as personal property belonging to the estate.

The similarity between the survival statutes in Connecticut and Iowa was recognized by the Iowa Supreme Court in Fitzgerald v. Hale, 78 N.W.2d 509 (1956). See also Lang v. United States and Morgan v. United States, 356 F. Supp. 546 (S.D. Iowa 1973) [consolidated opinion].

Section 2033 of the Code provides that the value of the gross estate shall include the value of all property to the extent of the interest therein of the decedent at the time of his death. Section 2041 requires that the value of all property with respect to which the decedent had a general power of appointment at the time of his death be included in the gross estate. For purposes of §2041, the term "general power of appointment" is defined as a power that is exercisable "in favor of the decedent, his estate, his creditors, or the creditors of his estate."

In several recent cases the Government unsuccessfully argued that the value of the proceeds of settlement or recovery under Connecticut's and Iowa's "survival" type wrongful death statutes was includible in the decedent's gross estate, for Federal estate tax purposes, pursuant to §2033 of the Code (as property owned by the decedent at the time of his death) or §2041 (as property with respect to which the decedent had at the time of his death a general power of appointment). See Connecticut Bank and Trust Company v. United States, 465 F.2d 760 (2d Cir. 1972); *Lang* and *Morgan*, above; and Vanek v. United States, 73-2 U.S. Tax Cas. (CCH) ¶12,943 (S.D. Iowa 1973). These cases hold that the wrongful death proceeds are not includible in the decedent's gross estate under either §2033 or §2041 because the wrongful death action cannot exist until the decedent has died. Thus, the decedent possessed neither a property interest in such cause of action nor a power of appointment over such cause of action at the time of his death.

The Internal Revenue Service will follow this line of cases. See Rev. Rul. 75-126 . . . with respect to Arizona law.

Accordingly, the Internal Revenue Service will no longer take the position under Connecticut, Iowa, or Arizona law, or under the law of any State having a wrongful death statute similar to the law of one of these states, that the value of wrongful death proceeds is includible in the decedent's gross estate. However, where it can be established that such proceeds represent damages to which the decedent had become entitled during his lifetime (such as for pain and suffering and medical expenses) rather than damages for his premature death, the value of these amounts will be includible in the decedent's gross estate.

Thus, since the death proceeds recovered by the executors in Situation 1 and Situation 2 included nothing for the pain, suffering, or expenses of the decedents during their lifetimes, the values of such proceeds are not includible in the gross estates of the decedents under §2033 or §2041 of the Code.

In *Connecticut Bank*, cited in Rev. Rul. 75-127, the decedents were assumed to have been killed instantaneously. In thinking about whether the exclusion of wrongful death recoveries is the right result, consider a couple of alternatives and try to determine what the tax consequences of those would be, and how the wrongful death case differs. First, what would the tax result be if either or both spouses survived the accident, at least for a demonstrable period of time? Compare Goodman v. Granger (reproduced at page 64), and Estate of Houston v. Commissioner, 44 T.C.M. (CCH) 284 (1982). Second, and not necessarily suggesting that the results would be different, what would be the tax consequences if the decedents were so severely injured that they no longer could work or enjoy a normal life and recovered a similar amount for their loss, but lived for many years before dying? Finally, how would these results or that in *Connecticut Bank* differ from the taxation of their estates if, over a normal lifetime, the decedents acquired the same amount of wealth through gainful employment (which, after all, is what the wrongful death recovery is meant to replace)? An important skill in tax lawyering is to ask the horizontal equity question: why should the taxation in these situations differ?

McDowell, A Few Dollars the IRS Won't Get[5]
Wall St. J., May 21, 1976, at 12

Last week Ted De Grazia gathered up 100 or so of his paintings, valued upwards to $1.5 million, and set out on horseback into the rugged Superstition Mountains east of Phoenix, Arizona.

---

5. Reprinted with permission of The Wall Street Journal, © Dow Jones & Company, Inc. 1976. All rights reserved.

Accompanying the 67-year-old artist on the grueling five hour journey were several journalists, several Mexican and Indian friends, and a 73-year-old prospector and longtime crony.

When they reached Angel Cliff, the ruins of ancient Indian cliff dwellings, De Grazia ignited the art works and watched with tears in his eyes as a roaring bonfire reduced them to ashes. Afterwards he marked the spot with two white Indian crosses.

What prompted this dramatic protest was De Grazia's opposition to federal inheritance taxes, which the artist complained could reach 77% of the assessed value of his works after he dies. "When I sell a painting and take in money, I expect to be taxed," he said. "But I don't think there should be a tax on paintings and other works of art that aren't sold. My heirs couldn't afford to inherit my works. . . ."

"I don't have any lawyers or accountants or estate planners advising me," says the man from whose studio rafters hang a half-dozen Bull Durham sacks to remind him of the days when he could not even afford tobacco. "I don't like them and I don't need them. For better or worse, this performance was my own idea. And I guess I'll just have to keep on thinning out my collection this way so the estate tax won't bankrupt my heirs, or until somebody does something about this unfair tax."

7.   *Testamentary Destruction.* If, instead of destroying the paintings inter vivos, Mr. De Grazia had directed in his will that they be destroyed, the direction, if challenged (by the Internal Revenue Service?), would almost certainly be held invalid as against public policy. See 2 A. Scott, THE LAW OF TRUSTS §124.7 (3d ed. 1967); Meksras's Estate, 63 Pa. D. & C.2d 371 (Ct. C.P. 1974) (direction that decedent's jewelry of considerable value be buried with her body held invalid); Everyman v. Mercantile Trust Co., 524 S.W.2d 210 (Mo. Ct. App. 1975), noted in 41 Mo. L. Rev. 309 (1976) (direction that decedent's house be razed); Will of Pace, 400 N.Y.S.2d 488 (Surr. Ct. 1977) (direction that two houses owned by decedent be razed); RESTATEMENT (SECOND) OF TRUSTS §124, comment g (1959). Thus, there would seem to be no escape from estate taxation by this route. Contrast, however, the newspaper report that the direction in the will of Sandra Ilene West, a Texas millionaire, that she be buried in her Ferrari sports car — seated "at a comfortable angle" and wearing her best lace nightgown — was upheld by a judge of the Los Angeles Superior Court. The judge was reported to have commented that her direction was "unusual, but not illegal." N.Y. Times, Apr. 13, 1977. See also National City Bank v. Case Western Reserve University, 369 N.E.2d 814 (Ohio Ct. C.P. 1976) (direction that decedent's residence be razed, upheld in the light of the testatrix's reasons for making the direction, as disclosed by her attorney's testimony).

8.   *Contraband; Stolen Goods.*   In TAM 9207004, the decedent, who had been suspected of smuggling illegal drugs, died when a plane he was piloting crashed, carrying a large amount of marijuana and some cash. The authorities confiscated the marijuana and cash, which were held to be contraband and therefore forfeited. The government ruled that if the decedent (1) had the possession and control of the drugs, and (2) could transfer them (or the proceeds of their sale), the decedent would be regarded as the owner of the drugs and they would be includible in the decedent's gross estate under §2033. Because the decedent owned the airplane and exercised possession of the drugs, the government assumed that the decedent was in control of the drugs and was entitled to their economic benefit. Thus, the government ruled that "the decedent's possession, control, and power of disposition over the marijuana were tantamount to his ownership of it for purposes of §2033 of the Code."

On the question of valuation, the government ruled that "it is reasonable to determine the fair market value of the marijuana based on the . . . retail street value of average grade marijuana (in the city at the time of the decedent's death)."

Finally, the government disallowed an estate tax deduction (claimed under §2053 and §2054) for the loss of the seized property on public policy grounds, citing cases disallowing *income tax* deductions for forfeited properties.

Was the government correct in including the marijuana and valuing it according to the price payable in an illicit market? If so, did the government correctly invoke public policy in denying an estate tax deduction for the seizure and forfeit?

In TAM 9152005, promulgated less than two months earlier, the government ruled that valuable art works, which were held at death but had been stolen by the decedent during and immediately after World War II while serving in the Army in France and Germany, were includible in his gross estate notwithstanding his lack of legal title to them. Regarding value, the only market in which some of the works could be sold was an illicit market, which was the market used in both TAMs. The government said that "the fact that the market is illicit does not obviate the existence of that market for estate tax valuation purposes." With that segue, we now direct our attention to the most difficult wealth transfer tax questions.

PART B. VALUATION

Code Reference: *Estate Tax: §2031*

9.   Under §2031, property that is included in a decedent's gross estate (whether "owned" by the decedent at death or otherwise) is valued "at the time of death" unless the decedent's executor elects to adopt the alternate valuation date under §2032 (as discussed in Part C of this chapter). The following case illustrates the connection between inclusion and valuation.

Goodman v. Granger
243 F.2d 264 (3d Cir. 1975)

KALODNER, J.: When does the federal estate tax attach? . . . .

That problem, of first impression, is presented by this appeal by the government . . . .

The District Court, subscribing to the taxpayer's contention, concluded as a matter of law that the decedent's contractual right was to be ". . . valued during decedent's lifetime and *at the moment before death* . . ." and made the factual finding that at such moment the contractual right was "valueless." . . .

The undisputed facts may be summarized as follows:

The decedent, Jacques Blum, for several years prior to his sudden death of a heart attack . . . was executive vice-president of Gimbel Brothers, Inc. ("Gimbels") in charge of its Pittsburgh store.

[The decedent's employment contract with Gimbels] provided for a basic salary of $50,000 per year, and for additional "contingent benefits" of [$6,000] per year for fifteen years "after the employee ceases to be employed" by the employer by reason of death or otherwise. The post-employment "contingent payments" were to be made only if the employee duly performed the services agreed upon and did not engage in a competing business within a specified period after termination of his employment; and they were to be reduced if his post-employment earnings from a non-competing business plus the contingent payments exceeded 75% of his yearly average compensation under the contracts. Any of the fifteen annual contingent payments which fell due after the employee's death were to be paid to his estate, or to a nominee designated in his will. . . .

After the decedent's death Gimbels paid the $6,000 annual installments . . . to the taxpayer in her capacity as administratrix as they became due. She filed with the Collector a timely federal estate tax return and included the three contracts at a value of $15,000. Upon audit of the return the Internal Revenue Agent in

Charge, Pittsburgh, increased the value of the three contracts from $15,000 to $66,710.34, the present worth of $90,000, payable in equal annual installments of $6,000 a year over a period of fifteen years. . . .

It is clear that the decedent's interest in the employment contracts was "property" includible in his gross estate under Section [2033]. Determination of the time when that interest is to be valued is the crux of the dispute. . . .

Since death is the propelling force for the imposition of the [estate] tax, it is death which determines the interests to be includible in the gross estate. Interests which terminate on or before death are not a proper subject of the tax. Assets may be acquired or disposed of before death, possibilities of the loss of an asset may become actualities or may disappear. Upon the same principle underlying the inclusion of interests in a decedent's gross estate, valuation of an interest is neither logically made nor feasibly administered until death has occurred. The taxpayer's theory of valuing property before death disregards the fact that generally the estate tax is neither concerned with changes in property interests nor values prior to death. The tax is measured by the value of assets transferred by reason of death, the critical value being that which is determined as of the time of death.

As was so succinctly stated by Judge Hartshorne in Christiernin v. Manning, 138 F. Supp. 923, 925 (D. N.J. 1956): "There can not be a decedent, till death has occurred. A decedent's estate is not transferred either by his will or by intestacy, till death has occurred. . . . And the decedent's interest in the property taxable is to be such interest 'at the time of his death.'" . . .

Here the employment contracts provided for additional "contingent" compensation of $6,000 per year for fifteen years to be paid to Blum or his estate after the termination of his employment by reason of death or otherwise. True, the right to these payments was forfeitable upon the occurrence of any of the specified contingencies. However, forfeiture as a result of the contingencies never occurred during Blum's lifetime, and any possibility of their occurrence was extinguished by his death. Gimbels has been making and the estate has been collecting the payment provided by the contracts. Valuation of the right to these payments must be determined as of the time of Blum's death when the limiting factor of the contingencies would no longer be considered. Death ripened the interest in the deferred payments into an absolute one, and death permitted the imposition of the tax measured by the value of that absolute interest in property. . . .

For the reasons stated the judgment of the District Court will be reversed with directions to proceed in accordance with this opinion.

Can you articulate how the exclusion from the gross estate of wrongful death benefit claims (Rev. Rul. 75-127, at page 59) is reconcilable with the holding in *Goodman* that the estate tax *value* of an asset included in the decedent's gross estate can be affected by the fact of the decedent's death? If you cannot articulate a principled distinction between these situations, which do you guess is wrong?

Assume that *X* was the sole shareholder and principal officer of Win All, Inc. Immediately prior to *X*'s death, the value of Win All was $500,000. *X*'s personal ability to attract customers was a major item in Win All's goodwill and *X*'s death caused a significant reduction in the value of the company to $320,000. The value of *X*'s stock will reflect this loss of a key person in determining the proper discount for estate tax purposes. On the other hand, assume the same facts *except* that *X* had retired from active participation in the business some years prior to death and none of the goodwill of Win All was attributable to *X*'s personal abilities or relationships with clients. Instead, *C* (*X*'s child) had become the dominant force in the business and, of the $500,000 value of Win All stock, $180,000 was attributable to the services and goodwill of *C*. *X*'s stock would not be valued for estate tax purposes with any kind of a discount for a key person (unless *C* also died when *X* did).

Note that Estate of McClatchy v. Commissioner, 147 F.3d 1089 (9th Cir. 1998), *rev'g* 106 T.C. 206 (1996), involved stock held at death that was subject during the decedent's life to restrictions under the Securities Act of 1933. Those restrictions depressed the value of that stock in the decedent's hands during the decedent's life, but those restrictions did not restrict the amount the estate — as compared to the decedent — could get on sale of that stock. As a result the Tax Court held that the stock should be valued for estate tax purposes at the higher value in the hands of the estate, without the securities law restrictions. The court on appeal found that to be error, holding instead that value should be determined in the hands of the decedent, albeit at death, rather than in the hands of the estate. As such it found that the restrictions still were relevant and should be considered. End of life death bed planning could have involved the decedent making a gift of the stock at the clearly reduced value, simply to avoid the need to litigate the question.

10. *Valuation Techniques.* Value is defined in Treas. Reg. §20.2031-1(b) as "the price at which the property would change hands between a willing buyer and a willing seller, neither being under any compulsion to buy or to sell and both having reasonable knowledge of relevant facts." The Code itself says nothing about estate tax valuation, although §2031(b) provides that, in determining the value of unlisted stocks and securities for which bid, asked, or sale prices are unavailable, the value of listed stocks and securities of corporations engaged in the same or a similar line of business should be taken into consideration.

With such a simplistic formulation, valuation is the source of more controversy than any other issue under the estate tax. For many estates the only issues raised on audit relate to valuation, usually because there is no established market for includible assets. Absent an actual sale between a willing and informed seller and buyer, the regulation posits a highly conjectural factual assumption. What a hypothetical knowledgeable and willing buyer would pay a hypothetical knowledgeable and willing seller is a question on which reasonable expert opinions may vary widely. Furthermore, it is a question to which a large number of factors — all the things that might seem important to any potential buyer or seller — are relevant.

For example, in valuing a trade or business, it may be necessary to appraise the strength of the national economy, the economic prospects for the specific business or segment of the industry, and the potential for future labor disputes, material shortages, or trade and market disruptions. It is not possible either to enumerate all the factors that may enter into the valuation of property or to specify the relative weight to be given these factors. Because valuation problems essentially are evidentiary issues, often it is desirable for a personal representative to secure expert appraisals, promptly after death, recognizing that contemporaneous expert appraisals may have greater probative value than any other evidence available at a later time. In other cases, however, actual sales even many months after death may prove more probative of value than any expert guesstimate of value. See, e.g., Gettysburg National Bank v. United States, 92-2 U.S. Tax Cas. (CCH) ¶60,108 (M.D. Pa. 1992) (arm's-length sale 16 months after death and 13 months after appraisal for 75% of the value reported for federal estate tax purposes was deemed the proper value under §2031). And see First National Bank of Kenosha v. United States, 763 F.2d 891 (7th Cir. 1985) (agreement to sell entered into 21 months after death but never consummated still was regarded as probative evidence of value).

The regulations, rulings, Audit Technique Handbook, and court decisions identify factors to be considered and prescribe procedures for determining values of various kinds of property. What follows is only a brief description of some of the more important of those procedures.

Stocks and Bonds For Which There Is a Market. If there is a market for corporate securities, either on a stock exchange or over the counter, Treas. Reg. §20.2031-2(b)(1) provides that the value of such securities is the mean between the highest and the lowest sales prices on the valuation date. If there were no sales on the valuation date (for example, because the decedent died on a weekend or holiday) but there were sales within a reasonable period before and after that date, value is determined by taking a weighted average of the means for the nearest date before and the nearest date after the valuation date on which there were sales. The average is weighted inversely by the number of trading days between the selling dates and the valuation date.[6]

If actual sale prices are not available within a reasonable period before and after the valuation date, value may be determined by taking either the mean between bona fide bid and asked prices on the valuation date or a weighted average of such means for the nearest trading dates for which such bid and asked prices are available, if within a reasonable period. Treas. Reg. §20.2031-2(c).

If actual sales or bid and asked prices are available for a date within a reasonable time before but not after the valuation date, or vice versa, then the mean between highest and lowest available sale prices or between available bid and asked prices may be taken as value. Treas. Reg. §20.2031-2(d).

Stocks and Bonds For Which There Is No Established Market. Securities of closely held corporations for which selling prices or bid and asked prices are unavailable must be valued on the basis of various relevant factors weighted according to the facts and circumstances of each case. Among the principal factors to consider in valuing bonds are the extent and soundness of any security, the interest yield, and date of maturity. Prominent factors in valuing shares of stock include the company's net asset value in liquidation, its prospective earning power and dividend-paying capacity as an on-going concern, and the value of comparable corporations. The regulations require that complete financial and other data upon which valuation is based be submitted with the return, including copies of reports by accountants, engineers, appraisers, or any other technical experts. Treas. Reg. §20.2031-2(f).

The valuation of closely held corporations is one of the most difficult problems under the wealth transfer taxes. See Rev. Rul. 59-60 for some valuation guidelines. Also, specific guidelines are available for specific businesses (e.g., Rev. Proc. 75-39 provides guidelines for valuing a radio or television station).

Valuation "Adjustments": Discounts and Premiums. These rules may be modified in their actual application if it can be shown that the

---

6. To illustrate, assume that sales of stock nearest the valuation date (Friday, July 4) occurred two *trading* days before (Wednesday, July 2) and three *trading* days after (Wednesday, July 9) and that on these days the mean sales prices per share were $10 and $15, respectively. A price of $12 is determined by formula as representing the fair market value of a share of the stock on the valuation date:

$$\frac{(3 \times 10) + (2 \times 15)}{5} = 12$$

value determined by them does not accurately reflect the value of the asset involved. For example, sales at or near the valuation date may be few or sporadic, and adjustments must reflect assets owned by an estate (1) that cannot be sold without depressing the market on which sales are made ("blockage"), (2) that are minority holdings subject to the whims of a majority shareholder, or (3) that represent control of a corporation, in each case making the market price only an initial indication of value. See Treas. Reg. §20.2031-2(e). The blockage concept can be applied in valuing all sorts of assets (including stock, art, bullion, or any other asset with a thin market). See, e.g., Estate of Smith v. Commissioner, 57 T.C. 650 (1972), *aff'd on another issue*, 510 F.2d 479 (2d Cir. 1975), and Estate of O'Keefe v. Commissioner, 63 T.C.M. (CCH) 2699 (1992) (both applying a blockage discount with respect to original artwork created by the decedent and owned by the decedent at death), and recall the failed effort by the Hunt brothers to corner the silver bullion market, as involved in Hunt v. Commissioner, 57 T.C.M. (CCH) 919 (1989) (distinguishing loans from gifts in the context of efforts undertaken to keep the taxpayer's children afloat as their silver buying endeavor went sour).

Johnson v. Commissioner, 74 T.C. 89 (1980) (income tax valuation of stock on the dates the taxpayer exercised a bargain-priced employee stock option) held that fair market value on a given date was determined by the mean price at which it was traded on that date, notwithstanding that corporate officers had deliberately misrepresented the earnings and profits of the corporation to cause the stock to sell at an inflated price. If a meaningful number of sales occur and blockage is not involved, the market price controls even if it is distorted; market price, because it is the best evidence of value, may be disregarded only in exceptional circumstances. The court did state that it would not rely on a market price that was controlled by a syndicate rather than merely influenced by publication of false information. Quaere whether control of the market should be distinguished from fraudulently influencing the market price.

The per-share value of a block of stock that constitutes control of a corporation may be greater than the value of noncontrolling stock. In contrast with this "control premium," a minority interest sometimes is valued by applying a discount factor for the lack of control. Although minority discounts and control premiums are opposite sides of the same coin, each reflecting the fact that ownership of an equity interest with control is more valuable than ownership without control, it is not necessarily the case that the two will match or produce an exact offset, and the sum of minority and controlling interest parts does not necessarily equal the value of the corporate whole. One possible reason for that inequality is that the presence of minority interests represents a potential nuisance for the controlling shareholders and may therefore cause the value of control itself to be discounted.

If *D* and *S* owned a block of stock as community property or in some other form of concurrent ownership, can either portion be assessed with a control premium merely because the block owned by them together constitutes a controlling interest? The Court of Appeals for the Fifth Circuit initially held in Estate of Bright v. United States, 619 F.2d 407 (5th Cir. 1980), that resolution of this question turns upon a factual determination whether a hypothetical willing seller would sell either portion separately or only as part of a control block sale. A majority of the court reversed this decision on a rehearing of the case en banc and held that the value of each block must be determined separately with each owner independently regarded as a solitary willing seller. Thus, the stock owned by any other shareholder is ignored in determining value, notwithstanding the relation of the concurrent owners. Estate of Bright v. United States, 658 F.2d 999 (5th Cir. 1981) (en banc).

Consider, then, the proper result if *D* and *S* own tenancy in common interests in a control block of stock and *D* placed half in a trust for the benefit of *S* for life, remainder to the same ultimate beneficiary who will receive *S*'s half at death. When *S* dies, if only *S*'s shares are taxable, must the ultimate recombination of the two halves be considered in determining the value of *S*'s shares? The Tax Court has not done so. See Estate of Pillsbury v. Commissioner, 64 T.C.M. (CCH) 284 (1992), and Mooneyham v. Commissioner, 61 T.C.M. (CCH) 2445 (1991). In TAM 9550002 the government asserted that certain marital trust property should be aggregated with property owned by the surviving spouse individually for valuation purposes, which was rejected with respect to one form of marital trust (a qualified terminable interest property — QTIP — trust) in Estate of Bonner v. United States, 84 F.3d 196 (5th Cir. 1996), and its progeny: Estate of Mellinger v. Commissioner, 112 T.C. 26 (1999), *acq.* AOD 1999-06, Estate of Lopes v. Commissioner, 78 T.C.M. (CCH) 46 (1999), and Estate of Nowell v. Commissioner, 77 T.C.M. (CCH) 1239 (1999), but accepted in another. Estate of Fontana v. Commissioner, 118 T.C. 318 (2002) (a general power of appointment marital deduction trust, the general power being equated with outright ownership; the §2041 taxation of general powers is considered in Chapter 3).

Similar types of discounts are available for undivided fractional interests, such as the decedent's share of a tenancy in common, representing that a willing buyer would not pay as much to become an undivided concurrent owner with the decedent's surviving property owners. For an excellent example of this see Estate of Baird v. Commissioner, 82 T.C.M. (CCH) 666 (2001), which involved undivided fractional interests in 16 parcels of Louisiana timberland. The estate produced a expert who was in the business of buying and selling fractional interests in Louisiana timber, who suggested "average" discount of 55%, which the court increased to

60% based on special family circumstances. A standard fractional interest discount in residential realty may run from 15% to double that amount.

These kinds of discounts are antithetical to the position the government asserted until 1993, that the value of a minority interest must reflect shares held by family members unless there is evidence of family discord. In Rev. Rul. 81-253, a donor who owned 100% of the stock of a corporation gave one third of the stock to each of three children. The government ruled that no minority discount was allowable in valuing those gifts because a hypothetical willing seller would not dispose of the stock to anyone outside the family without selling all the stock held by family members. Asserting that judicial precedent on this issue was in conflict, the government expressly stated that it would not follow those cases, including the en banc decision in *Estate of Bright*, that allow a minority discount even if there is family control and no family discord. Finally, in Rev. Rul. 93-12, the government indicated that it will no longer assert the family attribution argument to deny a minority discount.

In TAM 8907002 the government approached this issue from a different perspective. The taxpayer and various members of the taxpayer's family owned all of the stock in a closely-held corporation. The taxpayer owned the controlling interest but relinquished that control through a redemption of shares. Considering the proceeds received by the taxpayer in exchange for the redeemed shares, the government argued that the taxpayer made a gift because a control premium was allocable to the taxpayer's interest. To illustrate, assume that the taxpayer owned 51% of the stock in a closely-held corporation and that two children owned equal amounts of the remaining stock. If the taxpayer gave 1% of the stock to each of those children, the issue would be whether the collective value of those gifts is (1) 2% of the total value of the corporation, (2) a discount from that amount because each child receives a minority interest, (3) an amount equal to 2/51 of the value of the taxpayer's 51% controlling interest, or (4) an even greater premium amount because, by virtue of the gifts, the taxpayer relinquished the control element represented by the 51% interest. The TAM indicates that (4) is correct: the entire control premium should be taxed as part of the gift that eliminates the taxpayer's controlling interest. Quaere, however, whether the donees received that value or whether it just disappeared. If the latter, is it proper to tax the value the taxpayer re-linquished if it did not pass to the donees?

These types of issues raise serious and largely unresolved wealth transfer tax policy questions and have been exploited by taxpayers seeking valuation discounts. For example, taxpayers would like to persuade the courts that it is possible to engage in voluntary transactions that create restrictions on enjoyment such that the value of property is significantly diminished, as if that value had been destroyed, meanwhile retaining the ability to restore that value at a later time — for example by placing marketable investments in an entity (such as a limited partnership or limited liability company) and later liquidating that wrapper, all without making a "transfer" as to which the gift tax would apply. Courts have wrestled with notions such as the taxpayer's evidence showing that a willing buyer would not pay much for such a restricted interest while the government's evidence shows that a willing seller would not part with the interest for anywhere near the discounted value the taxpayer alleges is the proper assessment. The jury is still out over many of these valuation conundrums. See Bogdanski, FEDERAL TAX VALUATION ¶¶2.01[2][d], 2.01[2][e], and 2.01[4][c][iv] (Supp. 2002); Pennell, *Valuation Discord: An Exegesis of Wealth Transfer Tax Valuation Theory and Practice,* 30 U. MIAMI INST. EST. PLAN. 9-1 to 9-70 (1996).

Notwithstanding the ill defined parameters of these debates, in proper cases the lack of a ready market makes a discount available in valuing shares of any closely held business, and a lack of control discount routinely is allowed as well, with the aggregate of these two most common adjustments sometimes approximating 50% of the otherwise determined cash flow or asset liquidation value.

Meanwhile, in determining the value of assets included in a decedent's gross estate, the government's position is that all includible assets are to be considered regardless of how they were owned at death. See, e.g., Rev. Rul. 79-7. In some cases this may backfire on the government. For example, a blockage reduction might apply to value stock that is included in a decedent's gross estate even if the decedent made a gift of some of those shares prior to death and even if the donated shares represent a small percentage of the corporation's outstanding stock, provided that those shares are includible at death (e.g., because the decedent retained an interest or power that triggers §2036 or §2038, as discussed in Chapter 5).On the other hand, shares of stock may be valued with a majority premium if the aggregate shares included in the decedent's gross estate represent a controlling interest in the corporation. In this respect it may matter whether the decedent originally owned the includible asset and made a transfer of it in such a way that causes inclusion at death, as opposed to the asset being includible at the decedent's death because of interests or powers granted to the decedent by a third party in a manner that, notwithstanding inclusion, denies the decedent the ability to deal with the assets effectively to realize that value.

Other issues remain to be resolved, such as whether estate tax valuation should consider the final destination of the includible portions as does gift tax valuation. At present a huge disparity exists between valuation for the two tax regimes because the testamentary destination of estate assets is not considered the way it is considered for gift tax valuation. This differential offers a significant planning opportunity to those with enough wealth to engage in inter vivos transfers that simply are not available to taxpayers who feel they must wait until death before making any transfers. For example, a decedent owning 100% of the stock in a family corporation at death would incur estate tax on the value of the business, with a control premium, even if that stock was left in equal shares to several children such that each received a minority, noncontrol block. But if the taxpayer made equal minority interest gifts of that stock to the same children shortly before death, the gift tax would be imposed on each slice individually, and the aggregate gift tax value of the respective transfers would be far lower than the undivided whole for estate tax purposes. Congress probably never intended nor considered these distinctions, and they provide meaning to the notion that the wealth transfer taxes are not yet properly unified. The hard question is: which result should apply for both tax purposes if a single rule were applicable — valuation of the niblets that ultimately land in the hands of the respective beneficiaries, or valuation of the diminution in net worth to the taxpayer by virtue of the total transfer?

Interests In an Unincorporated Business Enterprise. Valuation poses similar problems to taxpayers who own interests in unincorporated business enterprises, either in partnership form, as a joint venture, or a sole proprietorship. Treas. Reg. §20.2031-3 provides that the value of a sole proprietorship or similar interest is to be determined essentially as it is for an incorporated business, looking at the value of all assets of the business, tangible and intangible, including goodwill, the demonstrated earning capacity of the business, and other relevant factors, specifically including those that are relevant to the valuation of stock for which selling prices or bid and asked prices are unavailable.

Effect of Buy and Sell Agreements. Interests in a closely held business — incorporated or unincorporated — frequently are subject to agreements to purchase the decedent's interest at a specified price. The question with respect to such agreements is whether they represent a term of the decedent's participation in the business enterprise that limits the value of the interest, a convenient arrangement for disposing of the decedent's interest at death or, worse, a mechanism designed to transfer ownership of the interest to family members in a manner that seeks to avoid or minimize wealth transfer tax.

For valuation purposes, Treas. Reg. §20.2031-2(h) states that little weight will be given to buy-sell agreements if the decedent was free to dispose of the interest to any buyer and at any price during life. Further, even if the decedent could not freely dispose of the interest during life, an agreement or option to purchase will be disregarded for valuation purposes unless it represents a "bona fide business arrangement and not a device to pass the decedent's shares to the natural objects of his bounty for less than an adequate and full consideration." Further restricting the effect of such an agreement on valuation is §2703, applicable with respect to agreements entered into after October 8, 1990; it provides that value is determined without regard to a buy-sell agreement or other option or similar right to acquire property at less than fair market value unless, in addition to codifying the bona fide business arrangement and not a device standards, the agreement also is "comparable to similar arrangements entered into by persons in an arm's-length transaction." Courts usually will accept the striking price as determinative of the estate tax value of the stock if the bona fide arrangement, not a device, and comparability standards are met and (1) the agreement is valid and enforceable, (2) the purchase price established was "reasonable," fixed, and determinable, (3) the decedent's estate was obligated to sell the stock at the striking price, and (4) the decedent was prohibited from selling the stock during life without first offering it to purchasers under the agreement at the striking price. If, as often is the case, the agreement was made between related parties (under Treas. Reg. §25.2703-1(b)(3), if 50% or more of the parties to the agreement are members of the seller's family or are natural objects of the seller's bounty), the very strong presumption is that the agreement is not effective to establish value. See, e.g., St. Louis County Bank v. United States, 674 F.2d 1207 (8th Cir. 1982) (a buy-sell agreement with decedent's corporation — a redemption agreement — that used a formula striking price that produced a value of $0 notwithstanding a book value of the corporation of over $200,000 was deemed ineffective for federal estate tax purposes notwithstanding a finding that the formula was reasonable when executed; the remaining shareholders were decedent's family, meaning the effect was to shift value tax free). For a more full discussion of buy-sell agreements, see Gamble, *Buy-Sell Transfer Restrictions and Section 2703: Have Buy-Sells Gone Bye-Bye?*, 50 N.Y.U. INST. FED TAX'N 19-1 (1992); and Gamble, *Will Chapter 14 Freeze Buy-Sell Agreements and Make Lapsing Rights Disappear?*, 26 U. MIAMI INST. EST. PLAN. ¶1300 (1992).

If the decedent's interest in a business is not subject to a binding option (and therefore the estate may retain the interest if the price set by the agreement is not sufficiently attractive), or if a buy-sell agreement simply is not respected because §2703 is applicable, the interest nevertheless may be subject to an agreement that it will not be sold unless it first is offered to a named buyer at a set price. In that case the price fixed by the restrictive agreement may bind the estate but will not be determinative of value. Although the striking price may be a factor to be considered in pre-1990 agreements, §2703 provides that the agreement will be ignored if the agreement was executed after October 8, 1990.

Temporal Interests: Annuities, Life Estates, Terms For Years, Remainders, and Reversions.   An annuity contract issued by a company regularly involved in the sale of annuities is valued at the price that the company charges for comparable contracts. Treas. Reg. §20.2031-8(a). Otherwise, the value of an annuity, life estate, term for years, remainder, reversion, or any other interest in property limited or postponed in time of enjoyment is determined by the use of formulas that are made up of interest rate and mortality assumptions. The interest rate assumptions are revised monthly and the mortality assumptions are revised every decade. See §7520(a), (c). The Actuarial Branch of the Internal Revenue Service's national office will perform valuations of this variety on request. See Treas. Reg. §§20.2031-7, -10 (both contain outdated tables but reveal the type of tables now found in the freestanding published actuarial value volumes promulgated by the government). Rather than use the government's phone-book sized tables, most serious planners today utilize reasonably priced computer programs that perform valuation computations using the government's own formulas and factors.

These rules, like others for the valuation of property, are subject to modification if it can be shown that they do not accurately reflect value in a particular case. See, e.g., Estate of Butler v. Commissioner, 18 T.C. 914 (1952); Huntington National Bank v. Commissioner, 13 T.C. 760 (1949). See also Estate of Christ v. Commissioner, 480 F.2d 171 (9th Cir. 1973). The government's position for all wealth transfer tax purposes regarding deviations from the use of tables in making actuarial valuations and from the use of interest rate assumptions is set forth in Treas. Reg. §§20.7520-3(b) and 25.7520-3(b) (effective December 13, 1995). For a similar approach applicable to the period prior to December 13, 1995, see Rev. Rul. 80-80.

Under the current regulations, the mortality tables cannot be employed for gift and for many estate and income tax purposes if the person who is the measuring life is "terminally ill" at the time of the transaction. The regulations provide that an individual is considered terminally ill if the individual "is *known* to have an incurable illness or other deteriorating condition . . . [and] if there is at least a 50% probability that the individual will die within 1 year." [Emphasis added.] If an individual survives for at least eighteen months after the date of the transaction, it is presumed that the individual was not terminally ill at the time of the transaction unless the contrary is established by clear and convincing evidence. Treas. Reg. §§1.7520-3(b)(3), 20.7520-3(b)(3), and 25.7520-3(b)(3). Use of the mortality tables is not precluded merely because the individual who is the measuring life is aged and subject to the general infirmities of old age. Consequently, an elderly person who has one or more illnesses, none of which, standing alone or considered together, is known to be life-threatening, will not be considered to be terminally ill. See T.D. 8630 (Dec. 13, 1995), which contains the Preamble to the final regulations.

In addition to the "terminally ill" exception, the mortality tables cannot be employed for estate tax purposes if the decedent and the person who is the measuring life die as the result of a common accident (or similar occurrence). See Treas. Reg. §20.7520-3(b)(3)(iii).

Although the "terminally ill" exception to the use of the mortality tables applies for most estate tax purposes, there are several estate tax provisions for which the "terminally ill" provision is inapplicable. Treas. Reg. §20.7520-3(b)(3)(ii). For example, for purposes of §§2037(b) and 2042(2), the valuation of a decedent's reversionary interest immediately before death is determined by the mortality tables without regard to the person's actual physical condition at that time. In addition, the "terminally ill" exception applies to §2013 (the credit for taxes on prior transfers) only in certain circumstances.

The valuation of annuity, income, or remainder interests is made by utilizing a rate of return (i.e., an assumed interest rate) that is determined according to a formula supplied by §7520. Under what circumstances would it be wrong to use the assumed rate of return because of the nature of the underlying investments or because of the speculative nature of the interest to be valued? The current regulations state that the §7520 income factor cannot be used to value a beneficiary's interest unless the effect of the governing instrument is to provide "the income beneficiary with that degree of beneficial enjoyment of the property during the term of the income interest that the principles of the law of trusts accord to a person who is unqualifiedly designated as the income beneficiary of a trust for a similar period of time." Treas. Reg. §§1.7520-3(b)(2)(ii)(A), 20.7520-3(b)(2)(ii)(A), 25.7520-3(b)(2)(ii)(A). It is likely that the interest component provided by the §7520 formula will be applied unless the party (the government or the taxpayer) objecting to its use shows that it will not provide an accurate evaluation. Cf. O'Reilly v. Commissioner, 973 F.2d 1403 (8th Cir 1992). For example, assume that the interest to be valued is an interest in a trust. One circumstance in which the interest component will be disregarded is if the trust assets include unproductive or underproductive property that must be retained by the trustee. See Treas. Reg. §20.7520-3(b)(2)(v) *Example 1*. However, the income component of the §7520 formula will apply if the unproductive or underproductive trust assets need not be retained by the trustee and if the income beneficiary can require the trustee to convert those assets to produce a return that is "consistent with income yield standards for trusts under applicable state law." See Treas. Reg. §§20.7520-3(b)(2)(v) *Example 2*, 25.7520-3(b)(2)(v) *Example 2*. There is one narrow exception for gift tax purposes because of the adoption of Chapter 14 (the "estate freeze" provisions that are discussed in Chapter 15 of this text): if the donor is also the life income beneficiary, the value of the donor's retained income interest may be zero by virtue of §2702. See Treas. Reg. §25.7250-3(b)(2)(v) *Example 2*.

If either the mortality tables or the interest component of §7520 is inapplicable, the fair market value of the interest will be determined by examining all of the facts and circumstances instead of relying on the valuation rules under §7520. See Treas. Reg. §20.7520-3(b)(1)(iii).

Realty Used In a Farm or Closely Held Business. The normal standard is to value realty in the light of the highest and best use to which the property could be put. The Internal Revenue Manual Audit Techniques Handbook at ¶620(2) defines this to mean

that reasonable and probable use that will support the highest present worth of the (improved) property as of the assessment date based on the highest net return that it can produce over a reasonably foreseeable period of time, such as the property's probable remaining useful life [considering] all zoning, deed restrictions, or other physical, economic, legal-governmental or locational restrictions preventing a higher income-producing use. . . .

This valuation practice may be unreasonable as applied to farmland (and to land used in a closely held business) that could be put to higher-income-productive use, because it penalizes the farmer (or the closely-held business owner) for not terminating the farming or business activities and selling the land and putting it to the highest income-productive use. Congress adopted the §2032A special use valuation provision to facilitate the continued use of realty for farming or other business purposes and to protect this land from taxation on speculative values. This complex provision, in very simplified and general terms, provides that the decedent's estate may elect to value qualifying real property that is devoted to farming or closely held business use based on the property's actual use as a farm or in the closely held business, rather than its highest and best use fair market value. The maximum reduction of a decedent's gross estate from the special use valuation is indexed for inflation (it was $820,000 in 2002). If, within ten years after the decedent's death, the specially valued realty is disposed of outside the decedent's family or the property ceases to be used for its qualifying farming or closely held business use, §2032A(c) "recaptures" the federal estate tax benefits derived from the special valuation election.[7]

11. *Postmortem Facts.* One of the hardest questions the courts have wrestled with is the applicability of postmortem facts to determine estate

---

7 Property transferred by an estate or trust in satisfaction of a pecuniary bequest or other obligation is treated as a sale or exchange for income tax purposes, which can cause the estate or trust to recognize gain or loss to the extent the transferred property has a fair market value different from its basis. Until repeal of the estate tax, basis under §1014 is federal estate tax value — which reflects the §2032A reduction in value. Congress realized that property valued under §2032A would have a date of distribution value different from (and usually substantially in excess of) its estate tax value (and therefore its basis) even if no post-valuation-date appreciation occurred. To preclude the unintentional recognition of phantom gain or loss, §1040 provides that the §2032A valuation is ignored and basis is deemed to be the *actual* fair market value of the property at the estate tax valuation date (rather than the special use value under §2032A). In effect, §1040 limits gain recognition on transfer of §2032A property to a §2032A(e)(1) qualified heir to actual appreciation of the property over its actual value on the applicable estate tax valuation date.

tax value. If admissible at all, at what point would new information cease to be relevant? Consider the following case.

United States v. Simmons
346 F.2d 213 (5th Cir. 1965)

WISDOM, J.: This taxpayer's suit for an estate tax refund grew out of executors' settling for $42,000 an estate's claim for an income tax refund of $60,000 listed in the estate tax return as having "no value" at the date of the decedent's death.

The decedent, B. Hill Simmons, died December 27, 1955. Some time before his death, the Internal Revenue Service began investigating, on a net worth basis, Simmon's income tax returns for the years 1941 through 1953. As a result of the investigation, the decedent paid a deficiency in the amount of $43,000. The decedent never entertained the idea of filing a claim for refund of these taxes. Shortly after Simmons's death, the executors of the estate employed an attorney, Mr. Louis B. Thompson, counsel for appellee, to investigate the decedent's tax affairs. By November 1956 the attorney decided that a claim for a refund should be filed for the decedent's taxable years 1941 through 1953. February 1, 1957, Mr. Thompson filed the claim for refund amounting to $60,000. Upon the Service's disallowing the claim, Mr. Thompson filed suit on behalf of the estate. In 1960, the Department of Justice approved the executors' offer of compromise for $41,187. Meanwhile, the taxpayer's attorney had filed an estate tax return listing the income tax claim as having no value, but had requested that the estate tax liability be held in abeyance pending the outcome of the claim. The Commissioner determined that the claim was includible in the decedent's estate and valued the claim at the amount of the settlement.

Under Section 2031 of the Internal Revenue Code of 1954, the federal estate tax includes "all property, real or personal, tangible or intangible" of the decedent. When Simmons died, his "property" included the claim for refund of federal income taxes. Both parties agree that the claim for refund of income taxes is a part of Simmons's gross estate. But as far as it is possible to disagree as to value, they disagree: the United States contends that the amount of the compromise, $42,000, fixed the estate tax value of the claim; the Estate of B. Hill Simmons (the taxpayer) contends the claim had *no* value when Simmons died. The taxpayer asserts that at the time of death the executors thought the claim was worthless and would have sold it for $1,000. Allegedly, a key factor in filing the claim was the discovery in October 1956 of a pencil memorandum tending to disprove fraud in that it showed the decedent's intention to report certain cotton sales that had not been reported. The executors paid the tax assessed against the estate and sued for a refund.

The district court submitted the issue of valuation to the jury. The jury found that the claim was valueless at the time of the decedent's death. The district court denied the Government's motions for a directed verdict, a judgment n.o.v., and a new trial. We hold that the trial court correctly denied the motions for a directed verdict and judgment n.o.v., but we reverse the judgment and remand the case for a new trial, because there was no rational basis for the jury's finding that the claim for an income tax refund was valueless on the date of the decedent's death.

I. . . . The Commissioner contends . . . that the trial judge should have directed the verdict in favor of the United States or granted a judgment n.o.v. because, as a matter of law, the amount of the compromise fixed the value of the claim for estate tax purposes.

The few decided cases in this area of tax law reject the Commissioner's contention. At one time the Board of Tax Appeals took the position that the amount later recovered on an income tax refund claim fixed the value of the claim for estate tax purposes. On appeal the Ninth Circuit reversed [the Board and] held that the decedent's claim for refund of income taxes was a part of the decedent's gross estate; that the value of the claim was the fair market value as between a willing buyer and a willing seller at the time of the decedent's death. Instead of determining the fair market value, the Board had arbitrarily used the amount of the recovery. . . .

The Treasury Regulation applies the "willing buyer and seller test" to all questions of valuation. Treas. Reg. §20.2031-1(b). When, as in this case, the claim cannot be lawfully sold or assigned, the test approaches the outer limits of an acceptable test. However, we cannot say that the regulation exceeds the statutory authority of the Treasury. And the test probably cuts across the board with a minimum of harm about as well as any other test that might be devised.

Applying the willing buyer and seller test to the claim for income tax refund, we see no reason for concluding that the amount of the settlement necessarily represents the fair market value of the claim at the date of death. The amount of the settlement is relevant but not conclusive.

The issue was a factual one for the jury. The record supports the trial judge's denial of the motions for a directed verdict and a judgment n.o.v.

II. . . . If the jury had found that, based on "a reasonable knowledge of relevant facts" (Treas. Reg. §20.2031-1(b)), the claim for a tax refund, at the moment of the decedent's death, had a much smaller value than the amount of the settlement, we would not question the jury's finding. But there is no rational basis in the evidence for the jury to bring in a verdict that the claim had no value. . . .

Reasonable knowledge of the relevant facts would have revealed to the decedent and his accountant, as later discovered by present counsel, that there were gross errors in the revenue agent's report sent to the decedent nine months before his death. And reasonable knowledge of decedent's record would have led the decedent, his accountant, attorney, and executors to know that a certain memorandum tended to rebut the Commissioner's finding of fraud. All of the records were in existence and among the decedent's papers when he died.

In similar circumstances the Tax Court has held that the later discovered facts determine the value of the property at the date of death. The Tax Court said: "Even if the executors were totally ignorant of the claim, we do not agree that it would for that reason be without value. An estate may possess many assets, tangible and intangible, of which the deceased's representative or even the deceased himself may be unaware, and which may not become apparent until the lapse of a substantial period of time after death. Such property is for that reason no less an asset of the estate, nor can it necessarily be said to be valueless at the date of death. This is particularly true where, as here, the asset is one which by its nature is discoverable in the ordinary course of administration of the estate." Estate of Baldwin v. Commissioner, P-H T.C. Memo ¶59,203 (1959).

The administration of every estate involves a delay before the succession representative knows all the relevant existing facts affecting the value of the property. The federal estate tax law is sufficiently flexible and realistic to take account of this delay.

The taxpayer contends that what brought the claim into being was a memorandum Mr. Thompson "discovered [October 1956] among a bunch of old papers that appeared to be of no value." This memorandum concerned the sale of seven bales of cotton for $5,954.80. In one corner, in the decedent's handwriting, were the words "income taxes." One of the executors testified that the memorandum showed that the decedent "had no intention to defraud, and it would be impossible for the agent to go further back than three years in the investigation."

This discovery may have affected the taxpayer's appraisal of the claim. But the claim existed wholly apart from the memorandum. The "willing buyer and seller" are a hypothetical buyer and seller having a reasonable knowledge of relevant facts. It is impossible to believe that Congress intended valuation to be tested subjectively according to the state of mind of the executor making the return in question, the valuation depending on whether he was diligent and efficient in examining the decedent's records.

In any event, the relevancy of the memorandum to the issue of valuation does not mean that all other evidence is irrelevant. The record shows conclusively that the claim had value and was considered to have value wholly aside from the memorandum. The original attorney for the estate, just a few days after the decedent's death, December 27, 1955, recommended that the executors employ Mr. Thompson to inquire into the possibility of income tax refunds. March 22, 1956, within three months after the date of death, the executors engaged Mr. Thompson to make "a detailed investigation into the financial affairs and transactions" of the decedent. A week later they authorized him to file claims for refund of income taxes. By that time he had been "going through the records . . . and had come up with some evidence that several mistakes had been made." April 5, 1956, the estate's preliminary estate tax notice referred to a "contingent claim pending for refund of taxes, penalties, and interest on Fed. and State income taxes." Thus, there is no doubt that before the discovery of the memorandum in October 1956, the executors knew that the estate had a claim worth something. The executors, attorneys, and accountants simply had not sufficiently examined the decedent's records to be able to make an intelligent guess as to the value of the claim and to support the claim with evidence. But the evidence was always there to be found. The revenue agents testified that as soon as the full facts were known to them or to their superiors, the value of the claim was accepted. Mr. Thompson testified that all of the relevant facts existed at the time of Simmons's death, and that with full knowledge of these facts he reluctantly recommended that the estate settle for $42,000. He would have discovered the agents' errors along with the memorandum had Simmons retained him. In short, ignorance of the value of an asset at the time of a decedent's death does not justify treating the asset as valueless, any more than ignorance of the existence of an asset, discovered after the date of death, justifies exclusion of the asset from the decedent's gross estate.

Finally, although we do not accept the extreme position taken by the Government, that the amount of the compromise was necessarily the value of the claim at the time of death, that amount is certainly highly indicative of the fact that the claim had value at the time of Simmons's death. . . .

Considering this case in its entirety, we conclude that the controlling facts make it utterly unreasonable for the jury to bring in a verdict that the refund claim had no value at the time of the decedent's death. The absence of any rational basis for the jury's verdict makes it a mistake of law for the trial judge to deny the motion for a new trial. . . .

The judgment below is reversed and remanded.

Should the asserted fact that federal law prohibits the assignment of an income tax claim require a finding that the claim has no fair market value because it is not possible for there to be any buyers or sellers? Although 31 U.S.C. §203 (Rev. Stat. §3477) provides that an assignment of a claim against the United States before it has been allowed is null and void, that provision applies only to protect the United States and does not affect the legality of an assignment in proceedings between the assignor and the assignee. See Martin v. National Surety Co., 300 U.S. 588 (1937).

On a related inquiry, consider the proper valuation of a long-term annuity payout to a winner of a state lottery, includible in the winner's gross estate, valued to reflect the fact that the right to receive the payments could not be transferred, anticipated, attached, or assigned. The hypothetical willing-buyer, willing-seller test posits sale in a market of knowledgeable and willing parties dealing at arm's length and, like *Simmons*, no such market exists. Marketability of a right to receive payments is not (and never has been) a factor in the valuation tables for income or annuity interests. Rather, the historic reality is that the right to receive payments for a term of years or for life has been determined under the valuation tables with no consideration of marketability, notwithstanding that most traditional trust interests are nonassignable by virtue of virtually boilerplate inclusion of spendthrift protection provisions. Compare Estate of Gribauskas v. Commissioner, 116 T.C. 142 (2001), and Estate of Cook v. Commissioner, 82 T.C.M. (CCH) 154 (2001), sharply disagreeing with Estate of Shackleford v. United States, 99-2 U.S. Tax Cas. (CCH) ¶60,356 (E.D. Cal. 1999), aff'd, 262 F.3d 1028 (9th Cir. 2001) (the court determined that it must *assume* the existence of a market and then concluded that a lack of marketability discount should be applied in the context of that hypothetical market, the net result being that the discounted present value of the stream of payments determined under the valuation tables was cut to almost exactly half that amount.

The effect of postmortem facts can work both ways. Imagine that *D* died owning ten acres of unimproved land in a sparsely populated town in a very dry and dusty backcountry location. Seven months after *D*'s death, substantial uranium deposits were discovered in the hills, twenty miles away. Because of the need to house personnel to mine the uranium, the value of land in D's town rose immediately after the uranium discovery. At the time of D's death, a competent appraiser (not knowing of the existence of the nearby uranium) would have valued D's land at $100,000. Once the presence of the uranium became known, a competent appraiser would appraise it at $400,000. D's personal representative knew of the existence of the uranium when D's estate tax return was filed nine months after D's death, and did not elect alternate valuation. At what value should the land be included in D's gross estate? If postmortem facts are relevant, how would you argue that the property was not worth the higher value?

Well, it is one thing to quibble over the value of the land where the uranium was discovered, because at death not all the facts that did exist at death were known about that particular property, and the postmortem facts helped to better understand the value that did exist at the date of death. Quite a bit different is the land in town, which did not change and about which no new facts were discovered. It was the same at all times before and after death, and the uranium discovery did not alter the fundamental nature of (or even what was known about) the land in question. The facts didn't expose the true value of the property at the date of death; instead, that value changed by virtue of other factors, all of which occurred postmortem and therefore should be irrelevant. In this regard consider Estate of Necastro v. Commissioner, 68 T.C.M. (CCH) 227 (1994). Five years after the decedent's death it was discovered that realty included in the decedent's estate had suffered environmental contamination. The estate filed a claim for refund, attributable to a reduction in value from that reported for federal estate tax purposes based on the facts that were known at the date of death, when the awareness and stringent oversight devoted to these issues today did not exist. The court noted that it was not clear when the contamination occurred, or whether a reasonable buyer could have discovered it and correspondingly discounted the value of the property. Nevertheless, based on the government's own expert revaluation, the court permitted a reduction of over 33% from the value of the property determined before the contamination was discovered. The opinion did not, however, address the substantive issue whether facts discovered after death may influence valuation if willing buyers and sellers would not have known the relevant facts as of the valuation date.[8]

That this postmortem discovery issue is particularly uncertain is illustrated by Rubenstein v. United States, 826 F. Supp. 448 (S.D. Fla. 1993), in which the existence of the includible asset was not even known at

---

8. Flanders v. United States, 347 F. Supp. 95 (N.D. Cal. 1972), is an important reminder, however, that valuation differentials (in that case attributable to postmortem donation of a conservation easement) will be ignored if postmortem developments changed the character of the property. See also TAM 8432012 (the value of real estate for alternate valuation purposes should not reflect the effect of a long-term lease that automatically was renewed postmortem).

the valuation date, much less its value. The court held that property (a cause of action) discovered only after the decedent's death was includible in the gross estate and that the best evidence of its value was the amount for which it was settled during the course of estate administration. But Estate of Davis v. Commissioner, 65 T.C.M. (CCH) 2365 (1993), which involved a cause of action that was in litigation prior to the decedent's death and produced a judgment prior to filing the estate tax return, required inclusion but stated that valuation should reflect only events subsequent to the valuation date that were reasonably foreseeable at the valuation date. On that basis, a recovery of several million dollars was valued for estate tax purposes at less than $300,000, rejecting the government's assertion that the amount actually recovered was the best evidence of value.[9]

That even this result is uncertain is well illustrated by Estate of Andrews v. United States, 850 F. Supp. 1279 (E.D. Va. 1994), in which the decedent was the leading author of a particular genre of fiction. The government successfully asserted that the decedent's name was a market-able asset that had a determinable value for inclusion in the decedent's gross estate. Postmortem facts relating to a publication contract under negotiation when the decedent died were deemed germane to the determina-tion of what a willing buyer would pay for the right to use the decedent's name on ghostwritten books that mimicked the decedent's unique writing style. The court held that these facts were reasonably foreseeable at death and that informed buyers and sellers would consider them in reaching an agreement regarding a purchase of the decedent's name. The fact that a postmortem ghostwriting endeavor proved to be successful was deemed not relevant, however, on the question of the degree of discount that was

---

9. Other cases that involve the valuation of contingent interests or claims owned by a decedent at death include American Nat'l Bank & Trust Co. v. United States, 594 F.2d 1141 (7th Cir. 1979) (value of a claim to collect accidental death insurance proceeds), Estate of Curry v. Commissioner, 74 T.C. 540 (1980) (contingent legal fees in litigation in progress at the decedent's death), Estate of Sharp v. Commissioner, 68 T.C.M. (CCH) 1521 (1994) (cloud on title not resolved until after the decedent's death), Estate of Crossmore v. Commissioner, 56 T.C.M. (CCH) 483 (1988) (value of a decedent's interest in the estate of a prior decedent that was under attack on will contest grounds), Estate of Bartberger v. Commissioner, 54 T.C.M. (CCH) 1550 (1988) (value of a ranch that was subject to an adverse ownership claim), Estate of Aldrich v. Commissioner, 46 T.C.M. (CCH) 1295 (1983) (contingent legal fees), Estate of Cobb v. Commissioner, 44 T.C.M. (CCH) 1281 (1982) (value of a decedent's elective share interest in a predeceased spouse's estate that was contested and litigated to the state supreme court), Estate of Biagioni v. Commissioner, 42 T.C.M. (CCH) 1663 (1981) (estate tax value of a claim made for flood damage, as reduced by the one-third amount that attorneys would receive), Rev. Rul. 61-88, 1961-1 C.B. 417 (value of a descendible future interest that was contingent upon death without issue of a 44-year-old childless life beneficiary), TAM 9349003 (interests adverse to the decedent's ownership in the form of deeds dated prior to but filed of record after the decedent's death, regarded by the government as irrelevant to estate tax value because the decedent's entitlement at death was unimpaired), TAM 8308001 (value of suits filed by the decedent's estate to collect the proceeds of several life insurance policies). Cf. Estate of Cartwright v. Commissioner, 183 F.2d 1034 (9th Cir. 1999) (income in respect of a decedent for the value of legal fees involving work in progress at death).

appropriate in valuing the decedent's name to reflect the substantial risk that the endeavor would fail instead.

See Chapter 10 on the related issue of the admissibility of post-mortem facts to value the decedent's debts for §2053 deduction purposes.

12.   *Liquidation Value Versus Replacement Cost.*   The reference in Treas. Reg. §20.2031-1(b) to "fair market value" raises the question of which market is the appropriate referent. A secondhand automobile, for example, will be sold to a used car dealer at a lower price than the dealer will charge a customer to purchase the same car. Treas. Reg. §20.2031-1(b) states that property that dealers buy at a lower price than that at which they sell must be valued at the higher retail price because property must be valued at the price at which it most commonly is sold to the general public. Rev. Proc. 65-19 indicated, however, that if tangible personal property is sold through advertisement in the classified section of a newspaper or at a public auction, the sale price may be determinative of the value of the item on the applicable valuation date if sale occurs within a reasonable time after the valuation date. Moreover, if the estate actually sells an asset to a dealer for less than its estate tax value, the estate *may* be granted an estate tax deduction for all or part of the difference. Treas. Reg. §20.2053-3(d)(2). See Chapter 10 for a discussion of other requirements of this deduction.

Another issue regarding the proper market for valuation of an asset is illustrated by assets subject to a restriction on marketability. The following case is an unusual aspect of that issue, and it prompted an unusual reaction from the government.

United States v. Cartwright
411 U.S. 546 (1973)

Mr. Justice WHITE delivered the opinion of the Court.

The Internal Revenue Code of 1954 requires that, for estate tax purposes, the "value" of all property held by a decedent at the time of death be included in the gross estate. 26 U.S.C. §2031. By regulation, the Secretary of the Treasury has determined that shares in open-end investment companies, or mutual funds, are to be valued at their public offering price or "asked" price at the date of death. Treas. Reg. §20.2031-8(b). The question this case presents is whether that determination is reasonable in the context of the market for mutual fund shares.

At the time of her death in 1964, Ethel B. Bennett owned approximately 8,700 shares of three mutual funds that are regulated by the Investment Company Act of 1940, 15 U.S.C. §80a-1 et seq. The 1940 Act seeks generally to regulate publicly held companies that are engaged in investing in securities. Open-end investment companies, or mutual funds, "dominate" this industry. Unquestionably, the unique characteristic of mutual funds is that they are permitted, under the Act, to market their shares continuously to the public, but are required to be prepared to redeem outstanding shares at any time. §80a-22(e). The redemption "bid" price that a shareholder may receive is set by the Act at approximately the fractional value per share of the fund's net assets at the time of redemption. §80a-2(a)(32). In contrast, the "asked" price, or the price at which the fund initially offers its shares to the public, includes not only the net asset value per share at the time of sale, but also a fixed sales charge or "sales load" assessed by the fund's principal underwriter who acts as an agent in marketing the fund's shares. §80a-2(a)(35). Sales loads vary within fixed limits from mutual fund to mutual fund, but all are paid to the fund's underwriters; the charges do not become part of the assets of the fund. The sales loads of the funds held by the decedent ranged from seven and eight percent to one percent of the fractional net asset value of the fund's shares.

Private trading in mutual fund shares is virtually nonexistent. Thus, at any given time, under the statutory scheme created by the Investment Company Act, shares of any open-end mutual fund with a sales load are being sold at two distinct prices. Initial purchases by the public are made from the fund, at the "asked" price, which includes the load. But shareholders "sell" their shares back to the fund at the statutorily defined redemption or bid price.

Respondent is the executor of the decedent's estate. On the federal estate tax return, he reported the value of the mutual fund shares held by the decedent at their redemption price, which amounted to about $124,400. The Commissioner assessed a deficiency based upon his valuation of the shares at their public offering or asked price, pursuant to Treas. Reg. §20.2031-8(b). Valued on that basis, the shares were worth approximately $133,300. Respondent paid the deficiency of about $3,100, including interest, filed a timely claim for a refund, and, when that claim was denied, commenced a refund action in Federal District Court on the ground that the valuation based on §20.2031-8(b) was unreasonable. . . .

We recognize that this Court is not in the business of administering the tax laws of the Nation. Congress has delegated that task to the Secretary of the Treasury, and regulations promulgated under his authority, if found to "implement the congressional mandate in some reasonable manner," must be upheld. But that principle is to set the framework for judicial analysis; it does not displace it. We find that the contested regulation is unrealistic and unreasonable, and therefore affirm the judgment of the Court of Appeals.

In implementing §2031, the general principle of the Treasury Regulations is that the value of property is to be determined by its fair market value at the time of the decedent's death. "The fair market value is the price at which the property would change hands between a willing buyer and a willing seller, neither being under any compulsion to buy or sell and both having reasonable knowledge of relevant facts." Treas. Reg. §20.2031-1(b). The willing buyer-willing seller test of fair market value is nearly as old as the federal income, estate, and gifts taxes themselves, and is not challenged here. Under this test, it is clear that if the decedent had owned ordinary corporate stock listed on an exchange, its "value" for estate tax purposes would be the price the estate could have obtained if it had sold the stock on the valuation date, that price being, under Treas. Reg. §20.2031-2(b), the mean between the highest and lowest quoted selling prices on that date. Respondent urges that similar treatment be given mutual fund shares and that, accordingly, their value be measured by the redemption price at the date of death, the only price that the estate could hope to obtain if the shares had been sold.

Respondent's argument has the clear ring of common sense to it, but the United States maintains that the redemption price does not reflect the price that a willing buyer would pay, inasmuch as the mutual fund is under a statutory obligation to redeem outstanding shares whenever they are offered. According to the Government, the only market for mutual fund shares that has both willing buyers and willing sellers is the public offering market. Therefore, the price in that market, the asked price, is an appropriate basis for valuation. The central difficulty with this argument is that it unrealistically bifurcates the statutory scheme for the trading in mutual fund shares. To be sure, the fund is under an obligation to redeem its shares at the stated price. §80a-22(e). But, at the time of the original purchases both the fund and the purchasers are aware of that duty and both willingly enter into the sale transactions nonetheless. . . .

In the context of the Investment Company Act, the redemption price may thus be properly viewed only as the final step in a voluntary transaction between a willing buyer and a willing seller. As a matter of statutory law, holders of mutual fund shares cannot obtain the "asked" price from the fund. That price is never paid by the fund; it is used by the fund when selling its shares to the public — and even then the fund receives merely the net asset value per share from the sale, with the sales load being paid directly to the underwriter. In short, the only price that a shareholder may realize and that the fund — the only buyer — will pay is the redemption price. In the teeth of this fact, Treas. Reg. §20.2031-8(b) purports to assign a value to mutual fund shares that the estate could not hope to obtain and that the fund could not offer.

In support of the Regulation, the Government stresses that many types of property are taxed at values above those which could be realized during an actual sale. For example, ordinary corporate stock is valued at its fair market price without taking into account the brokerage commission that a seller must generally pay in order to sell the stock. Respondent does not contend that that approach is inappropriate or that, for example, the value of ordinary stock in an estate should be the market price at the time less anticipated brokerage fees. But §20.2031-8(b) operates in an entirely different fashion. The regulation includes as an element of value the commission cost incurred in the hypothetical *purchase* of the mutual fund shares already held in the decedent's estate. If that principle were carried over to the ordinary stock situation, then a share traded at $100 on the date of death would be valued, not at $100 as it now is, but at, say, $102, representing the "value" plus the fee that a person buying the stock on that day would have to pay. It hardly need be said that such a valuation method is at least inconsistent with long-established Treasury practice and would appear at odds with the basic notions of valuation embodied in the Internal Revenue Code. See Estate of Wells v. Commissioner, 50 T.C. 871, 880 (1968) (Tannenwald, J., dissenting).

Even if it were assumed that the public offering price were somehow relevant to the value of mutual fund shares privately held, there would still be the difficulty that shares so held are, in important respects, similar to ordinary corporate stock held subject to a restrictive agreement (such as a first-refusal right at a specified price). With respect to the value of such stock, the Treasury Regulations have provided that the price that may be obtained in the marketplace does not control. Rather, so long as the restriction is a bona fide one, the value of the shares in the hands of the restricted stockholder is determined in accordance with the terms of the restriction. Treas. Reg. §20.2031-2(h). Outstanding mutual fund shares are likewise held subject to a restriction, as the Court of Appeals noted. 457 F.2d. at 571. Those shares may not be "sold" at the public offering price. By statute, they may be "sold" back to the mutual fund only at the redemption price. We see no valid justification for disregarding this reality connected with the ownership of mutual fund shares.

The Government nevertheless argues that Treas. Reg. §20.2031-8(b) reasonably values the "bundle of rights" that is transferred with the ownership of the mutual fund shares.[10] For this argument, heavy reliance is placed on this Court's decision in Guggenheim v. Rasquin, 312 U.S. 254 (1941); Powers v. Commissioner, 312 U.S. 259 (1941); United States v. Ryerson, 312 U.S. 260 (1941), which held that the cash-surrender value of a single-premium life insurance policy did not necessarily represent its only taxable value for federal gift tax purposes. In *Guggenheim*, the lead case, the taxpayer purchased single-premium life insurance policies with an aggregate face value of one million dollars for approximately $852,000 and, shortly thereafter, gave the policies to her children. On the gift tax return, the policies were listed at their cash-surrender value of about $717,000 — admittedly the only amount the donor or the donees could receive, if the policies were surrendered. But the Commissioner valued the gift at the cost of the policies, and this Court upheld that valuation: "the owner of a fully paid life insurance policy has more than the mere right to surrender it; he has the right to retain it for its investment virtues and to receive the face amount of the policy upon the insured's death. That these latter rights are deemed by purchasers of insurance to have substantial value is clear from the difference between the cost of a single-premium policy and its immediate or early cash-surrender value. . . ." 312 U.S. at 257. Because the "entire bundle of rights in a single-premium policy" is so difficult to give a realistic value to, the Court deferred to the Commissioner's determination and permitted valuation to be based on cost: "Cost is cogent evidence of value." Id. at 258. But as the District Court observed, 323 F. Supp. at 773, shares in mutual funds are quite unlike insurance policies, particularly in light of the policyowner's right to receive the full face value of the policy upon the insured's death. Moreover, mutual fund shares present no analogous difficulties in valuation. On any given day, their commercial value may be determined by turning to the financial pages of a newspaper. Obviously, with respect to mutual funds, there are "investment virtues" and the prospects of capital gains or dividends. But that is true of any corporate security. Nonetheless, shareholders in mutual funds are singled out by the Regulation and their holdings

---

10.　The Government argues that, as a practical matter, an estate would rarely be hurt by valuation of mutual fund shares at the asked price, because Treas. Reg. §20.2053-3(d)(2) permits an estate to deduct the difference between the asked and bid prices if the shares are sold to pay certain enumerated expenses. By its terms, however, that regulation applies only if "the sale is *necessary*" to pay those expenses. [Emphasis added.] In any event, the regulation is inapplicable altogether if the shares are transferred in kind to an heir or legatee.

valued at an unrealistic replacement cost — which includes "brokers' commission" — while other shareholdings are valued without regard to such commissions. . . .

We recognize that normally "Treasury regulations must be sustained unless unreasonable and plainly inconsistent with the revenue statutes." But even if the Regulation contested here is not, on its face, technically inconsistent with §2031, it is manifestly inconsistent with the most elementary provisions of the Investment Company Act of 1940 and operates without regard for the market in mutual fund shares that the Act created and regulates. Congress surely could not have intended §2031 to be interpreted in such a manner. The Regulation also imposes an unreasonable and unrealistic measure of value. We agree with Judge Tannenwald, who stated at the very outset of the dispute over Treas. Reg. §20.2031-8(b), that "it does not follow that, because [the Commissioner] has a choice of alternatives, his choice should be sustained where the alternative chosen is unrealistic. In such a situation the regulations embodying that choice should be held to be unreasonable." Estate of Wells v. Commissioner, 50 T.C. at 878 (dissenting opinion).

The judgment of the Court of Appeals is affirmed.

Mr. Justice STEWART, with whom the Chief Justice and Mr. Justice REHNQUIST join, dissenting. . . .

. . . [A]s both the District Court and the Court of Appeals noted, the only practical means of disposing of mutual fund shares once acquired is redemption, and redemption cannot be deemed a sale of the sort described in the general rule since the party purchasing (the issuing company) is under an absolute obligation to redeem the shares when tendered, and the party selling has no practical alternative, if he wishes to liquidate his holdings, other than to offer them to the issuing company for redemption.

This being the case, the Commissioner was faced with the problem of establishing a method of valuing the shares most nearly equal to their inherent worth. In doing so, he chose not to treat their redemption value as dispositive of this question. In promulgating his Regulation, he might rationally have considered that "on demand" redemption at net asset value is but one of many rights incident to the ownership of mutual fund shares.

For example, in the case of Mrs. Bennett's shares, her estate had not only the right to redeem them "on demand," but also to retain them; and if it had done so it would have possessed not only the normal dividend and capital gains rights associated with most investments, but also the right to have such dividends and capital gains as accrued applied toward the purchase of additional shares at a price below that which a member of the general public would have had to pay for such shares. . . .

The Commissioner has determined that the proper method of valuing *all* the rights, both redemptive and otherwise, incident to the ownership of mutual fund shares is to determine what a member of the general public, acting under no constraints, would have had to pay for these rights if purchased on the open market. And, as noted earlier, although no such market exists for mutual fund shares *once issued* to an investor, a perfectly normal market of willing buyers and sellers does exist with respect to such shares prior to their issuance. Thus, the Commissioner took the price at which the shares would have sold on this market as fairly reflective of their inherent worth. I cannot say that this method of valuation adopted by the Commissioner, and embodied in Treas. Reg. §20.2031-8(b), is so unreasonable and inconsistent with the statute as to render it invalid.

The respondent's claim that the regulation is invalid is grounded upon two principal arguments. First, he says, the estate is being taxed on an amount in excess of what it can, as a practical matter, realize from the disposition of the mutual fund shares. But this is equally true of many other assets subject to taxation under our estate tax laws. For example, real property passing into an estate is taxed upon its full fair market value, despite the fact that as a practical matter the estate must usually pay some percentage of that sum in brokerage fees if it wishes to dispose of the property and receive cash in its stead. This attack upon the Regulation thus amounts to no less than an attack upon the whole system of valuation embodied in the Treasury Regulation on Estate Tax, based as it is upon fair value in an open market. I am not ready to hold that this long-established and long-accepted system is basically invalid. . . .

Given the peculiar characteristics of mutual fund shares, it is arguable that the Commissioner might reasonably have adopted a method of valuation different from that which he has chosen. But that is a question that is not for us to decide. "[We] do not sit as a committee of revision to perfect the administration of the tax laws. Congress has delegated to the Commissioner, not to the courts, the task of prescribing 'all needful rules and regulations for the enforcement' of the Internal Revenue Code. 26 U.S.C. §7805(a). In this area of limitless factual variations, 'it is the province of Congress and the Commissioner, not the courts, to make the appropriate adjustments.' " United States v. Correll, 389 U.S. at 306-307.

I would reverse the judgment of the Court of Appeals and sustain the validity of the Regulation.

Following *Cartwright* the Treasury Department amended the estate tax and the gift tax regulations, but only to adopt liquidation value for the limited case of shares in open-end-load mutual funds. Treas. Reg. §§20.2031-8(b); 25.2512-6(b). The Treasury Department has *not* amended the regulations pertaining to the valuation of any other property. Life insurance owned on the life of another, for example, is still valued at replacement cost. Is there an adequate justification for treating shares in open-end-load mutual funds differently from other assets? Does the Court's adoption of redemption price as the value of such shares constitute different treatment from that accorded to other assets? These issues relating to the parameters of *Cartwright* remain to be litigated, and the case for finding a regulation to be invalid is daunting.

In general, the challenging issue is whether liquidation value is a more appropriate figure than replacement cost for the estate tax valuation of all assets. The majority opinion in *Cartwright* analogized the position of a holder of mutual fund shares to that of a shareholder of corporate stock subject to a restrictive agreement, such as a right of first refusal at a specified price. The Court asserted that Treas. Reg. §20.2031-2(h) would determine the estate tax value of such shares according to the terms of the restrictive agreement. If the holder of the decedent's mutual fund shares was not *obliged* to sell those shares, the Court was not correct when it assumed that a restrictive agreement would have determined the estate tax value of the shares. See Worcester County Trust Co. v. Commissioner, 134 F.2d 578 (1st Cir. 1943); Lowndes, Kramer, & McCord, ESTATE AND GIFT TAXES §18.45 at 561-562 (3d ed. 1974). Note that, since 1990, restrictive agreements do not determine estate tax value unless the conditions of §2703(b) are satisfied.

Consider the situation involved in TAM 9235005 in light of *Cartwright*. The will involved specified that the decedent's child could select art objects from the estate not to exceed in value the amount of that child's share of the estate. The will also directed that any art not selected was to be sold and the proceeds added to the estate for distribution. All the art was sold at auction because the child selected none of it. Responding to a question regarding the value of the art, the government ruled that it was determined by the price paid by the successful bidder at auction, which included a 10% premium or commission assessed against the buyer to compensate the auctioneer. The estate argued on the basis of *Cartwright* that value should be what the selling estate realized rather than what the buyer paid in gross, to which the government correctly responded that numerous authorities stand for the proposition that value is replacement cost (what a buyer would pay) rather than liquidation value (what the seller realizes). According to the TAM, the estate could have sold the art without the assistance of the auctioneer and might have received the full price paid by the willing buyer without incurring the selling commission, making the total price paid by the buyer at auction the true reflection of what the art was worth in the open market. The government did concede, however, that if the sale met the requirements of §2053(a)(2) and Treas. Reg. §20.2053-3(d)(2) (sale was necessary to pay the decedent's debts, expenses of administration, or taxes, to preserve the estate, or to effect distribution), then the commission paid to the auctioneer would be an allowable deduction that would subject only the net amount actually received by the estate to tax. The TAM concluded, however, that sale was not necessary in this estate to effect distribution to the extent the child could have taken the art in kind; thus, to that extent, sale "was primarily for the benefit of" the child and could not support a deduction for the auctioneer's commission. It was not stated, but presumably the decedent's direction to sell the balance of the art would justify a deduction for any commission incurred on the sale of art in excess of what the child could have received in kind. Moreover, the government ruled that sales the estate could prove were necessary to generate funds to pay estate expenses, debts, or taxes also would generate deductible commissions.

In conjunction with the replacement cost concept, consider how the government views the issue illustrated by the next Ruling:

Revenue Ruling 55-71

Advice has been requested whether the Federal excise tax on jewelry, furs and related articles of personal property should be considered in determining the fair market value of such property for Federal estate and gift tax purposes. . . .

While the determination of fair market value is a question of fact, the question of which criterion or standard should be used in determining the value of property for estate or gift tax purposes is a question of law.

In Publicker v. Commissioner, 206 F.2d 250 (3d Cir. 1953), it was held that where jewelry was purchased at retail by a taxpayer and made the subject of gifts, the Federal excise tax should be included in ascertaining the value of the jewelry for Federal gift tax purposes. The court stated that in view of the irreconcilable conflict of testimony of the expert witnesses, the cost of the jewelry, including that part of the donor's cost of the gifts which represented the Federal excise tax, was considered as the best evidence of value. To the same effect, see Duke v. Commissioner, 200 F.2d 82 (2d Cir. 1952), and Estate of Gould v. Commissioner, 14 T.C. 414 (1950).

In Guggenheim v. Rasquin, 312 U.S. 254 (1941), it was held that the value of single premium life insurance policies, which were irrevocably assigned simultaneously with issuance, is cost to the donor rather than their cash surrender value at the time of the transfer. The Court states, "Presumptively the value of these policies at the date of the gift was the amount which the insured had expended to acquire them. Cost is cogent evidence of value. And here it is the only suggested criterion which reflects the value to the owner. . . . Cost in this situation is not market price in the normal sense of the term. But the absence of market price is no barrier to valuation." See also Estate of DuPont v. Commissioner, 18 T.C. 1134 (1952), wherein the Tax Court held that, for estate tax purposes, the proper measure of the value of certain insurance policies, owned by the decedent on the life of his father, was the replacement cost thereof or, in the absence of such replacement cost, the respective interpolated terminal reserve value thereof.

The existence of the Federal excise tax on jewelry, furs, and other related articles of personal property sold by dealers, is an item which will tend to increase the amount at which an individual or an estate would be willing to sell such property. It is an element which affects the general market for that type of property.

In view of the foregoing, it is held that the Federal Excise tax on jewelry, furs, and related articles of personal property is a relevant factor which should be considered in determining the fair market value of such property for Federal estate and gift tax purposes.

See Treas. Reg. §25.2512-7. See also Estate of Robinson v. Commissioner, 69 T.C. 222 (1977), in which the court held that the value of an installment obligation that was included in a decedent's gross estate is not discounted by estimated income taxes on gain payable by the estate or the beneficiaries on collecting future installment payments.

The issue whether built-in income tax liabilities should be considered in estate (or gift) tax valuation is difficult to evaluate, and case law has been all over the map on a number of different issues. For example, if X were the owner of stock in a closely held business that was a going concern, and the assets owned by that business were highly appreciated (such that a buyer who planned to liquidate the business would incur a large capital gains tax), (1) is that potential income tax liability too contingent to be reflected at all, (2) should the potential cost reduce the value of the business dollar for dollar (and if so, based on what rate of tax, and discounted from what assumed date of liquidation), (3) should the possible tax be one among a number of factors in determining the net asset value of the business, which might be just one among several methods used to determine the overall value of the stock (the other common method being to value the cash flow as a going concern), or (4) should the tax situation be reflected in determining any discount to the underlying value of the business (determined using going concern and net asset values, without considering this element) to reflect a lack of marketability discount? Authority can be found on each side of this issue, with respect to each of these positions. Similar questions arise if a business qualifies for S Corporation status but a potential buyer might not qualify, in which case a going concern valuation based on income flow appropriately might consider the tax attributable to the expected income flow. And what about other forms of built in tax liability — such as a piece of farmland that was §2032A special use valued in a prior decedent's estate and as to which a recapture tax liability would apply if material participation were to cease before expiration of the recapture period? These questions are just beginning to come to the courts, so stay tuned for the "Paul Harvey" (rest of this story).

PART C.   ALTERNATE VALUATION

Code References: *Estate Tax: §2032*
                       Generation-Skipping Transfer Tax: §§2624, 2642(b)(2)

13.   The §2031(a) value of all property included in a decedent's gross estate (even property not owned by the decedent at death) is determined at the decedent's date of death, unless the decedent's executor[11] elects the §2032 alternate valuation method. This alternative is available only if the gross estate is large enough to require that an estate tax return be filed under §6018. Treas. Reg. §20.2032-1(b)(1). In addition, §2032(c) requires that the election result in a reduction of both the gross estate and the aggregate tax imposed under the estate and generation-skipping transfer taxes — after applying all credits that further reduce the tax payment obligation. Why was Congress concerned about the election being made in a zero-tax estate, and why would anyone make this election if it did not reduce the value of the gross estate? The answers lie in the applicable exclusion amount and unlimited marital deduction, which may cause a larger estate to be tax free, and the new basis at death rule in §1014. As well, taxpayers sometimes reduce the size of the estate of the first spouse to die in anticipation of the amount that may be includible in the estate of the surviving spouse. Keep these kinds of issues in mind as you analyze the alternate valuation date opportunity as part of an overall genre of planning known as "postmortem estate planning." Tax planning doesn't cease just because the taxpayer did!

If the executor properly elects alternate valuation, the applicable date for valuing each item in the decedent's gross estate (including property not owned by the decedent at death) is determined according to the following rules:

---

11.   For estate tax purposes, the term "executor" is broadly defined by §2203 to refer to the executor or administrator of the decedent's estate or, if none is appointed who is qualified and acting within the United States, to any person in actual or constructive possession of any of the decedent's property.

(1) The general rule is that property is valued six months after the decedent's death. If the sixth month after the month of the decedent's death does not have a date corresponding to the date of the decedent's death (for example, the decedent died on March 31 or August 30), the alternate valuation date is the last day of the sixth month following the decedent's death (for example, September 30 or February 28 — or February 29 in a leap year — in the prior example). Rev. Rul. 74-260.

(2) An exception to the general rule is that property distributed, sold, exchanged, or otherwise disposed of within six months after the decedent's death is valued on the date of that disposition. Thus, although most people refer to the "six-month valuation rule" as a shorthand reference to the alternate valuation date, the proper valuation date may precede six months and can be affected by actions engineered by the personal representative to lock-in earlier values. Such as to freeze some values during a rising market.

(3) There is a special rule for any interest or asset, the value of which is affected by a mere lapse of time. This type of property is valued at the decedent's death (instead of on the alternate valuation date), with an adjustment to reflect any difference in value on the alternate valuation date that is not due to the mere lapse of time. Thus, for example, life estates, remainders, reversions, patents, leaseholds, and similar interests that are time-sensitive are valued in a way that reflects changes in the value of underlying assets but not changes that reflect the passage of time, as illustrated in Treas. Reg. §§20.2032-1(f)(1) and -1(f)(2). Notice the difference between §2032(a)(3) and the flush language in §2032(b). Let's look at an illustration of this last factor:

Assume that D transferred assets in trust to pay income to S for life, remainder to C, who died ten years later and bequeathed the remainder to R. At C's death S was 50 years and four months old, and the value of the trust assets was $130,000; assume the life estate factor for that month (based on the fluctuating §7520 interest rate) was .66666. C's personal representative made a *valid* alternate valuation election. To simplify the facts, assume that no distributions were made from the trust and no income was earned or received by the trust between the date of C's death and the alternate valuation date. Also assume the factor for S's life estate on the latter date was .60000 (which reflects the fact that S got older and it also reflects a different §7520 interest rate assumption on the later date). Using the same §7520 mortality rate as at C's death but the current interest rate assumption on the later date, the factor on the alternate valuation date would be .62500. The issue would be the includible value in C's gross estate under §2033 in each of the following circumstances:

(a) Six months after C's death the value of the trust assets was $100,000 and S was alive and healthy. Here the proper factor to value S's life estate would be .625 so the value of C's remainder is the antithesis, .375 multiplied against $100,000. Can you explain why?

(b) S died five months after C's death. The date of C's death value of the trust assets was $150,000; six months later it was $140,000. The issue here is whether the death of S is a change attributable to the mere lapse of time, such that it cannot be reflected in a valuation of the life estate at $0 and therefore the remainder at 100% of the trust value. Notwithstanding that this is the quintessential lapse of time for C, it is not the kind of change contemplated by the rule, so the proper inclusion would be 100% of $140,000. See Estate of Hance v. Commissioner, 18 T.C. 499 (1952), *acq.*; Rev. Rul. 55-379. Compare Rev. Rul. 63-52.

Another factor to consider in alternate valuation is to compare apples to apples, between the date of death and the alternate valuation date. Which is to say that changes in the asset itself, as opposed to the value of the same asset, may not be reflected. So assume that D owned an automobile with a date of death fair market value of $13,600. Two months after D's death, the automobile was totaled in an accident; its salvage value was $3,000 and the loss was not insured, nor could damages be collected in reimbursement of the loss. D's personal representative made a valid alternate valuation election. How the automobile should be reported on D's estate tax return may be a function of a number of factors. First, is the wreck the "same asset" as the car owned at death such that §2032 is even available? Let's assume it is so regarded. Next: what amount of casualty loss may D's personal representative deduct from D's gross estate under §2054? And third, pursuant to §642(g), if D's personal representative filed a waiver of the right to deduct the casualty loss as an estate tax deduction under §2054 to instead claim a §165(c) casualty loss income tax deduction, how will valuation affect these postmortem planning options? See §165(b) and recall §1014 new basis at death. The imponderable is whether a reduced estate tax value is preferable to a date of death value and either a §165 or §2054 deduction.

14. *Distribution, Sale, Exchange, or Other Disposition.* Any transaction that removes an asset from the decedent's estate (or from the ownership of any person who acquired the asset from the decedent — e.g., a surviving joint tenant) will trigger §2032(a)(1). Some transactions (such as a tax-free exchange of securities pursuant to a corporate reorganization) are regarded as a mere change in form and not dispositions that accelerate the alternate valuation date. Treas. Reg. §20.2032-1(c)(1). But transactions that remove the property and its value from the estate, such as distributions from the probate estate, constitute dispositions that establish the valuation date.

Property is considered as distributed upon settlement of the estate or an earlier entry of an order or decree of distribution, if the order or decree subsequently becomes final. Distribution also is deemed to occur on the segregation or separation of property from an estate or trust if it becomes unqualifiedly subject to the demand or disposition of the distributees, or upon the actual payment or delivery of property to a distributee, whichever first occurs. Treas. Reg. §20.2032-1(c)(2). In a pour-over will estate plan in which the personal representative is also trustee of the following trust, distribution will be just a bookkeeping entry moving the asset from one ledger to the other, but acceleration nevertheless occurs as if the asset had been sold or otherwise disposed of. As a consequence, the alternate valuation rules can affect a personal representative's decision whether to make partial distributions of estate assets within six months of the decedent's death. This in turn increases the duties imposed on a personal representative in a taxable estate in which alternate valuation might be relevant.

In addition to actions by a personal representative, §2032(a)(1) may be put in play by a trustee, by any donee to whom the decedent transferred property during life in a way that required inclusion in the gross estate under §§2036 through 2038 or §2041, or by an heir, devisee, or other owner (such as a surviving joint tenant or tenant by the entirety) to whom title passed directly under local law. Treas. Reg. §20.2032-1(c)(3). However, the passage of both title and the right to possess real property to the decedent's heirs or devisees immediately upon the decedent's death under state law does not constitute an accelerating distribution if the property remains subject to the executor's right of possession to satisfy claims. See Rev. Rul. 78-378. A binding contract for the sale, exchange, or other disposition of property is regarded as a disposition on the effective date of the contract (normally the date it is entered into, unless the contract specifies a different effective date), if the transaction subsequently is carried out substantially in accordance with the contract terms. Treas. Reg. §20.2032-1(c)(3).

Consider now an illustration about the all-or-nothing nature of the alternate value election. Assume that D died owning Blackacre and 10,000 shares of stock in a publicly held corporation. The value of the rest of D's assets was negligible. A year before death, D transferred Whiteacre to Y, reserving a §2036(a)(1) legal life estate therein. D made no other inter vivos gifts. At the date of D's death, the fair market value of the 10,000 shares of stock was $700,000, the fair market value of Blackacre was $450,000, and the fair market value of Whiteacre was $425,000. Three months after D's death, Y sold Whiteacre to an unrelated party for its then value of $426,500. Five months after D's death, D's personal representative distributed Blackacre, then worth $452,000, to the fiduciary designated to serve as trustee of a trust created by D's will. The fair market value of the corporate stock six months after D's death was $680,000. One month later, when D's personal representative distributed this corporate stock to the fiduciary serving as D's testamentary trustee, it was worth $685,000.

(a) If D's personal representative made a valid alternate valuation election the estate tax values of D's three assets would be $680,000, 452,000, and 426,500, for a total of $1,558,500, or a total decline of $16,500.

(b) If *D*'s estate qualified for a $600,000 charitable deduction the original $1,575,000 estate would no longer be taxable and alternate value would not be an option. Nor would it be available if the stock had not changed in value. Be certain that you understand why *D*'s personal representative might want to elect alternate valuation in such a situation.

15. *Treatment of Income.* Alternate valuation involves only the valuation of items includible in the gross estate and not the initial identification of which items are includible. Regardless of whether the personal representative elects the alternate valuation method, the items of property to be included in the gross estate must be identified as of the date of death. For this purpose, income derived from includible property is regarded as a separate item of property. Thus, for example, interest accrued on a bond at the date of the decedent's death is inventoried separately from the principal amount of the bond, and each is valued separately whether the personal representative elects the alternate valuation method or the date of death valuation method. Moreover, interest that accrues after the decedent's death but before the alternate valuation date also is a separate property item and it is not includible in the gross estate and is not reflected in either valuation method because it did not exist on the date of death. Is this the right result, or does date of death valuation implicitly reflect the income generating capacity of an asset so that post-mortem income actually *is* reflected in that value? If this is true, should income earned post-mortem be includible in the gross estate for alternate valuation purposes? Consider the following materials in answering this question.

A owned a bond that pays 6% interest semi-annually (on June 30 and December 31), and died on January 31, not having collected the interest due on December 31. At death the bond was selling at par ($1,000). The personal representative collected the accrued interest on March 4 and sold the bond on May 31 for a cash price of $1,020 (which included interest accrued after December 31). The bond and interest should be inventoried and valued as shown in the following table.

Inventory Item	Date of Death Value	Date for Alternate Value	Alternate Value
Bond Principal	$1,000	May 31	$995*
Bond Interest Accrued and Payable on Dec. 31	$30	March 4	$30
Accrued Interest for Jan.1 — Jan. 31	$5	May 31	$5

* This figure is $1,020, less five months accrued interest

Similarly, with respect to leased property, rent accrued to the date of death should be included in the gross estate, regardless of the valuation method elected, but rent accrued thereafter is excluded under both methods.

16.   Dividends. Should the same treatment apply to postmortem dividends? Consider, for example, whether dividends that reflect capital gain do and should differ from ordinary dividends, as explained by the following Ruling.

Revenue Ruling 76-234

Advice has been requested whether capital gains dividends of regulated investment companies (mutual funds) are includible in computing the value of a decedent's gross estate under §2032 under the circumstances described below.

The decedent died owning shares of stock in various regulated investment companies. The estate's representative elected to use the alternate valuation method in determining the value of the decedent's gross estate. Between the date of the decedent's death and the alternate valuation date, capital gains dividends were declared and paid on the stock. These dividends were attributable solely to gains on stock held by the companies at the decedent's death. The amount of dividends represented approximately 5% of the value of the securities as of the alternate valuation date. . . .

Under Treas. Reg. §20.2032-1(d) property interests are divided into "included property" and "excluded property" when the estate's representative elects the alternative valuation method. "Included property" encompasses all property interests existing at the date of the decedent's death that form a part of the decedent's gross estate as determined under §§2033 through 2044 and are valued in accordance with the provisions of §2032. "Excluded property" is composed of property earned or accrued (whether received or not) after the decedent's death and during the alternate valuation period with respect to any property interest existing at the date of the decedent's death, that does not represent a form of "included property" itself or the receipt of "included property."

Treas. Reg. §20.2032-1(d)(4) provides that ordinary dividends out of earnings and profits declared to stockholders of record after the decedent's death are excluded property. However, if dividends are declared to stockholders of record after the decedent's death with the effect that the shares of stock at the subsequent valuation date do not reasonably represent the same "included property" of the gross estate as existed at the date of the decedent's death, the dividends are "included property," except to the extent that they are out of earnings of the corporation after the date of the decedent's death. . . .

These regulations reflect the decision in Maass v. Higgins, 312 U.S. 443 (1941), 1941-1 C.B. 434. In that decision, the Supreme Court of the United States held that ordinary dividends, rents, and interest received during the alternate valuation period are commonly considered income and not to be included in the value of the gross estate under the optional (alternate) method of valuation.

A distribution to an estate from a regulated investment company in the form of a capital gains dividend, which is declared and paid to stockholders of record after the decedent's death, is estate income subject to the Federal income tax. Such a dividend is not "included property" within the contemplation of Treas. Reg. §20.2032-1(d)(4) unless, as a result of the distribution, the shares of stock at the subsequent valuation date do not "reasonably represent" the same "included property" of the gross estate as existed at the date of the decedent's death. . . . The facts in the present case indicate that the shares of stock owned by the estate at the alternate valuation date reasonably represent the same "included property" at the date of death because the dividend was not extraordinary in any sense.

Accordingly, the capital gains dividend paid to the estate by the regulated investment company is not includible in computing the value of the decedent's gross estate under §2032.

17.   Other Forms of Earnings.   In the following case the notion of postmortem earnings was stretched by the taxpayer. Consider how the hydrocarbon extraction differed from ordinary income production.

Estate of Johnston v. United States
779 F.2d 1123 (5th Cir. 1986)

POLITZ, J.: This case presents the *res nova* question whether proceeds from interests in oil and gas properties, received by a decedent's estate between the date of death and the alternate valuation date authorized by §2032(a), are includible in the gross estate, in whole or in part, for the purpose of determining the federal estate tax. The district court held that no portion of such proceeds was includible in the gross estate. The government appeals. We reverse and remand.

. . . Nellie S. Johnston died testate on January 27, 1974. Her will named Robert B. Payne as executor. Payne exercised the option authorized by §2032(a) and chose to value Johnston's estate as of six months after her death rather than on the date of her death. Johnston died owning various working and royalty interests in numerous oil and gas properties, most of which were located in Texas. In the six months after her death her interests generated net income of $156,011 on which the estate paid income tax after deducting the statutory allowance for depletion. Following an audit by the Internal Revenue Service, this entire income was included in Johnston's gross estate under §2032(a)(1), and a net deficiency of $278,941.59 in estate taxes was assessed.[12] . . .

The Internal Revenue Code of 1954 imposes an excise tax on the transfer of an estate at death. The statutory scheme and regulations provide that the contents of a decedent's gross estate are fixed as of the moment of death. Treas. Reg. §20.2032-1(a). The variable allowed relates only to the valuation of the estate; it does not affect the inventory of assets which becomes inviolate at the death of the owner. Under the statute and regulations, assets sold continue as included property "even though they change in form." The issue before us is whether the proceeds received after Nellie Johnston's death are to be considered as in her estate at the time of her death, subsequently appearing in a changed form, or whether these proceeds are income of the estate wholly severed from taxable estate assets.

Under the government's rationale, the oil and gas payments are nothing more than a change in the form of estate assets from in-place oil and gas reserves to money. Since the in-place reserves were in the estate at Johnston's death, the payments, representing a conversion of those reserves to money, are likewise in the estate. Treas. Reg. §20.2032-1(d).

The argument advanced by the estate, accepted by the district court, is based on its reading of the Supreme Court's decision in Maass v. Higgins, 312 U.S. 443 (1941). In *Maass* and its companion cases, the Court reviewed an IRS regulation . . . [that] directed that when an estate was valued on the alternate valuation date, all rents, royalties, interest, and dividends received by the estate after the decedent's death, and not accrued prior to date of death, were to be fully included in the taxable estate. The petitioners in the *Maass* litigation challenged the inclusion in the gross estate of such rental and dividend income received between the date of the decedents' deaths and the alternate valuation dates. The Court agreed with the petitioners' arguments.

---

12. The bulk of the deficiency was attributed to an alleged undervaluing of the estate's oil and gas interests, not to the exclusion of the subject income. The dispute over the valuation of these assets was part of this suit but was settled. The only issue remaining is the question of the includibility of the income received during the six months post-death.

In upholding the contention of the taxpayers-petitioners in *Maass*, the Court referred to the "common understanding [that] rents, interest, and dividends are income." *Id.* at 447. The Court expressly rejected as "unreal and artificial" the theory behind the IRS regulation that for purposes of estate tax valuation the asset consisted of two elements, "one the right of ownership the other the right to receive the income." *Id.* Instead, the Court held that the value of an asset is to be determined by viewing all of its components, including the income stream, "as an entirety." *Id.* at 448.

The government argues that *Maass* and its progeny are inapposite, maintaining that the contents of the estate are fixed as of the moment of the decedent's demise. This point is not in dispute. From this linchpin the government contends that, unlike the proceeds in *Maass*, the proceeds at bar are nothing more or less than a change in the form of the asset reserves to cash. Analogies to cases involving dividend income from stock or bond investments or rentals from leased property are not applicable because those proceeds would not be in the estate on the date of decedent's death. Finally, the government urges that the existence of the oil and gas depletion allowance in the income tax code is recognition by the Congress that revenues derived from the production of oil and gas reserves are commonly understood to be different from dividends or rental income.

We perceive *Maass* as directing a review of each case on its own facts, with an eye toward determining the common understanding whether the proceeds in question truly represent income produced by the estate or, rather, are the translation of the corpus of the estate into another form. The former would not be included in the estate tax inventory, the latter would. One might suggest that the result in *Maass* derives as much from intuition as logic. All investment income, from whatever source, represents to some extent a portion of the investment principal. As a matter of "common understanding," however, rents, dividends, and the like represent an income stream separate from the principal. The value of the principal is determined by viewing it as an "entirety," factoring in the income stream. This common understanding results in large measure from the apparent perception that the principal generating the dividends and rentals is not diminished by the use which produced the income. This perception of non-wasting principal is slightly fogged.[13] The tax system recognizes wasting by

---

13. It cannot be gainsaid that a building held for rent is "used up" in some physical sense in return for the rental payment. Regardless of the accuracy of the forecast of the economic life of a structure, at some point that life ends.

providing for depreciation. The critical difference, however, is that a fully depreciated building or piece of personal property generally survives its tax-depreciation life-span and continues to provide use or an income stream, whereas a fully depleted mine or well produces nothing but storage space.

Applying the foregoing, we must determine which party's position is unreal and artificial and which comports with our common understanding. To do so we recast the arguments.

The government argues that when Nellie Johnston died she owned interests in X amount of in-place oil and gas reserves. That amount, fixed as of the moment of her death, is the property interest within the inventory of her estate for estate tax purposes. During the six months between the date of Johnston's death and the alternate valuation date, that estate was depleted by the removal of some of the reserves, identified as Y. On the alternate valuation date the amount of in-place reserves was X-minus-Y. The value which must be included in the federal estate tax is the fair market value of X, not the diminished value of X-minus-Y.

The executor argues that at Johnston's death her estate included various mineral interests from which the estate derived income generated by the production of oil and gas. Conceding that the contents of the estate are necessarily fixed as of the date of death, the executor contends that on the alternate valuation date the estate contained the exact interests, i.e., mineral interests which generated income from the production and sale of oil and gas. The estate maintains that it had not sold any of the contents of the estate, it still owned the same fractional mineral interests; it had merely realized income from one of the estate's assets.

We conclude that the estate's position is artificial and that the government's position comports with common understanding. Under the theory advanced by the estate, if one died possessed of $10,000,000 in oil and gas reserves and, during the ensuing six months, the entirety was produced so that on the alternate valuation date there was no reserves whatever, there would be no federal estate tax. We cannot give the statute or regulations that anomalous interpretation. The quantity of the reserves are determined as of the date of the decedent's death; only the value to be assigned to that quantity of reserves may be changed by market variances when severed before the alternate valuation date.

The estate makes additional arguments that merit some discussion. It urges that acceptance of the government's position would defeat the legislative purpose behind §2032. The district court accepted this argument. We do not. The alternate valuation date was not enacted to permit an estate to reduce its tax liability by disposing of estate assets. The purpose behind §2032 is neither elusive nor uncertain. The statute was designed to mitigate the hardship resulting when the value of a decedent's assets between the date of death and the date the estate tax became due was significantly reduced. The raison d'etre of §2032 does not suffer by our decision today; it remains to protect estates with oil and gas interests when the value of those interests declines during the six-month grace period. In the not-too-distant past that likelihood was considered remote. Not so today, considering the volatile forces extant in the world oil and gas industry.

. . .

This leads then to the final question necessary to the resolution of this appeal: What portion of the proceeds are to be included in the gross estate? Appraising oil and gas interests presents unique problems. . . .

We are persuaded, and now hold, that the appropriate value to be assigned to oil and gas produced during the interim period, for inclusion in the gross estate, is the in-place value of that oil and gas on the date of its severance. The Johnston inventory included interests in oil and gas reserves. The value for estate tax purposes is the value of those reserves in place. In accordance with §2032(a)(1), if the alternate valuation date is chosen the estate includes the in-place value of the reserves remaining on the alternate valuation date, valued as of that date, together with the in-place value of all oil and gas produced during the intervening six months, valued as of the dates of severances. Valuation of oil and gas reserves, both as to quantity and value, albeit complex, is a matter routinely done for myriad reasons, business, finance, inheritance, divorce, contract litigation, and taxes, to name a few. It is a matter within the competence of the experts. It readily may be done here.

On the present record it is not possible to determine the in-place value of the oil and gas produced as of the dates of severance. The case must be remanded for the development of evidence reflecting those values, which are then to be included in the inventory for estate tax purposes, together with the reserves remaining on the alternate valuation date.

18.   *Method and Effect of Electing Alternate Valuation.*   The election to use the alternate valuation method must be exercised by the decedent's personal representative on an estate tax return filed within one year after the time prescribed to timely file the return. See §2032(d). The election is an all-or-nothing proposition; it is not available on an asset-by-asset basis. The value of property determined under §2032 is the federal estate tax value at the decedent's death for all purposes under the income and the estate tax laws. See §1014(a)(2); Treas. Reg. §20.2056(b)-4. In determining whether to elect alternate valuation, the personal representative must consider both the effect on the value of the gross estate and the likely effect of altering the basis of the property (for example, the effect on recipients of property included in the gross estate if the property is transferred in a transaction that generates gain or loss for income tax purposes, or if it is depreciable property), as discussed in Part D below.

Generation-Skipping Transfers.   An alternate valuation election applies to the generation-skipping tax as well as the estate tax.

PART D.   BASIS OF PROPERTY INCLUDED IN THE DECEDENT'S GROSS ESTATE

Code References: *Income Tax: §§1014, 1015*

19.   For income tax purposes, property received gratuitously as an inter vivos gift or a bequest or inheritance is excluded under §102 from the gross income of the recipient. Under current law, however, these transfers have an income tax significance to the donee or legatee because of the so-called *basis* rules. "Basis" refers to the amount a taxpayer is *deemed* to have invested in an asset and that, among other consequences, serves as the baseline from which to determine gain or loss if the taxpayer sells or exchanges the asset. A taxpayer's gain or loss on the sale or exchange of an asset is the difference between basis in the asset and the "amount realized" on its sale or exchange. See §1001(a). Property that is the subject of an inter vivos gift has a basis in the hands of the donee equal to the donor's basis. Under §1015, gifts thus have a "carryover" basis. But with only a few exceptions, property included in a decedent's gross estate for estate tax purposes obtains a new basis under §1014 equal to the federal estate tax value of the property.[14] This new basis at death rule of §1014 applies to almost any property included in a decedent's gross estate, even if the decedent no longer owned the property at death. Thus, property transferred inter vivos by the decedent but brought back into the gross estate by any of

---

14.   Congress in 2001 adopted legislation that would repeal the estate and generation-skipping transfer taxes in the year 2010, with a "pay back" loss of §1014 and replacement with a §1022 carryover of basis rule that largely would match the §1015 gift tax rule (with certain adjustments). It is widely believed that the system Congress adopted, in a hurry, at the last minute, as part of the 2001 legislative process is so significantly flawed that, should repeal ever occur, Congress will need to revisit this legislation and cure certain problems. Stay tuned.

§§2035 through 2042 acquires this new basis. Between the date of the gift and the decedent's death, the donee's carryover basis in the transferred property would be that of the donor. When the decedent dies, however, that basis would be changed under §1014.[15]

The new-basis-at-death rule of §1014 often influences the choice of assets transferred inter vivos because highly appreciated assets might better be retained by an elderly donor to generate an income tax-free increase in basis when the donor dies. If feasible, donors choose to give away appreciated assets whose value and basis differ to the smallest possible extent.

An exception to §1014 is contained in §1014(e), applicable if a decedent held appreciated property at death that was received as a gift within one year before death. If this property passes from the decedent back to the original owner (or that owner's spouse), §1014(e) provides that the basis of the property is a carryover of the decedent's adjusted basis immediately before death. Were it not for this exception, donors could move property into the estate of an impending decedent and generate an income tax-free adjustment to basis. This would have been desirable if the decedent's estate would not be taxable because it would qualify for the marital deduction or would be below the applicable exclusion amount that can pass estate tax-free under the unified credit.

Another exception to the new basis at death rule is found in §1014(c), relating to income in respect of a decedent (IRD). Were it not for this exception, IRD would receive a basis at the decedent's death that would preclude the income from being taxed for income tax purposes. This would frustrate the legislative intent of §691 to preserve the character of these items as taxable income after the decedent's death.

---

15. See Treas. Reg. §1.1014-6. The basis of property acquired by a transferee prior to the decedent's death will reflect depreciation deductions allowed the transferee prior to the decedent's demise.

Chapter 3

POWERS OF APPOINTMENT

Part A.   Property Law and Historical Background
Part B.   Post-1942 General Powers
Part C.   Power of Appointment Planning

PART A.   PROPERTY LAW AND HISTORICAL BACKGROUND

Most wealth transfer tax case books proceed straight through the Code, meaning the "string" provisions of §§2035-2038 come next after studying inclusion under §2033. That is not the preference here. One reason is because those rules are not very important any longer, following unification in 1976 and a gift tax that largely stifles inter vivos transfers that may trigger those rules. Alas, it is too soon to explain either of those realities, but we'll come back to both concepts in Chapters 13 and 14. The more important reason why this book deviates from that straight-through approach is because §§2033 and 2041 are at opposite ends of the inclusion spectrum, the former requiring inclusion of property a decedent owns at death and the latter requiring inclusion of property the decedent *never* owned and *never will*. We go a long way toward appreciating the wealth transfer tax system when we understand why §2041 inclusion makes sense, notwithstanding this seeming impropriety.

1.   *Primer on Powers of Appointment.* In addition to having owned property at death, a decedent may have held a "power of appointment" over property not owned. A power of appointment is defined in §11.1 of the RESTATEMENT (SECOND) OF PROPERTY (Donative Transfers) (1986) as "the authority, other than as an incident of the beneficial ownership of property, to designate the beneficial interests in property." Under the unique power of appointment terminology, the person who created the power of appointment is the *donor*. The holder of the power — the person in whom the power was created and who may exercise it — is the *donee*. That is confusing to many people, so the Restatement will refer in the future to the *powerholder*. Other parties are the *appointees* (the persons in favor of whom the powerholder exercised the power); the *objects* or *permissible appointees* (the persons to whom or in whose favor the powerholder may exercise the power); and the *takers in default* (the persons designated by the donor to receive any property not effectively appointed). Not every power of appointment designates default beneficiaries. It also is not always clear to whom or on what terms the powerholder may exercise the power. Moreover, the powerholder normally is not obligated to exercise the power.

Ordinarily a power of appointment is personal to the powerholder. The power lapses — it ceases to exist — to the extent the powerholder dies without having validly exercised it. Thus, except under extraordinary circumstances as specified in the document granting the power, a power-holder cannot pass the power to others, nor does it descend by intestacy. Thus the estate taxation of powers of appointment is easiest to understand in terms of termination of a power of appointment at death, either due to exercise, release, or lapse.

Unlike §2033, under which expiration of a property interest at death (such as a life estate that terminates) precludes estate taxation, §2041 taxes expiration of the power at death. The powerholder would have the appointive property if the power were exercised in favor of the powerholder, and §2033 would apply at death. If the power were exercised in favor of anyone else a gift tax would have been imposed on exercise inter vivos. So it is only in the case in which the powerholder does *not* exercise the power that §2041 is needed, and it applies at death because at that time it is clear that the powerholder will not *ever* own the property subject to the power. Nevertheless, Congress regards the opportunity to acquire the property as adequate to attract the tax, which is imposed on the "transfer" that occurs when the power no longer can be exercised — at death. In this light, it is easy to question whether the "transfer" requirement for a constitutional tax on wealth really means anything! In that regard, it is best to think of the "transfer" as the decedent no longer having something rather than in terms of someone else having acquired that something.

A donor may transfer property inter vivos and retain a power over the property. *Retained* powers, however, are *not* our concern in this chapter. See Treas. Reg. §20.2041-1(b)(2). Retained powers are subject to §§2036(a)(2) and 2038(a)(1), as discussed in Chapter 5. Our study here of §2041 only reaches *conferred* powers of appointment — powers granted to the powerholder by another.

Powers of appointment may differ in other respects. The holder of a *collateral* power has no additional interest in the appointive property. Collateral powers are commonly held by independent trustees who are not beneficiaries of the appointive property. The holder of a power *in gross* has an interest in the appointive property that will not be affected by exercise of the power. A classic example is a trust beneficiary with an income interest for life and a testamentary power to appoint the remainder interest. This is the most common form of power of appointment. Finally, the holder of a power *appendant* has an interest in the appointive property that will be affected by exercise of the power. It is commonly assumed that powers appendant to a powerholder's property interest are invalid, because the power merges into the property interest held by the powerholder and ceases to have any separate existence. See RESTATEMENT (SECOND) OF PROPERTY (Donative Transfers) §12.3 (1986). Consequently, if an income beneficiary has a power to transfer the corpus of a trust to others, an exercise could have unexpected gift tax or generation-skipping transfer tax consequences. See Chapter 14.

A second differentiation is suggested by terms used in the prior paragraph. *Testamentary* powers only authorize the powerholder to exercise the power by will, while *presently exercisable* powers permit the powerholder to exercise the power by either an inter vivos instrument or by will. Although it is possible for a donor to disallow the exercise by will of a presently exercisable power, rarely is this done. However, some powers are inherently exercisable only inter vivos, the best example being a power conferred on a trust income beneficiary to withdraw trust corpus. This withdrawal or invasion power cannot normally be exercised by the powerholder's will. Cf. Connecticut General Life Insurance Co. v. First National Bank, 262 N.W.2d 403 (Minn. 1977); Annot., 81 A.L.R.3d 959 (1977). But cf. Estate of Lowry, 418 N.E.2d 10 (Ill. App. Ct. 1981). Another example of a power only exercisable during life is a power to revoke or to amend the terms of a trust.

The third, and for our purposes most important, differentiation is between general and nongeneral powers. Section 11.4 of the RESTATEMENT (SECOND) OF PROPERTY (Donative Transfers) (1986) generally embraces the same definition as does §2041(b)(1). It defines a *general* power as one that is exercisable in favor of the powerholder, the powerholder's estate, creditors of the powerholder, or creditors of the powerholder's estate. A nongeneral power (sometimes also referred to as a "special" or a "limited" power) is any power that is not a general power, meaning that it can be made exercisable in favor of any class of permissible appointees, large, small, or unlimited, as long as it cannot be exercised in favor of the power-holder, the powerholder's estate, or creditors of either. A power exercisable in favor of anyone in the world except the powerholder, the powerholder's estate, or creditors of either is sometimes called a *statutory power* because it is as broad a nongeneral power as §2041 will permit without it being taxable.

For a more extensive exegesis on powers of appointment from the nontax side of the law, see Medlin, *A Primer on Powers*, 2 HOFSTRA PROP. L.J. 165 (1988).

Sample Language Creating a Power of Appointment. A full-scale version of language creating a general power of appointment might read:

Upon the death of A [the income beneficiary], the principal and any accrued and undistributed income of the trust shall be held in trust hereunder or distributed to or in trust for such appointee or appointees (including the estate of A), with such powers and in such manner and proportions as A may appoint by A's will making specific reference to this power of appointment. Upon A's death, the trustee shall distribute the principal and any accrued and undistributed income of the trust not effectively appointed to A's then living descendants by representation.

A's power is a general testamentary power of appointment. Because A is the life tenant, the power would be a power in gross. Because A may appoint to A's own estate, it is a general power. The phrase "by A's will" makes this a testamentary power, and the specific reference requirement is designed to preclude inadvertent exercise. A presently exercisable power would probably be drafted to require exercise by a written instrument delivered to the trustee during A's life and would probably *also* permit exercise by will.

If A's power were limited to "such appointee or appointees other than A, A's estate, or creditors of either," or if the power defined the class of permissible appointees, such as "any one or more of A's descendants and their spouses," then A's power would be nongeneral.

Powers of Appointment Compared With Ownership and Powers of Attorney.   A power of appointment does not make the powerholder the owner of the appointive property (although holders of general powers may make themselves or their estates the owner by exercising the power in favor of themselves or their estates). Comment b to §318 of the RESTATEMENT OF PROPERTY (1940) describes the essential difference between ownership and a power of appointment as follows:

The owner of property ordinarily has the power to create interests in another person by a transfer . . . to such other person. Thus if A effectively devises Blackacre to B, B acquires the power to transfer Blackacre to C; and, if this power is exercised, C thereby becomes B's transferee. The donee of a power of appointment likewise has the power to create interests in other persons; but it is the underlying dogma of the law of powers of appointment that such interests constitute transfers from the donor of the power, not from the donee. As stated in this Section, the donee has only the "power to designate the transferees" of the donor.

The notion that, upon exercise of a power of appointment, the appointed interest passes directly from the donor to the appointee is called the "relation back" doctrine. The idea is that the powerholder's appointment is viewed as relating back to and becoming part of the donor's original instrument. If *A* in the above example exercised the power in favor of *B*, the effect is as if the original disposition were to *B* and not to *A*'s descendants. In this respect, the powerholder is the donor's agent, effectively altering the donor's estate plan. The relation of donor and powerholder is not, however, governed by the law of agency.

Comment f to §11.1 of the RESTATEMENT (SECOND) OF PROPERTY (Donative Transfers) (1986), distinguishes a power of *attorney* from a power of *appointment* as follows:

> A power of attorney creates the relationship of principal and agent between the one who gives the power and the one who holds the power. This relationship is generally terminated by the death of the principal and may be terminated (depending on controlling local law) by the incompetency of the principal. A power of appointment does not create an agency relationship between the creator of the power and the powerholder, and a power of appointment may be created that is exercisable after the death of the creator of the power. The holder of a power of attorney is exercising for the present owner of property, as the owner's agent, one or more of the incidents of ownership of the property of such owner. By contrast, the holder of a power of appointment is completing the terms of a disposition made by a transferor.

As we will see, a power of attorney may constitute a power of appointment for tax purposes, but the converse would not be true, notwithstanding the theory of the relation back doctrine.

2.   *Taxation of Powers of Appointment Before 1951.* The Revenue Act of 1916, in which the modern estate tax originated, contained no provision specifically dealing with property subject to a power of appointment. The Supreme Court in United States v. Field, 255 U.S. 257 (1921), held that property subject to an exercised general testamentary power of appointment was not included in the powerholder's gross estate under that Act.

Revenue Act of 1918 added §402(e), a specific provision taxing powers of appointment, which governed the federal estate taxation of powers of appointment until 1942. The general thrust of the 1918 provision was that property subject to a *general* power was subject to estate taxation only to the extent the power was *exercised* by will (or by an inter vivos exercise of such a nature that, had the property been owned by the powerholder and had the powerholder transferred it under the same terms, it would have been included in the powerholder's gross estate) and the property actually *passed* under the powerholder's exercise. In Helvering v. Grinnell, 294 U.S. 153 (1935), the Court held that the passing requirement was not met when the appointees — who also turned out to be the takers in default — renounced the appointment and elected to take as default takers instead.

Although the 1918 provision did not define the term "general power of appointment," the regulations declared:

Ordinarily a general power is one to appoint to any person or persons in the discretion of the donee of the power, or, however limited as to the persons or objects in whose favor the appointment may be made, is exercisable in favor of the donee, his estate, or his creditors. [Treas. Reg. 80, art. 24 (1937).]

The Supreme Court approved this definition in Morgan v. Commissioner, 309 U.S. 78 (1940), and also held that a power exercisable only in conjunction with another person who had no interest in the property adverse to its exercise was a general power.

Dissatisfaction with the 1918 provision led in 1942 to the next stage in the development of estate taxation of powers of appointment.[1] Congress changed the statute in 1942 so that the gross estate included the value of property over which the decedent had at death any power of appointment, exercisable by the decedent either alone or in conjunction with any other person, regardless of whether the power was exercised. There were two exceptions: fiduciary powers, and powers to appoint among a class that included no one other than the powerholder's spouse, the donor's spouse, descendants of the powerholder or of the powerholder's spouse, descendants (other than the powerholder) of the donor or of the donor's spouse, spouses of such descendants, and charitable organizations. As to this latter exception, the House bill had designated a narrower class (excluding the donor's spouse, descendants of the donor or of the donor's spouse, and spouses of those descendants), but the class was expanded in the Senate. S. Rep. No. 1631, 77th Cong., 2d Sess. 55-56, 232-234 (1942), in 1942-2 C.B. 504, 549-550, 674-676.

The 1942 amendments were in effect until 1951. The final step was taken in the Powers of Appointment Act of 1951, the matter to which we now turn.

PART B. POST-1942 GENERAL POWERS

Code References: *Estate Tax: §§2041, 2207*
                       Income Tax: §678

3.   *The Estate Tax Burden.*   The current treatment of powers of appointment, contained in §2041, was enacted in the Powers of Appoint-

---

1.   Compare Griswold, *Powers of Appointment and the Federal Estate Tax*, 52 HARV. L. REV. 929 (1939), with Leach, *Powers of Appointment and the Federal Estate Tax — A Dissent*, 52 HARV. L. REV. 961 (1939).

ment Act of 1951. Section 2041 contains a dual rule, one for powers of appointment created before October 22, 1942 (called "pre-42 powers"), and one for powers of appointment created after October 21, 1942 ("post-'42 powers"). Under §2041(a)(1), the value of property subject to a pre-42 power is includible in the powerholder's gross estate only to the extent the power was exercised by will (or by an inter vivos exercise of such a nature that, had the property been owned by the powerholder and had the powerholder transferred it under the same terms, it would have been included in the powerholder's gross estate). Under §2041(a)(2), the value of property subject to a post-'42 power is includible in the powerholder's gross estate if the powerholder possessed the power at death, regardless of whether the power was exercised. With certain exceptions that we will explore, general powers whenever created are defined in §2041(b) as powers exercisable in favor of the powerholder, the powerholder's estate, creditors of the powerholder, or creditors of the powerholder's estate.

Under §2207, unless the powerholder directs otherwise by will, that portion of the estate tax attributable to the inclusion of appointive property in the powerholder's gross estate may be recovered by the powerholder's executor from "the person receiving such property by reason of the exercise, nonexercise, or release of a power of appointment." Section 2207 originated in the Revenue Act of 1942 and was intended "to achieve a fair and equitable apportionment of the tax burden attributable in part to appointive property." H.R. Rep. No. 2333, 77th Cong., 1st Sess. 161 (1942), in 1942-2 C.B. 372, 490; S. Rep. No. 1631, 77th Cong., 2d Sess. 233-234 (1942), in 1942-2 C.B. 504, 675. Estate tax payment and apportionment in general is considered in Chapter 13.

Income Taxation: the Mallinckrodt Doctrine. Before moving to more technical matters, one final piece in the legislative framework of taxing powers of appointment was added in 1954. The congressional purpose of equating a general power of appointment with ownership of the appointive property is furthered by §678. A person who owns property is taxed on the income derived from that property. Section 678(a)(1) declares the same rule for trust property over which a powerholder holds "a power exercisable solely by himself to vest the corpus or the income therefrom in himself." Often called the "Mallinckrodt" doctrine because it originally was established in Mallinckrodt v. Nunan, 146 F.2d 1 (8th Cir. 1945), without the benefit of legislation, this provision is an application of the "Clifford" theory for taxing grantor trusts.

4.   *Incapacitated Donee.*   Should a general power cause inclusion if the powerholder is unable to exercise it and seize its benefits? The answer is yes! Consider why that makes sense. Also pay particular attention to the judicial reasoning and approach employed in *Alperstein*. Judge Friendly has a well deserved reputation as a first rate jurist, and it shows in this opinion. Also consider the road map that the author of the legal briefs may have crafted in arguing this case. This was fine lawyering as well.

Estate of Alperstein v. Commissioner
613 F.2d 1213 (2d Cir. 1979)

FRIENDLY, J.: . . . Fannie Alperstein died . . . after surviving her husband, Harry, who had . . . established a trust for the benefit of the decedent which was to contain the maximum portion of his adjusted gross estate that was [then] allowable as a marital deduction, I.R.C. §2056. Fannie Alperstein was to receive all the net income from the trust payable at frequent intervals for the duration of her life, and was granted a testamentary power to appoint the principal of the trust free of any restrictions.[2] If the decedent failed to exercise her testamentary power of appointment, Mr. Alperstein's children or their issue would take in default.

On January 16, some six months before Harry Alperstein's death, Fannie Alperstein had entered a nursing home where she remained until shortly before her death. On December 27, 1967, a New York court declared Fannie to be incompetent and appointed her daughter, Rosalind A. Greenberg, to manage her person and property. Although the judicial determination of the decedent's incompetence followed the death of Mr. Alperstein by almost six months, the parties have stipulated that from her husband's death until her own death, the decedent lacked the capacity to execute a will under New York law, did not purport to exercise the power of appointment granted by her husband's will, and was legally incapable of exercising that power.

Rosalind A. Greenberg, the decedent's executrix, filed a federal estate tax return that did not include in the decedent's gross estate the value of the property over which the decedent had been granted testamentary power of appointment by her husband's will. The Commissioner asserted a deficiency based on his determination that the decedent possessed at death a general power of appointment within the meaning of §2041(a)(2), which required the inclusion of the entire value of the property subject to that power

---

2. In relevant part, Article Fourth of Mr. Alperstein's will provided:

   If my wife, Fannie Alperstein, shall survive me, I give and bequeath unto my Trustees . . . IN TRUST, to pay to my said wife all the net income therefrom quarter-annually or at more frequent intervals during her life, and *upon her death she shall have the power by her last Will and Testament to appoint the entire principal of this trust fund then remaining in the hands of my said Trustees to her estate, free of any trust, or to or in trust for the benefit of anyone else.* [Emphasis added.]

within her gross estate. . . . Appellant does not question that, so far as language is concerned, the power of appointment conferred by Article Fourth of Harry Alperstein's will, see note 2 supra, met the statutory test. The claim is that, despite this, §2041(a)(2) is inapplicable because, under the stipulated facts, Fannie Alperstein was never able to exercise the power vested in her by her husband's will — a situation allegedly not present in any of the cases that have sustained the taxability of powers against attacks of the same general sort as that mounted here.[3]

I. We start, as always, with the words of the statute. The operative verb in §2041(a)(2) is "has." Beyond cavil Mrs. Alperstein "had" a general power of appointment at the time of her death. This had been granted by her husband's will and nothing done by the New York courts purported to take it away. Even if we assumed that the judgment of Fannie Alperstein's incompetency conclusively established her inability to exercise this power, that judgment was subject to being vacated if her mental condition changed for the better. The argument is rather that although Mrs. Alperstein "had" such a power, it was not "exercisable" at the time of her death since she had long since been declared incompetent and in fact had been so ever since her husband had died. However, the word "exercisable" is found not in the operative portion of the statute but in a section addressed to how broad a power must be in order to be "general." The natural meaning of the words is that "exercisable" is shorthand for "which by its terms may be exercised," and does not mean that §2041(a)(2) is limited to cases where the decedent could in fact exercise the power at the moment of death — something which, in the absence of a will or similar instrument could rarely occur.

---

3. In fact Mrs. Alperstein's inability ever to have exercised the power is not so clear as appellant's counsel asserts. Harry Alperstein's will was executed on September 23, 1953. The stipulation that Mrs. Alperstein was incompetent to execute a valid will after her husband's death on July 6, 1967, does not negate her capacity to have exercised the power prior to his death. Absent contrary specification by the donor, New York law does not require the donee of a testamentary power to provide for its exercise in a will executed subsequent to the donor's death. See N.Y. Est., Powers & Trusts Law §10-6.1 (McKinney). Indeed, Mrs. Alperstein could have exercised the power by a will made even before Harry's will was executed. See, e.g., In re Tucker's Trust, 167 N.Y.S.2d 211 (S. Ct. 1957), aff'd, 175 N.Y.S.2d 559 (App. Div. 1958), aff'd, 161 N.E.2d 391 (N.Y. 1959). However, we do not find it necessary to rest decision on this ground.

[EDITOR'S NOTE: The proposition that the holder of a power of appointment can exercise the power in a will executed before the donor's death — indeed, even in a will executed before execution of the donor's will — is not peculiar to New York law. See RESTATEMENT OF PROPERTY §344 (1940). This is true only in the absence of a restriction to the contrary expressly imposed by the donor, which can be imposed without jeopardizing the marital deduction in the donor's estate. See Treas. Reg. §20.2056(b)-5(g)(4).]

II. The meaning which thus emerges from the words of the statute is strongly reinforced by the legislative history. Section 2041 reflects, in all respects here relevant, the Powers of Appointment Act of 1951, 65 Stat. 91. The latter was a substantial amendment of the amendments to §811 of the Internal Revenue Code of 1939 that were included in the Revenue Act of 1942, 56 Stat. 798, 942. . . .

The 1942 amendments extended the policy of taxing powers, regardless of exercise, to general powers created before the enactment of the amendments. See 1942 amendments, supra, §403(d)(1). However, the amendments sought to mitigate the retroactive impact of this by allowing a grace period in which all holders of general powers might release their power without estate tax consequences, id. §403(d)(3), and by extending this grace period in the case of holders who were "under a legal disability to release such power" until six months after the termination of their disability, id. §403(d)(2). . . . Senate Report No. 1631, [77th Cong., 2d Sess. 232 (1942)], suggested that legal incompetents such as insane people, minors, and unborn children might be expected to benefit from this exemption. Id. at 234. Beyond demonstrating that when Congress wished to make a dispensation for incompetents, it has known how to say so, the fact that the 1942 Congress felt it necessary to include this provision strongly suggests its belief that the existence of a legal disability by the holder of a general power would not prevent inclusion of property subject to that power in the estate. Although the provision in question related only to pre-1942 powers, there is no reason to suppose that Congress intended a different rule with respect to incompetency for post-1942 powers.

Until the 1951 Act, Congress extended taxpayer deadlines for releasing pre-1942 powers on numerous occasions, but left the treatment of post-1942 powers unchanged. In the case of pre-1942 powers, the 1951 Act returned to the criterion of pre-1942 law by taxing only those general powers that had been exercised. 1951 Act, supra, §2(a). However, the 1951 Act continued the policy of taxing post-1942 general powers regardless of their exercise, and its legislative history contains no indication that Congress intended to alter the treatment of legally disabled holders of post-1942 powers. To the extent that the 1951 Act dealt more liberally than its predecessor with post-1942 powers, it did so only by shrinking the class of taxable powers to those that fall within its definition of "general powers" — a definition that looks primarily to the terms of the trust instrument and not at all to the status of the donee of the power.

This conclusion is also buttressed by one of the Act's broader purposes, namely, to provide "a test of taxability which is simple, clearcut, and easy to apply." S. Rep. No. 382, 82d Cong., 1st Sess. 2, [1951] U.S. Code Cong. & Ad. News 1530, 1531. Linking an interpretation of "exercisable" to decedents' disabilities under local law would hardly simplify the 1951 test, particularly since the Act provides no basis for distinguishing decedents adjudged to be legally incompetent from those who were otherwise barred from exercising their powers. . . .

Further support for the construction that the 1951 Act embraced all general powers regardless of the donee's capacity to exercise them is furnished by a provision in the marital deduction . . . now codified as amended in I.R.C. §2056(b)(5). This provides that property passing in trust to a surviving spouse will qualify for exclusion from the decedent's estate, inter alia, if the surviving spouse is entitled to all income from the property for life; if the surviving spouse has the power to appoint such property in favor of herself or the estate; and if the power to appoint such property, "whether exercisable by will or during life, is exercisable by such spouse alone and in all events." The Internal Revenue Service has long held that competency under local law is irrelevant for determining whether a power is "exercisable" within the meaning of the marital deduction. Rev. Rul. 55-518, 1955-2 Cum. Bull. 384; Rev. Rul. 75-350, 1975-2 Cum. Bull. 367. This conclusion is virtually dictated by the consideration that "[o]therwise, in view of the possibility that any given person may become legally incompetent during his or her lifetime, no trust could ever qualify under §2056(b)(5)." Rev. Rul. 75-350, 1975-2 Cum. Bull. at 368. The implication of accepting this most sensible construction of "exercisable" in the marital deduction context is that at the time the 1951 Powers of Appointment Act was passed, a determinant legislative meaning as to what constitutes an "exercisable" power of appointment already existed in both the powers of appointment and marital deduction provisions of the Code. Still more persuasive is the evidence that Congress intended the marital deduction as a deferral of tax on property which, however, would eventually be subject to a gift or an estate tax paid by the surviving spouse or by her estate. . . . Given that this purpose was served in 1948 by adopting the same use of "exercisable" in the marital deduction that had already existed in the corresponding powers of appointment provision, Congress can [not] be thought to have abandoned sub silentio the intended interaction between these two provisions a mere three years later and thereby to have created a situation, such as concededly would exist here if appellant were to prevail, wherein property escapes estate tax at the time of the death of the donor of the power because the competency of the donee is immaterial and also at the time of the death of the donee because competency is held to be crucial. The 1951 Powers of Appointment Act must be read not in isolation but as a part of a comprehensive statutory scheme.[4]

III. We find no basis for a contrary view in the Service's rulings and regulations.

The Service first addressed the relationship between incompetency and §2041(a)(2) in Rev. Rul. 55-518, 1955-2 Cum. Bull. 384, which ruled on the estate of a surviving spouse who had enjoyed an unrestricted lifetime power of appointment over a testamentary trust created by her husband. In a dual holding, the Service determined that the husband's estate qualified for a marital deduction and the wife's estate was taxable for her power even though the wife was incompetent from the date of her husband's death until the time of her own death. Id. at 385. The Service reasoned that the wife could have exercised her power with the aid of a local court and, therefore, "possessed" the power at the time of her death even if she could not have freely exercised it at any time. Id. . . .

[The court rejected the taxpayer's contention that the fact that the final regulations for §2041 did not include a provision dealing with the incompetency of a donee, despite the fact that such a provision had been part of the prior Proposed Regulation, supported the taxpayer's position. —ED.]

. . . [T]he Service has never withdrawn from the position it originally expressed in Rev. Rul. 55-518. Rev. Rul. 75-350, 1975-2 Cum. Bull. 367, the Service's most recent pronouncement on the relationship between incompetency and the possession of a general power within the meaning of §2041, extends the Service's original determination of taxability to a legally incompetent holder of a testamentary power who is indistinguishable from Mrs. Alperstein in all relevant respects. This ruling abandons any reliance on the possibility that a legally incompetent holder of a power might be able to exercise his power with the aid of a court or anyone else. Instead, it concludes:

> Just as incapacity or incompetency does not render property owned outright by a decedent exempt from estate taxation, neither is property subject to a general power of appointment exempt in such circumstances, unless *by the terms of the grant of the power* such circumstances have

---

4. We recognize that a general power of appointment can be conferred in contexts other than a marital deduction trust. However, now that property subject to such a power is taxable to the estate of the donee, use of the general power in the marital deduction trust must be far and away the principal one.

caused the existence of the power itself to cease prior to the decedent's death.

Id. at 368 (emphasis original).

IV. Although appellant may be right in contending that no decision upholding the estate taxation of property subject to a general power of appointment has presented facts quite so humanly appealing in favor of the donee as this, the general thrust of the case law in appellate courts is decidedly unfavorable to her.

While the Supreme Court has not had occasion to rule on the effect of incompetency of the holder of a general power on taxability under §2041, C.I.R. v. Estate of Noel, 380 U.S. 678 (1965), strongly indicated the Court's probable approach. *Noel* required a construction of I.R.C. §2042, which provides inter alia that a decedent's estate is taxable for the proceeds of insurance policies on the life of the decedent "with respect to which the decedent possessed at his death any of the incidents of ownership, exercisable alone or in conjunction with any other person." Immediately before boarding a plane doomed to a fatal crash, the decedent in *Noel* purchased several flight insurance policies which he left with his wife on the ground. The decedent's estate contended that on these facts there had been no exercisable incidents of ownership within the meaning of the statute. While acknowledging that "there was no practical opportunity" to exercise ownership power, the Court concluded:

It would stretch the imagination to think that Congress intended to measure estate tax liability by an individual's fluctuating, day-to-day, hour-by-hour capacity to dispose of property which he owns. We hold that estate tax liability for policies "with respect to which the decedent possessed at his death any of the incidents of ownership" depends on a general, legal power to exercise ownership, without regard to the owner's ability to exercise it at a particular moment.

Id. at 684.

Three courts of appeals have considered the effect upon taxability under §2041 of the inability of the holder of a power to exercise it; all have ruled in favor of the Government. . . . [The court cited and discussed Fish v. United States, 432 F.2d 1278 (9th Cir. 1970); Estate of Bagley v. United States, 433 F.2d 1266 (5th Cir. 1971); and Pennsylvania Bank and Trust Co. v. United States, 597 F.2d 382 (3d Cir. 1979). —Ed.]

Against this array of unfavorable decisions by the Supreme Court and courts of appeals, all of which emphasize the creation of rights and pay scant regard to the possibility of their exercise, taxpayer relies on four recent decisions of courts of first instance that are now under appeal to the Court of Appeals for the Fifth Circuit: Finley v. United States, 404 F. Supp. 200 (S.D. Fla. 1975); Estate of Gilchrist v. C.I.R., 65 T.C. 5 (1977); Williams v. United States, 78-2 U.S. Tax Cas. (CCH) ¶13,264 (W.D. Texas 1978); and Estate of Reid v. Commissioner, 71 T.C. 816 (1979). Whether correctly decided or not, *Gilchrist* is readily distinguishable; it dealt not with a testamentary power of appointment but with a clause conferring on the widow "full rights to transfer all the remainder of my property, both real and personal, so long as she may live." The court held that under Texas law the appointment of guardians transformed, for the period of incompetency, Mrs. Gilchrist's general power over corpus to one limited by an ascertainable standard within §2041(b)(1). 69 T.C. at 15-19. *Estate of Reid*, which relies heavily on *Gilchrist*, is even more remote from the instant case, as it deals with the effect of legal incompetence on taxation under I.R.C. §2036(a)(2). In our view, *Finley* and, if the decedent in *Williams* possessed a testamentary power of appointment, that case also, were wrongly decided.

In sum we hold, on the basis of statutory language, legislative history (particularly the interaction of §2041(a)(2) with the marital deduction, §2056(b)(5)), administrative interpretation and case law, that when an instrument has conferred a testamentary power which by its terms can be exercised in favor of the donee's estate, the property subject to the power is part of the donee's gross estate even though the donee, by virtue of incompetency, was unable to make a valid will at any time after the power was granted.

Affirmed.

Alperstein stopped short of declaring that *Gilchrist* was wrongly decided by the Tax Court, but Pennsylvania Bank & Trust Co. v. United States, 597 F.2d 382, 383 (3d Cir. 1979), declared that *Gilchrist* and *Finley* (the *Williams* case was not discussed) were wrongly decided, and the lower courts in all three ultimately were reversed. Estate of Gilchrist v. Commissioner, 630 F.2d 340 (5th Cir. 1980); Williams v. United States, 634 F.2d 894 (5th Cir. 1981); Finley v. United States, 612 F.2d 166 (5th Cir. 1980) (vacated on jurisdictional grounds). *Finley* was vacated because a petition filed in the Tax Court deprived the district court of jurisdiction. Subsequently, the Tax Court decided *Finley* under a different name — Estate of Whitlock v. Commissioner, 43 T.C.M. (CCH) 1389 (1982).

In *Whitlock*, the Tax Court cited *Alperstein* with approval and held that a powerholder's general testamentary power caused inclusion of the property in her gross estate even though she was mentally incompetent from the time that she acquired the power until her death. See also Boeving v. United States, 650 F.2d 493 (8th Cir. 1981); Estate of Freeman v. Commissioner, 67 T.C. 202 (1976) (the value of appointive property was includible notwithstanding that the decedent was unaware of the power's existence).

Thus, to date, the government has scored a clean sweep on this issue. However, although *Gilchrist* and *Williams* ultimately were decided for the government, the Court of Appeals for the Fifth Circuit did not adopt the *Alperstein* rule. Instead of holding that property subject to a general power is includible in the powerholder's gross estate regardless of the power-holder's capacity to exercise the power, the Fifth Circuit ruled that the appointive property is includible "unless the [powerholder's] estate can show that the power could not be exercised at all on the [powerholder's] behalf by any person in any capacity." *Williams*, 634 F.2d at 895; *Gilchrist*, 630 F.2d at 344. The appointive property was held to be includible in both cases because the estates were unable to make the required showing; the power in each case was inter vivos, not testamentary, and the controlling local law provided the powerholder's guardian with authority to exercise the power on the powerholder's behalf.

How would the *Williams/Gilchrist* rule apply to the facts of *Alperstein*? Which approach implements the more desirable tax policy?

Incapacity by Reason of Minority.   In addition to a mentally incompetent powerholder, a holder of a power of appointment who is a minor at the time of death may lack the legal capacity to exercise a power. Rev. Rul. 75-351 stated that inclusion of the value of appointive property is not precluded by the powerholder's incapacity by reason of minority, and Estate of Rosenblatt v. Commissioner, 633 F.2d 176, 180–181 (10th Cir. 1980), upheld the government, stating:

The final blow to [the estate's] argument that Utah's limitations on decedent's ability to exercise her power should cause the property subject to it to be excluded from her estate is found in I.R.C. §§2056(b)(5), 2503(c).

I.R.C. §2056(b)(5) provides that property passing in trust to a surviving spouse can qualify for exclusion from the decedent's estate if, among other things, the surviving spouse has the power to appoint such property in favor of herself or her estate. Competency under local law has been determined to be "irrelevant for determining whether a power is 'exercisable' within the meaning of the marital deduction." Alperstein v. Commissioner, 613 F.2d 1213, 1217 (2d Cir. 1979), *cert. denied*, 100 S. Ct. 1852 (1980).

I.R.C. §2503(c) states the conditions under which transfers to minors will be considered gifts of present interests sufficient to qualify for the [annual] gift exclusion available under I.R.C. §2503(b). Unless the property is made payable to the minor's estate in case of his death, §2503(c)(2)(B) requires that the minor be given a general power of appointment over the property transferred to him in trust in order to qualify for the §2503(b) exclusion. Treas. Reg. §25.2503-4(b) explicitly makes incapacity to exercise the power due to the donee's minority irrelevant to the determination of whether the minor possesses a power for purposes of §2503(c).

These two treatments of incapacity to exercise a power, in light of the fact that the federal estate and gift tax laws "are in pari materia and must be construed together," Estate of Sanford v. Commissioner, 308 U.S. 39, 44 (1939), suggest that the question of capacity should not be treated any differently under §2041.

Minority, like mental incompetency, is not pertinent to a determination of whether a decedent had a general power of appointment for purposes of I.R.C. §2041. In this case the instrument creating the trust granted decedent a general power of appointment and did not, by its terms, limit its exercise. The property subject to that power is part of decedent's gross estate under §2041(a)(2).

5. *Conditional Powers.* According to Treas. Reg. §20.2041-3(b), "a power which by its terms is exercisable only upon the occurrence during the decedent's lifetime of an event or a contingency which did not in fact take place or occur during such time is not a power in existence on the date of the decedent's death." In Rev. Rul. 75-350, alluded to in *Alperstein*, the government suggested that the appointive property would not be includible in the powerholder's gross estate if *by the terms of the grant of the power* the powerholder's incapacity had caused the power itself to cease prior to the powerholder's death. As a planning matter, would it be advisable to embrace the government's suggestion by imposing in instruments creating a general power of appointment a condition that the powerholder have capacity to exercise the power?

In Rev. Rul. 55-486, the government ruled on the following fact situation:

A trust created in 1923 by the decedent's mother provides that if the decedent predeceases her sister A, the principal of the trust is to be distributed, on the death of A, in equal shares to such brother or sister of the decedent as shall survive A. If no brother or sister survives A, the principal is to be distributed on the death of A, to such persons as the decedent appoints by deed or by will. . . . The decedent did not appoint by deed. Her will, however, provides that the residue of her estate is to be distributed in equal shares to her sister A, her sister B and her brother C. . . . The decedent died survived by A, B and C.

The government ruled:

> [T]he condition in the trust instrument relating to the deaths of *B* and *C* prior to that of *A* did not in any way restrict the exercise of the power; it merely qualified the property interest subject to the power. Accordingly, the decedent possessed at her death a general power of appointment within the meaning of section [2041(a)(1)]. *Held further*, . . . the decedent is deemed to have exercised the power of appointment despite the lack of a specific reference thereto in her will. . . .

The case addressed by the Ruling involved exercise to default takers and a condition not met, making the Ruling arguably *doubly* wrong. See Keating v. Mayer, 236 F.2d 478 (3d Cir. 1956). Notice that the decedent was not either A nor B nor C, so it was possible when the decedent died that the condition still might be met.

6. A further look at conditional powers is provided by the following opinion. Notice what it says about the analogous but distinct situation of a donor who reserves a power — not a §2041 situation but instead a §2036(a)(2) or §2038(a)(1) analog. Should inclusion be easier in one case or the other? Notice also in reading that the issue involves a "five or five" power in the nonmarital trust, which many planners wrongly assume to be totally without tax consequence. That notion also is wrong — but only for estate tax purposes in the year of death (and for ongoing income tax purposes under §678, which need not concern us). See if you can read §§2514(e) and 2041(b)(2) and ascertain why this is true. We return to that planning in Chapter 14.

Estate of Kurz v. Commissioner
101 T.C. 44 (1993)

PARKER, Judge: . . . The issue is whether, at the time of her death, Ethel H. Kurz (decedent) had a general power of appointment over a portion of a family trust that would cause such portion of the trust to be included in her gross estate under §2041(a)(2). . . .

At the time of decedent's death, decedent was a beneficiary of . . . the Ethel Hull Kurz Trust Fund (the Marital Trust Fund) and the Family Trust Fund. . . .

The trust instrument [gave decedent an unlimited power to withdraw all or part of the Marital Trust Fund at any time or times during her life and] . . . the trust instrument also granted decedent the following power over the principal of the Family Trust Fund:

> In addition to income, commencing with the first day of January following the tenth anniversary of . . . [Mr. Kurz's]

death the trustee also shall pay to . . . [decedent] such amounts from the principal of the Family Trust Fund as she from time to time may direct by writing filed with the trustee, except that (1) no payments shall be made to her pursuant to this subparagraph until the principal of the . . . [Marital Trust Fund] has been completely exhausted, and (2) during any calendar year no payments shall be made to her pursuant to this subparagraph at any time when the aggregate payment or payments theretofore made to her during such calendar year pursuant to this subparagraph equal or exceed 5% of the current value of the principal of the Family Trust Fund then held hereunder and the maximum payment which may be made to her at any other time during such calendar year pursuant to this subparagraph shall not exceed an amount equal to 5% of the current value of the principal of the Family Trust Fund then held hereunder minus the aggregate payment or payments theretofore made to her during such calendar year pursuant to this subparagraph, if any. . . . The rights to withdraw principal of the Family Trust Fund during any given calendar year bestowed upon . . . [decedent] by this subparagraph shall lapse at the end of such year.

. . . The estate tax return included in decedent's gross estate the full value of the Marital Trust Fund but did not include in decedent's gross estate any portion of the value of the Family Trust Fund.

Respondent issued a notice of deficiency determining that, at her death, decedent possessed a general power of appointment over 5% of the Family Trust Fund. As a result, respondent determined that 5% of the value of the Family Trust Fund was includable in decedent's gross estate under §2041. . . .

I. Section 2041. Property subject to a power of appointment held by a decedent may be included in such decedent's gross estate under §2041. . . .

A. General Power of Appointment. . . . The power to consume the principal of a trust is a general power of appointment. Therefore, decedent's right to demand principal from the Family Trust Fund constitutes a general power of appointment. The issue, however, is whether the power existed on the date of decedent's death.

B. Existence of Power at Decedent's Death. The regulations provide [that] a power which by its terms is exercisable only upon the occurrence during the decedent's lifetime of an event or a contingency which did not in fact take place or occur during such time is not a power in existence on the date of the decedent's death. For example, if a decedent was given a general power of appointment exercisable only after he reached a certain age, only if he survived another person, or only if he died without descendants, the power would not be in existence on the date of the decedent's death if the condition precedent to its exercise had not occurred. Treas. Reg. §20.2041-3(b).

It is the interpretation and application of this regulation that is the focus of the controversy in this case. Under the trust instrument, decedent could receive up to 5% of the principal of the Family Trust Fund in any given year, provided the principal of the Marital Trust Fund had been completely exhausted. At the time of decedent's death, the Marital Trust Fund had assets valued in excess of $3 million.

II. Positions of the Parties. Petitioner argues that, . . . because decedent's power to withdraw 5% of the principal from the Family Trust Fund was exercisable only upon the occurrence during decedent's lifetime of an event or a contingency (complete exhaustion of the entire principal of the Marital Trust Fund), which did not in fact occur during decedent's lifetime, the power did not exist on the date of decedent's death. . . . Petitioner takes the position that the express language of Treas. Reg. §20.204[1]-3(b) excludes from decedent's gross estate property subject to a contingent power unless the event or contingency has in fact occurred, regardless of the substance of the event or contingency.

. . . Respondent argues that, because at the time of decedent's death decedent had the power to exhaust the principal of the Marital Trust Fund, she could control the occurrence of the event or the contingency placed on her right to receive 5% of the principal of the Family Trust Fund. Therefore, respondent concludes, on the date of decedent's death, decedent had a general power of appointment over 5% of the principal of the Family Trust Fund, causing that portion of the fund to be includable in her gross estate. Respondent takes the position that property subject to any contingent power otherwise includable under §2041 is includable in a decedent's gross estate unless the event or contingency is beyond the decedent's control.

While we think respondent's interpretation is too broad, we also think petitioner's interpretation is too narrow. This is essentially an issue of first impression. There are no cases that address this issue. . . .

IV. The Language of Section 2041. Respondent argues that Congress intended that powers of appointment be considered to exist even where the holder of the power is required to perform an act prior to the exercise of the power. Respondent contends that Congress did not intend §2041 to be avoided by the use of conditions or contingencies within the control of the holder of the power.

In support of that position, respondent cites the last sentence in §2041(a)(2), which provides that:

> For purposes of this paragraph (2), the power of appointment shall be considered to exist on the date of the decedent's death even though the exercise of the power is subject to a precedent giving of notice or even though the exercise of the power takes effect only on the expiration of a stated period after its exercise, whether or not on or before the date of the decedent's death notice has been given or the power has been exercised. . . .

[The] legislative history clearly indicates that Congress intended to eliminate what it considered an abusive technique for avoiding the application of certain taxes; i.e., by the use of minor restrictions that did not affect the decedent's "practical, if not technical, ownership" of the property. However, we can find nothing in the legislative history, or the language of the statute, that would indicate that Congress equated this precedent-notice or period-of-delay language with a broad proscription against all conditions precedent within the control of a decedent. . . .

V. The Language of the Estate Tax Regulations. Both parties argue that their positions are supported by Treas. Reg. §20.2041-3(b), which defines when a power of appointment is considered to exist on the date of a decedent's death. That regulation begins with a restatement of the statutory precedent-notice or period-of-delay language. In support of its position that the event or contingency must in fact occur, petitioner cites the language of Treas. Reg. §20.2041-3(b), that immediately follows:

> However, a power which by its terms is exercisable only upon the occurrence during the decedent's lifetime of an event or a contingency which did not in fact take place or occur during such time is not a power in existence on the date of the decedent's death. . . .

Respondent asserts that the examples immediately following the above-quoted regulation language support her position that the event or contingency must be beyond the decedent's control:

> For example, if a decedent was given a general power of appointment exercisable only after he reached a certain

age, only if he survived another person, or only if he died without descendants, the power would not be in existence on the date of the decedent's death if the condition precedent to its exercise had not occurred.

Respondent reasons that, because all the conditions in the examples are beyond the decedent's control, the regulation was intended to apply only to such contingencies. A review of the evolution of the regulation does not support respondent's overly broad interpretation. . . .

Treas. Reg. §20.2041-3(b) was promulgated by T.D. 6296, 1958-2 C.B. 432, 527. In that same Treasury decision, respondent promulgated Treas. Reg. §20.2038-1(b), applicable to retained powers and determining whether a power to alter, amend, or revoke exists on a decedent's date of death. T.D. 6296, 1958-2 C.B. at 507.

Prior to the issuance of T.D. 6296 the regulation applicable to retained powers provided that a power to alter, amend, revoke, or terminate was considered to exist on the date of a decedent's death even though "the exercise of the power was restricted to a particular time which had not arrived, or the happening of a particular event which had not occurred, at decedent's death." T.D. 6296 specifically considered and changed the standard to exclude from a decedent's gross estate retained powers subject to a contingency beyond the decedent's control.

T.D. 6296 also revised the regulation applicable to powers of appointment to specifically address contingent powers which were not addressed in the prior regulation applicable to powers of appointment.

In 1958, T.D. 6296 included the language "beyond the decedent's control" in Treas. Reg. §20.2038-1(b) with regard to retained powers. In contrast, although the regulations are otherwise similar, T.D. 6296 did not include the words "beyond the decedent's control" in Treas. Reg. §20.2041-3(b) with regard to powers of appointment. There is no indication that the omission was inadvertent.

Furthermore, we think that the omission is reasonable, and that different treatment for a power of appointment as opposed to a retained power is warranted. In order for a decedent to remove from his gross estate for Federal estate tax purposes property that he previously owned and has transferred, a decedent must place such property irrevocably beyond his control. In such cases, retaining a small amount of control will cause the property to remain in the decedent's estate. In contrast, a decedent must be granted a greater amount of control or power over property not previously owned by the decedent before that property becomes includable in his gross estate.

This difference is reflected in the general application of sections 2038 and 2041. For example, a decedent who transfers property to a trust, retaining the right to appoint such property among his children, but not to himself, his estate, his creditors, or creditors of his estate, is required to include the entire property in his gross estate under section 2038. Estate of Porter v. Commissioner, 288 U.S. 436, 443 (1933). On the other hand, if another person grants the decedent the same power over property that the decedent did not previously own, the property is not included in the decedent's gross estate under either section 2038 or section 2041. Estate of Resch v. Commissioner, 20 T.C. 171, 183 (1953); Treas. Reg. §20.2041-1(c)(1)(*b*)

The regulations under these two sections reflect this difference. Under the language of Treas. Reg. §20.2038-1(b), any contingency must be "beyond the decedent's control" before it will serve to keep retained-powers property out of a decedent's estate. Under the language of Treas. Reg. §20.2041-3(b) there is no requirement that the contingency be "beyond the decedent's control".

Neither the statute (last sentence of §2041(a)(2)) nor the pertinent regulation (§20.2041-3(b)) expressly requires that the event or contingency be "beyond the decedent's control." We are not persuaded by respondent's efforts to construct such a requirement from bits and pieces of other regulations either defining a type of power of appointment or governing retained powers (§2038) rather than powers of appointment (§2041). Since respondent added such a requirement to the retained powers regulation (§20.2038-1(b)) and at the same time failed to include that language in the powers of appointment regulation (§20.2041-3(b)), we decline to engraft this language into the regulation. . . .

[A]lthough we decline to read into the statute a requirement that the event or contingency must necessarily be beyond a decedent's control, the event or contingency must not be illusory and must have some significant non-tax consequence independent of the decedent's ability to exercise the power. The legislative history, however, clearly indicates that all property of which the decedent on the date of his death had practical, if not technical, ownership is to be included in his estate. We think any illusory or sham restriction placed on a power of appointment should be ignored. An event or condition that has no significant non-tax consequence independent of a decedent's power to appoint the property for his own benefit is illusory. For example, for purposes of §2038, a power is disregarded if it becomes operational as a mere by-product of an event, the non-tax consequences of which greatly overshadow its significance for tax purposes. See Bittker & Lokken, FEDERAL TAXATION OF INCOME, ESTATES AND GIFTS ¶126.5.4, at 126–64 (2d ed. 1984). If the power involves acts of "independent significance," whose effect on the trust is "incidental and collateral," such acts are also deemed to be beyond the decedent's control. See Rev. Rul. 80-255, 1980-2 C.B. 272 (power to bear or adopt children involves act of "independent significance," whose effect on a trust that included after-born and after-adopted children was "incidental and collateral"); see also Estate of Tully v. United States, 528 F.2d 1401, 1406 (Ct. Cl. 1976) ("In reality, a man might divorce his wife, but to assume that he would fight through an entire divorce process merely to alter employee death benefits approaches the absurd"). Thus, if a power is contingent upon an event of substantial independent consequence that the decedent could, but did not, bring about, the event is deemed to be beyond the decedent's control for purposes of §2038.

We do not think that, where the general power of appointment is the right to withdraw principal from a trust, Congress intended that application of §2041(a)(2) could be avoided by stacking or ordering the withdrawal powers; i.e., exercising the power to withdraw a certain number of dollars before the power to withdraw the next portion comes into operation. A condition that has no significant non-tax consequence independent of a decedent's power to appoint the property for her own benefit does not prevent practical ownership; it is illusory and should be ignored. We conclude that for purposes of §2041, although the condition does not have to be beyond the decedent's control, it must have some significant non-tax consequence independent of the decedent's power to appoint the property. Petitioner has not demonstrated that withdrawing principal from the Marital Trust Fund has any significant non-tax consequence independent of decedent's power to withdraw principal from the Family Trust Fund. Such condition is illusory and, thus, is not an event or a contingency contemplated by Treas. Reg. §20.2041-3(b).

We hold that, if by its terms a general power of appointment is exercisable only upon the occurrence during the decedent's lifetime of an event or contingency that has no significant non-tax consequence independent of the decedent's ability to exercise the power, the power exists on the date of decedent's death, regardless of whether the event or contingency did in fact occur during such time. Because petitioner has failed to demonstrate any significant non-tax consequence independent of decedent's right to withdraw principal from the Family Trust Fund, we hold that, on the date of her death, decedent had a general power of appointment over 5% of the Family Trust Fund that causes that portion to be includable in her estate under §2041.

Decedent's power of appointment over 5% of the Family Trust Fund was in existence on the date of her death regardless of the fact that the principal of the Marital Trust Fund had not been completely exhausted by that date. Hence, 5% of the Family Trust Fund was includable in her gross estate.

In thinking about conditional powers, assume that D created a testamentary trust to pay income to S for life; at S's death, the corpus was payable to named individuals, with a proviso that:

the Trustee shall first pay from income or principal to the personal representative of S's estate such sums as needed, in addition to and after exhaustion of the property of S's estate, to pay all claims, expense of administration, and taxes as may be allowed by the court having jurisdiction of S's estate as properly chargeable against S's estate.

S's own assets at death were sufficient to cover all claims, expenses of administration, and taxes chargeable against S's estate, so nothing could have been paid from the trust. Think about why any portion of D's trust nevertheless should be includible in S's gross estate. See Treas. Reg. §20.2041-1(c)(1); PLR 8049011. Would anyone spend themselves into insolvency to obtain the ability to have taxes, expenses, and claims paid from such a trust?

Let's alter the facts such that D was beneficiary of a trust that contained a provision that merely authorized payment of any estate taxes caused by inclusion of that trust in D's estate. That clause operating on its own would not cause inclusion of any portion of the trust in D's gross estate. See TAM 8551001. Why are these different?

Now assume that Child (C) is empowered under a springing durable power of attorney for property management created by C's parent (P) to make distributions to P's descendants to take advantage of the gift tax annual exclusion. This authority applies only after the power of attorney "springs," which requires a determination that P no longer is able to manage normal business affairs, as certified by an independent physician. From a tax policy perspective, should any portion of the property subject to the power be includible in C's gross estate if C dies before a determination of P's inability to manage business affairs is certified? The easy conclusion is that no inclusion should result if P clearly was able to manage business affairs. But if the fact was otherwise, would it be appropriate to allow the tax consequence to turn on whether anyone had sought to obtain the requisite determination or certification?

7.   *Joint Powers.* These didn't used to be very common, but a renewed use of "trust protectors" and individual cofiduciaries has caused the following issue to resume significance.

Estate of Towle v. Commissioner
54 T.C. 368 (1970)

[The decedent was the income beneficiary of insurance settlement contracts that accorded the decedent a noncumulative right to withdraw $13,500 per year from the principal and the right (unexercised at the date of death) to withdraw at any time all of the principal with the consent of the First National Bank of Chicago as trustee under the will of Charles W. McNear, the decedent's father. Upon the decedent's death, any remaining principal was payable to the trustee.]

TANNENWALD, J.: . . . Petitioner [argues] that the power of withdrawal by the decedent of the entire proceeds of the insurance settlement contracts was not a general power of appointment within the meaning of §2041(b)(1) and that therefore the amount of those proceeds, in excess of that subject to the noncumulative annual right of withdrawal, is not includible in the decedent's gross estate under §2041(a) [for the following reasons]:

. . . (1) First National, albeit concededly as a trustee, held a direct remainder interest under the insurance settlement contracts and consequently had an "interest in the property, subject to the power"; (2) because of the fiduciary duty imposed upon First National to protect the interests of the remaindermen of the residuary trust under the will of Charles W. McNear, its "interest" was "substantial" and "adverse"[5] within the meaning of subsection (C)(ii) of §2041(b)(1); and (3) First National was simply an agent of the grandson remainderman decedent. We disagree.

As a general rule, the interest of a nonbeneficiary trustee is neither substantial nor adverse. Reinecke v. Smith, 289 U.S. 172 (1933), so holds with respect to the income tax and its principles

---

5.   Petitioner makes no claim that its financial interest, derived from its prospective administration of any insurance proceeds with the resulting administration charges, constitutes a substantial adverse interest. See Miller v. United States, 387 F.2d 866, 870 (3d Cir. 1968), *rev'g* 267 F. Supp. 182 (W.D. Pa. 1967), holding that a right of compensation for serving as trustee is not a substantial adverse interest within the meaning of §2041(b)(1)(C)(ii).

are fully applicable to the estate tax. Northern Trust Co. v. United States, 389 F.2d 731 (7th Cir. 1968); New England Merchants Nat'l Bank v. United States, 384 F.2d 176 (1st Cir., 1967); Welch v. Terhune, 126 F.2d 695 (1st Cir. 1942); Steward v. Commissioner, 28 B.T.A. 256 (1933), *vacating* 27 B.T.A. 593 (1933), *aff'd sub nom.* Witherbee v. Commissioner, 70 F.2d 696 (2d Cir. 1934). This conclusion is further supported by the following statement in the committee reports which accompanied the original enactment of the pertinent portion of §2041 . . . :

> a future joint power is totally exempt if it is not exercisable by the decedent except with the consent or joinder of a person having a substantial interest, in the property subject to the power, which is adverse to the exercise of the power in favor of the decedent, his estate, his creditors, or the creditors of his estate. A taker in default of appointment has an interest which is adverse to such an exercise. Principles developed under the income and gift taxes will be applicable in determining whether an interest is substantial and the amount of property in which the adversity exists. A coholder of the power has no adverse interest merely because of his joint possession of the power nor merely because he is a permissible appointee under a power, since neither the power nor the expectancy as appointee is an "interest" in the property. . . .

(See H. Rep. No. 327, to accompany H.R. 2084, 82d Cong., 1st Sess. 5-6 (1951); S. Rep. No. 382 to accompany H.R. 2084, 82d Cong., 1st Sess. 5 (1951). [And see Treas. Reg. §20.2041-3(c)(2) — Ed.])

In *Reinecke v. Smith* the Supreme Court stated:

> In approaching the decision of the question before us it is to be borne in mind that the trustee is not a trustee of the power of revocation and owes no duty to the beneficiary to resist alteration or revocation of the trust. Of course he owes a duty to the beneficiary to protect the trust res, faithfully to administer it, and to distribute the income; but the very fact that he participates in the right of alteration or revocation negatives any fiduciary duty to the beneficiary to refrain from exercising the power. . . .

See 289 U.S. at 176–177.

Petitioner seeks to avoid the application of the principles announced in *Reinecke v. Smith* by claiming that First National had a direct remainder interest in the insurance proceeds and that its fiduciary obligations arose only under the will of Charles W. McNear *after* it had collected the insurance proceeds. In essence, petitioner asserts that First National was a beneficiary of those proceeds in its own right. But a beneficiary is one who has a beneficial interest of his own and not one who administers property for the benefit of others. See Reinecke v. Smith, 289 U.S. at 174. Clearly, First National fits the latter category. We do not think its status as the remainderman of the insurance proceeds so enlarged its interest as to place it outside the rationale of *Reinecke v. Smith*. Nor does petitioner's recital of numerous authorities under State law with respect to the requirement of good faith imposed upon the exercise of discretionary powers by a trustee or the ability of a beneficiary to enforce the requirement by injunction, surcharge, or otherwise have any bearing on the issue before us. New England Merchants Nat'l Bank v. United States, 384 F.2d at 180.

Petitioner admits that, "No provision in the Will of Charles W. McNear in express terms directs or controls the exercise of the Trustee's power to permit the withdrawal of the retained funds by [the decedent]." Petitioner argues that the testamentary objective of Charles W. McNear was to assure that the principal of his estate would pass to his grandson or his heirs and that the trustee had a special duty to see that such objective was accomplished. But on this record it is at least equally, if not more, plausible to conclude that Charles W. McNear considered the insurance settlements to be separate from the residuary trust in order that the decedent would have funds adequate to meet her reasonable desires during her lifetime, as she saw them, and that the corporate trustee had merely the usual fiduciary responsibility to guard against the capricious exhaustion of the insurance principal.

We think that the phrase "substantial interest in the property, subject to the power, which is adverse to exercise of the power in favor of the decedent," as used in §2041(b)(1)(C)(ii), was intended at the very least to require that the third person have a present or future chance to obtain a personal benefit[6] from the property itself. Cf. Latts v. Commissioner, 212 F.2d 164, 167 (3d Cir. 1954); Commissioner v. Prouty, 115 F.3d 331, 335-336 (1st Cir. 1940), *aff'g in part and rev'g and rem'g in part* 41 B.T.A. 274 (1940).[7] Compare also

---

6. Whether such benefit includes, not only the possibility of direct realization, but also the possibility of indirect realization through a power affirmatively to dispose of an interest in the property to others is a question we are not now required to decide. See 5 Mertens, Law of Federal Gift & Estate Taxation §34.68 at 302.

7. The rationale of the *Prouty* case as to what constitutes an adverse interest has been accepted by this Court. See Estate of Gillette v. Commissioner, 7 T.C. 219, 222 (1946). See also Strite v. McGinnes, 330 F.2d 234, 240 (3d Cir. 1964), *aff'g* 215 F. Supp. 513 (E.D. Pa. 1963), where the court accepted without discussion the proposi-

the provisions of §2041(b)(1)(C)(iii), which exclude, on an allocable basis, a portion of property subject to a power which would otherwise be a general power of appointment, but which is exercisable "in favor of" a person whose consent is required.

As the final element in . . . its argument, petitioner asserts that First National was simply the agent of the grandson remainderman under the will of Charles W. McNear in granting or withholding its consent to the invasion of the insurance principal by decedent.[8] We can find nothing in the record herein to support such an assertion. Clearly, First National's relationship to the grandson was simply that of a trustee to a beneficiary and, in this context, our previous analysis refutes petitioner's contention. . . .

Decision will be entered for the respondent.

For further elaboration on when a joint powerholder will be considered to have a substantial interest in the appointive property, adverse to its exercise in favor of the decedent, see Treas. Reg. §20.2041-3(c). See also Estate of Maxant v. Commissioner, 40 T.C.M. (CCH) 1328 (1980); Rev. Rul. 79-63; Rev. Rul. 75-145.

In PLR 9030032, the decedent was the life income beneficiary of a bypass trust, with remainder to the decedent's children. The decedent and one of those children as cotrustees had the unrestricted power to distribute corpus to the decedent. According to the government, the child as cotrustee was an adverse party, which precluded treating the power as a general power of appointment. If a remainder beneficiary is entitled to only an equal share of the remainder along with the other children, why is that beneficiary adverse with respect to more than just that portion of the trust? Cf. Treas. Reg. §§20.2041-3(c)(2) and -3(c)(3).

In Rev. Rul. 82-156, the decedent, D, created a testamentary marital deduction trust that granted S, D's spouse, a power, commencing at D's death and continuing throughout S's overlife, to appoint trust corpus in such amounts and at such times as S chose in favor of S or S's creditors. D's will provided further that any corpus remaining in trust at S's death will pass to A and B in equal shares. The will provided that any proposed exercise of the power of appointment by S must be preceded by notice to A and B and, if either objected to a proposed exercise of the power of appointment, the matter was to be submitted for resolution to the trustee of the testamentary trust, a bank, whose decision was binding. The government ruled:

---

tion that a corporate trustee, who was a coholder of a power of appointment, was a nonadverse party where the remaindermen were the decedent's nieces and nephews.

8. We note that if the consent of [the remainder beneficiary] was directly required for invasion of the insurance principal, his interest in the proceeds as remainderman would be termed substantially adverse. See Treas. Reg. §20.2041-3(c)(2) *Example (1)*.

S's power was exercisable, in effect, either with the joint consent of *A* and *B*, or with the consent of the trustee. The consent of *A* and *B* made the consent of the trustee unnecessary and, conversely, the consent of the trustee made the consent of *A* and *B* unnecessary. Since the trustee had no adverse interest for purposes of §2041, and since *S* could freely exercise the power of appointment as long as the trustee consented, *S* had a general power of appointment within the meaning of §2041.

Joint Power With the Donor.   Under §2041(b)(1)(C)(i), a power held jointly with the creator of the power — the donor — is not considered a general power of appointment. However, it is likely that the full value of the property subject to the power will be includible in the donor's gross estate under either §2036(a)(2) or §2038(a)(1), or both. See Chapter 5.

8.   *Powers Exercisable Only During Life.*   The decedent's power of withdrawal over the principal in *Estate of Towle*, reproduced at page 133, was a power that by its nature was exercisable only while the decedent was alive; it was not exercisable by will. Did this power meet the §2041(a)(2) requirement that the decedent have the power at the time of death? Under §2033, property interests that expire at the instant of a decedent's death (such as a life estate) are not includible in the decedent's gross estate because, at the time of death, the decedent no longer had an interest in the property.

The issue regarding a power exercisable only inter vivos was raised in Jenkins v. United States, 428 F.2d 538 (5th Cir. 1970). The court held that the appointive property was includible under §2041(a)(2) but gave no satisfactory explanation of how it was able to say that the decedent had such a power at the time of death. The court failed to cite the House committee report, H.R. Rep. No. 2333, 77th Cong., 1st Sess. 160-161 (1942), in 1942-2 C.B. 372, 490, accompanying the 1942 Act, which contains the following statement:

The term [power of appointment] includes powers to appoint exercisable only during the decedent's lifetime and terminable at his death. A power of appointment is deemed to exist at the date of the decedent's death where the time for the exercise of the power is determined by the date of his death.

Essentially the same statement is repeated in the committee reports accompanying the Powers of Appointment Act of 1951. See H.R. Rep. No. 327, 82d Cong., 1st Sess. 6 (1951); S. Rep. No. 382, 82d Cong., 1st Sess. 6 (1951).

Section 2033 operates differently because it is aimed at property that the decedent can transfer at death. Section 2041 is aimed at property over which the decedent could have exercised dominion. The key to §2041 is that it reaches powers that lapse because of death — either because a testamentary power cannot be exercised by will after the powerholder dies or because it is an inter vivos power that expires at death. A power that lapses before death will trigger §2514 gift taxation.

9.   *Powers Subject to an Ascertainable Standard.*   A huge exception to §2041 exposure is found in §2041(b)(2)(A) as revealed in the following case.

Brantingham v. United States
631 F.2d 542 (7th Cir. 1980)

CAMPBELL, Senior District Judge: . . . C. Alan Brantingham died testate . . . a resident of Massachusetts . . . and his will was probated there. The will, which had been drawn seventeen years prior to his death, contained the following provision:

> I hereby give, devise and bequeath unto my children, share and share alike, per stirpes, all of my property and estate of whatsoever kind or nature, now or hereafter acquired, subject, however, to the life use thereof, which I hereby give unto my wife, Beatrice F. Brantingham, and as such life user, my said wife shall have and is hereby given the uncontrolled right, power and authority to use and devote such of the corpus thereof from time to time as in her judgment is necessary for her maintenance, comfort and happiness.

Section 2056 . . . provides for a marital deduction for certain interests passing to the spouse of the decedent. . . . The Commissioner determined that the life estate devised to Beatrice Brantingham did not provide her with unlimited power of appointment, and therefore did not qualify for the deduction. Since Mrs. Brantingham could dispose of the principal of the life estate only for purposes of her "maintenance, comfort and happiness," she lacked the requisite control to qualify for the exception contained in 26 U.S.C. §2056(b)(5). . . .

John Brantingham, the executor of Beatrice Brantingham's estate, did not include the [property subject to the] life estate in question as part of the decedent's gross estate on her federal estate tax return. The Commissioner determined that the [property subject to the] life estate should be included and issued a notice of deficiency. . . .

The Commissioner based the inclusion of the [property subject to the] life estate in Beatrice Brantingham's gross estate on . . . 26 U.S.C. §2041(a)(2). The Commissioner reasoned that, in allowing his widow to "devote such of the corpus . . . as in her judgment is necessary for her maintenance, comfort and happiness," Alan Brantingham had given her a general power of appointment over the [property subject to the] life estate in question. Thus, the Commissioner concluded, the corpus of the life estate was part of Beatrice Brantingham's gross estate, and was subject to estate tax again.

As is the case with any rule, and particularly those found in the Internal Revenue Code, there are exceptions. Property over which the decedent has a general power of appointment is not included in the decedent's gross estate if the power to dispose of that property is "limited by an ascertainable standard relating to the health, education, support, or maintenance of the decedent." 26 U.S.C. §2041(b)(1)(A). Presumably, the theory behind this exception is that if the decedent has been constrained in the manner in which she may dispose of property during her lifetime, it should not be considered part of her estate at death. . . .

The District Court, on recommendation of the United States Magistrate, entered summary judgment for defendant as to both the taxpayer's claim for reimbursement and the government's counterclaim for interest due. We reverse.

The taxpayer initially presents two arguments on appeal. First, the taxpayer argues that Congress intended that §§2056 and 2041 be read as interdependent parts of a single statutory pattern. He contends that Congress did not intend that a property interest be included in the original testator's estate and again in the spouse's estate. The spouse either exercises a sufficient degree of control over an interest to qualify for the marital deduction, in which case the remaining portion of that interest would be included in her gross estate; or she lacks sufficient authority over the interest to qualify for the deduction and the interest will not be included in her gross estate. Since the marital deduction was disallowed at the time of Alan Brantingham's death, the life estate would not be included in his widow's estate under this theory. The second argument advanced by petitioner is that the government is estopped from including the [property subject to the] life estate of Beatrice Brantingham's estate by the prior inclusion of that interest in her husband's gross estate.

Were these the only arguments in support of the taxpayer, we would affirm the entry of summary judgment. While §§2056 and 2041 both discuss powers of appointment, there is nothing in either provision which suggests that they should be construed in pari materia. Nor is there any discussion in the legislative history which suggests such a result.

The taxpayer's estoppel argument is similarly without merit. In order to assert estoppel against the Commissioner, there must be some reasonable reliance on the Commissioner's statements or actions. The taxpayer suggests that the Commissioner's ruling that the assets of the C. Alan Brantingham estate subject to the life-use by Beatrice Brantingham could not be allowed as a marital deduction to Alan's estate estops the Commissioner from including the [property subject to the] life estate in Beatrice Brantingham's estate. Yet, the Commissioner's disallowance of the marital deduction simply stated:

> Your claim for refund is rejected in its entirety. Under the provisions of the decedent's Will, it does not appear that the surviving spouse had such right to consume property subject to her use as to qualify for the marital deduction.

There is nothing in this statement which even remotely suggests any disposition as to the inclusion of the [property subject to the] life estate in Beatrice Brantingham's estate.

The taxpayer apparently elected not to pursue the argument that Beatrice Brantingham's power of appointment over the [property subject to the] life estate is limited by an ascertainable standard. Government counsel, however, have brought the ascertainable standard exception to our attention in their brief. We believe that Beatrice Brantingham's power to invade the corpus of the life estate is limited by an ascertainable standard, and that her interest in the corpus of that estate should not be included in her gross estate.

Section 2041 and similar provisions of the tax code designate which property interests are included in a decedent's estate and subject to Federal Estate Tax. Section 2041(b)(1)(A) excludes from Federal taxation interests in which the decedent's power of appointment is limited by an "ascertainable standard." The determination as to what legal rights and interests are created by a specific instrument is a question of state law. Morgan v. Commissioner, 309 U.S. 78, 80 (1940); Estate of Gartland v. Commissioner, 293 F.2d 575, 580 (7th Cir. 1961). Thus, to determine whether the [property subject to the] life estate left to Beatrice Brantingham by her husband is subject to Federal taxation, we must look to state law.

Alan Brantingham was a resident of Massachusetts at the time of his death. His estate was probated in Massachusetts. Accordingly, Massachusetts law defines all interest created in Alan

Brantingham's will. The government urges that Beatrice Brantingham was granted virtually unlimited authority to dispose of the [property subject to the] life estate, and therefore her power of appointment cannot be considered limited by any standard, much less an ascertainable one.[9] . . .

Our review of Massachusetts law reveals that any interest to which the decedent places limitations on the spouse's power of appointment is considered by the Courts as a limited interest. In Homans v. Foster, 121 N.E. 417 (Mass. 1919), a widower inherited his wife's estate for life "with the full power to dispose of the whole or any part of said property . . . by deed or otherwise, if he may deem it conducive to his comfort so to do." 121 N.E. at 418. The Court construed the husband's life estate as a limited one. The Court noted that there were purposes for which the husband could not part with the property and that this was sufficient to construe his interest as a limited one.

In Nunes v. Rogers, 30 N.E.2d 259, 261 (Mass. 1940), a widow took a life estate in her deceased husband's property "with power to sell, mortgage or otherwise dispose of so much . . . of (the) estate as in her judgment shall be necessary for her comfortable support and maintenance." 30 N.E.2d at 260. The Court found "the power of disposal was limited by its very terms and could be exercised for no other purpose than therein stated." 30 N.E.2d at 261.

We point to these cases simply to demonstrate that Massachusetts Courts have, even prior to the adoption of the tax code, viewed a life estate such as the one in the instant case as a limited interest. . . .

Turning to more recent Massachusetts case law construing testamentary instruments for purposes of determining Federal tax liability, we conclude that Beatrice Brantingham's [power to withdraw the property subject to her] life estate was not only limited, but limited by an ascertainable standard as well. In Pittsfield Nat'l Bank v. United States, 181 F. Supp. 851 (D. Mass. 1960), the District Court interpreted a similar life estate for purposes of determining whether the taxpayer's right to invade principal was limited by an ascertainable standard. The decedent had the right to "all or such part of the principal of same as he may from time to time request, he to be the sole judge of his needs." The Court relied on the inclusion of the words "needs" in finding that the

---

9. While we are not concerned with the Commissioner's disallowance of the marital deduction in the estate of Alan Brantingham, we note that this position appears to contradict the Commissioner's prior ruling.

decedent's power to invade the principal of the life estate was limited by an ascertainable standard within the meaning of §2041(b)(1)(A). In Woodberry v. Bunker, 268 N.E.2d 841 (Mass. 1971), the Court found that a trustee's power to dispose of principal for comfortable support, medical care "or other purposes which seem wise to my trustees" was a limited and enforceable standard. Id. at 844.

The Government seeks to distinguish these cases on the ground that [the] right of invasion of principal is based on some notion of need, whereas in the present case invasion is permitted for the widow's "happiness." The prerequisites for invasion of corpus in these cases do not seem to differ significantly from the language of Beatrice Brantingham's [power over the property subject to her] life estate. Yet even assuming that "happiness" is so broad a term to distinguish the above cases, Dana v. Gring, 371 N.E.2d 755 (Mass. 1971), resolves any doubt that the Massachusetts Courts would construe Beatrice Brantingham's power of invasion as limited by an ascertainable standard. In that case the trustees were authorized to invade principal as they deemed "necessary or desirable for the purpose of contributing to the reasonable welfare or happiness of (the settlor's) daughter or her immediate family." Id. at 759. While recognizing that happiness is a broad term the Massachusetts Court did not consider it evidence of intent to establish a trust for the decedent's daughter with fee simple powers. Rather, in looking at the entire instrument, the Court concluded that the settlor's intent was to preserve the principal of the fund for his lineal descendants alive at the time of his death. The Court found the trustee's right to distribute principal was limited by "an objective, ascertainable standard." Id. at 761.

The language found in Alan Brantingham's Will also reflects an intent to preserve the principal of his estate for his children. . . . The bequest in the instant case is virtually indistinguishable from that in Dana v. Gring.

We conclude, as we believe that any Massachusetts Court would conclude, that Beatrice Brantingham's power to invade the principal of the life estate was limited by an ascertainable standard. The Massachusetts cases discussed herein leave no doubt that the §2041(b)(1)(A) exception to a general power of appointment applies, and that the corpus of the life estate was erroneously included in Beatrice Brantingham's gross estate. . . . Accordingly, the entry of summary judgment is Reversed and Remanded to the District Court with instructions to enter judgment for plaintiff in accordance with the views expressed herein.

Case law and statutes in a broad number of jurisdictions purport to assist taxpayers to avoid general power of appointment treatment. Some define a wide range of terms as ascertainable under state law in an effort to protect their citizens from the type of issue involved in *Brantingham*. Others purport to cut back the power of a trustee who is a beneficiary to a power that will not constitute a general power of appointment by preventing indirect benefits to the trustee through principal and income allocations or from distributions that would discharge the trustee's legal obligation of support. In Rev. Proc. 94-44 and a wide array of private letter rulings the government has held that application of this type of limitation to pre-existing irrevocable trusts is effective, and the Procedure concluded also that it does not constitute the lapse of a general power of appointment for purposes of §2041(b)(2) or §2514(e). See 3 Casner & Pennell, ESTATE PLANNING §12.1 nn.9, 10, 13 (2002). Quaere whether state law that varies from one jurisdiction to another (and perhaps from one year to another) should provide such a powerful federal tax exemption. If so, why don't more states embrace such legislation?

Absent state legislation defining terms to be ascertainable, the ability to predict whether a power is limited by the requisite standard is remote unless the government's own terminology from Treas. Reg. §20.2041-1(c)(2) is utilized. And, as the following sampler is designed to illustrate, this is no place for a drafter to use a thesaurus. The only safe manner to draft a guaranteed ascertainable standard is to use terms the regulation has blessed. A wide collection of cases deliberating the effects of various terms is collected in 3 Casner & Pennell, ESTATE PLANNING §12.3.2.4 (2002). Just to illustrate how arbitrary or technical the distinctions can be, consider just a handful of the legion of determinations made by courts and the government involving seemingly synonymous terminology but reaching different results.

TAM 9125002 determined that "health, support *and* reasonable comfort, best interest and welfare" is not an ascertainable standard. The phrase "support *in* reasonable comfort" is an ascertainable standard under Treas. Reg. §20.2041-1(c)(2), and it may have been the settlor's intent to use that phrase but a stenographic error occurred in the preparation of that portion of the provision used; nevertheless, according to the regulations, "best interest and welfare" are not ascertainable standards. Pyle v. United States, 766 F.2d 1141 (7th Cir. 1985), held "comfort" to be ascertainable under Illinois law while PLRs 9030032 and 8523071 deemed "comfort" standing alone to be nonascertainable, again based on the regulations. PLR 9203047 involved "maintenance, support and comfort, in order to defray expenses incurred by reason of sickness, accidents and disability, and whether used for medical, dental, hospitals, nursing and institutional costs . . . ." Distinguishing cases such as Vissering v. Commissioner, 96 T.C. 749 (1991) ("comfort" used alone deemed not an ascertainable standard), the government determined that use of the term in relation to amounts required to defray health related costs was ascertainable and protected the decedent from general power of appointment treatment. The analogy was made to use of the phrase "support in reasonable comfort" in which the phrase used in relation to "health, education, support, or maintenance" also is ascertainable. On appeal in *Vissering*, 990 F.2d 578 (10th Cir. 1993), the court held that, although the controlling state (Florida) court would regard "comfort" alone to be nonascertainable, that term was ascertainable in the context in which it was used ("required for the continued comfort") in conjunction with distributions for support, maintenance, and education. The court distinguished standards allowing invasion as "desired" by the fiduciary and accepted the analogy of the "required for the continued comfort" standard to "support in reasonable comfort," which is ascertainable under the regulations. PLR 9235025 involved the terms "comfort, emergencies, and serious illness," which the government held were nonascertainable.

TAM 8339004 held that "emergency" is not ascertainable under Georgia law, but Estate of Sowell v. Commissioner, 708 F.2d 1564 (10th Cir. 1983), *rev'g* 74 T.C. 1001 (1980), and dated almost the same day as the TAM, held that "emergency" is ascertainable under New Mexico law. Hunter v. United States, 597 F. Supp. 1293 (W.D. Pa. 1984), held that "for the comfortable support and maintenance of any beneficiary . . . or should any emergency arise" was ascertainable under Pennsylvania law and that it was even less liberal than the clearly ascertainable standard of "support in an accustomed manner of living." PLR 9012053 held that "to relieve emergencies" is an ascertainable standard but TAM 9044081 held that "emergency condition of any exigencies which may make the distributable income from such fund insufficient for [Decedent's] reasonable needs" is not an ascertainable standard. According to the TAM, "Decedent's power could be exercised in case of emergencies which did not otherwise relate to her needs for health, maintenance, and support, such as financial setbacks that would not otherwise jeopardize the Decedent's ability to support herself," and thus did not "reasonably relate to Decedent's health, education, maintenance and support" as required by §2041(a)(2) and Treas. Reg. §20.2041-1(c)(2). The decedent was also given a power to withdraw corpus for "support, maintenance and medical payments," which provided an indication that the "emergency" power was meant to give a broader authority. Although the reference to the decedent's "reasonable needs" provided some limitation on the power of withdrawal, it was not regarded as sufficient to qualify as an ascertainable standard. Similarly, TAM 8121010 held "needs from time to time, in the broadest sense" to be not ascertainable.

PLR 9148036 involved "maintenance, care, and support." Finding no state law on the issue whether the term "care" is an ascertainable standard, and the regulations being silent on the issue, the government relied on Rev.

Rul. 76-547, which involved the terms "care, maintenance, health, and enjoyment." According to the PLR, "care" is ascertainable, stating that Rev. Rul. 76-547 "singles out the word 'enjoyment' and states that 'enjoyment' indicates that the trust could be invaded for purposes other than health, education, support, or maintenance. The revenue ruling does not discuss the word 'care' because 'care' is an ascertainable standard relating to health, education, support, or maintenance."

TAM 8901006 held that the decedent possessed a general power of appointment under a will that gave the decedent the right to use as much or all of certain property as necessary for sickness, hospitalization, doctor's care, medication, support, maintenance, welfare, and general comfort in keeping with the manner and mode of living to which the decedent was accustomed. But TAM 7836008 held that "reasonable health, education, support, and maintenance needs consistent with a high standard and quality of living" is ascertainable.

On the drafting of powers in general and the use of external standards, see generally Lowndes, Kramer, & McCord, FEDERAL ESTATE TAXES §12.6 (3d ed. 1974); Stephens, Maxfield, Lind, & Calfee FEDERAL ESTATE & GIFT TAXATION ¶4.13[4][a] (8th ed. 2002); Pennell, *Estate Planning: Drafting and Tax Considerations in Employing Individual Trustees*, 60 N.C. L. REV. 799 (1982), abridged and reprinted in 9 EST. PLAN. 264 (1982).

In Rev. Rul. 76-368, *D*'s testamentary trust gave the corporate trustee a power to invade the corpus for *S* in the trustee's discretion for *S*'s medical care, comfortable maintenance, and happiness. The government ruled that the trust was not includible in *S*'s gross estate. At one time the government asserted that the result would differ if the trust conferred on *S* the power to remove the trustee and appoint a new corporate trustee to administer the trust. See Rev. Rul. 95-58, revoking Rev. Rul. 81-51 and Rev. Rul. 79-353. See also Estate of Wall v. Commissioner, 101 T.C. 300 (1993); and Estate of Vak v. Commissioner, 973 F.2d 1409 (8th Cir. 1992).

10. *Nonobvious Applications of §2041.*

The "Delaware Tax Trap." A little known and frequently misunderstood provision, §2041(a)(3), constitutes a trap in some cases but represents a valuable planning opportunity in other situations in which only a nongeneral power of appointment is involved. This provision is a classic illustration of the fact that sometimes a *nongeneral* power of appointment will generate tax liability. It also illustrates the unfortunate reality that sometimes you need to understand what the Code is telling you before you can read it and understand what it says. Try reading §2041(a)(3). If you glean even as little as that the Rule Against Perpetuities somehow seems to be involved, you have mastered the most difficult aspect of this arcane provision!

Under §2041(a)(3) (with its gift tax counterpart in §2514(d)), property subject to a nongeneral power of appointment is taxable as if the power were a general power of appointment to the extent the power is exercised[10] to create another power of appointment that has the effect of postponing the period of the Rule Against Perpetuities. Thus, to understand §2041(a)(3), it is necessary to learn a bit about the Rule Against Perpetuities.

The common law Rule as applied to trusts generally requires contingent future interests to be certain to vest (or fail to vest, i.e., for the contingency to be resolved one way or the other) no later than 21 years after the death of some person who was alive when the trust was created.[11] Neither a general testamentary power nor a nongeneral power is regarded as a vested property interest for perpetuities purposes. Nor can any of these forms of power be exercised in a manner that extends the original perpetuities period. In most jurisdictions, however, a presently exercisable general (PEG) power of appointment is regarded as a vested property interest. This is because the holder of such a power may immediately appoint the subject trust property to himself or herself personally, meaning that alienation of the property is no longer suspended.[12] Under the common law Rule, if the new powerholder may presently exercise the power to appoint the property in further trust, a new perpetuities period will begin with that exercise.[13]

Sections 2041(a)(3) and 2514(d) were originally enacted as part of the Powers of Appointment Act of 1951 to prevent estate tax avoidance by exploiting a special Delaware statute[14] that allowed the absolute ownership of property to be suspended indefinitely through successive exercises of, and creation in others of new, nongeneral powers of appointment. Like a growing number of states, Delaware has since amended its law to totally repeal the Rule Against Perpetuities. Still, these Code sections continue to apply to the creation, by exercise of a nongeneral power, of a presently exercisable general power of appointment (the PEG power) if, under the

---

10.   "Exercise" includes either an actual exercise by the powerholder during life or by the powerholder's will, or a disposition during life of such a nature that, if it had been a transfer of the powerholder's own property, it would have caused estate tax inclusion under §§2035, 2036, or 2037. Curiously, §2038 is not one of the sections noted in this provision.

11.   Some states impose different perpetuities periods and the Uniform Statutory Rule Against Perpetuities, enacted in nearly half the states, revises the common law rule in a number of useful respects.

12.   See 6 AMERICAN LAW OF PROPERTY §§24.31, 24.33 (1952).

13.   See, e.g., 6 AMERICAN LAW OF PROPERTY §§24.31, 24.33 (1952). Although not universally the rule, most states also allow exercise of a nongeneral power of appointment to create a new trust (or extend the term of the original trust) and grant to a permissible object of the original nongeneral power a new, general power of appointment, on the theory that the property could have been given to that appointee directly and then the appointee could have disposed of the property in any manner the appointee might choose. See 5 AMERICAN LAW OF PROPERTY §23.49 (1952).

14.   Del. Code tit. 25, §501.

local Rule Against Perpetuities, creating the new PEG power begins a new perpetuities period without regard to the creation of the original nongeneral power.[15] This is the case under most states' Rule Against Perpetuities.[16] In addition, these provisions may apply to the exercise of any power in any manner that extends the duration of a trust in any state in which the Rule Against Perpetuities does not exist.

To illustrate, assume that Parent created a trust for the benefit of Child, giving Child a nongeneral power to appoint the remainder at death among Child's descendants in such shares as Child selects, either outright or in further trust, and allowing creation of new powers of appointment. Without exercise of this nongeneral power, eventually the trust must vest to avoid violation of the Rule Against Perpetuities (except in states in which the Rule does not operate to restrict the duration of trusts). But assume that, consistent with the terms of the nongeneral power and with local law, Child's will exercises the nongeneral power to extend the trust and grants a PEG power of appointment to Child's youngest living descendant. By this simple exercise, Child begins a new period for purposes of the Rule Against Perpetuities, applicable with respect to the extended trust. Under §2041(a)(3), several commentators contend that Child's exercise of the nongeneral power causes the trust property subject to the new PEG power to be includible in Child's estate as if Child had a general power of appointment, even though the trust property would not otherwise be includible in Child's estate (that is, if the power had been exercised in some other manner or not at all). If those commentators are correct, then, arming Child with this nongeneral power of appointment in a generation-skipping trust allows Child to decide whether to allow the generation-skipping transfer tax to apply or, by proper exercise, to cause the trust property to be includible in Child's estate to the extent Child creates a PEG power of appointment in another beneficiary.[17] In states without the Rule Against Perpetuities, exercise to extend the duration alone may trigger inclusion.

11. Like the Delaware Tax Trap, there can be other unexpected sources of general power of appointment exposure even in simple planning. To illustrate, consider the government's likely arguments in the following examples:

(a) *P* is acting as custodian of an account created for *P*'s minor child by a third party under the Uniform Transfers to Minors Act. As custodian,

---

15. See H.R. Rep. No. 327, 82d Cong., 1st Sess. 6-7 (1951); S. Rep. No. 382, 82d Cong., 1st Sess. 6 (1951), making it clear that §2041(a)(3) is not limited to just the Delaware opportunity.

16. See 6 AMERICAN LAW OF PROPERTY §§24.31, 24.33 (1952); Uniform Statutory Rule Against Perpetuities §§1, 2 (1986).

17. For more on this particular use, see Blattmachr & Pennell, *Adventures in Generation-Skipping, or How We Learned to Love the "Delaware Tax Trap,"* 24 REAL PROP., PROB. & TRUST J. 75–94 (1989).

P may distribute any part or all of the principal of the account directly to or for the benefit of the child's health, education, maintenance, or support. See Treas. Reg. §20.2041-1(c)(1) (third sentence); Pennell, *Custodians, Incompetents, Trustees and Others: Taxable Powers of Appointment?*, 15 U. MIAMI INST. EST. PLAN. ¶1600 (1981). Note that §14(c) of the uniform act provides: "A delivery, payment, or expenditure under this section is in addition to, not in substitution for, and does not affect any obligation of a person to support the minor."

(b) Assume that *P* was acting as trustee of a trust for the benefit of *P* and *P*'s children and was authorized to make distributions that were not limited by an ascertainable standard. *P* resigned as trustee when advised that inclusion would result when *P* died if still acting as trustee, but *P* continued as income beneficiary of the trust. As we will see when we study Chapter 5, if the release had been a transfer of *P*'s own property into the trust, that income interest would have caused §2036(a)(1) inclusion of the transferred property in *P*'s gross estate at death. See the second clause of §2041(a)(2), and de Oliveira v. United States, 767 F.2d 1344 (9th Cir. 1985).

(c) *S* was the income beneficiary of a §2056(b)(5) all income, general power of appointment marital deduction trust and of a bypass trust. Both trusts owned stock in a closely held corporation. The trustee engaged in a corporate recapitalization that caused the stock in the marital deduction trust to decline in value and the stock in the bypass trust correspondingly to rise in value. *S*, as beneficiary of the marital trust, consented to the transaction, resulting in a gift of the value of the remainder interest in the amount effectively shifted from the marital to the bypass trust. This gift was effectively a release of *S*'s general power to appoint that transferred value of the marital trust. See the second clause of §2041(a)(2) and Rev. Rul. 86-39.

(d) When *B* died, *B* had a right to purchase assets from a trust created by a third party at a purchase price that was less than 20% of the property's fair market value. See Treas. Reg. §20.2041-1(b)(1) and TAM 8330004. What amount should be includible in *B*'s gross estate at death?

(e) Consider a power to withdraw the greater of $5,000 or 5% of the value of the corpus (sometimes called a *Crummey* power). What are the estate tax consequences if, to negate the trustee's need to provide the beneficiary with notice of the annual right of withdrawal, the beneficiary simply notifies the trustee in the first year of the trust's existence that "I do not intend to exercise my power of withdrawal" or words to that effect? Read §§2041(b)(2) and 2514(e) carefully. Is this a lapse, or a release? Cf. TAM 9532001, which concluded that a beneficiary's letter directing the trustee not to send further notices was sufficient to preclude present interest treatment for annual exclusion purposes, which at a minimum tells us that the government doesn't like these efforts to simplify the trustee's life.

12.   Forced Share of a Surviving Spouse. Every state except Georgia and the nine legitimate community property jurisdictions confers on a surviving spouse a right to elect to take a designated share of a decedent's estate in lieu of or in addition to any provision for the surviving spouse in the decedent's will. See, e.g., Uniform Probate Code §§2-201 to 2-214 (1993). Rev. Rul. 74-492 ruled that this right of election constitutes a general power of appointment within the ambit of §2041. Under the facts of that ruling, the surviving spouse died without having exercised the election but before the time limit for making the election had expired. The ruling stipulated that, under local law, the right of election was personal and nondelegable and, therefore, expired when the spouse died; it could not be exercised by the spouse's personal representative.

Although expiration of the general power when the surviving spouse died would not prevent it from being deemed held at the time of the spouse's death, the government nevertheless ruled that the property subject to the unelected forced share was not includible in the surviving spouse's gross estate. The theory was that the spouse's failure to elect the forced share constituted a disclaimer of the general power rather than a lapse or a release thereof, as defined in Treas. Reg. §20.2041-3(d)(3). The ruling was promulgated, however, before Congress enacted §§2046 and 2518, which now govern disclaimers of property interests and powers. Is the theory of Rev. Rul. 74-492 still valid in view of these new sections, which recognize only "qualified disclaimers" and require them to be in writing and filed within a certain time limit? If it is questionable, a surviving spouse's personal representative (or the surviving spouse, while still living) might prevent incurring transfer tax consequences as a result of an unelected forced share by making an actual disclaimer. Cf. Estate of Rolin v. Commissioner, 588 F.2d 368 (2d Cir. 1978), and the 1990 version of Uniform Probate Code §2-801(a).

13.   Power of Appointment or Property Interest? Some situations raise the issue whether the decedent had a property interest includible under §2033, or a power of appointment subject to §2041, or both. We already encountered this question in connection with wrongful death recoveries and the surviving spouse's right to elect a forced share. The following materials raise the same question.

In Second National Bank v. Dallman, 209 F.2d 321 (7th Cir. 1954), the decedent was the beneficiary of a life insurance policy settlement option (the insured had predeceased the decedent) that, in simplified form, provided for the decedent to receive interest on the proceeds for life and provided for the remainder of the settlement account to be paid to the decedent's "executors, administrators or assigns." In concluding that the proceeds were not includible in the decedent' gross estate, the court held that the decedent had neither a remainder interest nor a power of appointment. Although the executor actually distributed the property in accordance with the decedent's will, the court felt that the executor was not compelled to do so. Compare Treas. Reg. §20.2056(c)-2(b)(1)(i).

Under a similar set of facts, the court in Keeter v. United States, 461 F.2d 714 (5th Cir. 1972), held that the insurance proceeds were includible in the decedent's gross estate under §2041(a)(1). The decedent's will contained a residuary clause that bequeathed "any property over which I may hold the power of appointment or distribution." In deciding that the decedent had a general power of appointment, which was exercised by this residuary clause, the court said: "We know of no state in which the executor is empowered to do whatever he chooses with a decedent's estate. Certainly Florida law required [the decedent's] executors to do precisely what [was] directed in [the decedent's] will."

For a discussion of the construction of bequests of corpus to the "estate" or to the "executors and administrators" of an income beneficiary, see Browder, *Trusts and the Doctrine of Estates*, 72 MICH. L. REV. 1507, 1524–1528 (1974).

If the *decedent* in these cases, not the decedent's executors, had *something*, are you satisfied with the *Keeter* conclusion that it was a general power of appointment? If not, what *was* it? Under what circumstances (if any) does the §2033 versus §2041 debate make a difference? Cf. §2207.

PART C.   POWER OF APPOINTMENT PLANNING

The following illustration demonstrates the extent to which enjoyment and control can be conferred on the beneficiary of a trust without causing the trust to be includible in the beneficiary's gross estate.

Under the provisions of a testamentary trust created by *A*'s parent, *A* will receive so much or all of the trust income or principal as *A*, who also is the trustee, deems appropriate for *A*'s health, maintenance, and support in reasonable comfort. At *A*'s death, the trust property will be delivered to such persons as *A* appoints under a nongeneral testamentary power of appointment exercisable in favor of anyone except *A*, *A*'s creditors, *A*'s estate, or creditors of *A*'s estate. In default of appointment, the trust property will be held in further trust for *A*'s children. Alternatively, the power of appointment could be limited to just those persons among the settlor's descendants (and perhaps their spouses) or for such charitable, scientific, or educational purposes as *A* appoints. In addition, *A* may be given the same powers to appoint trust income or principal exercisable during life, and a noncumulative power to withdraw principal not to exceed in any calendar year the greater of $5,000 or 5% of the value of the trust at the time of withdrawal. (We will consider §§2041(b)(2) and 2514(e), which encourage the use of such "five or five" powers, in Chapter 14.)

If done properly, no part of the principal of this trust will be includible in A's gross estate at death. See Rev. Rul. 79-373. This is true even though A was the trustee. See Rev. Rul. 78-398. Although special added precautions might be required if any minor children are beneficiaries during A's tenure as trustee, often this is not the case because all the children are grown and emancipated when the testator, A's parent, dies. See Rev. Rul. 79-154. The same extended benefits may be created for A's children, who also could be made trustee, in lieu of or after the death of A, with similar estate tax avoidance.

It was this form of planning that led Congress in 1976 to enact the generation-skipping transfer tax that we study in Chapter 16. Although it was changed substantially in 1986, it remains in force to preclude a form of abuse by which trust beneficiaries enjoy property held in trust without incurring estate or gift tax liability when the beneficial interest passes to younger generations.

Chapter 4

TRANSFERS PROXIMATE TO DEATH

Part A.   Transfers by the Decedent
Part B.   Transfers to the Decedent

PART A.   TRANSFERS BY THE DECEDENT

Code References: *Estate Tax: §§2001(b), (d), & (e), 2035*

1.   *Historical Introduction.*

The 1916 Provision. Congress has recognized since inception of the federal estate tax in 1916 that an obvious way to avoid the tax is to transfer property inter vivos. To plug that hole in the estate tax system, Congress provided in the 1916 Act that the value of certain property transfers that it regarded as will substitutes — inter vivos alternatives to testamentary transfers — must be included in the decedent's gross estate.[1] The category of transfer that is the subject of this chapter, involving §2035, stands out as different from the other will substitutes (addressed in §§2036 through 2040 and 2042) because, in a §2035 transfer, the decedent retains no interest in or power over the transferred property. Prior to the Tax Reform Act of 1976, §2035 differed in another important respect. It provided that the gross estate included property the decedent gratuitously transferred "in contemplation of death," thus gearing inclusion to the subjective motives of the decedent in making the transfer, rather than to the objective nature of the transfer itself.

The 1950 Amendments. The contemplation of death rule enacted in 1916 contained a rebuttable presumption that any transfer made by the decedent within two years of death of "a material part" of the decedent's property was in contemplation of death and therefore was includible in the decedent's gross estate at death. The rebuttable presumption period was expanded from two years before death to three in 1950. The requirement

---

1.   As detailed in Chapter 14, Congress did not adopt a separate gift tax until 1924 (eight years after the estate tax was first adopted), and it was repealed in 1926. A revised version of the gift tax was adopted in 1932 and has been retained ever since.

that the transfer be of a material part of the decedent's property was deleted, and Congress specified that transfers made more than three years before death were excluded from operation of the rule. This three-year rule limited the focus of the inquiry, but it did not solve the problem of divining the decedent's subjective intent in making transfers proximate to death. Moreover, because the statutory phrase "in contemplation of death" was not defined by the Code, the problem of determining its scope was left to the courts. The principal guide to its meaning was the following formulation in United States v. Wells, 283 U.S. 102 (1931):

> [T]here can be no precise delimitation of the transactions embraced within the conception of transfers in "contemplation of death." There is no escape from the necessity of carefully scrutinizing the circumstances of each case to detect the dominant motive of the donor in the light of his bodily and mental condition, and thus give effect to the manifest purpose of the statute.

Congress recognized as early as 1926 that, despite the rebuttable presumption, the contemplation of death rule was "very ineffective in practical administration." H.R. Rep. No. 1, 69th Cong., 1st Sess. 15 (1925), in 1939-1 C.B. (pt. 2) 315, 325. It therefore sought to deal with this problem in the Revenue Act of 1926 by eliminating the issue of intent. The House Committee described the purpose of the change as one providing that "all . . . transfers made within two years of the decedent's death without a fair consideration will be included in the gross estate regardless of whether . . . they are made in contemplation of death." *Id.* The actual statutory language, however, was couched in the form of a conclusive presumption that any transfer exceeding $5,000 to any one person within the statutory period was in contemplation of death and therefore includible. The statute was struck down by the Supreme Court in Heiner v. Donnan, 285 U.S. 312 (1932), which held this conclusive presumption to be so arbitrary and unreasonable as to violate the due process clause of the Fifth Amendment. Congress restored the rebuttable presumption in 1932, and so things stood, with the exception of the 1950 changes, until 1976. During this period, in litigating the subjective and rebuttable presumption of a decedent's contemplation, the government lost many more cases than it won.[2]

At the same time that the contemplation of death rule was undergoing these changes, a parallel property law issue was confronting the state courts, involving the statutory forced share of a surviving spouse that can be taken against a decedent's probate estate. In your trusts and estates course, you may have studied the ways legislatures and state courts in

---

2. See Lowndes, Kramer, & McCord, FEDERAL ESTATE AND GIFT TAXES §5.17 (3d ed. 1974).

noncommunity property states have protected surviving spouses from inter vivos transfers designed to defeat this statutory entitlement. The earliest mechanism that was created by state courts for this purpose rested on a "fraudulent intent" test, which evaluated the decedent's subjective motives in making nonspousal transfers. Either the value of the transfer or the transferred property itself was made subject to the forced share if the intent was to "disinherit" the surviving spouse. More recently, most courts have abandoned what proved to be an unworkable effort to divine the decedent's motives and have adopted objective approaches such as an "illusory transfer" test that looks to the decedent's retained interests in or powers over the transferred property. See generally T. Atkinson, THE LAW OF WILLS §32 (2d ed. 1953).

More recently still, the Uniform Probate Code has established an elective share with respect to a decedent's "augmented estate," which is a statutory formulation defined in §§2-203 through 2-207 that clearly is informed by and patterned in many respects after §§2036 through 2040 and 2042 of the Code. Thus, in each case, the law looking to whether a decedent's inter vivos transfers will be respected at death has moved away from subjective determinations and toward more objective formulations. Congress further refined the analogue when it eliminated the subjective application of §2035 in 1976.

The 1976 Amendments.   The Tax Reform Act of 1976 eliminated the need to discover the decedent's dominant motive for making a gift within three years of death. This time, however, Congress eschewed the conclusive presumption approach and instead eliminated the "in contemplation of death" requirement itself. Now §2035(a) simply provides that all transfers made by a decedent within three years of death are includible in the decedent's gross estate,[3] subject to several objective exceptions that nearly swallow the rule. Congress also added §2035(b) to eliminate the incentive for making deathbed taxable gifts that exclude the resulting gift tax from the donor's transfer tax base. As explained in Chapter 14, excluding gift tax from the transfer tax base means that, even after the 1976 Act nominally established a single unified rate schedule for both inter vivos and testamentary transfers, the marginal effective gift tax rates continue to be lower than the marginal effective estate tax rates.[4] In enacting the §2035(b) "gross

---

3. Is §2035 constitutional as amended in 1976? The House Ways and Means Committee thought so, "even assuming [*Heiner v. Donnan*] would be followed today." See H.R. Rep. No. 1380, 94th Cong., 2d Sess. 14 (1976). See also Peat, *The Constitutionality of New Section 2035: Is There Any Room for Doubt?*, 33 TAX L. REV. 287 (1978). But cf. In re Estate of Cavill, 329 A.2d 503 (Pa. 1974); Estate of French, 365 A.2d 621 (D.C. 1976).

4. Prior to 1977, substantial tax savings could be achieved by making sizeable gifts shortly before death, even if the transferred property ultimately was included in the decedent's gross estate under §2035, because the gift tax paid was a credit against the estate tax liability and it escaped both gift and estate taxation. This tax saving opportunity

up" rule in 1976, Congress determined that this preferential treatment of inter vivos gifts should not be available for gifts made within three years of death. Accordingly, §2035(b) requires inclusion in the decedent's gross estate of any gift tax paid by the decedent (or by the decedent's estate) on any gift made by the decedent or by the decedent's spouse within three years of the decedent's death. As explained by H.R. Rep. No. 1380, 94th Cong., 2d Sess. 14 (1976):

This "gross-up" rule for gift taxes eliminates any incentive to make deathbed transfers to remove an amount equal to the gift taxes from the transfer tax base. The amount of gift tax subject to this rule would . . . not, however, include any gift tax paid by the [decedent's] spouse on a gift made by the decedent within 3 years of death which is treated as made one-half by the spouse, since the spouse's payment of such tax would not reduce the decedent's estate at the time of death.

The gross up rule does not bring back into the gross estate any state gift tax paid on gifts made at any time; §2035(b) specifically refers only to gift taxes paid under Chapter 12 of the Internal Revenue Code.[5] The initial impression may be that this exclusion of state gift taxes is beneficial to taxpayers, but the overall effect may not be. Under unification, a properly paid state gift tax may be regarded as the equivalent of prepaying state death taxes, for which §2011 traditionally permitted a credit to be taken against the federal estate tax (and, effective in 2005, §2058 permits a deduction). Because §2035(b) does not apply to state gift taxes, however, no credit under §2011 or deduction under §2058 is allowed for any state gift taxes paid, even if they are treated under state law as a prepayment of state death taxes. Estate of Owen v. Commissioner, 104 T.C. 498 (1995); Rev. Rul. 81-302. The effect is to trade avoidance of federal transfer tax on state gift tax payments for loss of the federal tax benefit that would have been available to the extent the state tax had been incurred at the decedent's death. It is a small matter, given how few states impose a gift tax, but a matter to consider in states that do.

2.   *Current §2035: the 1981 Amendments.* Section 2035 was amended five times in the six years between 1976 and 1982.[6] In 1997 the

---

sometimes is referred to as "the DuPont effect," after In re DuPont, 194 A.2d 309 (Del. Ch. 1963).

5.   In addition, in Rev. Rul. 81-302, the government capitulated on the issue whether gift taxes paid to a state should be included in a decedent's gross estate under §2033. Prior arguments for inclusion focused on state law, regarding those taxes as a credit against the estate's inheritance or estate tax liability to the state at death; the government argued that the tax already paid was tantamount to an asset that should be included in the decedent's gross estate.

6.   The Tax Reform Act of 1976 eliminated the rebuttable presumption that a transfer made within three years of death was a gift in contemplation of death and replaced it with

entire section was restated to make it more understandable and to cure a major defect by adding §2035(e). Because the restatement reordered most of §2035 you must be very careful in reading older opinions and regulations or rulings because the substance may be the same but the paragraph reference may not be. For example, §2035(b) today was §2035(c) and the gist of §2035(a)(2) used to be §2035(d)(2). Overall, the most significant changes were made by the Economic Recovery Tax Act of 1981, which added certain important exceptions that make §2035(a) not apply to the estates of most decedents. That change reflected the fact that the unified rate structure, adopted in 1976, eliminated most of the need that previously existed for §2035(a). Insofar as inter vivos outright transfers of property were concerned, §2035 served only to require inclusion of the transferred property at its estate tax value rather than its gift tax value; that was not of sufficient significance to justify the complexity that the retention of §2035 would have caused. However, there is a continuing need to prevent a taxpayer from reducing transfer taxes by giving away retained interests or powers that would cause inclusion in the donor's gross estate of a much larger amount of property if retained. So, §2035(a)(2) retains the application of §2035(a) to such "balloon value" transfers. More on this at page 165. Also, §2035(b), dealing with gift tax payments, has been retained and is important for reasons already noted.

One potentially significant detriment to taxpayers of the general inapplicability of §2035(a) relates to the basis rules for income tax purposes under current law. Property included in a decedent's gross estate receives a basis under §1014 that usually equals its estate tax value. But property that is transferred inter vivos and that is not included in the donor's gross estate has a basis under §1015 that is a carryover of the donor's basis, adjusted to include the amount of any gift tax paid with respect to any appreciation in the donated property. If the federal estate tax value is roughly the same as the gift tax value, §2035(a) inclusion would not be significant for wealth transfer tax purposes but might generate a significant change in basis from the donor's carryover basis to the federal estate tax value.

To illustrate, assume that after 1981 and within three years of death, *D* gave securities worth $100,000 to *A*. *D*'s adjusted basis in the securities was $70,000 and the gift qualified for the gift tax annual exclusion. If §2035(a) does not apply the federal estate tax value of the securities is not included in *D*'s gross estate, but the value of the taxable gift ($90,000) is included in *D*'s adjusted taxable gifts calculation. Only the gift tax paid on the gift would be included in *D*'s gross estate under §2035(b), and *A*'s basis

---

an absolute inclusion rule (subject to an annual exclusion exception), and adopted the gross up rule in §2035(b). The Technical Corrections Act of 1978 clarified the annual exclusion exception as an "all or nothing" proposition. The Technical Corrections Act of 1979 granted a special election, relative to the annual exclusion exception, for gifts made in 1977. The Economic Recovery Tax Act of 1981 effectively revoked most of the three year rule. And the Technical Corrections Act of 1982 made further refinements.

in the securities equals the carryover basis of $70,000 plus any gift tax attributable to appreciation in the gifted securities. See §1015(d)(6). If the estate tax were applicable *A*'s basis would become the federal estate tax value, which could wipe out a good deal of capital gain tax. Loss of the annual exclusion would need to be weighed in any calculation of which approach is preferable.

The Transfer Requirement. One year before death, *D* was adjudged mentally incompetent and an appointed conservator successfully petitioned the appropriate court for an order directing that gifts of $100,000 be made to each of *D*'s three children. *D* previously had exhausted the §2505 unified credit but had not made gifts to the children earlier in the year to take advantage of the annual exclusion. If the gift is a valid transfer under state law, $300,000 less three times the annual exclusion is the amount includible in *D*'s adjusted taxable gifts, and the gift tax payable on the gift is includible in *D*'s gross estate under §2035(b). See City Bank Farmers Trust Co. v. McGowan, 323 U.S. 594 (1945); Estate of Himmelstein v. Commissioner, 73 T.C. 868 (1980). Cf. Rev. Rul. 56-408. If instead of a conservator the gifts had been made by *D*'s attorney in fact under a durable power of attorney the issue of the validity to make gifts would be more debatable under most state laws. See Estate of Ridenour v. Commissioner, 65 T.C.M. (CCH) 1850 (1993), *aff'd*, 36 F.3d 332 (4th Cir. 1994); Estate of Collins v. United States, 94-1 U.S. Tax Cas. (CCH) ¶60,162 (E.D. Mich. 1994); Townsend v. United States, 889 F. Supp. 369 (D. Neb. 1995); Estate of Gaynor v. Commissioner, 82 T.C.M. (CCH) 379 (2001); Estate of Casey v. Commissioner, 58 T.C.M. (CCH) 176 (1989), *rev'd*, 948 F.2d 895 (4th Cir. 1991), *citing* Estate of Bronston v. Commissioner, 56 T.C.M. (CCH) 550 (1988), *and* Estate of Gagliardi v. Commissioner, 89 T.C. 1207 (1987); TAMs 9403004, 9347003, 9342003, and 9231003, and PLR 9410028 (all dealing with the question whether holders of powers of attorney had authority under the power or state law to make gifts).

About nine months before death, *D* made a significant gift to *C*, who agreed to a condition that *C* pay *D*'s gift tax on the transfer. See page 831 regarding the income and gift tax consequences of making such a net gift. The issue is whether *D*'s estate is entitled to a §2001(b)(2) offset for the gift tax paid by *C*, and whether the amount of the gift tax paid by *C* is includible in *D*'s gross estate under §2035(b). Consider the answer to both questions in the following opinion, which gives special insight into the role of the court when Congress failed to foresee an issue.

Estate of Sachs v. Commissioner
88 T.C. 769 (1987), *aff'd on the issue herein*, 856 F.2d 1148 (8th Cir. 1988)

COHEN, J. . . . [D]ecedent gave 14,000 shares of Sachs Holding Co. to each of three irrevocable trusts established for the benefit of his grandchildren (the trusts). Article ninth of the trust instrument provided, in relevant part, that decedent's gift was "made subject to and upon the conditions . . . that the Trustees shall promptly pay, or cause to be paid, any and all gift taxes which may be found to be due to the United States because of the making of such gifts."

Decedent and his wife reported the gifts as split, net gifts . . . .

Pursuant to §2035, the shares transferred to the trusts were included in decedent's gross estate at date of death value ($2,196,180) reduced by the amount of gift tax ($612,700) paid by the donee trusts. Although the gift tax paid by the trusts was not included in the gross estate, in the computation of estate tax it was deducted under §2001(b)(2) from the tentative estate tax computed under §2001(b)(1). In his notice of deficiency, respondent determined that the gift tax paid by the trusts is included in decedent's gross estate pursuant to §2035[(b)]. . . .

Petitioners contend that §2035[(b)] does not "gross-up" decedent's estate to include gift tax paid by the donee on a net gift made within 3 years of decedent's death. Petitioners maintain that gift tax paid by the donee trusts is not tax paid by "the decedent or his estate" and argue that the "concise and unambiguous" language of the statute thus dictates our decision. . . .

The Supreme Court has stated:

> There is, of course, no more persuasive evidence of the purpose of a statute than the words by which the legislature undertook to give expression to its wishes. Often these words are sufficient in and of themselves to determine the purpose of the legislation. In such cases we have followed their plain meaning. When that meaning has led to absurd or futile results, however, this Court has looked beyond the words to the purpose of the act. Frequently, however, even when the plain meaning did not produce absurd results but merely an unreasonable one "plainly at variance with the policy of the legislation as a whole" this Court has followed that purpose, rather than the literal words. [United States v. American Trucking Associations, 310 U.S. 534, 543 (1940).]

The Supreme Court has recently reaffirmed this "familiar rule, that a thing may be within the letter of the statute and yet not within the statute, because not within its spirit, nor within the intention of its makers."

Thus, although we are not "free . . . to twist [the Code] beyond the contours of its plain and unambiguous language in order to comport with good policy," we may go beyond the literal language of the Code if reliance on that language would defeat the plain purpose of Congress. Because "words do not have an immutable meaning," we have interpreted the Code in a manner contrary to its literal wording where necessary to implement clearly expressed congressional intent. . . .

Application of the literal language of §2035[(b)] would dictate a result inconsistent with the architecture of the transfer tax system. This case thus presents circumstances "plainly at variance with the policy of the legislation as a whole" that warrant our search for unequivocal evidence of the purpose of §2035[(b)]. . . .

The 1976 Tax Reform Act (the 1976 Act), did much to reduce the disparity of treatment between lifetime gifts and transfers at death. The act established a unified cumulative rate schedule and a unified credit to replace the separate rate schedules and exemptions of prior law. . . .

The 1976 Act also sharpened the distinction between lifetime gifts and "deathbed" gifts, i.e., gifts made within 3 years of the taxpayer's demise. . . .

Congress carefully distinguished "deathbed" gifts from other lifetime gifts because, although the 1976 Act reduced the disparity of treatment between gifts and transfers at death, the act retained several provisions favoring lifetime gifts. The annual gift tax exclusion . . . was retained. Donors of lifetime gifts continued to avoid tax on appreciation that might accrue between the date of a gift and the date of the taxpayer's death. The 1976 Act also left undisturbed prior law under which funds used to pay gift tax are not included in the transfer tax base. . . .

Insistence on the literal language of §2035[(b)] would distort the framework erected by the Tax Reform Act of 1976. The act retained some of the prior law's preferences for lifetime gifts; however, these preferences were not made available to deathbed gifts. Petitioners' construction of §2035[(b)] extends the benefit of one such preference to deathbed net gifts. Mechanical application of §2035[(b)] would completely remove from the transfer tax base all funds used to pay gift tax on such gifts. This interpretation of the statute is wholly inconsistent with Congress' goal of sharply distinguishing deathbed gifts from other gifts and eliminating the disparity of treatment between deathbed gifts and transfers at death. . . .

Our analysis is also consistent with the Supreme Court's holding in Diedrich v. Commissioner, 457 U.S. 191 (1982). In *Diedrich*, the Court held that a donor's gross income includes the excess of gift tax paid by the donee over the donor's basis in the given property. . . . Decedent was primarily liable for payment of the gift tax. As donor of a net gift, he may be deemed to have paid the tax by ordering the donee to pay it over to the Internal Revenue Service on his behalf in satisfaction of his gift tax liability. Decedent gave property worth $2,399,044 to the trusts. Because the trusts paid gift tax in the amount of $612,700, decedent and his wife reported the three net gifts at an aggregate value of $1,786,340 (sic). The funds used to pay the gift tax were thus excluded from the transfer tax base pursuant to §2512(a). When decedent died, the shares transferred to the trusts were included in his estate at date of death value reduced by the amount of gift tax paid by the donee trusts. But for §2035[(b)], $612,700 transferred within 3 years of decedent's death would escape the transfer tax system altogether.

Section 2035[(b)] speaks of gift taxes "paid . . . by the decedent or his estate" rather than gift taxes "paid" without modification because payment of tax on gifts described in §2035(a) does not always remove funds from the transfer tax base. . . .

. . . Although the language selected for this purpose does not, in isolation, describe net deathbed gifts, our analysis of §2035[(b)], its legislative history, and the framework erected by the 1976 Act persuades us that Congress did not intend to distinguish net deathbed gifts from other deathbed gifts. . . .

HAMBLEN, J., concurring. I concur with the majority opinion, and I think it appropriate to respond to Judge Chabot's concurring and dissenting opinion as to the §2035 issue in that it fails to recognize that a net gift is merely a conduit for the payment of the donor-decedent's tax liability. The net gift concept is a gift made on condition that the donee or a third party pay the tax imposed on the donor of the gift. Consequently, when the donee or other party pays the tax, it is simply an indirect payment by the donor which was reserved as a condition of the gift. As such, the tax paid should be included in the gross-up. Overall congressional intent reflected in the structure of the estate tax provisions of the Revenue Act of 1976 would be frustrated otherwise, and a loophole would be created. . . .

Indeed, if the majority opinion has a fault, it is in devoting too much attention to the charge that our rationale departs from the statute. I believe we are simply adhering to the elementary principle of not exalting form over substance. In any realistic view, the gift tax at issue was paid by the donor and, therefore, falls squarely within the statutory language of §2035[(b)].

SIMPSON, J., concurring in part and dissenting in part. I agree with the majority's conclusions concerning the . . . includability in the estate of the gift taxes paid by the donees. I should like to add that, in my judgment, the conclusion that the gift tax is includable in the estate reflects a responsible effort to carry out the legislative objective. Tax legislation is generally carefully drafted, and the complex procedures for enacting such legislation provide many opportunities for perfecting it; nevertheless, oversights do occur, and in my judgment, it is the proper role and responsibility of a court to assist Congress by filling in the niches where possible. In our scheme of Government, Congress has been assigned the responsibility for making policy, and once it has exercised its authority and declared a policy, it then becomes our responsibility to carry out that policy. There can be no genuine doubt over the result intended by §2035. If we do not hold that the gift tax paid by the donees is includable in the estate, it will simply be necessary for Congress to enact further legislation to achieve its objective. . . .

CHABOT, J., concurring and dissenting. . . . The majority hold that "the literal language of §2035[(b)]" would "dictate a result" for petitioner (i.e., no gross-up of tax paid by donees of decedent's gifts), that this result is "plainly at variance with the policy of the legislation as a whole," and that "unequivocal evidence of the purpose of §2035[(b)]" appears in H.R. Rep. No. 1380 (1976), 1976-3 C .B. (Vol. 3) 735, 772–774.

The majority conclude that the statutory language is "plainly at variance" with the congressional intent and profess to find "unequivocal evidence" of that intent. Shortly after the enactment of the Tax Reform Act of 1976, it became apparent that the legislation included many typographical and technical drafting errors. . . . [T]itle VII of the Revenue Act of 1978 — Technical Corrections of the Tax Reform Act of 1976 . . . encompassing 47 pages of the Statutes at Large consists of corrections of drafting errors. Fourteen of these 47 pages are devoted to corrections of errors in the estate and gift tax provisions of the Tax Reform Act of 1976. Remarkably, no one brought to the attention of the Congress the error that the majority conclude is plain, the error of which the majority find unequivocal evidence. . . .

. . . Congress amended §2035 in four different statutes in the 6 years after enacting the provision we apply in the instant case. In two of these statutes, the Congress' avowed purpose was to be sure the words of the 1976 Act did not deviate from the policy of that act. In the 1981 Act, the Congress reexamined and revised the policy of the 1976 Act. Then, in the 1982 Act, the Congress "flyspecked" the 1981 Act's revision.

Now, more than 10 years later, the majority announce "unequivocal evidence" that the 1976 Act's language is "plainly at variance" with that act's policy.

I would conclude that the unequivocal evidence — the Congress' careful, almost contemporaneous, reexaminations of both the "literal language" and the policy of the 1976 Act, together with its actual amendments of [various] subsections . . . and its failure to amend subsection [(b)] of §2035 — is that the literal language of §2035[(b)] is not plainly at variance with the policy of the 1976 Act.

Before the amendments made by the Tax Reform Act of 1976, the gross estate was not increased by the amount of gift tax paid by the decedent. As the majority note, the Ways and Means Committee report (and the corresponding "Blue Book," 1976-3 C.B. (Vol. 2) 1, 539) state that this resulted in tax savings, which the Congress sought to eliminate. Accordingly, under the heading "Reasons for change," the Ways and Means Committee report states as follows, "To eliminate this tax avoidance technique, the committee believes that the gift tax paid on transfers made within 3 years of death should in all cases be included in the decedent's gross estate." H.R. Rep. No. 1380, at 12 (1976), 1976-3 C.B. (Vol. 3) at 746; Staff of the Joint Committee on Taxation, General Explanation of the Tax Reform Act of 1976, at 527 (1976), 1976-3 C.B. (Vol. 2) at 539.

However, after stating the "Reasons for change," the Ways and Means Committee proceeded to present a detailed "Explanation of provisions." As the majority note, the explanation provides a somewhat different view of the statute. The explanation does not state that "the gift tax paid should in all cases be included." Rather, the explanation states that "The amount of gift tax subject to this rule would include tax paid by the decedent or his estate on any gift made by the decedent or his spouse after December 31, 1976. It would not, however, include any gift tax paid by the spouse on a gift made by the decedent within 3 years of death which is treated as made one-half by the spouse, since the spouse's payment of such tax would not reduce the decedent's estate at the time of death." H.R. Rep. No. 1380, at 14 (1976), 1976-3 C.B. (Vol. 3) at 748; Staff of the Joint Committee on Taxation, General Explanation of the Tax Reform Act of 1976, at 529 (1976), 1976-3 C.B. (Vol. 2) at 541.

From this, we may conclude that, although the general policy ("Reasons for change") apparently would be served by the gross-up that the majority's opinion requires, it is not clear that the legislative articulation of the detailed policy ("Explanation of provisions") is served by the gross-up.

It is not unusual for the Congress to determine a general policy, or focus on a specific problem, but then write its statute differently from its general policy or from what we would think is the intended legislative response to the specific problem. . . . In the instant case, for all we can tell from the legislative history, the Congress had a general intention but intended to deviate from that when it came time to focus on the specifics.

We cannot tell from the legislative history whether the differences between the "Reasons for change" and the "Explanation of provisions" were intended or accidental. Under these circumstances, I respectfully suggest that we do not have such "unequivocal evidence" of intent as to justify departing from what the majority concede to be the meaning of the statute's language. . . .

. . . I would hold for petitioner that the statute provides the answer — no gross-up since the gift tax was not paid by decedent or petitioner. The statute should control over the Congress' unclear intent. . . .

Exceptions.   Section 2035 still applies to two sets of transfers. One set is covered by §2035(a)(2), and the items included in the set have as a common denominator transfers within three years of the decedent's death of interests that "balloon" in value for federal estate tax purposes at the decedent's death. The other set of transfers is covered by §2035(c), and the included items have in common transfers that in some way take advantage of, or seek an advantage under, special rules *not* primarily related to inclusion of property in the decedent's gross estate. Most of these ancillary rules involve a threshold requirement that relates to the size of the decedent's gross estate, but one (§2035(c)(1)(C)) is included simply because it was a convenient place to put it; it does not relate to the rest of the exclusions in that section. Its significance is illustrated by the following summary of the transaction that was addressed in PLR 9339010 and that, had it worked, would have permitted serious tax avoidance.

The decedent whose estate was involved in PLR 9339010 probably knew that death was not far away. Imagine, therefore, your client asking you if there is any way to reduce transfer tax by transactions near the very end of her life, and you suggest giving away as much of her estate as possible, so that all she retains is the gift tax due on these transfers. This decedent did just that, making substantial gifts and paying over $1.8 million in gift tax. The decedent lived for a little less than three years after making the gifts. Because of §2035(b), the gift tax payment of more than $1.8 million was included in her gross estate. That produced an estate tax of over $900,000, which substantially exceeded the amount of the decedent's probate estate, which was all that the estate had available for payment of the liability. Who pays this estate tax if the decedent's estate is insolvent? The government opined that the donees of the gifts should pay, citing no authority for that result but stating that it was dictated by state law, which almost certainly was not true (at least a computer search turned up no such state tax apportionment rule). Nevertheless, the government reached a desirable result, albeit for the wrong reason.

Because the tax due under §2035(b) is not a gift tax (instead, it is the estate tax generated by inclusion of the gift tax paid), the §6324(b) gift tax transferee liability rule is not applicable. And the estate tax transferee liability rule under §6324(a)(2) provides that estate tax liability may be imposed on any "beneficiary, who receives, or has on the date of the decedent's death, property included in the gross estate under §§2034 to 2042, inclusive, to the extent of the value, at the time of the decedent's death, of such property." In this case, if there is a "beneficiary," it is the federal government, which received the gift tax dollars on which the estate tax liability is incurred. Nevertheless, the estate tax transferee liability rule is applicable as if the donees received the transferred property from the decedent's estate, by virtue of the obtuse rule in §2035(c)(1)(C), which deems the donated property to be includible in the gross estate under §2035(a). Thus, the donees are the proper transferees for all the estate tax attributable to the transfer, as imposed under §§6321 through 6326 (Subchapter C of Chapter 64 of the Code). For sure, this is one of those rules that, if you did not already know what it was saying, you could not figure it out from reading the Code (and there are no regulations on point). The PLR did not even mention §2035(c)(1)(C), which probably means that the author of the PLR did not know what it was about either.

3.   *Section 2035(a)(2)* deals with interests in property that, if retained until death, would cause inclusion in a decedent's gross estate under §§2036 (retained interests or powers), 2037 (retained reversions), 2038 (retained powers), or 2042 (insurance on the decedent's life). Because these all constitute interests that typically have a much lower gift tax value than the value that would be includible at death if no transfer were made, §2035(a)(2) makes them subject to the three-year prior to death rule of §2035.

For example, if a decedent had retained a life estate in previously transferred property, a subsequent release or transfer of just what remains of the life estate within three years of the decedent's death would require inclusion, for gift tax purposes, of only the value of the life estate, something (perhaps much) less than 100% of the value of the originally transferred property, based on actuarial tables reflecting the decedent's remaining life expectancy. If no transfer had been made, however, that interest would have caused inclusion under §2036(a)(1) of the full estate tax value of the property producing the life estate.

Similarly, if a life insurance policy on a decedent's life, with a low gift tax value, were transferred during the last three years of the decedent's life, §2042 inclusion of the full face value of the proceeds would be avoidable were it not for §2035(a)(2). Extensive precedent noted in Chapter 8 wrestles with the overlap of §§2035(a) and 2042 with respect to inclusion of the full value of life insurance proceeds on the decedent's life. As with each provision listed in §2035(a)(2), the rationale for preserving exposure to §2035(a) with respect to transfers of life insurance policies within three years of the insured's death is that the value of a life insurance policy is *certain* to appreciate — often dramatically — between the date of even a death bed gift of the policy and the date of the insured's death.

In all of the situations listed in §2035(a)(2), the "appreciation" element, or difference between gift tax and potential estate tax value, is simply too significant to be allowed to escape transfer taxation by a disposition within three years of a decedent's death. Consequently, §2035(a)(2) makes the §2035(a) general inclusion rule apply, meaning that a transfer taxed at the low gift tax value of a relinquished interest will not prevent inclusion at death of the full value that would have been includible had no transfer been made.[7] Consequently, §2035(a) continues to apply in those cases representing the greatest possibility for appreciation between gift and estate tax values.

Interests that do not pose the same potential for appreciation have been omitted from §2035(a)(2). For example, §2041 (powers of appointment) was included in the §2035(a)(2) list prior to 1983; its removal by the Technical Corrections Act of 1982 reflects the fact that the value of the property subject to the power for §2514 gift tax purposes should be the same as for §2041 estate tax purposes. Similarly excluded from the list of interests subject to §2035(a)(2) are interests that, if held at death, would cause inclusion in a decedent's gross estate under any of §§2033, 2039, 2040, or 2044. With respect to each, the same rationale justifies their exclusion from the three-year rule; they are not interests that dramatically balloon in their taxable value upon a decedent's death.

So, for example, assume *D* was the life income beneficiary of a post-1942 trust that was created by *R* and that gave *D* a nongeneral power of appointment, which *D* released within three years of death. The release would not be taxable as a gift and there are no estate tax consequences in *D*'s estate. If *D*'s power were general the release would be taxable, but §2035(a) need not apply because the gift taxable value would not differ from that which would be taxed at *D*'s death.

---

7.   With respect to each of the listed exceptions, the determination whether §2035(a)(2) applies is made at the time of the decedent's death, with the inquiry being whether the interest transferred within the three-year period prior to death would have caused inclusion if still held at death. Thus, the time for determining whether a §2037 reversion exceeds the 5% value required by §2037(a)(3) is immediately before death, not at the time of the prior relinquishment of that interest. Rev. Rul. 79-62 (reversion worth more than 5% at relinquishment but less than 5% at the decedent's death, resulting in no inclusion). Similarly, if a retained interest or power is relinquished by the decedent but otherwise would have expired or terminated independent of that transfer, inclusion should be avoided by virtue of the interest not existing at the decedent's death.

An enticing but illusory means of avoiding §2035(a) inclusion following a transfer of an interest itemized in §2035(a)(2) is to qualify for the §2035(d) exception for transfers made for full and adequate consideration in money or money's worth. See Chapter 6. To preclude an obvious abuse under this exception, full and adequate consideration is measured against the value that would be included if no transfer were made, *not* against the value of the interest or power relinquished. See, e.g., United States v. Allen, 293 F.2d 916 (10th Cir. 1961), reproduced at page 244; Estate of Pritchard v. Commissioner, 4 T.C. 204 (1944). Because of the special nature of interests subject to §2035(a)(2), which have a low gift tax value relative to the estate tax value if inclusion occurs, it is not likely that §2035(a)(2) will be avoided by application of §2035(d) because it is unlikely that anyone would pay the balloon inclusion value for an interest worth only the gift tax value at the time of the transfer.

Unfortunately, there are a couple of circumstances in which §2035(a)(2) may still apply when arguably it should not. For example:

(a) *D* created an irrevocable inter vivos trust for a handicapped child and retained powers that would trigger §§2036(a)(2) and 2038(a)(1) inclusion of the trust principal in *D*'s gross estate at death. The trust terminated and was distributed to *D*'s other children when the handicapped child died, less than three years before *D*'s death. Is §2035(a) applicable? See TAM 9032002, which held that the child's death was not a transfer and thus did not trigger §2035(a)(2). Is that a proper result?

(b) In making an original transfer to an irrevocable inter vivos trust, *D* inadvertently retained a power that would cause §2036(a)(2) or §2038(a)(1) inclusion in *D*'s gross estate. Upon discovery of this glitch, *D* immediately relinquished the offending power but died within three years thereafter. No inclusion would result if *D* had made a complete, no strings attached transfer and died within three years thereafter. Should this situation differ? Would it make any difference if *D* paid gift tax on creation of the trust on the full value, based on the assumption that nothing of value was retained?

(c) If you were presented with a situation involving such an incomplete transfer, would it be better to revoke the original transfer, if possible, and start over, with a 100% complete transfer the second time rather than completing the originally defective transfer by releasing the power?

To legislatively overrule the result in Estate of Jalkut v. Commissioner, 96 T.C. 675 (1991), *acq.*, Congress adopted §2035(e) to eliminate an unintended distinction between transfers by a donor out of a revocable trust. For example, in *Jalkut*, the decedent created a revocable trust that was funded with the decedent's entire estate, including his personal residence, bank and brokerage accounts, and publicly traded stocks. That trust was subject to §§2036(a) and 2038(a) and transfers were made from it to third parties within three years of the decedent's death. Those transfers were no different than if the decedent had gifted probate estate assets that would be §2033 includible, and the Tax Court agreed with the taxpayer that the gift transfers should not be includible. Unfortunately, the court could not justify that result with respect to the bulk of the transfers made, and regarded them as includible. In the process the court squirmed up a distinction not now worth mentioning but that impelled Congress to add the more logical §2035(e) protection. That result essentially mirrors the prior decision in McNeely v. United States, 16 F.3d 303 (8th Cir. 1994), in which the court rejected the artificial distinction in *Jalkut* and simply held that §2035(a)(2) did not apply. Involved were distributions to descendants of the settlor, made pursuant to the settlor's direction from a revocable inter vivos trust that authorized distributions either to the settlor or as the settlor directed. Citing *Jalkut* and Estate of Barton v. Commissioner, 66 T.C.M. (CCH) 1547 (1993), the court just outright rejected the application of §2035(a)(2) in this circumstance because it contradicted the government's admission that there would have been no estate tax inclusion if the distributions had been made directly to the settlor who then made the gift. In addition, the court held that it could not require inclusion under the three year rule found in the last clause of §2038(a)(1) because it refers to relinquishment of the power to revoke within three years of the settlor's death and, with respect to the transferred property, the power in *McNeely* was exercised, not relinquished. Then the court held that §2035(a)(2) could not apply because it would produce a result that is inconsistent with its holding under §2038(a)(1).

4.   *Split Gifts Within Three Years of Death.*   Section 2001(b) provides relief from double taxation to the extent that property transferred inter vivos by the decedent subsequently is included in the decedent's gross estate. In determining the size of the adjusted taxable gifts base for tax computation purposes under §2001(b)(1)(B), the last sentence of §2001(b) excludes gifts that are includible in the gross estate. In addition, §2001(b)(2) provides an offset against the tentative estate tax determined under §2001(b)(1) in the amount of gift tax that would be payable on the transferred property at current rates. Together, these provisions guarantee that the same property will be taxed only once (includible for estate tax purposes in §2001(b)(1)(A) and purged from the adjusted taxable gift base of §2001(b)(1)(B)), and that any tax dollars already paid effectively will be treated as a down payment on the decedent's tax bill at death. See page 186.

But what happens in a case in which the decedent's spouse split the gift under §2513? Indeed, what if the spouses split gifts and the *consenting* spouse dies within three years? The easy part of this question relates to the gross up rule. If *D*, the donor spouse, transferred property to a third party and *S*, the non-donor consenting spouse made the gift splitting election under §2513, §2035(b) would apply equally with respect to *D* and *S* — without regard to the nature of the interest transferred or to which spouse made the transfer. The statute requires that any gift taxes paid by *D* be added to D's gross estate if D dies within three years of the transfer, and any gift taxes paid by S be added to S's gross estate if S dies within three years of the transfer. For this purpose, it does not matter whether the gift on which the gift tax was paid was made by the decedent or by the decedent's spouse. Notwithstanding the fact that the gift was made solely by D, and that the §2513 election has the effect of treating the gift as made half by S for purposes of the gift tax, §2035(b) specifically directs inclusion of "any tax paid under chapter 12 by the decedent . . . on any gift made by the decedent or [the decedent's] spouse." Thus, if S, the non-donor consenting spouse, were to die within the three-year period, gift taxes paid by S would be added to S's gross estate. However, there is no addition for taxes paid by the other spouse. Rev. Rul. 82-198. So, if D paid all the gift taxes owed by both D and S, nothing would be added to S's gross estate if S died within the three-year period. On the other hand, the full amount paid would be added to D's gross estate if D died within three years of the gift.

Another easy application of these rules arises if S dies within three years of the split gift. Because §2513 applies only for gift tax purposes, §2035(a) cannot apply at S's death, even if the interest D transferred was one listed in §2035(a)(2). Thus, if it would be desirable to utilize S's unified credit before S dies, or to incur tax to be paid by S, it can be useful for D to make a gift with S's consent to split even if S's death is imminent. If §2035(a) is applicable, because the transfer is of an interest listed in §2035(a)(2), the gift will cause full inclusion in D's gross estate if D dies within three years of the transfer but no inclusion to S even if S dies within three years of the transfer. Rev. Ruls. 82-198, 81-85, and 54-246.

With respect to D, several adjustments are provided for tax computation and payment purposes. As already noted, with respect to any gift as to which §2035(a) applies, the gift is purged from D's adjusted taxable gifts base under §2001(b)(1)(B), and D is entitled to an offset under §2001(b)(2) for gift taxes payable on D's taxable gift. In addition, by virtue of §2001(d), D is entitled to a §2001(b)(2) offset for any gift taxes payable by S on the gift. This treatment is appropriate if the full amount of the gift is brought back into D's gross estate by §2035(a). To avoid double taxation, D must be credited with the full gift tax payable on the gift. However, to prevent a double benefit from the gift tax payable by S, that tax is purged by the last clause of §2001(e) from the §2001(b)(2) offset available upon S's subsequent death. Moreover, because the gift is fully included in D's gross estate as if the transfer had not been made, §2001(e) also purges the gift from S's adjusted taxable gifts base.

An important and quite inappropriate omission from this system of adjustments is that the gift that S is treated as having made because of a §2513 consent is included in the sum of S's gifts for preceding taxable years when computing the gift tax on gifts that S makes in years subsequent to the split gift. Thus, S may be boosted into a higher gift tax bracket by virtue of the split gift, even if it is treated for estate tax purposes on the death of D as if it never was made. Curiously, Congress knew about this consequence, and its failure to remedy it was not inadvertent. See H.R. Rep. No. 1380, 94th Cong., 2d Sess. 13 (1976): "[W]here the transfer . . . is included in the decedent's gross estate and was considered to have been a transfer made in part by the surviving spouse under the gift-splitting provisions . . . , there is to be no restoration of any portion of the unified credit used against gift taxes paid by the surviving spouse"; S. Rep. No. 745, 95th Cong., 2d Sess. 89 (1978): "[A]ny unified credit used is not restored and the amount of aggregate taxable gifts for prior periods is not adjusted." Cf. Ingalls v. Commissioner, 336 F.2d 874 (4th Cir. 1964); Norair v. Commissioner, 65 T.C. 942 (1976); this defect existed under the lifetime exemption system, before adoption of the unified credit regime that replaced it.

Notwithstanding this gift tax computation flaw, by virtue of §§2001(d) and (e), property that was given by D and split with S and that is included in D's gross estate under §2035(a) will have no effect on S's future *estate* tax computation. There is no *estate* tax disincentive to S for making the election to split gifts with D. But there is the gift tax disincentive to S. These are among the most convoluted rules in all the wealth transfer tax, so you should read them and re-read them, and then work through the following illustrations.

(a)   In Year 1, D gave a life insurance policy insuring D's life to C. The value of the policy on the date of the gift was $50,000, the face value of the policy was $110,000, and D's spouse, S, consented under §2513 to have this gift treated as made half by each. Neither D nor S had made any prior gifts to C in Year 1, but both previously had exhausted their full unified credits under §2505. There is no need for any adjustment if S dies three months after the gift, when the value of the policy is $50,500, and D dies in Year 5. Only §2035(b) will apply to cause the gross up of any taxes paid by S on the split gift. But what if the order of their deaths were reversed, D dying three months after the gift and S in Year 5? This is when §§2001(d) and (e) apply.

(b)   Rather than a life insurance policy, suppose that the subject matter of the Year 1 gift in **(a)** had been securities worth $50,000 at the date of the gift, that the securities were worth $50,500 at S's death, and that their value was $110,000 at D's death. Your answers to **(a)** would differ because no estate tax inclusion rule would apply and no adjustment would be required. Only §2035(b) would be relevant and it requires no special application.

(c)   If neither D nor S had made any gifts previously, the resulting gift tax liability of each would be offset by their respective unified credits under §2505. If D died within three years later, survived by S, nothing would restore S's unified credit used on the gift for future gift tax purposes. But §2001(e) *does* effectively restore the credit for S's subsequent estate tax calculation. Be sure you see how it does this through reference to §2001(b)(1)(B).

5.   *Section 2035(c): Special Applications of the Three Year Rule.* When it repealed most of the §2035(a) inclusion rule Congress added special rules, now incorporated in §2035(c) retaining application of the three-year rule for purposes of §§303 (nondividend treatment on stock redemption), 2032A (special use valuation), Subchapter C of Chapter 64 (relating to liens for taxes), and 6166 (installment payment of estate tax). Because already discussed earlier in this chapter, §2035(c)(1)(C) is not addressed any further here.

The balance of §2035(c) provides that, with the exception of certain gifts for which no gift tax return was required, transfers for less than full and adequate consideration within three years of a decedent's death are treated as subject to §2035(a) when applying the qualification requirements of §§303, 2032A, and 6166. For example, transfers made within three years of death are ignored for purposes of qualifying a decedent's estate for special treatment under §§303 and 2032A if they reduce the amount of nonqualified assets and thereby increase the percentage of qualified assets remaining in the decedent's gross estate. These transfers are not, however, brought into the gross estate for any other purpose. For example, they are not entitled to a new basis at death under §1014(b). And, although qualifying stock transferred within three years of death is brought back for purposes of determining whether the estate qualifies for §303 treatment, the redemption of the transferred stock after the decedent's death is not entitled to favorable nondividend treatment.[8] Only other qualifying stock that was included in the decedent's gross estate may be redeemed with the special protection that §303 provides.

Unlike §2035(c)(1), which can permit transfers within three years of death to be brought back into the gross estate to help qualify for special treatment, §2035(c)(2) requires the estate to qualify for §6166 treatment both with and without application of §2035(a). This means that the percentage of §6166 qualifying stock actually included in the decedent's gross estate at death must exceed the 35% threshold of §6166(a)(1) *and* the estate must qualify after all transfers within three years of death of both qualifying stock and nonqualifying assets have been considered. In essence, the decedent's estate cannot be assisted by §2035(c)(2) in qualifying for §6166, and may be disqualified by it. Further, it now appears reasonably clear that §2035(c)(2) applies only for purposes of testing the initial qualification of a decedent's estate for §6166 installment payments, but not otherwise.

Section 2035(c) applies only if the annual exclusion exception of §2035(c)(3) does not. This all-or-nothing rule provides that transfers not

---

8.   Section 2035(c)(1)(A) specifically regards the transferred stock as part of the estate *only* for purposes of meeting the eligibility requirements of §303(b). The transferred stock is not so regarded for purposes of §303(a), which provides favorable tax treatment to qualifying stock.

exceeding the annual exclusion amount may be ignored in applying §2035(c) if — not to the extent — the transfer does not require the filing of a gift tax return. As a consequence, a client who wishes to reduce the size of the estate for estate tax purposes by transferring assets that otherwise would qualify at death for special treatment under §§303 or 2032A, but also wants the benefit of special treatment under those provisions if death occurs within three years of the transfer, can walk both sides of the street by transferring sufficient assets to require filing a gift tax return to report a gift of as little as $1 in excess of the annual exclusion (for example, a $11,001 transfer). Because §2035(c)(3) applies only to a transfer for which no gift tax return is required, if the decedent were to transfer no more than the annual exclusion amount, the transferred property would not qualify for special treatment if the decedent died within three years; but, by increasing the size of the gift to just over that amount, the decedent can retain that advantage. This kind of planning will not work to obtain §6166 qualification because of the special requirement in §2035(c)(2) that the estate qualify for §6166 purposes both without application of §2035(a) as well as with it.

Valuation. In formulating the §2035(c) exceptions, the Senate Finance Committee proposed that the gift tax value of transferred assets be used rather than the federal estate tax value. S. Rep. No. 144, 97th Cong., 1st Sess. 138-139 (1981). The conference committee chose not to adopt the Senate Finance Committee's proposal. H.R. Rep. No. 215, 97th Cong., 1st Sess. 255 (1981). As a consequence, §2035(c) requires that property that does *not* balloon in value at death nevertheless must be revalued at the federal estate tax valuation date, which preserves various complications inherent in valuing completed gifts at a date other than at the date of the gift. Specifically, (1) what assets are to be valued if the donee no longer owns the property on the federal estate tax valuation date, and (2) does the federal estate tax value of the donated property include income generated or other distributions with respect to the property made between the date of the gift and the federal estate tax valuation date? The following materials, although involving pre-1982 law, continue to be relevant under post-1981 law because of this complication. They are also relevant to the valuation of property included in a gross estate by §2035(a)(2), although most of those properties will be held in trust, for which a special valuation rule is applied.

Revenue Ruling 72-282

Advice has been requested as to the valuation of property required to be included in the donor-decedent's gross estate under §2035 where the property transferred was sold by the donee prior to the donor's death.

Two years before her death, decedent transferred 5,000 shares of *Y* Company stock to her son. At the time of the transfer, the value of this stock was 50x dollars. The son thereupon sold the entire 5,000 shares. With the proceeds he purchased 2,500 shares of stock in another corporation for 50x dollars. . . .

At date of death the fair market value of the stock transferred by the decedent was 55x dollars. The stock purchased by the son with the proceeds of his sale of the Y Company stock had increased in value to 75x dollars. . . .

The value of the transferred property as of the proper valuation date is the amount includible in the decedent's gross estate. Any increase in value resulting from actions of the donee is not taken into consideration in determining the value of the included interest. Treas. Reg. §20.2035-1(e). Where the donee has dissipated the property so that there is nothing left as of the date of the transferor's death, the amount includible is not what actually exists but rather the present value of the property originally transferred. Estate of Humphrey v. Commissioner, 162 F.2d 1 (5th Cir. 1947). In that case, the court stated: ". . . The evident purpose [of §2035] is to make the transferred property cause the same tax result as if the decedent had kept it till he died instead of transferring it. We do not accede to the argument that if the transferee injures or makes way with it, it shall be considered that he has acted as the agent of the decedent, or that he may substitute it by other property of less value. What is to be valued at the time of decedent's death is the very property which the decedent transferred. . . ."

In the present case, the transferred property has been sold by the donee. He has substituted therefor property that has increased in value. The fair market value of the 2,500 shares of stock actually owned by the decedent's son on the date of death was considerably greater than the value of the shares originally transferred. The value of stock acquired by subsequent independent actions of the donee is not that which is includible in the decedent's gross estate, despite the fact that the stock now owned by the donee can be attributed to the proceeds of sale of the transferred property. Rather, what is includible is the present value of the property originally transferred by the decedent.

Accordingly, it is held that the value includible in the decedent's gross estate under §2035 of the Code is the fair market value as of the decedent's death of 5,000 shares of Y Company stock, or 55x dollars.

Non-trust Gifts. In *Humphrey*, cited in Rev. Rul. 72-282, the decedent gave cash, which the donees combined with their own money and, by their own ineptitude prior to the decedent's death, lost about half of the total. Because cash does not fluctuate in value for wealth transfer tax purposes (notwithstanding that the value of the dollar fluctuates in the world monetary market), and because the proper amount includible is the value of the transferred property, the court held that the cash amount of the gift was the amount includible under §2035(a), notwithstanding the events and losses after the transfer. See also Rev. Rul. 76-235 (within three years of death, *D* gave real property to a child who mortgaged it as security for a loan; the value of the property without reduction by the amount of the unpaid mortgage was includible).

As noted by Rev. Rul. 72-282, the value of any additions or enhancements made by the transferee after the decedent's transfer is not includible. Treas. Reg. §20.2035-1(e) (prior law). It is often a challenge to identify the various elements that constitute the value of the total property owned at the decedent's death.

Trusts. The government's position with respect to the amount includible if the transfer involves a trust differs from the foregoing traditional valuation rules. Rather than look to the underlying trust investments at the time of the transfer to determine what should be regarded as includible at the decedent's death, the government's position is that the value of the trust itself is includible, regardless of changes made in investments constituting the trust corpus. See, e.g., Estate of Kroger v. Commissioner, 145 F.2d 901 (6th Cir. 1944); Igleheart v. Commissioner, 77 F.2d 704 (5th Cir. 1935). Virtually all interests, other than insurance, that are subject to §2035(a)(2) inclusion will involve trusts, making this rule of particular continuing significance.

Aggregation. By including the transferred asset as if no transfer had been made, the government takes the position that includible transferred interests may be aggregated with interests retained in determining value. For example, if the decedent owned 51% of Family Co. stock and made a transfer of 1.1% of it, as to which §2035(a) is applicable, no discount for the 49.9% minority interest remaining at death would be allowable because §2035(a) inclusion would be coupled with the retained shares to produce the same 51% ownership interest that would have existed had no transfer been made. Rev. Rul. 79-7. For §§303 and 2032A qualification purposes this is a favorable result if the transferred property is the property as to which qualification is sought. A similar result is not available under §6166, however, because §2035(c)(2) requires qualification with and without inclusion of the transferred property.

Income. A third valuation aspect involves income earned during the three year period prior to death:

Commissioner v. Estate of Gidwitz
196 F.2d 813 (7th Cir. 1952)

SWAIM, J. . . . When Gidwitz died the total assets in the trust had a value of $341,102.02. The original shares of stock transferred to the trust had a valuation of $140,610. The difference of $200,492.02 represented the value of accrued income and property purchased for the trust with accrued income.

The Commissioner, while admitting that the statute places in the gross estate only property *transferred* by the decedent, bases the Government's claim that the valuation of the gross estate should include all income received by the trust prior to the decedent's death on the theory that the property transferred to the trust in 1936 included not only the ownership of the 83⅓ shares of stock but also a separate property right to receive the income on the stock. It is argued that the value of this property right to receive income is measured by the income accumulated in the trust prior to the decedent's death.

The same theory advanced by the Commissioner in this case was rejected by the Supreme Court in Maass v. Higgins, 312 U.S. 443 (1941). The *Maass* case involved two estates where the executors had elected to have the gross estates valued as of one year after the decedents' deaths, pursuant to §[2032]. During the year after the decedents' deaths the executors had collected interest and dividends on bonds and stocks belonging to the estates. The Commissioner determined tax deficiencies against the estates for failures to include these collections as part of the gross estates. A Treasury regulation, then being enforced, required the return and inclusion of such income as a part of the gross estate. The Supreme Court, while recognizing that a bond embodies two promises to pay — one to pay the principal at maturity and the other to pay interest periodically — and while recognizing that the income factor affects the value of a security, said, 312 U.S. at 448: "But these elements are not separately valued in appraising the worth of the asset at any given time." The Supreme Court there, 312 U.S. at 447, agreed with the taxpayer: ". . . that the Government's position is unreal and artificial; that it does not comport either with economic theory or business practice; and that the regulation is an unwarranted extension of the plain meaning of the statute and cannot therefore, be sustained."

In Estate of Humphrey v. Commissioner, 162 F.2d 1 (5th Cir. 1947), the donees of an inter vivos gift made in contemplation of death, by an improvident investment, lost one-half of the amount of the gift. It was contended that the half of the property lost should not be included in the decedent's gross estate. The Court held, however, that it was the *transferred* property which was to be valued at the time of the decedent's death. The Court said, 162 F.2d at 2: "What is to be valued at the time of decedent's death is *the very property which the decedent transferred.*" (Our emphasis.)

In Burns v. Commissioner, 177 F.2d 739 (5th Cir. 1949), *aff'g* Estate of Frizzell v. Commissioner, 9 T.C. 979 (1947), a father established an irrevocable trust and, in contemplation of death, made an inter vivos gift of certain shares of the stock of the Coca-Cola Company to the trust. The trustee invested part of the income from the trust in other stocks and bonds prior to the donor's death. The court accepted the conclusion of the Tax Court that the part of the corpus of the trust which represented income received prior to the death of the donor, or property acquired with such income, had not been *transferred* by the decedent and, therefore, should not be included in the decedent's gross estate for estate tax purposes. The court said, 177 F.2d at 741: "The tax statute in question should be strictly construed in favor of the taxpayer, and since it does not expressly provide for the inclusion of income derived from the *transferred* property in the gross estate, it is not our prerogative, by judicial fiat, to give it that effect." (Our emphasis.)

As against the principles announced in the above cases the Commissioner cites decisions involving other provisions of the Internal Revenue Code which admittedly deal with transfers intended to take effect in possession or enjoyment at or after death, or in which the grantor had retained until death the power to designate the persons who would enjoy the property, or in which the grantor had retained until death the power to alter, amend or revoke. The Commissioner admits that such transfers are included in the gross estate on the theory that such a transfer does not become complete and effective until death, whereas a transfer in contemplation of death is included because of the motive inducing it. The Commissioner argues that the same rules should apply in both classes of cases. Such an argument ignores the realities of the two types of transfers.

In transfers made in contemplation of death, such as in the instant case, the donor has made an actual transfer during life. The transfer became effective at that time. The transfer was irrevocable. The terms of the trust agreement expressly prohibited any change in the provisions of the agreement which would in any manner effect a change relating to the distribution, disposition, possession or enjoyment of the trust property. Here the income was paid to the trust because it belonged to the trust, not to Gidwitz. The income was payable to the trust and belonged to the trust as an incident of the ownership by the trust of the stock transferred to the trust by Gidwitz in 1936. The Tax Court correctly held that such income and the property acquired with such income should not be included in the decedent's gross estate for estate tax purposes.

The Commissioner acquiesced to *Gidwitz* and *Frizzell*. See Treas. Reg. §20.2035-1(e) (prior law). Quaere: should it have done so? *McGehee* deals with a different form of yield acquired after a §2035(a) transfer.

McGehee v. Commissioner
260 F.2d 818 (5th Cir. 1958)

JONES, J. . . . From a stipulation of facts it appears that Delia Crawford McGehee made gifts in the years 1947, 1948, and 1949 of shares of the stock of Jacksonville Paper Company. She died on February 6, 1950. In 1948 and 1949 the corporation declared stock dividends. Stock certificates evidencing the dividends on the stock which had been the subject of the prior gifts were issued and delivered to the donees. These dividends represented a capitalization of current earnings. The issuance of such dividends was in keeping with the policy of the corporation. It had capitalized current earnings by the distribution of a stock dividend in each of the years 1941 through 1949. The company had never declared a dividend payable in cash or property. The executor conceded that the transfers of the shares of stock made by Mrs. McGehee were . . . included as a part of her estate for Federal estate tax purposes. The Commissioner of Internal Revenue asserted and the Tax Court held that shares issued as stock dividends were also to be included. A minority of the Tax Court disagreed. The executor, in his petition for review of the Tax Court's decision, insists that this holding is erroneous.

The Tax Court decision is apparently the only reported American case upon the stock dividend question. In the English case of Attorney General v. Oldham, 1 K.B. 599 (1940), *aff'd,* 3 All Eng. Rep. 450, upon facts similar to those here present, it was held that a stock dividend declared and paid after an inter vivos gift of stock made in contemplation of death was not a part of the gift subject to the estate tax imposed with respect to the estate of the donor.

The Tax Court majority were of the belief that the gift of stock transferred a proportional interest in the assets, business, and affairs, and that this interest, so transferred, was unaffected by the dividends paid in stock. In support of this view the Tax Court cited Eisner v. Macomber, 252 U.S. 189 (1920). This is the leading case holding that a dividend paid in stock of the same kind as that upon which it is declared is not subject to taxation as income to the stockholder. . . . We do not think that because a stock dividend is not taxed as income to the stockholder it must necessarily be included as a part of a gift made [within three years] of death, of the shares upon which it was declared. There are, we would say, substantial differences between the two situations.

. . . It is the interest of the decedent of which a transfer has been made which is to be included in the taxable estate of the donor. It seems unnecessary to decide whether the subject matter of the transfer was regarded as a "proportionate interest in the corporation, its business and its assets," as the Tax Court held it to be, or as "specific shares of stock" which the Tax Court held it was not. The stock dividends were declared out of profits of the corporation earned subsequent to the gifts and hence were not a proportionate part of the corporation's assets at the time of the gift. This being so, it follows that the deceased donor never had any interest in the shares which were distributed as stock dividends or in the corporate earnings which the dividends capitalized. Although the tax is to be measured by the value of the transferred property as of the date of the donor's death, this does not mean that, for the purpose of determining what property was transferred, the gifts should be regarded as having been made as of the date of death. It has been held, and properly so, that income earned by previously taxed property should not be regarded as previously taxed property. So also, we think, a stock dividend distributed as a capitalization of income of a corporation earned subsequent to a gift of the shares upon which the dividend was declared should not be regarded as a part of the gift.

We conclude that of the stock of Jacksonville Paper Company, only 774 shares should have been included in the gross estate of the decedent. Cases involving stock splits or stock dividends capitalizing corporate profits earned prior to the transfer might require different treatment. . . .

Reversed and Remanded.

See also Tuck v. United States, 282 F.2d 405 (9th Cir. 1950); English v. United States, 270 F.2d 876 (7th Cir. 1959). But cf. Treas. Reg. §20.2032-1(d)(4); Estate of Schlosser v. Commissioner, 277 F.2d 268 (3d Cir. 1960). *Compare* the Revised Uniform Principal and Income Act §6(a). The following Ruling indicates the extent of the government's disagreement with *McGehee*.

Revenue Ruling 80-336

. . . In January 1979, *D*, the decedent, gratuitously transferred 500 shares of stock of *X* Corporation to *A*. The stock of *X* Corporation is publicly traded.

In December 1979, *X* Corporation declared a stock dividend of one share of stock for every two shares owned.

At *D*'s death in 1980 *A* owned 750 shares of *X* Corporation stock. However, on the federal estate tax return, the executor included only 500 shares. The executor stated that the 250 shares acquired from the stock dividend were not part of the original transfer.

Section 2035 of the Code provides, in part, that the value of all property that the decedent gratuitously transferred during the three-year period ending on the date of the decedent's death is includible in the decedent's gross estate.

The value of property includible in the gross estate under §2035 is the fair market value as of the decedent's death. Neither income received subsequent to the transfer nor property purchased with such income is considered in determining the value of the property. Treas. Reg. §20.2035-1(e). Rather, only the value of the property originally transferred by the decedent is includible in the gross estate under §2035. See Rev. Rul. 72-282.

A stock dividend, in which common stock is proportionately distributed according to the number of common shares held, does not alter the fractional interests of the stockholders. In Eisner v. Macomber, 252 U.S. 189, 202 (1920), a case involving the federal income tax, the Court quoted from a previous case in describing the nature of a stock dividend as follows: "A stock dividend really takes nothing from the property of the corporation, and adds nothing to the interests of the shareholders. Its property is not diminished, and their interests are not increased. . . . The proportional interest of each shareholder remains the same. The only change is in the evidence which represents that interest, the new shares and the original shares together representing the same proportional interest that the original shares represented before the issue of the new ones. . . . In short, the corporation is no poorer and the stockholder is no richer than they were before."

Similarly, for estate tax purposes, the stock acquired through such a pro rata, common stock dividend is regarded as part of the interest held in the corporation prior to the dividend. See Estate of Schlosser v. Commissioner, 277 F.2d 268 (3rd Cir. 1960), considering the treatment of a common stock dividend for alternate valuation purposes, and Rev. Rul. 80-142, holding that, for purposes of §2040 of the Code, a common stock dividend declared on jointly owned stock is considered the contribution of the tenant who originally created the tenancy. Compare McGehee v. Commissioner, 260 F.2d 818 (5th Cir. 1958). In *McGehee*, the parties stipulated that the stock dividend was generated by profits that were earned after the transfer. In view of the analysis discussed above, the analysis of *McGehee* would not be followed even if the stock dividend could be attributed to post-transfer income.

In the present situation, since the common stock dividend was distributed to common shareholders on a pro rata basis, the *X* Corporation shares held by *A* at *D*'s death represent the same fractional interest in the corporation transferred by *D*. Thus, the 250 shares are not distinguishable from the 500 original shares, for purposes of §2035.

The fair market value of the 750 shares of *X* Corporation is includible in *D*'s gross estate as property transferred by *D* within three years of death.

PART B.   TRANSFERS TO THE DECEDENT

Code Reference: *Income Tax: §1014(e)*

6.   *Income Tax Basis.*   The Economic Recovery Tax Act of 1981 added §1014(e) to prevent abuse of the basis rules. As explained in H.R. Rep. No. 201, 97th Cong., 1st Sess. 188 (1981):

> Because an heir receives property from a decedent with a stepped-up basis, an heir can transfer appreciated property to a decedent immediately prior to death in the hope of receiving the property back at the decedent's death with a higher basis. The donor-heir might pay gift taxes on the fair market value of the gift (unless it qualified for the marital deduction or the amount of gift is less than the donor's annual exclusion or unified credit) but will pay no income tax on the appreciation. Then, upon the death of the donee-decedent, the donor-heir could receive back the property with a stepped-up basis equal to its fair market value. The stepped-up basis would permanently exempt the appreciation from income tax.
>
> Because the [1981 Act] provides an unlimited marital deduction and substantially increases the unified credit, the committee believes that there would be an even greater incentive to plan such deathbed transfers of appreciated property to a donee-decedent.

Because the committee believes that allowing a stepped-up basis in this situation permits unintended and inappropriate tax benefits, [§1014(e)] provides that the stepped-up basis rules should not apply with respect to appreciated property acquired by the decedent through gift within [1 year[9]] of death where such property passes from the decedent to the original donor or the donor's spouse.

To illustrate, consider two examples:

(a) Early last year, *O* gave Blackacre (then worth $195,000) to *P*. *O*'s adjusted basis in Blackacre on the date of the gift was $70,000, and *O* had sufficient unified credit to offset the gift tax on the taxable gift. *P* died intestate six weeks later and *O*'s spouse, *C*, was *P*'s sole heir at law. The fair market value of Blackacre on the date of *P*'s death was $200,000. The value of *P*'s taxable estate, including Blackacre, was $225,000, and *P*'s unified credit was fully available. Notice how §1014(e)(1)(B) makes reference to the donor or the donor's spouse. *C*'s basis is a carryover from *P*.

(b) Early last year, *S* gave Blackacre (then worth $195,000) to *S*'s spouse, *D*. *S*'s adjusted basis in Blackacre on the date of the gift was $70,000, and the transfer qualified for the unlimited gift tax marital deduction. *D* died six weeks later, and *S* received Blackacre as the sole legatee of *D*'s validly executed will. The fair market value of Blackacre on the date of *D*'s death was $225,000 and the full value of *D*'s gross estate, including Blackacre, qualified for the estate tax marital deduction. This too is subject to §1014(e)(1) and *D*'s basis is a carryover of *S*'s basis.

Section 1014(e) is the opposite of §2035 in that it applies to property the decedent *received*, rather than *transferred*, proximate to death. Also different from §2035 is use of a one-year rather than three-year period, making the rule less encompassing. Nevertheless, §1014(e) is harder to avoid than §2035 because it has no broad exceptions. Section 1014(e) reaches any appreciated property acquired by gift (not a bona fide sale for full and adequate consideration in money or money's worth), including the gift element in a part-sale, part-gift transaction. The rule presumably does not apply to property acquired by the decedent upon termination of a joint tenancy, to the extent the decedent contributed the property for acquisition of the joint tenancy and termination is not, therefore, a gift. Further, the rule is relevant only with respect to "appreciated property," reaching only an asset whose fair market value at the time of the gift exceeded the donor's adjusted basis.

---

9. The House bill, H.R. 4242, set the period at three years, but the time was reduced to one year by the conference committee. See H.R. Rep. No. 215, 97th Cong., 1st Sess. 256 (1981). — ED.

In an effort to prevent abuse of the rule through artifice or indirection, §1014(e) applies to certain cases in which acquired assets do not pass directly back to the decedent's donor or the donor's spouse. For example, the rule will apply if an acquired appreciated asset is sold by the decedent, by the decedent's estate, or by a trust of which the decedent was the grantor, to the extent the sale proceeds pass back to the donor or the donor's spouse. §1014(e)(2)(B). The rule also is meant to apply if the appreciated asset or its proceeds pass "indirectly" back to the donor or to the donor's spouse. Thus, for example, a pecuniary bequest to the donor constitutes an indirect benefit "to the extent that the inclusion of the appreciated property in the estate of the decedent affects the amount that the donor receives under the pecuniary bequest."[10] Staff of the Joint Committee on Taxation, 97th Cong., 1st Sess., General Explanation of the Economic Recovery Tax Act of 1981 at 265 (Comm. Print 1981). Because this special rule would be unnecessary if the appreciated asset were actually distributed in funding the pecuniary bequest, the indirect benefit rule must be applicable even if the appreciated asset is not itself available or used for funding.

Problem areas and unanswered questions abound under §1014(e). For example, if the property acquired by the decedent was fungible and matched property already owned by the decedent, will a tracing rule, a pro rata presumption, a first-in-first-out (FIFO), a last-in-first-out (LIFO), or a worst-in-first-out (WIFO) regime dictate whether any of that property is conveyed back to the donor or to the donor's spouse? For example, O gave 10 shares of Family Co. stock to D at a time when D already owned another 90 shares of that stock. On D's death within one year after the gift, D bequeaths 50 shares of Family Co. stock to O. Has O received all 10 of D's acquired shares under a LIFO rule, only five shares under a pro rata presumption, no shares of the stock under a FIFO regime, the 10 shares with the lowest basis under a WIFO rule, or must O somehow prove what became of the 10 acquired shares under a tracing rule?

Second, with the rule's reference to a "sale" of the acquired property and return of the proceeds to the donor or to the donor's spouse, does it *not* apply to a tax free exchange of the acquired property followed by return of the proceeds of that exchange? Whether in a tax free reorganization, contribution to a corporation or partnership in exchange for stock or a transferable partnership interest, or in a §1031 like-kind exchange, §1014(e) ought to apply if the decedent's estate has a substituted basis in the proceeds of the exchange.

Third, to the extent gain is partially recognized by the decedent's estate after death, should any corresponding adjustment to basis be reflected in the

---

10.   Quaere whether a fractional bequest (as opposed to a pecuniary bequest) was meant to be excluded, and whether the government is likely to adopt any of the passing concepts embodied in Treas. Reg. §§20.2056(e)-1 or -2 as additional forms of indirect application of §1014(e). See pages 613-615.

basis upon reacquisition by the donor or the donor's spouse, notwithstanding the rule's dictate that the reacquired basis will be the same as the decedent's basis immediately before death? See §1014(e)(1) (last clause).

The ultimate effect of §1014(e) for basis purposes is as if no gift had occurred: the decedent having received the donor's basis on the original transfer, and the donor or the donor's spouse having reacquired the property with the decedent's premortem basis. Nevertheless, no adjustment is made under §§2001 or 2502 to purge the donor's adjusted taxable gifts base to place the donor in the same position for future wealth transfer tax purposes as if no gift had been made. Any unified credit that was used is not reinstated. Nor is the decedent's estate treated as if the acquired property had not passed through it. For basis purposes as well, by acquiring the decedent's premortem basis, the donor or the donor's spouse is subjected to the potential of incurring gain as a result of depreciation or depletion taken by the decedent during the period of the decedent's ownership prior to death. And no basis adjustment like that allowed under §1015(d)(6) for gift taxes attributable to appreciation in donated property is allowed for any transfer tax incurred by the decedent in passing the property back to the donor or to the donor's spouse, even though the result for basis purposes is as if the decedent had made an inter vivos gift of the property.

Chapter 5

WILL SUBSTITUTES: THE STRING PROVISIONS

Part A.   Retained Life Estates and Similar Interests
Part B.   Reversionary Interests in Principal
Part C.   Retained Powers
Part D.   Proposals for Transfer Tax Revision

1.   This chapter addresses transfers that sometimes are referred to as "will substitutes" — inter vivos transfers in which the transferor (also known as a settlor when a trust is involved but referred to herein as the "grantor" for consistency, because that is the term the income tax rules always use) retained some "string" over the property, in the form of one or more retained property interests, or powers, or both. The term "will substitute" covers different types of transfers, but all are inter vivos in form and to one degree or another are "testamentary" in substance, in the sense that the grantor doesn't completely let go until death.

The federal tax system, consisting in this instance of the income, gift, and estate taxes, is not fully coordinated in how it treats will substitutes. Ideally, a transfer that is categorized as testamentary in substance would be treated for all tax purposes as if no transfer occurred during life. The transfer would not be subject to the gift tax, would be subject to the estate tax, and the post-transfer income would be taxed to the grantor as if it was still owned until death. This is how the most common and most pure will substitute of all, the garden variety revocable inter vivos trust with a retained income interest, *is* treated. The post-transfer income (both ordinary income and capital gains) is taxed to the grantor under §§677(a)(1) and 676, the creation of the trust is treated as an incomplete gift for gift tax purposes under Treas. Reg. §25.2511-2(c), and the full value of the property is included in the grantor's gross estate under either §2036 or §2038.

Moving away from the garden variety revocable inter vivos trust with a retained income interest, however, coordination of the three taxes begins to break down. For example, some will substitutes that are included in the grantor's gross estate under one or another of the string provisions might nevertheless be subject to the gift tax when the transfer was made, and the grantor might be taxed on only part or none of the post-transfer income.

The unification of the gift and estate taxes in 1976 offered Congress an opportunity at least to eliminate or reduce the inconsistency within the transfer tax system itself, by assuring that no transfer would be subject to both the gift and estate taxes. Both the Treasury Department and the American Law Institute previously worked out such systems. They are summarized in Part D of this chapter. Instead, Congress retained the existing substantive rules under which a transfer could be subject to both the gift and estate taxes, and attempted to eliminate double taxation by adopting the "purge and credit" mechanism that appears in §2001(b): it purges the gift from the grantor's adjusted taxable gifts and provides an offset against the tentative estate tax for any gift taxes already incurred.

To take a simple illustration, suppose that a grantor creates an irrevocable inter vivos trust with a retained income interest. Because the grantor retained the income interest, the full value of the property is included in the grantor's gross estate under §2036. Because the trust was irrevocable, however, the transfer of the remainder interest was subject to gift taxation when the trust was created. See Treas. Reg. §§25.2511-1(e), -1(h)(7). [Beginning in 1990, because of the special valuation rules of §2702, which are discussed in Chapter 15, the remainder interest might be treated for gift tax purposes as having a value equal to the value of the entire trust.] At death, the purge and credit mechanism kicks in to eliminate the gift of the remainder interest from the grantor's adjusted taxable gifts and to offset the gift tax payable on the gift against the grantor's tentative estate tax. As we will see, there is an argument that the purge and credit mechanism does not work perfectly, because the §2001(b)(2) offset for gift tax payable does not reflect the time value of money, i.e., the offset does not account for interest for the government's use of the taxpayer's money received in the form of the gift tax. From this perspective, the taxpayer is worse off than if he or she had simply made the transfer by will.

This imperfection in the purge and credit mechanism caught Judge Easterbrook's ire in Grimes v. Commissioner, 851 F.2d 1005 (7th Cir. 1988), in which Jesse Grimes was deemed to have made a gift with a retained life estate when his wife predeceased him and he became contractually obligated to fulfill the terms of their joint and mutual will. The government successfully argued that, when his wife died, Jesse incurred a gift tax on the value of the remainder interest in *his* property that became subject to the will contract. The government also successfully argued that the full value of his property that was subject to that will contract was included in his gross estate under §2036 because, as we will learn, he had retained a life estate in his own property. He was allowed a §2001(b) purge of his adjusted taxable gifts base and an offset for the gift taxes payable on the gift of the remainder interest. But the court characterized this treatment as inadequate relief:

It should be apparent, however, that . . . [if] there had never been a gift, the estate tax due in 1985 would have been $200,000 in 1985 dollars. Because of the gift in 1975, the IRS received

$100,000 in 1975 dollars — which, given the 7.17% rate of interest, *is identical to $200,000 in 1985 dollars*.[1] That is the amount either the Commissioner or the taxpayer could have produced by investing $100,000 in 1975 and reinvesting all interest until 1985. To levy a gift tax of $100,000 in 1975, and a net estate tax of $100,000 in 1985, is to collect on the one parcel a full tax of $300,000 in 1985 dollars. Why? The taxpayer did not become wealthier by making the gift in 1975; in either case he used the property during his life, and his children received it on his death. . . .

. . . . [T]he difficulty we have sketched is . . . a source of inequitable treatment in the computation of the estate tax. Crediting the interest on the gift tax (actual or imputed) against the estate tax would be one solution, for such a credit would state both taxes in the value of money as of the time of death.

This chapter examines transfers in which the grantor has retained an interest, such as a life estate (part A) or a reversionary interest (part B), or some power over the property (part C). A power to revoke the transfer and have the property return to the grantor is an obvious example of such a power, but the matter is broader than that and, as we will see, the retention of even nonbeneficial powers that are limited to shifting the beneficial interests in the property among persons other than the grantor — or even certain administrative powers — may cause the transfer to be treated as testamentary for wealth transfer tax purposes. Although the gift tax valuation of many of the transfers discussed in this chapter will be affected by §§2701 and 2702, we will largely ignore those provisions in this chapter and defer an examination of them to chapter 15.

The estate tax string provisions that deal with these types of transfers — §§2036, 2037, and 2038 — are outgrowths of a single statutory provision contained in the Revenue Act of 1916. They evolved into their present form largely because of congressional dissatisfaction with the way courts, principally the Supreme Court, interpreted the 1916 provision, which is set forth below.

Revenue Act of 1916

39 Stat. 756, 777

Be it enacted . . .

Sec. 202. That the value of the gross estate of the decedent shall be determined by including the value at the time of his death

---

1. Something made clear in Jesse Grimes's case because the Commissioner wants to collect, in 1985, about twice the principal of the tax that would have been due in 1979. (Note that in all of these computations we disregard income taxes payable on interest.)

of all property, real or personal, tangible or intangible, wherever situated. . . .

(b)   To the extent of any interest therein of which the decedent has at any time made a transfer, or with respect to which he has created a trust, . . . intended to take effect in possession or enjoyment at or after his death. . . .

PART A.   RETAINED LIFE ESTATES AND SIMILAR INTERESTS

Code References: *Estate Tax: §2036(a)(1)*
Gift Tax: §§2503(b), 2514; Treas. Reg. §§25.2511-1, 25.7520
Income Tax: §§652, 662, 671, 673, 677, 678

2.   Under the doctrine of estates, *D* makes an inter vivos transfer of a remainder interest to *X* if *D* transfers real estate to *X* by deed, reserving a life estate in the property. The same is true if *D* deeds the property to *T*, in trust, directing the trustee to pay the net income from the property to *D* for life and the principal after *D*'s death outright to *X*. Either transfer occurs when *D* delivers the deed, because *X* acquires an existing (although not a possessory) interest in the property: a future interest that has all the incidents of a possessory property interest (except the right to possession or enjoyment before *D* dies). During *D*'s life, *X* can transfer the remainder by sale, gift, or (assuming the remainder is not subject to an express survivorship condition) by will if *X* predeceases *D*.

In some respects, however, *D*'s transfer to *X* is testamentary, in the sense that *D* retains enjoyment of and income from the property until death. *X*'s possession of the property does not begin until *D* dies. Enjoyment of the property by both *D* and *X* is similar to what they would have if *D* merely retains complete ownership of the property until death and devises it to *X* by will. This explains why transfers with retained life estates often are referred to as will substitutes.

Property law permits form to control over substance to a great extent because the property law issue is merely the validity of the document of transfer. By respecting the form of transfer, courts have permitted greater flexibility in the transfer of wealth than otherwise might be possible. For example, it is extremely unlikely that *D*'s transfer would be said to be sufficiently testamentary that it should be treated as invalid unless it complies with the technical formalities of the Statute of Wills. Instead, property law permits property owners to avoid probate by the use of inter vivos transfers in which the grantor can reserve far greater control than the mere reservation of a life estate or a reversionary interest, all without causing the transfer to be treated as incomplete or invalid. About the only exception to this rule arises in some states in connection with the forced share of a surviving spouse, which is an area in which countervailing policy may be more important than is the interest of preserving the integrity of transfers that sidestep the Statute of Wills. Under the Uniform Probate Code, for example, a surviving spouse is entitled to an elective share of the "augmented estate," which is a statutory concept defined in §2-205(2)(i) to include property subject to a retained life estate.

Although property law focuses mainly on form, shifting to substance only in limited circumstances, tax law purports to focus mostly on substance. This is understandable, in that manipulation of tax consequences by merely formal transactions violates one of the fundamental tax goals of treating taxpayers in similar positions similarly: the principle of "horizontal equity" (to say nothing of avoiding substantial revenue loss to the government). The difficulty in characterizing a transaction according to its substance is that a grantor may retain some substantive rights but dispose of others: what retained ownership rights should warrant treating the transfer as testamentary? The answers to this question vary for purposes of applying different federal taxes according to the policies underlying each tax. Thus, the estate tax, the income tax, and the gift tax each provide different, albeit overlapping, criteria for treating a grantor as the owner of "transferred" property.

Although the committee reports that accompanied the Revenue Act of 1916 contain no direct statement to this effect, it nevertheless seems clear that one transfer — if not the central one — that Congress intended to subject to the estate tax under §202(b) was a transfer with a retained life estate. See Commissioner v. Estate of Church, 335 U.S. 632, 637-639 (1949). In fact, §202(b) was copied from the death tax statutes of several states whose courts had held that this language reached such transfers. See, e.g., Reish v. Commonwealth, 106 Pa. 521 (1884). Moreover, §202(b) was competently drafted to cause the inclusion of these transfers in the grantor's gross estate if the provision had been properly construed. Although property law would say that *X received* a remainder interest when *D* delivered the deed, §202(b) would describe *X*'s remainder as an interest *that is to take effect in possession or enjoyment* at *D*'s death.

Nevertheless, the Supreme Court took a hostile attitude toward the estate tax in its early days. And a unanimous Court, in May v. Heiner, 281 U.S. 238, 243 (1930), held that a transfer with a retained life income interest was not subject to the federal estate tax. The opinion was brief; the Court explained its position in the following passage:

[The transfer] was not testamentary in character and was beyond recall by the decedent [Mrs. May]. At the death of Mrs. May no interest in the property held under the trust deed passed from her to the living; title thereto had been definitely fixed by the trust deed. The interest therein which she possessed immediately prior to her death was obliterated by that event.

Everything the Court said in this passage is correct from a property law perspective; but these points should have been irrelevant for transfer tax purposes. The Court ignored the fact that the statute was expressly geared to the time when an interest was intended to take effect in possession or enjoyment, not to the time it was created or transferred.

Mrs. May's retained life estate was not the primary life estate; it was a secondary life estate following a life estate in her husband. She was to receive the net income only for the balance of her life after his death. The Court noted that the record did not disclose whether Mrs. May survived her husband, but held that this was of no special importance. The government's hope that *May* meant that only the reservation of a secondary life estate would escape the estate tax was dashed the following year when the Court rendered three per curiam decisions, based solely on the authority of *May*, that transfers with a reserved primary life estate also were not subject to the estate tax. Burnet v. Northern Trust Co., 283 U.S. 782 (1931); Morsman v. Burnet, 283 U.S. 783 (1931); McCormick v. Burnet, 283 U.S. 784 (1931).

The congressional response was swift: The day after the three per curiam decisions were announced, Congress passed and the President signed a joint resolution drafted by the Treasury Department, which added language to the 1916 provision that specifically included "a transfer under which the grantor has retained for his life or for any period not ending before his death (1) the possession or enjoyment of, or the income from, the property . . . ." 46 Stat. 1516. The following year Congress passed the Revenue Act of 1932, which brought §2036(a)(1) to its current form. The Committee Reports accompanying the 1932 Act explained Congress' reason for adding and altering some of the 1931 language:

The purpose of this amendment . . . is to clarify in certain respects the amendments made . . . by the joint resolution of . . . 1931, which were adopted to render taxable a transfer under which the decedent reserved the income for his life. The joint resolution was designed to avoid the effect of decisions of the Supreme Court holding such a transfer not taxable if irrevocable and not made in contemplation of death. Certain new matter has also been added, which is without retroactive effect.

(1) The insertion of the words "or for any period not ascertainable without reference to his death" is to reach, for example, a transfer where decedent reserved to himself semiannual payments of the income of a trust which he had established, but with the provision that no part of the trust income between the last semi-

annual payment to him and his death should be paid to him or his estate, or where he reserves the income, not necessarily for the remainder of his life, but for a period in the ascertainment of which the date of his death was a necessary element.

(2) The insertion of the words "or for any period which does not in fact end before his death" [in place of the words "or for any period not ending before his death,"] which is to reach, for example, a transfer where decedent, 70 years old, reserves the income for an extended term of years and dies during the term, or where he is to have the income from and after the death of another person until his own death, and such other person predeceases him. This is a clarifying change and does not represent new matter.

(3) The insertion of the words "the right to the income" in place of the words "the income" is designed to reach a case where decedent had the right to the income, though he did not actually receive it. This is also a clarifying change.

H.R. Rep. No. 708, 72d Cong., 1st Sess. 46-47 (1931), in 1939-1 C.B. (pt. 2) 457, 490-491; S. Rep. No. 665, 72d Cong., 1st Sess. 49-50 (1931), in 1939-1 C.B. (pt. 2) 496, 532.

In Commissioner v. Estate of Church, 335 U.S. 632 (1949), the Supreme Court upheld the constitutionality of §2036(a)(1), and in Helvering v. Bullard, 303 U.S. 297 (1938), and Hasset v. Welch, 303 U.S. 303 (1938), held that the 1931 and 1932 amendments were not to apply retroactively. But it was *Church* that caused Congress to act once again, because the Supreme Court overruled *May* and held that a transfer with a reserved life estate was taxable under the original 1916 language. Thus, even transfers before adoption of the 1931 joint resolution were deemed subject to the estate tax. Congress again reacted swiftly, passing the forerunner of what is now the effective date rule in §2036(c). Technical Changes Act of 1949, §7, as amended by the Technical Changes Act of 1953, §207. See H.R. Rep. No. 894, 83d Cong, 1st Sess. (1953), in 1953-2 C.B. 513.

Neither the gift nor the income taxes underwent these major shifts in direction. No special problems were presented by retained life estates for income tax purposes and §677, like its predecessors, applies to the extent transferred property produces income to which the grantor is entitled. This general principle has been incorporated explicitly in the Code since 1924.

The gift tax also has been stable since its original enactment in 1924. See T.D. 3648, Treas. Reg. 67, arts. 1 and 7(7), 26 Treas. Dec. Int. Rev. 1163, 1169 (1924). There is an immediate taxable gift of the remainder interest to the extent the grantor completely parts with all interests in the transferred property other than the retained life estate. Treas. Reg.

§§25.2511-1(e), -1(h)(7). The gift does not qualify for the annual exclusion because the remainder is a future interest.[2]

To the extent that §2036(a)(1) requires inclusion of the transferred property, the flush language of §2001(b) will apply to purge the original transfer from the grantor's adjusted taxable gifts for purposes of §2001(b)(1)(B) (if the transfer was made after 1976) in computing the grantor's estate tax at death, and §2001(b)(2) allows an offset for the gift tax payable on the transfer. In this manner double taxation is meant to be avoided, although Judge Easterbrook's opinion in *Grimes* shows that these adjustments do not perfectly equate the tax on inter vivos transfers with those on testamentary dispositions.

3. *Summary of the Tax Consequences of an Inter Vivos Transfer with a Retained Life Estate.* Assume that, after 1976, *D* transferred property to *T* in an irrevocable trust, directing the trustee to pay the net income from the property to *D* for life and the remainder at *D*'s death outright to *X*.

Gift Tax Consequences: At the time of the transfer, *D* made a taxable gift to *X* of the remainder interest in the property. Treas. Reg. §§25.2511-1(e), -1(h)(7). This gift of a future interest does not qualify for the §2503(b) gift tax annual exclusion.

Income Tax Consequences: Under §677(a)(1) *D* will continue to be taxed on the ordinary income generated by the property, although *D* will not be taxed on any capital gains realized by the trust that properly are allocated to principal. Treas. Reg. §§1.677(a)-1(g) *Example (1)*; 1.671-3(b).

Estate Tax Consequences: When *D* dies, the full value of the trust principal will be includible in *D*'s gross estate under §2036(a)(1). Because of this inclusion, *D*'s inter vivos gift to *X* of the remainder interest will be purged from *D*'s adjusted taxable gifts under the flush language of §2001(b), and any gift tax payable on the inter vivos gift to *X* will be an offset against *D*'s tentative estate tax under §2001(b)(2). If *D*'s transfer occurred within three years of death, any gift taxes paid by *D* or *D*'s estate on the gift of the remainder interest will be includible in *D*'s gross estate under §2035(b). Rev. Rul. 81-229.

Split Gifts Included in the Donor Spouse's Gross Estate under §2036(a)(1). If *D*'s spouse, *S*, consented under §2513 to split the

---

2. If the transferor retains a secondary life estate, the primary life estate is a present interest and qualifies for the annual exclusion.

gift to X, §2036(a)(1) inclusion in D's gross estate will affect the computation of S's estate tax if S dies after D. Unfortunately, §2001(e) is flawed and will not apply, although §2001(d) does (all as explored in more detail at page 168). No offset under §2001(b)(2) is available to S's estate for any gift tax incurred by D or by S on the gift, but D's estate is entitled to a credit under §2001(b)(2) for any gift tax on the split gift incurred by S. See §2001(d). This inadequate treatment is a good reason to avoid gift splitting if a transfer may trigger string provision inclusion at the grantor's death.

4.   *The Three Statutory Periods of §2036.*

Secondary or Contingent Life Estates.   Gross estate inclusion under §2036(a)(1) arises only if the right to the income from or the possession or enjoyment of the transferred property is retained for at least one of the three described periods. When Congress reacted against *May v. Heiner* (and its progeny) in 1931 by passing the predecessor of §2036(a)(1), it made it clear that the reservation of a primary life estate causes inclusion of the value of the transferred property.

If the Transferor Survives the Primary Life Tenant.   Since 1931 there does not seem to be any doubt about the includibility of property subject to a reserved *secondary* life estate *if* the grantor survived the primary life tenant and therefore was the current life tenant at death.

If the Transferor Predeceases the Primary Life Tenant.   The situation that produced greater confusion, however, is if the grantor who reserved a secondary life estate predeceased the primary life tenant. An early ruling, E.T. 5, 1934-2 C.B. 369, drew a negative implication from the committee reports accompanying the Revenue Act of 1932 concerning change (2), and held that §2036(a)(1) was triggered only if the grantor survived the primary life tenant. A few years later, however, the government reversed its position and amended the regulations accordingly. T.D. 4729, 1937-1 C.B. 285. The following year an amendment changed the regulation to say that the "not ascertainable without reference to his death" period "may be illustrated by" this secondary life estate situation. T.D. 4868, 1938-2 C.B. 356.[3] See Treas. Reg. §20.2036-1(b)(1).

---

3.   Accord, Statement of the Managers (of the Technical Changes Act of 1949), on the Part of the House after Conference, H.R. Rep. No. 1412, 81st Cong., 1st Sess. 5 (1949), in 1949-2 C.B. 295, 300:

The expression "not ascertainable without reference to his death" . . . includes the right to receive the income from transferred property after the death of another person who in fact survived the transferor; but in such a case the amount to be included . . . does not include the value of the outstanding income interest in such other person.

The Tax Court initially agreed with the government's original construction of the statute, holding that §2036(a)(1) was not triggered if the grantor predeceased the primary life tenant, embracing both the negative implication articulated in E.T. 5 and an additional theory that the grantor never had a "right" to the income. Estate of Curie v. Commissioner, 4 T.C. 1175, 1182-1184 (1945). A subsequent Tax Court decision that followed *Curie* was reversed in Commissioner v. Estate of Nathan, 159 F.2d 546 (7th Cir. 1947), in which the court of appeal said:

We think it clear that . . . the contingent estate retained by Nathan was . . . *for a period which does not in fact end before his death.* . . .

The doubt, if any exists in this case, is over the question . . . was the period during which his contingent estate . . . existed ascertainable without reference to his death . . . ?

Notwithstanding some doubt (in view of the discussion in the *Curie* case) we hold the language of the statute must be so construed as to impose an estate tax on the property covered by this trust less the value of the life estate of the [primary life tenant]. . . .

. . . The transfer in which the deceased retained a contingent estate was held by him for a period which did not in fact end before his death. . . .

The factual difference between the instant case and the usual trust agreement . . . did not take the transfer out of the reach of the language of §[2036(a)(1)] which controls our decision. We cannot lessen the effect or the meaning of the words because the settlor's interest was less certain or the enjoyment of the estate reserved more remote.

Subsequent decisions were in accord with *Nathan* and it is now well settled that the value of property subject to a reserved secondary life estate is includible under §2036(a)(1), even if the decedent predeceases the primary life tenant. See Lowndes, Kramer, & McCord, FEDERAL ESTATE AND GIFT TAXES §9.10 n.9 (3d ed. 1974). However, if the primary income beneficiary is living at the decedent's estate, the value of that primary income interest is not included in the decedent's estate. Treas. Reg. §20.2036-1(b)(1)(ii). Neither *Nathan* nor the committee report accompanying the 1949 Act quoted in footnote 3 explained why the value of the outstanding income interest in the primary life tenant is excluded from the amount includible. Is there a proper reason for its exclusion, and what is the proper §2001(b) purge from the decedent's adjusted taxable gifts? To illustrate, assume that *D* created a trust providing: (1) income to *A* for life, (2) then income to *B* for life, (3) then income to *D* for life, (4) then on the death of the survivor of

A, *B*, and *D*, principal to *R*. *D* predeceased both *A* and *B*. The full value of the trust is included in *D*'s gross estate, reduced by the value of both *A* and *B*'s superior life estates.

What type of retained income interest would fit within the period (a) "for life" but not within the other two periods; (b) "not in fact end before his death" but not the other two periods; (c) "not ascertainable without reference to his death" but not the other two periods? Would anyone create such interests? Consider the following:

Estate of Honigman v. Commissioner, 66 T.C. 1080 (1976), extinguished any notion that the "not in fact end before his death" period applies only to a retention that evidences the decedent's intent that the period should extend for the duration of the decedent's life, stating:

In National Bank of Commerce v. Henslee, 179 F. Supp. 346 (M.D. Tenn. 1959), the court determined that the corresponding provision (§811(c)(1)(B) of the 1939 Code) required gifts to be included in a transferor's estate only when the facts showed that his possession, enjoyment, or right to income — which *in fact* was retained until his death — was *intended* at the time of the gift to *endure for his lifetime*. The district court relied both on the legislative history of the Revenue Act of 1932 (S. Rep. No. 665 and on Treasury Regulations interpreting the 1939 Code (Regulations 105, sec. 81.18, as amended by T.D. 5834, 1951-1 C.B. 72, 81, ¶8(A)). We find the cited legislative history to be inconclusive and subsequent reenactments have not been accompanied by clarification of congressional intent on this issue. Significantly, Treas. Reg. §20.2036-1(a) . . . no longer makes intention a test of includability under §2036. . . . Although there is some indication in the legislative history that Congress was thinking of situations where the period of retention was such as to evidence an intention that decedent's possession or enjoyment should continue for his life, the wording of §2036 itself is clear and unambiguous and reflects no such qualification. Such being the case, we find ourselves unable to adopt a loose construction in order to aid this petitioner (see Lowndes, Kramer and McCord, FEDERAL ESTATE AND GIFT TAXES 201-202 (3d ed. 1974)) — a course which could open up a Pandora's box of litigation.

5.   *The Transfer and Retention Requirements.* Unless the owner of a life insurance policy has designated otherwise, upon the insured's death, the beneficiary has the option of taking the insurance proceeds in a lump sum or instead to elect a different option. Consider whether §2036(a)(1) would apply on *O*'s death if *O* is the primary beneficiary of a

$100,000 insurance policy on *I*'s life (and owned by *I*) in the following alternative situations:

(a) When *I* died, *O* selected an "interest only" settlement option that pays *O* an annual amount equal to a designated rate of return on the proceeds held by the insurer and, when *O* dies, pays the proceeds to *I*'s children in equal shares.

(b) Before *I* died, *O* and *I* concluded that the settlement option in **(a)** was desirable and *I* alone signed the instrument selecting this option.

See Pyle v. Commissioner, 313 F.2d 328 (3d Cir. 1963); National City Bank v. United States, 371 F.2d 13 (6th Cir. 1966). The answer lies in the following question: Did *O* transfer any property as required by §2036?

6. *Reciprocal Transfers.* An important concept with much broader application is illustrated by the following landmark decision. The reciprocal transfer doctrine applies well beyond the string provisions, which just happen to be where it originated.

United States v. Estate of Grace
395 U.S. 316 (1969)

MARSHALL, J.: This case involves the application of §[2036(a)(1)] to a so-called "reciprocal trust" situation. After Joseph P. Grace's death in 1950, the Commissioner of Internal Revenue determined that the value of a trust created by his wife was includible in his gross estate. A deficiency was assessed and paid and, after denial of a claim for a refund, this refund suit was brought. The Court of Claims, with two judges dissenting, ruled that the value of the trust was not includible in decedent's estate under §[2036(a)(1)] and entered judgment for respondent. . . . We reverse.

. . . On December 15, 1931, decedent executed a trust instrument, hereinafter called the Joseph Grace trust. Named as trustees were decedent, his nephew, and a third party. The trustees were directed to pay the income of the trust to Janet Grace during her lifetime, and to pay to her any part of the principal which a majority of the trustees might deem advisable. Janet was given the power to designate, by will or deed, the manner in which the trust estate remaining at her death was to be distributed among decedent and their children. The trust properties included securities and real estate interests.

On December 30, 1931, Janet Grace executed a trust instrument, hereinafter called the Janet Grace trust, which was virtually identical to the Joseph Grace trust. The trust properties included the family estate and corporate securities, all of which had been transferred to her by decedent in preceding years.

The trust instruments were prepared by one of decedent's employees in accordance with a plan devised by decedent to create additional trusts before the advent of a new gift tax expected to be enacted the next year. Decedent selected the properties to be included in each trust. Janet Grace, acting in accordance with this plan, executed her trust instrument at decedent's request.

Janet Grace died in 1937. The Joseph Grace trust terminated at her death. Her estate's federal estate tax return disclosed the Janet Grace trust and reported it as a nontaxable transfer by Janet Grace. The Commissioner asserted that the Janet and Joseph Grace trusts were "reciprocal" and asserted a deficiency to the extent of mutual value. Compromises on unrelated issues resulted in 55% of the smaller of the two trusts, the Janet Grace trust, being included in her gross estate.

Joseph Grace died in 1950. The federal estate tax return disclosed both trusts. The Joseph Grace trust was reported as a nontaxable transfer and the Janet Grace trust was reported as a trust under which decedent held a limited power of appointment. Neither trust was included in decedent's gross estate.

The Commissioner determined that the Joseph and Janet Grace trusts were "reciprocal" and included the amount of the Janet Grace trust in decedent's gross estate. . . .

The doctrine of reciprocal trusts was formulated in response to attempts to draft instruments which seemingly avoid the literal terms of §[2036(a)(1)], while still leaving the decedent the lifetime enjoyment of his property. The doctrine dates from Lehman v. Commissioner, 109 F.2d 99 (2d Cir. 1940). In *Lehman*, decedent and his brother owned equal shares in certain stocks and bonds. Each brother placed his interest in trust for the other's benefit for life, with remainder to the life tenant's issue. Each brother also gave the other the right to withdraw $150,000 of the principal. If the brothers had each reserved the right to withdraw $150,000 from the trust that each had created, the trusts would have been includible in their gross estates as interests of which each had made a transfer with a power to revoke. When one of the brothers died, his estate argued that neither trust was includible because the decedent did not have a power over a trust which he had created.

The Second Circuit disagreed. That court ruled that the effect of the transfers was the same as if the decedent had transferred his stock in trust for himself, remainder to his issue, and had reserved the right to withdraw $150,000. The court reasoned: "The fact that the trusts were reciprocated or 'crossed' is a trifle, quite lacking in practical or legal significance. . . . The law searches out the reality and is not concerned with the form." 109 F.2d at 100. The court ruled that the decisive point was that each brother caused the other to make a transfer by establishing his own trust.

The doctrine of reciprocal trusts has been applied numerous times since the *Lehman* decision. It received congressional approval in §6 of the Technical Changes Act of 1949, 63 Stat. 893.[4] The present case is, however, this Court's first examination of the doctrine.

The Court of Claims was divided over the requirements for application of the doctrine to the situation of this case. Relying on some language in *Lehman* and certain other courts of appeals' decisions, the majority held that the crucial factor was whether the decedent had established his trust as consideration for the establishment of the trust of which he was a beneficiary. The court ruled that decedent had not established his trust as a quid pro quo for the Janet Grace trust, and that Janet Grace had not established her trust in exchange for the Joseph Grace trust. Rather, the trusts were found to be part of an established pattern of family giving, with neither party desiring to obtain property from the other. Indeed, the court found that Janet Grace had created her trust because decedent requested that she do so. It therefore found the reciprocal trust doctrine inapplicable.

The court recognized that certain cases had established a slightly different test for reciprocity. Those cases inferred consideration from the establishment of two similar trusts at about the same time. The court held that any inference of consideration was rebutted by the evidence in the case, particularly the lack of any evidence of an estate tax avoidance motive on the part of the Graces. In contrast, the dissent felt that the majority's approach placed entirely too much weight on subjective intent. Once it was established that the trusts were interrelated, the dissent felt that the subjective intent of the parties in establishing the trusts should become irrelevant. The relevant factor was whether the trusts created by the settlors placed each other in approximately the same objective economic position as they would have been in if each had created his own trust with himself, rather than the other, as life beneficiary.

We agree with the dissent that the approach of the Court of Claims majority places too much emphasis on the subjective intent of the parties in creating the trusts and for that reason hinders proper application of the federal estate tax laws. It is true that there

---

4. See S. Rep. No. 831, 81st Cong., 1st Sess. 5-6 (1949); H.R. Rep. No. 920, 81st Cong., 1st Sess. 5 (1949).

is language in *Lehman* and other cases that would seem to support the majority's approach. It is also true that the results in some of those cases arguably support the decision below. Nevertheless, we think that these cases are not in accord with this Court's prior decisions interpreting related provisions of the federal estate tax laws.

Emphasis on the subjective intent of the parties in creating the trusts, particularly when those parties are members of the same family unit, creates substantial obstacles to the proper application of the federal estate tax laws. As this Court said in Estate of Spiegel v. Commissioner, 335 U.S. 701, 705-706 (1949): "Any requirement . . . [of] a post-death attempt to probe the settlor's thoughts in regard to the transfer, would partially impair the effectiveness of . . . [§§2035-2037] as an instrument to frustrate estate tax evasions." We agree that "the taxability of a trust corpus . . . does not hinge on a settlor's motives, but depends on the nature and operative effect of the trust transfer." Id. at 705. . . .

We think these observations have particular weight when applied to the reciprocal trust situation. First, inquiries into subjective intent, especially in intrafamily transfers, are particularly perilous. The present case illustrates that it is, practically speaking, impossible to determine after the death of the parties what they had in mind in creating trusts over 30 years earlier. Second, there is a high probability that such a trust arrangement was indeed created for tax-avoidance purposes. And, even if there was no estate tax-avoidance motive, the settlor in a very real and objective sense did retain an economic interest while purporting to give away his property.[5] Finally, it is unrealistic to assume that the settlors of the trusts, usually members of one family unit, will have created their trusts as a bargained-for exchange for the other trust. "Consideration," in the traditional legal sense, simply does not normally enter into such intrafamily transfers.[6]

For these reasons, we hold that application of the reciprocal trust doctrine is not dependent upon a finding that each trust was created as a quid pro quo for the other. Such a "consideration" requirement necessarily involves a difficult inquiry into the subjective intent of the settlors. Nor do we think it necessary to

---

5. For example, in the present case decedent ostensibly devised the trust plan to avoid an imminent federal gift tax. Instead of establishing trusts for the present benefit of his children, he chose an arrangement under which he and his wife retained present enjoyment of the property and under which the property would pass to their children without imposition of either estate or gift tax.

6. The present case is probably typical in this regard. Janet Grace created her trust because decedent requested that she do so; it was in no real sense a bargained-for quid pro quo for his trust. . . .

prove the existence of a tax-avoidance motive. As we have said above, standards of this sort, which rely on subjective factors, are rarely workable under the federal estate tax laws. Rather, we hold that application of the reciprocal trust doctrine requires only that the trusts be interrelated, and that the arrangement, to the extent of mutual value, leaves the settlors in approximately the same economic position as they would have been in had they created trusts naming themselves as life beneficiaries.[7]

Applying this test to the present case, we think it clear that the value of the Janet Grace trust fund must be included in decedent's estate for federal estate tax purposes. It is undisputed that the two trusts are interrelated. They are substantially identical in terms and were created at approximately the same time. Indeed, they were part of a single transaction designed and carried out by decedent. It is also clear that the transfers in trust left each party, to the extent of mutual value, in the same objective economic position as before. Indeed, it appears, as would be expected in transfers between husband and wife, that the effective position of each party vis-à-vis the property did not change at all. It is no answer that the transferred properties were different in character. For purposes of the estate tax, we think that economic value is the only workable criterion. Joseph Grace's estate remained undiminished to the extent of the value of his wife's trust and the value of his estate must accordingly be increased by the value of that trust.

The judgment of the Court of Claims is reversed and the case is remanded for further proceedings consistent with this opinion.

It is so ordered.

DOUGLAS, J., dissenting: The object of a reciprocal trust, as I understand it, is for each settlor to rid himself of all taxable power over the corpus by exchanging taxable powers. Each retained a sufficient power over the corpus to require the inclusion of the corpus in his or her taxable estate. Each settlor, as one of the three trustees, reserved the right to alter the trust by paying to the chief beneficiary "any amounts of the principal of the said trust, up to and including the whole thereof, which the said Trustees or a majority of them may at any time or from time to time deem advisable." I have quoted from Janet Grace's trust. But an almost identical provision is in the trust of Joseph P. Grace.

---

7. We do not mean to say that the existence of "consideration," in the traditional sense of a bargained-for exchange, can never be relevant. In certain cases, inquiries into the settlor's reasons for creating the trusts may be helpful in establishing the requisite link between the two trusts. We only hold that a finding of a bargained-for consideration is not necessary to establish reciprocity.

I would conclude from the existence of this reserved power that the corpus of the Janet Grace trust was includible in her estate for purposes of the estate tax. Lober v. United States, 346 U.S. 335 (1953).

That is to say the use of a reciprocal trust device to aid the avoidance of an estate tax is simply not presented by this case.

I would dismiss the petition as improvidently granted.

The still relevant — and largely unanswered — question is how different must the terms of two trusts be, or how far apart in time must they be created, to avoid the interrelated standard in *Grace*? For example, if Joseph had granted Janet a nongeneral testamentary power of appointment in the trust he created for her benefit but she had not granted him a power of appointment at all, Estate of Levy v. Commissioner, 46 T.C.M. (CCH) 910 (1983), would say the reciprocal trust doctrine does not apply. Would it suffice if they each created powers with different classes of permissible appointees? The trusts in *Grace* were created 15 days apart. Would it be adequate to avoid the doctrine if they had been created 15 months apart? What about 150 days apart? Because there are so few guideposts on this road, usually it is best simply to avoid the issue entirely. Some aspects of the rule *are* clear. For example, what happens if the two transfers differ in size, as illustrated next below? That is *not* a viable way to avoid reciprocity!

Revenue Ruling 74-533

. . . On August 15, 1960, *H* transferred $400,000, of which he was the sole owner, to an irrevocable trust which he created on that day. The terms of the trust required the corporate trustee to pay the annual income to *W* for the balance of her lifetime and to pay, at her death, the trust principal to the issue of *H* and *W*. On the same day, *W* established a separate trust and transferred to it $300,000, of which she was the sole owner. The terms of *W*'s trust were identical to those of her husband's trust, except the income from her trust was payable to *H* for the rest of his life and, at his death, the trust principal was payable to the issue of *H* and *W*. . . .

At the death of *H* on January 15, 1971, the value of the principal of *W*'s trust, which had grown from $300,000 to $500,000, was paid over to the children of *H* and *W* at that time. The value of the principal of *H*'s trust had increased from $400,000 to $600,000 when the death of *W* occurred on June 2, 1971. The children of the two settlors also received the principal of *H*'s trust.

Pursuant to . . . United States v. Estate of Grace, 395 U.S. 316 (1969), the executors of the estates of *H* and *W* included in each decedent's gross estate the principal of the trust created by the other spouse to the extent of the mutual value of the reciprocal transfer. The gross estate of *H* thus included the full value, $500,000, of the principal of *W*'s trust as of the date of death of *H*, since the principal of *W*'s trust was initially smaller than that of *H*'s trust.

Three-fourths of the value of the principal of *H*'s trust, as of the date of death of *W*, was included in her gross estate, since the value of the principal of *H*'s trust was greater than that of *W*'s trust at the time of the original transfer. The amount includible, $450,000, was properly determined by multiplying the value of the principal of *H*'s trust at the death of *W* by the ratio of the original value of the principal of the smaller *W*'s trust to that of the larger *H*'s trust. See Rev. Rul. 57-422. . . .

The reciprocal trust doctrine in *Grace* involved the issue whether the nominal grantors retained income interests in transferred property for §2036(a)(1) purposes. But the issue also can arise in other settings. For example, assume that *A* created a trust for *X* with *B* as trustee, and *B* created a trust for *X* with *A* as trustee. If the standards for applying the doctrine are met, each trustee may be regarded as having retained powers over property deemed transferred by the trustee under the reciprocal trust doctrine, causing it to be includible in the trustee's gross estate under either §2036(a)(2) or §2038(a)(1) (see Part C of this chapter) as if the trustee transferred the property. In this example *A* would be treated as having transferred the property as to which *A* is trustee and *B* would be regarded as having transferred the trust property as to which *B* is trustee. See Estate of Bischoff v. Commissioner, 69 T.C. 32 (1977). This application of the doctrine is made questionable by the following decision in *Green*, dealing with application of the reciprocal trust doctrine to trusts with crossed powers that would have triggered §§2036(a)(2) and 2038 if retained by the grantors.

Estate of Green v. United States
68 F.3d 151 (6th Cir. 1995)

KRUPANSKY, J.: Plaintiff-Appellee, the Estate of Jack Green, challenged the ruling of the Internal Revenue Service ("IRS") that the reciprocal trust doctrine required that the property transferred in a trust created by Jack Green for the benefit of his granddaughter be included in his gross estate. The district court concluded that the reciprocal trust doctrine did not apply, and the IRS appealed.

Jack Green and his wife, Norma Green, had two grandchildren, Jennifer Lee Goodman and Greer Elizabeth Goodman. Jennifer and Greer were sisters and the couple's only grandchildren. On December 20, 1966, Jack and Norma Green executed two trust agreements for the benefit of their grandchildren. As settlor of the "Jennifer" trust, Jack Green designated his wife Norma trustee and Jennifer as its beneficiary. Norma Green, the settlor of the "Greer" trust, named her husband as the trustee and Greer as its beneficiary.

The trusts were substantially identical. The authority vested in each trustee was the same: the trustees could not alter, amend, revoke or terminate their respective trusts. The only retained authority by each trustee was the discretion to reinvest and time the distribution of trust corpus and income until each respective beneficiary reached her 21st birthday. Under the terms and conditions of the trusts, neither Jack or Norma Green, directly or indirectly, retained or reserved any economic benefit from the assets or income of the trusts.

The government posits that the limited discretionary power to reinvest and time the distribution of trust corpus and income to third party beneficiaries invoked the reciprocal trust doctrine to un-cross the trusts and subject the trusts to taxation pursuant to §§2036(a)(2) and 2038(a)(1). The estate has countered the application of the reciprocal trust doctrine by citing to the Supreme Court decision in United States v. Grace, 395 U.S. 316 (1969), wherein the Court, in a simple one-sentence statement defined, to the exclusion of all other standards, the criteria to be considered in applying the doctrine:

> Rather, we hold that application of the reciprocal trust doctrine requires *only* that the trusts by interrelated, and that the arrangement, *to the extent of mutual value*, leaves the settlors in *approximately the same economic position* as they *would have been in had they created trusts naming themselves as life beneficiaries.*

Id. at 324 (emphasis added).

In the instant case, the government seeks to rewrite *Grace* by a strained and attenuated interpretation of language that needs no interpretation. It argues as it has since the Tax Court's 1977 decision in Bischoff v. Commissioner of Internal Revenue, 69 T.C. 32 (1977), a decision rejected by every circuit which has considered the application of the reciprocal trust doctrine, that interrelated trusts are taxable by virtue of the doctrine pursuant to §2036(a)(2) and §2038(a)(1). The government asserts that the only condition precedent required to apply the doctrine and uncross the trusts is a finding of retained settlor/trustee fiduciary powers even if the retained fiduciary powers are not coupled with retained settlor/trustee economic benefits which leave "the settlors in approximately the same economic position as they would have been in had they created trusts naming themselves as life beneficiaries." The Supreme Court in *Grace* explained that "(f)or purposes of the estate tax, we think that *economic value is the only workable criterion*." *Grace*, 395 U.S. at 325 (emphasis added). See also Lehman v. Commissioner, 109 F.2d 99 (2nd Cir. 1940), the progenitor of the reciprocal trust doctrine; Krause v. Commissioner of Internal Revenue, 57 T.C. 890 (1972), *aff'd,* 497 F.2d 1109 (6th Cir. 1974); Exchange Bank & Trust Company v. United States, 694 F.2d 1261 (Fed. Cir. 1982), wherein, without exception, retained settlor/trustee discretionary, fiduciary power was coupled with retained settlor/trustee retained economic benefit.[8]

Without considering the district court's findings that the trusts here in issue were not interrelated,[9] this court concludes that the

---

8. In citing to *Lehman*; *Hill's Estate*; *Warner*; *Krause*; *Exchange Bank*; *Moreno's Estate*; and *Glaser*, the dissent neglects to distinguish those cases from the instant controversy by disclosing that, without exception, each case involved a retained identifiable position that left the settlors/trustees in the same economic position they would have been in had they created trusts naming themselves as life beneficiaries. In *Lehman*, which preceded *Grace*, each brother retained present economic enjoyment of the property for his lifetime. In *Hill's Estate*, which predated *Grace*, the retained economic benefits were also life estates. Likewise, in *Krause*, the grandmother and grandfather retained a discretionary right to receive trust income themselves during their lifetime. In *Exchange Bank*, the transferors retained a present economic power to satisfy their own present legal obligations. In *Morena's Estate*, which predated *Grace*, the economic interests retained were contingent life estates, the fruits of which one spouse would enjoy if the spouse survived the other spouse. In *Glaser*, which also predated *Grace* and which did not involve reciprocal trusts directly, the decedent and his wife merely exchanged one piece of property for another of equivalent value, thus remaining in a similar economic position. The sole case cited by the government which supports application of the reciprocal trust doctrine without an economic benefit, *Bischoff*, itself indicates that virtually every pre-*Grace* case and every post-*Grace* case in which reciprocal arrangements were challenged involved retention of "very substantial economic benefits." *Bischoff*, 69 T.C. at 45.

9. The dissent totally misconstrues and reflects a misunderstanding of the concept and elements of the reciprocal trust doctrine generally and its limited application as dictated by the Supreme Court in *Grace*. Consequently, it misconstrues completely the thrust and reasoning of the Supreme Court in *Grace* as adopted, virtually verbatim, by the majority opinion.

Assuming, arguendo, the contrary to the district court's conclusion, the trusts in the instant case were interrelated as urged by the dissent, the reciprocal trust doctrine would nevertheless be inapplicable for the simple reason that the settlor's trustee's retained fiduciary powers to reinvest income and time distribution of trust income and corpus until the beneficiaries reached 21 years of age did not rise to the level of a retained economic benefit that satisfies the *core* mandate of *Grace*, "that the arrangement, to the *extent of mutual value*, leaves *the settlors in approximately the same economic position as they would have been in had they created trusts naming themselves as life beneficiaries.*" *Grace*, 395 U.S. at 324 (emphasis added).

settlor/trustee retained fiduciary powers to reinvest income and time distribution of trust income and corpus until the beneficiaries reach 21 years of age do not constitute a retained economic benefit that satisfies the *core* mandate of *Grace* "that the arrangement, to the *extent of mutual value,* leaves the settlors in *approximately the same economic position as they would have been in had they created trusts naming themselves as life beneficiaries.*" *Grace*, 395 U.S. at 324 (emphasis added).[10]

For the foregoing reasons, the decision of the district court is AFFIRMED.

JONES, J. dissenting.

Because I believe that trusts in this case satisfy the requirements set forth by the Supreme Court in United States v. Estate of Grace, 395 U.S. 316 (1969), I dissent.

First, I conclude that the trusts created by Jack and Norma Green were interrelated. The district court held that the trusts in this case were not substantially similar because each trust named a different granddaughter as beneficiary. Each of the grandparent trustees could act only to benefit one of the granddaughter beneficiaries. The district court held that this differentiation in the trustees' powers prevented the trusts from being substantially similar. I find the court's conclusion to be in error.

Identity of beneficiaries is not a prerequisite to a finding that two trusts are substantially similar or interrelated. There is no mention of such a factor in *Estate of Grace*. In fact, the beneficiaries of the trusts in *Grace* were not identical. In *Krause*, we

---

Apart from a conclusory statement, the dissent fails to articulate any factual support or explanation for its generalization that the settlors/trustees were in the same economic position they would have been in had they created trusts naming themselves as life beneficiaries.

Having resolved this case in controversy by adopting the core dictates of the Supreme Court in *Grace*, this Court need not address the correctness of the district court's finding that the trusts here in issue were not "interrelated." A court of appeals may affirm the decision of a lower court on any basis supported by the record, even if the appellate court's reasoning differs from the lower court's reasoning. Brown v. Allen, 344 U.S. 443 (1953).

10. Having reviewed and considered the Supreme Court's decision in Commissioner of Internal Revenue v. Holmes, 327 U.S. 813 (1946), and Lober v. United States, 346 U.S. 335 (1953), both of which predate its decision in *Grace*, this court concludes that the effect of those cases upon ultimate tax inclusion in the instant case, if any, would be relevant only if the reciprocal trust doctrine as interpreted in *Grace* required the trusts in the instant case to be uncrossed. Stated differently, the rationale of *Estate of Holmes* and *Lober* cannot be relied upon to extend the reciprocal trust doctrine to include retained non-economic discretionary fiduciary powers including powers to reinvest and time distribution of trust income and corpus until the core mandate of retained economic benefits by the settlor/trustee has been satisfied.

approved the application of the doctrine where the husband named the couples' children as beneficiaries and the wife named their grandchildren. 497 F.2d at 1110. Similarly, in Lehman v. Commissioner, 109 F.2d 99 (2d Cir. 1940), the original case applying the reciprocal trust doctrine, each trust named only one brother as beneficiary. See *Lehman*, 109 F.2d at 100 (two brothers named each others' children as beneficiaries); see also Estate of Hill v. Commissioner, 229 F.2d 237, 239-241 (2d Cir. 1956) (applying doctrine to trusts naming different sisters as beneficiaries); Commissioner v. Warner, 127 F.2d 913, 915-916 (9th Cir. 1942) (same). In Estate of Bischoff v. Commissioner, 69 T.C. 32 (1977), the case on which the district court relied, the trustees did have the identical power to act on behalf of each and every beneficiary. Nevertheless, the cases applying the doctrine demonstrate that identity of beneficiaries is not dispositive.

Interrelatedness depends on a number of factors including: the similarity in the terms of the trusts, see Lehman v. Commissioner, 109 F.2d 99, 100 (2d Cir. 1940); the dates on which the trusts were created; see *Grace*, 395 U.S. at 323; similarity or identify of trusts assets, id.; and whether the trusts appeared in pursuance of a prearranged plan of gifting, see Exchange Bank and Trust v. United States, 694 F.2d 1261, 1266 (Fed. Cir. 1982).

In this case, the trusts were simultaneously executed and amended under the same terms and funded with the same amounts of money. The trusts also contained the same operative terms and identical addenda. In addition, the trusts mirrored each other in the sense that each grandparent was a trustee of the trust the other created, and each was a trustee for one grandchild. These factors can point only to the conclusion that the trusts were interrelated. Therefore, I would reverse the district court's holding that these trusts were not interrelated.

In addition to the requirement that trusts be "interrelated" in order to be reciprocal, *Estate of Grace* imposes the requirement that the trusts "leave[ ] the settlors in approximately the same economic position as they would have been in had they created trusts naming themselves as life beneficiaries." 395 U.S. at 324. The majority opinion focuses solely on this element of the *Grace* test, which the district court never addressed.

The majority, in my opinion, mistakenly concludes that the retained economic benefits did not "satisf[y] the *core* mandate of *Grace*," although "the settlor/trustee retained fiduciary powers to reinvest income and time distribution of trust income and corpus until the beneficiaries reach 21 years of age." To the contrary, I believe that this is precisely the sort of arrangement that this court has previously found to be prohibited under the reciprocal trust doctrine. See Krause v. Commissioner, 497 F.2d 1109, 1112 (6th Cir. 1974) (affirming Tax Court's holding that reciprocal trust doctrine applied where husband and wife taxpayers created cross-trust arrangements whereby husband transferred property in trust for the benefit of the couple's children, whereas wife transferred property in trust for benefit of the couple's grandchildren).

In this case, if the decedent had named himself as the trustee of the Jennifer trust, his Estate would be liable for taxes on the value of the trust. . . . [under §2036].

In United States v. O'Malley, the Supreme Court held that the retained power to determine when payments of income or principal would be made to the beneficiary is sufficient to trigger inclusion of the trust assets in the estate of the decedent. 383 U.S. 627, 631 (1966).

Had Green named himself trustee of the Jennifer trust, he would have retained the powers to deny his granddaughter immediate enjoyment and thus the power to designate. Therefore, the value of the trust would be included in his gross estate. The same would apply to the trust created by Norma Green if she were the named trustee. Instead, Green and his wife named each other as trustees of their respective trusts, and under the majority's holding, were able to avoid the inclusion of the trusts assets in their estates and avoid additional estate taxes.

In *Grace*, the Supreme Court concluded that application of the reciprocal trust doctrine was appropriate because the transactions left the parties in the same economic position as they were before the creation of the trusts. 395 U.S. at 324. The same has occurred with the Greens. The parties in *Grace* maintained their economic positions through retention of a life estate, where the Greens maintained their economic positions through retention of the power to designate whom (sic) would enjoy the trust assets. Retaining either of these economic interests subjects a party to estate taxes under §2036.

The Tax Court has previously applied the reciprocal trust doctrine to an arrangement identical to the Greens' crossed trusts. In Bischoff v. Commissioner, the Tax Court applied the reciprocal trust doctrine to trusts in which parties retained the power to accumulate or distribute trust income and corpus to the trust beneficiaries in their sole discretion. 69 T.C. 32 (1977). In Exchange Bank & Trust v. United States, [694 F.2d 1261 (Fed. Cir. 1982)], the Federal Circuit adopted the court's reasoning from *Bischoff*, and concluded that the settlor's retention of a substantial economic interest is not a prerequisite to applying the doctrine. . . .

The majority holds that the reciprocal trust doctrine does not apply because the Greens' trust arrangement did not leave the parties in the same economic position as they would have been in if they had created trusts naming themselves as life beneficiaries. I do not agree that this is the core mandate of the reciprocal trust doctrine. . . . Rather I find the Court's pronouncement limited to the facts of *Grace*. In *Grace* the Court was presented with a situation in which the parties sought to circumvent the estate tax on their retained life estates. In the present case, we are presented with parties attempting to avoid the estate taxes on their retained powers to designate. This distinction I do not choose to minimize. Thus, instead of looking to the fact specific language requiring the parties to be in the same position if they had named themselves beneficiaries of the estate, I look to the Court's broader pronouncements on economic position.

I find that the Greens' trusts were interrelated and that the trusts arrangements failed to disturb the grandparents' economic positions with respect to their granddaughters. I would apply the reciprocal trust doctrine to uncross these trusts and include the value of the trust property in Jack Green's estate. I respectfully dissent.

If the dissent in *Green* is correct and the reciprocal trust doctrine applies, which of the two trusts (the "Jennifer" trust or the "Greer" trust) is includible in Jack Green's gross estate? The answer lies in the traditional application of the doctrine, which "uncrosses" the trusts at the grantor level. So Jack would be regarded as grantor of the trust Norma created for Greer, of which Jack was trustee.

In TAM 8029001 the reciprocal trust doctrine was applied in a case involving two trusts, both created by *P*, one with child *A* as trustee for child *B* and the other with child *B* as trustee for child *A*. Although normally the doctrine causes uncrossing at the grantor level, here that would produce no change because *P* created both trusts, so they were uncrossed at the trustee level, causing *A* to be deemed trustee of the trust created for *A*'s benefit and *B* as trustee of the trust for the benefit of *B*. Obviously, this ruling is at odds with the decision in *Green* immediately above. The presumption applied by the government is that each trustee will accommodate the wishes of the other in anticipation of the other trustee doing the same for the first. See PLR 9235025.

In a reciprocal trust situation, is there any danger that the value of *both* trusts will be included in the gross estate of either decedent? In *Grace*, for example, the facts revealed that at Janet's death a deficiency was asserted leading to a settlement by which 55% of the Janet trust was included in her gross estate. And the dissent in *Grace* suggested that Joseph retained sufficient powers over the Joseph trust for Janet's benefit that §2036(a)(2) or §2038(a)(1) might be applicable. What if Joseph had retained a secondary life estate in the Joseph trust in which Janet was the primary life tenant? The Tax Court in Estate of Guenzel v. Commissioner, 28 T.C. 59, 63 (1957), *aff'd on another ground*, 258 F.2d 248 (8th Cir. 1958), stated: "We see no reason to go into the applicability of the [reciprocal trust] doctrine when the transfer in trust, which the decedent made in this case, is plainly includible in his estate under the statute." Is the reciprocal trust doctrine a fall back approach, to be used only if some other, more direct, form of inclusion is not applicable, or could both trusts be includible in the decedent's gross estate under different provisions or theories? Given the age and history of the doctrine, it is a bit odd — and disconcerting — that we still have no answer to these questions. What relief might be available against the potential double taxation of each trust?

The reciprocal trust doctrine has been applied under the income tax grantor trust rules as well as for estate tax purposes. See, e.g., Krause v. Commissioner, 57 T.C. 890 (1972), *aff'd*, 497 F.2d 1109 (6th Cir. 1974). It most recently has been applied in the gift tax annual exclusion arena. To illustrate, consider *A* and *B,* who are brothers. Each has two children. This year, *A* gave $11,000 to each of *A*'s children and $11,000 to each of *B*'s children. *B* gave $11,000 to each of *B*'s children and $11,000 to each of *A*'s children. *A* and *B* must file gift tax returns as if each gave $22,000 to their own children and zero to their nephews and nieces. See Estate of Schuler v. Commissioner, 80 T.C.M. (CCH) 934 (2000), *aff'd* (8th Cir. 2002), *following* Sather v. Commissioner, 251 F.3d 1168 (8th Cir. 2001); Schultz v. United States, 493 F.2d 1225 (4th Cir. 1974); Furst v. Commissioner, 21 T.C.M. (CCH) 1169 (1962); TAM 8717003.

As revealed in *Sather,* the reciprocal trust doctrine is not limited to trusts created (or other transfers) by only two parties. For example, assume partners *A, B,* and *C* each created identical trusts, each for the benefit of their respective children, to which annual contributions will be made that they hope will be covered by the annual exclusion. To increase the amount that may be contributed tax free, *A*'s trust grants Crummey powers of withdrawal (see Chapter 14) to *A*'s children and to *B* and to *C.* *B*'s trust grants withdrawal powers to *B*'s children and to *A* and to *C.* And *C*'s trust grants withdrawal powers to *C*'s children and to *A* and to *B.* Do you have any reason to doubt that the reciprocal transfer doctrine will apply? Compare Estate of Cristofani v. Commissioner, 97 T.C. 74 (1991), *acq. in result,* with Rev. Rul. 85-24. See page 897 for more on this topic.

More Than One Grantor. Suppose that two or more persons (including the decedent) contributed property to a single trust in which the decedent had a property interest or a power of the type that triggers §§2036(a)(2), 2037, or 2038(a)(1). Or a transfer is made to an existing trust to which one or more other persons previously made transfers? How is the amount includible in the decedent's gross estate to be calculated? In Estate of Bell v. Commissioner, 66 T.C. 729, 736-737 (1976), *acq.*, the government argued that a percentage of the value of the trust principal based on values determined on the date of the decedent's contribution to the trust should be applied to calculate the amount includible. The court said:

Where property so transferred by the several grantors of a trust is commingled with other property and cannot be identified, the formula advocated by [the government] may have merit. See Estate of Karagheusian v. Commissioner, 23 T.C. 806, 812-813 (1955), *rev'd on other grounds*, 233 F.2d 197 (2d Cir. 1956). See also Estate of Thompson v. Commissioner, 58 T.C. 880, 890-891 (1972), *aff'd*, 495 F.2d 246 (2d Cir. 1974). If specific property transferred by a decedent is capable of identification, however, the value of such specific property should be included in the gross estate. Estate of Kinney v. Commissioner, 39 T.C. 728, 733-734 (1963). Conversely, where someone other than the decedent has transferred specific assets to a trust which can be identified or traced, it is only reasonable that their value should be excluded in making the required allocations.

Rev. Rul. 78-74 announced the government's support of the result in *Bell*. But Treas. Reg. §26.2654-1(a)(2) provides a fractionalization approach for generation-skipping transfer tax purposes if contributions are made to a single trust by several grantors. The single trust is divided into separate trusts, based on the value of a person's contribution immediately after the contribution was made, divided by the value that the single trust had at that time.

7.   *Retention.*   To apply, §2036 requires a transfer with *retained* enjoyment or powers. Notwithstanding that it is a fundamental requisite, it almost never is called into question. The following case shows that it seldom needs to be.

Estate of Wyly v. Commissioner
610 F.2d 1282 (5th Cir. 1980)

GARZA, J.: We are squarely confronted in these three federal estate tax cases with a single question of law, a question answered by way of what is alleged to be dicta thirty years ago in Commissioner v. Estate of Hinds, 180 F.2d 930 (5th Cir. 1950). Is §2036(a)(1) (hereinafter referred to as "the Act"), applicable automatically to any gift of property from a decedent to his or her spouse in Texas, solely because the decedent by unavoidable operation of Texas law is left with a residue of interest in any income generated by such gifted property?

If the answer is affirmative, then it is clear that a portion of the property will by the Act be includable in the gross estate of the decedent. The Government and other parties hereto, and even separate decisions of the Tax Court differ on what fraction of the value of gifted property should be included.[11]

We will not answer the collateral question, for we hold today that the Act does not automatically render some portion of the value of property gifted by one Texas spouse to another includable in the giving spouse's gross estate, solely on the basis of Texas community property law. In so holding, we mean to breathe new life into the "dicta" of *Hinds*, to follow the intention of Congress in enacting this provision, and to accord with the great weight of authority handed down by the courts of Texas.

DISPOSITION BELOW

The cases arrive from different courts and bring different holdings. The facts and disposition of each must be summarized in some detail.

Estate of Wyly v. Commissioner, 69 T.C. 227 (1977), comes to us from the Tax Court. The case involved an irrevocable trust created by Charles J. Wyly and his wife, in March of 1971, funded with shares of stock which were community property of the Wylys. The trustees were to distribute the income to Mrs. Wyly, and upon her death the corpus was to be divided and held in trust for grandchildren. The trustees were given the power to invade the corpus for the benefit of Mrs. Wyly, and she could withdraw up to $5,000 of it annually.

Mr. Wyly died in 1972 and a deficiency was assessed against his estate following an audit of the estate tax return. The Commissioner determined that the Act applied to the trust on a theory that the decedent retained an interest in community property trans-

---

11. In *Hinds*, the Tax Court held that one-fourth of the total value of property transferred was includable, that fraction representing one-half of the one-half community property interest conveyed. The Commissioner maintained there, and in the three cases before us, that the full one-half community property interest should be included. The estates of Wyly, Castleberry, and Frankel argue that the one-fourth fraction would be correct if any portion is includable. In *Castleberry*, the Tax Court followed the one-fourth measure, but in *Wyly*, it held the full one-half includable, basing its decision upon the "reciprocal trust doctrine" and trust features of that case. In *Frankel*, the Government sought to obtain a full one-half, but the district court held no portion of the transfers value includable.

ferred to the trust. The Tax Court sustained this position by its decision under review.

In Estate of Castleberry v. Commissioner, 68 T.C. 682 (1977), the Tax Court confronted the applicability of the Act to gifts of community property between Texas spouses on facts free of the complicating trust provisions present in *Wyly*. Prior to Mr. Castleberry's death in 1971, he made gifts to his wife of his one-half community interest in several municipal bonds. On its federal estate tax return, petitioner did not include any portion of the value of these bonds in decedent's gross estate. The Commissioner determined that a portion of their total fair market value was includable, under the Act. The Tax Court ruled in the Commissioner's favor.

Frankel v. United States comes not from the Tax Court but from a District Court, and brings a ruling directly contrary to those of the Tax Court. The decedent, Jules R. Frankel, died in July of 1973. Between 1960 and 1972 he made seven transfers, giving his community property interest in certain assets to his wife. The taxpayer brought this estate tax refund case to avoid inclusion. The District Court granted partial summary judgment for the taxpayer on that issue, without discussion of its reasoning.

THE COMPETING CONTENTIONS

The Government's rationale for the applicability of the Act to these transfers is based upon provisions of Texas community property law which will be examined in detail below. The crucial portions of that body of Texas law are those which cause the income from the separate property of a spouse to be the community property of both spouses. The Government contends that the Act applies because it requires inclusion in a decedent's gross estate of the value of any property transferred to another if there was retained a "right to the income" from such property. On the facts before us, the Government maintains that a gift from one spouse to another becomes the separate property of the donee, but that any income from the gift automatically becomes the community property of both, the resultant interest in the donor triggering the Act. The Tax Court so held, and further found, as prerequisites to its applicability ruling, that such an interest was "retained" within the meaning of the Act, and that it was retained "under" these transfers.

The taxpayers do not dispute that the donors became automatically possessed of a community property interest in the income from their gifts, but contend that the resultant interests were so "limited, contingent, and expectant" that they did not approach the level required to come within the Act. They argue further that these interests were neither "retained" within the Act, or "under" the gift transfers. . . .

Against this background, and recognizing that state law determines the natures of a property interest while federal law determines whether it is subject to taxation, Morgan v. Commissioner, 309 U.S. 78 (1940), we proceed to an analysis of the community property law of Texas, and its impact on the application of the Act.

TEXAS COMMUNITY PROPERTY LAW

The basic concept underlying the Texas community system of marital property is derived from the Spanish Civil Law, a heritage of Spanish-Mexican sovereignty. Its fundamental precept is that marriage is a partnership in its tangible incidents as well as in the ideal personal relationship. Under the system, the rights and duties of a spouse with regard to specific property may vary as to ownership, the right to control, and corresponding liability. . . .

Article 16 §15 of the Texas Constitution sets out two basic classifications of marital property. "Separate property" of a spouse is specifically defined as that acquired by its owner before marriage, or "that acquired afterward by *gift*, devise, or descent" (emphasis added). Community property is all other property acquired by a spouse during marriage. Thus, a gift of property from one spouse to another or a gift of a spouse's one-half community interest to the other spouse results in separate ownership in the donee, by the mandatory constitutional definition. Story v. Marshall, 24 Tex. 305 (1859).

However, by the equally mandatory operation of the same provision, the *income* from separate property becomes the community property of both spouses. Arnold v. Leonard, 273 S.W.2d 799 (Tex. 1925). Neither spouse may change the character of such income from community property to separate property before the income comes into existence. Burton v. Bell, 380 S.W.2d 561 (Tex. 1964). Thus, the only way spouses could cause such income to become separate property is to partition it after it comes into existence, and the community property interest has automatically vested in both. In our cases, it is undisputed that the donor spouse had imposed upon him a community property interest in the income from the transferred property.

. . . .

[O]ur next inquiry [is]: as these interests were created by operation of law, were they "retained" within the Act "under" the transfers? We hold they were not. It is conceded that if they were not, the Act does not apply. . . . In Texas, on the facts of our cases, the donors did all they could do to transfer the totality of their interest and control. Nevertheless, the constitutional definition of community property imposed such an interest on them. . . .

We do not believe that an interest, created solely by operation of law as the unavoidable result of what was in form and within the intendment of the parties the most complete conveyance possible, is a retention within the Act. There must be some act or omission on the part of the donor, such as an express or an implied agreement between donor and donee at the time of the transfer, which provides for retention. . . .

We are persuaded that this interest arose simply by operation of law, and not "under" the transfers of property we have before us, within the Act.

CONCLUSION

For the reasons stated in detail above, it is our conclusion that §2036(a)(l) does not sweep the value of these transfers into the donor's gross estate. To summarize our review of federal and state law, we have held that the donor's community property interest in the income produced by these transferred properties . . . arises only by operation of a mandatory definition contained in the Texas constitution which spouses may not circumvent, and that thus it is neither "retained" within the meaning of the Act, nor arisen "under" the transfers concerned. . . .

Accordingly, the judgments of the United States Tax Court in *Estate of Wyly v. Commissioner* and *Estate of Castleberry v. Commissioner* are reversed, and those causes are remanded to that court for proceedings consistent with this opinion. The judgment of the District Court in *Frankel v. United States* is affirmed.

The government subsequently adopted a position not reproduced here from the Fifth Circuit opinion in *Wyly* that, under Texas community property law, a decedent's interest in income from separate property of the decedent's spouse does not qualify as an income interest under §2036. Rev. Rul. 81-221. The ruling did not address the "retention" issue, which was the basis of the rationale shown above in *Wyly*.

A different form of retention issue was involved in PLR 200101021, in which spouses created a joint settlor trust that provided for both of them during their joint lives and for the survivor until the second death. The first spouse to die was given a general testamentary power to appoint all of the trust property, which caused §2038(a)(1) or §2041(a)(2) inclusion of the entire trust in the estate of whomever died first. By virtue of that inclusion the survivor's benefit in the ongoing trust was not regarded as having been "retained" for §2036(a)(1) purposes but, instead, it was treated as having passed from the deceased spouse, meaning that the survivor would not suffer §2036(a)(1) retained interest inclusion of any part of that trust when the survivor dies. That result is much like the position taken in Treas. Reg. §25.2523(f)-1(f) *Example 11* regarding the cleansing effect of §2044 inclusion of an inter vivos QTIP marital trust in the estate of the donee spouse, followed by a secondary life estate in the donor spouse. Either treatment avoids §2036(a)(1) inclusion when the original donor spouse dies, because estate tax inclusion in the donee spouse's estate cleanses the survivor's involvement with the trust. It is as if there was no retention of enjoyment by the survivor.

Yet another situation arises in which the retention issue is implicated, in this case involving a provision that the government on occasion insists that a trust grantor include in a trust to reimburse the grantor for any income tax liability imposed by the grantor trust income tax rules. PLR 200120021 held that such a reimbursement provision does not constitute a sufficient retention of benefits to trigger §2036(a)(1) estate tax inclusion. Quaere: can you justify that result?

A final useful illustration is PLR 9729024, in which the taxpayer owned two lots that once were one, with a common driveway that served both. Upon a gift of one of those lots the taxpayer reserved an easement to use that driveway to access the other lot, which the government ruled was not a retention of enjoyment such as to trigger §2036(a)(1) inclusion of the transferred lot (although the value of the easement was said to be §2033 includible). It was as if the easement was a totally separate asset than the lot that was conveyed away.

8.   *Prearrangements.*   Imagine that *A* made a gift of $500,000 to *B*, who later placed the $500,000 in a trust under which the income is to be paid to *A* for life, remainder to *A*'s children in equal shares. Upon *A*'s death, will §2036(a)(1) require inclusion of the value of this trust in *A*'s gross estate? Does it matter what "later" means in this situation, or how *B* transferred the property back into trust for *A*? See the last sentence of Treas. Reg. §20.2036-1(a) and compare PLR 9141027 and TAM 9128005. As the following material shows, these cases arise often, usually in unplanned situations.

Estate of McNichol v. Commissioner
265 F.2d 667 (3d Cir. 1959)

STEEL, J.: More than nine years before his death, the decedent purported to convey certain income-producing real estate to his children. Thereafter, pursuant to an oral understanding with his children, the decedent continued to receive the rents from the properties until his death. The Tax Court held that the properties were includable in the decedent's gross estate under §[2036(a)(1)]. 29 T.C. 1179. That decision is before us for review.

The following findings by the Tax Court are supported by the record and are accepted as a basis for our decision:

Between 1939 and 1942 the decedent, a Pennsylvania resident, executed general warranty deeds to his children for income-producing real estate, together with the rentals therefrom, which he owned in Pennsylvania. The deeds were recorded. They reserved no interest in the realty or rents to the decedent, and the decedent received no consideration in connection with the transaction. Following the execution of the last deed the grantees, as owners-landlords entitled to the rental income, registered the properties with the O.P.A.

Contemporaneously with and subsequent to the execution of the deeds, it was orally understood between the decedent and his children that the decedent should retain for his lifetime the income from the real estate. In accordance with this understanding the decedent actually received all of such income from the dates of the deeds to the time of his death.

In his federal income tax returns for 1948 to 1950, inclusive, and for the period from January 1, 1951 to the time of his death on June 17, 1951 the decedent reported the rents as his personal income.[12] In the same returns the decedent claimed as deductions depreciation, taxes and water rent applicable to the properties.

The petitioners contended before the Tax Court that under Pennsylvania law the deeds conferred upon the children a fee simple title, that the Pennsylvania statute of frauds barred the grantor from enforcing his oral understanding against his children, and that the grantor therefore had retained no "right" to the income "under" the transfer within the meaning of the statute. The Tax Court rejected this argument and held that Pennsylvania law was immaterial, and that the test of gross estate includability under §[2036(a)(1)] was a factual one; i.e., whether a decedent in reality had retained possession or enjoyment of the property. Finding that the collection of the rents by decedent pursuant to his under-standing with his children constituted a factual enjoyment of the properties under the transfer, the Tax Court held that the properties were properly included in decedent's gross estate.

Petitioners argue that §[2036(a)(1)] is inapplicable to a transfer with a retained income interest unless that interest is reserved in

---

12. The record fails to reveal how the rents were treated in prior periods.

the instrument of transfer. This argument is based upon the statutory provision that the income must be retained *"under"* the transfer. This is too constricted an interpretation to place on the statute. The statute means only that the life interest must be retained in connection with or as an incident to the transfer. That the reservation need not be expressed in the instrument of transfer is implicitly recognized by the reciprocal trust decisions. Orvis v. Higgins, 180 F.2d 537 (2d Cir. 1950); Estate of Cole v. Commissioner, 140 F.2d 636 (8th Cir. 1944); Estate of Moreno v. Commissioner, 260 F.2d 389 (5th Cir. 1948). They hold that when two persons separately create equivalent trusts simultaneously, with income payable from each trust to the settlor of the other, the property transferred by each settlor is nevertheless subject to §[2036(a)(1)] even though neither trust instrument reserves any interest in the income to its settlor or refers to the companion trust. Petitioners' argument is irreconcilable with these holdings. . . .

Next, petitioners point out that the statute speaks of the retention of "the right to the income." Emphasizing the word "right," petitioners argue that Congress has decreed that §[2036(a)(1)] is applicable only if a transferor reserves to himself an enforceable claim to the income. Since, according to petitioners, the statute of frauds of Pennsylvania would foreclose judicial enforcement of the oral understanding between the decedent and his children, petitioners conclude that the decedent had no "right" to the income from the property.

It is not necessary for us to delve into Pennsylvania law, for the question is not one of local law. Rather, it is whether Congress intended that §[2036(a)(1)] should subject to an estate tax property conveyed under circumstances which here prevail. While state law creates legal interests and rights, it is the federal law which designates which of these interests and rights shall be taxed. Morgan v. Commissioner, 309 U.S. 78, 80-81 (1940); Helvering v. Stuart, 317 U.S. 154, 162 (1942).

In seeking to discover the type of transfers at which §[2036(a)(1)] is aimed, the words "right to the income" are not entitled to undue emphasis. Section [2036(a)(1)] states that property which has been transferred inter vivos is includable in the gross estate of a decedent when the decedent "has retained for his life . . . the possession or enjoyment of, or the right to the income from the property. . . ." Thus, the statute deals with two things: retention of "possession or enjoyment" and retention of "the right to the income."

The history of the statute discloses that "the right to the income" clause was not intended to limit the scope of the "possession or enjoyment" clause used in §[2036(a)(1)]. Section [2036(a)(1)] derives directly from §302(c) of the Act of 1926, as amended in 1931 and 1932. . . . The amendment of 1931 included for the first time express language taxing property which had been transferred inter vivos with a lifetime retention of "the possession or enjoyment of, or the income from" the property. This amendment said nothing about the "right to" income. The words "right to" were inserted for the first time by the 1932 amendment, and the language of the 1932 amendment was carried over into §[2036(a)(1)]. This insertion was to make clear that Congress intended that the statute should apply to cases where a decedent was entitled to income even though he did not actually receive it. [The court cited and quoted from the committee reports.] Hence, the "right to income" clause, instead of circumscribing the "possession or enjoyment" clause in its application to retained income, broadened its sweep.

The conclusion is irresistible that the petitioners' decedent "enjoyed" the properties until he died. If, as was said in Estate of Church, 335 U.S. at 645, the most valuable property attribute of stocks is their income, it is no less true that one of the most valuable incidents of income-producing real estate is the rent which it yields. He who receives the rent in fact enjoys the property. Enjoyment as used in the death tax statute is not a term of art, but is synonymous with substantial present economic benefit. Commissioner v. Estate of Holmes, 326 U.S. 480, 486 (1945). Under this realistic point of view the enjoyment of the properties which the decedent conveyed to his children was continued in decedent by prearrangement and ended only when he died. The transfers were clearly of a kind which Congress intended that §[2036(a)(1)] should reach. . . . Since Congress barred resort to formal trust agreements with reserved life estates as a means of circumventing the payment of death taxes, it is unreasonable to conclude that it intended to permit the accomplishment of the same result by an oral agreement having an identical effect. : . . .

The decision of the Tax Court will be affirmed.

9. *Implied Understandings.* A footnote to a passage in *McNichol* not reproduced said: "We intimate no opinion as to whether we would have [reached a contrary result] if, in the case before us, the decedent had received the rents following the transfer without an agreement with his children that he might do so." In Estate of McCabe v. United States, 475 F.2d 1142 (Ct. Cl. 1973), the decedent established an irrevocable inter vivos trust of certain property, naming his longtime friend and business associate as trustee and his wife as income beneficiary. Portions of the trust principal were paid over to the decedent on several occasions despite the absence of any provision in the trust instrument empowering the trustee to do so. In holding the value of the trust includible in the decedent's gross estate under §2036(a)(1), the court concluded that the dealings between the decedent and the trustee and the decedent's wife created an inference of an abdication to the decedent's interests and of a prearrangement that the decedent was entitled to control and enjoyment for life.

In Estate of Hendry v. Commissioner, 62 T.C. 861, 872-873 (1974), the court said:

> The retained interest of the decedent can arise from an implied understanding between the decedent and the person to whom the transfer was made . . . and such an agreement or understanding may be inferred from the facts and circumstances of the transfer and the subsequent use of the property. . . . Since §2036(a)(1) applies only in situations where the possession or enjoyment of, or the right to income from, the property is retained by the decedent at the time the transfer is made, the circumstances that inferentially establish an agreement must demonstrate that such an understanding occurred contemporaneously with the transfer. . . .
>
> In a case such as this, particularly where the circumstances imply a prearrangement, the burden of proof is on the petitioner to establish that an implied understanding or arrangement did not in fact exist. . . . We realize that this burden requiring the taxpayer to disprove the existence of an intrafamily prearrangement is a heavy one. . . . However, as this Court [previously] stated . . . "such difficulty does not justify exclusion from the operation of §2036(a)(1)." This section is designed to include in the gross estate of the decedent, all property of decedent which was the subject of an incomplete inter vivos transfer. . . . The mandate underlying the includability of an interest pursuant to §2036(a)(1) is broad. . . . Consequently, we cannot countenance an attempt to circumvent the perimeters of this section by relieving the taxpayer of the burden of negating the existence of an agreement and, concurrently, requiring the [government] to establish that such understanding did exist.

The most common form of retained enjoyment is illustrated next and, as the note that follows it shows, these can range from exclusive enjoyment to co-occupancy with a spouse or children.

Estate of Linderme v. Commissioner
52 T.C. 305 (1969)

TANNENWALD, J.: . . . Decedent executed a quitclaim deed to [his] residence to his three sons in 1956. At that time, he delivered the deed to his son Emil. While the other two sons were not made aware of the delivery until after the father's death, we think it a reasonable assumption that Emil's actions in accepting the deed and in dealing with the decedent in respect of subsequent treatment of the property coincided with their views. Although the deed had been recorded prior to delivery, it was put into a file with decedent's other papers — a factor perhaps of more significance if there were an issue as to whether any gift was made, but also having some bearing on the existence of an understanding with respect to decedent's interest in the property. Decedent continued in *exclusive* possession of the residence until he entered [a] nursing home. The residence was unoccupied from that time until his death about a year and a half later. There was neither consideration of any sale or rental of, nor any effort to sell or rent, the residence during that interval, thus indicating that the property was being held available for decedent's possible return. From the date of the quitclaim deed until his death, decedent's funds were used to pay all the expenses relating to the property, including real estate taxes, insurance premiums, and costs of maintenance. Even after the property was sold, part of the proceeds of sale were used to pay the obligations of decedent's estate. [T]his factor . . . is a further indication, when taken into account with the other elements involved herein, of a retained interest in decedent.

Petitioner claims that the application of §2036(a)(1) under the foregoing circumstances would unjustifiably extend the frontiers of that section contrary to the mandate of the decided cases and particularly our decision in Estate of Gutchess v. Commissioner, 46 T.C. 554 (1966), *acq.* We disagree. Petitioner correctly concludes that it is neither necessary that the proscribed retained interest be expressed in the instrument of transfer nor necessary that the decedent have a legally enforceable right to possession or enjoyment. Petitioner, however, points out that, in all of the decided cases in which §2036(a) was held applicable to situations similar to that involved herein, the property was income-producing . . . and that, in all of the decided cases which refused to apply that section, the property involved was non-income-producing. . . . Petitioner then seeks to parlay the foregoing decisions into the negative proposition that, unless income-producing property is involved, no agreement or understanding with respect to a decedent's retention of "possession or enjoyment" can be inferred.

To be sure, the factual distinction emphasized by petitioner does exist in these cases. But a more significant element seems to have been the fact that there was no withholding of occupancy from the donee. In the absence of such withholding, the continued co-occupancy of the property by the donor with the donee was considered, in and of itself, an insufficient basis for inferring an agreement as to retained possession or enjoyment. See *Estate of Gutchess*, 46 T.C. at 556-557. The presence of income from the property was simply a useful ancillary tool for decision rather than a limiting principle imposed as a matter of law. The retention of income was thus only an example, albeit a very clear one, of "possession or enjoyment." . . .

In the instant case, the decedent continued to occupy the residence to the exclusion of the donees or anyone else whose status stemmed from their rights to the property. Surely that occupancy was as much an "economic benefit" as if decedent had rented the property and obtained the income therefrom. . . . Additionally, such *exclusive* occupancy, while not necessarily determinative, should be accorded greater significance than co-occupancy in the process of evaluating the various facets of a particular situation in order to determine whether an understanding existed whereby a decedent would retain possession or enjoyment.

In Commissioner v. Estate of Church, 335 U.S. 632 (1949), the Supreme Court, in dealing with the predecessor of §2036, in the context of transfers in trust, cut the shackles of earlier decisions and stated (335 U.S. at 645-646): "An estate tax cannot be avoided by any trust transfer except by a bona fide transfer in which the settlor, absolutely, unequivocally, irrevocably, and without possible reservations, parts with all of his title and all of his possession and all of his enjoyment of the transferred property. After such a transfer has been made, the settlor must be left with no present legal title in the property, no possible reversionary interest in that title, and no right to possess or to enjoy the property then or thereafter. In other words such a transfer must be immediate and out and out, and must be unaffected by whether the grantor lives or dies."

We take our cue from this mandate for a broad inclusion within the gross estate pursuant to §2036(a)(1). The burden of proof is on the taxpayer and, in cases of this type, that burden may be a heavy one. . . . But such difficulty does not justify exclusion from the operation of §2036(a)(1). On the basis of the entire record herein, we are satisfied as our ultimate finding of fact reflects that, beyond the mere existence of the family relationship and the mere occupancy of the premises, decedent did have an understanding whereby he retained the exclusive use of the residence until his death. The property in question is thus includible in decedent's gross estate under §2036(a)(1). . . .

10.   *Co-occupancy With the Donee.* In *Linderme* the decedent continued after the transfer in *exclusive* occupancy of the residence until his death. The government's position that §2036(a)(1) applies in similar situations was established in Rev. Rul. 70-155 and has been sustained in numerous other decisions. See, e.g., Estate of Maxwell v. Commissioner, 98 T.C. 594 (1992), *aff'd*, 3 F.3d 591 (2d Cir. 1993) (alleged sale with leaseback recharacterized as gift with retained life estate); Estate of Callahan v. Commissioner, 42 T.C.M. (CCH) 362 (1982); Estate of Bianchi v. Commissioner, 44 T.C.M. (CCH) 422 (1982); Estate of Rapelje v. Commissioner, 73 T.C. 82 (1979) (almost exclusive occupancy); but see Estate of Powell v. Commissioner, 63 T.C.M. (CCH) 3192 (1992) (decedent transferred only 60% and ceased occupancy before death, when decedent was required by health considerations to move to a nursing home).

The results are not so uniform if the decedent does not continue to occupy the transferred residence exclusively but instead occupies it with the donee. The courts have held §2036(a)(1) to be inapplicable if the donee was the decedent's spouse. Union Planters National Bank v. United States, 361 F.2d 662 (6th Cir. 1966); Estate of Gutchess v. Commissioner, 46 T.C. 554 (1966), *acq.* The government acquiesced in *Gutchess* and explicitly conceded that "co-occupancy, where the donor and donee are husband and wife, does not of itself support an inference of an agreement or understanding as to retained possession or enjoyment by the donor." Rev. Rul. 70-155. *Union Planters* emphasized that continued co-occupancy with a donee-spouse is a natural incident to the marriage and that the government's attempted inclusion is as illogical as it would be to suggest that personal property, such as an automobile, should be included in the donor-spouse's gross estate merely because the donee-spouse allowed the donor to use that property. Today the marital deduction probably makes the spouse cases irrelevant and, indeed, §2036(a)(1) inclusion with a §2056 marital deduction at death might be a good result for basis adjustment purposes.

The results under §2036(a)(1) are much less predictable if the donee with whom the decedent continued to occupy the residence was not the decedent's spouse, although some courts have held that inclusion is not warranted. Diehl v. United States, 68-1 U.S. Tax Cas. (CCH) ¶12,506 (W.D. Tenn. 1967); City National Bank v. United States, 78-1 U.S. Tax Cas. (CCH) ¶13,219 (D. Conn. 1977) (jury finding); Estate of Roemer v. Commissioner, 46 T.C.M. (CCH) 1176 (1983). Rev. Rul. 78-409 stated that the government will not follow *Diehl* and will continue to press for inclusion in co-occupancy cases not involving spouses. The donee in the Ruling was the decedent's child, and the decedent continued to occupy the residence with the donee and the donee's spouse, which is not such an unusual transaction if the child is induced to care for the decedent in exchange for a present gift of the residence, which the child is unwilling to risk receiving only under the decedent's will. Such a case also would raise full and adequate consideration possibilities. See the parenthetical in §2036(a), and the discussion next below in *Maxwell*.

Would the government's case be stronger or weaker if the donees with whom the donor continued to occupy the residence were the donor's *minor* children, and would it matter whether they still were minors when the donor died?

In Revenue Ruling 79-109 the decedent, *D*, owned a residence that *D* used for vacation purposes during December, January, and February, and leased to others during the rest of the year. *D* conveyed the residence to *D*'s adult children, reserving the right to use or lease the residence each year during the month of January. The rental value for the months of December, January, and February was twice the rental value for the balance of the year, so *D*'s month was 2/15ths, not 1/12th, of the total value of the property using that measure. Because the amount includible is only the value of the retained portion, the government ruled that *D*'s retained right to use the property or receive the rent for January represented 13.3% of the fair market value of the property and required inclusion of that percentage of the federal estate tax value of the property, which represented "that portion of the property that would be necessary to yield the retained income right." The notion of determining how much of a prior transfer is needed to generate an income flow is a familiar issue that we will encounter again. But first, let's look at the full and adequate consideration exception.

Estate of Maxwell v. Commissioner
3 F.3d 591 (2d Cir. 1993)

LASKER, District Judge: This appeal presents challenges to the tax court's interpretation of §2036(a) of the Internal Revenue Code, relating to "Transfers with retained life estate." The petitioner, the Estate of Lydia G. Maxwell, contends that the tax court erred in holding that the transaction at issue (a) was a transfer with retained life estate within the meaning of §2036 and (b) was not a bona fide sale for adequate and full consideration under that statute.

The decision of the tax court is affirmed.

On March 14, 1984, Lydia G. Maxwell (the "decedent") conveyed her personal residence, which she had lived in since 1957, to her son Winslow Maxwell, her only heir, and his wife Margaret Jane Maxwell (the "Maxwells"). Following the transfer, the decedent continued to reside in the house until her death on July 30, 1986. At the time of the transfer, she was eighty-two years old and was suffering from cancer.

The transaction was structured as follows:

1) The residence was sold by the decedent to the Maxwells for $270,000;[13]

2) Simultaneously with the sale, the decedent forgave $20,000 of the purchase price (which was equal in amount to the annual gift tax exclusion to which she was entitled);

3) The Maxwells executed a $250,000 mortgage note in favor of decedent;

4) The Maxwells leased the premises to her for five years at the monthly rental of $1800; and

5) The Maxwells were obligated to pay and did pay certain expenses associated with the property following the transfer, including property taxes, insurance costs, and unspecified "other expenses."

While the decedent paid the Maxwells rent totalling $16,200 in 1984, $22,183 in 1985 and $12,600 in 1986, the Maxwells paid the decedent interest on the mortgage totalling $16,875 in 1984, $21,150 in 1985, and $11,475 in 1986. As can be observed, the rent paid by the decedent to the Maxwells came remarkably close to matching the mortgage interest which they paid to her. In 1984, she paid the Maxwells only $675 less than they paid her; in 1985, she paid them only $1,033 more than they paid her, and in 1986 she paid the Maxwells only $1,125 more than they paid her.

Not only did the rent functionally cancel out the interest payments made by the Maxwells, but the Maxwells were at no time called upon to pay any of the principal on the $250,000 mortgage debt; it was forgiven in its entirety. As petitioner's counsel admitted at oral argument, although the Maxwells had executed the mortgage note, "there was an intention by and large that it not be paid." Pursuant to this intention, in each of the following years preceding her death, the decedent forgave $20,000 of the mortgage principal, and, by a provision of her will executed on March 16, 1984 (that is, just two days after the transfer), she forgave the remaining indebtedness.

The decedent reported the sale of her residence on her 1984 federal income tax return but did not pay any tax on the sale because she elected to use the once-in-a-lifetime exclusion on the sale or exchange of a principal residence provided for by §121.

She continued to occupy the house by herself until her death. At no time during her occupancy did the Maxwells attempt to sell the house to anyone else, but, on September 22, 1986,

---

13. The parties have stipulated that the fair market value of the property on the date of the purported sale was $280,000.

shortly after the decedent's death, they did sell the house for $550,000. . . .

There are two questions before us: Did the decedent retain possession or enjoyment of the property following the transfer. And if she did, was the transfer a bona fide sale for an adequate and full consideration in money or money's worth. . . .

In numerous cases, the tax court has held, where an aged family member transferred her home to a relative and continued to reside there until her death, that the decedent-transferor had retained "possession or enjoyment" of the property within the meaning of §2036.

. . . [T]he tax court found as a fact that the decedent had transferred her home to the Maxwells "with the understanding, at least implied, that she would continue to reside in her home until her death." This finding was based upon the decedent's advanced age, her medical condition, and the overall result of the sale and lease. The lease was, in the tax court's words, "merely window dressing" — it had no substance.

The tax court's findings of fact are reversible only if clearly erroneous. Bausch & Lomb, Inc. v. Commissioner, 933 F.2d 1084, 1088 (2d Cir. 1991). We agree with the tax court's finding that the decedent transferred her home to the Maxwells "with the understanding, at least implied, that she would continue to reside in her home until her death," and certainly do not find it to be clearly erroneous. The decedent did, in fact, live at her residence until she died, and she had sole possession of the residence during the period between the day she sold her home to the Maxwells and the day she died. There is no evidence that the Maxwells ever intended to occupy the house themselves, or to sell or lease it to anyone else during the decedent's lifetime. Moreover, the Maxwells' failure to demand payment by the estate, as they were entitled to do under the lease, of the rent due for the months following decedent's death and preceding their sale of the property, also supports the tax court's finding. . . .

For the reasons stated above, we conclude that the decedent did retain possession or enjoyment of the property for life and turn to the question of whether the transfer constituted "a bona fide sale for adequate and full consideration in money or money's worth."

Section 2036(a) provides that even if possession or enjoyment of transferred property is retained by the decedent until her death, if the transfer was a bona fide sale for adequate and full consideration in money or money's worth, the property is not includible in the estate. Petitioner contends that the Maxwells paid an "adequate and full consideration" for the decedent's residence, $270,000 total, consisting of the $250,000 mortgage note given by the Maxwells to the decedent, and the $20,000 the decedent forgave simultaneously with the conveyance.[14]

The tax court held that neither the Maxwells' mortgage note nor the decedent's $20,000 forgiveness constituted consideration within the meaning of the statute.

. . . As to the $250,000 mortgage note, the tax court held that:

> Regardless of whether the $250,000 mortgage note might otherwise qualify as "adequate and full consideration in money or money's worth" for a $270,000 or $280,000 house, the mortgage note here had no value at all if there was no intention that it would ever be paid.

> The conduct of decedent and the Maxwells strongly suggest that neither party intended the Maxwells to pay any part of the principal of either the original note or any successor note.

There is no question that the mortgage note here is a fully secured, legally enforceable obligation on its face. The question is whether it is actually what it purports to be — a bona fide instrument of indebtedness — or whether it is a facade. The petitioner argues not only that an allegedly unenforceable intention to forgive indebtedness does not deprive the indebtedness of its status as "consideration in money or money's worth" but also that "[t]his is true even if there was an implied agreement exactly as found by the Tax Court." . . .

We agree with the tax court that where, as here, there is an implied agreement between the parties that the grantee would never be called upon to make any payment to the grantor, as, in fact, actually occurred, the note given by the grantee had "no value at all." We emphatically disagree with the petitioner's view of the law as it applies to the facts of this case. As the Supreme Court has remarked,

> The family relationship often makes it possible for one to shift tax incidence by surface changes of ownership without

---

14. As noted above, the parties have stipulated that the fair market value of the property on the date of the purported sale was $280,000. The Estate contends that $270,000 was full and adequate consideration for the sale, with a broker, for a house appraised at $280,000. We assume this fact to be true for purposes of determining whether the transaction was one for "an adequate and full consideration in money or money's worth."

disturbing in the least his dominion and control over the subject of the gift or the purposes for which the income from the property is used.

Commissioner v. Culbertson, 337 U.S. 733, 746 (1949). There can be no doubt that intent is a relevant inquiry in determining whether a transaction is "bona fide." As another panel of this Court held recently, construing a parallel provision of the Internal Revenue Code, in a case involving an intrafamily transfer:

> when the bona fides of promissory notes is at issue, the taxpayer must demonstrate affirmatively that "there existed at the time of the transaction a real expectation of repayment and an intent to enforce the collection of the indebtedness." . . .

Flandreau v. Commissioner, 994 F. 2d 91, 93 (2d Cir. 1993), slip op. at 3481 (May 26, 1993) (case involving §2053(c)(1)). In language strikingly apposite to the situation here, the court stated:

> it is appropriate to look beyond the form of the transactions and to determine, as the tax court did here, that the gifts and loans back to decedent were "component parts of single transactions."

The tax court concluded that the evidence "viewed as a whole" left the "unmistakable impression" that

> regardless of how long decedent lived following the transfer of her house, the entire principal balance of the mortgage note would be forgiven, and the Maxwells would not be required to pay any of such principal.

The petitioner's reliance on Haygood v. Commissioner, 42 T.C. 936 (1964), not followed by Rev. Rul. 77-299, 1977-2 C.B. 343, Kelley v. Commissioner, 63 T.C. 321 (1974), not followed by Rev. Rul. 77-299, 1977-2 C.B. 343, and Wilson v. Commissioner, 64 T.C.M. (CCH) 583 (1992),[15] is misplaced. Those cases held only that intent to forgive notes in the future does not per se disqualify such notes from constituting valid consideration. In contrast, in the case at hand, the decedent did far more than merely "indicate[ ] an intent to forgive the indebtedness in the future." *Wilson*, 64 T.C.M. (CCH) 583, 584 (1992).

---

15. Apart from all of the other distinctions outlined below, *Wilson* is not a tax court opinion but a tax court memorandum; moreover, the decision in *Wilson* succeeded the tax court decision in this case.

In *Haygood*, *Kelley*, and *Wilson*, the question was whether transfers of property by petitioners to their children or grand-children in exchange for notes were completed gifts within the meaning of the Internal Revenue Code. None of the notes was actually paid by the grantees; instead the notes were either forgiven by petitioners at or about the time they became due (*Haygood* and *Kelley*) or the petitioner died prior to the date when the note was due (*Wilson*). In those circumstances, the tax court held that the notes received by petitioners, secured by valid vendor's liens or by deed of trust on the property, constituted valuable consideration for the transfer of the property.

The *Kelley* court made no finding as to intent to forgive the notes. In *Haygood*, although the court did find that the "petitioner had no intention of collecting the debts but did intend to forgive each payment as it became due," it also found that the transfer of the property to the children had been a mistake.[16] And, the *Wilson* court found that:

> The uncontradicted testimony in this case establishes that petitioner and her children intended that the children would sell the property and pay the note with the proceeds.

Wilson, 64 T.C.M. (CCH) at 584.

By contrast, in the case at hand, the tax court found that, at the time the note was executed, there was "an understanding" between the Maxwells and the decedent that the note would be forgiven. . . .

If *Haygood* is read as holding that the intent to forgive notes has no effect on the question of whether the notes constitute valid consideration, it appears to be inconsistent with controlling tax principles and tax court decisions. For example, in Deal v. Commissioner, 29 T.C. 730 (1958),[17] the tax court held that the notes

---

16.   The court stated that it was "eminently clear from the testimony that it was petitioner's intent to give only a $3,000 interest [in the property] to each of her sons" that year but her lawyer accidentally structured the transaction to give the entire property to the petitioner's sons. Haygood v. Commissioner, 42 T.C. 936, 942 (1964).

17.   *Deal* involved a conveyance by the taxpayer of a remainder interest in real property to a trust for the benefit of her four daughters. The taxpayer forgave a $3,000 portion of each note to each daughter in the year of the transfer of the property, and a similar portion of each note in the two subsequent years, and the remaining balance of the note in the following year. The tax court held that the taxpayer had made a gift of the remainder interest to the children.

The petitioner claims that *Deal* "may have been wrongly decided." However, *Deal* is still good law. Although *Haygood* reached a different conclusion, the court was careful not to overrule *Deal* but to distinguish it on its facts. Haygood v. Commissioner, 42 T.C. 936, 944 (1964).

executed by the children were not intended as consideration for the transfer, holding that:

> After carefully considering the record, we think that the notes executed by the daughters were not intended to be enforced and were not intended as consideration for the transfer by the petitioner, and that, in substance, the transfer of the property was by gift.

29 T.C. at 746, quoted by *Haygood*. See also Rev. Rul. 77-299, 1977-2 C.B. 343. Even *Kelley* stated that notes "in proper legal form and regular on their face" are only "prima facie" what they purport to be. *Kelley*, 63 T.C. at 324-325.

We also agree with the tax court that, as to the $20,000 which was forgiven simultaneously with the conveyance,

> In the absence of any clear and direct evidence that there existed an obligation or indebtedness capable of being forgiven . . .

the $20,000 item had "no economic substance."

To conclude, we hold that the conveyance was not a bona fide sale for an adequate and full consideration in money or money's worth.

. . . The petitioner argues finally that the tax court should be reversed because, under §2043, if there was any consideration in money or money's worth paid to the decedent, even if the payment was inadequate, the Estate is at least entitled to an exclusion pro tanto. The argument has no merit in the circumstances of this case. The tax court held, and we do also, that the transfer was without *any* consideration. Section 2043 applies only where the court finds that some consideration was given.

[The dissenting opinion of Judge WALKER is omitted.]

11.   *Discretionary Trusts and Trusts for Support.* One of the most difficult questions in all of wealth transfer taxes is whether D has retained a sufficient "right" to trust income to trigger §2036(a)(1) in the case of a discretionary trust or a trust for support. You will also discover in analyzing the various authorities that the respective income, gift, and estate tax rules are not consistent — they are not in pari materia. To illustrate:

(a) D transferred property in trust, directing the trustee (a Bank) to pay D so much or all — or none — of the income as the trustee in its unfettered discretion deems appropriate, accumulating and adding to principal any income not distributed annually. At D's death, the corpus (including accumulated income) is to be distributed to D's living children, in equal shares. Courts quite simply have split on whether this trust is subject to §2036(a)(1) inclusion in *D*'s gross estate at death. Compare Estate of Skinner v. United States, 316 F.2d 517 (3d Cir. 1963), with In re Estate of Uhl, 241 F.2d 867 (7th Cir. 1957), *rev'g* 25 T.C. 22 (1955); Estate of German v. United States, 85-1 U.S. Tax Cas. (CCH) ¶13,610 (Ct. Cl. 1985); Estate of Wells v. Commissioner, 42 T.C.M. (CCH) 1305 (1981); TAM 8213004; PLR 8037116. As a surrogate for answering how much enjoyment is enough to cause inclusion, courts have used an easier determination of inclusion in some cases, being whether *D*'s creditors would be able to reach the income interest of this trust. See Estate of Paxton v. Commissioner, 86 T.C. 785 (1986); RESTATEMENT (SECOND) OF TRUSTS §§147 and comment *c*, 156(2) (1959); and 2A Scott & Fratcher, THE LAW OF TRUSTS §156.2 (4th ed. 1987). If the answer is yes, because a spendthrift provision is not effective to hold the grantor's own creditors at bay, then courts easily find for inclusion. The converse remains to be tested, with the government to date only having opined that an effective self-settled spendthrift trust constitutes a completed gift on creation but not whether the retained enjoyment is adequate to generate estate tax liability. See 2 Casner & Pennell, ESTATE PLANNING §7.3.4.2 (6th ed. 1999).

For income tax purposes, *D* need not retain a "right" to trust income to cause §677(a)(1) grantor trust taxation to *D* of trust income not distributed to *D*.

Note that the amount of *D*'s gift in this case may exceed the value of the remainder interest. Compare Treas. Reg. §25.2511-2(b) with Rev. Ruls. 62-13, 77-378, and 76-103 and see also §2702 as discussed in Chapter 15.

(b) Courts have an easier time in these cases if the trustee's discretion is subject to an enforceable ascertainable standard because it is harder to argue that the taxpayer has no "rights" in the trust. It is arguable that the grantor is entitled to *more* enjoyment, not less, if the grantor's entitlement is not defined by an ascertainable standard, albeit enforceability may be harder. See Treas. Reg. §20.2041-1(b). Compare Estate of Green v. Commissioner, 64 T.C. 1049 (1975), with Rev. Rul. 76-368.

12.   *Transfers with Retention of Indirect Benefits.* An even harder case exists if *D* transferred property in trust, directing the trustee to pay the net income to *D*'s spouse, *S*, for life, principal upon *S*'s death to their children in equal shares. The trust instrument also directs the trustee to pay *D* any income needed by *D* to maintain *D*'s current standard of living to the extent *D*'s other sources of income are inadequate. Consider the following discharge of obligation materials.

The tax laws easily could be circumvented if a taxpayer could escape estate and income taxation by directing that the income from property transferred into trust be used to discharge the taxpayer's legal obligations rather than being paid directly to the taxpayer. This will not succeed.

For estate tax purposes, Treas. Reg. §20.2036-1(b)(2) interprets the §2036(a)(1) phrase "the possession or enjoyment of, or the right to the income from" the transferred property as including the right that the income or property be applied toward the discharge of legal obligations of the grantor (including the elusive legal obligation to support a dependent), or otherwise for the grantor's pecuniary benefit. There is ample judicial support for this interpretation.

Similarly, for income tax purposes, the phrase in §677(a)(1) treating the grantor as the owner of any portion of a trust "whose income . . . is . . . distributed to the grantor or the grantor's spouse," is interpreted in Treas. Reg. §1.677(a)-1(d) as including payments in discharge of a legal obligation of the grantor. Indeed, that explains why §677(b) is useful as a limit on an otherwise even broader income tax liability. Again there is ample judicial authority supporting this interpretation.

Transfers of Encumbered Property. In Estate of Hays v. Commissioner, 181 F.2d 169 (5th Cir. 1950), a few years before her death in 1943 the decedent irrevocably transferred Mississippi farmland to herself as trustee for the benefit of her four adult children. The trust was to terminate upon her death and the farmland was to be distributed in kind to the children in equal shares. The land, valued at roughly $107,000 at the time of the transfer and at the time of the decedent's death, was encumbered by about $36,000 of debt secured by mortgage notes. The land was transferred to the trust subject to these encumbrances, and the trust directed the trustee to service the debts using trust income. (Under the law generally, as well as under the law of Mississippi, the transferee of encumbered property who assumes the mortgage debt is primarily liable for the debt and the mortgagor becomes secondarily liable, even absent the mortgagee's concurrence.) When the decedent died the government argued unsuccessfully that the value of the trust property was includible in her gross estate under the forerunner of §2036(a)(1). The court of appeals said:

> The Tax Court held that there was nothing in the trust agreement or elsewhere in the evidence to indicate that the grantor intended for the trustee to assume the primary obligation of the mortgage notes. We agree with the petitioner that this ruling was erroneous as a matter of law. The trust instrument expressly provided that the trustee was therein authorized and directed to pay the indebtedness secured by the liens out of the income that might be derived from said lands or in such manner as she deemed to the best interest of the beneficiaries. . . . It is elementary that the grantee in an instrument who accepts such a trust is bound by its obligations . . . .

The indebtedness secured by liens on the land conveyed by decedent to the trust, although originally incurred by her, constituted no charge upon her capital assets after the conveyance. Thereafter, the decedent's liability for said indebtedness was contingent, not only upon the failure of the trust to pay the same, but upon the existence of a deficiency after a foreclosure sale of the land and the application of the proceeds of the sale to the payment of the indebtedness. The possibility of decedent's liability for said debts was so remote that her direction that the trust pay the same did not constitute a reservation of income by her from the land conveyed in trust. Such possibility of liability was too remote to come within the meaning of the statute. . . .

Although the payments made on the mortgage notes benefited the trust, the Tax Court held that they were also for the benefit of the grantor. . . .

It is not a general or indefinite benefit but a pecuniary benefit that is necessary for a transaction to constitute a reservation of income, and in this case no pecuniary benefit resulted to the decedent by the trustee's payment of the mortgage notes. A pecuniary benefit means an increase in one's net worth by the receipt of money or property. The payment of the mortgage notes did not and could not increase the decedent's net worth; she received no money; she received no property; none of her property was thereby enhanced in value or released from liens or encumbrances. The payment of the mortgage debts resulted in pecuniary benefit to the trust alone, in that the net worth of its land was increased to the extent of the payments made. There was no legal obligation upon the decedent to discharge this debt except in case of a deficiency being due after there had been a sale of the land upon foreclosure of the mortgage.

Income and Gift Tax Consequences of Transfers of Encumbered Property. Do you remember your income tax course? *Estate of Hays* treated the encumbrance as a debt of the trust rather than the grantor's obligation, which is consistent with federal income tax principles treating a transfer of property subject to an outstanding obligation as a *sale* in which the grantor's amount realized includes the encumbrance. Under Crane v. Commissioner, 331 U.S. 1 (1947), a transfer subject to a debt is treated as if the obligation had been repaid by the transferee, who then undertook a new obligation of equal amount. Thus, the grantor's amount realized includes the amount of the debt, and the transferee's cost basis also includes the debt that encumbers the property. Although the transfer in *Estate of Hays* was a gift for gift tax purposes, it would be characterized as a part-sale, part-gift transfer for income tax purposes because the grantor received consideration of about $36,000 (the amount of the mortgage debt).

If the grantor's basis in the property (i.e., the investment in the land as determined for income tax purposes) was less than this amount, the grantor would have recognized gain equal to the difference. See Diedrich v. Commissioner, 457 U.S. 191 (1982); Estate of Levine v. Commissioner, 634 F.2d 12 (2d Cir. 1980); Treas. Reg. §1.1001-2(a).

In *Estate of Hays* the decedent filed a gift tax return reporting a gift of roughly $71,000, which was the appropriate gift tax treatment.

Liabilities Imposed by Law — Duties of Support.   State law traditionally imposes upon one or both parents a duty to support their minor children, upon a married person a duty to support the spouse, and upon specified relatives a duty to support indigent family members. The nature and extent of such duties are determined by state law. Can a parent establish and fund a trust for the support of minor children and escape estate and income taxation by shifting the primary support obligation to the trust? In other words, can the principle in *Estate of Hays* be utilized in this setting? In this connection, see National Bank of Commerce v. Henslee, 179 F. Supp. 346, 352-354 (M.D. Tenn. 1959), in which the court said:

It is not disputed that a reservation of the right to have the trust income applied in the discharge of the settlor's legal obligation is equivalent to "retaining the right" to the income within the meaning of §[2036(a)(1)]. . . .

It is plaintiff's contention that decedent was required, under the terms of the settlement agreement between him and his wife, and as a part of the consideration therefor, to establish a trust to insure the support and maintenance of Laura Ann during her minority; that "the terms of the trust require the payment of the income for such support and maintenance and thus, to that extent, is a release of Frederick Smith from his legal obligation to support"; and that such release is a consideration in money or money's worth within the meaning of §[2043]. . . .

In support of this contention, plaintiff relies upon Estate of McKeon v. Commissioner, 25 T.C. 697 (1956), and the cases therein cited. The court has considered the decisions in these cases and finds that they are not applicable to the facts in the present case. In *Estate of McKeon v. Commissioner*, and in four of the five cases cited therein,[18] the wife was given custody of the children, and the agreement or transfer in trust was for the purpose

---

18. McDonald's Trust v. Commissioner, 19 T.C. 672 (1953), *aff'd sub nom.* Chase National Bank v. Commissioner, 225 F.2d 621 (8th Cir. 1955); Estate of Phillips v. Commissioner, 36 B.T.A. 752 (1937); Hooker v. Commissioner, 10 T.C. 388 (1948), *aff'd*, 174 F.2d 863 (5th Cir. 1949); Commissioner v. Weiser, 113 F.2d 486 (10th Cir. 1940).

of providing income, to be paid to the wife, for the children's support. The decision in each case was predicated upon a finding that the agreement or transfer involved effected a release of the father from his legal obligation to support his minor children, and the court's holding was that such release was a consideration in money or money's worth. The fifth case cited in *Estate of McKeon v. Commissioner*[19] involved a gift tax . . . . In that case the Commissioner conceded that a part of the fund was transferred for an adequate consideration represented by a discharge of the father's obligation to support his minor daughter.

In the case at bar, the facts are directly opposite. The decedent was given custody of the minor child, thereby continuing his legal obligation to support her. Neither the agreement between decedent and his wife nor the transfer in trust released or purported to release the decedent from that obligation.

The court, therefore, finds that the transfer creating the Laura Ann Smith Trust was not made for a consideration in money or money's worth, within the meaning of §[2043], and that plaintiff's insistence in this respect is not well taken.

Instead of establishing a trust, if the grantor had transferred the trust assets outright to the children, had himself appointed their guardian, and in that capacity had used the income from the funds for their support, the issue squarely presented would be whether the grantor retained *any* personal enjoyment.

In that regard, the government has asserted §2036(a)(1) indirect retained beneficial ownership (and in analogous cases §2041(a)(2) general power of appointment inclusion) with respect to any donor (or any third party) acting as trustee or custodian over assets held for their own dependents. The government's theory is that the parent is the indirect beneficiary of funds that may be used to support or maintain a person the parent is legally obligated to support or maintain. See Treas. Reg. §§20.2036-1(b)(2), 20.2041-1(c)(1). This discharge of obligation of support theory is significantly misunderstood and not supportable under the law of most states, which typically provides that a trust or custodial account created for a dependent child may *not* be used to discharge or satisfy the legal obligation of the child's parent to support or maintain the child. See, e.g., Cohen v. Cohen, 609 A.2d 57, 60 (N.J. Super. 1992); Weiss v. Weiss, 1996 WL 91641, 1996 U.S. Dist. LEXIS 2471 (S.D. N.Y. 1996) (unreported); Sutliff v. Sutliff, 528 A.2d 1318 (Pa. 1986); Erdmann v. Erdmann, 226 N.W.2d 439, 442-443 (Wis. 1975). In the context presented, this inability to use assets held for the benefit of a minor should

---

19. Commissioner v. Converse, 5 T.C. 1014, 1016 (1945), *aff'd*, 163 F.2d 131 (2d Cir. 1947).

mean that §2036(a)(1) indirect enjoyment should not be deemed to exist. This is because distributions from the account may not have the effect of satisfying the parent's legal obligation of support. Moreover, the theory upon which the government's discharge theory rests is wrong, and the trust or custodianship assets should not be included in the parent's gross estate.[20] Indeed, the improper assertion of the discharge of obligation theory for wealth transfer tax purposes is all the more interesting in light of the income tax regulations, which very carefully avoid use of the terms "discharge" or "satisfaction" in conjunction with the obligation of support.[21]

Even if the *Henslee* court was correct to regard the income as retained by the decedent by virtue of it being used to discharge the decedent's legal obligation, a further estate tax question raised by transfers in trust for the support of a decedent's minor child is whether that right has been retained for one of the three statutory periods. If the decedent survives the child's emancipation the answer clearly is no. The question arises only if the child is a dependent when the parent dies. That and another matter may suffice to explain the result in *Douglass*, next below. Consider carefully whether the decedent had any "rights" that could be ascertained.

---

20. The government understands and accepts this analysis. See FSA 199930026 (absent application of an exception, authority to distribute funds to a dependent is not sufficient to cause §2041 general power of appointment inclusion to the powerholding fiduciary).

21. In the income tax context, the discharge of an obligation is required before income will be taxed to a person who is obligated, and the regulations recognize that it would be unusual for a discharge to occur. Treas. Reg. §1.662(a)-4 states that:

The term "legal obligation" includes a legal obligation to support another person if, and only if, the obligation is not affected by the adequacy of the dependent's own resources. For example, a parent has a "legal obligation" within the meaning of the preceding sentence to support his minor child if under local law property or income from property owned by the child cannot be used for his support so long as his parent is able to support him. On the other hand, if under local law a mother may use the resources of a child for the child's support in lieu of supporting him herself, no obligation of support exists within the meaning of this paragraph, whether or not income is actually used for support.

This is consistent with the grantor trust rules, under which a "discharge" of obligation is not required before income is attributable to the settlor, presumably because such a requirement would be greater than Congress wanted to impose before causing trust income to be taxable to the trust's settlor. For example, in §677(b), the Code refers to income being taxable to the trust's settlor if it was "distributed for the support or maintenance of a beneficiary . . . whom the grantor is legally obligated to support or maintain," and the concept of a discharge or satisfaction of that obligation is not presented. It is only in Treas. Reg. §§1.677(a)-1(d), 1.677(b)-1(d) (first sentence), and 1.678(a)-1(b) that the "discharge" or "satisfaction" concepts are introduced and with an apparent lack of appreciation for the distinction here discussed or for the fact that the discharge theory is not properly applicable under the law of most states.

Commissioner v. Estate of Douglass
143 F.2d 961 (3d Cir. 1944)

GOODRICH, J.: In 1935 the decedent, Payson Stone Douglass, set up a trust for the benefit of his four children. Neither grantor nor beneficiaries were among the three trustees named. The settlor died in 1938. One of the children at the time was a minor. One paragraph of the trust gave the trustees permission to apply the income of the minor's share, to the extent that the trustees deemed advisable, for the maintenance, education and support of the minor. The Commissioner claims that one-fourth of the value of the corpus of the trust is to be included in the decedent's gross estate for the purpose of estate tax. This was denied by the Tax Court. 2 T.C. 487 (1943). The Commissioner seeks reversal of that ruling in this Court.

The Commissioner's claim is based on §[2036(a)(1)]. The Commissioner's argument also cites [Treas. Reg. §20.2036-1(b)(2), which] language is only helpful to the Commissioner's case if the phrase "is to be applied" is read to mean "may be applied." We think this is a strained interpretation of the language used in the Regulations. If that language is applicable at all, it is rather in the direction of a conclusion opposed to that which the Commissioner now urges. We get no help from the Regulations, except to note that the theory of tax liability now urged goes beyond that which was conceived when the Regulations were promulgated.

The real argument for the Commissioner, however, is based upon the doctrine of constructive receipt following the decisions in income tax cases beginning with Douglas v. Willcuts, 296 U.S. 1 (1935), and with special emphasis on Helvering v. Stuart, 317 U.S. 154 (1942). It is urged that since, under §[677(a)(1)] of the income tax law, the income of the trust, to the extent that it could have been used for the support of a minor child and thus relieve the settlor therefor, was taxable as part of the settlor's income, so the portion of the corpus which provided such income should be included in the gross estate at his death. . . .

In addition to the theory thus advanced the Commissioner's argument cites Helvering v. Mercantile-Commerce Bank & Trust Co., 111 F.2d 224 (8th Cir. 1940). This involved a trust for a wife created by a husband in his lifetime. The income was to be paid to her for family expenses and her own maintenance and support. The Eighth Circuit held that the corpus of the trust was to be included as part of his estate for estate tax purposes. The decision is, obviously, not an authority on the question before us in this litigation. There is certainly an important difference of fact between the trust set up for the very purpose of providing for the settlor's legal obligation to his wife and the one in which disinterested trustees have an option to apply a portion of the income for the support of the settlor's minor child.

Under the section of the estate tax law already quoted, the settlor's estate is subject to the tax if he retained the possession or enjoyment of the income from the property or the right to designate the persons who should enjoy it. But he did neither. He granted the property to trustees, retaining nothing. The Commissioner's argument that these trustees would be likely to do what he asked of them about assigning income for the support of a minor child departs from the "practical" and "realistic" approach we are asked, in the same argument, to take. We have no notion what the trustees would have done had such a request been made. It is apparent, from the terms of the instrument, that the settlor could not direct or control the matter, once the trust settlement had become effective. The set of facts here presented is not therefore within the language [of §2036(a)(1)], nor, as already stated, of the Regulations concerning that section.

To impose liability we should have to transfer the case law on the concept of constructive receipt, which has grown up under the different terminology of [§677(a)(1)] of the income tax law, over to §[2036(a)(1)] of the estate tax law. The suggestion has a certain smooth plausibility. If the fruit can be taxed to the settlor as income, why may not the tree be taxed to his estate? The answer is that Congress has imposed liability for estate tax and income tax in different language. The Commissioner himself points out that Congress has shown no intention completely to integrate income and estate tax laws. See the many instances cited in Higgins v. Commissioner, 129 F.2d 237 (1st Cir. 1942). The "constructive receipt" doctrine is an artificial concept originated and applied, like fictions of the common law, to attain a desirable result. But like other fictions, it should not be taken out of its context and applied in a different situation. If this addition to tax law is to be made, the Congress, not the courts should make it.

The decision of the Tax Court is affirmed.

Section 677(b) was first enacted in 1943 and was thus not taken into consideration by the court in *Estate of Douglass*. That limitation on the amount taxable to the grantor applies only to legal obligations of support (of persons other than the grantor's spouse), and not to legal or contractual obligations in general. Treas. Reg. §1.677(b)-1(d). Note that the result in *Douglass* might have differed if the grantor had been one of the trustees under either §2036(a)(1) or §2036(a)(2).

With *Douglass* compare Estate of Gokey v. Commissioner, 72 T.C. 721 (1979), in which the Tax Court held §2036(a)(1) to be applicable. The trusts in question were established for the benefit of the decedent's children, who were still minors when the decedent died in 1969. The trust instruments stated that the trustee (the decedent's surviving spouse) "shall use such part or all of the net income . . . for the support, care, welfare, and education of the beneficiary. . . ." The court said:

> We believe the language of the children's trusts . . . clearly manifests decedent's intent to require the trustees to apply the income for the stated purpose. In our view, it is impossible to construe the instrument as one which gives the trustees discretion as to whether or not income shall be used for "support, care, welfare, and education."

After reviewing applicable state law decisions, the court further held that "we must reject petitioners' argument that the term 'welfare' in the phrase allows the trustee to make nonsupport payments because 'welfare' is broader than 'support' under Illinois law." The court then concluded: "We are satisfied that the instrument before us provides an ascertainable standard under Illinois law. Accordingly, we find that decedent's gross estate includes the value of [the children's] trusts since we find them to be support trusts within the meaning of §2036(a)(1) and Treas. Reg. §20.2036-1(b)(2)." The difference may be the distinction between mandatory distribution in *Gokey* for ascertainable purposes and much less certainty in *Douglass*.

To cap this discharge and indirect enjoyment discussion, consider how many ways your appreciation for §2036(a)(1) is challenged by the following opinion:

Estate of Sullivan v. Commissioner
66 T.C.M. (CCH) 1329 (1993)

GERBER, J.: [The decedent created an irrevocable inter vivos trust providing that

> During the lifetime of Christine Sullivan, wife of the Settlor, the Trustees shall pay to said Christine Sullivan the entire net income from the Trust Estate in quarterly or more frequent installments so long as she shall live, and in addition to such payments of net income, the Trustees shall pay to or expend for the benefit of said Christine Sullivan such sum or sums from the principal of the Trust Estate as the Trustees, in the exercise of their discretion, may deem necessary or advisable from time to time to provide for her proper care, support, maintenance and health, taking into

consideration her needs and the other sources of financial assistance, if any, which may be or may become available for such purposes.

When the decedent died the trust was worth just over $1 million.]

. . . The issue for our consideration is whether within the meaning of §2036(a) Virgil C. Sullivan (decedent) retained the possession or enjoyment of, or the right to the income from, transferred trust assets. In resolving these questions we consider: (1) Whether decedent retained a right to use the income of the trust to discharge a legal obligation to support his wife, and (2) whether decedent retained an interest in the trust corpus. . . .

Respondent's position is that decedent retained the right to use both trust income and corpus to discharge his legal support obligations within the meaning of Treas. Reg. §20.2036-1(b)(2). Respondent contends that this retained right constitutes "possession and enjoyment" and, therefore, trust income and corpus are includable in the gross estate under §2036(a)(1). Petitioner maintains that decedent retained no rights in trust income and further argues that §2036(a)(1) does not apply to retained interests in the corpus of income-producing property.

1. The Application of §2036 — Trust Income. The trust income would be considered as retained by the decedent under §2036 if it could be applied toward discharging decedent's legal obligation to support his spouse during his lifetime. Treas. Reg. §20.2036-1(b)(2). . . .

It is well established that one spouse may make a gift to the other spouse without affecting their duty of support, and there is no presumption that such a gift is in discharge of the donor's marital duty. Colonial-American National Bank v. United States, 243 F.2d 312, 314 (4th Cir. 1957). However, where it is clear from the trust document that the trust property is to be applied to discharge a support obligation, the trust property is includable in the decedent's gross estate. Commissioner v. Estate of Dwight, 205 F.2d 298 (2d Cir. 1953), rev'g 17 T.C. 1317 (1952). . . .

The circumstances here lead us to conclude that the Trust was not designed to discharge or relieve the decedent of his legal obligation to support his wife. The disposition clause of article I in clear and unambiguous language directs the trustee to pay the income to the wife. It is an unconditional gift and is not limited for support. A grantor is not deemed to have retained a right to trust income where, as here, it is payable to a wife or child without any restriction that it be used for the beneficiary's support or applied toward the discharge of a legal obligation of the grantor. Estate of

Lee v. Commissioner, 33 T.C. 1064, 1067, 1069 (1960) (and cases cited therein). . . .

2. The Application of §2036 — Trust Corpus. . . . [W]e proceed to consider whether decedent retained the power to use trust corpus to discharge his duty of support. Petitioner contends that the Trust was not a support trust and the principal of the Trust was not to be so applied. Petitioner asserts that the Trust agreement requires the trustees to consider other resources available to Christine and that . . . [if] we find that a portion of the Trust is includable in the gross estate, . . . the amount includable is limited to the portion needed to discharge decedent's support obligation. Respondent counters that where a possibility of corpus invasion exists, inclusion of the entire interest is warranted. Respondent contends that remoteness and improbability of the exercise of the right does not preclude the application of §2036(a)(1). . . .

Petitioner's argument that distributions in discharge of decedent's support obligations were effectively precluded because the trustees were required to consider Christine's other resources is misplaced. The trustees' ability to consider other sources of funds is not a bar to the exercise of discretion. Instead, it is a consideration or guideline in the exercise of that discretionary authority. . . .

The likelihood that decedent would actually use the trust funds to satisfy his support obligations is irrelevant. If the decedent, as trustee, has the power to discharge his legal obligations, that power triggers the applicability of §2036(a)(1). Estate of Pardee v. Commissioner, 49 T.C. 140, 148-149 (1967). Section 2036(a)(1) does not require that the transferor pull the "string" or even intend to pull the string on the transferred property; all that is required is that the string exist. Estate of Pardee v. Commissioner, 49 T.C. at 148; Estate of McNichol v. Commissioner, 29 T.C. 1179, 1183 (1958). . . .

Having held that §2036(a)(1) is applicable, we must consider what portion of the assets are properly includable. Petitioner contends that inclusion is limited to that portion of trust assets necessary to satisfy decedent's support obligation. Respondent argues that the entire trust corpus is includable.

Petitioner relies upon Estate of Pardee v. Commissioner, wherein we stated:

> the right retained "for any period which does not in fact end before his death" under §2036(a)(1) was the right to satisfy his legal obligation of $500 per month for the two children under 18, and so much of the corpus necessary to generate this amount is includable in his gross estate.

49 T.C. at 150. . . .

In this case there is a qualification with respect to the amount of corpus invasion. Decedent, as trustee, had the power to use corpus for his wife's support, but only after considering her needs and her other sources of "financial assistance." Here, Christine's needs and her other sources of income have been shown with sufficient clarity to permit a valuation of the terms set forth in the trust for purposes of the inclusion of a discrete amount in decedent's gross estate. . . .

[The court determined that Christine's living expenses were about $26,000 annually, her fixed sources of income were approximately $6,000 annually, and that the decedent's net obligation to support Christine under the terms of the trust therefore would not exceed about $20,000 annually. Then, applying the Treas. Reg. §20.2031-7 valuation tables in effect at the decedent's death, it applied a 10% factor to conclude that $200,000 of trust principal was required to finance the decedent's $20,000 annual obligation to support Christine. That amount of the trust principal was deemed includible in the decedent's gross estate.]

The *Sullivan* opinion stated that "[t]he trust income would be considered as retained by the decedent under §2036 if it could be applied toward discharging decedent's legal obligation to support [a] spouse," 66 T.C.M. at 1332, without evaluating the underlying assumption that, under state law, a spousal support obligation can be discharged by trust distributions. Can it? Notwithstanding that the law in most states specifies that trust distributions do *not* have the effect of discharging a legal obligation of support unless the trust was created for the express purpose of supplanting that obligation, no taxpayer ever has litigated the propriety of the discharge theory on that ground.[22] The court also held that Christine's mandatory income entitlement would not trigger §2036(a)(1) because the trust "was not designed to discharge or relieve" the donor's support obligation. Do you find in the Code or the regulations authority for the notion that intent is relevant to the discharge theory?

A third curious aspect of the court's opinion was that, in determining Christine's unmet support needs, trust income was not considered along with other sources of fixed income, notwithstanding that the trust required the trustees to consider the donee's "needs and the other sources of financial assistance, if any, which may be or may become available for" her support. Because trust income is not what triggered application of §2036(a)(1), should it have been ignored for purposes of determining her needs?

---

22.   See 2 Casner & Pennell, ESTATE PLANNING §7.3.4.2 n.140 et seq. and accompanying text (6th ed. 1999) and authorities cited therein.

Finally, and most mystifying about *Sullivan*, is the fact that the decedent's estate fought inclusion, notwithstanding its new basis at death benefit, which is hard to understand, given the fact that by all appearances the trust was capable of qualifying for the marital deduction if the personal representative made a §2056(b)(7)(B)(v) qualified terminable interest property election.

The discharge theory is *so* uncertain that knowing what the law is today is hard enough, without trying to know what a court might conclude in uncharted waters. To consider one situation that may become more common as people live longer, imagine that A's parents lacked sufficient funds to support themselves. Applicable local law imposes upon adult children a duty to support parents who are indigent. A transferred $300,000 in trust to use the income for the support and maintenance of A's parents and, on the death of the survivor of them, to distribute to A's children. As grantor of the trust, is trust income taxable to A? Compare Treas. Reg. §1.662(a)-4 (reproduced in footnote 21 at page 235) and §677(b). Is (or should) the result be different under §§677 and 2036? Would §2036(a)(1) require inclusion of the property in A's gross estate, assuming A predeceases at least one of the parents? Only time will tell how these questions will be answered.

13.   *Funded Life Insurance Trusts.* As revealed in Chapter 8, the grantor of a funded life insurance trust typically designates the trustee to be the beneficiary of insurance policies on the grantor's life, assigns ownership of the policies to the trustee, and transfers other property such as cash or securities to the trustee, directing that income therefrom be used to pay premiums on the policies. Section 677(a)(3) specifies that income available in the discretion of a nonadverse party to be so used is taxable to the grantor. Burnet v. Wells, 289 U.S. 670 (1933), upheld the constitutionality of attributing income to the grantor in these circumstances. *Wells* involved a typical funded life insurance trust, except that the policies had not been assigned to the trustee. The opinion contained the following passage:

[The settlor], by the creation of these trusts, did more than devote his income to the benefit of relatives. He devoted it at the same time to the preservation of his own contracts, to the protection of an interest which he wished to keep alive. The ends to be attained must be viewed in combination. True he would have been at liberty, if the trusts had not been made, to put an end to his interest in the policies through nonpayment of the premiums, to stamp the contracts out. The chance that economic changes might force him to that choice was a motive, along with others, for the foundation of the trusts. In effect he said to the trustee that for the rest of his life he would dedicate a part of his income to the preservation of these contracts, so much did they mean for his peace of mind and happiness. Income permanently applied by the act of the taxpayer to the maintenance of contracts of insurance made in his name for the support of his dependents is income used for his benefit in such a sense and to such a degree that there is nothing arbitrary or tyrannical in taxing it as his.

Insurance for dependents is today in the thought of many a pressing social duty. Even if not a duty, it is a common item in the family budget, kept up very often at the cost of painful sacrifice, and abandoned only under dire compulsion. It will be a vain effort at persuasion to argue to the average man that a trust created by a father to pay premiums on life policies for the use of sons and daughters is not a benefit to the one who will have to pay the premiums if the policies are not to lapse. Only by closing our minds to common modes of thought, to everyday realities, shall we find it in our power to form another judgment.

In a case like *Wells*, should §2036(a)(1) cause the value of the property transferred to the trust to be includible in the grantor's gross estate? See Rev. Rul. 81-164.

If the result under §2042 will not vary by virtue of the grantor's paying premiums on the policies, and if funding a life insurance trust does not prevent the trust income available to pay premiums from being taxed to the grantor, are there any tax advantages in creating a funded life insurance trust rather than one that is unfunded — that is, one in which the grantor continues to pay the premiums out of after tax income after creation of the trust and assignment of the policies to the trustee? This issue will be considered in Chapter 8.

14. *Relinquishing Retained Interests.* A devilish issue can arise in the following kinds of scenarios. Imagine that, 15 years before death, *D* transferred property in trust, retaining a right to the trust income for life. Would the value of the trust principal be includible in *D*'s gross estate if:

(a) *D* gave the income interest to *A* five years before dying?

(b) *D* gave the income interest to *A* five months before dying?

Rev. Rul. 56-324 held that the full value of the trust principal in the latter circumstance is includible in *D*'s gross estate under §2035(a)(2). Because §2035(a) requires that "the value of all property to the extent of any interest therein" that was transferred within three years of death — in this case, *D*'s life estate — be included in the grantor's gross estate at its estate tax value, how can §2035(a) cause inclusion of more than a zero value? The answer is to apply §2035(a)(2) to ignore the transfer within three years of death and then to apply §2036 as if that was the reality of the case.

(c) Now comes the hardest question: Would the case for inclusion in **(a)** or **(b)** be stronger or weaker if *D* sold the income interest for its actuarial value, or if the trustee commuted the trust by distributing the value of D's income interest to D and distributing the remainder early? In addition to *United States v. Allen*, reproduced next below, see Estate of Cuddihy v. Commissioner, 32 T.C. 1171, 1177 (1959). Would it affect your analysis, particularly with respect to situation **(a)**, if D promptly purchased from an insurance company a nonrefund, single life annuity contract with the proceeds of the sale or commutation? What if D exchanged the life estate, not for cash, but for a private straight life annuity? See Rev. Rul. 79-94, which held that §2036(a)(1) requires inclusion in the decedent's gross estate of a trust in which the decedent, more than three years before death, exchanged a retained income interest for a private annuity promise from the decedent's children that they would remit to the decedent all income paid to them by the trustee and, in any year in which the income fell below a stated dollar amount, they would pay the deficiency out of their own pockets.

What about the §2035(d) exception for bona fide sales for adequate consideration; how is it meant to apply in a case such as this? The following decision deals with that issue.

United States v. Allen
293 F.2d 916 (10th Cir. 1961)

Murrah, C.J.: This is an appeal from a judgment of the trial court awarding plaintiff-executors a refund for estate taxes previously paid.

The pertinent facts are that the decedent, Maria McKean Allen, created an irrevocable trust in which she reserved 3/5ths of the income for life, the remainder to pass to her two children, who are the beneficiaries of the other 2/5ths interest in the income. When she was approximately seventy-eight years old, the trustor-decedent was advised that her retention of the life estate would result in her attributable share of the corpus being included in her gross estate, for estate tax purposes. With her sanction, counsel began searching for a competent means of divesture, and learned that decedent's son, Wharton Allen, would consider purchasing his mother's interest in the trust. At that time, the actuarial value of the retained life estate, based upon decedent's life expectancy, was approximately $135,000 and her attributable share of the corpus, i.e., 3/5ths, was valued at some $900,000. Upon consultation with his business advisers, Allen agreed to pay $140,000 for the interest, believing that decedent's actual life span would be sufficient to return a profit to him on the investment. For all intents and purposes, he was a bona fide third party purchaser — not being in a position to benefit by any reduction in his mother's estate taxes. The sale was consummated and, upon paying the purchase price, Allen began receiving the income from the trust.

At the time of the transfer, decedent enjoyed relatively good health and was expected to live her normal life span. A short time thereafter, however, it was discovered that she had an incurable disease, which soon resulted in her untimely death. As a result of the death, Allen ceased receiving any trust income and suffered a considerable loss on his investment.

The Internal Revenue Commissioner determined that 3/5ths of the corpus, less the $140,000 purchase money, should be included in decedent's gross estate because (1) the transfer was invalid because made [within three years] of death, and (2) the sale was not for an adequate and full consideration.

Plaintiff-executors paid the taxes in accord with the Commissioner's valuation of the estate, and brought this action for refund, alleging that the sale of the life interest was for an adequate consideration; and that, therefore, no part of the trust corpus was properly includible in the gross estate.

The trial court held [that] the consideration paid for the life estate was adequate and full, thereby serving to divest decedent of any interest in the trust, with the result that no part of the corpus is subject to estate taxes.

Our narrow question is thus whether the corpus of a reserved life estate is removed, for federal estate tax purposes, from a decedent's gross estate by a transfer at the value of such reserved life estate. In other words, must the consideration be paid for the interest transferred, or for the interest which would otherwise be included in the gross estate?

In one sense, the answer comes quite simply — decedent owned no more than a life estate, could not transfer any part of the corpus, and Allen received no more than the interest transferred. And, a taxpayer is, of course, entitled to use all proper means to reduce his tax liability. . . . It would thus seem to follow that the consideration was adequate, for it was in fact more than the value of the life estate. And, as a practical matter, it would have been virtually impossible to sell the life estate for an amount equal to her share in the corpus. Cf. Sullivan's Estate v. Commissioner, 175 F.2d 657 (9th Cir. 1949).

It does not seem plausible, however, that Congress intended to allow such an easy avoidance of the taxable incidence befalling reserved life estates. This result would allow a taxpayer to reap the benefits of property for his lifetime and, [within three years] of death, sell only the interests entitling him to the income, thereby removing all of the property which he has enjoyed from his gross estate. Giving the statute a reasonable interpretation, we cannot believe this to be its intendment. It seems certain that in a situation like this, Congress meant the estate to include the corpus of the trust or, in its stead, an amount equal in value. I.e., see Helvering v. Hallock, 309 U.S. 106 (1940); Commissioner v. Wemyss, 324 U.S. 303 (1945); Commissioner v. Estate of Church, 335 U.S. 632 (1949).[23]

The judgment of the trial court is therefore reversed and the case is remanded for further proceedings in conformity with the opinion filed herein.

BREITENSTEIN, J. (concurring in result): . . . Trustor-decedent in 1932 created an irrevocable trust and received no consideration therefor. She retained for life the right to income from 3/5ths of the property which she placed in the trust. By the plain language of the statute that portion of the property held in the trust and devoted to the payment to her of income for life is includible within her gross estate. Such property is an "interest" of which she made a transfer with the retention of income for life.

The fact that the transfer of the life estate left her without any retained right to income from the trust property does not alter the result. As I read the statute the tax liability arises at the time of the inter vivos transfer under which there was a retention of the right to income for life. The disposition thereafter of that retained right does not eliminate the tax liability. The fact that full and adequate consideration was paid for the transfer of the retained life estate is immaterial. To remove the trust property from inclusion in decedent's estate there must be full and adequate consideration paid for the interest which would be taxed. That interest is not the right to income for life but the right to the property which was placed in the trust and from which the income is produced.

As the 1932 trust was irrevocable, trustor-decedent could thereafter make no unilateral transfer of the trust property. Granting that she could sell her life estate as that was a capital asset owned by her, such sale has no effect on the includibility in her gross estate of the interest which she transferred in 1932 with the retention of the right to income for life.

---

23. In his treatise, . . . 34 Minnesota Law Review 50, 70, 71, Professor Lowndes says: "(T)he adequacy of the consideration which will prevent a tax when an incident of ownership in connection with a taxable inter vivos transfer is relinquished [within three years] of death, will be measured against the value of the interest which would be taxable apart from the transfer [within three years] of death, rather than the property interest which is transferred. . . . [T]he determination of what interest is transferred [within three years] of death and what is adequate consideration to prevent a transfer [within three years] of death from being taxable, should be made on the basis of the tax effect of the transfer and the effect of the consideration on the transferor's taxable estate, rather than by the comparatively irrelevant rules of property law."

For the reasons stated I would reverse the judgment with directions to dismiss the case.

(d)   The government conceded in *Allen* that the proportional part of the trust principal that was included in the decedent's gross estate should have been reduced by the $140,000 received by her for the sale of her retained life estate. See §2043(a). Rev. Rul. 79-94 held that there was no reduction in the amount includible for the value of the annuity the decedent received in exchange for the relinquished life estate because the "annuity" was actually the income interest in disguise. The government ruled that, in fact, the decedent received no consideration. Is that determination different from the question in *Allen* of whether the decedent's gross estate should have been reduced by $140,000?

(e)   The concurring opinion of Judge Breitenstein in *Allen* described the decedent's retained life estate as a capital asset. For income tax purposes, the $140,000 she received for the sale of her retained life estate would be treated as capital gain. See McAllister v. Commissioner, 157 F.2d 235 (2d Cir. 1946); TAMs 200304025 and 200252092. Presumably §1001(e) is applicable to deny her any basis, making the full amount received taxable in the year of sale. At capital gain rates that might be a good alternative to receiving the income over time, taxable at ordinary income rates.

(f)   If Judge Breitenstein is right in *Allen*, would that mean that an inadvertent retention of an interest in trust property that the grantor thought was transferred completely could never be relinquished for tax purposes — that the grantor never would be able to get rid of estate tax exposure? Stated differently, should it matter if a grantor uses two documents to transfer a full fee simple interest in property to a trust instead of one? Certainly you would like to avoid the issue, but §2035(a)(2) puts a three year premium on doing it right, the first time.

(g)   Read §2519 regarding the effect of a surviving spouse's assignment of any part of the qualified income interest in a QTIP marital deduction trust. As illustrated by Treas. Reg. §§25.2519-1(g) *Example 4* and 20.2044-1(e) *Example 5*, assignment of less than all the income interest will cause §2036(a)(1) to apply to a portion of the trust at the surviving spouse's death. The gift made under §2519 will be valued by using §2702. See Chapters 11 and 15 for a discussion of how these various rules operate. The net result probably dictates that a surviving spouse should assign the entire qualified income interest in a QTIP trust or none at all, *unless* the object is to just get the gift tax dollars out of the spouse's estate (to the extent §2035(b) will not apply).

(h)   What amount would be includible if *D* transferred property to a trust during life and retained an annuity rather than an amount equal to all income payable annually? See Rev. Rul. 82-105, holding that only the amount of the trust needed to produce an annual income equal to that annuity would be includible. The government doesn't like that result and wants to apply §2039 instead. See TAM 200210009 and FSA 200036012. Quaere whether this result differs from the situation in which *D* purchases a commercial annuity payable for *D*'s life.

(i) Consider the difference in wealth transfer tax treatment if *D* has $100x with which to provide for *D*'s needs until death and then for the benefit of *D*'s surviving family members and either (a) transfers the full $100x to an inter vivos trust, retaining a life estate valued at $20x and naming the family members as remainder beneficiaries, or (b) transfers only $80x to a trust for the family members, retaining no interest therein, and uses the remaining $20x to purchase a single life, no refund, annuity payable to *D* for life. These produce wildly different wealth transfer tax consequences. What justification is there for the difference?

15. *Exercise or Release of Powers of Appointment.* And now, just because it should be possible to understand it for the first time, consult the second clause of §2041(a)(2), as illustrated next:

Fish v. United States
432 F.2d 1278 (9th Cir. 1970)

TAYLOR, J.: . . . The stipulated facts reveal that Clarence G. Blagen, the husband of Minnie C. Blagen, died on May 28, 1951. The residuary clause of his will established a trust, the terms of which provided that Minnie C. Blagen should have, during her lifetime, the right in any calendar year to demand payment to her of all or part of the net income of the trust for that year, but that any income not so claimed by her would be added to the corpus of the trust. . . .

Minnie C. Blagen (decedent) never exercised or released her power over the income of the trust in any year from the inception of the trust until her death on July 13, 1960, except insofar as the annual lapse of the power, if any such lapse occurred, constituted a release of the power as a matter of law under §2041(b)(2) of the Internal Revenue Code. The Commissioner, in assessing the tax deficiency, included in the decedent's gross estate the net . . . accumulated income which had been added to the trust . . . .

The Commissioner determined that the decedent possessed a general power of appointment over the trust income and that the failure of the decedent to exercise this power constituted a lapse of the power in each year in which it was not exercised. The Commissioner contends that the lapse constitutes a release of the power under §2041(b)(2) in such a way that, if it were a transfer of property owned by the decedent, the property would have been includible in the decedent's gross estate as a transfer with a retained life estate under §2036(a)(1).[24]

The taxpayer agrees that the decedent possessed a general power of appointment, and that the "transfer" each year, had the property been owned by the decedent, would be a transfer with a retained life estate. The taxpayer contends, however, that the decedent was incompetent for some seven years prior to her death and her general power of appointment could not have been lawfully exercised or released by her or by anyone acting in her behalf and that therefore the annual expiration of her power over the trust income was not a "lapse" and thus not a release of the power within the meaning of §2041(b)(2). Alternatively, the taxpayer contends that, if the incompetency of the decedent is immaterial and a lapse of the power occurred in each year, the Commissioner and the District Court erred in computing the allowable exemption under §2041(b)(2) on the basis of five per cent of the net income of the trust instead of, as taxpayer contends, five per cent of the total trust assets.

We agree with the District Court that the competency of the decedent is immaterial in determining whether a lapse or release of the power occurred. The statute provides, without equivocation, that a lapse of the power shall be considered a release, and does not purport to qualify the manner in which the lapse occurs. . . .

The taxpayer next contends that the District Court erred in computing the exemption allowed under §2041(b)(2). That section allows as an exemption to the amount includible in the taxable estate an amount equal to five per cent of "the aggregate value of the assets out of which, or the proceeds of which, the exercise of the lapsed powers could have been satisfied," or the sum of $5,000, whichever is the greater. The District Court, in determining the amount of the exemption, computed the exemption on the basis of five per cent of the trust income. Since for each year in question, the sum of $5,000 was greater than five per cent of the trust income, the District Court allowed an exemption of $5,000 for each year, as the Commissioner had done. The taxpayer argues that the exemption should be $5,000 or five per cent of the total trust assets . . . . The taxpayer argues that since the income

---

24. As income was added to the trust each year as a result of the decedent's inaction, that income generated additional income in following years which was subject to the decedent's lifetime power of appointment, and thus the "transfer" each year by the decedent was one which left her with a lifetime interest in the property. Such a transfer, resulting from the exercise or release of a power of appointment, becomes includible in the gross estate of the decedent under the provisions of §2041(a)(2) of the Internal Revenue Code.

payable to the decedent, had she demanded it, would have been payable either from corpus or income, the entire trust represents "assets out of which, or the proceeds out of which, the exercise of lapsed powers could be satisfied," and thus the entire trust assets should serve as the basis for the five per cent computation. We do not agree. Even if the trustee could have satisfied a demand for income out of either corpus assets or income funds, a point which we do not here decide, the distribution would necessarily have been a distribution of income as a matter of federal tax law or as a matter of trust accounting, since the decedent had no power whatever to invade the corpus of the trust.

While the language of §2041(b)(2)(B), like much of the statutory tax law, is hardly a model of precision and clarity on the point, we are satisfied from the reading of the statute together with its legislative history that the applicable basis for computation of the allowable exemption is the trust or fund in which the lapsed power existed.[25] The District Court correctly determined that the power of appointment in the instant case existed only with respect to the trust income, and properly allowed an exemption of $5,000 for each year in question.

Accord, Rev. Rul. 66-87.

The result would differ if the trust had required accumulation and addition to principal of the net income and conferred on Minnie an annually exercisable power to demand principal equal to the net accumulated income of the trust for that year. But the more important issue is whether §2041(a)(2) would apply at all. In that regard, Treas. Reg. §§20.2041-3(d)(3) and -3(d)(4) should help to clarify the §2036(a)(1) analog. See also Treas. Reg. §20.2041-3(d)(5).

PART B.   REVERSIONARY INTERESTS IN PRINCIPAL

Code References: *Estate Tax: §§2033, 2037*
Gift Tax: Treas. Reg. §§25.2511-1(e), (f); 25.2512-5;
25.7520-1
Income Tax: §673

16.   A person who creates a revocable inter vivos trust, retaining an income interest for life, is not trying to save income or estate taxes. But there are non-tax reasons for creating such a trust. Prior to 1986, taxpayers often created irrevocable inter vivos trusts and retained only a reversionary interest that would not "reasonably be expected to take effect in possession

---

25.   S. Rep. No. 382, 82d Cong., 1st Sess., 6-7 (1952). . . .

or enjoyment within 10 years" of creation and, in so doing, avoided §673 grantor trust treatment while shifting trust income for the trust's initial term. These planning opportunities were eliminated in 1986, and today a donor would more likely achieve an income shifting objective by transferring outright ownership of income producing property to a donee or to a trust in which the donor retains no property interests or powers. As a consequence, it is much less likely today that a decedent will own a reversion that was created intentionally. Section 673 for income tax and §2037 for estate tax purposes, if they arise at all, are likely to be unanticipated. Indeed, it is so uncommon to encounter either provision, there probably isn't much reason to even *mention* these rules. But, sure enough, it's what you don't know that will bite you — so herewith is just a bare overview of something you should know to avoid and, if you do know it, you shouldn't ever have trouble with §2037. First, let's set the stage:

Robinette v. Helvering
318 U.S. 184 (1943)

BLACK, J.: . . . In 1936, the petitioner, Elise Paumgarten (neé Robinson), was thirty years of age and was contemplating marriage; her mother, Meta Biddle Robinette, was 55 years of age and was married to the stepfather of Miss Robinson. The three, daughter, mother and stepfather, had a conference with the family attorney, with a view to keeping the daughter's fortune within the family. An agreement was made that the daughter should place her property in trust, receiving a life estate in the income for herself, and creating a second life estate in the income for her mother and stepfather if she should predecease them. The remainder was to go to her issue upon their reaching the age of 21, with the further arrangement for the distribution of the property by the will of the last surviving life tenant if no issue existed. Her mother created a similar trust, reserving a life estate to herself and her husband and a second or contingent life estate to her daughter. She also assigned the remainder to the daughter's issue. The stepfather made a similar arrangement by will. The mother placed $193,000 worth of property in the trust she created, and the daughter did likewise with $680,000 worth of property.

The parties agree that the secondary life estates in the income are taxable gifts, and this tax has been paid. The issue is whether there has also been a taxable gift of the remainder of the two trusts. The Commissioner determined that the remainders were taxable, the Board of Tax Appeals reversed the Commissioner, and the Circuit Court of Appeals reversed the Board of Tax Appeals. 129 F.2d 832. . . . [The taxpayers argued that] "in computing the value of the remainders herein, allowance should be made for the value of the grantor's reversionary interest." Here, unlike [Smith v.

Shaughnessy, 318 U.S. 176 (1943)], the government does not concede that the reversionary interest of the petitioner should be deducted from the total value. In the *Smith* case, the grantor had a reversionary interest which depended only upon his surviving his wife, and the government conceded that the value was therefore capable of ascertainment by recognized actuarial methods. In this case, however, the reversionary interest of the grantor depends not alone upon the possibility of survivorship but also upon the death of the daughter without issue who should reach the age of 21 years. The petitioner does not refer us to any recognized method by which it would be possible to determine the value of such a contingent reversionary remainder.[26] It may be true, as the petitioners argue, that trust instruments such as these before us frequently create "a complex aggregate of rights, privileges, powers and immunities and that in certain instances all these rights, privileges, powers and immunities are not transferred or released simultaneously." But before one who gives his property away by this method is entitled to deduction from his gift tax on the basis that he had retained some of these complex strands it is necessary that he at least establish the possibility of approximating what value he holds. Factors to be considered in fixing the value of this contingent reservation as of the date of the gift would have included consideration of whether or not the daughter would marry; whether she would have children; whether they would reach the age of 21; etc. Actuarial science may have made great strides in appraising the value of that which seems to be unappraisable, but we have no reason to believe from this record that even the actuarial art could do more than guess at the value here in question. Humes v. United States, 276 U.S. 487, 494.

The judgment of the Circuit Court of Appeals is affirmed.

See Treas. Reg. 25.2511-1(e); Rev. Rul. 76-275, in which the government said that "if a governing instrument provides the trustee with a totally discretionary power to divest a retained interest, then the donor's retained interest is not severable from the gift portion of the transferred property since no known formula has been advanced for ascertaining the value of the retained interest." Cf. Holbrook v. United States, 575 F.2d 1288 (9th Cir. 1978). In Rev. Rul. 77-99, the government further ruled that

when a trust instrument provides that capital gains . . . must be allocated to income and capital losses . . . must be allocated to principal, then under the rationale of *Robinette v. Helvering* . . . and Rev. Rul. 76-275, [a donor's reversionary interest in a trust to pay

---

26.   A what? — ED.

income to a third party for a term over 10 years is incapable of valuation and consequently] the entire value of property transferred is subject to the gift tax. . . .

As a result of these valuation realities, the situation in which a §2037 reversion exists often will involve a prior transfer in which 100% of the value of the property was subjected to gift tax, which makes the purge and credit mechanism of §2001(b) all the more important to avoid double taxation of the same property.

17. *Tips on Distinguishing §2037 Circumstances from §2033.* If the decedent's reversionary interest does not terminate on his or her death, then the value of that reversionary interest will be included in the decedent's gross estate under §2033. It is unlikely that §2037 will apply in such a case, because it would be highly unusual for the possession or enjoyment of any interest in the property to depend upon surviving the decedent.[27] However, if the decedent's reversionary interest terminates on his or her death, then nothing will be includible in the decedent's gross estate under §2033. In that case, §2037 *might* apply[28] to cause inclusion in the decedent's gross estate of those interests (if any) in the property the possession or enjoyment of which could be obtained only by surviving the decedent. Note that, for a person's interest in the property to escape inclusion in the decedent's gross estate under §2037, it is not sufficient that the person's interest can become *vested* without surviving the decedent; it is necessary that the person can *possess or enjoy* the property without surviving the decedent.

A rule of thumb that might be useful is that: if the decedent's reversionary interest is not terminated by death, §2033 will apply and §2037 likely will not; if the decedent's reversionary interest is terminated by death, then §2033 will not apply, and careful inquiry should be made to see

---

27. It is possible for §2037 to apply in such cases, but the circumstances are not likely to occur. Consider this example. *D* transferred property in trust to pay the income to *X* for 10 years. At the end of the 10-year period, the corpus is to be distributed to *D* (or to *D*'s estate) if *G* is living at that date. If *G* is not living at the end of the 10-year period, the corpus is to be distributed to *F* if *D* is alive at the end of the 10-year period, or to *P* if *D* is not then living. *D* dies three years after the trust was created, survived by *X*, *G*, *F*, and *P*. *D* had a reversionary interest in the trust at *D*'s death that is contingent upon *G* being alive seven years later. That reversionary interest does not terminate on *D*'s death. *D* can bequeath that interest to whomever *D* chooses. So, the value of *D*'s reversionary interest is included in *D*'s gross estate under §2033. Also, *P* could not obtain possession of the property unless *P* survived *D*. If the actuarial value of *D*'s reversionary interest immediately before *D*'s death exceeded 5% of the value of the trust, §2037 will include the value of *P*'s remainder interest in *D*'s gross estate. It therefore is possible that both the value of *D*'s reversionary interest and the value of *P*'s remainder interest will be included in *D*'s gross estate. But, the terms of the disposition in the trust that gave rise to this result are contorted and are very unlikely to occur.

28. For §2037 to apply, the actuarial value of the decedent's reversionary interest must satisfy the more than 5% of value requirement of §2037(a)(2).

if §2037 does apply. An additional point to remember is: if §2033 applies the amount includible is the value of the reversion. If §2037 applies the amount includible is the full value of the property in which the reversion exists — reduced by any intervening interests. Given the potentially vast difference in the amount includible, it is fitting that §2033 is easy but §2037 is hard to trigger with a reversion.

Keep in mind that a grantor will not often expressly retain a reversionary interest. However, there will be a reversion to the grantor (or to the grantor's estate) by operation of law if there is a gap in the dispositive provisions of the governing instrument of a trust or other transfer document. The grantor may not have intended to retain a reversion and may be totally unaware that the entire fee simple was not conveyed. The unintended reversion can cause transfer tax consequences (and also income tax consequences by causing a trust to be a grantor trust under §673). For estate tax purposes, §2037 might apply; or §2033 might apply. In many cases in which §2037 applies, the cause will be a reversion that was not planned.

The genesis of §2037 was §202(b) of the Revenue Act of 1916. The language of §2037, however, bears little resemblance to the 1916 provision, and it came to have its present shape after a long process of Supreme Court decisions and congressional reactions. Very briefly, this was the chain of events: The 1916 language remained the relevant statutory provision until 1949, during which time the Supreme Court interpreted it as requiring retention of a reversionary interest. This interpretation was reached with difficulty, as shown by Helvering v. Hallock, 309 U.S. 106 (1940), which reviewed and overruled some earlier decisions. In the Technical Changes Act of 1949, Congress replaced the 1916 language with a more specific provision that, as to pre-October 8, 1949, transfers, required inclusion only if the grantor *expressly* retained a reversionary interest that, immediately before death, was worth more than 5% of the value of the transferred property; transfers made after October 7, 1949, were includible regardless of whether a reversionary interest was retained, but only if the beneficiary had to survive the grantor to possess or enjoy the property. The last change occurred in 1954, when present §2037 replaced the 1949 provision and reinstated the requirement that the decedent had a reversionary interest of more than a de minimis value in the property. For more detail, see Lowndes, Kramer, & McCord, FEDERAL ESTATE AND GIFT TAXES Ch. 6 (3d ed. 1974).

18. *The Doctrine of Worthier Title.*[29]   Three property law rules that originated in the English feudal system survived and were accepted in the

---

29. This discussion concerns only the "inter vivos branch" of the doctrine of worthier title. The "testamentary branch" of that doctrine is of little, if any, significance today, and it is of no tax significance. See generally Morris, *The Wills Branch of the Worthier Title Doctrine*, 54 MICH. L. REV. 451 (1956).

United States as part of the common law: the rule of destructibility of contingent remainders and the Rule in Shelley's Case do not concern us here, but the doctrine of worthier title does. In its original form the doctrine (like the other two rules) was a rule of law (sometimes called a rule of property) that would not yield to a contrary intention of the grantor, no matter how strongly expressed. Moreover, because of their feudal origins, the doctrine of worthier title and the two rules applied only to interests in real property. The doctrine of worthier title declared that a grantor could not by an inter vivos transfer create a future interest in the grantor's own heirs; an attempt to do so was void or ineffective. Thus, an inter vivos transfer of real property, for example, "to A for life, remainder to my heirs" was read as if it said "to A for life." Because the transferor only parted with a life estate, a reversion was retained. It is believed that the purpose of the doctrine (like the Rule in Shelley's Case) was to force the property to pass by intestacy rather than "by purchase," preserving the feudal dues to a lord. The reason for the doctrine ceased to exist when the feudal system crumbled and, along with the two rules, the doctrine has long been abolished by statute in England.

All three rules were rooted in feudalism, so they never served any purpose in the United States; nevertheless, they were accepted here as part of the common law. The rule of destructibility and the Rule in Shelley's Case have been widely abolished by statute, but not the doctrine of worthier title. Indeed, the doctrine was rejuvenated by the New York Court of Appeals in its well known decision, Doctor v. Hughes, 122 N.E. 221 (N.Y. 1919). The opinion, written by Judge Cardozo, said that "the rule persists today, at least as a rule of construction, if not as one of property." As Cardozo may have expected, and probably intended, the courts in New York and many other states henceforth viewed the doctrine as merely a rule of construction. See RESTATEMENT (SECOND) OF PROPERTY (Donative Transfers) §30.2(1) (1988). In only a very few jurisdictions is it still followed as a rule of law. Conversely, about 20% of the states (including New York) have abolished the doctrine altogether, mostly by legislation. See, e.g., Uniform Probate Code §2-710.

A rule of construction is supposed to carry out the ordinary intention of a grantor who uses certain words. Thus, under *Doctor v. Hughes*, it is possible for a grantor to create a future interest in the grantor's own heirs. But the grantor must indicate this intention more strongly than merely saying "remainder to my heirs." Unless a contrary intention can be shown, the phrase "remainder to my heirs" is taken to mean "reversion in myself." As a rule of construction, moreover, the doctrine applies to interests in personal as well as real property, and to equitable as well as legal interests. Thus, it applies to one of the most frequently created types of estate planning arrangements — inter vivos trusts of personal property.

The presumption that a grantor who says "remainder to my heirs" means "reversion in myself" is overcome if the grantor adds words such as, "and such persons to take as purchasers" (which is quite uncommon). Apart from an explicit statement of contrary intention, various features of an instrument have been held to rebut the presumption. Although this topic is too complicated to go into here, it is worth noting that the reservation of a power of appointment by the grantor usually has rebutted the presumption, as has use of the term "heirs" in the instrument in a nontechnical sense. On this latter point, see, e.g., Estate of Graham v. Commissioner, 46 T.C. 415 (1966).

See generally Simes & Smith, THE LAW OF FUTURE INTERESTS §§1601-1613 (2d ed. 1956); Waggoner, ESTATES IN LAND AND FUTURE INTERESTS IN A NUTSHELL ch. 12 (2d ed. 1993); Johanson, *Reversions, Remainders, and the Doctrine of Worthier Title*, 45 TEX. L. REV. 1 (1966).

(a)   Assume that *D* created a trust under which income was payable to *A* for life and then the principal would revert to *D*. *A* was 46 years old and already quite wealthy when the trust was created. *D* transferred $1 million to the trust, named a corporate fiduciary as sole trustee, and authorized principal distributions to *A* to provide for *A*'s "comfort and benefit." The government audited *D*'s gift tax return and asserted that *D* made a gift of the full $1 million because of the inability to value the potential for distributions to *A*. In such a case *D* would be wise to give the reversion to *D*'s children (and hope to outlive the §2035(a)(2) exposure).

(b)   Five years ago, *D* created an irrevocable inter vivos trust to pay the income to *D*'s child, *A*, for life, then to *A*'s spouse, *B*, for life, and on the death of the survivor of *A* and *B*, to distribute to *A*'s then-living children. At the time of the transfer, *D* was 55 years old, *A* was 35, *B* was 37, and *A*'s two children were 15 and 10. *A* and *A*'s oldest child were killed in an automobile accident two years ago, and *D* died a few weeks ago. Nothing is includible in *D*'s gross estate by virtue of §2037 but there is a §2033 inclusion. See Treas. Reg. §20.2037-1(e) *Example (1)*. That result would be avoidable if *D* directed the trustee to distribute the principal "to my heirs at law" in the event that no child of *A* was living at the death of the survivor of *A* and *B*.

19.   *The Survivorship Requirement of §2037*   is illustrated by the following simple example:

Revenue Ruling 78-15

On September 27, 1972, the decedent, *A*, entered into an employment contract with *X* Corporation. The contract provided that, in consideration of *A*'s performance of services, the corporation would pay a death benefit of a stated amount to the decedent's spouse, *B*, provided *A* was in the employment of *X* Corporation at the time of death. If *B* predeceased *A*, the death benefit was to be paid to *A*'s estate.

Upon *A*'s death, the death benefit was paid to *B* pursuant to the terms of the contract. The value of *A*'s reversionary interest in the death benefit payment, immediately before *A*'s death, exceeded 5% of the value of the payment. See Rev. Rul. 76-178 for a discussion of the principles applicable in valuing a reversionary interest for purposes of §2037.

Revenue Ruling 76-304 holds that the transfer requirements of §2038(a)(1) are satisfied where the decedent, by entering into an employment contract, procures the transfer by the decedent's employer of a death benefit to the decedent's surviving spouse in return for the performance of services by the decedent during the course of employment.

The discussion contained in Rev. Rul. 76-304 pertaining to §2038(a)(1) is equally applicable to a transfer of a death benefit made in conjunction with the employment contract where the inclusion of the death benefit is sought under §2037. See Estate of Bogley v. United States, 514 F.2d 1027 (Ct. Cl. 1975).

Held, by entering into the employment contract, *A* has effected a transfer within the purview of §2037. *B* had to survive *A* in order to receive the payment that was the subject of the transfer. Further, *A* retained a reversionary interest in the death benefit payment and the value of the reversionary interest immediately before *A*'s death exceeded 5% of the payment. The value of the death benefit is therefore includible in *A*'s gross estate under §2037.

Try your hand at it: Assume that *D* transferred a significant amount of property in trust. If *D* dies while *A* is still alive, will the value of any part of the property be includible in *D*'s gross estate if the trust had the following alternative terms? See Treas. Reg. §§20.2037-1(b), -1(e).

(a) Income to *A* for life, remainder to *D*'s children who survive *A* and, if none, then to *D*. No children must survive *D*.

(b) Income to *A* for life, remainder to *D* if living, otherwise to *B*. Quaere: must *B* survive *D*?

(c) Income to *A* for life, remainder to *B* if living, otherwise to *D* if living, otherwise to *C*. *D* was survived by *A*, *B*, and *C*. *B* does not need to survive *D*. Must *C*?

20.   *The 5% Rule of §2037.*   H.R. Rep. No. 1412, 81st Cong., 1st Sess. 7 (1949), in 1949-2 C.B. 295, 297:

In determining whether the value of the reversionary interest exceeds 5%, it is to be compared with the entire value of the transferred property, including interests which are not dependent upon survivorship of the decedent. . . .

The decedent's reversionary interest is to be valued by recognized valuation principles, pursuant to regulations prescribed by the Commissioner . . . and, of course, without regard to the fact of the decedent's death. The value shall be ascertained as though the decedent were, immediately before his death, making a gift of the property and retaining the reversionary interest. The rule of *Robinette v. Helvering*, under which a reversionary interest not having an ascertainable value under recognized valuation principles is considered to have a value of zero, is to apply.

See also Treas. Reg. §§20.2037-1(c)(3), -1(c)(4).

H.R. Rep. No. 1337, 83d Cong., 2d Sess. 90 (1954); S. Rep. No. 1622, 83d Cong., 2d Sess. 123 (1954):

[Property will be includible in the decedent's] estate only if he still had . . . immediately before his death a reversionary interest in the property exceeding 5% of its value, that is, prior to his death, had 1 chance in 20 that the property would be returned to him.

See also Estate of Cardeza v. United States, 57-1 U.S. Tax Cas. (CCH) ¶11,681 (E.D. Pa. 1957), *aff'd*, 261 F.2d 423 (3d Cir. 1958).

Revenue Ruling 76-178

. . . Pursuant to the terms of a trust agreement executed in 1961, the decedent (a male) gave A (a female) a life interest in Blackacre, a parcel of income-producing real property. The trust agreement provided that Blackacre would revert to the decedent if the decedent survived A; but, if A survived the decedent, then upon A's death Blackacre should pass to the decedent's child or to the child's estate.

The decedent died on July 1, 1973, survived by A and decedent's child. At the date of decedent's death both the decedent and A were aged 88. The fair market value of Blackacre on such date was $100,000. . . .

The decedent's reversionary interest is described as the present worth of the right of the decedent (a male aged 88) to receive $100,000 upon the death of A (a female aged 88), provided the decedent survives. The actuarial factor representing this described reversionary interest is 0.43194. (This factor cannot be found in the tables contained in Treas. Reg. §20.2031-10(f). Rather, it is a special factor that will be computed by the National Office upon submission of the information specified in Treas. Reg. §20.2031-10(f).)

Using the factor of 0.43194 applicable in the present case the value of the decedent's reversionary interest is $43,194 ($100,000 x 0.43194). In determining whether the value of the decedent's reversionary interest exceeds 5% of the value of the transferred property, A's life estate is not excluded from such value for purposes of making this determination under Treas. Reg. §20.2037-1(c)(4). Since the value of the decedent's reversionary interest exceeds 5% of the value of Blackacre, the percentage requirement of §2037 is satisfied.

The value of the reversionary interest determines the applicability of §2037, but this is not the interest includible in the decedent's gross estate. See H.R. Rep. No. 1412 (Conf.), 81st Cong., 1st Sess. 7 (1949), 1949-2 C.B. 297; S. Rep. No. 831, 81st Cong., 1st Sess. 9 (1949), 1949-2 C.B. 294, and H.R. Rep. No. 1337, 83d Cong., 2d Sess. 90 (1954); S. Rep. No. 1622, 83d Cong., 2d Sess. 123 (1954). Since the decedent's child's possession or enjoyment of the underlying property, through ownership of the remainder interest, is dependent on surviving the decedent, the value of such property less the value of the outstanding life estate in A is includible in the decedent's gross estate. Klein v. United States, 283 U.S. 231 (1931).

Accordingly, §2037 requires the inclusion of the entire trust corpus at its date of death value of $100,000 less the value of A's life estate; or using the remainder factor applicable to a female aged 88, as specified in Table A(2) of Treas. Reg. §20.2031-10(f), the includible interest is the present worth of the right to receive $100,000 upon the death of a female aged 88 or $81,569 ($100,000 x 0.81569).

Hall v. United States
353 F.2d 500 (7th Cir. 1965)

MAJOR, J.: . . . The decedent, on February 20, 1928, created an irrevocable trust under which the net income was to be paid to the settlor for life, with remainders to her daughter and son or to the survivor of them. The instrument provided that should the settlor's son and daughter predecease her the trust should immediately terminate and be paid over to the settlor. Julia Jean Hall, the decedent's daughter, predeceased, and William S. Hall, the son, survived her. The date of birth of Helen S. Hall (decedent) was April 10, 1888, and that of William S. Hall, December 15, 1910. At the time of her death, decedent was about 72, and William S. Hall about 49 years of age. . . .

The District Court found:

9. The decedent's life expectancy immediately prior to death on February 18, 1960, without regard to the fact of death, did not exceed three years.

10. William S. Hall's life expectancy on such date was not less than fifteen years.

11. The value of the decedent's reversionary interest immediately before her death on February 18, 1960, without regard to the fact of her death, was not more than 2.61% of the value of the trust property.

. . . Plaintiffs introduced a large amount of medical testimony relating to the decedent's physical and mental condition, covering a period of many years. Also, testimony was given relating to the physical condition of William S. Hall, the trust beneficiary. Plaintiffs also introduced the testimony of actuarial experts who determined from the medical history of the two persons the life expectancy of each. Using this determination in connection with the mortality table, as suggested by the Treasury Regulations, these expert witnesses concluded that the value of decedent's reversionary interest was not more than 2.61% of the value of the trust property. On the other hand, defendant introduced the testimony of its expert, an employee of the Internal Revenue Service, who testified that the value of decedent's reversionary interest was 9.413% of the value of the trust property. This conclusion was based solely on United States Life Table 38.

In view of the narrow question for decision, there is no point in relating in detail the medical testimony as it relates to the state of health of either the decedent or William S. Hall. The same may be said as to the actuarial testimony determining the life expectancy of each based on their medical history, and in fixing the value of decedent's interest in the trust. This is so because defendant objected to the admission of such testimony solely on the ground that it was irrelevant and immaterial. If it was properly admitted, no question is raised but that it supports the findings made by the court. . . .

Section 2037(b), with reference to the valuation of reversionary interest, in pertinent part provides, ". . . shall be determined . . . *by usual methods of valuation*, including the use of tables of mortality and actuarial principles, under regulations prescribed by the Secretary or his delegate." (Italics supplied.) It is plain that the statute does not contemplate that valuation shall be determined in all cases solely by the use of tables of mortality and actuarial principles prescribed by the Secretary, as is argued by defendant. What the statute provides is that such valuation shall be determined "by usual methods of valuation," including mortality tables prescribed by the Secretary.

The interpretation of this provision urged by defendant would eliminate the italicized phrase so that it would read, "the value . . .

shall be determined . . . by the use of tables of mortality and actuarial principles, under regulations prescribed by the Secretary. . . ." Defendant's contention is emphasized by the testimony of its expert witness who concluded that the value of decedent's reversionary interest was 9.413%, based entirely upon U.S. Life Table 38, set forth in the Treasury Regulations. He completely ignored, as defendant does on brief in this court, the statutory provision that such valuation shall be determined "by usual methods of valuation."

We think no good purpose could be served in setting forth the lengthy and complicated Treasury Regulations designed to cover a wide variety of situations. Particularly is this so in view of defendant's statement on brief: "The value is ascertained in accordance with recognized valuation principles for determining the value for estate tax purposes of future or conditional interests in property. See Treas. Reg. §§20.2031-1, 20.2031-7, and 20.2031-9."

Treas. Reg. §20.2031-1 provides: "Valuation of Property in General . . . All relevant factors and elements of value as of the applicable valuation date shall be considered in every case."

Defendant's admission that value is ascertained "in accordance with recognized valuation principles" and the regulation lastly quoted, "[a]ll relevant factors and elements of value . . . shall be considered in every case," are consistent with the statutory provision that value shall be determined "by usual methods of valuation, including the use of tables of mortality . . . under regulations prescribed by the Secretary. . . ."

Even so, defendant on brief, as did its expert witness, places its reliance on Treas. Reg. §20.2031-7, which provides that value shall be computed upon the basis of mortality Table 38 of United States Life Tables published by the United States Department of Commerce. We do not understand this regulation to require that value be determined solely on the mortality table. If so, it contravenes not only the statutory provision but is inconsistent with Treas. Reg. §20.2031-1, which provides that all factors and elements of value be considered in every case. Thus, even under the Treasury Regulations, we think that the District Court correctly considered factors other than the age of the decedent, such as her physical and mental condition, in determining the value of her reversionary interest. . . .

There can hardly be doubt on this record but that "usual methods of valuation" require or at least permit taking into consideration the life expectancies of the parties involved. The mortality table solely relied upon by defendant is based upon the life expectancy of the average or normal person. In the instant case, the decedent for nine years prior to her death, the last four of which were spent in a hospital, was in a progressively declining state of health until at the time immediately before her death she had, as found by the court, a life expectancy not to exceed three years. More than that, the value of her reversionary interest was further limited by the highly improbable contingency that she outlive her son, William S. Hall, who had a life expectancy of not less than fifteen years.

To hold, as defendant would have us do, that these circumstances must not be taken into consideration in valuing decedent's reversionary interest is to ignore realism and common sense. Certainly we are not persuaded that Congress intended such a result. . . .

The judgment appealed from is affirmed.

Although not specifically mentioning *Hall*, the government repudiated it in Rev. Rul. 66-307, which stated that "in computing the value of a decedent's reversionary interest for the purposes of §§2037(b) and 2042(2) . . . Congress has provided a rule of administrative convenience which requires the application of actuarial tables notwithstanding the facts of the decedent's death or the facts surrounding his death." See also Treas. Reg. §20.2037-1(c)(3). The position promulgated by the government in Rev. Rul. 66-307 was adopted in Estate of Roy v. Commissioner, 54 T.C. 1317 (1970), and in Robinson v. United States, 632 F.2d 822 (9th Cir. 1980), and Estate of Allen v. United States, 558 F.2d 14 (Ct. Cl. 1977). The Tax Court said in *Roy* that, if the position of Rev. Rul. 66-307 were to be rejected, it would mean that §2037 would "be applicable only in cases of sudden death; e.g., when a healthy individual dies as the result of a sudden coronary." 54 T.C. at 1323.

Rev. Rul. 80-80 updated the government's position in this area by making the following statements:

In view of recent case law, the resulting principle is as follows: the current actuarial tables in the regulations shall be applied if valuation of an individual's life interest is required for purposes of the federal estate or gift taxes unless the individual is known to have been afflicted, at the time of transfer, with an incurable physical condition that is in such an advanced stage that death is clearly imminent. Death is not clearly imminent if there is a reasonable possibility of survival for more than a very brief period. For example, death is not clearly imminent if the individual may survive for a year or more and if such a possibility is not so remote as to be negligible. If the evidence indicates that the decedent will survive for less than a year, no inference should be drawn that death will be regarded as clearly imminent, because this question depends on all the facts and circumstances.

The above principle is applicable to every situation that involves valuation of an interest that is dependent upon the life of one or more individuals for federal estate or gift tax purposes, including valuation with respect to deductions allowable under §2055 or §2522, with the exception of determinations involving a decedent's own life expectancy under §§2037 and 2042(2). The Service adheres to the conclusion, stated in Rev. Rul. 66-307, that the actuarial tables must be applied in every case where a decedent's reversionary interest must be valued under §§2042(2) or 2037. See the discussion in Estate of Roy v. Commissioner, 54 T.C. 1317 (1970), which declined to follow Hall v. United States, 353 F.2d 500 (7th Cir. 1965). See also Estate of Allen v. United States, 558 F.2d 14 (Ct. Cl. 1977).

Since 1989, for federal tax purposes, the values of temporal interests in property, including estimates of mortality, are determined under §7520. The regulations under §7520 require that, for purposes of §2037(b), the valuation of a decedent's reversionary interest is to be determined by using the government's mortality tables, regardless of the condition of the decedent's health prior to death. Treas. Reg. §20.7520-3(b)(3). Mortality tables are not to be used for most tax purposes if a person whose life expectancy is to be determined for tax purposes is terminally ill at the measuring date; there are several exceptions to that general rule and a determination for purposes of §2037(b) is one of them. Id. Treas. Reg. §20.7520-3(b)(3)(ii) repeats the position stated in Rev. Ruls. 66-307 and 80-80 that ". . . the value of a decedent's reversionary interest under §2037(b) . . . shall be determined without regard to the physical condition, immediately before the decedent's death, of the individual who is the measuring life."

The government's position that mortality tables must be used in §2037(b) cases does not always disfavor the taxpayer. The valuation of a reversion may depend upon the life expectancy of two or more persons — not solely upon that of the grantor. For example, if D has a reversionary interest conditioned upon D surviving Y, the shorter Y's life expectancy is, the greater will be the value of D's reversion. If Y was terminally ill at the time of D's death, the tables (in lieu of considering Y's actual life expectancy) will not allow the value of D's reversion to be higher.

Ignoring differing perceptions of proper tax policy or congressional intent, does *Hall* have a good point insofar as the statutory language of

§2037(b) is concerned? Estate of Allen v. United States, 558 F.2d 14, 19 (Ct. Cl. 1977), addressed this problem as follows:

> [N]ot all reversionary interests can be valued actuarially.[30] As such, we believe that the provisions' "usual methods of valuation" and "without regard to the fact of the decedent's death" only apply to interests which cannot be valued actuarially. When a reversionary interest can be valued actuarially, we interpret the Code to allow exclusive use of actuarial principles. This interpretation of the statutory language not only gives effect to all provisions in §2037(b) but also harmonizes Treas. Reg. §20.2031-1 with §§20.2031-7 and 20.2031-10.

See also Robinson v. United States, 632 F.2d 822, 827-829 (9th Cir. 1980).

21.   *Burden of Proof Under the 5% Rule.* Valuation is critical but not often easy. The 1997 change in the burden of persuasion does not alter the burden to produce valuation evidence. See, e.g., Estate of Thacher v. Commissioner, 20 T.C. 474, 482-483 (1953):

> [T]he record contains no evidence that the reversionary interest based upon the contingency of divorce or legal separation cannot be valued. . . . The burden was upon the [estate] to produce evidence that the value of such reversionary interest, immediately before the death of the decedent, could not be determined or that its value was not in excess of 5% of the value of the corpus of the trust. The court must assume, therefore, that the value did exceed the necessary 5%.

H.R. Rep. No. 1337, 83d Cong., 2d Sess. A 314 (1954); S. Rep. No. 1622, 83d Cong., 2d Sess. 469 (1954):

> The decedent's reversionary interest is to be valued by recognized valuation principles and without regard to the fact of the decedent's death. Where it is apparent from the facts that property could have reverted to the decedent under contingencies that were not remote, the reversionary interest is not to be necessarily regarded as having no value merely because the value thereof cannot be measured precisely.

---

30. For example, actuarial principles cannot value a reversionary interest contingent on death without issue. See Commissioner v. Estate of Sternberger, 348 U.S. 187 (1955); Humes v. United States, 276 U.S. 487 (1928).

Estate of Tarver v. Commissioner, 26 T.C. 490, 500 (1956), *aff'd*, 255 F.2d 913 (4th Cir. 1958), *acq.*:

Here there is no showing that the value of the reversionary interest immediately before the death of the decedent did not exceed 5% of the value of the property comprising the corpus of the trust. The burden of proof in this respect was upon the [estate] and in the absence of such proof we must assume that the value did exceed the necessary 5%.

Estate of Graham v. Commissioner, 46 T.C. 415, 427 (1966):

[W]e find that, since the decedent's [reversionary interest] cannot be ascertained by the use of any recognized valuation principles, the power must be accorded a value of zero. Estate of Cardeza v. United States, 261 F.2d 423 (3d Cir. 1958); Estate of Slade v. Commissioner, 190 F.2d 689 (2d Cir. 1951), *rev'g* 15 T.C. 752 (1950). No part of the trust assets can thus be included in decedent's gross estate under §2037.

Cf. Rev. Rul. 79-117: "[T]he value of *D*'s reversionary interest [for purposes of §2042(2)] is less than 5% of the policy value as of the moment immediately before *D*'s death, because it was subject to *B*'s right to change the beneficiary."

22. *The General Power Exception to §2037.* Read the last sentence of §2037(b). Such a general power of appointment would not exist in a normal trustee discretion, nor with respect to a power exercisable only after the decedent's death, but a presently exercisable general power to appoint the remainder and divest the decedent's reversion would be effective.

23. *Relinquishing the Reversionary Interest.* Although the Economic Recovery Tax Act of 1981 effectively repealed much of §2035(a) for the estates of donors who die after 1981, one of the §2035(a)(2) exceptions to this repeal is with respect to any transfer of an interest in property within three years of the grantor's death if the property would have been included in the grantor's gross estate under §2037 if the grantor had retained the interest until death. In this regard recall United States v. Allen, 293 F.2d 916 (10th Cir. 1961), reproduced at page 244. The following Ruling shows an added element of a consistent valuation principle:

Revenue Ruling 79-62

In 1950, *D* transferred property in trust with the income payable to *A* during *A*'s life. The remainder interest in the trust property was to revert to *D*, if *D* survived *A*. If *D* predeceased *A*, the remainder interest was to vest in *C*. In 1975, *D* . . . assigned the reversion to *C*. At the time of the assignment, the value of the trust property was 150x dollars, and the value of the reversionary interest exceeded 5% of the value of the trust property. *D* died in 1976, survived by *A*. Immediately before *D*'s death, the value of the trust property was 155x dollars. If *D* had not assigned the reversionary interest, the value of that interest at the time of *D*'s death would have been less than 5% of the value of the trust property.

. . . If *D* had not assigned *D*'s reversionary interest in the trust property, the first two requirements of §2037(a) would have been met. *C* could obtain possession or enjoyment of the trust property only by surviving *D*. See Treas. Reg. §20.2037-1(e) *Example (3)*. Further, under the terms of the trust instrument, there was a possibility that the trust property would return to *D* under certain circumstances. The third requirement of §2037(a) would not have been satisfied, because the present value of the reversionary interest immediately before *D*'s death was less than 5% of the value of the trust property. Thus, if *D* had retained until death the reversionary interest in the trust property, none of the property would have been includible in *D*'s gross estate under the provisions of §2037(a).

. . . Therefore, none of the trust property is includible under §2035 even though the decedent transferred the reversionary interest [within three years] of death.

PART C.   RETAINED POWERS

Code References: *Estate Tax: §§2036(a)(2), 2036(b), 2038*
Gift Tax: Treas. Reg. §§25.2511-2, 25.7520
Income Tax: §§671, 672, 674-677

Property law and tax law share the perception that policy considerations are served by treating some inter vivos transfers as testamentary. Under both property law and tax law, a grantor who retains sufficient control over property in the form of certain *powers* (as opposed to retained enjoyment of *interests* in the property, such as a life estate or a reversion), has not made a sufficiently "complete" transfer to be treated as having made an effective inter vivos gift. The actual transfer, therefore, is deemed to occur, or become complete, only when the grantor's retained powers expire — usually when the grantor dies. Thus, a transfer that is in form inter vivos may be testamentary in substance, and be so treated by either or both sets of laws.

24.   *Beneficial Powers.*   For tax purposes, a grantor who reserves a beneficial — or general — power (such as a power to revoke the transfer and reacquire the property) has not made an effective transfer, because the beneficial power to revest the property represents substantive ownership of the property to which the power relates. For property law purposes, however, retention of a beneficial interest — such as a life estate or a reversionary interest — ordinarily is not sufficient to cause an inter vivos transfer to be treated as testamentary. The same is true of a retained power of revocation, if the question is merely the formal sufficiency of the document of transfer under the Statute of Wills. RESTATEMENT (SECOND) OF TRUSTS §57 (1959). A revocable trust has proven to be a popular planning tool even though it provides no tax benefits.

Property law's emphasis of form over substance provides desirable flexibility in family property settlements. Absent additional problems in a given case, there is no persuasive reason to invalidate will substitutes, such as revocable trusts, merely because the transfer was not effected in accordance with the statutory will execution formalities. Nevertheless, for some purposes, even property law regards reserved powers to revoke as sufficient to make a transfer incomplete. In one of these — the principle that the period of the Rule Against Perpetuities does not begin to run until the power to revoke expires — the shift from form to substance can be viewed as furthering flexibility, not contracting it. In other circumstances, countervailing policies control the treatment.

For example, in some states revocable transfers are subject to a surviving spouse's statutory forced share, as is the case under the 1990 version of Uniform Probate Code §2-205(2)(i), the "augmented estate" concept, which includes property subject to a retained power of revocation. Similarly, some states overrule by legislation the common law rule that, absent a fraudulent conveyance, creditors of the grantor have no claim to property subject to a power of revocation. See also federal bankruptcy law, which regards a bankrupt's estate as including all property subject to powers the debtor may exercise for the debtor's own benefit.

Although property law focuses mainly on form, the tax principle of "horizontal equity" requires that persons in similar substantive positions be treated similarly. Thus, virtually from the original version of the tax law, the notion has been that a transfer is not complete to the extent the grantor has retained a beneficial power. The Revenue Act of 1924 introduced income tax provisions substantially similar to present §§676(a) and 677, an estate tax provision substantially similar to present §2038(a)(2), and a gift tax provision substantially similar to present §2501(a). The income tax provision explicitly declared that the existence of a power to revoke was sufficient to render a transfer incomplete, so that the post-transfer income from the property was attributed to the grantor regardless of to whom it actually was paid.[31] The estate tax provision required inclusion of the transferred property in the grantor's gross estate if the power was still held at death).[32]

The gift tax provision, unlike its income and estate tax counterparts, did not expressly state that certain gifts are incomplete when made. Instead, the statute simply provided, as it still does today, that a tax is imposed on the transfer of property by gift. Moreover, because the gift tax was introduced from the floor in both houses of Congress, the committee reports that accompanied the 1924 Act contained no guidance as to congressional intent; nor did the floor debates yield any helpful comments. It was left to the government initially and ultimately to the courts to work out the overall approach of the gift tax.

The government lost little time issuing a regulation in 1924 providing that transfers with retained powers to revoke were not taxable transfers for gift tax purposes. This "interpretation" of the gift tax was resisted by the taxpayer in Burnet v. Guggenheim, 288 U.S. 280 (1933), in which a revocable trust (created prior to enactment of the gift tax) was made irrevocable by release in 1925 of the power to revoke. In accordance with the regulation, the government determined that a taxable gift was made when the power was released. The Court held:

The tax upon gifts is closely related both in structure and in purpose to the tax upon those transfers that take effect at death. What is paid the one is in certain circumstances a credit to be applied in reduction of what will be due upon the other. The gift tax [and] the estate tax . . . are plainly in pari materia. . . . The tax upon estates, as it stood in 1924, was the outcome of a long process of evolution; it had been refined and perfected by decisions and amendments almost without number. The tax on gifts was something new. Even so, the concept of a transfer, so painfully developed in respect of taxes on estates, was not flung aside and scouted in laying this new burden upon transfers during life. Congress was aware that what was of the essence of a transfer had come to be identified more nearly with a change of economic benefits than with technicalities of title. . . .

---

31.   The income tax provision was declared to be constitutional in Corliss v. Bowers, 281 U.S. 376 (1930), in which the grantor was taxed on income from a revocable inter vivos trust that was payable to the grantor's spouse for life, with a remainder to their children.

32.   The estate tax provision contained in the Revenue Act of 1916 taxed transfers "intended to take effect in possession or enjoyment at or after" the transferor's death. The applicability of this language to revocable transfers was confirmed in Reinecke v. Northern Trust Co., 278 U.S. 339 (1929), but Congress in 1924 adopted the more explicit language of what is now §2038(a)(2) to remove any doubt about the matter.

The [taxpayer] finds comfort in the provisions . . . governing taxes on estates. He asks why such a provision should have been placed in [the estate tax] and nothing equivalent inserted in [the gift tax] if powers for purposes of the one tax were to be treated in the same way as powers for the purposes of the other. . . . No doubt the draftsman of the statute would have done well if he had been equally explicit in the drafting of [the gift tax]. This is not to say that meaning has been lost because extraordinary foresight would have served to make it clearer. Here as so often there is a choice between uncertainties. We must be content to choose the lesser. To lay the tax at once, while the deed is subject to the power, is to lay it on a gift that may never become consummate in any real or beneficial sense. To lay it later on is to unite benefit with burden. We think the voice of Congress has ordained that this be done.

Compare Treas. Reg. §20.2041-1(e) and *Example (1)*; Lowndes, Kramer, & McCord, FEDERAL ESTATE AND GIFT TAXES §9.5 (3d ed. 1974).

There were no committee reports to which the Supreme Court in *Guggenheim* could turn for assistance in determining the intent of Congress in enacting the 1924 gift tax. But in reenacting the gift tax in the Revenue Act of 1932 (the 1924 version was repealed in 1926), Congress expressly provided that revocable transfers were subject to gift tax upon relinquishment of the power, and the reports of both the House Ways and Means Committee and the Senate Finance Committee expressly noted that revocable transfers were not intended to be subject to the gift tax when made.[33] Although the *Guggenheim* opinion did not allude to the 1932 enactment or to the committee reports, the statute had been enacted and the reports had been issued before *Guggenheim* was argued. Subsequently, the Revenue Act of 1934 repealed the 1932 provision because *Guggenheim* was thought to have made it unnecessary.[34]

To summarize, notwithstanding that the gift tax was (and is) unspecific insofar as revocable transfers are concerned, the tax was construed by the government and the courts to be in pari materia with estate tax law. Although we will return to a more detailed consideration of the tax treatment of revocable transfers, it is sufficient at this point to note that all three taxes treat revocable transfers as if the grantor still owns the property: No gift tax is imposed; the post-transfer income earned from the property is taxed to the grantor; each payment of income to a beneficiary other than the grantor is subject to gift tax; and the value of the property is includible in the grantor's gross estate.

---

33. H.R. Rep. No. 708, 72d Cong., 1st Sess. 28 (1932), in 1939-1 C.B. (pt. 2) 457, 477; S. Rep. No. 665, 72d Cong., 1st Sess. 40 (1932), in 1939-1 C.B. (pt. 2) 496, 524-525.

34. H.R. Rep. No. 704, 73d Cong., 2d Sess. 40 (1934), in 1939-1 C.B. (pt. 2) 554, 584; S. Rep. No. 558, 73d Cong., 2d Sess. 50 (1934), in 1939-1 C.B. (pt. 2) 586, 624.

25. *Nonbeneficial Powers.* Nonbeneficial powers are limited to shifting beneficial interests in transferred property among persons other than the grantor. The proper tax treatment of nonbeneficial powers is a more complex issue than the treatment of beneficial powers because it cannot properly be said that no transfer has occurred; something substantial has been transferred even while something has been retained. The question is whether the grantor retained so much control over the transferred property that the grantor should be treated as still owning it, or was sufficient enjoyment and control transferred that the transferee should be treated as owning it? This same question arises in the income and estate tax areas in the case of retained property interests.

Under the gift tax, the transfer is bifurcated if a value can be placed upon what the grantor retains. Thus, if the grantor retained a life income interest, for estate tax purposes the grantor is treated as the owner of the entire property until death; and the income from the property is taxed to the grantor under §677 as it is earned by the trust. But for gift tax purposes the grantor is treated as having transferred the remainder interest during life, with double transfer taxation on that value being eliminated by the §2001(b) purge and credit in computing the gross estate tax.

No gift tax bifurcation is possible, however, in the case of retained nonbeneficial powers because (as to the interest as to which the power applies) there is no viable way to value what is retained and what is transferred. Thus, the gift tax is forced into an all-or-nothing posture. The grantor must be treated as having transferred all of the property or none of it. In the early income tax, the only provisions dealing with retained powers were the forerunners of present §§676(a) and 677, which only apply to beneficial powers. But this is not how the tax law later evolved.

The nonbeneficial power issue first came to the Supreme Court in an estate tax case, Porter v. Commissioner, 288 U.S. 436 (1933). Unlike the income tax, the 1924 estate tax predecessor of present §2038(a)(2) referred to a power to "alter, amend, or revoke." Despite the "or," which clearly seems to indicate that Congress intended to treat beneficial and nonbeneficial powers alike for estate tax purposes, the committee reports accompanying the Revenue Act of 1924 were equivocal. At one point those reports state that the full value of transferred property is includible in the grantor's gross estate if the grantor retains until death a power "to change the enjoyment of a property interest," thereby having "substantial control over the disposition of the property, through the power to change the enjoyment thereof." Yet the very next sentence suggested that these statements were limited to beneficial powers, saying that "this provision is in accord with the principal of §[671(a),] which taxes to the transferor the income of a revocable trust."[35] Federal courts disagreed over this question.

---

35. H.R. Rep. No. 179, 68th Cong., 1st Sess. 28 (1924), in 1939-1 C.B. (pt. 2) 241, 261; S. Rep. No. 398, 68th Cong., 1st Sess. 34-35 (1924), in 1939-1 C.B. (pt. 2) 266, 290.

Brady v. Ham, 45 F.2d 454 (1st Cir. 1930), and Cover v. Burnet, 53 F.2d 915 (D.C. Cir. 1931), held that the estate tax caught only revocable transfers, while Porter v. Commissioner, 60 F.2d 673 (2d Cir. 1932), held that the existence of a nonbeneficial power in the grantor also caused estate tax inclusion of the property subject to the power.

The Supreme Court reviewed *Porter* to resolve this conflict. Before certiorari was granted in *Porter*, however — indeed, over a year before the court of appeals rendered its decision — Congress almost casually took action that bore directly on the policy issue involved. On March 3, 1931, the joint resolution that introduced the forerunner of present §2036 was rushed through Congress in reaction to three per curiam decisions of the Supreme Court that made it clear that the Court meant what it said in May v. Heiner, 281 U.S. 238 (1930) — that transfers under which the grantor retained an income interest for life were not covered by the statutory phrase taxing transfers "intended to take effect in possession or enjoyment at or after" the grantor's death. Although the principal purpose of the joint resolution was to provide explicitly that transfers with retained enjoyment were includible in the grantor's gross estate, Congress also adopted what is now §2036(a)(2). This provision covered retained nonbeneficial powers over the income from transferred property. Thus, although the joint resolution did not govern the construction of the predecessor of §2038(a)(2), it did indicate that Congress no longer confined the estate tax to beneficial powers, if indeed it ever intended to do so.

In *Porter* the grantor reserved a power to change the trust in any manner except to benefit the grantor or the grantor's estate. Without alluding to the joint resolution, the Court in *Porter* decided in favor of inclusion of the value of the property subject to the nonbeneficial power, relying heavily on the statutory language:

. . . [The taxpayer] argues that, as decedent was without power to revoke the transfers or to alter or modify the trusts in favor of himself or his estate, the property is not covered by [§2038(a)(2)]. But the disjunctive use of the words "alter," "modify" and "amend" negatives that contention. We find nothing in the context or in the policy evidenced by this and prior estate tax laws or in the legislative history of [§2038(a)(2)] to suggest that conjunctive use of these words was intended, or that "alter" and "modify" were used as equivalents of "revoke" or are to be understood in other than their usual meanings. We need not consider whether every change, however slight or trivial, would be within the meaning of the clause. Here the donor retained until his death power enough to enable him to make a complete revision of all that he had done in respect of the creation of the trusts even to the extent of taking the property from the trustees and beneficiaries named and transferring it absolutely or in trust for the benefit of others. So far as concerns the tax here involved, there is no difference in principle between a transfer subject to such changes and one that is revocable. The transfers under consideration are undoubtedly covered by [§2038(a)(2)].

[The taxpayer] contends that so construed [§2038(a)(2)] is repugnant to the due process clause of the Fifth Amendment. . . . They maintain that inclusion of the transfers in question would be to measure decedent's tax by property belonging to others, a thing condemned in Heiner v. Donnan, 285 U.S. 312 (1930), and Hoeper v. Tax Commission, 284 U.S. 206 (1931), and would be to tax gifts inter vivos that were fully consummated prior to the enactment of [§2038(a)(2)] and therefore would be confiscatory under Nichols v. Coolidge, 274 U.S. 531 (1927), and *Heiner v. Donnan*.

They treat as without significance the power the donor reserved unto himself alone and ground all their arguments upon the fact that deceased, prior to such enactment, completely divested himself of title without power of revocation. It is true that the power reserved was not absolute as in the transfer considered in Burnet v. Guggenheim, 288 U.S. 280 (1933), in which this court, in the absence of any provision corresponding to [§2038(a)(2)], held that the donor's termination of the power amounted to a transfer by gift within the meaning of [§2501]. But the reservation here may not be ignored, for, while subject to the specified limitation, it made the settlor dominant in respect of other dispositions of both corpus and income. His death terminated that control, ended the possibility of any change by him, and was, in respect of title to the property in question, the source of valuable assurance passing from the dead to the living. That is the event on which Congress based the inclusion of property so transferred in the gross estate as a step in the calculation to ascertain the amount of what in [§2001] is called the [taxable] estate. Thus was reached what it reasonably might deem a substitute for testamentary disposition. United States v. Wells, 283 U.S. 102, 116 (1931). There is no doubt as to the power of Congress so to do. Reinecke v. Northern Trust Co., 278 U.S. 339 (1929); Chase National Bank v. United States, 278 U.S. 327 (1929); Tyler v. United States, 281 U.S. 497 (1930); Klein v. United States, 283 U.S. 231 (1931); Gwinn v. Commissioner, 287 U.S. 224 (1932).

The estate tax treatment of nonbeneficial powers spread to the income tax, which underwent a partial modification. The early income tax legislation contained provisions attributing post-transfer income to any grantor who retained a beneficial power, but there was no such provision regarding nonbeneficial powers. Indeed, the income tax distinction between beneficial and nonbeneficial powers eventually was supported by lower federal court authority. Knapp v. Hoey, 104 F.2d 99 (2d Cir. 1939). But the landmark Supreme Court decision in Helvering v. Clifford, 309 U.S. 331 (1940), came hard on the heels of *Knapp* and very soon thereafter the majority of federal courts (including the *Knapp* court) concluded that retention of nonbeneficial powers would cause post-transfer income to be attributed to the grantor. See Lowndes, Kramer, & McCord, FEDERAL ESTATE AND GIFT TAXES §28.4 n.32 (3d ed. 1974). This position was solidified in the 1945 Clifford regulations, the principles of which subsequently were codified in §674, which establishes the general principle that the grantor must report the income from property transferred with retained nonbeneficial powers (although §§674(b)-(d) contain many specific exceptions for various enumerated retained powers).

The gift tax question came to the Supreme Court in the companion cases of Estate of Sanford v. Commissioner, 308 U.S. 39 (1939), and Rasquin v. Humphreys, 308 U.S. 54 (1939), which involved retained powers similar to those held by the grantor in *Porter*. Curiously, the government conceded that it was advocating inconsistent positions in the two cases, arguing that the transfer was complete when made in *Humphreys* but not complete until the power is released in *Sanford*, because it was unable to determine which construction of the gift tax statute would be more advantageous in terms of revenue collected. Without delving into an analysis of which construction would yield the higher revenue, the Court followed the pattern set by *Guggenheim* of reading the estate tax view into the gift tax law, saying in *Sanford*:

There is nothing in the language of the statute, and our attention has not been directed to anything in its legislative history to suggest that Congress had any purpose to tax gifts before the donor had fully parted with his interest in the property given, or that the test of the completeness of the taxed gift was to be any different from that to be applied in determining whether the donor has retained an interest such that it becomes subject to the estate tax upon its extinguishment at death. The gift tax was supplementary to the estate tax. The two are in pari materia and must be construed together. Burnet v. Guggenheim, 288 U.S. 280, 286 (1933). An important, if not the main, purpose of the gift tax was to prevent or compensate for avoidance of death taxes by taxing the gifts of property inter vivos which, but for the gifts, would be subject in its original or converted form to the tax laid upon transfers at death.

. . . We are concerned here with a question to which Congress has given no answer in the words of the statute, and it must be decided in conformity to the course of judicial decision applicable to a unified scheme of taxation of gifts whether made inter vivos or at death. If Congress, for the purpose of taxing income, has defined precisely the amount of control over the income which it deems equivalent to ownership of it, that definition is controlling on the courts even though without it they might reach a different conclusion, and even though retention of a lesser degree of control be deemed to render a transfer incomplete for the purpose of laying gift and death taxes.

Section [2012] provides that, when a tax has been imposed by [§2501] upon a gift [made prior to 1977], the value of which is required by any provision of the statute taxing the estate to be included in the gross estate, the gift tax is to be credited [against] the estate tax. The two taxes are thus not always mutually exclusive as in the case of gifts made in contemplation of death which are complete and taxable when made, and [were] also required to be included in the gross estate for purposes of the death tax. But [§2012] is without application unless there is a gift inter vivos which is taxable independently of any requirement that it shall be included in the gross estate. Property transferred in trust subject to a power of control over its disposition reserved to the donor is likewise required by [§2038(a)(2)] to be included in the gross estate. But it does not follow that the transfer in trust is also taxable as a gift. The point was decided in the *Guggenheim* case where it was held that a gift upon trust, with power in the donor to revoke it is not taxable as a gift because the transfer is incomplete, and that the transfer whether inter vivos or at death becomes complete and taxable only when the power of control is relinquished. We think, as was pointed out in the *Guggenheim* case that the gift tax statute does not contemplate two taxes upon the gift when a trust is created or when the power of revocation, if any, is relinquished, and another on the transfer of the same property at death because the gift previously made was incomplete.

See Treas. Reg. §25.2511-2(c).

From a policy perspective, it is arguable whether the present transfer tax system supports the *Porter* position. Should transfers over which the grantor retains nonbeneficial strings be taxed when the property is transferred or when the strings are relinquished or lapse? Under the current system a transfer is not immune from gift tax when made merely because the transferred property will be subjected to an estate tax when the grantor dies, and the purge and credit mechanism in §2001(b) is meant to ameliorate the double taxation that otherwise would result. If bifurcation of a transfer is not possible, because of the impossibility of valuing the retained nonbeneficial power, the all-or-nothing approach forced on the gift tax resulted in the Court reaching a "nothing" decision in *Sanford*. But later Robinette v. Helvering, 318 U.S. 184 (1943), held that a grantor who retained a property interest that cannot be valued is deemed to have transferred the entire property — an "all" decision. That easy-to-complete gift tax position now is embodied in Treas. Reg. §25.2511-1(e).

The *Sanford* Court seemed to base its "nothing" decision on the notion that Congress did not intend that a single transfer of property (other than a transfer made in contemplation of death) should be subject to both an estate tax and a gift tax, based on the Court's theory that the estate tax credit for gift taxes paid was intended only for gifts made in contemplation of death.[36] But on the same day *Robinette* was decided, the Supreme Court held in Smith v. Shaugnnessy, 318 U.S. 176, 178-179 (1943), albeit in the context of a different type of transfer, that the two taxes could be applied to a single transfer that was not made in contemplation of death; consequently, the fact that an estate tax would be imposed when the grantor died was not a bar to subjecting the transfer to a gift tax:

> The taxpayer's principal argument here is . . . that in the *Sanford* case we intimated a general policy against allowing the same property to be taxed both as an estate and as a gift.
>
> This view, we think, misunderstands our position in the *Sanford* case. As we said there, the gift and estate tax laws are closely related and the gift tax serves to supplement the estate tax.[37] We said that the taxes are not "always mutually exclusive," and called attention to [§2012] there involved . . . which charts the course for granting credits on estate taxes by reason of previous payment of gift taxes on the same property. The scope of that provision we need not now determine. It is sufficient to note here that Congress plainly pointed out that "some" of the "total gifts subject to gift taxes . . . may be included for estate tax purposes and some not." H.R. Rep. No. 708, 72d Cong. 1st Sess. 45. Under the statute the gift tax amounts in some instances to a security, a form of down-payment on the estate tax, which secures the eventual payment of the latter; it is in no sense double taxation as the tax payer suggests.

---

36. The question in *Sanford* was whether a gift tax would be imposed under the Revenue Act of 1924. It is noteworthy that, when *Sanford* was decided, the credit for gift taxes was limited to the *basic* estate tax on the donated property and could not be applied against the larger tentative tax that was then applicable. This may have been a factor in the Court's assumption that the credit played such a limited role.

37. The gift tax was passed not only to prevent estate tax avoidance, but also to prevent income tax avoidance through reducing yearly income and thereby escaping the effect of progressive surtax rates. H.R. Rep. No. 708, 72d Cong. 1st Sess. 28; Brandeis, J., dissenting in Untermyer v. Anderson, 276 U.S. 440, 450 (1928); Stone, J., dissenting in Heiner v. Donnan, 285 U.S. 312, 333 (1932).

The position taken in *Sanford* is therefore somewhat anomalous when placed against the way the wealth transfer tax system subsequently developed. Nevertheless, there has been no retreat from the holding of *Sanford* that the retention of a nonbeneficial power to shift property interests from one donee to another prevents a transfer from being complete for gift tax purposes, and this still constitutes an integral part of gift tax law. See Treas. Reg. §25.2511-2(c).[38]

Noting this anomaly does not imply that an ideal transfer tax system should not develop a single standard by which transfers would be subjected to the transfer tax once and only once. Discussion of that idea is postponed, however, until Part D of this chapter, which considers proposals for transfer tax revision. Interestingly, in adopting the unified transfer tax system in the Tax Reform Act of 1976, Congress did not seek to change this aspect of the law. Only the following statement on this question appears in the 1976 House Ways and Means Committee Report: "In general, the rules established under present law [are] retained as to when a gift is considered to be completed for gift tax purposes and as to when property is included in a decedent's gross estate for estate tax purposes." H.R. Rep. No. 1380, 94th Cong., 2d Sess. 12 (1976).

26.   *Estate, Gift, and Income Tax Points of Inconsistency.* Notwithstanding general principles shared by all three tax structures, when each is viewed individually it is clear that they are neither coordinated nor mutually exclusive in their operation. Overlapping yet different tests of completeness have been developed in the estate, the gift, and the income tax areas, so that some transfers with retained powers are not treated consistently. This state of affairs caused Judge Frank to remark in Commissioner v. Estate of Beck, 129 F.2d 243, 246 (2d Cir. 1942), that Congress might be well advised to "use different symbols to describe the taxable conduct in the several statutes, calling it a 'gift' in the gift tax law, a 'gaft' in the income tax law, and a 'geft' in the estate tax law."

To be specific, it is easier in two respects for a transfer with a retained power to be treated as complete for gift tax purposes than it is for estate tax purposes; consequently, despite what was said by the Supreme Court in *Sanford*, some transfers are subject to both a gift tax (at the time of the transfer) and an estate tax (at the donor's death). And, recall Judge Easterbrook's argument in Grimes v. Commissioner, 851 F.2d 1005 (7th

---

38.   Under this regulation, if a transferor's power to change beneficial interests in donated property is limited to a temporal interest in the property, such as an income interest, then only the value of that temporal interest is excluded from the gift tax. Note that this result constitutes a departure from the rationale adopted by the Supreme Court in *Sanford* in that a retained power over the income interest would cause inclusion of the entire property in the transferor's gross estate and yet the transferor would be subjected to a gift tax on the value of the remainder interest when the gift was made.

Cir. 1988) (reproduced at page 186), that the double transfer tax is not totally eliminated by the §2001(b) purge and credit regime.

Although the easy or hard to complete approaches of the estate and gift taxes can be compared, the income tax grantor trust rules defy efforts at comparison. In some respects it is easier for income tax purposes to complete a transfer than it is for purposes of either or both transfer taxes; in some respects it is harder. Thus, it is wrong to assume that the income tax treatment of a transfer will coordinate with the estate or gift tax treatment. The income from transferred property may be taxable to the grantor even if the transfer incurred a gift tax when it was made but, conversely, the grantor may escape income tax exposure even if a transfer tax liability does not arise until the donor's death (i.e., the transfer is subject only to the estate tax).

27. *Tax Consequences of Retained Powers to Revoke.* A transfer subject to an unrestricted power of revocation is not complete for gift tax purposes. Only when and to the extent a portion of the transferred property or the income from that property is released from the grantor's power to revoke does the transfer become complete for gift, income, and estate tax purposes (and relinquishing a power to revoke within three years of death may trigger §2035(a)(2) notwithstanding that the release was a completed gift). The gift, income, and estate tax consequences of revocable inter vivos transfers can be itemized in two distinct scenarios: if the grantor retains a life estate and if the grantor does not.

Tax Consequences of Revocable Transfer with Retained Life Estate. D transferred property to T, in trust, directing T to pay the net income from the property to D for life, remainder at D's death to X. D retained a power to revoke the trust at any time, which would return the trust property to D or as D directs. The tax consequences of D's transfer are:

(1) Gift Tax: Because of the retained power to revoke, D's transfer at creation of the trust of the remainder interest to X is not a completed taxable gift. Treas. Reg. §25.2511-2(c).

(2) Income Tax: D will continue until death to be taxed on both the ordinary income generated by the trust property and any capital gains (or losses) realized by the trust. §§677(a)(1), 676; Treas. Reg. §1.671-3(b).

(3) Estate Tax: The full value of the trust principal will be includible in D's gross estate at death, under either §2036(a)(1) or §2038(a)(1).

In actual practice this trust is prototypical of the most commonly created inter vivos trust. Obviously the trust is not created for tax purposes because nothing has changed: the tax laws treat this as if no transfer were made by D until death.

Tax Consequences of Revocable Transfer With No Retained Life Estate. *D* transferred property to *T*, in trust, directing *T* to pay the net income from the property to *A* for *A*'s life, remainder at *A*'s death to *X*. *D* retained a power to revoke the trust at any time, which would return the trust property to *D* or as *D* directs. The tax consequences of *D*'s transfer are:

(1) Gift Tax: Upon creation of the trust, *D* transferred a life income interest to *A* and a remainder to *X*, but neither gift is complete, due to *D*'s retained power to revoke. Therefore, creation of the trust involved no taxable gifts. Treas. Reg. §25.2511-2(c). During continuance of the trust, however, each payment of income from the trust to *A* is considered to be a completed taxable gift from *D* to *A*. Treas. Reg. §25.2511-2(f). These income payments are present interests that qualify for the §2503(b) gift tax annual exclusion.

(2) Income Tax: D will continue until death to be taxed on both the ordinary income generated by the trust property and any capital gains (or losses) realized by the trust. §676; Treas. Reg. §1.671-3(b). The income payments to *A* are treated as a direct gift from *D* that are not includible in *A*'s gross income. §102.

(3) Estate Tax: The full value of the trust principal will be includible in *D*'s gross estate at death under §2038(a)(1). In addition, §2035(b) will require inclusion in *D*'s gross estate of any gift tax payable on any of the income payments made to *A* within three years of *D*'s death.

28. *Powers to Revoke in the Future.* The tax consequences described above may differ if a grantor's power to revoke is not exercisable, or if a current exercise is not effective, until some time in the future. Working from the template above, it should be possible to describe the gift, income, and estate tax consequences in the two examples below. As you work through those tax consequences, consider whether they present conditional powers or whether the powers are exercisable immediately but the effect of exercise is postponed, and what difference this distinction should make. See Treas. Reg. §§25.2511-2(b) and -2(c) with respect to the gift tax, §676(a) with respect to the income tax, and §2038(b) and Treas. Reg. §20.2038-1(b) with respect to the estate tax.

(a) *D* transferred property in trust, income payable to child, *C*, until *C* reaches the age of 35, when principal is distributable to *C*. *D* reserved a power to revoke the trust, but any exercise of this power is not effective until *C* becomes 21 years old. *D* died when *C* was 18 years of age, without having exercised the power.

(b) Assume the same facts except that *D* died when *C* was 25 years old, again without having exercised the power.

29. *Scope of a Power to Revoke.* Ordinarily a grantor will expressly retain both a power to revoke the trust and a power to amend its terms. Does a power to revoke, expressly retained, include the power to amend the trust? According to the RESTATEMENT (SECOND) OF TRUSTS §331, Comments g and h (1959):[39]

[I]t is a question of interpretation to be determined in view of the language used and all the circumstances. . . . Ordinarily a general power to revoke the trust will be interpreted as authorizing the settlor not only to revoke the trust in part by withdrawing a part of the trust property from the trust (see §330, Comment n), but also to modify the terms of the trust, and it will be unnecessary for the settlor first to revoke the trust and then to create a new trust. If, however, the effect of the modification is to add to or vary the duties of the trustee, this is a ground for permitting the trustee to resign as trustee. See §106. If the settlor reserves power to revoke the trust "as an entirety," he cannot modify the trust, although he can revoke the trust and if he so desires create a new trust.

With respect to whether it is possible to create an irrevocable trust but reserve a power to amend the trust terms, the RESTATEMENT further provides that:

[I]f the settlor reserves a power to modify the trust, it is a question of interpretation to be determined in view of the language used and all the circumstances whether and to what extent the power is subject to restrictions. If the power to modify is subject to no restrictions, it includes a power to revoke the trust.

In most states the common law rule has been that a trust is irrevocable unless the grantor has expressly retained a power to revoke. Some states, however, follow the opposite rule. E.g., Cal. Prob. Code §§15400, 15401; Iowa Code Ann. §633.3102(1); Okla. Stat. tit. 60, §175.41; Tex. Prop. Code §112.051, and RESTATEMENT (THIRD) OF TRUSTS §63 (T.D. 3 2001) and the Uniform Trust Code propose to reverse the common law presumption. State law is controlling for tax purposes on this point. Estate of Hill v. Commissioner, 64 T.C. 867 (1975).

State law in several cases has permitted the grantor of an irrevocable trust to rescind or reform the trust on the ground of mistake regarding the tax consequences of the transfer. See 4 Palmer, THE LAW OF RESTITUTION §§18.6, 18.7 (1978); 4 Scott & Fratcher, THE LAW OF TRUSTS §333.4 (4th ed. 1989); Berger v. United States, 487 F. Supp. 49 (W.D. Pa. 1980) (in a

---

39. Copyright © 1959 by the American Law Institute. Reprinted with the permission of the American Law Institute.

state court proceeding based on a unilateral mistake, the grantor of an irrevocable inter vivos trust successfully reformed the instrument to make the trust revocable, and then successfully sued the government for a refund of gift taxes paid on creation of the trust). Compare Rev. Rul. 73-142; Rev. Rul. 76-309.

Savings account trusts (also called "Totten" trusts) usually are held to be revocable and the value of the account includible in the depositor's gross estate under §2038(a)(1). Estate of Sulovich v. Commissioner, 587 F.2d 845 (6th Cir. 1978); Estate of Wilhelm v. United States, 76-1 U.S. Tax Cas. (CCH) ¶13,114 (D. N.J. 1975).

Some transfers not in trust nevertheless are revocable, in the sense that they are voidable. For example, in Estate of Casey v. Commissioner, 948 F.2d 895 (4th Cir. 1991), *rev'g* 58 T.C.M. (CCH) 176 (1989), gifts made under a durable power of attorney that did not specifically authorize gratuitous transfers were held to be voidable by the grantor and therefore subject to estate tax inclusion. See also Townsend v. United States, 889 F. Supp. 895 (D. Neb. 1995); Estate of Collins v. United States, 94-1 U.S. Tax Cas. (CCH) ¶60,162 (E.D. Mich. 1994); Estate of Gaynor v. Commissioner, 82 T.C.M. (CCH) 379 (2001); TAM 9231003; but see Estate of Bronston v. Commissioner, 56 T.C.M. (CCH) 550 (1988), and Estate of Gagliardi v. Commissioner, 89 T.C. 1207 (1987).

30.   *The Estate Tax Maze: Duplications and Differences in §§2036(a)(2) and 2038.*   One reality is that the gift, income, and estate tax rules are not well coordinated. Worse, even within the estate tax itself, there are unexpected duplications and a few instances of dissonance, attributable to the existence of two estate tax provisions that deal directly with powers over transferred property: §§2036(a)(2) and 2038(a)(1).[40] Although the language of §2041 (covering powers of appointment) is broad enough to apply to retained powers over transferred property as well as to powers conferred by a third party upon a donee, Treas. Reg. §20.2041-1(b)(2) limits the scope of §2041 to donee powers and makes §§2036 and 2038 the primary focus with respect to retained powers. Don't make the rookie mistake of trying to apply §2041 to transferor retained powers, which properly are the subject of the succeeding materials.

In many (perhaps most) cases, §§2036(a)(2) and 2038(a)(1) overlap and yield the same result. That is, many grantor powers trigger the application of both sections and each requires inclusion of the same amount in the decedent's gross estate. In those cases it makes little practical difference which section is applicable. See §2207B for one obvious ancillary

---

40.   In some circumstances a retained power also can raise a §2037 inclusion issue, because the term "reversionary interest" under §2037(b)(2) is deemed to include a power of disposition held by the transferor. This backwater aspect of retained powers is not pursued here, having already been discussed in Part B of this chapter.

difference (of no significance to the government, however). The government frequently will assert both provisions as support for its position and either or both provisions will cause the same amount to be included in the grantor's gross estate (only once, not double).

Many of the estate tax cases we study in this Part arose under a forerunner of §2038(a)(2), which is applicable with respect to transfers made before June 23, 1936. Nevertheless, a comparison of that provision to §§2038(a)(1) and 2036(a)(2) discloses that the general principles also apply to the latter two sections. In that regard you may consider both parts of §2038(a) as two peas from the same pod.

Differences.   Although there is much duplication between §§2036(a)(2), 2038(a)(1), and 2038(a)(2), there also are significant differences between these provisions, both as to applicability and as to the amount of property includible in the grantor's gross estate.[41] The primary reason it is worth knowing the differences between these provisions is because the amount includible in the grantor's gross estate may be greater under one provision (typically §2036(a)(2)) than the other. Briefly, some of the differences between §§2036(a)(2) and 2038(a)(1) are:

(1)   Section 2036(a)(2) requires inclusion of the same amount that would be included if the grantor had retained enjoyment of trust income until death, typically the full value of the entire trust. Section 2038(a)(1) only requires inclusion of the value of the interest that is subject to the grantor's power. Thus, under §2038, a power to defer enjoyment of income only would require inclusion of only the value of the income interest, and a power limited to changing the remainder beneficiary would cause inclusion of only the value of the remainder interest.

(2)   Section 2038(a)(1) applies to powers created by the grantor and held at the date of death (or released within three years thereof) regardless (with a few exceptions[42]) of how it came about that the grantor acquired or reacquired the power (for example, by a third party's exercise of a power of appointment or designation of the grantor as a successor trustee); §2036(a)(2) applies only to powers "retained" by the grantor. Thus, questions of prearrangement are important under §2036(a)(2) but not under §2038(a)(1),

---

41.   One difference of no great significance for obvious reasons is that a transfer prior to March 4, 1931, is subject only to §2038 because of the express limitation in §2036(c), and transfers before June 23, 1936, are subject to §2038(a)(2) rather than §2038(a)(1) by virtue of their express terms.

42.   See Estate of Skifter v. Commissioner, 468 F.2d 699 (2d Cir. 1972).

because only the former requires that the power be retained rather than just created and later held by the grantor at death.[43]

(3) Section 2036(a)(2) involves retained powers to affect or designate the enjoyment of an interest that would cause §2036(a)(1) inclusion if enjoyed or retained by the grantor personally. Thus, the power must exist for one of the periods that would cause §2036(a)(1) to apply: (a) for life, (b) for a period not ascertainable without reference to the grantor's death, or (c) for a period that does not in fact end before the grantor's death. In addition, §2036(a)(2) applies only with respect to powers over income or over the possession of nonincome producing property; a power that affects only the enjoyment of income-producing principal and not the income so produced is not subject to §2036(a)(2) (for example, a power to distribute principal to the income beneficiary). By way of contrast, §2038(a)(1) can apply to powers over either income or principal. See Treas. Reg. §20.2036-1(b)(3).

(4) Section 2038(a)(1) involves a grantor's power to alter, amend, revoke, or terminate enjoyment of any interest that was transferred, meaning that a negative power — to *prevent* enjoyment — will suffice. Section 2036(a)(1) requires an affirmative power "to designate the persons who shall possess or enjoy" the income or the nonincome producing principal.

(5) Unlike the prior differences, all of which make it easier to trigger §2038(a)(1) than §2036(a)(2), one difference works the opposite way: §2038(a)(1) does not apply to powers subject to an unmet contingency or condition that was beyond the grantor's control at death, but §2036(a)(2) may apply to contingent or conditional powers even if not exercisable at the grantor's death.

As you study the succeeding materials, consider the extent to which courts tend to ignore the differences in statutory language between §§2036(a)(2) and 2038(a)(1).

---

43. However, indirect control over enjoyment will suffice, even for §2036(a)(2), as illustrated by Rifkind v. United States, 84-2 U.S. Tax Cas. (CCH) ¶13,577 (Ct. Cl. 1984) (a trust created by the decedent distributed income to a foundation of which the decedent was a director, and in that capacity the decedent possessed control over the ultimate recipients of that income).

Of much less practical importance are differences between §§2038(a)(1) and 2038(a)(2). The 1936 amendment to the antecedent of §2038(a)(1) mostly involved the addition of certain words and phrases to the language of what is now §2038(a)(2). One inconsequential addition was the word "other," so that instead of saying "in conjunction with any person" (see §§2036(a)(2) and 2038(a)(2)), §2038(a)(1) says "in conjunction with any *other* person." Additional differences in language between §§2038(a)(1) and 2038(a)(2) will be examined at appropriate points in the succeeding materials to determine the extent to which the two subsections differ substantively.

Similarities. There are a number of similarities between §§2036(a)(2) and 2038(a)(1) that are worthy of note:

(1) Both sections contain exceptions for transfers made for full and adequate consideration in money or money's worth.

(2) Both sections regard joint powers and veto rights as tantamount to sole powers and direct powers to act, even if shared with an adverse party. Treas. Reg. §§20.2036-1(b)(3)(i); 20.2038-1(a).

(3) Both sections regard a grantor's power to remove the trustee and appoint the grantor as successor trustee as tantamount to possessing the trustee's powers. Treas. Reg. §§20.2036-1(b)(3); 20.2038-1(a)(3). The government initially asserted that a power to remove and replace a trustee at will, even if the grantor cannot be named as a successor trustee, produces the same result. After losing several cases, the government conceded that the power to remove a trustee and substitute an individual or corporation who is not related or subordinate to the decedent (within the meaning of §672(c)) does not give the decedent the trustee's powers, and therefore does not trigger §2036 or §2038. Rev. Rul. 95-58. See also PLR 9607008.

(4) Existence of a grantor's power will suffice under both sections, regardless of the grantor's capacity to exercise it.

(5) A power merely to alter the time of a beneficiary's enjoyment alone is sufficient under each section. For example, a power to accumulate income for future distribution will suffice to trigger each section.

(6) Discretion is required under each provision, meaning that a definite external objective standard (similar to, but not as inflexible as, a §2041 ascertainable standard) will protect against inclusion exposure under each. Thus, purely administrative or ministerial powers will not trigger either provision.

The following materials in this Part explore these similarities and differences, putting a little more meat on these bones.

The Amount Includible. One potential difference between §§2036(a)(2) and 2038(a)(1) is the amount required to be included in the gross estate. For example, a retained power to spray income among a group of income beneficiaries would trigger both sections, with §2036(a)(2) requiring inclusion of the value of the entire trust principal. (It is not accurate, however, to assume that §2036(a)(2) always requires inclusion of the full value of the trust principal, because it is necessary to exclude the value of any interest that precedes the interest subject to the grantor's power.) On the other hand, if §2036(a)(2) were inapplicable for some reason §2038(a)(1) would catch only the value of the income interest outstanding at the grantor's death. See if you can detect the subtle difference in statutory language upon which these disparate tax consequences rest, by studying the following materials and then the examples that follow.

Commissioner v. Estate of Hager, 173 F.2d 613 (3d Cir. 1949). In 1924 the decedent and his wife established five irrevocable inter vivos trusts, each spouse contributing half of the principal of each trust. The decedent was trustee of all five trusts, which were administered as a single unit and experienced considerable appreciation before the decedent died. The income beneficiary of each trust was a different child or grandchild of the decedent and each had a power to appoint the remainder of his or her trust. Each trust authorized the trustee to apportion realized appreciation to income rather than to principal as normally would be the case under state law, and permitted the trustee to pay or accumulate trust income in the trustee's sole discretion.

The court agreed with the government that the decedent as trustee held a §2038(a)(2) power to alter or amend the trust. The proper amount includible was a more troublesome issue. The court easily concluded that the value of "(1) the increments to corpus which had come by the profitable buying and selling of securities, and (2) income of the life tenant which the grantor-trustee could withhold or pay over at his discretion" was includible, and then proceeded to consider whether to include the full value of the decedent's half of the entire trust, as advocated by the government. As to this issue, the court stated:

. . . This question the court did not have in [Commissioner v. Estate of Holmes, 326 U.S. 480 (1946)]. There the power to alter or amend by terminating the trust certainly cut across the entire corpus. That is not quite this case. Here the trustee, as explained above, could withhold income from a life tenant, reassign it to corpus and then assign it out again. He could allocate profits from buying and selling trust securities to either corpus or income. He could buy speculative securities if he chose. He was expressly empowered to exercise in dealing with the trust estates "each and every right that might be exercised by one holding the same as his individual property." But we take it that in spite of this clause he could not willfully eliminate the interests of the remaindermen.

Our legal question, therefore, is whether such a limitation on the power of a grantor has the effect of limiting the power of the United States to levy its estate tax based on the value of the whole trust. . . . In Commissioner v. Bridgeport City Trust Co., 124 F.2d 48 (2d Cir. 1941), the court upheld a claim by the Commissioner to the inclusion of the income beneficiaries' interest in a trust where a settlor had reserved to himself the power to reallocate the disposition of the income. It is to be noted, however, that the Commissioner got, by this holding, all that he had claimed. Therefore, the question whether the value of the entire estate could have been subject to the estate tax was not before the court. And in Helvering v. Proctor, 140 F.2d 87 (2d Cir. 1944), the [court] held that, where the settlor had reserved an estate for life with remainders over, the principal was not includible in the gross estate for estate tax purposes. The discussion by the court, of course, turned around May v. Heiner, 281 U.S. 238 (1930), and its children and collateral relatives. Since *May v. Heiner* has now disappeared through the decisions of the Supreme Court in Commissioner v. Estate of Church, 335 U.S. 632 (1949), and Estate of Spiegel v. Commissioner, 335 U.S. 701 (1949), any structure based upon *May v. Heiner* has, obviously, lost its foundation. Our conclusion is that the grantor of these trusts retained to himself as trustee a sufficient power to alter or amend to affect very substantially the interests of the life tenants and the remaindermen, even though he could not, unless he lost all the money of the trusts by unfortunate investments, completely eliminate the remaindermen. He could certainly affect them by many of the things he kept power in himself to do. We think there is enough retained to bring the grantor within the wording of the statute and that the Commissioner's contention, therefore, must be upheld.

United States v. O'Malley
383 U.S. 627 (1966)

WHITE, J: . . . Edward H. Fabrice, who died in 1949, created five irrevocable trusts in 1936 and 1937, two for each of two daughters and one for his wife. He was one of three trustees of the trusts, each of which provided that the trustees, in their sole discretion, could pay trust income to the beneficiary or accumulate the income, in which event it became part of the principal of the trust.[44] Basing his action on [§§2036(a)(2) and 2038(a)(1)] the Commissioner included in Fabrice's gross estate both the original principal of the trusts and the accumulated income added thereto. He accordingly assessed a deficiency, the payment of which

---

44. The following provision in the trust for Janet Fabrice is also contained in the other trusts:

> The net income from the Trust Estate shall be paid, in whole or in part, to my daughter, Janet Fabrice, in such proportions, amounts and at such times as the Trustees may, from time to time, in their sole discretion, determine, or said net income may be retained by the Trustees and credited to the account of said beneficiary, and any income not distributed in any calendar year shall become a part of the principal of the Trust Estate.

prompted this refund action by the respondents, the executors of the estate. The District Court found the original corpus of the trusts includable in the estate, a holding not challenged in the Court of Appeals or here. It felt obliged, however, by Commissioner v. Estate of McDermott, 222 F.2d 665 (7th Cir. 1955), to exclude from the [gross] estate the portion of the trust principal representing accumulated income and to order an appropriate refund. 220 F. Supp. 30 (N.D. Ill. 1963). The Court of Appeals affirmed, 340 F.2d 930 (7th Cir. 1964), adhering to its own decision in *Estate of McDermott* and noting its disagreement with Round v. Commissioner, 332 F.2d 590 (1st Cir. 1964), in which the Court of Appeals for the First Circuit declined to follow *McDermott*. Because of these conflicting decisions we granted certiorari. 382 U.S. 810. We now reverse the decision below.

The applicability of [§2036(a)(2)], upon which the United States now stands, depends upon the answer to two inquiries relevant to the facts of this case: first, whether Fabrice retained a power "to designate the persons who shall possess or enjoy the property or the income therefrom"; and second, whether the property sought to be included, namely, the portions of trust principal representing accumulated income, was the subject of a previous transfer by Fabrice. . . . [The Court noted that the first condition was satisfied in this case.]

The dispute in this case relates to the second condition to the applicability of [§2036(a)(2)] — whether Fabrice had ever "transferred" the income additions to the trust principal. Contrary to the judgment of the Court of Appeals, we are sure that he had. At the time Fabrice established these trusts, he owned all of the rights to the property transferred, a major aspect of which was his right to the present and future income produced by that property. Commissioner v. Estate of Church, 335 U.S. 632, 644 (1949). With the creation of the trusts, he relinquished all of his rights to income except the power to distribute that income to the income beneficiaries or to accumulate it and hold it for the remaindermen of the trusts. He no longer had, for example, the right to income for his own benefit or to have it distributed to any other than the trust beneficiaries. Moreover, with respect to the very additions to principal now at issue, he exercised his retained power to distribute or accumulate income, choosing to do the latter and thereby adding to the principal of the trusts. All income increments to trust principal are therefore traceable to Fabrice himself, by virtue of the original transfer and the exercise of the power to accumulate. Before the creation of the trusts, Fabrice owned all rights to the property and to its income. By the time of his death he had divested himself of all power and control over accumulated income which had been added to the principal, except the power to deal with the income from such additions. With respect to each addition to trust principal from accumulated income, Fabrice had clearly made a "transfer" as required by [§2036(a)(2)]. Under that section, the power over income retained by Fabrice is sufficient to require the inclusion of the original corpus of the trust in his gross estate. The accumulated income added to principal is subject to the same power and is likewise includable. . . .

Respondents rely upon two cases in which the Tax Court and two circuit courts of appeals have concluded that, where an irrevocable inter vivos transfer in trust, not incomplete in any respect, is subjected to tax as a gift [within three years] of death under [pre-1982 §2035], the income of the trust accumulated prior to the grantor's death is not includable in the gross estate. Commissioner v. Estate of Gidwitz, 196 F.2d 813 (7th Cir. 1952), *aff'g* 14 T.C. 1263 (1950); Burns v. Commissioner, 177 F.2d 739 (5th Cir. 1949), *aff'g sub nom.* Estate of Frizzell v. Commissioner, 9 T.C. 979 (1947). The courts in those cases considered the taxable event to be a completed inter vivos transfer, not a transfer at death, and the property includable to be only the property subject to that transfer. The value of that property, whatever the valuation date, was apparently deemed an adequate reflection of any income rights included in the transfer since the grantor retained no interest in the property and no power over income which might justify the addition of subsequently accumulated income to his own gross estate. Cf. Maass v. Higgins, 312 U.S. 443 (1941).

This reasoning, however, does not solve those cases arising under other provisions of [the estate tax]. The courts in both *Burns* [nee Frizzell], 9 T.C. 979, 988-989, and *Gidwitz*, 196 F.2d 813, 817-818, expressly distinguished those situations where the grantor retains an interest in a property or its income, or a power over either, and his death is a significant step in effecting a transfer which began inter vivos but which becomes final and complete only with his demise. *McDermott* failed to note this distinction and represents an erroneous extension of *Gidwitz*.[45] In both *McDermott* and the case before us now, the grantor reserved the power to accumulate or distribute income. This power he exercised by accumulating and adding income to principal and this same power

---

45. The Court of Appeals in *McDermott* was clearly wrong in saying that the transfer there involved was as complete as was the transfer in *Gidwitz*. In *Gidwitz* the transfer was in trust and the grantor was one of the trustees but there was a specific direction to accumulate with no discretionary powers in the trustees over either income or principal. In *McDermott*, as in this case, the grantor retained the power, with other trustees, to accumulate or distribute trust income.

he held until the moment of his death with respect to both the original principal and the accumulated income. In these circumstances, [§2036(a)(2)] requires inclusion in Fabrice's gross estate of all of the trust principal, including those portions representing accumulated income.

Reversed.

STEWART, J., with whom HARLAN, J., joins, dissenting. In the 1930's Edward Fabrice made an irrevocable transfer of certain property to trusts for the benefit of his wife and daughters. Twelve years later he died. Because of the provisions of [§2036(a)(2)] . . . , the value of the property Fabrice has irrevocably transferred was nonetheless included in his gross estate for estate tax purposes. The respondents do not question the correctness of that determination. But in this case the Court holds that the accumulated income which that property generated during the 12 years that elapsed after Fabrice had irrevocably transferred it is also to be included in his gross estate under [§2036(a)(2)]. I think the Court misreads the statute.

By its terms the statutory provision applies only to property "of which the decedent has at any time made a transfer." Fabrice "made a transfer" only of the original trust corpus. He never "made a transfer" of the income which the corpus thereafter produced, whether accumulated or not.[46] I can put the matter no more clearly than did the Court of Appeals for the Seventh Circuit in Commissioner v. Estate of McDermott, 222 F.2d 665, 668 (7th Cir. 1955):

> Irrespective of all other considerations, property to be includible must have been transferred. Obviously, the accumulations here involved were not transferred by the decedent to the trustee. It is true, of course, that the accumulations represented the fruit derived from the property which was transferred but, even so, Congress did not make provision for including the fruit, it provided only for the property transferred. If it desired and intended to include the accumulations, it would have been a simple matter for it to have so stated.

. . . Nothing in the legislative history persuades me that the statute should not be applied as it was written, and I would therefore affirm the judgment.

---

46. The value of the original trust corpus at the time of transfer and at the time of Fabrice's death no doubt reflected its income-producing capacity.

Considering the point of disagreement between Justice White for the majority and Justice Stewart for the dissent, would it be possible to argue that, when a power to accumulate is retained, the value of all the post-transfer income is includible — even if it is not accumulated?

D created a trust to pay the income annually to *A* for 15 years and then distribute the principal to *A*. *D* retained a power to distribute principal to *A* during the trust term. *D* died 4 years after creating the trust and the government acknowledged that the amount includible in *D*'s gross estate under §2038(a)(1) is the value of *A*'s *remainder* interest, valued at *D*'s death. Thus, the value of *A*'s remaining 11-year income interest is not includible. Walter v. United States, 341 F.2d 182 (6th Cir. 1965); Rev. Rul. 70-513.

Now for those examples: Assume that *D* created a trust to pay the income to *A* for life and the remainder at *A*'s death to *B*. *A* was an adult. If *D* dies before *A*, the amount includible in *D*'s gross estate under §§2036(a)(2) and 2038(a)(1), respectively, in the following circumstances is:

(a) *D* retained a power to appoint the remainder interest; *B*'s remainder was in the form of a gift in default of effective exercise of that power. Only §2038 is applicable and only the value of *B*'s remainder interest is includible. See Treas. Reg. §20.2036-1(b)(3). It would make no difference whether *D*'s power was exercisable in favor of *D* or *D*'s estate.

(b) *D* retained a power to distribute trust principal to *B* during *A*'s life. Now both sections would apply and §2036(a)(1) would require inclusion of the full trust value. Is the Treas. Reg. §20.2036-1(b)(3) interpretation of the word "property" in §2036(a)(2) supported by the statute itself?

(c) *D* retained a power to distribute trust principal to *A*. Only §2038 would apply, as in **(a)**. See Walter v. United States, 341 F.2d 182 (6th Cir. 1965); Rev. Rul. 70-513.

(d) *D* retained a power to accumulate income and add it to principal. Both sections would apply, as in **(b)**. While you're at it, consider the gift and income tax consequences of these transfers and retained powers.

Creation of the Power: When and By Whom?   In Estate of Skifter v. Commissioner, 468 F.2d 699 (2d Cir. 1972), the decedent assigned in 1961 all his interest in nine insurance policies on his life to his wife, who died several months later leaving a will that directed that her residuary estate, including the nine insurance policies, be placed in a trust for the primary benefit of their daughter for life. The decedent, as trustee of the trust, had discretion to invade principal for the daughter and the government determined that, when he died, the insurance proceeds should be included in the decedent's gross estate under §2042(2), on the theory that he possessed "incidents of ownership" in the policies as trustee of the trust. The term "incidents of ownership" is undefined in the statute and there has been considerable litigation over its meaning. In a part of the opinion reproduced at page 468, Judge Lombard analyzed the legislative history of §2042(2) and concluded that Congress intended it to "operate to give insurance policies estate tax treatment that roughly parallels the treatment that is given to other types of property by §2036 (transfers with retained life estate), §2037 (transfers taking effect at death), §2038 (revocable transfers), and §2041 (powers of appointment)." Section 2036 could not apply because the decedent had not transferred the insurance and "retained" the powers he possessed as trustee when he died. The discussion then centered on §2038, Judge Lombard saying:

Until now, the discussion has assumed that §2038 only applies when the power possessed by the decedent was reserved by him at the time he divested himself of all interest in the property (other than life insurance) subject to the power. This necessitates a brief discussion of the language of §2038, which provides in pertinent part: "The value of the gross estate shall include the value of all property to the extent of any interest therein of which the decedent has at any time made a transfer . . . , by trust or otherwise, where the enjoyment thereof was subject at the date of his death to any change through the exercise of a power (in whatever capacity exercisable) . . . (*without regard to when or from what source the decedent acquired such power*), to alter, amend, revoke, or terminate . . ." (emphasis added). The emphasized language would appear to indicate that §2038 would apply even when the power was acquired under circumstances such as are present here. However, there is no indication that the Commissioner has ever made such an argument and we have been able to find no case applying §2038 in this manner.

The noted language was added to the predecessor of §2038 in 1936 in response to the decision in White v. Poor, 296 U.S. 98 (1935). In that case, the decedent had created an inter vivos trust and conferred on the trustee the power jointly to terminate the trust. Subsequently, the decedent was appointed a successor trustee. Therefore, at death decedent possessed this power to terminate and the Commissioner attempted to apply the predecessor to §2038; but the Supreme Court held this was impermissible because decedent had not retained the power at the time of transfer but had received it later. It was for the purpose of changing this result that Congress added the emphasized language. However, this language appears never to have been applied to a power other than one that the decedent created at the time of transfer in someone else and that later devolved upon him before his death. In essence, the language has been applied strictly to change the result in *White v. Poor.*

We need not here consider the reasons for applying §2038 to powers such as that involved in *White v. Poor*. Nor need we speculate whether or not such a power would trigger §2042, for that question is not before us. What is significant for our purposes is that §2038 has not been applied when the power possessed by decedent was created and conferred on him by someone else long after he had divested himself of all interest in the property subject to the power. Therefore, because of our view that Congress did not intend §2042 to produce divergent estate tax treatment between life insurance and other types of property, we conclude that the fiduciary power that Skifter possessed at this death did not constitute an "incident of ownership" under §2042; hence, that provision does not require that the life insurance proceeds at issue be included in Skifter's estate.

Although §2036(a) specifically requires that an offending interest or power be "retained" by the grantor under the original transfer, §2038(a) does not contain the same explicit requirement. Nevertheless, in the wake of the Supreme Court's decision in *White v. Poor*, it was included in Treas. Reg. §20.2038-1(c) for transfers made before the effective date of the 1936 amendment.

Congress responded to *White v. Poor* by enacting the 1936 amendment that produced what is now §2038(a)(1), explicitly waiving a "retention" requirement by including the parenthetical phrase "without regard to when or from what source the decedent acquired such power." In view of this quite broad language, is the qualification imposed by *Skifter* justified? It has been accepted by Hunter v. United States, 474 F. Supp. 763 (W.D. Mo. 1979), *aff'd*, 624 F.2d 833 (8th Cir. 1980); Estate of Reed v. United States, 75-1 U.S. Tax Cas. (CCH) ¶13,073 (M.D. Fla. 1975); and rejected by Adolphson v. United States, 90-2 U.S. Tax Cas. (CCH) ¶60,048 (C.D. Ill. 1990).

Remember that estate tax inclusion is not always a bad thing. For example, assume that D created an irrevocable inter vivos trust for A, in which the corporate trustee was given the power to accumulate income and to name its successor trustee if it should cease to serve. Shortly before D's death, when the value of the trust principal was only 60% of its original value, the corporate trustee (on the advice of counsel and with the written consent of A) resigned as trustee and transferred the trust assets to D as successor trustee. When D died shortly thereafter, D's personal representative contended that the value of the trust is includible in D's gross estate. Why would it be advantageous to D's estate if this contention is correct? An additional example of similar planning would be if the value of D's property had not changed since creation of the trust but the income tax basis was quite low. Inclusion for §1014 new basis would be advantageous if the gift and estate tax consequences would be nearly the same.

White v. Poor also prompted addition of the parenthetical phrase "in whatever capacity exercisable" in §2038(a)(1). Notwithstanding that *White* was somewhat unclear and arguably held that the value of the transferred property was not includible in the decedent's gross estate because the power was held only in a fiduciary capacity, the government takes the position in Treas. Reg. §20.2038-1(c) that this parenthetical phrase is applicable under §2038(a)(2) also. Although the Supreme Court has not considered this question, the government's position has been upheld. See the cases collected in Lowndes, Kramer, & McCord, FEDERAL ESTATE AND GIFT TAXES §8.6 n.51 (3d ed. 1974). Notwithstanding that §2036(a)(2) does not contain this phrase, the government's interpretation in Treas. Reg. §20.2036-1(b)(3)(ii) is that the capacity in which the power is exercisable is irrelevant, which has not been seriously challenged.

On occasion the government seeks to impose taxation based on a reality that differs from what the document provides. For example, assume that ten years before death *D* created an irrevocable inter vivos trust for a child for life, remainder to grandchildren. The trustee, a corporation, was given the discretionary power to pay income or principal to the child but, in fact, the trustee exercised this authority only upon receiving *D*'s oral or written instruction. Estate of Goodwyn v. Commissioner, 32 T.C.M. (CCH) 740 (1973), concluded that §2036(a)(2) was not applicable to tax trust principal in the grantor's gross estate because no formal power was retained. The fiduciary was, at most, just committing a breach of trust. Beware, however, of prearrangement and implied retained powers.

If *P* transferred stock outright to a three-year-old child and then was appointed guardian of the child's property, the stock would not be includible in *P*'s gross estate even if *P* died while the child was a minor. The result would differ, however, if the gift was made to a Uniform Gifts or Uniform Transfers to Minors Act account of which *P* was custodian for the child.

If *D* transferred individually owned securities to *D* as custodian for a child under the Uniform Transfers to Minors Act and filed a gift tax return that elected pursuant to §2513 to treat the gift as made half by *D* and half by *D*'s spouse, *S*, only *D* is the transferor for estate tax purposes. The gift split only applies for gift tax purposes. So, no part of the value of the custodial property would be includible in *S*'s gross estate under §2036 or §2038 if *S* was appointed successor custodian several years later when *D* became incapacitated and resigned, and then *S* died before the child reached the age of majority. See Rev. Rul. 74-556. Regardless of whether *S* had split the gift, the other source of possible inclusion would be §2041, relying on the questionable governmental discharge of legal obligation of support theory.

Contingent Powers.   One of the easiest traps to avoid is illustrated by the following case. But the larger issue relates to more than just the common trustee replacement contingency.

Estate of Farrel v. United States
77-1 U.S. Tax Cas. (CCH) ¶13,185 (Ct. Cl. 1977)

DAVIS, J., delivered the opinion of the court: The stipulated facts in this tax refund suit thrust upon us a narrow but knotty issue of estate tax law under §2036(a)(2). In 1961 Marian B. Farrel established an irrevocable trust with a corpus of various securities and her grandchildren as beneficiaries. Two individuals were named as trustees. They were given discretionary power to pay or apply all or part of the net income or principal to or for the benefit of any one or more of the beneficiaries (and their issue). The instrument also provided for a "time of division" when the corpus was to be divided into various portions, each of which (according to specified circumstances) was either to be paid over immediately to a specified beneficiary, or held in a new trust with the trustees having discretionary power to make payments to or for the benefit of specified beneficiaries until a later time when required payments were to be made. No provision was made in the trust for any distribution to Mrs. Farrel in any circumstances.

The trust called for two trustees at all times, and provided for Mrs. Farrel to appoint a successor trustee if a vacancy occurred in that position through death, resignation or removal by a proper court for cause. However, neither the instrument nor Connecticut law (which governed the trust) permitted Mrs. Farrel to remove a trustee and thereby create a vacancy. The trust was silent as to whether Mrs. Farrel could appoint herself as a successor trustee in the event of a vacancy, but neither the trust instrument nor Connecticut law would have prevented her from doing so.

Two vacancies occurred in the office of trustee during Mrs. Farrel's life. In 1964 a named trustee died and Mrs. Farrel appointed a third person as successor trustee. In 1965 that successor trustee resigned and Mrs. Farrel, as settlor, appointed another individual to succeed him.

Mrs. Farrel died in October 1969. Her estate, plaintiff here, filed in 1971 a federal estate tax return which did not include the trust property in the gross estate, and paid the tax shown on the return. In 1973 the Internal Revenue Service assessed a deficiency on the ground that the trust property should have been included in the gross estate under §2036(a)(2). Plaintiff paid the deficiency, filed a timely refund claim, and after the appropriate waiting period instituted the present refund suit.

Both parties agree that (a) the trustees had "the right, either alone or in conjunction with any person, to designate the persons who shall possess or enjoy the property or the income therefrom" within the meaning of §2036(a)(2); (b) Mrs. Farrel, the decedent-settlor, could lawfully designate herself (under the trust and Connecticut law) as successor trustee if a vacancy occurred during her life; (c) the occurrence of a vacancy in the office of trustee was a condition which Mrs. Farrel could not create and which was beyond her control; and (d) Mrs. Farrel had the opportunity, before her 1969 death, to appoint a successor trustee only during the two periods in 1964 and 1965 mentioned above. The legal conflict is whether the right of the trustees (as to who should enjoy or possess the property or income) should in these circumstances be attributed to the decedent under §2036(a) for any of the three periods designated in that statutory provision — her life; any period not ascertainable without reference to her death; any period which does not in fact end before her death. The government's answer is yes and the plaintiff of course says no.

Only §2036(a) is now before us but taxpayer's presentation emphasizes a comparison of that provision with §2038 (a cognate but separate part of the estate tax). Plaintiff's primary point is that (i) it is now and has long been settled that §2038 does not cover a power or right subject to a conditional event which has not occurred prior to and does not exist at the decedent's death, such as a discretionary power to distribute income or principal under specified conditions which have not occurred before the death, and (ii) the same rule has been and is applicable to §2036(a).

There is no question that taxpayer is correct as to the construction of §2038. . . .

The initial and fundamental question we have to face is whether this settled understanding of §2038 necessarily governs §2036(a), as it now stands. We think not for two reasons which we shall consider in turn: first, that the critical points-of-view of the two provisions differ and, second, that the regulations governing the two sections take diametrically opposed positions on the narrow issue of contingent rights and powers of the kind involved here.

The two separate provisions appear to diverge sharply in their perspective — the point from which the pertinent powers and rights are to be seen. Section 2038(a) looks at the problem from the decedent's death — what he can and cannot do at that specific moment. Excluded are contingent rights and powers (beyond the decedent's control) which are not exercisable at that moment because the designated contingency does not exist at that time. Section 2036(a), on the other hand, looks forward from the time the decedent made the transfer to see whether he has retained any of the specified rights "for his life or for any period not ascertainable without reference to his death or for any period which does not in fact end before his death." This language makes the transferor's death one pole of the specified time-span but the whole of the time-span is also significant. Because of the statute's reference to the time-span, differences of interpretation are quite conceivable. It is possible, for instance, to hold the words to mean that the retained right has to exist at all times throughout one of the periods, but it is also possible to see the language as covering contingencies which could realistically occur at some separate point or points during the designated periods — always including the moment of decedent's death. We take it (from the argument's insistence on the parallel to §2038) that the taxpayer would not stand on the former ("at all times") interpretation if a vacancy in the trusteeship existed and had not been filled at Mrs. Farrel's death. But under the language of §2036(a) there is no compelling reason why the moment of death has to be exclusively important. Unlike §2038, this provision seems to look forward from the time of transfer to the date of the transferor's death, and can be said to concentrate on the significant rights with respect to the transferred property the transferor retains, not at every moment during that period, but whenever the specified contingency happens to arise during that period (so long as the contingency can still occur at the end of the period).

There is nothing unreasonable about this latter construction, which accords with Congress' over-all purpose to gather into the estate tax all transfers which remain significantly incomplete — on which the transferor still holds a string — during his lifetime. It is hard to believe, for instance, that, whatever may be true of §2038, §2036(a) would have to be seen as failing to cover a trust where the trustee, with discretionary powers, could be removed by the settlor, and the settlor substituted as trustee, whenever economic conditions fell below a stated level (e.g., a designated level on a certain stock exchange index or a level of earnings of the trust) even though fortuitously that condition did not happen to exist at the time of death. In a case like that, the lifetime link between the decedent and the trust property (and income) would be so strong as plainly to measure up to both the letter and the spirit of §2036(a) if the Treasury chose to see it that way. This case, though perhaps less clear, falls into the same class of a continuing substantial tie.

The other element which leads us to reject plaintiff's attempt to equate §2036(a) with §2038, for this case, is that the Treasury has affirmatively chosen to separate the two sections — there is a Treasury regulation under the former §20.2036-1 which, to our mind, clearly covers this decedent's situation (in contrast to the regulation under §2038 which excludes it). Taxpayer urges us to read the regulation otherwise, and if we cannot to hold it invalid.

The regulation says flatly . . . that it is immaterial "(iii) whether the exercise of the power was subject to a contingency beyond the decedent's control which did not occur before death (e.g., the death of another person during the decedent's lifetime)." This would seem on its surface to blanket this decedent's position under her trust, but plaintiff would read it very literally and narrowly to apply only where the contingency relates to the "exercise" of an already existing power, and conversely, to be inapplicable where the power only springs into existence when a trustee vacancy occurs. Similarly, taxpayer sees in the broad sweep of the last sentence of Treas. Reg. §20.2036-1(b)(3) . . . the implied negative pregnant that a restricted power in the decedent to appoint herself a substitute trustee only in the event of a vacancy lies outside §2036(a). We cannot accept these strained (if not casuistic) analyses of the regulation because they go directly counter to its apparent purpose to cover just such contingencies as we have here. If proof of that objective is needed it is fully supplied by the companion regulation under §2038 (Treas. Reg. §20.2038-1(b)) which declares in coordinate terms that "§2038 is not applicable to a power the exercise of which was subject to a contingency beyond the decedent's control which did not occur before his death (e.g., the death of another person during the decedent's life). *See, however, §2036(a)(2) for the inclusion of property in the decedent's gross estate on account of such a power*" (emphasis added).

We are required, then, to consider whether Treas. Reg. §20.2036-1(b)(3) should be overturned as invalid. Recognizing the deference due Treasury Regulations (Commissioner v. South Texas Lumber Co., 333 U.S. 496, 501 (1948); Bingler v. Johnson, 394 U.S. 741, 749-751 (1969)), we cannot take that step. We have pointed out that §2036 is not the same as §2038 in its wording or in the viewpoint from which it appraises the decedent's link to the transferred property. We have also said that it is not unreasonable to regard §2036(a), in the way the Treasury does, as a blanket overall sweeping-in of property over which the decedent still has at death some significant, though contingent, power to choose those who shall have possession or enjoyment. . . .

We end by noting that the contingent right of Mrs. Farrel to make herself a trustee in the event of a vacancy — unlike the de facto "powers" involved in United States v. Byrum, 408 U.S. 125 (1972) and in Estate of Tully v. United States, 528 F.2d 1401 (Ct. Cl. 1976) — was a legally enforceable right, in effect imbedded in the trust instrument, which bore directly on the designation of the persons to possess or enjoy the trust property or income. That the exercise of this right was foreseeable when the trust was created — that it was a real right, neither insignificant nor illusory — is shown by the fact that Mrs. Farrel had two opportunities to exercise it in eight years and, if she had lived, may well have had more.

CONCLUSION. For these reasons, we hold that plaintiff is not entitled to recover and the petition is dismissed.

The estate tax consequences of a grantor's retention of the right to substitute trustees but not to appoint the grantor are discussed at page 310.

A condition is disregarded for gift tax purposes if the grantor can control the condition to which a retained power is subject. Rev. Rul. 54-537. If the happening of the contingency is not within the grantor's control, however, the question whether the power should be disregarded is not resolved. Compare Lowndes, Kramer, & McCord, FEDERAL ESTATE AND GIFT TAXES §28.11 (3d ed. 1974), with Stephens, Maxfield, Lind, & Calfee, FEDERAL ESTATE AND GIFT TAXATION ¶10.01[5][b] (7th ed. 1997).

What Constitutes a Power in the Decedent?

Joint Powers: Unanimity Requirement

The RESTATEMENT (SECOND) OF TRUSTS §194 (1959) provides: "If there are two or more trustees, the powers conferred upon them can properly be exercised only by all the trustees, unless it is otherwise provided by the terms of the trust." Comment *a* adds a few qualifications to this principle:

If one of [the co-trustees] refuses to concur in the exercise of a power, the others cannot exercise the power. In such a case, however, if it appears to be for the best interest of the trust that there should be an exercise of the power, the court may on the application of a co-trustee or beneficiary direct its exercise. The court may remove a trustee who unreasonably refuses to concur in the exercise of a power if such removal would be for the best interest of the trust. . . . One or more of several trustees can properly exercise powers conferred upon the trustees if there is an emergency making action necessary for the carrying out of the purpose of the trust of such a character that the consent of the others or of the court cannot be obtained before such action is taken. . . .

In reading the following decision remember that §§2038(a)(1) and 2038(a)(2) functionally are the same.

Helvering v. City Bank Farmers Trust Co.
296 U.S. 85 (1935)

ROBERTS, J.: . . . The questions for decision are whether [§2038(a)(2)] requires inclusion in the gross estate of the value of the corpus of a trust established in 1930 where the creator reserved a power to revoke or modify, to be exercised jointly with a beneficiary and the trustee; and whether, if such value is to be included in the gross estate, the section offends the Fifth Amendment.

By a writing dated February 21, 1930, Gertrude Feldman James, a non-resident citizen, transferred securities to the respondent as trustee, the trust to last during the lives of her two daughters or the survivor of them. The income was to be paid to her until her death, or until the termination of the trust, whichever should first occur. After her death, her husband surviving, the income was to be paid to him. If he did not outlive her, or upon his death, the income was to be distributed amongst their issue per stirpes. At the termination of the trust the corpus was to be delivered to the husband, if he were alive; if not, to the settlor, if living, or, if she were dead, to the beneficiaries at that time entitled to receive the income; if there were none such, to the heirs at law of the husband. The trust was irrevocable save that the settlor reserved the right to modify, alter or revoke it, in whole or in part, or to change any beneficial interest, any such revocation or alteration to be effected with the written consent of the trustee and her husband or, if the husband were dead, of the trustee and her husband's brother. If they could not agree the decision of the husband or of the brother, as the case might be, was to be final. Samuel James, the husband, survived the grantor, whose death occurred before the termination of the trust, and he is in receipt of the income.

The petitioner included the value of the corpus of the trust in Mrs. James' gross estate and determined a deficiency of tax. The Board of Tax Appeals reversed, holding that [§2038(a)(2)] did not apply. The Circuit Court of Appeals affirmed the Board's decision. We granted the writ of certiorari because the decision below conflicts with that in another circuit. We hold that the section covers this case and as so applied is valid. . . .

The respondent says that [§2038(a)(2)] ought to be construed in the light of the analogous [§676]. The latter, part of the income tax title, is "Where the grantor of a trust has, at any time during the taxable year, either alone or in conjunction with any person not a beneficiary of the trust, the power to revest in himself title to any part of the corpus of the trust, then the income of such part of the trust for such taxable year shall be included in computing the net income of the grantor." The two sections have a cognate purpose but they exhibit marked differences of substance. The one speaks of a power to be exercised with one not a beneficiary; the other of a power to be exercised with any person. The one refers to a power to revest the corpus in the donor; the other has no such limitation. It is true, the Report of the Ways and Means Committee on [§2038(a)(2)] said "this provision is in accord with the principle of §[676] which taxes to the grantor the income of a revocable trust." [H.R. Rep. No. 179, 68th Cong., 1st Sess. 28.] But to credit the assertion that the difference in phraseology is without significance and in both sections Congress meant to express the same thought would be to disregard the clear intent of the phrase "any person" employed in [§2038(a)(2)]. We are not at liberty to construe language so plain as to need no construction, or to refer to Committee reports where there can be no doubt of the meaning of the words used. The section applies to this transfer.

. . .

The respondent insists that a power to recall an absolute and complete gift only with the consent of the donee is in truth no power at all; that in such case the so-called exercise of the power is equivalent to a new gift from the donee to the donor. And so it is claimed that the statute arbitrarily declares that to exist which in fact and law is nonexistent. The position is untenable. The purpose of Congress in adding [§2038(a)(2)] was to prevent avoidance of the tax by the device of joining with the grantor in the exercise of the power of revocation someone who he believed would comply with his wishes. Congress may well have thought that a beneficiary who was of the grantor's immediate family might be amenable to persuasion or be induced to consent to a revocation in consideration of other expected benefits from the grantor's estate. Congress may adopt a measure reasonably calculated to prevent avoidance of a tax. The test of validity in respect of due process of law is whether the means adopted are appropriate to the end. A legislative declaration that a status of the taxpayer's creation shall, in the application of the tax, be deemed the equivalent of another status falling normally within the scope of the taxing power, if reasonably requisite to prevent evasion, does not take property without due process. But if the means are unnecessary or inappropriate to the proposed end, are unreasonably harsh or oppressive when viewed in the light of the expected benefit, or arbitrarily ignore recognized rights to enjoy or to convey individual property, the guarantee of due process is infringed. . . .

In view of the evident purpose of Congress we find nothing unreasonable or arbitrary in the provisions of [§2038(a)(2)] as applied in the circumstances of this case. It was appropriate for Congress to prescribe that if, subsequently to the passage of that Act, the creator of a trust estate saw fit to reserve to himself jointly with any other person the power of revocation or alteration, the transaction should be deemed to be testamentary in character, that is, treated for the purposes of the law as intended to take effect in possession or enjoyment at the death of the settlor.

The judgment is reversed.

Justices VAN DEVANTER, MCREYNOLDS, SUTHERLAND, and BUTLER are of opinion that the judgment should be affirmed.

See Treas. Reg. §20.2038-1(a). Compare Helvering v. Helmholz, 296 U.S. 93 (1935), the principle of which, embodied in Treas. Reg. §20.2038-1(a)(2), is that a decedent's power is of no consequence in applying §2038 if the power can only be exercised with the consent of all parties having an interest (contingent or vested) in the transferred property. Should that principle also apply to §2036(a)(2)? There is no gift or income tax principle comparable to the *Helmholz* principle because a transfer is not rendered incomplete for gift and income tax purposes by the grantor retaining a power jointly with an adverse party.

In Rev. Rul. 70-513 the decedent (*D*) had created an inter vivos trust to pay the income to *D*'s child for life, although the trustees had discretion to terminate the trust at any time by distributing the principal to the income beneficiary. *D* was not one of the trustees but *D*'s written consent was required for a termination to be effective during *D*'s life. Citing Estate of Grossman v. Commissioner, 27 T.C. 707 (1957), the government said:

While a power to consent to or to veto an action is distinct from a power to initiate, where the power is in the grantor there is little practical difference between the two for trust purposes. . . . The fact that the power could be exercised only after the trustees had taken action does not alter its basic nature as a joint power exercisable by the decedent in conjunction with other persons within the meaning of §2038 . . . . The amount includible under §2038 is limited to the value of the property interest that was subject to the decedent's power. Walter v. [United States], 341 F.2d 182 (6th Cir. 1965). Accordingly, as the enjoyment of the life estate in this case was not subject to change through the exercise of the decedent's power, only the value of the remainder interest is includible in the gross estate.

See also Lowndes, Kramer, & McCord, FEDERAL ESTATE AND GIFT TAXES §8.4 (3d ed. 1974).

A generally accepted property law principle is that a trust can be terminated prematurely and the principal distributed among the beneficiaries if every potential beneficiary joins in the petition and if no "material purpose" of the trust would be defeated by early distribution. The material purpose requirement is not applicable, however, if the grantor joins in the petition. With this in mind, if *G* created an irrevocable inter vivos trust to pay the income to *A* for life and, upon *A*'s death, the principal is distributable to *G*'s heirs at law, could *G* and *A* successfully petition a court for termination of the trust? The problem is *G*'s heirs and would preclude termination. What if a living identifiable remainder beneficiary could join the grantor? Would *G* be regarded as having a §2038 power "in conjunction with any other person" if *G* died while the trust was in existence? See Treas. Reg. §20.2038-1(a)(2), which states that this "control" is not adequate to cause §2038 inclusion. There is no comparable regulation under §2036 but there is no reason to think that it should apply — in most respects §2038 is the easier provision to trigger.

The next case involves an even harder power to exercise:

Estate of Tully v. United States
528 F.2d 1401 (Ct. Cl. 1976)

KUNZIG, J.: The single issue presented in this estate tax case is the includibility in decedent Edward A. Tully, Sr.'s gross estate of death benefits paid directly to Tully's widow by his employer. Plaintiffs (co-executors) move for partial summary judgment claiming that no estate tax provision compels such treatment. Defendant's cross-motion counters that the death benefits must be added to the gross estate as required either by §2038(a)(1) or §2033. We agree with plaintiffs and hold the sum at issue not includable in Tully's gross estate.

The facts in this case are uncontested. Before his death, Tully was employed by Tully and DiNapoli, Inc. (T & D), a company owned 50% by decedent and 50% by Vincent P. DiNapoli. On July 1, 1959, Tully, DiNapoli, and T & D entered into a contract whereby T & D promised to pay death benefits to the Tully and DiNapoli widows. Later, in October 1963, the same parties amended the 1959 agreement to limit the maximum amount of death payments to $104,000. On March 7, 1964, Tully died. T & D paid his widow the $104,000 called for in the contract.

Because the death benefits were paid directly by T & D to the widow, plaintiffs did not include this sum in Tully's gross estate when they filed the estate tax return. On audit, the [government] concluded that the $104,000 was part of Tully's gross estate and assessed an estate tax deficiency. . . .

In essence, plaintiffs say §2038(a)(1) is inapplicable because Tully never transferred an interest in the death benefits, either at the time of their creation or thereafter, and even if he had, he kept no power to "alter, amend, revoke, or terminate" the interest. Further, plaintiffs assert, decedent had no "interest" in the death benefits at the time of his death within the meaning of estate tax

§2033. Defendant takes an opposing viewpoint. It contends that Tully made a transfer of his interest in the benefits prior to his death, but kept a power to "alter, amend, revoke, or terminate" such transfer until the time of his death. Defendant claims this power requires addition of the benefits to Tully's gross estate under §2038(a)(1). Alternately, the government argues, Tully still had sufficient "interest" in the benefits at the time of his death to force the $104,000 into his gross estate under §2033. . . .

Defendant's contentions, specifically its argument that §§2038(a)(1) and 2033 must be treated as virtually identical, suggest at the outset that we consider the basic philosophy of estate tax law. As enacted by Congress, the primary purpose of the estate tax is to tax "the transfer of property at death." Lowndes, Kramer, & McCord, FEDERAL ESTATE AND GIFT TAXES §2.2 (3d ed. 1974). If sufficient incidents of ownership in an item of property are given away before death, no tax will be imposed. Since all estate tax statutes are directed at taxing property transferred at death, it can become easy to confuse their operation or to apply them in an overlapping fashion.

Within this context, the estate tax sections involved in the instant case, 2038(a)(1) and 2033, both impose a tax on property transferred at death. However, they are directed at two different situations. Section 2038(a)(1) is specific in its terms. It taxes property which an individual has given away while retaining enough "strings" to change or revoke the gift. Section 2033 is more general in its approach, and taxes property which has never really been given away at all.

Certain of defendant's arguments misconstrue this basic difference between §2038(a)(1) and §2033. By suggesting that the same "controls" over property which might represent a §2038(a)(1) "power" can be viewed as a §2033 "interest," the government attempts to turn §2033 into an estate tax "catch all." This was not the intent of Congress in enacting §2033. Congress has provided a "catch all" in the income tax statutes.[47] It has not done so in the estate tax area. Therefore, defendant's efforts to treat the two sections as virtually identical by the "catch all" method are misplaced.

In accordance with this analysis, our inquiry takes two avenues. First, did Tully transfer the death benefits but keep a power to change or revoke them until the time of his death? If so,

---

47. Int. Rev. Code §61 provides: ". . . [G]ross income means all income from whatever source derived. . . ."

§2038(a)(1) applies. Second, did Tully have an "interest" in the benefits at his death? If he had an "interest," §2033 applies.

We find that Tully effectively transferred his interests in the death benefits before his death, determine that he did not keep any significant powers to "alter, amend, revoke or terminate" the transfer, and conclude that he had no "interest" in the benefits at the time of his death. We, therefore, hold that the death benefits at issue here were not includable in Tully's gross estate.

I. SECTION 2038(A)(1)

Defendant argues that Tully transferred an interest in the death benefits at some point prior to his death and kept a §2038(a)(1) power to "alter, amend, revoke, or terminate" the enjoyment of the benefits after the transfer until his death. Plaintiffs counter that there was no "transfer" in the 1959 contract or thereafter because decedent never had any interest in the benefits which he could transfer. Even if a transfer is found, plaintiffs claim Tully did not keep a §2038(a)(1) "power" after such transfer.

Contrary to plaintiffs' position, Tully did transfer an interest in the death benefits to his wife by executing the 1959 contract. In one of the three death benefit plans at issue in Estate of Bogley v. United States, 514 F.2d 1027 (Ct. Cl. 1975), the decedent (an employee, officer, director, and 34% shareholder) entered into an enforceable contract with his employer. In consideration of decedent's past and future services, the employer promised to pay decedent's *widow* or the estate two years' salary after his death. We found that where decedent was married at the time of the execution of the contract he ". . . did make a transfer of his interest to his wife during his lifetime by making the contract with [the employer]." *Bogley*, 514 F.2d at 1039. In the instant case, the basic facts are nearly identical. The 1959 agreement looked to Tully's past and future services to T & D for consideration. The benefits here were also payable to the "widow" and decedent was married at the time of the 1959 contract. Tully in substance, if not in form, made a gift of a part of his future earnings to his wife.

However, within the meaning of §2038(a)(1), Tully did not keep a power to "alter, amend, revoke, or terminate" the death benefit transfer after the 1959 contract. There was no express reservation of such power in either the 1959 or 1963 contracts and no indication in the record of any other express agreements in which Tully obtained a §2038(a)(1) power.

The government implies that Tully's 50% stock ownership of T & D gave him unfettered power to change the death benefit plan to suit his own tastes. The facts do not bear this out. To the contrary, Tully's every movement could have been blocked by the other 50% shareholder. Tully did not have individual control of T & D and could not by himself alter the terms of the death benefit agreement.[48] As stated by the court in Harris v. United States, 72-1 U.S. Tax Cas. (CCH) ¶12,845 (C.D. Cal. 1972), §2038(a)(1) powers must be *demonstrable, real, apparent, and evident*, not speculative. We agree with this test and find Tully did not have a §2038(a)(1) power to "alter, amend, revoke, or terminate" through his 50% stock ownership in T & D at the time of his death.

Moreover, the death benefits are not includable in Tully's gross estate despite the fact that Tully *might* have altered, amended, revoked, or terminated them in conjunction with T & D and DiNapoli. A power to "alter, amend, revoke, or terminate" expressly exercisable in conjunction with others falls within §2038(a)(1), but "power" as used in this section does not extend to *powers of persuasion*. If §2038(a)(1) reached the possibility that Tully might convince T & D and DiNapoli to change the death benefit plan, it would apply to *speculative powers*. Section 2038(a)(1) cannot be so construed. In addition, if §2038(a)(1) applies to situations where an employee *might* convince an employer to change a death benefit program, it would sweep all employee death benefit plans into the gross estates of employees. It would always be at least possible for an employee to convince the employer that it would be to their mutual benefit to modify the death benefit plan. In light of the numerous cases where employee death benefit plans similar to the instant plan were held not includable in the employee's gross estate, we find that Congress did not intend the "in conjunction" language of §2038(a)(1) to extend to the mere possibility of bilateral contract modification. Therefore, merely because Tully might have changed the benefit plan "in conjunction" with T & D and DiNapoli, the death benefits are not forced into Tully's gross estate.

Tully also did not obtain a §2038(a)(1) "power" from the remote possibility that he could have altered the amount of death benefits

---

48. In effect, defendant asks us to hold that corporate control constitutes a §2038(a)(1) "power." In United States v. Byrum, 408 U.S. 125 (1972) (Justices White, Brennan, and Blackmun dissenting), the Supreme Court rejected the government's arguments that the corporate control could provide a §2036 right to alter beneficial enjoyment of trusts. The Court specifically noted the vagaries and uncertainty which a corporate control test would produce in the estate tax area. Id. at 138 n.13.

Since we find that Tully did not have *control* of T & D, we need not reach the equally complex question of whether corporate control might give rise to a §2038(a)(1) "power."

payable to his widow by changing his compensation scheme. The death benefits here were to be paid based on decedent's annual salary. From this, defendant reasons that, up until the time of his death, Tully could have accepted lesser compensation or terminated his employment in order to alter or revoke the death benefits. In practical terms, we reject this *possibility*. This is not a factor which rises to the level of a §2038(a)(1) "power." An employee might accept lesser compensation or terminate his employment for a myriad of reasons, but to conclude that a motive for such action would be the death benefit plan itself is not only speculative but ridiculous. And we have already made clear that a §2038(a)(1) "power" cannot be speculative, but must be *demonstrable, real, apparent, and evident*. In addition, modification of Tully's employment contract would have required the cooperation of T & D or a breach by Tully. Neither of these two events constitutes a §2038(a)(1) "power." Further, it is a common practice to "peg" employee death benefit plans to the employee's salary. To our knowledge, no court has ever held that such practice subjects death benefits to inclusion in the employee's gross estate. On the contrary, in Estate of Whitworth v. Commissioner, 22 T.C.M. (CCH) 177 (1963), the court concluded that, although the decedent could have terminated his widow's benefits by leaving his employ or by breaching his employment contract, the death benefits at issue were *not* includable in his estate as a §2038(a)(1) revocable transfer. Due to the practicalities of death benefit contracts and using the rationale of the *Whitworth* case, we hold that no §2038(a)(1) power was created by the remote possibility that Tully might have changed the amount of death benefits prior to his death.

Finally, Tully did not retain a §2038(a)(1) "power" to revoke or terminate the transfer to his wife by virtue of the *possibility* that he could have divorced her. The contract called for T & D to make the death benefit payments to Tully's *widow*. It might be argued that Tully could have divorced his wife to terminate her interest in the death benefits, but again such an argument ignores practicalities, reduces the term "power" to the speculative realm, and is not in accord with prior cases. In reality, a man might divorce his wife, but to assume that he would fight through an entire divorce process merely to alter employee death benefits approaches the absurd. Further, in various cases, death benefits payable to the "widow," Estate of Porter v. Commissioner, 442 F.2d 915 (1st Cir. 1971), or "wife," Kramer v. United States, 406 F.2d 1363 (Ct. Cl. 1969), were not thereby held includable in the gross estate. The possibility of divorce in the instant situation is so de minimis and so speculative rather than *demonstrative, real, apparent and evident* that it cannot rise to the level of a §2038(a)(1) "power." Thus the use of "widow" in the death benefit contract did not give Tully a real power to revoke or terminate the death benefit transfer to his wife.

In short, in the 1959 contract Tully transferred certain interests to his wife by obtaining T & D's promise to pay death benefits. While it may be argued that Tully kept a certain de minimis association with the death benefit plan, such association never rose to the dignity of a power to "alter, amend, revoke or terminate" the transfer. In *Kramer*, we held that a substantially similar plan did not create §2038(a)(1) powers. The facts here are not significantly different. Therefore, §2038(a)(1) does not operate to compel inclusion of the death benefits in decedent's gross estate.

II. SECTION 2033

Nor does §2033 require addition of the benefits to Tully's gross estate. The government argues that corporate control, "pegging" the benefits to Tully's salary, and naming "widow" as a beneficiary constituted §2033 "interests" kept by Tully until his death. We found above that these facts did not give rise to a §2038(a)(1) "power." We also determine that they did not create a §2033 "interest."

Having found that Tully transferred the death benefits to his wife and that he could not reach them for his own use, he could not have kept a §2033 "interest." The de minimis associations Tully may have still had with the benefits are not strong enough to force a conclusion that decedent never transferred his interests in the benefits to his wife.

Defendant would use §2033 as a "catch all." The simple answer to this is that §2033 is not a "catch all," but applies to situations where decedent kept so much control over an item of property that in substance he still owns the property. "Interest" as used in §2033 connotes a stronger control than "power" as used in §2038(a)(1). If controls over property cannot rise to the dignity of §2038(a)(1) "powers" they equally cannot create §2033 "interests." In the instant case, having failed to establish that corporate stock ownership, "pegging" the benefits to Tully's salary and naming the "widow" as beneficiary created §2038(a)(1) "powers," defendant equally fails to demonstrate that the same facts create §2033 "interests."

The value of the death benefit would have been includible under §2038(a)(1) if Edward Tully's contract with T & D had expressly granted Tully the power to change the beneficiary and if he still held this power at death. See Rev. Rul. 76-304, which stated:

[T]he corporation's promise to pay the death benefit was given in consideration of the decedent's promise to render future services, which the decedent discharged on a day-to-day basis during the course of decedent's employment career with [the] corporation . . . . [T]he transfer requirement of §2038(a)(1) is satisfied where the decedent procured the transfer by the decedent's employer of a death benefit to the decedent's surviving spouse in return for the performance of services during the course of employment.

The result would have been different if Edward Tully's contract with T & D had expressly granted Tully the power to change the beneficiary, even if only with the written approval of T & D. See Estate of Siegel v. Commissioner, 74 T.C. 613 (1980), in which the employee's agreement expressly reserved the right of the parties to modify the death benefit. The taxpayer contended that this "reservation" merely restated the right that contracting parties always have to modify their contract and added nothing to the terms of the agreement. See Treas. Reg. §20.2038-1(a)(2). The Tax Court determined that, although third-party beneficiaries to a contract acquire rights that limit the power of the contracting parties to modify their agreement, a reserved power to modify the contract bars the beneficiaries of the contract from acquiring those rights. Thus, the court applied §2038(a)(1).

Tully also would have been decided differently if Edward Tully had owned a control interest in the voting stock in the corporation. See Estate of Levy v. Commissioner, 70 T.C. 873, 880-882 (1978) (decedent was held to have incidents of ownership under §2042 in a policy insuring the decedent's life that was held by a corporation in which decedent owned 80.4% of the stock).

As an aside, consider the gift tax consequences of executing a death benefits only contract. A married employee who executes an enforceable contract providing for a death benefit payable to the employee's surviving spouse makes a transfer for estate tax purposes. Indeed, *Tully* held that the employee "in substance, if not in form," transferred part of the employee's future earnings. Is this transfer taxable for gift tax purposes and, if so, when is the gift complete? Recall Rev. Rul. 81-31 and Estate of DiMarco v. Commissioner, 87 T.C. 653 (1986), *acq. in result*, alluded to at page 54 with respect to §2033 and covered in detail at page 867 with respect to gifts, in which the court rejected the notion that an employee makes a transfer in a case in which the employee is not in control of the employer, and further held that, even if a gift were made, it was complete at the time of the agreement and not later at the employee's death, notwithstanding that the value of the gift could not be determined until death.

Also dealing with joint powers is:

Revenue Ruling 79-177

Is property transferred in trust includible under §2036(a)(2) or §2038(a)(1) if the grantors retained the right to change the interests of the beneficiaries and if the decedent is the surviving grantor?

Situation 1. In 1965, *A* and *D* created an irrevocable trust, and each contributed an undivided one-half interest in Blackacre to the trust. . . . According to the terms of the trust instrument, the grantors reserved the right to make such changes in the trust instrument as they deem proper with respect to the character and form of the investments. The grantors also reserved the rights to vary the interests of the beneficiaries and to make any other changes that in the opinion of the grantors would be in the best interests of the beneficiaries. The trust instrument is silent as to whether the power is exercisable by the surviving grantor after the death of one grantor. *A* died in 1970, and *D* died in 1976. . . . The trust instrument is governed by the laws of State *X*. Under the laws of State *X*, the death of one holder of a joint power extinguishes the power, unless a contrary intention is evident from the instrument creating the power.

Situation 2. The facts are the same as above, except that the trust instrument is governed by the laws of State *Y*. State *Y* has a statute providing that a power vested in several people must be exercised by all. The statute further provides that, if any one or more of them dies, is legally incapacitated, or releases the power, the power may be exercised by the others, unless otherwise stated in the terms of the governing instrument.

. . .

In the instant case, the grantors retained the right to change the trust instrument in any manner that the grantors determined would be in the best interests of the beneficiaries. The grantors also retained the right to change the interests of the trust beneficiaries. These powers over the trust property are the type that would cause inclusion of transferred property in the decedent's gross estate under §2036(a)(2) or §2038(a)(1).

In *Situation 1*, under the laws of State *X*, the joint power does not survive the death of one holder of the power. Therefore, *D*'s retained powers terminated when *A* died. At the time of *D*'s death, *D* had no power to change the interests of the beneficiaries. Because the powers did in fact terminate six years before *D*'s death, *D* had no powers over the trust property that would cause inclusion of the property in *D*'s gross estate under §2036(a)(2) or §2038(a)(1).

In *Situation 2*, under the laws of State *Y*, the joint power may be exercised by the survivor after the death of one holder of the power. After *A*'s death, *D* alone could have changed the interests of the trust beneficiaries. *D* retained for life the power to designate the persons to enjoy the trust property or its income. *D* also possessed at death the power to alter, amend, revoke, or terminate the beneficial enjoyment of the trust property. *D* originally transferred one-half of the property into the trust and retained sufficient powers over the transferred property to require its inclusion under §2036(a)(2) or §2038(a)(1). Therefore, in *Situation 2* . . . the value of one-half of the trust property at *D*'s death is includible in *D*'s gross estate.

The law of most states is in accord with that of State *X* in *Situation 1*. See RESTATEMENT (SECOND) OF TRUSTS §194. James v. United States, 448 F. Supp. 177 (D. Neb. 1978), held the jointly held power did not survive the death of one of the grantors and thus was not held by the surviving grantor. See also Estate of Webster v. Commissioner, 65 T.C. 968 (1976).

In Rev. Rul. 79-177, don't overlook the estate tax consequences in *A*'s gross estate.

Jointly Held Powers: Gift and Income Taxes.

The estate tax position established in *City Bank Farmers Trust* (reproduced at page 297) differs markedly from the rule applicable under the gift and income taxes: for those purposes a transfer is not incomplete by reason of a power retained by the grantor that is held jointly with a third party who has a substantial beneficial interest in the property that could be affected adversely by exercise or nonexercise of the power. Treas. Reg. §25.2511-2(e); §§672(a), 674(a), 675, 676(a), 677(a). It is important therefore in applying those taxes that a determination be made as to whether a co-holder of a power with the transferor is a person who has a substantial adverse interest. Under neither tax is an independent trustee considered to be a party who has a substantial adverse interest. See Treas. Reg. §§25.2511-2(e) and 1.672(a)-1(a), the latter of which states further that an interest is substantial "if its value in relation to the total value of the property subject to the power is not insignificant." And Treas. Reg. §1.672(a)-1(b) provides that a beneficiary is an adverse party, but only as to the portion or to the extent the beneficiary's right to income or principal is affected by exercise of the power. Similarly, the interest of a remainder beneficiary is adverse to the exercise of any power over the principal of a trust, although it may not be adverse to the exercise of a power affecting only an income interest preceding the remainder.

With these principles in mind, consider the gift and estate tax consequences of the following transfer: Four years ago, *D* created an inter vivos trust to pay the income to *A* for life and, upon *A*'s death, to distribute the principal to *B*. *D* retained a power to revoke the trust, but only with the consent of *A*. *D* has now died, survived by *A* and *B*. For gift tax purposes the joint power is not enough of a retained control to prevent completed gift treatment, even if the power is exercisable only with the consent of a person who is substantially adverse to its exercise. See Treas. Reg. §25.2511-2(e). So *D* incurs an immediate gift tax upon creation. Yet for estate tax purposes there is no exception for powers that are jointly held, even if the other party is adverse to exercise, so §2038(a)(1) inclusion also will result.

Power to Substitute Trustees. We saw in *Estate of Farrel v. United States* (reproduced at page 293) that a grantor to a trust who retains the power to name the grantor as trustee at any time (e.g., as a replacement for the current trustee or as an additional trustee) is deemed to possess all powers granted to the trustee for purposes of §§2036(a)(2) and 2038. Treas. Reg. §§20.2036-1(b)(3), 20.2038-1(a)(3). Under §2036(a)(2) but not under §2038, this attribution of trustee powers to a grantor occurs even if the grantor's power to appoint the grantor as a trustee is contingent, such as on the death or resignation of the existing trustee, and even if the contingency has not been met. Rev. Rul. 73-21; Treas. Reg. §20.2036-1(b)(3); *Estate of Farrel*. Thus, if the trustee's powers are such that they would cause §2036(a)(2) inclusion in the grantor's gross estate if the grantor possessed those powers at death, the power just to name successor trustees is sufficient to trigger §2036(a)(2) if the grantor can be named as a successor trustee, even if there is no vacancy to fill when the grantor dies. See Heckerling, *Tax Aspects of Power to Remove, Substitute and Appoint Trustees*, 8 REAL PROP., PROB. & TR. J. 545 (1973).

At one time the government wanted to go farther with this concept but eventually retreated — although not all the way, as revealed by their third Revenue Ruling on the topic, next below:

Rev. Rul. 95-58

The Internal Revenue Service has reconsidered whether a grantor's reservation of an unqualified power to remove a trustee and appoint a new trustee (other than the grantor) is tantamount to a reservation by the grantor of the trustee's discretionary powers of distribution. This issue is presented in Rev. Rul. 79-353, 1979-2 C.B. 325, as modified by Rev. Rul. 81-51, 1981-1 C.B. 458. An analogous issue is presented in Rev. Rul. 77-182, 1977-1 C.B. 273. The reconsideration is caused by the recent court decisions in Estate of Wall v. Commissioner, 101 T.C. 300 (1993), and Estate of Vak v. Commissioner, 973 F.2d 1409 (8th Cir. 1992), *rev'g* 62 T.C.M. (CHH) 942 (1991).

. . . [I]f a decedent transferred property in trust while retaining, as trustee, the discretionary power to distribute the principal and income, the trust property will be includible in the decedent's gross estate under §§2036 and 2038. The regulations under §§2036 and 2038 explain that a decedent is regarded as having possessed the powers of a trustee if the decedent possessed an unrestricted power to remove the trustee and appoint anyone (including the decedent) as trustee. Sections 20.2036-1(b)(3) and 20.2038-1(a).

Rev. Rul. 79-353 concludes that, for purposes of §§2036(a)(2) and 2038(a)(1), the reservation by a decedent-settlor of the unrestricted power to remove a corporate trustee and appoint a successor corporate trustee is equivalent to the decedent-settlor's reservation of the trustee's discretionary powers.

Rev. Rul. 81-51 modifies Rev. Rul. 79-353 so that it does not apply to a transfer or addition to a trust made before October 29, 1979, the publication date of Rev. Rul. 79-353, if the trust was irrevocable on October 28, 1979.

Rev. Rul. 77-182 concludes that a decedent's power to appoint a successor corporate trustee only in the event of the resignation or removal by judicial process of the original trustee did not amount to a power to remove the original trustee that would have endowed the decedent with the trustee's discretionary control over trust income.

In *Estate of Wall*, the decedent had created a trust for the benefit of others and designated an independent corporate fiduciary as trustee. The trustee possessed broad discretionary powers of distribution. The decedent reserved the right to remove and replace the corporate trustee with another independent corporate trustee. The court concluded that the decedent's retained power was not equivalent to a power to affect the beneficial enjoyment of the trust property as contemplated by §§2036 and 2038. See also Estate of Headrick v. Commissioner, 93 T.C. 171 (1989), *aff'd*, 918 F.2d 1263 (6th Cir. 1990).

In *Estate of Vak*, the decedent had created a trust and appointed family members as the trustees with discretionary powers of distribution. The decedent reserved the right to remove and replace the trustees with successor trustees who were not related or subordinate to the decedent. The decedent was also a discretionary distributee. Three years later, the trust was amended to eliminate both the decedent's power to remove and replace the trustees and the decedent's eligibility to receive discretionary distributions.

The issue considered in *Estate of Vak* was whether the decedent's gift in trust was complete when the decedent created the trust and transferred the property to it or, instead, when the decedent relinquished the removal and replacement power and his eligibility to receive discretionary distributions. The Eighth Circuit concluded that the decedent had not retained dominion and control over the transferred assets by reason of his removal and replacement power. Accordingly, the gift was complete when the decedent created the trust and transferred the assets to it.

In view of the decisions in the above cases, Rev. Rul. 79-353 and Rev. Rul. 81-51 are revoked. Rev. Rul. 71-182 is modified to hold that even if the decedent had possessed the power to remove the trustee and appoint an individual or corporate successor trustee that was not related or subordinate to the decedent (within the meaning of §672(c)), the decedent would not have retained a trustee's discretionary control over trust income.

See also PLR 9607008. The gist of Rev. Rul. 95-58 is that the government wants to argue that a power to remove and replace that does not preclude related or subordinate successors is still a viable source of §2036 or §2038 exposure. There have been no cases to test that refined proposition and, aside from saving face by not just abandoning the ill advised Rev. Rul. 79-353 concept entirely, it is likely that Rev. Rul. 95-58 puts the whole concept to rest.

Third-Party Powers. In the preceding material the grantor either held a tainted power alone or in conjunction with another party. Should a transfer be regarded as incomplete under any circumstances if the grantor does not hold the power at all — because it was conferred solely on another person or persons? Would it be significant — as it is sometimes in the case of jointly held powers — whether the person upon whom the power is conferred has a substantial interest in the property that could be adversely affected by exercise or nonexercise of the power? And what if the putative adverse party is a member of the grantor's immediate family, such as a spouse or a child? Finally, would it be relevant whether the power is exercisable in favor of the grantor?

Estate Tax

Sections 2036(a)(2) and 2038(a)(1) expressly speak of including in the gross estate the value of property subject to tainted powers only if held by the grantor either alone or in conjunction with another person. Thus, these sections do not appear to present promising grounds for inclusion in the circumstances now under consideration.[49]

---

49.   As noted previously, those provisions can apply if the transferor has the unrestricted power to remove or discharge the trustee at any time and to appoint the transferor as trustee, even if the power is subject to the occurrence of some contingency. Rev. Rul. 73-21; Treas. Reg. §20.2036-1(b)(3). A similar rule applies under the income tax (Treas.

Take as an example a discretionary trust created by *D* for *D*'s own benefit, with an independent trustee that has complete discretion to distribute income or principal to *D*. If the trustee's discretion relates to *income*, it is likely that §2036(a)(1) will apply under the principles we studied in Part A of this chapter, at least if the income actually was paid to *D* or if the trustee's discretion was subject to an ascertainable standard.

Section 2037 may apply if the trustee's discretion relates to *principal*. See Part B of this chapter. The government would seem to have a strong argument if the power is subject to an ascertainable standard, because this would give *D* an enforceable albeit contingent right that would qualify as a reversionary interest, and there are cases holding that transfers with such contingent retained rights are intended to take effect at death. See Toeller v. Commissioner, 165 F.2d 665 (7th Cir. 1948); Blunt v. Kelley, 131 F.2d 632 (3d Cir. 1942). These cases predate enactment of the 5% requirement of §2037(a)(2). Does the fact that such a reversionary interest may not be subject to actuarial valuation prevent §2037 from applying? If the government overcomes this problem, could §2037 apply even if there is no ascertainable standard governing the trustee's power — that is, if exercise of the power is completely discretionary? See Treas. Reg. §20.2037-1(c)(2). The reality is that §2037 has not been a focus of government concern.

Account also must be taken of Estate of McCabe v. United States, 475 F.2d 1142 (Ct. Cl. 1973), which applied §2036(a)(1) to a situation in which the government proved that there was a prearrangement that a third-party power to invade corpus for the benefit of the grantor would be exercised.

Are there grounds for applying §2038(a)(1) to a discretionary trust established by the grantor for the grantor's own benefit? The Commissioner seems to think so. See Rev. Rul. 76-103, reproduced at page 314. Before addressing that ruling, however, we consider briefly application of the gift tax to transfers that confer tainted powers on third parties alone.

Gift Tax

Third party powers have not caused a transfer to be deemed incomplete and nontaxable unless an unrestricted power can be exercised for the benefit of the grantor. The grantor has effectively retained an interest in a discretionary trust for the grantor in which the trustee's discretion is limited by an external standard, such that the ascertainable value may be subtracted from the present value of the otherwise completed gift. See Rev. Ruls. 54-538 and 62-13. The value of the donor's retained interest may be subject to

---

Reg. §1.674(d)-2(a)), but it is not as broad as the estate tax rule. Does the rule also apply under the gift tax? It has been urged that it should, but the point seems not to have been decided. See Lowndes, Kramer, & McCord, ESTATE AND GIFT TAXES §28.12 (3d ed. 1974); Heckerling, *Tax Aspects of Power to Remove, Substitute and Appoint Trustees*, 8 REAL PROP., PROB. & TR. J. 545, 557 (1973). See Estate of Edmonds v. Commissioner, 72 T.C. 970, 985-990 (1979); Rev. Ruls. 77-182 and 79-353.

gift tax treatment by the special valuation rules of §2702, which are discussed in Chapter 15. Absent an external standard, however, Rev. Rul. 62-13 held that the transfer will be considered incomplete and not taxable at all under the gift tax if the trustee's "power to invade income and corpus for the benefit of the grantor is so great that under the circumstances there is no assurance that anything of value will be paid to any beneficiary other than the grantor." See also Gramm v. Commissioner, 17 T.C. 1063 (1951), *acq.*; Estate of Holtz v. Commissioner, 38 T.C. 37 (1962), *acq.*; Commissioner v. Vander Weele, 254 F.2d 895 (6th Cir. 1958), *aff'g* 27 T.C 340 (1956), *acq.* But see Treas. Reg. §25.2511-2(b). Without current gift tax, the net result is going to be estate tax inclusion, and the government seems to have shifted its position to the one adopted in Rev. Rul. 76-103.

Revenue Ruling 76-103

Advice has been requested whether a completed gift has been made, for the purposes of the Federal gift tax, where an irrevocable trust is created under the circumstances described below.

The grantor created an irrevocable inter vivos trust on September 2, 1975. During the lifetime of the grantor, trust income may, in the absolute discretion of the trustee, be paid to the grantor or accumulated and added to principal. Any amount of trust principal may be distributed to the grantor at any time, in the absolute discretion of the trustee. Upon the death of the grantor, any remaining principal is payable to the issue of the grantor. The surrounding facts indicated that the trust had not been created primarily for the benefit of the grantor.

The trust was created in State *X* and has been administered under the laws of that State from the date of the transfer. The terms of the trust include, however, a provision allowing the trustee, in its absolute discretion, to move the situs of the trust to any other State.

Under the law of State *X*, the trust is a "discretionary trust" and the entire property of the trust may be subjected to the claims of the grantor's creditors, whenever such claims may arise.

The question presented is whether the transfer in trust is an incomplete gift for Federal gift tax purposes because the assets of the trust are subject to the claims of creditors of the grantor. . . .

In Paolozzi v. Commissioner, 23 T. C. 182 (1954), *acq.*, a grantor empowered the trustees to determine how much of trust income should be distributed, in their absolute discretion, in the best interest of the grantor. Any unpaid income was to be added to principal. The Tax Court agreed with the petitioner's interpretation of Massachusetts law as allowing both prior and subsequent creditors of the grantor to reach the maximum amount of income that the trustees could in their discretion pay out to the grantor. The grantor could thus effectively enjoy all the trust income by relegating the creditors to the trust for settlement of their claims. Therefore, the court held that no taxable gift of trust income had been made.

In the present case, the law of State *X* is similar to that of Massachusetts when the *Paolozzi* case, above, was decided. As long as the trustee continues to administer the trust under the law of State *X*, the grantor retains dominion and control over the trust property.

Accordingly, in the instant case, the grantor's transfer of property to the trust does not constitute a completed gift for Federal gift tax purposes.

If and when the grantor's dominion and control of the trust assets ceases, such as by the trustee's decision to move the situs of the trust to a State where the grantor's creditors cannot reach the trust assets, then the gift is complete for Federal gift tax purposes under the rules set forth in Treas. Reg. §25.2511-2. . . .

Furthermore, if the grantor dies before the gift becomes complete, the date of death value of the trust corpus will be includible in the grantor's gross estate, for Federal estate tax purposes, under §2038[(a)(1)] because of the grantor's retained power to, in effect, terminate the trust by relegating the grantor's creditors to the entire property of the trust.

Accord on the gift tax point, Outwin v. Commissioner, 76 T.C. 153 (1981), *acq.*; Vander Weele v. Commissioner, 27 T.C. 340 (1956), *aff'd*, 254 F.2d 895 (6th Cir. 1958). On the estate tax point, Estate of Uhl v. Commissioner, 25 T.C. 22 (1955), is in accord with the result reached above, but that decision rested on §2036(a)(1), not on §2038(a)(1), and was reversed. 241 F.2d 867 (7th Cir. 1957).

Rev. Rul. 77-378 concluded that there would be a completed gift of the entire value of the property transferred to a trust like the one in Rev. Rul. 76-103 if local law precluded the grantor's creditors from reaching trust principal. When it was issued it was doubtful whether local law in any state so provided; instead, the local law upon which Rev. Rul. 76-103 was founded was widely accepted: the grantor's creditors can reach the maximum amount of income or principal that the trustee could distribute to the grantor in the exercise of its maximum discretion. 2 Scott & Fratcher, THE LAW OF TRUSTS §156.2 (4th ed. 1987). This principle is qualified in most jurisdictions only by the requirement that "creditors must first exhaust their remedies at law before resorting to equitable execution" on trust assets. Id. §147. This important point means that the assumption underlying Rev. Rul. 76-103 is questionable in states in which this qualification is respected. That is, the well-accepted principle that the grantor's creditors can reach the maximum amount of income or principal that is subject to the trustee's discretion does not necessarily mean that the grantor effectively can enjoy all the trust income or principal by incurring debts and relegating creditors to the trust for settlement of their claims: while the grantor is solvent the trustee has no duty to pay the grantor's debts. Note, however, that a Massachusetts grantor's creditors are not required to exhaust their remedies at law before resorting to equitable execution on trust assets; consequently, *Paolozzi* is not vulnerable to this charge. Outwin v. Commissioner, 76 T.C. 153 (1981), *acq.*, also turned on Massachusetts law.

Much more importantly, since issuance of these rulings, a handful of American jurisdictions have engaged in a race to become the "haven of choice" for property owners interested in asset protection through the use of self-settled trusts that are afforded state law spendthrift protection. See Alaska Stat. §34.40.110 and Del. Code Ann. tit. 12, §§3570-3576, each of which was amended in 1997 to provide the same asset protection benefits of a spendthrift clause for a third party with respect to a grantor's own interests in a trust, provided that creation of the trust was not a fraudulent transfer or otherwise intended to hinder, delay, or defraud then existing creditors. Subsequently Nev. Rev. Stat. §166.040 and R.I. Gen. Laws §18-9.2 were enacted to provide similar benefits. Mo. Rev. Stat. §456.080 affords similar benefits and apparently existed long before Alaska and Delaware started the current trend. Allegedly Colo. Rev. Stat. §38-10-111 affords creditor protection against any but existing creditors as well, but In re Cohen, 8 P.3d 429 (Colo. 1999) (dicta in a lawyer discipline case) casts doubt on that interpretation. It is too early to determine whether creditors from states other than these will be able to obtain judgments against the trust that a court in one of these states will respect under the full faith and credit provisions of the United States Constitution. And there has been no determination to date regarding the effect of any of these statutes on the gift or estate taxation of the creation of such a trust or the grantor's subsequent death. How would you assess these questions: if a client were to inquire, would you recommend the use of such a trust, and what tax compliance would you advise as necessary or advisable?

If *D* transfers assets to an irrevocable trust under which the trustee has discretion to distribute income or principal to *D* subject only to the written consent of *D*'s spouse, will the transfer constitute a completed gift if *D*'s spouse is a contingent beneficiary of the trust if the spouse survives *D*? *Outwin* held that the transfer was incomplete, again relying on Massachusetts law governing the rights of creditors. Remember that the ploy is to accelerate tax as a gift tax and then be done with the wealth transfer tax system. Historically the government resisted such efforts because they amounted to an estate freeze, which is what Chapter 14 of the Code eventually was enacted to preclude. Quaere whether the government should care when property is made subject to the tax: in a world of flat tax rates and issues regarding the time-value of the dollars lost "early" through payment of gift tax (rather than waiting to pay estate tax at death), is this acceleration of tax advisable? This question is part of the larger debate that underlies the "easy" versus "hard" to complete conundrum that informs the really fundamental question of when is the proper time to impose the wealth transfer tax on dispositions that are not no-strings-attached "complete." As either a policy or an economic matter, which result is preferable? Why has Congress avoided providing a clear and unequivocal answer to that question?

Income Tax

The income tax deals with third-party powers more specifically than do the estate and the gift taxes. In general any power that would trigger the grantor trust rules if held by the grantor (or by the grantor jointly with a nonadverse party) and cause income from the transferred property to be attributed to the grantor has the same consequence if held by a nonadverse third party. See §§674, 675, 676, and 677(a). In this respect the income tax follows a harder-to-complete rule than either the gift or the estate taxes. But there are a few specific and important exceptions to this principle:

> *Certain powers of independent trustees.* Powers enumerated in §674(c), held by an independent trustee (not the grantor or the grantor's spouse and no more than half of whom are related or subordinate parties who are subservient to the wishes of the grantor — §672(c) defines the term "related or subordinate party"), do not cause attribution of income from transferred property to the grantor.

> *Powers to allocate income or principal, limited by a standard.* Sections 674(b)(5)(A) and 674(d) ignore powers to distribute principal and income, respectively, if limited by a reasonably definite external standard specified in the trust instrument. Under §674(b) anyone may be trustee, but §674(d) applies only if the trustee is not the grantor or the grantor's spouse. The standard is similar to but more flexible than an ascertainable standard for §2041(b)(1)(A) purposes.

None of these §674 exceptions is applicable if any person can add beneficiaries other than to provide for afterborn or afteradopted children. They also are inapplicable if the grantor may remove, substitute, or add trustees in a way that would preclude satisfaction of these requirements. Treas. Reg. §1.674(d)-2(a). For example, in evaluating whether the requirements of §674(c) are met, the grantor may have the power to replace a trustee with another independent trustee, but not with the grantor or any related party (unless the independent trustee requirement still would be satisfied).

> *Obligation of support.* A third exception found in §677(b) permits anyone (including the grantor as trustee) to possess a power to distribute income (but not principal) for the support or maintenance of a beneficiary (other than the grantor's spouse) whom the grantor is legally obligated to support or maintain. Income is taxed to the grantor only to the extent income actually is distributed for such support or maintenance.

Neither the estate nor gift tax is as well coordinated as these income tax provisions, which makes this an area that is fraught with danger if inter vivos transfers are meant to be excluded from a taxpayer's gross estate. By way of example, assume that D created a trust naming D and two others as trustees. There always must be three trustees, and they are authorized to act only by majority vote. None of the trustees has a beneficial interest in the trust. For gift and estate tax purposes, D is regarded as having the powers conferred on the trustees. See Jennings v. Smith, 161 F.2d 74 (2d Cir. 1947); Estate of Gilman v. Commissioner, 65 T.C. 296 (1975), *non acq.* Cf. Morton v. United States, 457 F.2d 750 (4th Cir. 1972). The income tax treatment of D would not be as harsh, due to the §674(c) definition of an independent trustee and the §674(b)(5)(A) exception. Quaere whether these results should differ.

Incompetency of the Transferor to Exercise the Power. Should a transfer subject to a retained power be regarded as complete if and when the grantor becomes mentally incompetent to validly exercise the power? In Round v. Commissioner, 332 F.2d 590 (1st Cir. 1964), the court said:

> In Hurd v. Commissioner, 160 F.2d 610, 613 (1st Cir. 1947), this court said: "The statute is not concerned with the *manner* in which the power is exercised, but rather with the existence of the power." So long as the powers retained by decedent *still existed in his behalf* the trust property was includible in his estate. What is required, this court said, is "some definitive act correlating the decedent's actual incompetence with his incapacity to serve as trustee." The court suggested that besides resignation and removal, an adjudication of mental incompetency might be sufficient to extinguish a trustee's interest in the trust, undoubtedly following the belief that under the circumstances of that case a legal determination of insanity was the least that was necessary if

the purpose of the statute was not to be defeated.[50] The Tax Court, however, has gone even further and has held that a judicial declaration of a trustee's incompetence was insufficient to terminate for tax purposes a power held under a trust where the New York law "specifically grants the Supreme Court of New York jurisdiction over the care of the person and property of an insane person." Estate of Inman v. Commissioner, 18 T.C. 522, 526 (1952), *rev'd on other grounds*, 203 F.2d 679 (2d Cir. 1953).

We do not need to go that far here. Suffice to say that decedent was never declared mentally incompetent. The appointment of a conservator did not remove the possibility that decedent could have recovered and resumed his position as co-trustee. A conservatorship "raises . . . no [conclusive] presumption of continued incapacity." Chase v. Chase, 103 N.E. 857, 858 (Mass. 1914). The trust instruments provided that upon incapacity the corporate trustee shall act as sole trustee, thus leaving decedent free to resume his duties as trustee upon the recovery of capacity. The definitive act required before a trustee's powers can be said to have been extinguished must certainly be more than an act which contains within it the possibility of a temporary incapacity. Estate of Noel v. Commissioner, 39 T.C. 466, 472 (1962); Estate of West v. Commissioner, 9 T.C. 736 (1947), *aff'd sub nom.*, St. Louis Union Trust Co. v. Commissioner, 173 F.2d 505 (8th Cir. 1949). To this, it may be added, as the Tax Court noted, that the Probate Court's adjudication of decedent's capacity to file the petition for conservatorship makes clear that he "would have had capacity to resign at that time had it been his intention to abandon the trusteeship." 40 T.C. 979.

Similar is Estate of Gilchrist v. Commissioner, 630 F.2d 340 (5th Cir. 1980), *rev'g* 69 T.C. 5 (1977) *and rev'g sub nom.* Estate of Reid v. Commissioner, 71 T.C. 816 (1979). Shortly before death, the grantor of an

---

50. In *Hurd* the decedent, as one of the trustees, had the power, together with the other trustee, to terminate the trust. The taxpayer argued that the decedent had been mentally incompetent for more than a year prior to death (although not adjudged incompetent in any legal proceedings) and, therefore, had been incapable of exercising the power at the time of his death. In rejecting this argument, the Tax Court said at 6 T.C. 823:

> . . . While the matter is one of first impression, we would think that some definitive action might well be necessary to terminate the retained power of the decedent before the purpose of the statute can be defeated. It is not unusual that during a protracted illness one might be incapable both physically and mentally of making normal decisions affecting property rights, and yet we wouldn't suppose that the statute did not apply in such cases. Petitioner's argument is a plausible one, but we are not convinced.

inter vivos trust was declared mentally incompetent by a Texas court and a guardian was appointed. Under the trust instrument, the grantor reserved powers that arguably would trigger §2036(a)(2). The court invoked the rule it promulgated for §2041 — that incapacity does not preclude inclusion if the power remains exercisable on the grantor's behalf by a guardian. The court also ruled that, under Texas law, a guardian could exercise the arguably tainted power with the approval of a Texas court, and remanded the case to the Tax Court to determine whether the retained power was in fact tainted for §2036(a)(2) purposes.

Powers to Alter the Time or Manner of Enjoyment. The following case was decided under the predecessor of §2038(a)(2), the theory underlying inclusion attributable to a power only to alter the timing or manner of enjoyment being that this is a power to "terminate" the trust. Although the word "terminate" appears in §2038(a)(1) and not in §2038(a)(2), the Supreme Court previously held that introduction of the one word by Congress in 1936 in producing what is now §2038(a)(1) was merely a declaration of prior law — that a power to "terminate" is the equivalent of a power to "alter, amend, or revoke," which already was the statutory language of §2038(a)(2).

Lober v. United States
346 U.S. 335 (1953)

BLACK, J: This is an action for an estate tax refund brought by the executors of the estate of Morris Lober. In 1924 he signed an instrument conveying to himself as trustee money and stocks for the benefit of his young son. In 1929 he executed two other instruments, one for the benefit of a daughter, the other for a second son. The terms of these three instruments were the same. Lober was to handle the funds, invest and reinvest them as he deemed proper. He could accumulate and reinvest the income with the same freedom until his children reached twenty-one years of age. When twenty-one they were to be paid the accumulated income. Lober could hold the principal of each trust until the beneficiary reached twenty-five. In case he died his wife was to be trustee with the same broad powers Lober had conveyed to himself. The trusts were declared to be irrevocable, and as the case reaches us we may assume that the trust instruments gave Lober's children a "vested interest" under state law, so that if they had died after creation of the trusts their interests would have passed to their estates. A crucial term of the trust instruments was that Lober could at any time he saw fit turn all or any part of the principal of the trusts over to his children. Thus he could at will reduce the principal or pay it all to the beneficiaries, thereby terminating any trusteeship over it.

Lober died in 1942. By that time the trust property was valued at more than $125,000. The Internal Revenue Commissioner treated this as Lober's property and included it in his gross estate. That inclusion brought this lawsuit. The Commissioner relied on [§2038(a)(2)]. That section, so far as material here, required inclusion in a decedent's gross estate of the value of all property that the decedent had previously transferred by trust "where the enjoyment thereof was subject at the date of his death to any change through the exercise of a power . . . to alter, amend, or revoke. . . ." In Commissioner v. Estate of Holmes, 326 U.S. 480 (1946), we held that power to terminate was the equivalent of power to "alter, amend, or revoke" it, and we approved taxation of the Holmes estate on that basis. Relying on the *Holmes* case, the Court of Claims upheld inclusion of these trust properties in the assumption that the trust conveyances gave the Lober children an indefeasible "vested interest" in the properties conveyed. The Fifth Circuit Court of Appeals had reached a contrary result where the circumstances were substantially the same, in Estate of Hays v. Commissioner, 181 F.2d 169, 172-174 (5th Cir. 1950). Because of this conflict, we granted certiorari.

. . .

We pointed out in the *Holmes* case that [§2038(a)(2)] was more concerned with "present economic benefit" than with "technical vesting of title or estates." And the Lober beneficiaries, like the Holmes beneficiaries, were granted no "present right to immediate enjoyment of either income or principal." The trust instrument here gave none of Lober's children full "enjoyment" of the trust property, whether it "vested" in them or not. To get this full enjoyment they had to wait until they reached the age of twenty-five unless their father sooner gave them the money and stocks by terminating the trust under the power of change he kept to the very date of his death. This father could have given property to his children without reserving in himself any power to change the terms as to the date his gift would be wholly effective, but he did not. What we said in the *Holmes* case fits this situation too: "A donor who keeps so strong a hold over the actual and immediate enjoyment of what he puts beyond his own power to retake has not divested himself of that degree of control which [§2038(a)(2)] requires in order to avoid the tax." Commissioner v. Estate of Holmes, 326 at 487.

Affirmed.

Justices DOUGLAS and JACKSON dissent.

See Treas. Reg. §20.2038-1(a).

Now we focus on §2036(a)(2), and ask whether there is any reason for doubting that it too is applicable to a power to alter only the timing or manner of enjoyment.

In Struthers v. Kelm, 218 F.2d 810 (8th Cir. 1955), the decedent was Mrs. Barney. She was one of three trustees of three trusts created by her in 1937 — one trust for each of her three children. Under the terms of each trust, the child was to receive the trust principal when the decedent died, along with any accumulated or unpaid income. During the decedent's life, the trustees had discretion to pay income to the child or to accumulate it and the power to distribute principal to the child. Noting that *Lober* was decided under the predecessor of §2038(a)(2), whereas this case was brought under the predecessor of §2036(a)(2), the court said in part:

> . . . [T]he gravamen of both [§2038(a)(2)] and [§2036(a)(2)] is the same. Both deal, in regard to the question before us, with the "enjoyment" or "possession" of the trust. Both sections adopt as the factor determinative of whether the trust shall be treated as a part of the donor's estate the existence or nonexistence of the power of the donor to "alter, amend, or revoke" [§2038(a)(2)] or to designate the person who shall "possess or enjoy" the property or its income [§2036(a)(2)]. The *Lober* opinion, quoting from Commissioner v. Estate of Holmes, 326 U.S. 480 (1946), states that [§2038(a)(2)] "was more concerned with 'present economic benefit' than with 'technical vesting of title or estates.'" . . . Lober's children, as beneficiaries of the trust, were granted no "present right to immediate enjoyment of either income or principal" without Lober's consent. In this case the beneficiary under Mrs. Barney's trust instrument was not granted the present right to immediate enjoyment of the income or principal without Mrs. Barney's permission, acting "in conjunction with" the other trustees. Since the *Estate of Holmes* case and the *Lober* case give controlling emphasis and effect to the present right of enjoyment of the trust by the beneficiary, rather than when the title to the trust property technically vested under state law, or the absence of power on the part of the donor to alter or amend that title, this case may not be distinguished from *Lober v. United States* and *Commissioner v. Estate of Holmes*.

Did *Struthers* ignore or at least overlook the express language of §2036(a)(2), which requires that the grantor must have retained the right to designate the *persons* who shall possess or enjoy the property or the income therefrom? No such express requirement appears in §2038(a). In trusts of the sort involved in *Lober* and *Struthers* there is a single beneficiary, whose interest is not conditioned on living to the end of the trust term and therefore might be classified in property law terms as an equitable fee simple absolute. See Browder, *Trusts and the Doctrine of Estates*, 72 MICH. L. REV. 1507 (1974). Thus, a retained power, say to accumulate income, can affect only the *timing* of the beneficiary's receipt of the income and not the beneficiary's ultimate right to it.

If, on the other hand, there were a condition of survivorship, so that the property classification might be an equitable fee simple defeasible, then presumably the "persons" requirement of §2036(a)(2) would be met. Was this the fact situation in United States v. O'Malley, 383 U.S. 627 (1966) (reproduced at page 285), or does *O'Malley* support *Struthers* despite the fact that this issue was not addressed by the Supreme Court? Estate of Lumpkin v. Commissioner, 474 F.2d 1092 (5th Cir. 1973) (involving inclusion of life insurance proceeds in the insured's gross estate), opined that *O'Malley* does support *Struthers*.

Is it arguable, even in a single-beneficiary case, whether the "persons" requirement of §2036(a)(2) is met? Consider the following statement from Estate of Rott v. United States, 321 F. Supp. 654, 655 (E.D. Mo. 1971): "By accumulating income, the [grantor] could determine whether the beneficiaries, their estates, or such persons as the beneficiaries had appointed by will would possess or enjoy the property or the income from the property transferred to the trusts." In this regard, note the Supreme Court's statement in *O'Malley* that such a power could deny "the beneficiaries the privilege of immediate enjoyment and condition their eventual enjoyment upon surviving the termination of the trust."

Most trusts for a single beneficiary are created for children. Frequently a custodianship under the Uniform Gifts or Uniform Transfers to Minors Act of the appropriate state is used instead of a trust, as was the case in Rev. Rul. 59-357:

> . . . any transfer of property to a minor under statutes patterned after either the Model Gifts of Securities to Minors Act or the Uniform Gifts to Minors Act constitutes a completed gift for Federal gift tax purposes to the extent of the full fair market value of the property transferred. Such a gift qualifies for the annual gift tax exclusion authorized by §2503(b). See Rev. Rul. 56-86 and Treas. Reg. §25.2511-2(d). No taxable gift occurs for Federal gift tax purposes by reason of a subsequent resignation of the custodian or termination of the custodianship.

> Income derived from property so transferred which is used in the discharge or satisfaction, in whole or in part, of a legal obligation of any person to support or maintain a minor is taxable to such person to the extent so used, but is otherwise taxable to the minor donee. See [§677(b) and] Rev. Rul. 56-484.

> The value of property so transferred is includible in the gross estate of the donor for Federal estate tax purposes if . . . the donor

appoints himself custodian and dies while serving in that capacity. See Rev. Rul. 57-366 and Treas. Reg. §20.2038-1(a). In all other circumstances custodial property is includible only in the gross estate of the donee. . . .

Although Rev. Rul. 59-357 relies exclusively on §2038 for inclusion of the value of custodial property as to which the donor acts as custodian, the government also has relied successfully on §2036. Estate of Prudowski v. Commissioner, 55 T.C. 890 (1971), *aff'd*, 465 F.2d 62 (7th Cir. 1972); Estate of Chrysler v. Commissioner, 44 T.C. 55 (1965), *rev'd on other grounds*, 361 F.2d 508 (2d Cir. 1966); Crocker Citizens National Bank v. United States, 75-2 U.S. Tax Cas. (CCH) ¶13,106 (N.D. Calif. 1975). Upon what basis would you guess that §2036 applies and, if §2036 properly applies, is there any basis for including the value of custodial property in the gross estate of a donor who is *not* the custodian? See the discussion at page 233 of the discharge of obligation of support theory for inclusion. Cf. Rev. Rul. 77-460 (a parent's right to petition a court to order a custodian to distribute custodial property to a minor beneficiary — a child who the parent was obligated to support — is not a §2041 general power of appointment; the parent's sibling was the donor).

Gift and Income Taxation of Powers to Alter Time or Manner of Enjoyment

Under *Lober* the estate tax hard-to-complete rule requires inclusion of property subject to a retained power by which the grantor may alter only the timing or manner of enjoyment but cannot shift the ultimate right to the property from one person to another. In general, it is somewhat easier to complete a transfer under the gift tax than it is under the estate tax, especially in a *Lober* type situation. A power to affect merely the timing or manner of enjoyment does not render a transfer incomplete for gift tax purposes. Treas. Reg. §25.2511-2(d).

With respect to powers to affect beneficial enjoyment, the income tax follows a much easier-to-complete approach than even the gift tax. Although it is difficult to characterize the income tax as following either an easier- or a harder-to-complete rule overall, §674(a) states a general rule that a grantor is treated as the owner of any portion of a trust as to which the grantor or any nonadverse party holds a power to alter the beneficial enjoyment of trust principal or income. Nevertheless, the balance of §674 establishes numerous specific exceptions that, for knowledgeable planners, swallow the rule. Thus, many transfers with retained powers that would trigger §2036 or §2038 estate tax inclusion do not cause post-transfer income from the transferred property to be attributed to the grantor. Indeed, the *Lober* type power comes within these exceptions. Thus, as under the gift tax, a retained power only to alter the timing or manner of enjoyment does not render the transfer incomplete for either gift or income tax purposes. See the relatively specific exceptions in §674(b)(5)(B) and (b)(6) and Treas. Reg. §§1.674(a)-1(b)(2), 1.674(b)-1(b)(5)(ii), and 1.674-1(b)(6). The more challenging task in estate planning is finding ways intentionally to cause grantor trust income taxation without exposing the grantor to §2036 or §2038 estate taxation at death. That is a very complex matter, better left for another day — it *may* be covered in your estate planning course or you may just need to cajole your instructor into providing an overview. Otherwise see 1 Casner & Pennell, ESTATE PLANNING §5.11.10 (6th ed. 1995).

Administrative Powers and Definite External Standards.

We learned in studying §2041 that an ascertainable standard would protect against inclusion. The same is not stated as true in §2036 or §2038, but case law says that the proper restrictions *will* similarly be applied. Because this exception is not defined by the statute or regulations, it requires a more careful analysis.

Restatement (Second) of Trusts (1959)[51]

§187. CONTROL OF DISCRETIONARY POWERS

Where discretion is conferred upon the trustee with respect to the exercise of a power, its exercise is not subject to control by the court, except to prevent an abuse by the trustee of his discretion.

COMMENT:

i. Reasonableness of trustee's exercise of judgment. If there is a standard by which the reasonableness of the trustee's judgment can be tested, the court will control the trustee in the exercise of a power where he acts beyond the bounds of a reasonable judgment, unless it is otherwise provided by the terms of the trust. . . .

This rule is applicable where the trustee is under a duty to exercise a power but the extent or manner of its exercise is left to the judgment of the trustee. Thus, if the trustee is empowered to apply so much of the trust property as he may deem necessary for the support of the beneficiary and the trustee does not apply at least the minimum amount which could reasonably be considered necessary for the beneficiary's support, the court will compel the trustee to pay the beneficiary at least that minimum amount. Similarly, if the trustee applies more than the maximum amount which could reasonably be considered necessary for the beneficiary's support, the court will interpose.

---

51. Copyright © 1959 by the American Law Institute. Reprinted with the permission of the American Law Institute.

§183. DUTY TO DEAL IMPARTIALLY WITH BENEFICIARIES

When there are two or more beneficiaries of a trust, the trustee is under a duty to deal impartially with them.

COMMENT:

a. . . . . By the terms of the trust the trustee may have discretion to favor one beneficiary over another. The court will not control the exercise of such discretion, except to prevent the trustee from abusing it. See §187.

As to successive beneficiaries, see §§232-241.

§233, Comment p. Terms of the trust. . . . The trustee may be given discretion in allocating receipts or expenditures to income or principal. The extent of the discretion thus conferred upon the trustee depends upon the interpretation of the trust instrument. Thus, his discretion may be limited to situations where he is in reasonable doubt whether under the law and the facts certain receipts or expenditures should be allocated to income or principal; or discretion may be conferred upon him to make such an allocation as in his opinion is fair and reasonable. The exercise by the trustee of the power thus conferred upon him is not subject to control by the court, except to prevent an abuse by the trustee of his discretion. See §187.

Old Colony Trust Co. v. United States
423 F.2d 601 (1st Cir. 1970)

ALDRICH, C.J.: The sole question in this case is whether the estate of a settlor of an inter vivos trust, who was a trustee until the date of his death, is to be charged with the value of the principal he contributed by virtue of reserved powers in the trust. The executor paid the tax and sued for its recovery in the district court. All facts were stipulated. The court ruled for the government, 300 F. Supp. 1032, and the executor appeals.

The initial life beneficiary of the trust was the settlor's adult son. Eighty per cent of the income was normally to be payable to him, and the balance added to principal. Subsequent beneficiaries were the son's widow and his issue. The powers upon which the government relies to cause the corpus to be includible in the settlor-trustee's estate are contained in two articles. . . .

Article 4 permitted the trustees to increase the percentage of income payable to the son beyond the eighty per cent, "in their absolute discretion . . . when in their opinion such increase is needed in case of sickness, or desirable in view of changed circumstances." In addition, under Article 4 the trustees were given the discretion to cease paying income to the son, and add it all to principal, "during such period as the Trustees may decide that the stoppage of such payments is for his best interests."

Article 7 gave broad administrative or management powers to the trustees, with discretion to acquire investments not normally held by trustees, and the right to determine what was to be charged or credited to income or principal, including stock dividends or deductions for amortization. It further provided that all divisions and decisions made by the trustees in good faith should be conclusive on all parties and, in summary, stated that the trustees were empowered "generally to do all things in relation to the trust Fund which the Donor could do if living and this Trust had not been executed."

The government claims that each of these two articles meant that the settlor-trustee had "the right . . . to designate the persons who shall possess or enjoy the [trust] property or the income therefrom" within the meaning of §2036(a)(2) . . . and that the settlor-trustee at the date of his death possessed a power "to alter, amend, revoke, or terminate" within the meaning of §2038(a)(1). . . .

If State Street Trust Co. v. United States, 263 F.2d 635 (1st Cir. 1959), was correctly decided in this aspect, the government must prevail because of the Article 7 powers. There this court, Chief Judge Magruder dissenting, held against the taxpayer because broad powers similar to those in Article 7 meant that the trustees "could very substantially shift the economic benefits of the trusts between the life tenants and the remaindermen," so that the settlor "as long as he lived, in substance and effect and in a very real sense . . . 'retained for his life . . . the right . . . to designate the persons who shall possess or enjoy the property or the income therefrom; . . .'" 263 F.2d at 639-640, quoting 26 U.S.C. §2036(a)(2). We accept the taxpayer's invitation to reconsider this ruling.

It is common ground that a settlor will not find the corpus of the trust included in his estate merely because he named himself a trustee. Jennings v. Smith, 161 F.2d 74 (2d Cir. 1947). He must have reserved a power to himself[52] that is inconsistent with the full termination of ownership. The government's brief defines this as "sufficient dominion and control until his death." Trustee powers given for the administration or management of the trust must be equitably exercised, however, for the benefit of the trust as a

---

52.   The number of other trustees who must join in the exercise of that power, unless the others have antagonistic interests of a substantial nature is, of course, immaterial. Treas. Reg. §§20.2036-1(a)(ii), -1(b)(3)(i); 20.2038-1(a).

whole. . . . Scott, THE LAW OF TRUSTS §§183, 232 (3d ed. 1967); RESTATEMENT (SECOND) OF TRUSTS §§183, 232. The court in *State Street* conceded that the powers at issue were all such powers, but reached the conclusion that, cumulatively, they gave the settlor dominion sufficiently unfettered to be in the nature of ownership. With all respect to the majority of the then court, we find it difficult to see how a power can be subject to control by the probate court, and exercisable only in what the trustee fairly concludes is in the interests of the trust and its beneficiaries as a whole, and at the same time be an ownership power.

The government's position, to be sound, must be that the trustee's powers are beyond the court's control. Under Massachusetts law, however, no amount of administrative discretion prevents judicial supervision of the trustee. Thus, in Appeal of Davis, 183 Mass. 499 (1903), a trustee was given "full power to make purchases, investments and exchanges . . . in such manner as to them shall seem expedient; it being my intention to give my trustees . . . the same dominion and control over said trust property as I now have." In spite of this language, and in spite of their good faith, the court charged the trustees for failing sufficiently to diversify their investment portfolio.

The Massachusetts court has never varied from this broad rule of accountability, and has twice criticized *State Street* for its seeming departure. Boston Safe Deposit & Trust Co. v. Stone, 203 N.E.2d 547 (Mass. 1965); Old Colony Trust Co. v. Silliman, 223 N.E.2d 504 (Mass. 1967). See also Estate of McGillicuddy v. Commissioner, 54 T.C. 315 (1970). We make a further observation, which the court in *State Street* failed to note, that the provision in that trust (as in the case at bar) that the trustees could "do all things in relation to the Trust Fund which I, the Donor, could do if . . . the Trust had not been executed," is almost precisely the provision which did not protect the trustees from accountability in *Appeal of Davis*.

We do not believe that trustee powers are to be more broadly construed for tax purposes than the probate court would construe them for administrative purposes. More basically, we agree with Judge Magruder's observation that nothing is "gained by lumping them together." State Street Trust Co. v. United States, 263 F.2d at 642. We hold that no aggregation of purely administrative powers can meet the government's amorphous test of "sufficient dominion and control" so as to be equated with ownership.

This does not resolve taxpayer's difficulties under Article 4. Quite different considerations apply to distribution powers. Under them the trustee can, expressly, prefer one beneficiary over another. Furthermore, his freedom of choice may vary greatly, depending upon the terms of the individual trust. If there is an ascertainable standard, the trustee can be compelled to follow it. If there is not, even though he is a fiduciary, it is not unreasonable to say that his retention of an unmeasurable freedom of choice is equivalent to retaining some of the incidents of ownership. Hence, under the cases, if there is an ascertainable standard the settlor-trustee's estate is not taxed. . . .

The trust provision which is uniformly held to provide an ascertainable standard is one which, though variously expressed, authorized such distributions as may be needed to continue the beneficiary's accustomed way of life.[53] Ithaca Trust Co. v. United States, 279 U.S. 151 (1929); cf. United States v. Commercial Nat'l Bank, 404 F.2d 927 (10th Cir. 1968); Blodget v. Delaney, 201 F.2d 589 (1st Cir. 1953). On the other hand, if the trustee may go further, and has power to provide for the beneficiary's "happiness," Merchants Nat'l Bank v. Commissioner, 320 U.S. 256 (1943), or "pleasure," Industrial Trust Co. v. Commissioner, 151 F.2d 592 (1st Cir. 1945), or "use and benefit," Newton Trust Co. v. Commissioner, 160 F.2d 175 (1st Cir. 1947), or "reasonable requirement[s]," State Street Bank & Trust Co. v. United States, 313 F.2d 29 (1st Cir. 1963), the standard is so loose that the trustee is in effect uncontrolled.

In the case at bar the trustees could increase the life tenant's income "in case of sickness, or [if] desirable in view of changed circumstances." Alternatively, they could reduce it "for his best interests." "Sickness" presents no problem. Conceivably, providing for "changed circumstances" is roughly equivalent to maintaining the son's present standard of living. But see Hurd v. Commissioner, 160 F.2d 610 (1st Cir. 1947). The unavoidable stumbling block is the trustees' right to accumulate income and add it to capital (which the son would never receive) when it is to the "best interests" of the son to do so. Additional payments to a beneficiary whenever in his "best interests" might seem to be too broad a standard in any event. In addition to the previous cases see Estate of Yawkey v. Commissioner, 12 T.C. 1164, 1170 (1949), where the court said: "We can not regard the language involved ['best interest'] as limiting the usual scope of a trustee's discretion. It must always be

---

53. Many of the cases we are about to cite consider whether there is an ascertainable standard with a different object in view, viz., whether the amount of uninvaded corpus there provided to go ultimately to charity could be reliably predicted, so as to permit an estate tax deduction under 26 U.S.C. §2055(a)(2). While the purpose of inquiry is different, we believe the existence and measurability of a standard to be the same. Cf. Treas. Reg. §20.2055-2(a); 4 Mertens, LAW OF FEDERAL GIFT & ESTATE TAXATION §28.38.

anticipated that trustees will act for the best interests of a trust beneficiary, and an exhortation to act 'in the interests and for the welfare' of the beneficiary does not establish an external standard." Power, however, to decrease or cut off a beneficiary's income when in his "best interests" is even more troublesome. When the beneficiary is the son, and the trustee the father, a particular purpose comes to mind, parental control through holding the purse strings. The father decides what conduct is to the "best interests" of the son, and if the son does not agree, he loses his allowance. Such a power has the plain indicia of ownership control. The alternative, that the son, because of other means, might not need this income, and would prefer to have it accumulate for his widow and children after his death, is no better. If the trustee has power to confer "happiness" on the son by generosity to someone else, this seems clearly an unascertainable standard. . . .

The case of Estate of Hays v. Commissioner, 181 F.2d 169 (5th Cir. 1950), is contrary to our decision. The opinion is unsupported by either reasoning or authority, and we will not follow it. With the present settlor-trustee free to determine the standard himself, a finding of ownership control was warranted. To put it another way, the cost of holding onto the strings may prove to be a rope burn.

Affirmed.

In accord with the court's decision regarding administrative or ministerial powers are Estate of Ford v. Commissioner, 53 T.C. 114 (1969), *nonacq.*, *aff'd per curiam*, 450 F.2d 878 (2d Cir. 1971), and cases cited therein. As to the income tax treatment of grantor administrative powers, see §675. On the gift tax, see Treas. Reg. §25.2511-2(g); Lowndes, Kramer, & McCord, FEDERAL ESTATE AND GIFT TAXES §28.13 at 728 (3d ed. 1974).

Sometimes the government goes out of its way to find powers or control that would require inclusion. To illustrate, assume that D created a trust that named D as one of three trustees. The trust principal included insurance policies on D's life and various income-producing assets. The trustees were instructed to pay the insurance premiums out of trust income and to pay any remaining income to D's adult child, C, until C reached the age of 35, when the trustees are to distribute the principal to C. At no time was income insufficient to pay the premiums. In D's individual capacity D also retained a power to substitute securities, property, and policies "of equal value" for those transferred to the trust. If D dies before the trust terminates, will the value of the trust be includible in D's gross estate because of D's power to substitute property of equal value and thereby control the timing of C's enjoyment? Estate of Jordahl v. Commissioner, 65 T.C. 92 (1975), *acq.*, held that fiduciary restraints would sufficiently constrain any action by D and that inclusion would not result.

Leopold v. United States
510 F.2d 617 (9th Cir. 1975)

GOODWIN, J.: . . . The . . . issue is the includability in the decedent's gross estate of the entire corpus and accumulated income of two inter vivos trusts, one for the primary benefit of his daughter Catherine, and the other for the primary benefit of his daughter Celeste.

The relevant portions of the trust for Catherine are quoted below. The trust for Celeste was identical except for the difference in names. Decedent designated himself and a friend as trustees of both trusts.

> First: The Trustees shall receive, hold, manage, sell, exchange, invest and reinvest such property and every part thereof in the manner hereinafter specified, and shall collect, recover and receive the rents, issues, interest and income thereof, hereinafter called "income" and, after deducting such expenses in connection with the administration of the trust as, in the opinion of the Trustees, are properly payable from income, shall pay the balance of the said income to Catherine J. H. de Schulthess, the daughter of the Donor, during the term of her natural life, at such intervals as the Trustees, in their sole discretion, may determine. During the minority of the said Catherine J. H. de Schulthess the said income may be accumulated or paid to Amelie de Schulthess, the mother of the said Catherine J. H. de Schulthess, or to the guardian of Catherine J. H. de Schulthess, for the support, education, maintenance and general welfare of the said infant, but such decision to accumulate or pay the income during such minority is to be made solely in the uncontrolled discretion of the Trustees. Any income accumulated when the said Catherine J. H. de Schulthess shall attain the age of twenty-one (21) years shall be paid over to her at that time.

> Second: Upon the death of the said Catherine J. H. de Schulthess, this trust shall terminate, and the principal thereof shall then be paid and distributed to the issue of the said Catherine J. H. de Schulthess, in equal shares per stirpes and not per capita. If the said Catherine J. H. de Schulthess shall die leaving no issue then the trust principal shall be paid and distributed to her sister. . . .

> Third: The Donor hereby authorizes and empowers the Trustees at any time during the continuance of the trust to pay to the said Catherine J. H. de Schulthess, or to apply

for her benefit out of the principal of the trust, such amounts, if any, as the Trustees may deem necessary or proper, and their judgment with respect to the time and amount of any such payments of principal shall be final and conclusive beyond any dispute or appeal. Any payment or payments of principal under this Article may only be made in the event both Trustees hereunder concur in such payment or payments, and such payment or payments may in no manner be applied, directly or indirectly, to the benefit of the Donor. . . .

Fourteenth: In case of the death, resignation, removal, disability or inability (for any reason whatsoever) further to act of any Trustee hereunder, the surviving or remaining Trustee shall have the right to appoint a successor Trustee from time to time, such successor Trustee, upon executing a duly acknowledged written acceptance of the trusteeship, to be and become vested with all the estate, title, authorities, rights, powers, duties, privileges, immunities and discretions granted to his predecessors, with like effect as if originally named as Trustee hereunder. . . .

On decedent's federal estate tax return, the trusts were identified, but no portion of either was included in the gross estate. The Commissioner determined that the entire corpus and undistributed accumulated income of each trust were includible under §§2036 and 2038 and asserted a deficiency in estate taxes. The district court, rejecting part of the Commissioner's determination, held that none of the accumulated income and only the actuarial value of the remainder interests (21.187% of the corpus of Catherine's trust and 20.021% of the corpus of Celeste's) was includible in the gross estate.

The appeal asserts the Commissioner's original position. The taxpayers have not cross-appealed from the district court's holding that the actuarial value of the remainder interests is includible, and that issue is not before us. . . .

The government contends that the powers of decedent and his co-trustee to distribute principal to decedent's daughters whenever they deemed such payments to be "necessary and proper" and to accumulate trust income or to pay it out in their "uncontrolled discretion" for the girls' "support, education, maintenance and general welfare" constituted a power "to alter, amend, revoke, or terminate" within the meaning of §2038. The government also contends that these powers gave the decedent the ability to shift income from his daughters to their heirs and, thus, to designate the persons who would receive the enjoyment of the property within the meaning of §2036(a)(2).

The district court concluded, and the taxpayers do not dispute, that since the decedent had the power to pay out principal as he deemed "necessary and proper," he retained sufficient control over the remainder interest of each trust to justify its inclusion in his gross estate. However, the court also held that the decedent had retained no power to affect the beneficial enjoyment of the income of either trust, except to the extent that such power was limited by an ascertainable, external, objective standard. Although the question is a close one, we agree with the district court that the standard was ascertainable. The Court of Appeals for the First Circuit has said: "The trust provision which is uniformly held to provide an ascertainable standard is one which, though variously expressed, authorizes such distributions as may be needed to continue the beneficiary's accustomed way of life. . . ." Old Colony Trust Co. v. United States, 423 F.2d 601, 604 (1st Cir. 1970).

The provision at issue here, authorizing payments of income for the "support, education, maintenance and general welfare" of decedent's daughters, requires the trustees to maintain the daughters in their accustomed way of life and, hence, provides a sufficiently objective standard. See Estate of Ford v. Commissioner, 450 F.2d 878 (2d Cir. 1971), *aff'g* 53 T.C. 114 (1969); United States v. Powell, 307 F.2d 821, 826-828 (10th Cir. 1962); Jennings v. Smith, 161 F.2d 74 (2d Cir. 1947); Lowndes, Kramer, & McCord, FEDERAL ESTATE AND GIFT TAXES §8.9 at 157-158 (3d ed. 1974). See generally Note, *The Doctrine of External Standards Under Sections 2036(a)(2) and 2038*, 52 MINN. L. REV. 1071 1968).

From this conclusion it follows that the present value of a portion of the income interests was properly excluded from the decedent's gross estate. At the time of decedent's death, the daughters had an enforceable right to enjoy that portion of the trust income necessary to maintain them in their accustomed way of life. The government has elsewhere conceded the propriety of excluding from the gross estate the present value of a fixed, indefeasible income right even though the decedent retained the power to pay corpus prematurely to the income beneficiary. See Walter v. United States, 295 F.2d 720 (6th Cir. 1961). See also Rev. Rul. 70-513, which holds that under §2038 only the value of the remainder interest, and not the entire corpus, of a trust is includible in the decedent's gross estate where the enjoyment of a life estate is vested in the beneficiary and is not subject to reduction through exercise of the decedent's reserved power to terminate the trust and to pay over the corpus to the life beneficiary.

But the daughters here had an enforceable right to enjoy currently only a *portion* of the full income stream prior to reaching twenty-one years of age — i.e., that amount necessary to maintain them in their accustomed way of life. With respect to the remaining income, the decedent had two options: he could either allow that income to accumulate until the girls reached 21, or he could provide for present enjoyment of the income by paying over the corpus with its full income-generating capacity. Thus, the decedent possessed a degree of control over the enjoyment of that segment of the future income he was not required to distribute currently which precludes exclusion of its actuarial value from his gross estate. See United States v. O'Malley, 383 U.S. 627, 631 (1966); Lober v. United States, 346 U.S. 335, 337 (1953).

The amount of previously accumulated income was properly excluded. Once the decision had been made to accumulate part of the income, this accumulation was placed beyond the reach of the trustees. The accumulated income would be paid to the children when they reached 21. Although the trustees could pay out the principal early, they could not prematurely distribute the accumulated income. Unlike the accumulated income held taxable in *United States v. O'Malley*, the accumulated income here did not become part of the trust principal and was not subject to the powers decedent reserved over the principal.

We hold, then, that under §§2036(a)(2) and 2038(a)(1) the decedent's reserved power to distribute the principal of the trusts at any time requires the inclusion of the corpus of each trust, reduced by the actuarial value of that segment of the future income stream which the decedent would be obligated to distribute currently to his daughters.[54] We further hold that the exclusion of previously accumulated income was proper. The case must be remanded to the district court for a factual determination of the amount of the includible sum.

Although the *Old Colony* opinion referred to an ascertainable standard with respect to limitations on distribution powers, the proper term is a "definite external standard" and a study of case law reveals it to be a more flexible limitation than the ascertainable standard as defined for general power of appointment purposes under §2041(b)(1)(A). In this respect, it is more like the §674(b)(5)(A) and §674(d) reasonably definite external standard. For

---

54. The government also contends that these trusts are includible in decedent's gross estate under §2036(a)(1), because the decedent retained the right to apply trust income in satisfaction of his legal obligation to support his daughters. See Treas. Reg. §20.2036-1(b)(2). However, this issue was never raised at the time of audit or in the district court, but only for the first time on this appeal. Since this issue presents genuine factual questions, we decline to consider it now. . . .

example, terms such as emergency, welfare, comfort, and happiness have been held to qualify, along with more conservative fare such as education, maintenance, support, and health or medical care. See United States v. Powell, 307 F.2d 821 (10th Cir. 1962) ("comfort" standing alone); Estate of Ford v. Commissioner, 53 T.C. 114 (1969) ("welfare and happiness"); Estate of Budd v. Commissioner, 49 T.C. 468 (1968) ("in the event of sickness, accident, misfortune or other emergency" and "education"); Estate of Pardee v. Commissioner, 49 T.C. 140 (1967), *acq.* ("education, mainte-nance, medical expenses, or other needs occasioned by emergency"); Estate of Kasch v. Commissioner, 30 T.C. 102 (1958), *acq.* ("proper care, support and medical attention . . . during the period of any illness or other incapacity"); Estate of Weir v. Commissioner, 17 T.C. 409 (1951) ("educa-tion"). More recent cases are difficult to find, but see PLRs 9118009 and 9049041. See Halbach, *Tax Sensitive Trusteeships*, 63 OR. L. REV. 381 (1984); Horn, *Whom Do You Trust: Planning, Drafting and Administering Self and Beneficiary-Trusteed Trusts*, 20 U. MIAMI INST. ON EST. PLAN. ¶500 (1986); Pennell, *Estate Planning: Drafting and Tax Considerations in Employing Individual Trustees*, 60 N.C. L. REV. 799 (1982).

How do you evaluate an unusual or untested standard, such as the following: *D* created an inter vivos trust to pay the net income to *A* for life, remainder to *B*. *D* served as a cotrustee of the trust, together with a corporate trustee. The trustees had discretion to invade principal to the extent necessary to provide "a home or business" for *A*. If *D* predeceases *A*, will any part of the trust be included in *D*'s gross estate? See Estate of Bell v. Commissioner, 66 T.C. 729 (1976), *acq.*, which held that the standard was not ascertainable. As noted with respect to the ascertainable standard exception to §2041, this is no place for a thesaurus, nor for untried approaches. How might the drafter have avoided this litigation while still accommodating the client's objectives?

31.   *Retained Power to Vote Stock.* The following case is self-explanatory and it spawned legislation to reverse its effect:

United States v. Byrum
408 U.S. 125 (1972)

POWELL, J: Decedent, Milliken C. Byrum, created in 1958 an irrevocable trust to which he transferred shares of stock in three closely held corporations. Prior to transfer, he owned at least 71% of the outstanding stock of each corporation. The beneficiaries were his children or, in the event of their death before the termina-tion of the trust, their surviving children. The trust instrument specified that there be a corporate trustee. Byrum designated as sole trustee an independent corporation, Huntington National Bank. The trust agreement vested in the trustee broad and detailed powers with respect to the control and management of the trust property. These powers were exercisable in the trustee's sole discretion, subject to certain rights reserved by Byrum: (i) to vote the shares of unlisted stock held in the trust estate; (ii) to disapprove the sale or transfer of any trust assets, including the shares transferred to the trust; (iii) to approve investments and reinvestments; and (iv) to remove the trustee and "designate another corporate Trustee to serve as successor." Until the youngest living child reached age 21, the trustee was authorized in its "absolute and sole discretion" to pay the income and principal of the trust to or for the benefit of the beneficiaries, "with due regard to their individual needs for education, care, maintenance and support." After the youngest child reached 21, the trust was to be divided into a separate trust for each child, to terminate when the beneficiaries reached 35. The trustee was authorized in its discretion to pay income and principal from these trusts to the beneficiaries for emergency or other "worthy need," including education.

When he died in 1964, Byrum owned less than 50% of the common stock in two of the corporations and 59% in the third. The trust had retained the shares transferred to it, with the result that Byrum had continued to have the right to vote not less than 71% of the common stock in each of the three corporations. There were minority stockholders, unrelated to Byrum, in each corporation.

Following Byrum's death, the Commissioner determined that the transferred stock was properly included within Byrum's gross estate under §2036(a) . . . because of the rights reserved by him in the trust agreement. It was asserted that his right to vote the transferred shares and to veto any sale thereof by the trustee, together with the ownership of other shares, enabled Byrum to retain the "enjoyment of . . . the property," and also allowed him to determine the flow of income to the trust and thereby "designate the persons who shall . . . enjoy . . . the income."

The executrix of Byrum's estate paid an additional tax of $13,202.45, and thereafter brought this refund action in District Court. The facts not being in dispute, the court ruled for the executrix on cross motions for summary judgment. 311 F. Supp. 892 (S.D. Ohio 1970). The Court of Appeals affirmed, one judge dissenting. 440 F.2d 949 (6th Cir. 1971). . . .

The Government relies primarily on its claim, made under §2036(a)(2) that Byrum retained the right to designate the persons who shall enjoy the income from the transferred property. The argument is a complicated one. By retaining voting control over the corporations whose stock was transferred, Byrum was in a position to select the corporate directors. He could retain this position by not selling the shares he owned and by vetoing any sale by the trustee of the transferred shares. These rights, it is said, gave him control over corporate dividend policy. By increasing, decreasing, or stopping dividends completely, it is argued that Byrum could "regulate the flow of income to the trust" and thereby shift or defer the beneficial enjoyment of trust income between the present beneficiaries and the remaindermen. The sum of this retained power is said to be tantamount to a grantor-trustee's power to accumulate income in the trust, which this Court has recognized constitutes the power to designate the persons who shall enjoy the income from transferred property.[55]

At the outset we observe that this Court has never held that trust property must be included in a settlor's gross estate solely because the settlor retained the power to manage trust assets. On the contrary, since our decision in Reinecke v. Northern Trust Co., 278 U.S. 339 (1929), it has been recognized that a settlor's retention of broad powers of management does not necessarily subject an inter vivos trust to the federal estate tax. Although there was no statutory analogue to §2036(a)(2) when Northern Trust was decided, several lower court decisions decided after the enactment of the predecessor of §2036(a)(2) have upheld the settlor's right to exercise managerial powers without incurring estate tax liability. In Estate of King v. Commissioner, 37 T.C. 973 (1962), a settlor reserved the power to direct the trustee in the management and investment of trust assets. The Government argued that the settlor was thereby empowered to cause investments to be made in such a manner as to control significantly the flow of income into the trust. The Tax Court rejected this argument, and held for the taxpayer. . . .

---

55.   United States v. O'Malley, 383 U.S. 627 (1966).

It is irrelevant to this argument how many shares Byrum transferred to the trust. Had he retained in his own name more than 50% of the shares (as he did with one corporation), rather than retaining the right to vote the transferred shares, he would still have had the right to elect the board of directors and the same power to "control" the flow of dividends. Thus, the government is arguing that a majority shareholder's estate must be taxed for stock transferred to a trust if he owned at least 50% of the voting stock after the transfer or if he retained the right to vote the transferred stock and could thus vote more than 50% of the stock. It would follow also that if a settlor controlled 50% of the voting stock and similarly transferred some other class of stock for which the payment of dividends had to be authorized by the directors, his estate would also be taxed. Query: what would happen if he had the right to vote less than 50% of the voting stock but still "controlled" the corporation? See n.[56], infra.

Essentially the power retained by Byrum is the same managerial power retained by the settlors in *Northern Trust* and in *King*. Although neither case controls this — *Northern Trust*, because it was not decided under §2036(a)(2) or a predecessor; and *King*, because it is a lower court opinion — the existence of such precedents carries weight. The holding of *Northern Trust*, that the settlor of a trust may retain broad powers of management without adverse estate-tax consequences, may have been relied upon in the drafting of hundreds of inter vivos trusts. The modification of this principle now sought by the Government could have a seriously adverse impact, especially upon settlors (and their estates) who happen to have been "controlling" stockholders of a closely held corporation. Courts properly have been reluctant to depart from an interpretation of tax law which has been generally accepted when the departure could have potentially far-reaching consequences. When a principle of taxation requires reexamination, Congress is better equipped than a court to define precisely the type of conduct which results in tax consequences. When courts readily undertake such tasks, taxpayers may not rely with assurance on what appear to be established rules lest they be subsequently overturned. Legislative enactments, on the other hand, although not always free from ambiguity, at least afford the taxpayers advance warning.

The Government argues, however, that our opinion in *United States v. O'Malley*, compels the inclusion in Byrum's estate of the stock owned by the trust. . . .

In our view, and for the purposes of this case, *O'Malley* adds nothing to the statute itself. The facts in that case were clearly within the ambit of what is now §2036(a)[(2)]. That section requires that the settlor must have "retained for his life . . . (2) the *right* . . . to designate the persons who shall possess or enjoy the property or the income therefrom." *O'Malley* was covered precisely by the statute for two reasons: (1) there the settlor had reserved a legal right, set forth in the trust instrument; and (2) this right expressly authorized the settlor, "in conjunction" with others, to accumulate income and thereby "to designate" the persons to enjoy it.

It must be conceded that Byrum reserved no such "right" in the trust instrument or otherwise. The term "right," certainly when used in a tax statute, must be given its normal and customary meaning. It connotes an ascertainable and legally enforceable power, such as that involved in *O'Malley*. Here, the right ascribed to Byrum was the power to use his majority position and influence over the corporate directors to "regulate the flow of dividends" to the trust. That "right" was neither ascertainable nor legally enforceable and hence was not a right in any normal sense of that term.

Byrum did retain the legal right to vote shares held by the trust and to veto investments and reinvestments. But the corporate trustee alone, not Byrum, had the right to pay out or withhold income and thereby to designate who among the beneficiaries enjoyed such income. Whatever power Byrum may have possessed, with respect to the flow of income into the trust, was derived not from an enforceable legal right specified in the trust instrument, but from the fact that he could elect a majority of the directors of the three corporations. The power to elect the directors conferred no legal right to command them to pay or not to pay dividends. A majority shareholder has a fiduciary duty not to misuse his power by promoting his personal interests at the expense of corporate interests. Moreover, the directors also have a fiduciary duty to promote the interests of the corporation. However great Byrum's influence may have been with the corporate directors, their responsibilities were to all stockholders and were enforceable according to legal standards entirely unrelated to the needs of the trust or to Byrum's desires with respect thereto.

The Government seeks to equate the de facto position of a controlling stockholder with the legally enforceable "right" specified by the statute. Retention of corporate control (through the right to vote the shares) is said to be "tantamount to the power to accumulate income" in the trust which resulted in estate tax consequences in *O'Malley*. The Government goes on to assert that "[t]hrough exercise of that retained power, [Byrum] could increase or decrease corporate dividends . . . and thereby shift or defer the beneficial enjoyment of trust income."[56] This approach seems to us not only to depart from the specific statutory language, but also to misconceive the realities of corporate life. . . .

There is no assurance that a small corporation will have a flow of net earnings or that income earned will in fact be available for

---

56.   The Government uses the terms "control" and "controlling stockholder" as if they were words of art with a fixed and ascertainable meaning. In fact, the concept of "control" is a nebulous one. Although in this case Byrum possessed "voting control" of the three corporations (in view of his being able to vote more than 50% of the stock in each), the concept is too variable and imprecise to constitute the basis per se for imposing tax liability under §2036(a). Under most circumstances, a stockholder who has the right to vote more than 50% of the voting shares of a corporation "controls it" in the sense that he may elect the board of directors. But such a stockholder would not control, under the laws of most States, certain corporate transactions such as mergers and sales of assets. Moreover, control — in terms of effective power to elect the board under normal circumstances — may exist where there is a right to vote far less than 50% of the shares. This will vary with the size of the corporation, the number of shareholders, and the concentration (or lack of it) of ownership. . . .

dividends. Thus, Byrum's alleged de facto "power to control the flow of dividends" to the trust was subject to business and economic variables over which he had little or no control.

Even where there are corporate earnings, the legal power to declare dividends is vested solely in the corporate board. In making decisions with respect to dividends, the board must consider a number of factors. It must balance the expectation of stockholders to reasonable dividends when earned against corporate needs for retention of earnings. . . .

We conclude that Byrum did not have an unconstrained de facto power to regulate the flow of dividends to the trust, much less the "right" to designate who was to enjoy the income from trust property. His ability to affect, but not control, trust income, was a qualitatively different power from that of the settlor in *O'Malley*, who had a specific and enforceable right to control the income paid to the beneficiaries. Even had Byrum managed to flood the trust with income, he had no way of compelling the trustee to pay it out rather than accumulate it. Nor could he prevent the trustee from making payments from other trust assets, although admittedly there were few of these at the time of Byrum's death. We cannot assume, however, that no other assets would come into the trust from reinvestments or other gifts.

We find no merit to the Government's contention that Byrum's de facto "control," subject as it was to the economic and legal constraints set forth above, was tantamount to the right to designate the persons who shall enjoy trust income, specified by §2036(a)(2). . . .

For the reasons set forth above, we hold that this case was correctly decided by the Court of Appeals and accordingly the judgment is affirmed.

[The dissenting opinion of Justice WHITE, joined by Justices BRENNAN and BLACKMUN, is omitted.]

It took several years, but the anti-*Byrum* rule of §2036(b) was adopted in 1976 and then amended, as described next. Does it seem odd to you that §2036(b) inclusion is under §2036(a)(1) as enjoyment, rather than under §2036(a)(2) as control? The following is from S. Rep. No. 745, 95th Cong., 2d Sess. 89-91 (1978). The Revenue Act of 1978 amended §2036(b), as explained by the Senate Finance Committee:

[PRIOR] LAW

Under prior law, the retention of certain powers or interests by a decedent in property transferred by the decedent during his lifetime resulted in the property being includible in his gross estate for estate tax purposes (§2036). The 1976 Act extended this rule to the retention of voting rights in stock of any corporation which was transferred by the decedent during his lifetime even if the corporation was not a controlled corporation. This rule is often called the "anti-*Byrum*" rule because it was intended to overrule the result reached in that case by the U.S. Supreme Court.

REASONS FOR CHANGE

The rule in the 1976 Act required the inclusion of any stock over which the decedent retained a power to vote regardless of whether the corporation was controlled by the decedent. The committee believes that the retention of voting power should result in the inclusion of the stock in the decedent's gross estate only where the decedent and his relatives own 20% or more of the voting stock of the corporation.

In addition, the committee believes that the rule should be clarified with respect to the retention of voting rights in certain indirect transfers as well as direct transfers of stock in a controlled corporation.

EXPLANATION OF PROVISION

[The Act] makes two amendments to the rule contained in the 1976 Act. First, [it] restricts the rule to stock in corporations which are controlled by the decedent and his relatives. Second, [it] clarifies the rule under the 1976 Act that indirect transfers are subject to the rule. . . .

A "controlled corporation" is defined to mean a corporation where the decedent and his relatives owned, or had the power to vote, stock possessing at least 20% of the total combined voting power of all classes of stock. The constructive ownership rules of §318 apply solely for purposes of determining whether the corporation is a controlled corporation. In addition, in order for the corporation to be controlled, the ownership of, or power to vote, 20% of the total combined voting power of all classes of stock had to occur any time after the transfer of the property and during the 3-year period ending on the date of the decedent's death.

The rule requiring inclusion in the gross estate of stock of a controlled corporation applies where the decedent retained the voting rights of the stock which was directly or indirectly transferred by him. Thus, where the decedent transferred cash or other property prior to his death to a trust of which he is trustee within 3 years of his death, and then the trust uses that cash or other property to purchase stock in a controlled corporation from himself, the value of the stock would be included in his gross estate. In addition, the indirect retention of voting rights in the case of reciprocal transfers of stock in trust would result in the inclusion of the stock with respect to which the decedent had voting rights as trustee. However, voting rights in stock transferred in trust by the decedent will not be considered to have been retained by the decedent merely because a relative was the trustee who voted the stock. In these cases, the voting rights would be considered to have been indirectly retained by the decedent if in substance the decedent had retained such voting rights, e.g., there had been an arrangement or agreement for the trustee to vote the stock in accordance with directions from the decedent.

The rule would not apply to the transfer of stock in a controlled corporation where the decedent could not vote the transferred stock. For example, where a decedent transfers stock in a controlled corporation to his son and does not have the power to vote the stock any time during the 3-year period before his death, the rule does not apply even where the decedent owned, or could vote, a majority of the stock. Similarly, where the decedent owned both voting and nonvoting stock and transferred the nonvoting stock to another person, the rule does not apply to the nonvoting stock simply because of the decedent's ownership of the voting stock. . . .

Taxpayers were quick to realize an easy way to avoid §2036(b), confirmed by the government in the following Ruling. Quaere: why have the rule?

Revenue Ruling 81-15

The Internal Revenue Service has been asked to reconsider Rev. Rul. 67-54, in view of the Supreme Court decision in United States v. Byrum, 408 U.S. 125 (1972), and the enactment of §2036(b).

In Rev. Rul. 67-54, the decedent transferred assets to a corporation which issued nonvoting preferred stock and debentures, for the full current value of the assets transferred. The corporation also issued 10 shares of voting and 990 shares of nonvoting common stock. The decedent transferred the 990 shares of nonvoting stock in trust for the benefit of his children. The trust owned the 990 shares at the date of decedent's death. Under the terms of the trust, the trustee could not dispose of the stock without the consent of the decedent. Under an alternative fact situation, the grantor designated himself as trustee.

Rev. Rul. 67-54 concludes that the decedent has retained control of the corporate dividend policy through retention of the voting stock and, thus, has retained the right to determine the income from the nonvoting stock. The decedent has also retained control over the disposition of the nonvoting stock, either as trustee or as a result of the restrictions on the trustee's power to dispose of the stock. The ruling holds that the decedent's retention of the right to control income and the restriction on disposition amount to a transfer whereby the decedent has retained for life or for a period which in fact did not end before death the right to designate the persons who shall enjoy the transferred property or income therefrom. Therefore, the property is includible in decedent's gross estate under §2036(a)(2) . . .

In *United States v. Byrum*, the Supreme Court addressed the issue of includibility of transferred stock where the decedent had transferred the stock in trust, retaining the right to vote the transferred shares, the right to veto the sale or acquisition of trust property, and the right to replace the trustee.

The court concluded that, because of the fiduciary constraints imposed on corporate directors and controlling shareholders,[57] the decedent "did not have an unconstrained de facto power to regulate the flow of dividends, much less the right to designate who was to enjoy the income." 408 U.S. at 143.

Thus, *Byrum* overruled the proposition on which Rev. Rul. 67-54 was based; that is, that a decedent's retention of voting control of a corporation, coupled with restrictions on the disposition of the stock, is equivalent to the right to designate the person who shall enjoy the income.

Section 2036(b)(1), added by the Tax Reform Act of 1976, as amended by the Revenue Act of 1978, provides that, for purposes of §2036(a)(1), the direct or indirect retention of voting rights in transferred stock of a controlled corporation shall be considered to be a retention of the enjoyment of transferred property.

The Senate Finance Committee Report relating to §2036(b)(1) provides . . . that the rule of that section will not apply to the transfer of stock in a controlled corporation where the decedent could not vote the transferred stock. Thus, the effect of *Byrum* on Rev. Rul. 67-54 is not changed by the enactment of §2036(b) of the Code.

---

57. Quaere: is *this* why *Byrum* held that §2036 would not apply? —Ed.

In view of *United States v. Byrum*, and the enactment of §2036(b) of the Code, Rev. Rul. 67-54 is revoked. . . .

To the same effect in a partnership setting is TAM 8611004, which disregards a grantor's ongoing control of a partnership as its general partner after making a gift of a partnership interest.

Section 2036(b) applies only to stock of a controlled corporation. A controlled corporation is one in which, after a decedent's inter vivos transfer of stock, at any time within the three-year period preceding the decedent's death, the decedent owned stock, or had the right to vote stock, possessing at least 20% of the voting power of the corporation's outstanding stock. §2036(b)(2). The stock attribution rules of §318 are applied for purposes of determining whether a corporation was controlled by a decedent, but only for that purpose. Section 318 treats a decedent as owning stock that actually is owned by other parties who bear a specified relation to the decedent. The related party can be a natural person or a fictional entity. Section 318 treats a person as the constructive owner of *stock*; it does not attribute raw voting power to anyone. For example, if *A* has a proxy to vote stock in which *A* has no ownership rights (actual or constructive), those voting rights will not be attributed to a person related to *A*.

It is worth emphasizing that the stock attribution rules of §318 are applied only for the purpose of determining whether a corporation was controlled within the meaning of §2036(b). The stock attribution rules are not applied to determine whether a grantor retained voting rights in the transferred stock, nor for valuation purposes. Prop. Treas. Reg. §20.2036-2(c).[58] For example, if *A* transferred voting stock to a trust for *A*'s children, the voting stock owned by the trust will be attributed to *A* by §§318(a)(2)(B) and (a)(1)(A). The stock constructively owned by *A* will be taken into account in determining whether the corporation is a controlled corporation. But, in determining whether *A* retained voting rights in the transferred stock (as required by §2036(b)(1)), the attribution rules will not be utilized. In other words, §318 cannot cause *A* to be deemed to have retained voting rights in the transferred stock.

Quaere the right result if the taxpayer's retained voting right is exercisable only in conjunction with another: Is shared voting power sufficient to trigger §2036(b)? TAM 199938005 predictably said that joint voting power is adequate, which is consistent with authority under §2036(a)(2) relating to retained control over transferred property. But joint powers are subject to the retained control provision by express language in §2036(a)(2) that is lacking in §2036(b). Moreover, §2036(b) provides explicitly that —

---

58. The proposed regulations under §2036(b) were promulgated in 1983, but have not yet been made final!

when it's provisions are met — the result is treatment of the taxpayer as having made a transfer with a §2036(a)(*1*) retained *interest* rather than a §2036(a)(*2*) retained *power*, making any reference or analog to the §2036(a)(2) joint power rule questionable.

Section 318 would be a relevant concern if *D* was the sole shareholder of *X* Corporation, which has always had only voting stock outstanding, and if *D* transferred 81% of the *X* voting stock to a trust for *D*'s children and retained the remaining 19% of the *X* stock. But §318 would *not* be a relevant concern if *D* and the sole trustee (a bank) orally agreed that the trustee would vote the stock only in accordance with *D*'s advice and that the trustee would first consult with *D* before voting and throughout the rest of *D*'s life the trustee did so. Instead, §318 will cause attribution to *D* of the stock in the trust for control purposes, but not to attribute to *D* the trustee's voting control. That is purely a function of the trustee's agreement and Rev. Rul. 80-346 said that it was sufficient, as does Prop. Treas. Reg. §20.2036-2(c), which reflects the penultimate paragraph of the Senate Finance Committee Report reproduced second next above.

Under the same facts except that the trust beneficiaries were nieces and nephews of *D*, §318 would not attribute to *D* any of the shares of stock held in the trust and the inquiry would end because §2036(b) would not apply.

32. *Relinquishing Retained Powers.* A final note raises the §2035(a)(2) reality that getting rid of retained powers cannot be a death bed plan. To illustrate, assume that *D* created an irrevocable inter vivos trust to pay income to *C* for life and the remainder to *GC*. *D* retained a power to direct distribution of principal to *GC* during *C*'s life, which *D* released shortly before death. *D*'s transfer became subject to the gift tax upon creation but the trust is includible in *D*'s gross estate at death under §2035(a)(2), the last clause of §2038(a)(1), and Treas. Reg. §20.2038-1(e)(1). Note that §2038(a)(2) speaks of "the decedent" having relinquished a retained power within three years of death, whereas §2038(a)(1) merely speaks of the power having been "relinquished" within three years of the decedent's death. Can you think of a fact situation in which this variation in language could be significant today? See Treas. Reg. §20.2038-1(e)(2).

Now assume that ten years ago *D* created two trusts, retaining a secondary life estate in Trust A and a power to change the beneficiary of the remainder interest in Trust B. Within three years of *D*'s death, *D* relinquished the power over the remainder in Trust B and transferred the retained secondary life estate in Trust A, both without consideration. At *D*'s death, *N*, the primary income beneficiary of Trust A, was alive. Section 2036(a)(1) would reach the secondary life estate in Trust A; §2038(a)(1) would reach the power over income producing corpus in Trust B (but §2036(a)(2) would not). In both cases the amount includible is the full value of each trust, in both cases reduced by the life estate in *N*. Don't forget the §2001(b) purge and credit rules!

PART D.   PROPOSALS FOR TRANSFER TAX REVISION

The three principal studies and proposals for wealth transfer tax revision — the 1969 Treasury Proposals, the American Law Institute's 1969 Project, and the American Bankers Association 1973 Discussion Draft — all agree on the desirability of enacting a single transfer tax standard governing when an inter vivos transfer with retained interests or powers should be regarded as sufficiently complete to attract the tax. They all agree that a single standard should be adopted to assure that any transfer would be taxed only once, thereby reducing complexity of the variety we have seen in this chapter and in the computation regime involving transfers that were taxed during life but were includible in the decedent's gross estate at death.

But there the agreement stops. Both the Treasury Proposals and the ALI Project favored a hard-to-complete rule with respect to some retained interests but otherwise an easy-to-complete rule, especially with respect to retained powers. See Treasury Department Studies and Proposals (pt. 3) 351-357, 360-377, 381-387; American Law Institute Recommendations 8, 41-47, 188-198. According to the ALI recommendations at 5 and 8-9:[59]

23.   A line between completed and uncompleted gifts should be definitively established, so that all lifetime arrangements would fall on one side of the line or the other, and so that there would be no area where the same transfer is subject to transfer taxation both as a lifetime transfer and a deathtime transfer, under . . . a unified tax.

24.   Under a unified tax, an easy-to-complete-gift rule should be adopted in the power cases which would eliminate the significance of a power in a lifetime arrangement to prevent a completed gift unless (a) the power can be exercised in favor of the transferor, and (b) the power is exercisable by the transferor alone or in conjunction with one who does not have a substantial interest that would be adversely affected by the exercise of the power.

26.   A transfer with current beneficial enjoyment retained by the transferor should be considered an incomplete gift as long as the transferor retains the current beneficial enjoyment, under . . . a unified tax.

---

59. Copyright © 1969 by the American Law Institute. Reprinted with the permission of the American Law Institute.

In addition, with respect to reversions, the Treasury Department proposals embraced a bifurcated rule at 364-365:

> If the reversionary interest is a contingent interest (i.e., the property will revert back to the transferor only if some contingency is satisfied) then the full value of the property will be taxed as an included transfer at the time of transfer. If the reversionary interest is not contingent but the property is certain to revert at some future date, then only the interests which precede the retained reversionary interest will be treated as included transfers. The reversionary interest and any interest which may follow it will be excluded transfers at the time of the initial conveyance.
>
> *Example 1.* — *A* makes a transfer in trust, the income to be paid to *B* for *B*'s life, then if *A* survives *B*, to *A* for *A*'s life, then the principal to go to *C*. If *A* dies before *B*, the beneficial enjoyment (i.e., the income) from the property will not revert to *A*. Thus, *A*'s reversionary interest is a contingent interest, and the entire amount of the property transferred by *A* is an included transfer.
>
> *Example 2.* — *A* transfers property in trust, the income to be paid to *B* for 10 years, then the principal to revert back to *A* and his heirs. Since the property is certain to revert back to *A* (or to his heirs if he should die) after 10 years (i.e., there is no contingency), only the 10-year interest in *B* is taxed as an included transfer at the time of the initial transfer.

A similar proposal was made by American Law Institute Recommendations Resolution 27 at 9, 43-44. The rationale for an easy-to-complete rule with respect to retained powers, as explained by the Treasury Proposals at 361, was that:

> [U]nder the unified transfer tax the overall tax cost of transfers will be approximately the same regardless of whether they are made during lifetime or at death. Since the excessive advantages under present law for lifetime gifts would be eliminated, the tax avoidance possibilities in attempting to have an incomplete transfer qualify as a completed lifetime gift would also be eliminated. Thus, transfers which under present law are not sufficient to remove the subject property from the transferor's estate may be treated as completed transfers under the unified transfer tax.

The Bankers proposal is interesting because, although also favoring a uniform rule under the unified transfer tax system, it urged that a hard-to-complete standard be applied for all purposes. American Bankers Association Discussion Draft 29-30, 42-46, 118-126 (1973). The rationale for this position, expressed at 118-124, proceeds as follows:

C. "Hard-to-Complete" v. "Easy-to-Complete" Rule.

The time when a tax will be imposed on a lifetime transfer depends upon whether a "hard-to-complete" or an "easy-to-complete" rule is adopted, since the property is taxed only when the transfer is deemed complete for transfer tax purposes. . . . The main distinction between these two approaches is in the area of retained control over the disposition of property as contrasted to retained beneficial interests in property. Under the "easy-to-complete" rule only retained beneficial interests in property prevent the immediate imposition of a transfer tax, while under the "hard-to-complete" rule retention of control over the property will also preclude an immediate tax. The ALI Project (page 42) summarized the "easy-to-complete" rule as follows: "It would allow a transferor to retain many strings on a transfer and nevertheless get the value of the future growth out from under transfer taxation, as long as the strings do not permit the transferor to pull the property back to himself."

From the transferor's viewpoint, this rule allows him to remove from his estate subsequent appreciation and income accumulated with respect to the taxed property, but he loses the use of the amount paid as tax at an earlier point in time.

Both the Studies (pages 361, 363-365, 384-387) and the ALI Project (pages 41-44, 45-46, 188-190) recommend an "easy-to-complete" rule. We believe that as a policy matter such a rule is wrong. An individual should not be permitted to insulate future appreciation or income accumulations from transfer tax when he retains control over the transferred property.

There is another reason why we oppose an "easy-to-complete" rule. It will involve changing present estate tax law which is now reasonably clear in its effect after many years of interpretation. Unless there is a provable advantage to the "easy-to-complete" rule, the time spent in shifting from existing law to the new approach is an unproductive use of time and money.

A shift to an "easy-to-complete" rule is usually justified on one or both of two premises. We believe that each of the premises is incorrect. The first premise is that, although we have struggled for many years to draw a line between complete and incomplete transfers using a "hard-to-complete" approach, we have the skill to draw an "easy-to-complete" line which is free from doubt. Our experience with tax law makes us doubt that this is true. A line between a taxable transaction and a nontaxable transaction is always hard to draw. We should not abandon the knowledge which we have painfully acquired over the years regarding the "hard-to-complete" rule.

The second premise is that, since all transfers will be subject to a single rate schedule, even an imprecise dividing line will not be productive of controversy. This is erroneous. If an individual makes a lifetime transfer and the property appreciates in value, it is to the government's advantage to take the position that the transfer is a deathtime rather than a lifetime transfer. Under existing law, increases in value between the time of transfer and the time of death, more than rate differentials, cause the government to challenge the time of completion of the transfer. An "easy-to-complete" rule will not change this situation unless the law is drafted so that if an individual makes a transfer during lifetime and pays a tax, the government is estopped from raising the question of the time of completion of the transfer for transfer tax purposes. Absent such an objective test as to the time of transfer, existing law is superior because of the knowledge acquired as to the time of transfer. Further, as a matter of sound tax administration, we do not think that the government should make such a concession. We believe that a "hard-to-complete" rule is more satisfactory from the standpoint of sound tax administration than an "easy-to-complete" rule.

. . . Under [the Bankers proposal] the transferor's retention of a right to receive the income from transferred property pursuant to the trustee's exercise of a discretionary power is sufficient to require inclusion of the property in his transfers at death. Thus, if an individual creates a trust with the trustee having a discretionary power to pay income (or principal) among a class consisting of himself and his descendants, the trust property will not be taxed upon the creation of the trust but will be included in his transfers at death . . . except to the extent that during his life payments of income or principal are made to his descendants, in which case the amounts of the payments are considered lifetime transfers by him.

The [Treasury Department] Studies (pages 384-385) and the ALI Project (pages 130-136) would apparently treat the type of trust transfer referred to in the preceding paragraph as complete (and taxable) when made because the transferor did not retain an absolute right to the current beneficial enjoyment. We believe this result is wrong and contrary to what is intended by most transferors in such a case. Also, not infrequently an individual will place his property in trust and give the trustee the discretion to pay the income to himself or to accumulate it. He does so "to protect himself" by placing the transferred property beyond his control, but he has no intention of foregoing the benefits of the property and does not expect a transfer tax to be imposed upon the creation of the trust. It is preferable to treat a retained right to income subject to a discretionary power in the same manner as a transfer with a retained life estate.

American Bankers Association Discussion Draft
29-30, 35 (1973)

§21. TRANSFERS WITH RETAINED INTEREST

(a) General Rule. — Except as provided in subsection (b), there shall be included in the transfers of an individual at death the value of all property as to which he has made a transfer and has retained until his death

(i)   a right or eligibility pursuant to the exercise of a power (other than a power taking effect upon the death of the person holding the power) to receive the property or the income from or the use of the property, which right or eligibility is not subject to a condition precedent (other than the exercise of such a power) immediately prior to his death; or

(ii)   a power, held in any capacity either alone or in conjunction with any person, to determine the persons (other than [qualified charities]) who shall receive the property, or the income from or the use of the property, or the time at which the property or the income from or the use of the property shall be received by any such person.

Any right, eligibility or power to which this section is applicable shall be deemed to relate first to amounts constituting income from the transferred property, notwithstanding any provision of the governing instrument or local law. As used in this section, the term "power" means an authority to do any act in relation to a beneficial interest in property, including but not limited to an authority whose exercise is limited by a fixed or ascertainable standard (whether or not such an authority is exercisable pursuant to such limitation at the death of the holder thereof).

(b) Exception for Certain Charitable Transfers. — The transfers of an individual at death shall not include the value of any property as to which he has made a transfer to a pooled income fund (as described in §642(c)(5)) or to a charitable remainder trust (as described in §664) if, after his death, no person other than [a qualified charity] has any interest in such property.

As explained by the Bankers Discussion Draft:

[Section 21] includes in the transfers of an individual at death the value of all property that he transferred and over which he retained (i) a right to receive the property or the income from or the use of the property, or (ii) a power to determine who shall receive the property, or the income from or the use thereof, or the time of receipt. It is intended to apply broadly to any retained right to a current benefit from the property and to any retained power to affect currently the beneficial enjoyment of the property. . .

Section 21 is a consolidation of §§2036 and 2038. . . . The terms "right" and "power" are to be interpreted broadly as under current law. . . . Section 21 encompasses a right subject to a discretionary power in another over whom the transferor has no control, but rights which are subject to a condition precedent immediately prior to the transferor's death other than the exercise of such a power are not so included. Thus, for example, the section will apply to a right in the transferor to receive income from a trust which he created as a member of a class of permissible recipients, even if the trustee has the discretion to retain any or all income in the trust, but it will not apply in a case where the transferor's income interest follows a life estate in another whom he predeceases. . . .

The general premise of the "hard-to-complete" rule in §21, which is more closely correlated with the income tax rules of §§671 through 677 than the "easy-to-complete rule," is that inclusion is appropriate in an individual's transfers at death where he has retained a right to current benefit from transferred property, or an existing or exercisable power to affect the enjoyment of the property. In either case, he has maintained a connection with, or a "string" over, the property which is not terminated until his death. In the case of a retained power, the final disposition of the transferred property is not fixed until the transferor's death.

. . . If a transferor retains a right to receive such amounts of the trust income as the trustee in his discretion may determine, §21 will apply because the transferor possesses a right to benefit currently from the property, even though this right is subject to a discretionary power lodged in the trustee. On the other hand, if the transferor has no interest in the trust income until he attains age 50 and he dies prior to attaining that age, his right is not a current right to share in the property and §21 will not be applicable. . . .

The amount includable under §21 is the full value at the transferor's death of the property which is the subject of his retained right or power.

Quaere whether taxation of appreciation under the Bankers Draft really benefits the government. For example, if property transferred inter vivos is worth $25x at the time of transfer and the tax is imposed immediately at a 40% rate, will the government receive less revenue than if the property doubles in value after the transfer and is taxed when the grantor dies? In answering, assume the tax is paid using the transferred property, that the tax rate remains at 40%, and that all dollars double in value between the date of the transfer and the grantor's death. Which system produces more revenue for the government and which is more favorable to the grantor: an easy-to-complete or a hard-to-complete rule?

If you perceive a disparity between these approaches, to what is that disparity attributable, and what assumptions were made in this example that are unreasonable? Finally, what does this exercise tell us about the design of a tax reform proposal that represents a clear improvement over current law?

For discussions of many of the problems considered in this chapter, and a plea for legislative revision, see Dodge, *Redoing the Estate and Gift Taxes Along Easy-to-Value Lines*, 43 TAX L. REV. 241 (1988); Peschel, *The Impact of Fiduciary Standards on Federal Taxation of Grantor Trusts: Illusion and Inconsistency*, 1979 DUKE L.J. 709.

Chapter 6

CONSIDERATION

Code Reference: *Estate Tax: §2043*

We need to interrupt our study of inter vivos transfers to address "consideration in money or money's worth." This concept pervades all inter vivos transfers, including several not yet studied, because a transfer made "for an adequate and full consideration in money or money's worth" will not be brought back into the decedent's gross estate for estate tax purposes, and will not be a gift for gift tax purposes. Note also that consideration is relevant in determining whether a deduction is allowable under §2053 for an outstanding debt, mortgage, or claim against a decedent's estate. Beginning with the meaning of the term "adequate and full consideration in money or money's worth," then we will consider the effect of receiving partial consideration for a transfer.

1. *Adequate and Full Consideration in Money or Money's Worth.* Consider first that the Code does not define the term "consideration in money or money's worth."

Commissioner v. Wemyss, 324 U.S. 303 (1945), held that, for gift tax purposes, a transferee's incurring a detriment does not constitute money's worth consideration; there must be a benefit to the transferor.

The §2043(a) "adequate and full consideration in money or money's worth" exception first appeared in the estate tax in the Revenue Act of 1926. According to Estate of Frothingham v. Commissioner, 60 T.C. 211, 215 (1973):

> The obvious purpose of the clause was to relieve of estate tax those transfers etc., in respect of which the decedent-transferor had *received* an equivalent amount of consideration. Thus, where the transferred property is replaced by other property of equal value received in exchange, there is no reason to impose an estate tax in respect of the transferred property, for it is reasonable to assume that the property acquired in exchange will find its way into the decedent's gross estate at his death unless consumed or otherwise disposed of in a non-testamentary transaction in much the same manner as would the transferred property itself had the transfer not taken place.

2.   *Marital and Support Rights.*   Added in 1932, §2043(b)(1) provides that "for purposes of [the estate tax], a relinquishment or promised relinquishment of dower or curtesy, or of a statutory estate created in lieu of dower or curtesy, or of other marital rights in the decedent's property or estate, shall not be considered to any extent a consideration 'in money or money's worth.'" Merrill v. Fahs, 324 U.S. 308 (1945), also held that the terms of §2043(b) apply to the gift tax because (at least in this instance) the estate and gift taxes are "in pari materia and must be construed together."

In 1984, Congress added §2043(b)(2) to incorporate by reference the §2516 deemed consideration rules relating to property settlements incident to divorce, but made it applicable only for §2053 estate tax deduction purposes. The §2053 deduction issue arises when part of the settlement was unpaid at the obligor's death. This leaves open the question whether a comparable rule will be applied to prevent inclusion in a transferor's gross estate of property transferred incident to a divorce in such manner that it otherwise would trigger one of the string provisions. The contention would be that the principle of §2516 should apply to treat the inter vivos transfer as having been made for adequate and full consideration in money or money's worth so that the string provisions will not apply. Reaching the same end in a different way was TAM 9826002, which found a divorce settlement trust to be §2036 includible with a §2056 offsetting deduction, supported by §2516 consideration, all in consideration of §2043(b)(2) establishing this as the appropriate legislative pattern (instead of saying that §2036 does not apply in the first instance). Quaere: without legislative authority, should the principle of pari materia be applied to construe the §2516 deemed consideration rules as applicable to the rest of the estate tax and not just to §2053?

The meaning of the reference in §2043(b)(1) to "other marital rights in the decedent's property or estate" remains somewhat in doubt. Neither the committee reports nor the regulations supply any assistance in this regard. There is authority for the proposition that the phrase refers to a surviving spouse's "rights of inheritance" on a decedent's death and not to a spouse's right to support during the joint lives of the decedent and the spouse. See Estate of Glen v. Commissioner, 45 T.C. 323, 339-342 (1966); Rev. Rul. 68-379; Rev. Rul. 71-67; Estate of Iverson v. Commissioner, 65 T.C. 391 (1975), *aff'd on that issue but rev'd on a different issue*, 552 F.2d 977 (3d Cir. 1977). In light of *Wemyss* and *Frothingham*, why distinguish support rights from "inheritance rights"? Well, because support payments actually reduce wealth as the person supported consumes it, while inheritance rights are a shift of wealth that does not necessarily get consumed. With respect to those, however, the question of consideration for transfers between spouses is academic, because of the unlimited gift tax marital deduction and perhaps it is better to govern these transfers with the marital deduction rules. The treatment of consideration in interspousal transfer cases is worth studying because some transfers between spouses do not qualify in form for a marital deduction, or they occur after the divorce. Moreover, the principles established in those cases can influence the consideration determination in other circumstances.

Revenue Ruling 71-67

Advice has been requested with respect to the allowance of a deduction from the gross estate for the commuted value of support payments due a decedent's wife under the circumstances described below.

In 1953 in anticipation of obtaining a final decree of divorce, the decedent and his wife entered into a separation agreement under the terms of which he was to pay her $7,500 annually for her lifetime or until she remarried. The agreement specifically provided that such payment was "in lieu of any claims of said wife to support and maintenance and/or alimony, past, present and future." Also, if he predeceased his wife, the support payments were to be a charge upon his estate. At the time the separation agreement was entered into, the decedent's income was approximately $40,000 a year. He was aged 57 years and she was aged 45 years. At decedent's death in 1969, she was aged 61 years. No divorce decree or judicial separation was ever obtained by the decedent or his wife.

In his will, the decedent gave all the residue of his estate to his executor in trust to pay the sum of $7,500 annually to his wife under the terms and provisions of the aforementioned separation agreement. On the Federal estate tax return filed for the estate, a deduction was taken on Schedule K for the amount of support that was payable during the lifetime or until the remarriage of the wife, as actuarially computed. The state of decedent's residence at the time of his death allowed a similar claim in the computation of the succession tax payable by his estate. This allowance was based upon a finding that the separation agreement was a valid and enforceable obligation under state law. . . .

With respect to the gift tax consequences of a transfer of property pursuant to a legal separation agreement, Revenue Ruling 68-379, 1968-2 C.B. 414, holds that where a husband transfers property to his wife in settlement of her support and property rights, such transfer is a taxable gift to the extent the value of the transferred property exceeds the value of the support rights that are surrendered. In other words, to the extent that the transferred property does not exceed the reasonable value of the relinquished support rights of the wife, it is to be treated as made for adequate and full consideration in money or money's worth. In Estate of Hundley v. Commissioner, 52 T.C. 495 (1969), the court reached the same conclusion with respect to a transfer of property pursuant to a negotiated settlement agreement between the husband and wife who were separated but not divorced.

While both the decision in *Hundley* and Revenue Ruling 68-379 involve the gift tax, their rationale is equally applicable to the estate tax. The Supreme Court of the United States has held the estate and gift taxes to be in pari materia from the standpoint of what represents adequate and full consideration in money or money's worth. Merrill v. Fahs, 324 U.S. 308 (1945).

Accordingly, it is held that the release by the decedent's wife of her right to support and maintenance is "consideration in money or money's worth" as that term is used in §2053(c)(1)(A). Therefore, the claim for payment after the death of the decedent, to the extent that it is based on such release, is deductible by the estate under §2053(a)(3) as a claim based upon an adequate and full consideration in money or money's worth to the extent of the value of the postponed support rights.

The question whether the amount of the claim is in excess of the wife's reasonable support rights is a matter for determination by the District Director after consideration of the facts and circumstances of the case. Elements to be considered are the amount of the husband's annual income, the extent of his assets, the relative ages of the parties and, where applicable, the probability of the wife's remarriage, etc. See Commissioner v. Estate of Nelson, 396 F.2d 519 (2d Cir. 1968).

It is to be noted that a wife's support rights are generally limited to the period of the joint lives of herself and her husband or until her earlier remarriage. Thus, where, as here, the support payments are to continue beyond the period of their joint lives, a determination must be made whether the lifetime payments were less than that to which she would have been entitled to receive as support under state law. It is the value of the postponed support rights to which the deduction allowable under §2053(a)(3) is limited (unless the value of the widow's claim is less than the value of the postponed support rights). For Federal estate tax purposes, the value of the portion of the wife's support rights which she agreed to have postponed is ascertained as of the date of the separation agreement. See United States v. Righter, 400 F.2d 344 (8th Cir. 1968).

The example below illustrates the computation of the values of the wife's postponed support rights and her claim against the estate. For this purpose, it is assumed that under local law the wife would have been entitled to receive $10,000 per year as support until her husband's death. The present worth of the right to receive an annuity of $1.00 per year during the joint lives of two persons aged 45 and 57 is $11.1080. The present worth of the right of a woman aged 61, just widowed, to receive an annuity of $1.00 per year until her death or remarriage is $10.6351. These factors are based on U.S. Life Table 38, with interest at 3½% and the American Remarriage Table.

(1)	Annual support rights	$10,000.00
(2)	*Less:* Contract payment	7,500.00
(3)	Excess	$ 2,500.00
(4)	*Multiply:* Annuity factors for joint lives	11.108
(5)	Value of postponed support rights	$27,770.00
(6)	Contract payment	7,500.00
(7)	*Multiply:* Age 61 remarriage annuity factor	10.6351
(8)	Value of widow's claim	$79,763.25
(9)	Allowable deduction (Lesser of 5 or 8)	$27,770.00

The Tax Court adopted the position asserted by the Commissioner in Rev. Rul. 71-67. Estate of Iverson v. Commissioner, 65 T.C. 391 (1975), *aff'd on that issue, but rev'd on another issue*, 552 F.2d 977 (3d Cir. 1977).

Why would the decedent's estate in Rev. Rul. 71-67 not be entitled to a marital deduction for the portion of the widow's claim that is not supported by adequate consideration? For example, if the decedent had died in 1996, why would a §2056(b)(7) election to qualify for the marital deduction not be effective?

In Sherman v. United States, 462 F.2d 577 (5th Cir. 1972), the decedent and his wife entered into a separation agreement that provided that he pay her $1,500 a month as alimony and for maintenance and support until her death or remarriage. The agreement further provided that his estate continue the payments if he predeceased her, which he did. The agreement referred to his previously established irrevocable inter vivos trust, under which the trustees had discretion to distribute principal and income to her and also recited his obligation to establish a testamentary trust that would require the trustees to distribute to her from income or principal an amount equal to the difference between the amount distributed from the inter vivos trust and $1,500 per month. The Commissioner disallowed the estate's deduction of the commuted value of a promise to pay $1,500 a month to a woman of the wife's age until her death or remarriage.

The district court held that the consideration for the husband's obligation was relinquishment of her support rights, which (unlike "marital rights" such as dower and the like) qualified under §§2043 and 2053 as full and adequate consideration in money or money's worth. In affirming, the Court of Appeals declared:

We cannot say that this finding is clearly erroneous. Under Georgia law the wife's right to support may be satisfied by periodic payments or given to her in a lump sum or by an interest in the husband's property. Bateman v. Bateman, 159 S.E.2d 387 (Ga. 1968); Harper v. Harper, 141 S.E.2d 403 (Ga. 1965). The husband's gross income of over $50,000 in the year of separation, the high standard of living of the husband and wife, the good state of health of both parties in spite of their ages of 69 and 70 years, and the fact that they had been married over 45 years, fully support the district court's finding that the obligation of the estate under the agreement was in consideration of the wife's relinquishment of support rights and not of her property or estate rights. We agree with the taxpayers that the hindsight knowledge that the husband died first is irrelevant to the value of the wife's support rights and thus to the adequacy of consideration.

Assume that D and S executed a premarital agreement under which D agreed that, if D died first and they were still married, D would establish a trust to provide S with $500 a month until S died or remarried. In return, S released the right to a statutory forced share of D's estate and any right to a year's support allowance for one year after D's death. D died, survived by S. D's will established the trust. The remainder of the trust was bequeathed to C. D's estate can deduct any portion of the obligation to pay $500 per month to S that is supported by consideration or that qualifies for the marital deduction. Remarriage is a problem on the latter score, and the statutory share is problematic as consideration, but what about the year's support right that was given up? Estate of Ellman v. Commissioner, 59 T.C. 367 (1972), held that it is like the elective share and not like the inter vivos duty to support a surviving spouse and therefore denied all claimed deductions.

3.   *Effect of a Divorce Decree.* Harris v. Commissioner, 340 U.S. 106 (1950), held that a wife's transfer to her divorced husband pursuant to a separation agreement was not a gift for gift tax purposes because the agreement was submitted to a divorce court, which incorporated the agreement into its decree. In Rev. Rul. 60-160, the government conceded that the *Harris* doctrine applied to the deductibility of a claim against a decedent's estate that was founded on a separation agreement that also was incorporated in the decree of a divorce court that had the power to alter the terms of the agreement. This position has been adopted in numerous cases. See, e.g., Robinson v. Commissioner, 63 T.C. 717 (1975). Thus, if D agreed to pay S (or cause to be paid to S) $10,000 per year until S dies or remarries (regardless of when D dies) in exchange for S's release of all marital rights, and if the terms of the agreement are included in the decree of divorce by a court that has the power to vary the terms of the agreement, after D's death the value of the estate's obligation to continue the payments to S will qualify as an estate tax deduction under §2053.

The gift tax also excludes transfers made in connection with a business transaction as defined in Treas. Reg. §25.2512-8. This exception has not been extended to the estate tax, although the Tax Court apparently considered the possibility in Estate of Glen v. Commissioner, 45 T.C. 323 (1966).

An exchange between persons acting at arm's length may be presumed to be equal for income tax purposes, as it was in United States v. Davis, 370 U.S. 65 (1962) (an income tax case in which a spouse's relinquishment of marital rights was deemed to be equal in value to the property received in exchange therefor). Despite several Tax Court decisions that appear to have indulged in that presumption, the great weight of authority is that the value of consideration received must be proved for estate tax purposes. E.g., United States v. Past, 347 F.2d 7 (9th Cir. 1965); Commissioner v. Nelson, 396 F.2d 519 (2d Cir. 1968); Estate of Iverson v. Commissioner, 65 T.C. 391 (1975), *rev'd on another ground*, 552 F.2d 977 (3d Cir. 1977); Rev. Rul. 71-67. The Tax Court's determination in *Iverson* that the value of the wife's support rights was not "adequate and full" consideration was reversed. In addition, the court hinted that it was dissatisfied with a rule that permits a full deduction if the divorce settlement is incorporated in the divorce decree but may deny a deduction in whole or in part if it is not. Estate of Fenton v. Commissioner, 70 T.C. 263, 274 (1978), found that the decedent's promise to leave his wife an income interest in half of his estate and to designate her as beneficiary of a life insurance policy was supported by adequate and full consideration in money's worth.

The government questions settlement agreements that courts really cannot change, as illustrated next:

Revenue Ruling 75-395

Advice has been requested whether a deduction under §2053(a)(3) is allowable for a decedent's indebtedness to his former spouse under the circumstances described below.

The following statute was enacted in 1972 in State A, with respect to separation agreements concluded by parties to actions for legal separation or dissolution of marriage:

(1) To promote amicable settlement of disputes between parties to a marriage attendant upon their separation or the dissolution of their marriage, the parties may enter into a written separation agreement containing provisions for maintenance of either of them, disposition of any property owned by either of them, and custody, support and visitation of their children.

(2) In a proceeding for dissolution of marriage or for legal separation, the terms of the separation agreement,

except those providing for the custody, support, and visitation of children, are binding upon the court unless it finds, after considering the economic circumstances of the parties and any other relevant evidence produced by the parties, on their own motion or on request of the court, that the separation agreement is unconscionable.

(3) If the court finds the separation agreement unconscionable, it may request the parties to submit a revised separation agreement or may make orders for the disposition of property, support, and maintenance.

(4) If the court finds that the separation agreement is not unconscionable as to support, maintenance, and property:

(a) Unless the separation agreement provides to the contrary, its terms shall be set forth verbatim or incorporated by reference in the decree of dissolution or legal separation and the parties shall be ordered to perform them;

(b) If the separation agreement provides that its terms shall not be set forth in the decree, the decree shall identify the separation agreement and state that the court has found the terms not unconscionable.

The decedent, H, died on March 3, 1974, after a lifetime of residence in State A. On January 24, 1973, H had entered into a written separation agreement with W, his wife at that time. The agreement required H to do the following upon the issuance of a final decree of dissolution of the marriage of H and W:

(1) H agreed to purchase and deliver to W a commercial annuity contract which would pay $500 each month to her for her life. In exchange for this promise, W agreed to surrender her right to support from H.

(2) H agreed to sell certain property and deliver the sale proceeds to W in consideration for which W agreed to relinquish all rights or claims which she might have against the property of the decedent by virtue of their marriage, including her dower interest or any statutory interest in the decedent's estate.

A final decree of dissolution of the marriage of H and W was issued by the proper court of State A on January 28, 1974. The court decree incorporated the separation agreement of the spouses verbatim. On January 31, 1974, H purchased and delivered to W the annuity contract as required by the first part of the separation agreement. The real property described in the second part of the agreement was sold by *H* on February 1, for $100,000. *H* failed, however, to deliver the sale proceeds to *W* before his death. The Federal estate tax return for *H*'s estate reflects a claimed deduction of $100,000 for the amount paid to *W* in satisfaction of *H*'s obligation to pay to her the sale proceeds. . . .

Under the statute of State *A* quoted above, a separation agreement between spouses is binding on the divorce court with respect to the settlement of their property interests unless the court finds the agreement to be unconscionable. This limitation on the powers of the divorce court is similar to that considered by the Tax Court in Estate of Barrett v. Commissioner, 56 T.C. 1312 (1971), and Estate of Bowers v. Commissioner, 23 T.C. 911 (1955), *acq.*, 1955-2 C.B. 4. There the Tax Court found that the State divorce court was bound by the property settlement agreement entered into by the parties, absent fraud, compulsion, or a violation of the confidential relationship of the spouses. The Tax Court held that this bound the divorce court sufficiently to make the obligation founded on the agreement, rather than on the divorce decree. Since in each case there was no showing that the obligation was contracted for adequate and full consideration in money or money's worth, the Tax Court disallowed the debt deduction sought by the estate.

As in *Barrett* and *Bowers* and pursuant to the principles set forth in Rev. Rul. 60-160, the divorce court's powers respecting the separation agreement between *H* and *W* in the instant case are circumscribed so completely that the court does not possess such control over the terms of the agreement that an indebtedness arising from the agreement can be considered as founded on the court decree incorporating it.

Since the indebtedness is founded on the separation agreement itself, a Federal estate tax deduction for such indebtedness is limited, under §2053(c)(1)(A) . . . , to the extent to which the indebtedness was contracted "bona fide" and for an adequate and full consideration in money or money's worth. A spouse's marital rights in the *property* of the other spouse, unlike the right to support, are not deemed to be "consideration in money or money's worth" for estate tax purposes, by virtue of §2043(b)[(1)]. Therefore, no deduction is allowable under §2053(a)(3) with respect to an indebtedness of a decedent which was created in exchange for the surrender of marital rights only and which is founded on a separation agreement that is binding on the divorce court under local law.

Accordingly, in the instant case, no deduction under §2053(a)(3) of the Code is allowable for the decedent's obligation to pay to his former spouse the proceeds from the sale of the real property since that obligation is founded on the decedent's property settlement agreement and was created in exchange for the surrender of marital rights not deemed to be consideration in money or money's worth under §2043(b)[(1)].

Accord, Gray v. United States, 541 F.2d 228 (9th Cir. 1976); Estate of Fenton v. Commissioner, 70 T.C. 263 (1978). See also Bowes v. United States, 77-2 U.S. Tax Cas. (CCH) ¶13,212 (N.D. Ill. 1977). In *Fenton*, the Tax Court again adopted the Commissioner's view that the *Harris* rule does not apply to an agreement that was incorporated into a divorce decree if the divorce court was not empowered to alter the terms of the agreement. The taxpayer contended in *Fenton* that every divorce court has the power to disregard a settlement because it has the power to refuse to approve and order performance of an agreement that it considers inequitable. The court determined, however, that a divorce court's power only to adopt or to reject a settlement is not sufficient to invoke the *Harris* rule; the divorce court must have the power to impose "its own settlement terms." *Fenton*, 70 T.C. at 272.

To put a partial end to the kind of hair-splitting illustrated by Rev. Rul. 75-395, Congress in 1984 finally incorporated the §2516 rules into §2043(b)(2), applicable to estates of decedents dying after July 18, 1984. Putting the estate and gift tax in pari materia for the first time, but only as to §2053 deductions, the change established a rule that qualifying transfers pursuant to divorce or legal separation are adequate and full consideration in money or money's worth. The change will not affect situations such as that in TAM 8526003, however, in which the decedent conveyed a remainder interest in property to children as part of a property settlement incident to divorce. Because that transfer was not for the support of the children nor as consideration for a release of their right to receive support payments, it was not supported by consideration in money or money's worth for purposes of either the estate or gift taxes. Nor does the 1984 amendment affect the situation represented by the decision in *O'Nan* below, because of the limitation on its application to deductions under §2053. There is a question whether the spirit of §2043(b)(2) [and note that §1041 was adopted at the same time] would lead a court to read the principle of §2516 into all of the estate tax to carry out the Congressional purpose of making marital settlements free of tax. Although that is possible, it does not appear a likely construction.

Estate of O'Nan v. Commissioner
47 T.C. 648 (1967), *acq.*

[Pursuant to a separation agreement that was promptly set forth and approved in a divorce decree, the decedent transferred the remainder interest in certain real estate to his wife, Tillie, retaining a life interest in it. On the decedent's death, the Commissioner sought to include the realty in his gross estate under §2036(a)(1). The principal issue was whether the decedent had received adequate consideration in money's worth for the transfer of the realty to qualify for the exception to inclusion in §2036(a)(1).]

HOYT, J.: . . . This question, in its several aspects, has recently been reviewed at considerable length by this Court in Estate of Keller v. Commissioner, 44 T.C. 851 (1965); Estate of Glen v. Commissioner, 45 T.C. 323 (1966); and Estate of Nelson v. Commissioner, 47 T.C. 279 (1966). These were all estate tax cases involving husband and wife transfers of properties made incident to divorce or pursuant to settlement agreements incident to divorce. We carefully reviewed the legislative and judicial history of §2043 and related sections of the Code, and applied the announced principles accordingly to the facts disclosed by the records therein.

In the *Keller* case, respondent conceded that the value of the wife's life estate in the transferred property, the only interest transferred to her pursuant to a divorce decree, was excludable from the gross estate under §2036(a) on the authority of Harris v. Commissioner, 340 U.S. 106 (1950); Estate of Watson v. Commissioner, 20 T.C. 386 (1953), *aff'd,* 216 F.2d 941 (2d Cir. 1954); and Rev. Rul. 60-160, 1960-1 C.B. 374. We held that the remainder interest in the property transferred to the two adult children was not excludable since the transfer of that interest was not related to the wife's surrender of marital rights in the property under the divorce decree. We said, after pointing out the confusion that has arisen in construing and applying §§2036(a) and 2043(b)[(1)]: "*However, it would seem that both a transfer with a retained life estate, and a claim based on a promise or agreement, will be deemed to be supported by an adequate and full consideration if they spring from a divorce decree, insofar as the decree effectively settles the property rights of the parties who are before the court, even though the wife has only marital rights to give up.* But we do not think this 'divorce as consideration' theory has yet been extended to provide a consideration for a transfer to third parties, not before the court in the divorce proceeding, simply because the divorce decree requires the transfer. [Emphasis supplied.]"

The same view was expressed in the *Glen* case. . . .

An exclusion from the gross estate was allowed in the *Nelson* case to the extent of the interest of the wife in a trust to which her husband transferred property under a divorce settlement agreement. The wife's relinquishment of her right to support, which had a value in excess of the determined value of her interest in the trust at the time of the transfer, was held adequate and full consideration in money or money's worth.

The crucial question here is whether the transfers to the wife were effected in consideration of Tillie's right to support or by the divorce decree, rather than in satisfaction of the wife's relinquishment of her dower, curtesy, or other marital rights in decedent's estate as respondent contends.

The Kentucky statutes and the cases decided by the courts of that State establish the right of a divorced wife to a fair and reasonable share of her husband's property.

[The Tax Court here examined and discussed Kentucky law.]

We are . . . unimpressed with respondent's arguments that the Kentucky divorce court had no power or authority to vary or alter the settlement agreement by its divorce decree. It has long been recognized in Kentucky that settlement agreements between the parties, if fair and made in contemplation of a permanent separation will be upheld. . . . However, it is clear that the parties in a divorce action cannot by their agreement take away the court's inherent and specifically conferred powers.

The divorce court here not only had power and authority to adjudge, and decree an alimony award to Tillie under KRS 403.060(1), but also under the express terms of KRS 403.065 to restore to decedent any property she had previously obtained from him. We conclude that the court had inherent and specific power, authority, and jurisdiction to alter, vary, accept, or reject the settlement agreement tendered to it by Tillie. We agree with petitioner's argument that there are few Kentucky cases discussing such a fundamental proposition because it is obvious as a practical matter that divorce courts are not going to freely and wantonly change or vary settlement agreements reached by the parties just to prove their undoubted authority. The fact that decedent and Tillie after lengthy arm's-length bargaining and negotiation had agreed upon a settlement or that decedent had deeded the properties in question to Tillie prior to entry of the decree has no real significance. The divorce court obviously could have varied the agreement to restore to decedent all of the real property which he had previously deeded to her and make an equitable award to Tillie from O'Nan's total property and estate. The fact that it did not do so and that the agreement of the parties was set forth in the decree and the rights of the parties were adjudged accordingly does not indicate at all that the court was powerless to do otherwise.

Here, instead of ignoring the arrangements worked out by the parties and applying its own equitable thumb, the court very properly accepted the negotiated agreement of the parties, incorporating it verbatim in the decree. The court then adjudged the rights and interests of the parties. . . . As in Pegram v. Pegram, 310 Ky. 86 (1949), the contractual agreement became merged into the judgment of the court and the transfers were then founded upon the divorce decree, sprang therefrom, and became final thereby.

We conclude and hold that until the divorce decree was entered there was no final settlement nor were effective and binding transfers previously made. Tillie's rights and the decedent's duties were then determined and fixed. . . .

We conclude that the divorce court had power to decree a settlement of all property rights between the parties and to vary the terms of the prior agreement if it saw fit to do so. Therefore, petitioner's reliance on *Harris v. Commissioner*, supra, puts him on sound ground here. As we observed in the *Glen* case, *Harris* stands for the principle that where an agreement settling marital property rights is incorporated into the divorce decree there is then deemed to be consideration for the transfers to the wife under the agreement. Once the decree issues, transfers made thereafter are not voluntary pursuant to the promise or agreement of the parties, but rather pursuant to judicial decree. We can see no valid distinction between transfers *thereafter* and *before* under the circumstances of this case. The same rule applies because the transfers were conditional upon the decree which the parties agreed would be obtained and which followed almost immediately as contemplated; the Kentucky court was not bound to accept the provisions of the agreement but free to order division and restoration to achieve an equitable result. Had O'Nan died after the decree and before he had transferred the farms to Tillie, her claim under the judgment would have been deductible for estate tax purposes. Commissioner v. Maresi, 156 F.2d 929 (2d Cir. 1946), *aff'g* 6 T.C. 582 (1946); E.T. 19, 1946-2 C.B. 166; Rev. Rul. 60-160, 1960-1 C.B. 374.

It is also clear that if O'Nan had effected the transfers outright and the respondent had asserted a gift tax, no gift tax liability would be found. . . .

While it is true that even respondent has long recognized that a release of support rights constitutes a money's-worth consideration and we have concluded here that the transfers in issue were obtained in exchange for Tillie's rights to support, the only right she had in Kentucky upon divorce, we are unable on the evidence before us to fix the value of those rights. We do not mean to imply that there must be a precise dollar-for-dollar matching of consideration paid with the value of the transferred property in order to conclude that a full and adequate consideration was furnished. See *Estate of Nelson*, supra. However, we cannot, as in *Nelson*, say here what Tillie's support rights were worth as of [the date of their divorce decree].

If we were here concerned with the income tax consequences of the transfer to decedent in the year of the settlement, United States v. Davis, [370 U.S. 65 (1962),] would dictate the conclusion that the release of Tillie's inchoate marital rights, the same under the State law there involved as under the Kentucky law here, were equal in value to the property for which they were exchanged. What the Supreme Court there said describes the situation here: "It must be assumed, we think, that the parties acted at arm's length and that they judged the marital rights to be equal in value to the property for which they were exchanged. There was no evidence to the contrary here. Absent a readily ascertainable value it is accepted practice where property is exchanged to hold, as did the Court of Claims in Philadelphia Park Amusement Co. v. United States, 126 F. Supp. 184, 189, (Ct. Cl. 1954), that the values 'of the two properties exchanged in an arm's-length transaction are either equal in fact or are presumed to be equal.' "

We believe that this method of evaluating interests such as here involved is particularly valid and should be applied under the facts of this case. There was long-standing marital discord, followed by 5 years of separation; the parties dealt at arm's-length and negotiated over a considerable period of time before reaching a settlement agreement; the reserved life interests (burdened with a lien to secure Tillie's annual payments and rights to farm products) as well as Tillie's remainder interests in the two farms were such that no readily ascertainable value of the properties exchanged can be attributed. We believe that here, too, on the record presented it should be concluded that the value of the rights surrendered by Tillie can be measured by and equated with the value of the property rights transferred to her by decedent so that full and adequate consideration in money or money's worth was provided for the transfer. There is certainly no hint or suggestion in this record that any donation or gift was intended or effected. The parties certainly judged that the rights given up by Tillie were equal in value to what she received from decedent. There was full consideration for the transfer.

We also conclude and hold that even without evidence to afford a yardstick to measure the consideration or without applying the rationale of *United States v. Davis*, supra, to equate the values of the properties exchanged, the exclusionary condition of §2036(a)[(1)] has been met with respect to the remainder interests in the two farms transferred to Tillie. We need not measure because here the divorce court had power to decree a settlement of all property rights in an equitable manner, to vary the terms of the prior agreement or to accept them and to restore to the decedent any and all property Tillie had obtained from him, including the interests in the farms. The court ratified and approved the agreement in every detail and adjudged the respective rights of the parties in all of their property accordingly. The transfers then became effective and final; they were founded upon the divorce decree and were therefore supported by an adequate and full consideration in money or money's worth. *Harris v. Commissioner,* supra; *Estate of Keller,* supra; Estate of Watson v. Commissioner, 20 T.C. 386 (1953), *aff'd,* 216 F. 2d 941 (2d Cir. 1954), *acq.* 1958-1 C.B. 6; E.T. 19, supra; Rev. Rul. 60-160, supra.

In the light of the foregoing, the respondent's determination cannot be sustained and the principal issue is decided for petitioner. . . .

4.   The following case anticipates challenging issues relating to the proper valuation of consideration for the transfer of a remainder interest (a topic that we will address at page 381 in *Gradow*) and the partial consideration application of §2043.

United States v. Past
347 F.2d 7 (9th Cir. 1965)

HAMLIN, J.: The decedent and Harry E. Rosedale were married for twenty-five years. In 1954, because of marital difficulties, complicated by the fact that decedent was addicted to alcohol, each employed independent legal counsel for the purpose of negotiating a property settlement. All of the property owned by the Rosedales was held as community property in which under California law each was an equal owner. For many years prior to 1954 decedent and her husband Harry obtained most of their income from a nursery business developed and managed by Harry. Decedent took no active part in the operation of the business. The principal assets of the community consisted of the common stock in two wholly-owned corporations, the Monrovia Nursery Company and Rosedale's Nurseries, Inc. In addition, the Rosedales owned real property referred to as "Huntington Drive property," upon which Rosedale's Nurseries conducted its business; a private residence; numerous insurance policies; furnishings; personal effects; and cash. Decedent and Harry had three children of their marriage, the youngest being a boy of five years.

Certain findings of fact of the district court [which gave judgment for the decedent's estate] provided inter alia as follows:

10. Decedent's husband wanted majority control of the two corporations for himself and desired that a substantial portion of their community property be preserved for their children. He did not wish that the decedent be permitted to have any part of their valuable community assets outright, particularly the business assets, because of her alcoholic condition; but he did desire that she be provided with an assured comfortable income. . . .

12. On December 17, 1954, after extensive negotiations, a property settlement involving a number of interrelated documents was agreed to. They included a property settlement agreement, a supplemental property settlement agreement, a declaration of trust, a lease and assignment of lease, a guarantee of said lease, and various deeds. . . .

13. Under the terms of the property settlement agreement, the decedent's husband received free from any claims by decedent, 55% of the stock he and decedent owned in Monrovia Nursery Company and Rosedale's Nurseries, Inc., plus various items of miscellaneous personal property of approximately $3,000 in value. The property settlement agreement further provided that an irrevocable spendthrift trust was to be created by the parties concurrently therewith, to which the parties would convey the remaining 45% of the stock they owned in the two companies, along with the Huntington Drive property and the residence. Decedent would receive the income for life from such trust, but the property itself would ultimately go to the children. She also received from the property settlement the right to use the residence for her life, and various items of personal property valued at $20,000 plus $1000 in cash. . . .

16. Concurrently with the execution of the property settlement agreement, and as part of the division of property thereunder, both the decedent and her husband executed a declaration of trust which created the irrevocable trust referred to in the property settlement agreement [and made the required transfers to the trust].

19. It was intended by both decedent and her husband and their respective counsel that all of the property transferred to the aforesaid trust was owned by both spouses equally at the time it was transferred, and that the transfer was a joint transfer by both decedent and her husband. All of said property transferred to said trust was in fact owned equally by the decedent and her husband, and the transfer

was in fact a joint one in which each transferred the one-half which he or she owned. The transfers were an integral part of a single larger transaction, to wit, a property settlement. . . .

24. The total value of all community property owned by the decedent and her husband at the time of the property settlement was $848,746.08. Of that amount, the decedent's husband received property valued at $293,887.74; the decedent received outright property valued at $21,000, in addition to the valuable life estate in the trust: the trust received property valued at $487,976; and the clean-up fund [which was used to satisfy certain obligations] received $45,880.34.

25. As of December 17, 1954, the decedent was 44 years of age, and in good health, other than for her addiction to alcohol. Decedent's life expectancy at said date was 28 years, 8 months. Her subsequent death was caused by murder.

On March 8, 1955, an interlocutory decree of divorce was granted to decedent and her husband, incorporating therein the property settlement agreement, and a final decree of divorce was granted March 13, 1956. Decedent remarried after the final decree and on December 25, 1956, was murdered by her then husband.

Harry died August 15, 1956.

In assessing a deficiency in decedent's estate tax, the government contended that the entire corpus of the trust at decedent's death valued at $642,788.66 should be included in decedent's estate, relying on §2036. . . .

The district court found: "The entire property settlement was an effort by the decedent and her husband to settle their marital and business relationships. It was a bona fide arm's-length bargained-for transaction." On the basis of this finding the district court held: "The transfer of property in trust by decedent . . . was, as a matter of law, made for an adequate and full consideration in money or money's worth, within the meaning of §2036 . . . ."

Therefore, the district court concluded that no part of the decedent's transfer to the trust was a transfer subject to §2036. In support of its decision, the district court cited Estate of McCoy v. Commissioner, 20 T.C.M. (CCH) 224 (1961). There, the husband and wife entered into a property settlement agreement incident to a divorce. Pursuant to the agreement, both spouses received life estates in separate trusts made up of property which had previously been jointly owned, with the remainder going to their children. The wife also relinquished her stock ownership in the family corporations and in certain other jointly owned property. Without mentioning the relative values of the properties received by the spouses, the tax court held that the transfers were bona fide sales for an adequate and full consideration for estate tax purposes. Therefore, upon the death of the husband, the value of the trust in which he possessed a life estate by reason of the property settlement was held not includible in his gross estate under §2036. The tax court seemed to assume that because the transfers were part of an arm's-length transaction settling both the marital and business affairs of the spouses that, as a matter of law, there was sufficient consideration for the purposes of §2036. We do not agree.[1] The fact alone that the transfer into the trust was part of a property settlement agreement incident to a divorce is not sufficient to make the transfer of the decedent one for an adequate and full consideration within the meaning of §2036. The value of what the decedent received under the trust must be measured against the value of the property she transferred to the trust. See Estate of Gregory v. Commissioner, 39 T.C. 1012 (1963).

The district court found that the decedent and her husband both joined in the transfer of the trust and that each contributed one-half of the property to the trust. This finding cannot be said to be clearly erroneous, and we accept it as a starting point in our calculations.

The property placed in the trust and its value was:

---

1. Absent donative intent, a transfer made in a bona fide bargained-for transaction is deemed to be for an adequate and full consideration for the purposes of the gift tax provisions of the Code. E.g., Rosenthal v. Commissioner, 205 F.2d 505 (2d Cir. 1953); Treas. Reg. §25.2512-8. Appellee maintains that the same principle applies equally for estate tax purposes. See Estate of Friedman v. Commissioner, 40 T.C. 714 (1963). In *Estate of Friedman*, a decedent, within three years of her death, transferred certain property to her stepchildren in compromise of a dispute. The decedent retained a life estate in the property. The Commissioner argued that the taxpayer was liable for a gift tax or, in the alternative, that the property should be included in her gross estate pursuant to §2035 or §2036. Relying on previous decisions holding that a compromise of a disputed claim constituted sufficient consideration for the purposes of §2512 of the gift tax, the court held that the taxpayer was not liable for estate taxes under either §2035 or §2036. The rationale of the decision was that the test of adequate consideration for the purposes of §2036 of the estate tax was that same test used in gift tax cases. We do not agree. Carried to its logical conclusion, the rationale of the *Friedman* and *McCoy* cases would nullify the effect of §2036 every time a life estate was retained as a result of a property settlement incident to a divorce. Moreover, the gift tax cases are readily distinguishable in that here the transaction was not free from donative intent.

(1) Huntington Drive property	$225,000
(2) Residence	25,000
(3) 45% of the stock of the Monrovia and Rosedale companies	237,978
Total	$487,978

Since each of the parties contributed one-half of the property to the trust, the value of the property contributed by the decedent thereto was $243,989.

The trust agreement provided that the decedent received a life estate in all of the property placed in trust. Her life expectancy at the time of the creation of the trust was 28 years 8 months. According to the computations prescribed by the government regulations, the value of the life estate to the decedent at the time of its creation was $286,691.95. The consideration received by the decedent was equal to the value of her right to receive the income for life from her husband's contribution, or $143,345.97, — one-half the value of the life estate in the entire trust corpus.[2]

From the above facts it appears that the decedent contributed $243,989 to the trust (one-half of the total property contributed to the trust). She received from the trust a life estate worth $286,691.95 (one-half of which came from decedent's contribution and one-half from her husband's contribution). Since the decedent's contribution to the trust was greater than the consideration she received in return (the difference between $243,989 and $143,346, or $100,643), she did not receive adequate and full consideration for the purposes of §2036.

In the alternative, the district court found: "Since the decedent received consideration in money or money's worth for her transfer to the trust, pursuant to the property settlement, even if such consideration had not been adequate and full, her estate would

---

2. Estate of Gregory v. Commissioner, 39 T.C. 1012 (1963). The taxpayer urges that the commuted value of the life estate in the entire corpus should be treated as consideration passing to the decedent for the purposes of §2036. In support of its contention, the taxpayer would have us draw an analogy from the gift tax area. For gift tax purposes, where a trust is created from community property contributed by both spouses and the wife receives income for life from the entire trust corpus, the amount of her taxable gift is calculated by subtracting the value of the entire life estate from the value of her share of community property transferred into the trust. See, e.g., Commissioner v. Siegel, 250 F.2d 339 (9th Cir. 1957). The gift tax situation is readily distinguishable. There, the retained life estate is not treated as consideration. Rather, since the donor is giving only the remainder interest, it is necessary to reduce the value of the donor's transfer by the value of the retained life estate in order to determine the value of the gift. See Estate of Gregory v. Commissioner, 39 T.C. 1012, 1016-1017 (1963).

nevertheless be entitled to a credit under §2043(a) to the extent of the consideration she actually received, which would be deducted from the value of any property that might be includable in her gross estate under §2036."

The district court then held: "A recomputation of the decedent's taxable estate would be required *in accordance with the foregoing Findings of Fact*, taking into account the property of the corpus actually transferred by decedent and the credit for consideration received along with all other allowable deductions, exemptions and credits. Such a recomputation would still result in no Federal Estate Tax or interest due." (Emphasis added.)

Since the decedent's transfer into the trust was subject to §2036, we agree with the district court that her gross estate would include one-half of the value of the trust corpus at her death[3] ($321,394.43) reduced by the credit allowed by §2043(a) for the consideration she received.[4] We have found that the consideration received by the decedent was equal to the value of her right to receive the income for life from her husband's contribution to the trust. Under the treasury regulations the consideration received by the decedent was $143,345.97.

Therefore, under the above reasoning and calculations, the amount to be included in decedent's gross estate would be the difference between the value of one-half of the trust corpus at the date of her death, $321,394.43 (one-half of $642,788.86) and the amount of consideration she received therefor, $143,345.97 (one-half of the value of the trust estate at its creation, i.e., one-half of $286,691.95), or the sum of $178,048.46. From this gross estate, of course, there should be deducted all allowable exemptions and deductions, including reasonable attorney fees. Also to be considered is the allowance, if any, of a gift tax credit.

The case is remanded to the district court for recalculation of taxes, if any, in accordance with this opinion.

[Judge Ely dissented on the manner in which the majority treated the partial consideration received by the decedent, but he agreed with the majority's determination that the decedent did not

---

3. The property transferred is to be valued at the date of decedent's death. See Estate of Vardell v. Commissioner, 307 F.2d 688, 693 (5th Cir. 1962). At the date of decedent's death, the value of the entire trust corpus was stipulated to be $642,788.86. One-half, or $321,394.43, is includable in the decedent's gross estate under §2036.

4. Estate of Gregory v. Commissioner, 39 T.C. 1012 (1963). The consideration received by the decedent is to be valued at the time of the transfer. Estate of Vardell v. Commissioner, 307 F.2d at 693.

receive adequate and full consideration within the meaning of §2036.]

In Pope v. United States, 296 F. Supp. 17 (S.D. Cal. 1968), the court applied §§2036 and 2038 to include in the decedent's gross estate property transferred by him to a trust in which his wife had the primary income interest, the decedent had a secondary income interest, and their children had the remainder interest. The wife predeceased the decedent. The court stated:

Assuming a transfer of the remainder to the children in 1936, plaintiffs cite United States v. Davis, 370 U.S. 65 (1962), for the proposition that under a pre-divorce property settlement agreement the support right released is presumed to be equal in value to the property exchanged. This case is inapposite here because (1) *Davis* only applies in cases where the value of the right released cannot be ascertained — here the right has been valued; and (2) *Davis* was an income tax case dealing with a different problem and presenting different tax policies. Moreover, the recent case of United States v. Past, 347 F.2d 7 (9th Cir. 1965), held that there is no presumption of full and adequate consideration in a §2036(a) or §2038 situation such as we have here. The court in *Past* distinguished *Davis* and similar cases. Therefore, in order to prevail plaintiffs would have to prove that decedent received partial consideration under §2043(a) in exchange for the remainder interest transferred.

Defendant concedes that the support right released by Clara qualifies as consideration "in money or money's worth" under the proviso in §2036(a) or §2038. However, the amount is disputed. Plaintiffs contend that the right was worth $39,000. Defendant argues that it was worth $25,000. Plaintiffs base their argument on the fact that Clara could receive $3,600 a year plus a medical allowance. Defendant contends that since Clara was only guaranteed $2,400 a year, this must be the basis for computation. There is no hard and fast rule regarding such an evaluation but it is safe to conclude that a California court would have given Clara an amount comparable to what she had previously lived on while separated from decedent. Prior to the 1936 agreement Clara had been receiving $4,200 a year under the terms of the 1930 trust. Therefore, it is a little unreasonable to conclude that the $2,400 a year figure should be used as a computational basis. Whatever the value, this dispute becomes academic when we apply the principle of partial consideration to the facts of the case.

The concept of partial consideration must be applied within the context of the entire transaction. In the normal situation involving

§2036(a) or §2038, the decedent transfers the remainder or corpus to the wife in exchange for some sort of consideration and retains a life estate or power to revoke. The life estate or power to revoke terminates at his death and is not taxed in his estate. However, the remainder or corpus is, to the extent decedent did not receive consideration for the transfer. If such were the case here, the value of the remainder or corpus would be reduced by approximately $39,000. But in the instant case, again assuming a transfer as plaintiffs contend, Clara exchanged $39,000 for the remainder *and* a life estate worth $39,000 (the valuation being identical). Defendant contends that what Clara released was offset or "washed out" by what she received as a life estate and that the remainder should now be taxed in decedent's estate.

Plaintiffs cite Estate of O'Nan v. Commissioner, 47 T.C. 648 (1967), and Estate of Glen v. Commissioner, 45 T.C. 323 (1966), in support of their contention that the life estate Clara received should be ignored and the remainder reduced by the value of the support right.

At the time of trial, *Glen* was on appeal. Since then the parties have reached a compromise and settled. The Ninth Circuit remanded the case with the suggestion that the Tax Court decision be vacated; therefore, plaintiffs find no support in this case.

The only other string in plaintiffs' bow is *O'Nan*; however, this case is distinguishable on many points. In *O'Nan* the husband transferred two farms to the wife, and retained a life estate in each. In addition, the husband agreed to provide the wife with alimony payments of $4,000 a year and various food products from the farms. The Government contended there, as here, that the alimony payments and the farm products equaled the value of the wife's support right, hence the remainder was includible in the husband's estate. The court rejected the argument because it was unable to place a value on the wife's support right. It based its holding on the fact that under Kentucky law the wife's support right is of an equitable nature. The court then concluded that since the divorce court incorporated the settlement agreement in toto it found full and adequate consideration. Indeed, state law provided for such a presumption. The court went on to analogize a §2036(a) situation with income tax cases such as *Davis*, supra.

A reading of *O'Nan* reveals that it is in direct conflict with *Past*. The Tax Court in *O'Nan* did exactly what this Circuit has stated it will not do, i.e., presume full and adequate consideration on a divorce decree. In *Past*, supra, the court correctly reasoned that such a rule would defeat the purpose behind §2036(a) and the provisions for partial consideration under §2043(a), as well as invite collusion by the parties.

Any solace plaintiffs find in the similarity of facts in *O'Nan* and the instant case is made illusory by the court's holding. In presuming full consideration the court never reached the issues that would follow from a piece-meal evaluation and a true balance sheet analysis. What's more, the facts in *O'Nan* indicate that there was no evidence of donative intent, such as we have here in the 1930 transfer, and there the remainder was transferred to the wife, not the children as in the instant case.

In short, plaintiffs have neither cited authority nor given any reason why this court should ignore the life estate Clara received when applying the principle of partial consideration under §2043(a). In the few cases actually coming to grips with the problem, the decedent did not transfer anything in addition to the remainder interest. For this court to divide an integrated transaction into two individual transfers, then disregard one for purposes of consideration, would result in an artificial distinction unwarranted by either the language of the statute or the cases decided under it. [296 F. Supp. at 23-25]

In Estate of Fenton v. Commissioner, 70 T.C. 263 (1978), the question arose as to the proper time to value a wife's claims against her deceased former husband's estate for the purpose of determining whether her prior release of her support rights constituted adequate and full consideration for the decedent's promise to leave her at his death an income interest in half of his taxable estate and to maintain certain life insurance policies on his life with his wife as beneficiary. The decedent's promise was made as part of a settlement agreement that was executed almost twelve years prior to his death. After decedent's death his personal representative claimed a deduction for the value of the former wife's claim against decedent's estate pursuant to the settlement agreement.

It was agreed by all parties that the value of her support rights was to be determined as of the date the settlement agreement was executed in determining the adequacy of the consideration furnished by the wife (i.e., the release of her support rights). The Commissioner maintained, however, that the value of the contractual rights granted to the wife to receive property on the decedent's death was to be valued when the decedent died 12 years later, when those rights blossomed into present interests. The consideration she provided would not be adequate if the value of the wife's support rights when the agreement was executed was compared with the date of death value of the interests she owned in December 1971 in both the decedent's estate and the insurance policies. The court, however, held that the value of the contractual rights the wife acquired from the decedent must be valued as of the date the settlement agreement was executed, taking into account the contingencies to which her claims were subject. By so valuing her contractual rights, the court found that the value of the consideration paid by the wife was greater than the value of the contractual rights she was granted by the decedent at that time. Accordingly, the court allowed the estate a deduction equal to the value of the wife's claims, determined as of the decedent's death. The court properly was not troubled by the fact that the amount of the deduction allowed the decedent's estate for the wife's claims was more than five times the value of the consideration she provided some twelve years prior to the decedent's death.

In Estate of Keller v. Commissioner, 44 T.C. 851 (1965), pursuant to a divorce decree that was founded on a jury verdict, the decedent retained a primary life estate and deeded a secondary life estate in realty to his divorced wife and deeded the remainder to their adult children. The decedent did not execute a settlement agreement prior to the verdict in the divorce case, but he did not contest the terms prepared by his wife for the jury's consideration. The Commissioner sought to include the value of the children's remainder interest in the decedent's gross estate under §2036. The government conceded that the value of the wife's secondary life estate (determined at the date of the decedent's death) was excluded from the decedent's gross estate under the *Harris* doctrine and Rev. Rul. 60-160. The Tax Court stated that the "divorce as consideration" theory applies only to transfers to the divorced spouse and does not apply to transfers to third parties. The court included the value of the remainder interest in the decedent's gross estate.

To what extent does or should the *Harris* principle apply to transfers made to children of a marriage? Consider the following:

(a) X promised in writing and under seal to a fifteen-year-old grand-child, Y, that X would give Y $10,000 on Y's twenty-first birthday. Under local law, a promise in writing under seal is enforceable even if no consideration is given. On Y's twenty-first birthday, Y requested the $10,000 from X, who reneged. Y then sued X for $10,000 and two years later obtained a judgment; X died before Y collected on the judgment, however. Y then collected $10,000 from X's estate in satisfaction of the judgment. Stephens, Maxfield, Lind, & Calfee at ¶5.03[5][e] state in a somewhat similar example that the estate's obligation is not deductible under §2053(a)(3) because, notwithstanding the judgment, Y's claim is founded on X's promise and no full and adequate consideration passed to X. If the debt is not deductible, is there a possibility that X's estate might be entitled to a gift tax offset in computing X's estate tax? In the example discussed in Stephens, Maxfield, Lind, & Calfee, Y's judgment was obtained against X's estate after X's death. Timing of the judgment should affect the gift tax consequences. For example, if Y obtained a judgment against X prior to X's death would X make a gift at that time (or later when making the payment)? If Y had become 21 one month after X's death and then obtained a judgment against X's estate, the claim would not be any more deductible.

Relevant to these questions is Rev. Rul. 79-384, in which *A* promised in writing to pay a child, *B*, $10,000 if *B* graduated from college. *B* graduated from college in 1977 and promptly demanded payment, which *A* refused to make. *B* sued *A* on the contract and obtained a judgment from a local court in 1978, which *A* paid on the same date. The Government ruled that *A* became unconditionally obligated to make payment upon *B*'s graduation from college in 1977. So, *A* was treated as having made a gift of $10,000 to *B* in 1977, rather than in 1978, when the judgment was entered and when payment was made.

(b) Policy considerations point toward excluding from the *Harris* principle transfers to children, even though made pursuant to a divorce decree, to the extent the transferor's obligation of support is not as great as the transfer made. In such a case one parent or the other probably made a gift and it may be the transferor's former spouse, who agrees to less marital property in exchange for a larger transfer to the children. For a related problem, see Bank of New York v. United States, 526 F.2d 1012 (3d Cir. 1975), reproduced at page 595.

(c) The *Harris* doctrine was applied to transfers to children of the marriage in Bowes v. United States, 77-2 U.S. Tax Cas. (CCH) ¶13,212 (N.D. Ill. 1977), in which a settlement agreement obligated the decedent to maintain $10,000 of insurance coverage on his life for each of his three sons until each son's twenty-fifth birthday. The agreement also made provision for the decedent's wife and was incorporated into a decree of a California divorce court. Contrary to the agreement and the decree, the decedent allowed the insurance policies to lapse. Upon the decedent's death, each of the three children (two of whom were minors at that time) lodged a claim for $10,000 against the estate, which the decedent's personal representative paid and sought to deduct as claims against the estate under §2053(a)(3). As to the claims of the two minor children, the district court essentially applied the *Harris* rule in granting summary judgment for the estate and allowing a deduction, noting that, although a California divorce court has no authority to alter the terms of an interspousal settlement, it may modify child support provisions included in an otherwise unalterable settlement agreement. However, a California divorce court has no authority to order support and maintenance for a child beyond what is needed for the child's minority. As to the two children who were minors at the decedent's death, the court treated their claims as being founded on the divorce decree rather than on the agreement, and allowed a deduction under what, in effect, constitutes an expansion of the *Harris* doctrine.

As to the child who had attained majority before the decedent's death, the divorce decree provision was unenforceable and the child's rights therefore sprang from the settlement agreement. The court held that the consideration for the decedent's promise to that child was the child's release of his support rights, and this consideration was held to be adequate and full in money's worth. The court accordingly granted summary judgment for the estate's claim to an estate tax deduction for that payment as well. Quaere: how, and when, did that child release those rights?

Putting a number of these concepts into context is the following Ruling. Quaere how realistic are the facts that the taxpayers missed both the *Harris* and §2516 safe harbors, made the transfers too late to qualify for the marital deduction, *and* messed up a full and adequate consideration exception too! Note also that today there would be §2702 implications, not relevant in this older Ruling. See Chapter 15 for that added agony.

Revenue Ruling 77-314

Advice has been requested as to the application of the Federal gift tax where one spouse, A, who has created a trust pursuant to an agreement made with the other spouse, B, in contemplation of divorce, makes the transfers described below, and B surrenders B's support rights.

In each of the following situations, A and B entered into a written agreement in contemplation of their obtaining a divorce. Except as specified below, each agreement contained a provision that, in exchange for the surrender by B of the right to support, A would transfer 100x dollars in cash to a trust upon issuance of a valid divorce decree. At the time of the agreement A and B had two adult children. In each case, the divorce occurred more than 2 years after the agreement was entered into, and the divorce decree was issued by a court that had no power to alter or invalidate the agreement.

Situation 1. Under the terms of the trust to which A transferred 100x dollars, the income is payable to B for life, and at B's death the principal is payable to the children of the two spouses. The children are adults whom A and B have no legal obligation to support. The present value of the right of support surrendered by B is 50x dollars at the date of A's transfer. The present value of the right to trust income for B's lifetime is 60x dollars as of that date. The present value of the remainder is 40x dollars.

Situation 2. The facts are the same as in Situation 1, except the terms of the trust provide that one-third of the trust income is payable to an adult child of A and B, and two-thirds of the income is payable to B. At the death of B, all income payments cease and the remaining principal is payable to the children of the two spouses. The children are adults whom A and B have no legal obligation to support. The present values of the adult child's and B's rights to income for the life of B are, respectively, 20x dollars and 40x dollars. In the course of negotiating the settlement agreement, A agreed to provide the child with the one-third income interest after B asserted a preference to receive an income interest of lesser value than *B* might otherwise demand, in view of the value of *B*'s support rights, in order to secure the income payments to their child.

Situation 3. The facts are the same as those of Situation 1, except the terms of the trust provide that, upon the death of *B* (to whom all income is payable), the trust will terminate and the remaining principal is payable to a sibling of *A*. The present value of *B*'s income interest is 60x dollars. The present value of the remainder interest is 40x dollars. The value of *B*'s surrendered right to support in this situation is 70x dollars, thus exceeding the value of *B*'s right to trust income by 10x dollars. *B* neither suggested nor was otherwise concerned with the naming of the person who would receive the remainder or the payment of trust principal after *B*'s death. *B*'s main concern was to avoid the possibility of any litigation or other delays; thus *B* settled for a monthly payment that was smaller than the amount *B* would have received if *B* had demanded and been paid the full value of support to which *B* was entitled. There is no indication that *B* agreed to receive the lesser amount in order to secure benefits to third parties. . . .

Rev. Rul. 68-379, 1968-2 C.B. 414, holds that the surrender of a spouse's right to support constitutes a consideration in money or money's worth and that a transfer of property in exchange for the surrender of support rights pursuant to a legal separation agreement results in a taxable gift to the extent of the excess of the value of transferred property over that of the support rights. Accord, Estate of Hundley v. Commissioner, 52 T.C. 495 (19691, *aff'd per curiam*, 435 F.2d 1311 (4th Cir. 1971).

In the case of Rohmer v. Commissioner, 21 T.C. 1099 (1954), the taxpayer transferred to the taxpayer's spouse one-half of certain rights that the taxpayer held in connection with the authorship of a novel. The taxpayer argued that the transfer to the spouse was made in consideration for the spouse's valuable services in assisting the taxpayer's literary endeavors. The court held that the entire value of the transfer was a taxable gift and stated, at page 1103, the following principle: "Consideration must be bargained for in order to support a contract and negative a gift; and 'nothing can be treated as a consideration that is not intended as such by the parties.' Fire Insurance Association v. Wickham, 141 U.S. 564, 579 (1891)."

See also Commissioner v. McLean, 127 F.2d 942 (5th Cir. 1942), where the married taxpayers failed to show that any agreement existed between themselves that each spouse's transfer in trust for the benefit of the other was made as consideration for the other spouse's reciprocal trust transfer.

In Wiedemann v. Commissioner, 26 T.C. 565 (1956), a divorce court ordered, at one spouse's request, that the one spouse create a trust for the benefit of the other spouse and an adult child. The value of the remainder interest transferred to the child was held to be a taxable gift, the court noting that the other spouse did not insist on providing for the child.

In the case of Estate of Hartshorne v. Commissioner, 48 T.C. 882 (1967), an estate tax deduction was claimed for a "debt" under §2053 where the decedent was required by a prior divorce agreement to create a testamentary trust providing remainder interests for the decedent's children. The court, in holding that no valuable consideration had been shown for the creation of the debt, stated the following (p. 896): "With respect to the quid pro quo argument, case law indicates that merely because a husband, in his divorce settlement agreement, makes transfers to his adult children, that fact alone does not mean that such transfers are made for consideration. . . . Thus the taxpayer must show that such transfers to adult children are made at the insistence of the wife and for consideration in money or moneys worth."

In Spruance v. Commissioner, 60 T.C. 141, 154 (1973), *aff'd*, 505 F.2d 731 (3d Cir. 1974), the court held that the taxpayer had not produced sufficient evidence that the taxpayer's former spouse had bargained away a portion of the spouse's rights in exchange for the taxpayer's designation of their adult children as persons to receive the remainder in a trust created pursuant to the divorce settlement. See also, Dixon v. United States, 319 F. Supp. 719 (E.D.N.Y., 1970).

Therefore, §2512(b) is applicable in those situations where the donor has not only received a valuable transfer but has received it as an inducement for the donor's own transfer that would otherwise constitute a taxable gift in its full amount. Where a donor has made more than one transfer or created interests in trust for more than one person, each such transfer or interest created must be separately examined to determine whether any consideration in money or money's worth was received by the donor as inducement for that particular transfer.

Accordingly, in the three situations described above, the following conclusions are reached:

Situation 1. Since the value of the trust income interest transferred by A exceeds the value of B's support rights surrendered by B, the amounts of A's gifts, for Federal gift tax purposes are: (1) 10x dollars, to B, the excess of the value of B's income interest over that of the support rights; and (2) 40x dollars, to the children of the spouses, the full value of the remainder interest.

Situation 2. In this situation, *B* bargained for a reduced income interest with the express purpose of securing an income interest in the trust for the adult child. Therefore, the excess (10x dollars) of the value of *B*'s support rights (50x dollars) over the value of the income interest received by *B* (40x dollars) is excludable from the value of the child's income interest (20x dollars) as consideration in money or money's worth under §2512(b). As a result, the amount of *A*'s gift to the child of the income interest is the excess of the value of the income interest transferred to the child over the value of consideration received by *A* for that transfer, or 10x dollars. It also follows that, since *B* transferred the excess value (10x dollars) of *B*'s support rights to secure the additional income interest to the child, *B* has made a taxable gift to the child of 10x dollars. The gift tax is also applicable to the full value, 40x dollars, of the remainder interest transferred by *A* to the child.

Situation 3. In this situation, transfer of the income interest to *B* was adequately met by valuable consideration; so no gift was made to *B*. The amount of the gift of the remainder interest from *A* to the younger adult sibling, however, is its full present value as of the date of the gift, or 40x dollars. Although *A* obtained a release by *B* of support rights that exceeded the income interest transferred to *B*, such excess value was not paid and received in order to secure, even partially, the transfer of the remainder interest to the sibling. Therefore, no amount is excludable under §2512(b) as consideration in money or money's worth from the value of the remainder interest transferred by *A* to the sibling.

However, the value of the support rights *B* surrendered to *A* exceeded by 10x dollars the income interest *A* transferred to *B*. *B*'s motives for releasing the excess value of the support rights (to avoid litigation and delay) are not consideration for purposes of the gift tax. . . . Therefore, under §2512(b), *B* has made a taxable gift to *A* of 10x dollars.

5.   *Partial Consideration.*   *Gradow* and the issue it addresses are both "challenged" and challenging. See if you can detect the court's error before reading about it in the notes following the opinion.

Gradow v. United States
11 Cl. Ct. 808 (1987), *aff'd,*
897 F.2d 516 (Fed. Cir. 1990)

BRUGGINK, Judge.   This case raises an issue with respect to whether §2036[(a)(1)] requires certain property in which decedent Betty Gradow had a life interest to be included in her gross estate. . . .

I. *Factual Background.* [Betty and Alexander Gradow were married and at all times were residents of a community property state. By his will Alexander intended to dispose of both halves of their community property by putting Betty to an election. If she rejected the will, she would receive nothing under his will. If she took under the will, she would transfer her half of the community property into a trust from which she would receive all the income for life. Betty elected to take under Alexander's will. The estate asserted that the value of her half of the community property transferred subject to this election was $461,610, that her lifetime income interest in Alexander's half of the community property was worth $192,039, that the total value of all the consideration she received under the election was $300,695, and that the value of the remainder interest was $211,367. The government and the estate stipulated that the value of Betty's share of the community property exceeded the actuarial value of a life estate in Alexander's share. When Betty died her estate tax return referred to the trust established under Alexander's will but did not include any of it in her gross estate. The estate regarded the transfer with retained life estate as being supported by adequate and full consideration within the meaning of §2036(a)(1) so that inclusion of Betty's half of the community was not required.]

II. *Discussion.* Section 2036(a)[(1)] provides that a gross estate includes the value of all property transferred in which a decedent has retained a life interest. In the case at bar, prior to elections under her husband's will, Betty owned one-half of the couple's community property. When she made her election, she contributed this property to the trust created pursuant to her husband's will. This entitled her to collect the income from the entire trust during her lifetime. Pursuant to the general operation of §2036(a)[(1)], therefore, the value of the community property she transferred to the trust would be brought into her estate — she made a transfer with a retained life interest.

There is an important exception in §2036(a)[(1)], however, and it is the parties' disagreement over its construction and application which is the primary source of their present controversy. Property transferred with a retained life interest is entirely excluded from the operation of §2036(a)[(1)] if the transfer is a "bona fide sale for an adequate and full consideration in money or money's worth." In valuing the respective halves of the "sale" which took place upon Betty's election, there is no question that, at a minimum, she received a life income in her husband's share of the community property. The precise question posed by the parties here is whether the consideration flowing from her was merely the remainder interest left to George Gradow, or the entire value of the property she placed into the trust, i.e., her half of the community property.

The parties have stipulated that the value of Betty's share of the community property exceeded the value of a life estate in Alexander's share. . . .

If defendant is correct, and Betty received less than she gave up, then under §2043[(a)], her estate is nonetheless entitled to an offset for the consideration she did receive. Case law generally supports the conclusion that this offset includes the actuarial value, at the time of election, of a life estate in Alexander's share. As plaintiff points out, however, the two Code sections operate in such a way that if the "adequate and full consideration" exception of §2036(a)[(1)] does not apply, the "time-of-election" valuation of the consideration she received is matched against time-of-death valuation of the included property. If property to be included in the gross estate increases in value after the election, the offset under §2043[(a)] can therefore dramatically lose its impact. Theoretically, a one dollar deficiency of consideration at the time of election would allow taxation in the estate of property, which although transferred, has increased in value far beyond the one dollar difference. Plaintiff is correct therefore that it is critical to maintain a distinction between the calculation of an offset under §2043[(a)] and the determination of adequacy of consideration under §2036(a)[(1)].

The issue raised in the motion has been considered by a number of courts, although not on precisely the facts here. The decision most directly on point is that of Estate of Gregory v. Commissioner, 39 T.C. 1012 (1963). As in the case at bar, the couple were California residents. The husband died first, leaving the wife to elect whether to take her interest in the community property plus a probate homestead and family allowance, or to receive a life interest in all the couple's community property. She chose the latter and put property worth approximately $65,000 into trust along with her husband's share. Based on her life expectancy at that time, the actuarial value of her income interest in the $60,000 contributed by her husband's estate was only $11,926. Since the court measured Mrs. Gregory's life interest in her husband's share against the larger amount that she put into the trust, the transaction was not excluded from §2036[(a)(1)] by the "full and adequate consideration" clause. Some consideration was received, however, so the court proceeded to analyze the transaction under §2043[(a)].

Similarly, in United States v. Past, 347 F.2d 7 (9th Cir. 1965), with virtually no discussion, the court cites *Gregory* for the proposition that the value of what the wife received must be measured against the value of the property she transferred to the trust. Id. at 12. . . .

. . . The net result of Alexander's will and of Betty's election here was to ensure Betty's lifetime needs and then move family property to another generation. If she had not made the election, the property she received upon Alexander's death would, unless disposed of in a non-testamentary fashion, have been included in her gross estate. By electing under the will she gets the same benefit from the property as if she had kept it, and simultaneously ensures its transfer to her son. If the measurement of consideration flowing from the surviving spouse in these circumstances was limited to the remainder interest, then, as long as the surviving spouse is not very elderly at the time of the election, it would be a simple matter for a couple to avoid estate tax on half of their property. . . .

The requirement that any transfer of property under these circumstances be a bona fide sale "for adequate and full consideration" preserves the purposes of the rest of §2306(a)[(1)], because it is based on the expectation that what is being added to the surviving spouse's assets will be subject to inclusion in the gross estate. Even if the consideration is fungible and easily consumed, at least theoretically the rest of the estate is protected from encroachment for lifetime expenditures. The only way to preserve the integrity of the section, then, is to view the consideration moving from the surviving spouse as that property which is taken out of the gross estate. . . .

Plaintiff argues that defendant's construction would gut the utility of the "bona fide sales" exception and uses a hypothetical to illustrate his point. . . . In the example a 40-year-old man contracts to put $100,000 into a trust, reserving the income for life but selling the remainder. Plaintiff points out that based on the seller's life expectancy, he might receive up to $30,000 for the remainder, but certainly no more. He argues that this demonstrates the unfairness of defendant insisting on consideration equal to the $100,000 put into trust before it would exempt the sale from §2036(a)[(1)].

There are a number of defects in plaintiff's hypothetical. First, the transaction is obviously not testamentary, unlike the actual circumstances here. In addition, plaintiff assumes his conclusion by focusing on the sale of the remainder interest as the only relevant transaction. Assuming it was not treated as a sham, the practical effect is a transfer of the entire $100,000, not just a remainder. More importantly, however, if plaintiff is correct that one should be able, under the "bona fide sale" exception to remove property from the gross estate by a sale of the remainder interest, the exception would swallow the rule. A young person could sell a remainder interest for a fraction of the property's worth, enjoy the property for life, and then pass it along without estate or gift tax consequences. . . .

III. *Conclusion.* For the purposes of evaluating whether plaintiff's election constituted full and adequate consideration within the meaning of §2036(a)[(1)], the consideration flowing from Betty Gradow consists of the property which would otherwise have been included in her gross estate by virtue of her retention of a life estate — i.e., her half of the community property.

Although *Gradow* involved community property and a "forced election" estate plan, the form of the transaction was not particularly relevant; *Gradow* is important because it speaks to any transfer of a remainder interest with a retained life estate in the subject property. The issue, as phrased by the court, was whether §2036(a)(1) required that "the consideration be paid for the interest transferred, or for the interest which would otherwise be included in the gross estate." Why does this reveal that the court had little appreciation for what was involved in the case? When the court stated that "[t]he only way to preserve the integrity of [§2036(a)(1)], then, is to view the consideration moving from the surviving spouse as that property which is taken out of the gross estate," what was the court assuming, and why was it incorrect?

The proof that the court did not understand the economics of the transaction is found in comparing the transaction involved (sale of a remainder) with its cousin, the split purchase of property.[5] For example, if S sold the full fee interest in the community property and received cash, and then invested a portion of the cash in a life estate in similar property, the transaction would not run afoul of §2036(a)(1). How would it differ from the *Gradow* transaction? Another clue to consider in wrestling with this concept is to ask yourself: what do we call today the interest that will be includible in Mrs. Gradow's estate by virtue of §2036(a)(1)? Hint: it is *not* a fee simple (or equivalent in trust) today. Compare what she sold for what would be includible. How do they differ?

The *Gradow* court was not without impressive precedent in reaching its conclusion that §2036(a)(1) "is a reflection of Congress' judgment that transfers with retained life estates are generally testamentary transactions and should be treated as such for estate tax purposes" and that "[f]or the

---

5. The split purchase "cousin" of the sale of remainder interest transaction is subject to §2702(c)(2), just as Treas. Reg. §25.2702-4(d) *Example 2* makes it clear that the government regards §2702(c)(1) as applicable to the *Gradow* form of transaction because it refers to the "transfer of an interest in property with respect to which there is 1 or more term interests."

purposes of evaluating whether plaintiff's election constituted full and adequate consideration within the meaning of §2036(a), the consideration flowing from [the surviving spouse] consists of the property which would otherwise have been included in her gross estate by virtue of her retention of a life estate."[6]

Not to be overlooked is the important question why the forced election transaction is desirable if the value of the property transferred by S will be includible in S's gross estate under §2036(a)(1). The answer is found in the fact that *Gradow* allowed S's estate a consideration offset under §2043 for the value of the income interest received from D's share of the community property as consideration for the transfer of S's remainder interest.[7] Although this consideration offset was valued (as required under §2043) at the time of the transaction (meaning that appreciation in the consideration was not excluded along with the underlying consideration itself), S's estate was reduced by the value of the income interest in D's property, granted in exchange for S's election. Normally D would give this interest to S anyway,

---

6. But see Estate of McLendon v. Commissioner, 66 T.C.M. (CCH) 946, 972 n.24 (1993) (without deciding the issue, the opinion noted that the validity of *Gradow* is open to question). Although *Gradow* is very wrongly decided, Congress clearly meant to codify its results in §2702 to preclude gaming with temporal interests. See Chapter 15. For a critique of *Gradow*, see Estate of D'Ambrosio v. Commissioner, 101 F.3d 309 (3d Cir. 1996), *rev'g* 105 T.C. 252 (1995), and Pennell, *Sale of Remainder Interest Triggers Section 2036(a)(1) Inclusion*, 13 PROB. NOTES 188-192 (1987). *Gradow* was followed in Estate of Magnin v. Commissioner, 71 T.C.M. (CCH) 1856 (1996), *rev'd and rem'd*, 184 F.3d 1074 (9th Cir. 1999), *on remand*, 81 T.C.M. (CCH) 1126 (2001), in a mindless decision in Pittman v. United States, 878 F. Supp. 833 (E.D. N.C. 1994), and again it was followed in Wheeler v. United States, 77 A.F.T.R.2d (P-H) 1405 (W.D. Tex. 1996), because facts indicated a disguised gift, and in Parker v. United States, 894 F. Supp. 445 (N.D. Ga. 1995), because the taxpayer failed in its burden of proof, the *Parker* court stating without specification that it had "some reservations about the correctness of *Gradow*"; the facts also indicated that the consideration allegedly received in *Parker* may have belonged to the taxpayer and therefore would not be consideration at all.

7. Other cases granting the §2043 offset in this context include Estate of Christ v. Commissioner, 480 F.2d 171 (9th Cir. 1973); In re Estate of Bomash v. Commissioner, 432 F.2d 308 (9th Cir. 1970); United States v. Gordon, 406 F.2d 332 (5th Cir. 1969); United States v. Past, 347 F.2d 7 (9th Cir. 1965); Estate of Vardell v. Commissioner, 307 F.2d 688 (5th Cir. 1962); Whiteley v. United States, 214 F. Supp. 489 (W.D. Wash. 1963); Estate of Simmie v. Commissioner, 69 T.C. 890 (1978); Estate of Steinman v. Commissioner, 69 T.C. 804 (1978); Estate of Bressani v. Commissioner, 45 T.C. 373 (1966); and Estate of Sparling v. Commissioner, 552 F.2d 1340 (9th Cir. 1977), which is consistent in that it denied a §2013 previously taxed property credit to S's estate for the income interest received from D because it was acquired by purchase rather than by gift, bequest, or inheritance (its value being less than the consideration given by S in exchange for it).

meaning that the *Gradow* forced election served to reduce *S*'s gross estate by the amount of this income interest, which would have been included in *S*'s estate in any event and otherwise would have generated no reduction in the amount includible in *S*'s gross estate. Because any gift tax paid on the original transfer constitutes a §2001(b)(2) credit against the estate tax at death and because the amount of any gift deemed made under the original transfer is purged from *S*'s adjusted taxable gifts base for computation of the estate tax in *S*'s estate,[8] the only detriment to this transaction is any income tax incurred on the transfer caused by the election and loss of the use of any gift tax paid at that time.[9]

Now, let's try an illustration. Pursuant to an agreement, *B* paid $50,000 to *A*, in exchange for which *A* transferred property valued at $100,000 to a trust, the income from which was payable to *A* for life, remainder to *B*. The value of *B*'s remainder interest in the trust, under the §7520 tables, was $47,000, so *B* made a gift to *A* of $3,000 (unless the business transaction exception is applicable). Let's assume that §2702 is not applicable. Did *A* make any gift to *B*? If not, then let's further assume that *A* died several years later when the value of the trust corpus was $160,000. Should any part of the trust corpus be includible in *A*'s gross estate? If §2036(a)(1) *does* apply *A* will have $160,000 includible and a $50,000 consideration offset under §2043. Does that seem right?

If, in this illustration, instead of creating a trust, *A* had deeded to *B* a remainder interest in the income-producing property and had retained a life estate interest therein, would any part of the property be includible in *A*'s gross estate? Recall *Estate of O'Nan v. Commissioner*, reproduced at page 362, in which the court apparently compared the consideration received with the value of the remainder interest the decedent deeded to his divorced wife to determine whether the consideration was adequate. Can there be any justification for treating a transfer of a remainder interest with a life estate reserved to the transferor differently from a transfer in trust in which the transferor has a life income interest?

6. *The Community Property Forced Election.* The consideration issue frequently arises in community property states in connection with a transfer by the surviving spouse pursuant to a forced election estate plan. See Westfall, *Estate Planning and the Widow's Election*, 71 HARV. L. REV. 1269 (1968); Kahn & Gallo, *The Widow's Election: A Return to Fun-*

---

8. See the flush language in §2001.

9. The gift tax paid may be more than anticipated if §2702 is applicable, because the effect of that provision is to treat the full value of *S*'s property transferred — not just the value of the remainder interest therein — as subject to gift tax.

damentals, 24 STAN. L. REV. 531 (1972); Johanson, *Revocable Trusts, Widow's Election Wills, and Community Property: The Tax Problems*, 47 TEX. L. REV. 1247 (1969).

In Estate of Vardell v. Commissioner, 307 F.2d 688 (5th Cir. 1952), Judge Wisdom dissented from the majority allowing *S*'s estate to deduct under §2043(a) the value of the income interest acquired in the transaction, but so far the courts have followed the view of the majority in that case. You need to be comfortable with the notion that the reduction conforms with the purposes of §2043(a). To do so, think about what the surviving spouse would have at death if the election were not made.

7.   *Time of Valuation.*   *D* transferred Blackacre to a trust in which *D* had the right to the income for life and *R* had the remainder interest. The value of Blackacre was $100,000. In exchange for this transfer, *R* gave *D* 100 shares of Bilt-Rite, Inc. stock, having an aggregate value of $20,000. The $20,000 consideration paid by *R* was not adequate, and therefore when *D* subsequently died the value of Blackacre was included in *D*'s gross estate under §2036(a)(1). *D* still owned the Bilt-Rite stock, which had an estate tax value of $60,000. Meanwhile, Blackacre had appreciated in value to $140,000. The amount included in *D*'s gross estate under §2036(a)(1) is $140,000 and the §2043(a) consideration offset is $20,000 — not §60,000.

That is, a literal reading of §2043(a) and Treas. Reg. §20.2043-1(a) suggests that Blackacre is includible in *D*'s gross estate at its federal estate tax value, less the value of the consideration received, as valued at the date of receipt, and the overwhelming weight of authority has so held. Thus, *D*'s estate includes the appreciated $140,000 value of Blackacre less the pre-appreciation $20,000 value of Bilt-Rite stock at the date of the exchange; the total included in *D*'s gross estate is $120,000 *plus* the value of the Bilt-Rite stock owned by *D* at death, another $60,000. E.g., United States v. Gordon, 406 F.2d 322, 344 n.19 (5th Cir. 1969); United States v. Righter, 400 F.2d 344, 347-348 (8th Cir. 1968); *United States v. Past*, reproduced at page 367; Estate of Vardell v. Commissioner, 307 F.2d 688, 693 (5th Cir. 1962); Estate of Iverson v. Commissioner, 65 T.C. 391, 398 n.2 (1975), *rev'd on another issue*, 552 F.2d 977 (3d Cir. 1977); Estate of Marshall v. Commissioner, 51 T.C. 696, 703 (1969); Estate of Davis v. Commissioner, 51 T.C. 269, 280-281 (1968) (reviewed by the entire court), *rev'd on a different issue*, 440 F.2d 896 (3d Cir. 1971); Estate of Gregory v. Commissioner, 39 T.C. 1012, 1021 (1963). In their treatise, Lowndes, Kramer, & McCord, ESTATE AND GIFT TAXES (3d ed. 1974) at 353-354, properly criticize this rule. It means in essence that the appreciation in both properties is includible in the decedent's estate, whereas Congress' purpose was to treat the decedent as if the less-than-adequate-consideration transaction never occurred. See also the dissent of Judge Ely in *Past*.

If you were preparing a legislative draft, what changes would you recommend be made in §2043(a), assuming that the construction of that statute in its current form has been determined by the cases cited above? Note that a botched full and adequate consideration transaction is worse in most cases than doing no transfer at all. Note also: this is not a "new" problem, although Congress has shown no proclivity to fix it.

Chapter 7

CONCURRENT OWNERSHIP

Part A. Creation of Concurrent Ownership
Part B. Termination of Concurrent Ownership at Death
Part C. Termination of Concurrent Ownership During Life

Code References: *Estate Tax: §2040*
Gift Tax: Treas. Reg. §§25.2511-1(e), -1(h)(4)
& -1(h)(5)
Income Tax: §§1014, 1015

1. *Property Law Aspects of Joint Tenancy and Tenancy by the Entirety.* Concurrent ownership gives each of several owners an undivided fractional interest in an asset. The forms of concurrent ownership developed by the common law still recognized today are joint tenancy, tenancy by the entirety, and tenancy in common. A tenancy by the entirety can exist only if the owners are married to each other, but no similar restriction attaches to the other two. In addition, ten states recognize in one form or another the community property system developed by the civil law countries. Like tenancies by the entirety, community property is a form of concurrent ownership that is available only to married couples.

Of the types of concurrent ownership, we are concerned in this chapter primarily with joint tenancy and tenancy by the entirety, because these have a principal characteristic — the right of survivorship — that requires special wealth transfer tax treatment. The other two forms of concurrent ownership — tenancy in common and community property — have no right of survivorship (although some states now recognize a form of survivorship community property that, for our purposes, essentially is joint tenancy), and are no different from other forms of outright ownership for wealth transfer tax purposes. The only special tax consideration that applies to the nonsurvivorship joint interests relate to valuation discounts for undivided fractional shares that have a lesser value than the fraction times the undivided value of the asset.

The right of survivorship means that the interest of one of the concurrent owners terminates at death and the entire property continues to be owned by the surviving owner(s). Thus, there is a similarity between the right of survivorship and a remainder interest conditioned on outliving a life tenant. For example, suppose that *A*, *B*, and *C* owned Blackacre as equal joint tenants with right of survivorship. If *A* were the first to die, *A*'s one-third interest would cease to exist in the same manner that a life estate terminates upon the life tenant's death. Also, upon *A*'s death, the interests of *B* and *C* grow from one-third to half each, which resembles the change in the remainder beneficiary's interest to include the right to possession. Because *A*, like a life tenant, no longer owns an interest in Blackacre at *A*'s death, no part of the value of Blackacre would be includible in *A*'s gross estate under §2033, and *A* would have no power to control its devolution by will. *B* and *C* would not await the settlement of *A*'s probate estate for their interests to be enlarged, nor would Blackacre be available to *A*'s estate creditors. Indeed, although there is some legislation to the contrary,[1] in most states *A*'s surviving spouse would have no forced share entitlement to such property.

The analogy between concurrently owned property with the right of survivorship and the life estate and remainder combination is even stronger in a few states that have abolished the joint tenancy estate, but in which an express provision in the title for survivorship rights (or, in some states, an explicit reference to joint tenancy ownership) is enforced judicially. The rationale often given is that the parties have created a tenancy in common for the life of each tenant, with a contingent remainder in favor of the survivor or survivors. It often is said, therefore, that a survivorship estate can *in effect* be created in virtually every state, including those that formally abolished the estate as such.

There may be differences between the traditional form of joint tenancy and the joint tenancy effected by construing the title as creating a tenancy in common for life with a contingent remainder in favor of the survivor or survivors. In its traditional form, a joint tenancy can be severed by any joint tenant acting unilaterally. That is, any joint tenant can terminate the survivorship rights of all cotenants by selling or otherwise disposing of the joint tenant's undivided property interest, or by petitioning a local court for partition of the property. If, however, the title's reference to survivorship rights is given effect as a tenancy in common for life with a contingent remainder in the survivors, it is possible that the survivorship rights of one joint owner cannot be terminated without the consent of the others. But see Nunn v. Keith, 268 So. 2d 792 (Ala. 1972). Another difference is that the creditors of one tenant have less to reach for payment of their claims than they would have in the case of a traditional joint tenancy. For transfer tax purposes, will the tenancy in common for life with a contingent remainder in the survivors construction be treated as a joint tenancy estate? It is virtually certain that it will. It is well established that the federal taxation of a

---

1. See, e.g., the 1990 version of Uniform Probate Code §2-205(1)(ii).

taxpayer's interest hinges on the substantive rights and obligations of the interest and not on the label given the interest by the local jurisdiction.

The tenancy by the entirety form of concurrent ownership with the right of survivorship, which is available only to spouses during their marriage, is distinguishable from a joint tenancy principally because it cannot be severed by either spouse acting unilaterally (either by partition or by an inter vivos disposition) other than by divorcing or making a conveyance to the other spouse. Also, in many jurisdictions, property held by the entirety is insulated from the claims of creditors of just one of the spouses.

Tenancies by the entirety are authorized in 60% of the states,[2] although the characteristics of the tenancy may differ among them.[3] In states that authorize tenancy by the entirety ownership, spouses can choose instead to hold property as joint tenants or as tenants in common. The language in a deed or other conveyancing instrument that creates a joint tenancy, tenancy in common, or tenancy by the entirety is determined by local law, and states that authorize tenancies by the entirety may apply a presumption that property titled exclusively in the names of spouses is held by the entirety unless a contrary intent is clearly evidenced. E.g., DeYoung v. Mesler, 130 N.W.2d 38 (Mich. 1964).

For a more extensive discussion of the property aspects of joint tenancy and tenancy by the entirety, see generally 7 R. Powell, THE LAW OF REAL PROPERTY, chs. 51, 52 (M. Wolf ed. 2000).

Joint Accounts.   Joint tenancy and tenancy by the entirety are not the only forms of concurrent ownership with the right of survivorship. Joint accounts at financial institutions (including various forms of bank or savings and loan checking and saving accounts and investment brokerage, security, or asset management accounts) also provide survivorship rights as a principal incident of ownership. Laws dealing with joint bank accounts are complex and subject to considerable confusion, with various theories — gift, joint tenancy, contract, or trust — employed to explain the nature of the account. Moreover, most states have legislation that affects or regulates joint accounts, the most widely adopted of which — passed in over half the

---

2.   See Schoenblum, MULTISTATE GUIDE TO ESTATE PLANNING Table 5.01 Part 1 (2001).

3.   Exclusion of a wife from income of the property was the common law rule, now changed in the United States but held constitutional in D'Ercole v. D'Ercole, 407 F. Supp. 1377 (D. Mass. 1976). See 2 AMERICAN LAW OF PROPERTY §6.6 at 27–28 (A.J. Casner ed. 1952); Johnston, *Sex and Property: The Common Law Tradition, The Law School Curriculum, and Developments Toward Equality*, 47 N.Y.U. L. REV. 1033, 1083–1089 (1972); Kahn, *Joint Tenancies and Tenancies by the Entirety in Michigan — Federal Gift Tax Considerations*, 66 MICH. L. REV. 431, 444–449 (1968); Phipps, *Tenancy by Entireties*, 25 TEMPLE L.Q. 24 (1951). State laws also differ as to whether or what kinds of personal property can be held by the entirety and, in some states, as to whether only certain kinds of personalty can be so held. See 7 R. Powell, THE LAW OF REAL PROPERTY ¶52.02[6] (M. Wolf ed. 2000); Annot., 22 A.L.R.4th 459 (1983); 64 A.L.R.2d 8 (1959).

states — provides that bank or saving and loan deposits made in the names of two or more persons, payable to either or to the survivor,[4] may be paid to any depositor regardless of whether a codepositor has died. A minority of states have joint tenancy statutes providing that opening such an account creates a joint tenancy. Legislation in still fewer states provides simply that the balance remaining in joint accounts at the death of any depositor is the property of the survivor(s).

Despite the complexity and confused nature of the law, a few general statements are possible. Regardless of the type of statute, and regardless of which theory is followed, surviving depositors typically are entitled to the funds,[5] just as with a joint tenancy or tenancy by the entirety. Unlike those concurrent ownership estates, however, joint account deposit agreements authorize each depositor to withdraw the *entire* balance, even if another depositor is alive. As among themselves, a result often reached is that each codepositor has the power to prevent another codepositor from acquiring absolute ownership of amounts in excess of the other's own contributions to the account. This result is achieved by permitting a codepositor to disclaim any intent to make or create a joint tenancy when the codepositor contributed assets to the account.

The Uniform Probate Code attempts to reform and clarify the law with respect to multiple-party accounts of various sorts, including joint accounts with the right of survivorship. Part 2 of Article 6 authorizes a financial institution to pay out any amount on the request of any party but provides that ownership of the account during the life of the parties is in proportion to the net unwithdrawn contribution of each, and that ownership following the death of any party is in the survivors if there is more than one. If one of the survivors is the decedent's surviving spouse, the spouse takes the decedent's share immediately before death; but if none of the survivors is the decedent's surviving spouse, then:

the amount to which the decedent, immediately before death, was beneficially entitled . . . belongs to the surviving parties in equal shares, and augments the proportion to which each survivor, immediately before the decedent's death, was beneficially entitled . . . , and the right of survivorship continues between the surviving parties.

---

4. A typical joint account agreement would include these terms: "When signed below, this account becomes a Joint Account payable to either during the lifetime of both or to the survivor. The bank may make payments from this account upon the orders or receipts of both or either and the bank's records for any payment so made shall be a sufficient acquittance therefor. Each of the undersigned appoints the other attorney with power to endorse (by rubber stamp or otherwise) for deposit to this account checks, drafts, notes, orders and receipts for the payment of all money belonging or payable to either or both of the undersigned." J. White & R. Summers, THE UNIFORM COMMERCIAL CODE §18-2 n.2 (3d ed. 1988).

5. Cf. Uniform Commercial Code §4-405.

On joint accounts, see generally Cone, *The Creation of Joint Tenancy in Bank Accounts: the Old, the New, and the Uncertain*, 44 ARK. L. REV. 199 (1991); Genello, *The Right of Survivorship in Joint Bank Accounts and Safe Deposit Boxes — the Search for a Solution*, 88 DICK. L. REV. 631 (1984); Kepner, *The Joint and Survivorship Bank Account — A Concept without a Name*, 41 CALIF. L. REV. 596 (1953); Kepner, *Five More Years of the Joint Bank Account Muddle*, 26 U. CHI. L. REV. 376 (1959); Annot., 43 A.L.R.3d 971 (1972). See also Wellman, *The Joint and Survivor Account in Michigan — Progress through Confusion*, 63 MICH. L. REV. 629 (1965).

United States Savings Bonds. A third type of arrangement with the right of survivorship incident is joint ownership of United States Savings Bonds, which is controlled by federal, not state, law. United States v. Chandler, 410 U.S. 257 (1973); Free v. Bland, 369 U.S. 663 (1962); Guldager v. United States, 204 F.2d 487, 489 (6th Cir. 1953). Registered ownership of Savings Bonds by natural persons is governed by 31 C.F.R. §315.7, which authorizes joint ownership with only two natural persons and 31 C.F.R. §315.5 states that "[t]he registration must express the actual ownership of, and interest in, the bond [and] is conclusive of ownership, except as provided in §315.49 [relating to errors in the registration]." Accord, Robertson v. United States, 281 F. Supp. 955, 962 (N.D. Ala. 1968); United States v. Dauphin Deposit Trust Co., 50 F. Supp. 73 (M.D. Pa. 1943). The only form of joint ownership registration authorized is in the form of "*A* or *B*," with no mention of a right of survivorship. But registration in this form generates survivorship because 31 C.F.R. §315.70 provides that, "if one of the coowners named on the bond has died the surviving coowner will be recognized as its sole and absolute owner . . . ." During the life of both parties, 31 C.F.R. §315.37 authorizes payment of jointly owned savings bonds to either owner, upon a separate request, and further provides that payment to one terminates any interest of the other in the bond. Because 31 C.F.R. §315.37 requires presentment and surrender of the bond itself to receive payment, any joint owner can prevent the other joint owner from cashing the bond and thereby becoming absolute owner of the full proceeds only by preserving physical possession of the bond.

Under 31 C.F.R. §315.15, "[s]avings bonds are not transferable . . . , except as specifically provided in these regulations and then only in the manner and to the extent so provided." But any owner can request payment of the bond and then transfer the proceeds. In addition, bonds can be transferred by having them reissued, although there are fairly restrictive limits on the power to do so. Except for a gift causa mortis,[6] reissuance of a bond

---

6. 31 C.F.R. §315.22(b) provides: "*Gift causa mortis.* A savings bond belonging solely to one individual will be paid or reissued on the request of the person found by a court to be entitled by reason of a gift causa mortis from the sole owner."

registered in the name of a natural person is authorized only for certain purposes, such as to add a joint owner or to name as registered owner a person related to the owner. §315.47. Subject to similar limitations, a bond registered in joint ownership form can be reissued under §315.51 only "upon the request of both" owners, although a bond registered in joint ownership form may be reissued in the name of one of the owners individually upon the request of only the one to be eliminated. Both state and federal courts agree that an attempted gift to a person who is not a registered owner is ineffective unless the transfer complies with the regulatory requirement of reissuance, and United States v. Chandler, 410 U.S. 257 (1973), held that the federal regulations also control as to an attempted gift from one owner to the other. Thus, a transfer from one owner to the other was not effective for estate tax purposes (nor, presumably, for gift tax or property law purposes) by mere physical delivery of the bond. Instead, the bond must be reissued or the owner must request payment of the bond. See Rev. Rul. 55-278; Rev. Rul. 68-269 (situations 5 and 6).

For some perspective on the amount of property placed in the various types of concurrent ownership with the right of survivorship, the following table was constructed from information contained in Internal Revenue Service, Statistics of Income — 1997 Estate Tax Returns 102, 107 (1999).

ESTATE TAX RETURNS FILED IN 1997

Size of Gross Estate (millions)	Joint Tenancy as Percentage of Gross Estate
$0.6 — $1.0	10.4%
$1.0 — 2.5	8.8%
$2.5 — 5.0	6.3
$5.0 — 10.0	5.3
$10.0 — 20.0	3.7
over $20	0.9
All estates	6.7

The most recent versions of the Statistics of Income report only for taxable estates and the incidence of concurrent ownership property likely is much greater in smaller estates — 20 years earlier (the last year for which it was available in small estates) it averaged 18.7% in all estates, ranging from a low of 3.3% in estates over $1.0 million, 21% in estates of $200,000 to $500,000, and roughly 30% in estates of $100,000 to $200,000 and again in those under $100,000. This data suggests that concurrent ownership with the right of survivorship is especially popular among persons with smaller estates.[7] One of the reasons for this popularity undoubtedly is probate avoidance: The right of survivorship ensures the avoidance of the delays — though not necessarily all the expenses[8] — of probate.

A negative consideration, however, is that these arrangements are inflexible, especially when contrasted with other probate-avoidance devices, such as inter vivos trusts. To be sure, as the preceding text illustrates, the inflexibility varies in degree, depending on the type of joint ownership involved. Tenancies by the entirety are extremely inflexible. As to joint tenancies, there are ways — albeit often awkward and costly — for a contributing party to reacquire outright ownership of at least a pro rata portion of the property held in joint tenancy, and typically the entire property held in a joint account and U.S. Savings Bonds to the extent of that joint owner's contributions. But inflexibility is derived both from the difficulty of reacquisition during life and from the rigid plan for disposition of the property upon another tenant's death. A significant percentage of jointly held property likely was placed in that form of ownership without the advice of sophisticated counsel, without a full consideration of the consequences of that form of ownership, and especially without an appreciation of the transfer tax consequences, all as compared to alternate forms of property ownership.

Most lawyers sophisticated in estate planning are of the view that, in the case of a taxable estate, it usually is undesirable for property to be held in concurrent ownership with the right of survivorship. E.g., Campfield, *Estate Planning for Joint Tenancies*, 1974 DUKE L.J. 669; Johnson, *Survivorship Interests with Persons Other Than a Spouse: The Costs of Probate Avoidance*, 20 REAL PROP., PROB. & TRUST J. 985 (1985); Rieker, *Joint Tenancy: The Estate Lawyer's Continuing Burden*, 64 MICH. L. REV. 801 (1966). The edge of this undesirability was blunted in some respects by the adoption of §2040(b) — the fractional interest rule for "qualified joint interests" of married tenants — as part of the 1976 Tax Reform Act and by the subsequent expansion of §2040(b) by the Economic Recovery Tax Act of 1981. But in other respects, those changes made concurrent ownership with right of survivorship *worse* than outright ownership. Because of the unlimited marital deduction, no estate tax consequences turn on the amount of property co-owned with a spouse that is included in the gross estate of

---

7. See also Stein, *Probate, Administration Study: Some Emerging Conclusions*, 9 REAL PROP., PROB. & TR. J. 596, 599 (1974); Hines, *Real Property Joint Tenancies: Law, Fact, and Fancy*, 51 IOWA L. REV. 582 (1966); Hines, *Personal Property Joint Tenancies: More Law, Fact, and Fancy*, 54 MINN. L. REV. 509 (1970). The government's petition in United States v. Chandler, 410 U.S. 257 (1973), stated that 75% of the approximately 500 million Series E Bonds (worth over $50 billion) then outstanding were registered in joint ownership form.

8. See Report of Subcommittee of Committee on Administrative Expenses, *Fiduciary Compensation and Legal Fees with Respect to Nonprobate Assets*, 8 REAL PROP., PROB. & TR. J. 1 (1973).

the first spouse to die. But if the co-owned property has appreciated in value, the greater the percentage of that property that is included in the gross estate of the first to die, the greater will be the increase in the property's basis under §1014. Because only 50% of qualified property jointly held by spouses will be included in the gross estate of the first to die, only half of that property will receive an increased basis.

The other significant hickey of concurrent ownership with right of survivorship is that it automatically qualifies for the estate tax marital deduction if held only with a decedent's surviving spouse. This denies the ability to use that property to shelter the unified credit of the first spouse to die, which is an increasingly significant issue as the applicable exclusion amount rises.

2.   *Characterization of the Property Interest for Federal Tax Purposes.* For federal tax purposes, the type of property interest a person holds and the rights attendant to those interests is determined by reference to local law. See, e.g., Harvey v. United States, 185 F.2d 463 (7th Cir. 1950). Although the manner in which property is titled often will control, title is not conclusive and tax considerations depend on beneficial interests in property rather than on legal title. Estate of Chrysler v. Commissioner, 361 F.2d 508 (2d Cir. 1966); Silverman v. McGinnes, 259 F.2d 731, 734 (3d Cir. 1958); Wilson v. Commissioner, 56 T.C. 579, 585-587 (1971), *acq. in result only.* Cf. Treas. Reg. §20.2033-1(a); Rev. Rul. 78-214.

PART A.   CREATION OF CONCURRENT OWNERSHIP

3. Purchasing property in joint names probably is the most common way that concurrent ownership is created. But the sole owner of property may grant a concurrent interest to another or may transfer the entire property to two or more donees as concurrent owners. And one concurrent owner may transfer his or her interest to another. Whichever method is employed, except for joint bank accounts and United States Savings Bonds, any difference between the value of the interest acquired by a concurrent owner and any consideration paid by that owner may constitute a gift for gift tax purposes. See Treas. Reg. §25.2511-1(h)(5). If the cotenants are spouses, any such gift will qualify for the marital deduction, and all such gifts typically will qualify for the gift tax annual exclusion.

To illustrate, if stock worth $100,000 is purchased in the names of *A* and *B* as joint tenants with the right of survivorship, if *A* and *B* are not spouses, and if state law permits any joint tenant acting alone to partition the property, the gift tax consequences in the following alternative circumstances are:

(a) If *A* provided the full $100,000 consideration for the purchase, then *A* has made a gift to *B* of $50,000.

(b) There is no gift on creation if *A* provided $50,000 of consideration and *B* provided the other $50,000.

(c) If *A* provided $35,000 of consideration and *B* provided $65,000, *B* has made a gift to *A* of $15,000 — the difference between actual contributions and equal contributions.

More dicey problems typically infect concurrent ownership and illustrate why there is nearly universal noncompliance with the gift tax consequences of creating concurrent ownerships. To wit:

Revenue Ruling 78-362

ISSUE Are a co-tenant's monthly payments of a mortgage debt on property held jointly regarded as gifts to the other joint tenants?

FACTS On January 15, 1974, *D*, the donor, paid 30x dollars as a down payment for the purchase of real property. *D* had title to the property conveyed to the joint ownership, with rights of survivorship, of *D*, *A*, and *B*. *A* and *B* were the children of *D*. The fair market value of the property was 150x dollars.

The property was subject to a mortgage of 120x dollars that was to be paid in monthly installments of 3x dollars. The payment included principal and interest on the mortgage plus escrow payments of local real property taxes and casualty insurance premiums. As each monthly payment to the mortgage became due, *A* and *B* lacked funds to contribute to the payment. Therefore, *D* made all of the monthly payments and at the time of each payment advised *A* and *B* that *D* did not expect any reimbursement from them.

Under local law, a joint tenant may unilaterally sever the joint tenant's interest in the jointly held property at any time. Interests of joint tenants are presumed to be owned in equal shares.

Local law provides that co-tenants are equally responsible for the payment of the expenses of jointly held property. A co-tenant who has paid all of the expenses of the property is entitled to reimbursement from the other joint tenants for their aliquot shares of the indebtedness.

LAW AND ANALYSIS . . . A transfer is taxable as a gift to the extent that the value of the property transferred exceeds the consideration in money or money's worth received by the transferor. See Treas. Reg. §25.2512-8. If an individual with the individual's own funds purchases property and has title conveyed to the individual and others as joint tenants with rights of survivorship, and any joint tenant acting alone may sever the joint tenant's interest, the individual is deemed to have made a gift to the other joint tenants of equal shares of the property. See Treas. Reg. §25.2511-1(h)(5).

In addition, the payment of money or property on behalf of an individual can result in a taxable gift. For example, the gratuitous payment of the debt of another person is a transfer subject to the gift tax. See Estate of Woody v. Commissioner, 36 T.C. 900 (1961), *acq.*

A mortgage debt on property that is subject to the mortgage is regarded as the obligation of the owner of the property in that the payment of the mortgage debt by someone else is equivalent to a cash payment directly to the owner of the property. Further, the value of the owner's interest in the property is increased as the mortgage debt on the property is reduced.

In the present situation, *D*, *A*, and *B* owned equal interests in the jointly owned property that could be unilaterally severed. Since *D* provided the funds for the down payment and received no consideration from *A* and *B*, *D* made taxable gifts of one-third interests to *A* and *B* when the property was purchased and placed in joint ownership. Inasmuch as the expenses of the property were the obligations of *D*, *A* and *B* in equal shares, *D*'s monthly payments to the mortgage were gifts to *A* and *B* when *D* paid their respective one-third shares of the obligations without the expectation of reimbursement from *A* and *B*.

HOLDING On January 15, 1974, *D* made gifts to *A* and *B*, valued at 10x dollars for each gift, of one-third interests in the net value of the property placed in joint ownership. Thereafter, *D* made monthly gifts to *A* and *B* of 1x dollars each, which is one-third of the total monthly payment to the mortgage lender.

The often little-known reality is that, under state law, the gift in a concurrently owned bank account does not occur on deposit but, instead, on withdrawal of more than the depositor contributed. So, for example, if *A* deposited the full balance in a joint bank account titled in the names of *A* and *B*, no gift occurs until *B* later withdrew an amount from the account. Under local law, if *A* had the right to require *B* to return the funds, but *A* never exercised that right, the failure to mandate the return would inform the time of *A*'s gift to *B*. Compare Treas. Reg. §25.2511-1(h)(4)[9] with Estate of Buchholtz v. Commissioner, 36 T.C.M. (CCH) 1610 (1977).

---

9.   Note that the same result would be reached under this regulation if *A* had purchased United States Savings Bonds payable to "*A* or *B*." See also Rev. Rul. 68-269 (situation 5). Moreover, the Commissioner has applied the theory of this regulation to the purchase of securities held in "street" name for a joint brokerage account titled in the names of the parties as joint tenants with the right of survivorship. Rev. Rul. 69-148. U.S. Treasury notes are to be distinguished from United States Savings Bonds. The extent to which, if

4. *Creation of Concurrent Ownership Interests by Spouses.*

Pre-1982 Creations.   The tax treatment of tenancies by the entirety and joint tenancies between spouses was quite complex under the law in existence prior to 1982. For cotenancies in personal property created prior to 1977, the determination of whether one spouse made a gift to the other, and if so in what amount, followed the same basic procedure used in the case of non-spousal tenancies: A comparison had to be made between the amount of consideration supplied by each spouse and the value of the interest received by that spouse. In the case of a destructible joint tenancy, the value of the interest received by each spouse was 50% of the value of the property. If, for example, *A* and *B* are married to each other and the tenancy was created before 1982, the solution to the illustration at page 399 would be unchanged: in (a) *A* made a gift to *B* of $50,000; in (b) no gift occurred; and in (c) *B* made a gift to *A* of $15,000. In the case of a tenancy by the entirety, however, the value of the interest received by each spouse was not necessarily equal to 50% because the absence of a unilateral right to sever made it necessary to make an actuarial valuation of each spouse's interest, which depended upon the age of each spouse and whether local law recognized a right in each spouse to 50% of the income from the property or gave the husband the right to all of the income. Thus, if *A* and *B* took title in the stock as tenants by the entirety rather than as joint tenants, if each spouse was entitled to 50% of the income from the stock, and if *A* was 60 years old and *B* was 50 years old, then using Table ET6 (promulgated by the government for this purpose), the value of *A*'s interest in the stock (rounded off to the nearest thousand dollars)[10] was $35,000 and the value of *B*'s interest (similarly rounded off) was $65,000. This would mean that in (a) *A* made a gift to *B* of $65,000, in (b) *A* made a gift to *B* of $15,000, and in (c) no gift occurred.

The gift tax treatment of the creation of spousal joint tenancies with right of survivorship in personal property was changed by the adoption in 1978 of §2515A, which was repealed in 1981. Once the existence and the amount of the gift was determined, the next question was whether it qualified for the §2503(b) gift tax annual exclusion and the marital deduction. In general, it qualified for both. The marital deduction did not always prevent gift tax consequences because of the limit on marital deductions that existed prior to 1982.

We have been discussing the gift tax consequences of creating a concurrent ownership in personal property. The wealth transfer tax consequences of creating concurrent ownership of real property was not always

---

any, the purchase of U.S. Treasury notes by *A* in the name of "*A* or *B* or the survivor" constitutes a gift for federal gift tax purposes depends on state law. See Rev. Rul. 78-215.

10.   In an actual case, it would be permissible to round off only to the nearest dollar.

the same. There were statutes providing for special gift tax treatment of cotenancies between spouses at various times between 1954 and 1982. The old version of §2515 addressed such cotenancies in realty, and later §2515A addressed personalty. The old version of both §§2515 and 2515A were repealed in 1981.[11] They were a mess. Compliance was even worse.

Post-1981 Creations. The Economic Recovery Tax Act of 1981 greatly simplified the tax treatment of concurrent ownership between spouses by repealing §§2515 and 2515A, removing the ceiling on the amount deductible under the gift tax marital deduction, and amending §6019 to provide that a gift tax return need not be filed if the gift is fully exempt from gift taxation by reason of either the annual exclusion or the gift tax marital deduction or both. The 1981 Act also expanded the scope of §2040(b) (which provides special estate tax treatment of spousal joint tenancies) so that it applies to all concurrent interests of spouses in property in which only the spouses have an interest. The significance of these changes is that, after 1981, spouses no longer need to consider gift tax consequences when they purchase or retitle property in concurrent ownership, because no *taxable* gift can ever occur, and no gift tax return need ever be filed.

As we're about to see, all this gift tax mumbo jumbo is good theory but everyone understands that it is hardly respected and the estate tax rules only make sense if you assume that the gift tax rules *were* ignored. Otherwise a compliant taxpayer would be facing double taxation with no obvious cure. So, for our understanding and peace of mind, you probably would do well to forget what we've just learned!

PART B. TERMINATION OF CONCURRENT OWNERSHIP AT DEATH

5.   Section 2040 governs the estate tax consequences of the death of any owner of a concurrent interest that has a survivorship feature. First enacted in 1916 the legislative history contains no statement as to why Congress thought it was necessary. Although it required inclusion of the value of transfers intended to take effect in possession or enjoyment at or after the transferor's death, apparently Congress was concerned that it was not applicable to property held jointly with the right of survivorship.[12] Notwith-

---

11.   For a detailed exegesis of §§2515 and 2515A during those years, see Plaine & Siegler, *The Federal Gift and Estate Tax Marital Deduction for Non-United States Citizen Recipient Spouses*, 25 REAL PROP., PROB. & TRUST J. 385, 436–443 (1991).

12.   Congress may have been correct in this, because the provision was borrowed from language in the death tax statutes of several states that was held inapplicable to property held jointly with the right of survivorship. E.g., McDougald v. Boyd, 159 P. 168 (Cal. 1916) (joint bank account).

standing application of §2033 to a decedent's share of property held as a tenant in common or as community property, a special rule is needed to tax the expiration of a decedent's concurrent interest in property with survivorship rights — joint tenancies, tenancies by the entirety, joint bank accounts and bonds, and other instruments payable to either the decedent or the survivor.

Section 2040(a) in its current form establishes two alternate methods to determine the amount includible in a decedent's gross estate: A percentage of consideration rule and a fractional interest rule. The percentage of consideration rule requires inclusion of that percentage of the value of property held jointly with the right of survivorship that corresponds to the percentage of consideration furnished by the decedent toward acquisition of the property. The fractional interest rule limits inclusion in a decedent's gross estate to a fraction of any property held in concurrent ownership with a right of survivorship when the cotenants acquired their interest gratuitously. In 1976 a fractional interest rule was enacted in §2040(b), applicable only with respect to "qualified joint interests" owned exclusively by married couples. Because both versions of the fractional interest rule are straightforward, and the consideration furnished rule is complex, let's dispose of the former rather summarily first and then turn our attention to the latter for most of this study.

Property Received Gratuitously.   Inclusion in a decedent's gross estate is limited to the decedent's fractional share of the property if the decedent and the other concurrent owners received the property in joint form with right of survivorship as a gift, bequest, devise, or inheritance, provided that the transfer was from someone who is not one of the concurrent owners. The decedent's interest in the property is treated the same as if it were a tenancy in common interest. The survivorship rights of the concurrent owners are ignored and an equal share is includible. See Treas. Reg. §20.2040-1(a)(1). To illustrate, assume that P purchased income-producing real property for $200,000 cash and placed the title in the names of a child, C, a grandchild, G, and a great-grandchild, GG, as joint tenants with the right of survivorship. State law grants each joint tenant the right to partition the property. G is a child of C, and GG is a child of G. In the following circumstances, the alternate valuation date was not elected in any case.

Ignoring the possibility that §2013 might apply, the wealth transfer tax consequences (including — getting ahead of ourselves — the generation-skipping transfer tax consequences) of P's purchase include:

(1) P made a taxable gift of one-third of the value of the property to each of the three concurrent owners at the time of original acquisition. P also made a generation-skipping transfer taxable direct skip of one-third to G and another one-third GG. Each gift may qualify for the gift tax annual exclusion, and for a zero inclusion ratio to that same extent

under the §2642(c) generation-skipping transfer tax counterpart (all as explained in Chapter 16).

(2) There were no added taxable events when P died survived by C, G, and GG because P was not a concurrent owner and retained no strings with respect to the property. The inter vivos gifts will be included in the adjusted taxable gift tax base for calculation of P's estate tax and any gift tax paid will be a credit against P's aggregate estate tax liability under §2001(b).

(3) When C subsequently dies, survived by G and GG, one-third of the value is includible in C's gross estate under §2040(a) because the property was acquired gratuitously from a third party donor (P). That inclusion protects against any generation-skipping transfer taxable event as a taxable termination of C's interest in the property, but half the value deemed to pass to GG constitutes a generation-skipping transfer taxable direct skip. If the property was valued at $375,000 there will be estate tax inclusion of $125,000 and a generation-skipping direct skip of $62,500. (With respect to a sliver of the property the inclusion ratio is zero attributable to the §2642(c) treatment in (1) but otherwise that direct skip will incur generation-skipping transfer tax).

(4) When G subsequently dies survived by GG, half the value of the property is includible in G's gross estate under §2040(a) but, because GG is only one generation below G there will be no generation-skipping transfer taxable direct skip and inclusion in G's gross estate means there can be no generation-skipping transfer taxable termination. If the property was then valued at $600,000 the only result will be estate tax inclusion of $300,000.

Notice that 100% of the value of the property was subject to tax when P made the original gift, an additional 83.33% has been subjected to estate tax at the deaths of C and G, and when GG dies the full value of the property will be subjected to §2033 inclusion in GG's estate. About the only way to make matters worse would be if P had purchased the property and became a joint tenant along with C, G, and GG, in which case the original gifts on creation would be limited to one-quarter to each of the three donees but 100% of the date of death value of the property would be includible in P's gross estate under §2040(a) — with an appropriate purge and credit under §2001(b) for the quarter interest gifts.

6.   "*Spousal Joint Interests.*"   Added by the Tax Reform Act of 1976 and greatly expanded by the Economic Recovery Tax Act of 1981, §2040(b) provides that the amount includible on the death of a married concurrent owner is just half the value of a "qualified joint interest," irrespective of the percentage of consideration provided by either spouse. This provision was enacted for the avowed purpose of "implicitly recogniz[ing] the services furnished by a spouse toward the accumulation of the jointly owned property even though a monetary value of the services cannot be accurately determined." H.R. Rep. No. 1380, 94th Cong., 2d Sess. 20 (1976). The congressional decision to expand the scope of §2040(b) in 1981 was explained as follows:

> The committee believes that a husband and wife should be treated as one economic unit for purposes of estate and gift taxes, as they generally are for income tax purposes. Accordingly, no tax should be imposed on transfers between a husband and wife.
>
> Moreover, the committee believes that the taxation of jointly held property between spouses is complicated unnecessarily. Often such assets are purchased with joint funds making it difficult to trace individual contributions. In light of the unlimited marital deduction adopted by the [Act], the taxation of jointly held property between spouses is only relevant for determining the basis of property to the survivor (under sec. 1014) and the qualification for certain provisions (such as current use valuation under sec. 2032A, deferred payment of estate taxes under secs. 6166 . . . , and for income taxation of redemptions to pay death taxes and administration expenses under sec. 303). Accordingly, the committee believes it appropriate to adopt an easily administered rule under which each spouse would be considered to own one-half of jointly held property regardless of which spouse furnished the consideration for the property.

S. Rep. No. 144, 97th Cong., 1st Sess. 127 (1981). The original version of §2040(b) had a narrow definition of "qualified joint interest," but the meaning of that term (and therefore the scope of the provision) was greatly expanded in 1981. For decedents dying after 1981, a qualified joint interest is any joint interest created after 1976[13] that is either a tenancy by the

---

13.   Gallenstein v. United States, 91-2 U.S. Tax. Cas. (CCH) ¶ 60,088 (E.D. Ky. 1991), *aff'd*, 975 F.2d 286 (6th Cir. 1992), followed in Hahn v. Commissioner, 110 T.C. 140 (1998), acq., AOD 2001-06, involved the income tax basis of property held in joint tenancy before the death of the taxpayer's spouse. The property was acquired before 1977 and had appreciated significantly when sold 33 years later. The effective date of the original adoption of §2040(b) applied to joint interests created after 1976. The effective date of the 1981 amendment was to estates of decedents who die after 1981. The taxpayer successfully argued that the effective date of the original version of §2040(b) was not altered by this 1981 amendment. Therefore, joint tenancies created prior to 1977 were not subject to §2040(b). The percentage of consideration rule applied if §2040(b) was inapplicable to the taxpayer's property. Application of that rule in *Gallenstein* required inclusion of 100% of the property in the estate of the taxpayer's spouse, which yielded a full §1014 step-up in basis, with no adverse estate tax consequence because of the unlimited marital deduction. Notwithstanding that the 1981 amendment of §2040(b) requires inclusion of 50% of the jointly held property on the death of the first spouse to die and notwithstanding that this amendment was made "applicable to estates of decedents dying after . . . 1981" (which was the case in *Gallenstein*), the court held that §2040(b) is inapplicable to a joint tenancy between spouses that was created before 1977. The court stated that the

entirety or a joint tenancy in which the only joint tenants are the spouses. To illustrate: assume that D and S were married in 1975. After 1981 D and S acquired stock as joint tenants with the right of survivorship. The stock was purchased for $90,000, all of which was paid with D's funds. At the time of D's death the value of the stock was $120,000. The amount includible in D's gross estate under §2040(b) is $60,000. That same amount is deductible from D's gross estate under §2056. See §2056(c)(5). Although D's purchase of the stock was a gift to S of $45,000, no taxable gift occurred and no amount was included in D's adjusted taxable gifts under §2001(b) because the full amount of the gift in excess of the amount allowed as an annual exclusion was deductible under §2523(d). Indeed, no gift tax return was required to be filed. See §6019. S's basis in the stock immediately after D's death is $105,000 ($60,000 determined under §1014 plus $45,000, the basis under §1015 that S obtained in the half interest that S acquired as a gift from D).

In such a situation S might be better off if, instead of registering title in the names of D and S as joint tenants with the right of survivorship, they had registered it in D's name as sole owner and D's will had bequeathed it to S. Indeed, S might be better off if Congress had not enacted §2040(b). That depends on whether D or S dies first.

The §2040(b) tax consequences would not differ if S had paid some, most, or all of the $90,000 purchase price, nor if S had died first, survived

---

effective dates of the 1976 and 1981 versions of §2040(b), one referring to the time of creation and one to the year of death, are not mutually exclusive and that the 1981 amendment did not override or repeal the effective date of the original adoption of §2040(b). The government argued that, given the fact that the 1981 version took the place of the 1976 version, there was an implied repeal of the effective date of the old provision by the new. The court rejected that contention because there is a strong judicial policy disfavoring implied repealers absent a "positive repugnancy" or irreconcilability between the two statutes, which the court found lacking. On appeal, the court stated that "[w]hen Congress wanted to repeal a particular section of the estate tax code, it did so expressly. We should not provide by judicial interpretation what Congress did not expressly enact." As thus interpreted, the court held that the 1981 version of §2040(b) applies only to a qualified joint tenancy that was both created after 1976 and held by a decedent who died after 1981.

The conclusion reached is quite favorable in those cases in which the spouse who provided all the consideration for acquisition of appreciated jointly held property dies first. It is not so desirable in the converse case and it is a gamble which spouse will die first — the bread winner who provided the consideration (or maybe the lucky inheritor of the wealth used for the purchase) or the less propertied spouse. In addition, §121 exclusion of gain on the most common concurrent ownership asset — a principal personal residence — may slacken the significance of this rule. In the favorable case of 100% inclusion the *Gallenstein* holding provides the surviving spouse with a full basis adjustment to fair market value without incurring any federal estate tax because of the unlimited marital deduction. In the latter case little or none of the property may be includible in the first estate, in which case the §2040(b) result would have been better. See generally 2 Casner & Pennell, ESTATE PLANNING §10.5.1 n.7 and accompanying text (6th ed. 1999).

by D. But a §2040(a) — or §2033 for that matter — result would be far different.

If S — recognizing the imminence of D's death — had transferred all right, title, and interest in the stock to D, and had received the stock back as a bequest on D's death, the income tax basis abuse avoidance rule in §1014(e) would preclude an increase in basis to the full fair market value of $120,000. Recall that discussion at page 180.

7.   *The Percentage of Consideration Rule.* The §2040(b) treatment of a qualified joint interest reduces the significance of the §2040(a) percentage of consideration rule because a large portion of properties held jointly with rights of survivorship is owned by married couples. Nevertheless, many concurrent ownership interests are held by individuals who are not married to each other, such as parents and their children, siblings, married couples with additional joint tenants, and committed partners who are not married. In these cases, unless the joint interests were obtained gratuitously, the percentage of consideration rule — also known as the consideration furnished rule — continues to apply. Its application on the death of one concurrent interest owner can be complex. Discussion of this rule comprises the balance of part B of this chapter.

If the percentage of consideration rule is applicable, §2040(a) presumes that the decedent provided all the consideration for the jointly held property and, therefore, that 100% of the value of the property is includible in the decedent's gross estate. The decedent's personal representative has the burden of proving the amount of any consideration in money or money's worth that was provided by other joint owners. Treas. Reg. §20.2040-1(a)(2). Only the portion of the jointly held property that is proportionate to the consideration shown to have been provided by the surviving joint tenants is excluded from the decedent's gross estate. Thus, if it is not possible to determine how much consideration each joint owner contributed to acquire the interest, 100% of the value of the property will be included in the gross estate of whichever joint owner dies first. On the death of the remaining joint owner(s), the same result may be repeated under §2040(a) or, in the last survivor's gross estate, under §2033.

The amount includible in a decedent's gross estate under §2040(a) is the percentage of the value of the property at the estate tax valuation date that equals the percentage of consideration not furnished by owners other than the decedent. The statute accomplishes this by including in a decedent's gross estate all of the jointly held property, less only that percentage that is proportionate to the percentage of consideration that was furnished by the surviving joint tenants. Computation of the amount *excluded* from the decedent's gross estate is determined by the following formula:

$$\frac{\text{consideration furnished by survivor(s)}}{\text{total consideration}} \times \text{estate tax value of property}$$

8.   *Property Originally Owned by One Concurrent Owner.* The entire value of property is includible in a decedent's gross estate if the decedent owned that property outright and caused it to be retitled in joint ownership with others without receiving consideration in money or money's worth. Conversely, no part of the property would be includible in the decedent's gross estate if the decedent died first and if someone else owned the property and caused it to be transferred into joint ownership in the names of the original owner and the decedent, who paid no consideration in money or money's worth for the transfer. If each new joint owner compensated the original owner for causing the property to be transferred into joint ownership, only a pro rata portion of the estate tax value of the property would be includible in the decedent's gross estate. Treas. Reg. §§20.2040-1(a)(2), -1(b), and -3(c).

Again, an illustration may help: Assume that P and an adult child, C, acquired stock as joint tenants with right of survivorship. The joint tenancy was destructible. The stock was purchased for $90,000, of which $60,000 was paid by P and $30,000 was paid by C. At P's death five years later, the federal estate tax value of the stock was $120,000.

The amount includible in P's gross estate under §2040(a) is $80,000, because P provided two-thirds of the consideration for the purchase. See Treas. Reg. §20.2040-1(c)(2). If C still owns the stock when C subsequently dies, 100% of the value of the stock at C's death will be includible in C's gross estate under §2033.

Note also that P made a gift to C of $15,000 when the stock was purchased. A portion of this gift may have been excluded from gift taxation under §2503(b), and the remaining taxable gift is excluded from P's adjusted taxable gifts base under the last clause of the flush language of §2001(b) because, under §2040(a), P's gross estate includes P's half interest in the joint tenancy plus the one-sixth interest P gave to C when the stock was acquired. This assumes P complied with the gift tax on creation — which experience shows is quite uncommon.

C's basis in the stock immediately after P's death is $110,000 (the $80,000 federal estate tax value of the portion includible in P's gross estate under §2040(a), determined under §1014, plus the $30,000 cost basis of the one-third that is not includible in P's gross estate).

If C had died first, survived by P, the amount included in C's gross estate under §2040(a) would be $40,000. P's basis in the stock immediately after C's death would be $100,000. If P still owned the stock at P's subsequent death, the full value of the stock would be includible in P's gross estate under §2033, and no part of the taxable gift P made to C when the joint tenancy was created would be purged from P's adjusted taxable gifts base under the last clause of the flush language of §2001(b).

The burden of proving the amount of consideration provided by surviving joint owner(s) can be difficult to meet. The Tax Court does not require that the decedent's personal representative demonstrate to an "absolute certainty" the amount of consideration provided by the surviving owners if there is reasonable evidence of approximately the amount contributed. The government's own instructions to its estate tax agents also recognize that the burden of proof does not require a demonstration to be made to an absolute certainty.

In Estate of Montagnino v. Commissioner, 26 T.C.M. (CCH) 133 (1967), the decedent and his brother, Joseph, purchased a building in 1910, resided in the building together, and operated a barber shop and a shoe shop in the building until the decedent died in 1963. They pooled their resources and engaged in a number of business ventures as partners. While several other family members were partners with them for various intervals, the decedent and Joseph were the only two partners in these ventures from 1956 until the decedent's death in 1963. At death, the decedent held some assets in joint tenancy with Joseph. The decedent's executor also treated some assets (realty, savings and loan accounts) held in the decedent's name alone and some assets held in Joseph's name alone as joint tenancy property and included only half of all the scheduled joint tenancy property (including the property nominally titled in the name of either the decedent or Joseph alone) in the decedent's gross estate. The court said:

> The principal issue relates to the various items in Schedule E ("Jointly Owned Property") of the estate tax return. The theory of the return and petitioner's theory before us is that the decedent and Joseph had pooled all their assets, that together they were equal members of a "partnership" in which all their assets were employed, and that such assets belonged to them in equal shares regardless of whether title was technically in one or the other of them or in their joint names. Accordingly, it is petitioner's position that only one-half of the value of the various assets in the decedent's name and only one-half the value of the assets in the joint names of decedent and Joseph are includable in decedent's gross estate. And consistently, the estate tax return included as well one-half of the value of assets in Joseph's name. The Government, on the other hand, takes the position that the full value of the assets in the decedent's name is includable in the gross estate as his property, and that the full value of the assets in joint names must likewise be included in the gross estate under §2040[(a)] of the 1954 Code.

> The problem is primarily one of fact, and the burden of proof is upon petitioner. The record before us is confused, and the principal witness, Joseph Montanio [sic], was hardly one to inspire confidence. Nevertheless, we are reasonably satisfied on this record that petitioner's position is correct, that the decedent and his brother in fact had an understanding whereby they pooled all their

resources, that the various assets here involved were in fact purchased out of such pooled resources to which each brother contributed equally, that the decedent thus had only a one-half interest in the various assets standing in his name, and that the assets in joint names were acquired with funds in which each brother similarly had a one-half interest.

In the circumstances, we conclude that the Commissioner erred in the adjustments whereby he attributed to the decedent the full value of the assets listed in Schedule E.

Internal Revenue Service, Audit Technique Handbook for Estate Tax Examiners

(10)33
Presumption as to Includibility — Non-Spousal Joint Tenancy

(1) IRC 2040[(a)] declares that all jointly owned property is includible in the gross estate "*except such part thereof as may be shown* to have *originally* belonged to such other person, and *never* to have been received or acquired by the latter from the decedent for less than adequate and full consideration in money or money's worth." The words "*except such part thereof as may be shown*" create the prima facie presumption; once it becomes clear that an asset or legal interest was jointly owned by the decedent and any other person or persons, the executor must present evidence proving contribution by the survivor or he/she must concede includibility.

(10)40
Claims of Contribution in General

(10)41
Dealing with Claims of Contribution

(1) The approach of the examiner in this area is simplicity itself; after the value of the jointly owned asset is established, you may propose includibility unless the executor can prove contribution by the survivor. You may discover that *some* contribution has been made by the survivor, although exact amounts cannot be determined.

(2) If the evidence indicates that a contribution by the survivor has been made, the executor's burden has been held to be met notwithstanding that the amount of the contribution could not be

computed with precision nor any portion thereof demonstrated to be specifically traceable to the survivor.

(3) When commingling prevents *precise* proof of the amount of contribution to specific items, an approximation could be made of the proportionate cost contributed by the survivor, as indicated by a preponderance of the available evidence. But, to the extent there is reasonable doubt of the percentage of contribution, the approximation should be made against the taxpayer and in favor of the Government. If we required positive evidence, many taxpayers would be deprived of substantial allowances to which they are entitled, and if an occasional error should be made against the Government, the effect would be small compared to the injustice of disallowing any contribution where the evidence strongly indicates some should be allowed.

(10)42
Positive Identification of the Source of Funds

If the taxpayer can trace and identify the source of the funds involved in the acquisition of jointly owned property and the evidence establishes that the survivor made a contribution from his/her own resources, the problem is, of course, simplified. But, as the regulations point out (in Example 4 of 20.2040-1(c)), if the decedent gave the survivor a sum of money or property prior to the acquisition of the jointly owned property and that money or property so given thereafter became the survivor's contribution, the entire value of the property is includible. Executors occasionally overlook the fact that the decedent's gift tax returns disclose substantial gifts. If you can establish a substantial gift at some time in the past from the decedent to the surviving joint owner, the taxpayer may be unable to sustain the burden of proof.

(10)43
Commingled Funds

Jointly owned property may have its immediate source in commingled funds, and the difficulties involved in tracing and identifying the respective contributions of the parties are enormous. Usually such commingling has continued for many years; possibly the records and control of the funds have been managed by the decedent, and the survivor is innocent of any intent to cause confusion. Reconstruction by a skilled accountant may be subject to challenge, involving controversial items and assumptions. Difficult though this problem is, a careful step-by-step analysis of the factual information will usually enable you to arrive at a reasonable determination of contribution.

(10)44
Ascertaining Separate Assets of Claimant

(1) In all cases where contribution is claimed by a surviving joint owner, . . . the proof required to satisfy the law and regulations falls into two parts. First, it must appear that the survivor contributed to the acquisition of the property in question. Secondly, it must appear that the contribution by the survivor had never been received at any time in the past from the decedent for less than adequate and full consideration. But the second part does not prove the first; for example, proof that the surviving tenant had separate funds which he/she *might* have contributed does not prove that such funds were in fact contributed. It remains up to the executor to prove that the funds *were* contributed, not just that they might have been contributed. Generally it is not your responsibility to prove that the separate funds were expended elsewhere and thus could not have been contributed to the joint property. The burden remains on the taxpayer as to both parts of the proof referred to above. However, once the executor has offered evidence which, if unchallenged, would support a contribution claim, the burden of "going forward with the evidence" (not the burden of proof) shifts to the Government.

(2) Accordingly, it is sometimes necessary to inquire about other assets of the surviving joint tenant in order to determine whether the alleged contribution was possible under the circumstances. . . . Thus, claims of contribution, which may appear reasonable at first glance, may be found unsupportable when it is discovered that the claimant has expended all separate funds for living expenses, for the acquisition of a separate estate, gifts to third persons, etc.

(3) This is an especially difficult problem when separate funds of both joint tenants were first deposited in a joint bank account, and then other joint property, such as real estate or securities, was purchased from the funds in this joint bank account. It may be immaterial which joint tenant of the bank account actually signed the check drawn for the purchase of joint real estate or securities. There is no easy solution to this problem; it may be necessary to inspect cancelled checks, deposit slips, bank statements and other records over a period of several years to analyze the case.

(10)50
Persons Claiming Contribution

The relationship between the decedent and the surviving joint owner frequently has a bearing on establishing a claim of contribution. The closer the relationship, the greater the likelihood that commingled funds were used for the acquisition of the joint property. Precise identification of sources of funds is more difficult where the joint owners were closely related, since record keeping and "accounting" between the parties is often informal or non-existent. Accordingly, the techniques you will employ in investigating a contribution claim may vary depending upon the degree of relationship between the decedent and the surviving joint owner.

9.   *Tracing of Consideration.* Congress was concerned that a party who wanted to acquire property in joint tenancy with another party (or to transfer separately held property into joint tenancy) might seek to do so in a manner that would circumvent the §2040(a) percentage of consideration rules that otherwise would apply. This might be attempted by giving cash or other property to the intended joint owner who would then apply the donated cash or other property as a contribution to purchase the jointly owned property. Alternatively, the property could be transferred outright to the intended joint owner, who subsequently would cause it to be transferred into joint ownership with the original donor. The "sham" or "step" transaction rules might be employed to treat the acquired contribution as made by the original donor. Cf. Treas. Reg. §§20.2036-1(a) (last sentence); 20.2038-1(c) (last sentence). But the factual basis for invoking those rules might be found inapplicable in some cases. Consequently, Congress adopted an "acquired consideration" rule for §2040(a) that minimizes the possibility of success for such schemes.

This provision requires that any contribution to jointly owned property be attributed to the original source of the contributed property. Thus, under §2040(a), to the extent property or cash nominally contributed to a joint ownership by one party (the "nominal contributor") was acquired by the nominal contributor for less than full and adequate consideration in money or money's worth from another party (the "original contributor"), the contribution is attributed to the original contributor. Although the proviso refers only to a *surviving* nominal contributor who acquired consideration *from the decedent* original contributor for less than adequate and full consideration in money or money's worth, it is clear that the same rule applies to the converse circumstance. Thus, although the statute does not so state, to the extent the *decedent's* contribution to the acquisition of the concurrent ownership property was acquired by the decedent as a gift *from the sur-*

viving original contributor, then the decedent's nominal contribution should be ignored and that portion of the value of the concurrently owned property should be excluded from the decedent's gross estate. Estate of Koussevitsky v. Commissioner, 5 T.C. 650 (1945), *acq.*; see Treas. Reg. §20.2040–1(c)(6).

Let's assume that *O* gave $10,000 to *N*, which *N* deposited in a money market fund registered in *N*'s name alone and into which *N* previously had deposited $10,000 of *N*'s own money. Later, *N* wrote a check for $10,000 on the money market fund account as *N*'s contribution toward the purchase of $20,000 worth of real property. *O* contributed the other $10,000 of the purchase price and *O* and *N* took title to the real property as joint tenants with right of survivorship. *O* died, survived by *N*, and the federal estate tax value of the real property was $24,000. The issue is how much, if any, of the $24,000 value can be excluded from *O*'s gross estate. What position would you expect the government to take on this question? See (10)44 of the Audit Technique Handbook, reproduced at page 412. Compare Lowndes & Stephens, *Identification of Property Subject to the Federal Estate Tax*, 65 MICH. L. REV. 105, 137 (1966):

This must be settled by means of a presumption. A number of presumptions which could be adopted but which make no particular sense come to mind, such as first-in, first-out, or last-in, first-out. . . . Perhaps the most equitable procedure in this situation would be to prorate any withdrawals from the fund in proportion to the respective contributions to the fund.

The problem of tracing funds that have been commingled arises frequently in restitution cases. As discussed in G. Palmer, THE LAW OF RESTITUTION §§2.16, 2.18 (1978), at least two methods of tracing are utilized, depending on the circumstances. One method applies if a thief's funds were commingled with stolen funds: all presumptions run against the thief and, to the extent possible, withdrawals are deemed to have been made from the thief's own contributions to the fund. Another method often applies if the funds of two innocent parties are commingled: withdrawals are deemed to be pro rata from the respective contributions. Should the estate tax analogize *N* to a thief or to an innocent party?

Income and Gains Generated by Acquired Consideration.
To set the stage for an even harder set of issues, imagine the following facts: When it had appreciated in value to $18,000, *M* transferred to *T* stock that *M* had previously purchased for $15,000. In consideration for which, *T* paid *M* $5,000. *M* reported having made a gift of $13,000 to *T* of which almost all was excluded by the annual exclusion. Eight years later *T* caused the stock, then valued at $24,000, to be titled in the names of *T* and *M* in joint tenancy with right of survivorship. *M* died four years after receiving this

joint tenancy interest and the federal estate tax value of the stock was $23,000. It is not clear that any amount included in M's adjusted taxable gifts base on account of the transfer of the stock to T 12 years before M's death will be purged from M's adjusted taxable gifts base under §2001(b). But the *real* controversy centers around the $6,000 of appreciation between the part-sale, part-gift from M to T and T's titling of the stock in joint tenancy. Does any part of it count as T's clean consideration?

Even though the contribution of property previously received as a gift from another joint owner is attributed to the original contributor, the *income* generated by donated property is treated as clean consideration provided by the nominal contributor. Treas. Reg. §20.2040-1(c)(5). So, assume that A gave a $10,000 bond to B, from which B received interest that B used to acquire with A unimproved Blackacre as joint tenants with right of survivorship, each contributing an equal amount to the purchase price. If A predeceased B, 50% of the value of Blackacre would be includible in A's gross estate. On the other hand, if X gave property to Y that Y later transferred into joint tenancy with right of survivorship with X, Y is deemed to have contributed none of the cost of the property irrespective of whether the property had appreciated in value before it was transferred to X and Y. Similarly, if Y did not cause the previously donated property to be titled in the names of X and Y as joint tenants, but instead Y and X purchased new property as joint tenants and Y's contribution to the cost of the new property was by transfer of the previously donated and appreciated property to the seller, X still would be deemed to have provided all of the consideration for the jointly held property. Treas. Reg. §20.2040-1(c)(4). Thus seen, the tax treatment accorded to the unrealized appreciation element in the contributed property is not consistent with the tax treatment accorded to the contribution of income generated by acquired property. As illustrated next, this regulation does *not* apply to a contribution by Y to the cost of jointly held property *if* the contribution constituted a taxable exchange by Y for income tax purposes. Gain realization is critical to cleansing the appreciation as Y's contribution.

Revenue Ruling 80-142

ISSUE What is the amount includible in the decedent's gross estate with respect to jointly owned stock, under the following circumstances?

FACTS The decedent, D, died in 1976. In 1970, D purchased 800 shares of X corporation common stock and placed the shares in a joint tenancy, with rights of survivorship, with A. The stock of X corporation is publicly traded.

In 1972, X corporation distributed a stock dividend of one share of X corporation common stock for every four shares of X corporation common stock owned.

Thereafter, *D* and *A* owned 1,000 shares jointly.

In 1974, *X* corporation declared a cash dividend of two dollars with respect to each share of stock held by the shareholders. The company offered to distribute additional shares of common stock in lieu of the cash dividends at the rate of forty dollars per share. *D* and *A* elected to receive additional shares rather than the cash dividend and therefore jointly acquired an additional fifty shares of stock.

At *D*'s death, 1,050 shares of *X* corporation common stock, with a value of 50 dollars per share, were owned jointly by *D* and *A*.

Under applicable local law, income produced by property held jointly is regarded as belonging to the joint tenants in equal shares.

LAW AND ANALYSIS . . . The 1972 common stock dividend represents a fragmentation of the original interest in the corporation which *D* transferred into joint tenancy rather than an increased interest therein. This reasoning, which is the basis for not taxing the dividends as income, is also the basis for including them in *D*'s estate under §2040[(a)]. Inclusion of the stock dividends on this basis is supported by the analysis of Estate of Schlosser v. Commissioner, 277 F.2d 268 (3rd Cir. 1960).

In *Schlosser*, the court stated that ordinary dividends, which change the shareholder's proportionate interest in the corporation or give him something different in kind from the original stock, would not be included in the property valued in the gross estate. See Tuck v. United States, 282 F.2d 405 (9th Cir. 1960), and English v. United States, 270 F.2d 876 (7th Cir. 1959).

In the situation of a common stock dividend issued with regard to common stock, the period to which the capitalized profits are attributable should not be controlling, and the analysis of McGehee v. Commissioner, 260 F.2d 818 (5th Cir. 1958), will not be followed.

In contrast to the 1972 dividend, the 1974 elective stock dividend constitutes something different in kind from the shares originally transferred by *D* into joint tenancy. Like a cash dividend, which is treated as the contribution by the survivor under Treas. Reg. §20.2040-1(c)(5), an elective stock dividend constitutes income to the recipient under §305(b)(1), and income tax considerations are relevant to the determination of includibility for estate tax purposes in this case. If a shareholder has the option to take cash or stock and decides to take stock the result is the same as if he had received a cash dividend and purchased additional stock. See, for example, Rev. Rul. 76-53, 1976-1 C.B. 87.

Under local law, each joint tenant is entitled to an equal share of the elective stock dividend. Therefore, each joint tenant would be taxed on the value of this property as income. See Rev. Rul. 56-519, 1956-2 C. B. 123.

HOLDING The amount includible in *D*'s gross estate is $51,250 or the value of 1,025 shares of the *X* corporation stock. The value of twenty-five shares, which constitute *A*'s share of the 1974 elective stock dividend, or $1,250, is excluded as the contribution of *A*.

Harvey v. United States
185 F.2d 463 (7th Cir. 1950)

[The surviving joint tenant had invested, sold, and reinvested property acquired by gift from the decedent, realizing substantial gains over the years. The surviving joint tenant had owned no other property and contributed the profits from those sales plus income earned from the property to acquire certain properties in joint tenancy with right of survivorship with the decedent. The government sought to include the entire value of the jointly held properties in the decedent's gross estate under the antecedent to §2040(a). The decedent's personal representative contended that the surviving joint tenant's contribution was not disqualified as acquired consideration and, therefore, that a portion of the jointly held properties should be excluded from the decedent's gross estate.]

LINDLEY, J.: . . . It seems clear that none of the cases cited contains any support for the novel proposition that income produced by gift property, after the gift has been completed, belongs to the donor and is property received or acquired from him by the donee; nor is there, in these cases, anything to impeach the conclusion of the trial court, or that of the Tax Court in the *Howard* case, that the income produced by property of any kind belongs to the person who owns the property at the time it produces such income and does not originate with a donor who has made a completed gift of that property prior to its production of the income. Similarly, they fail to sustain the contention that the statute should be interpreted as excepting from inclusion in the gross estate such part of the jointly held property "as may be shown to have originally belonged to such other person and never to have been received or acquired *or produced by property which was received or acquired* by the latter from the decedent for less than an adequate and full consideration in money or money's worth." . . .

Although it concedes that the case of Estate of Howard v. Commissioner, 9 T.C. 1192 (1947), *acq.*, supports the decision of the District Court insofar as it relates to dividends, rentals and interest, the government contends that the case "apparently" supports its position with respect to profits derived from the sale of property previously received by the surviving joint tenant as a gift from the decedent. This contention is founded on the court's statement that "If the proceeds from the sale of this stock had been deposited in the joint bank account, that would be another matter." Placing these words in context, however, it is obvious that all the Tax Court was saying was that if gift property is converted into another form of property, which is then placed in joint tenancy, the converted property is not within the [consideration furnished] exception provided for in §[2040(a)]; its statement can not logically be interpreted as meaning that "profits" or "gains," as distinguished from "proceeds" or "property received in exchange," do not fall within the scope of the exception. Moreover, no reason is suggested for holding that one form of income, . . . profit gained through a sale or conversion of capital assets, . . . is outside the exception, whereas other forms of income, such as dividends, rentals and interest, fall within its terms. It follows that the government's contention that the full value of the property held in joint tenancy by decedent and [the surviving joint tenant] at the time of his death should have been included in decedent's gross estate must be rejected. . . .

The judgment is affirmed.

The holding in *Harvey* was adopted in subsequent cases and by the government in Rev. Rul. 79–372. *Harvey* treats the profit realized on the sale of acquired consideration as "income" — and therefore as clean consideration — for purposes of §2040(a). However, the opinion in *Harvey* did not indicate the manner in which profits should be measured. For income tax purposes, a donee's basis in donated property typically is equal to the donor's basis at the time of the gift.[14] Any pre-transfer gain is deferred until the donee disposes of the property because a donor usually does not realize a gain on making a gift of appreciated property and because of the donee's carryover of the donor's basis. Thus, if the donee subsequently sells acquired consideration for a taxable gain, some part (and maybe all) of that

---

14.   §1015. If the donor paid a gift tax, the donee's basis may be increased by a portion of the amount of such tax. §1015(d). The donee's basis for purposes of determining a loss on a subsequent sale of the donated property cannot exceed the fair market value of the donated property at the date the gift was made. §1015(a). If a gift is made in the form of a bargain sale, the donee's basis is the greater of the consideration paid or the donor's basis, possibly increased by a portion of the gift tax paid by the donor. Treas. Reg. §1.1015-4.

gain may reflect appreciation in the donor's hands that was passed to the donee. Swartz v. United States, 182 F. Supp. 540 (D. Mass. 1960), determined that, for purposes of §2040(a), clean consideration "income" from a sale of previously donated property is limited to the amount received for appreciation in value *in the hands of the donee*. Accord, Estate of Goldsborough v. Commissioner, 70 T.C. 1077 (1978), *aff'd in an unpublished opinion* (4th Cir. 1982); Rev. Rul. 79-372.

Illustrations

(a) X owned Blackacre with a basis of $10,000 and gave it to Y; its value at the date of the gift was $15,000. Y later sold Blackacre for $22,000 and recognized a gain of $12,000 on the sale for income tax purposes. Y placed the proceeds of the sale in a joint bank account in the names of Y and X. If X dies before Y, Y's clean consideration is the $7,000 of realized post-gift gain and 15/22 of the joint bank account is includible in X's gross estate. The gift of Blackacre will be purged from X's adjusted taxable gifts base.

(b)   The facts are the same as in (a) except that X's basis in Blackacre was $20,000 at the time of the gift. Consequently, although Blackacre appreciated in value by $7,000 in Y's hands, Y recognized a gain for income tax purposes of only $2,000 on the sale of Blackacre. The same portion of the joint bank account is includible in X's gross estate. What counts is realization of the post-gift gain and not how much of that gain is subject to income tax to Y.

(c)   If Y, not X, died first after the sale proceeds were placed in the joint bank account, 7/22 of the joint bank account would be includible in Y's gross estate and there would be no purge under §2001(b).

Income from Jointly Held Property.   Endicott Trust Co. v. United States, 305 F. Supp. 943 (N.D. N.Y. 1969), addressed the question whether the income from jointly held property, which had been created by one of the joint tenants, is attributable only to the person who created the original joint tenancy. From 1946 to 1954, the decedent purchased 256 shares of IBM stock at a cost of over $32,000, all in the names of the decedent and another as joint tenants with right of survivorship. The IBM stock was sold in 1954 for more than $68,000, yielding a profit of over $36,000. The full proceeds were deposited in a joint checking account of the decedent and the other joint tenant. These funds were withdrawn from the checking account in 1956 to purchase 500 shares of Fruehauf Trailer stock and 100 shares of IBM stock; these stocks also were held in the names of the decedent and the other person as joint tenants with right of survivorship. The IBM stock appreciated greatly in value before the decedent died and the government sought to include all of the value of the Fruehauf and the IBM stock in the decedent's gross estate under §2040(a). The decedent's personal representative contended that half of the $36,000 of gain recognized in 1954 was profit earned by the other joint tenant that did not constitute acquired consideration and thus should be counted as clean consideration paid for the stock purchased in 1956. The district court rejected this contention and included 100% of the jointly held stock in the decedent's gross estate, saying:

The property in question was held in joint tenancy at time of death, hence it is all includible in the gross estate unless an applicable exception can be found to §2040[(a)]. The plaintiff cites Treas. Reg. §20.2040-1(c)(5); Harvey v. United States, 185 F.2d 463 (7th Cir. 1950); Swartz v. United States, 182 F. Supp. 540 (D. Mass. 1960); and First National Bank of Kansas City v. United States, 223 F. Supp. 963 (W.D. Mo. 1963), in support of its position.

However, neither the Regulation nor the cases cited support the position of the plaintiff. In the cases above-cited, the income, profits, appreciation or gain that was treated as the contribution of the survivor, resulted from the ownership by the survivor of property which the decedent had given to the survivor as an *outright*, "no-strings attached" gift; consequently, the "income belonged to [the survivor]." The interest of the survivor herein in the capital gain resulting from the sale of the initial IBM stock, never "belonged to" her in that sense. It was always joint property, subject to a right of survivorship in the other joint tenant (the decedent).

The plaintiff's claim is founded on the concept of a gift of one-half of the jointly held original IBM shares under local New York property law. This does not afford a firm foundation: "The obvious scheme of §2040[(a)] is to recapture the entire value of jointly held property into a decedent's gross estate, notwithstanding the fact that the decedent may have made a gift under local law of one-half of the property. Section 2040[(a)] looks to the source of the consideration represented by the property and disregards legal title." Estate of Peters v. Commissioner, 386 F.2d 404, 407 (4th Cir. 1967).

The surviving [joint tenant] and the decedent at all times held their property as joint tenants with a right of survivorship. Changing the character of the property but not the character of the ownership will not or should not permit an escape from taxation as joint property, unless so excepted by statute.

In this case, the decedent chose to consistently keep practically his entire estate in the form of joint ownership with a right of survivorship in his [joint tenant]. Having done so, his property must be taxed as such upon his death. To have avoided taxation as joint property, decedent was obliged to avoid this form of ownership.

Compare Estate of Ensley v. Commissioner, 36 T.C.M. (CCH) 1627 (1977), *aff'd in an unpublished opinion* (7th Cir. 1979). Citing *Endicott Trust*, the Tax Court said: "Since decedent apparently supplied all the consideration for the purchase of the jointly owned . . . property, which would have been fully included in his gross estate if retained, §2040[(a)] cannot be avoided by disposing of the property and converting it into other joint property." In *Ensley*, however, it is unclear from the facts given by the court whether the proceeds from the sale of one parcel of joint tenancy property were deposited into a joint bank account before they were reinvested in another parcel of property held in joint tenancy.

Suppose the proceeds of the 1954 sale in *Endicott Trust* had been divided equally between the decedent and the joint tenant, and that each half was placed in a separate checking account in the name of that joint tenant alone. If they withdrew those funds in 1956 and used the funds to purchase new stock as joint tenants, would the survivor's contribution of the gain from the 1954 sale be treated as acquired consideration? Note that Rev. Rul. 80-142, reproduced at page 415, treated taxable dividends on stock held in joint tenancy as income belonging to each tenant equally.

10.   *Purchase Money Obligations.*   Often property held in joint ownership is purchased in part with debt in the form of a personal obligation of the owners to pay at some future date(s). Typically the debt is secured by a mortgage that encumbers the property, which the joint owners either take subject to, assume, or give. In these cases, determining the consideration provided by each joint owner becomes quite difficult. To the extent the debt is satisfied before any owner dies, the issue is whether any actual cash payments constitute consideration provided by the owner who made that payment or whether the personal undertaking of each owner constitutes consideration provided by that owner, regardless of which owner(s) actually service the debt.

Bremer v. Luff, 7 F. Supp. 148 (N.D. N.Y. 1933), is the only direct judicial authority that discusses this issue.[15] At death, the decedent and another owned several parcels of realty jointly with the right of survivorship. With one exception, the parcels were purchased by a partial payment in cash by the decedent alone, with the balance of the purchase price being satisfied by the decedent and the other owner assuming an existing mortgage, or giving a new purchase money mortgage, or both. At the decedent's death, part of the original mortgage debt had been repaid, presumably by the decedent alone, although the court did not make a direct

---

15.   In Estate of Awrey v. Commissioner, 5 T.C. 222 (1945), *acq.*, the decedent purchased real property in joint tenancy with another, financed in part by a mortgage note signed by both joint tenants. The decedent discharged the mortgage debt before death and the court held that the full value of the joint tenancy property was includible in his gross estate. *Bremer v. Luff* was not cited, and the question addressed by *Bremer* was not discussed.

finding to this effect. Information concerning the parcels, the original mortgage indebtedness, the outstanding balance of the mortgages at the decedent's death, and other pertinent information was summarized by the court, which sustained the personal representative's contention that the surviving owner provided part of the consideration for the several parcels held at the decedent's death, so that a portion of the value was not includible in the decedent's gross estate. Part of the court's opinion follows:

It is not disputed that . . . the question here must be determined by the amount of the contributions of the [concurrent owners] "in the first instance" . . . , that is, at the time of the original purchase. . . .

Turning now to the mortgage debt given and assumed, it has been shown that the amount of such debt is $143,500. The mortgage indebtedness so jointly assumed or given must, because the separate estates of both [owners] are liable, be deemed to be equal contributions to the purchase price by each, asserts the plaintiff.

That the mortgages were given or assumed "in the first instance," that is, at the time of the original purchase, is without doubt. That the mortgages given and assumed are separate as well as joint obligations is also without doubt.

But upon the question of whether or not the joint giving and assuming mortgages was a joint and equal contribution to the original purchase price, no satisfactory authorities are cited in the briefs.

There is no mere presumption of joint ownership as in [the] case of [a] joint bank account.

The joint and several liability of both [owners] for such mortgage indebtedness is positive, fixed, and irrevocable, except for fraud, under the state law. That each signed the bonds and mortgages is certified by the notary public. The joinder of both in the bonds and mortgages was necessary, since title was taken in the name of both. The consideration (the title) passed to both, and the obligation to pay the balance secured by mortgage was that of both. The facts are inconsistent with the view that the [surviving owner] was a nominal or accommodation party.

The statute says the whole estate shall be taxed except such part thereof as "may be shown to have originally belonged to such other person and never to have been received or acquired by the latter from the decedent for . . . money or money's worth."

[T]he regulation states the same thing in slightly different language, but the same meaning. It says: "So much of the property as originally belonged to the other joint owner and which at no time in the past had been received or acquired by the latter from the decedent for less than an adequate consideration in money or money's worth, forms no part of the decedent's gross estate."

Surely no part of this property . . . was received or acquired by the [surviving owner] from the [decedent], for the property came to them as such tenants from a third person, and their interests therein have always remained the same.

What their interests were, in the first instance, or at the time of the original purchase, seems to be controlling, regardless of what, if anything, happened thereafter to the property or to [their] interests. . . .

Since the mortgages given and assumed are part of the consideration given at the purchase of these properties, the plaintiff is right and is entitled to exemption to the extent of such mortgage indebtedness given and assumed, less the amount unpaid, which has already been deducted from the gross estate.

It is not overlooked that such construction permits evasion of the statute by [concurrent owners] taking title to real estate [jointly], giving a mortgage for the whole consideration and the [decedent] paying the mortgage thereby exempting the property from the federal estate tax. . . .

Would *Bremer* be followed today and, if it was, with what gift tax consequence if the decedent serviced the debt alone? As indicated by Rev. Rul. 79-302, next below, the Commissioner does not accept the *Bremer* analysis.

Revenue Ruling 79-302

ISSUES 1. If a decedent and *B* owned property jointly and paid part of the mortgage indebtedness before the decedent's death, what amount is includible under §2040[(a)]?

2. What amount is deductible under §2053 with respect to the mortgage indebtedness that remained outstanding at the death of the decedent?

FACTS . . . [T]he decedent, *A*, and [another], *B*, purchased a residence as joint tenants with rights of survivorship. The purchase price of the property, which is located in State *X*, was $100,000. Each [joint tenant] contributed $10,000 in cash toward the purchase, and the balance was obtained through a mortgage for $80,000, on which the [joint tenants] were jointly and severally liable.

After the residence was purchased, *A* made all mortgage payments, in a total amount of $20,000, until *A* died. . . . At *A*'s death the fair market value of the residence was $100,000. The outstanding mortgage indebtedness at that time was $60,000.

Under the law of State *X*, *A* and *B* were jointly and severally liable on the mortgage debt and thus each cotenant was personally and primarily liable for the entire debt. Under State *X* law, if either cotenant was required to satisfy more than one-half of the debt, the cotenant paying more than one-half the debt would be entitled to contribution from the other cotenant to the extent of the excess of the amount paid over one-half of the amount of the debt. Upon *A*'s death, *B* succeeded to sole ownership of the residence and, under local law, *A*'s estate and *B* became jointly and severally liable for the mortgage debt.

LAW AND ANALYSIS Section 2040(a) provides that, in general, the full value of property in which the decedent had an interest as a joint tenant with rights of survivorship is includible in the decedent's gross estate, except for that portion of the property value that is attributable to the surviving joint owner's contributions toward the purchase of the property. . . .

Although the assumption, by both joint tenants, of liability on a mortgage in connection with the purchase of property is a contribution by each tenant to the extent of one-half of the mortgage liability amount, subsequent payments to the mortgage by one cotenant are counted as that person's contributions for the purposes of §2040[(a)]. See Estate of Awrey v. Commissioner, 5 T.C. 222 (1945).

Therefore, for the purposes of §2040[(a)], if the owners of property in joint tenancy were jointly and severally liable on a mortgage on the property and if, at the death of a joint tenant, the mortgage is outstanding, the surviving joint tenant's total contribution to the purchase of the property is the sum of the surviving joint tenant's actual payments with respect to the purchase of the property or with respect to subsequent mortgage payments and one-half of the mortgage indebtedness that remained outstanding at the decedent's death.

Section 2053 provides for deductions with respect to, among other things, claims against the decedent's estate (subsection (a)(3)) and unpaid mortgages on property that is included in the decedent's gross estate without reductions by the amount of the mortgage (subsection (a)(4)). The deduction allowed by §2053 in the case of claims against the estate or unpaid mortgages is limited by §2053(c)(1) to the extent that they are contracted bona fide and for adequate and full consideration in money or money's worth.

Under Treas. Reg. §20.2053-4, only those amounts that represent personal obligations of the decedent and that are enforceable against the decedent's estate are deductible as claims against the estate. In addition, a deduction will be allowed for a claim against the estate only if the estate has paid or will pay the claim. See Estate of Courtney v. Commissioner, 62 T.C. 317 (1974).

If, under applicable local law, the estate of a deceased joint owner is jointly and severally liable, with the surviving joint owner, on a mortgage debt the estate would be obligated to pay one-half of the debt with a right of contribution for any payments in excess of one-half of the debt. If this is the case and if the probate estate is actually expected to pay one-half of the debt, a deduction is allowable, under 2053(a)(3) of the Code, with respect to such an indebtedness as a "claim against the estate."

Subsection 2053(a)(4) allows a deduction with respect to unpaid mortgages on property includible in the gross estate. Treas. Reg. §20.2053-7 provides that, if the decedent's estate is liable for the amount of the mortgage, the full value of the property must be included in the gross estate and the amount of the mortgage liability is allowable as a deduction. If the estate is not so liable, then the value of the property less the mortgage debt is included in the gross estate.

In the case of joint property where both cotenants are equally liable on the mortgage (with the result that one-half of the mortgage is included in the estate in the form of contribution under §2040[(a)]), the corresponding portion deductible would be one-half, whether or not the overall contribution ratios under §2040 for the two cotenants are equal.

HOLDINGS 1. The amount includible in A's gross estate under §2040[(a)] is $60,000. This is the value of the property at the date of A's death, reduced by the value of B's contributions, computed as follows:

Initial cash contributions by B	$10,000
Subsequent mortgage payments by B	0
One-half of mortgage balance outstanding	30,000
Total contributions by B	$40,000
Divided by purchase price of property	100,000
Proportion of B's contributions to total	.40
Times value of property at date of death	$100,000
Portion attributable to B's contributions	$40,000

2. The amount deductible from A's gross estate, under either §2053(a)(3) as a claim against the estate or under §2053(a)(4) as an unpaid mortgage on includible property, is one-half of the balance due, or $30,000, as that amount is the extent to which the

estate is ultimately liable for payment on the mortgage, under the law of State *X*, in view of the joint and several liability of *A* and *B*.

3. If, in the above case, the joint property had appreciated to $200,000 by the date of *A*'s death, the amount includible in *A*'s gross estate under §2040 would be computed as follows:

Proportion of *B*'s contributions to total	.40
Times value of property at date of death	$200,000
Portion attributable to *B*'s contributions	$80,000
Amount includible in *A*'s gross estate ($200,000, value at death, less $80,000, *B*'s contributions)	$120,000

See also Rev. Rul. 81-183; Rev. Rul. 81-184.

The law of most states is in accord with the assumption about local law made in Rev. Rul. 79-302. Some states, however, follow a rule that the surviving joint tenant becomes solely liable on the mortgage debt, with no right of contribution from the deceased joint tenant's estate. See, e.g., Annot., 76 A.L.R.2d 1004 (1961). If local law were to this latter effect, *B*'s contribution would be larger and the §2053 deduction would be zero. Here the percentage of contribution provided by *B* would be 70% (an initial contribution of $10,000 plus the balance due on the mortgage at *A*'s death of $60,000, divided by the $100,000 purchase price, and 70% of the estate tax value of the property would be excluded from *A*'s estate. See generally Young, *Joint Tenancy: Headaches in Estate Planning*, 1 U. MIAMI INST. EST. PLAN. ¶706 (1967); Dean, *Jointly-Owned Property: Problems and Techniques*, 2 U. MIAMI INST. EST. PLAN. ¶1805 (1968). Consider the validity of this proposition from Dean: "Of course, if the decedent had directed — by will or codicil — the remainder of the mortgage to be paid off by the estate, then the entire value of the property should be included in his estate with a deduction under §2053 for the mortgage debt assumed." No authority was cited for this proposition.

Suppose in Rev. Rul. 79-302 that the parties had purchased the property subject to the mortgage and were not personally liable for repayment of the debt? See the Young article at ¶706 n.18, and consider the discussion in Chapter 10 regarding nonrecourse debt.

In Drummond Estate v. Commissioner, 75 F. Supp. 46 (E.D. Ark. 1947), a third party gave income-producing real property to *A* and *B* jointly with the right of survivorship. The income from this property was divided by *A* and *B* between them and kept separate. *A* and *B* later combined their respective shares of this income to make the down payment on other real property that they took jointly with the right of survivorship. They also combined their respective shares of that income to make the mortgage payments thereon. The court held that, as to this latter property, each party furnished half of the consideration.

11.   *Contribution to Improvements.* Another source of complexity to §2040(a) is ongoing additions by way of renovations or additions:

Estate of Peters v. Commissioner
386 F.2d 404 (4th Cir. 1967),
aff'g 46 T.C. 407 (1966), *acq.*

WINTER, J.: The question we must decide is: Where, by gift, decedent created a joint tenancy with inherited property that had appreciated in value, and thereafter both decedent and the surviving joint tenant made capital expenditures on the property, the capital improvements not having been shown to have appreciated in value from the time of making until decedent's death, does §2040[(a)] require the entire date-of-death value of the property to be included in the decedent's gross estate, less only the capital contributions of the surviving joint tenant? The Tax Court decided in the affirmative, and we affirm.

Briefly stated, the facts are that the decedent inherited certain real property, known as the Mt. Olivet Road property, from her husband in 1942, at which time its fair market value was $33,650. Six years later, at a time when the value of the property had increased to over $64,000, she created a joint tenancy with her son, T. Graham Peters. From 1948 until her death in 1960, the decedent contributed $10,168.31 toward capital improvements on the property, while her son expended $16,485.19. The property was appraised in Mrs. Peters' estate at $95,000. The record established, and the Tax Court found, that the value of the improvements contributed by the son at the date of decedent's death was the cost to the son at the time of his contribution.

Applying literally the terms of §2040[(a)], the Tax Court held that the entire value of the jointly owned property ($95,000) was includable in the gross estate of the decedent, except the $16,485.19 contributed by her son. . . .

The obvious scheme of §2040[(a)] is to recapture the entire value of jointly held property into a decedent's gross estate, notwithstanding the fact that the decedent may have made a gift under local law of one-half of the property. Section 2040[(a)] looks to the source of the consideration represented by the property and disregards legal title. In a case like that before us, the value of property is includable in the decedent's gross estate to the extent that the decedent furnished the consideration for acquiring the property; to the extent that present value was supplied by consideration in money or money's worth flowing from the other joint tenant, that value is excluded from decedent's estate. The Tax Court's determination literally meets the language of §2040[(a)] that the entire value of the jointly-owned property at the date-of-death of the decedent ($95,000.00) should be included in her gross estate, except "... such part ... shown to have originally belonged to such other person and never to have been received or acquired by the latter from the decedent for less than an adequate and full consideration in money or money's worth. ..." In the case at bar, the excluded portion was $16,145.19, which the record showed was the cost as well as the present value of the son's contribution.

The Tax Court opinion in *Peters* contains the following statement:

> Limiting ourselves strictly to the facts of the instant case, it is our opinion that the record before us warrants a conclusion that the sum of money which fairly represents the property or interest originally belonging to the surviving joint tenant is the amount of money actually expended by him therefor or $16,485.19. There has been no showing by the petitioner that such property or interest has appreciated in value over its cost[16] and no testimony adduced by respondent to weaken the evidence of cost as representing value. It follows that the amount to be included in decedent's gross estate on account of the value of the property "held as joint tenants by the decedent" and the surviving joint tenant is $78,514.81 ($95,000 minus $16,485.19).

Notice that, in *Peters,* all they were fighting over was whether to apportion any part of the appreciation post-contribution to the joint tenancy, as if the survivor's contribution acquired some part of it. What effect would it have on the amount included in the decedent's gross estate if it could be proven that the value of the improvements contributed by the surviving tenant (the decedent's son) in *Peters* had appreciated in value at the time of the decedent's death? What would be the effect if the improvements made by both the decedent and the son had appreciated or depreciated in value? In Lowndes, Kramer, & McCord, ESTATE & GIFT TAXES §11.2 at 273 (3d ed. 1974), *Peters* is described as holding that "where the contribution of the surviving joint tenant was in the form of funds expended for improvements and additions, only the funds actually expended ... may be excluded from the decedent's gross estate."

12.   *Transfers of Joint Interests.* Assume that *A* is a joint tenant who provided all the consideration to acquire property and that the percentage of consideration rule would cause the full value of the property to be included in *A*'s gross estate under §2040(a). What will be the tax

---

16. If such a showing had been made it might have been necessary for us to devise a formula or ratio of our own.

consequences of A's transferring A's entire interest in the property inter vivos in such manner as to cause the transferred property to be included in A's gross estate under some other inclusion provision?

The issue could arise in connection with a variety of transfers of joint tenancy interests: a transfer of the jointly held property subject to a retained life income interest; a change of the form of ownership from a joint tenancy to a tenancy in common; or a transfer of the jointly held property to a trust that is revocable by A. It is only in the case of a transfer to a revocable trust that the government has succeeded in including more than the value of the transferred interest in the decedent's gross estate, and the government has virtually conceded this issue in the case of the other types of transfers. See Rev. Rul. 69-577.

For example, A paid $100,000 for Blackacre, which A acquired in joint tenancy with right of survivorship with B. As a result, A made a taxable gift to B in the amount of $50,000 less one annual exclusion. If Blackacre remained in joint tenancy ownership until the death of A or B, the estate tax consequences would depend upon which one died first. If A died first, the full estate tax value of Blackacre would be includible in A's gross estate under §2040(a), and the taxable gift would be purged from A's adjusted taxable gifts. If B died first, no part of the value of Blackacre would be includible in B's gross estate. Now, suppose that A and B decided not to retain ownership of Blackacre in joint tenancy form. Instead, they:

(a)   severed the joint tenancy and converted their ownership of Blackacre into an equal tenancy in common; or

(b)   transferred Blackacre to an irrevocable trust, directing the trustee to pay the income to them in equal shares during their joint lives and thereafter all to the survivor for life.

In either case, if A dies first, 50% of the estate tax value of Blackacre will be includible in A's gross estate (under §2033 in (a); under §2036(a)(1) in (b)). Estate of Sullivan v. Commissioner, 175 F.2d 657 (9th Cir. 1949); United States v. Heasty, 370 F.2d 525 (10th Cir. 1966); Glaser v. United States, 306 F.2d 57 (7th Cir. 1962); Rev. Rul. 69-577. Cf. Rev. Rul. 81-227. The taxable gift presumably would remain part of A's adjusted taxable gifts base for computation of the estate tax under §2001(b).

In either (a) or (b), if B dies first, 50% of the estate tax value of Blackacre will be includible in B's gross estate (under §2033 in (a); under §2036(a)(1) in (b)). Rev. Rul. 76-348. Cf. Rev. Rul. 81-227.

(c)   If the trust in (b) was revocable rather than irrevocable, and A died first, Estate of Horner v. Commissioner, 130 F.2d 649 (3d Cir. 1942), *aff'g* 44 B.T.A. 1136 (1941), held that the full value of Blackacre was includible in A's gross estate. Presumably this means that A's adjusted taxable gifts base would be purged of the taxable gift made by A upon creation of the joint tenancy. If B died first, Estate of May v. Commissioner,

37 T.C.M. (CCH) 137 (1978), held that no part of the value of Blackacre was includible in B's gross estate.

Suppose that (instead of any of the foregoing transactions) A and B joined in giving Blackacre to C in fee simple absolute. A and B each filed a gift tax return reporting a gift to C of 50% of the gift tax value of Blackacre. Both portions of the gift qualify for the gift tax annual exclusion (as if this was a split gift by spouses). Upon the respective deaths of A and B, the amount of the taxable gift each made to C would be included in each donor's adjusted taxable gifts base under §2001(b).[17] In addition, the gross estate of either A or B (or both) who dies within three years of the gift to C would include the §2035(b) amount of any gift tax paid by that decedent (or his or her estate) on the gift.[18]

13. *Simultaneous Death of Joint Tenants.* This topic is confusing and complex. Think about how you would fashion a proper tax-policy based but easy result. Consider the §2013 previously taxed property credit. Also think about the proper application of §2040(a) if the tenants who die under these circumstances are spouses: would it matter?

Revenue Ruling 76-303

The Internal Revenue Service has reconsidered the holdings of Rev. Rul. 66-60, 1966-1 C.B. 221, with regard to the includibility of the value of the property held in [joint] tenancy . . . in the gross estate of the [joint tenants].

In Rev. Rul. 66-60, [joint tenants] were killed in an automobile accident under circumstances wherein there was not sufficient evidence as to which [joint tenant] may have died first. [One of the joint tenants, A,] furnished the entire consideration for the purchase of certain realty which was held by them. . . . The decedents resided and perished in a state which has adopted the [original] Uniform Simultaneous Death Act, and the property in question was located in that state. Section 3 of the Act provides that "[w]here there is no sufficient evidence that two joint tenants or tenants by the entirety have died otherwise than simultaneously the property so held shall be distributed one-half as if one had survived and one-half as if the other had survived." . . .

Rev. Rul. 66-60 holds that inasmuch as the estate of the [other joint tenant, B,] is entitled to a half interest in the property, one-half

---

17. A's adjusted taxable gifts base also would include the taxable gift A made to B when the joint tenancy originally was created.

18.   If A were to die within three years of the original creation of the joint tenancy, §2035(b) would also include in A's gross estate the amount of any gift tax paid on the taxable gift to B.

of the value of the property is includible in [*B*'s] gross estate under §2033 of the Code.

Rev. Rul. 66-60 also holds that, inasmuch as the property in question was held in [joint] tenancy . . . at the time of [*A*'s] death and since there is no evidence to indicate that [*B*] furnished any consideration for the property, the full value of the property is includible in [*A*'s] gross estate under §2040[(a)] of the Code.

However, in order for any of the value of jointly held property . . . to be includible in a decedent's gross estate under §2040[(a)] of the Code, the decedent must be survived by a joint tenant. . . . Under the [original] Uniform Simultaneous Death Act, [*A* and *B*] are each considered to have survived with respect to one-half of the property. Thus, §2040[(a)] will be applicable for determining the includibility of the value of one-half of the property in each of their gross estates. Since there is no evidence to indicate [that *B*] furnished any consideration for the property, the value of one-half of the property with respect to which [*B*] is considered to have survived is includible in [*A*'s] gross estate under §2040[(a)]. Since [*A*] furnished all the consideration for the property, none of the value of the one-half of the property with respect to which [*A*] is considered to have survived is includible in [*B*'s] gross estate under §2040[(a)].

In addition, since each is considered to have survived as to one-half of the property, each is considered to have acquired an absolute, sole ownership interest in one-half of the property before death. Thus, the value of one-half of the property is includible in each of their gross estates under §2033 of the Code.

Rev. Rul. 66-60 stated that the value of one-half of the property was includible in [*B*'s] gross estate under §2033 of the Code because [*B*'s] estate was entitled to a half interest in the property. However, the mere fact that property becomes part of a decedent's estate does not make the property includible in a decedent's gross estate under §2033. See Rev. Rul. 75-126, 1975-1 C.B. 296; Rev. Rul. 75-127, 1975-1 C.B. 297; and Rev. Rul. 75-145, 1975-1 C.B. 298, where the decedent had no interest in the property at death. In the instant case, the requirement of §2033 is satisfied with respect to the one-half of the property as to which [*B*] is deemed to have survived and which [*B*] therefore is considered to have owned at death.

Thus, the result here is the same as in Rev. Rul. 66-60, that is, inclusion of the full value of the property in [*A*'s] gross estate and inclusion of the value of one-half of the property in [*B*'s] gross estate. However, the basis for inclusion in each of the gross estates is different.

Rev. Rul. 66-60 is hereby modified.

If *A* and *B* had employed a presumption of survivorship that overcame the original Uniform Simultaneous Death Act, would the better tax result be generated by presuming *A* to have survived, or *B*? The Uniform Simultaneous Death Act was revised in 1991. Section 4 of the revised USDA provides that, if it is not established by clear and convincing evidence that one joint tenant survived the other by 120 hours, half of the property passes as if one joint tenant had survived the other and the other half passes as if the other had survived. Also consider whether the results should differ if *A* or *B* survived by 121 hours.

PART C.   TERMINATION OF CONCURRENT OWNERSHIP DURING LIFE

The preceding material demonstrates that the transfer or "termination" of concurrently owned property interests before death may have both estate and gift tax consequences. This final part focuses more closely on just the gift tax consequences. One of the difficulties of exploring this subject is that much of the stated law on the question was contained in the regulations that were promulgated under §2515, which was repealed. Some of those regulations were not interpretive of the provisions of §2515 itself, and would seem to have continuing validity.

Concurrent ownership is "terminated" if (1) the tenants become tenants in common in the property, or (2) all or a portion of the property is sold, exchanged, or otherwise disposed of. An increase in the indebtedness encumbering property held jointly constitutes a partial termination of the tenancy in the amount of the increase, except to the extent the increase is offset by additions to the jointly held property made within a reasonable time after the increase was incurred. Treas. Reg. §25.2515-1(d)(2).

Basically, gift tax consequences on termination can arise in two directions: There may be a gift from one tenant to another tenant, there may be a gift by one or more tenants to a third person, or there may be both. Let's explore each of these directions with respect to a joint tenancy in which the tenants are not married to each other, and then in which they are.

14.   *Termination of Non-Spousal Tenancies.*

Gift From One Tenant to the Other.   A gift between concurrent owners occurs to the extent that any proceeds received by them on termination is disproportionate to the ratio of the actuarial value of their respective interests in the property immediately prior to the termination. A joint tenancy commonly can be severed by either tenant unilaterally, in which case the value of the tenants' interests is equal.[19] Thus, if *A* and *B* own stock as joint tenants, a sale of the stock for $100,000 would constitute a gift from one tenant to the other to the extent the proceeds were not divided equally — $50,000 each.[20] If *A* received $35,000 of the proceeds, however, and *B* the remaining $65,000, then *A* would have made a gift to *B* of $15,000. Because of the gift tax annual exclusion, the amount of *A*'s *taxable* gift might be less; this would depend upon the extent to which, if any, *A* previously had made annual exclusion gifts to *B* during the year.

Gifts From Tenants to Third Parties. If the concurrent owners give the property to a third party, the full value of the property constitutes a gift in whatever proportion each concurrent owner chooses to report on a gift tax return; to the extent an owner's reported gift to the third party is less than the owner's proportionate entitlement, however, the owner is deemed to make a gift to the other concurrent owner(s). The rationale for this treatment is that the owners are treated as having divided the proceeds of a termination between themselves and then having transferred those proceeds as individual gifts to the third party or the other owner(s). Cf. Treas. Reg. §25.2515-1(d)(3). There is a deemed gift to the other concurrent owner(s), in addition to the gift to the third party to the extent the amount that each concurrent owner reports as a gift to the third party is less than the actuarial value of that owner's interest in the property immediately prior to the gift.

To illustrate, suppose that *A* and *B* own stock worth $100,000 as joint tenants, which they give to *C*. *A* files a gift tax return reporting a $30,000 gift to *C* (which may be reduced by reflecting the gift tax annual exclusion, to the extent available); *B* files a gift tax return reporting a $70,000 gift to *C* (which also may be reduced by reflecting the gift tax annual exclusion, to the extent available). In addition, *A* is treated as having made a gift to *B* of $20,000 (which may be reduced by reflecting the gift tax annual exclusion, to the extent available). If, on the other hand, *A* and *B* each filed gift tax returns reporting gifts to *C* of $50,000 each (which may be reduced by reflecting the gift tax annual exclusion, to the extent available), there would be no gifts as between *A* and *B*.

In the common case of a joint tenancy that is terminable by any owner's unilateral action, any tenant may make a gift to a third party and thereby terminate the joint tenancy. If less than all tenants make such a gift, the transaction is treated for gift tax purposes as if the donor tenant(s) received the value of their interests as the proceeds of a termination and made gifts

---

19.   In the much less common case of a joint tenancy that cannot be severed by either tenant alone, and in the case of a tenancy by the entireties, the value of each tenant's interest must be determined actuarially as of the date of termination.

20.   Similarly, no gift would occur if the tenants severed the joint tenancy by transforming it into a tenancy in common in which each had an equal share.

thereof, but the nondonor tenant(s) retained their interests in the property as the proceeds of a termination. Cf. Treas. Reg. §25.2515-1(d)(3). Because no tenant has the power to transfer more than their interest, however, a unilateral termination will not constitute a gift from one tenant to the other.

15.   *Termination of Spousal Tenancies.*

Gifts Between the Spouses.   If a tenancy by the entirety or a joint tenancy in which the only joint tenants are married to each other is terminated by selling the property or by converting the form of ownership to a tenancy in common, theoretically the same analysis outlined above is applicable to determine whether division of the property or its proceeds constitutes a gift from one spouse to the other. As a practical matter, however, the exercise is pointless and need not be undertaken. The gift tax marital deduction (and the annual exclusion) prevents any gift from being *taxable* and, under §6019, no gift tax return needs to be filed reporting gifts that are fully covered by the deduction or exclusion or both.

In the event of an automatic severance of a tenancy by the entirety upon divorce, or the severance of a joint tenancy by order of the divorce decree, §2516 might not apply, because the "transfer" was not made pursuant to a written agreement, but the *Harris* doctrine should prevent gift tax consequences.

Gifts to Third Parties.   If instead of selling the property the spouses join in giving it to a third party, each spouse can file a return reporting a gift in any amount as long as their combined gifts equal the full value of the property. The spouses need not be concerned about having made taxable gifts between themselves, because of the gift tax marital deduction. In addition, each spouse may be entitled to a gift tax annual exclusion for his or her portion of the gift to the third party, regardless of whether they split their gifts under §2513.

If spouses hold property as joint tenants and either spouse can terminate the tenancy unilaterally, either spouse is empowered to make a gift to a third party of his or her interest in the property and that spouse would make such a gift measured simply by the value of the interest transferred to that party, reduced by any allowable annual exclusion. The other spouse could (but need not) split that gift under §2513.

Chapter 8

LIFE INSURANCE

Code References: *Estate Tax: §§2035, 2042, 2206*
Gift Tax: Treas. Reg. §25.2512-6(a)
Income Tax: §101
States: Revised Uniform Estate Tax Apportionment Act

Life insurance is a major source of wealth in many decedents' estates and presents some of the few truly effective planning opportunities available for shifting wealth and providing estate liquidity. Regrettably, the planning pitfalls are as numerous and substantial as are the benefits. Fortunately, however, most of the law has become reasonably well-settled and is relatively cognizable, as this Chapter reveals.

In case you are not familiar with insurance terminology, we begin with a description of the parties. An "insurer" issues insurance policies on the lives of "insureds." The "policyholder" owns the policy and the economic rights in it and powers over it (e.g., the right to surrender the policy for cash, to borrow against the policy, to name the beneficiary, etc.). The policyholder designates the "beneficiaries," who receive the proceeds of the insurance when the policy "matures." The policyholder and the insured usually are one and the same, but not always. In sophisticated plans, the policy often is owned by a trustee of a trust created by the insured or members of the insured's family. Typically that trust is irrevocable — an irrevocable life insurance trust (ILIT) — although it might be amendable by a trust protector or other third party.

The basic attribute of life insurance is risk shifting — it insures against the risk that the insured will die during a stated period. In that respect "life" insurance is a misnomer because this product insures against *dying* too soon. Life insurance is designed to compensate for the financial loss that beneficiaries of a policy will suffer when the insured dies. The cost of this risk coverage (the pure insurance cost of a policy) is determined roughly in the manner below.

Assume the insured, I, is X years old and in good health. To underwrite $1,000 of life insurance for a one-year period, assume that the insurer's actuarial tables indicate that 1% of persons of X age will die during that year. Thus, a premium charge of approximately 1% ($10) will cover the risk of I's death for that year. In addition, the insurer has management and selling expenses that will be passed on to policyholders, so I's premium will be somewhat greater than $10. If the insurer is a profit-making "stock" company, the premium may include an allowance for a profit to pass to its shareholders. If the insurer is a "mutual" company (meaning its policyholders own the company and are like shareholders, in that they participate in the insurer's earnings), the company will charge a larger premium than it reasonably expects to need and, at the end of each year, will return the amount that exceeds its actual needs as a "dividend." Policies that pay dividends are said to "participate." Some stock companies now offer participating insurance to be competitive with mutual companies.

"Term insurance" provides pure insurance coverage for a stated term (usually one year). In the case of I, the annual premium of a $1,000 term policy was a little more than $10. If I wishes to continue that coverage for an additional year, the premium will be higher because the percentage of persons $X + 1$ years of age who will die during the year is greater than the percentage of persons only X years of age. Thus, under straight term insurance, the premium cost will increase each year. Term insurance purchased for a specific term, such as one or five years, typically has additional rights, such as an automatic right to renew the policy at the end of each term without evidence of insurability, and also may have a right to convert the policy into another form of insurance — permanent — that does not lapse.

The premium cost of term insurance will increase as the insured grows older and eventually the premium becomes prohibitively expensive. As an alternative to this steady increase in the annual premium, the insured can purchase life insurance for a term certain (such as 20 years) and pay a level premium each year for a smaller amount of insurance. Thus, the annual premium remains constant but the amount of insurance coverage declines. This type of coverage is referred to as "declining term" or "decreasing term" insurance. It often is tied to an outstanding debt (such as a mortgage or car loan) so that the term and face amount of the policy and the outstanding balance of the debt match; such "credit life" insurance is designed to leave the insured's beneficiaries debt free if death occurs unexpectedly.

A second type of life insurance, "ordinary" or "permanent" life (sometimes called "straight life" or "whole life"), combines the purchase of pure risk coverage with an investment element. Part of the premium is charged for the pure insurance coverage (including the company's expenses), and part of the premium is treated as an investment with (or perhaps "in" is more accurate) the insurer. Referred to as the policyholder's "reserve" in the policy, this investment is an equity interest that appreciates in value each year, often at no less than a minimum rate guaranteed by the insurer. The terms "straight life" or "whole life" refer to how long the premium is payable (every year until death, often subject to a maximum period) and are to be compared to such alternatives as "65-pay life" or "20-year-pay life" (which mean all premiums needed to fully finance the pure insurance and investment portions of the policy for life will be paid by the age of 65 or over a 20-year term certain).

A modified form of permanent life coverage is "variable life" insurance, which may pay a fluctuating amount of coverage and may exceed a guaranteed minimum. The policyholder's reserve and the death benefit that it finances vary according to the relative success or failure of the insurer's investment program. As a modern creation, variable life insurance has not yet become as popular as ordinary life insurance and presents a degree of risk to the policyholder that is not present in the more traditional coverage; it is very attractive when the economy is strong and investment results are favorable, but it provides less coverage than needed (or hoped) if investment returns are below the insurer's expectations or representations.

Another variation of ordinary life is "universal life" insurance, which is a form of coverage that combines a volatile rate of interest on the investment reserve with a term insurance component. A typical high-yield policy has a pure term insurance death benefit that is smaller than the investment portion of the policy, with the total amount payable at death being the sum of this pure death benefit and the accumulated reserve. Universal life policies permit the insured to increase or decrease the pure death benefit (within certain defined limits) from time to time, and appreciation in the reserve fluctuates depending upon market conditions. At one time, the investment return on universal life was higher than that generated by most other types of insurance; but in a sluggish economy this product, like variable life insurance, will perform more poorly than will a traditional permanent insurance policy.

Many universal life policies also specify that premiums can be paid with a portion of the investment return and were sold under projections that showed such strong returns that the premium "vanished" early in the policy life. In fact, however, they performed so poorly that the policyholder was obliged to pay premiums for a longer period and in a greater amount than anticipated. Indeed, some were so expensive and the projections so unrealistic that the policyholder was unable to shoulder the burden that the investment performance was supposed to carry and had to allow the policy to lapse. The projected advantages of universal life (higher yields on the investment portion, greater flexibility in choosing the amount of pure death risk coverage, and lower commission costs) must be weighed against these risks, and the desirability of this type of coverage also depends upon whether the policy qualifies as insurance for income tax purposes, which is discussed beginning at page 440.

The policyholder's premiums generate little or no reserve in the policy in the first several policy years of most ordinary life policies because the initial premiums are allocated by the insurer to pay the company's expenses, including the selling agent's commission. After this start-up period, the reserve begins to increase due to appreciation in the established reserve and because the policyholder pays additional premiums. Because the amount payable at death typically is a fixed amount, the insurance risk coverage purchased by the policyholder is the difference between the amount payable at death and the policyholder's reserve. The reserve (which represents the policyholder's equity) increases each year, so the policyholder purchases less true insurance each year and the premiums for the policy can remain constant (indeed, they may even decline). In effect, the policyholder combines an investment program with a relatively secure rate of return with declining term life insurance coverage.

A policyholder may borrow against the policy reserve, or may surrender the policy for its cash value. Because of administrative costs, the amount that can be realized (the "cash surrender value") by surrendering the policy or borrowing on it is slightly less than the total reserve. The cash surrender value at a given date typically can be determined from tables included in the policy itself and, after approximately five years from the date a policy was issued, the cash surrender value will be close to the policyholder's reserve and can be used as an approximation of the reserve for planning purposes. Upon request, the insurer will provide the policyholder with a statement of the current value of the reserve, which is the more accurate value.

When the insured dies, the policy proceeds are payable according to the settlement option elected by the policy owner or, if none was selected, by the beneficiary (typically after the insured's death). These settlement options permit an election either to have the insurance proceeds paid in one lump sum or to have the insurance company retain the proceeds (which earn interest for the beneficiary) and pay them under one of the following general types of options (or some combination thereof):

(1) *Interest only (deposit) option.* Interest is paid currently to the beneficiary, who is entitled to change to any other settlement option (including a lump-sum payment); some policies require the beneficiary to make such an election within a stated period after the insured's death, but many policies permit the election to be made at any time. The purpose of the deposit option is to provide interest on proceeds left with the insurer while the beneficiary decides which other settlement to elect.

(2) *Fixed period option.* The proceeds are paid in installments of no less than a specified amount over a fixed period and, if the policy earns more than the minimum guaranteed interest for any installment period, the installments paid to the beneficiary for that period are increased accordingly.

(3) *Fixed amount option.* The proceeds are payable in a specified minimum number of installments of a fixed amount. If the policy earns more than the guaranteed minimum income, the number of payments is increased, but the amount of each installment payment remains constant.

(4) *Straight life annuity.* A periodic payment of a fixed dollar amount for the life of the beneficiary. Recently, some life insurance companies have offered a variation of the straight life annuity, called the "variable life annuity," under which the periodic payments vary according to the company's investment experience.

(5) *Self and survivor annuity.* An annuity of a specified amount, paid periodically to the primary beneficiary for life, and then to a named secondary beneficiary for life (often in an annuity amount that is smaller than the primary beneficiary's annuity).

(6) *Joint and survivor annuity.* An annuity for the joint lives of two beneficiaries and for the life of the survivor. (The term "joint and survivor annuity" sometimes is used improperly to describe a self and survivor annuity option).

(7) *Annuity with a refund or guaranteed payment.* A refund feature provides that, if less than a specified amount has been paid when the last annuitant dies, the difference is payable in a lump sum to a designated beneficiary. A guaranteed payment annuity provides that payments will be made for no less than a specified period of time regardless of when the beneficiaries die.

Although these settlement options are not as flexible as investing the proceeds in a trust, they are not entirely inflexible. For example, a fixed period option may provide larger installment payments for part of the period than at others, but the size of the payments typically must be fixed when the election is made.

From this attenuated description of the types of life insurance policies available and their various features, three economic components of life insurance are identifiable: (1) the *term insurance coverage component* (coverage against the risk of the insured's death within the period covered by the last premium paid); (2) the *right of continuation component* (the right to continue having insurance coverage at a fixed price, regardless of the insured's health, beyond the period covered by the last premium); and (3) the *equity or terminal reserve component.* Not all life insurance policies consist of all three components. Nevertheless, it is important to keep these components in mind because they are crucial to the analysis of the proper tax treatment of assignments of life insurance policies.

Illustration: Think back to §2036(a)(1). *I* was the owner and the insured of a life insurance policy. On *I*'s death, *B* was entitled to the life insurance proceeds but elected a deposit option under which *B* receives interest income from the insurer for life and, at *B*'s death, the proceeds are payable to *B*'s child. The proceeds will be included in *B*'s gross estate as if *B* received them and set up a trust. If instead *I* had elected a deposit option for *B* prior to *I*'s death (and if *B* did not have the right to elect a different settlement option within the one-year period after *I*'s death allowed by many policies), then §2036(a)(1) would not apply. See pages 195-196. Note that §2039 might cause part of the proceeds to be included in *B*'s gross estate if *B* had elected an installment option with payments over in certain cases to a named beneficiary (e.g., a self and survivor annuity, an annuity with either a refund feature or a guaranteed number of payments, or a fixed-sum or a fixed-period option). See Chapter 9.

No amount of the trust corpus will be included in *B*'s gross estate if *I* elected a settlement option under which the income is payable to *B* for life and the corpus is payable to *I*'s children upon *B*'s death. If *B* were given the power during life to appoint the trust corpus to those adult children whom *B* had no obligation to support, that power also would not cause the corpus to be includible in *B*'s gross estate under §2041 (although exercise might trigger a gift tax, as noted at page 919. See Rev. Rul. 79-154).

1.   *Income Tax Exclusion of Proceeds from Gross Income.*
Section 101 excludes life insurance proceeds from the beneficiary's gross income, subject to the §101(a)(2) "transfer for value" exception (noted in a moment). Proceeds payable in a lump sum present no problems under the §101 exclusion. The exclusion becomes more complicated if the proceeds are retained by the insurer under a settlement option. For obvious reasons, interest paid to the beneficiary on those proceeds is includible in the beneficiary's gross income. Payments made to a beneficiary in installments (e.g., under an annuity option, or a fixed amount or fixed period option), contain a principal portion that is excluded from the beneficiary's gross income and an interest element, which is includible in the beneficiary's gross income.[1]

Transfer for Value Rule.   An important exception to the general exclusion of lump-sum insurance payments from gross income is the §101(a)(2) "transfer for value" rule. If a life insurance policy was acquired for valuable consideration (other than from the insurer) the amount of proceeds excluded from gross income is limited to the consideration and premiums paid by the policyholder. This rule does *not* apply if a transferee

---

1.   The exclusions of the principal portion of installment payments continues after the amount so excluded exceeds the face amount of the insurance. Take an example in which the face amount of a matured life insurance policy is $100,000, and the beneficiary elected to receive $12,000 per year for life and the beneficiary has a 10-year life expectancy. Of each payment, $2,000 is taxable income and $10,000 is excluded from income. After 10 years the beneficiary will have excluded a total of $100,000, which equals the face amount of the insurance. If the beneficiary outlives the life expectancy, $10,000 of the $12,000 payment received in the eleventh year still is excluded from the beneficiary's income. For commercial annuities beginning after 1986, §72(b)(2) terminates the exclusion once the cost has been recovered. No change was made to §101, however, and it appears that the amendment of §72 will not be deemed to have amended §101 by inference. See §101(d) and Treas. Reg. §1.101-4 for a discussion of the manner in which the interest portion of such payments is determined.

received the policy without consideration, or if the transferee was (1) the insured, (2) a partner of the insured, (3) a partnership in which the insured was a partner, or (4) a corporation in which the insured was a shareholder or officer. Curiously, other shareholders of a corporation are not granted the same protection from §101(a)(2) as are other partners in a partnership of which the insured was a partner. Nor is the insured's spouse granted the same protection. Thus, for example, in Estate of Rath v. United States, 608 F.2d 254 (9th Cir. 1979), the insured's surviving spouse purchased a policy on the insured's life from a corporation of which the insured was a major shareholder and §101(a)(2) was applicable, making the proceeds of the policy (less consideration and premiums paid by the spouse) includible in the spouse's gross income.[2] Converting a tax free flow of insurance proceeds into an income taxable amount is a huge mistake if done by inadvertence, and often can be avoided with a little forethought and proper attention to detail.

Appreciation of the Reserve. A policyholder's reserve or equity interest in an ordinary life insurance policy appreciates over time. To the extent this appreciation is not attributable to the payment of additional premiums it constitutes "earnings" from the policyholder's investment, but these earnings are not taxed to the policyholder during life.[3] The rationale given for not taxing this "internal build-up" to the policyholder is that the income has not been realized in a tax sense. See Cohen v. Commissioner, 39 T.C. 1055 (1963). On the death of the insured, the face amount of the proceeds payable to the beneficiary includes this appreciation, but the full proceeds still are excluded from the beneficiary's gross income. As just this abbreviated introduction shows, life insurance holds special tax benefits if certain obvious mistakes are avoided.

---

2. An interesting question is whether the underlying purpose of §1041 (excluding recognition of gain or loss from transfers between spouses) will be applied to §101(a)(2) and affect the treatment of a spouse. Section 1041 was adopted after the court of appeal decided *Rath*. Although §1041 does not address this issue, it might influence a court's application of §101(a)(2).

3. A participating insurance policy dividend paid by the company to the policyholder each year is regarded as a return of premiums previously paid and is not an income item that is includible in the policyholder's gross income. Even dividends paid on paid-up policies for which no further premium payments are due are excluded from gross income because those dividends are treated as a reduction of premiums paid in prior years. If, however, the policyholder does not withdraw the dividends from the insurance company but instead leaves them on deposit with the insurer to earn interest, the interest credited to the accumulated dividends is included in the policyholder's gross income just like interest credited to a savings account deposit.

A policyholder who sells an insurance policy to a third party will recognize a gain on the sale if the amount realized exceeds basis in the policy. Although all premiums previously paid by the policyholder (less dividends received) are included in basis, the value of the policy due to appreciation may be greater. The amount realized therefore easily could exceed the seller's basis.

2.   *Estate Tax Policy.*   In evaluating the appropriate wealth transfer tax treatment of life insurance, the proper and widely acknowledged view is that, when the insured dies, the policyholder's investment in the policy (the reserve or equity) passes to the named beneficiaries and, in addition, the insurer pays those beneficiaries the proceeds of the pure risk coverage of the policy as well.[4] Thus, the beneficiaries receive the policyholder's equity interest and a death benefit payment, which conforms with the actuarial determination of the premiums charged for a policy as the amount needed to purchase pure risk coverage for the difference between the face amount of the policy and the policyholder's equity in it.

Insurance proceeds receivable by the insured's personal representative ("executor" under the Code terminology) are included in the insured's gross estate under §2042(1), which has been part of the federal estate tax since 1918. The explicit reference to amounts payable to the insured's executor, although not entirely free of ambiguity, has been deemed to encompass proceeds payable to, on behalf of, or available to the insured's estate. See Treas. Reg. §20.2042-1(b). Although the 1916 estate tax contained no special provision concerning life insurance, the Commissioner had no difficulty including the proceeds of life insurance payable to an insured policyholder's executor under the original predecessor to §2033. H.R. Rep. No. 767, 65th Cong., 2d Sess. 22 (1918), in 1939-1 C.B. (pt. 2) 86, 101, explained that the 1918 enactment of what is now §2042(1) was a clarification that proceeds "payable to the executor or to the estate" are includible. Moreover, it stated that enactment would "serve the further purpose of putting on notice those who acquaint themselves with the statute for the purpose of making more definite plans for the disposition of their property."

Insurance proceeds in well-planned estates are not often made payable to or for the benefit of an insured's personal representative. Some insurance is made available in this way for liquidity or similar purposes, but only if the insured was the policyholder and the proceeds would have been included in the insured's gross estate anyway. If a third party as policyholder named the insured's estate as beneficiary of a policy on the insured's life, however, it is likely that the proceeds would not be includible in the insured's gross estate under §2033. See page 59 and Connecticut Bank & Trust Co. v. United States, 465 F.2d 760 (2d Cir. 1972), involving the receipt of wrongful death damages by the decedent's personal representative. If §2033 does not apply, then §2042(1) serves a greater purpose than mere clarification.

The original version of §2033 was inadequate to deal with the situation now covered by §2042(2), which was the primary motivation for enactment in 1918 of the special provision addressing life insurance. Again, House Ways and Means Committee H.R. Rep. No. 767, 65th Cong., 2d Sess. 22 (1918), in 1939-1 C.B. (pt. 2) 86, 101–102, explained this point:

---

4.   See, e.g., Old Kent Bank & Trust Co. v. United States, 430 F.2d 392 (6th Cir. 1970).

The provision with respect to specific beneficiaries has been included for the reason that insurance payable to such beneficiaries usually passes under a contract to which the insurance company and the individual beneficiary are the parties in interest and over which the executor exercises no control. Amounts passing in this way are not liable for expenses of administration or debts of the decedent and therefore do not fall within the existing provisions defining the gross estate.[5] It has been brought to the attention of the committee that wealthy persons have and now anticipate resorting to this method of defeating the estate tax. Agents of insurance companies have openly urged persons of wealth to take out additional insurance payable to specific beneficiaries for the reason that such insurance would not be included in the gross estate.

Under the 1918 Act, proceeds receivable by beneficiaries other than the insured's executor were includible in the insured's gross estate only if the insurance was "taken out by the decedent upon his own life," which was not clear, but it soon was accepted that the statute did not require the insured to apply initially for the policy.

The regulations vacillated as to whether the insured must have paid premiums on the policy or must have died possessing "incidents of ownership" in the policy. The 1929 regulations took the position that both the premium payment and the incidents of ownership requirements had to be satisfied, but the 1934 regulations stated that satisfaction of either requisite was sufficient. Again in 1941 the regulations were changed to provide that premium payment was the exclusive requirement, which lasted only until 1942, when Congress took the matter out of the hands of the Commissioner by amending the statute in several respects. It eliminated the requirement that the policies be "taken out by the decedent upon his own life." In its place Congress adopted essentially the position taken by the Commissioner in the 1934 regulations — that satisfaction of either the premium payment or the incidents of ownership requirement was sufficient to cause inclusion of the proceeds. It further provided that a retained reversion was not an "incident of ownership" and that, if only the premium payment test were satisfied, only a fraction of the proceeds comparable to the portion of all premiums paid by the insured would be included.[6]

The latest alteration came in the 1954 Code, which made the incidents of ownership requirement the exclusive test for inclusion of insurance proceeds payable to a person other than the insured's executor. The premium

---

5.   Nor would such amounts have met a third requirement of the predecessor to §2033, that the assets be "subject to distribution as part of [the decedent's] estate." —ED.

6.   The constitutionality of the premium payment test was upheld in United States v. Manufacturers National Bank, 363 U.S. 194 (1960).

payment test was eliminated. Section 2042(2) also expressly treats certain reversionary interests owned by an insured in a policy on the insured's life as an incident of ownership, thereby reversing the position taken in 1942.

3.   *Elimination of the Premium Payment Test.*   The really important change was that Congress eliminated the premium payment test in 1954. It did so because "no other property is subject to estate tax where the decedent initially purchased it and then long before his death gave away all rights to the property and to discriminate against life insurance in this regard is not justified." H.R. Rep. No. 1337, 83d Cong., 2d Sess. 91 (1954).

H.R. Rep. No. 1337, 83d Cong., 2d Sess. B14 (1954), a dissenting report, stated in part:

> It is sought to justify this change as merely putting life insurance on a par with other property which may be given away free from estate tax. . . . But life insurance is not like any other property. It is inherently testamentary in nature. It is designed, in effect, to serve as a will, regardless of its investment features. Where the insured has paid the premiums on life insurance for the purpose of adding to what he leaves behind at his death for his beneficiaries, the insurance proceeds should be included in his taxable state.

Lowndes, Kramer, & McCord, ESTATE & GIFT TAXES 327–328 (3d ed. 1974)[7], a highly-regarded treatise, is critical of the elimination of the premium payment test:

> Life insurance should not be taxed like other property because it is not like other property. Regardless of whether or not life insurance is "inherently testamentary," which, after all, depends on how one defines "inherently testamentary," the abolition of the premium payment test opens the door for substantial estate tax avoidance. A man can pass along unlimited amounts of property at his death without encountering the estate tax by investing in life insurance and divesting himself of all incidents of ownership in the insurance during his life.

> It is true that a man can avoid an estate tax if he makes a complete gift of other kinds of property during his life. He will, however, incur a gift tax on the property given away. Moreover, he will suffer the inconvenience which the loss of the property entails. Life insurance may be given away before it has built up any substantial reserve values with little or no gift tax. The principal present enjoyment which an insured derives from life insurance is

---

7. Copyright © by the West Publishing Company. Reprinted with permission.

the thought that it will take care of his dependents after his death. In the ordinary case this will not be diminished by an assignment of the insurance to the intended beneficiary. It is true that a man who irrevocably assigns his insurance during his life cannot cash in the insurance to meet financial emergencies which may later arise. This detriment may, however, be more theoretical than actual, since the assignee will normally be one of the insured's intimate family group who will readily re-assign the insurance should the need arise.

Special considerations apply if a policy is assigned within three years of the donor's death, or if the donor pays any of the post-assignment premiums within that period; these are discussed beginning at page 485. Putting that aside to question whether elimination of the premium payment test opens a tax loophole, consider the following gifts of life insurance policies that were not made within three years of the donor's death and in which the donee pays all premiums post-assignment:

(a) Insured, I, owned a fully paid-up $50,000 policy insuring I's life, which I gave to P. The cash surrender value of the policy at the date of the gift was $42,000 and, because the policy was fully paid up, no further premiums were due. I died four years later, the $50,000 of proceeds were paid to P, and nothing was includible in I's gross estate. The value of the gift (less the gift tax annual exclusion) was included in I's adjusted taxable gifts base under the unified rate system. If the premium payment test was applicable and if the policy qualified as insurance (see Treas. Reg. §§20.2042-1(a)(2), 20.2039-1(d)), $50,000 of the proceeds would be includible in I's gross estate. From a tax policy perspective, which result is more appropriate? In evaluating this, ask yourself: if P had surrendered the policy to the insurer shortly after the gift and invested the proceeds in stocks valued at $50,000 when I died, what amount would be includible in I's wealth transfer tax calculation?

I's assignment of the policy constituted a completed gift for gift tax purposes of the value of the policy. The method for valuing a life insurance policy is discussed later, and for now it is sufficient to state that the gift tax value of the policy would have been close to (but not the same as) its $42,000 cash surrender value. For estate tax purposes, is there any reason to distinguish the assignment of a life insurance policy from a gift of other property, such as stock, bonds, or real estate?

Lowndes, Kramer, & McCord apparently believed that the abuse in the current estate tax treatment of life insurance proceeds occurs most flagrantly if life insurance is "given away before it has built up any substantial reserve values with little or no gift tax." Consider the validity of that concern in light of the following examples.

(b) In Year One, X acquired a permanent life policy insuring X's life in the amount of $100,000. The premium for the policy was $2,500 per year. After making the first two premium payments X assigned ownership of the policy to Y, who paid the premiums thereafter. The gift tax value of the policy (approximately $300) was well below the gift tax annual exclusion, so X incurred no gift tax liability. When X died more than three years after the assignment, Y had made only three additional premium payments and collected $100,000 of proceeds. Under §2042(2), no part of this wealth is includible in X's gross estate. If a premium payment test were applicable, 40% of the proceeds (X paid two out of five premiums) would be includible in X's gross estate.

Is there a connection between the two premium payments made by X and Y's collection of the insurance proceeds? Each premium payment made by X purchased both risk insurance coverage for the year involved and an equity interest. The equity interest (roughly the $300 cash surrender value) was given to Y when the policy was assigned and should not be included in X's gross estate. The risk coverage was acquired in one year term increments only and the risk coverage paid for by X expired at the end of the second year. What generated the remaining $99,700 of insurance proceeds? A relatively small portion of it (several thousand dollars perhaps) is attributable to the premiums paid by Y that were allocated to Y's investment (the reserve in the policy), and no part of Y's premium payments should be included in X's gross estate. Thus, this amount of the reserve should be excluded. The balance of the proceeds (approximately $95,000) is attributable to the risk coverage purchased by Y's payment of the premium in the year of X's death. Is there any justification for taxing the proceeds of risk coverage acquired by Y in the gross estate of X?

X gave Y something more than the reserve value of the insurance. X gave Y the right to purchase risk coverage on X's life at a contractually fixed price. If X was in good health the assignment of that right would have no value because anyone with an insurable interest could purchase risk coverage on X's life for a premium of equal amount (actually, for the same amount plus any start-up administrative costs, but those are de minimis and can be ignored). If, however, X were in poor health at that time, the right to purchase risk coverage at a cost set for a healthy insured would be of tangible value to Y. Perhaps this extra benefit should affect the value of X's gift. But neither should alter the estate tax analysis, because the risk coverage that actually matured was purchased by Y and any extra benefit assigned by X was given away more than three years prior to X's death.

(c) In Year One, S took out a $100,000 policy insuring the life of S's sibling, I. S had an insurable interest in I and was named as beneficiary of the policy. S paid all premiums on the policy for five years, and then I died. None of the proceeds are includible in I's gross estate, and even the premium payment test would not cause inclusion of any of the proceeds in I's estate. If, instead, I had taken out the policy in Year One, paid one premium, and assigned the policy to S, is there any justification for taxing a portion of the proceeds in I's gross estate? In both situations, the insurance proceeds are largely attributable to the risk coverage purchased under the policy, and *I*'s death causes the policy to mature; should the fact that in one situation *I* paid one year's premium and in the other *I* paid none warrant different estate tax consequences?

(d)   If *I* never owned a policy on *I*'s life, never possessed any incidents of ownership, and never paid any premiums for the policy, could Congress constitutionally require inclusion anyway? Think back to page 3 and consider what impediment might exist to a simple but effective rule that the proceeds of insurance on the life of the decedent are includible, regardless of any other factor.

4.   *State Death Taxes.*   Many freestanding state death tax statutes (those that do not *just* impose a pick-up tax) follow the federal scheme of distinguishing between proceeds of life insurance receivable by the insured's executor and proceeds receivable by other beneficiaries, with only the former being subject to state estate taxation while the latter frequently are not taxed at all or are taxed only to the extent they exceed a specified amount. See, e.g., Cal. Rev. & Tax. Code §§13723, 13724 (1992).

5.   *Definition of Life Insurance.*

Commissioner v. Treganowan
183 F.2d 288 (2d Cir. 1950)

CLARK, J.: The Commissioner of Internal Revenue here seeks review of a decision of the Tax Court . . . which expunged a deficiency he had assessed against the taxpayer executrix on the ground of her failure to include the proceeds of life insurance in the gross estate of her decedent for the computation of the estate tax. . . . The sum in question, claimed by the Commissioner but denied by the Tax Court majority to be the proceeds of insurance, is $20,000 paid to the decedent's widow on his death by the "Trustees of the Gratuity Fund" of the New York Stock Exchange.

From 1925 until his death in 1944, decedent was a member of the New York Stock Exchange. Since 1873 the Exchange has had a plan providing for the payment by the surviving members of a certain sum to the families of deceased members. The constitution of the Exchange sets up for this purpose a Gratuity Fund and provides that before any one may be elected to membership in the Exchange he must make a contribution to the Gratuity Fund of $15. By the constitution the member also "pledges himself to make, upon the death of a member of the Exchange, a voluntary gift to the family of each deceased member in the sum of fifteen dollars." The constitution also pledges the faith of the Exchange to pay, out of these assessments, $20,000, or so much thereof as may have been collected, to the persons named in the next section of the document. . . . No member has at any time had the right to name, select, or designate any beneficiary or beneficiaries other than those named above, nor may the proceeds be assigned or pledged for the payment of any debt.

Although the constitution provides that the beneficiaries of a deceased member are to receive the full $20,000 only if that amount is collected, practically it is certain that the full amount will be paid. Under Art. X, §5, of the constitution of the Exchange, members are subject to loss of their seats for failure to meet any assessment, including the contribution due on decease of a member. When the assessments against all 1374 living members are met, the Exchange has actually received $610 more than is necessary to cover the payment of $20,000; thus default of more than forty members would be required before the benefit would be decreased, and in fact the full amount has invariably been paid. Moreover, the Fund itself has reached such an amount that the Exchange in 1941 took steps for its reduction by the device of foregoing such contributions. . . .

"Insurance" is not defined by statute, and Treasury interpretation of the term has never gone beyond a statement that [§2042] is applicable to "insurance of every description, including death benefits paid by fraternal beneficial societies operating under the lodge system." Treas. Reg. 105, §81.25, 26 C.F.R. 81.25. In deciding whether the $20,000 paid to decedent's widow is insurance within the statutory meaning, the Tax Court looked, rather naturally, to the test announced in the leading case of Helvering v. Le Gierse, 312 U.S. 531, 539 (1941) . . . that "historically and commonly insurance involves risk-shifting and risk-distributing." The Tax Court concluded that the Exchange's plan does not shift the risk of premature death, and that the plan is not insurance. With this conclusion we cannot agree.

. . . [T]he *Le Gierse* case . . . [involved] an ingenious transaction whereby an uninsurable prospect did obtain a policy of life insurance. The device was the purchase by the uninsurable risk (in the particular instance a woman of 80) of both a life insurance and a life annuity contract upon the payment of single premiums for each, sufficient together to avoid all loss by the insurer; for the nature of these contracts is such that, whatever the time of death, any loss upon one will be necessarily offset by the gain on the other. The Court therefore held that when the two contracts were put together there was no "insurance risk." The holding really highlights the situation here where the payment is actually conditioned upon death, whenever occurring, in the true terms of insurance.

"From an insurance standpoint there is no risk unless there is uncertainty or, to use a better term, fortuitousness. It may be uncertain whether the risk will materialize in any particular case. Even death may be considered fortuitous, because the time of its occurrence is beyond control." 8 Encyc. Soc. Sc. 95. That fortuitousness, whether we speak of death generally or premature death, as the Tax Court wished to emphasize, seems perfectly embodied here to fit both branches of the Supreme Court's test. As a critical commentator on the decision below well states it:

> Risk shifting emphasizes the individual aspect of insurance: the effecting of a contract between the insurer and insured each of whom gamble on the time the latter will die. Risk distribution, on the other hand, emphasizes the broader, social aspect of insurance as a method of dispelling the danger of a potential loss by spreading its cost throughout a group. By diffusing the risks through a mass of separate risk shifting contracts, the insurer casts his lot with the law of averages. The process of risk distribution, therefore, is the very essence of insurance.

Note, *The New York Stock Exchange Gratuity Fund: Insurance That Isn't Insurance*, 59 YALE L.J. 780, 784 (1950).

Here the risk of loss from premature death is effectively shifted from the individual to the group of other members of the Exchange. If the individual member dies prematurely, the amount paid to his kin will exceed the amount of assessments which he himself has paid in, the difference representing the loss caused by his premature death which the group has had to bear. Had he not been a member of the plan, he would have saved the amount of assessments against him before his death, but his beneficiaries would be $20,000 poorer. Thus they would have borne this loss which, through the Exchange plan, he has shifted to the group. And manifestly this plan provides a distribution of the risk, for because of the plan the risk of premature death is borne by the 1373 other members of the Exchange, rather than by the individual.

The Tax Court stressed such matters as the lack of adjustment of premiums to health or age or living habits of the member, of any requirement as to the passing of a physical examination, of any fixing of the amount of the "gift" with reference to his life expectancy as determined by the *mortality tables*. But these do not appear to be essentials. As Judge Opper well said, in dissenting for himself and Judge Turner in the Tax Court: "Modern level-premium life insurance contracts issued by great companies engaged primarily in that business have become so commonplace that the contention can now be made, and apparently with success, that nothing else is 'life insurance.' I venture to suggest, however, that neither legal authority nor ordinary usage justifies even today so narrow a construction of the term."...

The finding that this plan is insurance does not alone ensure taxability of the sum in question here, for the other requirements of the statute must also be fulfilled. The insurance must result from contracts wherein the insured either "possessed at his death any of the incidents of ownership" or which he had "purchased with premiums, or other consideration, paid directly or indirectly by the decedent."...[A] majority of the court is of the view that the deceased member did possess some at least of the incidents of ownership so as to render the entire sum taxable....

[Judge Hand dissented from that part of the majority opinion that held that the decedent possessed "incidents of ownership" in the insurance at his death.]

Treas. Reg. §§20.2042-1(a)(2) and 20.2039-1(d) incorporate the Supreme Court's decision in *Le Gierse* (discussed in *Treganowan*) that a single-premium life insurance policy purchased with an annuity contract pursuant to an integrated plan is not life insurance. The government was unsuccessful, however, in trying to apply §2036 to such plans. See Fidelity-Philadelphia Trust Co. v. Smith, 356 U.S. 274 (1958). Nevertheless, the government has successfully applied §2039 to such transactions and also has imposed income tax consequences on the beneficiary's receipt of the insurance proceeds. See Estate of Montgomery v. Commissioner, 56 T.C. 489 (1971), *aff'd per curiam*, 458 F.2d 616 (5th Cir. 1972); Kess v. United States, 451 F.2d 1229 (6th Cir. 1971).

In the context of insurance product development and a modern trend toward promulgation of policies that compete favorably with market investments, some attention must be devoted to the fundamental issue whether the product offered is in fact insurance — as that term is defined for federal income tax purposes. If that definition is not met, two significant detriments will be experienced: The proceeds received on the insured's death will not be excluded from the beneficiary's income under §101, and the internal build-up in the policy will be immediately taxable to the owner, in an amount equal to the excess of the cash surrender value over total premiums paid.

Section 7702 provides that a policy qualifies as life insurance only if it is considered under state law to provide a single integrated death benefit (not an annuity or investment vehicle, and not a product that can be divided into several separable items). In addition, the policy must meet either the cash value accumulation test or both of the guideline premium and cash value corridor requirements. According to those who are far more sophisticated about insurance, even if you could figure out what §§7702(b), (c), (d), and (f) actually provide, you cannot realistically expect to determine whether a particular insurer's product complies. Instead, at best you can only ask for a verification from the company that the policy meets these requirements and, if the policy is of sufficient size, indemnification of the insured and the beneficiaries from the adverse tax consequences that will attach if these definitions are not met.

Given the abuse that sometimes exists in the insurance market — with some companies wrapping what clearly are investment mutual funds with insurance to obtain insurance policy internal tax free build-up, sometimes fueled with loan provisions that drive premium payment — it should be expected that the government will take a hard look at coverage that is "too good to be true." Protection to knowledgeable clients may come only at the cost of avoiding policies that are based on unrealistic assumptions and those that are issued by newer or less reputable or reliable companies.

In Commissioner v. Estate of Noel, 380 U.S. 678 (1965), the Supreme Court held that flight insurance and accidental death insurance constituted "life insurance" within the meaning of §2042. The Court reversed a decision that life insurance referred to an agreement to pay a specified sum upon the occurrence of an *inevitable* event (death of the insured) and that the term did not encompass accident insurance that covered a risk that "is *evitable* and not likely to occur." The Court rejected the significance given by the lower court to the distinction between "evitable" and "inevitable" events. If the taxpayer (the decedent's widow) had prevailed in her contention in *Noel* that flight insurance does not qualify as life insurance under §2042, would the proceeds have been excluded from income taxation under §101? See Treas. Reg. §1.101-1(a)(1).

6. ***Proceeds Receivable by the Insured's Executor.*** Section 2042(1) requires the inclusion of life insurance proceeds in the insured's gross estate to the extent "of the amount receivable by the executor" of the insured. Rev. Rul. 83-44 illustrates the breadth of this provision: the decedent was required by state law to maintain no-fault automobile liability insurance that included a death benefit payable to the estate of every person killed in an accident involving an automobile; because it was payable to a decedent's estate, the death benefit was deemed subject to §2042(1).

The phrase "receivable by the executor" refers to proceeds payable to, on behalf of, or available to the insured's estate, regardless of who is the nominal recipient. Treas. Reg. §§20.2042-1(a)(1) and -1(b)(1), the latter of which states that, if the proceeds are receivable by a beneficiary other than the insured's estate:

but are subject to an obligation, *legally binding upon the other beneficiary*, to pay taxes, debts, or other charges enforceable against the estate, then the amount of such proceeds required for the payment in full *(to the extent of the beneficiary's obligation)* of such taxes, debts, or other charges is includible in the [insured's] gross estate. [Emphasis added]

Consider the following: The insured assigned all incidents of ownership in a $100,000 life insurance policy and transferred certain securities to an irrevocable trust more than three years prior to death. The trustee was named the beneficiary of the policy and was directed to and did pay all subsequent premiums on the policy out of income generated by the securities. The insured had no power over the trust assets. In each of the following factual circumstances the issue is the amount of the $100,000 insurance proceeds payable to the trustee that is includible in the insured's gross estate under §2042.

(a)   When the insured died the value of the securities held in trust was $200,000 and the trustee collected $100,000 of proceeds from the insurer. The trustee was instructed to pay the insured's debts, expenses, and taxes using trust assets selected by the trustee. The total amount paid by the trustee was $60,000 and the balance of the trust estate was distributed to the insured's children. It does not matter whether the trustee used the insurance proceeds to pay the debts, expenses, and taxes, or sold securities and used those proceeds exclusively to pay those amounts. $60,000 is includible.

(b)   The same facts as in (a) except the trustee was authorized, not required, to pay the estate's debts, expenses, and taxes. If the trustee does not pay them, there is authority that §2042(1) does not apply. Estate of Wade v. Commissioner, 47 B.T.A. 21 (1942); Rev. Rul. 77-157. Dictum in Hooper v. Commissioner, 41 B.T.A. 114 (1940), states that §2042(1) applies to the extent the trustee does pay them, although the court relied on a case in which the trustee was *directed* to pay the debts, expenses, and taxes in making this statement.

(c)   The same facts as in (a) except the trustee was instructed to pay the estate's debts, expenses, and taxes only to the extent the estate's assets were insufficient to meet those obligations. If the estate's assets were $35,000 short and the trustee made up the difference, just that $35,000 amount would be includible. Nothing would be includible if the estate's assets were sufficient.

(d)   How would your answers differ if, instead of the trustee being either directed or authorized to pay the estate's debts, expenses, and taxes, the trustee was authorized, but not required, to lend the estate proceeds not in excess of the amount of the debts, expense, and taxes? It is doubtful whether §2042(1) would reach this case unless the loan provided a substantial benefit to the estate, such as because it was unsecured, bore interest at a below-market interest rate, or was repayable only on demand.

Try another: Imagine that your client, *C*, will have a liquidity problem at death, based on your estimate that, if *C* were to die within the next four years, the estate would need another $100,000 of liquid assets to pay its debts, expenses, and taxes. Over a sufficient number of years, C could collect enough liquid assets, but there is a risk of a liquidity shortage if C dies in the near-term future. The liquidity problem is reduced, but not removed, if the estate can defer the payment of the estate tax under §§6161(a)(2) and 6166. You recommend that C purchase $100,000 of life insurance to protect against this risk. However, if C purchases and owns a $100,000 policy, the proceeds will be included in C's gross estate, thereby increasing the estate taxes. Only the excess of the proceeds over the added estate tax burden will be available for liquidity needs. One potential remedy is to have C create an irrevocable family trust that will acquire the necessary insurance, in which C will have no incidents of ownership. How would you plan this arrangement to provide the needed liquidity to C's estate without causing the proceeds to be includible in C's gross estate? A hint: your answer might differ if §1014 new basis at death no longer exists. See Pennell, *Life Insurance Owned by a Third Party: Estate Planning Considering Income, Gift and Generation-Skipping Taxes*, 18 HOUSTON L. REV. 103 (1980).

Finally, assume that in Year One X assigned a $100,000 life insurance policy insuring X's life to an irrevocable trust, and the trustee paid the premiums thereafter. That assignment was treated as a gift of $24,000 for gift tax purposes. When X died in Year Five the trustee paid the $100,000 proceeds to the government as partial payment for X's estate tax, as instructed in the trust instrument, and this caused the $100,000 proceeds to be includible in X's gross estate under §2042(1). Is the $24,000 gift of the insurance policy purged from X's adjusted taxable gifts base under the flush language of §2001(b)? Cf. Peters v. United States, 572 F.2d 851 (Ct. Cl. 1978), which held that premiums paid by an insured within three years of death on a policy previously assigned were not includible in the gross estate under §2035 if the proceeds of the policy were includible in the gross estate under §2042.

7. *Proceeds Not Receivable by the Insured's Executor: Incidents of Ownership.*

Section 2042(2) provides that life insurance proceeds receivable by beneficiaries other than the insured's executor are includible in the insured's gross estate if the insured possessed at death any incidents of ownership in the policy, whether exercisable by the insured alone or in conjunction with any other person. A reversionary interest in a policy is treated as an incident of ownership if the value of a reversion (determined in the same manner as for §2037, using actuarial tables without regard to the death of the decedent) exceeds 5% of the value of the policy immediately before the insured's death.

The term "incidents of ownership" was used from time to time in the regulations under the 1918 Act, but it did not appear as part of the statutory language until 1942. H.R. Rep. No. 2333, 77th Cong., 2d Sess. 163 (1942), in 1942-2 C.B. 372, 491; S. Rep. No. 1631, 77th Cong., 2d Sess. 235 (1942), in 1942-2 C.B. 504, 677, stated:

There is no specific enumeration of incidents of ownership, the possession of which at death forms the basis for inclusion of insurance proceeds in the gross estate, as it is impossible to include an exhaustive list. Examples of such incidents are the right of the insured or his estate to the economic benefits of the insurance, the power to change the beneficiary, the power to surrender or cancel the policy, the power to assign it, the power to revoke an assignment, the power to pledge the policy for a loan, or the power to obtain from the insurer a loan against the surrender value of the policy. Incidents of ownership are not confined to those possessed by the decedent in a technical legal sense. For example, a power to change the beneficiary reserved to a corporation of which the decedent is sole stockholder is an incident of ownership in the decedent.

Compare this statement with the definition of "incidents of ownership" that now appears in Treas. Reg. §20.2042-1(c)(2). They differ, but you can see how the regulation was crafted from the committee report. That is very common, and illustrates how committee reports can be a fruitful and typically reliable resource prior to promulgation of regulations.

The phrase "in conjunction with any other person" includes veto powers in the insured (as we will study shortly). It even includes powers held with persons with interests adverse to exercise of an incident of ownership by the insured. Gesner v. United States, 600 F.2d 1349 (Cl. Ct. 1979); cf. Helvering v. City Bank Farmers Trust Co., 296 U.S. 85 (1935).

In Commissioner v. Estate of Noel, 380 U.S. 678 (1965), the facts found that Mrs. Noel drove her husband to the airport, where he signed applications for two round-trip flight insurance policies aggregating $125,000 that named Mrs. Noel as beneficiary. Mrs. Noel testified that she paid the premiums of $2.50 each on the policies and that her husband instructed the sales clerk to "give them to my wife. They are hers now, I no longer have anything to do with them." The clerk gave Mrs. Noel the policies, which she kept, and Mr. Noel departed on his flight. Less than three hours later, his plane crashed and he was killed. The companies paid Mrs. Noel the $125,000 face value of the policies, but the proceeds were not included in the estate tax return filed for his estate. The Supreme Court held that flight insurance constitutes "life insurance" within the meaning of §2042 and then considered whether Mr. Noel held incidents of ownership in the policies at his death:

While not clearly spelled out, the contention that the decedent reserved no incident of ownership in the policies rests on three alternative claims: (a) that Mrs. Noel purchased the policies and therefore owned them; (b) that even if her husband owned the policies, he gave them to her, thereby depriving himself of power to assign the policies or to change the beneficiary; and (c) even assuming he had contractual power to assign the policies or make a beneficiary change, this power was illusory as he could not possibly have exercised it in the interval between take-off and the fatal crash . . . .

(a)　The contention that Mrs. Noel bought the policies and therefore owned them rests solely on her testimony that she furnished the money for their purchase, intending thereby to preserve her right to continue as beneficiary. Accepting her claim that she supplied the money to buy the policies for her own benefit (which the Tax Court did not decide), what she bought nonetheless were policy contracts containing agreements between her husband and the companies. The contracts themselves granted to Mr. Noel the right either to assign the policies or to change the beneficiary without her consent. Therefore the contracts she bought by their very terms rebut her claim that she became the complete, unconditional owner of the policies with an irrevocable right to remain the beneficiary.

(b)　The contention that Mr. Noel gave or assigned the policies to her and therefore was without power thereafter to assign them or to change the beneficiary stands no better under these facts. The contract terms provided that these policies could not be assigned nor could the beneficiary be changed without a written endorsement on the policies. No such assignment or change of beneficiary was endorsed on these policies, and consequently the power to assign the policies or change the beneficiary remained in the decedent at the time of his death.

(c)　Obviously, there was no practical opportunity for the decedent to assign the policies or change the beneficiary between the time he boarded the plane and the time he died. That time was too short and his wife had the policies in her possession at home. These circumstances disabled him for the moment from exercising those "incidents of ownership" over the policies which were undoubtedly his. Death intervened before this temporary disability was removed. But the same could be said about a man owning an ordinary life insurance policy who boarded the plane at the same time or for that matter about any man's exercise of ownership over his property while aboard an airplane in the three hours before a fatal crash. It would stretch the imagination to think that Congress intended to measure estate tax liability by an individual's fluctuating day-by-day, hour-by-hour capacity to dispose of property which he owns. We hold that estate tax liability for policies "with respect to which the decedent possessed at his death any of the incidents of ownership" depends on a general, legal power to exercise owner- ship, without regard to the owner's ability to exercise it at a particular moment. Nothing we have said is to be taken as meaning that a policyholder is without power to divest himself of all incidents of ownership over his insurance policies by a proper gift or assignment, so as to bar its inclusion in his gross estate under §2042(2). What we do hold is that no such transfer was made of the policies here involved.

Relying on the unlimited marital deduction that was adopted in 1981, an assignment of insurance to a spouse will have no significance for transfer tax purposes unless the spouse is not the beneficiary (e.g., because the spouse predeceases the insured, which could occur with flight insurance if, for example, a round trip is covered and the insured is killed on the return trip after the death of the spouse). The *Noel* principle continues to be significant if the policy is assigned to a person who is not the insured's spouse. See §2035(a)(2). Inability to exercise incidents of ownership due to incapacity also does not preclude application of §2042(2). See Estate of Rockwell v. Commissioner, 49 T.C.M. (CCH) 331 (1984), *rev'd on another ground*, 779 F.2d 931 (3d Cir. 1985).

Ownership and Incidents Thereof. Would the proceeds have been included in Mr. Noel's gross estate if Mrs. Noel could have and had applied for the flight insurance policy, as well as being named beneficiary and having paid the premiums for the policy? Flight insurance is not anything worth considering these days, but the notion of acquisition of insurance that will be kept out of the insured's gross estate is a cottage industry. In that regard, think about the advice you would give as to the manner in which insurance should be purchased and held. Also note, the Supreme Court may not have been correct in holding that Mr. Noel's assignment to Mrs. Noel was ineffective. According to R. Brown, THE LAW OF PERSONAL PROPERTY §8.3 (3d ed. W. Raushenbush 1975), "the overwhelming weight of authority . . . is that a manual delivery with the requisite donative intent of . . . life insurance policies constitute good gifts . . . of the insurance contract." Furthermore, Treas. Reg. §20.2042- 1(c)(5) provides that "as an additional step in determining whether or not a decedent possessed any incidents of ownership in a policy or any part of a policy, regard must be given to the effect of the State or other applicable law upon the terms of the policy." If an insured were to make a valid assignment of a flight insurance policy before embarking on a fatal flight, would the proceeds be excluded from the insured's gross estate? See Berman v. United States, 487 F.2d 70 (5th Cir. 1973), excerpted at page

487: today the issue is §2035(a)(2), which always is a problem if the insured owned the policy first.

Prichard v. United States

397 F.2d 60 (5th Cir. 1968)

[Smith, a resident of a community property state, sought permanent mortgage financing for a shopping center he proposed to construct. Great Southern, an insurance company, required as a condition of making the loan that Smith purchase $250,000 of insurance on his life from the company and that the policy be assigned to the company as collateral for the loan. The company issued a $250,000 policy insuring Smith's life, with Mrs. Smith named as sole owner and beneficiary of the policy. Seven months after purchase of the policy the company made the permanent take-out loan to the Smiths and, as agreed, the Smiths assigned the policy to the company. Mr. Smith was killed, the unpaid balance of the mortgage loan exceeded the face amount of the policy, and that entitled the company to the entire $250,000 of proceeds. Nevertheless, the company released $150,000 to Mrs. Smith and applied only the $100,000 balance against the debt. The Commissioner sought to include Mr. Smith's community property half of the proceeds ($125,000) in his gross estate. The district court agreed with the Commissioner. The estate appealed.]

GODBOLD, J.: Under Texas law a conveyance by husband to wife makes the property conveyed the wife's separate property, so that the quantum of Mrs. Smith's ownership of the policy, as a matter of state title law, was complete and sole. . . . But we do not close our eyes to the realities. From the initial statement by Great Southern of what its conditions would be, and up to the time of Smith's death, the insurance policy and the loan were indispensable parts of an integrated transaction. The negotiations and the course of the loan transactions, the correspondence, and the other documents, admit of only one conclusion. Although Mrs. Smith was designated as owner we would be wholly unrealistic to conclude anything other than that she was named as owner under the understanding, agreement and arrangement that the policy must be assigned when the community loan was ready to be closed. The requirement that the policy be obtained and assigned was imposed before application was made for the insurance. The intent that it be assigned was reported by the agent on the original application, which was before the matter arose of Mrs. Smith's being named owner. Without an assignment by her there could be no loan . . . .

Appellant emphasizes that the loan was closed eight months after Mrs. Smith was named owner, that had the loan never been closed the policy would have remained in force so long as the premiums were paid, that had Smith died before the loan was closed the policy would have been the property of Mrs. Smith, and had she died before the loan was closed, her husband surviving, the cash surrender or replacement value of the policy would have been includible in her estate. A husband may unconditionally make his wife the owner and beneficiary of an insurance policy on his life when it is issued, or later if he desires, so as to bar inclusion of it in his estate. . . . The lapse of eight months, and the rights of the wife during that time, are evidentiary only; they are of little force here, since this was the period during which the center was being built under interim financing which was to be paid off out of the Great Southern loan upon completion.

Also appellant seems to contend that as a matter of law there was no incident of ownership in Smith at his death because the assignment had been made two years previously and any power or control that he may have had over the policy had been exhausted when the assignment was executed and delivered. But the arrangement existed for such a pledge or assignment to be made, and it was made, and the substantial economic benefit to the husband of having the policy stand as collateral for the community debt then commenced and continued up to his death. Smith's separate property could be liable for the community debt, and the assigned policy stood between his estate and that possible liability. . . .

. . . Under different circumstances than in this case a wife who has become the absolute owner of an insurance policy on her husband's life, her husband no longer having any incidents of ownership therein, could assign it as collateral for a community debt and the husband would commence enjoying economic benefit from the time the assignment is made. Whether this alone would bring the policy within the husband's estate is a question for another case. It is not what happened in this case where in the total transaction there were incidents of ownership at all times, an unconsummated arrangement for eight months followed by the continuing economic benefit of the completed assignment. . . . The decision of the district court is affirmed.

Would any part of the proceeds have been included in Mr. Smith's gross estate if he had died after his wife acquired the insurance policy but prior to the date on which the company made the loan and the policy was assigned to it? Would any part of the proceeds have been included in Mr. Smith's gross estate if Mrs. Smith had owned the life insurance policy for some years prior to the negotiations with the company for the loan and if the company had not required Mrs. Smith to assign the policy to it as security but she had done so voluntarily to assist in obtaining the loan? See Bintliff v. United States, 462 F.2d 403 (5th Cir. 1972), holding that half of the insurance proceeds used to satisfy a community debt were included in the deceased spouse's gross estate under §2042(1) as proceeds payable for the benefit of the insured's estate to the extent of the decedent's share of the debt.

Not all community property states accept that the mere designation of one spouse as the owner of a life insurance policy is a clear, definite, and convincing demonstration of the parties' intent that the policy qualify as that spouse's separate property. See Kern v. United States, 491 F.2d 436 (9th Cir. 1974); Estate of Meyer v. Commissioner, 66 T.C. 41 (1976). If the policy is treated as community property, then half the proceeds likely will be included in the insured's gross estate even if the surviving spouse is named as the beneficiary.

In addition to giving some insight into what are incidents of ownership, and who owns them, the following case reveals an ugly reality that sometimes the estate argues that a mistake was made by the insurance agent or the insurer, and sometimes it is true that a policy was issued to the wrong party. As you read the case, think about what you should do when you discover such an error.

United States v. Rhode Island Hospital Trust Co.
355 F.2d 7 (1st Cir. 1966)

COFFIN, J.: . . . The facts, undisputed, are of two kinds: "intent facts" — those relating to the conduct and understanding of the insured and his father, who was the instigator, premium payer, and primary beneficiary of the policy; and the "policy facts" — those revealed by the insurance contract itself.

Decedent's father, Charles A. Horton, was a textile executive, a prominent businessman in his community, and, according to the testimony, "a man with strong convictions and vigorous action." Charles and his wife, Louise, had two sons, decedent and A. Trowbridge Horton. In 1924, when decedent was 18 and Trowbridge 19, their father purchased an insurance policy on the life of each boy from Massachusetts Mutual Life Insurance Company. The policies were identical, each having the face amount of $50,000, the proceeds being payable to Charles and Louise, equally, or to the survivor.

Charles Horton's purpose was to assure that funds would be available for his wife, should he and either son die. Charles kept the policies in his safe deposit box and paid all premiums throughout his life. Under the policies, however, the right to change beneficiaries had been reserved to the sons. In January 1952, the boys' mother, Louise, died. In March, 1952, Charles told each of his sons to go to the insurance company's office and sign a change of beneficiary form. The amendment executed by decedent named his father as primary beneficiary, with decedent's wife, brother, and the executors or administrators of the last survivor being the successive beneficiaries. After this amendment, decedent continued to retain the right to make further changes, but none was made. Decedent died on April 1, 1958, survived by his wife and father. His father died on October 2, 1961.

The father, Charles, regarded the policies as belonging to him, saying at one point that it would be "out of the question" for the sons to claim them. Decedent's brother never discussed the policies with his father, never asked for a loan based on the policies, obediently signed the change of beneficiary form at his father's request, and considered the policy on his life as the property of his father. Decedent's widow recalled only that decedent had once told her that his father had a policy on himself and his brother but that "in no way did it mean anything to us or would it ever. It was completely his." She added that her husband, the decedent, had wanted more insurance of his own, but was not able to obtain it.

Coming to what we call "policy facts," a careful reading of the policy, captioned "Ordinary Life Policy — Convertible," reveals the following rights, privileges, or powers accorded to the decedent.

- Right to change beneficiary. . . .
- Assignment. . . .
- Dividends. The insured had the option to have dividends paid in cash, used to reduce premiums, used to purchase paid-up additions, or accumulate subject to withdrawal on demand.
- Loans. On condition that the unlimited right to change the beneficiary was reserved, as in this case, the company would "loan on the signature of the insured alone."
- Survival. Should no beneficiary survive the insured, the proceeds were payable to his executors and administrators.
- Alteration. The policy could be altered only on the written request of the insured and of "other parties in interest." . . .

The plaintiffs contend that the district court properly held that decedent possessed no incidents of ownership in the policy; that the term "incidents of ownership" refer[s] to the rights of insured or his estate to the economic benefits of the policy; that the question of possession of such incidents is one of fact; that such possession depends upon all relevant facts and circumstances, including the intention of the parties; and that these facts and circumstances clearly establish that decedent's father was the real owner of the policy, while decedent was merely the nominal owner, having no real economic interest in it.

The government asserts that, as a matter of law, the facts bring this case squarely within the reach of §2042, as applied by the cases, notwithstanding the evidence as to the intentions and extra-policy circumstances of the parties, and the lack of economic benefit to decedent. . . .

Taking the subsidiary facts as presented to the district court, we differ with its conclusion that "the decedent's father was actually the real owner of the various incidents of ownership in said policy." But in differing we recognize that early holdings and occasional dicta, early and late, have invited litigation. This is the kind of case where the government enters, appearing to seek its pound of flesh on the basis of petty technicality, while the taxpayer's decedent generally appears as a person who had very little to do with the insurance policy which is causing so much trouble to his estate. . . .

. . . What power did decedent possess? This is the relevant question — not how did he feel or act. Did he have a capacity to do something to affect the disposition of the policy if he had wanted to? Without gaining possession of the policy itself, he could have borrowed on the policy. He could have changed the method of using dividends. He could have assigned the policy. He could have revoked the assignment. Should he have gained possession of the policy by trick (as by filing an affidavit that the policy was lost), force, or chance, he could have changed the beneficiary, and made the change of record irrevocable. Other such possibilities might be imagined. We cite these only to evidence the existence of some power in decedent to affect the disposition of the policy proceeds. In addition, he always possessed a negative power. His signature was necessary to a change in beneficiary, to a surrender for cash value, to an alteration in the policy, to a change in dividend options. Even with this most limited power, he would be exercising an incident of ownership "in conjunction with" another person. . . .

The existence of such powers in the decedent is to be distinguished from such rights as may have existed in decedent's father or duties owed the father by decedent. It is, therefore, no answer that decedent's father might have proceeded against him at law or in equity. The company made it clear in the contract that it bore no responsibility for the validity of an assignment, that it could pay a beneficiary without recourse, and that it was under no obligation to see to the carrying out of any trust. It even made clear that a beneficiary need only write to the home office to receive payment. Should a third party — for example, an innocent creditor who had given valuable consideration to decedent — receive the proceeds of the policy, the proceeds of a loan on the policy, or the cash value, it could not be said that the transaction between decedent and such third person would in all such cases be nugatory. For decedent had some powers — perhaps not rights, but powers — which could, if exercised alone or in conjunction with another, affect the disposition of some or all of the proceeds of the policy.

Nor is it a compelling argument that decedent lacked physical possession of the policy. Commissioner v. Estate of Noel, 380 U.S. 678 (1965). Moreover, as we have noted, some rights could be exercised without physical possession of the policy.

The cases arising from similar facts over nearly a quarter of a century give little support, in their holdings, to plaintiffs. Even Estate of Doerken v. Commissioner, 46 B.T.A. 809 (1942), heavily relied upon by plaintiffs, turned on the issue whether or not decedent (as opposed to a corporation in which he had a one-fourth interest) had "taken out" the policy on decedent's life. It was not a decision that decedent possessed no incidents of ownership. Decisions in subsequent cases have, on the evidence presented, almost uniformly held the "policy facts" (reservation of rights in the policy) impregnable to attack from the "intent facts." . . .

To the principle of heavy predominance of the "policy facts" over the "intent facts" there must be added the caveat that, where the insurance contract itself does not reflect the instructions of the parties, as where an agent, on his own initiative, inserts a reservation of right to change a beneficiary contrary to the intentions which had been expressed to him, no incidents of ownership are thereby created. The case before us presents no such issue, for the right in decedent to change beneficiaries was recognized on the one occasion when it was exercised and this right continued thereafter.

While decisions against the estate of a passive but power-possessing decedent may often conflict with the honest intentions and understanding of premium-paying beneficiaries and insureds, the alternative of abandoning the insistence on the governing nature of the contract, in most cases, is less desirable. The drawing of a useful line would be impossible; there would be a much wider range of varying decisions on similar facts; and there would be an invitation to unprincipled estate manipulation. As government counsel has pointed out, there could always be a formally executed side agreement under which the insured clearly surrenders to the beneficiary all his rights to the policy, such agreement to be brought to light only in the event of the decedent's dying before the beneficiary. . . .

Judgment will be entered vacating the judgment of the district court and ordering judgment for the defendant.

Veto Powers. The court stated in *Rhode Island Hospital Trust* that a negative or veto power over matters such as a change in the beneficiary, when held by the insured at his death, constitutes an incident of ownership exercisable "in conjunction with" another person. The Tax Court, in Schwager v. Commissioner, 64 T.C. 781 (1975), adopted the same view. In *Schwager* an insurance policy on the life of the insured was owned by the insured's employer. The beneficiary of the policy was the insured's spouse. The employer, as owner of the policy, held all the powers over the policy, with one exception: it could not change the beneficiary without the consent of the insured. In holding that the proceeds of the policy were includible in the insured's gross estate, the Tax Court, citing *Rhode Island Hospital Trust*, said:

[I]t is not the number of powers possessed that is the determining factor. Rather, it is the existence of even a "fractional" power not the "probability" of its exercise that controls. . . . The distinction between the power to make changes and the power to bar change by the expedient of denying permission was found insufficient to alter the result in the Estate of Karagheusian [233 F.2d 197 (2d Cir. 1956),] where the Court of Appeals stated that it made "no difference whether under the trust instrument the decedent may initiate changes or whether he must merely consent to them." . . .

The decedent was the named insured to a policy on his life. The proceeds from the policy were to be paid to his wife. No alteration of this scheme was possible without his consent. By declining to consent to any change in the designation, a valuable economic benefit was available to the decedent. The term, incidents of ownership, "has reference to the right of the insured or his estate to the economic benefits of the policy." Treas. Reg. §20.2042-1(c)(2) . . . .

See also Estate of Rockwell v. Commissioner, 49 T.C.M. (CCH) 331 (1984), *rev'd,* 779 F.2d 931 (3d Cir. 1985); Estate of Dimen v. Commissioner, 72 T.C. 198, 204 (1979).

In Rev. Rul. 75-70, the insured-decedent, *I*, assigned all interests in a policy to *I*'s spouse as owner and beneficiary but (by the terms of a rider *I* caused to be added to the policy before the assignment) *I*'s spouse could not change the beneficiary or assign the policy to anyone who did not have an insurable interest in *I*'s life unless the spouse first obtained *I*'s written consent. The Commissioner found that there was no person other than the spouse who had an insurable interest in *I*'s life. The Commissioner also determined that it was very unlikely that *I* would have exercised this power to veto any action of the spouse. Nevertheless, *I*'s possession of the veto power was deemed an incident of ownership that caused inclusion of the proceeds of the policy in *I*'s gross estate.

The Commissioner has taken the same position with respect to the applicability of §2038 to property over which a decedent had a veto power. See Rev. Rul. 70-513; Lowndes, Kramer, & McCord, ESTATE & GIFT TAXES (3D ED. 1974) at 147–148.

In Rev. Rul. 79-46, the decedent's employer owned a policy insuring the decedent's life, and the decedent's spouse was designated as beneficiary of the policy. Under the decedent's employment agreement with the employer, if the employer chose to discontinue paying the premiums or to surrender the policy for its cash value, the decedent had the right to purchase the policy from the employer for its cash surrender value. The Commissioner ruled that the decedent's power to prevent the employer from surrendering the policy and thereby canceling it constituted a veto power that qualified as an incident of ownership. The Commissioner ruled that the proceeds of the policy less the cash surrender value at the decedent's death were includible in the decedent's gross estate. The Tax Court expressly repudiated Rev. Rul. 79-46 in Estate of Smith v. Commissioner, 73 T.C. 307 (1979), and held that a power to purchase the policy in that circumstance did not constitute an incident of ownership. The Commissioner acquiesced only in that result, which suggests that the Commissioner disagrees with the Tax Court's reasoning in *Smith*. The employer named itself as beneficiary of the policy, but that should not be a factor in determining whether life insurance held by the insured's employer should be includible in the insured's gross estate.

In First National Bank v. United States, 358 F.2d 625 (5th Cir. 1966), the insured was one of four equal shareholders who executed a cross-purchase buy-sell agreement by which the surviving shareholders were granted an option to purchase the stock of a deceased shareholder at a price fixed by a formula in the contract. Several years later the four executed an additional agreement, which stated:

Each of the parties hereto carries [$15,000 of] life insurance under a group policy arrangement made with the National Association of Security Dealers. [Each shareholder named the others as equal beneficiaries of that insurance.] It is understood and agreed that the said beneficiaries shall use the net proceeds of such insurance toward the purchase of the common stock [of the company] owned by a decedent, his lawful heirs, or estate, in accordance with the terms of the contract.

When the insured died the three surviving shareholders first indicated to the insured's executor their intention to exercise their purchase options and they deposited the $15,000 insurance proceeds with the estate. Subsequently, however, by mutual consent, the shareholders withdrew their offer, and their deposit was returned to them. The corporation then purchased the insured's stock. The government sought to include in the insured's gross estate the $15,000 of insurance proceeds paid to the three surviving shareholders, and the district court granted summary judgment for the government. In reversing, the appellate court said, in part:

[Did the decedent] possess any "incident of ownership in the policy"? As we read the applicable Alabama law, he did not.

The . . . contract mandatorily committed the proceeds of the insurance. The only possible positive guarantee supporting that commitment would be the inability of the parties to defeat the agreement by changing the beneficiaries in the policies. The purpose of the contract, the specific purpose which the parties were arranging to achieve, would have immediately been defeated if any one of them could have changed the beneficiary in any one of the policies. We are thus inescapably driven to the conclusion that by these contracts all the parties, including the decedent, did contractually surrender the power to change the beneficiary . . . . Although as the Government says, this did not appear in the contracts in express language, the implication that the parties so agreed . . . leaves this as the truly logical construction. Since, at death, [the decedent] possessed no right to change the beneficiary and no right to direct the expenditure of the proceeds, that having been expressly dedicated to a particular purpose which neither he nor his Executor had the power to change, we must hold that he possessed no incident of ownership in the fifteen thousand dollars.

It is true that after [the decedent's] death the surviving partners did pay the proceeds of the insurance policies to the estate in accordance with the . . . agreement. We find no importance in the fact that by mutual agreement the corporation was later allowed to step in and buy the stock. Obviously the estate had the unconditional power to keep that which had been paid to it. It was under no duty to do otherwise. . . . What the Executor . . . did with the stock, since the net result to the estate was the same, amounted to no more than any other transaction it might have seen fit to make in the handling of the property. The estate collected the full value of the stock . . . and the Government collected estate taxes in full on that value.

We accordingly find it unnecessary to elaborate upon the argument . . . that the contract . . . gave rise, or did not give rise, to a claim against the estate. Nor is it necessary to consider the contention of appellant that taxing the transfer of the entire value of the estate as well as the fifteen thousand dollars proceeds of the insurance policy would constitute double taxation.

Cf. *Morton v. United States*, 457 F.2d 750 (4th Cir. 1972).

Rhode Island Hospital Trust and *First National Bank* appear irreconcilable. *First National Bank* might appear to invite the use of a contract surrendering the insured's rights to the beneficiary, such contract to be brought forth only if the insured predeceases the beneficiary. Note the reference to the possible resort to such contracts in *Rhode Island Hospital Trust*. As a practical matter it is unlikely that a court would regard such a sub rosa agreement to be valid.

Incidents Held in a Fiduciary Capacity. Treas. Reg. §20.2042-1(c)(4) states that a decedent has incidents of ownership in a life insurance policy if the decedent alone, or in conjunction with others, has the power "as trustee or otherwise" to change the beneficial interests in the policy or in the proceeds, "even though the decedent has no beneficial interest in the trust." See also Rev. Rul. 76-261. Is this statement consistent with Treas. Reg. §20.2042-1(c)(2), which makes reference to the right of the insured to "economic benefits" of the policy? Consider the effect of the following:

Revenue Ruling 84-179

In 1960, *D*, the decedent, purchased an insurance policy on *D*'s life and transferred all incidents of ownership to *D*'s spouse. The spouse designated their adult child as the policy beneficiary.

The spouse died in 1978 and, by will, established a residuary trust for the benefit of the child. *D* was designated as trustee. The insurance policy on *D*'s life was included in the spouse's residuary estate and was transferred to the testamentary trust. The drafting of the spouse's will to provide for the residuary trust and the appointment of *D* as trustee were unrelated to *D*'s transfer of the policy to the spouse.

As trustee, *D* had broad discretionary powers in the management of the trust property . . . . Under the terms of the policy, the owner could elect to have the proceeds made payable according to various plans, use the loan value to pay the premiums, borrow on the policy, assign or pledge the policy, and elect to receive annual dividends. The terms of the will did not preclude *D* from exercising these rights, although *D* could not do so for *D*'s own benefit. *D* paid the premiums on the policy out of other trust property.

D was still serving as trustee when *D* died . . . .

Section 20.2042-1(c)(4) of the regulations provides that a decedent is considered to have an incident of ownership in a policy held in trust if under the terms of the policy the decedent (either alone or in conjunction with another person) has the power (as trustee or otherwise) to change the beneficial ownership in the policy or its proceeds, or the time or manner of enjoyment thereof, even though the decedent has no beneficial interest in the trust.

The legislative history of §2042 indicates that Congress intended §2042 to parallel the statutory scheme governing those powers that would cause other types of property to be included in a decedent's gross estate under other Code sections, particularly §§2036 and 2038. S. Rep. No. 1622, 83d Cong., 2d Sess. 124 (1954). See Estate of Skifter v. Commissioner, 468 F.2d 699 (2d Cir. 1972).

Sections 2036(a)(2) and 2038(a)(1) concern lifetime transfers made by the decedent. Under these sections, it is the decedent's power to affect the beneficial interests in, or enjoyment of, the transferred property that required inclusion of the property in the gross estate. Section 2036 is directed at those powers retained by the decedent in connection with the transfer. Section 2038(a)(1) is directed at situations where the transferor-decedent sets the machinery in motion that purposefully allows fiduciary powers over the property interest to subsequently return to the transferor-decedent, such as by an incomplete transfer.

In accordance with the legislative history of §2042(2), a decedent will not be deemed to have incidents of ownership over an insurance policy on decedent's life where decedent's powers are held in a fiduciary capacity, and are not exercisable for decedent's personal benefit, where the decedent did not transfer the policy or any of the consideration for purchasing or maintaining the policy to the trust from personal assets, and the devolution of the powers on decedent was not part of a prearranged plan involving the participation of decedent. This position is consistent with decisions by several courts of appeal. See Estate of Skifter; Estate of Fruehauf v. Commissioner, 427 F.2d 80 (6th Cir. 1970); Hunter v. United States, 624 F.2d 833 (8th Cir. 1980). But see Terriberry v. United States, 517 F.2d 286 (5th Cir. 1975); Rose v. United States, 511 F.2d 259 (5th Cir. 1975), which are to the contrary. Section 20.2042-1(c)(4) will be read in accordance with the position adopted herein.

The decedent will be deemed to have incidents of ownership over an insurance policy on the decedent's life where decedent's powers are held in a fiduciary capacity and the decedent has transferred the policy or any of the consideration for purchasing and maintaining the policy to the trust. Also, where the decedent's powers could have been exercised for decedent's benefit, they will constitute incidents of ownership in the policy, without regard to how those powers were acquired and without consideration of whether the decedent transferred property to the trust. Thus, if the decedent reacquires powers over insurance policies in an individual capacity, the powers will constitute incidents of ownership even though the decedent is a transferee.

In the present situation, D completely relinquished all interest in the insurance policy on D's life. The powers over the policy devolved on D as a fiduciary, through an independent transaction, and were not exercisable for D's own benefit. Also, D did not transfer property to the trust. Thus, D did not possess incidents of ownership over the policy for purposes of §2042(2) of the Code.

. . .

In addition to what the following case tells us about the special incidents-held-as-fiduciary issue, pay attention to the §2038 analog that was mentioned in Rev. Rul. 84-179 as well. It may be a good review of what you learned in Chapter 5.

Estate of Skifter v. Commissioner
468 F.2d 699 (2d Cir. 1972)

LOMBARD, J.: . . . In 1961 Hector Skifter, the decedent, assigned all his interest in nine insurance policies on his life to his wife Naomi, effectively making her the owner of those policies. Skifter retained no interest in the policies and retained no power over them. Several months later, Naomi died and left a will directing that her residuary estate, which included the nine insurance policies, be placed in trust. She directed that the income was to be paid to their daughter, Janet, for life and, upon Janet's death, there were provisions for the distribution of corpus and income to other persons.

Naomi appointed Skifter as trustee . . . . The essential issue before this Court is whether the broad fiduciary powers that were granted to Skifter under Naomi's will constitute "incidents of ownership" within the meaning of §2042(2). We hold that they do not, and thus affirm the decision of the Tax Court.

In enacting the predecessor of §2042(2), the Senate and House Committee Reports of the Seventy-seventh Congress acknowledged that, while the new provision introduced the term "incidents of ownership," it failed to suggest a definition of it. The

Reports then went on to list the sort of powers and interest that the Congress was concerned with:

> Examples of such incidents are the right of the insured or his estate to the economic benefits of the insurance, the power to change the beneficiary, the power to surrender or cancel the policy, the power to assign it, the power to revoke an assignment, the power to pledge the policy for a loan, or the power to obtain from the insurer a loan against the surrender value of the policy.

See 1942-2 C.B. 491, 677. The Treasury relied on this legislative history in promulgating its regulations on §2042(2). . . . It seems significant to us that the reference point in the regulation for "incidents of ownership" is "the right . . . to the economic benefits of the policy," since there was no way in which Skifter could have exercised his powers to derive for himself any economic benefits from these insurance policies. . . .

The core of the controversy here centers on the decedent's power, as trustee, to prefer the current income beneficiary over the remainderman and all later income beneficiaries through payment of the entire trust corpus. He did not have the power to alter or revoke the trust for his own benefit and he could not name new, additional, or alternative beneficiaries. In this regard, Reg. §20.2042-1(c)(4) provides:

> A decedent is considered to have an "incident of ownership" in an insurance policy on his life held in trust if, under the terms of the policy, the decedent (either alone or in conjunction with another person or persons) has the power (as trustee or otherwise) to change the beneficial ownership in the policy or its proceeds, or the time or manner of enjoyment thereof, even though the decedent has no beneficial interest in the trust.

The Commissioner contends that this regulation requires that the proceeds of the policies here be included in decedent's estate.

The Tax Court declined to interpret that regulation so as to make it applicable here, but concluded that, since the power could not be exercised to benefit the decedent or his estate, it would not cause the proceeds to be included in his estate. If the power had been exercisable for the benefit of decedent, or for the benefit of whomever the decedent selected, it would have been necessary to include the proceeds in the estate; for there would be a powerful argument that this was an incident of ownership since he would have had the equivalent of a power of appointment, which under

§2041 would cause other types of property to be included in the estate of the holder of such a power. . . .

The power that the decedent possessed was over the entire trust corpus, which included property other than the insurance policies. But there is no serious doubt that this power did not result in this other property being in decedent's estate for tax purposes. This type of power would fall under both §2036 and §2038. The former provision is clearly not triggered in this case because it only applies to a power retained by the grantor over the income from property when he transferred it to another. Thus, for purposes of §2036, it would not matter that the decedent effectively had the power to deprive later income beneficiaries of the income from the corpus in favor of an earlier income beneficiary. However, the . . . Commissioner has pointed to many cases holding that such a power would result in the property interest over which the power could be exercised being included in the estate of the holder of the power. Therefore, he argues, this power must be an incident of ownership for §2042 purposes also.

But the Commissioner's reliance on §2038 cases exposes the fatal flaw in his position. The cases he cites dealt with powers that were retained by the transferor or settlor of a trust. That is not what we have here; the power the decedent had was given to him long after he had divested himself of all interest in the policies — it was not reserved by him at the time of the transfer. This difference between powers retained by a decedent and powers that devolved upon him at a time subsequent to the assignment is not merely formal, but has considerable substance. A taxpayer planning the disposition of his estate can select the powers that he reserves and those that he transfers in order to implement an overall scheme of testamentary disposition; however, a trustee, unless there is agreement by the settlor and/or beneficiaries, can only act within the powers he is granted. When the decedent is the transferee of such a power and holds it in a fiduciary capacity, with no beneficial interest therein, it is difficult to construe this arrangement as a substitute for a testamentary disposition by the decedent. . . .

Accordingly, we conclude that, although such a power might well constitute an incident of ownership if retained by the assignor of the policies, it is not an incident of ownership within the intended scope of §2042 when it has been conveyed to the decedent long after he had divested himself of all interest in the policies and when he cannot exercise the power for his own benefit. We justify this interpretation of "incidents of ownership" on the apparent intent of Congress that §2042 was not to operate in such a manner as to discriminate against life insurance, with regard to estate tax treatment, as compared with other types of property. We also note that our conclusion comports with the views expressed by the Sixth Circuit in Estate of Fruehauf v. Commissioner, 427 F.2d 80, 84–85 (6th Cir. 1970). Therefore, we must reject the contention of the Commissioner that the language of §2042 requires that it be given a broader scope of operation than the statutes covering other types of property.

Until now, the discussion has assumed that §2038 only applies when the power possessed by the decedent was reserved by him at the time he divested himself of all interest in the property (other than life insurance) subject to the power. This necessitates a brief discussion of the language of §2038, which provides in pertinent part:

> The value of the gross estate shall include the value of all property to the extent of any interest therein of which the decedent has at any time made a transfer . . . , by trust or otherwise, where the enjoyment thereof was subject at the date of his death to any change through the exercise of a power (in whatever capacity exercisable) . . . *(without regard to when or from what source the decedent acquired such power)*, to alter, amend, revoke, or terminate . . . (emphasis added).

The emphasized language would appear to indicate that §2038 would apply even when the power was acquired under circumstances such as are present here. However there is no indication that the Commissioner has ever made such an argument and we have been able to find no case applying §2038 in this manner.

The noted language was added to the predecessor of §2038 in 1936 in response to the decision in White v. Poor, 296 U.S. 98 (1935). In that case, the decedent had created an inter vivos trust and conferred on the trustee the power jointly to terminate the trust. Subsequently, the decedent was appointed a successor trustee. Therefore, at death decedent possessed this power to terminate and the Commissioner attempted to apply the predecessor to §2038; but the Supreme Court held this was impermissible because decedent had not retained the power at the time of transfer but had received it later. It was for the purpose of changing this result that Congress added the emphasized language. However, this language appears never to have been applied to a power other than one that the decedent created at the time of transfer in someone else and that later devolved upon him before his death. In essence, the language has been applied strictly to change the result in *White v. Poor*.

. . . What is significant for our purposes is that §2038 has not been applied when the power possessed by decedent was created and conferred on him by someone else long after he had divested himself of all interest in the property subject to the power. Therefore, because of our view that Congress did not intend §2042 to produce divergent estate tax treatment between life insurance and other types of property, we conclude that the fiduciary power that Skifter possessed at his death did not constitute an "incident of ownership" under §2042; hence, that provision does not require that the life insurance proceeds at issue be included in Skifter's estate. . . .

In addition to those authorities rejecting the government's position noted in Rev. Rul. 84-179, the Court of Appeals for the Third Circuit adopted the *Skifter* position in Connelly v. United States, 551 F.2d 545 (3d Cir. 1977), and the cited opinion in *Hunter* was consistent with the earlier Eighth Circuit position established in Estate of Margrave v. Commissioner, 618 F.2d 34 (8th Cir. 1980). The government's only success on this issue came in the Court of Appeals for the Fifth Circuit; Rev. Rul. 84-179 does not entirely concede that the Fifth Circuit cases were wrongly decided, and it would not be safe planning today to name an insured as fiduciary over policies on the insured's life unless added precautions are taken.

In Rev. Rul. 81-166, *D* created a revocable unfunded trust providing that the trust income was to be distributed to *B* for life, remainder to *E* and *F*. *B* purchased a 20-year term insurance policy on the life of *D* and designated the trustee as beneficiary of the policy. Under applicable state law, this beneficiary designation was sufficient to support creation of the trust. As the owner of the policy, B retained all incidents of ownership, particularly including the right to change the beneficiary, and *B* paid all premiums on the policy. Nevertheless, as settlor of the trust with a power to revoke *D* had certain control over the trust, which was beneficiary of the insurance. *D* died while *B* was still alive, and the insurance proceeds were paid to the trust. The government ruled that *B* made a completed inter vivos transfer when *D* died, and that none of the insurance proceeds were included in *D*'s gross estate. Although not well articulated, the rationale for the government's holding is telegraphed by the first sentence in the following extract of the Ruling:

B's initial designation of the trustee as the beneficiary of the insurance proceeds payable on the death of *D* was not a transfer of any interest in the proceeds at the time of designation. *B*, until the death of *D*, possessed all the incidents of ownership in the policy, including the right to change the beneficiary. *B* made a completed gift on *D*'s death, at which time the identity of the beneficiary became fixed and the trustee became indefeasibly entitled to the proceeds.

Under the terms of the trust, *B* will receive all the income from the trust corpus for life. Thus, the value of the gift is the fair market value of the property less the present value of *B*'s life estate, as determined under Treas. Reg. §25.2512-9.

In Margrave v. Commissioner, 618 F.2d 34 (8th Cir. 1980), the court held that, under similar facts, the insurance proceeds were not included in the insured's gross estate under either §2041 or §2042 of the Code. In the *Margrave* situation, the Service will no longer advance the position that the insurance proceeds are includible in the insured's gross estate under §2041 or §2042 of the Code. . . .

Further, for purposes of §2036 of the Code, *B* transferred the policy proceeds to the trust under the terms of which *B* retained the right to income for life. Under §2036(a)(1) of the Code, if *B* does not relinquish *B*'s income interest in the trust, then that portion of the trust corpus attributable to *B*'s contributions will be includible in *B*'s gross estate at *B*'s death. Therefore, assuming that no third parties make contributions to the trust, the value of the entire trust corpus will be includible in *B*'s gross estate at death.

If the situation described in Rev. Rul 81-166 took place today, the value of the gift made by *B* on *D*'s death would be affected by §2702.

Indirect Powers. Prior to changes adopted in 1974, Treas. Reg. §20.2042-1(c)(2) provided that the term "incident of ownership" included "a power to change the beneficiary reserved to a corporation of which the decedent is a sole shareholder." Rev. Rul. 71-463 sought to expand this provision to cover life insurance owned by a corporation in which the insured had voting control even though the proceeds were payable to the corporation as beneficiary. In response to strong criticism of the ruling, the government promulgated Rev. Rul. 72-167, which retracted Rev. Rul. 71-463 and announced that the regulations were being reconsidered. In 1974, Treas. Reg. §§20.2042-1(c)(2), -1(c)(6), and 20.2031-2(f) were amended by striking the quoted provision and adopting the current language. The regulations do not have the same effect advocated by Rev. Rul. 71-463 because they only cause insurance proceeds payable to the corporation to be reflected only in valuing the insured's corporate stock. See Estate of Huntsman v. Commissioner, 66 T.C. 861, 874–875 (1976), *acq.*, in which the Tax Court rejected the government's contention that the value of the stock of a *sole* shareholder under Treas. Reg. §20.2031-2(f) should be determined by first finding the value of the stock without the life insurance proceeds and then adding those proceeds to that value:

In determining the price a willing buyer would pay, it is obvious that life insurance proceeds must be given "consideration," but it is equally obvious that the price paid by a willing buyer would not necessarily be increased by the amount of the life insurance proceeds. A buyer would take into consideration such proceeds in the same manner as he would consider other liquid assets of the corporation. If the corporation is operating a going business, the willing buyer will be influenced by the prospective earning power and dividend-earning capacity of the business, as well as its net worth, including any life insurance proceeds. . . . Even if the value of the stock is based on the net worth of the corporation, such value may not be increased concomitantly by the amount of life insurance proceeds payable to the corporation. . . . [T]he interpretation urged by the Commissioner would treat the life insurance proceeds differently than other nonoperating assets. [66 T.C. at 874–875]

In Estate of Levy v. Commissioner, 70 T.C. 873 (1978), the decedent owned 80% of the voting stock of Levy Bros, which owned a policy insuring the decedent's life. The face amount of the policy was $250,000, of which $50,000 was payable to Levy Bros. and the remaining $200,000 was payable to the decedent's surviving spouse. Treas. Reg. §20.2042-1(c)(6) provides that, in such a case, $200,000 of the proceeds (those *not* paid to the corporation) are includible in the decedent's gross estate, which the Tax Court upheld as valid.

Consider some illustrations of how this regulation works:

(a) The decedent owned 60% of the outstanding stock of *XYZ, Inc.*, which owned assets valued at $200,000 when the decedent died. *XYZ* also owned a $120,000 policy insuring the decedent's life, the proceeds of which were payable to a trustee of a trust for the benefit of the decedent's surviving spouse. Under an agreement among the trustee, *XYZ*, and the decedent, the trustee delivered to *XYZ* the stock owned by the decedent, and the insurance proceeds were treated as payment for those shares. Those insurance proceeds are not includible in the decedent's gross estate under Treas. Reg. §20.2042-1(c)(6) because the redemption effected by this arrangement effectively is tantamount to payment to the corporation. Rev. Rul. 82-85.

(b) The decedent owned 55% of the outstanding stock of Win All, Inc. The decedent and the corporation contracted that Win All would redeem the decedent's stock when the decedent died. The decedent's executor was required to surrender the decedent's shares to the corporation at a redemption price of 55% of six times the average net income of Win All for the three years prior to the decedent's death. This contract was bona fide, at arm's length, and the formula price was reasonable. Prior to the 1974 amendments to the regulations and to the adoption of §2703 in 1990, the price established in the contract would have conclusively established the value of the decedent's stock for estate tax purposes. See Kahn, *Mandatory*

Buy-Out Agreements for Stock of Closely Held Corporations, 68 MICH. L. REV. 1, 5–6 (1969). Under the formula established in the contract, the price for the decedent's stock is $300,000, and Win All paid that amount to the decedent's estate, funded in part with the proceeds from a $100,000 policy insuring the decedent's life, under which Win All was the owner and beneficiary. Under Treas. Reg. §§20.2042-1(c)(6) and 20.2031-2(f), no part of the proceeds paid to Win All at the decedent's death will be includible in the decedent's gross estate under §2042. But they will increase the value of the decedent's stock and may inform the value of the decedent's shares if §2703 is applicable. See Part C of Chapter 15 at page 969.

(c) The decedent owned 20% of the outstanding stock of Bilt-Rite, Inc. At death the decedent was a vice-president and director of Bilt-Rite. The corporation purchased $100,000 of insurance on the decedent's life because the decedent's services were valuable to the corporation and because loss of the decedent's personal goodwill with customers would cause a loss of business at the decedent's death. Commonly known as key person insurance, the policy was acquired to compensate the corporation for its loss if the decedent died prematurely. Bilt-Rite was the owner of the policy, possessed all its incidents of ownership, and was beneficiary of all the proceeds. Because the decedent did not control the corporation, none of the proceeds are includible in the decedent's gross estate under §2042. Decedent's role as an officer or director will not change that result.

(d) *E* is a valued employee of Peerless, Inc., and a 60% shareholder. To provide additional compensation to *E* the corporation is considering adoption of a split-dollar insurance plan by which the benefits and costs of an ordinary life insurance policy would be split between Peerless and *E*. Like most split-dollar plans, Peerless would pay that part of the annual premium that equals the current year's increase in the cash surrender value of the policy, and *E* would pay the balance (if any) of the premium. If *E* dies while the plan is in effect, the insurance proceeds would be divided between Peerless and *E*'s designated beneficiary; Peerless would receive an amount equal to the greater of the aggregate premiums it paid and the cash surrender value of the policy at *E*'s death, and the balance of the proceeds would be paid to *E*'s beneficiary. Peerless would receive the full cash surrender value if the policy is surrendered prior to *E*'s death. There are two types of split-dollar plans — endorsement plans and collateral assignment plans. In an endorsement plan, Peerless would own the policy and *E*'s interests would be protected by endorsements added to the policy. In a collateral assignment arrangement the policy would be owned by someone other than Peerless (e.g., by *E*, a member of *E*'s family, or a trustee) and Peerless' interests in the policy would be secured by a collateral assignment of the policy by *E*. Would you recommend that Peerless adopt an endorsement plan or a collateral assignment plan for *E*'s split-dollar insurance: might it matter? The preamble accompanying the final 1974 amendments to the regulations noted that the proposed regulations were criticized because of their apparent applicability to both split-dollar and group term life insurance. Because the final version of the amendments excluded certain group term life insurance from its coverage but made no specific mention of split-dollar life insurance, it appears that the government intended to subject split-dollar insurance to the terms of the final regulations. See Simmons, *Final Regs on Corporate Owned Life Insurance: Greatly Improved but Still Questionable*, 41 J. TAX'N 66, 67–68 (1974). The government's position on the extent to which split-dollar life insurance is includible in an insured shareholder's gross estate is established by Rev. Rul. 76-274, modified by Rev. Rul. 82-145. The government's position on the extent to which a corporation's contribution to the premium for split-dollar life insurance for the benefit of a principal shareholder results in a taxable dividend from the corporation to the shareholder is stated in proposed regulations that most specifically address the income tax treatment of split-dollar insurance. See Prop. Treas. Reg. §§1.61-2(d)(2)(ii)(A), 1.61-22, 1.83-3, 1.83-6(a)(5), 1.301-1(q), and 1.7872-15.

Rev. Rul. 83-147 held that Treas. Reg. §20.2042-1(c)(6) is applicable with respect to a partnership that owns insurance on one of three equal partners, stating that any incidents of ownership held by the partnership effectively are held by its partners as individuals. The absence of control was not discussed.

Group Term Life Insurance. Term life insurance often is offered to members of a group, such as employees of an organization, alumni of a university, or members of a professional or trade association. If the group is sufficiently large the risk shifting character of the coverage allows all members to qualify for coverage without regard to medical condition. Many employers provide group term life insurance for their employees, and often the employer will pay most or all of the premium. One explanation for this popular benefit is that, although clearly compensation for services, the fringe benefit enjoys a special income tax advantage: the premium cost of up to $50,000 of group term life insurance coverage is excluded from the employee's gross income by §79.

Group term life insurance is like any other in that the proceeds are includible in the gross estate of an insured who possessed any incident of ownership at death. Estate of Lumpkin v. Commissioner, 474 F.2d 1092 (5th Cir. 1973), held that an employee's right to select a settlement option is an incident of ownership even if the employee could not change the person who would receive the benefits and only could affect the timing of distributions. Connelly v. United States, 551 F.2d 545 (3d Cir. 1977), rejected the *Lumpkin* rationale and held that a settlement option of that type does not constitute an incident of ownership. Rev. Rul. 81-128 announced that the government will not follow *Connelly* in cases arising outside the Third Circuit.

The question for planning purposes is whether an employee can successfully assign incidents of ownership in a group policy to escape §2042. In Rev. Rul. 76-490, an employee assigned a group term policy to an irrevocable trust and the employer was not contractually obligated to pay the premiums thereon; the government ruled that the employer's voluntary premium payments were indirect gifts made by the employee. The premium payments will be gifts of future interests for which no annual exclusion is allowed unless the trust is a so-called "Crummey" trust (a trust in which beneficiaries have powers of withdrawal for a brief period of time after a contribution to the trust was made, as discussed beginning at page 887). Rev. Rul. 79-47. If the trust provides *Crummey* powers, an annual exclusion likely will be allowed and, in many cases, premium payment will be gift tax free. See PLRs 8103074, 8021058, and 8006109. If done properly this plan may avoid *all* wealth transfer tax, as illustrated next.

Revenue Ruling 69-54

Advice has been requested whether the value of the amount received under a group term life insurance policy is includible in an employee's gross estate for Federal estate tax purposes under each of the situations discussed herein. . . .

In determining whether the decedent possessed an incident of ownership in the policy, consideration must be given to the effect of State or other applicable law. See Treas. Reg. §20.2042-1(c)(5). The decedent's rights in the policy are generally determined by local insurance or property laws.

The insurance laws of most States require that an employee have the right to convert his group insurance into individual insurance within a specified time after termination of his employment. The conversion privilege is a safeguard for the insured and cannot be deleted from the policy. Moreover, as a provision required by statute it cannot be waived by mutual consent of the parties to the contract, unsupported by consideration.

The application of §2042 to amounts received under group term life insurance policies is illustrated by three factual situations, as follows:

Situation 1. The decedent at the time of his death was insured for 50x dollars under a group term life insurance policy wholly paid for by his employer. Neither the group term policy nor State law gives the employee the right to convert his group insurance into individual insurance upon termination of his employment. The policy provides that each employee's coverage ceases upon termination of his employment. The employee makes an irrevocable assignment of his insurance under the group policy.

The value of the proceeds of the policy is includible in the gross estate of the insured employee since he had the power to cancel the insurance by terminating his employment, and any power to effect such a cancellation is an incident of ownership with respect to the policy. See Treas. Reg. §20.2042-1(c)(2). It is also evident that the assignee of the policy had no means of preventing a termination of the decedent's employment from causing a loss of such assignee's interest in the policy and thus effectively controlling its ultimate disposition.

Situation 2. The decedent at the time of his death was insured for 50x dollars under a group term life insurance policy wholly paid for by his employer. As required by State law, the employee is granted under the terms of the policy the right to convert his group insurance into individual upon termination of his employment. Both the policy and State law permit absolute assignment of the group insurance including the conversion privilege. The policy provides that coverage under the group policy shall cease upon termination of employment. The employee makes an irrevocable assignment of his insurance under the group policy, but retains the conversion privilege.

The value of the proceeds of the group term life insurance is includible in the gross estate of the insured. The decedent has effectively retained the power to control the disposition of the insurance through an exercise of the conversion privilege upon any termination of his employment and has thus retained an incident of ownership with respect to the policy. If either the group policy or local law prohibits an assignment of the conversion privilege, the same result follows notwithstanding any purported assignment of the conversion privilege.

Situation 3. The facts are similar to those in *Situation 2*, in that both the group policy and the State law permit the employee to make an absolute assignment of all of his incidents of ownership in the policy. The policy provides that coverage thereunder shall cease upon termination of employment. Upon such termination of the insured's employment, the assignee acting alone could convert to a 50x dollar individual policy. The employee made an irrevocable assignment of all of his incidents of ownership in the policy, including the conversion privilege. The insured could not have effected cancellation of the insurance coverage by terminating his employment. Consequently, the insured decedent did not die possessed of any incidents of ownership in the policy.

No part of the value of the proceeds of the group insurance is includible in the insured's gross estate under §2042. Under the circumstances, the assignee's right to the amount of the group term coverage could not have been defeated by any action within the control of the assignor.

Revenue Ruling 68-334 is hereby superseded. . . .

This next Ruling modifies the last:

Revenue Ruling 72-307

The Internal Revenue Service has given further consideration to Revenue Ruling 69-54, 1969-1 C.B. 221, insofar as it relates to whether the value of the proceeds receivable under a group term life insurance policy is includible in an employee's gross estate under the circumstances described in Situation 1 of that Ruling. . . .

An insured's power to cancel his insurance coverage by terminating his employment is a collateral consequence of the power that every employee has to terminate his employment. The examples in Treas. Reg. §20.2042-1(c), on the other hand, concern powers that directly affect the insurance policy or the payment of its proceeds without potentially costly related consequences. Where the power to cancel an insurance policy is exercisable only by terminating employment, it is not deemed to be an incident of ownership in the policy.

Accordingly, it is held that under the circumstances of *Situation 1* of Revenue Ruling 69-54, the value of the proceeds of the group insurance is not includible in the insured's gross estate under §2042 of the Code.

Revenue Ruling 69-54 is hereby modified.

See also Rev. Rul. 75-415, and the dissenting opinion of Judge Learned Hand in Commissioner v. Treganowan, reproduced at page 447, which involved a New York Stock Exchange plan to make payments to the surviving families of Exchange members. The court held that the plan constituted life insurance. The court also held that the power to terminate the insurance by selling the member's seat on the Exchange constituted an incident of ownership, to which Judge Hand dissented:

I think [incidents of ownership] covers those policies which the insured has reserved some power to change; it means that he can change the beneficiary; that he can borrow on them; that he can surrender them; that he can influence their obligation by acts directed to them alone. It does not mean, I submit, that he can affect them by transactions in which they are at best only an incident, and a relatively unimportant one at that.

Estate of Smead v. Commissioner, 78 T.C. 43 (1982), rejected the government's argument in Situation 2 of Rev. Rul. 69-54 that an employee's right to convert a group term policy into an individual policy upon termination of employment is an incident of ownership. The government distinguished Rev. Rul. 72-307 because it dealt with an employee's right to cancel rather than to convert a group term policy, to which the Tax Court replied: "If quitting one's job is too high a price to pay for the right to cancel an insurance policy, it is likewise too high a price to pay for the right to convert to another policy." Notwithstanding its acquiescence to *Smead* in Rev. Rul. 84-130, the government again asserted that a conversion privilege is an incident of ownership in TAM 9141007 because of the added fact in the TAM that the power was exercised within three years of the insured's death, implicating §2035(a)(2). The next case speaks to these issues.

Landorf v. United States
408 F.2d 461 (Cl. Ct. 1969)

[At death the decedent was president of Sam Landorf and Company. He held half the voting common stock, William Glottstein, executive vice-president of the corporation, held the remaining shares of voting common stock, and the non-voting common stock was held by the decedent's wife, Lillian, and his two sons. In 1959 a noncontributory group life insurance policy was issued to the company, providing that the company would pay annually the renewal premiums for term insurance for each covered employee, all of whom received a "certificate" to evidence participation in the plan. The policy had no cash surrender or loan value. The decedent designated Lillian as beneficiary of his $200,000 policy coverage. In 1961 the decedent executed the insurance company's "Assignment of Insurance" form, gratuitously assigning the policy to Lillian. It assigned the insurance, all future additional insurance, and all interests and benefits under the policy.]

LARAMORE, J.: . . . Mrs. Landorf, as beneficiary, received the $200,000 proceeds of the group policy from the insurance company. The executors of the estate, however, excluded the proceeds from the decedent's gross estate subject to Federal estate taxes. Upon audit, the District Director of the Internal Revenue Service did include the proceeds in the taxable estate . . . and a deficiency was assessed. . . .

Basically, plaintiffs argue that the decedent was neither a legal nor equitable owner at the time of his death because he had irrevocably and absolutely assigned to his wife his entire title to, and his interest and rights in, both the policy and the proceeds. . . .

Several aspects of this case involve issues of first impression. . . . On the basis of the specific facts before us, we conclude that plaintiffs are entitled to recover a refund.

I. SECTION 2042

. . .

The group policy in this case gave each insured employee the right to designate a beneficiary; the right to elect among optional modes of settlement (to be agreed upon by the insured and the insurance company); the power to assign the policy; and in the event of termination for any reason, the right to convert the group coverage into an individual life insurance policy of equal amount, without providing evidence of insurability. Defendant argues that, in addition to these rights, decedent had a right to surrender or cancel the group policy and also that he had a reversionary interest in the policy in excess of 5% of the value of his policy. Defendant argues that if, despite a transfer of all of his rights in the policy, the decedent nevertheless retained any one of these incidents of ownership, either because applicable local law proscribes the assignment of a particular right or for any other reason, all of the proceeds of the policy are includible in the taxable gross estate.

(a) Right to Convert the Term Insurance to Ordinary Life Insurance The problems raised by the Federal estate tax consequences of an absolute, written assignment of all rights in a group life insurance policy have been considered by many commentators. These same problems, however, have not been resolved by Congress, and they have been considered by very few courts. . . .

Under Treas. Reg. §20.2042-1(c)(5) (and Revenue Ruling 68-334) we must, where appropriate, give effect to applicable state or local law in deciding whether the decedent possessed any incident of ownership. Specifically, we must look to the insurance and property law of the State of New York (which the parties agree is applicable) to determine whether an employee may assign his coverage and rights under a group life insurance policy, including the right to convert. Ultimately, the question of incidents of ownership is one of Federal tax law, but this decision, as the Regulations and Revenue Ruling state, may turn on state law. . . .

As a general rule, ordinary life insurance policies are assignable under New York law. . . . Whether a *group* policy and its conversion privilege may be assigned, however, is unclear. Neither the courts of the State of New York nor its legislature has directed itself to these specific questions. . . .

Our conclusion, therefore, is that local law neither prohibits nor approves assignments of group policies. As noted above, there is no decision of the New York Court of Appeals on this point. We can find nothing to prohibit an assignment and, therefore, conclude that group life insurance policies are no less assignable under New York law than ordinary life insurance policies.

This determination, however, is merely the first step of our analysis. We must now find whether, under both local law and the Federal tax laws, decedent possessed any other right in the policy or proceeds which may be deemed an incident of ownership.

(b) Right to Terminate Employment Defendant argues that decedent could at any time terminate his employment and thereby force the assignee to exercise the conversion privilege. The decedent's ability to terminate his employment, however, did not control his assignee's rights in the policy because, as we said above, Mrs. Landorf could exercise the conversion privilege and obtain the same amount of coverage. The only adverse effect on the assignee would be that she must pay a higher premium for the new policy.

A similar argument was made in Estate of Whitworth v. Commissioner, 22 T.C.M. (CCH) 177 (1963). Defendant argued that a transfer was revocable (under §2038) because the employee could at all times cease his employment and terminate the rights to pension benefits that he had transferred to his wife. The court thought that this argument leads to an absurd result; it found that Congress could not have intended to make the right to terminate one's employment a power to revoke within §2038. In our case, even if Mr. Landorf had quit, the only effect on the policy would be to make the conversion privilege exercisable. Moreover, we do not believe that Congress intended to include the power to terminate employment, a right which everyone can exercise at any time, to be an "incident of ownership" in property simply because the property involved is somehow related to the employment. The exercise of the right to terminate employment in no way derogates the rights in the property assigned. Accordingly, we find that decedent's right to terminate his employment is not an incident of ownership within the meaning of §2042.

(c) Reversionary Interest Defendant argues that, under §2042(2), decedent had a reversionary interest in the proceeds of the policy. A reversionary interest in either the policy or the proceeds of the policy, whether it arises by virtue of the terms of

the policy or another instrument, or by operation of law, is an incident of ownership, if immediately prior to the death of the decedent, the value of the reversionary interest exceeds 5% of the value of the policy. "Reversionary interest" is defined in §2042(2) as including "a possibility that the policy, or the proceeds of the policy, may return to the decedent or his estate, or may be subject to a power of disposition by him."

Defendant argues that the decedent had a reversionary interest because, under the terms of the policy, the proceeds would have been paid to his estate if his wife had predeceased him. This would have occurred because his wife was the sole designated beneficiary under the policy; there were no contingent beneficiaries who would take the proceeds if the wife had predeceased the insured. This becomes important because the group policy provided that in the absence of a designated beneficiary who survives the employee the proceeds of the policy shall be paid to the executors of the employee's estate. Therefore, argues defendant, there is a possibility that the proceeds of the policy will return to the decedent's estate and that possibility is an incident of ownership in the policy. (Defendant asks the court to return the case to a trial commissioner for a factual determination of whether the reversionary interest represents 5% of the value of the policy.)

The government's argument presupposes that the insured retained some rights under the contract as an "employee." As we have decided above, all of the rights to which he might have been entitled were assigned to his wife. Therefore, any proceeds originally payable to the "employee" are, subsequent to the assignment, payable to the assignee. If the wife had predeceased the decedent, the proceeds of the policy would be payable to *her* estate because, upon the subsequent death of the employee, the proceeds originally payable to the employee's estate instead would be paid to the assignee's estate. We find, therefore, that the decedent did not retain any reversionary interest under the terms of the policy.

(d)　Rights to Revoke the Assignment and to Terminate the Policy　We turn now to the last of defendant's arguments on this issue. They are that the decedent could have acted either together with his wife to revoke the assignment, or together with Mr. Glottstein, his co-stockholder, to cancel the entire group policy; these are rights exercisable in conjunction with another person and, therefore, incidents of ownership within the meaning of §2042.

Defendant makes the conclusory statement that decedent probably could have revoked the gratuitous assignment by himself under local law and that, in any event, he could have revoked the assignment together with his wife. . . .

It is, of course, possible for the assignee and the assignor to agree to revoke the assignment. If, however, this possibility is sufficient to establish an incident of ownership within §2042(2), it is difficult to see how any assignment, no matter how complete and irrevocable, could effectively remove property from the provisions of §2042.

The cases relied on by defendant to support its proposition are inapposite. They stand only for the general proposition that if a decedent can exercise some affirmative or negative control over the policy (whether alone or in conjunction with someone else) the proceeds of the policy are includible in his estate. In these cases, however, the powers of control are obvious and they are in no sense comparable to the possibility posed by defendant, i.e., that the assignee and assignor could agree to revoke the assignment. . . .

Defendant's last "incident of ownership" argument is that the decedent, as president and owner of 50% of the voting stock of the corporation, could have surrendered or cancelled the policy by acting together with Mr. Glottstein (who owned the other 50%), and thereby terminate all rights under the contract, including those of the assignee. In addition, he had the power to prevent Mr. Glottstein from canceling the entire policy. Defendant points out that Mr. Landorf, as president, signed the amendment which made the policies assignable. Moreover, he remained as president with power to cancel the policy (whether or not such cancellation would be wrongful). Equally damaging in defendant's view, is the fact that the policy limited the amount of coverage obtainable in the event of a termination of the entire policy to $2,000 and, therefore, the decedent retained power to control the *amount* of insurance which an exercise of the conversion privilege could obtain (either $2,000 or $200,000).

By virtue of the special stock-ownership position of Mr. Landorf, he had rights which an insured employee generally would not have. This issue is, we admit, a very close question. However, we are not convinced by defendant's arguments because we cannot conclude that Congress intended to impose special difficulties on the insured-employee who is also a stockholder of the corporation. If the mere ownership of stock in the corporation is a barrier to assignability, defendant's argument would be equally applicable to employees with substantially lower percentages of ownership because they, too, *could* terminate the policy if they were to obtain the agreement of other stockholders. In effect, the ownership of a small percentage of stock (as is frequently the case) combined with the possibility of agreement among sufficient stockholders to terminate the policy would prevent the assignment of any employee group policy rights. The net effect, we believe, is beyond the pale of what Congress intended should be the thrust of §2042. This may not be the case, however, if the corporation is wholly-owned or if it is proved that a particular stockholder has control over a sufficient number of other stockholders to effectuate a cancellation at his will. Of prime importance is the fact that there is no proof that this is the situation in our case. Defendant has not proved that decedent could have caused the corporation to act at his will. The mere fact of stock ownership is insufficient. We conclude that decedent did not have this alleged incident of ownership.

Defendant states . . . that a failure to pay the premium for a particular employee would terminate that employee's coverage. There is no proof, however, that the insurance company would refuse to accept a payment of the premium by the assignee, and the record before us is inadequate for a determination that decedent had an incident of ownership on this basis. . . .

Accordingly, plaintiffs are entitled to recover the amount set forth in their claim for refund, together with interest as provided by law.

Treas. Reg. §20.2042-1(c)(6) now provides that a corporation's powers to surrender or cancel a group term life insurance policy will not be attributed to a decedent through stock ownership.

8. *Transfers Within Three Years of Death.* If Mr. Landorf's assignment had taken place after 1976 and if he had died within the next three years, §2035(a)(2) would require the proceeds of the policy to be included in his gross estate. *Landorf* itself found the pre-1977 version of §2035 inapplicable because the assignment was not made "in contemplation of death," but that requirement no longer exists. Now we must confront this pervasive impediment to end-of-life efforts to move what often is a large sum of proceeds out of the gross estate at a much lower gift tax cost.

Revenue Ruling 80-289

The decedent, *D*, was an active employee of the *X* corporation until the date of death on November 16, 1977.

In 1970, *X* corporation entered into a group term life insurance arrangement with the *Y* insurance company. Under the plan, a master insurance policy was issued to the *X* corporation and individual insurance certificates were issued to the *X* corporation employees. All premiums were paid by the *X* corporation. The *Y* insurance company master policy provides, among other things, that an insured employee may assign all rights in the insurance policy to any person with such an assignment to be effective upon written notification to, and acceptance by, the Y insurance company.

In 1971, D assigned all rights under the insurance policy issued by the Y insurance company to D's spouse. The employer was duly notified of the assignment, and the Y insurance company received and accepted the assignment. Before making the assignment, D executed a written agreement with D's spouse stating that the assignment would vest in the assignee-spouse not only D's rights under the current policy issued by the Y insurance company, but also D's rights under any arrangement for life insurance coverage of the employees of X corporation.

On January 17, 1977, less than 3 years before D's death, the X corporation terminated the insurance arrangement with the Y insurance company and obtained a new master contract from the Z insurance company. Notice of the termination of coverage under the master policy of the Y insurance company was properly given to the employees and their assignees. Upon termination, the new master policy of the Z insurance company came into effect. The terms of the new master policy and the individual employees' certificates of insurance were, in all relevant aspects, identical to the terms of the previous arrangement with the Y insurance company. Two weeks after the Z insurance company coverage came into effect, the decedent executed an assignment of all rights under the new policy to the decedent's spouse.

Rev. Rul. 79-231 concluded under identical facts that the anticipatory assignment in 1971 was not effective as a present transfer of the decedent's rights in the group term life insurance policy issued by the Z insurance company and that the time of transfer for purposes of §2035 was in 1977. The Internal Revenue Service maintains the view that the anticipatory assignment was not technically effective as a present transfer of the decedent's rights in the policy issued by Z. Nevertheless, the Service believes that the assignment in 1977 to D's spouse, the object of the anticipatory assignment in 1971, should not cause the value of the proceeds to be includible in the gross estate of the decedent under §2035 where the assignment was necessitated by the change of the employer's master insurance plan carrier and the new arrangement is identical in all relevant aspects to the previous arrangement with Y. . . .

The value of the proceeds from the group term life insurance policy is not includible in the gross estate of the decedent under §2035.

It is not known how close to identical the policies must be for an automatic or individuated assignment of a replacement policy to avoid §2035(a)(2).

In Berman v. United States, 487 F.2d 70 (5th Cir. 1973), the court stated in part:

> Before boarding an airplane at the Jackson, Mississippi, airport, Joseph Emile Berman, a 67-year-old food broker and lawyer, purchased a $30,000 flight insurance policy on his life for one dollar, naming his son as beneficiary. The ownership of the policy was immediately assigned to the son. The plane crashed shortly thereafter and Berman was killed. . . .
>
> The assignment of the life insurance policy by Berman to his son was a transfer of property. The value of property transferred [within three years] of death is included in a donor's gross state for estate tax purposes. 26 U.S.C.A. §2035. In the case of an insurance policy, the entire death benefit is the policy's fair market value to be included, not merely the amount of the premiums paid. Bel v. United States, 452 F.2d 683 (5th Cir. 1971); Rev. Rul. 71-497, 1971-2 C.B. 329.

See also Treas. Reg. §20.2042-1(a)(2).

The proceeds of the policy would not have been included in Berman's gross estate if Berman's son had purchased the flight insurance policy insuring Berman's life and had used his own dollar to pay the premium. Should the result differ if Berman had given his son the dollar to purchase the flight insurance? Remember that the premium payment test no longer applies.

Subject to one exception, gratuitous transfers made after 1976 and prior to 1982 were included in the gross estate of a donor who died within three years after making the gift. See Chapter 4. Prior to 1977, transfers within three years of death were included in a decedent's gross estate only if made in contemplation of death. A gratuitous assignment of a life insurance policy made prior to 1977 often was determined to have been made in contemplation of death (there being few lifetime motives for ownership or transfer of life insurance). If the gratuitous assignment was made after 1976, it was not even necessary to show that the motive for the assignment was death-oriented; virtually any assignment of an insurance policy by an insured within three years of death therefore would trigger §2035(a) and cause inclusion of the proceeds in the insured's gross estate as if no transfer had occurred.

The automatic inclusion rule was repealed by the Economic Recovery Tax Act of 1981, but this repeal does not apply to certain transfers itemized in §2035(a)(2), one of which is transfers of property that would be subject to estate tax inclusion under §2042. Thus, an insured's gratuitous assignment of a life insurance policy within three years of death continues to be subject to §2035(a). The stated rationale for this exception is that life insurance typically has a much lower gift tax value than the amount that would be includible under §2042 if held until death, and deathbed transfers should not permit movement of this wealth without the appropriate gift or estate tax.

This background sets the stage for an odyssey that has taken some very interesting turns and that today allows well-advised taxpayers to move significant amounts of wealth in the form of life insurance proceeds for little or no wealth transfer tax. The progress of this saga is as important as the final word, which we'll get to soon enough. Please bear with the prologue:

Revenue Ruling 71-497

The Internal Revenue Service has given further consideration to the position set forth in Revenue Ruling 67-463, 1967-2 C.B. 327, relating to the amount includible in a decedent's gross estate by reason of the payment by him [within three years] of death, of premiums on an insurance policy on his life owned by another. Consideration has also been given to the question whether the proceeds of insurance on the life of the decedent in each of the situations described below are includible in his gross estate.

Situation 1. Four years prior to his death a decedent purchased and transferred to his wife all incidents of ownership in a whole life insurance policy and a five-year term policy on his life. However, he continued to pay the premiums on the policies until the time of his death.

Situation 2. Nine months before he died by accidental means, the decedent purchased an accidental death insurance policy on his life for a one-year term, designating his children as owners and beneficiaries. He paid the full premium from his individual funds.

. . .

Revenue Ruling 67-463 holds that each premium payment made by a decedent on an insurance policy on his life owned by another was a transfer of an interest in the policy measured by the proportion the premium so paid bears to the total premiums paid. Accordingly, the value of the proportionate part of the insurance proceeds that is attributable to those premiums paid within three years of death is includible in decedent's gross estate under §2035 of the Code. However, First National Bank of Midland v. United States, 423 F.2d 1286 (5th Cir. 1970), . . . rejected the rationale of the Revenue Ruling in a substantially identical factual situation and held that no part of the proceeds of the policies was includible under §2035.

The Service will follow the decision in *Midland*, insofar as that decision holds that payment, by a decedent, of premiums on a whole life insurance policy on his life that had been owned by another for more than three years prior to his death, is not a transfer of an interest in the policy.

Accordingly, it is held with respect to *Situation 1* that no part of the proceeds of the whole life policy on the life of the decedent is includible in his gross estate. The same conclusion is equally applicable to the five-year term policy that the decedent had transferred more than three years before his death. . . .

In *Situation 2*, on the other hand, the purchase by the decedent of a one-year term policy on his life, designating his children as beneficiaries and owners, constituted a transfer of the policy to his children just as the purchase of any other asset in their names would have effected a transfer. In Chase National Bank v. United States, 278 U.S. 327 (1929), the Supreme Court of the United States upheld the constitutionality of [§2042] as applied to tax the proceeds of a life insurance policy taken out by decedent on his own life, as a tax on the indirect transfer of the proceeds from decedent to the beneficiaries, reasoning as follows:

> Obviously, the word "transfer" in the statute or the privilege which may constitutionally be taxed, cannot be taken in such a restricted sense as to refer only to the passing of particular items of property directly from the decedent to the transferee. It must, we think, as least include the transfer of property procured through expenditures by the decedent with the purpose, effected at death, of having it pass to another. [Section 2035] taxes [certain] transfers made [within three years] of death. It would not, we assume, be seriously argued that its provisions could be evaded by the purchase by a decedent from a third person of property, a savings bank book, for example, and its delivery by the seller directly to the intended beneficiary on the purchaser's death, or that the measure of the tax would be the cost and not the value of proceeds at the time of death.

The Supreme Court's analysis of the "transfer" of life insurance proceeds for estate tax purposes indicates that the estate tax provisions extend to the proceeds of a life insurance policy that are transferred only indirectly by the decedent to the beneficiaries, that the real subject of the estate tax is the shifting of the economic benefits of property at death, and that [§2035] cannot be evaded by decedent's purchase of property from a third person and the delivery of the property by the seller directly to the intended beneficiary.

Thus, in *Situation 2*, the economic benefit that the decedent did in substance transfer to his children by the purchase of the insurance policy was not the use of the cash amount of the premium payment, but the right to the insurance coverage for the one-year period of the contract. This coverage matured into the proceeds of the policy at his death. Accordingly, it is held that the value of the insurance in this situation is includible in his gross estate under §2035. See Treas. Reg. §2042-1(a)(2).

Consistent with Situation 2 in the Ruling is Bel v. United States, 452 F.2d 683 (5th Cir. 1971), which adopted a "beamed transfer" approach that treated the insured as the assignor of a policy purchased at the insured's initiative and paid for with funds provided by the insured. Commencing in October 1957, the decedent, John Albert Bel, purchased annually an accidental death policy on his own life in the principal amount of $250,000. Each policy covered a term of one year, and the last such policy was acquired in October 1960, less than one year prior to the decedent's death. While the decedent himself executed the original insurance application and paid, with community funds, all of the premiums, the policies from their inception were owned solely by the decedent's three children. The October 1960 policy matured as a result of the decedent's accidental death, and his three children, as beneficiaries under the policy, received the $250,000 proceeds. The court held that Bel's community share of the proceeds was includible in his gross estate.

In our opinion the broad legal principle enunciated by the Supreme Court . . . is that the word "transfer" is not limited to the passing of property directly from the donor to the transferee, but encompasses a donation "procured through expenditures by the decedent with the purpose, effected at his death, of having it pass to another." Like the Supreme Court, we perceive little seriousness in the argument that a decedent should be permitted to evade the provisions of §2035 by funneling property to various beneficiaries through a third-party conduit. Judicial sanctioning of such evasion, we think, would so frustrate the attempted taxation of testamentary substitutes that §2035 would stand emaciated and skeletonized beyond congressional recognition. We recognize, of course, that John Bel never formally possessed any of the incidents of owner-ship in the accidental death policy. . . . [H]owever, we conclude that §2042 and the incidents-of-ownership test are totally irrelevant to a proper application of §2035. We think our focus should be on the control beam of the word "transfer." The decedent, and the decedent alone, beamed the accidental death policy at his children, for by paying the premium he designated ownership of the policy and created in his children all of the contractual rights to the insurance benefits. These were acts of transfer. The policy was not procured and ownership designated and designed by some goblin or hovering spirit. Without John Bel's conception, guidance, and payment, the proceeds of the policy in the context of this case would not have been the children's. His actions were not ethereally, spiritually, or occultly actuated. Rather, they constituted worldly acts which by any other name come out as a "transfer." Had the decedent, within three years of his death, procured the policy in his own name and immediately thereafter assigned all ownership rights to his children, there is no question but that the policy proceeds would have been included in his estate.

In our opinion the decedent's mode of execution is functionally indistinguishable.

In Detroit Bank & Trust Co. v. United States, 467 F.2d 964 (6th Cir. 1972), the decedent created a trust with the Detroit Bank and Trust Company as trustee, to which the decedent transferred $9,600 to acquire $100,000 of insurance on the decedent's life, payable to the decedent's children as beneficiaries. The trust was irrevocable and beyond the decedent's control but provided for the decedent to contribute to the trust for premium payment purposes and the trust confined the trustees to expending contributed funds solely for the described purpose. The decedent died about six months later. The court said:

We believe that what this appeal presents is still another method of evading a portion of the federal estate tax. At oral argument counsel for appellee bank did not seriously dispute this characterization, but contended that the device employed made use of an existing loophole in the federal tax statutes and that his client should be allowed full benefit of that loophole until, when, as, and if Congress elected to close it.

We do not deny the force of this argument. . . . Yet it appears to us that the congressional purpose was clearly to sweep into the estate tax gifts of insurance made [within three years] of death and to value such gifts in terms of the transfer of the proceeds at death rather than at the purchase or premium cost.

If the dominant purpose of §2035 is "to reach substitutes for testamentary disposition and thus to prevent evasion of the estate tax" (United States v. Wells, [283 U.S. 102 (1931)]), we feel justified in holding that the trustee in this case was an agent for purchase of the insurance and that the trust device was a "substitute for testamentary disposition."

Note, please, that in the next case "spouse owned" insurance no longer makes sense — rather than transfer it to the spouse to prevent estate tax inclusion in the estate of the insured, with subsequent wealth transfer taxation to the *spouse*, the decedent instead could retain ownership of it, name the spouse as beneficiary, generate a marital deduction in the insured-decedent's estate, and still incur no wealth transfer tax until disposition by the spouse — and the insured need not relinquish control of the policy in the latter alternative. Either way, avoidance of wealth transfer tax in *both* estates is possible only if *neither* spouse owns the policy or its proceeds (which is what the irrevocable life insurance trust is used to accomplish). Still, as part of our study, Mr. and Mrs. Slade's plan is worthy of your time.

First National Bank v. United States
488 F.2d 575 (9th Cir. 1973)

CHOY, J.: . . . In 1966 the decedent [Mr. Slade] had his wife sign the applications for two 20-year term insurance policies on his life. This was done at the urging of his insurance agent, who explained that such a purchase could exempt the proceeds from federal estate taxation. The policies were issued to Mrs. Slade as owner and beneficiary, but all the premiums were paid by Mr. Slade. Within three years Mr. Slade died.

Section 2035 of the Internal Revenue Code provides that *transfers* of interests in property made for less than adequate consideration and within three years of death are . . . includible in a decedent's gross estate. . . . The sole issue on appeal is whether the property interest transferred was the proceeds of the policies, as the district court held, or only the premiums advanced by Mr. Slade, as appellant contends.

We agree with *Detroit Bank and Trust Co.* that where life insurance policies are procured at the instance of the decedent within the [§2035] period and where the premiums are paid by the deceased, the gross estate includes the proceeds of the policies.

Appellant argues that, since Mr. Slade never owned the policies, he could not have "transferred" them to Mrs. Slade. We cannot sanction such a technical reading of the statute. . . . There is only a formal difference between a decedent first buying a policy, then transferring it to the beneficiary, and the beneficiary purchasing the policy at the urging of the decedent and with the decedent's funds. . . . No policy, except one of tax evasion, supports this formalistic distinction. We decline to adopt it.

Not only would appellant's interpretation of §2035 be unduly technical, it would also undermine its statutory goal . . . to reach substitutes for testamentary dispositions and thus to prevent the evasion of the estate tax." An insured pays the premiums on a life insurance policy in order to leave the proceeds to his beneficiaries;

thus, where a policy is both procured at the behest of the decedent within the statutory period and where all the premiums are paid by the deceased [within three years] of death, the gift must necessarily be one of the property interest in the policy. In short, what is intended with the purchase of a life insurance policy in circumstances like these is the passing of the proceeds at death. That is the equivalent of a testamentary disposition, and its taxation is precisely the object of §2035.

Finally, acquiescing in appellant's interpretation would create an anomalous exception to §2035 in the case of life insurance policies. The normal rule under §2035 is that property transferred [within three years] of death is valued as of the decedent's death, not as of the date the property was transferred. Treas. Reg. §20.2035-1(e). . . . But taxing only the premiums paid on life insurance as gifts [within three years] of death would mean ignoring the increase in value the premiums purchased — namely, the value of the proceeds.

Our holding does not, as appellant argues, impermissibly raise the old "premium payment" test "phoenix-like from the language" of §2035. . . . Congress eliminated this harsh rule in adopting §2042 dictating that life insurance proceeds are includible in the gross estate when the insured possesses at his death "any of the incidents of ownership" of the policy. Appellant argues that the adoption of §2042 wholly put to rest the "premium payment" test, and that a holding employing it for the limited purpose of determining the value of a gift [within three years] of death contravenes that congressional intent.

However, the legislative history of §2042 demonstrates that the test was eliminated only as a standard for the inclusion of insurance proceeds under that section. Both the House and Senate committee reports stated that §2042 "revises existing law so that payment of premiums is no longer a factor in determining the taxability *under this section* of insurance proceeds." H.R. Rep. No. 1337, 83d Cong., 2d Sess. A316 (1954); S. Rep. No. 1622, 83d Cong., 2d Sess. 472 (1954) (emphasis added). Congress jettisoned the "premium payment" test under §2042 because "no other property [was] subject to estate tax where the decedent initially purchased it and then long before his death gave away all rights to the property." H.R. Rep. No. 1337, supra at 91. The purpose was to end discrimination against insurance as a form of property, not to affect the treatment of insurance proceeds — or indeed favor insurance over other types of property — under §2035.

In Estate of Kurihara v. Commissioner, 82 T.C. 51 (1984), the decedent created an irrevocable life insurance trust to own a policy of one year renewable term insurance on the decedent's life. Although the trustee actually applied for the insurance and was its original owner, the decedent transferred funds to the trustee in the year of the trust's creation in the exact amount of the premium due for the year, specifically designating that the funds were to provide the premium to be paid for that year. When the decedent died later in the same year, the government successfully argued that the decedent's contribution of funds to pay the premium should be treated as direct payment thereof by the decedent. Further, because of the renewable term nature of the policy, the government argued that the decedent's premium payment within three years of the decedent's death should be regarded as an acquisition and transfer of the insurance by the decedent in the year of the decedent's death. The consequence, according to the government, was that §2035(a)(2) should cause inclusion of the proceeds of the insurance in the decedent's gross estate, as if the decedent had died owning the policy and §2042(2) had applied at death.

Subsequently, in Estate of Baratta-Lorton v. Commissioner, 49 T.C.M. (CCH) 770 (1985), and the factually identical case of Estate of Hass v. Commissioner, 51 T.C.M. (CCH) 453 (1986), the decedent's spouse owned the policy and used community property income to pay premiums on the policy. Notwithstanding that the decedent did not apply for the policy and never owned it (and the parties had agreed that it would be the spouse's separate property), the court required §2035 inclusion of *half* the proceeds because (1) the policy was obtained within three years of the decedent's death, (2) because community income was used to pay policy premiums, the decedent had effectively paid half the premiums, and (3) premium payment was deemed sufficient to constitute a "transfer" of the right to half the proceeds for §2035 purposes.

And then the tide began to turn against the government. In Estate of Clay v. Commissioner, 86 T.C. 1266 (1986), the government lost what appeared to be the noncommunity property clone of *Baratta-Lorton*. In *Clay*, the insurance was spouse-owned but premiums were paid out of a joint bank account, to which the decedent-insured had contributed 73% of the account balance. To the government's predictable tracing argument that 73% of the proceeds should be includible under §2035, the court replied that tracing was reminiscent of the defunct premium payment test under the pre-1954 version of §2042, which the court would not reinstate. The court characterized premium payments using joint account monies withdrawn with the decedent's knowledge and consent as a transfer of those funds that terminated the decedent's interest in those funds and precluded a characterization as the decedent's premium payment through an agent. It may have been important to the court that the facts established that the decedent was not instrumental in securing the insurance and that no facts would support an allegation that the decedent's spouse, as owner of the policy, was acting as the decedent's agent.

Then, completing its total turnaround on this issue, *Clay* was followed by the Tax Court in Estate of Schnack v. Commissioner, 52 T.C.M. (CCH) 1107 (1986), *rev'd*, 848 F.2d 933 (9th Cir. 1988), in which Husband owned a policy of insurance on the life of Wife. Wife had paid the initial premium on the policy, using funds from a joint tenancy bank account established by Husband and Wife, and died within three years thereof. Holding that Wife was acting only as manager of the joint account, the Tax Court found that Wife paid the premium as Husband's agent, at his request, and that her consent to his use of joint funds was tantamount to her making a gift to Husband of that amount. Thus, the court held that the premium payment was not a joint payment, tracing could not apply, and no part of the insurance proceeds were includible in Wife's estate.

Next came the cases discussed below, which cast an entirely new light on this topic.

Estate of Headrick v. Commissioner
93 T.C. 171 (1989) (reviewed by the court),
aff'd, 918 F.2d 1263 (6th Cir. 1990), *acq.*

NIMS, Chief Judge: . . . The issue for decision is whether the proceeds of a life insurance policy purchased within three years of the decedent's death by a trust established by the decedent are properly includible in the decedent's gross estate under §2035(a). . . . Resolution of this issue requires us to determine whether the decedent directly or indirectly possessed incidents of ownership over the life insurance policy during his lifetime. [§§2035[(a)](2) and 2042].

. . . As part of his personal estate planning, the decedent, then 30 years of age, skillfully drafted an irrevocable trust agreement (Trust Agreement) of which decedent was grantor. The Trust Agreement designated decedent's wife and children as primary beneficiaries, conferred on the trustee by reference to Tennessee statutes most of the fiduciary powers recognized in that state, specifically permitted the trustee to accept additional contributions of property, reserved to decedent the right to remove any trustee at will and appoint a successor bank trustee, granted trust beneficiaries a limited power to withdraw trust property within 30 days of the contribution of such property and authorized the trustee to hold life insurance policies as trust principal. Regarding the power of the trustee to hold life insurance as a trust investment, the Trust Agreement specifically provided:

> 2.3 Life Insurance as Trust Principal: The trustee may accept the contribution of a life insurance policy on my life or on a beneficiary or on a person in whom I or a beneficiary have an insurable interest as Trust Principal. Like-

wise, the trustee may purchase insurance on my life, or on a beneficiary or on a person in whom there is an insurable interest, and hold each such policy as Trust Principal.

2.4 Payment of Premiums: The trustee may pay the premium on each policy of insurance held as Trust Principal from either Trust Principal or income, and such payment is an authorized expenditure. However, if the trustee does not have sufficient funds with which to pay a premium, it may:

(i) borrow money to pay the premium;

(ii) use such part of the cash surrender value of a policy (including a policy other than the one on which the premium is due) as is necessary to pay the premium; or

(iii) refuse to pay the premium and either convert the policy to a paid up policy or retain full coverage for an extended definite term or, if term insurance, permit the policy to lapse.

The decision of the trustee on which course of action to take is binding upon each beneficiary.

2.5 Ownership of Insurance: The trustee must own each policy of insurance purchased by, or contributed to, it. The trustee alone shall exercise each incident of ownership over each such policy.

Prior to executing the Trust Agreement, decedent met with life insurance agent William Turner to price life insurance policies. One of the policies discussed was offered by Massachusetts Mutual Life Insurance Company.

. . . On December 18, 1979, decedent . . . met with James C. Brewer (Brewer), the president of CBT, who up to that time had had no experience in the trust and estates field and was unfamiliar with the procedures of opening trusts. Decedent and Brewer generally discussed the trust for about 30 minutes. From the discussion, Brewer believed decedent intended the trust to function as an "insurance trust for [decedent's] family." The decedent did not, however, condition the establishment of the trust on CBT's commitment to acquire life insurance with the funds contributed to corpus. During the meeting the Irrevocable Trust Agreement of Eddie L. Headrick was executed . . . .

Schedule A of the executed Trust Agreement indicated that decedent irrevocably assigned $ 5,900 to CBT contemporaneously with the execution of trust. On December 18, 1979, the date the trust was established, Lucille Bonderud Headrick, wife of decedent, executed on behalf of herself and her minor children a fully informed waiver of the beneficiaries' right to withdraw any portion of her husband's $ 5,900 contribution to trust principal. . . .

On December 19, 1979, Brewer, president of trustee CBT, executed Part I of [a] Massachusetts Mutual Life Insurance Company Application . . . for the purpose of obtaining a $ 375,000 insurance policy on the life of the decedent. The application stated that the policy owner would be Cleveland Bank & Trust Co. of Cleveland, Tenn., Trustee u/a Eddie Lynn Headrick dated December 18, 1979, their successors in trust or assigns. Similarly, the application designated Cleveland Bank & Trust Co. of Cleveland, Tenn., Trustee u/a Eddie Lynn Headrick dated December 18, 1979, their successors in trust or assigns as beneficiary. Decedent signed Part I of the application as the insured. . . .

On December 20, 1979, the day after CBT executed part I of the application, decedent submitted to the medical examination required in Part 2 of the application, an examination performed by Marvin R. Batchelor, M.D.

CBT's application for insurance on the life of decedent was approved. . . . On December 30, 1980, decedent made a second contribution to the trust corpus of $ 5,500. On December 22, 1981, decedent made a third and final contribution of $ 2,000. No beneficiary elected to withdraw any portion of decedent's second or third contributions. The total contributions of $ 13,400 covered all premium payments made by the trust.

Part 3 of the policy issued to CBT described the rights of the owner as follows:

> While the Insured is living, the Owner may exercise all rights given by this policy or allowed by us. These rights include assigning this policy, changing Beneficiaries, changing ownership, enjoying all policy benefits and exercising all policy options.

No ownership rights were conferred by the policy on the decedent. Likewise, no ownership rights in the policy were indirectly acquired by the decedent via a reserved power in the Trust Agreement. On the contrary, as discussed above, the agreement articulated that "the trustee alone shall exercise each incident of ownership over each [life insurance] policy."

Approximately three months after the trust was established, decedent joined CBT's board of directors and as a director became a member and chairman of CBT's trust committee. One of the trust committee's responsibilities was to review and discuss new trust accounts and the investments in those trusts. The Trust Agreement was first reviewed by the bank's trust committee on April 30, 1980.

Thereafter, the trust was reviewed every three or four months as part of the bank's routine trust administration procedure. . . .

The decedent, age 33, tragically died in an automobile accident on June 19, 1982, a date which was within three years of the trust's purchase of the life insurance policy. Decedent was survived by his wife and three minor daughters.

Upon decedent's death, Massachusetts Mutual Life Insurance Company paid $ 378,701.93 in death benefits to the trustee as owner of the policy. The life insurance proceeds were not included in decedent's gross estate on the estate tax return filed by the executors of his estate. Respondent determined in the statutory notice of deficiency that:

> The proceeds of [the] Massachusetts Mutual Life Insurance Company policy transferred to Cleveland Bank & Trust Company as trustee, constitute a transfer within the meaning of §2035(a) of the Internal Revenue Code, and is therefore includible in the decedent's taxable estate. . . .

The issue before the Court is whether the proceeds of a life insurance policy purchased by a trust within three years of the insured grantor's death must be included in the trustor's gross estate under §2035(a). Simply stated, petitioners contend that §2035(a), as amended by the Economic Recovery Tax Act of 1981 (ERTA), does not apply to the insurance proceeds because the decedent never possessed any incident of ownership in the policy within the meaning of §2042.

Respondent, on the other hand, while conceding at trial that "In this particular case the matter was structured so that the incidents of ownership were not legally or technically held by the decedent," contends that decedent's dominance over the trust arrangement indicates that the trustee was substantively acting as decedent's agent in acquiring insurance on decedent's life. (We perceive no reason to question the appropriateness of respondent's concession.) Respondent reasons that decedent thereby acquired a transferable interest in the policy and the §2042 incident of ownership requirement of §2035([a])(2) is therefore satisfied.

We think the result in this case is controlled by our decision in *Estate of Leder v. Commissioner*, 89 T.C. 235 (1987), *aff'd*, 893 F.2d 237 (10th Cir. 1989). Briefly stated, the facts in *Estate of Leder* were as follows: a wife, within three years before her husband's death, purchased a life insurance policy on his life and signed the original application as owner. The husband's wholly-owned corporation paid all of the premiums on the policy directly to the insurance company.

In the case before us, a husband created an irrevocable trust with a bank as trustee, naming his wife and the couple's three minor children as beneficiaries. As permitted by the trust agreement, the bank, as trustee, purchased an insurance policy on the husband's life and paid the periodic premiums out of trust corpus donated by the husband.

In *Estate of Leder v. Commissioner* we held that the proceeds from the policy in that case were not includible in the gross estate of the insured where the insured did not possess at the time of his death, or at any time within the three years preceding his death, any of the incidents of ownership in the policy because (1) the conditions of §2042 were never met; [and] (2) the §2035[(a)](2) exception . . . is not applicable because the proceeds of the policy were not includible under §2042 (or any of the other sections cited in §2035[(a)](2)) . . . . We think this holding applies here.

We construe respondent's concession, quoted above, to mean that the decedent, Eddie L. Headrick, did not retain, under the provisions of the trust agreement created by him, any incidents of ownership in the life insurance policy acquired by the bank as trustee. Consequently, our inquiry is limited solely to the question of whether, under §2042, Eddie Headrick ever owned the policy acquired by the trustee. . . .

The gravamen of respondent's grievance is the charge that Eddie Headrick indirectly paid the insurance premiums. However, under the terms of the trust agreement the bank, as trustee, was permitted but was not required to buy an insurance policy on Eddie Headrick's life and pay the periodic premiums out of the trust corpus contributed by Eddie Headrick or the income therefrom. We do not think this creates a sufficient nexus to support a finding that Eddie Headrick himself paid the life insurance premiums. The record as a whole supports a finding that CBT did not act as Headrick's agent in acquiring the policy.

But in any event Congress long ago changed the test for including life insurance proceeds in the gross estate from a tracing of premiums paid to an evaluation of whether the decedent retained incidents of ownership in the policy. . . . Today, some 35 years after the enactment of the 1954 Code, §2042 remains unchanged from its 1954 version . . . . Furthermore, courts have consistently held that with the enactment of the 1954 Code, Congress abolished payment of premiums as a factor in determining the taxability of life insurance proceeds under §2042. In more modern times, we have continued to recognize that the premium payment test is "now abandoned" under §2042.

In *Estate of Kurihara v. Commissioner*, 82 T.C. 51 (1984), the decedent-insured was the creator of a trust under an agreement which contained the words "The Grantor, the initiator of a policy of insurance on his life * * * hereby assigns to the Trustees all of his right, title, and interest in and to such policy of insurance * * *." 82 T.C. at 62. From these words it would be difficult not to conclude, as we did in *Kurihara*, that the decedent, Kurihara, initially owned the policy. Decedent having died three months thereafter, the policy was unquestionably includible in his gross estate under §§2035([a])(2) and 2042.

In discussing the events surrounding the acquisition of the insurance policy in *Kurihara*, we drew attention to the fact that the decedent-insured wrote a check to one of the trustees for the exact amount of the first premium, which the trustee then endorsed over to the insurance company. *Kurihara* should not, however, be read to suggest that payment of premiums has now become a talisman for includibility of insurance proceeds under §2042.

In *Estate of Leder v. Commissioner* we examined the law of Oklahoma to determine whether under the law of that State the mere fact that an individual is an insured under a policy gives him or her a beneficial interest in the policy, even though someone else is shown as the owner of the policy on the insurance application. Our examination of Oklahoma law satisfied us that the answer to that question would be in the negative. We reached a similar conclusion under the law of Arizona in *Estate of Chapman v. Commissioner*, T.C. Memo. 1989-105. In this case we have similarly examined the law of Tennessee, where the policy in question was issued, to determine whether a different result would be reached under the law of that State, and have satisfied ourselves that no different result would obtain.

Respondent asks us to apply an agency or "beamed transfer" theory to impute to Eddie Headrick a transfer of the life insurance policy acquired by the trust. In support of his position, respondent cites Bel v. United States, 452 F.2d 683 (5th Cir. 1971); Detroit Bank & Trust Co. v. United States, 467 F.2d 964 (6th Cir. 1972); and *Estate of Kurihara v. Commissioner*, see also Hope v. United States, 691 F.2d 786 (5th Cir. 1982); and Estate of Clay v. Commissioner, 86 T.C. 1266 (1986). However, all of these cases were decided under various versions of §2035 prior to its amendment by ERTA. As we have already pointed out, in *Estate of Leder* we construed §2035[(a)] as requiring us to first analyze the life insurance transaction under §2042, so as to ascertain the existence or non-existence of any incident of ownership. In *Estate of Leder*, we concluded that the beamed transfer approach was not germane to the §2042 determination, and we apply the same rationale here.

In summary, we conclude that the decedent never possessed any incidents of ownership in the policy on his life under §2042, and consequently that the proceeds therefrom are not includible in his gross estate under . . . §2035(a).

Reviewed by the Court.

CHABOT, PARKER, KORNER, SHIELDS, HAMBLEN, COHEN, CLAPP, SWIFT, JACOBS, GERBER, WRIGHT, PARR, WILLIAMS, WELLS, RUWE, WHALEN, and COLVIN, JJ., agree with this opinion.

Like *Cristofani*, reproduced at page 888, a unanimous reviewed Tax Court opinion is extraordinary.

It is widely believed that the premium payment, deemed agency, and beamed transfer theories for inclusion of life insurance owned by a third party no longer are viable as a consequence of the 1981 amendment of §2035 by ERTA and by the Tax Court's decisions in *Headrick* and *Leder*. Note that the government acquiesced in the Tax Court's decision in *Headrick*.

If the three year rule *does* apply, there is a court sanctioned ploy available to minimize its consequence. Estate of Silverman v. Commissioner, 61 T.C. 338 (1973), *aff'd*, 521 F.2d 574 (2d Cir. 1975), *acq.*, dealt with the effect to be given to the payment of premiums by an assignee of a life insurance policy that was made by the insured within 3 years of death. At age 60, Morris Silverman purchased a $10,000 policy insuring his life. The premiums on the policy were payable monthly. Almost five years later, Morris assigned the policy to his son, Avrum Silverman, and Morris died within six months of making that assignment. Avrum paid the monthly premiums that became due after the assignment. On the question of the amount to be included in Morris's gross estate, the Tax Court said:

The transfer of a life insurance policy [within three years] of death normally requires inclusion in the gross estate at face value. In the instant case, however, the petitioner paid all the insurance premiums after the assignment. Of total premiums amounting to $3,261.20, petitioner paid $368.20 or 11.29% and the decedent paid $2,893 or 88.71%. Under these circumstances we feel that the petitioner contributed to the value of the policy, and it would be inappropriate to include in the gross estate that portion of the value which petitioner contributed.

Throughout its existence, including the time of transfer, the policy had a face value of $10,000. At the time of the decedent's death, however, a certain number of premiums were required to keep the face value intact. It is apparent, therefore, that at the time the decedent transferred the policy, only a portion of the premiums necessary to maintain the face value payment on death had in fact been paid. The petitioner's continued premium payments were thus a vital part of the consideration necessary to secure full payment on the insurance policy on decedent's death. To hold otherwise would tax the estate on an asset greater than that which the decedent transferred. We are further bolstered in our decision by Treas. Reg. §20.2035-1(e), which states: "However, if the transferee has made improvements or additions to the property, any resulting enhancement in the value of the property is not considered in ascertaining the value of the gross estate." We therefore hold that the decedent's estate must include that portion of the face value of the life insurance policy which the decedent's premium payments bore to all premium payments.

The result of the Tax Court's decision in *Silverman* was that only 88.71% of the proceeds were includible in the decedent's gross estate. The decedent's executor argued that only the cash surrender value of the policy ($1,120) or only the amount of premiums paid by the decedent within three years of death ($1,525) should be included in the gross estate, but was rejected on both contentions.

PLR 8724014 involved application of the *Silverman* rule to group term insurance. The important aspect of the ruling was that premiums paid from inception of the policy, not just in the year of the decedent-insured's death, would be used in the *Silverman* rule determination. Although this was not favorable to the taxpayer (who would have liked for the final premium — paid by a third party — to be treated as the sole premium for acquisition of the policy that matured, so that the entire proceeds would be excluded), presumably it is the correct result under *Silverman* if the term insurance is automatically renewable, in which case it is not proper to consider the insurance payable in the year of death as having been newly acquired with that year's premium payment. The ruling also was instructive because, although the decedent actually paid the annual premiums, the decedent's children reimbursed these payments. The ruling treated the reimbursement program as if the children had been the original payors for purposes of the *Silverman* rule. There was no indication of how quickly or often the children reimbursed the decedent.

The policy justification for the apportionment adopted by the Tax Court in *Silverman* is hard to garner. The insured transferred a policy that had a value at least equal to its equity reserve. Surely no part of that equity reserve should be excluded from the insured's gross estate. Moreover, if an insured became seriously ill two years after acquiring a life insurance policy and promptly assigned it to another, who paid premiums for two additional years before the insured died, it hardly seems appropriate to exclude half the proceeds from the insured's gross estate. The proration of insurance proceeds seems no more rational in this circumstance than it was in the context of the premium payment test that was rejected in the 1954 Code. Under the prior version of §2035, Kahn & Waggoner, *Federal Taxation of the Assignment of Life Insurance*, 1977 DUKE L.J. 941, 975–981, noted that, if the insured had kept the policy and paid all the premiums, the insured's gross estate would include the full proceeds but would not include the money expended to pay the premiums on the policy. To match that result, the authors argued that the amount includible at death should be the full proceeds reduced only by the amount of any premiums paid by third parties after the transfer (premiums paid by the insured already being out of the decedent's estate).

Before we leave this important area, let's come back to imputed incidents under Treas. Reg. §20.2042-1(c)(6) and coordinate its application with the three year rule.

Revenue Ruling 90-21

. . . If, within 3 years of death, a stockholder, for less than adequate and full consideration, disposes of the controlling interest in a corporation that owns a life insurance policy on the stockholder's life, and if the life insurance proceeds are payable to a third party for other than a business purpose within the meaning of Treas. Reg. §20.2042-1(c)(6), are the insurance proceeds includible in the deceased stockholder's gross estate under §2035?

. . . *D* owned 80% of the voting stock of *X* corporation. In 1982, *X* corporation acquired a life insurance policy on *D*'s life payable to *D*'s child *B*. . . . [In 1987 *D* transferred to *C* 40% of the shares of *X*.] *D* died in 1988, and the proceeds of the policy were paid to *B*. . . .

. . . Under §2035[(a)](2), §2035(a) applies to a transfer of an interest in property which is included in the value of the gross estate under §2036, 2037, 2038, or 2042, or would have been included under any of those sections if the interest had been retained by the decedent until death. . . .

Treas. Reg. §20.2042-1(c)(6) . . . explains that, if a decedent is the controlling stockholder in a corporation that holds a life insurance policy on the decedent's life, and the proceeds of the policy are payable to a third party for nonbusiness purposes, the incidents of ownership held by the corporation will be attributed to the decedent through the decedent's stock ownership and the proceeds will be included in the decedent's gross estate under §2042 . . . .

Includibility of life insurance proceeds under §2042 depends on the decedent's possession of incidents of ownership of the policy at death. However, includibility of life insurance . . . based on . . . §2035[(a)](2) will apply if the decedent transferred an incident of ownership in the life insurance policy during the 3-year period before death.

Rev. Rul. 82-141, 1982-2 C.B. 209, considers whether the value of life insurance proceeds is includible in a decedent's gross estate under §2035. In 1980, within 3 years of the decedent's death, the decedent's controlled corporation had transferred ownership of a policy on the decedent's life. The decedent owned more than 50% of the voting stock in the corporation at the time the policy was transferred. The Ruling states that "the principle underlying the attribution rule of Treas. Reg. §20.2042-1(c)(6) mandates that the incidents of ownership possessed by [the controlled corporation] be attributed to [the decedent] for purposes of §2035." The Ruling holds that the entire value of the insurance proceeds is includible. . . .

. . . [A] similar rationale applies [here]. The incidents of ownership in a life insurance policy on *D*'s life were transferred within 3 years of *D*'s death, within the meaning of §2035[(a)](2), as a result of the transfer of 40% of the stock of *S* corporation. Although the policy itself was not transferred, . . . the result is the same. As a result of the transfer of stock, *D* no longer held a controlling interest in *X* corporation. *D* thereby effectively released the incidents of ownership in the policy attributed to *D* as the controlling shareholder and such release is a transfer within the meaning of §2035[(a)](2). Accordingly, the value of the policy proceeds is includible in *D*'s gross estate under §2035(a).

Technical Advice Memorandum 8806004

. . . [T]he decedent formed her own wholly owned corporation, known as X Inc, [which owned a $1 million policy of ordinary life insurance on the life of the decedent.] . . .

On January 1, 1982, the decedent owned 85% of X Inc. . . .

On March 24, 1982, X Inc. transferred ownership of the life insurance policy in equal one-third shares to each of the decedent's two sons and to an irrevocable insurance trust created January 2, 1982, with the decedent's husband as primary beneficiary. X Inc. continued to pay insurance policy premiums.

. . . The face amount of the policy . . . was greatly in excess of any consideration that the decedent's sons provided. . . .

The decedent died on January 7, 1984, 23 months after the transfer of the insurance policy by the corporation. . . .

The fact that the life insurance policy may have been transferred for consideration equal to its reserve value does not preclude inclusion of the entire value of the policy proceeds under §2035[(a)](2). Under the principles of cases such as United States v. Allen, 293 F.2d 916 (10th Cir. 1961), and United States v. Past, 347 F.2d 7 (9th Cir. 1965), if a property interest which would be includible in the gross estate under §2036, 2037, 2038, or 2042 is transferred prior to death, any consideration received for such transfer is not adequate and full unless it is equal to the value at which such property would be included in the gross estate had it been retained by the decedent. In the present case . . . the consideration received is . . . wholly inadequate since such consideration is measured against the value at which the property is includible in the decedent's estate, or $1,000,000. Accordingly, the entire value of the policy proceeds minus the value of any consideration received by the decedent's controlled corporation is includible in her estate. . . .

9.   *Apportionment of Estate Taxes.*   In re King, 239 N.E.2d 875, 876 (N.Y. 1968), described, in general terms, the allocation of jurisdiction between state and federal law for the apportionment of estate taxes.

Generally speaking, apportionment of taxes among the beneficiaries of an estate, or among persons receiving property which is included within an estate for tax purposes, is a matter of state law. . . . There are, however, two exceptions to this general rule. The apportionment of taxes attributable to nonexempt insurance proceeds and property subject to a power of appointment is governed by Federal law.

The federal law to which *King* referred is §§2206 (dealing with §2042 life insurance) and 2207 (dealing with §2041 powers of appointment). Subsequent to *King*, §§2207A (dealing with §2044 qualified terminable interest property) and 2207B (property includible under §2036) were added. First introduced by the Revenue Act of 1918, along with §2042, the reimbursement authorized by §2206 has not been substantially changed since. Unless the decedent's will directs otherwise, §2206 authorizes the personal representative to collect from the beneficiaries of the insurance policy the proportionate amount of federal estate tax attributable to inclusion of insurance proceeds in the insured's gross estate. The right to reimbursement does not apply to insurance proceeds for which a marital deduction is allowed. The House Ways and Means Committee, in recommending enactment of the 1918 Act, described §2206 as a slight modification in procedure that was being made "for the sake of insuring more equitable, uniform, and efficient administration of the law." H.R. Rep. No. 767, 65th Cong., 2d Sess. 23 (1918), in 1939-1 C.B. (pt. 2) 86, 102–103. Congress apparently does not view §2206 as a significant intrusion of federal law into the arena of state apportionment of the tax burden.

Quaere how badly §2206 would operate if the settlement option selected is not a lump-sum payment. There is no corresponding reimbursement right for §2039 annuities, which we study in Chapter 9, and perhaps it is for just this reason.

10. *Valuation.*

General Principles. A life insurance policy given to another must be valued to determine the gift tax consequences of the transfer. Similarly, the value of a policy insuring the life of another that is includible in the owner's gross estate under §2033 must be established for estate tax purposes.

For wealth transfer tax purposes the value of a life insurance policy is determined by the price an insurer would charge for a comparable contract. Treas. Reg. §§20.2031-8(a), 25.2512-6(a). Thus, if the policy is paid up, the value of the policy is the single premium the company would charge for a comparable contract of insurance "on the life of a person of the age of the insured." Treas. Reg. §§20.2031-8(a)(3) *Example (2)*; 25.2512-6(a) *Example (3)*. To qualify, Rev. Rul. 78-137 states that the replacement policy "must provide the same economic benefits as the policy owned by the decedent" or the donor, including the same cash surrender value.

The price of comparable contracts is not available if the policy has been in force for some years but further premiums must be paid to the insurer, making that method of valuation unavailable. In such cases, the regulations provide that "the value may be approximated" by using the interpolated terminal reserve method (not the cash surrender value, which is less but often an easy and not so wildly inaccurate surrogate), but even this method cannot be used if, "because of the unusual nature of the contract, such an approximation is not reasonably close to the full value of the contract." Treas. Reg. §§20.2031-8(a)(2); 25.2512-6(a). A reference here to a policy's "interpolated terminal reserve method" of valuation means the "interpolated terminal reserve" of the insurance policy plus the unused portion of the premium for that year. The interpolated terminal reserve method is illustrated in Treas. Reg. §§20.2031-8(a)(3) *Example (3)*; 25.2512-6(a) *Example (4)*.

Estate of Wien v. Commissioner

441 F.2d 32 (5th Cir. 1971)

GOLDBERG, J.: The taxpayers and the government both seek us to referee this mortal combat involving the taxation of life insurance policies. We have examined both sides in their polarization and, forsaking their extreme positions, pitch our tent of conclusion midway between their extremes. Thus in remanding we satisfy neither party in our solution to this necrological dilemma.

On June 3, 1962, Sidney and Ellen Wien, domiciliaries of Atlanta, Georgia, were killed in an airplane crash at Orly Field, Paris, France. It was stipulated that the circumstances of the crash were such that it was impossible to determine whether Ellen or Sidney Wien died first or whether they died at the same moment. At the time of their deaths the Wiens were married and the parents of two children, Joan Wien and Claire Wien Morse. Joan was killed with her parents in that fatal crash, leaving Claire Wien Morse as their sole survivor.

At the time of her death Ellen Wien owned fifteen insurance policies having a face value of $150,000 on the life of her husband. In each policy Ellen was named primary beneficiary, and the children were named secondary beneficiaries. Similarly, at the time of his death Sidney Wien owned seven insurance policies having a face value of $100,000 on the life of his wife. In each policy Sidney was named the primary beneficiary, and the children were named secondary beneficiaries.

At the time of the Wien tragedy Georgia law provided that where an insured and a beneficiary are killed in a common disaster under circumstances where it cannot be established who died first, the proceeds of the policy shall be distributed as if the insured had survived the beneficiary [and, in this case, the owner as well]. As a result, after the Wiens' death had been established, the insurance companies paid the proceeds of the policies directly to the only surviving beneficiary, Claire Wien Morse. The funds never went to either Sidney's or Ellen's estate. Consequently this case is not concerned with the taxation of proceeds accruing to the beneficiary of an insurance policy. Both the government and the taxpayers agree that neither deceased had any taxable interest by virtue of their status as a beneficiary. The argument instead concerns the ownership interest which each deceased owned in the various insurance policies on the life of the other.

In the estate tax return filed by [each] estate, the Executor included . . . the value of the interpolated terminal reserves of those policies. . . . The Commissioner sent each estate a notice of deficiency, alleging that the value of [each] ownership interest in the policies . . . was . . . the total proceeds paid . . . .

The taxpayers contested these deficiencies assessed by the Commissioner, and suit was brought in the Tax Court. Before that court the taxpayers went one step further and demanded a refund for the amount they had actually included in the respective estates, asserting that no amount should be included as a result of the decedent's ownership interests in the various insurance policies.

The Tax Court, basing its decision on its earlier opinion in Estate of Chown v. Commissioner, 51 T.C. 140 (1968), *rev'd*, 428 F.2d 1395 (9th Cir. 1970), held that "the absolute and unrestricted owner of life insurance policies on the life of another possesses at the instant of his simultaneous death with the insured, property rights which are includible in his 'gross estate' at a value equal to the entire proceeds payable under the terms of the policies." . . . The taxpayers have appealed from this decision, and we reverse.

We begin our discussion by examining the estate tax liability which accrues as a result of an ownership interest in the normal situation when the owner of an insurance policy on the life of another predeceases the insured. While courts have disagreed about the proper value to assign to the ownership interest in such a policy, it has always been supposed that the ownership rights, i.e., the power to borrow against the policy, the power to change the beneficiary, and the power to surrender the policy for cash, constituted a valuable property interest. . . . Consequently, when the owner of such a property interest predeceased the insured, the value of this ownership interest was included in the estate of the deceased under I.R.C. §2033 or its predecessors. . . .

The taxpayers have argued, however, that since Mr. and Mrs. Wien died in a common disaster these normal estate tax consequences are inapplicable. The taxpayers contend instead that neither Ellen nor Sidney possessed any ownership interest in the policies which passed through their estates at death [because] . . . the ownership interest in an insurance policy is extinguished or terminated when the policy matures as a result of the death of the insured. . . . While we agree with the taxpayers' premise that ownership rights are extinguished at the moment the insured dies, we think the taxpayers' conclusion that nothing was left in either owner's estate results from failure to appreciate the consequences of the Georgia simultaneous death act [under which] . . . Ellen, as the owner-beneficiary of the policies on Sidney's life, is treated for property purposes as if Sidney still survived at the instant of her death. Since it is Sidney's death alone which could have caused the extinguishment of Ellen's ownership rights, it is clear that under state law Ellen's ownership rights were intact and in her estate at the moment of her death. The same is true with regard to Sidney's ownership interest in the policies insuring Ellen's life, for Ellen's death alone could extinguish those ownership rights. Since Sidney, as the owner-beneficiary, is treated as if he predeceased Ellen, his ownership interest in the policies insuring Ellen's life was intact and in his estate at the moment of his death.

. . . [T]hese state law consequences govern what the decedent owns for purposes of estate taxation. The federal taxing statutes merely determine how that interest shall be taxed. . . .

Applying these principles to the instant case we conclude that Ellen, as the owner-beneficiary of policies insuring Sidney's life, had under Georgia law at the time of her death an ownership interest which was a valuable property right, and that the value of this interest must be included in her estate under §2033. Similarly, we conclude that Sidney, as the owner-beneficiary of policies insuring Ellen's life, had at the moment of his death an ownership interest which was a valuable property right, and that the value of that interest must be included in his estate under §2033.

Having once determined that both decedents at the moment of death had existing ownership interests in the policies insuring the life of the other, the value of which is includible in their respective estates, it becomes necessary to determine the value of those respective ownership rights. The answer to this question is not without doubt because, as we noted earlier, the courts dealing with the normal situation, not complicated by a common disaster, have found it difficult to agree on a method of valuation. Some courts have determined that the cash surrender value of the policy is the amount which ought to be included in the estate of the deceased owner. . . . Others have concluded that it is the cost or replacement cost of the policy which should be included . . . or, if the policy cannot be purchased, then the value is to be based on the interpolated terminal reserve. . . . We think that those courts which have used cost, replacement cost or the interpolated terminal reserve have employed the proper method of valuation. In Guggenheim v. Rasquin, [312 U.S. 254 (1941),] the Supreme Court, in adopting cost as a proper measure of the value of a recently purchased single premium policy, clearly indicated its disapproval of the cash surrender method of valuation. . . .

The Supreme Court in a related case held that where a substantial period of time had elapsed between the purchase of a single premium policy and the date of the gift of that policy, the ownership rights were to be valued at their replacement cost at the date of the gift. United States v. Ryerson, [312 U.S. 260 (1941)]. In short, the Court has indicated that market value measured in various ways at the date of valuation is the proper standard to be used. The Commissioner has followed these instructions in the regulations concerning the valuation of ownership rights in policies where a gift tax is involved, Treas. Reg. §25.2512-6, and where the estate tax is involved, Treas. Reg. §20.2031-8. However, the Commissioner has also recognized the distinction noted by the Supreme Court in *Guggenheim v. Rasquin* between a single premium policy, where the cost or replacement cost can be determined by the sale of comparable contracts, and the ordinary life insurance policy, such as those involved here, where the contract has been in force for some time and further premiums are due. For the latter type of policy the Commissioner has provided that the taxpayer may approximate market value by relying on the interpolated terminal reserve since the value cannot be conveniently determined by the sale of comparable contracts. . . .

The parties here, both the Commissioner and the taxpayers, have argued, however, that the method of valuation provided in Treas. Reg. §20.2031-8(a)(2) is not applicable to the present situation because the owner and the insured died in a common disaster. The Commissioner, while admitting that Treas. Reg. §20.2031-8(a)(2) would apply if either decedent had predeceased the other, asserts that in this common disaster situation the ownership interest should be valued at the full amount of the proceeds paid as a result of the death of the insured. His argument is that because the parties died at the same instant the owner had at the moment of death the power to control the disposition of the full proceeds, and thus his ownership interest was worth the full proceed value. This proceed value, the Commissioner asserts, constitutes the market value of the ownership interest. In rejecting this argument the [Ninth Circuit] in *Chown v. Commissioner* said: "The Tax Court held the regulation inapplicable . . . because the deaths of Harriet and Roger were . . . simultaneous. It stated the proposition in this way: 'We find that 20.2031-8(a)(1) states the general rule that fair market value is to be used, and that paragraph (a)(2) is intended only to provide an approximation, in limited circumstances, of the value that would result from the general rule. Under the circumstances of this case, we hold the approximation under paragraph (a)(2) is obviously improper because it results in a valuation that is not consistent with the actual fair market value of the policy at the time of Harriet's death, which under the facts we hold to be an amount equal to the proceeds payable under the policy. As we see it, at the time Harriet died, the policy must be treated as fully matured.' [51 T.C. at 143.] The primary difficulty with this reasoning is that it must be based upon the assumption that Roger died first; nothing but Roger's death could 'fully mature' the policy. And when that happened, Harriet's ownership interest disappeared; her rights to change the beneficiary, surrender the policy, assign it, or borrow on it had vanished. The only conceivable interest that she could have by reason of Roger's death was as beneficiary, but that interest never came to fruition as the Tax Court correctly held. Yet the Tax Court's reasoning is based upon the proposition that the policy became fully matured at the instant of Roger's and Harriet's deaths, thereby giving to her ownership interest the full value of the proceeds, which, for that fleeting instant, became the fair market value of her ownership interest. The notion that any one would have paid such an amount, or any amount at all, for that fleeting interest is a bit of metaphysics that we cannot accept. It rests on an assertion that what one at the same instant 'acquires' and 'loses' one *has* rather than *has not* at that instant" . . . 428 F.2d at 1398.

We agree with this reasoning. Estate taxation is not based on such "now you see it, now you don't" concepts. . . .

An even more fundamental difficulty exists in the Commissioner's argument. In essence he is arguing that to value the interest of the owner it is permissible to look at the fact that the insured died at the same moment. . . . [T]he principal issue is whether it is proper to investigate the imminence of the insured's death in determining the value of the owner's interest. If such a peek at the insured is not permitted, the Commissioner's entire argument fails.

The taxpayers, while arriving at a different conclusion as to value, have in effect followed the Commissioner's major premise and have looked to the fact that the insured died in valuing the ownership interests. They conclude that a buyer would have paid nothing for the ownership rights in the policies because those interests were going to be immediately extinguished by the death of the insured. In short, the taxpayers argue that because the parties died in a common disaster the real value of the ownership interests were zero.

We think that both parties have erred in looking at the fact of the insured's death in valuing the ownership rights, and that the disparity in their valuation determinations are a consequence of this error. We note that Treas. Reg. §20.2031-8 makes no distinction in valuation based on the imminence of the insured's death. The only exception stated in the regulation concerns an alternate value if the contract is unusual. Here, from all that appears, we are dealing with perfectly ordinary life insurance contracts. The Commissioner applied a different value to the ownership rights, not because the contracts were unusual, but because the *facts* surrounding the death of the owner and the insured were unusual. We note further, as did the court in *Chown*, that no court has ever held that the interpolated terminal reserve method provided in the regulations was improper because the insured could be expected to die shortly. The court [of appeals] in *Chown* noted: "No case has been called to our attention in which the executor's method of valuation was held to be improper because the insured's death was imminent at the time of the death of the owner of the policy. Yet we find it hard to believe that such cases have not occurred. The occurrences of such fatal illnesses as heart attacks, unsuspected but incurable cancer, and many others, followed by a brief period of life, but with early death a virtual certainty, are too frequent for us to think otherwise." 428 F.2d at 1399.

We think that the principles of estate taxation preclude consideration of such facts as the actual state of the insured's health or peril in valuing the owner's property interest. Indeed it would bring virtual disaster upon the integrity of estate taxation if the value of an ownership interest fluctuated with the probable longevity of the insured. Any valuation method depending upon such an uncertain measure as the day-by-day health of an individual insured would be impossible to enforce accurately. There are simply no actuarial computations which can be applied to an individual illness or accidental circumstance which will accurately predict the probability of death. For this reason the standard mortality tables on which the interpolated terminal reserve is based, rather than ad hoc medical prognosis, have always been the norm for estate tax valuations. Yet here because there is a common disaster involved both the Commissioner and the taxpayers suggest that we depart from the norm and value the policy on the basis of the individual insured's probability of death. We think considerations of this sort are as unmanageable when a common disaster is involved as they are in the ordinary case. . . .

Treas. Reg. §20.2031-8 has relieved us of the burden of calculating such imponderables and provides a stable method of estimating the value of an ordinary insurance policy. We think that this regulation is applicable both to the ordinary situation, where the owner dies leaving the insured surviving, and to the unusual situation, where the insured and the owner-beneficiary perish in a common disaster. The regulation bases its value on the interpolated terminal reserve of the insurance policy. . . .

We conclude, therefore, that Mrs. Wien's estate tax liability for the ownership interest in insurance policies insuring Mr. Wien's life should be valued according to the procedures outlined in Treas. Reg. §20.2031-8(a)(2). Mr. Wien's estate tax liability for his interest in those policies on Mrs. Wien's life should be valued in like manner. We remand this case to the court below for a determination of the estate tax liability in accordance with this opinion.

Reversed and remanded.

[The dissenting opinion of Judge Tuttle is omitted.]

The government subsequently conceded the valuation of cross-owned life insurance if the order of death of the insured and the beneficiary cannot be proved and local law establishes a presumption that the insured survived the beneficiary. Rev. Rul. 77-181 (the proceeds of each policy were paid to the contingent beneficiary, which was the estate of the policyholder, but valued at the interpolated terminal reserve). Although local law usually applies in valuing assets for federal estate tax purposes, what result do you think a court would reach in a case like *Wien* if there is clear evidence that the husband died one day prior to the wife but state law provided that, when a beneficiary died within 120 hours of the insured, the proceeds are distributed as if the beneficiary predeceased the insured?

The *Wien* court rejected the notion that the valuation of life insurance could rest on an ad hoc consideration of the insured's health or similar factors. Should such ad hoc inquiries be barred? Consider the following factual circumstances: *O* purchased a single premium policy on the life of *I*. Several years later, *O* and *I* discovered that *I* had an incurable disease from which the doctors predicted *I* would die within six months. *O* then assigned the policy to an irrevocable trust. The amount payable on the policy at *I*'s death was $100,000, and the price the insurer would have charged for a single premium comparable policy issued at the time of the assignment was $34,000. This price does not reflect *I*'s health condition because the company would not have issued a policy on *I*'s life at all, once the illness was discovered. Should the value of *O*'s gift to the trust be *only* $34,000? Perhaps the court's reluctance to consider *I*'s health should apply only to policies that are not paid up. If the policy owned had not been paid up and if the value of the policy under the interpolated terminal reserve method had been $34,000, the policy should be valued at no less than that figure for gift tax purposes. Note that this is an extreme case — usually poor health means an insured is "rated" — meaning that the cost of the insurance is higher and that would be an appropriate result for valuation purposes. Also remember that, if the proceeds from the insurance policy are not included in *O*'s gross estate, the value of the gift made by *O* to the trust is included in *O*'s estate tax base under §2001(b).

Assume that O purchased a policy on the life of I. Because I was overweight and had a history of hypertension, the insurance company "rated" the policy — it charged a higher premium than would be charged for a perfectly healthy individual of I's age. Four years later, O assigned the policy to a trust. For gift tax purposes, a policy valued under the interpolated terminal reserve method would reflect this greater premium payment requirement and should not again be valued with respect to I's health. Thus, valuation without special reference to I's health is appropriate and the last sentence in the first paragraph of Treas. Reg. §25.2512-6(a) should not be relevant.

Finally, imagine that C owned a policy insuring the life of P in the face amount of $60,000. C predeceased P, and C's personal representative elected the alternate valuation date under §2032. At C's death, the value of the policy on P's life under the interpolated terminal reserve method was $28,000; five months after C's death, the value of the policy under that method was $29,000. No premiums were paid after C's death, and P died five months and one day following C's death. C's personal representative collected the $60,000 insurance proceeds. That amount is included in C's gross estate because that change in value was not due to the mere lapse of time (other than to P, for who it is the quintessential lapse of time!) See Rev. Rul. 63-52. If C's will bequeathed the insurance policy to C's surviving spouse, the amount of marital deduction allowable would be only the $28,000 date of death value. See §2032(b), which refers to ignoring changes in value due to the (non)occurrence of a contingency — which includes death.

11. *Life Insurance Trusts.* For an insured who is reluctant to have the proceeds of life insurance payable to a beneficiary in one lump sum and wishes instead to provide for some sort of management of the proceeds, or who wishes to provide for two or more beneficiaries successively (e.g., income from the proceeds to a surviving spouse for life, then the proceeds themselves to their descendants), the choice is between electing one of the settlement options provided by the terms of the policy and having the proceeds payable to a trust. A life insurance trust directs the trustee to collect the proceeds of the policy when the insured dies and to administer the proceeds in accordance with the provisions of the trust agreement. The trustee is entitled to the proceeds as the designated beneficiary of the policy; in some cases the trustee also is the policy owner.

Life insurance trusts and settlement options share the advantages that accrue to any beneficiary other than the insured's estate. If the insurance proceeds are not included in the insured's probate estate, the proceeds ordinarily are not subject to claims of the insured's creditors nor to the forced share of the insured's surviving spouse (although the 1990 version of the Uniform Probate Code changes this treatment as to the rights of a surviving spouse who elects against the will). Moreover, the proceeds are not reduced by added fees nor is distribution delayed by the probate process. Finally, many state death tax statutes exclude insurance proceeds payable to an insurance trust, as well as to a beneficiary other than the insured's estate.

Although these advantages are shared by each form of beneficiary designation, there are important differences in both the property and the federal tax law treatment of life insurance trusts and settlement options. Some settlement options are selected by persons who are unaware of the availability of the trust as an alternative device, or by individuals who want to avoid the trouble and expense of establishing a trust. The election between a settlement option and an insurance trust should be made only after weighing the relative merits and costs of each in light of the needs and goals of the policy owner.

Settlement options often provide a secure investment with a stable rate of return, albeit sometimes it is a relatively low rate. The advantage of such security is evidenced by a comparison of the returns on settlement options with the performance of institutional trustees. Also, the cost of managing funds left with an insurer under a settlement option is built into the rate of return and thus borne proportionately by all beneficiaries, which is of particular benefit to beneficiaries of relatively small amounts.

The principal non-tax benefit of a life insurance trust is the flexibility it provides both in dispositive arrangements and in investments. Trusts facilitate discretion to be exercised with respect to the relative needs of beneficiaries. Although some flexibility is available under some settlement options, insurance companies do not have the staff to make the discretionary judgments that a trustee can be expected to exercise, and insurers will not accept the obligation to make those judgments. The availability of flexibility is particularly valuable if the beneficiaries are minors.[8]

Another aspect of the flexibility of trust arrangements is that the beneficiaries of an insurance trust may be able to force a deviation from the dispositive terms of the trust when changed circumstances so warrant[9] but even changed circumstances may not permit beneficiaries to force a change from the terms of a settlement option.[10] Whether alteration of a trust is desirable may depend on the dead-hand wishes of the insured, although alterations may be necessary to effectuate the owner's testamentary scheme.

---

8. Note, however, that although trusts afford greater flexibility, they must comply with the Rule Against Perpetuities, whereas the Rule is inapplicable to insurance settlement options. Doyle v. Massachusetts Mutual Life Insurance Co., 377 F.2d 19 (6th Cir. 1967); Holmes v. John Hancock Mutual Life Insurance Co., 41 N.E.2d 909 (N.Y. 1942). This may be especially desirable if a generation-skipping disposition is appropriate and the proceeds will be made totally exempt using the generation-skipping transfer exemption.

9. E.g., Post v. Grand Rapids Trust Co., 238 N.W. 206 (Mich. 1931); RESTATEMENT (SECOND) OF TRUSTS §168 (1959).

10. Pierowich v. Metropolitan Life Insurance Co., 275 N.W. 789 (Mich. 1937).

Trusts also may permit the trustee to tailor an investment portfolio to the beneficiaries' needs, although more insurance companies now offer so-called variable annuity options that permit greater variety in the investment focus of some settlement options.

An important detriment of insurance trusts is the fee of a professional fiduciary compared to the shared management cost imposed by an insurer. This detriment may be offset by a greater rate of return on trust assets if the trustee's investments are successful, but the greater rate of return also reflects the increased risk of loss that trust beneficiaries may incur. Because most professional trustees impose a minimum fee, the cost of managing a small trust may be excessive relative to lower cost settlement options. See Gelfand, *Trusts without Trustees*, 115 TR. & EST. 8 (1976).

The owner need not regard insurance trusts and settlement options as mutually exclusive and may divide the insurance proceeds between those two by having a portion paid to a trust and the balance held or distributed under a settlement option.

An insured can avoid the imposition of federal estate tax on life insurance proceeds only by avoiding ownership of the policy. If another individual owns it, the policy or its proceeds will be subject to tax in that owner's hands and the insured has no protection against a surrender of the policy for its cash value before the insured's death. But the insured usually can avoid these risks by assigning the policy to a life insurance trust. That trust need not be irrevocable or unamendable, but the insured should not retain either power and must be careful to whom such authority is granted.

Payment of any subsequent premiums due on the policy must be considered. Typically, the insured will pay the premiums when due or will transfer sufficient assets to the trust to permit the trustee to pay the premiums. The trust commonly is called a *funded* insurance trust if other assets are transferred to the trust in addition to the insurance policy. It commonly is referred to as an *unfunded* insurance trust if only the insurance policies are transferred or the trust owns nothing and is merely the designated beneficiary.

The transfer of a life insurance policy to an individual is a gift of the interpolated terminal reserve value plus the unearned portion of the premium for that year. That gift is a *present* interest and may qualify for the §2503(b) annual exclusion. However, assignment to an irrevocable trust is a gift to the trust beneficiaries that constitutes a *future* interest for which no annual exclusion is allowable. Treas. Reg. §25.2503-3(c) *Example (2)*. If Crummey withdrawal powers are granted to beneficiaries of the trust, however, any property subject to the power will constitute a *present* interest for which the annual exclusion will be available, but with potential gift tax (and income tax) problems for the powerholders if their withdrawal powers lapse. Refer to page 919. Payment of the premium due on a policy owned by another is a gift that raises the same present interest annual exclusion issues, as is a transfer of assets to a funded insurance trust.

To illustrate, what are the gift tax consequences if O irrevocably designated B as the beneficiary of policies O owned insuring O's life or if O releases the power to surrender the policy but retains the power to borrow against its equity reserve? In either case B has not yet acquired anything of value that would constitute a completed gift (except to any extent in the latter case that O cannot borrow the full value of the trust and therefore leaves benefit in the trust for B's eventual enjoyment). Similarly, there are no gift tax consequences of O's payment of premiums on the policy after irrevocably designating B as the beneficiary if O continues to own the policy. If, however, O transfers the policy to B as well, then the value of the policy itself is a completed gift, as are future premium payments, and because B owns the policy each will qualify as a present interest for annual exclusion qualification purposes.

An individual who pays premiums on a policy that was assigned to a trust usually uses "after-tax" dollars (net income after payment of income tax). If, instead, that individual creates a funded life insurance trust, the trustee might use trust income to pay premiums on the policies, but §677(a)(3) nevertheless causes the trust's grantor to be taxed on any trust income that is (or in the discretion of a nonadverse party may be) used to pay premiums for policies insuring the life of the grantor or the grantor's spouse. Thus, there is no income tax advantage or disadvantage to funding the trust if the grantor is the insured or the insured's spouse. There probably is a gift tax advantage to using the unfunded trust approach because premiums paid annually probably will generate more annual exclusion entitlements, but that assumes the owner is not making annual exclusion transfers otherwise.

Finally, if an insured transfers a life insurance policy more than three years prior to death, the proceeds will not be included in the insured's gross estate unless there are retained powers over or interests in the policy or in a trust that holds the policy. Subsequent premium payments made by the insured or by the assignee usually will not cause adverse estate tax consequences to the insured. If, however, within three years of death, the insured pays the final premium on an automatically renewable accidental death policy, the proceeds of that policy may be includible in the insured's gross estate. Under §2001(b), premiums paid on any policy owned by another will be included in the payor's adjusted taxable gifts base to the extent that they did not qualify for the gift tax annual exclusion.

Chapter 9

ANNUITIES AND EMPLOYEE DEATH BENEFITS

Part A.   Annuities
Part B.   Employee Death Benefits

PART A.   ANNUITIES

Code References: *Estate Tax: §2039*
Gift Tax: §2517

1.   *Non Refund Single Life Annuities.* *D* recently bought an annuity contract for $125,000, providing for the payment of $12,000 at the end of each year for the balance of *D*'s life. Will anything be includible in *D*'s gross estate at death by reason of this annuity contract? The answer is yes and no. To the extent that *D* does not consume the annual payments in ways that leave no value at death, those benefits that were paid to *D* and increased *D*'s net worth will be included in *D*'s gross estate under §2033. And even if *D* consumes these funds, other assets that *D* otherwise might have consumed may remain at death. So the unconsumed value of the annuity inflates *D*'s net worth and it is taxable.

But the answer with respect to the annuity contract itself is no, if the annuity *D* purchased is a *non refund single life (or straight life) annuity* that terminates when *D* dies. The annuity ceases to exist at the moment of *D*'s death. A purchase of this type of annuity (especially from a commercial company engaged in selling annuities, but also from a private individual if proper valuation techniques are employed and full and adequate consideration is paid) does not incur either gift taxation at the time of purchase or estate taxation at the time of death. At neither time has the purchaser of the annuity gratuitously transferred any property. The transfer of cash for the annuity is merely an exchange for full and adequate consideration, an investment really, by which *D* acquires a wasting asset. If *D* lives longer than the mortality tables predict, *D* will receive a larger amount than *D* invested in the contract. If *D* dies prematurely, the issuer of the annuity contract comes out ahead. Either way, nothing remains for inclusion.

The issue in the first case below is whether this no-inclusion result is justified, given the nature of the investment "package" — a combination of insurance and an annuity. It also shows why, ultimately, Congress thought

§2036 was not adequate to cause inclusion of certain annuities and therefore adopted §2039.

Fidelity-Philadelphia Trust Co. v. Smith
356 U.S. 274 (1958)

WARREN, Chief Justice: The question before the Court is whether the proceeds of certain insurance policies on the life of the decedent, payable to named beneficiaries and irrevocably assigned by the insured, should be included in the estate of the decedent for the purposes of the federal estate tax. The facts are not in dispute. In 1934 decedent, then aged 76, purchased a series of annuity-life insurance policy combinations. Three single-premium life insurance policies, at face values of $200,000, $100,000, and $50,000 respectively, were obtained without the requirement of a medical examination. As a condition to selling decedent each life insurance policy, the companies involved required decedent also to purchase a separate, single-premium, nonrefundable life annuity policy. The premiums for each life insurance policy and for each annuity policy were fixed at regular rates. The size of each annuity, however, was calculated so that in the event the annuitant-insured died prematurely the annuity premium, less the amount allocated to annuity payments already made, would combine with the companion life insurance premium, plus interest, to equal the amount of insurance proceeds to be paid. Each annuity policy could have been purchased without the insurance policy for the same premium charged for it under the annuity-life insurance combination.

The decedent's children were primary beneficiaries of the insurance policies; the Fidelity-Philadelphia Trust Company, as trustee of a trust established by decedent, was named beneficiary of the interests of any of decedent's children who predeceased her. In the year of purchase, decedent assigned all rights and benefits under two of the life insurance policies to her children and under the other to the Fidelity-Philadelphia Trust Company as trustee. These rights and benefits included the rights to receive dividends, to change the beneficiaries, to surrender the policies, and to assign them. Dividends were received but, as far as the record discloses, none of the other rights was exercised. A gift tax on these transfers was paid by the decedent in 1935. In 1938 decedent amended the above-mentioned trust so that it became irrevocable. As the Government concedes, the decedent retained no beneficial or reversionary interest in the trust.

The insured died in 1946. The proceeds of the three insurance policies were not included in her estate in the estate tax return. The

Commissioner of Internal Revenue determined that these proceeds should have been included and assessed a deficiency accordingly. The adjusted tax was paid by the executors, and when claim for refund was denied, this action for refund followed. The District Court entered judgment for the taxpayers, but [was] reversed. 241 F.2d 690 (3d Cir. 1957).

It is conceded by the parties that the question of whether the proceeds should be included in the estate is not determinable by the federal estate tax provision dealing with life insurance proceeds. Cf. *Helvering v. Le Gierse*, 312 U.S. 531 (1941). To support the decision below, the Government argues that the proceeds are includible in the estate under §[2036(a)]. . . . The Government contends that the annuity payments, which were retained until death, were income from property transferred by the decedent to her children through the use of the life insurance policies.

On the other hand, petitioners, executors of the estate, assert that the annuity payments were income from the annuity policies, which were separate property from the insurance policies, and that since decedent had assigned away the life insurance policies before death, she retained no interest in them at death.

The Government relies on *Le Gierse*, where this Court also had before it the issue of the taxability of proceeds from a life insurance policy in an annuity-life insurance combination. After holding that the taxability of these proceeds was not to be determined for estate tax purposes according to the statutory provisions dealing with life insurance, the Court held that the proceeds were includable in the estate under [an antecedent of §2036(a)] because they devolved on the beneficiaries in a transfer which took "effect in possession or enjoyment at or after . . . death." 312 U.S. at 542. However, in reaching this conclusion the decision did not consider the problem in the case at bar, for in *Le Gierse* the insured had retained the rights and benefits of the insurance policy until death. The facts in the instant case on this point are fundamentally different. Prior to death, the decedent had divested herself of all interests in the insurance policies, including the possibility that the funds would return to her or her estate if the beneficiaries predeceased her. The assignees became the "owners" of the policies before her death; they had received the right to the immediate and unlimited use of the policies to the full extent of their worth. The immediate value of the policies was always substantial. In the year of assignment their total cash surrender value was over $289,000; in the year of death it was over $326,000. Under the assignment, the decedent had not become a life tenant who postpones the possession and enjoyment of the property by the remaindermen until her death.[1] . . . On the contrary, the assignees held the bundle of rights, the incidents of ownership, over property from which the decedent had totally divorced herself. . . . [T]he Government's position that the annuities were income from property which the insured transferred to her children under the life insurance policies is not well taken.

To establish its contention, the Government must aggregate the premiums of the annuity policies with those of the life insurance policies and establish that the annuity payments were derived as income from the entire investment. This proposition cannot be established. Admittedly, when the policies were purchased, each life insurance-annuity combination was the product of a single, integrated transaction. However, the parties neither intended that, nor acted as if, any of the transactions would have a quality of indivisibility. Regardless of the considerations prompting the insurance companies to hedge their life insurance contracts with annuities, each time an annuity-life insurance combination was written, two items of property, an annuity policy and an insurance policy, were transferred to the purchaser. The annuity policy could have been acquired separately, and the life insurance policy could have been, and was, conveyed separately. The annuities arose from personal obligations of the insurance companies which were in no way conditioned on the continued existence of the life insurance contracts. These periodic payments would have continued unimpaired and without diminution in size throughout the life of the insured even if the life insurance policies had been extinguished.[2] Quite clearly the annuity payments arose solely from the annuity

---

1.   Nor are the assignees like second annuitants in survivorship annuities or joint annuitants in joint and survivor annuities. The donor's and donee's annuities have a common fund as the source so that if the source of the donor's annuity is extinguished, the donee's annuity is destroyed. The entire economic enjoyment of the second annuitant must, realistically speaking, await the death of the first annuitant, and a substantial portion of the surviving joint annuitant's enjoyment is similarly postponed. Cf., e.g., Commissioner v. Estate of Wilder, 118 F.2d 281 (5th Cir. 1941); Commissioner v. Clise, 122 F.2d 998 (9th Cir. 1941); Estate of Mearkle v. Commissioner, 129 F.2d 386 (3d Cir. 1942).

2.   Where a decedent . . . has transferred property to another in return for a promise to make periodic payments to the transferor for his lifetime, it has been held that these payments are not income from the transferred property so as to include the property in the estate of the decedent. E.g., Estate of Bergan v. Commissioner, 1 T.C. 543 (1942), *acq.*; Security Trust & Savings Bank v. Commissioner, 11 B.T.A. 833 (1928); Estate of Johnson v. Commissioner, 10 B.T.A. 411 (1928); Hirsh v. United States, 35 F.2d 982 (Ct. Cl. 1929); cf. Welch v. Hall, 134 F.2d 366 (1st Cir. 1943). In these cases the promise is a personal obligation of the transferee, the obligation is usually not chargeable to the transferred property, and the size of the payments is not determined by the size of the actual income from the transferred property at the time the payments are made.

policies. The use and enjoyment of the annuity policies were entirely independent of the life insurance policies. Because of this independence, the Commissioner may not, by aggregating the two types of policies into one investment, conclude that by receiving the annuities, the decedent had retained income from the life insurance contracts.

Accordingly, the judgment of the Court of Appeals is reversed.

Mr. Justice BURTON, with whom Mr. Justice BLACK and Mr. Justice CLARK join, dissenting. For the reasons stated by the court below, 241 F.2d 690 . . . it seems to me that, for federal estate tax purposes, this case is indistinguishable from one in which a settlor places a sum in trust under such terms that he shall receive the income from it for life, and the principal shall be payable to designated beneficiaries upon his death. As the principal, in that event, would be includable in the settlor's estate for federal estate tax purposes, so here the proceeds of the insurance policies should be included in this decedent's estate. Accordingly, I would affirm the judgment of the Court of Appeals.

Just as an aside, the insurance proceeds received on the death of the decedent by the beneficiary of an integrated life insurance-annuity plan are not excluded by §101 from the beneficiary's gross income for income tax purposes. Kess v. United States, 451 F.2d 1229 (6th Cir. 1971); Rev. Rul. 65-57. Nor are the annuity payments to the decedent during life excluded by §101 from the decedent's gross income. Indeed, if no part of these payments constitutes a return of principal, no amount is excluded by §72 either. Rev. Rul. 75-255.

Notice that the government sought to include the package investment under §2036. Today would §2039(a) apply without the government's attempt to aggregate the annuity with the life insurance plan? Because the answer is no, it does not appear that anything was accomplished by adoption of §2039 without that additional important element, as shown in *Montgomery*, next.

Estate of Montgomery v. Commissioner
56 T.C. 489 (1971), *aff'd per curiam*,
458 F.2d 616 (5th Cir. 1972)

WITHEY, J.: . . . In a simultaneous step transaction, decedent on May 4, 1964, created two irrevocable trusts in favor of his grandchildren and on the next day applied to National for an annuity on his life and paid therefor a premium of $2,200,000. Also on May 5, 1964, the trustees of each of the two trusts applied to National for life insurance on the life of decedent in the amount of $1 million each. On the next day, May 6, 1964, both the annuity policy and the two life insurance policies were issued by National.

Each of the trusts paid a single annual premium to National in the amount of $132,938, the exact amount of a gift made to each trust by decedent. Under the terms of the annuity, decedent received for each month of his life after its issuance, the amount of $22,682. This payment ceased with the last payment preceding his death. No refund of premium was to be made thereafter nor was any provision made in the annuity policy for survivorship benefits.

By purchase of the annuity, decedent acquired the additional right to either purchase life insurance on his life in the aggregate amount of $2 million or to permit the purchase thereof by the two trusts referred to. Without this right, such insurance would not have been obtained as decedent was then of such advanced age and in such precarious health as to be uninsurable.

National would not have issued the policies of "life insurance" to the two trusts without the consent of the decedent and likewise would not have done so unless decedent had purchased the annuity. He gave that consent prior to the issuance of the policies and in substance further consented by paying the first annual premium on each through the trusts as conduits.

National, decedent, and the trustees of the two trusts carried through the above transactions as an integrated step transaction as a result of an understanding between them. National suffered no risk of loss as a result of the transactions after decedent's purchase of the annuity, regardless of whether the "life insurance" policies were purchased.

Respondent's primary position is based upon §2039. His contention is that the "life insurance" involved herein is not life insurance within the meaning of the parenthetical exception contained in §2039; that therefore the proceeds of "life insurance" policies herein are includable in decedent's gross estate as: "the value of . . . [an] other payment receivable by any beneficiary by reason of surviving the decedent under any form of contract or agreement . . . if, under such contract or agreement, an annuity or other payment was payable to the decedent . . . for his life or for any period not ascertainable without reference to his death. . . ." The key to the applicability of §2039 rests upon the determination whether his premise is correct.

The word "insurance" is not defined in the 1954 Code or respondent's regulations and we therefore resort to case law for its definition. The word has been discussed by the Supreme Court, particularly with respect to annuity-insurance combinations, in Helvering v. Le Gierse, 312 U.S. 531 (1941). . . .

In a companion case to *Le Gierse*, Estate of Keller v. Commissioner, 312 U.S. 543 (1941), *aff'g* 113 F.2d 833 (3rd Cir.

1940), the Supreme Court differentiated with some particularity between an investment risk by an insurance company which it held had no bearing upon the question whether its policy is one of life insurance and an insurance risk which it held to be indispensable to a life insurance contract. It was also there held that, in using the word "insurance" in the section of the Code there under consideration, Congress had in mind the economic rather than only the contractual aspects of the word. . . .

The basic test in determining whether the integrated transactions before us involved life insurance is whether National in settling its obligations thereunder was exposed to a financial loss. We have found as a fact, based on the evidence before us, that National bore no insurance risk of any kind. It is true that on an annual basis, National was bound to pay decedent $6,308 as annuity payments more than it received as premium payments on "life insurance policies" but the only risk involved was an investment risk, *Le Gierse* and *Estate of Keller*, for it had received from decedent as the price of the annuity an amount of $2,200,000 which it was free to invest, to say nothing of the so-called life insurance premiums. Even invested at 1%, interest on that amount would far exceed the $6,308 excess. We agree with National's president that, reading the annuity and insurance contracts as one integrated transaction, National bore no risk with respect thereto, be it insurance risk or economic risk.

Having so concluded, it is clear that §2039 applies. It is stipulated that decedent, under the annuity contract, not only possessed the right but actually did receive monthly annuity payments which ceased with the last such payment prior to his death. His grandchildren, who were beneficiaries of the two trusts, each received in trust an "other payment" in the form of life insurance proceeds by reason of surviving the decedent. We have found that the transaction here involved grew out of an understanding or agreement between decedent, National, and the trustees of the trusts which in our view fits the [§2039(a)] phrase "under any form of contract or agreement." The language of the statute is clear and unambiguous and for that reason we apply its literal wording to the facts before us.

Section 2039 and acts amendatory thereof are new provisions which first appear in the 1954 Code. The congressional history thereof[3] indicates clearly that Congress thereby sought to include in a decedent's gross estate for estate tax purposes *the full value* of any contract or agreement whereby an annuitant who received

---

3. H.R. Rep. No. 1337, 83d Cong., 2d Sess. A314 (1954). S. Rep. No. 1622, 83d Cong., 2d Sess. 470 (1954).

lifetime annuity benefits by contribution to the purchase price thereof, at his death left value in or as a result of the agreement remaining to his beneficiaries either by way of lump-sum or periodic payments.

Both houses of Congress in their committee reports on §2039 used the same language in describing one of the contracts to which the section applies, as follows: "A contract under which the decedent immediately before his death was receiving or was entitled to receive for the duration of his life an annuity, or other stipulated payment, with payments thereunder to continue after his death to a designated beneficiary if surviving the decedent." Immediately following the examples is the following: "The amount to be included in the gross estate is the value at the decedent's death of the annuity or other payment receivable by the survivor of the decedent, and it is immaterial whether the payments to the survivor are payable in a lump sum, in installments, in the same, or in a greater or lesser amount than the annuity or payment to the decedent."

Inasmuch as we have held §2039 to be controlling herein, we do not discuss authority cited by petitioner which pertains only to §2035. The only authority cited and relied on by petitioner with respect to the §2039 issue is Fidelity-Philadelphia Trust Co. v. Smith, 356 U.S. 274 (1958). In that case, the Supreme Court had before it an issue arising under [§2036(a)] as to whether annuity payments received by decedent and retained until her death "were income from property transferred by the decedent to her children by the use of the life insurance policies." Section 2039, relating as it does specifically to "an annuity or other payment" did not exist at the date of the transaction which gave rise to that decision, and for that reason, the decision is not controlling with respect to the issue before us. It is true that in *Fidelity-Philadelphia Trust Co.* the Supreme Court found an insurance-annuity arrangement, to some extent the same as that before us, involved two separate items of property, the proceeds from which were not to be aggregated in an estate tax computation under §[2036(a)], but even though the annuity and the insurance policies here in controversy might be said to have separate entities and values, they each came into being as the result of a single integrated "form of contract or agreement" not dealt with in the Code until the advent of §2039.

In our view, the arrangement before us consists, in essence, of a single contract for the investment by decedent with National of the aggregate amount of $2,465,876 (annuity premiums plus insurance premiums for 1 year) in return for a fixed monthly payment to decedent for his life with a provision, at his death, that

$2 million of the invested sum devolve to his beneficiaries. Application of §2039 to these facts calls for inclusion of the proceeds of the life insurance herein in decedent's gross estate. We so hold.

Accord, Sussman v. United States, 76-1 U.S. Tax Cas. (CCH) ¶13,126 (E.D. N.Y. 1975). Under current law, if a taxpayer purchased a single life annuity and a policy insuring the taxpayer's life as an integrated transaction, and if the taxpayer then assigned ownership of the life insurance policy to an individual, the government might successfully apply §2702 to impose a special value for gift tax purposes to the assignment of the policy.

2. *Refund Annuities.* A single life annuity may provide for a refund of a portion of the cost of the annuity if the annuitant dies prematurely. That refund may be payable to the annuitant's estate or to a designated beneficiary. The value of such a refund is includible in the annuitant's gross estate under §2033 if it is payable to the annuitant's estate. Section 2039 is the relevant provision if the refund is payable to a designated beneficiary. Also, if the beneficiary designation that the annuitant made was irrevocable, and if the annuitant had no power to terminate the annuity contract, the making of an irrevocable designation of the annuity constitutes a gift of a future interest for gift tax purposes. On the annuitant's death, the gift caused by an irrevocable designation will be purged from the annuitant's adjusted taxable gifts under §2001(b) if a refund is payable. It will not be purged if no refund is payable. Quaere, in that regard: if the decedent lived long enough to receive sufficient payments that the refund feature does not apply, doesn't that mean the wealth is includible under §2033 and the same purge should apply?

3. *Survivorship Annuities.* Survivorship annuities fall into two basic categories: *joint and survivor annuities* and *self and survivor annuities.* The former provides for payments to be made to the primary annuitant and another person during their joint lives and, upon the death of either, continuation of the payments (at the same or a lower level) to the survivor for life. The self and survivor annuity differs in that the payments are made only to the primary annuitant for life, and then to the designated beneficiary after the primary annuitant's death. The distinction between these two types of annuities is not always noticed, and both are referred to on occasion as joint and survivor annuities.

If the primary annuitant purchased the self and survivor contract and dies first, §2039 requires the value of the survivor's right to future payments to be included in the primary annuitant's gross estate. The same result was reached under the predecessors of §2036 or §2037 prior to the adoption of §2039 in 1954. See Forster v. Sauber, 249 F.2d 379 (7th Cir.

1957), and cases cited therein; Stephens, Maxfield, Lind, & Calfee ¶4.11[7] (8th ed. 2002); Lowndes, Kramer, & McCord, FEDERAL ESTATE AND GIFT TAXES §10.2 (3d ed. 1974).

The committee reports accompanying the 1954 Code suggest the same §2039 result in the case of a joint and survivor contract if the annuitant who purchased the contract dies first. See H.R. Rep. No. 1337, 83d Cong., 2d Sess. A314 *Example (2)* (1954); S. Rep. No. 1622, 83d Cong., 2d Sess. 470 *Example (2)* (1954). The same result was reached prior to 1954 in a few cases under the predecessors of §2036 or §2037 or both in combination. Estate of Mearkle v. Commissioner, 129 F.2d 386 (3d Cir. 1942); Grant v. Smyth, 123 F. Supp. 771 (N.D. Cal. 1954).

An election or purchase of a survivor annuity may cause gift tax consequences. In a self and survivor annuity, the designation of a person to receive payments that commence when the primary annuitant dies is a gift of a future interest, from the primary annuitant, effective when the designation becomes irrevocable. Treas. Reg. §25.2512-6(a) *Example (5)* (self and survivor annuity, incorrectly labeled a joint and survivor annuity); Rev. Rul. 70-514; cf. Roberts v. Commissioner, 143 F.2d 657 (5th Cir. 1944). There appears to be no direct authority on the gift taxation of joint and survivor annuities, but the gift tax should apply with respect to those annuities also.

4.   *Partial Consideration.* H.R. Rep. No. 1337, 83d Cong., 2d Sess. A314 (1954); S. Rep. No. 1622, 83d Cong., 2d Sess. 470 (1954):

[Section 2039] applies only to that part of the value of the annuity or other payment receivable by the surviving beneficiary which the decedent's contribution to the purchase price of the contract or agreement bears to the total purchase price thereof. For example, assume that the value of the annuity to the beneficiary at decedent's death is $20,000 and that the decedent contributed one-half of the purchase price of the contract. In such case, $10,000 would be includible in the decedent's gross estate.

Contributions by an employer are regarded as payments of compensation to the employee who then made the full premium contribution. §2039(b); Treas. Reg. §20.2039-1(c).

5.   *Private Annuities.* Annuities purchased from someone not in the business of selling annuities are private annuities and usually cover only a single life. For example, suppose that *D* purchased a single life annuity contract from a child, *C*, and paid $200,000 for the right to receive $12,000 per year for the rest of *D*'s life, and that the actual value of that annuity was $125,000. The issue is whether anything will be includible in *D*'s gross estate at death as a result of this private annuity contract. Section 2039 will not apply because no payment will be made after *D*'s death. See GCM

38593 (May 7, 1986). It also seems that §2036 will not apply to cause inclusion of the transferred property, because the annuity payments are not required to be made out of the transferred property, but rather are a general obligation of *C*. See Fidelity-Philadelphia Trust Co. reproduced at page 520; *accord*, Estate of Becklenberg v. Commissioner, 273 F.2d 297 (7th Cir. 1959); Cain v. Commissioner, 37 T.C. 185 (1961). *Compare* Lazarus v. Commissioner, 513 F.2d 824 (9th Cir. 1975); Greene v. United States, 237 F.2d 848 (7th Cir. 1956); Rev. Rul. 68-183. Nevertheless, regardless of whether a portion of the property is includible in *D*'s gross estate, *D* made a gift subject to gift taxation to *C* to the extent the $200,000 consideration exceeded the $125,000 value of the annuity. The value is the amount *D* would have paid a commercial annuity company for a comparable annuity. Rev. Rul. 69-74. Furthermore, if *D* died within three years of purchasing the annuity, gift tax incurred by *D* on the gift of the excess consideration would be included in *D*'s gross estate under §2035(b). See Treas. Reg. §20.7520-1 to value noncommercial annuities.

A number of these rules and principles are brought to bear in the context of several pronouncements that indicate the government is preparing to litigate a new issue regarding the scope and application of §2039 to a form of private annuity developed in response to §2702, which we study in Part B of Chapter 15. You may want to note that a Field Service Advice is rendered in the context of litigation support. and generally these are a bit aggressive. That definitely characterizes FSA 200036012, which is the government's effort to improve on the inclusion result that otherwise *ought* to occur under §2036(a)(1) if a taxpayer creates a grantor retained annuity trust (GRAT) interest and dies before the retained term expires. On the other hand, a Technical Advice Memorandum is delivered as advice to a government attorney in the field and is normally thought to be more balanced, but TAM 200210009 hews the same line.

In the FSA the government correctly determined that a GRAT that survives the settlor's death would cause an amount to be includible under §2036(a)(1) as determined by Rev. Rul. 82-105, being that portion of the trust needed to generate the annual annuity payment. In many cases that would be 100% of the trust, because the annuity was larger than the annual income generated by the entire trust. But in a case in which the trust is more than adequate to generate the annual annuity payment (and, therefore, only that portion of the trust needed to generate the annuity is includible under §2036(a)(1)) the government nevertheless would like to cause 100% inclusion, and that is what the Advice and subsequently the Memorandum assert to be the proper result, under language in §2039(a) referring to "the value of an annuity *or other payment receivable* by any beneficiary by reason of surviving the decedent" (emphasis added*)*. The "other payment receivable" under the facts of these pronouncements was the *remainder* interest in the GRAT, passing to remainder beneficiaries on the taxpayer's death before expiration of the term interest retained by the grantor.

Although no court has addressed this issue yet, the government almost certainly is wrong in its reliance on the quoted language, for two reasons: one is that the remainder interest did not pass by virtue of surviving the taxpayer; it passed on creation of the trust, as a future interest that was a complete and taxable transfer upon initial validity of the GRAT itself. The second reason is because that remainder is not the type of interest that the Code envisions when it speaks of "an annuity or other payment"; that language is designed to reach traditional annuities and similar *ongoing* payments that may differ from a vanilla annuity but that have the same functional effect. It is the *annuity* (or its functional equivalent, like a lump sum refund payment in lieu of a survivor's annuity) that the taxpayer retained *and that passes to another* at death that triggers §2039(a), not the underlying corpus that was used to purchase the stream of payments.

Notwithstanding this defect in its reasoning, the government raises an interesting question regarding the proper application of the Code in general. Should anything be includible in a taxpayer's gross estate if the taxpayer creates a no-refund, single-life annuity such that nothing remains at death? By way of example, if T transfers property to a third party vendor of commercial annuity contracts, in exchange for an annuity that pays for life and then ceases, would the underlying corpus used to purchase that annuity be includible in T's gross estate? Certainly the annuity payments received and not completely consumed with no lingering value would be includible. But the amortization of wealth represented by that transfer would not otherwise trigger inclusion of the fund used to purchase that annuity.

Should this uncontroversial and clear result differ if T transfers the same wealth to a trust created by T's child (a private annuity), in exchange for the same annuity? If the commercial vendor is no different than the child's trust in such a case, and if inclusion does not result in either case, would the answer somehow differ if T instead transfers the same wealth in exchange for the same annuity, the only change being that the transferee is a trust created by T? If the annuity is the same in each case, the inclusion result should not differ; indeed, why would either of §2036(a)(1) or §2039(a) properly be applicable?

Another thought that should inform this evaluation is that, in a commercial annuity setting, there should be no inclusion under §2036(a)(1) to the extent the full and adequate consideration exception applies. Thus, there is no §2036(a)(1) exposure at death if T transfers $1 million during life for a lifetime annuity worth $1 million. Indeed, if T lives to the exact life expectancy that informed the cost of that annuity, and received all the contractual annuity payments, T would have received $1 million of replace-ment value (the full and adequate consideration), which prevents any reduction in net worth that otherwise would escape taxation, and that replacement value would be includible under §2033. There might be a difference in the size of T's estate given that the annuity issuer makes a profit and depending on whether T's actual life exceeded or fell short of the mortality assumption. But in the case of annuities the law does not care about these actualities in valuation – the Code and regulations engage in the notion that the tables must be applied in all but terminal illness cases, and it is understood that cases that deviate from the "average" will offset each other, some involving longer lives and some shorter. So that dissonance is ignored.

The important point is that §2036(a)(1) should not apply at all in any case involving a commercial annuity with a straight life entitlement that constitutes full and adequate consideration for the money used to purchase it. *If*, on the other hand, *T* as the decedent/annuitant did not receive full and adequate consideration – for example, because the annuity payable to *T* was reduced because there was a refund or survivor benefit payable to another person – then §2036 would (and should) apply to the differential. But only the difference between what *T* transferred to acquire the annuity and the value of the consideration (the annuity) personally received back by *T* should be subject to §2036(a)(1) inclusion in *T*'s gross estate. (That's the theory, although we know that the full transfer would be includible and the §2043 consideration offset would apply, which can create a dissonance that also is not relevant to this consideration. Recall this discussion in Chapter 6). If the government is right that §2039(a) is simply meant to take the place of §2036(a)(1) in such a situation, then it too should apply only to the differential. But the government is arguing for a totally different result.

Notice that there is no full and adequate consideration exception in §2039(a), as there is in §2036(a). That is not a problem because §2039(a) only purports to tax the value of a survivor's benefit – which is the differential referred to above. In that light, §2039(a) should not purport to tax the full value of the underlying property that was transferred in exchange for the annuity payments. That is a critically important point because §2039(a) by its terms only taxes the value of any "annuity or other payment receivable by any beneficiary by reason of surviving the decedent." The impropriety in the government's approach is that it is trying to tax under §2039(a) the full value of the property transferred – more than just any survivor's benefit. Put another way, the government is suggesting that it can tax the *remainder* – the full value at death of the property transferred in exchange for the annuity contract in its entirety. Note that §2039(a) does not support that result unless the term "other payment receivable" properly includes the original consideration transferred, and not just the survivor benefit, and that would destroy the functional symmetry between §§2036(a)(1) and 2039(a).

6. *Income Taxation of Annuities.* Each payment made under a commercial annuity may consist partly of a return of the consideration paid for the annuity and partly of income earned on that consideration, until the expected annuity term is reached. Under §72(b)(1), only a percentage of each annuity payment (the "exclusion ratio") is excluded from the recipient's gross income. The exclusion ratio is a fraction, the numerator of which is the investment in the annuity contract and the denominator of which is the total expected return from the annuity over the annuity term. For example, assume that 56 year old D purchased for $125,000 a single life annuity that will pay $12,000 per year in monthly installments until D dies. D's expected return from the annuity is $332,400 ($12,000 x 27.7, which is the number of years of D's life expectancy under Table V in Treas. Reg. §1.72-9). Using the cost ($125,000) as the numerator and the expected return ($332,400) as the denominator, the exclusion ratio is slightly less than 38%. Thus, slightly more than 62% of each monthly payment is included in gross income.

The exclusion ratio applies only until the annuitant's total investment in the contract is recovered, after which all amounts received are includible in gross income. Thus, D will recoup the original $125,000 investment by exclusion from gross income just before D reaches the age of 84; thereafter D must include in gross income the full amount received every year. In this sense, D is not rewarded under the tax laws for outliving the mortality tables prescribed in the regulations. Alternatively, if D dies before fully recovering the $125,000 investment, any unrecovered investment is allowable as a deduction on D's final income tax return, which would be filed by D's personal representative. This economic realism is applicable with respect to any annuity that started after 1981.[4]

The income tax consequences of buying and selling private annuities is more complex than that of commercial annuities. The government's position is set forth in Rev. Rul. 69-74.

PART B.   EMPLOYEE DEATH BENEFITS

7.   *Background.*   Although §2039 has had some impact on the estate taxation of commercial and private annuities not connected with employment, the primary purpose of §2039 was to deal with employee death benefits. H.R. Rep. No. 1337, 83d Cong., 2d Sess. 90-91 (1954); S. Rep. No. 1622, 83d Cong., 2d Sess. 123 (1954):

Under present law the value at the decedent's death of a joint and survivor annuity purchased by him is includible in his gross estate. It is not clear under existing law whether an annuity of that

---

4.   Older annuities retain their original exclusion ratio for the life of the annuitant, with neither a deduction for unrecovered amounts nor a change to full inclusion when the full investment is recovered, reflecting a prior congressional policy that D should not be forced to readjust to a lesser after-tax income after receiving an annuity for a number of years to reflect increased gross income due to a changed exclusion ratio when D has outlived the mortality assumptions. See H.R. Rep. No. 1337, 83d Cong., 2d Sess. 10 (1954); S. Rep. No. 1622, 83d Cong., 2d Sess. 11 (1954).

type purchased by the decedent's employer, or an annuity to which both the decedent and his employer made contributions is includible in the decedent's gross estate.

[Section 2039] requires the inclusion of a joint and survivor annuity in the gross estate to the extent that the decedent contributed to its cost and, for the purpose of determining the extent of the decedent's contribution, the payments made by the employer . . . are to be taken into account.

Prior to the enactment of §2039, the Commissioner experienced great difficulty in trying to include the value of employee death benefits in an employee's gross estate. The Commissioner was forced to rely on the forerunners of §§2035 through 2038 unless the death benefit was payable to the employee's estate and §2033 applied. A major obstacle to their application was their universal threshold requirement of a "transfer" of "property." To illustrate, consider how substantially different the following situations are: (1) Employee X, who is paid $20,000 per year by employer E, each year uses $2,000 of after-tax income to buy a self and survivor annuity from a commercial insurance company, with payments beginning when X reaches the age of 68; (2) Employee Y's wages are $18,000 per year, plus a fringe benefit costing E $2,000 per year, consisting of an annuity of the same type purchased by employee X. Employee X's transaction clearly is a transfer of property, and the value of the survivor's benefit would have been includible in X's gross estate even before 1954. Whether employee Y had property and, if so, whether Y transferred it was never resolved prior to the adoption of §2039. Moreover, even if a transfer of property occurred, the courts surprisingly rejected the notion that Y retained an interest that was adequate to trigger the forerunners of either §2036 or §2037.[5]

Section 2039 dispenses with the formal wealth *transfer* tax requirement of a *transfer* of *property*, which reflects a congressional judgment that a property transfer occurs by virtue of employee and employer contributions to employee death benefit plans. Moreover, although Congress did not require a formal finding of a property transfer, it nevertheless drew heavily from §§2036 and 2037 in fashioning the §2039 requirements. For example, §2039 applies only to contracts or agreements entered into after March 3, 1931, which is when the joint resolution that introduced §2036 was passed,

---

5. See, e.g., Commissioner v. Estate of Twogood, 194 F.2d 627 (2d Cir. 1952), *aff'g* 15 T.C. 989 (1950); Estate of Higg v. Commissioner, 184 F.2d 427 (3d Cir. 1950), *rev'g* 12 T.C. 280 (1949). In 1949 Congress deleted the retention of a reversionary interest requirement from the predecessor of §2037. See Rev. Ruls. 158 and 260. But before this position could be tested adequately in court, Congress in 1954 restored that reversionary interest requirement to §2037 and added new §2039 to deal directly with employee death benefits.

and it employs the three "timing" notions of §2036, as discussed beginning at page 538.

The employee's contributions are taken into account under §2039 and the includibility of benefits directly traceable to employee contributions probably was not in doubt even before 1954. The innovation in 1954 was the explicit attribution to the employee of employer contributions made "by reason of [the employee's] employment." §2039(b). According to H.R. Rep. No. 1337, 83d Cong., 2d Sess. A315 (1954); S. Rep. No. 1622, 83d Cong., 2d Sess. 471 (1954):

the contributions of an employer . . . shall be considered to have been made by reason of [the] decedent's employment if, for example, the annuity or other payment is offered by the employer as an inducement to employment, or a continuance thereof, or if the contributions are made by the employer in lieu of additional compensation or other rights, if so understood by employer and employee whether or not expressly stated in the contract of employment or otherwise.

This attribution of employer contributions to employees was not universal: it did not apply to benefits payable under certain qualified plans and annuities specified in §2039(c) until 1983 and then not entirely until after 1984, when §2039(c) finally was repealed and exempt retirement and death benefits became fully subject to wealth transfer tax like other forms of a decedent's net worth. A special transition date rule is applicable with respect to a decedent who retired before 1983 or before 1985 with respect to the two reductions, respectively. See Rev. Rul. 92-22 for more details. With the adoption of §4980A in 1986, imposing a 15% supplemental estate tax on certain "excess" benefits accumulated at death, employee death benefits went in four short years from the most favored form of a decedent's wealth to the most heavily taxed, especially when the income taxation of these benefits is considered. Fortunately, §4980A subsequently was repealed but, with income tax liability, employee death benefits still count as the most expensive wealth a decedent can leave to beneficiaries at death. It makes a fine asset to leave to charity, however! See Hoyt, *The Family Wins When IRD is Used for Charitable Bequests — How to Do It*, 36 U. MIAMI INST. EST. PLAN. ¶400 (2002).

8.   *Gift Taxation of Irrevocable Beneficiary Designations.* As noted previously, an irrevocable beneficiary designation by the purchaser of a survivorship annuity can constitute a taxable gift; the same principle applies to employee death benefits.

9.   *Includibility under Other Sections.* S. Rep. No. 1622, 83d Cong., 2d Sess. 472 (1954):

The provisions of [§2039] shall not prevent the application of any other provisions of law relating to the estate tax. For example, if a contract provides for a refund of a portion of the cost thereof, in the event of the decedent's premature death, payable to the decedent's estate, the amount thereof shall be treated as any other property of the decedent. This section does not, however, apply to insurance under policies on the life of the decedent to which §2042 is applicable.

See also Treas. Reg. §20.2039-1(a). We have studied several cases in which the government tried to tax employee death benefits under other estate tax provisions, with some success. See, e.g., Estate of Bogley v. United States, excerpted at pages 52-53 (§2037), and Estate of Tully v. United States, reproduced at page 301 (§2038), which found that the threshold property transfer requirement was met. The government's success depended on compliance with the other requirements of the pertinent provision.

10. *Life Insurance Not Includible under §2039.*

All v. McCobb
321 F.2d 633 (2d Cir. 1963)

[The decedent was an eligible employee under an Annuity Plan funded by employer contributions. The decedent also participated in a Supplemental Annuity Plan that augmented the retirement allowance at the joint expense of the employer and the decedent. Finally, the employer adopted a Death Benefit Plan to supplement Social Security benefits provided to dependents of annuitants under the Annuity Plan. This unfunded plan was financed wholly by the employer and provided for twelve equal payments to a beneficiary designated in the plan (an annuitant had the right, with written approval of the employer, only to exclude persons from the stated classes of eligible beneficiaries). The decedent's surviving spouse was entitled to these payments, and the government determined that they were includible in the decedent's gross estate.

MARSHALL, J.: The district court held that they represented insurance that was excludible and ruled for the taxpayer. The government appealed.]

The district court held, upon cross-motions for summary judgment, that the Commissioner acted improperly in requiring that the payments made to the widow under the Death Benefit Plan be included in her husband's gross estate for purposes of federal estate taxation. Judgment was entered against the District Director and in favor of the taxpayer in the amount of $5,356.39. It is from that judgment that the District Director has taken this appeal. . . .

The district court held that §2039 was not applicable because the payments to the decedent's widow were "functionally 'insurance'," 206 F. Supp. at 903, and therefore fell within the parenthetical exclusion of the section. Because we have concluded that the payments here in question are clearly taxable to the decedent's estate under §2039, as the Commissioner has from the first contended, the decision of the district court must be reversed.

Putting to the side for the moment the question of whether the payments to the widow may properly be regarded as insurance, the operative facts in this case otherwise satisfy each of the conditions of the statute. The Treasury Regulations interpreting and implementing §2039 . . . provide that "The term 'annuity or other payment' as used with respect to both the decedent and the beneficiary has reference to one or more payments extending over any period of time. The payments may be equal or unequal, conditional or unconditional, periodic or sporadic." Treas. Reg. §20.2039-1(b)(1)(ii). The twelve equal payments received by the widow during each of the twelve months immediately following the decedent's death were thus an "annuity or other payment" within the meaning of the statute, and they were "receivable" by the widow under the terms of the Death Benefit Plan "by reason of [the widow's] surviving the decedent." That the Death Benefit Plan constituted a "form of contract or agreement" within the meaning of §2039 also is made clear by Treas. Reg. §20.2039-1(b)(1)(ii), which goes on to state, "The term 'contract or agreement' includes any arrangement, understanding or plan, or any combination of arrangements, understandings or plans arising by reason of the decedent's employment." The Death Benefit Plan, a formal document specifying the obligations of the company and the rights of the employees' surviving beneficiaries, falls directly within this language. . . . It is not disputed that the retirement allowance received by the decedent prior to his death had been "payable" to him under the Annuity Plan. Finally, for purposes of determining the applicability of §2039, the Annuity Plan and the Death Benefit Plan are to be considered as having been integrated into a single plan. "All rights and benefits accruing to an employee and to others by reason of the employment . . . are considered together in determining whether or not §2039(a) and (b) applies. The scope of §2039(a) and (b) cannot be limited by indirection." Treas. Reg. §20.2039-1(b)(2) *Example (6)*.

The statute thus clearly calls for inclusion in the decedent's gross estate of the death benefits paid to the widow, unless these benefits can be found to have been insurance, as the district court found. It based this finding upon the ground that "the payments in this case were designed to provide partial protection for one year to her as a dependent beneficiary against loss of retirement allowances to her husband through his untimely death." 206 F. Supp. at 903. We hold that this finding is without support and cannot be sustained. The fact that a payment is designed to afford a widow partial protection against the difficulties presented by her husband's death does not, ipso facto, convert that payment into insurance. The function of providing partial protection to widows is characteristic of a great many survivorship annuities and payments which nevertheless are not insurance for purposes of federal estate taxation and which are includable within a decedent's gross estate and taxable as such under §2039. See Comment, 66 YALE L.J. 1217, 1238–1248 (1957). It is thus necessary to carry the analysis beyond the point of merely concluding that the payments to the widow provided her with partial protection after the death of her husband, because that conclusion cannot logically be dispositive. . . .

Judged by the standards of [Helvering v.] Le Gierse, [312 U.S. 531 (1941)], and [Commissioner v.] Treganowan, [183 F.2d 288 (2d Cir. 1950)], the Death Benefit Plan bears no resemblance to a life insurance program. The Plan was unfunded and the company did not make periodic contributions to it in the employee's name. "Premium payments [were] not required, nor [was] there a shifting and spreading of the risk of death in any meaningful sense." Essenfeld [v. Commissioner], 311 F.2d 208, 209 (2d Cir. 1962). The decedent in no way shifted to the company the risk that his death would come prematurely and before the company, as insurer, had received premiums by or on his account in a sum equal to the amount required to be paid to the beneficiary. The company in no way gambled with the decedent that he would live a long life and that it would recover by periodic assessments before his death the amount to be paid to the beneficiary. It made no difference to the company, so far as any fund was concerned, whether the decedent died prematurely or not. Cf. Old Colony Trust Co. v. Commissioner, 102 F.2d 380 (1st Cir. 1939). Nor did the company in any way undertake to distribute among a larger group of employees, on the basis of actuarial data from which the appropriate size of a terminal reserve could be computed, the risk of the premature death of a single employee. The company did nothing more than promise to pay a sum certain to a named beneficiary upon the death of a retired employee. If payments resulting from such a promise were under the present facts to be regarded as insurance, the effectiveness and significance of §2039 would be greatly diminished, if not vitiated.

Even if the Death Benefit Plan were to be considered together with the Annuity Plan as a "coordinated system of payments to employees in consideration for their services," *Essenfeld*, 311 F.2d at 209, the result would remain the same. The Treasury Regulations provide that "A combination annuity contract and life insurance policy on the decedent's life (e.g., a 'retirement income' policy with death benefits) which matured during the decedent's lifetime so that there was no longer an insurance element under the contract at the time of the decedent's death is subject to the provisions of §2039(a) and (b)." Treas. Reg. §20.2039-1(d).

This disposition makes it unnecessary to consider the holding of the district court that the payments to the widow were also not taxable, as the Government had contended in the alternative, under several other sections of the Code.

Reversed.

The benefit in *McCobb* would not be includible in the decedent's gross estate under §2039 *or* §2042 if the employer had purchased group term life insurance from an insurance company that provided for payment to the decedent's beneficiary under the same terms (essentially denying the employee any control) as provided by the employer. Recall *DiMarco*, reproduced at page 857.

The death benefit in *McCobb* might have qualified as life insurance if the plan had provided that the amount payable to a retired employee would be reduced by 10% on the employee's 69th birthday, by 20% on the employee's 74th birthday, by 30% on the employee's 79th birthday, etc. Does that make the conclusion reached seem arbitrary?

11.   *The Decedent's Annuity or Other Payment.* S. Rep. No. 1622, 83d Cong., 2d Sess. 470-472 (1954):

Your committee has revised this section so as to make it clear that the provisions of [§2039] apply not only to cases where an annuity was payable to a decedent but also to contracts or agreements under which a lump-sum payment was payable to the decedent or the decedent possessed the right to receive such a lump-sum payment in lieu of an annuity. . . . The provisions of this section are applicable to annuities or other payments payable to the decedent, or which the decedent possessed the right to receive, either alone or in conjunction with another for his life or for any period not ascertainable without reference to his death or for any period which does not in fact end before his death. The rules applicable under §2036 in determining whether the annuity or other payment was payable to the decedent, or whether he possessed the right thereto, for his life or such periods shall be applicable under this section.

Applying the §2036 rules creates an anomaly. Consider: D entered into a contract with D's employer, a corporation in which D was an officer and a major shareholder, that provided for the payment to D upon retirement of a lump sum of $100,000 and the payment of $70,000 to D's spouse S upon D's death. If D was not yet entitled to the $100,000 when D died (for example, before retiring) the payment to S would be includible because the right to D's payment did not end before death. But if D was paid the $100,000 when D retired and lived another five years, the corporation's $70,000 payment to S would not be includible in D's gross estate under §2039. See Treas. Reg. §20.2039-1(b)(2) *Example (5)*. Quaere whether this makes any sense.

Kramer v. United States
406 F.2d 1363 (Ct. Cl. 1969)

[The decedent, Abraham Kramer, entered into a contract with his employer, paragraph (1) of which provided that Mr. Kramer would be general manager of the company at an annual salary of $12,000. The contract continued, in part:

> (2) In the event of illness and/or in the event that due to any circumstances which may make it impossible for Mr. Kramer to continue to act as General Manager, the Company agrees that he shall remain with it as an Advisor and Counsellor and to assist the officers and Employees in formulating plans and programs for the continuation of the business, for the remainder of his life. That during such services being rendered, he shall receive an annual salary of $12,000, payable in regular weekly installments.

> (3) In the event of Mr. Kramer's decease, and while serving the Company either under the provisions of Paragraph (1) or (2), and in the event his wife, Carrie Kramer, shall survive him, then the Company agrees that she shall receive as compensation the sum of $150.00 per week, as long as she lives.

Mr. Kramer died in 1961 while serving as general manager of the company. His executors did not include in his gross estate the value of Mrs. Kramer's right to $150 per week for life.]

NICHOLS, J.: . . . There have been very few cases that have dealt with §2039, but a reading of them indicates that all of the requirements of the section must be met for the payments such as those received by Mrs. Kramer to be includable in a decedent's gross estate. See Bahen v. United States, 305 F.2d 827, 158 Ct. Cl. 141 (1962). There must be an "annuity or other payment receivable by any beneficiary by reason of surviving the decedent" and the payments under subsection (b) must be by reason of the decedent's employment. We think that the $150 per week paid to Mrs. Kramer constituted an "annuity or other payment" which was paid by reason of the decedent's employment, and under paragraph 3 of the agreement she had to survive Mr. Kramer to receive the payments.

An annuity or other payment also must have been payable to the decedent or he must have possessed the right to receive the payment. It is this requirement that is in issue in this case, and we do not believe that it has been met. Under the agreement the only payments Mr. Kramer had a right to receive were in the form of compensation for services rendered. There is nothing in the agreement or stipulated facts that leads us to believe anything different was intended. In *Bahen* the issue of whether or not salary was meant to be included in the definition of "other payment" was discussed. In that case, the decedent's beneficiary was to receive at his death an amount equal to three months' salary of the deceased. The Government had argued that "other payment" included salary, but we said: ". . . Since employees normally receive salary or wages, defendant's interpretation would effectively obliterate, for almost all employees, the express requirement in §2039 of 'an annuity or other payment' to the decedent." *Bahen*, 305 F.2d at 834. In considering this same issue in Estate of Fusz v. Commissioner, 46 T.C. 214 (1966), the Tax Court approved of our reasoning in *Bahen* and concluded that salary was not included in the meaning of "other payments" but that "the phrase 'other payment' is qualitatively limited to post-employment benefits, which at the very least, are paid or payable during decedent's lifetime." *Fusz*, 46 T.C. at 218.

The defendant argues that Mr. Kramer's agreement with the Company was really a retirement arrangement. We cannot agree. Because the parties chose to stipulate the facts in this case, we have a rather sparse record on which to base our decision, but we find in it nothing to indicate that this was a scheme to pension off Mr. Kramer while at the same time avoid the impact of §2039. The facts we do have indicate the opposite. Mr. Kramer worked seven hours a day, five and one-half days a week as General Manager of the Company, which would hardly appear to be a retirement schedule. The defendant argues that, as part of the retirement process, the decedent had even turned over stock control of the corporation. But the facts as stipulated show that decedent never did have stock control of the Company; the most he ever owned was 20.25 shares out of the 250 shares issued.

Under paragraph 2 of the agreement decedent was to serve as "Advisor and Counsellor" if it became impossible for him to perform the duties of General Manager. Defendant considers that paragraph a disability arrangement providing for contingent payments similar to the disability payments the decedent in the *Bahen* case had a contingent right to receive. We held in that case that contingent rights to receive payments that qualified as "other payments" came within the meaning of "possessed the right to receive" of §2039 and their value was includable in the decedent's gross estate. *Bahen*, 305 F.2d at 830–832. Thus, the fact that Mr. Kramer died while serving under paragraph 1 would not affect the significance of paragraph 2, even though it never became operative, were we to find those payments qualified as "other payments" which he possessed the right to receive. Paragraph 2 of the agreement provided that plaintiff was to receive his salary "during such services [those of Advisor and Counsellor] being rendered."

Because of Mr. Kramer's interest in and close ties to the Company and its management, the defendant argues that he would have been expected to remain available for advice anyway, and thus the payments under paragraph 2 were really retirement or disability payments. But we do not find defendant's argument persuasive. Again we have only the stipulated facts — but they reveal no basis for defendant's argument. It seems just as reasonable to conclude from this record that decedent's advice might have been preempted by others who would have been willing to have paid decedent for it had the Kramer Supply Company been getting it for nothing.

The result in this case turns entirely on the stipulation and under different stipulated or proven background facts, an identical contract might have different tax consequences. . . . Here, defendant wants us to infer from the stipulated family relationship that the agreement really imports something different from what it says. It invokes the presumption in favor of the Commissioner's decision and reminds us that the burden of proof is on plaintiff. However, the submission via stipulation, of a contract, without more, satisfies the burden of establishing that the parties agreed to what the contract says. One who intends to argue that there were side agreements, oral, implied, or merely understood, should not stipulate a basic contract alone. There are all sorts of families, and among those who are close by blood or marriage, every relationship may be found from love and affection to bitter hostility. There is no stipulation into which category these people fell. There is nothing in the stipulated facts to disprove that Mr. Kramer exacted the agreement precisely because he mistrusted the love and affection of his kin as assuring support for him in his twilight years.

We think paragraph 2 of the agreement means that on the contingency contemplated Mr. Kramer was to assist the officers and employees in formulating plans and programs for the continuation of the business, to the extent he was able and such assistance was needed. We have no clue how much it would have been needed. We know nothing about the character of the business which would show whether this responsibility was light or onerous. Having no facts to warrant any other view, we can only suppose it was worth the $12,000 per annum consideration that was proposed. Cf. Tasty Baking Co. v. United States, 393 F.2d 992 (Ct. Cl. 1968), in which we held it to be presumed that the future loyal adhesion of officers and employees was worth the value of the property placed in a pension trust to obtain it. A majority of us do not believe that Mr. Kramer could have advised and consulted for an hour and then have told the officers and employees to be gone, though still seeking advice and consultation. Such behavior, we think, would have breached the agreement and forfeited the $12,000 honorarium. If the parties had intended to pay $12,000 for little or nothing they could just as well have omitted paragraph 2 and allowed Mr. Kramer, though sick, to hold the title of General Manager until his decease, and by doing so they would have avoided any issue under §2039.

The stipulation recites that there was no other agreement between decedent and the Company that provided for payment of any amounts to the decedent or to anyone else by reason of surviving him. This is somewhat ambiguous, and may not mean to say there was no contract or agreement at all between decedent and the Company prior to the agreement set forth. At any rate, he was employed as President. It is all the more impossible to draw inferences beyond the text of the writing itself, when one does not know what it replaced, or what claims, demands, or choses in action Mr. Kramer then had against the Company, other than the moral ones recited in the preamble.

Estate of Wadewitz v. Commissioner, 339 F.2d 980 (7th Cir. 1964), affirms the Tax Court, 39 T.C. 925 (1963), in holding that a somewhat similar arrangement was covered by §2039. Decedent had an agreement with his Company calling for payment of specified sums for 15 years, to him beginning with his retirement, to his wife and daughter if he died before retiring, and if he died after retirement but before the full sums were paid, the balances were to go to the wife and daughter. Both courts considered that §2039 required inclusion of the unpaid balance in the gross estate. There were clauses prescribing what decedent was to do after retiring; he was to "keep himself reasonably available for consultation" but mostly the clauses sought to bar him from competing with the

Company or aiding others to do so. The agreement is called a "retirement contract," 339 F.2d at 981. Both courts refer to our *Bahen* case with approval and there is no suggestion of any conflict. It is therefore clear that neither court gave any serious consideration to the possibility that the post-employment payments were primarily for affirmative services during the "retirement" period and evidently this was not urged. In *Wadewitz*, as here, facts were presented by stipulation, precluding any comparison in depth of the background circumstances. As we see no reason to call the paragraph 2 period in Mr. Kramer's contract a post-employment period, as the word "retirement" is not used, and as apparently the parties contemplated that Mr. Kramer would render services worth $12,000, we do not see *Wadewitz* as an applicable precedent.

We hold that §2039 does not require inclusion of the commuted value of the annuity in the gross estate, reiterating that this result turns on the facts as suspected, speculated, or inferred by the defendant. Any court, construing a similar contract, will not regard this case as a precedent if it appears that the services to be rendered were nominal or pro forma or that the prescribed payments were really a retirement annuity. . . .

DAVIS, J. (dissenting): Although this case was stipulated, the claimants still bear the double burden — first in their capacity as plaintiffs in a refund suit, and second as taxpayers seeking to overturn a determination of the Internal Revenue Service — of proving that they are entitled to recover. See Boehm v. Commissioner, 326 U.S. 287, 293–294 (1945). Gaps in the stipulation should not be filled in their favor. Under this standard, they have failed to persuade me that they fall outside of §2039.

The only real issue is whether the payments to be made to Mr. Kramer under the second paragraph of the Memorandum of Agreement with the Company constituted "an annuity or other payment [which] was payable" to him or which he "possessed the right to receive" for his life. In Estate of Bahen v. United States . . . we held that this term "an annuity or other payment" does not include "the decedent-employee's regular salary." See also Estate of Fusz v. Commissioner, 46 T.C. 214 (1966). Here the court interprets the $12,000 payable to Mr. Kramer "[i]n the event of illness and/or in the event that due to any circumstances which may make it impossible for [him] to continue to act as General Manager" as equivalent to the "regular salary" of which we spoke in *Bahen*. On the other hand, I see these payments as "post-employment benefits" to Mr. Kramer (*Estate of Fusz*, 46 T.C. at 218), close kin to an ordinary retirement annuity or retirement payment.

The Memorandum of Agreement makes it absolutely plain that these payments were to be made after the decedent had stopped being general manager (for which he was also being paid $12,000 per year), and that he was nevertheless to "remain" with the company for "the remainder of his life." His illness was expressly contemplated, as were "any circumstances which may make it impossible for Mr. Kramer to continue to act as General Manager." In other words, he could be totally disabled for active participation in the business but would still continue to receive $12,000 each year for the rest of his life.[6]

True he was to be "an Advisor and Counsellor" and was "to assist the officers and Employees in formulating plans and programs for the continuation of the business." Also, he was to receive his $12,000 "during such services being rendered." But for me the significant aspect of the agreement is that nothing whatever was specified as to how much advice and counsel he was to give each year — or how often. Unlike the retiree in Estate of Wadewitz v. Commissioner, 339 F.2d 980 n.2 (7th Cir. 1964), our decedent did not even promise to "keep himself at all times reasonably available for consultation by the officers and directors of the company." If this were somehow to be implied, there is no indication that the company was expected to call upon him for any substantial amount of advice. Perhaps a day or two a year of pro forma consultation would be all; since this was a small family corporation, my guess is that, especially if the paterfamilias fell ill, no one anticipated more than a minimal exchange, just enough to say that "services" were "being rendered" during the year.

In essence, the agreement, as phrased, was clearly open to being used as a device for paying Mr. Kramer $12,000 so long as he lived even though, because of the state of his health or his age, he could do very little for the firm. This was in fact a "post-employment benefit," not a "regular salary" such as was paid him as general manager. I repeat that we should read the lacunae in the contract and the stipulation against the taxpayers, not against the Government as the court prefers.

What the court does in this case is contrary to what was actually held in *Wadewitz*, though the precise issue appears not to have been raised in that case and there is therefore no direct conflict. But I find it significant that in that instance all assumed that

---

6.   The Agreement gives no hint of the other "circumstances" which might make it "*impossible* for Mr. Kramer to continue to act as General Manager" (emphasis added), and the stipulation gives us no light. It is fair to assume that these other "circumstances," making it "impossible" for him to continue as general manager, would be comparable to a disabling illness.

the payments were not "regular salary" within the meaning of *Bahen*. If the rule laid down for Mr. Kramer were generalized, it would afford an easy device by which businesses could actually pension off their officers while protecting the latter's estates by exacting amorphous undertakings from them to give "advice" when called upon. The court's stress on the stipulated nature of the present case, and the adverse inferences it draws from the Government's willingness to stipulate, gives me hope that we are not declaring any such general proposition.

LARAMORE, J., joins in the foregoing dissenting opinion.

The Commissioner acquiesced in the Tax Court opinion in *Fusz*, cited by the *Kramer* opinion.

An illustration might be helpful: Isidor Hetson entered into a contract with Purity Paint Products Corporation (a closely held corporation) in 1960. The contract provided that Hetson would continue to receive a salary in an amount not greater than that being paid to his sons and that "such salary may be paid to Hetson regardless of the amount of time devoted by him to the Corporation's business and regardless of his being disabled, incapacitated, or otherwise unable to perform services for the Corporation." The contract further provided that, in the event of Hetson's death, "the Corporation shall forthwith make payment of a pension to Fannie [Hetson's wife] in the sum of $13,000.00 per annum, in consideration and in recognition of the many years of devoted and valuable services by Hetson to the Corporation." Hetson died in 1963 at the age of 77 after about a nine-month illness. He was absent from work throughout his illness. The value of the payments to Fannie was held to be includible in Hetson's gross estate. The Court of Claims held that Hetson had the right to a non-salary payment at the time of his death because he had an enforceable right to receive the "salary" from the corporation even if he was disabled. Therefore, §2039 was applicable to the pension payable to Fannie. Hetson v. United States, 75-2 U.S. Tax Cas. (CCH) ¶13,098 (Ct. Cl. Trial Div. 1975), *adopted*, 76-1 U.S. Tax Cas. (CCH) ¶13,124 (Ct. Cl. 1976).

12. *Any Form of Contract or Agreement: Combining Plans.* As indicated in *All v. McCobb*, reproduced at page 535, the statement in Treas. Reg. §20.2039-1(b)(1) and (2) *Example (6)* that an employer's various plans may be treated as one in determining whether the requirements of §2039 are met has been upheld by the courts. The leading decision on this point is Estate of Bahen v. United States, 305 F.2d 827 (Ct. Cl. 1962), in which the court, referring to the regulation, said:

Effect must be given to this declaration, adopted pursuant to the Treasury's recognized power to issue regulations and not challenged by plaintiff, since it does not violate the terms or the spirit of §2039. In view of the general purpose of the statute to cover a large share of employer-contributed payments to an employee's survivors, it is not unreasonable to lump together all of the employer's various benefit plans taking account of the employee's death (except those qualified under §401(a), which are excepted by the statute . . .) in order to decide whether and to what extent §2039 applies to his estate. There is no immutable requirement in the legislation that each plan separately adopted by a company must be considered alone. One good ground for rejecting that position is to prevent attempts to avoid the reach of the statute by a series of contrived plans none of which, in itself, would fall under the section.

The Commissioner has ruled that the principle requiring plans to be combined does not require qualified and nonqualified plans to be lumped together. Thus, if an employer has both a "qualified" and a "nonqualified" plan, the benefits accruing under each plan are to be considered separately for purposes of §2039. Rev. Rul. 76-380. Compare Rev. Rul. 77-183.

In Estate of Schelberg v. Commissioner, 612 F.2d 25 (2d Cir. 1979), *rev'g* 70 T.C. 690 (1978), the court essentially rejected the *Bahen* doctrine. The decedent in *Schelberg* died while employed by IBM and had been covered during his employment by a variety of employee benefit plans: a Group Life Insurance Plan, a Retirement Plan, a Sickness and Accident Income Plan, and a Total and Permanent Disability Plan. The decedent died within one week after his fatal illness was discovered and at the time of death was not receiving benefits under any of the plans. Pursuant to the Group Life Insurance Plan, the employer paid a monthly benefit to the decedent's widow after the decedent's death. The government contended that the commuted value of that annuity was includible in the decedent's gross estate under §2039. The issue in dispute was whether, at the time of death, and under the same contract that provided the Group Life Insurance benefit, the decedent possessed the right to receive an annuity or other payment for life or for any period not ascertainable without reference to the decedent's death, or for any period that did not in fact end before the decedent's death. The Commissioner, relying inter alia on *Bahen*, sought to combine the monthly death benefit from the Group Life Insurance Plan with the decedent's right to payments under one of the other employee benefit plans, to satisfy the "other payment" under the same contract requirement.

As a qualified plan, the Retirement Plan provisions could not be used to satisfy the "other payment" requirement. See Rev. Rul. 76-380. The Sickness and Accident Income Plan provided IBM employees full salary payments (less worker's compensation payments) while absent from work on account of sickness or accident for up to 52 weeks in any 24-month period. The application of §2039 turned on whether the decedent's rights under the Permanent Disability Plan constituted a right to "other payments" within the meaning of §2039, because salary continuation payments are like an employee's basic salary payments and therefore also do not qualify as "other payments." See Rev. Rul. 77-183.

The Disability Plan provided monthly benefits to an IBM employee who was determined to have a total and permanent disability. The payments under the Disability Plan commenced after expiration of a five week period, during which payments were made to the employee under the Sickness and Accident Income Plan. The disability payments continued until the employee's death or until the employee attained normal retirement age, at which date payments were made to the employee under the Retirement Plan. The amount of the monthly payments under the Disability Plan depended upon the amount of the employee's regular compensation prior to disability. Only one-fourth of 1% of IBM's employees qualified for benefits from the Disability Plan.

Reversing the Tax Court, the Court of Appeals for the Second Circuit held that the decedent's rights under the Disability Plan "were too dissimilar in nature from an 'annuity or other payment' and too contingent to meet the condition of §2039(a)." While seeking to distinguish *Bahen*, the court indicated its disapproval of it, stating:

We here decide only that to consider a deceased employee's potential ability to have qualified at some future time for payments under a plan protecting against total and permanent disability — a disagreeable feat that had been accomplished as of January 1, 1974, by only a quarter of 1% of IBM's employees — as meeting the condition in §2039(a) that there must be a contract or agreement under which the decedent received or be entitled to receive "an annuity or other payment," is such a departure from the language used by Congress, read in the light of the problem with which it was intending to deal, as to be at war with common sense. Cf. United States v. American Trucking Associations, Inc., 310 U.S. 534, 543 (1940). The only decision by which we are bound, All v. McCobb, 321 F.2d 633 (2d Cir. 1963), does not come near to the problem here presented. Of the other decisions cited to us, there are clear grounds of distinguishing all with the possible exception of the leading one, Estate of Bahen v. United States, 305 F.2d 827 (Ct. Cl. 1962), and the certain exception of Gaffney v. United States, 200 Ct. Cl. 744 (1972). Although we have been able to distinguish the cases other than *Gaffney* and possibly *Bahen* on grounds that seem to us sufficient, we would not wish to be understood as necessarily agreeing with all of them or with the general approach taken in *Bahen*. See 305 F.2d at 833. Some other case may require complete rethinking whether courts, under the influence of the *Bahen* opinion, have not unduly eroded the condition in §2039(a), as is pointedly suggested by Judge Aldisert's dissent in Gray v. United States, 410 F.2d 1094, 1112–1114 (3d Cir. 1969); on the other hand, Congress might decide to cast its net more widely and eliminate or broaden the condition, as it could have done in 1954. We simply decline to carry the erosion of the condition to the extent here urged by the Commissioner.

In Looney v. United States, 569 F. Supp. 1569 (M.D. Ga. 1983), the government again failed in its attempt to aggregate various benefits under IBM plans, in that case the Disability Plan and the Survivor Benefit Plan. The court originally held that the contingent, potential entitlement under the Disability Plan would cause otherwise excludible benefits under the Survivor Benefit Plan to be subject to §2039 inclusion. Pointing to Treas. Reg. §20.2039-1(b)(1)(ii), which provides that an employee benefit contract or agreement includes "any combination of arrangements, understandings or plans" and that "all rights and benefits accruing . . . by reason of the employment . . . are considered together in determining whether . . . §2039(a) . . . applies," the court determined that the plain language of the regulation dictated aggregation of the several plans as component parts of a united corporate employee benefit plan, resulting in §2039 inclusion. In a subsequent hearing, however, the court vacated its inclusion judgment and entered a verdict for the taxpayer.

13.   *Voluntary Payments.*   In Chapter 2, we saw that death benefits paid voluntarily by an employer are not includible in the employee's gross estate under §2033. See Rev. Rul. 65-217. Does the same principle apply to §2039? In Estate of Barr v. Commissioner, 40 T.C. 227 (1963), *acq. in result only*, the Tax Court held that the survivor's annuity or other payment must be payable under a contractual obligation. The court stated:

The repeated reference (in both subsections (a) and (b) [of §2039]) to the requirement for some form of contract or agreement, indicates that the rights of both the decedent and the survivor must be enforceable rights; and that voluntary and gratuitous payments by the employer are not taxable under §2039. This is expressly recognized in Treas. Reg. §20.2039-1(b)(2) *Example (4)*. However, this same example does state that where the terms of an enforceable retirement plan have been modified by consistent practice of the employer, the annuity received pursuant to such modification will be considered to have been paid under a "contract or agreement." We do not think that the latter statement was intended to mean that where there was no enforceable arrangement, contract, or agreement whatever, the mere consistency of an employer in making voluntary or gratuitous payments would be sufficient to supply the essential "contract or agreement." Congress, for reasons satisfactory to it, has made the existence of some form of "contract or agreement" an indispensable prerequisite to the application of §2039.

In PLR 8006013, *D* and the firm of which *D* was a principal had not entered into a formal contract providing either retirement or death benefits. Nevertheless, after *D*'s death the firm sent *D*'s surviving spouse, *S*, a letter summarizing certain benefits to which *S* was entitled, including a right to an annual payment until the first to occur of *S*'s death or remarriage. This benefit was payable under a resolution adopted by the firm several years earlier, subject to modification or withdrawal.

The firm's handbook for partners outlined a retirement allowance for partners and principals, but *D* died prior to retirement. With the exception of partners and principals who retired early or who withdrew from the firm, all partners and principals had received retirement benefits upon retirement and surviving spouses of the five other partners or principals who died before retirement over the previous ten years all received the same form of allowance specified in the letter to *S*. In ruling that §2039 required inclusion in *D*'s gross estate of the value of *S*'s survivorship benefit, the government said:

Because of the consistent method in which the decedent's firm has paid retirement benefits to its partners and principals and their surviving spouses, and the expectancies which the firm provides to such partners and principals, the elements in issue here of "contract or agreement" and the decedent "possessing the right to receive" an annuity at the time of death are present so as to include the full survivorship benefits in the decedent's estate under §2039.

In a similar situation, Courtney v. United States, 84-2 U.S. Tax Cas. (CCH) ¶13,580 (N.D. Ohio 1984), rejected the government's inclusion argument on the ground that §2039(a) must be interpreted as applicable only to payments made under an *enforceable* contract or agreement and held that the arrangement was not enforceable. Notwithstanding that *D* retired as chairman of the board of the corporation making the payment, the court held that *D* lacked actual control over the corporation and that only an agreement founded on consideration would be an enforceable contract. Because the arrangement in *Courtney* was conceded by the government to be gratuitous, inclusion was deemed to be improper. That raised the type of issue addressed in *Neely*:

Neely v. United States
613 F.2d 802 (Ct. Cl. 1980)

BENNETT, J.: . . . The decedent, Mr. Neely, worked for Blocker Storage & Transfer Company (Blocker) from the mid-1930s until his retirement on January 1, 1973. . . . From October 1964 until the time of his death, Mr. Neely held approximately 51% of the stock of Blocker and, during the same period, his wife held approximately 20% of the stock of Blocker. All of the remaining stock of Blocker was held by the Neelys' two daughters and their husbands. These six stockholders constituted Blocker's entire board of directors from 1966 up to the time of Mr. Neely's death, and the remaining five stockholders have been the only directors since that time. Additionally, since 1966 all of the officers of the corporation have been drawn from this group of stockholder-directors.

In the mid-1960s, Mr. Neely reduced his day-to-day contact with Blocker. At the same time, Mr. Neely's two sons-in-law began to assume more of the responsibility for Blocker's operation. The minutes of Blocker's board of directors for December 28, 1972, indicate that the following actions were taken:

> Chairman Neely announced his retirement as of January 1, 1973. After discussion it was decided that Mr. Neely would be retained as Chairman of the Board and as a consultant at a total compensation of $100.00 per month and paid a pension of $1,000.00 per month which in event of his death, is to be paid to his wife until her death, then cease. This pension is for his long faithful employment of 42 years with the company.

Effective January 1, 1973, Mr. Neely retired from the employment of Blocker. After his retirement, Mr. Neely performed the minimal duties required of him as a consultant, for which he was paid $100 per month for 3 months. Mr. Neely also received his pension of $1,000 per month from Blocker for the first 3 calendar months of 1973. On April 11, 1973, Mr. Neely died. He did not suffer from any debilitating illness for any length of time prior to his death. After Mr. Neely's death, Blocker continued to make the monthly payments to Mrs. Neely.

The funds utilized to pay Mr. Neely and, later, Mrs. Neely, came from Blocker's operating revenues. No annuity contract was purchased by Blocker to pay Mr. Neely's pension, nor did Blocker make any contributions to a separate fund established to pay annuities to employees.[7] Blocker claimed a business expense deduction on its 1973 and 1974 federal income tax returns for the payments to Mr. and Mrs. Neely, and the payments received by

---

7.   It is immaterial to the application of §2039 that the employer did not formally make "contributions" to a separate fund, or actually purchase annuity or like contracts. Estate of Bahen v. United States, 305 F.2d 827, 833 (Ct. Cl. 1962).

them were included in gross income on their federal income tax returns. . . .

I.R.C. §2039 is the sole ground asserted by defendant for the inclusion in Mr. Neely's gross estate of the value of the annuity payable to Mrs. Neely after his death. Plaintiff offers two arguments in support of her contentions that no amount should be included in decedent's gross estate because of the annuity passing to her. First, plaintiff argues that one critical element of §2039(a), the presence of a contract or agreement, is missing. Second, under §2039(b) the amount to be included in the gross estate depends on whether the payments by Blocker were "made by reason of his [decedent's] employment." Plaintiff argues that payments in recognition of past services are not made by reason of the decedent's employment.

. . . There is no dispute between the parties regarding the presence of most of the elements necessary for the application of §2039(a). The payments made to Mr. Neely during his lifetime and to Mrs. Neely after his death are annuity payments in the traditional sense of the term. The annuity was receivable by Mrs. Neely by reason of surviving Mr. Neely. While it is not so clear that Mr. Neely possessed a right to receive the annuity, the satisfaction of the alternative test is not in doubt since Mr. Neely received annuity payments for a period which did not in fact end before his death.

Plaintiff contends that under Florida law the payments to Mrs. Neely (and presumably also to Mr. Neely) were gratuitous and not enforceable by her (or him) and that therefore the annuity was not receivable "under any form of contract or agreement" as required by the statute. Somewhat similar resolutions of the boards of directors of three closely held corporations were considered in Estate of Bogley v. United States, 514 F.2d 1027 (Ct. Cl. 1975).[8] These resolutions in general provided that, in consideration of past services and services to be rendered by the decedent and other officers, the corporation was authorized upon the death of any of these officers to pay an amount equivalent to 2 years' salary to the decedent's estate or named beneficiary. Based on principles of general contract and corporation law, two of the resolutions were held to be merely expressions of intention or corporate policy, and not contracts or offers to contract which would bind the corpora-

---

8. Defendant in *Bogley* did not attempt to include the payments in decedent's gross estate under §2039 and, unlike the present case, conceded that, if the corporations were not contractually obligated to make the payments, no inclusion should be made. Defendant's approach in *Bogley* was dictated by the absence of any payments, or any right to receive payments, other than salary on the part of the decedent. Section 2039 does not apply in such situations. Estate of Fusz v. Commissioner, 46 T.C. 214 (1966), *acq.*

tion. Only the third resolution, which expressed an intent to impose a contractual obligation on the corporation, was held to be a binding promise and offer to make payments to the decedent's estate or beneficiary. In the present case, the resolution of Blocker's board of directors contains no clear expression of an intent to impose a contractual obligation. In addition, plaintiff contends that, unlike the resolutions in *Bogley*, Blocker's resolution was solely in recognition of past services and that past consideration is insufficient to support a contract. See Williston, CONTRACTS §142 (3d ed. 1957). Defendant argues that, even if Mrs. Neely could not enforce the payment of her annuity, the requirement of a contract or agreement should be deemed to be satisfied. We agree although our reasoning differs somewhat from that of defendant.[9]

Treas. Reg. §20.2039-1(b)(1) provides in pertinent part:

> . . . The term "contract or agreement" includes any arrangement, understanding or plan, or any combination of arrangements, understandings or plans arising by reason of the decedent's employment. An annuity or other payment "was payable" to the decedent if, at the time of his death, the decedent was in fact receiving an annuity or other payment, whether or not he had an enforceable right to have payments continued. The decedent "possessed the right to receive" an annuity or other payment if, immediately before his death, the decedent had an enforceable right to receive payments at some time in the future, whether or not, at the time of his death, he had a present right to receive payments. In connection with the preceding sentence, the decedent will be regarded as having had "an enforceable right to receive payments at some time in the future" so long as he had complied with his obligations under the contract or agreement up to the time of his death.

Based on the second sentence quoted above, defendant argues that there is no need for an enforceable contract in cases in which an annuity was being paid to the decedent as opposed to cases in which the decedent had only a right to receive payments in the future. While defendant relies upon the lack of any need for enforceability by the decedent, plaintiff focuses on the need for enforceability by the surviving beneficiary because of the requirement of a "contract or agreement." The second quoted sentence purports to deal only with the "payable" test while the first quoted

---

9.   Therefore, we do not reach the question of whether either Mr. or Mrs. Neely could enforce the payment of his or her annuity.

sentence defines the term "contract or agreement." Nevertheless, if the regulation is to be construed in a harmonious fashion, the second quoted sentence must be considered as putting a gloss on the requirement of a "contract or agreement," at least as applied to payments to the decedent. This gloss is an appropriate interpretation of the statute since no estate tax is imposed until it is determinable whether the decedent in fact received payments up to the time of his death. If he did, the fact that he could not enforce such payments is no longer relevant.

Because the statute uses the term "contract or agreement" twice, to refer to the payments to both the decedent and to the beneficiary, it might be inferred that the same gloss should be applied in "payable" cases with respect to the enforceability of the contract or agreement by the beneficiary. We reject any such inference however. The requirement of a "contract or agreement" must be given a flexible interpretation to meet the differing situations of the decedent and the beneficiary.[10] If §2039 applies to an annuity, the present value of the future payments to the beneficiary will be included in the gross estate of the decedent. In contrast to the situation of a decedent in a "payable" case, the enforceability of the future payments by the beneficiary is still very much relevant. It would be entirely inappropriate to judge the requirement of a "contract or agreement" as applied to the payments to the beneficiary by a lesser standard in "payable" cases than in "right to receive" cases. Which of the two alternative tests was met by the interest held by decedent has no relevance to the question of whether the beneficiary's interest is sufficiently "vested" to warrant the inclusion of the annuity in the gross estate.[11]

We therefore must look to the first, and not the second, sentence quoted above to decide whether a contract enforceable by the beneficiary is required by the regulation. In using the words "any arrangement, understanding or plan," the regulation clearly seeks to encompass more than just enforceable contracts.[12]

---

10.   The Government itself in Treas. Reg. §20.2039-1(b)(2) *Example (6)* takes the view that a survivor's annuity paid by an employer of the decedent may be includible even though it was not paid under the same contract or agreement as the annuity paid to the deceased employee. The courts have agreed with this flexible approach. Gray v. United States, 410 F.2d 1094, 1104–1106 (3d Cir. 1969); All v. McCobb, 321 F.2d 633, 636 (2d Cir. 1963); Estate of Bahen v. United States, 305 F.2d at 835.

11.   See C. Lowndes, R. Kramer & J. McCord, FEDERAL ESTATE AND GIFT TAXES 250–251 (3d ed. 1974), which considers this problem of reconciling the regulations interpreting the "payable" and "contract or agreement" requirements, but which reaches a different conclusion.

12.   The examples in Treas. Reg. §20.2039-1(b)(2) reinforce this conclusion. In *Example (2)* a survivor's annuity which was forfeitable upon the remarriage of the

Treasury regulations must be held valid unless unreasonable or inconsistent with the statute. They are entitled to respectful consideration and will not be overruled except for weighty reasons.

The statute reads "any form of contract or agreement." By using the words "any form" and "agreement" instead of the word "contract" alone, Congress intended to broaden the scope of §2039(a).[13] While in one sense of the word the term "agreement" is synonymous with the term "contract," it also means "an arrangement as to a course of action." WEBSTER'S NEW COLLEGIATE DICTIONARY (1977). The committee reports[14] accompanying the enactment of §2039 state:

> . . . Under present law the value at the decedent's death of a joint and survivor annuity purchased by him is includible in his gross estate. It is not clear under existing law whether an annuity of that type purchased by the decedent's employer, or an annuity to which both the decedent and his employer made contributions is includible in the decedent's gross estate.

Thus, the focus of §2039 was employment-related annuities which often are not as formal as annuity contracts with an insurance or investment company. Attempts to tax the survivor's

---

survivor was held to be includible under §2039, and the element of forfeitability was deemed to be significant only with respect to the valuation of the annuity. In *Example (4)* an employee died prior to retirement, which disqualified his designated beneficiary from receiving an annuity. The employer nevertheless paid an annuity to the beneficiary. Because of the absence of a legal obligation to pay, it was held that the annuity was not paid under a "contract or agreement." However, it was further stated that the annuity would be considered paid under a "contract or agreement" if the employer had consistently paid an annuity under such circumstances.

13.   The court in Gray v. United States, 410 F.2d at 1106, stated that §2039 is a departure from common law notions and that Congress did not necessarily intend that the words "contract or agreement" should be considered in terms of traditional property or contract law. However, since the court found the contract to be enforceable, it did not decide whether "in using the phrase 'contract or agreement' in §2039 Congress intended to create a unique, 'federal' type of contract relationship limited to estate tax purposes. . . ." The Tax Court in Estate of Barr v. Commissioner, 40 T.C. 227, 235–236 (1963), *acq. in result only*, has taken a contrary view and stated: "The repeated reference (in both subsections (a) and (b) to the requirement for some form of contract or agreement, indicates that the rights of both the decedent and the survivor must be enforceable rights; and that voluntary and gratuitous payments by the employer are not taxable under §2039. . . . Congress, for reasons satisfactory to it, has made the existence of some form of 'contract or agreement' an indispensable prerequisite to the application of §2039."

14.   S. Rep. No. 1622, 83d Cong., 2d Sess. 123 (1954). See also H.R. Rep. No. 1337, 83d Cong., 2d Sess. 90 (1954).

benefits under the predecessors of §§2033, 2035, and 2038 would fail if the employee's rights were forfeitable, so that he had only an "expectancy" as distinguished from a "vested interest."[15] Congress apparently intended to sweep at least some of these less formal employment-related annuities into the gross estate through §2039. Since the exact extent to which Congress intended to reach is not clear, the discretion of the Commissioner in interpreting the statute through regulations should be affirmed.

Therefore, our decision hinges on whether the resolution of Blocker's board of directors should be considered to be an "arrangement, understanding or plan" within the meaning of Treas. Reg. §20.2039-1(b)(1). None of the prior decisions under §2039 are helpful in this regard. With only one exception, Estate of Barr v. Commissioner, 40 T.C. 227 (1963), *acq. in result only*, all of the cases under §2039 appear to have involved an enforceable contract which clearly was an "arrangement, understanding or plan."[16] The facts presented in *Barr* differ greatly from those here. The decedent was an employee of Eastman Kodak Company and had no significant interest in the company as a stockholder. Because the decedent died before the close of the year, neither he nor his estate had a right to the wage dividend usually paid to employees by the company. However, in such situations, the board of directors, after investigation into the financial circumstances of the deceased employee's family, "would usually, but not always, approve payment of an amount equivalent to the wage dividend the employee would have received if he had lived and otherwise qualified therefor." 40 T.C. at 229. The Tax Court found that there was no "contract or agreement" because the decedent and surviving beneficiary had no enforceable rights.[17]

---

15. C. Lowndes, R. Kramer & J. McCord, Federal Estate and Gift Taxes 241–242 (3d ed. 1974).

16. The plan under which payments were made was expressly found to be irrevocable in Estate of Bahen v. United States, 305 F.2d at 830, and enforceable in Gray v. United States, 410 F.2d at 1106. The agreement in Hetson v. United States, 76-1 U.S. Tax Cas. (CCH) ¶ 13,124 (Ct. Cl. 1976), involved reciprocal promises between stockholders in a family corporation and would appear to have been enforceable although there is no specific holding on this point.

17. The Tax Court in *Barr* stated that an enforceable contract was a prerequisite to the application of §2039. See note 13 supra. Such statements must be regarded as obiter dictum since the decision in *Barr* is not necessarily inconsistent with Treas. Reg. §20.2039-1(b)(2) *Example (4)*, which held that a consistent practice of making payments may be sufficient. See note 12 supra. The Commissioner in acquiescing with the result only of the *Barr* decision, is apparently now of the view that greater consistency than that found in *Barr* is necessary before the arrangement becomes a "contract or agreement."

Unlike the *Barr* case, any requirement of enforceability here would be an empty formality. After Mr. Neely's death plaintiff held approximately 70% of the stock of Blocker either personally or as the personal representative of Mr. Neely's estate. Her daughters and sons-in-law held the remainder. These same persons were the officers and directors of the corporation. Any possibility that the annuity payments to plaintiff would cease other than through a voluntary renunciation is extremely remote.[18] We need not explore the outer boundaries regarding the extent to which §2039(a) may apply to legally unenforceable arrangements, but to allow the annuity in this case to escape inclusion under §2039(a) would seriously erode that section with regard to pensions and death benefits paid by a closely held corporation with any knowledgeable tax planning.[19]

Plaintiff argues that no portion of the value of the annuity should be included under §2039(b) because payments in recognition of past services are not made by reason of the decedent's employment. Plaintiff's argument is based on S. Rep. No. 1622,[20] which states:

> The contributions of an employer . . . shall be considered to have been made by reason of decedent's employment if, for example, the annuity or other payment is offered by the employer as an inducement to employment, or a continuance thereof, or if the contributions are made by the employer in lieu of additional compensation or other rights, if so understood by employer and employee whether or not expressly stated in the contract of employment or otherwise.

---

18.   Plaintiff has cited Frank v. Anthony, 107 So. 2d 136 (Fla. Dist. Ct. App. 1958), to show that a majority stockholder may not summarily dismiss the directors of the corporation. Families do sometimes disagree, and it is possible that in the short run the other directors of Blocker could terminate Mrs. Neely's annuity, but such a possibility is negligible because of the control which Mrs. Neely could exercise over the corporation in the long run.

19.   Plaintiff's last argument is that a decision based on the closely held nature of Blocker would cause a dual inclusion, i.e., the value of the business at death undiminished by the later voluntary payment, plus the amount of the postdeath payment. Acceptance of plaintiff's argument would cause an underinclusion since the estate tax was imposed on only 51% of the value of Blocker. The valuation of the stock of Blocker is not before the court in this action, but we are convinced that if there is any merit to plaintiff's argument, the elimination of any dual inclusion should be done through the valuation of the stock and not through the exclusion of the annuity.

20.   S. Rep. No. 1622, supra note 14, at 471.

Defendant argues that inducement is not necessary and that the appropriate test is whether the payments would not have been made "but for" the decedent's employment. Treas. Reg. §20.2039-1(c) similarly adopts an expansive interpretation of §2039(b) by requiring the inclusion of any amount attributable to a contribution "made by his [decedent's] employer (or former employer) for any reason connected with his employment. . . ." Plaintiff does not appear to dispute that the "but for" test (if appropriate) is met in this case.[21]

We agree with defendant that the "but for" test should be used. The examples given in the legislative history were not intended to be exhaustive. The purpose of the ratio created by §2039(b) is well illustrated by Treas. Reg. §20.2039-1(c) *Example (1)*. In the example, the amount includible in the gross estate was held to be one-half of the value of the survivor's annuity where the decedent and his wife had each contributed equal amounts towards the purchase of a joint and survivor annuity. In enacting §2039(b) Congress concluded that it would be inappropriate to include in the gross estate the value of an annuity attributable to contributions by the surviving beneficiary or contributions from another as a gift. The value attributable to such contributions does not represent accumulated wealth of the *decedent* which should be subject to the estate tax. However, the value attributable to contributions by an employer which would not have been made but for the decedent's employment represents taxable wealth of the decedent accumulated through his labor. Such value should not be attributed to the survivor or treated as a gift.

Accordingly, we hold that the value of the survivor's annuity is includible in the decedent's gross estate under §2039(a) and that, in calculating the amount includible under §2039(b), all payments by Blocker should be treated as made by reason of decedent's employment.

14.   *Favored to Disfavored Status of Qualified Plan Distribution.*

Employee benefits paid prior to 1983 from qualified plans were exempt from federal estate taxation. By changes made in 1982 and 1984, Congress first reduced to $100,000 and then entirely eliminated this exclusion by repealing §2039(c) through (f). In 1986, Congress increased the tax ultimately imposed on tax-deferred employee income by adding §4980A, the supplemental income and estate tax on excess qualified plan retirement accumulations. Although §4980A ultimately was repealed in 1997, the

---

21.   As noted above, the resolution of the board of directors approving the payments to the Neelys expressly states that the pension is for Mr. Neely's long, faithful employment of 42 years with the company.

remaining income tax burden, coupled with wealth transfer tax, makes deferred compensation an expensive asset to hoard for future enjoyment — and that is the idea: Congress wants this wealth to provide essentially for retirement, not for inheritance. In that regard, the wealth transfer taxation of annuities and other employee benefits has been relatively stable as compared to the amount of change that has occurred with respect to the income tax rules that apply to these assets. Income tax changes have been especially significant and frequent since Congress adopted the Employee Retirement Income Security Act of 1974 (ERISA). A detailed study of this matter is well beyond the scope of this book, so what follows is a brief general description of the key requirements of *qualified* plans, designed to provide only the most basic overview of the topic.

The amount of wealth controlled by private pension plans in America is staggering and grows exponentially. The principal reason for this investment is the favorable income tax advantages granted to all parties involved with qualified plans. In exchange for these benefits, Congress imposes detailed qualification rules. For starters, a tax-favored plan must satisfy all the qualification requirements of §401, the minimum participation standards of §410, the minimum vesting standards of §411, the minimum funding standards of §412, and the limitations on benefits and contributions of §415. A qualified plan must exist for the exclusive benefit of employees and their beneficiaries and have as its sole objective providing these individuals with a share of profits or an income after retirement. Death benefits can be only an incidental feature of a qualified plan. In addition, participation in, contributions to, and benefits provided under a qualified plan may not unduly discriminate in favor of officers, shareholders, or highly compensated employees. Because the definitions of what constitutes a discriminatory plan are among the elements that tend to vary from one amendment to another, the most recent version of these rules should be the focus of study by those crafting a plan but, fortunately, these are not rules that we need to know.

The income tax consequences to the employer-sponsor of a qualified plan are relatively straightforward. Under §404, the employer's contributions to the plan are deductible currently from its income as an immediate business expense. Nevertheless, the employer's contributions to the plan are not taxed currently as income to the employee-participant. Instead, taxation of this form of compensation is deferred until benefits are distributed or made available to the participant (or to designated beneficiaries). The tax advantages of deferring this income include: (1) Usually it is anticipated that the participant will be in a lower income tax bracket in the years after retirement when distributions are received, so the hope is that the benefits will incur a lower overall income tax liability. (2) If the participant is over the age of 65 when taxable distributions are received, an additional standard deduction will be available to offset this income (and additional deductions also may be available on account of the participant's spouse, if any). (3)

Perhaps the most important advantage of deferral is that income invested in the plan is unreduced by income tax, and appreciation earned in the plan between the time of contribution and the time of distribution is exempt from income tax until distribution. This "tax-free internal build-up" applies to contributions by the employer and the participant alike and allows a significant increase in the earning and growth potential of the invested wealth — the taxpayer gets to invest the government's share (the tax dollars) that otherwise reduce the wealth most folks can invest.

Nonqualified plans differ from qualified plans in one significant respect. Under §404(a)(5), the employer may not deduct contributions to a nonqualified plan until the year in which the participant includes the benefit in income, meaning that the benefit of a deduction prior to the employee's "matching" inclusion is not available. The participant's inclusion, however, normally is not affected. See §§402(b), 403(c) and 83(c)(1); the fact that nonqualified plans typically are not funded or vested normally precludes current §83 taxation to the employee. Notwithstanding this deferred deduction to the employer, nonqualified plans are relatively popular, for a number of reasons. For example, nonqualified plans need not meet the rigid funding, minimum participation, minimum vesting, nondiscrimination, and other technical rules that apply to qualified plans. Thus, a nonqualified plan can target benefits to certain favored officers and employees and need not be funded currently; and certain incidental administrative costs of maintaining qualified plans may be reduced or avoided entirely. Although the participant in a nonqualified plan incurs risks that are meant to be minimized by the federal requirements that apply to qualified plans, nonqualified deferred compensation may be an attractive benefit. Further, as discussed immediately below, the §401(a)(9) "required beginning date" rules do not apply, meaning that there is more flexibility in determining when to receive the benefit; the penalties under §§4974 and 72(t) for early or late receipt of benefits are not applicable either.

15.   *Rules Governing Distributions.*   The income tax treatment of employee benefit distributions is a source of significant complexity. It is not appropriate to describe the income tax rules that apply during a participant's life, but some knowledge of the operation of income taxation during life is helpful to a full appreciation and understanding of the options that are available for postmortem distribution, especially if payout began during the participant's life.

In a nutshell, the income taxation of benefits during life can be described as following a "not too early, not too late" pattern. Congress sought to insure that participants and their beneficiaries receive benefits in a way that provides a retirement income during the full duration of their "retirement years," receiving the amounts not too quickly or early in life and not too slowly or late in life. Indeed, Congress especially wants to insure that, in normal cases, the benefits are paid to the participant rather than left to accumulate tax free for disposition to future generations.

Section 401(a)(9) provides the "required distribution" rules, imposing conditions for qualified plan status that mandate distributions to begin by a certain time and to be made within certain periods. This "not too late" aspect is enforced by means of the §4974(a) 50% penalty tax on the amount of any deficiency in meeting these minimum distribution standards. Under §401(a)(9)(C), distributions must begin no later than April 1 of the calendar year following the later of the year the participant reaches the age of 70½ or the year the participant retires. For many participants payments will begin years before that, due to the default distribution rules of §401(a)(14), which apply unless the participant affirmatively elects to defer distributions. Coupled with the §72(t) 10% penalty that applies if distributions begin before age 59½ (the "not too soon" aspect, which applies unless distribution is on account of death, disability, separation from service, other hardships, or as a life annuity), the window of time during which distributions usually begin is approximately 12 years for participants who retire before reaching 70½.

These rules are important because, once payments begin, the benefit must be paid in certain minimum annual amounts. The longer the delay in beginning distribution, the larger the amounts must be to avoid the minimum distribution penalty. This will have a carryover effect on distributions received after death. Under §401(a)(9)(A)(ii), benefits distributed during life must be paid over one of the following periods: (1) the life of the participant, (2) a term certain that does not exceed the actuarial life expectancy of the participant, (3) the joint lives of the participant and a designated beneficiary, or (4) a term certain that does not exceed the actuarial life expectancy of the participant and a designated beneficiary. The real significance of the income tax distribution rules lies in §401(a)(9)(B), which applies if the participant dies before the entire interest is distributed, and in §408(a)(6), which provides that IRA distributions must follow the same rules as those imposed by §401 for other qualified plans. If distributions had begun before death, then §401(a)(9)(B)(i) requires that the entire benefit be distributed after death at least as rapidly as under the distribution program that was begun during life. If distributions had not begun before death, then §401(a)(9)(B)(ii) requires that the entire interest must be distributed before the sixth new year after the participant's death. Two exceptions to this required distribution rule exist and, in many cases, swallow the rule.

First, if payments begin by the end of the first full year after the year of the participant's death, §401(a)(9)(B)(iii) permits the participant to elect a benefit payable over the life expectancy of a designated beneficiary or a term certain that does not exceed the actuarial life expectancy of the designated beneficiary. Section 401(a)(9)(E) defines "designated beneficiary" as any individual, so distribution to the participant's estate will not qualify. See Treas. Reg. §1.401(a)(9)-4 A-3. A trust may be a designated beneficiary if the trust is valid under state law, it is irrevocable as of the participant's death, all trust beneficiaries who conceivably might enjoy benefits are individuals (that is, none are charities or estates), and a copy of the trust instrument or a list of the trust beneficiaries is on file with the plan. Treas. Reg. §§1.401(a)(9)-4 A-5(b) and A-6(b). If these requirements are met, the trust beneficiaries will be treated as the designated beneficiaries; the beneficiary with the shortest life expectancy is used to determine the payout period.

The second exception applies only if the designated beneficiary is the participant's surviving spouse. Section 401(a)(9)(B)(iv) provides that the payments may be deferred to begin no later than the time when the participant (not the spouse) would have reached age 70½, and may extend for the life expectancy of the spouse or a term certain that does not exceed the life expectancy of the spouse. Further, if the surviving spouse also dies before distributions begin, then the benefits must be paid following the spouse's death according to the foregoing rules, as if the spouse were the participant.

Finally, §402 establishes the income tax treatment of distributions to participants and their beneficiaries. The default treatment, if no other elections are made, is distribution of accumulated benefits in the form of an annuity, with income taxation imposed under §72. The fundamental alternative to annuity treatment is §402(e) lump sum distribution of the participant's entire remaining interest in the plan, with payment within one taxable year of the participant or designated beneficiary. Not all plans permit a lump sum distribution, and not all participants (or their designated beneficiaries) will qualify; but, if properly elected, lump sum distributions may qualify for §402(c)(9) "rollover" election available if the designated beneficiary is the participant's surviving spouse. The advantage of the rollover election is that it permits the spouse to place a portion or all of a distribution in another eligible tax deferred plan such as an IRA, with deferral of all income tax on the benefit itself and on any internal build-up in the receptacle plan until distribution. In many cases this is the option of choice, but evaluation of the various options often requires a computer analysis and typically entails an accountant or pension consultant, in addition to the participant or beneficiary's lawyer.

Chapter 10

DEDUCTIONS FOR ADMINISTRATION AND FUNERAL EXPENSES, DEBTS, LOSSES, AND RELATED ITEMS

Part A.   Expenses and Losses Incurred After Death
Part B.   Expenses and Debts Incurred Before Death

Code References: *Estate Tax: §§2053, 2054*
Generation-Skipping Tax: §2622(b)
Income Tax: §§212, 213, 642(g), 691(b)

1.   *The Taxable Estate.* We have completed our study of the inclusion of assets in a decedent's *gross estate*. Now we need to consider deductions that are allowable in computing the *taxable estate*. The estate tax is determined by applying the appropriate tax rates to the taxable estate, which is computed by subtracting deductions from the *gross estate*.

This chapter focuses primarily on deductions allowed under §§2053[1] and 2054 for (1) expenses and losses incurred in connection with disposition of the decedent's body and the administration and distribution of estate assets and (2) obligations incurred by the decedent before death. These provisions have been part of the estate tax in some form since its inception in 1916.

PART A.   EXPENSES AND LOSSES INCURRED AFTER DEATH

2.   *Deductible Expenses and Losses.* A decedent's estate may deduct allowable funeral expenses and, subject to certain limitations, expenses of administering property that is included in the gross estate. Uncompensated casualty and theft[2] losses incurred during estate administra-

---

1. Note that §2622(b) permits a generation-skipping transfer tax deduction "similar to . . . §2053 . . . for amounts attributable to property with respect to which [a] taxable termination has occurred." No regulation or other guidance exists with respect to this provision.

2. A theft loss is relatively rare in an estate administration. Estate of Meriano v. Commissioner, 142 F.3d 651 (3d Cir. 1998), *rev'g* 71 T.C.M. (CCH) 2060 (1996) (excessive fees that a state court ordered to be returned never were repaid, in part pursuant to a settlement reached with the estate), addressed the meaning of "theft" for

tion are deductible to the extent not reflected in estate valuation under the alternate valuation rule. Note that §2054 is needed because alternate valuation may not be available, but the converse is not true. Why might a taxpayer elect alternate valuation for a postmortem loss if a §2054 deduction is available instead?

3.   *Funeral Expenses.*   Funeral expenses are deductible from the gross estate pursuant to §2053(a)(1). Funeral expenses include the cost of (1) interment, (2) a burial lot or vault for the decedent and the decedent's family, (3) a grave marker, (4) payments made for future care of the grave site, and (5) transportation for the one person needed to bring the body to the place of burial. See Treas. Reg. §20.2053-2. The transportation cost for one member of the decedent's family to attend the setting of the decedent's grave marker is a deductible funeral expense because it is an integral part of the decedent's burial and the presence of a family member is deemed necessary to ensure completion of that task. However, transportation costs for other family members, to attend the funeral or otherwise, are deemed not necessary to the decedent's funeral and are not deductible expenses. Estate of Berkman v. Commissioner, 38 T.C.M. (CCH) 183 (1979).

Deductible expenses must be reasonable and they must be "allowable" under local law, meaning that they are a proper payment out of the probate estate. An order of a local court approving the payment of a funeral expense typically will be sufficient evidence that it is allowable, but a probate court order is not required. See Treas. Reg. §20.2053-1(b)(2); Underwood v. United States, 407 F.2d 608 (6th Cir. 1969). Some states have statutory restrictions on the amount allowable for funeral expenses, but a larger expense typically is allowed if the decedent's will directs that the funeral expenses should not be so restricted. Nevertheless, the government routinely reduces or disallows certain expenses, such as for a wake or meals provided incident to the funeral.

The deduction for funeral expenses is limited to the amount actually expended by the estate. Any Veterans Administration reimbursement will offset the deduction, but a death benefit paid to the surviving spouse under the Social Security Act will not offset the deduction because the Social Security Act does not require that the benefit be used for funeral expenses. If a spouse does not survive, however, the Social Security Act limits the death benefit to the payment of funeral expenses, and Rev. Rul. 66-234 holds that the benefit must be offset against the deduction in those cases.

---

§2054 purposes and derived guidance from §165. The Tax Court labeled the case merely a fee dispute and denied the claimed theft loss deduction; the court on appeal concluded that it was the wrongdoer's frame of mind and not the estate's effort to "cut its losses" that was relevant. Although the estate's failure to exert reasonable efforts to collect the amounts owed might disqualify its deduction, the estate's efforts were irrelevant to the question whether there was a theft in the extraction of excessive fees.

Assume that *D* died in a state whose law requires a surviving spouse to pay the funeral expenses of a deceased spouse unless the decedent's will provides otherwise. Although *D*'s will did not waive the spouse's obligation, *D*'s personal representative used *D*'s probate assets to pay the funeral expenses, notwithstanding that *D* was survived by a spouse who could afford to pay for the funeral. If the will did not direct payment, and the spouse is able to pay, *D*'s funeral expenses will not be allowed as an estate tax deduction. See Rev. Rul. 76-369. Even if a local probate court approved the personal representative's payment of the expenses. Nor would it matter whether *D*'s residuary estate passed to the surviving spouse (although perhaps a marital deduction could be claimed in that case, as if the payment was an indirect distribution to the spouse, who then paid those expenses individually).

4.   *Administration Expenses.*   Administration expenses are deductible regardless of whether the decedent died testate or the estate went through probate. DeNivoco v. United States, 561 F.2d 653 (6th Cir. 1977); Pitner v. United States, 388 F.2d 651 (5th Cir. 1967). Deductibility turns on the nature of the expenditure and not on its classification by local law or, in most cases, by whom or in what capacity the expense was incurred. Nevertheless, under §2053, administration expenses are divided into two categories: (1) expenses incurred in the administration of "property subject to claims," which the government regards as meaning property constituting the decedent's estate that is subject to probate administration (and often referred to as the "probate estate" or "probate assets") and (2) expenses incurred in the administration of property "not subject to claims," which the government regards as meaning nonprobate property included in the decedent's gross estate (such as property held in a revocable inter vivos trust, life insurance proceeds payable to someone other than the decedent's estate, or jointly owned property passing by right of survivorship).

With respect to property not subject to claims, only expenses attributable to the decedent's death are deductible, such as expenses flowing from the need to file a Form 706 estate tax return and to value nonprobate assets for estate tax inclusion, and expenses incurred in selling nonprobate assets to pay taxes allocable to them. The key is to identify those expenses paid from nonprobate property that relate to administration of the decedent's estate, such as for the collection of assets, payment of debts and taxes, and distributions triggered by the decedent's death. As illustrated by TAM 9121002, other expenses attributable to nonprobate property that would have been incurred regardless of the decedent's death are not deductible unless actually and properly imposed upon and paid by the decedent's probate estate.

The major difference between the deduction of administration expenses attributable to the probate estate and those incurred with respect to nonprobate assets is that the latter are deductible under §2053(b) only to the extent they are paid prior to expiration of the estate tax limitation period for assessing estate tax against the property, which generally is three years after the estate tax return is filed. §6501. Unless an extension under §6161(a) is obtained, the return is due nine months after the decedent's death. §6075(a). For probate assets, there is no requirement that expenses be paid by any particular date although, if the total expenses and debts exceeds the value of the probate estate, the excess is deductible only if paid with nonprobate assets prior to the due date (including any extensions) for filing the return. See §2053(c)(2). Thus, if total expenses and debts exceed the probate estate, deductions will be maximized if items paid prior to the due date of the return are paid out of nonprobate assets. See Treas. Reg. §20.2053-1(c)(2) *Example (2)*.

To illustrate, Estate of Snyder v. Commissioner, 99-2 U.S. Tax Cas. (CCH) ¶60,357 (Ct. Fed. Cl. 1999), involved a funded inter vivos trust that owned an interest in a landfill that was identified as a Superfund site five months before the decedent died. A postmortem settlement of the estate's liability for the cleanup cost was claimed as a deduction under §2053(a)(3) as a claim against the estate, which the government disallowed to the extent payment occurred after the estate tax return was filed and exceeded the size of the probate estate. Fortunately the court read the statute carefully and held that the §§2053(b) and 2053(c)(2) reference to "property subject to claims" is not necessarily the same as the probate estate, as implied by the regulation, and concluded that the property subject to claims in this case included trust funds used to pay the liability. This appears to be a reasonable interpretation given the fact that Superfund liability is a direct lien against the contaminated property itself (along with other assets of the landowner). That application is obvious.[3]

It may be that the same result would be reached in many other cases. For example, PLR 9123024 involved interest on a deferred estate tax payment that was deductible under §2053(a)(2) and the government regarded it as allowable even though it was the decedent's revocable inter vivos trust that would pay the installments and the interest thereon, long after the time for filing the estate tax return. The limitations of §§2053(b)

---

3. S. Rep. No. 1622, 83d Cong., 2d Sess. 474 (1954), provides an additional illustration of the §2053(c)(2) exception for "property subject to claims":

For example, if the decedent's estate includes only property held by the decedent and his surviving spouse as tenants by the entirety, such items as funeral expenses, debts and other valid claims if allowable under local law and paid by the spouse prior to the time for filing the estate tax return, will be allowed by this section.

It may be that concurrent ownership property is subject to claims against a decedent's estate. See, e.g., In re Granwell, 228 N.E.2d 779 (N.Y. 1967) (creditors may reach a decedent's half of joint tenancy property with respect to debts that were not extinguished at the decedent's death, at least to the extent other assets of the decedent were insufficient to meet these obligations; moreover, the entire transfer could be set aside for the benefit of creditors if the transfer into joint tenancy was in fraud of creditors).

and 2053(c)(2) were deemed not applicable because, under state law, the trust corpus was subject to any claims of the settlor's creditors and creditors of the settlor's estate, meaning that payment from that property at any time was adequate to permit the §2053(a) deduction.

Attorney fees to litigate an estate tax deficiency or refund claim are deductible if paid within three years after filing the estate tax return. Treas. Reg. §20.2053-3(c)(2). Moreover, attorney fees incurred in litigating estate tax issues in the Tax Court are deductible under §2053(b) if paid within 60 days after the decision of the Tax Court becomes final, even if payment occurs more than three years after filing the estate tax return. See Rev. Rul. 61-59. Relying on §6215(a), however, the government ruled that no deduction will be allowed for the payment of attorney fees after the Tax Court's decision is final unless the Tax Court decision expressly allows an additional deduction for costs of litigation paid within 60 days after the court's decision becomes final. Rev. Rul. 78-323.

Expenses incurred in the administration of probate and nonprobate property are deductible if necessary for (1) the collection and preservation of those assets, (2) the payment of estate debts, or (3) the distribution of those assets to the proper beneficiaries. Many factual issues regarding deductible expenses arise within these parameters. One of the issues that arises frequently is the binding effect of state law or a court order allowing payment of an expense. Treas. Reg. §20.2053-3(d)(2) states that the expenses of selling estate property, including brokers' commissions and related costs, are deductible only "if the sale is necessary in order to pay the decedent's debts, expenses of administration, or taxes, to preserve the estate, or to effect distribution." This regulatory restriction is an application of the principle in Treas. Reg. §20.2053-3(a) that an expense for the individual benefit of a beneficiary of the estate (as contrasted with an expense for the proper settlement of the estate itself) is not deductible. These regulations relate to the issue whether property included in a decedent's gross estate should be valued at liquidation value or at replacement cost. See *Cartwright,* reproduced at page 85, and TAM 9235005, discussed at page 92. But the litigation flowing from them highlights a more significant principle.

The Necessity Requirement. In Estate of Park v. Commissioner, 475 F.2d 673 (6th Cir. 1973), overruled en banc by Estate of Millikin v. Commissioner, 125 F.3d 339 (6th Cir. 1997), the assets owned by the decedent at death included a residence and a cottage that passed to four sons, as residuary beneficiaries. The sons decided that they did not wish to retain either property. They requested the decedent's personal representative to sell them, which the personal representative was empowered by the will to do. Expenses were incurred in connection with those sales (principally brokerage fees), which the Michigan Probate Court approved as proper to administration of the estate. Nevertheless, the government disallowed a deduction of those expenses under §2053. The Tax Court, which sustained the Commissioner, was revered on the ground that deductibility is governed by state law alone. On that issue the Court of Appeals for the Sixth Circuit stood alone for two dozen years and then, in *Millikin*, it finally reversed itself and now all courts accept the government's position that distinguishes between what is necessary for the estate and what is for the individual benefit of the beneficiaries.

By way of example, Treas. Reg. §20.2053-3(c)(3) was amended in 1979 to provide that no deduction is allowable for attorneys' fees incurred by beneficiaries incident to litigation relating to their respective interests that is not essential to the proper settlement of the estate. The regulation stresses that no deduction is allowable even if the expense is approved by a probate court as payable or reimbursable by the estate. Another notable example is Hibernia Bank v. United States, 581 F.2d 741 (9th Cir. 1978), in which a bank executor chose to prolong administration of an estate so that it could liquidate the decedent's mansion. The bank encountered substantial difficulty in disposing of the mansion, and incurred substantial expense to carry the asset. To do so the bank elected to borrow funds and, in doing that, it also incurred interest that it sought to deduct. Notwithstanding a state court approval of these expenses, the federal court disallowed the deduction, holding that:

[I]n addition to showing that the claimed expense is allowable under state law, "the taxpayer must show that the claimed administrative expense was a reasonable, necessary administrative expense within the meaning of federal law."

There is no dispute in this case as to whether the interest rate was reasonable or as to the total amount of interest payments. . . .

[But the] district judge found that the estate had been kept open *much* longer than necessary, thereby rendering the loans and interest payments made during the excess period also unnecessary. Specifically, the judge found as a matter of fact that . . . Hibernia had failed "Factually [to] demonstrate an existing necessity to keep the estate open for seven years." The district judge reasoned that since it was wholly unnecessary to keep the estate open during the period of the loans, the loans and interest payments were therefore also unnecessary to the administration of the estate. The implication is that the estate was left open in order to sell the mansion not because the sale was necessary for the administration of the estate, but rather because the heirs preferred to have cash . . . . Thus, the expenses were not deductible.

III. We agree with the district judge that allowability under state law is not the sole criterion for determining the deductibility of a particular expenditure under §2053(a)(2).

In Pitner v. United States, 388 F.2d 651 (5th Cir. 1967), the Fifth Circuit held that "[i]n the determination of deductibility under §2053(a)(2), it is not enough that the deduction be allowable under state law. It is necessary as well that the deduction be for an 'administration expense' within the meaning of that term as it is used in the statute, and that the amount sought to be deducted be reasonable under the circumstances. These are both questions of federal law and establish the outside limits for what may be considered allowable deductions under §2053(a)(2)." Id. at 659.[4] See also Estate of Smith v. Commissioner, 510 F.2d 479 (2d Cir. 1975).[5]

. . . Affirmed.

DUNIWAY, J. (concurring): I write only to point out that there are sound practical reasons . . . which require that we construe §2053(a)(2) as permitting the deduction of those expenditures only which are expenses of administration within the meaning of federal estate tax law.

First, in California, and I suspect in most other states, probate proceedings are essentially ex parte in character. While the Probate Code requires an executor or administrator wishing to borrow money to obtain an order of court authorizing the borrowing, and while an executor or administrator must account to the court for all receipts and expenditures, there is no requirement that

---

4. In *Pitner*, the court did observe, and we agree, that in most instances "the state law may be relied upon as a guide to what deductions may reasonably be permitted for federal estate tax purposes." 388 F.2d at 659. As the court explained, however, deference to state law as a guide cannot justify the deduction of expenses which simply are not "administration expenses" within the meaning of federal estate tax law.

5. In *Estate of Smith* the decedent's executors sought to deduct commissions paid on the sale of certain estate assets. Even though all of the commission payments had been allowed by the state probate court, the Tax Court permitted the deduction of only about half of the commissions. The Tax Court concluded that the sale of assets beyond what was needed to pay the estate's debts, expenses, and taxes was not necessary for the administration of the estate. 57 T.C. 650 (1972).

The Second Circuit affirmed, holding: "In the present case, appellants' claims for administration expenses were not contested in the Surrogate's Court and there is some question as to whether some of these expenses were in fact incurred for the benefit of the estate in accordance with the general purpose of §2053 rather than for the benefit of individual beneficiaries. In such circumstances, the federal courts cannot be precluded from reexamining a lower state court's allowance of administration expenses to determine whether they were in fact necessary to carry out the administration of the estate or merely prudent or advisable in preserving the interests of the beneficiaries." Id. at 482-483 (footnote and citations omitted).

personal notice be given to any party interested in the estate. Notice is given by posting a notice by the clerk at the courthouse and is required to be mailed to an interested party only if that party has filed a request for a special notice. . . . In this case only one person interested in the estate filed a request for notice and the administrator, because of that notice, regarded that person as "uncooperative." The petitions for orders of the court authorizing the administrator to borrow, and the accounts of the administrator, were not contested by anyone. There is no inducement to a California state court to restrict the allowance of claimed administrative expenses in order to prevent improper reductions of the federal estate tax. Indeed, many state judges would probably be pleased to assist the representative of the estate and the heirs in thus reducing the estate tax.

Second, . . . the Hibernia Bank was on every possible side of the probate proceedings in this case. It was the administrator with the will annexed of the decedent's estate; it was the trustee of the . . . testamentary trusts that were each to receive one quarter of the residue of the estate; it borrowed $625,000 from itself, and paid itself over $130,000 in interest. A large block of its stock was the most valuable single asset of the estate, and Hibernia's management had an interest in not having that stock sold. As administrator, Hibernia had a duty to hold down expenses. As the lender, it had a duty to its shareholders to obtain the highest interest rate that it could lawfully obtain. As the trustee, it had a duty to compel itself as administrator to close the administration of the estate as soon as practicable. As lender, its interest was to have the estate kept open and continue to borrow money and pay interest. As administrator, it owed beneficiaries a duty to minimize estate taxes. No matter which way it turned, it met itself. There was nobody actually before the probate court to question the validity or propriety of any of its expenditures, or to object to any phase of its administration of the estate. Certainly the interest of the United States in collecting its estate tax was not represented before the probate court, and it is doubtful that the United States would have been recognized had it attempted to appear before that court. Moreover, the United States would be likely to find itself in a hostile forum if it did appear.

I cannot believe that it was the intention of the Congress in adopting §2053(a)(2) to place the federal fisc at the mercy of an essentially ex parte probate proceeding in a California court in which it is possible for one institution to play so many and such inconsistent roles. I do not believe that Congress intended to give the game away in that fashion

To illustrate how fine a line this sale for the benefit of the beneficiary or for the estate issue can be, in Estate of Vatter v. Commissioner, 65 T.C. 633 (1975), *aff'd per curiam*, 77-2 U.S. Tax Cas. (CCH) ¶13,169 (2d Cir. 1976), the Tax Court allowed an administration expense deduction for costs incurred in selling rental dwellings that were part of the decedent's residuary estate, which was devised to a testamentary trust. The dwellings were old and required maintenance and repairs, and the trustee did not wish to manage them as part of the trust corpus. The court held that the sale was not for the benefit of the trustee but rather was necessary to effect distribution of the residuary estate, noting that the decedent did not specifically devise the rental dwelling, that the will did not indicate that the decedent contemplated a distribution of them in kind, and that the personal representative was empowered by the decedent's will and by state law to sell the property. The court emphasized that the selling expenses were allowable administration expenses under the laws of New York, where the estate was administered. In holding that the sale was "necessary," the court stated:

> The trustee did not wish to accept as trust property the rental real estate which comprised a substantial portion of the decedent's residuary estate. Thus, in order for the residuary estate to be distributed to the trustee named in decedent's will, it was necessary for the executrix to sell the rental real estate. Therefore, the selling expenses were necessarily incurred to effect the distribution of the residuary estate to the testamentary trust within the meaning of Treas. Reg. §20.2053-3(d)(2).

Unfortunately, *Vatter* may be wrongly decided, because state law authorized distribution in kind of the estate property, notwithstanding the trustee's desires. See N.Y. E.P.T.L. §11-1.1(20). So the sale really was not necessary. Quaere: was that an error of fact, generally not subject to appellate review, or of law?

The Reasonableness Requirement, and the Effect of a State Court Determination.   Assume that a personal representative petitions the local probate court for approval of its fees and that the court consents, perhaps with the approval of the heirs or other beneficiaries. The issue is whether that approval is determinative of the reasonableness of the fees for purposes of claiming a §2053(a)(2) deduction. In PLR 8636100 the government opined that it *is* determinative under either of two circumstances: (1) the state court passed on all the facts and circumstances surrounding the fee request and the determination was made in a genuinely adversarial proceeding involving those fees, or (2) the state court entered a consent decree that constitutes a bona fide settlement by the parties of a valid dispute or claim regarding fees.

In other situations, the Ruling said the court order will not necessarily bind the government, nor must the government accept a local court decree that is at variance with state law (for example, if the awarded fees exceed statutory fees, with no special justification for the excess). United States v. White, 853 F.2d 107 (2d Cir. 1988), involved the government's subpoena of attorney White's time records, which White refused to provide. The district court determined that the government, under Treas. Reg. §20.2053-1(b)(2), was bound to accept the state court determination of fees unless there was prima facie evidence of fraud, overreaching, or some other reason to believe that the court had not passed on the factors upon which deductibility depends. Further, the court held that the burden is on the government, particularly if the state court determination took into account all of the factors the government would consider. No added requirement was imposed that the determination be made in a genuinely adversarial proceeding, nor that it be a bona fide settlement of a valid dispute regarding fees.

In reversing, the Court of Appeals for the Second Circuit stated that:

> We do not read [§2053(a)(2)] as giving state trial court decrees preclusive effect with regard to IRS investigations. To be sure, the plain language of §2053(a)(2) indicates that the federal deductibility of estate administrative expenses is governed by state law. [But] . . . the deductibility of such expenses nonetheless remains a federal question. The statute does not address the effect of state trial court approval of estate administrative expenses under federal law. In the absence of preclusive language in the statute, we are not persuaded that Congress unambiguously intended to make state trial court decrees determinative of the federal deductibility of such expenses to the exclusion of any federal inquiry.
>
> . . .
>
> We believe the holding in [Commissioner v. Estate of] Bosch [387 U.S. 456 (1967)] supports the view that the Surrogate's decree is not conclusive and binding on the IRS under I.R.C. §2053(a)(2). . . . We conclude that, with regard to the federal deductibility of White's fees, the IRS is entitled to make an independent assessment of the validity of White's fees under applicable state law as determined by the state's highest court [and is not precluded] from investigating the deductibility of White's fees under state law.

853 F.2d at 113-114. According to the court, the government would be bound by state law factors that are to be applied in determining the allowability of fees, but would not be bound by a lower state court's application of those factors in a particular case. Moreover, a government summons to investigate the attorney's records is enforceable, to help make

an independent determination of the allowability of those fees. Finally, the court held that Treas. Reg. §20.2053-1(b)(2) is not inconsistent with its reading of §2053(a)(2), allowing an inquiry into the question whether the proper factors were properly considered under state law; thus, the government had a legitimate purpose in investigating White's fees and the time records that were relevant to a determination of reasonableness.

Meanwhile, in Estate of DeWitt v. Commissioner, 54 T.C.M. (CCH) 759 (1987), the government had challenged the deductibility of certain expenses of administration, all of which had been allowed by the Surrogate's Court for state law purposes. In allowing most of the deductions on motion for summary judgment, the Tax Court stated:

> [A] court decree ordinarily controls the deductibility under the Federal estate tax [but] . . . the [taxpayer] . . . must show that all the facts necessary for deductibility under Federal estate tax were considered and found pursuant to the state court's inquiry.
>
> In most instances the interest of the federal government in protecting its revenues will coalesce with the interest of the state in protecting its citizens, and state law may be relied upon as a guide to what deductions may reasonably be permitted for federal estate tax purposes. In some cases, however, the state law on its face or in its application may not be responsive to the interests traditionally protected by the state. . . . [Thus,] . . . we are not stating as a rule of law a Surrogate's Court decree establishes deductibility of administration expenses . . . .

54 T.C.M. at 762. Only those deductions not proven by the taxpayer were denied on the motion for summary judgment, although the taxpayer was given the opportunity to present evidence to support their deductibility.

The important issue in Estate of Love v. United States, 923 F.2d 335 (4th Cir. 1991), was whether federal or state law should govern the deductibility of a payment to buy out a partner to a "foal sharing" horse breeding agreement. The payment ultimately was regarded as an investment related item, not an administration expense, and therefore was deemed to be nondeductible under §2053, notwithstanding that it was approved by the state court as a proper estate expenditure. In reaching its conclusion, the Court of Appeals for the Fourth Circuit said that it was joining the majority courts in holding that federal law is determinative, citing *Smith*, *Pitner*, *Hibernia*, and Treas. Reg. §20.2053-3(a). *Love* properly held that federal law controls the determination of what is an administration expense for §2053 deductibility. Federal law establishes the criteria to determine whether an expense is deductible, and the appropriate determination ought to be whether, in allowing an administration expense, a state court appropriately considered the factors that establish federal deductibility. If the proper factors were applied by the state court, however, the expense should be deductible under §2053(a)(2) and a federal court should not redetermine whether the particular expense was reasonable and necessarily incurred in the proper administration of the estate and therefore meets those federal criteria. The *Love* court determined that the expenditure, although approved by the state court as a legitimate administration expense for state law purposes, did not meet the definition of an administration expense for federal estate tax purposes, which is the proper approach.

A case frequently but mistakenly cited as supporting the majority approach on this issue is Estate of Streeter v. Commissioner, 491 F.2d 375 (3d Cir. 1974) (en banc). The decedent made a specific bequest to a testamentary trust of a valuable collection of books, maps, historical manuscripts, and similar properties relating to American history. The decedent's will directed the trustees to sell the Americana collection, the time of sale to be determined by the trustees. After receiving the collection from the executors, the trustees sold the collection through a gallery, incurring commissions that the estate sought to deduct as an administration expense. The Tax Court denied the deduction because the trust and the estate were separate entities and the wrong entity sold the collection. On appeal, the court stated:

That by choosing a testamentary trust rather than directing a sale by his executors the decedent has lost a large estate tax deduction which might otherwise be available may seem a harsh result. But we cannot redraft the instrument chosen by the decedent. The decision of the Tax Court will be affirmed.

How would you have provided for the sales to be made to maximize tax benefits if the decedent had employed you to plan the estate and had explained to you that the collection would be sold item by item over a period of six years to maximize the amount realized?

For Whose Benefit Incurred?   Would the decision in *Hibernia* have been influenced if the decedent's will had directed the personal representative to sell such assets as the legatees requested or had directed that all assets be sold and that the estate be distributed in cash? In the latter case, it is a well-established principle that a legatee can elect to take the property in kind rather than in cash. 4 Scott & Fratcher, THE LAW OF TRUSTS §346 (4th ed. 1989).

Assume that D's will bequeathed the residuary estate to a testamentary trust, the income from which was to be distributed to X and Y. The will was ambiguous as to whether trust income was required to be divided equally between X and Y or whether the trustee had authority to sprinkle the income between them in such proportions as the trustee might determine. X and Y brought suit to construe the testamentary trust. Although D's personal representative and the trustee participated in the suit, *D*'s personal representative paid all the legal fees incurred in that suit on behalf of the estate, the trust, and *X* and *Y*. Notwithstanding that the local probate court approved the payments, the legal fees are not deductible under §2053 to the extent they are deemed to have been incurred for the benefit of *X* and *Y*. See Treas. Reg. §20.2053-8(d) *Example (2)*.

In Estate of Reilly v. Commissioner, 76 T.C. 369 (1981), litigation arose about who was the owner of property the decedent transferred to the decedent's spouse prior to death or that was held by the decedent and the spouse in joint tenancy at the decedent's death. The decedent's spouse, personal representative, and trustee of a testamentary trust were parties to the suit. The parties executed a compromise agreement that was approved by the probate court, under which the testamentary trust was required to pay the attorney fees of the spouse and the estate. The Commissioner conceded that the trust's payment of the attorney fees was equivalent to payment by the estate, but determined that the fees were incurred primarily for the benefit of the surviving spouse and were not deductible. The Tax Court held that the fees were deductible under Treas. Reg. §20.2053-3(a) because whether the estate or the surviving spouse owned the assets in question was essential to proper settlement of the estate. As an alternative holding, the court treated the expenses as deductible under §2053(a)(3) as an expense incurred in settling a claim against the estate by the surviving spouse.

Examples of Deductible Expenses. Estate of Joslyn v. Commissioner, 500 F.2d 382 (9th Cir. 1974), held that an estate tax deduction will be allowed for expenses incurred in making a secondary offering of corporate stock (including the underwriters' fees and the cost of registering the stock with the Securities and Exchange Commission) made to raise funds needed to pay extraordinary expenses incurred in administering the decedent's estate. Stock must be sold at a discount to attract sufficient buyers if a large block of stock is offered for sale in a market that does not have sufficient buyers to purchase all of the stock at its quoted price. This blockage price reduction is reflected in valuing the stock for estate tax purposes, and the estate tax agent who valued the decedent's stock in *Joslyn* used the actual expenses incurred by the estate to make a secondary offering as the measure of the blockage element. The government then challenged the estate's §2053(a)(2) deduction of the secondary offering expense on the ground that the reduction in the value of the stock already incorporated the blockage element. According to the government, the estate's claim for a §2053(a)(2) deduction would constitute a double allowance of the same amount, which the Tax Court accepted. In reversing on appeal, the court held that valuation techniques are too imprecise to warrant treating the selling expenses as already having been allowed by the valuation discount, and that holding is not comparable to allowing a double benefit for expenses incurred in selling estate assets. Can you explain why?

Estate of Webster v. Commissioner
65 T.C. 968 (1976)

[The Service challenged the estate tax deduction of two forms of interest expenses incurred by the estate. One was for delayed payment of a gift tax liability that the estate disputed. The other was for interest on a loan obtained by the decedent during life that was not repaid by the estate until some time after the decedent's death. The decedent died a resident of Massachusetts.]

WILES J. . . .

III. POSTDEATH INTEREST ON GIFT TAX LIABILITY The [first] issue is whether interest on the gift tax liability accruing subsequent to decedent's death is deductible as an administration expense under §2053(a)(2).

In Estate of Smith v. Commissioner, 57 T.C. 650, 660-661 (1972), aff'd, 510 F.2d 479 (2d Cir. 1975), this Court stated two conditions which must be met before the deduction of administration expenses under §2053(a) will be allowed: (1) The expenses must be "allowable by the laws of the jurisdiction . . . under which the estate is being administered," and (2) the various requirements of respondent's regulations must be satisfied. We need deal with only the first of these conditions since the parties have agreed that interest on the gift tax liability accruing subsequent to decedent's death is deductible as an administration expense under §2053(a) if allowed by the law of Massachusetts as an administration expense.

The record does not indicate that, at the time of trial, postdeath interest had been allowed by a Massachusetts probate court. But this is not fatal to petitioner's cause since §2053(a) says "as are allowable," not "as have been allowed." Furthermore, "a reasonable expense of administration will not be denied because no court decree has been entered if the amount would be allowable under local law." Treas. Reg. §20.2053-1(b)(2).

The first question is whether a Massachusetts probate court would have jurisdiction over the type of expense involved herein. . . . There is no serious question that the type of expenses involved herein would not be within the jurisdiction of the proper Massachusetts probate court.

The next question is whether, granting jurisdiction, the court would allow such an expense as postdeath interest. "Under administration expenses would, of course, come any reasonable and proper liabilities incurred by the executor or administrator in the course of settling the estate." 1 Newhall, Settlement of Estates and Fiduciary Law in Massachusetts, §185, at 533 n.3 (4th ed. 1958). . . . There is nothing in the record to indicate that petitioner has unduly delayed the payment of the gift tax (thus causing an increase in interest). There was a serious question whether any gift tax was owing at all. Petitioner could, of course, have paid the gift tax and sued for a refund, but it chose instead to dispute the matter in this Court, where prepayment of an alleged tax liability is not required. That is its right. We think that a proper Massachusetts probate court would allow the postdeath interest as a reasonable expense of administration. In light of the parties' stipulation, we hold the postdeath interest deductible under §2053(a).

IV. POSTDEATH INTEREST ON LOANS MADE DURING DECEDENT'S LIFETIME   The executor paid $43,649.38 in interest which accrued subsequent to decedent's death on loans outstanding at the time of her death. . . . Respondent disallowed the deduction.

There are three conditions for allowability under §2053(a): The expense must be (1) actually and (2) necessarily incurred in administration of the decedent's estate, and (3) the expense must be allowable as an administration expense under local law.

Certainly there is no doubt that the interest payments were actually made; the parties have so stipulated. Nor do we see any problem with the condition of "necessarily incurred." Decedent had made these loans before her death. When the executors were appointed, the debts and the interest thereon became their obligation. The record does not reveal whether, upon their appointment, the executors could have immediately retired the debt and stopped further running of interest, but even if they could have retired the debt, we see no requirement for them to do so. The unpaid balance on the loans was over $3.5 million at decedent's death. Considering the various items of major value in the estate, as for example, stocks and bonds, the executors would perhaps have lost money had they tried to raise such a great sum. We think it was eminently reasonable for them to pay the interest instead.

The third condition is whether the postdeath interest would be allowable as an administration expense under Massachusetts law. We have reviewed most of the pertinent material in the discussion of the previous issue. Here we need only add that in Massachusetts it has been held that an executor may borrow money and that the interest paid thereon is allowable. . . . [W]e think the proper Massachusetts probate court would allow this interest as a proper expense. As already stated, the loans and interest thereon became the obligation of the executors on their appointment. They had to pay the interest, unless, of course, they could have retired the debt on their appointment. Even if they could have retired the debt upon their appointment, there was no necessity for them to do so. We accordingly hold that the postdeath interest . . . is deductible under §2053(a).

The government acquiesced in result only to the Tax Court's allowing a deduction for postmortem interest on the decedent's gift tax liability in *Webster* (Issue III), but nonacquiesced to the court's allowing a deduction for interest arising after the decedent's death on loans made during the decedent's life (Issue IV). In Rev. Rul. 77-461, the government denied a deduction for postmortem interest payable on loans made to the decedent during life because the loans were not essential to estate administration. However, the government also held that, if the executor extended the term of an outstanding loan to avoid a sacrifice sale of estate assets, any *additional* interest incurred as a consequence of that extension may qualify as an estate tax deduction. This distinction was repudiated by the Tax Court in Estate of Wheless v. Commissioner, 72 T.C. 470 (1979), *non acq.*, in which the court allowed an estate tax deduction for interest that accrued after the decedent's death on a loan obtained by the decedent during life. The *Wheless* debt was not extended beyond maturity by the estate but it was not repaid prior to maturity, for reasons that related to proper estate administration.

Interest on a debt incurred by the decedent during life is deductible and interest accruing after the decedent's death for which the estate is liable also may be deducted under §§2053(a)(3) or 2053(a)(4). See Treas. Reg. §§20.2053-4 and 20.2053-7.

Other impediments to deduction may arise and present taxpayers with challenging administration issues. Consider:

Pickett v. United States
90-2 U.S. Tax Cas. (CCH) ¶60,030 (N.D. Fla. 1990)

VINSON., J. . . . On August 16, 1986, plaintiff submitted a claim for a partial refund of federal estate tax. One of the bases for the claim was that plaintiff had incurred additional deductible administrative expenses due to sizable interest payments made during 1985 and 1986 upon a loan from the Federal Land Bank. The loan was obtained and used to pay . . . estate taxes. On April 29, 1987, plaintiff received a refund in the amount of the entire claimed refund, plus interest.

Plaintiff submitted a second claim for partial refund of federal estate taxes, postmarked on June 30, 1987. This second claim concerned additional interest payments made during 1987 on the same Federal Land Bank loan. On November 13, 1987, the Internal Revenue Service denied her refund request because her claim was not timely filed.

The parties agree that the refund claim submitted in 1987 was filed outside of the limitations period set out in §6511, [which] requires such refund claims to be filed within three years from the date the tax return was filed, or two years from the date the taxes were paid, whichever is later. . . .

Plaintiff concedes that the 1987 claim was filed more than three years after the original return was filed, but nevertheless argues [that] she had no choice but to file her claim outside the limitations period, because she was not permitted to claim esti-mated future interest payment obligations in the original return or in the 1986 claim. . . .

An estate cannot claim a present estate tax deduction for estimated future interest expense, even though such an expense would otherwise be deductible under §2053(a)(2) and Treas. Reg. §20.2053-3(a). If installment payment of the tax is approved [see §§6161, 6163, and 6166], then Rev. Rul. 80-250 allows the deductions to be claimed "at the time of the annual dates prescribed for payment under §6166." But if the estate elects to borrow the funds and pay the tax when due, as did the plaintiff here, there is no set way for the estate to claim the interest as an estate tax deduction.[6] Thus, plaintiff claims there is a "Catch 22" between the limitations period of §6511(a) and the Service's treatment of future interest accruals.

As defendant correctly points out, however, plaintiff could have filed a "protective claim" for a refund of the estimated amounts *within* the limitations period, and then supplemented the protective claim with a formal claim when the 1987 interest payment amounts became definite. This later formal claim would relate back to the original protective claim. The case law authorizes this method of making the claim even though the Service apparently has not formalized a "protective claim" procedure in the Regulations, nor does the Code itself authorize it. It is well settled that where the taxpayer has knowledge of future deductions and yet fails to file such a protective claim, a later claim outside the limitations period is barred. . . .

---

6. The interest expense would presumably be utilized as an estate income tax deduction if not claimed on the estate tax [return].

Since there are no material issues of fact relating to the late filing of this refund claim, . . . the defendant's motion for summary judgment is granted.

5.   *Community Property.* If a decedent who is survived by a spouse held community property at death, the expenses incurred in administering the entire community property (both the decedent's and the survivor's shares) are deductible only to the extent of the decedent's percentage interest therein. United States v. Stapf, 375 U.S. 118 (1963). But expenses specifically allocated to the decedent's share of the community are fully deductible. Estate of Lang v. Commissioner, 97 F.2d 867 (9th Cir. 1938). See Rev. Rul. 78-242.

6.   *Double Deductions.* Some §2053 administration expenses also qualify as an income tax deduction under §§163, 212, 213, or elsewhere in computing the income tax liability of the decedent's estate (which is a separate income taxpaying entity, under Subchapter J, §§641 through 682). With the exception of §691(b) "deductions in respect of a decedent," §642(g) prevents the use of such expenses for both tax purposes by denying an income tax deduction for amounts allowed as an estate tax deduction under §2053 or §2054. Thus, the personal representative must elect whether to deduct these expenses for estate tax or for estate income tax purposes. Because this prohibition also applies to expenses of selling estate assets, the personal representative must decide whether to claim selling expenses (such as a broker's commission) as an estate tax deduction or as a reduction of the amount realized by the estate on sale (to reduce the estate's gain or increase its loss for income tax purposes). Rev. Rul. 70-361 permits apportionment of all of these items partly to the income tax return and partly to the estate tax return, as the personal representative chooses, but usually they will be taken all on one return or the other.

An income tax deduction for certain expenses is allowable only to the extent that the expenses exceed a specified figure, which may be determined as a percentage of some amount such as the "adjusted gross income" of the taxpayer. For example, under §67, a taxpayer's so-called "miscellaneous itemized deductions" are deductible only to the extent that the aggregate amount of such items exceeds 2% of the taxpayer's adjusted gross income. Thus, if a taxpayer, having adjusted gross income of $100,000 for a taxable year, had $8,000 of miscellaneous itemized deductions, the taxpayer is permitted to deduct only $6,000 of those items because that is the amount of those items ($8,000) that exceeds 2% of the taxpayer's adjusted gross income ($2,000). Similar circumstances can arise in connection with other income tax provisions (such as §213 medical expenses of the decedent's final illness) for which only the amount that exceeds a floor figure can be deductible.

If an estate incurs an expense that is deductible for either estate tax or income tax purposes (a so-called "swing item"), and if an income tax deduction of that item is subject to a nondeductible floor, the personal representative cannot deduct the amount of the expense that exceeds the floor as an income tax deduction and take the balance of the expense (i.e., the "floor" amount) as an estate tax deduction. The purpose of §642(g) is to prevent the *use* of an expense for both estate tax and income tax purposes. Thus, in the prior example, the "floor" amount ($2,000) was "used" for income tax purposes because it enabled the taxpayer to deduct $6,000 of the $8,000 of expenses. Because the $8,000 of expenses is utilized to create a $6,000 income tax deduction, the personal representative cannot then use the $2,000 amount as an estate tax deduction. That is, the $2,000 of miscellaneous itemized "deductions" that the taxpayer is not permitted to claim for income tax purposes nevertheless is deemed used for income tax deduction purposes; they serve to satisfy the "floor" that must be met to deduct the remaining $6,000 of those items, and the full $8,000 of income tax deductible expenses is lost as estate tax deductions. See Rev. Rul. 77-357, dealing with the similar floor applicable to the deduction of medical expenses in the final income tax return filed on behalf of the decedent. See §213(c).

If an expense that constitutes a miscellaneous itemized deduction, or some other income tax deduction that is subject to a floor, also qualifies for an estate tax deduction, the personal representative can elect to take the *entire* amount of the expense as an estate tax deduction. The floor that applies to taking the item as an income tax deduction does *not* apply to the estate tax deduction.

For these and a number of other reasons, often the better choice is to use swing item deductions for estate tax purposes. Yet often the election is made to claim them for income tax purposes. Why might that seem better?

PART B.   EXPENSES AND DEBTS INCURRED BEFORE DEATH

7.   *Debts and Mortgages.* Debts incurred by the decedent before death, including interest accrued to the date of death, are deductible under §2053(a)(3) as a claim against the estate, even if the debt is not yet mature at the decedent's death, provided that the decedent had personal liability on the debt. On the other hand, mortgage obligations that encumber property and for which the decedent had no personal obligation to repay (nonrecourse debt) reduce the includible value of the encumbered property. Treas. Reg. §20.2053-7. The effect essentially is equivalent to allowing a deduction for the debt.

Debts are deductible only if bona fide and, if founded on a promise or agreement, only to the extent incurred for "adequate and full consideration in money or money's worth."[7] The government will scrutinize a transaction closely if the "creditor" is a relative of the decedent to determine whether the decedent actually intended the "loan" to be repaid or merely disguised a donative transfer in the form of an allegedly deductible debt.

8. *Admissibility of Postmortem Facts.* Treas. Reg. §20.2053-4 states that only claims enforceable against the estate are allowable as deductions. Estate of Hagmann v. Commissioner, 60 T.C. 465 (1973), *aff'd per curiam*, 492 F.2d 796 (5th Cir. 1974), a decision reviewed by the entire Tax Court, denied a deduction for a bona fide debt of a decedent that became void and unenforceable after the decedent's death but prior to filing the estate tax return because the creditor failed to file a timely claim against the estate as required by local law.[8] The Tax Court held that events occurring after the decedent's death may be considered in determining the deductibility of a debt, although postmortem facts may not be considered to determine the amount of the deduction.[9] More recently, Estate of Smith v. Commissioner, 198 F.3d 515 (5th Cir. 1999), *rev'g* 108 T.C. 412 (1997), *nonacq.*, held that postmortem facts may not be considered and that the Tax Court's distinction between a review of postmortem developments for purposes of determining whether the debt was enforceable rather than its value was bankrupt. Consider the issue as it informs the following decision:

Estate of Kyle v. Commissioner
94 T.C. 829 (1990)

COHEN, J. . . . Decedent was involved in a business transaction in 1981. Decedent died in 1983, and his estate tax return was filed in 1984. In 1984, decedent's business associate, Walden, filed a claim against the estate for $4.8 million. Also in 1984, Walden initiated a lawsuit against the estate in Federal court. In 1985, when the Federal court action was dismissed for lack of diversity of citizenship, Walden filed suit in an Oklahoma district court. In 1986, the Oklahoma trial court granted the estate's motion for summary judgment on the grounds that Walden's bankrupt corporation was the real party in interest. Finally, in 1989, the State court action

---

7. The concept of an "adequate and full consideration in money or money's worth," which cuts across many areas of wealth transfer taxation, is considered in Chapters 6 and 14.

8. The estate also may have recognized cancellation of indebtedness income for income tax purposes. See Estate of Bankhead v. Commissioner, 60 T.C. 535 (1973).

9. Contra, Russell v. United States, 260 F. Supp. 493 (N.D. Ill. 1966); Winer v. United States, 153 F. Supp. 941 (S.D. N.Y. 1957); cf. Estate of Lester v. Commissioner, 57 T.C. 503 (1972).

became final when the Oklahoma Supreme Court denied Walden's petition for certiorari.

On its Federal estate tax return, petitioner claimed an estate tax deduction for a claim against the estate in the amount of $1.2 million. Respondent disallowed the claimed deduction. . . .

1. *Relevance of Post-Death Events* The starting place for any discussion of the effect of post-death events on deductibility must be Ithaca Trust Co. v. United States, 279 U.S. 151 (1929). In *Ithaca Trust*, the decedent left substantial sums in trust for his widow, with a remainder to charity. Ordinarily, an estate tax return would have been filed claiming a charitable deduction based on the estimated actuarial value of the charitable remainder based on the widow's life expectancy. The widow, however, died before the filing of the estate tax return. The estate therefore claimed a charitable deduction based on the actual amount passing to charity because of the widow's early demise, a larger sum than the actuarial estimate. The Court of Claims upheld the larger deduction based on actual post-death events, but the Supreme Court reversed. The Supreme Court observed:

> The first impression is that it is absurd to resort to statistical probabilities when you know the fact. But this is due to inaccurate thinking. The estate so far as may be is settled as of the date of the testator's death. * * * Therefore the value of the thing to be taxed must be estimated as of the time when the act is done. * * * Like all values, as the word is used by the law, it depends largely on more or less certain prophecies of the future, and the value is no less real at that time if later the prophecy turns out false than when it comes out true. * * * Tempting as it is to correct uncertain probabilities by the now certain fact, we are of the opinion that it cannot be done * * * [279 U.S. at 155.]

Notwithstanding *Ithaca Trust*, lower courts have frequently considered post-death events in determining the deductibility of claims.

In Estate of Van Horne v. Commissioner, 78 T.C. 728 (1982), *aff'd*, 720 F.2d 1114 (9th Cir. 1983), this court observed that "all of the cases in this field dealing with post-death evidence are not easily reconciled with one another, and at times it is like picking one's way through a minefield in seeking to find a completely consistent course of decision." 78 T.C. at 736-737. There appear to be two broad categories of cases that have considered post-death events: (1) Cases concerning the valuation of claims that are certain and enforceable at the time of death and (2) cases concerning the enforceability of disputed or contingent claims against the estate.

At the time of her death, the decedent in *Estate of Van Horne* was obligated to pay spousal support to her surviving ex-husband for the remainder of his life. The ex-husband, however, died approximately 7 months after decedent and approximately 2 months before the estate tax return was filed.

Because the obligation at issue was fully enforceable as of the date of the decedent's death, that court again held that the estate was entitled to a deduction for the actuarial value of the debt computed without regard to events occurring subsequent to the date of death. Thus, the lifetime spousal support obligation was valued at the date of decedent's death even though the surviving ex-spouse died prior to the filing of the estate tax return.

In *Estate of Van Horne* we analyzed these cases and concluded that we must consider post-death events in cases concerning the enforceability of claims against the estate. We also concluded, however, that the general principle announced in *Ithaca Trust* is applicable in cases involving the valuation of claims against the estate. . . .

The dispute in this case involves enforceability or validity of Walden's claim, not just valuation of a valid claim. Thus we look to post-death events to determine whether the Walden claim was a valid claim against decedent's estate.

2. *Enforceability of the Walden Claim* Petitioner argues that the estate's victory as a result of unexpected procedural blunders by Walden is not evidence as to the existence, enforceability, or value of the claim and therefore should not be considered. . . . Specifically, petitioner argues that uncontroverted evidence in the record shows that decedent misled and manipulated Walden, demonstrating bad faith dealings throughout their business transaction. . . .

The attorney who represented the estate in the State court testified that the victory in the State appellate court was unexpected. . . . He did not, however, provide any evidence that the claim was *valid*. . . .

Petitioner has the burden of proving the validity of the claimed deduction. Petitioner is, in effect, asking us to render summary judgment in Walden's favor in a dispute that reeks of uncertainty and material issues of fact. The State courts, on records including evidence from the estate factually refuting Walden's claim, decided against him. We are not persuaded that these State court decisions can be cast aside, as petitioner seeks, as merely based on a procedural error by Walden. . . .

Petitioner has presented no evidence from which we can determine that Walden would have prevailed if he had not encountered the difficulties reflected in the records of the Federal and State court proceedings. It is illogical to conclude that his claim should be treated as valid and valuable where the only evidence is from cases that he lost.

Petitioner has not carried its burden of proving that the Walden claim was a valid, enforceable claim against the estate at the date of decedent's death and, therefore, no estate tax deduction is allowable for the claim. . . .

Estate of Cafaro v. Commissioner, 57 T.C.M. (CCH) 1002 (1989), provides a comprehensive summary of cases the *Kyle* court characterized as falling into the two primary categories. Postmortem developments are relevant in determining whether a debt was enforceable at the decedent's death. But the value of the debt for deduction purposes must be determined based on the facts and circumstances that existed at the decedent's death. In these cases postmortem facts may be relevant to determine the date of death value, but postmortem events or circumstances that change the value of the debt may not be considered. *Cafaro* determined that the issue was enforceability of various unmatured, contingent, and contested claims, thus making it permissible to consider events after the decedent's death. Several claims against the decedent's estate were based on alleged debts that were never proven in probate although they were presented and settled at less than their alleged face amount. The court considered these postmortem settlements and allowed a deduction only for the amount paid, not for the amounts alleged to be owing, stating that postmortem events such as settlement of a claim for less than the amount petitioned to the probate court are relevant in determining whether the claim was for a sum certain and legally enforceable at the date of the decedent's death. Several other debts were based on guarantees or accommodations made by the decedent, which raised the question whether the decedent was liable to make good on those debts and again postmortem events were treated as relevant. In several of these situations the decedent cosigned for loans received by partnerships or corporations as the primary debtors and deductions claimed for those debts were denied because the decedent's estate was not the primary borrower and had not been required to make good on the decedent's guarantees.

Increasing the uncertainty generated by these distinctions is the government's own uneven approach to the entire issue of postmortem facts for inclusion valuation or for deduction valuation purposes. For example, a claim against another at the time of the decedent's death is includible in the decedent's gross estate at a value determined according to the facts that exist at death. Yet the *Gowetz* court (in a decision reproduced at page 587) suggested that facts occurring after death may be considered to a limited extent in determining the deduction allowable for a claim *against* a decedent's estate. Is there a justification — either in statutory language or in policy, or in both — for adopting a different rule for the deduction of claims against a decedent's estate? See generally Committee Report, *Estate Tax Deductions for Claims*, 9 REAL PROP., PROB. & TR. J. 492 (1974).

The decedent in TAM 9321004 guaranteed a lease for a wholly owned corporation. When the decedent died the corporation was solvent and not in default on the lease, but it failed after the decedent's death and the landlord timely filed a claim against the estate to collect on the guarantee. The claim was allowed by the local probate court and payments were made by the estate, raising the question whether a §2053(a)(3) deduction was available notwithstanding that there was no more than a contingent or unmatured possibility of a claim at the date of death. The government advised that the postmortem payments were a legitimate indicator of the answer to that question and a deduction was allowed for the amount paid after death. In theory, the amount deductible should be the value of the liability as of the date of death, which need not match either the amount owed or actually paid. In practice, the amount paid in an arm's length dispute is likely to be the best indicator of the value of the claim as well as the likelihood of its being asserted. If the deduction had been disallowed in this case, another alternative available to the estate to reflect this contingent liability was to reflect it in valuing the corporate stock.

The courts have not been totally consistent either. For example, Estate of Sachs v. Commissioner, 856 F.2d 1158 (8th Cir. 1988), *aff'g in part and rev'g in part* 88 T.C. 769 (1987), is the converse of these cases. After the decedent's death but before the decedent's personal representative filed the estate tax return, the Sachs estate paid income tax on the basis of the United States Supreme Court decision in Diedrich v. Commissioner, 457 U.S. 191 (1982), and claimed that payment as a §2053(a)(3) deductible debt of the decedent. Two years later, Congress adopted legislation limiting *Diedrich* to only a prospective application, which generated a refund of the estate's previously paid income tax. The estate argued and the Tax Court agreed that, because valuation is determined as of the date of death, deductibility under §2053 also should be based on the facts and circumstances that exist at that time. The court on appeal rejected this argument on the ground that valuation and deduction are different, noting that some §2053 deductions do not even exist as of death — such as funeral expenses and expenses of administration. In this respect the court's logic was sound. The court also stated that "a federal statute which dissolves a tax obligation changes the law which imposed the estate's liability in the first place, and does so, as a practical matter, with retroactive effect," 856 F.2d 1162. The court quoted its much earlier decision in Jacobs v. Commissioner, 34 F.2d 233, 235 (8th Cir. 1929), which said:

The claims which Congress intended to be deducted were actual claims, not theoretical ones. . . . It was . . . claims presented and allowed or otherwise determined as valid against the estate and actually paid or to be paid that Congress had in mind, when it provided for the deduction from the gross estate . . . .

34 F.2d at 235. Thus, the court determined that, if "subsequent events establish that money deducted under §2053(a)(3) does indeed belong to the estate, there is no legislative purpose . . . to preserve the fiction of the testator's original" indebtedness. 856 F.2d at 1162. Unstated by the court was when a redetermination of deductibility based on subsequent events will be foreclosed: when the estate tax return is filed, when a closing letter is issued, when the statute of limitation expires, or at some other time. How would you answer that question? As they say, the postmortem facts imbroglio is a quintessential slippery slope. Would an absolute hard and fast rule be preferable for inclusion and deduction purposes? If so, which hard and fast rule should apply?

As long as we're talking about valuation, consider the taxpayer's dilemma in the following case:

Gowetz v. Commissioner
320 F.2d 874 (1st Cir. 1963)

ALDRICH, J.: The question raised in this petition to review a decision of the Tax Court is what deduction may be made from the gross estate of a Massachusetts decedent because of an obligation to pay alimony to his former wife. Prior to a divorce the decedent had entered into a separation agreement to pay $500 a month to his wife for life as long as she remained unmarried. It was not expressly stated that the obligation would continue after the husband's death. The ensuing divorce decree did not in terms incorporate the agreement, but notice was taken thereof and no independent financial provision was made for the wife.[10] In the estate tax return the executors, present petitioners, claimed a deduction in a sizable amount because of the future requirements of the agreement. It is conceded that their figure was supported by accepted actuarial tables as being the fair discounted value, as of the date of decedent's death, of an obligation to pay $500 a month to a woman of the former wife's then age for life or until she

---

10.   The government has not contended that the claim is founded on an agreement and to any extent lacked consideration in money or money's worth. See §§2043(b), 2053(c)(1)(A); Rev. Rul. 60-160, 1960-1 C.B. 374, *modifying* E.T. 19, 1946-2 C.B. 166; cf. Harris v. Commissioner, 340 U.S. 106 (1950); McMurtry v. Commissioner, 203 F.2d 659 (1st Cir. 1953). We are not to be taken as ruling that this was a necessary concession.

remarried. At the same time, vis-a-vis the former wife, they denied all liability, and resisted suit in the state court. No Massachusetts case had passed on the precise question and we accept the executor's assertion that they believed in good faith that there was a reasonable possibility that their defense would be successful. During the pendency of that suit the wife remarried. This, of course, terminated any future rights, and in effect reduced the estate's maximum obligation for monthly payments to a much lower figure than the one indicated by the actuarial tables. Thereafter the executors lost the state court suit, Taylor v. Gowetz, 339 Mass. 294 (1953). The Commissioner limited the deduction to the amount actually payable, and the Tax Court sustained that determination.

Expressly rejecting the broad arguments the government now urges, the Tax Court stated that the executors' total asserted deduction would have been proper . . . had it not been for the fact that the estate's liability was contested. . . . In its opinion the court distinguished uncontested claims with respect to which the amount eventually payable could be approximated by the use of actuarial tables, and "disputed," "contingent" and "potential" claims not so measurable. It described the present claim prior to the final state court decision as "contingent," but rather than saying that initially the deduction was not allowable because it had not been determined that anything would ever be paid, it concluded that until the state court had acted "[t]he value of the claim for deduction purposes was not reasonably ascertainable."

Although we agree with its result we do not altogether adopt the court's reasoning. We question whether, viewing the claim as of the date of death, its value as a claim was necessarily unascertainable. Even a disputed claim may have a value, to which lawyers who settle cases every day may well testify, fully as measurable as the possible future amounts that may eventually accrue on an uncontested claim. If the court was to rest its decision on ascertainable value we think it would have been more appropriate to point out that the executors failed to ascertain it for the reason that in taking a figure based on actuarial tables only, with no allowance for the fact that liability was contested, they made a totally unrealistic appraisal. Obviously a disputed claim is of less value than one which is uncontested.[11]

The executors are on the horns of a dilemma. If they are correct in saying that Ithaca Trust Co. v. United States, 279 U.S. 151 (1929),

---

11.   As the court said in Ithaca Trust Co. v. United States, 279 U.S. 151, 155 (1929), "[T]he value of property at a given time depends upon the relative intensity of the social desire for it at that time, expressed in the money that it would bring in the market."

requires the claim to be valued as of the date of death irrespective of future events, they have failed to prove its then value. If they wish to relax that principle to the extent of looking to subsequent events to eliminate the question of liability, they cannot object to the government's looking at least that far into the future to remove the other uncertainty.

We need decide no more. At the same time we must observe that the executors' basic position appears in conflict with the statutory scheme, which has frequently been construed to encompass after events rather than to require valuation as of date of death. See, e.g., Commissioner v. State Street Trust Co., 128 F.2d 618 (1st Cir. 1942); Commissioner v. Estate of Shively, 276 F.2d 372 (2d Cir. 1960); Jacobs v. Commissioner, 34 F.2d 233 (8th Cir. 1929), Estate of Metcalf v. Commissioner, 7 T.C. 153 (1946). How far into the future it may be appropriate to go we need not determine.

Judgment will be entered affirming the decision of the Tax Court.

Accord, Estate of Chesterton v. United States, 551 F.2d 278 (Ct. Cl. 1977). Compare the decisions in *Gowetz* and *Hagmann* with *Ithaca Trust*.

9.   *Unpaid Gift Tax.* The government is a creditor of a decedent's estate if the decedent made a gift prior to death but did not pay the gift tax before death. The entire unpaid gift tax is deductible, even if the decedent's spouse elected "split gift" treatment under §2513. Treas. Reg. §20.2053-6(d). Split gift treatment means that half of the gifts made by either or both spouses is treated as made by each spouse and the other half of such gifts is deemed to have been made by the other spouse. See Part D of Chapter 14. If the decedent's spouse made a gift prior to the decedent's death that the decedent's personal representative consented to split, the decedent's resulting gift tax liability for the half of the gift treated as made by the decedent is not deductible, because the decedent had no liability for the gift tax at the time of death. Proesel v. United States, 585 F.2d 295 (7th Cir. 1978) (the fact that the decedent's will authorized her personal representative to consent to split gift treatment did not alter the fact that the decedent was not liable at death).

Under Treas. Reg. §20.2053-6(d), a deduction is available only to the extent the government enforces gift tax liability against the decedent's estate and the estate has no effective contribution right against the donor spouse. Would the decedent's share of the unpaid gift tax qualify as a §2053(a)(3) deduction if the decedent in *Proesel* had consented to split gift treatment prior to death? A decedent's agreement to pay any liability is deductible only to the extent supported by adequate and full consideration in money or money's worth. Would a liability for gift tax, assumed voluntarily, be deductible? The result embraced by the government is that the liability is deductible to the extent paid and there is no enforceable contribution right.

See also Rev. Rul. 78-271, which disallowed a deduction for a surviving spouse's claim for compensation for full time services provided to the decedent's sole proprietorship prior to the decedent's death. Under applicable local law, a married person could not collect for services rendered to the spouse's business in the absence of a bona fide compensation agreement. In effect, the services of one spouse to the other's business were presumed to be gratuitous. Because the surviving spouse's claim was not enforceable under local law, it did not represent a personal obligation of the decedent at the time of death and was not deductible.

10.   *Enforceability.* In Rev. Rul. 75-24, a valid and enforceable claim was informally presented to a personal representative and paid with the approval of the estate's beneficiaries. The claim was not allowable under local law because the creditor failed to present it in accordance with the statutory requirements, but the beneficiaries' consent immunized the personal representative from the risk of a surcharge for paying the claim without proper presentment. The government allowed the deduction because the law should not require persons to do a vain act; there was no need for the probate court to approve the payment because the personal representative was protected by the beneficiaries' consent.

11.   *Decedent's Personal Obligation.* A §2053(d) deduction is allowed for unpaid mortgages or indebtedness on property included in the decedent's gross estate to the extent the full value of the encumbered property (and not merely the decedent's equity interest therein) is included in the gross estate for estate tax purposes. The value of included property is not reduced by a mortgage or debt thereon if the decedent was personally liable to pay the debt at the time of death. Alternatively, with respect to nonrecourse debt on which the decedent had no personal liability, only the equity interest in the property is included in the gross estate and no deduction is allowed for the debt. A decedent is considered personally liable for a debt if the creditor could obtain a deficiency judgment against the decedent following a sale of the property that produces insufficient proceeds to satisfy the debt. See Treas. Reg. §20.2053-7; Estate of Fawcett v. Commissioner, 64 T.C. 889 (1975), *acq.*

There is a difference in certain very limited circumstances between (1) including the entire value of mortgaged property in the decedent's gross estate and then allowing a deduction for the mortgage, and (2) including only the decedent's equity of redemption in the gross estate. Although the *taxable* estate will be the same in most cases (it was not in Estate of Fung v. Commissioner, 82 T.C.M. (CCH) 4244 (2001), due to §2106(a)(1)), the size of the *gross* estate may affect items such as the amount of the foreign death tax credit allowed to the estate under §2014 or qualification for certain entitlements such as §2032A special use valuation or §6166 deferred payment of estate tax.

Personal obligation is a concept explored by the following Ruling:

Revenue Ruling 76-113

... Under the terms of a decree of divorce by a court with power under local law to decree a settlement of all marital property rights, the decedent was required to name the decedent's spouse as beneficiary of certain life insurance policies on the decedent's life. The decedent was also required to maintain and keep the policies in full force and effect with all premiums until death. After death, the proceeds were paid directly to the decedent's former spouse by the insurance company in conformity with the terms of the insurance contracts and never became part of the probate estate in the hands of the decedent's executor. However, as the possibility existed that the policy proceeds might return to the decedent or the decedent's estate or be subject to a power of disposition by the decedent if the former spouse should either die or remarry prior to the decedent's death, the decedent held a reversionary interest that exceeded 5% of the value of the policies immediately before death. This reversionary interest was an incident of ownership in the policies and, accordingly, the value of the proceeds is includible in the decedent's gross estate under §2042(2). ...

The divorce court in this case, pursuant to local law, determined property rights in the insurance proceeds. The former spouse was, by the terms of the divorce decree, ensured the status of a beneficiary of the insurance proceeds and possessed all the property rights attendant upon that status. However, the decedent was not personally obligated to provide the former spouse with funds in the amount of the face value of the insurance. The decedent's only obligation was to keep the policies in full force and effect with all premiums paid for as long as the former spouse should live and remain unmarried. The decedent in fact discharged this obligation with the result that no obligation survived the decedent's death.

Therefore, no deduction is allowable under §2053(a)(3) for the amount of proceeds of insurance on the life of the decedent paid to the decedent's divorced spouse.

This is to be distinguished from the case where the divorce decree provided for the payment, upon the decedent's death, to the decedent's former spouse of a specific sum of money and the decedent provided funds therefor by the purchase of life insurance. In such a case, the payment of the required amount would be a personal obligation of the decedent and, should the insurance company be unable to meet its obligation, would be payable from the decedent's estate. Thus, the payment to the decedent's former spouse would be deductible from the decedent's gross estate under §2053(a)(3).

In the present case, the payment of insurance proceeds to the former spouse represents the satisfaction of an indebtedness created in settlement of the decedent's marital obligations. Since the insurance proceeds are includible in the decedent's gross estate at full value (by reason of the decedent's reversionary interest in the proceeds of the policy), the obligation to pay the proceeds to the decedent's former spouse is an indebtedness against property included in the value of the gross estate for purposes of §2053(a)(4).

Accordingly, in the present case, since the insurance proceeds were payable pursuant to a divorce decree issued by a court having the power to decree a settlement of all marital property rights, a deduction is allowable under §2053(a)(4).

Rev. Rul. 76-113 was promulgated after the Tax Court adopted an identical position in Robinson v. Commissioner, 63 T.C. 717 (1975). The government in *Robinson* argued that the limitation in §2053(c)(1)(A) was applicable because the express statutory provision in §2043(b) meant the decedent's debt to the surviving spouse was not founded on a promise for adequate and full consideration in money or money's worth. The Tax Court rejected this contention and, because it is not mentioned in Rev. Rul. 76-113, it appears that the government has abandoned it. Because the obligation is under a decree it is not subject to the §2053(c)(1)(A) requirement. See Rev. Rul. 75-395; *Harris v. Commissioner*, reproduced at page 841; Rev. Rul. 60-160; Gray v. United States, 541 F.2d 228 (9th Cir. 1976) (*Gray*).

If a divorce court approves a separation agreement, the provisions adopted by the court for transfers of property or the designation of one spouse as the beneficiary of life insurance will be deemed to be supported by adequate and full consideration in money or money's worth, provided that the divorce court had the power to alter the terms of the agreement. See, e.g., Rev. Rul. 75-395; *Gray*; Estate of Fenton v. Commissioner, 70 T.C. 263 (1978) (*Fenton*). If the court lacked the power to alter the terms of the separation agreement, transfers of property or the payment of insurance proceeds can qualify as deductible debts under §2053 if the surviving spouse relinquished support rights as consideration for those provisions, to the extent the value of the released support rights was equal to the value of rights obtained by the surviving spouse under the agreement. See, e.g., *Fenton* and *Gray*, 440 F. Supp. 684 (C.D. Cal. 1977), on remand from 541 F.2d 228 (9th Cir. 1976). With respect to transfers incident to divorce, see also §2516 (discussed in Chapter 14), and §2043(b)(2).

Assume that *D* and *S* executed a separation agreement under which *D* agreed to maintain $50,000 of insurance on D's life, payable to *A* and *B* (the minor children of *D* and *S*) as beneficiaries of the policy until the youngest child attained the age of 18 years, after which *D* could name whomever D wished as beneficiary. The separation agreement was incorporated in the divorce court's decree and *D* and *S* were divorced within two years after entering into the agreement. *D* died five years later and the proceeds of the policy were paid to *A* and *B*, neither of whom had attained 18. The full amount of the policy proceeds was included in *D*'s gross estate because *D* possessed incidents of ownership in the policy. See Chapter 8. Rev. Rul. 78-379 (involving similar facts) determined that no deduction was allowable to *D*'s estate for the proceeds paid to the children because there was no consideration in money or money's worth for *D*'s promise; *S*'s support rights were satisfied by other transfers, these proceeds were not transferred to *S* (so §2516, even if it had been in the Code at the time, would not have been applicable), and *D*'s obligation to support *A* and *B* terminated on *D*'s death. The government further ruled that incorporation of the agreement in the divorce court's decree did not qualify payment of the proceeds to the children as a deductible item, stating:

[I]t has been held that where a divorce court has authority to adjudicate all marital property rights or to vary the terms of the prior property settlement and the court incorporates the agreement in the divorce decree, an indebtedness arising out of the settlement is not based on a promise or agreement but on the divorce decree. Rev. Rul. 60-160, 1960-1 C.B. 376; Harris v. Commissioner, 340 U.S. 106 (1950); Rev. Rul. 76-113, 1976-1 C.B. 276. However, the rule in Rev. Rul. 60-160 and *Harris* applies only to obligations incurred with respect to adjudications of marital rights between spouses and does not extend to provisions in a divorce decree requiring payments to children. See Estate of Keller v. Commissioner, 44 T.C. 851 (1965).

Such payments to children, if required to be made after the death of the decedent, are generally in the nature of testamentary dispositions. In addition, the fact that the promise or court order to provide for children may be enforceable by them does not necessarily mean that it is based on adequate consideration. Lovering v. Commissioner, 318 F. Supp. 215 (S.D.N.Y. 1970). However, an indebtedness arising out of a divorce decree ordering payments to children upon the decedent's death is not regarded as testamentary in nature when the indebtedness is based upon an agreement between the parties to the divorce and the payments were contracted for a full and adequate consideration. Rosenthal v. Commissioner, 205 F.2d 505 (2d Cir. 1953). . . .

Since the spouse's support rights were surrendered for a lump sum payment of equal value and the provisions for child support were consistent with the decedent's legal obligation, that portion of the agreement that provided for payment of the insurance policy proceeds to minor children was not contracted for a consideration in money's worth. Consequently, even if the divorce decree was in accordance with state law in requiring the decedent to provide for a transfer of property to the decedent's children at death, the maintenance of the life insurance policy was a testamentary disposition since it was neither in satisfaction of a legal duty to support the children nor contracted for a full and adequate consideration.

Accordingly, the value of the life insurance payable to the decedent's minor children is not deductible from the decedent's gross estate under §2053.

Because the agreement was incorporated in a decree of a court having the power to alter its terms, why should it matter whether the recipient of the insurance proceeds is someone other than the spouse? Even though the transfer is a product of the court's decree rather than of the spouse's voluntary agreement, *Estate of Keller v. Commissioner* stated that the "'divorce as consideration' theory" does not extend to transfers to a person who is not the spouse of the transferor. 44 T.C. at 859. See *Bank of New York v. United States*, reproduced at page 595.

12.   *Will Contracts.* A promised bequest in exchange for services rendered to the decedent is deductible as a debt to the extent the services constituted adequate and full consideration in money or money's worth. The amount received by the promisee is gross income for income tax purposes to the same extent. In Wolder v. Commissioner, 493 F.2d 608 (2d Cir. 1974), the decedent bequeathed certain stocks to an attorney in exchange for legal services. How would the tax consequences have differed if, when the legal services were rendered, the decedent had given the attorney a remainder interest in the stocks and retained a life estate therein, triggering §2036(a)(1) at death? Could the decedent have conditioned the attorney's remainder interest on continued performance of legal services for the decedent's remaining life?

If a decedent breaches a promise to bequeath certain property to a natural object of the decedent's bounty and if the promisee enforces the contract against the decedent's estate, will the estate tax deductibility of the promisee's claim turn solely upon whether the promise was given in exchange for adequate and full consideration in money or money's worth? This question arises frequently in connection with divorce settlements by which a divorced spouse promises to bequeath property to the couple's children. As noted below, it arises in other contexts as well. In *Bank of New*

York, the court adopted an additional requirement for deductibility — that the claim be founded on an agreement on which the parties had bargained at arm's length.

Bank of New York v. United States
526 F.2d 1012 (3d Cir. 1975)

ADAMS, J.: . . . This appeal poses the question whether the cost to an estate of settling a claim set forth in a lawsuit brought by third-party donee beneficiaries and grounded on an alleged breach of contract to make mutual and reciprocal wills qualifies as a deductible claim under §2053 when the sole consideration supporting the contract passed between friendly spouses.

The genesis of this appeal is to be found in wills executed over twenty-five years ago by Manuel E. and Ellen G. Rionda. The Riondas were husband and wife, with no children. In 1948, when Mrs. Rionda had assets of at least $400,000 and Mr. Rionda had assets of at least $600,000, they each executed a will.

Mr. Rionda's will, dated May 14, 1948, left his entire estate to Mrs. Rionda, but provided that if she predeceased him, half of his personal effects, specified real estate and stocks, and 24 per cent of his residuary estate should pass to Enrique Ervesun, his second cousin. Further, in that event, 14 per cent of the residuary estate was to go to Mary Ellen Baldwin, the daughter of a family employee.

Mrs. Rionda's will, dated June 2, 1948, was substantially similar. It left her entire estate to Mr. Rionda, but provided, should Mr. Rionda predecease her, for dispositions to Mr. Ervesun, Mrs. Baldwin, and to other legatees identical to the dispositions in Mr. Rionda's will.

When Mr. Rionda died in 1950, his estate of more than $515,000 passed to Mrs. Rionda in accordance with his will of May 14, 1948. Thereafter, however, Mrs. Rionda executed several more wills and codicils before she died in 1966. Her last will was dated August 1, 1963, and was significantly different in its terms from her 1948 will. The primary beneficiaries of her 1963 will were Mrs. Rionda's physician, Dr. John J. Bolton, and his family. Mr. Ervesun was left $5,000 and Mrs. Baldwin was left nothing.

Presumably because they did not have standing as heirs, neither Mr. Ervesun nor Mrs. Baldwin filed a caveat to the probate of Mrs. Rionda's will or appealed from its probate. Each of them, however, swiftly brought suit against Mrs. Rionda's estate in the Chancery Division of the New Jersey Superior Court and these suits were consolidated. The complaints alleged: (a) that in 1948

Mr. and Mrs. Rionda had entered into a contract to make mutual and reciprocal wills, each devising substantially all of his estate to the survivor, who was in turn to leave his estate to certain legatees, including Mr. Ervesun and Mrs. Baldwin; (b) that Mrs. Rionda had not devised her estate in accordance with the agreement; and (c) that, consequently, Mrs. Rionda's estate was liable to Mr. Ervesun and Mrs. Baldwin, as third-party beneficiaries, for Mrs. Rionda's breach of the contract to make mutual and reciprocal wills.

The lawsuit was vigorously contested. Then, in 1968 Mr. Ervesun and Mrs. Baldwin filed a second suit in New Jersey Superior Court against the estate, the Boltons, and the Bank of New York as executor, alleging fraud, duress, undue influence, and tortious interference with contract rights.

Trial on the breach of contract action began on September 17, 1968 and was settled the next day, along with the other suit. The settlement provided that Mrs. Rionda's estate would pay $250,000 to the complainants: two-thirds to go to Mr. Ervesun and one-third to Mrs. Baldwin. They, in turn, agreed to release all their claims against the estate and the Boltons, including Mr. Ervesun's $5,000 legacy under the 1963 will.

Having made payment to Mr. Ervesun and Mrs. Baldwin under the terms of the settlement, Mrs. Rionda's estate filed a claim in April 1970 for the refund of estate taxes. The estate had paid taxes in excess of $800,000, and sought a refund of more than $100,000 on the basis of the settlement achieved in connection with the claim that had been asserted against the estate. The claim of the estate was disallowed by the District Director of the Internal Revenue Service, and on January 10, 1972, the estate brought this suit for a refund in the district court. Both the estate and the government moved for summary judgment.

The district judge ruled in favor of the estate, finding that the claim was deductible under §2053(a) of the Internal Revenue Code or that, in the alternative, the sum of $250,000 was not includible in the gross estate of Mrs. Rionda. The government has appealed from the judgment of the district court. We reverse. . . .

In our view of the matter, the pivotal issue in this appeal is whether the consideration that supported the claims against Mrs. Rionda's estate satisfied the requirements of the Internal Revenue Code. Section 2053 permits the deduction of claims against the estate, subject to the limitations that claims bottomed on promises or agreements must be "contracted bona fide and for an adequate and full consideration in money or money's worth." It is our conclusion that the claims paid by the estate in this case, even if supported by consideration adequate to make them enforceable

under the law of New Jersey, do not meet the statutory requirements for a deduction under §2053. Because we decide this issue
in favor of the government, we do not address the government's
other contention that the consideration must have proceeded from
the claimants to the decedent to satisfy the requirements of the
Code.

The claims against the estate advanced by Mr. Ervesun and
Mrs. Baldwin were based on Mrs. Rionda's alleged agreement with
her husband to make mutual and reciprocal wills. The government
does not deny that the claims were colorable. Rather, the issue
between the government and the estate is whether the
consideration underlying the agreement was "adequate and full"
and "in money or money's worth."

The estate contends that the same consideration on which a
New Jersey court would rely to declare Mrs. Rionda's agreement
with her husband to make mutual wills enforceable was "adequate
and full consideration in money or money's worth" as required by
the Code. We need not rest our decision on an interpretation of the
New Jersey law regarding consideration in mutual wills. To decide
this appeal, the Court must look to the federal law of estate
taxation.

One purpose of the consideration provisions of §2053 is to
prevent the depletion of the estate for estate tax purposes by
transfers couched in contractual form but serving a donative intent.
Transactions among members of a family have been particularly
subject to scrutiny in this regard, even when they have been
supported by monetary consideration. Although there are no cases
squarely on point, an examination of the decisions, including those
in cognate areas of tax law, permits the inference that the value of
the claim settled by the estate may not be deducted if the
agreement on which the claim was based was not bargained at
arm's length.

The authorities upholding the deductibility of claims against the
estate appear to involve the sort of agreements that arise between
parties separated by divergent interests. The clearest cases are
those . . . which deal with settlements between estranged spouses.
It is reasonable to assume that each element of the agreement in
such situations contains advantages bargained for by concessions
on other matters, so that the final accord reflects a trade-off
between the rights of each party. Even a family agreement,
although achieved without apparent bitterness, has been regarded
as bargained for when members of the family had interests contrary to those of other members of the family. Where legal rights of
family members are in conflict, each member may have to surren-

der rights he would otherwise keep in order to secure rights that he wishes to obtain. To classify this sort of family arrangement as an arm's-length bargain seems within the compass of reasonableness.

That type of bargained-for arrangement among contending family members is substantially different from the situation with which we are dealing in this case. It would appear that Mr. and Mrs. Rionda were of one mind when they made their mutual wills; they agreed that the estate of the first to die should go to the survivor and then to certain specified legatees. The purpose of their mutual wills was simply to make the ultimate disposition of the property in effect irrevocable, which was to the advantage of each of them. There is nothing in the record to support a finding that the mutual wills here were executed as the result of an arm's-length bargain of any sort.

When the interests of family members are not divergent, but coincide so that the elements of a transaction advance the separate concerns of each, we are unable to find the arm's-length bargain mandated by the Code. This Court has adhered to the distinction between family arrangements bargained for at arm's length and family arrangements that reflect a community of interests. Tax advantages are not permitted when an agreement between members of a family could be regarded as a cooperative attempt to make a testamentary disposition rather than as an arm's-length bargain.

To effectuate the policy underlying the federal estate tax requires that courts look beneath the surface of transactions to discover the essential character of each transfer. Even where a claim is ultimately satisfied by the operation of law, the courts will determine the nature of the claim for federal tax purposes by examining the particular status of the claimant that enabled him to impose his claim on the estate.

In this case the initial intention of both Mr. and Mrs. Rionda was to make a gift, first to the survivor of them, but ultimately to certain third parties. Without an arm's-length bargain and absent consideration in money or money's worth, Mr. and Mrs. Rionda entered into a mutual will arrangement to make those gifts secure. That Mrs. Rionda may have been obliged by New Jersey law to carry out her original intention, despite her change of mind, does not alter the nature of her original intention. Mr. Ervesun and Mrs. Baldwin were required to proceed by an action at law in order to secure recovery, but there can be no doubt that the basis of their claims was the friendly agreement between Mr. and Mrs. Rionda to make a gift, and the status of Mr. Ervesun and Mrs. Baldwin under the agreement was that of donees. The policy of §2053 is to deny a deduction where the underlying transaction was "essentially donative in character."

Although there is no reason to suspect that the original intent of the Riondas, or that the final intention of Mrs. Rionda, was to establish a situation permitting the evasion of estate taxes, to sanction a deduction in this type of case could encourage tax avoidance. Some persons might be tempted to renege on irrevocable mutual wills in the hope that their intended beneficiaries would then take as claimants rather than as heirs, to the tax advantage of the estate.

Two issues remain in this appeal, but they do not require extensive commentary.

The estate has defended the deductibility of the claims on the alternative basis of Treas. Reg. §20.2053-4. That regulation provides, inter alia, that: "Liabilities imposed by law or arising out of torts are deductible." The estate reasons that Mrs. Rionda did not propose, at the time of her death, to make a gift to Mr. Ervesun and Mrs. Baldwin; the amounts paid to them by the estate were in settlement of a contested lawsuit; thus the claims were imposed by law and deductible under §20.2053-4. Such reliance on the regulation is misplaced.

If the deduction of the claim against the estate cannot be upheld on the basis of the statute, it cannot be upheld on the basis of the Treasury Regulation promulgated pursuant to that statute. Treasury Regulations must be interpreted in the context of the statute they are designed to explicate; "there is no power to amend [a statute] by regulation."

Section 20.2053-4 is itself quite explicit that claims founded on a promise or on an agreement are limited to the extent that the liability was "contracted bona fide and for an adequate and full consideration in money or money's worth," a provision identical to that in the statute. The subsequent sentence, on which the estate would rely, must be taken to refer to claims imposed by law other than those founded on promise or agreement.[12] As such, it is inapposite in the circumstances in this case.

---

12. This distinction of obligations arising from promises and agreements and other obligations imposed by law is confirmed by the legislative history of the limitation of §2053. That limitation was described as a clarifying provision limiting the consideration requirement to "liabilities founded on contract." This was regarded as necessary to avoid the erroneous interpretation that all claims, even if imposed by law or arising out of torts, must be supported by adequate and full consideration.

See H.R. Rep. No. 708, 72d Cong., 1st Sess. 48 (1931) (reprinted in 1939-1 C.B. (Part 2) 457, 491); S. Rep. No. 665, 72d Cong., 1st Sess. 51 (1931) (reprinted in 1939-1 C.B. (Part 2) 496, 533).

A final ground put forth by the estate for upholding the judgment of the district court is that Mrs. Rionda's power over the property received from the estate of Mr. Rionda, the unconsumed portion of which she was obligated to pass on to Mr. Ervesun and Mrs. Baldwin, was not sufficient to warrant its inclusion in the gross estate.

Whatever its merit, this rationale is not available to the taxpayer in the present proceeding. It has been established that "in the absence of a waiver by the government . . . or a proper amendment, petitioner [will be] precluded . . . from resting its claim on another ground [as distinguished from those advanced in the claim for refund]." An examination of the original claim in this case reveals that the estate asserted entitlement to a "deduction of $250,000 . . . in determining the taxable estate for the purposes of the federal estate tax."

A mere reference to the taxable estate is not sufficient to advance a claim regarding the calculation of the gross estate. Moreover, a claim for a refund based on a deduction would appear to concede that the amount in question was a part of the gross estate. No theory regarding the size of the gross estate was set forth in any way in the refund claim. That being so, there cannot now be used to support an order permitting a refund a theory based on the recalculation of the gross estate.

Accordingly, the judgment of the district court will be reversed.

See also *Luce v. United States*, 444 F. Supp. 347 (W.D. Mo. 1977). Compare Rev. Rul. 78-379; *Estate of Keller v. Commissioner*, 44 T.C. 851 (1965).

Chapter 11

THE ESTATE TAX MARITAL DEDUCTION

PART A.   HISTORY, PURPOSE, AND STRATEGIC USE OF THE MARITAL DEDUCTION

Code References: *Estate Tax: §§ 2032, 2044 2056, 2207A*
Gift Tax: §§2518, 2519
Income Tax: §§642(g), 678, 1014

Section 2056 permits a deduction of the estate tax value of property included in a decedent's gross estate that passes from the decedent to the decedent's surviving spouse. Originally, §2056 imposed a statutory cap on the amount that could be deducted, but that cap was removed in 1981.[1] Similarly, an unlimited gift tax marital deduction is allowable for gifts from one spouse to the other if the gift complies with the requirements of §2523, as discussed in Chapter 14. Coupled with §1041 for income tax purposes the federal tax law essentially makes transfers between spouses tax neutral (the one exception being §1014 new basis even if no estate tax is incurred — otherwise spouses are treated as a single economic unit for all these tax purposes).

---

1. For decedents dying before 1977, the cap was an amount equal to half the value of the decedent's adjusted gross estate. From 1977 through 1981 the marital deduction was capped at the greater of $250,000 or half the value of the decedent's adjusted gross estate. The "adjusted gross estate" is a tax concept that no longer applies to the marital deduction but is still employed in sporadic other places, like in §§6166(a)(1) and 6166(b)(6). In general, with a few modifications, the adjusted gross estate was defined as the value of a decedent's gross estate (as determined for estate tax purposes) reduced by the aggregate amount of deductions allowed by §§2053 (expenses, debts, and taxes) and 2054 (casualty and theft losses). ERTA'81 eliminated the cap on the amount deductible, effective (generally speaking) for estates of decedents dying after 1981.

1. *Origin of the Marital Deduction.* The original purpose of the marital deduction (when enacted in 1948) was to grant married citizens of noncommunity property law states tax treatment similar to that accorded to married citizens of community property states. The ceiling originally placed on the amount deductible — half the value of the decedent's adjusted gross estate — was a key ingredient in achieving this objective.

Prior to 1942, the progressive tax rates of the federal estate, gift, and income tax laws worked to give the married citizens of community property states generally more favorable treatment than the married citizens of noncommunity property law states. The operation of the property laws differ among the nine "legitimate" community property states,[2] but in most of those states the spouses are treated as equal owners of their community property. The federal tax laws contained no provisions dealing specifically with community property, and the property system in each state controlled the application of the federal tax laws. Thus, in general, community property couples were treated for tax purposes as if each spouse owned half of their community property separately; half of their community earnings was taxed to each spouse for income tax purposes; only half of their community property was includible on the death of either spouse for estate tax purposes; a transfer of community property to the sole ownership of either spouse was deemed a gift of half the value of the property by the other spouse; and community property given by the couple to a third party was deemed a gift of half made by each spouse.

There was no serious disparity in tax treatment as between couples in community property and noncommunity property jurisdictions if the spouses individually produced roughly the same amount of income and had amassed roughly the same amount of wealth. But this seldom occurs because, in most marriages, one spouse produces more income or amasses greater wealth than the other. The application of federal taxes to spouses with disparate income and wealth was unfair to citizens of the non-community property states because, under the progressive income, estate, and gift taxes, income of the primary income producer was taxed to that spouse alone, all of the wealthier spouse's property was subject to estate tax in that spouse's estate and, if the wealthier spouse made a gift to the poorer spouse or to a third party during life, the entire value of the transferred property would be subject to gift tax.

In 1942, Congress sought to mitigate this disparity by adopting an estate and a gift tax treatment of community property that is somewhat similar to the treatment accorded jointly held property. Because that legislation did not change the income tax treatment of community earnings, which was regarded as the most important tax advantage of residing in a

---

2.   Arizona, California, Idaho, Louisiana, Nevada, New Mexico, Texas, Washington, and Wisconsin. Alaska has a form of "voluntary community property" that has yet to be tested to determine whether it will be respected for its intended tax benefits.

community property state, citizens of the noncommunity property states continued to feel disadvantaged. Consequently, between 1942 and 1948, five noncommunity property states adopted a community property system and other states (including New York) were considering that move. Because Congress felt that the federal tax laws should not influence a state's selection of its property law, Congress repealed the 1942 legislation in 1948, returning the tax treatment of community property to the pre-1942 rules. At the same time, Congress adopted the estate and gift tax marital deductions, the split gift provision for gift tax purposes, and the split income provision for joint income tax returns — all aimed at granting citizens of noncommunity property states tax treatment similar to (but not identical with) that accorded to citizens of community property states.[3] The income tax provision is not a topic for this book, but the marital deduction and split gift provisions are central to our purposes. This chapter examines the estate tax marital deduction. The gift tax marital deduction and the split gift provision are taken up in Chapter 14.

2.   *The "Single-Unit" Theory of the Unlimited Marital Deduction.* In 1981 Congress removed the cap on the amount deductible. By necessity that change shifted the theory of the marital deduction. Without the cap, the theory of the marital deduction can no longer be to equalize the tax treatment of married couples in community and noncommunity property states. Instead, for spouses everywhere, the current theoretical basis for the deduction, stated succinctly by the Senate Finance Committee report accompanying ERTA'81, is that "a husband and wife should be treated as one economic unit for purposes of estate and gift taxes. . . . Accordingly, no tax should be imposed on transfers between a husband and wife." S. Rep. No. 144, 97th Cong., 1st Sess. 127 (1981). A correlated principle is that the wealth transfer tax *should* apply when property is transferred out of the marital unit, because the marital deduction should not permanently exempt qualified transfers from the transfer tax system. The wealth transfer tax imposed on the transfer is deferred until the property leaves the marital unit, which inevitably will occur no later than at the death of the surviving spouse.

Transitional Rule for Certain Pre-1981 Formula Bequests. In general, the unlimited marital deduction applies to the estates of decedents dying after 1981. A transitional rule prevents the removal of the cap from distorting a decedent's dispositive plan that was formulated with the old cap in mind. If you encounter a pre-1981 estate plan, be sure to

---

3. For a further discussion of the purposes of and the historical events leading to the enactment of these provisions, see generally H.R. Rep. No. 1274, 80th Cong., 2d Sess. 421-426 (1948), in 1948-1 Cum. Bull. 241, 243-244, 257-261; S. Rep. No. 1013, 80th Cong., 2d Sess. 26-29 (1948), in 1948-1 Cum. Bull. 285, 303-306.

inspect the transition rules elaborated upon in 3 Casner & Pennell, ESTATE PLANNING §13.0.3 (2002) or a similar resource.

3.   *Division of Marital Assets Between Spouses.*   A married couple has the ability to decide how much of their aggregate wealth to have taxed in the estate of the first spouse to die. If it is important to maximize the amount of assets passing to their ultimate beneficiaries when the surviving spouse dies, what allocation between their taxable estates will minimize the tax burden on their aggregate wealth? Putting it differently, what allocation between the spouses will permit the maximum amount of wealth to pass into the hands of their beneficiaries? Minimizing taxes (or maximizing the amount of wealth transferred to the beneficiaries) is only one factor in crafting an estate plan and, in many cases, considerations such as personal wishes of the parties, liquidity problems, and other concerns will take priority. Nevertheless, it is important to determine how the tax burden will fall under alternate plans so that an informed decision can be made.

A factor in determining the tax costs of alternative plans is that the §1014 (if it remains the law long enough — it is slated for repeal in 2010 when the estate tax is slated for repeal) new basis of property that is subject to estate tax on the death of a surviving spouse equals the estate tax value of that property: It will be "stepped-up" if the property has appreciated (or stepped down if investment value has been lost). The new basis may reduce gain or loss recognized on a subsequent disposition of that property and provide greater or smaller depreciation deductions for depreciable property that is included in the surviving spouse's gross estate. Moreover, there are psychological considerations in this planning, such as whether a surviving spouse's willingness to make inter vivos gifts will be influenced by the amount of property the spouse owns.

The principal question is whether to provide, on the death of the first spouse to die, for a marital deduction bequest of all of the decedent's property, an amount that will "equalize" the two estates or their respective tax brackets or burdens (notice that those concepts — equalizing estates, brackets, or tax burdens — are not likely to be the same unless the estate tax is a flat tax — such as after 2005 under the 2001 tax legislative changes), or the smallest amount necessary to reduce the decedent's taxable estate to the maximum level at which the least estate tax is payable (sometimes inaccurately called a "reduce-to-zero" provision). Another option is to leave nothing to the surviving spouse, although that may prompt the spouse to elect against the decedent's estate plan and take any statutory elective share that is provided under state law.

Formula Clause.   The idea of using a formula to define the amount passing to the decedent's surviving spouse — rather than a predetermined dollar amount — was spawned by the statutory cap on the amount deductible under pre-1982 law. Then, as now, deductible property passing from the decedent to the surviving spouse is effectively excluded from the decedent's taxable estate, but will be subject to estate taxation in the surviving spouse's gross estate (unless consumed in a manner that has no residual value at death). Before 1982, property passing to a surviving spouse that was not deductible because it exceeded the statutory cap "overqualified" the deduction and caused taxation in both the decedent's estate and the survivor's estate.[4] To avoid overqualification and double tax, many decedents imposed a ceiling on the marital bequest so that the amount passing to the surviving spouse would be no greater than the maximum allowable deduction. At the same time, to prevent "underqualification," the marital bequest would provide for no less than the maximum amount allowable. Before 1982 the favored way of avoiding overqualification and underqualification was to construct a formula marital bequest equal in value to the exact amount needed to provide the decedent with the *maximum marital deduction allowable* — no more, no less. Thus, the survivor's interest was determined by a stated formula, rather than by a specified dollar amount or a fixed percentage of the decedent's estate.

The formula amount needed to qualify the estate for the maximum marital deduction and no more could be stated in various ways, illustrated by the provisions enclosed in brackets in the following sample clause:

an amount equal to [the maximum amount allowable as a marital deduction for federal estate tax purposes] *(or)* [50% of my adjusted gross estate as finally determined for federal estate tax purposes], reduced by the value for federal estate tax purposes of all interests passing or having passed to my spouse outside of this provision to the extent that those interests qualify for the marital deduction.

Now that there is no statutory limit on the amount deductible, it is not possible to overqualify for the marital deduction, at least not in the sense of giving the surviving spouse a greater amount *than can be deducted*. It is still possible to overqualify, however, if the amount that could have been exempted (for example, by the unified credit or other deductions) is passed to the surviving spouse in a form that qualifies for the marital deduction and therefore causes inclusion in the surviving spouse's transfer tax base. It may be preferable to pass this amount — the nonmarital or "credit shelter" amount — in a manner that prevents inclusion in the surviving spouse's transfer tax base. This goal also can be achieved by using a formula

---

4. If the surviving spouse died within ten years after the decedent, the double tax incidence would be mitigated (or possibly eliminated) by the credit allowed under §2013 for previously taxed property.

bequest, often described in terms of the maximum amount that can pass to someone other than the surviving spouse without causing an increase in the decedent's federal estate tax.

My personal representative shall allocate to the Nonmarital Trust all assets available for distribution that would not qualify for the federal estate tax marital deduction if allocated to the Marital Deduction Trust, plus the largest pecuniary amount, if any, that will not thereby increase federal estate taxes payable by reason of my death. In determining the pecuniary amount my personal representative shall consider the credit or deduction for state death taxes allowable to my estate only to the extent those taxes are not thereby incurred or increased, shall assume that none of the Nonmarital Trust qualifies for a federal estate tax deduction, and shall assume that all of the Marital Trust hereafter established (including any part thereof disclaimed by S) qualifies for the federal estate tax marital deduction. My personal representative shall allocate to the Marital Trust the residue of my estate. It is my intent that the Marital Trust will qualify for the federal estate tax marital deduction and that it not exceed the smallest amount that would result in the least possible federal estate tax payable by reason of my death.

This form of planning often is referred to as "optimum" rather than "maximum" marital deduction planning. However, that terminology should not be taken literally. Dividing assets in a manner that provides a zero estate tax for the first spouse to die is not necessarily "optimal." The "optimum" division turns on a number of considerations, of which deferral of the estate tax and minimization of the aggregate death taxes on both estates are merely two among many factors to consider.

[*]A quiet note about gender references may be useful here: Throughout this chapter and in sample drafting provisions the first spouse to die or the donor spouse is referred to as D and the surviving spouse or the donee spouse is S, without making assumptions with respect to gender. Statistically, although husbands still are more likely to die first, the gender gap for mortality is shrinking and it likely will disappear entirely in your generation.

Now let's think about planning for a couple of situations. Assume D and S have aggregate estimated wealth of the amounts indicated below and that neither has made any previous taxable gifts. What amount should D leave to S for marital deduction purposes if tax minimization is their sole object?

Combined Estates

(a) Under the Applicable Exclusion Amount

(b) Between one and two times the Applicable Exclusion Amount

(c) Exceeding double the Applicable Exclusion Amount

How does the answer to this question depend on division of the combined assets between *D* and *S*? Would the ages and health of *D* and *S* matter? Consider the suitability of using an equalization clause as discussed beginning at page 710.

4.   *Basis of Deductible Property.* Under §1014, property that is included in *D*'s gross estate receives a basis equal to its federal estate tax value, even if the value of the property qualifies for the estate tax marital deduction. This may have the consequences — enhanced by removal of any limitation on the amount deductible under §2056 — of providing *D*'s personal representative with an incentive to inflate the value of gross estate assets and of providing the Internal Revenue Service with an incentive to reduce that value on the ground that it is excessive! In this connection, the §6662 "accuracy related penalty" must be taken into account. Under §6662(d) a penalty applies if a substantial overstatement of the value of a decedent's property reduces income tax (e.g., from new basis), just as §6662(g) imposes a penalty if a substantial understatement of the value of a decedent's property reduces estate or gift taxes.

5.   *Election for Deducting Administration Expenses.* The value of *D*'s gross estate at death in Year One was $3,000,000. *D* bequeathed this entire estate to *S*. Expenses of administering *D*'s gross estate paid in Year One totaled $30,000. *D*'s estate was closed and distributed on March 10 of Year Two. The estate earned income of $40,000 in Year One (meaning that the estate could use the entire $30,000 of deductions to offset taxable income). What §642(g) election would you recommend that *D*'s personal representative make concerning the administration expenses, and would your answer differ if *D* bequeathed only an optimum marital deduction amount to *S* (meaning that it reduces estate tax to zero and causes the balance of the estate to pass into the nonmarital trust) and left the residue in a discretionary trust for *S* for life, with remainder to *D*'s children by a former marriage (meaning that the remainder beneficiaries may be in conflict with the best interests of the current income beneficiary)? If you were drafting *D*'s will, what provision (if any) would you make concerning the §642(g) election? See generally Dobris, *Equitable Adjustments in Postmortem Income Tax Planning: An Unremitting Diet of* Warms, 65 IOWA L. REV. 103 (1979).

PART B.   QUALIFICATIONS FOR DEDUCTION

Code Reference: *Estate Tax: §2056*

6.   *Some Preliminary Requirements for Qualification.*

Citizenship.   Before 1988, no marital deduction was available unless *D* was a citizen or resident of the United States at the time of death.[5] Surprisingly, *S* was not required to be either a U.S. citizen or resident. Adoption of §§2056(d), 2106(a)(3), and 2523(i) changed both rules.[6] Now §2106(a)(3) allows a marital deduction for property situated in the U.S. that was owned by a nonresident who was not a U.S. citizen if it was included in that nonresident decedent's U.S. gross estate, provided that the other requirements of §2056 to qualify for the marital deduction are met. But no marital deduction is allowable if *S* is not a U.S. citizen unless the bequest is crafted to qualify as a qualified domestic trust (QDOT) under §§2056(d)(2) and 2056A, and no gift tax marital deduction is allowable at all if S is not a U.S. citizen (although the annual exclusion is ten-fold (indexed for inflation) under §2523(i)(2), with no special transfer requirements).

The Survivorship Requirement.   To qualify for an estate tax marital deduction, Treas. Reg. §20.2056(a)-1(b) requires that there be a *surviving* spouse and that property *pass* to that surviving spouse. Usually there is no difficulty in establishing either of these requirements. In some cases it may be difficult to determine which spouse died first, such as if a married couple die in a common accident. Actual survival for any period of time, no matter how brief, will suffice if it can be proven.

Nearly all states have enacted a version of the Uniform Simultaneous Death Act (USDA) to resolve cases of "simultaneous" deaths. The original USDA, promulgated in 1940 and revised slightly in 1953, provided that if there is no sufficient evidence of the order of two persons' death each decedent is deemed to have survived the other for purposes of distributing that person's estate. Thus, for example, if *H* and *W* are killed in a common accident, and there is no sufficient evidence of the order of their deaths, *H*'s

---

5.   See Treas. Reg. §20.2056(a)-1(a), subsequently amended. This was because §2056 allowed a marital deduction for the "purposes of the tax imposed by §2001," which applies a tax only to the transfer of an estate of a decedent who was a citizen or resident of the United States. The estate of a nonresident not a citizen is taxed, if at all, under §2101.

6.   Sections 5033(a)(1) and (c) of TAMRA'88, P.L. 100-647, 100th Cong. 2d Sess. (1988), applicable to decedents dying after November 10, 1988, and §5033(b), disallowing the gift tax marital deduction for gifts made after July 13, 1988, to spouses who are not citizens of the United States.

estate is distributed as if he survived W and W's estate is distributed as if she survived H. This gives a sensible result, because H's property goes to H's beneficiaries and W's property goes to W's beneficiaries, rather than the other way around. It also avoids probate of all their property twice.

The problem with the USDA is that it does not apply to near-simultaneous deaths. Thus, for example, if it could be established that H survived W by a few hours, or even by a few seconds, a carelessly drafted plan would cause W's property to pass to H's estate. Then H's estate, which would now include W's property, would go to H's beneficiaries. Nothing would go to W's beneficiaries.[7] To prevent this from happening, the revised USDA (which is incorporated into the Uniform Probate Code as §2-702) treats anyone who fails to survive another by 120 hours as if that person predeceased the other,[8] unless the decedent's will (or other governing instrument) provides otherwise.[9]

When it comes to marital deduction planning, it may be advisable to reverse the USDA presumption *for the more wealthy spouse*. Unless the presumption is reversed, the marital deduction could be lost in a case of near-simultaneous deaths. Treas. Reg. §20.2056(c)-2(e) allows the state law presumption to be reversed,[10] by language such as: "For purposes of [this will] [the marital deduction gift made in Article ____], S shall be deemed to have survived me if the order of our deaths cannot be proved. S need not survive me for any fixed period of time."

Here is an example showing the numbers: Suppose that D owned property valued at $3 million and that S owned little or no property. Suppose further that D and S were killed — by all appearances instantly and simultaneously — in an airplane crash during 2003 and that D's will bequeathed an optimum marital deduction amount to S (for illustration purposes, assume that D's full unified credit was available, that no other assets passed to S for marital deduction purposes, that D's estate had no

---

7.   See, e.g., Janus v. Tarasewicz, 482 N.E.2d 418 (Ill. App. 1985), in which W survived H, but only by 48 hours. As a result, insurance owned by H on H's own life that named H's mother as contingent beneficiary if W did not survive passed to W and through her estate to her surviving father. Had the revised USDA governed this case, H's insurance proceeds would have gone to H's mother, not W's father.

8.   See Halbach & Waggoner, *The UPC's New Survivorship and Antilapse Provisions*, 55 ALB. L. REV. 1091, 1091-1099 (1992).

9.   Both the USDA and the Uniform Probate Code allow the maker of a will, living trust, or other dispositive document to create a different presumption as to the order of deaths and thereby preserve the marital deduction by generating transfers between spouses.

10.   Treas. Reg. §20.2056(c)-2(e) provides:

If the order of deaths of the decedent and his spouse cannot be established by proof, a presumption (whether supplied by local law, the decedent's will or otherwise) that the decedent was survived by his spouse will be recognized as satisfying [the requirement that the decedent be survived by his spouse], but only to the extent that [the presumption] has the effect of giving to the spouse an interest in property includible in her gross estate. . . .

other deductions or credits, and that the amount of the bequest therefore was $2 million). Absent a provision in *D*'s will expressly requiring that *S* be treated as having survived *D* in this circumstance, the original or revised USDA would treat *S* as having predeceased *D*, for purpose of the distribution of *D*'s estate; thus, nothing would pass to *S*. On a taxable estate of $3 million, after reflecting the unified credit, *D*'s personal representative would pay an estate tax of $930,000. If, however, *D*'s will required that *S* be treated as the survivor, the $2 million optimum marital deduction bequest would pass to *S* and qualify for the marital deduction. *D*'s estate would pay no estate tax and, assuming *S* has no more than this $2 million bequest and also had not used the unified credit previously, *S*'s estate would pay $435,000. Thus, the inclusion of a presumption of *S*'s survival achieves a tax savings of $495,000.

A presumption of a spouses' survival should apply only if the order of deaths cannot be determined. If the evidence shows that the decedent's spouse actually predeceased the decedent, however briefly, no marital deduction will be allowed.

Presumptions of Survivorship.

(a) State law would determine in what instrument you would need to include a provision to reverse the USDA presumption with respect to a tenancy by the entirety interest in realty. In most cases it would not be effective in a will. See Racca v. Commissioner, 76 T.C. 416 (1981); Estate of Ohre v. State Department of Revenue, 585 P.2d 920 (Colo. App. 1978); Keegan v. Estate of Keegan, 384 A.2d 913 (N.J. Super. 1978). In addition, care must be exercised to insure that both spouses use consistent presumptions (except in unusual cases) and that the presumptions are in the proper documents (e.g., a will provision probably would not govern a dispositive direction in an inter vivos trust, and vice versa).

(b) The following provision was included in *D*'s will, in which *D* left property to *S* if *S* survived *D*: "If *S* and I die as a consequence of a common disaster, the terms of this Will shall be applied as if *S* survived me." What is wrong with this provision? Carefully compare Treas. Reg. §§20.2056(c)-2(e) and 20.2056(b)-3(c). Some drafters, probably informed by §2056(b)(3)(A), refer to deaths "as a result of a common disaster resulting in the death" of both spouses. A presumption of survivorship in this situation may not be respected. For example, if both *D* and *S* were injured in the same automobile accident, with *S* dying immediately and *D* lingering before dying, the "common disaster" provision would be met but, because the actual order of their deaths could be proved, a presumption that *S* survived would be ineffective for federal estate tax purposes. The document might leave property to *S*, but no marital deduction would be allowed. Further, a common disaster provision may raise problems of construction as to whether the deaths were the result of a common disaster or, instead, were from independent causes.[11]

(c) In connection with drafting survivorship presumptions for a testator's will, consider Estate of Gordon v. Commissioner, 70 T.C. 404 (1978), *acq.* In *Gordon, D*'s will provided that *S* should be "presumed" to have survived if the order of deaths of *D* and *S* were "doubtful." *D* shot *S* and then committed suicide. The order of deaths depended upon how long each survived after being shot, and the available evidence, which one expert described as "skimpy," was not sufficient to prove who survived. The court held that the taxpayer has the burden of proving that there is insufficient evidence to establish the order of deaths but, once that burden is satisfied, the presumption in *D*'s will that *S* survived is conclusive for estate tax purposes (as to the property passing to *S* under *D*'s will). The court construed the term "presumed" in *D*'s will to mean that *S* should be *deemed* to have survived, and rejected the government's suggestion that the term "merely established an evidentiary presumption" that disappeared when any contrary evidence was introduced.

More importantly, the court rejected the government's contention that *D*'s estate had the burden of disproving the notice of deficiency, which asserted that *S* predeceased *D*. The court agreed that a notice of deficiency carries a "presumption of correctness," but that presumption does not require the taxpayer to disprove all factual statements made in the notice. Under Treas. Reg. §20.2056(c)-2(e), once the taxpayer proved that the order of deaths could not be established, the provision in *D*'s will that *S* should be deemed to have survived was dispositive; the government could not alter the jural significance of *D*'s testamentary provision by the manner in which the notice of deficiency was worded.

(d) A testator may presume survivorship as to certain properties that is different from the presumption employed for other properties. Why might a testator wish to do this?

(e) Presumptions of survivorship and qualification for the marital deduction do not always produce desirable results. For example, in Estate of Acord v. Commissioner, 93 T.C. 1 (1989), *D*'s will specified that *S* would not receive *D*'s estate if *S* "dies before I do, at the same time that I do, or under such circumstances as to make it doubtful who died first." The apparent intent in this community property estate was to preclude "estate stacking" if *D* and *S* died in a common disaster. As it turned out, *S* died 38 hours after *D*'s death as a result of injuries suffered in a common disaster. The government argued successfully that *S* was entitled to take under the specific terms of *D*'s survivorship provision and that the will, by virtue of

---

11. See, e.g., In re Davis Estate, 61 N.Y.S.2d 427 (Surr. Ct. 1946), *aff'd*, 69 N.Y.S.2d 327 (1947).

that provision, overcame the 120-hour survival rule of the Uniform Probate Code because it specifically addressed simultaneous deaths.

As a result of the court's holding, D's estate passed to S and qualified for the estate tax marital deduction. Because D's estate incurred no estate tax, S's estate received no §2013 credit, the effect being that D's share of their community property was stacked on top of S's own property and all of it was taxed in S's taxable estate at a higher progressive marginal tax bracket, causing more tax to be incurred than if the Uniform Probate Code's 120-hour rule had applied. This result was particularly egregious because the planning goal in any community property estate should be to avoid "unsplitting" the estates of the spouses if they die in rapid succession. See the last illustration in this chapter (at page 718) for a better tax motivated result in such a case.

Marital Status.   Still looking at easy qualification requirements, implicit in the surviving spouse requirement is that the survivor be married to the decedent at the decedent's death. S. Rep. No. 1013, 80th Cong., 2d Sess. (1948), 1948-1 C.B. 335. A legal separation or judicial action short of a final divorce decree terminating the marriage prior to the decedent's death does not affect the decedent's marital status for §2056(a) purposes. Rev. Rul. 56-368; Eccles v. Commissioner, 19 T.C. 1049 (1953), *acq.*

Recognition of common law marriages and the validity of divorce decrees normally turn on state law. Rev. Rul. 58-66. Sometimes questions about a beneficiary's status as a decedent's surviving spouse turn on the validity of a divorce from a prior marriage, as illustrated next.

Revenue Ruling 67-442

The taxpayer obtained an ex parte divorce in Mexico in 1961. His divorce was promptly challenged by his first wife and subsequently declared invalid in 1963 by a state court with personal jurisdiction of the parties and jurisdiction of the subject matter of the action. A marriage entered into by the husband following the Mexican divorce was also declared to be invalid. . . .

The Internal Revenue Service generally will not question for Federal income tax purposes the validity of any divorce decree until a court of competent jurisdiction declares the divorce to be invalid. However, where a state court, in a proceeding in which there is personal jurisdiction of the parties or jurisdiction of the subject matter of the action, declares the prior divorce to be invalid, the Service will usually follow the later court decision rather than the divorce decree for Federal income tax purposes for such years as may not be barred by the statute of limitations. In this regard the Service will not follow the decisions in Estate of Borax v. Commissioner, 349 F.2d 666 (2d Cir. 1965), and Wondsel v. Commissioner, 350 F.2d 339 (2d Cir. 1965).

Furthermore, the Service will not follow the *Borax* and *Wondsel* decisions in the disposition of cases involving questions of marital status for Federal estate and gift tax purposes, such as questions pertaining to the marital deductions . . . .

See also Rev. Rul. 76-155. *Borax* and *Wondsel* both held that the validity of a divorce for federal tax purposes was to be determined under a "rule of validation" that treats a putative divorce as valid in virtually all cases. The purpose of this validation rule was to promote certainty and uniformity, which the court regarded as important goals of the federal tax system. Estate of Goldwater v. Commissioner, 64 T.C. 540 (1975), *aff'd*, 539 F.2d 878 (2d Cir. 1976), held that a New York court's determination that the decedent's Mexican divorce was invalid rendered the decedent's first wife his surviving spouse. The forced share she obtained from the decedent's estate therefore qualified for the estate tax marital deduction and the decedent's bequest to the decedent's second wife did not.

The court distinguished Estate of Spalding v. Commissioner, 537 F.2d 666 (2d Cir. 1976). Charles and Elizabeth Spalding were married for 17 years in Connecticut, until Charles (who was then living in New York) obtained a Nevada divorce. Four years later a New York court ruled in favor of Elizabeth that the divorce was invalid. Nevertheless, two months later, Charles married Amy in California, where they resided until Amy's death. The Tax Court held that the bequest from Amy to Charles did not qualify for the estate tax marital deduction because the New York decree meant that Charles was not divorced from Elizabeth and therefore could not be married to Amy. The appellate court reversed the Tax Court because the estate was administered in a state other than the one that decreed the divorce to be invalid, and because it was the decedent's surviving spouse (Charles), not the decedent (Amy), who was the party to the former marriage and the invalid divorce decree purportedly terminating it.

Similar to *Spalding*, Estate of Steffke v. Commissioner, 64 T.C. 530 (1975), *aff'd*, 538 F.2d 733 (7th Cir. 1976), held that a decedent's bequest to his "wife" could not qualify for the estate tax marital deduction because her Mexican divorce from her first husband was invalid. The interesting feature of *Steffke* is that the validity of the Mexican divorce was not challenged during the decedent's life. Instead, the supreme court in the state of the decedent's domicile determined after his death that his purported wife did not qualify as a widow for state inheritance tax purposes, which distinguished the facts from *Spalding* and which the Tax Court regarded as dispositive for marital deduction purposes as well.

The "Passing" Requirement. Under §2056(a), the estate tax marital deduction is only allowed for property that "passes or has passed from" D to S. Although §2056(c) defines this requirement as having been met "if and only if" the transfer comes within one or more of seven specified categories, the Senate Finance Committee report accompanying the 1948 Act declared that the concept of passing is defined so that "interests which commonly would be considered as passing from the decedent" are included; the definition "is broad enough to cover all the interests included in . . . the decedent's gross estate." S. Rep. No. 1013 (pt. 2), 80th Cong., 2d Sess. 2-3 (1948), in 1948-1 C.B. 331, 332-333. Accordingly, Treas. Reg. §§20.2056(c)-1 and 20.2056(c)-2 represent that the passing requirement will be construed liberally and that passing includes transactions that are not expressly listed in §2056(c). For example, S's interest in an annuity is deemed to have passed from D to the extent that it was included in D's gross estate under §2039. A support allowance awarded to S during administration of D's estate is treated as having passed from D. Treas. Reg. §20.2056(c)-2(a). And property received as a consequence of S's election against a will — e.g., a dower or curtesy interest or a statutory forced share of D's estate — is treated as having passed from D. Thus, property bequeathed or devised to S who renounced D's estate plan and elected to take a forced share is deemed not to pass to S, but the elective share received instead qualifies for the marital deduction. Conversely, if S does not renounce D's estate plan, the property bequeathed or devised to S is deemed to pass from D to S and the elective share that otherwise was available is not. Cf. Rev. Rul. 74-492.

Note that the Uniform Probate Code's elective share does not require an electing spouse to renounce the decedent's estate plan. Instead, property that the decedent transfers to the spouse counts toward satisfying the elective share. The transfer must be in a qualifying form to be deductible.

In addition, an interest renounced by a third party to whom it otherwise would pass from D may be deemed to pass from D directly to S as default recipient of the rejected property if the renunciation meets the §2518 qualified disclaimer requirements. Conversely, no marital deduction is available for an interest that passes to a third party by virtue of S's §2518 qualified disclaimer. In either case, care is required to identify a qualified disclaimer (which is an irrevocable and unqualified refusal to accept an interest), because failure to meet the §2518 requirements is deemed to be an acceptance of the property that passed to the disclaimant, who then made a gift of it. Treas. Reg. §20.2056(d)-1(a).[12] In addition to satisfying the

---

12. As first adopted, the estate tax marital deduction did not apply to an interest that passed to S as a consequence of a disclaimer made by a third party who otherwise would have taken the interest from D. In 1966 Congress amended what was then §2056(d)(2) to permit a deduction if the third party did not accept the interest before attempting to disclaim it and the disclaimer was made prior to "the date prescribed for the filing of the estate tax return." The Tax Reform Act of 1976 repealed that provision because it became redundant when Congress enacted §2518, which now is the operative provision for all transfers creating an interest in the disclaimant.

passing requirement, qualified disclaimers are used with some regularity to qualify transfers for the marital deduction that were defective in some form. For example, TAMs 9119047 and 9003007 involved trusts that benefited *S* and others, which violated a requirement that *S* be the exclusive current beneficiary. By virtue of qualified disclaimers by and on behalf of those third parties (some of whom were minors or unborn or unascertainable, represented by a guardian ad litem), the trusts were purified and made to qualify for the marital deduction. As illustrated by Rev. Rul. 90-110, however, the proper party must make the disclaimer. In that situation a trustee attempted to relinquish its power to make disqualifying distributions to third parties, which was ineffective because the third party beneficiaries did not ratify the trustee's action and neither the document nor state law granted the trustee the authority to relinquish its distributive powers and thereby diminish the beneficiaries' rights.

Inclusion in *D*'s Gross Estate. The allowable estate tax marital deduction cannot exceed the estate tax value of the interest passing to *S*. §2056(a). Thus, an interest that passes to *S* must be included in *D*'s gross estate to qualify for the marital deduction. For example, the interests in **(a)** and **(b)** pass to *S* and all of the property in **(a)** but only half of the property in **(b)** qualify for the estate tax marital deduction. Do you see why the interest in **(c)** does not qualify for the deduction?

(a) *D* owned a policy of insurance on *D*'s life and named *S* as beneficiary. On *D*'s death, the proceeds of the policy were paid to *S* by the insurer, and the value of the proceeds was included in *D*'s gross estate under §2042.

(b) *D* and *S* own their residence as tenants by the entirety. On *D*'s death, *S* became the sole owner of the residence by survivorship. Because only half the value of the property is included in *D*'s gross estate under §2040(b), only half the value of the property qualifies for the estate tax marital deduction.

(c) *P* died ten years ago, leaving property in trust to pay income to *P*'s child, *D*, for life. Upon *D*'s death, the trust estate is distributable to such persons as *D* appoints by will other than *D*, *D*'s estate, or creditors of either. *D* exercised the power in favor of *S*.

PART C.   TERMINABLE INTERESTS

Code Reference: *Estate Tax: §2056*

7.   *The Nondeductible Terminable Interest Rule.* Treas. Reg. §20.2056(a)-2 provides that an interest passing to *S* is a "nondeductible interest" for estate tax purposes to the extent that:

(1)   it is not included in *D*'s gross estate; or

(2)   an estate tax deduction is allowed for that interest under either §2053 (the deduction for expenses and indebtedness) or §2054 (the deduction for casualty and theft losses); or

(3)   it constitutes a terminable interest for which a marital deduction is disallowed by §2056(b).

If it was not repealed so quickly the same thing would be true if a §2057 qualified family owned business interest deduction was allowed for qualifying stock given to a surviving spouse.

As we will see, a hugely important concept is that *not all terminable interests are nondeductible*. A terminable interest in property is an interest that "will terminate or fail on the lapse of time or on the occurrence or the failure to occur of some contingency." Treas. Reg. §20.2056)b)-1(b). It is essential to distinguish between "property" and an "interest in property"; a terminable interest is one of several interests in an underlying property. Thus, the regulation provides several examples of interests in property that are terminable and those that are not. "Life estates, terms for years, annuities, patents, and copyrights" are all said to be terminable interests, but "a bond, note or similar contractual obligation, the discharge of which would not have the effect of an annuity or a term for years, is not a terminable interest." See §2056(b)(1) (flush language). Moreover, the patent or copyright would qualify for the deduction without more, as might the annuity. Our challenge is to know first what a terminable interest is (that usually is easy) and then whether it is a nondeductible variety of terminable interest.

Let's try a conceptual question first: *D* loaned $10,000 to *Y*, for which *Y* gave *D* a personal note payable in five equal annual installments, plus interest. The note is said not to be a terminable interest. What is the difference between a note payable in installments and an annuity payable for a specified number of years? Is such an annuity a terminable interest? In that regard, Rev. Rul. 79-224 held that an installment contract obtained as partial payment for the sale of land was a terminable interest. The contract, which provided for 30 annual payments to be made by the buyer, was analogized to an annuity for years. If that is correct, what type of "bond, note, or similar contractual obligation" is *unlike* an annuity for years? Would the contract not be a terminable interest if it provided for only two installment payments? If it provided for only one payment at maturity? Even though the Commissioner classified the contract as a terminable interest, it was not deemed to be nondeductible. This is a very important notion, to which we now turn.

Deductibility of Terminable Interests. This is such an important concept that it bears repeating: NOT ALL TERMINABLE INTERESTS ARE NONDEDUCTIBLE. Section 2056(b)(1) provides that a terminable interest passing to the surviving spouse is *nondeductible* only if (1) an interest in the underlying property passes or has passed for less than full and adequate consideration in money or money's worth, (2) from *D*, (3) to any person other than *S* (or *S*'s estate), (4) possession or enjoyment by that other person follows the termination or failure of *S*'s interest, and (5) no statutory exception to the nondeductible terminable interest rule applies. In addition, entirely independent of those requirements, a terminable interest that is acquired for *S* by *D*'s personal representative or trustee pursuant to *D*'s direction is not deductible.

Why did Congress distinguish terminable interests that are acquired by *D*'s fiduciary from all other terminable interests, and is the distinction desirable as a matter of tax policy? Indeed, what is the justification for the nondeductible terminable interest rule? See Abrams, *A Reevaluation of the Terminable Interest Rule*, 39 TAX L. REV. 1 (1983), who suggests that the rule is nonsense.

D purchased a self and survivor annuity that paid a fixed monthly income for *D*'s life and thereafter for the life of *S*. If the total payments made under the annuity during the joint lives of *D* and *S* were less than $100,000, the contract called for a lump sum refund payment to a child of *D* and *S*. When *D* died, this annuity was subject to §2039 inclusion in *D*'s gross estate. *S* survived *D*. Is *S*'s right to the annuity payments a nondeductible terminable interest if total payments made to *D* pursuant to the annuity contract totaled (a) $87,000 or (b) $121,000? The answer is yes, and no. Consider *Jackson*, reproduced at page 618, in connection with this question and these answers.

Family Allowances. First, let's be sure we understand what was involved in *Jackson*. Many states provide an allowance to a surviving spouse similar to that guaranteed by Uniform Probate Code §2-404 (the pre-1990 version was §2-403):

(a) In addition to the right to homestead allowance and exempt property [provided in §§2-402 and 2-403], the decedent's surviving spouse and minor children whom the decedent was obligated to support and children who were in fact being supported by the decedent are entitled to a reasonable allowance in money out of the estate for their maintenance during the period of administration, which allowance may not continue for longer than one year if the estate is inadequate to discharge allowed claims. The allowance may be paid as a lump sum or in periodic installments. It is payable to the surviving spouse, if living, for the use of the surviving spouse and minor and dependent children; otherwise to the children, or persons having their care and custody. If a minor child or dependent child is not living with the surviving spouse, the allowance may be made partially to the child or his [or her] guardian or other person having the child's care and custody, and partially to the spouse, as their needs may appear. The family allowance is exempt from and has priority over all claims except the homestead allowance.

(b) The family allowance is not chargeable against any benefit or share passing to the surviving spouse or children by the will of the decedent, unless otherwise provided, by intestate succession, or by way of elective share. The death of any person entitled to family allowance terminates the right to allowances not yet paid.

Rev. Rul. 76-166 concluded that the Uniform Probate Code's homestead allowance (which is not a typical provision for homestead but, rather, a flat amount of money) and exempt property allowance qualify as deductible interests. The following material addresses the question whether the Uniform Probate Code's family allowance also qualifies for the estate tax marital deduction, which is a question upon which the government has not ruled.

Jackson v. United States
376 U.S. 503 (1964)

Mr. Justice WHITE delivered the opinion of the Court. . . .

The question raised by this case is whether the allowance provided by California law for the support of a widow during the settlement of her husband's estate is a terminable interest.

[The decedent's widow was granted an allowance of $3,000 per month for 24 months, payable from the corpus of the estate for her support and maintenance. Under the Probate Court order, an allowance of $42,000 had accrued during the 14 months since her husband's death. That amount, plus an additional $3,000 per month for the remainder of the two-year period, made a total of $72,000, which in fact was paid to the widow and claimed as a marital deduction on the decedent's estate tax return. That deduction was disallowed, which the district court upheld and the court on appeal affirmed.]

In enacting the Revenue Act of 1948 with its provision for the marital deduction, Congress left undisturbed §812(b)(5) of the 1939 Code, which allowed an estate tax deduction, as an expense of administration, for amounts "reasonably required and actually expended for the support during the settlement of the estate of those dependent upon the decedent." 26 U.S.C. §812(b)(5) (1946). As the legislative history shows, support payments under §812(b)(5) were not to be treated as part of the marital deduction allowed by [§2056]. The Revenue Act of 1950, however, repealed

§812(b)(5) because, among other reasons, Congress believed the section resulted in discriminations in favor of States having liberal family allowances. Thereafter allowances paid for the support of a widow during the settlement of an estate "heretofore deductible under §812(b) will be allowable as a marital deduction subject to the conditions and limitations of section [2056]." S. Rep. No. 2375, 81st Cong., 2d Sess. 130 [1950].

The "conditions and limitations" of the marital deduction under [§2056] are several but we need concern ourselves with only one aspect of [§2056(b)(1)], which disallows the deduction of "terminable" interests passing to the surviving spouse. It was conceded in the Court of Appeals that the right to the widow's allowance here involved is an interest in property passing from the decedent within the meaning of [§2056(c)], that it is an interest to which the terminable-interest rule of [§2056(b)(1)] is applicable, and that the conditions set forth in [§2056(b)(1)(A) and (B)] were satisfied under the decedent's will and codicils thereto. The issue, therefore, is whether the interest in property passing to Mrs. Richards as widow's allowance would "terminate or fail" upon the "lapse of time, upon the occurrence of an event or contingency, or upon the failure of an event or contingency to occur."

We accept the Court of Appeals' description of the nature and characteristics of the widow's allowance under California law. In that State, the right to a widow's allowance is not a vested right and nothing accrues before the order granting it. The right to an allowance is lost when the one for whom it is asked has lost the status upon which the right depends. If a widow dies or remarries prior to securing an order for a widow's allowance, the right does not survive such death or remarriage. The amount of the widow's allowance which has accrued and is unpaid at the date of death of the widow is payable to her estate but the right to future payments abates upon her death. The remarriage of a widow subsequent to an order for an allowance likewise abates her right to future payments.

In light of these characteristics of the California widow's allowance, Mrs. Richards did not have an indefeasible interest in property at the moment of her husband's death since either her death or remarriage would defeat it. If the order for support allowance had been entered on the day of her husband's death, her death or remarriage at any time within two years thereafter would terminate that portion of the interest allocable to the remainder of the two-year period. As of the date of Mr. Richards' death, therefore, the allowance was subject to failure or termination "upon the occurrence of an event or contingency." That the support order was entered in this case 14 months later does not, in our opinion, change the defeasible nature of the interest.

Petitioners ask us to judge the terminability of the widow's interest in property represented by her allowance as of the date of the Probate Court's order rather than as of the date of her husband's death. The court's order, they argue, unconditionally entitled the widow to $42,000 in accrued allowance of which she could not be deprived by either her death or remarriage. It is true that some courts have followed this path, but it is difficult to accept an approach which would allow a deduction of $42,000 on the facts of this case, a deduction of $72,000 if the order had been entered at the end of two years from Mr. Richards' death and none at all if the order had been entered immediately upon his death. Moreover, judging deductibility as of the date of the Probate Court's order ignores the Senate Committee's admonition that in considering terminability of an interest for purposes of a marital deduction "the situation is viewed as at the date of the decedent's death." S. Rep. No. 1013, Part 2, 80th Cong., 2d Sess. 10 [1948]. We prefer the course followed by both the Court of Appeals for the Ninth Circuit in Estate of Cunha v. Commissioner, 279 F.2d 292 (9th Cir. 1960), and by the Court of Appeals for the Eighth Circuit in United States v. Quivey, 292 F.2d 252 (8th Cir. 1961). Both courts have held the date of death of the testator to be the correct point of time from which to judge the nature of a widow's allowance for the purpose of deciding terminability and deductibility under [§2056]. This is in accord with the rule uniformly followed with regard to interests other than the widow's allowance, that qualification for the marital deduction must be determined as of the time of death.

Our conclusion is confirmed by [§2056(b)(3)], which saves from the operation of the terminable-interest rule interests which by their terms may (but do not in fact) terminate only upon failure of the widow to survive her husband for a period not in excess of six months. The premise of this provision is that an interest passing to a widow is normally to be judged as of the time of the testator's death rather than at a later time when the condition imposed may be satisfied; hence the necessity to provide an exception to the rule in the case of a six months' survivorship contingency in a will. A gift conditioned upon eight months' survivorship, rather than six, is a nondeductible terminable interest for reasons which also disqualify the statutory widow's allowance in California where the widow must survive and remain unmarried at least to the date of an allowance order to become indefeasibly entitled to any widow's allowance at all.

Petitioners contend, however, that the sole purpose of the terminable-interest provisions of the Code is to assure that interests deducted from the estate of the deceased spouse will not also escape taxation in the estate of the survivor. This argument leads to the conclusion that, since it is now clear that, unless consumed or given away during Mrs. Richards' life, the entire $72,000 will be taxed to her estate, it should not be included in her husband's. But as we have already seen, there is no provision in the Code for deducting all terminable interests which become nonterminable at a later date and therefore taxable in the estate of the surviving spouse if not consumed or transferred. The examples cited in the legislative history make it clear that the determinative factor is not taxability to the surviving spouse but terminability as defined by the statute. Under the view advanced by petitioners all cash allowances actually paid would fall outside [§2056(b)(1)]; on two different occasions the Senate has refused to give its approval to House-passed amendments to the 1954 Code which would have made the terminable-interest rule inapplicable to all widow's allowances actually paid within specified periods of time.

We are mindful that the general goal of the marital deduction provisions was to achieve uniformity of federal estate tax impact between those States with community property laws and those without them. But the device of the marital deduction which Congress chose to achieve uniformity was knowingly hedged with limitations, including the terminable-interest rule. These provisions may be imperfect devices to achieve the desired end, but they are the means which Congress chose. To the extent it was thought desirable to modify the rigors of the terminable-interest rule, exceptions to the rule were written into the Code. Courts should hesitate to provide still another exception by straying so far from the statutory language as to allow a marital deduction for the widow's allowance provided by the California statute. The achievement of the purposes of the marital deduction is dependent to a great degree upon the careful drafting of wills; we have no fear that our decision today will prevent either the full utilization of the marital deduction or the proper support of widows during the pendency of an estate proceeding.

Affirmed.

Mr. Justice DOUGLAS dissents.

==Let's see if we can divine the law from what the Court held in *Jackson*.==

(a) *D* created a testamentary trust to pay half the income to *S* for life. *S* also had a presently exercisable nongeneral power to appoint trust corpus to any descendant. *S* renounced the will and received a statutory one-third share of D's estate. This statutory share is deductible under the relation back principle, which regards S's entitlement as vested as of D's death. See Treas. Reg. §20.2056(c)-2(c). Does the timing rule (determine qualification at the moment of death) in *Jackson* suggest that a statutory forced heir share should be a nondeductible terminable interest?

(b) S as the designated beneficiary of insurance on the life of D (which is includible in D's gross estate under §2042) elected to receive a life annuity with a refund feature if payments made over S's remaining life do not exceed a designated amount, rather than receiving the proceeds in a lump sum as designated by D. At S's designation, any refund payable at S's death will be distributed to a child of D and S. The full amount of the insurance proceeds qualifies for the marital deduction in D's estate because S chose the settlement option.

(c) In Estate of Green v. United States, 441 F.2d 303 (6th Cir. 1971), the decedent's widow received a distribution from the decedent's estate of $18,000 as a "widow's allowance" under Michigan law. The sole issue was whether the allowance qualified for a marital deduction. After discussing and quoting from the Supreme Court's decision in *Jackson*, the court held that, under then Michigan law, a widow's right to one year's allowance vested at the decedent's death, is not terminated by her subsequent death or remarriage, and so is not a terminable interest. (In 1979, the Michigan widow's support allowance was replaced by a family allowance provision.)

The support allowance provided for a surviving spouse has been held to qualify for the marital deduction in a few other states. Miller v. United States, 74-2 U.S. Tax Cas. (CCH) ¶13,039 (N.D. Ohio 1974); Molner v. United States, 175 F. Supp. 271 (N.D. Ill. 1959); Estate of Watson v. Commissioner, 94 T.C. 262 (1990) (Miss.); Estate of Radel v. Commissioner, 88 T.C. 1143 (1987) (Minn.); Estate of Moss v. Commissioner, 43 T.C.M. (CCH) 582 (1982) (Neb., dicta). In most cases, however, the marital deduction has been denied. E.g., Estate of Abely v. Commissioner, 60 T.C. 120 (1973), *aff'd*, 489 F.2d 1327 (1st Cir. 1974) (Massachusetts); Hamilton National Bank v. United States, 353 F.2d 930 (6th Cir. 1965) (Tennessee); United States v. Edmondson, 331 F.2d 676 (5th Cir. 1964) (Georgia); Connecticut National Bank v. United States, 76-1 U.S. Tax Cas. (CCH) ¶13,132 (D. Conn. 1976); Iowa-Des Moines National Bank v. United States, 306 F. Supp. 320 (S.D. Iowa 1969); Stephens v. United States, 270 F. Supp. 968 (D. Mont. 1967); Wachovia Bank & Trust Co. v. United States, 234 F. Supp. 897 (M.D. N.C. 1964); Estate of Snider v. Commissioner, 84 T.C. 75 (1985) (Texas); Estate of Rubinow v. Commissioner, 75 T.C. 486 (1980) (Conn.).

(d) D's will directed payment of $1,000 per month to S for the period beginning on D's death and ending when administration of D's estate was complete. Even though the payments were to be made irrespective of whether S died or remarried during that period, this bequest is a nondeductible terminable interest because there is no knowing at death how many payments will be made. Cf. Estate of Fried v. Commissioner, 445 F.2d 979 (2d Cir. 1971). That factor may, however, be irrelevant, but only to the extent the estate passes to S. Do you see why? Consider, then, this final example: *D*'s will left one-third of the residue of *D*'s estate to *S* and the other two-thirds to *D*'s child. The local probate court awarded *S* an allowance of $1,000 a month, commencing as of *D*'s death and continuing until *S*'s death or remarriage or completion of administration of *D*'s estate, whichever occurred first. *S* received nine payments, totaling $9,000, and then the administration was completed. To what extent, if any, is the $9,000 paid to *S* a nondeductible terminable interest? See Treas. Reg. §20.2056(b)-1(g) *Example (8)*.

Meyer v. United States
364 U.S. 410 (1960)

Mr. Justice WHITTAKER: . . .

Two policies of life insurance are involved, but since they are in all material respects identical, we need deal with only one of them. The policy obligated the insurer to pay a death benefit of $25,187.50, and that sum was included by the executors in the federal estate tax return and the tax thereon was paid. The decedent had selected an optional mode of settlement which provided for the payment of equal monthly installments to his wife for her life, with 240 installments guaranteed, and further provided that if the wife should die before receiving the 240 installments his daughter would receive the remainder of them, but if both the wife and the daughter died before receiving the 240 installments the commuted value of those unpaid was to be paid in one sum to the estate of the last one of them to die.

Of the total proceeds of the policy of $25,187.50, the insurer determined that $17,956.41 was necessary to fund the 240 monthly payments to the wife, the daughter, or to the estate of the last survivor of them, and that the remaining $7,231.09 was necessary to fund the monthly payments to the wife so long as she might live beyond the 240 months. Accordingly, the insurer made such entries on its books.

Thereafter petitioners, as executors, timely filed a claim for refund of the amount of the tax paid upon the $7,231.09 which the insurer had shown upon its books as necessary to fund the monthly payments to the wife for her actuarial expectancy beyond the 240 months certain, on the theory that the insurer's treatment of that sum on its books created a separate "property" or fund payable to the wife alone, and hence it qualified for the marital deduction under [§2056]. The claim was denied, and this suit was brought to recover the tax that had been paid on that sum.

Petitioners correctly concede that if the Policy constitutes but one "property," within the meaning of the statute, it would not qualify for the marital deduction because the wife's interest in it would be a "terminable" one, within the meaning of the statute, inasmuch as the wife may die before receipt of the 240 guaranteed installments, in which event the unpaid ones must go to the daughter if then living. They concede, too, that the $17,956.41, shown on the insurer's books as necessary to fund the monthly payments for the 240 months certain, does not qualify for the marital deduction for the same reasons. But they contend that, although the policy made no provision therefor, the insurer's bookkeeping entries constituted a real division of the insurance proceeds into, and created, two "properties" — one of $17,956.41 and the other of $7,231.09 — and that the latter qualifies for the marital deduction under the statute because it is payable, if at all, only to the wife — during her lifetime beyond the 240 months — and no other person has any interest in it.

Whether a policy of life insurance may create several "properties" or funds, either terminable or nonterminable or both, we need not decide, for we think the policy here involved constituted only one property, and made only so much of its proceeds payable to the wife as she might live to receive in equal monthly installments, and made any guaranteed balance payable to the daughter. Hence, under the terms of the policy, the "interest passing to the surviving spouse [may] terminate or fail" and a "person other than [the] surviving spouse . . . may possess or enjoy [a] part of such property after such termination or failure of the interest so passing to the surviving spouse; . . ." Therefore the policy and its proceeds — considered apart from petitioners' claim that the insurer's bookkeeping division of the proceeds of the policy into two parts created two "properties" — are disqualified for the marital deduction by the express provisions of [§2056(b)].

The legislative history of the section further supports and compels this conclusion. Illustrating applications of the terminable interest rule, the Senate Committee Report gave an example that is in no relevant way distinguishable from this case, and makes it very clear that the marital deduction is not allowable in the case of an annuity for the surviving spouse for life if "upon the death of the surviving spouse, the payments are to continue to another person (not through her estate) or the undistributed fund is to be paid to such other person. . . ."

We think petitioner's argument — that the insurer's book-keeping division of the proceeds of the policy into two parts created two properties — cannot withstand the provisions of the policy and the actual facts respecting the insurer's bookkeeping division of its proceeds, under the clear terms of the statute and its legislative history. The policy made no provision for the creation of two separate properties — one a property sufficient to provide payments for 240 months, to the wife while she lived and any remainder to the daughter, and another property sufficient to provide an annuity to the wife for the period of her actuarial expectancy beyond the 240 months — and no such separate properties were in fact created. The allocations made were merely actuarial ones — mere bookkeeping entries — made by the insurer on its own books for its own convenience after the insured, the other party to the contract, had died. The wife and the daughter were, respectively, primary and contingent beneficiaries of the policy alone. Neither of them had any title to, nor right to receive, any special fund, and indeed none was actually created. The bookkeeping entries made by the insurer no more created or measured their rights than the insurer's erasure of those entries — which it was free to make at any time — would destroy their rights. Their rights derive solely from the policy. . . .

The proceeds of the policy were not payable to the wife (or to her estate or appointee) alone and at all events, but were payable in monthly installments to her for life, and if any obligation under the policy remained undischarged at her death it was payable to the daughter if living or, if not, to the estate of the last of them to die. It follows that the "interest passing to the surviving spouse [may] terminate or fail" and that a "person other than [the] surviving spouse . . . may possess or enjoy [a] part of such property after such termination or failure of the interest so passing to the surviving spouse; . . ." and hence the property is disqualified for the marital deduction by the express provisions of [§2056(b)(1)].

Affirmed.

Mr. Justice DOUGLAS, with whom Mr. Justice CLARK and Mr. Justice BRENNAN concur, dissenting. . . .

Concededly the amount necessary to make the 20-year payments does not qualify as a marital deduction because it may "terminate or fail" within the meaning of the Code, the daughter being entitled to any remaining payments during that term should the wife die before it terminates. The daughter, however, has no *interest* in the annuities payable beyond the 20-year period. And it seems to me that the wife's "interest" in that part of the insurance contracts does not "terminate or fail" within the meaning of [§2056(b)].

If the decedent had taken out *one group of policies* to pay installments for 20 years to his wife or, if she died within that period, to his daughter, and *another group of policies* to pay installments to his wife for life if she lived more than 20 years, the former would be nondeductible, but the latter would qualify for the marital deduction. Does then the continuation of the two types of insurance in one policy change the result? The Government maintains that it does because in its view the entire insurance proceeds of each policy are a single "property" as that term is used in the statute; and the Court so holds. Yet, with all deference, that conclusion is wide of the mark.

. . . These insurance policies created, of course, no fund or res. The sum . . . representing the wife's terminable *interest* and [that] representing her other *interest* were, of course, no more segregated in the insurance companies' assets than a customer's checking account is segregated in a commercial bank. Yet that seems immaterial. Each represented a chose in action. The wife or daughter, as the case might be, could sue for the one during the 20-year period. Only the wife could enforce the claim here in question. . . .

My conclusion is that where the "interest" that accrues to the surviving spouse is, as here, shared with no one else and is subject to no termination except her own death, it qualifies for a marital deduction under this statute, even though another "interest" of hers in the same annuity contract would not qualify.

(a) Following up on the notion in *Meyer* that a bequest to *S* is indivisible for qualification purposes, what would happen if, in Year One, *D* owned Blackacre, having a fair market value of $100,000, and assigned a remainder interest in Blackacre to *X*, reserving a 15-year term interest in the property. The value of the remainder interest assigned to *X* was $42,000, and *X* paid *D* $21,000 for that interest. *D* died in Year Five, devising the remaining 10-year term in Blackacre to *S*. Is a marital deduction allowable for half of that devise? What harm would exist if the property were regarded as two equal pieces, both subject to the terms of the transaction with *X*, one of which qualifying for the deduction?

Just to make the nondeductible terminable interest rule seem even more arbitrary (as if that was possible), assume that *D*'s parent transferred the remainder interest in Blackacre to *X* and at the same time gave *D* the 15-year term interest. How must your answer differ?

(b) Now consider that *D* died of cancer and bequeathed *D*'s estate to *S*, provided that *D* and *S* did not die as a consequence of a common disaster and provided also that S survived the period in which D's estate was subject to probate administration. D's personal representative completed the administration in four months and distributed the entire estate to S at that time. Why does this bequest not qualify for a marital deduction? See Treas. Reg. §20.2056(b)-3(d) *Example (4)*; Estate of Fried v. Commissioner, 445 F.2d 979 (2d Cir. 1971); Dunn v. United States, 80-1 U.S. Tax Cas. (CCH) ¶13,347 (M.D. Fla. 1980).

In TAM 8816001, S was required to be alive when the estate was distributed, which might occur after the permissible six-month survivorship period of §2056(b)(3). The government disallowed the deduction, notwithstanding a state statute providing that a survivorship condition in excess of six months would be cut back to just six months if the marital deduction was involved. According to the TAM, the statute did not apply because it required that a definite survival period in excess of six months be specified and the condition stated might not exceed six months and was not a specific period. That result was mirrored in Estate of Heim v. Commissioner, 56 T.C.M. (CCH) 146 (1988), in which S similarly was required to survive distribution of the estate and the state statute was deemed inadequate to save the bequest because it was regarded as applicable only to "marital deduction gifts" involving a "survivorship requirement . . . in excess of six months" and the subject provision made no reference to the marital deduction and did not specify a definite period of survivorship that was in excess of six months. (It may be that *Heim* was the same case that generated the TAM.) See also Rev. Rul. 88-90.

(c) D's will bequeathed half of D's residuary estate to S, but D's will provided that none of D's property was to pass to S if they died as a consequence of a common disaster. In the wee hours of January 1 D and S were riding in a car that was struck by a drunk driver. D was killed instantly, and S was seriously injured. What does the *Jackson* timing rule say if, by the time of the final audit of D's estate tax return, S had improved and was given a 70% chance of recovery. Is a marital deduction allowable to D's estate? See Treas. Reg. §20.2056(b)-3(c).

See Rev. Rul. 70-400 for the method of computing the six-month period for purposes of §2056(b)(3).

Earlier in this discussion we learned that substantial taxes may be saved by providing that one spouse is presumed to be the survivor if they die under circumstances such that the order of their deaths cannot be established by proof. In light of this, why might you utilize §2056(b)(3) by putting a provision in D's will that requires S to survive by six months to receive a bequest? Indeed, why might D validly create a presumption of S's survival for some of D's property and a requirement that S survive for six months to take the balance of D's property? Typically these decisions are informed by nontax factors, but can you think of a more effective method of accomplishing those results?

PART D.   POWER OF APPOINTMENT TRUST

Code Reference: *Estate Tax: §2056(b)(5)*

8.   *Trust Interests.* Many people prefer to create a trust for their surviving spouse rather than to leave property outright. Sometimes this attitude reflects a desire to deny the spouse control over the property, but often it reflects concerns about the spouse's ability or willingness to manage the funds, potential incapacity, or the desire to provide protection from predators (such as creditors, greedy relatives, overbearing charities, or just plain crooks). Whatever the motivation, absent special statutory dispensation, the only type of trust that would not run afoul of the nondeductible terminable interest rule is the so-called estate trust discussed at page 677, a device that often is viewed as undesirable. Not wishing seriously to impede a testator's choice among dispositive approaches, Congress included the forerunner of §§2056(b)(5) and 2056(b)(6) in the 1948 legislation. Enactment of the 1954 Code broadened the §2056(b)(5) exception to authorize transfers of a legal life estate to a spouse (as contrasted with a life income interest in a trust). See H.R. Rep. No. 1337, 83d Cong., 2d Sess. 91-92 (1954); S. Rep. No. 1622, 83d Cong., 2d Sess. 125 (1954). And in 1981 Congress added §§2056(b)(7) and 2056(b)(8). These sections permit additional forms of transfers in trust to qualify for the marital deduction. Because of the history behind their adoption, and because many requirements are the same, we will consider §2056(b)(5) first and then explore §2056(b)(7). In practice the alternatives authorized by §§2056(b)(6) and 2056(b)(8) seldom are employed, so we will not devote more than a moment's attention to either.

9.   *Life Insurance and Annuity Proceeds.* Here is that moment with respect to §2056(b)(6), which provides an exception to the non-deductible terminable interest rule for installment or interest payments made directly to a surviving spouse under a life insurance, endowment, or annuity contract if the payments are made no less frequently than annually and must commence within 13 months after the decedent's death. Other statutory requirements (similar to those imposed by §2056(b)(5) on power of appointment trusts) also must be satisfied and are best studied in that more popular and common forum because the §2056(b)(6) exception rarely is used or even encountered.

10.   *Life Interest With General Power of Appointment.* The conditions to qualify for the §2056(b)(5) exception to the nondeductible terminable interest rule have all been strictly construed:

(1) S must be entitled for life to all of the income from the trust (or from a specific portion thereof), payable no less frequently than annually;

(2) *S* must have a power to appoint the entire trust (or the specific portion thereof), to *S* or to *S*'s estate, exercisable alone and in all events, either inter vivos or by will, or both; and

(3) no person other than *S* may be a beneficiary during *S*'s overlife and no one other than *S* may have any power to appoint any part of the trust (or the specific portion thereof) to any person other than *S*.

11.   *Power of Appointment Comparison With §2041.* Although the power of appointment required by §2056(b)(5) is a general power of appointment that will cause estate or gift tax to *S*, compare the language of §§2056(b)(5) and 2041: there is a significant difference. The unfortunate fact is that *S*'s power could fail to meet the requirements of §2056(b)(5) but still cause the appointive property to be included in *S*'s gross estate under §2041(a)(2). See, e.g., Condon National Bank v. United States, 349 F. Supp. 755 (D. Kan. 1972), and read again footnote 9 at page 141, in the *Brantingham* opinion. The converse does not, however, appear to be true.

To illustrate, imagine that *D* bequeathed property in a trust to pay the income quarterly to *S* for life. *S* also had an inter vivos power of appointment, authorizing *S* to direct the trustee during *S*'s life to transfer all of the trust corpus to any person or persons other than *S* or *S*'s estate. At *S*'s death, any remaining trust corpus is distributable to the children of *D* and *S* but *S* has no testamentary power of appointment. Notwithstanding that this transfer will cause inclusion in *S*'s gross estate at death, it does not qualify for the §2056(b)(5) marital deduction. Do you see the crack that the drafter fell into? Now suppose that, in addition to the inter vivos power, *S* also had a general testamentary power to appoint the remainder interest to *S* or *S*'s estate. With this change *D*'s trust will satisfy the §2056(b)(5) general power of appointment requirements. See E.T. 23, 1950-1 C.B. 133; Treas. Reg. §20.2056(b)-5(g)(5); S. Rep. No. 1013 (pt. 2), 80th Cong., 2d Sess. 17 (1948), in 1948-1 C.B. 331, 343.

Consider how the following added facts affect marital deduction qualification of *D*'s trust:

(a) If *S* also has a power to invade trust corpus for *S*'s own benefit, which would constitute an inter vivos general power of appointment;

(b) If a disinterested trustee has the power to invade trust corpus for *S*'s benefit, but only in the case of need and always considering *S*'s other available sources of income; this would be neutral for all tax purposes;

(c) If a disinterested trustee has the power to distribute trust corpus to *S*'s adult children, this would disqualify an otherwise qualifying trust;

(d) If a disinterested trustee has the power to distribute trust corpus to *S*'s minor children, in fulfillment of *S*'s legal obligation of support, this would constitute an indirect benefit to *S* that would not salvage an otherwise nonqualifying trust but it should not disqualify an otherwise permissible trust.

See Treas. Reg. §20.2056(b)-5(j); Estate of McCabe v. United States, 73-1 U.S. Tax Cas. (CCH) ¶12,912 (Ct. Cl. 1973); see also Rev. Rul. 69-56. The impact of income tax §678 (taxing capital gain to S even if it is allocable to trust corpus) should be considered in evaluating the advisability of inserting the power described in (a) in a marital deduction trust.

Consider the sense of the following: D bequeathed property in a trust to pay the income quarterly to S for life. S also had an inter vivos general power to withdraw trust corpus any time within the first three years after D's death. Any assets not withdrawn remain in the trust for the balance of S's life. At S's death, the assets then held in trust are distributable to their children, A and B, in equal shares. This bequest does not qualify for the §2056(b)(5) exception to the nondeductible terminable interest rule. Cf. Estate of Tompkins v. Commissioner, 68 T.C. 912 (1977), *acq.*; S. Rep. No. 1013 (pt. 2), 80th Cong., 2d Sess. 17 (1948), in 1948-1 C.B. 331, 343; Rev. Rul. 66-38. Is there any *policy* reason why D's estate should not be entitled to a marital deduction? Consider §§2041 and 2514: will the property that otherwise would benefit from the marital deduction escape payback taxation to S inter vivos or by inclusion in S's gross estate?

12.   ***Qualification of the Amount Subject to a "5 or 5" Withdrawal Power.***   In Estate of Hollingshead v. Commissioner, 70 T.C. 578 (1979), D's will created a testamentary trust for S, to pay all trust income to S quarterly and allowing the disinterested trustee to invade principal for S's comfort, welfare, maintenance, or support. S also was granted a noncumulative annually lapsing power to withdraw the greater of $5,000 or 5% of the value of the trust corpus. The amount equal to 5% of the trust corpus was $9,503.60 for the short year immediately following D's death. D's estate claimed a marital deduction under §2056(b)(5) for the present value of S's right to withdraw 5% of the trust corpus every year for the balance of S's life expectancy. The government conceded that the estate was entitled to a marital deduction equal to 5% of the value of the trust corpus at D's death ($9,503.60) but disallowed the additional deduction, which the Tax Court sustained. The government's concession as to the qualification of 5% of the corpus for the marital deduction was strange in that the government had ruled to the contrary on that issue in Rev. Rul. 66-38. Cf., PLR 8202023. However, the government had previously made the same concession in a 1969 district court case. Guiney v. United States, 295 F. Supp. 789 (D. Md. 1969), *rev'd on other grounds*, 425 F.2d 145 (4th Cir. 1970).

No deduction was allowable on account of S's power to withdraw trust corpus in years following the first short year beginning with D's death, because S had to live another year to exercise additional installments of the power. Thus, the power was not exercisable "in all events" as required by §2056(b)(5). Because the government conceded that an amount equal to 5% of the initial trust corpus qualified under §2056(b)(5), the court expressly refrained from ruling whether *S*'s power for that first short year was exercisable in all events. What abuse opportunity would exist if *D*'s estate plan gave *S* the requisite income interest for life, a five or five withdrawal right that lapses after the first year, and makes a QTIP election to qualify the remaining 95% of the trust? We study QTIP trusts shortly and you will discover then that the 95% will be includible in *S*'s gross estate at death under §2044. What is the §2514 related issue with the remaining 5% of the trust as to which the marital deduction otherwise would be granted?

If *D*'s will created a testamentary trust to pay income annually to *S* for life, corpus to such persons as *S* appoints by will, there is a state law question upon which marital deduction qualification turns. The issue is what "such persons" means, and whether it includes *S* or *S*'s estate. The trust would not qualify if *S*'s testamentary power of appointment could be exercised only (for example) if *S* did not remarry. See Estate of Edmonds v. Commissioner, 72 T.C. 970, 993-996 (1979). But the trust would qualify even if *S* were incompetent to make a valid will at the time of *D*'s death and at all times thereafter, assuming the power was a proper general power. See *Estate of Alperstein v. Commissioner*, reproduced at page 116.

13.   *Transfer Tax Consequences of Inter Vivos Exercise of Nongeneral Power to Invade Corpus.* Assume that, in the second paragraph of **11-11** at page 629, *S* was given the right to receive trust income for life, a nongeneral inter vivos power to appoint the trust corpus, *and* a general testamentary power over the remainder interest. Suppose that, after *D*'s death, *S* (then age 60) exercised the nongeneral inter vivos power by directing the trustee to pay $100,000 of trust corpus to an adult child. Would that exercise be subject to gift tax? Tax policy suggests that it should be. Otherwise, property qualifying for the marital deduction in *D*'s estate would escape inclusion in *S*'s transfer tax base. Yet, as we will see in Chapter 14, the inter vivos exercise of a nongeneral power is not ordinarily taxable under §2514, which is the gift tax version of §2041. Does this mean that *S*'s appointment of $100,000 escapes transfer taxation? The government's position is that it does not, because it regards *S*'s appointment as different from exercising a garden variety nongeneral power. See Treas. Reg. §25.2514-1(b)(2). Rather, *S*'s exercise is a taxable gift consisting of two elements: (1) a transfer of the right to income from the $100,000 for the balance of *S*'s life, taxable under §2511, and (2) a release of *S*'s testamentary general power to appoint the remainder interest in that $100,000, taxable under §2514(b). Under Treas. Reg. §25.2512-5, the value of the two components equals $100,000.

Although there is some uncertainty concerning the validity of the government's position regarding the first element, the government has the better side of that debate and, until this issue is discussed at page 920, you should assume that the government's position is valid.

14.   *Will Contracts.*   A bequest to a surviving spouse that is absolute in form may be treated similarly to a life estate with a power of consumption or disposition if the spouses made a contract regarding the ultimate transfer of their properties upon the death of the survivor. Even if such a contract is not expressly made by the spouses, some cases have held that the fact that the bequest is contained in a joint will (a single instrument executed by two persons as the will of each) or in mutual wills (separate wills, but with reciprocal or mirror image provisions) generates a presumption that a contract exists. See generally B. Sparks, CONTRACTS TO MAKE WILLS ch. 2 (1956). Contra, the 1990 version of Uniform Probate Code §2-514. Joint wills are rare but mutual wills are quite common, especially among married couples. It is desirable to include a provision in each will explicitly negating the existence of a contract if mutual wills are employed but the parties do not wish the survivor to be contractually bound not to revoke the will. If no binding contract was made, a bequest in joint or mutual wills to a surviving spouse may qualify for the marital deduction. See, e.g., Estate of Aquilino v. Commissioner, 31 T.C.M. (CCH) 906 (1972). If a contract does exist, however, problems may arise under §§2056(b)(4) and (b)(5). The former is considered later in this chapter. The latter is the subject of *Opal*:

Estate of Opal v. Commissioner
450 F.2d 1085 (2d Cir. 1971)

FRIENDLY, C.J.: The Estate of Edward N. Opal appeals from a decision reviewed by the Tax Court holding that a bequest by the decedent to his wife under a joint will constituted a terminable interest under I.R.C. §2056(b)(1) which was not within the exception provided by I.R.C. §2056(b)(5) and therefore did not qualify for the marital deduction provided for by I.R.C. §2056(a).

The joint will, executed on August 29, 1961, began by reciting that:

> We, Edward N. Opal and Mae Opal, his wife, . . . do make, publish and declare this to be our joint Last Will and Testament, hereby agreeing, each of us with the other in consideration of the dispositive provisions hereinafter set forth, that this Will shall be irrevocable by either of us without the written consent of the other and hereby revoking any and all former Wills and Codicils by us or either of us at any time heretofore made.

It continued:

> Second: In the event Edward N. Opal predecease Mae Opal.

A. We direct that his just debts and funeral expenses be paid as soon after his decease as may be practicable;

B. All the rest, residue and remainder of the estate of Edward N. Opal, real, personal and mixed, and wheresoever the same may be situate, is hereby given, devised and bequeathed unto the said Mae Opal, absolutely and forever;

C. Thereafter and upon the death of said Mae Opal, and after payment of her just debts and funeral expenses, all the rest, residue and remainder of the estate of said Mae Opal, real, personal and mixed, and wheresoever the same may be situate, is hereby given, devised and bequeathed unto our beloved son Warren Ian Opal, absolutely and forever.

There was a precisely similar provision, mutatis mutandis, to cover the event in which Mae predeceased Edward. Edward died on November 16, 1961; Mae survived. The estate tax return claimed the maximum marital deduction. The Commissioner disallowed this, a divided Tax Court affirmed, 54 T.C. 154 (1970), and this appeal followed.

If [§2056(b)(1)] stood alone, it would be plain that the bequest to Mae did not qualify. The language in the preamble of the joint will is so clear as to render supererogatory any citation of New York authority that a binding contract was created. Despite the gifts to the surviving spouse "absolutely and forever," the manifest intention of the spouses was that everything the survivor owned on death should go to their son. It would be absurd to read these clauses as dictating the devolution of the property the surviving spouse owned of her or his own right, but not that which such spouse had received from the other. While a subsequent will made by the survivor in breach of the contract would be admitted to probate, a New York court would compel the executors to perform the contract. Tutunjian v. Vetzigian, 299 N.Y. 315, 319 (1949); Rich v. Mottek, 11 N.Y.2d 90 (1962). It follows from this that "on the occurrence of an event or contingency," to wit, Mae's death, her interest in any of Edward's property that she still owned would necessarily pass to Warren regardless of any contrary desire on her part, and Warren might "possess or enjoy" such part of Edward's estate. With respect to any property of Edward's remaining in Mae's hands at her death, she would have had, and was intended to have, only a life interest. Although this portion of Edward's property might ultimately prove to be small or even nonexistent, §2056(b)(1) looks at the possibilities as of the date of the first death.

Congress somewhat tempered the severity of the "general rule" by an exception, §2056(b)(5). . . .

This provision in the 1954 Code replaced §812(e)(1)(F) of the Internal Revenue Code of 1939 as amended by the Act of April 2, 1948. The 1948 statute was generally similar except that in terms it was limited to property left in trust with the life income payable to the surviving spouse where such spouse had power "to appoint the entire corpus *free of the trust* (exercisable in favor of such surviving spouse, or of the estate of such surviving spouse, or in favor of either, whether or not in each case the power is exercisable in favor of others) . . ." (emphasis supplied). In Estate of Pipe v. Commissioner, 241 F.2d 210, 213 (2d Cir. 1957), a case governed by the 1948 statute, this court dealt with a will giving the widow, during her natural life, "full power to use, enjoy, sell or dispose of the income and principal" of the residuary estate "for such purposes or in such manner, as she in her uncontrolled discretion may choose, it being my desire to place no restraint on her in any respect concerning the absolute right of full disposition and use of the whole or any part of said income or principal of my residuary estate, except that she shall have no power over the disposition of such part thereof as remains unexpended at the time of her death." This interest was of the same sort as Mrs. Opal's under what we believe would be a New York court's construction of the joint will. This court held that the bequest did not qualify under §812(e)(1)(F) since, in order to comply with that provision, "the surviving spouse must be able to appoint the entire corpus 'free of the trust' to herself or her estate." Mrs. Pipe could not do that "because as long as any of the corpus of her estate remains, it will be held 'in trust' for the named remaindermen." 241 F.2d at 213 (footnote omitted). . . .

The legislative history shows that the changes made in §812(e)(1)(F) of the 1948 amendment of the 1939 Code in the course of its transformation into §2056(b)(5) of the 1954 Code were meant to accomplish two objectives. One was to provide that the exception should be available for legal life estates as well as trusts, an issue over which this court had been troubled in *Estate of Pipe* but which we assumed in the taxpayer's favor; the other was to make clear "that a right to income plus a general power of appointment over only an undivided part of the property will qualify that part of the property for the marital deduction." See House Report No. 1337, 83d Cong., 2d Sess. in 3 U.S.C.C.A.N. 4118-4119, 4461-4462 (1954), and Senate Report No. 1622, id. at 4758-4759, 5118-5119. Although the former purpose required elimination of the words "free of the trust," the committee reports make it plain that Congress did not intend to abandon the requirement, stated plainly enough in the new statute, that, in order for the bequest to qualify for the marital deduction, the surviving spouse must have power not only to consume the property or to give it to others but to vest it in herself or her estate, either during her life or by will. Under what we believe would be a New York court's reading of the joint will, Mrs. Opal could not do this. Any lifetime "gift" of Edward's property to herself would have been meaningless, since she already had complete power to consume it or, even taking a view of New York law most favorable to the appellant, to give it away, whereas any unconsumed portion of the "gift" to herself would remain part of her estate and would pass to Warren. Still more plainly she could not give the property to her estate, either by deed or by will, in any meaningful sense, since she had agreed that her entire estate should pass to Warren. As the statute requires that she have power to vest the property in herself or her estate, we need not consider whether, as urged by the Commissioner, New York law would forbid her giving the property to someone else in a manner that would frustrate the joint plan. See Rastetter v. Hoenninger, 214 N.Y. 66, 74 (1915).

Appellant fares no better if we look to the Estate Tax Regulations, although these do treat the problem in a curiously convoluted fashion. Treas. Reg. §20.2056(b)-5(g)(1)(i) says that the statutory test is not met unless the power falls within one of several categories, including:

> (i) A power so to appoint fully exercisable in her own favor at any time following the decedent's death (as, for example, an unlimited power to invade). . . ."

If this were all, the interest here bequeathed to Mae would qualify, since the will imposed no restrictions on her devoting Edward's property to her own use. However, what this subsection would seem to give, others take away. Treas. Reg. §20.2056(b)-5(g)(2) says:

> (2) The power of the surviving spouse must be a power to appoint the entire interest . . . as unqualified owner (and free of the trust if a trust is involved, or free of the joint tenancy if a joint tenancy is involved) or to appoint the entire interest . . . as a part of her estate (and free of the trust if a trust is involved), that is, in effect, to dispose of it to whomsoever she pleases. . . .

And Treas. Reg. §20.2056(b)-5(g)(3) says, among other things, that:

> (3) . . . in order for a power of invasion to be exercisable in all events, the surviving spouse must have the unre-

stricted power exercisable at any time during her life to use all or any part of the property subject to the power, and to dispose of it in any manner, including the power to dispose of it by gift (whether or not she has power to dispose of it by will).

The "power to appoint the entire interest . . . as unqualified owner" must include the power to appoint to one's self or one's estate in such a manner that the property will be free of conditions imposed by the testator upon the devolution of the property on the survivor's death. Since Mrs. Opal did not have this, the exception does not apply.

Affirmed.

Accord, Estate of Krampf v. Commissioner, 464 F.2d 1398 (3d Cir. 1972), *aff'g per curiam* 56 T.C. 293 (1971); Estate of Siegel v. Commissioner, 67 T.C. 662 (1977); Estate of Abbruzino v. Commissioner, 61 T.C. 306 (1973).

Would either the estate of Edward Opal or Mae Opal's estate be entitled to a deduction under §2053? See *Bank of New York v. United States*, reproduced at page 595.

The *Opal* court relied heavily on the analysis in Estate of Pipe v. Commissioner, 241 F.2d 210 (2d Cir. 1957). *Pipe* held that a legal life estate coupled with a power of consumption or disposition did not qualify for the marital deduction under the forerunner of §2056(b)(5) because that property arrangement does not allow the surviving spouse to "devise or bequeath any unconsumed corpus at her death to beneficiaries of her own choice." 241 F.2d at 213. Accord, Pyle v. United States, 766 F.2d 1141 (7th Cir. 1985), *rev'g* 581 F. Supp. 252 (C.D. Ill. 1984); Stockdick v. Pinney, 65-2 U.S. Tax Cas. (CCH) ¶12,351 (S.D. Tex. 1965); Estate of Vermilya v. Commissioner, 41 T.C. 226 (1963); Estate of Field v. Commissioner, 40 T.C. 802 (1963); TAM 9023004. Tyler v. United States, 468 F.2d 959 (10th Cir. 1972), disagreed with the *Pipe* analysis. The court found that, under applicable state law, the life tenant's power of disposition permitted gifts and that this was sufficient to qualify the arrangement for the estate tax marital deduction. Accord, Estate of Salter v. Commissioner, 77-1 U.S. Tax Cas. (CCH) ¶13,170 (5th Cir. 1977); Rev. Rul. 77-30.

How does the power to make gifts to others qualify as a power "exercisable in favor of such surviving spouse, or of the estate of such surviving spouse, or in favor of either, whether or not in each case the power is exercisable in favor of others"? Consider this statement from Estate of Field v. Commissioner, 40 T.C. 802 (1963), a case that is in accord with *Pipe*:

[T]he power to dispose of trust corpus in any manner, including the power to dispose of it by gift, [does not] necessarily qualif[y] the spouse's interest as a life estate with power of appointment within the meaning of the statute. Under the language of the statute and Treas. Reg. §20.2056(b)-5(g)(1), the interest of the spouse does not qualify for the marital deduction unless the spouse has the power to appoint the trust corpus to herself during her lifetime or to her estate at her death free of the trust. We do not find that either the will of the decedent in this case, as construed under Ohio law, or the decree of the Probate Court goes that far.

The *Opal* problem can be finessed by making a QTIP election under §2056(b)(7). Instead, usually it will be preferable not to make a will contract (and not to employ a joint will) and thereby avoid the problem altogether. Quaere whether the following Ruling carries the government's issue too far, albeit in a different direction.

Revenue Ruling 71-51

Advice has been requested as to the treatment, for Federal estate tax purposes, of jointly owned property and the proceeds of life insurance under the circumstances described below.

A husband and wife owned certain property as joint tenants. The husband owned several insurance policies on his life in which his wife was designated beneficiary. In 1955 they executed a joint, mutual, and contractual will that provided that all property, real as well as personal, of whatever kind and wherever situated at the time of the death of either, was to be held by the survivor during his or her life with the right to the income therefrom for life. Upon the death of the survivor, the remainder interest in the property was to be distributed to their children.

In 1964 the husband died. His gross estate consisted mainly of the aforementioned jointly held property and the proceeds of the policies of insurance.

The surviving wife died in 1968. The property originally held jointly with her husband and the insurance proceeds remained substantially intact and were distributed to the children as required by the terms of the joint and mutual will.

The following specific questions arose.

Question 1. In view of the outstanding joint and mutual will, does the interest in property that passed to the surviving wife upon the death of her husband qualify for the marital deduction?

Question 2. Is the value of property originally held jointly with her husband and the value of the proceeds of the insurance on his life includable in the deceased wife's gross estate?

. . .

Under the general rule relating to joint tenancies, a joint tenant who survives does not take the interest of the other tenant from him as his successor, but takes it by right under the instrument by which the tenancy was created. Thus, joint tenancy property passes outside of a will even though the interest that vests in the surviving tenant is limited by the terms of the instrument. Similarly, the proceeds of life insurance pass to the named beneficiary by reason of the designation in the insurance contract and not under the will or pursuant to any contractual provision in the will. Any restriction limiting the surviving tenant's (beneficiary's) interest to a life estate is not placed on the property by the decedent, but arises out of the contract voluntarily entered into by the survivor. Estate of Awtry v. Commissioner, 221 F.2d 749 (8th Cir. 1955), McLean v. United States, 224 F. Supp. 726 [E.D. Mich. 1963], aff'd, 65-2 U.S. Tax Cas. (CCH) ¶12,326 (6th Cir. 1965), and United States v. Ford, 377 F.2d 93 (8th Cir. 1967).

Accordingly, it is held in answer to Question 1 that complete ownership of the jointly held property and the proceeds of insurance passed from the decedent to the surviving wife within the meaning of 2056[(c)] of the Code. Such complete ownership is a nonterminable interest that qualifies for the marital deduction under §2056(a) of the Code notwithstanding that such property is subject to the restriction of the joint and mutual will as to its ultimate distribution.

The surviving wife's survivorship interest in the jointly held property and the insurance proceeds ripened into absolute ownership upon the death of her husband. However, under the contractual aspects of the joint and mutual will that were irrevocable at the death of the husband, the wife's fee interest in the property was reduced to a life estate, the remainder interest passing to the children. Thus, the wife is deemed to have made a transfer in 1964 of the entire value of the property, under which she retained for her life the right to the income from the property.

Accordingly, it is held in answer to Question 2 that the entire value of the remainder of the property held jointly with her husband and the proceeds of insurance on his life is includible in the deceased wife's gross estate under §2036 of the Code.

Awtry and *McLean* involved only property held jointly with the right of survivorship. *Ford* involved both jointly held property and life insurance. None of those cases dealt with Question 2 in the above ruling — inclusion of the property in *S*'s gross estate. On this question, compare Olson v. Reisimer, 271 F.2d 623 (7th Cir. 1959) (in similar circumstances only half of jointly held property was includible in *S*'s gross estate).

The Commissioner subsequently advanced the theory of Rev. Rul. 71-51 to the further conclusion that, at *D*'s death, *S* makes a taxable gift of the remainder interest (following a retained life estate) in the property subject to the contractual will. Accord, Grimes v. Commissioner, 851 F.2d 1005 (7th Cir. 1988), *aff'g* 57 T.C.M. (CCH) 1 (1987); Pyle v. United States, 766 F.2d 1141 (7th Cir. 1985), *rev'g* 581 F. Supp. 252 (C.D. Ill. 1984). If *S* is deemed to have a power to sell, consume, or dispose of the property subject to a contractual will, as *Opal* held, would this negate a present gift of the remainder interest? See Treas. Reg. §25.2511-2(c) and Estate of Lidbury v. Commissioner, 800 F.2d 649 (7th Cir. 1986), *aff'g* 84 T.C. 146 (1985).

With respect to the jointly held property, Rev. Rul. 71-51 was predicated on pre-1982 law. If *D* died after 1981, only half — not all — of the jointly held property would be includible in *D*'s gross estate. See §2040(b). Moreover, for post-1981 decedents, it may be possible to qualify *S*'s receipt of contractually restricted property by having *D*'s personal representative make a QTIP election under §2056(b)(7). Nevertheless, as illustrated by Hess, *The Federal Transfer Tax Consequences of Joint and Mutual Wills*, 24 REAL PROP., PROB. & TRUST J. 469 (1990), joint wills are a tax disaster and knowledgeable planners do not use them.

15.   *Income for Life.* A second condition of §2056(b)(5) is that *S* be entitled for life to all income from the interest (or a specific portion of the interest), payable no less frequently than annually. The regulations state that this condition is satisfied if *S* is given "substantially that degree of beneficial enjoyment of the trust property during . . . life which the principles of the law of trusts accord to a person who is unqualifiedly designated as the life beneficiary of a trust." Treas. Reg. §20.2056(b)-5(f)(1). This simple description belies the number of issues that arise with respect to the required income interest. Moreover, because this "all income annually" requisite is the primary entitlement for §2056(b)(7) qualified terminable interest property (QTIP) trusts, and because Treas. Reg. §20.2056(b)-7(d)(2) essentially incorporates by reference the Treas. Reg. §20.2056(b)-5(f) principles regarding qualifying income interests, this segment of marital deduction qualification constitutes a significant element of our study. Additional issues unique to the QTIP trust income interest are raised later in this chapter.

In reading this material, ask yourself the question: what is the purpose of the "all income annually" requirement?

Delay in Payment of Income.   *D* bequeathed property in trust for the life of *S*, with income from the trust payable as follows:

One year after the trust has been created and the net income from the trust for the past year has been determined, such income shall be quarterly paid to S as long as S may live, and this shall continue by paying in each year the net income of the past year.

D also provided S with a general testamentary power to appoint the trust corpus. Rev. Rul. 72-283 ruled that the bequest did not qualify for the estate tax marital deduction, saying:

The one-year delay in the payment of trust income conflicts with . . . the requirements that the income be payable annually or at more frequent intervals. In order that this condition be satisfied, it is required that the income be *currently* distributable to the surviving spouse. Where there is a mandatory delay of at least a year before income may be paid out, such payment of income is not considered current. Consequently, the trust does not comply with [Treas. Reg. §20.2056(b)-5(a)(2)].

Does any *policy* reason justify denial of a marital deduction in this case? Compare Treas. Reg. §20.2056(b)-5(f)(9). Note that, in addition to issues regarding the meaning of "reasonably" in that regulation, the entire exception for delayed income applies only with respect to estate income and not income of an inter vivos trust during the same postmortem administration period.

Fiduciary Powers.   Drafters of marital deduction trusts must insure that powers granted to the trustee do not impinge on S's right to the income, payable at least annually. See Treas. Reg. §§20.2056(b)-5(f)(3) and -5(f)(4). Rev. Rul. 69-56 describes a number of fiduciary powers that are permissible under §2056(b)(5) and, by extrapolation, those same powers should be permissible under §2056(b)(7) as well.

Consider the following cases in which D created a trust giving S the right to the income, payable at least annually, and a general testamentary power to appoint the remainder interest. In the case of each administrative power described below, only **(b)(2), (c)(1), and (c)(2)** will prevent qualification of a bequest to the trust for the marital deduction under §2056(b)(5) or §2056(b)(7).

(a) *Administrative powers*

(1) The trustee has complete discretion to allocate receipts between income and principal. Cf. Englund v. First National Bank, 381 So. 2d 8 (Ala. 1980); Old Colony Trust Co. v. Silliman, 223 N.E.2d 504, 507-508 (Mass. 1967).

(2) The trustee's fees are to be paid exclusively from trust income. See Revised Uniform Principal and Income Act §§13(a)(5) and 13(c)(1),

which call for a trustee's "regular compensation" and "all expenses reasonably incurred for current management of principal and application of income" to be charged half to income and half to principal.

(b) *Investment powers*

(1) The trustee is authorized to invest in mutual funds.

(2) The trustee is authorized to "retain any property originally constituting the trust or subsequently added to it, and to invest and reinvest trust corpus in any manner the trustee chooses, including, without limitation, stocks, bonds, mortgages, notes, bank deposits, limited partnership interests, shares of registered investment companies and real estate investment trusts, collectibles of all types, precious metals or stones, cash, real estate (including unimproved land), puts, calls, options, hedges, straddles, and other financial derivatives, domestic or foreign, without regard to restrictions relating to the type, qualify, marketability, or diversification requirements otherwise imposed on a fiduciary's investment authority." Cf. Estate of Smith v. Commissioner, 37 T.C.M. (CCH) 745 (1978).

(3) The disqualification in **(b)(2)** would be avoided if the trust instrument also contained the following provision: "Anything contained herein to the contrary notwithstanding, *S* may require the trustee to invest the trust estate so that it will produce such income as is consistent with the value of the trust corpus and with its preservation." If that provision were included in the trust instrument and *S* failed to exercise the power to force the trustee to convert unproductive property held in the trust, would *S*'s failure to exercise the power cause gift tax consequences?

(c) *Accumulation of income.* Rather than granting *S* the right to the income, payable annually:

(1) The trustee is directed to accumulate trust income and add it to corpus.

(2) The trustee is given discretion to distribute trust income to *S* or to accumulate it and add it to corpus.

(3) In **(c)(1)** or **(c)(2)**, disqualification would be avoided if *S* was given a general power exercisable inter vivos but not at death to appoint all or any part of the trust income or corpus to *S* or to any other person or persons. Would it matter if *S*'s power could be exercised only once a year? See Treas. Reg. §§20.2056(b)-5(f)(8), -5(g)(1).

(d) *Facility of payment.* To permit the trustee to avoid making distributions directly to a beneficiary and instead to expend amounts required or authorized under other provisions directly for the beneficiary or to reimburse others for amounts they expended for the beneficiary, a provision like the following authorizes the trustee to do such things as pay the beneficiary's rent, utility, and grocery bills rather than to give the beneficiary amounts needed for those living expenses.

If income or discretionary amounts of principal become payable to a minor or to a person under legal disability or to a person not adjudicated disabled but who, by reason of illness or mental or physical disability, is in the opinion of the trustee unable properly to manage his or her affairs, then that income or principal shall be paid or expended only in such of the following ways as the trustee deems best: (a) directly to the beneficiary or his or her attorney in fact; (b) to the legally appointed guardian of the beneficiary; (c) to a custodian for the beneficiary under a Uniform Transfers or Gifts to Minors Act; (d) by the trustee directly for the benefit of the beneficiary; (e) to an adult relative or friend in reimbursement for amounts properly advanced for the benefit of the beneficiary.

Particularly useful about this provision are the statements in (d) that the trustee may pay items directly for the beneficiary and in (e) that amounts paid to others are in reimbursement for amounts already expended for the beneficiary, along with the absence of any language that might imply that this provision itself is a principal distribution authority that is inappropriate for tax purposes. Rev. Rul. 85-35 provides that a standard facility of payment provision does not disqualify a §2056(b)(5) marital deduction trust, and TAM 8706008 draws the same conclusion for QTIP trusts. Compare, however, TAMs 9318002 and 8901008, in which facility of payment clauses disqualified the marital deduction because, for example, they granted the trustee discretion to accumulate income if *S* became incapacitated.

16.   *Saving Clauses.* These are very important and potentially useful additions that attempt to protect a drafter from inadvertent failure to comply with marital deduction requirements. The following discussion is not relevant *only* to §2056(b)(5) trusts or to the all-income-annually requirement, but this is a convenient place to study the issue.

Sometimes savings clauses are used in the context of an abuse transaction, which causes the government to distrust their use universally. They are quite common in marital deduction drafting, albeit their reach and effect can be uncertain. At a minimum, the decedent's statement of intent to qualify for the marital deduction, "any other provision in the document notwithstanding," is helpful guidance of interpretation. Is there anything to lose for inclusion of such a statement of intent? If not, would the following provision in *D*'s will be helpful in obtaining a marital deduction for bequests to a testamentary trust?

The trustees shall have all the powers and discretions granted to them under the terms of this Will and applicable state law, except those that would deprive my estate of a federal estate tax marital deduction for any bequest or devise made to the trust under this Will.

In this connection, consider the following materials. The Ruling arose in the charitable deduction arena but is analogous for marital deduction concerns.

Revenue Ruling 65-144

. . . The donor taxpayer established an irrevocable trust. The trust agreement directs the trustees to distribute the net income to, or for the use or benefit of X for life, thereafter to Y for such time as he survives, and thereafter to Z for such time as he survives the survivor of the first two named persons. The trust will terminate upon the death of the survivor of the above-named income beneficiaries and, at that time, the then trust assets and accumulated or undistributed income, if any, are to be distributed to certain educational institutions and hospitals.

The trust agreement provides, in part, that the trustees shall hold and manage the trust estate with the following powers and authorities:

G. In their discretion to allocate to either principal or income or between them any and all taxes (especially capital gains taxes) which they may be required to pay on behalf of this trust estate; notwithstanding the local rule of construction, the Trustee shall have the power to determine whether any expense, charge, or loss is to be borne by income or principal, or partly by income and partly by principal. . . .

J. To apportion stock, extraordinary and liquidating dividends and profits on sales, received by them between income and principal in such manner as they may deem fit and to determine what constitutes such dividends. The Trustee shall not be bound by local practice or the provisions of the Uniform Principal and Income Act. His determinations shall be final and binding upon all parties concerned. . . .

N. If, as a result of any Treasury Ruling or provisions of the Internal Revenue Code or the Regulations promulgated thereunder, the powers, authorities or discretions vested in the trustees herein are construed or considered to render the charitable remainder provided herein as nonseverable or not subject to specific ascertainment, the powers, authorities and discretions of the trustees are hereby revoked to the extent necessary to make them consistent and conform to said rulings, Code provisions, or Regulations to the end that the charitable remainder provided herein shall be deductible for Federal Tax purposes.

Treas. Reg. §25.2522(a)-2(a) provides, in part, that if a trust is created or property is transferred for both a charitable and a private purpose, deduction may be taken of the value of the charitable beneficial interest only insofar as that interest is presently ascertainable, and hence severable from the noncharitable interest.

In Commissioner v. Procter, 142 F.2d 824 (1944), one of the issues involved the taxpayer's denial of liability for Federal gift tax because the trust indenture contained the following provision:

> Eleventh: The settlor is advised by counsel and satisfied that the present transfer is not subject to Federal gift tax. However, in the event it should be determined by final judgment or order of a competent federal court of last resort that any part of the transfer in trust hereunder is subject to gift tax, it is agreed by all the parties hereto that in that event the excess property hereby transferred which is decreed by such court to be subject to gift tax, shall automatically be deemed not to be included in the conveyance in trust hereunder and shall remain the sole property of Frederic W. Procter free from the Trust hereby created.

As to this issue, the United States Circuit Court of Appeals for the Fourth Circuit said, in part: "We do not think that the gift tax can be avoided by any such device as this. Taxpayer has made a present gift of a future interest in property. He attempts to provide that, if a federal court of last resort shall hold the gift subject to gift tax, it shall be void as to such part of the property given as is subject to the tax. This is clearly a condition subsequent and void because contrary to public policy. A contrary holding would mean that upon a decision that the gift was subject to tax, the court making such decision must hold it not a gift and therefore not subject to tax. Such a holding, however, being made in a tax suit to which the donees of the property are not parties, would not be binding upon them and they might later enforce the gift notwithstanding the decision of the Tax Court. It is manifest that a condition which involves this sort of trifling with the judicial process cannot be sustained."

The court held that the condition in the case was contrary to public policy for three reasons: first, it has the tendency to discourage the collection of tax by the public officials charged with its collection, since the only effect of an attempt to enforce the tax would be to defeat the gift; second, the effect of the condition would be to obstruct the administration of justice by requiring the courts to pass upon a moot question; and third, because the condition is to the effect that the final judgment of a court is to be held for naught because of the provision of an indenture necessarily before a court when the judgment is rendered.

In the instant case, under the provisions of paragraphs G and J of the trust agreement, it is clear that all or portions of the trust corpus may be diverted from charitable to noncharitable uses, and that, consequently, without the saving provisions of paragraph N of the trust agreement, none of the charitable beneficial interests are presently ascertainable, and hence severable, from the noncharitable interests within the meaning of Treas. Reg. §25.2522(a)-2(a). It is further evident, by virtue of essentially the same basic considerations relied upon in the *Procter* case, that paragraph N of the trust agreement constitutes a mere attempt to impose a condition subsequent with respect to certain powers otherwise granted to the trustees therein named which is wholly void and ineffective in law because of being contrary to public policy.

Therefore, it is held that no deduction under §§2522(a) and 170(c) of the Internal Revenue Code of 1954 may be allowed in the instant case with respect to the present worth of the charitable remainder interests in the trust estate for Federal gift and income tax purposes.

Compare King v. United States, 544 F.2d 700 (10th Cir. 1976), in which the court sustained a saving clause in connection with a sale of stock to a trust that provided that, if the government determined that the value of the stock was higher than the price determined, the trust would pay the higher price, thereby avoiding any gift tax consequences. The government concluded in TAMs 200245053 and 9309001, and the Tax Court held in Estate of McLendon v. Commissioner, 66 T.C.M. (CCH) 946 (1993), that such a provision indicates the lack of a bona fide agreement because unrelated parties dealing at arm's length never would agree to a post sale adjustment of this variety. In the course of its opinion, the Tax Court cast grave doubt on the factual conclusion reached in *King* that the parties were acting at arm's length and free of donative intent, which makes *King* and its form of saving clause unreliable for future planning.

Uniform Trustees' Powers Act §3(b)

In the exercise of his powers including the powers granted by this Act, a trustee has a duty to act with due regard to his obligation as a fiduciary, including a duty not to exercise any power under this Act in such a way as to deprive the trust of an otherwise available tax exemption, deduction, or credit for tax purposes or deprive a donor of a trust asset of a tax exemption, deduction, or credit or operate to impose a tax upon a donor or other person as owner of any portion of the trust. "Tax" includes, but is not limited to, any federal, state, or local income, gift, estate, or inheritance tax.

For a discussion of §3(b) by the chair of the committee that drafted the Act, see Horowitz, *Uniform Trustees' Powers Act*, 41 WASH. L. REV. 1, 13-16 (1966). In considering Rev. Rul. 65-144, the author said: "It is to be noted that §3(b) . . . is a statutory prohibition upon the exercise of power and is not merely contained in a private instrument. Unless §3(b) is constitutionally invalid (it is submitted that it is not), the statute must be applied." 41 WASH. L. REV. at 16 n.86. In 2002 the Uniform Trustees' Powers Act had been enacted in 16 states and others have similar provisions. E.g., N.C. Gen. Stat. §32-26.

The following Ruling did not involve a saving clause per se, but the concept employed is analogous. In it *D*'s gross estate was valued at $1 million. Pursuant to a premarital agreement, *D* bequeathed $100,000 to *S* and left the residue of *D*'s estate to a child. *S* sued to set aside the will, to have the premarital agreement declared void, and to claim a statutory forced heir share of half of *D*'s estate under state law. This suit was settled by a bona fide compromise under which *S* received $400,000 from the estate, subject to the condition that *S* would return $300,000 to *D*'s estate if the government disallowed the estate's claim for a $400,000 marital deduction. Revenue Ruling 76-199 instead allowed the estate's claim to a $400,000 marital deduction, saying in part:

A condition inserted in a compromise agreement with a surviving spouse to the effect that the Service must make a favorable Federal estate tax marital deduction determination, before the payment received as the settlement of a bona fide right to take against the decedent's will and obtain the spouse's dower is to become final, neither adds to nor detracts from the otherwise unquestionably qualified nature of the spouse's interest under the marital deduction provisions of the Code. This situation is distinguishable from the mala fide circumstances present in the condition subsequent type of savings clauses considered in Rev. Rul. 65-144, 1965-1 C.B. 442, and Commissioner v. Procter, 142 F.2d 824 (4th Cir. 1944), where saving clauses were used to negate questionable powers or transfers in the event of adverse action by the Internal Revenue Service occasioned by such powers or transfers.

Does the following fall under the same umbrella? Consider how it informs the proper drafting of saving clauses:

Revenue Ruling 75-440

Advice has been requested whether, under the circumstances described below, a marital deduction is allowable under §2056 of the Internal Revenue Code of 1954 with respect to a testamentary trust created by the decedent.

In his will, the decedent created [a] marital deduction trust for his wife [with the following provision]:

> . . . In no event shall there be included in this transfer in trust any asset, or the proceeds of any asset, which will not qualify for the marital deduction [for] Federal estate tax purposes. . . .

In reference to the marital deduction trust, the will stated:

> My Trustees shall pay all of the net income of the Marital Trust, in convenient installments, not less frequently than semiannually, to my wife, A, as long as she shall live. All of the income of the Marital Trust not so distributed shall be accumulated and added to corpus.

The decedent-testator also established a residuary trust in the will, naming a child as the beneficiary.

Thereafter, the will set out the powers granted to the trustees of both trusts. The powers were set out only once rather than being separately stated for each trust. One of the powers granted was the power:

> To take out and carry policies of insurance on the life of the beneficiary of the trust hereunder, or on the life of any person or persons in which such beneficiary may at any time have an insurable interest, provided that the policies for such insurance shall be owned by the trust, and that the proceeds of such insurance shall be payable to the trust.

After setting out the trustee powers, the will stated:

> Notwithstanding anything herein contained to the contrary, any power, duty, or discretionary authority granted to my Fiduciary hereunder shall be absolutely void to the extent that either the right to exercise or the exercise thereof shall in any way affect, jeopardize or cause my estate to lose all or any part of the tax benefit afforded my estate by the Marital Deduction under either Federal or State Laws.

Section 2056(b)(5) of the Code allows a marital deduction for an interest in property passing to the surviving spouse if (1) the spouse is entitled for life to all the income from the property interest, payable annually or more frequently, (2) the spouse has an unqualified power to appoint the property interest to himself (or herself) or to his (or her) estate, and (3) no one can appoint the property interest away from the surviving spouse.

Treas. Reg. §20.2056(b)-5(f)(4) states in part:

> Provisions granting administrative powers to the trustee will not have the effect of disqualifying an interest passing in trust unless the grant of powers evidences the intention to deprive the surviving spouse of the beneficial enjoyment required by the statute. Such an intention will not be considered to exist if the entire terms of the instrument are such that the local courts will impose reasonable limitations upon the exercise of the powers. . . .

Treas. Reg. §20.2056(b)-5(f)(4) also states, by way of an example, that the trustees of a marital deduction trust may have the power to retain unproductive property as trust assets if the spouse can require that the trustee either make the property productive or convert it within a reasonable time.

There is no question that life insurance policies are not income producing property within the general meaning of the term. On the contrary, additional funds are normally required to pay periodic premiums. Thus, a beneficiary of a trust owning such assets would not be entitled to all of the income from the trust, or from a specific portion thereof, as required by §2056(b)(5). See Smith v. Commissioner, 23 T.C. 367 (1954).

The trustees' power under the will of the decedent to invest in insurance policies is expressly and unconditionally granted by the decedent and, hence, would not be subject to any general requirement of law that trust property be fully productive. Nor is either trust beneficiary empowered to demand that the trust property be made fully productive along the lines indicated in Treas. Reg. §20.2056(b)-5(f)(4).

A marital deduction will be allowed in this situation only if it is determined that the decedent-testator intended that the disqualifying trustee power apply to the residuary trust and not to the marital deduction trust. The intent of the testator in such situations is to be determined by reading the entire instrument. See Treas. Reg. §20.2056(b)-5(f)(4); RESTATEMENT OF PROPERTY §242 comment c; Estate of Todd v. Commissioner, 57 T.C. 288 (1971), acq., 1973-2 C.B. 4; Virginia Nat'l Bank v. United States, 307 F.

Supp. 1146 (E.D. Va. 1969), *aff'd on other grounds*, 443 F.2d 1030 (4th Cir. 1971).

A reading of the entire will in this particular case evidences an intent on the part of the decedent-testator to restrict the power to invest in unproductive property to only the trustees of the residuary trust. The saving clause is not a saving clause in the strict sense of the term, but is an aid in determining the testator's intent; that is, the existence of a saving clause that would "void" a disqualifying power given to the trustees of the marital deduction trust is relevant here only because it helps indicate the testator's intent not to give those trustees a disqualifying power.

Accordingly, a marital deduction is allowable under §2056 of the Code with respect to the value of the interest passing in the marital deduction trust.

The above analysis can be used only in situations in which it is initially unclear whether a disqualifying power applies to the trust for which an estate tax marital deduction is sought.

The saving clause involved here is to be distinguished from the condition subsequent saving clause in Rev. Rul. 65-144, 1965-1 C.B. 442. That saving clause sought to revoke a power that was clearly applicable to the trust for which the deduction was sought in the event of an adverse action by the Internal Revenue Service.

Rev. Rul. 65-144 distinguished.

See also Boston Safe Deposit & Trust Co. v. Children's Hospital, 351 N.E.2d 848 (Mass. 1976); TAM 7916006.

There is legislation in nearly 40% of the states authorizing trustees to invest in life insurance policies or annuities. See 3 A. Scott & W. Fratcher, THE LAW OF TRUSTS §227.8 n.9 (4th ed. 1988); G. Bogert & G. Bogert, THE LAW OF TRUSTS AND TRUSTEES §§616-667 (2d rev. ed. 1980). What do such statutes suggest for the lawyer drafting wills and trusts?

In addition to Rev. Rul. 75-440, see Guiney v. United States, 425 F.2d 145 (4th Cir. 1970), in which *D*'s will contained a provision that said:

I want to make it clear that I am giving [S] a general power of appointment over this trust in order that one half of my estate may qualify for the marital deduction . . . as it is fully my intention to take advantage of the marital deduction as provided by the Internal Revenue Code of 1954, or amendments made thereafter.

The obstacle to marital deduction qualification in that case arose because of a peculiarity in the applicable local law concerning the scope of powers of appointment. See, e.g., Frank v. Frank, 253 A.2d 377 (Md. 1969); Rev.

Rul. 76-502. On the strength of the clause indicating *D*'s intention to qualify for the marital deduction, the court held that the will conferred a general power of appointment on *S* and that the trust qualified for the marital deduction.

In Estate of Pierpont v. Commissioner, 336 F.2d 277 (4th Cir. 1964), the same obstacle to qualification arose but the will contained no saving clause similar to the one in *Guiney*. Although there was extrinsic evidence indicating *D*'s intention to qualify the trust for the marital deduction, the deduction was denied.

In Estate of Ellingson v. Commissioner, 92-1 U.S. Tax Cas. (CCH) ¶60,101 (9th Cir. 1992), rev'g 96 T.C. 760 (1991), income payable to *S* could be accumulated to the extent it exceeded what the trustee deemed necessary for *S*'s "needs, best interests, and welfare." The court never-theless allowed the marital deduction over the government's argument that the trust violated the all income requirement, because "[t]he Commissioner's reading of the Trust Agreement causes the agreement to self-destruct in defiance of the settlor's obvious intent." Loss of the marital deduction would have generated taxes that would have necessitated liquidation of the principal trust asset (a family farm), which would not have been in the "best interests" of *S*, as that standard was used in the accumulation provision itself. Thus, the accumulation provision was deemed not to apply in a manner that would disqualify the trust for the marital deduction. The court cited with approval Estate of Todd v. Commissioner, 57 T.C. 288 (1971), which allowed the marital deduction for a trust that required distribution to *S* of only so much income as "should be so expended to accomplish the purposes of this trust"; because a stated trust purpose was qualification for the marital deduction, that provision was deemed to require distribution of all trust income to *S* annually. Obviously, although the use of saving clauses cannot guarantee qualification for the marital deduction, it cannot hurt either. On the advisability of using saving clauses, see Johanson, *The Use of Tax Saving Clauses in Drafting Wills and Trusts*, 15 U. MIAMI INST. EST. PLAN. ¶2100 (1981).

Now, don't be lulled into complacent — and negligent – drafting by the potential ability to protect the marital deduction with such a provision. As the following case reveals, at a minimum litigation may result, the cost of which may fall on an inept drafter's malpractice liability insurer, and the deduction still may be lost. The following involves a spendthrift provision — notice how the drafter used a belt and suspenders approach to the issue and went too far by adding a second provision to address the perceived problem. Mae West is quoted as saying that "too much of a good thing . . . is wonderful!" But maybe only in the right circumstances!

Virginia National Bank v. United States
443 F.2d 1030 (4th Cir. 1971)

[*D*'s estate claimed a marital deduction for Trust A created under *D*'s will, which the government disallowed. The district court rejected the government's argument and the government appealed.]

BOREMAN, J.: The sole issue on this appeal is whether property willed to decedent's surviving husband in Trust A qualified for the marital deduction under §2056(b)(5) of the Internal Revenue Code of 1954. Resolution of this question depends upon an interpretation of decedent's will. . . .

Clause Third of the will established Trust A for the benefit of the surviving husband and Trust B for the benefit of the surviving husband and children. The parties are agreed that Trust B does not qualify for the marital deduction. Trust A directed the trustee "To pay to my said husband . . . so much or all of the principal thereof as he, by his sole act, may, from time to time and by request to my Trustee, require." Taken by itself, this clause would qualify Trust A for the marital deduction since it gives the surviving husband the unlimited right to invade the corpus of the trust.

However, clause Sixth of the will contained severely limiting language, apparently conflicting with the provisions of Trust A. Clause Sixth consisted of two paragraphs, the first being a "spendthrift" provision and the second being a "forfeiture" provision. This clause reads as follows:

> *Notwithstanding anything herein to the contrary,* no interest of any beneficiary in income or principal of the *trusts* [sic][13] created by this will shall be subject to pledge, encumbrance, assignment, sale, transfer, or alienation in any manner by any such beneficiary, nor shall any beneficiary have power in any manner to anticipate, charge or encumber such interest nor shall such interest of any beneficiary be in any manner liable for or subject to the debts, contracts, liabilities, engagements or torts of such beneficiary.

---

13. [The [sic]s were added to highlight the different ways the drafter chose to refer to the subject of this clause. A fundamental drafting principle is to be consistent and, when you mean the same thing, to use the same language — including the same punctuation or, in this case, the plural or singular. Should the drafter's malpractice liability insurer be required to pay the costs of litigation to establish the right to the marital deduction in this case? —ED.]

If at any time a beneficiary hereof shall attempt to pledge, encumber, assign, sell, transfer or alienate all or any part of his interest in the income or principal of the trust [sic] created by this will, or if a petition in bankruptcy shall be filed by or against any such beneficiary, or if any creditor, tort claimant, dependent or other person or persons, natural or corporate, or any Government, shall attempt by proceedings in any court or by any statutory process to subject all or any part of the interest of a beneficiary hereunder in the income or principal of the trusts [sic] created by this will, to the payment of any claim or demand whatsoever, including without limitation upon the generality of the foregoing, a claim for alimony, then *the entire interest of such beneficiary in such trust [sic] shall immediately cease and determine.* Thereafter, during the life of such beneficiary or until the prior termination of the trust [sic], the Trustee may pay to or expend for the care and support of such beneficiary such amounts only as the Trustee may from time to time in its discretion deem proper, from either the income or principal of the Trust Estate [sic] to which the beneficiary would be entitled but for this provision, and any surplus income not so used may in the discretion of the Trustee be expended for the support and maintenance of the spouse, lineal descendants and dependents of such beneficiary or any one or more of such persons or in the discretion of the Trustee, any such surplus income may be retained by the Trustee and added to the principal from which such income was derived. [Emphasis supplied.]

The parties agree that the first paragraph alone, the "spendthrift" provision, would not disqualify Trust A for the marital deduction, but the Government contends that the second paragraph, containing the "forfeiture" provision, applies to Trust A and limits the trust to the extent that it cannot qualify for the marital deduction. It is agreed by the parties that if the "forfeiture" provision of clause Sixth does apply to Trust A, it cannot qualify for the marital deduction.

The district court held that clause Sixth was not intended to apply to Trust A because to so apply it would defeat the intention of the decedent, as expressed in clause Third, to give her surviving husband an unfettered right to invade the corpus of Trust A. The court found that clause Third gave the surviving husband an interest equivalent to a fee simple estate in Trust A, and that to allow clause Sixth to invalidate or restrict this interest would be contrary to Virginia law under which any restriction in a will upon the right of the owner to alienate the fee or the right to control the disposition of any portion of the estate is void as being repugnant to the estate of the tenant in fee. The district court further held that clause Sixth should not be deemed to apply to Trust A because the language creating the surviving husband's fee in Trust A was clear and unambiguous and should prevail over the more general language employed in clause Sixth under the Virginia rule of construction that a specific provision in a will should prevail over a general Provision where two such provisions are inconsistent. Thus, within the "four corners of the will," the district court concluded that clause Sixth was not intended to apply to Trust A. . . .

We find ourselves unable to agree with the district court that the will may be clearly interpreted within its four corners. While clause Third taken alone would appear to give the surviving husband an unfettered right to invade the corpus of Trust A, clause Sixth would appear to be repugnant thereto and to create an ambiguity. Clause Sixth begins with the prefatory phrase, "Notwithstanding anything herein to the contrary," which would support a construction that clause Sixth would control over any other provision in the will. Thus, there are two clauses in decedent's will which are wholly inconsistent, thereby rendering the will ambiguous and the testator's true intent unascertainable from the will alone.

Where the provisions of a will are ambiguous Virginia law sanctions the admission of parol evidence of attendant facts and circumstances at the time the will was written to show the meaning of the language used by the testator. Pitman v. Rutledge, 95 S.E.2d 153 (Va. 1956). However, it is not proper to admit direct parol "evidence of the testator's actual intention, such as his declarations of intention, his informal memoranda for his will, his instructions for its preparation, and his statements to the scrivener or others as to the meaning of its language." Coffman's Adm'r v. Coffman, 109 S.E. 454, 457 (Va. 1921). Thus, we must sift through the parol evidence proffered at trial to determine what portion, if any, was admissible for purposes of clearing up the facial ambiguity in the will. Since *Coffman* held that direct evidence of a testator's actual intention as stated in his declarations of intention or instructions for his will's preparation is inadmissible, the district court was correct in refusing to accept *evidence of what the decedent actually said to the trust officer or to the attorney* who assisted her in the preparation of her will. However, the court should have received and considered, as evidence of attendant facts and circumstances, *the testimony as to what the trust officer and the attorney advised and told the decedent*, since such testimony does not involve her own direct expressions of intention.

Both the trust officer and the attorney testified that they had advised the decedent to create Trust A so that her surviving husband would have an unfettered right to reach the corpus, thereby qualifying Trust A for the marital deduction and consequently effecting a reduction of estate taxes. Both the trust officer and the attorney testified that they had advised the decedent that the completed will established Trust A in such manner that her surviving husband would have an unrestricted right to invade the corpus of Trust A, and that Trust A would qualify for the marital deduction. Both the trust officer and the attorney testified that they did not specifically discuss clause Sixth with the decedent although the attorney told her that clause Sixth was a "spendthrift" clause, that it had been approved by the bank, that he had usually included such a provision in wills which he had drawn. The trust officer testified that he had told the decedent that the completed will would give her surviving husband the unrestricted right to the property transferred to him by her will and would minimize estate taxes by qualifying Trust A for the marital deduction.

We hold that such parol evidence was admissible since it does not violate *Coffman*'s admonition and teaching that parol evidence of a testator's own *direct* expression of intent is inadmissible to show what was meant by language used in a will. This admissible proffered testimony clearly shows that the decedent was repeatedly and consistently advised and assured that Trust A would qualify for the marital deduction. From our experience in the practice of the law and as judges we recognize that utmost care and consideration must be given to the choice of language employed in the preparation of legal documents. The ordinary layman cannot be expected to grasp the meaning of technical words and phrases employed in the creation of even a simple trust estate with a "spendthrift" clause designed primarily for the protection of the trust beneficiary or the creation of a trust designed to provide tax benefits flowing from the statutory marital deduction. He or she must, of necessity, rely upon the advice and assurances of those trained in such matters. It appears from the proffered testimony that decedent was advised by the trust officer and the attorney, persons upon whose advice she relied, that Trust A would qualify for the marital deduction. No explanation was made of the possible effect on Trust A of subsequent language supplied by the attorney as "boiler plate." From these circumstances the intent of the decedent is clear that Trust A should qualify for the marital deduction. That intent should be given effect. . . .

Affirmed.

Compare Estate of Mittleman v. Commissioner, 522 F.2d 132 (D.C. Cir. 1975); Estate of Holland v. Commissioner, 64 T.C. 499 (1975), *acq.* (in which the courts readily resorted to extrinsic evidence). As the court indicated in *Virginia National Bank*, usually there must be an ambiguity in the express terms of the instrument for extrinsic evidence to be admissible. See also Gall v. United States, 75-1 U.S. Tax Cas. (CCH) ¶13,067 (N.D. Tex.), *aff'd*, 521 F.2d 878 (5th Cir. 1975). The RESTATEMENT (THIRD) OF PROPERTY — WILLS AND OTHER DONATIVE TRANSFERS §11.1 (1995) defines an ambiguity as "an uncertainty in meaning that is revealed by the text or by extrinsic evidence other than direct evidence of intention contradicting the plain meaning of the text."

On the question of the *type* of extrinsic evidence admissible to clear up an ambiguity, compare Estate of Trunk v. Commissioner, 77-1 U.S. Tax Cas. (CCH) ¶13,175 (2d Cir. 1977), in which the court said:

It would seem that the most compelling evidence of a testator's intent would be his own statements concerning it. Yet, this is the type of extrinsic evidence which has been most often rejected, the theory being that its admission would accomplish the oral testamentary devolution of property and encourage fraud and perjury. However, even here, the tendency is towards greater liberality in admissibility, 7 Warren's Heaton, Surrogates' Courts §30(1)(b) (1976), particularly in cases involving latent ambiguities. . . . Although some state courts continue to reject testimony of this nature where the ambiguity is patent, . . . we see little justification, in a proceeding before the Tax Court, for applying different evidentiary rules to latent and patent ambiguities. Proceedings before that court are equitable in nature; and, because the court is concerned with substance and realities rather than form, its search for the truth is not rigidly restricted to the contents of writings.

On remand, the Tax Court received testimony concerning *D*'s statements from the attorney who drew the will and allowed the marital deduction on the basis of that testimony. Estate of Trunk v. Commissioner, 37 T.C.M. (CCH) 497 (1978).

Compare Estate of Craft v. Commissioner, 68 T.C. 249 (1977), *aff'd per curiam*, 80-1 U.S. Tax Cas. (CCH) ¶13,327 (5th Cir. 1979), in which the Tax Court said:

[We hold] that in those instances where we are called upon to make a state law determination as to the existence and extent of legal rights and interests created by a written instrument, we must look to that state's parol evidence rule in deciding whether or not to exclude extrinsic evidence that bears on the disputed rights and interests under the instrument.

To hold otherwise could conceivably lead to an anomalous situation in which, because we had admitted and found convincing parol evidence that would have been excluded by a state court, we might determine and cause to be taxed certain interests and rights that a state court applying state law would find to be nonexistent. Such a result would do violence to that fundamental principle of tax law that state law creates legal rights and property interests while the Federal law determines what, and to what extent, interests or rights, so created, shall be taxed.

The RESTATEMENT (THIRD) OF PROPERTY — WILLS AND OTHER DONATIVE TRANSFERS §10.2 comment (1995) authorizes the use of direct and circumstantial evidence of intention, including the donor's direct declarations of intention

PART E.   THE QTIP EXCEPTION

Code References: *Estate Tax: §§2056(b)(7), 2044, 2207A*
                    Gift Tax: §§2518, 2519

17.   *Qualified Terminable Interest Property.* Before 1982, the following disposition would not have qualified for the estate tax marital deduction:

The trustee shall pay the trust income to S in convenient installments, at least annually, for life. On the death of S the trustee shall distribute the trust estate, including any accrued but undistributed income, to such of my descendants as S may appoint by will. To the extent this power is not validly exercised, on the death of S the trustee shall distribute the balance of the trust estate per stirpes to my then living descendants.

This is a nondeductible terminable interest: *S* is granted only a naked life estate that terminates at death, and an interest in the property (the remainder) passes to someone other than *S* or *S*'s estate after *S*'s death. *S* is granted only a nongeneral power of appointment that cannot be exercised in favor of *S* or *S*'s estate. Therefore, this trust does not qualify as a §2056(b)(5) exception to the nondeductible terminable interest rule.

Before enactment of the unlimited marital deduction rule in 1981, the existing dispositive vehicles to secure the marital deduction — e.g., outright gifts, estate trusts, and §2056(b)(5) power of appointment arrangements (or the §2056(b)(6 counterpart) — all required that *S* be given control that could alter devolution of the property after *S*'s death. Considering in particular the situation of a subsequent marriage and children of *D* by a former spouse (who *S* might not favor), Congress enacted the §2056(b)(7) exception to the nondeductible terminable interest rule to permit marital deduction qualification without granting *S* testamentary control over the deductible property, stating its purpose as follows:

[T]he committee believes that the [pre-1982] limitations on the nature of interests qualifying for the marital deduction should be liberalized to permit certain transfers of terminable interests to qualify for the marital deduction. Under [pre-1982] law, the marital deduction [was] available only with respect to property passing outright to the spouse or in specified forms which [gave] the spouse control over the transferred property. Because the surviving spouse [had to] be given control over the property, the decedent [could not] insure that the spouse [would] subsequently pass the property to his children. Because the maximum marital deduction [was] limited under [pre-1982] law to one-half of the decedent's adjusted gross estate, a decedent [could] at least control disposition of one-half of his estate and still maximize current tax benefits. However, unless certain interests which do not grant the spouse total control are eligible for the unlimited marital deduction, a decedent would be forced to choose between surrendering control of the entire estate to avoid imposition of estate tax at his death or reducing his tax benefits at his death to insure inheritance by the children. The committee believes that the tax laws should be neutral and that tax consequences should not control an individual's disposition of property. Accordingly, the committee believes that a deduction should be permitted for certain terminable interests. [H.R. Rep. No. 201, 97th Cong., 1st Sess. 159-160, 1981-2 C.B. 377-378.]

This §2056(b)(7) exception causes the illustrated trust to qualify for the marital deduction unless *D*'s personal representative elects to opt out of qualified terminable interest property (QTIP) treatment. Otherwise, property settled in qualifying trust and scheduled on *D*'s estate tax return as marital deduction property will generate a marital deduction in *D*'s estate under §2056(b)(7) and, by virtue of §§2044 and 2519, will be taxed as a transfer by *S* upon release or assignment of the income interest during life or upon termination of the income interest at death, all notwithstanding that *S* has been given only a naked life estate.[14]

---

14. Estate tax inclusion under §2044 essentially is the clone of §2041 inclusion of a §2056(b)(5) trust, and §2519 is the counterpart for gift tax purposes of §2514. A right of

To be a qualifying income interest for life, §2056(b)(7) requires that the property must "pass" from D, S must be entitled to enjoyment of the property for life (i.e., an income interest of the same type as that required for a §2056(b)(5) power of appointment trust), no other beneficiary has any rights in the trust during S's overlife, and an irrevocable QTIP election must be made (actually, an election is deemed to have been made if the treatment on the estate tax return indicates that one was intended). Because the passing requirement is the same as for all other marital deduction purposes, no added attention need be devoted to it.

Qualifying Income Interest for Life. The QTIP exception requires that S be granted a "qualifying income interest for life," which has the same requirements as are demanded of §2056(b)(5) trusts. By regulation, all of the well-established §2056(b)(5) rules with respect to guaranteeing the income interest are adopted by reference. Treas. Reg. §20.2056(b)-7(d)(2). Thus, unproductive property should not be held for more than a reasonable time without S's consent (or one of a trio of other cures), income should be paid at least annually, and an income interest that terminates on remarriage (or on any other contingency during S's life) does not qualify.

One notable difference between the §2056(b)(5) and QTIP income requirements spawned some controversy. Unlike a §2056(b)(5) qualifying trust, in which S must be given a general power to appoint any accrued but undistributed income at death ("stub" income earned before S's death but not yet distributed under the fiduciary's periodic distribution procedure), the QTIP regulations provide that stub income of a QTIP trust at S's death need not be subject to such a power, nor must it be paid to S's estate. Treas. Reg. §20.2056(b)-7(d)(4). Instead, although the stub income will be subject to §2044 inclusion in S's gross estate at death, along with the rest of the QTIP trust property, it may be distributed in the same manner as the QTIP trust corpus. Treas. Reg. §20.2044-1(d)(2). As a result, S need not be given control over its devolution.

Unfortunately, notwithstanding that it is favorable to most taxpayers, the validity of this stub income regulation has been questioned. While the regulation was still in proposed form, the government's position was declared invalid in Estate of Howard v. Commissioner, 91 T.C. 329 (1988), rev'd, 910 F.2d 633 (9th Cir. 1990).[15] The Tax Court declared that there is

---

reimbursement exists under §2207A for the taxes caused by either section, much the same (although with significant differences) as §2207 applies to §2041, §1014(a)(10) provides a basis adjustment at S's death, and §2044(c) regards property includible under §2044 as passing from S for all wealth transfer tax purposes. No similar provision appears in §2519, presumably because the legislative history of §2056(b)(7) indicates that Congress thought that S cannot make a transfer of the corpus in a QTIP trust during life.

15. The genesis of *Howard* and the litigation posture of the parties was somewhat unusual. Mrs. Howard died less than three weeks after Dr. Howard's personal

no statutory support for the government's treatment and that, to comply with the all-income requirement of §2056(b)(7), the "stub" income must be subject to S's control either by requiring that it be paid to S's estate or by giving S a general power to appoint it. Because S had no control over the stub income in *Howard*, the Tax Court held that the entire marital deduction was lost to D's estate. Based on legislative history to the effect that the §2056(b)(7)(B)(ii)(I) all income annually requirement was meant to mirror the same requirement under §2056(b)(5), the Tax Court held that the position stated in the proposed regulation was inconsistent with established §2056(b)(5) rules. Finding no indication in the legislative history of a Congressional intent to deviate from those requirements, the court disallowed the marital deduction. The Tax Court dismissed the contrary proposed regulation on the ground that proposed regulations are "not entitled to judicial deference and carry no more weight than a position advanced on brief." 91 T.C. at 337. Subsequent to that decision, the regulation was finalized, without change on this score.

In reversing the Tax Court, the Court of Appeals for the Ninth Circuit upheld the government's position as a valid interpretation of the Code, consistent with the legislative history behind §2056(b)(7), stating:

> As long as the income is payable at least annually and the spouse is entitled to all regular distributions as long as she lives, the statutory test is met. . . .
>
> The statute did not impose . . . the requirement that the spouse hold a power of appointment over the stub income. All that was required was that the spouse be entitled to all the income at the time of its annual or more frequent distribution. . . .
>
> The whole purpose of the QTIP provision was to dispense with the requirement of a power of appointment as a condition of entitlement to the marital deduction. Since the power of appoint-

---

representative filed his estate tax return, which claimed a QTIP marital deduction. After running some computations, the personal representative of Mrs. Howard's estate determined that almost $675,000 less tax would be paid over both estates if Dr. Howard's estate did not qualify for the marital deduction, instead incurring tax in his estate that would support a §2013 previously taxed property credit in Mrs. Howard's estate based on the value of her life estate in the trust. See the illustration at pages 718-719 for an example of this result. Because she died within 10 months after his death, income paid to her pursuant to that life estate increased the value of her estate very little but, under the applicable actuarial tables, generated a significant credit for a portion of the taxes caused by inclusion of the trust assets in Dr. Howard's estate. Therefore, his estate sought to reverse the QTIP election. Because it could not revoke that irrevocable election, Dr. Howard's personal representative filed an amended return claiming that the trust did not qualify as QTIP property because a provision in the trust instrument specified that accrued but undistributed income at Mrs. Howard's death would be paid to the next income beneficiary of the trust. The government argued that the trust did qualify because, under the proposed regulation, this income need not be paid to her estate or be made subject to a general power of appointment.

t is not required, there is no need to require a power of
osal of the undistributed income.

F.2d 633, 635, 636-637 (9th Cir. 1990). Notwithstanding the logic of
this holding, the Tax Court again held (in a 9-6 reviewed decision) in Estate
of Shelfer v. Commissioner 103 T.C. 10 (1994) (reviewed by the court),
rev'd, 86 F.3d 1045 (11th Cir. 1996), that failure to pay the stub income to
S's estate or make it subject to a general power of appointment in *S* meant
that the marital trust failed to meet the QTIP requirements and, as a
consequence, §2044 inclusion would not occur. The Tax Court noted in
Shelfer that the proposed regulation had been finalized but that its effective
date did not apply to the decedent's estate in that case. The Tax Court
expressly declined to indicate how it will decide a case to which the final
regulation applies.

The Tax Court's decision in *Shelfer* was reversed. Because the
government's position in the final regulation is binding on the government,
taxpayers need not worry about disallowance even if the stub income is not
payable or subject to a general power of appointment in *S*. Moreover, if the
QTIP trust is silent about the stub income issue, the state Principal and
Income Act may cover the issue and mandate distribution of the stub income
to *S*'s estate, meaning this issue may exist only in documents that alter state
law by specifically addressing the issue.

A bill that would have codified the government's regulation and permit
stub income to be distributed without impairing a QTIP qualification was
introduced but never was enacted. Revenue Reconciliation Act of 1995
§11613, H.R. 2491.

No General Power of Appointment Is Required. Unlike a
§2056(b)(5) trust, *D* need not give *S* a general power to appoint QTIP trust
corpus or, for that matter, any control over the remainder interest. Thus, the
QTIP trust is attractive to many clients who want to "handcuff" *S* while at
the same time qualifying for the marital deduction. This does not preclude *D*
from granting *S* a power to appoint the property at death (but not during
life) to or among a class of permissible appointees specified by *D*, nor does
it preclude giving *S* a power to withdraw QTIP trust corpus during life, so
long as there is no restriction on withdrawal that *S* must make a gift (which
could constitute a constructive power of appointment in violation of the
statute, as discussed next).

No Other Beneficiaries During S's Life. Although the trustee
may invade principal for the benefit of *S*, no one (according to the

legislative history, not even $S)^{16}$ may have a power to divest S of any interest in the trust. For example, TAM 8526009 determined that a power granted to the trustee to distribute principal to S for "comfortable support, maintenance, health and/or [sic] education *and that of the settlor's issue under [S's] care and supervision*" (emphasis added) would not disqualify an otherwise valid QTIP trust. The government noted the fact that distributions could be made only to S (notwithstanding the determination of needs used to measure the amount to be distributed) and that S could choose to retain the funds or disburse them in S's sole discretion. TAM 8701004 retracted that advice because the government determined that, under state law, S was deemed to be under a fiduciary obligation with respect to distributions made for the needs of D's issue and therefore could be compelled to use funds received from the trust for the exclusive benefit of those individuals. Accordingly, because those indirect beneficiaries were not persons to whom S necessarily owed an obligation of support, the government determined that "[t]he terms of the . . . Trust authorized the trustee to appoint trust property to persons other than [S]" in violation of §2056(b)(7)(B)(ii)(II).[17] The marital deduction ought to be allowed if the distribution power is limited to distributions measured by the needs of persons S is obliged to support, or if the trust negates any fiduciary obligation otherwise imposed on S to pass any distributions received along to the descendants whose needs were the measure of those distributions. See Parasson v. United States, 87-1 U.S. Tax Cas. (CCH) ¶13,708 (N.D. Ohio 1987).

If D wants to add flexibility to a QTIP trust, D may give S a withdrawal right during life and give anyone a power of appointment exercisable at or after S's death, all without violating the sole beneficiary restriction in §2056(b)(7)(B)(ii) (flush language). In addition, D could make S the trustee of the QTIP trust.

Assume that D bequeathed property in trust, directing the trustee to pay the income quarterly to S for life, remainder to D's children by a former marriage. See if you can explain the distinction between the following qualified and nonqualifying powers and interests:

(a) S may have a testamentary power to alter the shares distributable to D's children.

---

16.   H.R. Rep. No. 201, 97th Cong., 1st Sess. 161 (1981) states that "there must be no power in any person (including the spouse) to appoint any part of the property subject to the qualifying income interest to any person other than the spouse during the spouse's life."

17.   To the same effect is TAM 9005002, in which the QTIP deduction was disallowed because the trust authorized distributions for S and "any child of mine who is dependent upon [S] for his or her support," because a dependent child of D might not be a person to whom S owed a legal obligation of support.

(b) *S* also may have a presently exercisable power to accelerate the remainder by making a nonqualified disclaimer but not by appointing trust corpus to such of *D*'s children as *S* selects. See H.R. Rep. No. 201, 97th Cong., 1st Sess. 161 (1981).

(c) *S* may have a power of withdrawal but may not have a presently exercisable power to appoint trust corpus to anyone else.

(d) *D*'s child may not purchase QTIP trust property for less than its fair market value or borrow from the trust at below market rates. See Estate of Rinaldi v. United States, 97-2 U.S. Tax Cas. (CCH) ¶60,281 (Ct. Fed. Cl. 1997); TAMs 9147065, 9139001, and 8843004.

(e) *D*'s sibling may have a testamentary power to appoint the remainder interest following *S*'s life estate to such of *D*'s children as the sibling selects. This power definitely is permissible if *S* dies before *D*'s sibling, but it is uncertain whether a power exercisable by a third party before the death of *S* and only effective at or after *S*'s death is permissible. See Joint Committee on Taxation, General Explanation of Economic Recovery Tax Act of 1981, 97th Cong., 1st Sess. 235 (1981). Based on tax *policy*, is there anything wrong with the power given to *D*'s sibling?

(f) Relative to **(c)**, TAM 8943005 advised that *S* may be given a presently exercisable *general* power of appointment without losing QTIP status. In that case *D* granted *S* an annually exercisable, inter vivos, general power to appoint to *S* or to anyone else the greater of $5,000 or 5% of the value of a QTIP trust. The government concluded that the power is permissible in a QTIP trust, noting that the logic underlying the §2056(b)(7)(B)(ii)(II) prohibition against powers of appointment in favor of anyone other than *S* is to "insure that the value of the property not consumed by the spouse is subject to tax upon the spouse's death (or earlier disposition) . . . ." The TAM stated that this logic is not violated by a general power because wealth transfer tax is not avoided, and concluded that denying this power would be unnecessarily restrictive:

[W]e believe the better reading of the legislative history would preclude a spousal power of appointment only where the exercise of the power would not be subject to transfer taxation; i.e., where the power is not a general power of appointment as defined in §2514 of the Code. An interpretation requiring that a spouse must first take physical possession of the property prior to a transfer to a third party would focus too much attention on the form of transaction. It is sufficient that the exercise of the power by the spouse in favor of a third party would be subject to transfer taxation.

Quaere, then, why the power of appointment should be restricted by a five or five limitation? Furthermore, would the same result apply if *S*'s power, as trustee of the marital trust, to appoint to *S* or others did not constitute a general power under §2514 because, for example, it was a joint power exercisable with an adverse party or a power subject to an ascertainable standard? Finally, is §2519 applicable, because any appointment of corpus will carry income away from *S*? The abuse to which §2519 is aimed is an assignment of income that permits avoidance of wealth transfer tax on corpus. That concern exists under the nongeneral, presently exercisable power of appointment scenario.

Legal Life Estates Can Qualify For QTIP Treatment. A QTIP disposition need not be in trust. A devise of Blackacre "to *S* for life, and on *S*'s death to my then living descendants by representation" would be in qualifying form and would constitute QTIP marital deduction property if listed on the appropriate Schedule to Form 706 (estate tax return) or Form 709 (gift tax return). See Treas. Reg. §20.2056(b)-7(h) *Example 1*. Thus, although legal life estates are rarely used in estate planning because of their inflexibility, the government has ruled that QTIP treatment is available for real property in which *S* has the full measure of enjoyment granted to a life tenant not in trust. This means, for example, that *D* must couple *S*'s right to occupy property for life with a life estate in any sale proceeds or the right to lease the property and enjoy the rent if *S* chooses not to enjoy the current right of occupation. See, e.g., Estate of Peacock v. United States, 914 F.2d 230 (11th Cir. 1990), *rev'g* 90-2 U.S. Tax Cas. (CCH) ¶60,050 (N.D. Ala. 1989); TAM 9040001; and PLRs 9242006, 9126020, 8352062, 8351141, 8351098.

Marital deduction qualification is not lost if obligations that are imposed on *S* are consistent with those ordinarily imposed on a life tenant, such as property taxes, payments under a deed of trust note, maintenance expenses, and costs of repairs. Estate of Novotny v. Commissioner, 93 T.C. 12 (1989); PLR 9046031. And in states that still recognize the common law dower estate or provide a comparable statutory substitute (i.e., a life estate in an undivided third of *D*'s lands), the dower estate may qualify for the marital deduction if a QTIP election is made. Otherwise, the dower interest will not qualify unless *S* receives its commuted value as a lump sum settlement. Indeed, by virtue of the last clause of §2056(b)(7)(B)(ii)(I), even the Louisiana form of usufruct in consumable or nonconsumable property qualifies for QTIP treatment if it is for the life of *S*.[18]

18.   *The QTIP Election.* For QTIP transfers to be deductible, §§2056(b)(7)(B)(v) and 2523(f)(4) require the executor to make an affirmative election. Nevertheless, the government encountered so much trouble with returns that compute the deduction but fail to make the

---

18.   See Darby v. Rozas, 580 So.2d 984 (La. App. 1991), explaining the difference between a "conventional" (testamentary or contractual) usufruct for life and the more limited "legal" usufruct that terminates on death or remarriage of the surviving spouse.

election[19] that it has adopted a more liberal administrative position. If property is scheduled on the return as deductible and the tax is computed with the deduction, the forms deem the election to have been made unless an affirmative election *out* of QTIP treatment is made.[20] Naturally this applies only with respect to transfers that otherwise are "QTIPable" because they would qualify if the election were made. Indeed, as to those interests, the government has gone so far as to presume at S's death that any interest that was QTIPable was allowed as a deduction in D's estate and therefore is includible under §2044 in S's gross estate unless proven to the contrary.[21]

------

19.   Before the November 1987 version of the Form 706 estate tax return moved the QTIP election to Schedule M (Bequests to Surviving Spouse), page 2 of Form 706 included six elections, of which number 4 was for "a marital deduction for an otherwise nondeductible interest under §2056(b)(7)," and Schedule M required only an inventory of items passing to S that qualified for the election. That separation of the election from Schedule M created many problems, and eventually the election was moved to Schedule M, but even there it was not uncommon for the return preparer to claim the deduction but not check the box to formally make the election. For some time the government's position was illustrated by TAM 8427004, in which the executor used a pre-1981 Form 706, which did not have a box for making the QTIP election. Notwithstanding that the terminable interest property was listed on Schedule M and a marital deduction was claimed, the government denied the deduction, stating:

The mere listing of the trust property on Schedule M does not constitute a clear manifestation that the executor is selecting between two alternatives that have such significant tax consequences. Rather, we believe the executor's actions in listing the property as a deductible interest, with no other explanation, was an equivocal act that could be subject to several interpretations.

Much more common was the kind of situation in which the executor checked "no" in the QTIP box on page 2 but listed a terminable interest on Schedule M and claimed a deduction for it. See, e.g., Estate of Robinson v. United States, 90-2 U.S. Tax Cas. (CCH) ¶60,045 (D.C. Ga. 1990) (QTIP deduction denied because of a failure to make an affirmative election on the federal estate tax return); Estate of McCants v. Commissioner, 61 T.C.M. (CCH) 2038 (1991) (QTIP deduction denied because the estate checked "no" to the QTIP question on the federal estate tax return). A third kind of error was illustrated by TAM 9117007, which also denied the marital deduction for failure to check the QTIP box on line 2 of Schedule M of the November 1987 version of Form 706. The estate claimed the marital deduction for the QTIP assets, but listed them on Part I of Schedule M, without referring to the QTIP election. The government now accepts that listing property on Schedule M and making a tax payment (or no tax payment) reflecting the marital deduction is a sufficiently "clear manifestation" of intent.

20.   The Form 706 (estate tax return) specifies on Schedule M that trust (or other) property that meets the requirements of qualified terminable interest property and that is listed on Schedule M and the value of which is deducted in the tax calculation is deemed to have been elected unless the executor specifically identifies property to be excluded from the election. There is no QTIP election box on Schedule M (other than to elect out of §2056(b)(7)(C) automatic QTIP treatment for annuities includible under §2039).

21.   Treas. Reg. §20.2044-1(c), which likely was promulgated to prevent another case like Estate of Letts v. Commissioner, 109 T.C. 290 (1997), in which the trust was not defective as QTIP property but the then required QTIP election never was made. The marital deduction was claimed and allowed in the estate of the first spouse to die but the surviving spouse's estate claimed that the trust was not includible as QTIP property because the election was lacking. The Tax Court applied a little used "duty of

For estate tax marital deduction purposes, the decedent's executor is responsible for the §2056(b)(7)(B)(v) election with respect to property includible in D's gross estate. Does it matter whether any property is not in that person's possession (i.e., property passing outside of probate)? See Treas. Reg. §20.2056(b)-7(b)(3). Consult Treas. Reg. §§20.2056(b)-7(b)(4) and 25.2523(f)-1(b)(4) to see how the election is made.

Formula Election. In making the election, the executor can, but need not, describe the assets or state the pecuniary amount deductible. Treas. Reg. §20.2056(b)-7(b)(2)(i) permits the executor to make a formula election, such as that fractional share "required to reduce the federal estate tax on the decedent's estate to zero." As stated in TAM 9217005, the government recognizes the fact that:

As a practical matter, the pecuniary amount of the property passing to the marital trust, the value of the property subject to the election, and the assets the executor selects to fund the marital trust will not be known until the value of the gross estate for estate tax purposes is finally determined and administration of the estate is complete. Further, any increase in the valuation of estate assets pursuant to an audit would, under the terms of the trust and formula election, increase the pecuniary amount passing to the trust, the value of the property subject to the election, the quantity of estate assets needed to fund the trust, and the election portion.

Thus, a QTIP formula election is permissible and, given the changes that can occur during audit of an estate, may be the smartest approach.

Protective QTIP Elections. Treas. Reg. §20.2056(b)-7(c) authorizes an executor to make a protective QTIP election if (and only if) at the time the federal estate tax return is filed there is a bona fide issue concerning whether an asset is includible in D's gross estate, or the amount or nature of the property S is to receive. Among other things, the protective election, which is irrevocable, must identify the basis for the protective election, which means the return must flag its questionable positions.

Authorizing the Election. A QTIP election can be made for all property that is qualified for the election or it can be made for only a portion of the qualified property. The portion can be defined as a set percentage of the qualified property or as a fraction defined by formula. Treas. Reg. §20.2056(b)-7(b)(2). When only a portion of the qualified property is elected for QTIP treatment, it is called a "partial election."

---

consistency" to prevent the taxpayer from benefiting from a position inconsistent with that taken in the earlier estate.

It is not wise in most cases for *D*'s will to direct the personal representative as to whether and to what extent a QTIP election should to be made. Instead, *D*'s will should authorize the personal representative to elect QTIP treatment or not in such amounts or proportions as the personal representative determines in its discretion. To the extent that any statement of direction is thought to be appropriate, the governing document should contain precatory language suggesting factors the personal representative may consider in deciding whether or to what extent to make an election. For example, it would be particularly unfortunate to direct that an election be made to qualify the maximum amount for the marital deduction if *D* and *S* should happen to die in quick succession in such circumstance that equalization would be the best tax-oriented result. A fine-tuned partial election could be used instead to minimize the aggregate tax payable by the two estates.

Complicating this issue, however, is the notion that a fiduciary's duty to maximize *D*'s estate by minimizing its taxes may make it imprudent for a personal representative ever to make a partial election if the effect is to cause *D*'s estate to pay a greater tax. Because the personal representative's duties run only to the single estate represented, the absence of an express authorization by the decedent might make it necessary to view the impact of a proposed election on *D*'s estate alone. The personal representative might be compelled to minimize the tax on *D*'s estate even though a partial election would be more prudent when viewing both spouses' estates together. See Ascher, *The Quandary of Executors Who Are Asked to Plan the Estates of the Dead: The Qualified Terminable Interest Election*, 63 N.C. L. REV. 1, 48 (1984). The wisest course would be for *D*'s will expressly to authorize the personal representative to consider the impact of an election on the estates of both spouses when determining the extent to which an election will be made, and to hold the personal representative harmless for the effects of this decision on any beneficiary.[22]

Partial QTIP Elections. The Code and regulations allow the decedent's executor to make a partial QTIP election. The practice is to include a provision in the decedent's will authorizing such an election.

---

22.   The clause recommended by Ascher, 63 N.C. L. REV. 1, 48 (1984) reads:

I hereby authorize my executor, in his sole discretion, to elect that none, any part, or all of any amount passing under this trust be treated as qualified terminable interest property for purposes of qualifying for the marital deduction allowable in determining the federal estate tax and any state death tax on my estate, regardless of the fact that such taxes are thereby increased or that there is a change in the proportions in which various persons (including my executor) share in my estate. The decision of my executor shall be binding and conclusive upon all persons interested in my estate, and my executor shall have no liability as a result of such decision.

Partial elections may be made by formula,[23] which is advisable to protect against the consequences of using a specific fraction or percentage if values or other factors change on audit, in which case the desired tax results might not be achieved. The availability of making a partial election by formula is important because, once made, the election is irrevocable. §2056(b)(7)(B)(v).

Self-adjusting formula fractional elections should be used. The numerator should specify the result sought (for example, the amount needed to reduce the estate tax incurred in the estate to the lowest amount possible) and the denominator should be the value of the fund against which the fraction is applied. Treas. Reg. §20.2056(b)-7(h) *Examples 7* and *8* provide illustrations of provisions that make qualifying partial elections. Instead of paying income to *S*, the regulations also permit the payment of a specified annuity to *S*. Treas. Reg. §20.2056(b)-7(h) *Examples 11* and *12*; and see Treas. Reg. §§20.2056(b)-5(c)(3) and -5(c)(5) *Example (1)* (relating to power of appointment trusts). Instead of using a reduce to zero formula (i.e., one that reduces *D*'s estate tax to zero), it appears to be permissible to adopt a formula that produces a taxable estate of a predetermined size. The flexibility of the formula approach permits a wide variety of arrangements.

Separate Shares Permitted

In addition to drafting a formula partial election properly, the executor should consider the effect that the partial election will have on other portions of the document. For example, is it clear that the tax arising on *S*'s death under §2044 will be payable only out of the elected portion of the trust, and that the tax arising on *D*'s death by virtue of making only a partial election will be paid out of the nonelected portion of the trust? To help obtain those results, Treas. Reg. §20.2056(b)-7(b)(2)(ii) permits separate trusts to be created by a partial election.

Even if separate trusts are not created when a partial election is made, Treas. Reg. §§20.2044-1(d)(3) and 25.2519-1(c)(3) authorize principal invasions for *S* during *S*'s life, first from the portion for which the QTIP election was made. See Treas. Reg. §20.2044-1(e) *Example 4*.

To accomplish this, the following language is thought to qualify under the present state of the law:

A portion of the Marital Trust, herein referred to as the "qualified terminable interest portion," shall qualify for the federal estate tax marital deduction. The value of the qualified terminable interest

---

23.　Treas. Reg. §20.2056(b)-7(b)(2) provides:

. . . any partial election must be made with respect to a fractional or percentage share of the property so that the elective portion reflects its proportionate share of the increase or decrease in value of the entire property for purposes of applying §2044 or §2519. The fraction or percentage may be defined by formula.

portion at any time may be determined by multiplying the value of the trust estate at that time by the fraction then in effect. Commencing with my death, and until the first distribution of principal pursuant to the provisions of section [*], the numerator of the fraction shall be equal to [the amount or formula desired], and the denominator shall be the value as finally determined for federal estate tax purposes of all interests in property included in the Marital Trust. The fraction shall be adjusted at the time of each payment of principal to my surviving spouse pursuant to the provisions of section [*], first by restating it so that the numerator and denominator are the values of the qualified terminable interest portion and of the trust estate, respectively, immediately prior to the payment, and then by subtracting the amount of the payment from each of the numerator and the denominator, except that the numerator shall not be reduced below zero.

The last sentence of this provision creates a "rolling fraction," which has the effect of treating any invasions of principal for the benefit of S (pursuant to section [*], permitting discretionary distributions by the trustee or withdrawals by S), as coming from the elected qualified terminable interest portion. The effect is to reduce the amount of property includible under §§2044 and 2519 on termination or disposition of S's income interest. To illustrate the effect of this, assume a partial fractional QTIP election made in 2004 for a trust having an initial value of $2.5 million. The initial elected fraction was 4/10 (which generated a $1.0 million marital deduction). A distribution of assets worth $100,000 is subsequently made to S at a time when the trust is valued at $3 million. The distribution reduced the value of the trust to $2.9 million. The QTIP fraction of the trust would be adjusted first by restating it as 4/10 × $3 million = 1.2/3.0 (million) and then subtracting $100,000 from both the numerator and the denominator = 1.1/2.9 = 37.93% of that trust, which fractional amount would be includible in S's gross estate. Compute the saving attributable to rolling the fraction if S dies when the trust is valued at $4.1 million, as against the $1,640,000 that would have been includible if the fraction had *not* been adjusted. Now consider the practical problem in trust administration created by a rolling fraction.

Contingent Income

Many estate plans direct that property not passing pursuant to a marital deduction bequest be held in a nonmarital trust, and many of those nonmarital trusts contain discretionary income distribution provisions. The nonmarital trusts are sometimes referred to as "bypass trusts" because one of the purposes of using them is to insulate the assets in such trusts from estate taxation when the surviving spouse dies — i.e., the trust "bypasses" inclusion in the surviving spouse's gross estate.

Some estate plans provide that the nonelected fraction of a QTIP trust pours over to the nonmarital trust. At one time the government asserted that such a pour-over provision violated the all-income requirement if income was not guaranteed to S in the pour-over trust. See Treas. Reg. §§20.2056(b)-7(d)(3), 20.2056(b)-7(h) *Example 6*, which applied to estates of decedents who die after March 1, 1994. Treas. Reg. §20.2056(b)-10. Indeed, the government's position was that a nonelected QTIP pour-over provision to a discretionary income trust would disqualify the entire QTIP trust for marital deduction purposes under §2056(b)(1), *even if the personal representative made a 100% QTIP election* so that no pour-over took place. The government reasoned that a pour-over provision means that on the happening of an event or contingency (the executor's partial QTIP election), S's mandatory income interest terminated or failed and an interest in the QTIP trust passes under D's estate plan to someone other than S or S's estate. Put another way, the government argued that failure to preserve the same dispositive provisions without regard to whether the QTIP election was made violated the government's interpretation that S's right to receive income cannot be contingent on the election's being made. In Estate of Clayton v. Commissioner, 97 T.C. 327 (1991), *rev'd*, 976 F.2d 1486 (5th Cir. 1992), the Tax Court agreed. In PLR 9224028 the government ruled that the marital deduction was not available for an otherwise QTIPable trust because any nonelected property was distributable to a nonmarital trust. According to the government, if the personal representative did not make the QTIP election, S would be divested of any interest in the QTIP trust, making the personal representative's power not to elect QTIP treatment tantamount to an impermissible power in the personal representative to appoint the QTIP property in violation of §2056(b)(7)(B)(ii)(II). A factually similar case to *Clayton*, Estate of Robertson v. Commissioner, 98 T.C. 678 (1992), *rev'd*, 15 F.3d 779 (8th Cir. 1994), was decided by the Tax Court within two weeks after release of PLR 9224028 and reached the same result for the same reason, as did Estate of Spencer v. Commissioner, 64 T.C.M. 937 (1992), *rev'd*, 43 F.3d 226 (6th Cir. 1995). However, in Estate of Clack v. Commissioner, 106 T.C. 131 (1996) (a reviewed decision), *acq in result only*, a majority of the Tax Court overruled the court's previously stated position (as expressed in *Clayton*, *Robertson*, and *Spencer*); the Tax Court repudiated the government's position and adopted the views of the three Circuit Courts of Appeals that reversed those earlier Tax Court cases.

The government relented and acquiesced to *Clack* once those three federal circuit courts of appeal and the Tax Court passed on this issue, and all four (the Tax Court and the 5th, 6th, and 8th Circuits) rejected the government's view. Ultimately the government amended Treas. Reg. §§20.2056(b)-7(d)(3), and -7(h) *Example 6*. The reasoning of the circuit courts is captured in the following extract from the decision on appeal in *Clayton*; it is helpful in appreciating the entire context and application of the QTIP election:

[L]ike other estate tax elections (and other exceptions to the terminable interest rules), the effect of the QTIP election is retroactive to the instant of death, irrespective of when it is actually made. Significantly, the party statutorily vested with the exclusive right to make the post-mortem QTIP election is not the surviving spouse, as one might expect, but the executor. Congress obviously did this as an extension of the testator's volition but with all of the guesswork removed.

. . . [T]here is nothing in the plain wording of the entire QTIP subsection which, when viewed in light of the definition of terms therein provided, even remotely supports the position of the Commissioner that if anything occurs after the death of the testator — such as the QTIP election — to prevent even a modicum of property which under the testament would have passed from the decedent to the surviving spouse, the deduction is unavailable for all otherwise eligible property. To reach that strained result, the Commissioner would have us ignore the overarching truism that many acts must be done and many facts must be determined after the death of the testator in order to determine the taxable estate. The question is not when those determinations are made or when those acts are performed but whether their effects relate back, ab initio, to the moment of death. For example, a qualified disclaimer by the Surviving Spouse has precisely the effect of the QTIP election here: Both are volitional acts; both can be made only after the death of the testator; both relate back, ab initio, to the date of death of the testator; and both have the effect of causing estate property which would otherwise pass to the Surviving Spouse to pass instead directly to or for the benefit of other parties. Likewise, while seldom volitional, the death of the Surviving Spouse within six months following the death of the testator who conditions the legacy on survivorship would have the same effect, but again retroactive to the moment of the testator's death.

. . . Congress was and is interested only in that portion of terminable interest property for which the QTIP election is made; it has no interest whatsoever in the portion of any terminable interest property for which the election is not made. . . .

From whence it came we know not, but the Tax Court here made the pronouncement that the QTIP election gave the executor "control over trust assets [that] is tantamount to a power to appoint property that was subject to the qualifying income interest." That unsubstantiated, conclusionary statement can only be the product of a circular argument — one that we reject. First, the QTIP election cannot vest the executor with control over "trust assets" before they become trust assets! The undivided interests in the securities for which the election is made are estate assets but they do not become trust assets until the trust is funded, even though the economic effect of funding is retroactive to the instant of death. Assets used to fund each testamentary trust get there by virtue of the provisions of the Will and the administration of the estate. The same analysis is applicable to that portion of the quotation from the Tax Court's opinion that refers to property that was subject to the qualifying income interest. No income interest is qualifying until it meets the full definition for QTIP, including the election prong. As we have just noted, one of the three essential elements in the definition of such property interest is that it be property for which — in the Tax Court's own words — "an election has been made." 976 F.2d at 1494-1495, 1498-1499.

Estate Tax Attributable to QTIP Trust

Section 2207A provides that, unless S's will contains a contrary provision, any tax attributable to inclusion of QTIP property in S's gross estate under §2044 (and any interest and penalties attributable thereto) is recoverable from the persons receiving the QTIP property (typically the corpus of a QTIP trust). The amount of tax attributable to the QTIP property, computed under §2207A(a)(1), is the difference between the amount of the actual estate tax in S's estate and the amount of estate tax that would be due if the QTIP property was not includible. Thus, §2207A allows a recovery of the amount S's estate tax is increased by inclusion of the QTIP, sometimes referred to as the "incremental" tax attributable to the QTIP. However, no recovery is granted for any state estate or inheritance taxes attributable to the QTIP property, nor for any amount of S's unified credit exhausted by the inclusion (because §2207A is for tax paid, not for tax payable). Treas. Reg. §§20.2207A-1(a)(1) (last two sentences) and 20.2207A-1(b).

An inequity can result under §2207A because QTIP property is taxed at the highest estate tax rate applicable to S's estate. Assume, for example, that D and S each have children by prior marriages and that they agree that their respective assets will be held for S for life and then pass to their respective families when S dies. Thus, the QTIP property will pass to D's remainder beneficiaries subject to the higher rates in S's estate tax calculation and S's property will pass to S's beneficiaries subject to the lower rates. How may these spouses overcome this result?

Failure to Exercise the Right of Recovery

Failure of S's estate to exercise the right to recover the tax under §2207A is a taxable gift "from the persons who would benefit from the recovery" (usually S's residuary beneficiaries) "to the persons from whom the recovery could have been obtained" (the QTIP remainder beneficiaries). Treas. Reg. §20.2207A-1(a)(2). No gift is made, however, to the extent that *S* either waived the right of recovery or authorized *S*'s personal representative to do so, and the personal representative did waive that right. See Treas. Reg. §20.2207A-1(a)(3). A gift made by failing to exercise a right of recovery is considered to be made when the right of recovery no longer is enforceable under local law, and any "delay" in exercising the recovery right "may be treated as an interest-free loan with appropriate gift tax consequences under §7872 depending on the facts of the particular case." Treas. Reg. §20.2207A-1(a)(2). No guidance exists with respect to the meaning of a "delay."

If waiver of the §2207A right of reimbursement is desirable, the requisite degree of specificity should be considered in light of *In re* Will of Gordon, 510 N.Y.S.2d 815, 817 (Surr. Ct. 1986), in which *S*'s tax clause read "I direct that all . . . taxes . . . imposed . . . by reason of my death with respect to any property includable in my estate . . . whether such property passes under or outside my will be paid out of my Residuary Estate . . . without apportionment." If the court had found that the §2207A reimbursement right had been waived by this provision, a charitable residuary bequest would have abated completely, which clearly was not *S*'s intent. Therefore, the court found that this provision was not adequate to work that result. For comparison purposes, in a case involving no "special" remainder beneficiary, the following language was adequate to waive the §§2206 and 2207 rights of reimbursement: "All estate taxes payable by reason of my death shall be chargeable against and payable out of my residuary estate without contribution by anyone." *In re* Bruce, 516 N.Y.S.2d 748 (A.D. 1987).

Note that New York E.P.T.L. §2-1.8(d-1) (1992) was subsequently amended to provide that a general direction in a will to pay all taxes imposed on account of the testator's death is not applicable to taxes imposed at the death of a surviving spouse as beneficiary of a QTIP trust unless the will specifically provides otherwise. A similar amendment to §2207A was enacted and now provides that the reimbursement right will not apply "to the extent that the decedent . . . *specifically indicates* an intent to waive any right of recovery . . . with respect to such property" (emphasis added).

If *S* assigns all or any part of a QTIP income interest during life, a gift is made of the full discounted present value of the remainder interest in the QTIP trust under §2519, in addition to the §2511 gift of the value of the assigned income interest. *S* is liable for the gift tax on both transfers, but is entitled under §2207A to recover the gift tax attributable only to the §2519 gift of the remainder interest. That right of reimbursement is from "the person receiving the property," which is the trustee if the property is held in trust. Treas. Reg. §25.2207A-1(e). *S* is regarded as making an *additional* gift to the trust remainder beneficiaries to the extent *S* declines or fails to exercise this right of recovery, thereby benefiting the persons who otherwise would have contributed to the payment of the tax. Although *S* is permitted to waive the §2207A right to recover *estate* taxes without causing additional estate or gift tax consequences at death, it is the government's position that *S*'s failure to recover gift taxes incurred under §2519 is an added gift. Based on that interpretation, the government reduces the §2519 gift by the amount of the gift tax that is §2207A recoverable from the trust (making the §2519 calculation more complex: it is a "net gift" computation on the discounted present value of the remainder interest). If *S* does not recover the tax that is the subject of the §2207A right of reimbursement, the ultimate effect is that the §2519 gift equals the full discounted present value of the remainder interest. See Prop. Treas. Reg. §25.2207A-1(b), which addresses the consequences of the exercise or failure to exercise the right to recover the gift tax. All this illustrates why an assignment of any portion of a QTIP income interest is tricky business.

19.   *Annuities, Employee Benefit Payments, and Individual Retirement Accounts.* An annuity payable to *S* will generally qualify for the marital deduction if there is no refund or survivor benefit payable, other than to *S*'s estate, that would cause the annuity to be a nondeductible terminable interest. See, e.g., Treas. Reg. §20.2056(b)-1(g) *Example (3)*. Furthermore, if the annuity is a terminable interest because there is an interest in a beneficiary other than *S*, automatic QTIP qualification will salvage the marital deduction if the annuity was includible in *D*'s gross estate under §2039 and *S* is the sole beneficiary during *S*'s remaining life. See §2056(b)(7)(C). Necessarily, such an annuity could not have been created by *D* at death or purchased by *D*'s fiduciary at *D*'s direction after *D*'s death, and therefore cannot run afoul of §2056(b)(1)(C).

These two forms of qualification cover many annuity situations, leaving as a major category only individual retirement accounts (IRAs) in which a QTIP trust is the sole designated beneficiary during *S*'s remaining life but a remainder benefit may be payable to a third party after *S*'s death. With respect to these IRAs, Treas. Reg. §20.2056(b)-7(h) *Example 10* and Rev. Rul. 2002-2 complicate the issue of annuity qualification because they presume annuity installment payments during *S*'s remaining life of the IRA corpus *plus* annual payment of an amount equal to all income earned by the entire undistributed IRA balance. The government has made clear, however, that this unusual form of payout is not the exclusive method of qualifying IRAs or other terminable interest annuities for the marital deduction.

In this respect, PLR 9317025 provides a veritable road map of how to draft an IRA with a QTIP trust as beneficiary and qualify for the marital deduction. In this ruling, (1) the IRA itself required annual distribution of an amount no less than all income generated in the IRA for the year, (2) the QTIP trustee was directed to exercise its authority to demand distributions from the IRA of no less than this amount if that mandate was not met, (3) *S* was given a power to compel the QTIP trustee to make that demand, and (4) the QTIP trustee was directed to allocate to trust income distributions received from the IRA equal to the income earned in the IRA. In addition, *S* was given a power to compel the QTIP trustee (5) to convert underproductive property to property producing a reasonable amount of income annually, or (6) to distribute QTIP trust amounts at least equal to the income that would be earned by assets producing reasonable income.[24] Another permissible alternative is to permit *S* to withdraw corpus equal to the same amount of income. Thus, it appears that annuity payments from an IRA to a QTIP trust will satisfy the QTIP marital deduction requirements if annual distributions from the QTIP trust to *S* will be no less than the amount of income earned in the IRA annually, and the arrangement cannot be used to deprive *S* of a reasonable enjoyment of the wealth held in the IRA.

20.   *QTIP and Charitable Remainder Trusts.* Although §§2056(b)(8) and 2523(g) were adopted along with §§2056(b)(7) and 2523(f) and are regarded by many planners as QTIP substitutes, they are not governed by the §§2056(b)(7) and 2523(f) QTIP rules. Instead, these provisions are additional, distinct exceptions to the nondeductible terminable interest rule and apply if (1) *S* is given a unitrust or annuity trust interest for life pursuant to the charitable remainder split interest rules of §664 and (2) *S* is the only private beneficiary of the trust (other than *D*, if an inter vivos transfer is involved).

If *D* creates a qualifying charitable remainder annuity trust or unitrust, *S*'s lead interest will qualify for the marital deduction under §2056(b)(8) and the charitable remainder will qualify for the charitable deduction under §2055. *D*'s estate will incur no tax on the total value of the trust and, because no QTIP election is involved, there will be no §2044 inclusion in *S*'s gross estate at death. Indeed, if properly structured, there will be no estate tax inclusion of the trust corpus under any Code section at *S*'s death and the trust property will pass unreduced by wealth transfer tax to the charitable remainder beneficiary.

The same objective can be achieved through conventional QTIP planning. As explained in the legislative history to §2056(b)(8), a charitable remainder deduction can be obtained through a normal QTIP trust:

---

24.   Some planners instead give *S* a right to withdraw the annuity from the QTIP trust, to convert it to a higher income producing asset, or they give *S* the power to compel the trustee to convert the annuity for the same purpose, but neither is as safe as a fiduciary accounting requirement that allocates an amount to income that will satisfy the all income requirement, because conversion of the annuity into a higher income producing asset may be impossible under the terms of the plan.

The general rules applicable to qualifying income interests may provide similar treatment where a decedent provides an income interest in the spouse for her life and a remainder interest to charity. If the life estate is a qualifying [§2056(b)(7)(B)(ii)] income interest, the entire property will . . . be considered as passing to the spouse. Therefore, the entire value of the property will be eligible for the marital deduction and no transfer tax will be imposed. Upon the spouse's death, the property will be included in the spouse's estate [under §2044] but, because the spouse's life estate terminates at death, any property passing outright to charity may qualify for a charitable deduction.

H.R. Rep. No. 201, 97th Cong., 1st Sess. 162 n.4 (1981). Thus, for example, a trust might provide that "the trustee shall pay the trust income to S at least quarterly for life. On S's death the trustee shall distribute the trust principal to [qualified charitable organization]." Being a qualified QTIP trust interest, the §2056(b)(7)(B)(v) QTIP deduction would apply to the extent D's estate reports the value of the trust principal on Schedule M to its Form 706 estate tax return. The entire trust corpus would qualify for a marital deduction in D's estate, it would cause §2044 inclusion in S's gross estate, and it would qualify for a §2055 charitable deduction in computing S's taxable estate.[25] Again, there would be no tax in either estate.

An advantage of the QTIP alternative over the §2056(b)(8) qualified charitable remainder trust approach is that it is not necessary to draft within the complicated confines of the §664 charitable remainder trust rules, and corpus distributions may be made to S from the QTIP trust. Alternatively, the §2056(b)(8) split interest trust approach provides a number of advantages over the QTIP alternative. For example, if created inter vivos, the §2523(g) inter vivos version of the §2056(b)(8) trust generates a §170 income tax deduction for D that the QTIP alternative would not generate. In addition, the tax character of the trust precludes ordinary income, capital gains, and income in respect of a decedent from being subject to income tax to the extent not carried out to S as beneficiary of the lead split interest trust payment. Nor must the trust distribute all its income annually to S or worry about satisfying the qualified income interest rules.[26] Indeed, under the authority of §664(f), the trust may be drafted to distribute to the qualified charitable remainder beneficiary prior to S's death, either because S's

---

25. By virtue of §2044(c), the remainder in a QTIP trust qualifies for a charitable deduction in S's estate because the interest is deemed to pass to the charity from S, in whose estate it is includible.

26. Because §2056(b)(8) provides that the nondeductible terminable interest rule of §2056(b)(1) does not apply at all, this trust is not an exception to that rule and need not meet the income payment requirements common to §§2056(b)(5) and 2056(b)(7) trusts.

interest is limited to a term of years[27] or is made terminable on a contingency such as remarriage.[28]

Although it is not likely to be relevant in garden variety estate planning, PLR 8730004 underscores a significant limitation on the availability of the §2056(b)(8) planning alternative. *D* created a 5% charitable remainder unitrust for *S* for life, followed by a similar interest for another private beneficiary, followed by a remainder to charity. This unitrust did not qualify for the combined marital deduction and charitable deduction under §2056(b)(8) because §2056(b)(8)(A) and Treas. Reg. §20.2056(b)-8(a)(1) require that *S* be the only private beneficiary (other than *D* in an inter vivos application) prior to the charity's interest. So, the personal representative attempted to elect §2056(b)(7) QTIP treatment for the entire trust, presumably assuming that the marital deduction would exclude the value of the entire trust from *D*'s taxable estate and correspondingly cause inclusion of the entire value of the trust in *S*'s gross estate, thereby allowing *S*'s estate to qualify for a charitable deduction of the value of the remainder after the intervening annuitant's interest.

The government, however, ruled that the §2056(b)(7) election was invalid, and the reasoning employed in that ruling raised doubts about the interchangeability of §§2056(b)(7) and 2056(b)(8) to accomplish essentially the same result. The Ruling stated:

> In the case of a qualified charitable remainder trust, Congress limited the allowance of the §2056 marital deduction to those trusts that satisfy the §2056(b)(8) requirements . . . [and] there is nothing in the legislative history of §2056(b)(8) to suggest that Congress intended §2056(b)(7) to be available in such cases. In the case of a qualified charitable remainder trust, with an annuity trust interest or a unitrust interest payable to the surviving spouse, no marital deduction is allowable for any portion of a qualified charitable remainder trust under §2056(b)(7) of the Code . . . . The existence of a charitable remainder interest in [the] Trust . . . precludes the estate from making a §2056(b)(7) election.

The taxpayer thus fell in an unintended crack between §§2056(b)(7) and 2056(b)(8): the former did not apply because this two life split interest trust was a qualified charitable remainder trust, notwithstanding that it failed to satisfy the sole beneficiary requirement for §2056(b)(8) qualification as well. Presumably to prevent this inappropriate result, Treas. Reg. §20.2056(b)-

---

27. Not, however, to exceed 20 years. Treas. Reg. §20.2056(b)-8(a)(2).

28. Although §664(f)(2) precludes the contingent acceleration of the charitable remainder from being reflected in valuing the remainder for charitable deduction purposes, it nevertheless may be *D*'s desire to terminate *S*'s enjoyment on the happening of such a contingency.

8(a)(1) provides: "If an interest in property qualifies for a marital deduction under §2056(b)(8), no election may be made with respect to the property under §2056(b)(7)." But "[i]n a case of a charitable remainder trust where the decedent's spouse is not the only noncharitable beneficiary . . . , the qualification of the interest as qualified terminable interest property is determined solely under §2056(b)(7) and not under §2056(b)(8)." Treas. Reg. §20.2056(b)-8(b). This appears to mean that a trust can be a qualified charitable split interest trust but not satisfy the §2056(b)(8) requirements and therefore not be precluded from qualifying for the §2056(b)(7) QTIP exception. The net result is that, in the context presented by PLR 8730004, the regulations appear to say that §2056(b)(8) overrides §2056(b)(7) only if both otherwise might be applicable.

The regulation fails to specify whether §2056(b)(7) is available in other circumstances in which the requirements of §2056(b)(8) are not met for reasons that do not relate to the sole beneficiary element. Although it still is possible for defective drafting or administration of a decedent's estate to result in loss of the marital deduction under both provisions, additional Rulings make it clear that qualification for the marital deduction under §2056(b)(7) is available if §2056(b)(8) is not applicable because, for example, the trust is not a qualified charitable remainder trust. It does not appear to be the government's intent to create a trap for the unwary.[29]

21. *Estate Trusts.*   Two topics require attention under the nondeductible terminable interest rule but neither fits precisely within either the Power of Appointment Trust or the QTIP Trust exception to the rule. Indeed, this first is the antithesis of both, because when it applies the nondeductible terminable interest rule does not, and therefore no exception to that rule is required. We're going to address them here in the organization of this chapter because, well, they "fit" here as well as they do anyplace else!

---

29. But see TAM 8742001, which involved *D*'s devise of a life estate in a personal residence to *S*, with remainder to charity, and the government went out of its way to state that "[a] marital deduction for the value of [*S*'s] annuity or unitrust interest in a *qualified* charitable remainder trust is allowable only under §2056(b)(8)" (emphasis added). Because this situation did not involve a trust, much less a qualified charitable remainder trust, it appeared at the time that perhaps the government was announcing a position that it intended to assert in the future. Numerous authorities indicate that it now seems to have backed away from creating such a trap. See, e.g., PLRs 8952024 (*S* received a legal life estate, not in trust, in artwork, with remainder to charity; not a qualified charitable split interest arrangement but *S*'s use and enjoyment, coupled with a power to sell, lease, encumber, or assign the life interest, made the artwork permissible QTIP property notwithstanding the charitable remainder); 9323039, 9144016, 9101010, 9047016, 9036040, and 9008017 (all QTIP marital deduction trusts with remainders to charity, none in qualified charitable remainder trust form; despite not complying with §2056(b)(8), the marital deduction was available under §2056(b)(7) for the full value of trust corpus, with §2044(c) inclusion and a §2055 charitable deduction available when *S* dies).

A so-called estate trust is an alternative to each of the all-income annually §2056(b) exceptions to the nondeductible terminable interest rule, such as a §2056(b)(5) general power of appointment trust or a §2056(b)(7) QTIP trust, and therefore provides yet another way to prevent disqualification under the nondeductible terminable interest rule. The estate trust is so named because it requires distribution of all trust corpus to S's estate[30] when S dies. Because no interest in any third party follows S's interest, the trust is not an exception to the nondeductible terminable interest rule; it is not a terminable interest at all. To illustrate, assume that D created a trust to pay income and principal to S or to accumulate income and add it to trust principal, all in the discretion of a disinterested trustee. On S's death, the trust corpus is distributable to S's estate. This trust qualifies for the marital deduction. See §2056(b)(1)(A); Treas. Reg. §§20.2056(b)-1(g) *Example (8)*; 20.2056(c)-2(b)(1)(i) and -2(b)(2)(i); Rev. Rul. 68-554. This trust still would qualify for the marital deduction even if the trustee was directed to accumulate the income and add it to principal throughout S's overlife (that is, even if the trustee had no power — discretionary or otherwise — to distribute any income to S).

As a policy matter, is there any reason to suggest that D's trust (under either variation) should not qualify for a marital deduction? That is to say, is there anything magical about a right to receive income that should inform the marital deduction requirements? In thinking about that issue it may help to consider when an estate trust might be preferable to a power of appointment or a QTIP trust as a device qualifying for the marital deduction — what kind of estates would benefit from having this alternative available?

Although a power of appointment is not required in an estate trust, is there any reason to question qualification for the marital deduction if the trust assets were subject to a general testamentary power of appointment in S, with the default distribution being made to S's estate? You might be inclined to think that the trust without a general power will qualify, and the power simply makes the trust a more useful or more valuable entitlement for the surviving spouse, so how could it be problematic. Nevertheless, Rev. Rul. 75-128 held that *this trust did not qualify* for the marital deduction, stating that, for purposes of Treas. Reg. §20.2056(c)-3, the permissible appointees were persons other than S to whom an interest in property passed from the decedent. Therefore, the trust was deemed to create a nondeductible terminable interest in S and, because S was not entitled to all

---

30. A bequest to S's "estate" may raise questions of construction for property or trust law purposes because property law does not treat an "estate" as a separate jural entity. These questions can be avoided merely by providing that, upon S's death, the trust assets are to be distributed to S. For a discussion of constructional problems that may be erected by a remainder to a person's estate, see Browder, *Trusts and the Doctrine of Estates*, 72 MICH. L. REV. 1509 (1974); Fox, *Estate: A Word to Be Used Cautiously, If At All*, 81 HARV. L. REV. 992 (1968); Huston, *Transfers to the "Estate" of a Named Person*, 15 SYRACUSE L. REV. 463 (1964).

the trust income for life, payable annually, the general power of appointment trust did not qualify for the §2056(b)(5) exception.

That analysis is questionable, because property law regards permissible appointees as having nothing more than an expectancy; they do not have a property interest. See RESTATEMENT OF PROPERTY §338, comment b (1940); but see RESTATEMENT (SECOND) OF PROPERTY (Donative Transfers) §11.2, comment d (1985). Cf. the House and Senate committee reports quoted at page 134 in *Towle*. Nevertheless, Treas. Reg. §20.2056(c)-3 declares to the contrary. What the Commissioner also overlooks is that *S*'s power of appointment is appendant to the gift in default. Consequently, under property law principles, *S*'s power of appointment is invalid. See RESTATEMENT (SECOND) OF PROPERTY (Donative Transfers) §12.3 (1984); RESTATEMENT OF PROPERTY §325 (1940). If *S*'s power of appointment is invalid, *D*'s bequest is an ordinary estate trust and ought to qualify for the marital deduction. Moreover, the government's conclusion is meritless from a tax policy perspective because there is no tax avoidance or abuse: the trust will be includible in *S*'s gross estate whether the power of appointment is exercised or lapses.

22. *Specific Portion.* This last item in this Part has an overarching significance: it is applicable to both the §§2056(b)(5) and 2056(b)(7) exceptions and therefore is a capstone of sorts in this discussion.

One requirement to qualify either a power of appointment trust or qualified terminable interest trust for a marital deduction is that *S* must be entitled for life to all the income (payable at least annually) from the entire interest or "a specific portion" of it. §§2056(b)(5), 2056(b)(7)(B)(iv). In the case of a power of appointment trust, the marital deduction is granted to the extent the surviving spouse's power of appointment coincides with the income entitlement in that entire interest or "specific portion." See Treas. Reg. §20.2056(b)-5(c)(5) *Example (2)*, illustrating the overlap computation. Note also that the term "specific portion" is used in the §2056(b)(6) exception to the nondeductible terminable interest rule provided for life insurance or annuity payments.

Prior to the adoption of §2056(b)(10) in 1992,[31] the meaning of "specific portion" was the subject of controversy and, ultimately, abuse. This ultimately led to legislation adopting the position previously found only in the regulations pertaining to power of appointment trusts, which state that a "specific portion" is a fractional or percentage share of a property interest. Treas. Reg. §20.2056(b)-5(c)(2). Thus, if a trust were funded with $1,000,000, a provision for payment to *S* of 40% of the income earned by the trust each year would be a specific portion, but a provision for the payment to *S* of $40,000 per year would not qualify as a specific

---

31.   See Treas. Reg. §20.2056(b)-7(e) to appreciate why this date is worth remembering.

portion. More importantly, a provision for payment to *S* of all income from the entire trust and granting *S* a general testamentary power to appoint (or as to which a partial QTIP election was made only with respect to) 40% of the trust would qualify for the marital deduction under the specific portion requirement, but a power of appointment or a partial election with respect to $400,000 would not. The validity of the regulations was the subject of the following Supreme Court decision. The dissenting opinion predicted the result in Estate of Alexander v. Commissioner, 82 T.C. 34 (1984), *aff'd*, 760 F.2d 264 (4th Cir. 1985), also excerpted below, and *Alexander* eventually prompted Congress to codify the prior regulatory position by adopting §2056(b)(10). The concept illustrated is vastly more important than just marital deduction qualification, so read with a more broad learning objective or horizon.

Northeastern Pennsylvania National Bank & Trust Co. v. United States
387 U.S. 213 (1967)

Mr. Justice FORTAS delivered the opinion of the Court.

The issue in this case is whether a bequest in trust providing for the monthly payment to decedent's widow of a fixed amount can qualify for the estate tax marital deduction under §2056(b)(5) . . . .

. . . The [decedent's] will provided that his widow should receive $300 per month until decedent's youngest child reached 18, and $350 per month thereafter. If the trust income were insufficient, corpus could be invaded to make the specific payments; if income exceeded the monthly amount, it was to be accumulated. The widow was given power to appoint the entire corpus by will.

. . . The Commissioner . . . determined that the trust did not qualify for the marital deduction because the widow's right to the income of the trust was not expressed as a "fractional or percentile share" of the total trust income, as the Treasury Regulations §20.2056(b)-5(c), require. . . .

. . . If this Regulation properly implements the Code, the trust in this case plainly fails to qualify for the marital deduction. We hold, however, that in the context of this case the Regulation improperly restricts the scope of the congressionally granted deduction.

In the District Court, the executor initially claimed that the entire trust qualified for the marital deduction simply because, at the time of trial, the corpus had not yet produced an income in excess of $300 per month, and that the widow was therefore entitled "to all the income from the entire interest." The District Court rejected this contention, observing that the income from the corpus *could* exceed $300 per month, and in that event the excess would have to be accumulated. The executor's alternative claim, which the

District Court accepted, was that the "specific portion" of the trust corpus whose income would amount to $300 per month could be computed, and a deduction allowed for that amount.

Resolution of the question in this case, whether a qualifying "specific portion" can be computed from the monthly stipend specified in a decedent's will, is essentially a matter of discovering the intent of Congress. The general history of the marital deduction is well known. The deduction was enacted in 1948, and the underlying purpose was to equalize the incidence of the estate tax in community property and common-law jurisdictions. . . .

The 1948 legislation required that the bequest in trust entitle the surviving spouse to "all the income" from the trust corpus, and grant a power to appoint the "entire corpus." These requirements were held by several lower courts to disqualify for the deduction a single trust in which the surviving spouse was granted a right to receive half (for example) of the income and to appoint half of the corpus. Since there was no good reason to require a testator to create two separate trusts — one for his wife, the other for his children, for example — Congress in 1954 revised the marital deduction provision of the statute to allow the deduction where a decedent gives his surviving spouse "all the income from the entire interest, or all the income from a specific portion thereof" and a power to "appoint the entire interest, or such specific portion." The House Report on this change states that "The bill makes it clear that . . . a right to income plus a general power of appointment over only an undivided part of the property will qualify that part of the property for the marital deduction." The Senate Report contains identical language. There is no indication in the legislative history of the change from which one could conclude that Congress — in using the words "all the income from a specific portion" in the statute, or the equivalent words "a right to income . . . over . . . an undivided part" in the committee reports — intended that the deduction afforded would be defeated merely because the "specific portion" or the "undivided part" was not expressed by the testator in terms of a "fractional or percentile share" of the whole corpus.

Congress' intent to afford a liberal "estate-splitting" possibility to married couples, where the deductible [portion] of the decedent's estate would ultimately — if not consumed — be taxable in the estate of the survivor, is unmistakable. . . .

. . . The Senate Report stated that the marital deduction would be available "where the surviving spouse, by reason of her [*sic*] right to the income and a power of appointment, is the virtual owner of the property." The Government's argument is that the deduction was intended only in cases where the equivalent of the outright ownership of a community property State was granted, and that this is what the Senate Report meant by the words "virtual owner." Actually, however, the words were not used in that context at all. The section of the Report from which those words derive deals with the rule that, with minor exceptions, the marital deduction does not apply where any person other than the surviving spouse has any power over the income or corpus of the trust. It is in this sense that the Report described the surviving spouse as a "virtual owner." . . .

The Court of Appeals advanced a somewhat different argument in support of the Government's conclusion. Without relying upon the validity of the Regulation, the Court of Appeals maintained that a "specific portion" can be found only where there is an acceptable method of computing it, and that no such method is available in a case of the present sort. The Court of Appeals noted that the computation must produce the "ratio between the maximum monthly income [producible by the whole corpus] and the monthly stipend [provided for in the trust]." . . . The Court of Appeals concluded . . . that the computation could not be made because "the market conditions for purposes of investment are not known" and, therefore, there are no constant investment factors to use in computing the maximum possible monthly income of the whole corpus.

It is with this latter conclusion that we disagree. To be sure, perfect prediction of realistic future rates of return is not possible. However, the use of projected rates of return in the administration of the federal tax laws is hardly an innovation. It should not be a difficult matter to settle on a rate of return available to a trustee under reasonable investment conditions, which could be used to compute the "specific portion" of the corpus whose income is equal to the monthly stipend provided for in the trust. . . .

The Government concedes, as it must, that application of a projected rate of return to determine the "specific portion" of the trust corpus whose income is equal to the monthly stipend allotted will not result in any of the combined marital estate escaping ultimate taxation in either the decedent's or the surviving spouse's estate. The Government argues, however, that if analogous actuarial methods were used to compute as a fixed dollar amount the "specific portion" as to which a qualifying power of appointment is given, where the power in fact granted extends to the whole corpus but the corpus is subject to measurable invasions for the benefit, for example, of a child, the result, in some cases, would be to enable substantial avoidance of estate tax. Whether, properly viewed, the Government's claim holds true, and, if so, what effect that should have upon the qualification of such a trust, is a difficult matter. Needless to say, nothing we hold in this opinion has reference to that quite different problem, which is not before us.

The District Court used an annuity-valuation approach to compute the "specific portion." This was incorrect. The question, as the Court of Appeals recognized, is to determine the amount of the corpus required to produce the fixed monthly stipend, not to compute the present value of the right to monthly payments over an actuarially computed life expectancy. Accordingly, we reverse and remand for further proceedings in conformity with this opinion.

Reversed.

Mr. Justice STEWART, whom Mr. Justice BLACK and Mr. Justice HARLAN join, dissenting.

. . . I must differ with the Court in its determination that the intent of Congress leads to the result the Court today reaches. For allowing the trust before us to qualify for the marital deduction will inevitably lead to the ironic and unjustified result of giving common-law jurisdictions more favorable tax treatment than community property States.

The Court holds that the widow in this case had an interest in "all the income from a specific portion" of the trust because the stream of payments to her could be capitalized by the use of assumed interest rates. This capitalized sum is then said to constitute the "specific portion" which qualifies for the marital deduction. A corollary of the Court's theory is that a trust which gave the widow the right to the income from a fixed amount (in dollars) of corpus and the right to appoint the entire corpus would support a marital deduction. But if such a bequest qualifies, then one which limits her power of appointment to only that amount of corpus with respect to which she has income rights will also qualify for the marital deduction. For under the statute, the survivor must have only the right to "all the income from a specific portion . . . with power in the surviving spouse to appoint . . . *such* specific portion." (Emphasis added.) The way in which such an estate allows a tax avoidance scheme not available to a community-property couple can be easily illustrated.

Assume a trust estate of $200,000, with the widow receiving the right to the income from $100,000 of its corpus and a power of appointment over that $100,000, and the children of the testator receiving income from the balance of the corpus during the widow's life, their remainders to vest when she dies. Now suppose that when the widow dies the trust corpus has doubled in value to $400,000. The wife's power of appointment over $100,000 applies only to make $100,000 taxable to her estate. The remaining $300,000 passes tax free to the children. Contrast the situation in a community property State. The wife's 50 per cent interest in the community property places $200,000 of the expanded assets in her estate and taxable as such; only $200,000, therefore, passes directly to the children. Thus, the Court's interpretation of "specific portion" affords common-law estates a significant tax advantage that community property dispositions cannot obtain.

By changing "specific portion" from the fractional share, which is both described in the Treasury Regulation and used as the basis for community property ownership, into a lump sum bearing no constant relation to the corpus, the Court allows capital appreciation to be transferred from the wife's to the children's interest in the estate without any tax consequence. . . .

Northeastern Penn is the "good" case involving the specific portion requirement, in the sense that there was no abuse involved and the Court's decision did not sanction planning that would do an injustice to the marital deduction concept. But there was a problem allegedly created by the Court's opinion, best illustrated by a hypothetical. Let's assume that *D* left $200,000 in trust for the life of *W*, to pay all of the trust income to *S* quarterly. The trust grants *S* a general testamentary power to appoint $100,000. Congress adopted §2056(b)(10) to make it clear that no part of this bequest will qualify for the marital deduction. The dissent in *Northeastern Penn* suggested the reason why this should be so, and the Tax Court's opinion below from *Estate of Alexander v. Commissioner*, 82 T.C. 34 (1984), was the call to arms that eventually lead to Congressional action:

DRENNEN, Judge. . . . The issue for decision is whether a bequest left to a residuary trust, which provided for the payment of all the income of the trust to decedent's widow and granted her a testamentary power of appointment over a specific dollar amount, qualifies for the Federal estate tax marital deduction. . . .

If there had not been so much judicial water over the dam on the invalidity of respondent's position, we would listen to his argument more sympathetically, because if the surviving spouse can appoint only the dollar amount of the interest given to her under her deceased spouse's will, only that amount will be taxable in her estate under §2041 and any increment in value of that interest between her death and the death of her husband will escape estate taxation. However, respondent has made the same argument in every case we have found that has come before the courts, and has lost the argument in every case. We therefore feel that if the statute is to be construed in accordance with respondent's regulation, it is up to Congress to change the language in the statute. . . .

. . . Congress used the same words "specific portion," which we find to be unambiguous, in stating the requirements with respect to both income and corpus to qualify for the marital deduction. Under the circumstances, we cannot say that Congress intended a different meaning to apply to the two categories. . . .

CHABOT, *J.*, concurring: The Supreme Court has interpreted the term "specific portion," as it is used the first time it appears in the first sentence of §2056(b)(5). *Northeastern Penn.* The majority hold that we must give the same content to that term when it is used the second time it appears in that same sentence.

Notwithstanding my concern that this interpretation may be bad tax policy (see the dissenting opinion of Simpson, J., infra), I agree that we are obligated to give the same content to each appearance of a term when the term appears twice in a single sentence, unless the statute itself (or perhaps unambiguous legislative history) gives clear instructions that the term is to have different meanings. . . .

SIMPSON, *J.*, dissenting: . . . It is said that "logical and practical consistency" requires that "specific portion" be given one interpretation for both income and corpus. In the *Northeastern* opinion, the Supreme Court stated that "nothing we hold in this opinion has reference to" the "quite different problem" of whether a power of appointment of a specific dollar amount of corpus satisfies the specific portion requirement. In the *Northeastern* case, the Court considered a bequest of the *income* from a specific mount of corpus, and its decision did not result in any of the appreciation of the value of the corpus escaping the estate tax since the power extended to the entire corpus. The Court was aware that in considering a limited power over corpus, different questions would arise, and the Court, explicitly and directly, told us that it was not deciding the corpus question and in effect directed us to consider that question separately on its merits.

It is not necessarily true that "specific portion" must have the same meaning wherever used: "A word is not a crystal, transparent and unchanged, it is the skin of a living thought and may vary greatly in color and content according to the circumstances and the time in which it is used." Towne v. Eisner, 245 U.S. 418, 425 (1918) (Holmes, J.). . . . We have not hesitated to ascribe different meanings to the same word used twice in one sentence of a section when necessary to effectuate the congressional intent. We must construe "specific portion" in the light of the objectives of the statute, and those objectives make it abundantly clear that we cannot adopt a single or consistent meaning of the term. Permitting a bequest of the income from a specific amount of corpus to qualify for the marital deduction does no violence to the congressional scheme of equality, but applying a similar rule to the corpus of a trust will frustrate the clear and important objective of equality of treatment of residents of community property and common law States. To carry out that objective, we must construe "specific portion," when applied to a power over corpus, to be limited in the manner prescribed by the regulations.

PART F. NON-CITIZEN SURVIVING SPOUSE

Code References: *Estate Tax: §§2106(a)(3), 2056(d), 2056A*

23. *Qualified Domestic Trusts.*

Citizenship Requirement. Prior to adoption of §2106(a)(3) in 1989, §2056(a) (through §2001(a)) required D to be a U.S. resident or citizen to qualify for the marital deduction; until passage of the Technical and Miscellaneous Revenue Act of 1988, no provision required that S be either.[32] Apparently Congress became persuaded that there is a significant possibility of D's estate qualifying for the marital deduction and then being removed from the United States' taxing jurisdiction before a noncitizen S's death, to avoid paying estate tax as the recompense for marital deduction qualification in D's estate.[33] Thus, §2056(d)(1) was enacted in 1988 to provide that, if S is not a U.S. citizen, the marital deduction under §2056(a) is not available unless the special requirements of §2056A are met.[34]

---

32. See Technical and Miscellaneous Revenue Act of 1988 §7815(d), P.L. 100-647, 100th Cong., 2d Sess. (1988) (hereafter TAMRA), Revenue Reconciliation Act of 1989, P.L. 101-239, 101st Cong., 1st Sess. (1989) (hereafter 1989 Act), and Revenue Reconciliation Act of 1990, P.L. 101-508, 101st Cong., 2d Sess. (1990) (hereafter 1990 Act), amending the marital deduction for estates of decedents dying after November 10, 1988.

33. See, e.g., Conf. Rep. to accompany H.R. 4333, H.R. Rep. No. 1104 at 114-115, indicating that special requirements under §§2056A(a)(1) and (a)(3) insuring collection of the tax were a special concern of Congress.

34. In addition, §2040(b) was made inapplicable by §2056(d)(1)(B) so that §2040(a) causes inclusion of joint tenancy property held by a decedent and a noncitizen surviving spouse based on their respective contributions to the property instead of including half the value of qualified joint property under §2040(b). By virtue of this provision, only that portion of a joint tenancy that is includible in D's gross estate under §2040(a) must meet the special §2056A rules to qualify for the marital deduction. Treas. Reg. §20.2056A-8(a)(3).

According to PLR 9021037, it is not adequate for *S* to have applied to become a citizen before *D*'s estate tax return is filed. To overcome disallowance of the marital deduction, §2056(d)(4) requires *S* to become a U.S. citizen before filing that return. Treas. Reg. §20.2056A-1(b) relaxes this rule by providing that a return filed early is deemed filed on the last date it is required to be filed, including extensions. More importantly, a return may be filed late and *S* may qualify by becoming a citizen before the return is filed. Therefore, the penalty for late filing may be worth incurring to avoid the §2056A requirements.

For purposes of a §2056(d)(4)(B) requirement that *S* was a resident at *D*'s death and until becoming a citizen, Treas. Reg. §20.2056A-1(b) adopts the Treas. Reg. §20.0-1(b)(1) definition of residence (rather than the §7701(b) income tax definition): domicile in the United States, which is acquired by living in a place "for even a brief period of time, with no present intention of later removing therefrom." However, "[r]esidence without the requisite intention to remain indefinitely will not suffice."

Also in 1988, §2523(i) was enacted to provide that the gift tax marital deduction is not allowable if *S* is not a U.S. citizen, with no §2056A-type exception to permit inter vivos marital deduction qualification. In its place, however, the §2503(b) gift tax annual exclusion was increased to ten times the normal amount per year (indexed for inflation) for gifts of present interests made to a spouse who is not a citizen, provided only that the gift otherwise would qualify for the gift tax marital deduction and meets the gift tax annual exclusion present interest requirements. §2523(i)(2).

Exceptions.   Section 2056(d) is subject to several exceptions. For example, transfers governed by wealth transfer tax treaties are exempt. Treas. Reg. §20.2056A-1(c). More importantly, §2056(d)(2) permits the estate tax marital deduction if a §2056A "qualified domestic trust" (QDOT) is utilized. Under this exception, property passing from a decedent directly to a QDOT will qualify for the estate tax marital deduction. So too will property passing to a surviving spouse who transfers or irrevocably assigns it to a QDOT before *D*'s estate tax return is filed and before the QDOT election is required. Treas. Reg. §§20.2056A-2(b)(2) and -4(b). It is not necessary that *D* create the QDOT; Treas. Reg. §20.2056A-2(b)(2) lists *S*, *D*, or *D*'s personal representative as potential creators (and does not purport to be exclusive) to receive such property. Treas. Reg. §§20.2056A-4(b)(5), and -4(d) *Examples 1, 5* illustrate the significantly adverse tax consequences that occur when a surviving spouse, after receiving property outright, then contributes that property to a QDOT. These examples illustrate that dramatically poor results are produced by having *S* make contributions to a QDOT. Because of this, it is extremely important (as a planning matter) to ascertain citizenship in the planning stage and craft the estate plan to create and fully fund a QDOT without the need for action by *S*.

In addition, a nonqualifying trust can be reformed to qualify under a procedure specified in §2056(d)(5). Unfortunately, because only an "explicit" trust can meet the QDOT requirements, entities such as qualified employee benefit accounts cannot be made to qualify and a special approach must be used to qualify "nonassignable annuities and other arrangements," such as an employee benefit spousal annuity payable to a surviving spouse who is not a U.S. citizen. See Treas. Reg. §§20.2056A-2(a) and -4(c).

24.   *QDOT Qualification Requirements.* A QDOT is a trust that satisfies the requirements of §2056(b)(5), 2056(b)(7) or 2056(b)(8), or is an estate trust, and that also satisfies special requirements that apply only to QDOTs. It probably is easiest to think of a §2056A(a) QDOT as a §2056(b)(5), §2056(b)(7), §2056(b)(8), or estate trust that meets the §2056A(a)(1) requirements, which are that at least one trustee be a U.S. citizen[35] or domestic corporation,[36] and that "no distribution (other than a distribution of income) may be made from the trust unless a trustee who is an individual citizen of the United States or domestic corporation has the right to withhold from such distribution the tax imposed by this section on such distribution." In addition, §2056A(a)(2) mandates that the QDOT must comply with any requirements prescribed by the regulations to ensure the collection of any tax imposed by §2056A(b). An election must be made on *D*'s last timely filed estate tax return or first late return.[37]

A bifurcated rule in Treas. Reg. §20.2056A-2(d)(1) imposes the requirement that a trust either (1) employ at least one trustee that is a §581 U.S. bank or trust company (i.e., a domestic law firm or other citizen acting as trustee will not suffice), (2) furnish a bond or security in an amount equal to 65% of the §2031 federal estate tax value of the trust corpus, or (3) if the §2031 value is no more than $2 million:[38] the trust instrument must prohibit investment of more than 35% of the annually determined fair

---

35.   To meet the U.S. citizen requirement, an individual trustee "must have a tax home . . . in the U.S." Treas. Reg. §20.2056A-2(d)(2). See §911(d)(3).

36.   Under Treas. Reg. §20.2056A-2(c), a domestic corporation is "a corporation created or organized" under state or federal law and, for reasons revealed in Treas. Reg. §20.2056A-2(d)(1)(i)(A), is likely to be a bank as defined in §581 (i.e., a bank, trust company, or savings and loan).

37.   Treas. Reg. §20.2056A-3(a). Note that §2056A(d) allows a late return to make the election only if it is no more than one year tardy; that limitation is reflected obliquely in the first clause of the regulation, reading "subject to the time period prescribed in §2056A(d)." Although partial QDOT elections are not allowed, the regulations recognize that a trust may be severed "in accordance with the applicable requirements of §2056(b)(7)" and only one of the trusts elected. Treas. Reg. §20.2056A-3(b). See Treas. Reg. §20.2056(b)-7(b)(2)(ii).

38.   Aggregation of multiple QDOTs for the same surviving spouse is required by Treas. Reg. §20.2056A-2(d)(1)(ii)(A) to determine whether the $2 million threshold has been exceeded.

market value in real estate located offshore, and all other assets must be held in the United States. See Treas. Reg. §20.2056A-2(d)(3). These "bank or bond" rules are designed to assure collection of the tax on a QDOT and require the trust to file annual reports that include information about trust investments and their annually determined fair market value. Treas. Reg. §20.2056A-2(d)(4).

25. *Taxation of QDOTs.* Wealth transfer tax is imposed on QDOTs in an unusual manner. Effectively, §2056A(b) treats a QDOT as not qualifying for a normal estate tax marital deduction in *D*'s estate but, rather, as deferring both the determination of the *amount* to be taxed and the liability for payment of the tax from *D*'s death until a later triggering event occurs. That is, the tax imposed under §2056A(b)(2)(A) is computed as if *D* had died at the time of the triggering event and the taxable property (determined at the time of the triggering event) was then includible in *D*'s estate.[39] The amount by which *D*'s taxes would have been increased by inclusion of such property is the amount of tax that is then to be paid by the QDOT with no imposition of interest for the deferral inherent in the delay between *D*'s death and the triggering event. There can be more than one triggering event, and the tax is imposed on the amount of property involved in each such event. In addition, because the QDOT also is subject to tax in *S*'s estate, §2056A(b)(10) makes benefits available to *S*'s estate as if *S* were a citizen or resident.

The deferred estate tax under §2056A is attractive in one potentially significant respect. Normal marital deduction planning shelters *D*'s unified credit and "stacks" the balance of *D*'s property on top of *S*'s estate in the form of a marital deduction bequest, causing taxation of that property at *S*'s marginal estate tax rates. This estate stacking does not occur with the QDOT approach. Instead, *D*'s property is taxed at *D*'s rates and *S*'s property is taxed at *S*'s rates. Thus, in effect, *D* enjoys a full "run through the brackets" and *S* enjoys a second run through the brackets. Overall, less tax will be paid under the QDOT approach if the estates are large enough to benefit from separate bracket runs and the estate tax is still a progressive impost.

Although the QDOT may be taxable in the estate of *S* as well (because it must comply with the normal marital deduction trust rules and will be subject to U.S. taxation if still in existence at *S*'s death), double tax under the QDOT regime is precluded by §2056(d)(3). It grants a special §2013 estate tax credit to *S*'s estate. The amount of the §2013 credit is based on taxes deemed paid by *D*'s estate with respect to a QDOT for that property.

---

39. See, e.g., the valuation rules in Treas. Reg. §20.2056A-5(b); only if the triggering event is *S*'s death is §2032 alternate valuation or §2032A special use valuation allowed, under Treas. Reg. §20.2056A-5(b)(2). See also Treas. Reg. §20.2056A-6(c)(5).

The percentage limitation that is normally imposed under §2013(a), based on the time elapsed between deaths, does not apply. §2056(d)(3) (flush language). Tax effectively is paid at whichever marginal bracket (*D*'s or *S*'s) is the highest, meaning that effective planning in this respect would insure that *D*'s bracket will be higher so as to preserve both bracket runs.

The triggering events for imposition of the §2056A(b) tax are *S*'s death, any termination of the qualified status of the trust, or any distribution from the QDOT during *S*'s remaining life *except* distributions of income and distributions of corpus "on account of hardship."[40] §2056A(b)(3)(A). Additional exceptions to the triggering events provision are set forth at Treas. Reg. §20.2056A-5(c)(3). Inter vivos distributions to *S* are taxed on a tax inclusive basis — i.e., the trustee must pay the tax on those distributions and that tax payment is regarded as another taxable distribution to *S*; the net result is that taxes paid by the trust by virtue of the distribution are also subjected to the tax. Treas. Reg. §20.2056A-5(b)(1).

The amount of tax is defined in §2056A(b)(2)(A)(i) as "the tax which would have been imposed under §2001 on the estate of the decedent if the taxable estate of the decedent had been increased by" the amount of the triggering distribution or the value of the trust property at the death of *S*. This tax is computed using the §2001 rates that were in effect at *D*'s death. Treas. Reg. §20.2056A-6(a). These tax computation rules can be avoided under §2056A(b)(12) if *S* becomes a citizen.

PART G. REDUCTIONS OF THE MARITAL DEDUCTION

Code References: *Estate Tax: §§2056, 2053, 4980A*
Income Tax: §642(g)

26. *Unidentified Assets.* If the pool of assets (or the proceeds of assets) from which the spouse's interest may be satisfied includes an asset or assets that constitute a nondeductible terminable interest (a "tainted" asset), then the deduction is reduced by the value of all such tainted assets. The presumption is that tainted assets are the first that will be distributed to *S* in satisfaction of *S*'s entitlement in the estate. §2056(b)(2); Treas. Reg. §20.2056(b)-2. For this reason a careful drafter precludes the use of any tainted assets (or the proceeds therefrom) in satisfying a bequest to a spouse.

---

40.   Treas. Reg. §20.2056A-5(c)(1) adopts the hardship definition found in Treas. Reg. §1.401(k)-1(d)(2)(i), allowing distributions that respond to an immediate and heavy financial need relating to *S*'s health, maintenance, or support, but only to the extent other resources (such as personally owned, publicly traded stock or a certificate of deposit that could be cashed in) are not reasonably available. Although not taxable, hardship distributions nevertheless must be reported as if they were, which allows the government to audit the claimed exemption. The application of the exception for distributions of income is described in Treas. Reg. §20.2056A-5(c)(2).

27. *Tax Payment.* An otherwise allowable estate tax marital deduction also is reduced by any death taxes that *may be* payable out of *S*'s interest. §2056(b)(4)(A); Treas. Reg. §20.2056(b)-4(c); Rev. Rul. 79-14. The extent to which an interest passing to *S* is subject to *D*'s death taxes may be determined variously by the terms of *D*'s will (if it directs *D*'s personal representative to use certain funds to pay those taxes) or other instrument, by a local or federal statute providing for tax apportionment (see §§2206, 2207, 2207A, and 2207B and the Uniform Estate Tax Apportionment Act), or by judicial equitable apportionment rules.[41]

It is customary to include a provision in *D*'s will exonerating all bequests to *S* from *D*'s death taxes to prevent reduction of the marital deduction if, under local law, a bequest to *S* is charged with a share of *D*'s death taxes. Fortunately, in most states the concept of equitable apportionment exonerates *S*'s share because only those bequests that generate tax are liable to contribute to that tax payment. Thus, for example, Estate of Sawyer v. Commissioner, 73 T.C. 1 (1979), accepted as controlling a decision of an Ohio lower court that the bequest to *S* of one third of *D*'s residuary estate was not burdened with any of *D*'s federal estate tax. Although no express provision for death taxes was made in *D*'s will and Ohio had not adopted an apportionment statute, the Ohio court found that *D* had an implied intent that *S*'s interest not be reduced by death taxes. See Sawyer v. Sawyer, 374 N.E.2d 166 (Ohio Ct. App. 1977). The Tax Court allowed a marital deduction for the entire unreduced third of *D*'s residuary estate. See also Elliot v. Elliot, 349 So.2d 1092 (Ala. 1977). Unfortunately there is no dearth of cases in which an intent to exonerate *S*'s interest is lacking and the marital deduction correspondingly is reduced. See, e.g., Estate of Swallen v. Commissioner, 65 T.C.M. (CCH) 2332 (1993); TAM 9313002.

The decedent in Estate of Ransburg v. United States, 91-1 U.S. Tax Cas. (CCH) ¶60,052 (S.D. Ind. 1990), clarified, 765 F. Supp. 1388 (S.D. Ind. 1991), directed payment of all taxes "which may be assessed as a result of my death and without regard to whether . . . payable by my estate or by any beneficiary," without indicating from what source payment was to be made. State law contained an equitable apportionment dictate that would cause each beneficiary to pay the tax attributable to his or her bequest, but that rule could be overcome if the will specifically directed otherwise or if payment of taxes was to be made from the residue of the estate. The *Ransburg* estate passed half to a surviving spouse, one-sixth to a qualified charity, and one-third to children of the decedent by a prior marriage. The government successfully argued that, because taxes were to be paid from the residue, the apportionment statute did not apply, taxes would come "off

---

41. See Kahn, *The Federal Estate Tax Burden Borne by a Dissenting Widow*, 64 MICH. L. REV. 1499 (1966). Note that the Uniform Estate Tax Apportionment Act is incorporated in §3-916 of the Uniform Probate Code and is the law in nearly half the United States.

the top" of the estate, and the amount ultimately distributable to the spouse and charity, qualifying for the marital and charitable deductions, should be reduced. The will failed to direct the source of tax payment as among the residuary takers and placed the tax payment provision before the actual distribution provision, making it appear that taxes were to be paid first, followed by distribution. As such, the court found that the tax clause negated the state equitable apportionment regime and resulted in a reduction of the amounts qualifying for each deduction.

28.   *Discretionary Power to Invade the Marital Trust to Pay Estate Taxes.* Assume that the residue of *D*'s residuary estate is divided into two equal shares: Share *A*, a power of appointment trust for the life of *S*, qualifies for the marital deduction; Share *B*, a bypass trust, does not qualify for the marital deduction. *D*'s will directs that all death taxes be paid out of Share *B*, but authorizes the personal representative to pay taxes out of Share *A* to the extent the personal representative determines in the exercise of discretion and business judgment that doing so would be more prudent. In fact, the personal representative paid all of the taxes using assets allocated to Share *B*. What is the rationale or statutory support for reducing the value of Share *A* for marital deduction purposes by the full amount of *D*'s death taxes? See Estate of Reno v. Commissioner, 916 F.2d 955 (4th Cir. 1990), *rev'd (en banc) on other grounds*, 945 F.2d 733 (4th Cir. 1991); Jeschke v. United States, 814 F.2d 568 (10th Cir. 1987); Adee Trust No. 1 v. United States, 52 A.F.T.R.2d ¶148,598 (D. Kan. 1983); Estate of Wycoff v. Commissioner, 506 F.2d 1144 (10th Cir. 1974); Rev. Rul. 79-14; PLRs 8622022, 8517036, 8508022, and 8450018; and cf. Pyne v. United States, 86-2 U.S. Tax Cas. (CCH) ¶13,677 (D. Me. 1986).

29.   *Other Encumbrances.* Any obligation imposed by *D* on *S*, or any encumbrance with respect to property passing to *S*, also reduces an otherwise allowable marital deduction. §2056(b)(4)(B). *United States v. Stapf*, the leading decision construing this section, arose when the marital deduction was limited to 50% of *D*'s adjusted gross estate. The result will not differ under the unlimited marital deduction applicable today:

United States v. Stapf
375 U.S. 118 (1963)

Mr. Justice GOLDBERG:

Lowell H. Stapf died testate on July 29, 1953, a resident and domiciliary of . . . a community property jurisdiction. At the time of his death he owned, in addition to his separate estate, a substantial amount of property in community with his wife. His will required that his widow elect either to retain her one-half interest in the community or to take under the will and allow its terms to govern the disposition of her community interest. If Mrs. Stapf were to elect to take under the will, she would be given, after specific bequests to others, one-third of her husband's separate estate. By accepting this bequest she would allow her one-half interest in the community to pass, in accordance with the will, into a trust for the benefit of the children. It was further provided that if she chose to take under the will the executors were to pay "all and not merely one-half" of the community debts and administration expenses.

The relevant facts and computations are not in dispute. . . . If Mrs. Stapf had not elected to take under the will . . . she would have received a net of $111,443.

In fact Mrs. Stapf elected to take under the will. She received, after specific bequests to others, one-third of the combined separate and community property, a devise valued at $106,268, which was $5,175 less than she would have received had she retained her community property and refused to take under the will. . . .

By electing to take under the will, Mrs. Stapf, in effect, agreed to accept the property devised to her and, in turn, to surrender property of greater value to the trust for the benefit of the children. This raises the question of whether a decedent's estate is allowed a marital deduction . . . where the bequest to the surviving spouse is on the condition that she convey property of equivalent or greater value to her children. The Government contends that, for purposes of a marital deduction, "the value of the interest passing to the wife is the value of the property given her less the value of the property she is required to give another as a condition to receiving it." On this view, since the widow had no net benefit from the exercise of her election, the estate would be entitled to no marital deduction. Respondents reject this net benefit approach and argue that the plain meaning of the statute makes detriment to the surviving spouse immaterial.

[Section 2056(a)] provides that "in general" the marital deduction is for "the value of any interest in property which passes ,. . . from the decedent to his surviving spouse." [§2056(b)(4)(B)] then deals specifically with the question of valuation . . . .

The disputed deduction turns upon the interpretation of (1) the introductory phrase "any obligation imposed by the decedent with respect to the passing of such interest," and (2) the concluding provision that "such . . . obligation shall be taken into account in the same manner as if the amount of a gift to such spouse of such interest were being determined."

The Court of Appeals, in allowing the claimed marital deduction, reasoned that since the valuation is to be "as if" a gift were being taxed, the legal analysis should be the same as if a husband had made an inter vivos gift to his wife on the condition that she give something to the children. In such a case, it was stated, the husband is taxable in the full amount for his gift. The detriment incurred by the wife would not ordinarily reduce the amount of the gift taxable to the husband, the original donor. The court concluded: "Within gift tax confines the community property of the widow passing under the will of the husband to others may not be 'netted' against the devise to the widow, and thus testator, were the transfer inter vivos, would be liable for gift taxes on the full value of the devise." 309 F.2d 592, 598.

This conclusion, based on the alleged plain meaning of the final gift-amount clause of [§2056(b)(4)(B)] is not supported by a reading of the entire statutory provision. First, [§2056] allows a marital deduction only for the decedent's gifts or bequests which pass "to his surviving spouse." In the present case the effect of the devise was not to distribute wealth to the surviving spouse, but instead to transmit, through the widow, a gift to the couple's children. The gift-to-the-surviving-spouse terminology reflects concern with the status of the actual recipient or donee of the gift. What the statute provides is a "marital deduction" — deduction for gifts to the surviving spouse — not a deduction for gifts to the children or a deduction for gifts to the privately selected beneficiaries. The appropriate reference, therefore, is not to the value of the gift moving from the deceased spouse but to the net value of the gift received by the surviving spouse.

Second, the introductory phrases of [§2056(b)(4)(B)] provide that the gift-amount determination is to be made "where such interest or property is encumbered in any manner, or where the surviving spouse incurs any obligation imposed by the decedent with respect to the passing of such interest. . . ." The Government, drawing upon the broad import of this language, argues: "An undertaking by the wife to convey property to a third person, upon which her receipt of property under the decedent's will is conditioned, is plainly an 'obligation imposed by the decedent with respect to the passing of such interest.'" Respondents contend that "encumbrance or obligation" refers only to "a payment to be made *out of* the property passing to the surviving spouse." Respondents' narrow construction certainly is not compelled by a literal interpretation of the statutory language. Their construction would embrace only, for example, an obligation *on* the property passing whereas the statute speaks of an obligation "*with respect* to the passing" gift. Finally, to arrive at the real value of the gift "such . . . obligation shall be taken into account. . . ." In context we think this relates the gift-amount determination to the net economic interest received by the surviving spouse.

This interpretation is supported by authoritative declarations of congressional intent. The Senate Committee on Finance, in explaining the operation of the marital deduction, stated its understanding as follows:

> If the decedent bequeaths certain property to his surviving spouse *subject*, however, to *her agreement*, or a charge on the property, for payment of $1,000 to *X*, the value of the bequest (and, accordingly, the value of the interest passing to the surviving spouse) is the value, reduced by $1,000, of such property. [S. Rep. No. 1013, 80th Cong., 2d Sess., Pt. 2, p. 6. (Emphasis added.)]

[Treas. Reg. §20.2056(b)-4(b) *Example (3)*] specifically includes an example of the kind of testamentary disposition involved in this case:

> A decedent bequeathed certain securities to his wife in lieu of her interest in property held by them as community property under the law of the State of their residence. The wife elected to relinquish her community property interest and to take the bequest. For the purpose of the marital deduction, the value of the bequest is to be reduced by the value of the community property interest relinquished by the wife.

We conclude, therefore, that the governing principle, approved by Congress and embodied in the Treasury Regulation, must be that a marital deduction is allowable only to the extent that the property bequeathed to the surviving spouse exceeds in value the property she is required to relinquish.

Our conclusion concerning the congressionally intended result under [§2056] accords with the general purpose of Congress in creating the marital deduction. The 1948 tax amendments were intended to equalize the effect of the estate taxes in community property and common-law jurisdictions. Under a community property system . . . the surviving spouse receives outright ownership of one-half of the community property and only the other one-half is included in the decedent's estate. To equalize the incidence of progressively scaled estate taxes and to adhere to the patterns of state law, the marital deduction permits a deceased spouse, subject to certain requirements, to transfer free of taxes one-half of his non-community property to his surviving spouse. Although applicable to separately held property in a community property state, the primary thrust of this is to extend to taxpayers in common-law States the advantages of "estate splitting" otherwise available only in community property States. The purpose, however, is only to permit a married couple's property to be taxed in two stages and not to allow a tax-exempt transfer of wealth into succeeding generations. Thus the marital deduction is generally restricted to the transfer of property interests that will be includible in the surviving spouse's gross estate. Respondents' construction of [§2056] would, nevertheless, permit one-half of a spouse's wealth to pass from one generation to another without being subject either to gift or estate taxes. We do not believe that this result, squarely contrary to the concept of the marital deduction, can be justified by the language of [§2056].

Furthermore, since in a community property jurisdiction one-half of the community normally vests in the wife, approval of the claimed deduction would create an opportunity for tax reduction that, as a practical matter, would be more readily available to couples in community property jurisdictions than to couples in common-law jurisdictions. Such a result, again, would be unnecessarily inconsistent with a basic purpose of the statute.

Since in our opinion the plain meaning of [§2056] does not require the interpretation advanced by respondents, the statute must be construed to accord with the clearly expressed congressional purposes and the relevant Treasury Regulation. We conclude that, for estate tax purposes, the value of a conditional bequest to a widow should be the value of the property given to her less the value of the property she is required to give to another. In this case the value of the property transferred to Mrs. Stapf ($106,268) must be reduced by the value of the community property she was required to relinquish ($111,443). Since she received no net benefit, the estate is entitled to no marital deduction. . . .

Was Mrs. Stapf's election to take under her husband's will a completed gift of $5,175 subject to gift taxation? See 1 Casner & Pennell, ESTATE PLANNING §3.7.1 (6th ed. 1995).

Note that costs that typically are borne by a life tenant can be borne by a surviving spouse who receives a life tenancy, without causing a reduction of the marital deduction. See Estate of Peacock v. United States, 914 F.2d 230 (11th Cir. 1990) (*D*'s bequest of a life estate in residential realty subject to *S*'s payment of property taxes, insurance premiums, and maintenance expenses did not reduce the allowable marital deduction); Estate of Novotny v. Commissioner, 93 T.C. 12 (1989) (*S*'s interest as life tenant of residential realty that was included in *D*'s gross estate qualified for the QTIP marital deduction notwithstanding that *S*'s tenure was conditioned on payment of mortgage installment obligations, property taxes, and costs of upkeep and repair, because these items were no greater than those imposed by state law on any legal life tenant).

30.   *Administration and Interest Expenses.*   Recall the brief discussion of §642(g) at page 607 regarding the personal representative's election to claim expenses of administering D's estate as an income tax or as an estate tax deduction. If these "swing item" administration expenses are taken as income tax deductions and if they exceed the amount of nonmarital property available for their payment, charging them against the marital share would trigger a §2056(b)(4)(B) reduction of the marital deduction. That reduction of the marital share could cause the estate to incur an estate tax that, if also charged against the marital share, would trigger another §2056(b)(4)(A) reduction of the marital deduction, which would further increase the estate tax, cause another reduction in the marital share and another increase in tax, culminating in a pyramiding whirlpool computation. That could cause a significant amount of estate tax in an estate that the planner may have thought would be tax free due to D's use of an optimum marital deduction bequest. All that estate tax can be avoided by having the personal representative elect to claim the administration expenses as estate tax deductions under §2053.

Will payment of administration expenses out of postmortem income of the estate prevent a reduction of a marital deduction? This issue was decided by the Supreme Court in the taxpayer's favor in Commissioner v. Estate of Hubert, 520 U.S. 93 (1997), and prompted a revision of Treas. Reg. §20.2056(b)-4(a) to establish a convoluted rule that distinguishes between typically recurring expenses to "manage" estate assets and "transmission" expenses incurred essentially on a one-time basis to administer the estate and make distribution. The government's position is that on-going management expenses are a proper charge to income earned postmortem but that transmission expenses ought to be paid from corpus of the estate. In addition, claiming certain expenses as a §2053 deduction will require reduction of the marital deduction under the no-double-deduction authority of §2056(b)(9). To illustrate, consider the following simple example: The decedent's estate was $3 million before taxes or expenses, the §2053 deductible expenses of administration are $200,000 (broken down into the regulation's management ($50,000) and transmission ($150,000) expenses) there is enough income earned postmortem to pay the full $200,000 of expenses if so desired, and the estate plan is a reduce-to-zero optimum marital bequest with residuary nonmarital.

There are several things going on in this example that make it hard to follow. One is the fundamental notion of expenses of administration that can be taken as estate tax deductions under §2053 *or* as estate income tax deductions by making the §642(g) election. When that occurs they show up as a zero on the §2053 line of the calculation shown below — simply because they were used for income tax purposes. Notice this occurs in the middle column. When they are used in this manner on the income tax return they reduce income taxes rather than estate tax, and that leaves more wealth (income after income tax is paid from it). That part of a comprehensive illustration is omitted — it would help decide which alternative is the better approach economically but shows us nothing about the marital deduction consequences of the *Hubert* regulation.

In that regard, the critical element in the calculation below is that estate transmission expenses paid from the marital share in the last column, and estate management or transmission expenses deducted under §2053 in the first and last columns, all cause a reduction in the marital deduction that otherwise would be allowed. That reduction in the deduction explains why there is a smaller marital deduction than the size of the marital bequest in the first and last columns. The tax generated by that reduction of the deduction is paid from the nonmarital trust to avoid further reduction in the marital deduction. That decision informs the reduced size of the nonmarital trust.

	Pay All with Nonmarital Corpus & Deduct on Estate Tax Form 706	Pay All with Nonmarital Corpus & Deduct on Income Tax Form 1041	Pay All Pro Rata with Income & Deduct on Estate Tax Form 706
Gross Estate	3,000,000	3,000,000	3,000,000
2003 Applicable Exclusion Amount	(1,000,000)	(1,000,000)	(1,000,000)
Transmission Expense (ETE)	(150,000)	(150,000)	(150,000)
Management Expense (EME)	(50,000)	(50,000)	(50,000)
§2053 Deduction	(200,000)	0	(200,000)
Optimum Marital Bequest	(1,800,000)	(2,000,000)	(1,800,000)
Marital Deduction	(1,767,857)	(2,000,000)	(1,680,000)
Taxable Estate	1,032,143	1,000,000	1,120,000
Nonmarital Trust Before Tax	1,000,000	800,000	1,200,000
Tax on Nonmarital Trust	13,179	0	49,200
Nonmarital Trust After Tax	986,821	800,000	1,150,800

Note that the first column entails loss of marital deduction because of prohibited §2053 deduction of the marital share of the EME. The third column entails loss of marital deduction because of payment of the ETE pro rata from the marital portion *and* because of prohibited §2053 deduction of the marital share of EME.

Calculations assume death in 2003 and a formula provision that does not self adjust to increase the marital bequest to the extent the marital deduction is reduced under the *Hubert* regulation

Pro rations are based on size of the marital and bypass trusts before tax payment from the nonmarital trust (to avoid circular calculations). Paying the tax from the nonmarital trust avoids further reduction of the marital deduction.

Notice that the last column leaves more wealth overall, simply because the expenses of administration were paid using income generated postmortem, rather than using a portion of the original $3 million estate corpus to pay the $200,000 of expenses of administration. This means that the last column shows more wealth in the nonmarital trust even after the marital deduction is reduced under the government's *Hubert* regulation. That also means that the estate tax will be less when the surviving spouse dies — wealth in the marital trust is taxable in the second estate, but not wealth in the nonmarital trust. When you crunch the numbers, what you will discover is that the last column — which is where the regulation inflicts the greatest punishment on the estate through reduction of the marital deduction and generation of the largest taxable estate — nevertheless is the best alternative to embrace.

Also notice what happened in the middle column: the least wealth remains when the estate uses the §642(g) swing items for income tax deductions rather than using them for estate tax deductions! That is what the government wants to happen — it is the choice the *Hubert* regulation encourages executors to make. It also is what many executors want, even though it produces the worst result. Can you think of a reason why? Here's a hint: most executors are (or cater to) the surviving spouse.

31. *Unascertainable Interest: Marital Funding.* The last major hurdle in marital deduction qualification involves a requirement that the interest passing to S must be ascertainable at D's death and not subject to a significant contingency. One context in which this requirement arises is when a "formula" is used to describe the property that will be used to fund the marital share. The choice of funding approach is an independent aspect of planning for the deduction — unrelated to the selection of the form of qualification for the marital share (i.e., outright, §2056(b)(5) general power of appointment trust, §2056(b)(7) QTIP trust, estate trust, or whatever). There are numerous variations available to express the nature and amount of the gift, but there are only two basic categories of formula clauses for funding purposes: pecuniary and fractional bequests.

A *pecuniary* formula clause makes a gift of money, using a provision like:

I give the smallest *pecuniary amount* that, if allowed as a federal estate tax marital deduction, would result in the least possible federal estate tax being payable by reason of my death.

This form of gift is analogous to a bequest of "$10,000 to my alma mater," although sophisticated marital pecuniary bequests are determined pursuant to a formula and the amount of the bequest is likely to be a tad larger.

A *fractional* share formula clause makes a gift of a fraction of the assets comprising the decedent's estate, using a provision like:

I give a *fractional share* of my residuary estate of which (a) the numerator is the smallest amount that, if allowed as a federal estate tax marital deduction, would result in the least possible federal estate tax being payable by reason of my death, and (b) the denominator is the value of my residuary estate as finally determined for federal estate tax purposes.

This form of gift is analogous to a bequest of the residuary estate "to my children, A and B, in equal shares," although the marital fractional share is likely to be determined pursuant to a formula and the fraction often is not as simple as ½ or ¼.

There are at least five basic types of pecuniary formula clauses and two types of formula fractional bequests, all tied to different mechanisms for accomplishing the funding. A variety of factors are relevant in evaluating the advantages and disadvantages of the available funding mechanisms. For example, which bequest (the marital, nonmarital, or neither) would be easier from an administrative perspective to constitute the residue of the estate, considering the need to value assets at the time they are distributed and concerns about flexibility in allocating assets between various shares? What is the likelihood that estate assets will appreciate or depreciate between the date of the decedent's death and the date(s) of funding, which may be several years later? In light of this, which of the marital or the nonmarital bequests ought to be funded and which should be the residue, and in what manner should it be funded to minimize any capital gain that may be realized in funding? If assets change in value before the date(s) of funding, which bequest should bear the loss from depreciation or benefit from appreciation, and with what effects? Several arcane income tax consequences must be considered, such as distributable net income (DNI) carry out and acceleration of income in respect of a decedent (IRD). Although we need not delve into all of these complications for purposes of this discussion,[42] a little familiarity may help understand more fundamental concerns.

With respect to assets distributed in kind (rather than being sold and the cash proceeds being distributed), the common law rule is that fair market value at the date(s) of distribution is used to measure the extent to which a distribution satisfies a pecuniary bequest.[43] This common law dictate generates the term "true worth" pecuniary that sometimes is applied to a date of distribution pecuniary funding provision. A significant disadvantage of the true worth pecuniary approach is that distribution of assets in kind, in satisfaction of the pecuniary amount, is deemed to be a sale or exchange for

---

42. For further study, consult Pennell, ESTATE TAX MARITAL DEDUCTION, 843 Estates, Gifts & Trusts Portfolio (Tax Mgmt. 2003), and 3 Casner & Pennell, ESTATE PLANNING §13.7 (6th ed. 2002).

43. See, e.g., In re Estate of Kantner, 143 A.2d 243 (N.J. Super. 1958); In re Gauff, 211 N.Y.S.2d 583 (1960); In re Burnett, 89 N.Y.S.2d 152 (1949).

income tax purposes.[44] Based on a theory that the pecuniary amount is a fixed obligation, funding is treated *as if* the fiduciary had sold the assets that actually were distributed in kind and had distributed the cash proceeds of the sale, which the recipient immediately used to purchase those same assets, giving them a new basis equal to fair market value in the distributee's hands. As a consequence, any appreciation or depreciation in distributed assets between their basis and their date of distribution value triggers realization of gain or loss. Fast funding — shortly after *D*'s death, before assets have fluctuated much in value — is one means of minimizing this problem.

To illustrate, if *D* bequeathed a pecuniary amount of $100,000 to *S* and eight months after *D*'s death the personal representative distributed Blackacre to *S* in satisfaction of that bequest (Blackacre having a value at that time of $100,000), that distribution would be treated as a sale or exchange of Blackacre for its fair market value. If Blackacre had a federal estate tax value and therefore a §1014(b) income tax basis of only $72,000, *D*'s estate would recognize a gain of $28,000 because the basis of Blackacre became $72,000 at *D*'s death due to its inclusion in *D*'s estate at that value for federal estate tax purposes.

Another mechanism to address the gain or loss realization problem is to utilize a pecuniary funding regime that avoids the consequence because the amount of bequest satisfied is equal to the fiduciary's basis in the distributed asset. This technique is known as a federal estate tax funded pecuniary, which deems assets to be worth their value for federal estate tax purposes and, because that is equal to the basis of assets included in *D*'s gross estate under §1014(b), the sale or exchange that is deemed to occur generates no gain or loss. Thus, for example, if the personal representative were satisfying the same $100,000 pecuniary bequest using Blackacre in the prior example and federal estate tax values were used in determining the amount of the bequest satisfied, the personal representative would be obliged to distribute additional property worth $28,000 to fully satisfy the bequest because Blackacre would be deemed to be worth only its $72,000 basis. There would be no gain or loss on the distribution, but an asset worth $100,000 would now be in the hands of the distributee and an additional distribution still would be required. This can cause overfunding of the pecuniary bequest because, in an appreciating estate, more assets are distributed than would be necessary if date of distribution values were used. The disadvantage of overfunding is that it increases the size of *S*'s gross estate.

---

44. See, e.g., Treas. Reg. §1.1014-4(a)(3); Kenan v. Commissioner, 114 F.2d 217 (2d Cir. 1940), *aff'g* 40 B.T.A. 824 (1939); Suisman v. Eaton, 15 F. Supp. 113 (D. Conn. 1935). The true worth pecuniary marital bequest frequently is referred to as a *"Suisman"* (pronounced Sussman) funded pecuniary after the *Suisman* case, which imposes this capital gain or loss treatment on its funding.

Authorizing the personal representative to satisfy a pecuniary bequest in this manner might permit postmortem manipulation by the personal representative's choosing only assets that have depreciated in value to satisfy the pecuniary bequest. For example, if Blackacre had been valued at $100,000 for federal estate tax purposes and had declined in value to only $72,000 on the date of distribution, its distribution would constitute a total satisfaction of the pecuniary bequest. This causes underfunding of the bequest. It was to prevent such manipulation that the Commissioner promulgated Rev. Proc. 64-19, which remains even today a very significant marital deduction pronouncement.

Revenue Procedure 64-19

SECTION 1. PURPOSE

The purpose of this Revenue Procedure is to state the position of the Internal Revenue Service relative to allowance of the marital deduction in cases where there is some uncertainty as to the ultimate distribution to be made in payment of a pecuniary bequest or transfer in trust where the governing instrument provides that the executor or trustee may satisfy bequests in kind with assets at their value as finally determined for Federal estate tax purposes.

SECTION 2. BACKGROUND

.01   The Internal Revenue Service has received inquiries concerning the amount of the marital deduction which should be allowed for a pecuniary bequest in a will or for a transfer in trust of a pecuniary amount where the governing instrument not only provides that the executor or trustee may, or is required to, select assets in kind to satisfy the bequest or transfer, but also provides that any assets distributed in kind shall be valued at their values as finally determined for Federal estate tax purposes. The question is the same whether the amount of the bequest or transfer is determined by a formula fixing it by reference to the adjusted gross estate of the decedent as finally determined for Federal estate tax purposes, or its amount is determined in some other fashion by which a fixed dollar amount distributable to S can be computed. Any bequest or transfer in trust described in subsection 2.01 is hereinafter referred to as a "pecuniary bequest or transfer" for purposes of this Revenue Procedure.

.02   Where, by virtue of the duties imposed on the fiduciary either by applicable state law or by the express or implied provisions of the instrument, it is clear that the fiduciary, in order to implement such a bequest or transfer, must distribute assets, including cash, having an aggregate fair market value at the date, or dates, of distribution amounting to no less than the amount of the pecuniary bequest or transfer, as finally determined for Federal estate tax purposes, the marital deduction may be allowed in the full amount of the pecuniary bequest or transfer in trust. Alternatively, where, by virtue of such duties, it is clear that the fiduciary must distribute assets, including cash, fairly representative of appreciation or depreciation in the value of all property thus available for distribution in satisfaction of such pecuniary bequest or transfer, the marital deduction is equally determinable and may be allowed in the full amount of the pecuniary bequest or transfer in trust passing to *S*.

.03   In many instances, however, by virtue of the provisions of the will or trust, or by virtue of applicable state law (or because of an absence of applicable state decisions), it may not be clear that the discretion of the fiduciary would be limited in this respect, and it cannot be determined that he would be required to make distribution in conformance with one or the other of the above requirements or that one rather than the other is applicable. In such a case, the interest in property passing from the decedent to his surviving spouse would not be ascertainable as of the date of death, if the property available for distribution included assets which might fluctuate in value. . . .

SECTION 4. SCOPE

.01   The problem here considered is restricted to the situation involving bequests and transfers in trust described in §§1 and 2.01. It does not arise in other cases, for example:

(1)   In a bequest or transfer in trust of a fractional share of the estate, under which each beneficiary shares proportionately in the appreciation or depreciation in the value of assets to the date, or dates, of distribution.

(2)   In a bequest or transfer in trust of specific assets.

(3)   In a pecuniary bequest or transfer in trust, whether in a stated amount or an amount computed by the use of a formula, if:

(a)   The fiduciary must satisfy the pecuniary bequest or transfer in trust solely in cash, or

(b)   The fiduciary has no discretion in the selection of the assets to be distributed in kind, or

(c)   Assets selected by the fiduciary to be distributed in kind in satisfaction of the bequest or transfer in trust are required to be valued at their respective values on the date, or dates, of their distribution. . . .

SECTION 5. FORM OF AGREEMENTS

.01 By Surviving Spouse

In the event of the allowance by or on behalf of the Commissioner of Internal Revenue of a marital deduction of a pecuniary bequest or transfer in trust to me or on my behalf of $_____, claimed in connection with the settlement of the Federal estate tax liability of the estate of_____, and as part of the consideration for this settlement, I hereby agree that in the event cash and other property accepted in full satisfaction of this bequest or transfer in trust is not fairly representative of my proportionate share of any net appreciation in the value, to the date or dates of distribution, of all property then available for distribution in satisfaction of such pecuniary bequest or transfer, the difference in value will be treated as a transfer or transfers by gift as of the date, or dates, of distribution, and a Federal gift tax return or returns with respect to such transfer or transfers by gift will be filed if required under the gift tax provisions of the Internal Revenue Code.

_____

Surviving Spouse of

_____

.02 By Executor or Trustee

In the event of the allowance by or on behalf of the Commissioner of Internal Revenue of a marital deduction for a pecuniary bequest or transfer in trust of $_____ claimed in connection with the settlement of the Federal estate tax liability of the estate of _____, and as part of the consideration for this settlement. I hereby agree that the assets to be distributed in satisfaction of this bequest or transfer in trust will be selected in such manner that the cash and other property distributed will have an aggregate fair market value fairly representative of the pecuniary legatee's (or transferee's) proportionate share of the appreciation or depreciation in the value to the date, or dates, of distribution of all property then available for distribution in satisfaction of such pecuniary bequest or transfer. I further agree that, within six months after the final distribution of cash and other property in satisfaction of the marital deduction pecuniary bequest or transfer in trust, I will file with the District Director of Internal Revenue, at _____, _____, a schedule showing the cash and other property distributed in satisfaction of the marital deduction pecuniary bequest or transfer in trust subsequent to the date of this agreement, the cash and other property available for distribution in satisfaction of the marital deduction pecuniary bequest or transfer at each date of distribution, and the fair market value of each such asset at each date of distribution.

_____

Trustee, or Executor of the Will of

_____

Many states have enacted legislation conforming with §2.02 of Rev. Proc. 64-19, but no such statute was applicable in Hurst v. First Kentucky Trust Co., 560 S.W.2d 819 (Ky. 1978). The will contained a pecuniary bequest to S that the personal representative was authorized to satisfy in cash or in kind, using assets selected in the personal representative's exclusive discretion and using values "as finally determined for Federal Estate Tax purposes." D's will contained no provision that complied with §2.02 of Rev. Proc. 64-19, notwithstanding that the will obviously was prepared by an attorney. Nevertheless, the court held that the personal representative's fiduciary duty to deal fairly and impartially with all beneficiaries required it to distribute assets in a manner that guaranteed "all distributions in satisfaction of the [marital bequest] will be fairly representative of appreciation or depreciation in the value of all property available for distribution." See also Estate of Hamelsky v. Commissioner, 58 T.C. 741 (1972); Pastan v. Pastan, 390 N.E.2d 2.53 (Mass. 1979).

32.　_Residuary and Pecuniary Marital Bequests._ In sizable estates, in which the marital bequest will be very large relative to the nonmarital residue, the potential for realization of capital gain on funding is significant under a true worth pecuniary format. To minimize the capital gain and administrative difficulties in an estate, the most recently developed marital deduction pecuniary funding approach calls for a nonmarital bequest to be funded by a pecuniary method, leaving the larger residue to qualify for the marital deduction, using a provision like the following:

My personal representative shall allocate to the Family Trust all assets available for distribution that would not qualify for the federal estate tax marital deduction if allocated to the Marital Deduction Trust, plus the largest pecuniary amount, if any, that will not thereby increase federal estate taxes payable by reason of my death. In determining the pecuniary amount my personal representative shall consider the credit or deduction for state death taxes allowable to my estate only to the extent those taxes are not thereby incurred or increased, shall assume that none of the Family Trust qualifies for a federal estate tax deduction, and shall assume that all of the Marital Deduction Trust hereafter established (including any part thereof disclaimed by S) qualifies for the federal estate tax marital deduction. My personal representative shall allocate to the Marital Deduction Trust the residue of my estate. It is my intent that the Marital Deduction Trust will qualify for the federal estate tax marital deduction and that it not exceed the smallest amount that would result in the least possible federal estate tax payable by reason of my death.

The terms "reverse pecuniary," "credit consuming pecuniary," "front end credit shelter pecuniary," and "residuary marital" all reflect this reversal of the traditional marital bequest.

Under this approach, the credit shelter bequest is segregated and funded, at the risk of incurring gain, carrying out DNI, accelerating IRD, etc. The marital portion, which is expected to be the larger amount, is not funded per se because it is the residue of the estate. The result does not completely avoid the drawbacks of traditional pecuniary marital deduction planning, although it minimizes the problems by funding the smaller nonmarital bequest rather than the larger marital deduction bequest. Nevertheless, it is necessary to consider the most appropriate funding mechanism as between the true worth and federal estate tax valuation approaches.

One possible issue involves the fact that, under the reverse pecuniary approach, capital gain can be incurred on funding the pecuniary nonmarital bequest, which gain will be taxed under normal state law principles to the estate residue, which is meant to qualify for the marital deduction. Therefore, the issue is whether this potential capital gain tax should reduce the marital deduction under §2056(b)(4)(B). Because it may not be known how large that tax will be until after final funding, which almost certainly will not occur until after final audit of the estate tax return, the issue is whether inability to determine the amount of the §2056(b)(4)(B) reduction makes the marital bequest itself unascertainable and therefore nondeductible. As it turns out, this concern makes sense only if there is "phantom gain" in a case in which there is no real appreciation, because the residue benefits from all appreciation and because the capital gain tax cannot consume the full appreciation. Thus, the marital residue is better off due to real appreciation in value, even though it pays any income tax on the gain. It is only if there is no real appreciation but gain is generated because of a reduction in basis (e.g., due to a depreciation or depletion deduction) that the residue is worse off by virtue of a realization of gain on funding, and that situation has not been addressed by the government.

In Rev. Rul. 90-3, the government concluded that a reverse pecuniary bequest funded using values at the date(s) of distribution qualifies for the marital deduction, notwithstanding the possibility that postmortem fluctuations in the fair market value of estate assets may diminish the amount the spouse received. According to the Ruling, this depreciation possibility does not create a Rev. Proc. 64-19 problem or cause the residuary bequest to be a nondeductible terminable interest. That conclusion was consistent with the conclusion in Rev. Rul. 81-20, which involved a charitable residue following a pecuniary bequest that could be satisfied in cash or in kind, using assets valued at the date(s) of distribution. Applying local fiduciary law, the government determined that the personal representative's discretion was limited to treating all beneficiaries in an impartial manner and permitted the charitable deduction for the residuary charitable bequest. Rev. Rul. 90-3 clarified Rev. Rul. 81-20, explaining that a personal representative's obligation under applicable state law to act impartially and fairly to all beneficiaries is satisfied if a pecuniary bequest is funded with assets valued at fair market value on the distribution date, provided that distribution is not unreasonably postponed (which would magnify the effect of consistent valuation fluctuations). The government also noted that the risk of depreciation of the spouse's interest is offset by the potential for appreciation of that interest.

33. *Valuation Quirks.* (a) If *D*'s personal representative elects alternate valuation, an odd rule in §2032(b) limits the marital deduction to the value as of *D*'s death with an adjustment for any difference in value on the alternate valuation date not attributable to the mere lapse of time or to the occurrence or nonoccurrence of any contingency. The rule is "odd" in that it does not take into account changes in value caused by the occurrence or nonoccurrence of a contingency even though such changes in value are taken into account for the purpose of determining the size of a decedent's gross estate when the alternate valuation was elected. §2032(a)(3). To illustrate, assume that *D* owned a $150,000 face value life insurance policy on the life of *D*'s parent that named *S* as primary beneficiary. *D* died in Year One, survived by the insured parent and survived by *S*. *D* bequeathed the policy to *S* and the residue of *D*'s estate to a trust for *D*'s children. At death, *D* owned stock valued at $1.2 million, land valued at $263,000, and the insurance with an interpolated terminable reserve value of $31,000. *D*'s personal representative elected alternate valuation under §2032 and the insured parent died during the six month alternate valuation period. Immediately prior to the insured parent's death the value of the policy was $32,000 and the $150,000 of proceeds from the insurance policy were paid to *S* immediately after the insured's death. After the alternate valuation date had passed *D*'s personal representative distributed the stock and the land, which were valued at $1.1 million and $261,000, respectively, six months after *D*'s death. Assume that *D* had no estate tax deductions allowable under §§2053 and 2054. What was the estate tax value of *D*'s gross estate if the insurance went up in value by $119,000 due to the parent's death, and the stock and land went down in value by $102,000; was the alternate valuation election valid? What amount of marital deduction was allowable on *D*'s estate tax return with respect to the insurance proceeds paid to *S*? See Rev. Rul. 63-52.

(b) The fair market value of *D*'s estate was $2 million when *D* died in 2003. *D*'s personal representative did not elect alternate valuation, but did elect to use the special valuation permitted by §2032A for farm property (Blackacre) that D owned with a fair market value of $1,000,000 but with a special use value under §2032A of only $600,000. Thus, although the fair market value of D's gross estate at death was $2 million, the estate tax value, using the special use valuation for Blackacre, was $1.6 million. D's will provided a pecuniary bequest to S in the minimum amount that would reduce the estate tax to the least amount possible. According to D's will, any property in kind that is distributed to S to satisfy that pecuniary bequest is to be valued at its fair market value at the date of distribution. D made no inter vivos gifts, and D's estate had no deductions under §§2053 or 2054. Given that the value of D's gross estate for estate tax purposes is $1.6 million and that the unified credit insulates $1 million of D's taxable estate from the estate tax, the amount of marital deduction needed to reduce the estate tax to zero is $600,000. If undivided ownership of a portion of Blackacre is distributed to S to fund the $600,000 pecuniary marital bequest (which percentage would fully satisfy that bequest because the terms of the will provide that the amount of property distributed in kind to S is the fair market value of that property at the date of distribution), should the amount of the marital deduction be $600,000 (the actual fair market value of the distributed property) or should the deduction be limited to the percentage ownership multiplied against the $600,000 estate tax value of Blackacre under the §2032A special valuation?

The government faced this issue in TAMs 8314001 and 8314005. It ruled that the marital deduction was based on the actual fair market value of that percentage of Blackacre ($600,000 in this hypothetical) and is not limited to the estate tax special use value of that portion of Blackacre. The rulings are correct. The amount added to S's estate is the full $600,000 actual value of that portion of Blackacre, and that is the amount of deduction that is allowed. The amount of assets that pass to the children tax free is $1.4 million. If the distributions were reversed so that the properties other than Blackacre were distributed to S to fund the $600,000 marital bequest and Blackacre was distributed to the children, the tax consequences would be identical to those reached by the government in the TAMs. D's estate tax would be zero; the amount added to S's estate would be $600,000; and the amount obtained by the children would be $1.4 million. There is no reason to treat the transaction differently when Blackacre is used to fund the marital bequest.

Even if a portion of Blackacre is distributed to S in satisfaction of a pecuniary bequest, the estate will not recognize any gain on making that transfer, and S's basis in Blackacre will be a portion of the $600,000 basis that the estate had therein, because appreciation that is attributable to the §2032A special use valuation election does not cause gain recognition when the property is distributed to a "qualified heir" as that term is defined in §2032A(e)(1). §1040(a). Thus, the allocation of Blackacre to S is advantageous because, when S dies, it could be special use valued again.

If, instead of using a formula funding arrangement, D had made a specific bequest of the requisite portion of Blackacre to S, the government has ruled that the amount of marital deduction allowed therefor would be limited to the estate tax value of the percentage portion multiplied against $600,000. PLR 8422011. A marital deduction is allowable for property passing to a surviving spouse only to the extent that the property is "included in determining the value of the gross estate." §2056(a). The government reasoned that, to the extent that the actual value of Blackacre exceeds its estate tax value, the excess was not included in determining the value of D's gross estate; so no marital deduction can be allowed for that excess. The ruling reaffirmed the government's view that the full value of such property qualifies for the marital deduction when it is distributed at fair market value in satisfaction of a pecuniary marital bequest, but maintained that a specific bequest of such property to the spouse is not entitled to the same treatment. Is the government justified in making that distinction?

(c) Assume that D's gross estate included 100% of the value of stock in a closely held business, and that 51% thereof is allocated to a pecuniary marital bequest. A control block premium is appropriate in valuing that stock for marital deduction purposes. See Estate of Chenoweth v. Commissioner, 88 T.C. 1577 (1987), and TAM 9050004. Note that, on the same principle operating in reverse the percentage of Blackacre needed to equal $600,000 in **(b)** would not be 60% — it would need to be a larger percentage due to fractional interest discounting.

(d) TAM 9403005 involved a control block of corporate stock included in D's gross estate. What are the respective marital and charitable deductions if it is bequeathed in equal shares to S and a charitable beneficiary, and what problem does this generate in D's estate?

For an excellent discussion of drafting errors and mistakes in funding of marital trusts, see J. Soled, D. Wolf, & N. Arnell, *Funding Marital Trusts: Mistakes and Their Consequences*, 31 Real. Prop., Probate and Trust J. 89 (1996).

PART H.   PLANNING STRATEGY

Code Reference: *Estate Tax: §2001*

34.   *Equalizer Provisions.*   If *D*'s assets are substantial but *S*'s assets are not, a formula bequest of half of *D*'s adjusted gross estate[45] would effect a rough equalization of the transfer tax base of each spouse. Until the progressive tax regime effectively becomes a flat tax (when the applicable exclusion amount and the threshold for the highest marginal rate converge), their equal estates would produce less tax than stacking *D*'s assets on top of *S*'s estate to be taxed at *S*'s marginal progressive tax rate. For example, if *D*'s gross estate is $3.2 million and *S*'s assets (as of *D*'s death) are zero, taxing *D*'s wealth in equal shares in two estates rather than lumping it all into *S*'s estate would reduce the maximum tax rate on all of it to 45% rather than taxing some of it at a higher maximum marginal rate.

If, however, both *D* and *S* have substantial but unequal estates, a more sophisticated form of equalizer is necessary. A formula provision can call for any of three different results: equalizing the marginal tax bracket applicable to each estate, equalizing each taxable estate, or equalizing the tax paid by each estate, in each case based on certain assumptions. Thus, for example, if *D* and *S* own $11 million of assets between them, (1) they could equalize brackets by taxing $2.5 million in *D*'s estate and $8.5 million in *S*'s estate (using the 2002 rate table, which reaches the maximum 50% rate at $2.5 million), (2) they could equalize their estates at $5.5 million, or (3) they could determine their respective prior gifts, credits available, and estimate the respective tax bills that would be generated based on various sized bequests from *D* to *S*. Fortunately, the difficult administration required under this last approach is not frequently justified by special planning needs.

The actual equalization clause used by some attorneys is set forth below.

If *S* survives me, I give to *S* the largest pecuniary amount[46] that, if allowed as a federal estate tax marital deduction, will cause the estate of *S* and my estate to be taxed in the same marginal federal estate tax bracket, determined as if *S* died immediately after my death and both estates were valued as of the date on,

---

45.   The document must define the term "adjusted gross estate" because it no longer is defined in §2056. For example, "As used in this document, 'adjusted gross estate' means the value of my gross estate (as finally determined for federal estate tax purposes), reduced by the aggregate amount of §§2053 and 2054 deductions allowed in computing my taxable estate as finally determined for federal estate tax purposes."

46.   Although a pecuniary marital approach is illustrated here, a fractional marital approach also could be utilized.

and in the manner in, which my estate is valued for federal estate tax purposes.

My personal representative shall accept the statement of *S* or *S*'s legal representative as to all information required in complying with this provision, without inquiring into any such information, and my personal representative's administration hereunder based on such information shall not be subject to question by any beneficiary. In determining the pecuniary amount my personal representative shall consider the credit or deduction for state death taxes only to the extent those taxes are not thereby incurred or increased and shall assume that none of the payments and devises under the preceding articles of this will qualify for a federal estate tax deduction.

For purposes of this gift, if *S* and I die under such circumstances that there is no sufficient evidence to establish the order of our deaths, *S* shall be deemed to have survived me.

This provision gives *S* an estate tax bracket equalizer marital deduction amount if *S* survives *D* (and, in the simultaneous death situation, *S* is presumed to survive *D*). It does not equalize the size of *D*'s and *S*'s taxable estates because that would require payment of more tax in *D*'s estate with no added tax saving benefit over both estates. This last principle will be illustrated shortly.

Upon *D*'s death, survived by *S*, will *D*'s assets that pass to the marital trust under this equalizer provision qualify for an estate tax marital deduction? Estate of Smith v. Commissioner, 565 F.2d 455 (7th Cir. 1977), *aff'g per curiam* 66 T.C. 415 (1976), rejected the government's assertion that the formula did not produce an amount that was ascertainable at *D*'s death and therefore was contingent and nondeductible. The government's rationale was that postmortem elections, valuation decisions, and inclusion issues all would affect the formula computation and might even result in *S* receiving nothing under the provision. According to the court:

Government counsel candidly admitted at the oral argument that there are no policy grounds for vitiating such a clause. This litigation was brought ostensibly because supposedly required by the literal language of §2056(b). . . . In his brief, the Commissioner stresses that, under this equalization clause, the trustee might have to allocate nothing to the marital deduction so that Mrs. Smith's interest would be zero. But, as . . . noted, in that event the entire value of the trust would be taxed in decedent's estate. There would be no marital trust to tax in Mrs. Smith's estate, and decedent's estate would have no marital deduction entirely independent of §2056(b)(1). (66 T.C. at 429.)

As the Tax Court explained, the purpose of the terminable interest rule in §2056(b)(1) forbidding a marital deduction is "to limit the marital deduction to the value of interests in property passing from the decedent to his surviving spouse which were interests of such a character that, unless consumed or disposed of prior to the surviving spouse's death, would be taxable in the surviving spouse's estate at her death" (66 T.C. at 423). That purpose is fully satisfied because Mrs. Smith's equalization clause share was taxable in her estate when she died in 1971. Because the purpose of §2056(b)(1) has been met, the Commissioner's dependence on any literal statutory language arguably contrary should not prevail, for in such an instance, form may not be elevated over substance. . . .

There being no possibility that the interest passing to Mrs. Smith might escape taxation altogether, the Tax Court properly refused to apply the terminable interest rule. Whether or not the value of the property left to Mrs. Smith might change under the equalization clause, the "interest passing" to her (§2056(b)(1)) would not terminate, so that even literally the terminable interest rule does not apply. . . .

Focusing on the issue of terminability at the time of the spouse's death, and guided on that issue . . . by the policies declared in Northeastern Pennsylvania Bank & Trust Co. v. United States, supra, which . . . emphasized "Congress' intent to afford a liberal 'estate-splitting' possibility to married couples," . . . we have determined that the Marital Portion was non-terminable at the date of the husband's death.

Accord, Estate of Meeske v. Commissioner, 72 T.C. 73 (1979); Estate of Laurin v. Commissioner, 645 F.2d 8 (6th Cir. 1981).

In Rev. Rul. 82-23, the Commissioner conceded the qualification of formula equalizer provisions for the marital deduction, saying:

The Internal Revenue Service will follow the decisions in *Smith*, *Laurin*, and *Meeske*, and will allow a marital deduction under §2056 of the Code for property passing under an "estate equalization clause" in which the executor has an option to value the spouse's estate, for equalization purposes, on the alternate valuation date, if that is elected for the valuation of *D*'s estate.

But see TAM 9010001, in which *D*'s will devised to a trustee "an amount equal to what my personal representative at the time of my death determines in his sole discretion will increase the total estate of my said husband to what my personal representative deems most desirable for reducing the total federal estate tax liability of our respective estates." Distinguishing the equalizer marital deduction cases, the government advised that no marital deduction was allowable because the provision provided no mechanism to determine at *D*'s death what was meant to pass to *S*. Thus, it was deemed to fail the passing requirement for marital deduction qualification.

Although Rev. Rul. 82-23 undoubtedly means that properly drafted equalizer bequests no longer endanger an estate's entitlement to a marital deduction, would it be desirable to provide for an equalizer bequest if *S* survives *D* by less than six months and to provide an additional amount to qualify a full optimum bequest if *S* survives *D* by six months? Would such a clause qualify for the marital deduction? With respect to the former question, consider the following illustrations.

In 2002 *D* and *S* have estates of $10 million and $1 million, respectively. A formula bracket equalizer marital bequest taxes $2.5 million[47] at *D*'s death and the balance of the aggregate wealth at *S*'s later death, generating the least tax over both estates consistent with maximum deferral of tax payment, as illustrated in the following computations. The amount of *D*'s estate that is not bequeathed to *S* or paid as estate taxes is bequeathed to a bypass trust.

Ignore for purposes of this discussion the promised repeal of estate tax in 2010 (or its reinstatement in 2011): it may never happen, the spouses both may die before then, and because one purpose of this discussion is to reveal the truth about a very common estate planning myth.

One assumption in analyzing any marital deduction planning approach that entails payment of estate tax in the estate of the first spouse to die is that use of the tax dollars deferred from the death of the first to die under an optimum approach will compensate for the difference in tax saved by avoiding estate stacking. That assumption is false. Two examples illustrate this, the second assuming time-value is reflected in the aggregate wealth doubling in value during the surviving spouse's overlife. For purposes of this illustration the source of this growth or the amount of time that it takes to occur is irrelevant.[48] What is relevant is that this doubling represents the enjoyment or use of the wealth over the surviving spouse's overlife and therefore illustrates the time-value of the deferred tax payment.

Baseline Example: Compared to an optimum marital deduction approach, the tax computations at the deaths of D followed by S (assuming deaths in 2002, no §2013 previously taxed property credit, and no changes in asset values) would look like:

---

47. This figure is chosen on the assumption that the maximum estate tax rate is 50%, beginning at $2.5 million.

48. Although there may be income tax differences whether this is due to income accumulation or capital appreciation, that factor is not considered because it is uncertain and therefore impossible to quantify. It also does not change the analysis.

	Optimum Marital	Taxable Estate Equalizer	Bracket Equalizer
D's gross estate	$10,000,000	$10,000,000	10,000,000
Marital deduction	9,000,000	4,500,000	7,500,000
D's taxable estate	1,000,000	5,500,000	2,500,000
Tentative estate tax	345,800	2,525,800	1,025,800
Unified credit	(345,800)	(345,800)	(345,800)
D's federal estate tax payable	0	2,180,000	680,000
amount of nonmarital trust remaining after *D*'s taxes	$1,000,000	$3,320,000	1,820,000

When *S* later dies:

	Optimum Marital	Taxable Estate Equalizer	Bracket Equalizer
S's taxable estate	$10,000,000	$5,500,000	8,500,000
Tentative estate tax	4,775,800	2,525,800	4,025,800
Unified credit	(345,800)	(345,800)	(345,800)
S's federal estate tax payable	4,430,000	2,180,000	3,680,000
Total tax over both estates	4,430,000	4,360,000	4,360,000

Compared to the optimum marital results, both equalizer approaches generate a $70,000 tax savings over both estates. To appreciate the meaning of this it is important to realize that the saving is attributable to a "full bracket run"; it represents the tax on $1.5 million at a 50% flat rate ($750,000) in the estate of S under the optimum approach, compared to the tax on $2.5 million less the tax on $1.0 million ($680,000) in the estate of *D* under the equalizer approach (that is, the incremental tax on the same $1.5 million added on top of the "normal" shelter of $1.0 million in *D*'s estate). Given the bracket assumptions, this $70,000 is the maximum saving available by sheltering the full amount that can be taxed at less than 50% in *D*'s estate.

Impressive about the middle and last column is that the total tax over both estates is the same $4,360,000, which represents the same total savings of $70,000 over an optimum marital bequest approach, but the bracket equalizer right column required payment of $1.5 million *less* tax in *D*'s estate. Overall that makes the bracket equalizer preferable to the taxable estate equalizer middle column because, although the aggregate tax paid over both estates is the same, the timing of the payments differs: the bracket equalizer defers until *S*'s death $1.5 million of the tax that would have been due at *D*'s death under the taxable estate equalizer. Moreover, it is just as desirable if all the wealth doubles during *S*'s overlife, as illustrated by the following time-value variation showing the tax at *S*'s subsequent death:

Time-Value Example: Many observers assume that if *S* outlives *D* by a sufficient period of time, the income earned in the optimum example on the estate tax that would be paid in *D*'s estate in either equalizer example will make up for any differential in tax illustrated in this comparison. Assuming (just to pick a number) a 7% after tax simple interest return on the tax deferred under an optimum plan (that is, the income that could be earned on the $2,180,000 of tax that would be paid under this equalizer plan on *D*'s death in the taxable estate equalizer column), many people would predict that the increase in taxes under the optimum plan would be earned back in less than six months — if S lives that long. And that is just about the time allowed as a survivorship condition under §2056(b)(3).

Naturally the after tax rate of return is not an item that is subject to ready estimation; this is just an illustration based on one arbitrarily selected assumption. In fact, a number of factors are relevant, including *S*'s health and overlife expectancy, the likely after tax return on the deferred taxes (which in turn depends on general rates of return and *S*'s income tax bracket), the effect of inflation, appreciation, and income accumulations that will increase (and invasions or depreciation that will dissipate) *S*'s estate, and the effect of other credits that may apply in one estate or the other. To minimize the effect of guesswork, the following illustration simply makes life easy by assuming that all the variables come together during the overlife of *S* so that between the deaths of *D* and *S* all property values double, which reflects the use of the money during *S*'s overlife. The same computations when S later dies now reveal:

	Optimum Marital	Taxable Estate Equalizer	Bracket Equalizer
	$10,000,000	$5,500,000	$8,500,000
	× 2	× 2	× 2
Double *S*'s taxable estate	$20,000,000	$11,000,000	17,000,000
Tentative estate tax	9,775,800	5,275,800	8,275,800
Unified credit	(345,800)	(345,800)	(345,800)
S's federal estate tax payable	9,430,000	4,930,000	7,930,000
Amount of marital trust after *S*'s taxes	10,570,000	6,070,000	9,070,000
Double the amount of nonmarital trust after *D*'s tax	2,000,000	6,640,000	3,640,000
Assets remaining for family	12,570,000	12,710,000	12,710,000

Compared to the optimum marital estate stacking results, both equalizers now generate a savings of $140,000 in tax, which is double the $70,000 saving attributable to the full bracket run in *D*'s estate under the baseline equalizer example. Notice that the time-value assumption is that the optimum marital approach is more economical—if *S* lives long enough and income yield is great enough—by investing tax that would be paid in the equalizer approaches to earn back the tax saving. Yet here the saving was not recovered to yield an overall better result with the optimum marital bequest: the saving doubled when the time-value of each approach was reflected. If the wealth involved had tripled to reflect even greater time-value, the saving still would not be earned back: it too would triple.

Put another way, the tax saving in *D*'s estate under an equalizer approach never is earned back under the optimum approach; it increases in value as the wealth itself increases in value, illustrating that the time-value bromide regarding these alternatives is, simply stated, just wrong. This is so critical—and so contrary to many advisors' understanding—that if you do not believe it, you literally should stop now and run the numbers personally, to be persuaded that time-value notions regarding deferred payment of taxes may be a viable notion for income tax purposes but it is exactly wrong for wealth transfer tax purposes.[49]

Under this analysis, the combination of income and growth — total portfolio performance — is considered as one element and, properly considered, here it illustrates that traditional notions about the time-value of taxes deferred from the death of D to the death of S and about an optimum approach being able to earn back the tax savings of an equalizer approach is a fallacy. The numbers involved are not compelling — in terms of prepayment of tax as against the many reasons to defer — and there are numerous legitimate reasons to defer the payment of estate tax in the combined estates of *D* and *S*, such as lack of liquidity or fear about too little wealth remaining for *S* to live on (or even the hope that repeal of the estate tax really will occur in 2010).

Although all of these examples assume that each estate will reach the highest marginal estate tax rate, the theory behind equalizer marital bequest planning holds true regardless of the marginal rates that actually will apply in the estates of *D* and *S*, provided that there *is* a tax saving from running through the lower marginal brackets When the estate tax becomes a flat tax (after 2005 if the 2001 changes to the tax rates and applicable exclusion amount remain the same) these benefits no longer will exist. Meanwhile, however, the ability to save taxes is available and is maximized in all cases to the extent the equalizer marital bequest causes *S* to be taxed in the same marginal bracket as *D*. If the spouses' estates otherwise would be taxed in the same bracket, then there is no need for — or saving attributable to — an equalizer approach. If there is a saving, however, it will be unaffected by appreciation if the property would appreciate at the same rate in either a

---

49. See Pennell & Williamson, *The Economics of Prepaying Wealth Transfer Tax*, 136 TRUSTS & ESTATES 49-60 (June 1997), 40-51 (July 1997), and 52-56 (August 1997), abridged and reprinted in 52 J. FIN. SERV. PROFS. 62 (Nov. 1998) and 53 J. FIN. SERV. PROFS. 42 (Jan. 1999).

marital or nonmarital trust, if appreciating assets must be used to pay the tax, and if the marginal rates remain the same.[50]

There is one final illustration that is worthy of consideration, involving an opportunity that entails a credit that we study in Chapter 13. Consider the example of TAM 8512004, in which *D*'s will bequeathed to S an amount equal to the maximum marital deduction allowable to *D*'s estate, and bequeathed *D*'s residuary estate to a nonmarital trust that gave *S* an income interest for life. *S* died three months after *D*, from causes not foreseeable at *D*'s death. *S*'s personal representative disclaimed the marital deduction bequest and *D*'s entire estate passed under *D*'s residuary clause to the nonmarital trust. Thus, a marital deduction was not available to *D*'s estate. Aggregate estate taxes over both estates were minimized, however, because the estate tax generated in *D*'s estate increased the §2013 previously taxed property credit available in *S*'s estate.

Most critically, *S*'s income interest in the nonmarital trust was sufficient to qualify for a §2013 credit, notwithstanding that no part of that trust was includible in *S*'s gross estate at death. Under the actuarial tables, the value of *S*'s life income interest (and the §2013 credit based thereon), far exceeded the income *S* actually received during the three months *S* survived D. Nevertheless, *S*'s estate was able to maximize the credit at a nominal cost because Rev. Rul. 80-80[51] required use of the actuarial tables (because *S*'s death was not clearly imminent due to an incurable physical condition that was known at *D*'s death).[52]

---

50. E.g., if *D*'s estate were $2x and the marginal estate tax rate were 50%, with no marital bequest a tax of $1x could be paid, leaving $1x in a nonmarital trust during *S*'s overlife. Alternatively, the $2x could be made to qualify for the marital deduction and the $1x of tax could be paid at *S*'s death, leaving the same $1x after *S*'s death. If all the wealth would double in value during *S*'s overlife it also would not matter whether the $1x in the nonmarital grew to $2x before *S* dies or the $2x in the marital trust became $4x and incurred a 50% tax when *S* dies and leaves the same $2x after tax in both estates.

51. Superseded by Treas. Reg. §20.7520-3(b)(3), which precludes use of the standard tables if the individual who is the measuring life is terminally ill (meaning that the individual is known to have an incurable illness or other deteriorating physical condition and there is at least a 50% probability of death within one year).

52. In a less well planned manner, essentially use of the §2013 credit is what generated a sizable savings in Estate of Howard v. Commissioner, 91 T.C. 329 (1988), *rev'd*, 910 F.2d 633 (9th Cir. 1990), dealing with the "stub income" issue in a QTIP trust, as discussed at pages 658-660. That substantial savings can be generated by the §2013 credit for a naked life estate in a bypass trust if the spouses die within several years of each other is easily illustrated by *Howard*, in which *S*'s estate claimed a credit that reduced its overall taxes by almost $675,000. But see Estate of Carter v. United States, 90-1 U.S. Tax Cas. (CCH) ¶60,003 (E.D. La. 1989), *rev'd*, 921 F.2d 63 (5th Cir. 1991), in which the issue was the proper value of *S*'s life estate (a usufruct) in *D*'s estate if both spouses died simultaneously. The lower court determined the value of *S*'s life estate based on (1) a state law presumption that the younger spouse was the survivor when they died under circumstances making proof of the order of their deaths impossible and (2) §2013(d), which determines the value of *S*'s life estate as of *D*'s death, at which moment *S* was deemed to be alive and well, notwithstanding that *S* died immediately after *D*. In Estate of Harrison v. Commissioner, 115 T.C. 161 (2000) (deemed simultaneous deaths of spouses

Example: *D* has an estate of $3.0 million and *S* has an estate of $1.5 million. *S* dies within nine months after *D*'s death (both in 2002) but, because *S* was not terminally ill when *D* died, valuation of *S*'s life estate in *D*'s property is based on the actuarial tables, as required by §7520 and Treas. Reg. §20.7520-3(b)(3).

	Optimum Marital	§2013 Maximizing Marital
D's gross estate	$3,000,000	$3,000,000
Marital deduction	2,000,000	544,479
D's taxable estate	1,000,000	2,455,521
D's federal estate tax	0	658,205.20
S's taxable estate	3,500,000	2,044,479

whose private aircraft never reached its destination and was presumed crashed with no survivors), and in Estate of Marks v. Commissioner, 94 T.C. 720 (1990) (a reviewed opinion involving facts virtually identical to *Carter*), the Tax Court held that the value of *S*'s life estate must reflect the simultaneous death, a result with which the Court of Appeals for the Fifth Circuit agreed in reversing *Carter*. According to the *Carter* opinion on appeal, simultaneous death rendered *S*'s life estate "worthless" for §2013 purposes because

the use of [the actuarial valuation] tables is subject to the underlying premise that what is sought to be achieved is value "as of the date of [D's] death on the basis of recognized valuation principles" [and] "recognized valuation principles" includes examination of facts known about [S] at the time of [D's] death. [W]e opt . . . to apply the maxim that certainty should be deemed a "recognized valuation principle." Just as it would be foolish to "predict" yesterday's weather, there is no reason to use uncertain valuation principles — regardless of how sophisticated — to "value" something for which a value in fact has already been indelibly fixed by the course of events.

921 F.2d at 67-68. The *Carter* opinion on appeal specifically stated that it was limited to "situations in which the transferee and transferor of an indeterminate interest such as a [life estate] die in a common disaster, because in this situation it is known with certainty that the transferee will die. . . ." Id. at 68. This is a disturbing statement for two reasons. First, it does not indicate what "common disaster" means, or whether it may differ from the situation presented in which the deaths occurred under such circumstances that the order of death could not be established by proof. Some common disaster deaths will not be such that the order of death is unproveable — such as if two individuals die as a result of injuries suffered in an automobile accident with one lingering longer than the other. In such a case perhaps actual facts and the survivor's short life expectancy will be considered because death is imminent and the tables will not apply.

    Second, when computing any §2013 credit for the value of a life estate, the length of *S*'s overlife always is known when the credit is being claimed in *S*'s estate, meaning that actual life always could be used if that were Congress' intent. The fact that §2013(d) instead requires valuation as of *D*'s death is a clear indication that valuation hindsight is not appropriate under a simultaneous death or any other situation. See Lee, *The Common Disaster: The Fifth Circuit's Error in* Estate of Carter v. United States *and the Glitch in the "Tax on Prior Transfer" Credit in Valuing Life Estates Created in a Common Disaster*, 40 EMORY L.J. 1269 (1991).

S's tax before §2013 credit	1,180,000	456,794.71
§2013 credit	(0)	(456,794.40)
S's tax after §2013 credit	1,180,000	.31
Tax over both estates	1,180,000	658,205.51

In this case D and S saved $521,794.49 in tax paid over both estates as compared to an optimum marital result—that is a 44% tax saving, representing almost 11.6% of the aggregate wealth of D and S.

This planning requires some balancing to insure that S has sufficient assets to generate enough tax to consume the §2013 credit produced from the tax on D's estate, and D's estate is large enough to produce enough tax to generate the necessary credit. Several computations may be needed to strike the proper balance, and more computational complexity will be encountered if a state death tax or alternate valuation election[53] is involved. Similar results to this example are available if S is not terminally ill, whether the marital bequest is outright or in trust and the marital deduction is fine tuned by formula, disclaimer of a portion of a marital bequest, or a partial qualified terminable interest election.

---

53. Rev. Rul. 81-118, 1981-1 C.B. 453, held that the value of a life estate created in a transferor's estate that elected to use the alternate valuation date should apply the actuarial life estate factor for the life tenant's age at the decedent's death, not at the alternate valuation date, but applied against the fair market value of the estate on the alternate valuation date.

Chapter 12

THE ESTATE TAX CHARITABLE DEDUCTION

Code References: *Estate Tax: §2055*
Income Tax: §§642(c)(5), 664

1. *Overview.* Unlike the marital deduction, which was first enacted in 1948, the §2055 charitable deduction originated in the Revenue Act of 1918 and is almost as old as the wealth transfer taxes themselves. Aside from minor tinkering, the deduction has also remained relatively unchanged except for one major amendment in 1969 when Congress tightened up all of the income, estate, and gift tax deductions for "split interest" charitable gifts.

Section 2055 is the estate tax counterpart of the §170 income tax charitable deduction; a gift tax counterpart is found in §2522. No special generation-skipping transfer tax charitable deduction is needed because of the operation of the generation assignment rule in §2651(e)(3). The income, estate, and gift tax deductions are very similar, but there are differences. A major difference is that the income tax deduction is subject to a percentage limitation, whereas the estate and gift tax deductions are unlimited. Other differences relate to perplexing variations in the language of the three provisions defining the type of entity that is an eligible recipient and describing the split interest trust rules, which are discussed beginning at page 736. Compare §§170(c), 2055(a), and 2522(a) generally, and see generally Lowndes, Kramer, & McCord, FEDERAL ESTATE AND GIFT TAXES §16.1 (3d ed. 1974), and then specifically compare §§170(f)(2)(B), 2055(e)(2)(B), and 2522(c)(2)(B), respectively. It is possible for an organization that qualifies as charitable for income tax purposes to fail to qualify for estate tax purposes. See, e.g., First National Bank of Omaha v. United States, 681 F.2d 534 (8th Cir. 1982).

2. *The Amount Deductible.* An estate tax limitation on the charitable deduction is the §2055(d) requirement that the transferred property interest must be includible in the decedent's gross estate. Thus, inter vivos and testamentary transfers to qualified charities are deductible under §2055 to the extent either involves property that is includible in the transferor's gross estate at death.

Only the net value of property passing to charity is deductible; as illustrated by the following case, under §2055(c) any federal, state, or foreign death taxes payable from the transferred property reduce the deduction, as do any administration expenses that are payable from the transferred property. Estate of Luehrmann v. Commissioner, 287 F.2d 10 (8th Cir. 1961); Alston v. United States, 349 F.2d 87 (5th Cir. 1965). The following case also reveals several very important aspects of the estate tax. Pay attention to those as well:

Estate of Bush v. Commissioner
618 F.2d 741 (Ct. Cl. 1980)

FRIEDMAN, C.J.: . . . Edyth Bush died testate on November 20, 1972, leaving a gross estate of $134,261,384. In her will, she made specific noncharitable bequests totalling $19,062,763. The residuary estate, after payment of expenses, was bequeathed to the Edyth Bush Foundation, a charitable organization. She provided for the payment of all federal and state death taxes out of this residue.

On its federal estate tax return, the estate claimed a charitable deduction of $91,885,201, although under the estate's computations the charity actually would receive only $82,157,034. It paid $20,021,002 in federal estate taxes. The Commissioner of Internal Revenue recomputed the charitable deduction at $46,425,856, which equalled the amount the charity actually would receive. . . . He assessed a deficiency . . . against the estate, which the estate paid. After the Commissioner denied its timely claim for refund, the estate brought this suit.

A.   Section 2055 of the Code provides that, in determining the value of a taxable estate, the amount of any charitable bequest is deducted from the value of the gross estate. The dispute in this case is over the amount of the charitable deduction. It arises because of the provision in the will that all death taxes were to be paid out of the residuary estate, here the charitable bequest. In such a situation, §2055(c) provides that the charitable deduction is calculated by subtracting the taxes payable out of the charitable bequest from that bequest. . . . Under the statute, the estate tax and the charitable deduction are mutually dependent variables. The size of the taxable estate, and therefore the amount of the estate tax, depends upon the amount of the charitable deduction, but the charitable deduction itself is calculated by reducing the charitable bequest by the amount of the taxes paid out of it.

The government interprets the statute as requiring that the charitable deduction equal the amount actually received by the charity. It provides two alternative but equivalent methods for achieving this result. One method uses a cyclical series of test computations, under which the residue available for charity is decreased on each cycle by the amount of the tax calculated on that cycle. This leads to another cycle on which the deduction is decreased, and the tax therefore increased, to reflect the residue calculated on the previous cycle. This process is repeated until the residue, or actual charitable donation, equals the deduction that produced it.[1] The second method reduces this process to a single algebraic formula. "The tax and the net charitable bequest must be determined simultaneously by algebraic formula so that the deduction for the net bequest will produce the tax which is used to compute that net bequest." . . .

In computing its estate tax, the plaintiff used a third method that adopted the first step of the government's cyclical system. But instead of repeating the cycles until the charitable deduction and the charitable contribution were equal, the plaintiff calculated the

---

1. For example: Assume an estate after all noncharitable deductions but before the charitable deduction of $100 million, specific noncharitable bequests of $10 million, provision in the will that all estate taxes be paid out of the residuary estate, bequest of that residuary estate to a qualifying charity, and a federal tax rate applicable to the entire estate of 77%. In such circumstances, the first several calculations under the cycling process would be as follows:

(1)	$100,000,000	Estate (as defined above)
	- 90,000,000	Initial trial charitable deduction (total residuary estate)
	= 10,000,000	Initial trial taxable estate x 77% Tax rate
	= 7,700,000	Trial gross estate tax
	82,300,000	Trial charitable donation (total residuary estate less taxes paid out of it)
(2)	$100,000,000	Estate
	- 82,300,000	Trial charitable deduction (trial charitable donation from previous calculation)
	= 17,700,000	Trial taxable estate x 77% Tax rate
	= 13,629,000	Trial gross estate tax
	76,371,000	Trial charitable donation
(3)	$100,000,000	Estate
	- 76,371,000	Trial charitable deduction
	= 23,629,000	Trial taxable estate x 77% Tax rate
	= 18,194,330	Trial gross estate tax
	71,805,670	Trial charitable donation

The 63rd such calculation yields a trial charitable donation of $56,521,743, which when used in the 64th calculation as a trial charitable deduction results in a trial taxable estate of $43,478,257 and a trial gross estate tax of $33,478,257. The payment of such a tax out of the residuary estate of $90,000,000 leaves $56,521,743 for the charity, which is the amount used as a charitable deduction, and thus on this calculation the requisite equality between these amounts is achieved.

gross federal estate tax by using a charitable deduction equal to the difference between the initial residue (gross estate less non-charitable bequests and fixed deductions) and an estate tax calculated as if the entire initial residue was deductible. (In the example in footnote 1, the plaintiff would stop after calculation (2), and take the charitable deduction and pay the tax there indicated.) This method produced a charitable deduction substantially larger than the actual amount donated to the charity — almost $10 million greater. The plaintiff argues that this method of determining the charitable deduction satisfies §2055.

B.   Although the plaintiff frames its objections to the Commissioner's calculations as directed against the computational method the Commissioner used — it states that "[t]he issue presented under §2055(c) is solely one of methodology" — its real quarrel is not with the Commissioner's methodology but with his interpretation of the statute as requiring an equivalence between the amount of the charitable deduction and the amount the charity receives. While plaintiff has suggested various alternative computations, including several presented in its post-argument submission, they either do not produce that equivalence or involve deviation from other Code provisions applicable to this estate.

The real issue in this case, therefore, is whether the statute intends the equivalence that the Commissioner's method of computation achieves. The language of the statute, its legislative history, and the consistent course of judicial decision require an affirmative answer.

1.   Section 2055(c) requires that the "amount deductible under [§2055(a)] shall be the amount of such bequests, legacies, or devises reduced by the amount of such taxes." The intendment is clear: The amount of the charitable deduction is to be the amount of the charitable bequest reduced by the amount of the estate taxes. Here, where the charitable bequest is the residuary estate, and all death taxes are to be paid out of that residuary estate, the statute will not permit a charitable deduction other than the amount of the residuary estate less the entire amount of death taxes paid. There is no indication that the estate taxes by which the charitable bequest is to be reduced are only the taxes upon the noncharitable bequest rather than the total amount of taxes paid. The Commissioner's method of calculating the charitable deduction, but not the plaintiff's method, reduces the residuary estate by the entire amount of the taxes paid on it. See Treas. Reg. §20.2055-3.

2.   Deductions for charitable testamentary transfers were first permitted in the Revenue Act of 1918, ch. 18, §403(a)(3). Pursuant to this statute, the Commissioner employed an algebraic formula to

calculate the tax due and the permissible charitable deduction when dealing with situations such as the one before us. Edwards v. Slocum, 264 U.S. 61, 63 (1924), rejected this formula. . . .

In the same year, however, Congress responded to this decision by enacting the predecessor of the present §2055(c). Revenue Act of 1924, ch. 234, §303(a)(3).[2] Congress stated (S. Rep. No. 398, 68th Cong., 1st Sess. 35 (1924), reprinted in 1939-1 C.B. pt. 2, 266, 290) that its intent was

> to make it clear that the amount deductible under these paragraphs on account of bequests, legacies, or devises for the specified benevolent purposes shall be the net amount distributable for such purposes, after estate, legacy, or inheritance taxes imposed in respect thereof have been deducted therefrom. It is evident that if a testator leaves a residuary estate of $1,000,000 to a charity, but the estate taxes payable out of the residue reduce the amount actually distributed to the charity to $950,000, only the latter amount should be deductible, in computing the amount of the net estate, as a bequest to charity.

This provision was eliminated in 1926, but was restored in the Revenue Act of 1932 . . . . Again the accompanying Senate Report explicitly stated that the amount of the charitable deduction would be the amount going to the charity less the taxes paid out of the charitable bequest (S. Rep. No. 665, 72d Cong., 1st Sess. 52 (1932), reprinted in 1939-1 C.B. pt. 2, 496, 534) . . . .

The congressional intent that "the amount deductible" for charitable bequests "shall be the net amount distributable" to the charity "after estate, legacy, or inheritance taxes imposed in respect thereof have been deducted therefrom" and that "the deduction for charitable bequests" be "limit[ed]" "to the amount which the decedent has in fact . . . bequeathed to charity" would be defeated if the amount of the charitable deduction exceeded the amount the charity received. The Commissioner's interpretation of the statute, but not the plaintiff's, achieves this legislative objective.

3.   The courts consistently have sustained the Commissioner's view that under §2055(c) and its predecessors the amount of the charitable deduction may not exceed the amount of the charitable

---

2. This was the first of four separate enactments of this provision. It was subsequently reenacted in the Revenue Act of 1932, ch. 209, §807, and was included as §812(d) in the 1939 Code and §2055(c) in the 1954 Code. The pertinent language has not changed since the original enactment, and any legislative or judicial comments on earlier enactments are equally applicable to §2055(c).

bequest. In Harrison v. Northern Trust Co., 317 U.S. 476 (1943), the Supreme Court upheld an application of the Commissioner's formula, citing the above-quoted legislative history as "conclusive in favor of the Government's contention that respondents are entitled to deduct only the amount of the residuary estate actually passing to the charitable beneficiaries after provision is made for the payment of the federal estate tax." Id. at 480. . . .

[The court here discussed with approval other cases that had reached the same conclusion as the Supreme Court had in *Northern Trust*.]

C. The plaintiff's arguments that the Commissioner's methods are arbitrary and unreasonable and that his "pyramidal computation method was without authority" do not withstand analysis.

1. The plaintiff refers to "the exceptional complexity of the calculations involved in the instant matter," states that "[o]ne's credulity strains at the idea that the draftsmen could consider describing [the use of such calculations] in such an indirect manner," and concludes that without explicit statutory authorization the calculations are impermissible.

The calculations involved here, however, are not so complex that their use is unreasonable. The plaintiff's own submissions so demonstrate. The method of calculation used in the Commissioner's cyclical recomputations is identical to that used in the plaintiff's one-cycle method. Performing that operation 60 or 70 times instead of once may be more time-consuming, but it is not more complex. Furthermore, the plaintiff's Submission Supplementing Oral Argument, prepared in the 15 days following argument in this case, contains an example of a repetitive recomputation involving 64 cycles. It also includes several examples of computations using the algebraic formula.

The plaintiff further suggests that the complexity of the computational methods leads to a "high possibility of computational error," and raises the possibility that the computations applied to the plaintiff may have been erroneous. There is no showing, however, that such error occurred here, and we can presume that, if computational error had occurred, the plaintiff, with its impressive battery of expert assistance, would have discovered it. In any event, such an error would not justify invalidating the Commissioner's computational method; it would warrant only an adjustment in the amount of the tax.

2. The plaintiff also argues that the Commissioner's methods impose "an effective tax rate upon non-charitable transferees which — because of the pyramiding consequence of the Govern-

ment's position — far exceeds 100%." (The gross federal estate tax assessed by the Commissioner is approximately 315% of the amount of the noncharitable bequests.) According to the plaintiff, this result violates the congressional judgment not to tax estates at rates higher than 77%, "is unreasonable and arbitrary, could not have been intended by Congress, and ought not to be permitted to stand in the absence of specific statutory authority."

This argument involves a misconception of the nature of the federal estate tax. The estate tax is "imposed on the transfer of the taxable estate," §2001(a), whose value is "determined by deducting from the value of the gross estate the exemption and deductions provided for in this part," §2051. As the plaintiff itself notes, the tax is not imposed on the receipt of property by the decedent's beneficiaries. In maximum bracket estates, the gross federal estate tax frequently will be several hundred percent of the amount actually received through nondeductible bequests, since by definition the tax is paid out of the taxable estate, and the amount of the tax is therefore included in the amount of the taxable estate. Under federal tax law this fact is irrelevant.

The Commissioner's methods conform to the definitions in §§2001 and 2051; the plaintiff's claim that the amount of tax due is to be determined by comparing it to the amount of the noncharitable bequests does not. . . .

Did you notice that, unlike the relatively "modest" rates at which most estates are taxed today, the highest marginal estate tax rate when *Bush* was decided was 77%? Also notable about *Bush* was the tax inclusive calculation, showing that the dollars used to pay the estate tax were themselves subject to the estate tax (and, prima facie, were not deductible).

Let's shift from the tax to another charge against the estate. To what extent will an estate's payment of administration expenses reduce the amount of charitable deduction allowable to the estate? Administration expenses are deductible for estate tax purposes under §2053(a)(2). Alternatively, the estate can elect not to take an estate tax deduction for those expenses and instead use them as an income tax deduction. §642(g). The amount paid for administration expenses will not be part of a charitable bequest. If an estate or income tax deduction is allowable for those payments, the amount of administration expenses that are paid out of the principal of the estate is excluded from any charitable deduction (and any marital deduction) that otherwise would be allowable.

The same issue involved in *Estate of Hubert* and its regulations, as discussed at pages 697-699, will apply to the extent that administration expenses are paid out of income earned by the estate (as contrasted to payments charged to the principal of the estate). Under the *Hubert* regulation payment and deduction of administration expenses is treated the same way for charitable and marital deduction purposes.

Now imagine that *D*'s will directed payment of all state and federal taxes from the residue of *D*'s estate. State law includes the Uniform Estate Tax Apportionment Act, which apportions taxes among all takers, subject to the concept of equitable apportionment (meaning that a portion that generates no tax should not bear any portion of the tax), but only to the extent that the will does not provide otherwise. The will made several preresiduary bequests and left the residue 25% to an individual and 75% to a qualified charity. In coordinating the will provision for tax payment with the equitable apportionment rule, the issue is the proper amount by which the charitable bequest should be reduced under §2055(c) for taxes payable from the residue. In a case such as this the government position is that the tax attributable to the preresiduary gifts is borne by every beneficiary of the residue, such that the charitable recipient would absorb 75% in this case. Not of the tax on the residue — that amount is charged entirely to the noncharitable residuary beneficiary — but the residue is calculated after payment of the tax on the preresiduary bequests and that reduction will come 75% from the charitable portion of the residue, with a corresponding reduction of the otherwise allowable charitable deduction. See Rev. Rul. 76-358 and TAM 9126005. Is there a drafting solution you might recommend if this result doesn't seem right to you?

3.   *Eligible Recipients and Uses.* Which, if any, of the following bequests qualify under §2055(a) for a charitable deduction?

(a) To the City of Gambrell to be used to modernize the offices of the mayor and city manager with the most up-to-date equipment. Does this satisfy the "exclusively for public purposes" requirement?

(b) To the XYZ Corporation to be used for research into ways of providing citizens of the United States with less expensive energy sources.

(c) To the Central Bank and Trust Company, as trustee, to provide scholarships for students who attend Center University, with a preference to be given to blood relatives of the decedent. See Estate of Sells v. Commissioner, 10 T.C. 692 (1948); TAM 7923001; cf. Griffin v. United States, 400 F.2d 612 (6th Cir. 1968).

(d) To an annuity trust to provide an annual payment of $X (which exceeds 5% of the value of the initial bequest), for the care of the decedent's cat for life, with a remainder to a qualified charity. Were it not for the identity of the annuitant (a cat), the bequest would qualify as a "charitable remainder annuity trust" under §2055(e)(2). See Rev. Rul. 78-105.

(e)   To Pals of the Planet, an earth watch organization, irrevocably and perpetually restricting the ability ever to develop the property subject to this conservation easement. See §§2031(c), 170(h), 2055(f), and 2522(d).

Bequests to entities were not deductible prior to the Tax Reform Act of 1976 if "carrying on propaganda, or otherwise attempting, to influence legislation" constituted a "substantial part" of the activity of the entity. See, e.g., League of Women Voters v. United States, 180 F. Supp. 379 (Ct. Cl. 1960). Sections 2055(a)(2) and 2055(a)(3) were amended in 1976 to preclude an estate tax deduction only if the entity is disqualified for income tax exemption under §501(c)(3) "by reason of attempting to influence legislation." Section 501(h) permits certain organizations to elect different treatment, subject to an excise tax if it exceeds certain limitations.

As the following material illustrates, the issue of qualification can be tricky. Most estate planners rely on a certification by the entity that it is exempt and provide an alternate disposition if the entity loses its exemption.

Dulles v. Johnson
273 F.2d 362 (2d Cir. 1959)

WATERMAN, J.: William Nelson Cromwell, a prominent New York City attorney, died in 1948. In addition to specific bequests, he provided in his will that the residue of his estate was to be divided into one hundred equal parts and distributed to various groups and organizations. Three of these parts were bequeathed to the New York County Lawyers Association, three parts to the Association of the Bar of the City of New York, and two parts to the New York State Bar Association. . . . Two parts were given to the Alumni Association of the School of Law of Columbia University and three parts to Russian War Relief, Inc. During administration of the estate the Surrogate's Court held that these latter two organizations were disqualified from taking, and thereafterwards the executors, acting under discretionary power given them in the will, reallocated these five parts to the Trustees of Columbia University. This appeal involves the disposition for federal estate tax purposes of these [thirteen] parts of the residual estate. . . .

I. BEQUESTS TO BAR ASSOCIATIONS

In order to secure a deduction for the bequests made to the Bar Associations plaintiffs must demonstrate that these bequests come within the language of §[2055] which permits as a deduction from the value of the gross estate "[t]he amount of all bequests, legacies, devises, or transfers . . . to or for the use of any corporation organized and operated exclusively for religious, charitable, scientific, literary, or educational purposes. . . ." The district court held that the executors failed to carry this burden . . . . The court appears to have based its conclusion on the following Association activities . . . : (1) regulation of the unauthorized practice of law; (2)

institution of disciplinary measures for professional misconduct of members of the bar and judiciary; [and] (3) recommendations with respect to judicial administration and procedure and the endorsement of candidates for judicial office. . . .

1.   Regulation of the Unauthorized Practice of Law. The three associations maintain committees to receive and investigate complaints dealing with unauthorized practice of law. The committees also present cases for prosecution to state or federal authorities, bring actions in behalf of the organizations, and initiate and support legislation — in order to prohibit the practice of the law by persons not admitted to the bar. We cannot say that this program does not benefit the public or that it does not serve charitable and educational purposes. Recognizing the need to protect the public, New York law makes it a misdemeanor for unauthorized persons to practice or hold themselves out as authorized to practice law. And the Bar Associations are empowered to commence proceedings for the punishment and restraint of such behavior. [T]he purpose of this regulation is "not to protect the bar . . . but to protect the public." If these activities were not undertaken by the Associations, the cost of this necessary regulation would descend upon the public. Hence we conclude that as to regulation of the unauthorized practice of law the Associations must be deemed "charitable."

2.   Disciplining of the Profession. The Associations maintain committees on discipline and grievance. The work of these committees has consisted of considering complaints filed against members of the bar by laymen and attorneys, of presenting to the courts charges against some of these attorneys, and of submitting requests to the Presiding Justice of the Appellate Division to appoint attorneys designated by the Bar Associations to prosecute disciplinary proceedings. Here again we think that the district court misconceived the purpose of these activities. Lawyers play a unique and important role in our society. In its dealings with lawyers the public must often act on faith. It is the function of bar associations to see that this faith is not misplaced. New York recognizes the need for this public service and confers upon bar associations statutory powers and obligations in connection therewith. While increased public esteem for lawyers may result in material advantage to members of the legal profession, the true benefit from a disciplined and socially responsive bar accrues directly to the public. Accordingly the present case is readily distinguishable from Better Business Bureau v. United States, 326 U.S. 279 (1945), cited by the Government, and relied upon by the court below. There it was "apparent beyond dispute that an important if not the primary pursuit of petitioner's organization

[was] to promote not only an ethical but also a profitable business community." 326 U.S. at 283. We agree with the case of Rhode Island Hospital Trust Co. v. United States, 159 F. Supp. 204, 205 (D. R.I. 1958), wherein a bequest to the Rhode Island Bar Association "to be used and employed by it for the advancement and upholding of those standards of the profession which are assumed by the members upon their admission to the Bar, and for the prosecution and punishment of those members who violate their obligations to the court and to the public," was held to be a gift to be used for charitable purposes within the meaning of section [2055].

3. Improving Court Procedure and Endorsement of Judicial Candidates. There is no dispute but that the associations have taken an active interest in improving legal and litigation procedure and judicial administration, and have probed into the qualifications of candidates for judicial office. In the past, for example, committees of the Associations have reported to the Judicial Council on a proposed revision of the procedure to review tax assessments on real property; they have made recommendations with respect to the Appellate Division rules; they have furthered proposals to unify and consolidate certain New York courts and proposals to increase the number of Judges in New York and Federal courts. Although such complaints have been happily few, committees of the Associations have investigated complaints of misconduct by judicial officers and employees. Recommendations concerning judicial candidates have been non-partisan and reflect primarily an evaluation of the professional experience and technical ability of the candidates. Here the committees perform a most valuable function, for lawyers are peculiarly well equipped to seek out and remedy flaws in the judicial machinery and to assess the performances and capabilities of judges. In today's immensely complex society they alone, perhaps, are alert to watch for and attempt corrections of manifest defects prior to the time when malfunctions become apparent to everyone. These activities clearly constitute a public service, and we fail to discern that they indicate that the Associations seek to achieve a selfish professional benefit thereby. . . .

Other activities of the Associations which the district court did not refer to and yet which are substantial in nature include maintaining libraries for legal research, sponsoring lectures and forums on the law, providing free legal service through participation in legal aid, and providing low cost legal service through participation in a legal referral system. All of these activities are, in our opinion, educational and charitable. The Associations do engage in certain other incidental activities, but these activities, some social in nature, are merely auxiliary to the charitable and educational purposes we have discussed.

"Organized and operated exclusively" means only that these unconforming activities be incidental in nature. Seasongood v. Commissioner, 227 F.2d 907 (6th Cir. 1955); 1 Paul, FEDERAL ESTATE AND GIFT TAXATION 668 (1946); cf. Better Business Bureau v. United States, 326 U.S. 279, 283 (1945). Such is the situation here.

Looking at the total operations of the three Bar Associations we hold that they are "charitable, scientific . . . [and] educational" within the meaning of section [2055] and that the district court erred in disallowing deductions for the bequests to them. The judgment is reversed with respect to the disallowance of the deductions.

II. BEQUESTS TO UNQUALIFIED LEGATEES

After the Surrogate's Court decreed that the Alumni Association of the School of Law of Columbia University and Russian War Relief, Inc. were disqualified from taking as legatees, the executors acted pursuant to that portion of the will which provided:

> Should any beneficiary named in this Article Eighth be disqualified or incompetent to receive the part or parts set opposite its name, or should not be in existence or be not functioning at the time of my decease, then and in such event, it is my specific will and absolute direction that the part or parts of such party or parties shall be distributed and disposed of by my Executors to such other party or parties named in this Article Eighth, and in such proportion, division and manner, as in their absolute judgment they may deem best.

The executors reallocated these bequests to the Trustees of Columbia University. It is conceded that Columbia qualified under §[2055], but the district court on the authority of Burdick v. Commissioner, 117 F.2d 972 (2d Cir. 1941), disallowed deduction on the ground that, inasmuch as the executors could have reallocated to the Associations which were not charitable, scientific or educational within the meaning of that section, the actual reallocation to the qualified corporation did not make the amount of the reallocated bequest deductible. Since we have reversed the district court's holding as to the Associations, Burdick is now inapplicable, and the denial of deduction for these two reallocated bequests is reversed. . . .

The Court of Appeals for the Eighth Circuit held that the St. Louis Bar Association is a qualified charity but that the St. Louis Medical Society is not. St. Louis Union Trust Co. v. United States, 374 F.2d 427 (8th Cir. 1967); Hammerstein v. Kelley, 349 F.2d 928 (8th Cir. 1965). The Commissioner nevertheless has ruled that unrestricted gifts and bequests to integrated state bars do not qualify for the income, gift, or estate tax charitable deduction. Rev. Rul. 77-232.

Rev. Rul. 67-235 disallowed a charitable deduction for a gift to an organization that provided recreational facilities that were open to only a portion of an entire community, on a racial basis. McGlotten v. Connally, 338 F. Supp. 448 (D. D.C. 1972), enjoined the government from allowing a deduction for gifts to fraternal organizations that exclude non-whites from membership. See Bittker & Kaufman, *Taxes and Civil Rights: "Constitutionalizing" the Internal Revenue Code*, 82 YALE L.J. 51 (1972). Compare McCoy v. Shultz, 73-1 U.S. Tax Cas. (CCH) ¶12,906 (D. D.C. 1973).

The government's position towards non-racial forms of discrimination appears to be quite tolerant. For example, it has allowed deductions for bequests to provide scholarships for deserving Jewish children of high academic ability or for male Protestant graduates of a specified high school. See TAMs 7744005 and 7744007. Those memoranda stated that religious and sexual limitations are permissible for a charitable bequest. See Rev. Proc. 75-50 §3.03. These pronouncements are discussed in Ginsburg, *Sex Discrimination and the IRS: Public Policy and the Charitable Deduction*, 12 TAX NOTES 27 (1980).

4.   *Who Is the Transferor?*   One of the more tricky aspects of the charitable deduction is whether the decedent made a charitable bequest or simply left precatory instructions to a private beneficiary, who made a charitable gift. In the latter case the deduction is the beneficiary's and the estate must pay estate tax. Sometimes the flow of money is even more complex:

Estate of Pickard v. Commissioner
60 T.C. 618 (1973), *aff'd*, 503 F.2d 1404 (6th Cir. 1974)

[The decedent bequeathed her residuary estate to the Pickard Trust, a revocable inter vivos trust that would pay the decedent's surviving mother an annuity of $3,000 for life, with remainder to the decedent's stepfather, who predeceased the decedent by about seven weeks. The stepfather's will bequeathed the residue of his estate to the Peterson Trust, under which the decedent's mother was the income beneficiary for life, remainder to qualified charities. An Ohio probate court held that the stepfather's remainder interest in the Pickard Trust passed under his residuary clause to the Peterson Trust. The decedent's estate claimed a charitable deduction for the value of the stepfather's remainder interest in the Pickard Trust because (as a consequence of the predeceased stepfather's will) it passed to the charitable remainder beneficiaries of the Peterson Trust.]

TANNENWALD, J.: We believe that . . . the "transfer . . . to or for the use of" such organization must be manifest from the provisions of the decedent's testamentary instrument.

The impact of the route of devolution has been considered in a variety of contexts. Thus, in Senft v. United States, 319 F.2d 642 (3rd Cir. 1962), property of the decedent, who died intestate, escheated to the Commonwealth of Pennsylvania. In denying the decedent a deduction under §2055, the Court of Appeals emphasized decedent's failure to make the transfer, as opposed to the property passing to the qualified recipient by another force, i.e., by operation of law.

In Cox v. Commissioner, 297 F.2d 36 (2d Cir. 1961), a deduction under the predecessor of §2055 was denied where the testatrix, with full knowledge of all relevant facts and her express approval of the ultimate recipient of the bequest, bequeathed part of her estate to her son, a priest, who had, prior to her death but subsequent to the making of the testatrix's will, taken solemn vows of poverty and renounced all his interests in property (including donations and legacies) in favor of the Society of Jesus, a qualified entity under the statute.

Similar reasoning formed the underpinning of the Supreme Court's decision in Taft v. Commissioner, 304 U.S. 351 (1938), where the decedent died with an outstanding but unfulfilled pledge of a charitable contribution which constituted a binding contractual obligation under local law. The Supreme Court denied a deduction for estate tax purposes on the grounds that . . . there was no bequest, legacy, devise, or transfer within the meaning of the predecessor of §2055.

In each of the foregoing cases, the fact that the designated portion of the decedent's estate inevitably inured to the benefit of the charity did not save the day. To be sure, they can be distinguished on their facts, but the common element which forms the foundation for decision is that the transfer to or for the use of the charity was not effectuated by a testamentary transfer on decedent's part but rather by the operation of an external force. The same is true herein, where it was the testamentary disposition of decedent's stepfather via the Peterson Trust which accomplished the transfer.

Concededly, the charities herein would not have received decedent's property if the decedent had not made the testamentary disposition to her stepfather. The lesson from the decided cases, however, is that a simple "but for" test is not, as petitioner would have us hold, sufficient. There must be something more, namely, the testamentary facts as gleaned from the decedent's own disposition must manifest the transfer to the charity. Commissioner v. Estate of Noel, 380 U.S. 678 (1965). In so stating, we do not imply that the decedent must specify the charitable recipient in so many words. But, at the very least, the instrument of testamentary disposition must sufficiently articulate, either directly or through appropriate incorporation by reference of another instrument, the manifestation of decedent's charitable bounty. See Y.M.C.A. v. Davis, 264 U.S. 47, 50 (1924). Such a situation simply does not obtain herein and, accordingly, the claimed deduction is not allowable.

Try to articulate the rationale for the stated results in each of the following alternative circumstances. Is *D*'s estate entitled to a charitable deduction if:

(a) *D* bequeathed *D*'s residuary estate to "such charities as my personal representative shall designate." The charitable deduction is allowable if the "charities" are §2055 qualified recipients. See Beggs v. United States, 27 F. Supp. 599 (Ct. Cl. 1939); Rev. Rul. 78-101.

(b) *D* bequeathed *D*'s residuary estate to *C*, with the suggestion that *C* "make such charitable gifts as *C* deems advisable." *C* gave the entire residue to a qualified charity but no deduction is allowable. See Rev. Rul. 55-335; Delaney v. Gardner, 204 F.2d 855 (1st Cir. 1953); Marine Midland Trust Co. v. McGowan, 233 F.2d 408 (2d Cir. 1955).

(c) *D* bequeathed $100,000 to *T* in trust to pay the income to *C* for life, remainder to such persons as *C* appoints by will. A qualified charity is the default beneficiary if *C* fails to make a valid appointment. *C* subsequently died without exercising the power. *D*'s estate is not entitled to a charitable deduction.

(d) *D* bequeathed $100,000 to *C* and the residue of *D*'s estate to a qualified charity. *C* filed a §2518 qualified disclaimer of the $100,000 bequest. Cf. Rev. Rul. 78-152. *D*'s estate *is* entitled to the charitable deduction in this case.

(e) *D* bequeathed property to a testamentary trust providing income to *C* for life, remainder to a qualified charity. The bequest did not qualify for the §2055(e)(2) split interest charitable remainder trust deduction. *C* instituted a will contest challenging the validity of the will, which resulted in a settlement by which the estate made outright distributions to *C* and to the charity of the commuted value of their respective interests. See Rev. Rul. 89-31 and the discussion of alternatives to reformation of trusts, all at pages 748-751.

(f) *D* bequeathed *D*'s residuary estate to *T*, in trust to distribute so much of the trust income and principal to *D*'s surviving spouse, *S*, for life, as *T* deemed to be in *S*'s best interests. Any balance of the trust funds remaining on the death of *S* pass to a qualified charity. *S* died prior to the due date for *D*'s estate tax return and before receiving a distribution of any trust funds and a charitable deduction is allowable. See §2055(e)(3)(F) and Shriners Hospitals for Crippled Children v. United States, 88-1 U.S. Tax Cas. (CCH) ¶13,744 (Ct. Cl. 1987), *rev'd*, 862 F.2d 1561 (Fed. Cir. 1988).

5.   *Charitable Split Interest Trusts.*   A bequest to a *corporation* is deductible only if the corporation was organized and is operated exclusively for charitable purposes. A bequest in trust, however, is not disqualified merely because the trust has private as well as charitable purposes. These "split interest" trusts most frequently provide current benefits to a private beneficiary, typically for life, and confer the remainder interest on a charity (thus, they are known as charitable remainder trusts); sometimes they provide current benefits to a charity for a term, and confer the remainder on a private beneficiary (these are charitable lead trusts). In each case the deduction is limited to the value of the charitable interest, which is a function of normal valuation concepts that focus on yield and duration. The law was changed substantially by the Tax Reform Act of 1969 to minimize the disparity between actual experience and the value determined under valuation presumptions, and thereby better match the deduction to what the charity is likely to receive. The following materials illustrate the general rules applicable prior to 1969 and then examine the additional requirements now imposed.

The Law Prior to the 1969 Act.   To say that the charitable deduction is allowable for the value of the interest passing to charity implies that it is possible to ascertain what the charitable and noncharitable interests are, how long it will be before a remainder interest vests in possession, and how much income is being generated relative to the lead interest. Because the charitable deduction is available under Treas. Reg. §20.2055-2(a) only to the extent the charitable interest is ascertainable and severable from the noncharitable interest, consider whether a deduction would be allowed in the following circumstances:

(a) *D* bequeathed $100,000 to *T* in trust to pay the income to *S* for life, remainder to a qualified charity. *S* is 60 years old at *D*'s death.

(b) Suppose in (a) that *D*'s trust provided that, upon the death of *S*, the corpus would be distributed to *X* (who was age 30 at *D*'s death), if living, and if not it would go to the charity. See Treas. Reg. §20.2055-2(b); Hamilton National Bank v. United States, 236 F. Supp. 1007 (D. Tenn. 1964), *aff'd per curiam*, 367 F.2d 554 (6th Cir. 1966).

(c) Suppose in (a) that *S* died in an automobile accident three months after *D*'s death. Should the result differ if *D*'s personal representative elected the alternate valuation date?

(d) Suppose in (a) that *S* died three months after *D*'s death as the result of a diagnosed terminal illness from which *S* was suffering when *D* died.

See Treas. Reg. §20.7520-3(b)(3)(i), which addresses the second issue in *Ithaca Trust*, next below.

Ithaca Trust Co. v. United States
279 U.S. 151 (1929)

HOLMES, J.: . . . On June 15, 1921, Edwin C. Stewart died, appointing his wife and the Ithaca Trust Company executors, and the Ithaca Trust Company trustee of the trusts created by his will. He gave the residue of his estate to his wife for life with authority to use from the principal any sum "that may be necessary to suitably maintain her in as much comfort as she now enjoys." After the death of the wife there were bequests in trust for admitted charities. The case presents two questions, the first of which is whether the provision for the maintenance of the wife made the gifts to charity so uncertain that the deduction of the amount of those gifts from the gross estate under [pre-1969 §2055], in order to ascertain the estate tax, cannot be allowed. . . . This we are of opinion must be answered in the negative. The principal that could be used was only so much as might be necessary to continue the comfort then enjoyed. The standard was fixed in fact and capable of being stated in definite terms of money. It was not left to the widow's discretion. The income of the estate at the death of the testator, and even after debts and specific legacies had been paid, was more than sufficient to maintain the widow as required. There was no uncertainty appreciably greater than the general uncertainty that attends human affairs.

The second question is raised by the accident of the widow having died within the [time] granted by the statute, §[6075], and regulations, for filing the return showing the deductions allowed by §[2055], the value of the net estate and the tax paid or payable thereon. By §[2055], the net estate taxed is ascertained by deducting, among other things, gifts to charity such as were made in this case. But as those gifts were subject to the life estate of the widow, of course their value was diminished by the postponement that would last while the widow lived. The question is whether the amount of the diminution, that is, the length of the postponement, is to be determined by the event as it turned out, of the widow's death within six months, or by mortality tables showing the probabilities as they stood on the day when the testator died. The first impression is that it is absurd to resort to statistical probabilities when you know the fact. But this is due to inaccurate thinking. The estate so far as may be is settled as of the date of the testator's death. The tax is on the act of the testator not on the receipt of property by the legatees. . . . Therefore the value of the thing to be taxed must be estimated as of the time when the act is done. But the value of property at a given time depends upon the relative intensity of the social desire for it at that time, expressed in the money that it would bring in the market. . . . Like all values, as the word is used by the law, it depends largely on more or less certain prophecies of the future; and the value is no less real at that time if later the prophecy turns out false than when it comes out true. . . . Tempting as it is to correct uncertain probabilities by the now certain fact, we are of opinion that it cannot be done, but that the value of the wife's life interest must be estimated by the mortality tables. Our opinion is not changed by the necessary exceptions to the general rule specifically made by the [Code].

In contrast to the Court's resolution of the first issue in *Ithaca Trust,* Merchants National Bank v. Commissioner, 320 U.S. 256 (1943), involved a decedent, *D,* who bequeathed the residue of *D's* estate in trust, income to *S* for life, remainder (less $100,000) to qualified charities. The trustee was authorized to invade the corpus "at such time or times as my said Trustee shall in its sole discretion deem wise and proper for the comfort, support, maintenance and/or happiness of [*S*] and it is my wish and will that . . . my said Trustee shall exercise its discretion with liberality to [*S*]." The government disallowed a charitable deduction for the value of the remainder interest, a position ultimately sustained by the Supreme Court, which said: "The salient fact is that the purposes for which [*S*] could, and might wish to have the funds spent do not lend themselves to reliable prediction." 320 U.S. at 262. See also Henslee v. Union Planters Bank, 335 U.S. 595 (1949). Now consider the notion of uncertainty:

Revenue Procedure 73-9

SECTION 1. PURPOSE

The purpose of this Revenue Procedure is to set forth procedures relative to the allowance of the charitable deduction for Federal estate tax purposes in certain cases where, by reason of the nature of the administrative or investment powers granted to the trustee, there is substantial doubt as to whether the value of an interest in trust passing from the decedent is ascertainable.

SECTION 2. BACKGROUND

.01 In the case of a charitable contribution of an income or remainder interest in a split-interest trust, the presence of certain administrative or investment powers exercisable by the trustee may render the value of the income or remainder interest unascertainable, with the result that no estate tax deduction is allowable. For instance, Revenue Ruling 60-385 holds that the charitable deduction for a remainder interest in trust is not allowable where the trustee is permitted, under the trust instrument, to invest in mutual funds and treat capital gains distributions (ordinarily held to be corpus) as income. In Revenue Ruling 67-33 the Internal Revenue Service extended that holding to cases where the power to allocate capital gains distributions to income is granted under applicable local law instead of the trust instrument. Similarly, Revenue Ruling 65-144 holds that the charitable deduction for a remainder interest in trust is not allowable where the trust instrument granted the trustee the power to allocate stock, extraordinary, and liquidating dividends, taxes, and other expenses between income and principal in his absolute discretion.

.02   Since the issuance of these Revenue Rulings, each of which illustrates a situation where the noncharitable beneficiary can be favored over the charitable beneficiary by the trustee's exercise of his administrative or investment powers, a number of cases have been litigated involving the allowance of the charitable deduction for an interest in a split-interest trust where the trustee is granted certain administrative or investment powers with respect to such matters as permissible investments or the characterization of receipts and disbursements. In many of these cases, the courts have concluded that in view of these powers the charitable interest could not be valued in a dollar amount and that the charitable deduction was, therefore, not allowable. These conclusions were based upon the finding by the courts that the trustees could shift substantial portions of the trust interests between charitable and noncharitable beneficiaries through exercise of the administrative or investment powers in a manner that would not be obviously inconsistent with the testamentary purpose of the decedent and that such exercise would not violate the standard of fairness and good faith to which a fiduciary is held. In other cases, the trustee's administrative or investment powers have been found to be strictly limited by an overriding duty of impartiality, thus enabling the value of the charitable interest to be ascertained.

03   The Tax Reform Act of 1969 amended §2055(e) to provide that no deduction will be allowed for a charitable contribution of an interest in a split-interest trust unless such interest is a remainder interest in a charitable remainder annuity trust (as described in §664(d)(1)), a charitable remainder unitrust (as described in §664(d)(2) and (3)), or a pooled income fund (as described in §642(c)(5)), or is a guaranteed annuity or a fixed percentage distributed yearly of the fair market value of the property (determined yearly). . . .

.04   In order to provide guidelines for settling cases governed by the provisions of §2055 in effect prior to the Tax Reform Act of 1969, the following procedure is established.

SECTION 3. INSTRUCTIONS TO TAXPAYERS AND SERVICE PERSONNEL

.01 Unless the Service determines that it is not clear whether the discretion of the trustee would be strictly limited by a duty of impartiality, the charitable deduction will be allowed.

.02 In cases where the Service determines that it is not clear whether the discretion of the trustee would be strictly limited by a duty of impartiality, the district director shall notify the estate of such determination and the charitable deduction may nevertheless be allowed for the value of the charitable bequest or transfer in trust if the appropriate parties enter into a prescribed agreement with the Service that the trustee of the trust will exercise enumerated administrative investment powers in an impartial manner and will not favor the interests of noncharitable beneficiaries as against those of charitable beneficiaries.

.03 The appropriate parties to the agreement must include the fiduciary of the decedent's estate, the trustees of the trust, and all charitable and noncharitable beneficiaries (both vested and contingent).

.04 If any of the charitable beneficiaries are not ascertainable, then the attorney general for the State that is the situs of the trust must also be a party to the agreement. Any unascertained noncharitable beneficiaries must be made parties to, or otherwise bound by, the agreement through appropriate process under the local law.

.05 If the trustee and other necessary parties fail to enter into such an agreement, then it will be necessary to determine whether the trustee's discretion is sufficiently limited under local law.

.06 The execution and performance of the agreement described in this Revenue Procedure will not be considered to be a gift.

SECTION 4. SCOPE

.01 The Service will not enter into such an agreement where §2055(e) applies. . . .

.02 The Service will not enter into such an agreement where the dispositive instrument clearly states, or the surrounding circumstances establish, an intention that the noncharitable beneficiaries should be favored over the charitable beneficiaries. See, e.g., Sachter v. United States, 312 F. Supp. 670 (S.D. N.Y. 1970). . . .

The Requirements Established by the 1969 Act. As stated in Rev. Proc. 73-9, the Tax Reform Act of 1969 imposed additional requirements for split interest transfers to qualify for the income, gift, and estate tax charitable deductions. These additional requirements emanated substantially from the Treasury Department's proposals for transfer tax revision and the concern that promoted their enactment was stated in similar terms by the Treasury Department in its Studies and Proposals and by the committee reports accompanying the 1969 Act. See Treasury Department Studies and Proposals (pt. 3) at 366–367, 381–382; S. Rep. No. 552, 91st Cong., 1st Sess. 86–93 (1969), in 1969-3 C.B. 423, 479–483; H.R. Rep. No. 413, 91st Cong., 1st Sess. (pt. 1) (1969) in 1969-3 C.B. 200, 237–240. The following excerpt is from the Treasury Studies; it was written before enactment of §7520(a) and its fluctuating interest rate rule for valuation purposes, but the principle is the same regardless of the applicable rate at any given time:

> Present rules provide that, in the case of split interest transfers, the income beneficiary's interest is to be valued on the assumption that the property will be invested to yield [x] percent interest per year. Obviously, the actual investment experience will rarely correspond to the . . . assumption. Abuses have arisen because of this fact. For example, assume a charity is the income beneficiary for a specified term, the property then to go to the transferor's grandchildren. The transfer is exempt for gift tax purposes to the extent of the value of the charity's interest, which is based on an assumed . . . return. But if the property is invested to maximize growth for the benefit of the transferor's grandchildren, then the charity will in fact get less than assumed. The result is that the transferor has paid less gift tax than he should have. If the charity gets the remainder and an individual has the income interest, then the abuse possibility is the reverse, i.e., the property can be invested to maximize the income yield, even at the risk of the principal. Again, a deduction for the charitable transfer has been permitted in a greater amount than in fact goes to charity. Another problem in cases where the charity has the remainder interest arises where discretionary powers are granted to divert principal from the charity to the income beneficiary under specified conditions. A great deal of litigation has been engendered under present rules to determine if such powers in fact reduce the charitable interest or not.

6.   *Charitable Remainder Trusts.* Section 2055(e)(2)(A) provides that no estate tax charitable deduction is allowable for any part of the value of transferred property if a remainder interest is transferred to a qualified charity and a beneficiary of any part of the preceding income interest is not a qualified charity, unless one of the following five conditions is satisfied:

(1) The transferred property is either a personal residence or a farm;[3] or

(2) The transferred property is realty in which a remainder interest is granted to certain (generally, publicly supported) charities for conservation purposes; or

(3) The transfer is made to a "charitable remainder annuity trust"; or

(4) The transfer is made to a "charitable remainder unitrust"; or

(5) The transfer is made to a "pooled income fund."

A *charitable remainder annuity trust* is a trust from which an annuity of at least 5% of the initial fair market value of all property transferred to the trust[4] is payable at least annually to beneficiaries, at least one of whom is not a charitable entity. It may be payable for a term of years not to exceed 20 or for the life or lives of the individual beneficiaries. When the annuity terminates the trust must be distributed to or for the use of a qualified charity, the value of the charitable remainder at inception of the trust must

---

3. According to Rev. Rul. 76-165, a personal residence does not include household furnishings that are not fixtures. Rev. Rul. 76-357 held that no deduction is allowed for the actuarial value of a charitable remainder if the personal residence is placed *in trust*. Rev. Rul. 76-544 opined that no deduction is allowable if, upon the life tenant's death, the personal residence goes to a charity and an individual as tenants in common; it was revoked by Rev. Rul. 87-37, which allowed the deduction for the charity's fractional interest in the remainder. And Rev. Rul. 76-543 denied the deduction if the personal residence is required to be sold on the life tenant's death and a part of the proceeds is to be paid to charity, although Rev. Rul. 83-158 allowed the deduction if state law allows the charity to prevent the sale and take the property in kind under the doctrine of equitable conversion. Moreover, notwithstanding that the personal residence was required to be sold on the life tenant's death and the full proceeds paid to charity, the Tax Court disagreed with Rev. Rul. 76-543 and allowed a deduction for the actuarial value of the remainder interest in Estate of Blackford v. Commissioner, 77 T.C. 1246 (1981).

4. The 5% minimum payout requirement was explained by the Senate committee report as follows:

> [R]equiring a charitable remainder trust to distribute currently at least the amount of its income (other than long-term capital gains), . . . and the requirement that the charitable remainder interest be valued by assuming at least a 5% payout to the income beneficiary will prevent a charitable remainder trust from being used to circumvent the current income distribution requirement imposed on private foundations. In the absence of these rules, a charitable remainder trust could be established which provided for a minimal payout to the noncharitable income beneficiary (substantially less than the amount of the trust income). Since the trust generally is exempt from income taxes this would allow it to accumulate trust income in excess of the payout requirement of the unitrust or annuity trust without tax for the future benefit of charity.

S. Rep. No. 552, 91st Cong., 1st Sess. 90 (1969), in 1969-3 C.B. 423, 481. Subject to limited transitional rules, §201(b) of the 1969 Act amended §642(c)(2) to preclude a charitable deduction for income permanently set aside for future distribution to a charity. In light of that amendment, the Senate committee's concern that accumulated income of a charitable remainder trust would go untaxed appears misplaced and the 5% minimum payout requirement unnecessary.

be at least 10% of the initial fair market value of the trust, and no other payments may be made to any noncharitable beneficiary. §664(d)(1).

A *charitable remainder unitrust* is the same as a charitable remainder annuity trust with three essential differences. The most important is that the minimum 5% payout fluctuates from year to year because it is based on the *annual* fair market value of the trust assets and not their *initial* fair market value. The second exception is that, in any year in which the trust income is less than the unitrust percentage payment, the document can provide for payment of the lesser all income amount. And third, if the all income cap is chosen and if it ever applies and if the document so provides, the trust may provide for distributions in future years of more than the unitrust payment if there is excess income in those years; these excess payments are permissible to the extent necessary to make up for any unrecovered unitrust payment deficiencies from prior years under the income only option. §§664(d)(2) and 664(d)(3). Rev. Rul. 74-19 held that a charitable remainder unitrust will not qualify for the charitable deduction if the trust instrument provides that any part of the trustee's fee will be paid out of the unitrust interest.

A *pooled income fund* is a trust created by a charity, to which multiple donors have contributed and from which the income is prorated among designated beneficiaries for their respective lives. After a beneficiary's death, the remainder in that portion of the commingled fund is freed from the trust and becomes available for the qualified purposes of the charity that manages the fund. §642(c)(5). In effect this is the mutual fund alternative to creating your own charitable remainder trust.

7.   *Combined Marital and Charitable Deductions.* The Economic Recovery Tax Act of 1981 added §2056(b)(8) to provide a marital deduction for the actuarial value of a surviving spouse's interest in a qualified charitable remainder annuity trust or unitrust if the trust has no noncharitable beneficiaries other than the surviving spouse. See page 764. Because the remainder interest qualifies for the charitable deduction under §2055, the marital deduction for the lead interest means that the full value of the trust is deductible and, because this trust will not be includible in the estate of the surviving spouse, no additional tax will be incurred when the spouse dies and the trust property passes to the charitable remainder beneficiary. As an alternative, it is possible instead to leave a traditional qualified terminable interest property (QTIP) trust that will qualify under §2056(b)(7) in its entirety for the marital deduction in the estate of the settlor, will cause inclusion of the full value of the trust in the surviving spouse's gross estate at death under §2044 and, by virtue of §2044(c), will qualify the full value of the trust (which at that time is the remainder interest, vested in possession) for the charitable deduction in the spouse's estate if a qualified charity is the designated remainder beneficiary.

With respect to the creation of split interest charitable remainder trusts, the government has promulgated forms of provisions that help guarantee that the charity's interest will not be diminished by trust administration choices and that allow the donor's contribution to be deductible in the amount of the value of the remainder interest at the time of creation rather than when the remainder vests in possession, provided only that the likelihood that the charity will not take the remainder is so remote as to be negligible. Treas. Reg. §20.2055-2(e)(1). That "so remote as to be negligible" standard generally is regarded as creating a 5% threshold, as illustrated next:

Revenue Ruling 78-255

Advice has been requested whether a deduction is allowable under §2055 for a contingent bequest, under the circumstances described below.

The decedent, *A*, died testate in 1975, survived by *B*, *A*'s wife. *A*'s last will, which was executed in 1972, provides for a preresiduary conditional bequest to *A*'s relative *C*, as follows:

> If my wife, *B*, dies prior to the expiration of thirty days after my death, I give the sum of 100x dollars to my relative *C*. If *B* survives the thirty day period following my death, then this 100x dollars shall become part of the residue of my estate.

The will further provides that if *A* is survived by *B*, then the residue of the estate is to be transferred to a charitable remainder unitrust. The terms of the trust provide that a unitrust amount, equal to 6% of the net fair market value of the trust assets, determined annually, shall be paid to *B*, for life. Upon the death of *B*, the trust will terminate and the trust corpus is to be paid to a designated charitable organization which meets the requirements of §2055(a).

B was aged 78 on the date of *A*'s death and *B* survived the thirty day period following *A*'s death. In addition, the charitable remainder unitrust created in *A*'s will meets the requirements of §664(d)(2).

The issue presented is whether the contingent preresiduary bequest, which passes into a charitable remainder trust meeting the requirements of §664(d)(2) upon *B* surviving for a period of 30 days after *A*'s death, qualifies for a charitable deduction under §2055.

. . . The rules pertaining to contingent gifts to charity are contained in Treas. Reg. §20.2055-2(b). The section, in part, provides:

> If, as of the date of a decedent's death, a transfer for charitable purposes is dependent upon the performance of some act or the happening of a precedent event in order that it might become effective, no deduction is allowable unless the possibility that the charitable transfer will not be-

come effective is so remote as to be negligible. If an estate or interest has passed to, or is vested in, charity at the time of a decedent's death and the estate or interest would be defeated by the subsequent performance of some act or the happening of some event, the possibility of occurrence of which appeared at the time of the decedent's death to be so remote as to be negligible, the deduction is allowable.

Rev. Rul. 70-452 states that, for purposes of the regulations, any possibility in excess of 5% that the contingency which will defeat the charitable interest will occur, is not considered so remote as to be negligible. Thus, in the case of a contingent bequest to a charity, if the possibility of the occurrence of the contingency which would defeat the charitable transfer does not exceed 5%, then the charitable bequest will qualify for a deduction under §2055(a). . . .

In the instant case, the bequest of 100x dollars will pass into the charitable trust if *B* does not die within thirty days after *A*'s death. Based upon Mortality Table LN contained in Treas. Reg. §20.2031-10(f), the probability that a female person aged 78 will die within the next thirty days is .005391, or less than 1%. Since the possibility that the contingency which will defeat the charitable bequest will occur does not exceed 5%, the contingent bequest meets the requirements of §2055(a).

In addition, *A*'s will provides that the residue of the estate is to be transferred to a charitable remainder unitrust which meets the requirements of §664 of the Code. Since the 100x dollar bequest falls into the residue upon the non-occurrence of the contingency, the charitable remainder interest in the bequest is in a trust which is a charitable remainder trust meeting the requirements of §664. Therefore, the charitable interest in the bequest meets the requirements of §2055(e)(2)(A).

Accordingly, since the possibility that the bequest will not fall into the charitable trust is so remote as to be negligible, the present value of the charitable remainder interest in the bequest is deductible under §2055.

Notice in the following Ruling that the government is *not* driven to results that favor the charity; even though charity may get more of an estate the government may conclude that the deduction is not available.

Revenue Ruling 76-291

Advice has been requested whether a deduction is allowable under §2055(a) with respect to a remainder interest in a testamentary trust payable to charity in the situations described below.

Situation 1. The decedent died in 1973. By the terms of a will executed in 1970, the decedent devised and bequeathed the residuary estate in trust. The trust provided that 5% of the net fair market value of the trust assets valued annually shall be paid annually in equal shares to *A* for life, to *B* for life, and to *C* until remarriage or death. Following this, the trust shall terminate and the assets distributed to the decedent's church and a hospital, both qualified organizations within the meaning of §2055(a).

Situation 2. Same facts as in Situation 1, except that in the event of *C*'s remarriage, *C*'s share shall be reduced to 1%, the balance of *C*'s share to be distributed to the charitable remainder beneficiaries. . . .

The terms "for life" or "for a term of years" in §664(d)(2) and Treas. Reg. §§1.664-1(a)(1)(i) and 1.664-3(a)(5) are specific and unambiguous. They do not mean a measuring period of a life subject to termination by a condition subsequent, such as marriage or remarriage. Thus, since in Situation 1 *C*'s interest may terminate by remarriage, the unitrust amount is not payable for the period of *C*'s life or for a term of years not to exceed twenty years, as required by the statute and regulations.

Accordingly, the testamentary trust created under the will of the decedent in Situation 1 does not qualify as a charitable remainder trust under §664. Therefore, the trust does not meet the requirements of §2055(e)(2) and no charitable deduction is allowable for Federal estate tax purposes under §2055(a).

On the other hand, in Situation 2 payment of the unitrust amount will continue throughout the lives of *A*, *B*, and *C*, as required by the statute and the regulations. Accordingly, the testamentary trust created under the will of the decedent in Situation 2 qualifies as a charitable remainder unitrust under §664 and a charitable deduction is allowable for the value of the charitable remainder interest. However, no deduction is allowable for the value of the contingent unitrust amount payable to charity upon the remarriage of *C*. See Rev. Rul. 76-225.

The strict attitude displayed by the government in Rev. Rul. 76-291 toward qualification of charitable remainder trusts for the charitable deduction is not atypical. As another example, see Rev. Rul. 76-310, in which an otherwise qualifying charitable remainder unitrust provided for the trust assets to be divided after the grantor's death into two equal parts, each to be operated separately, to pay *A* the lesser of the annual income or 5% of the net fair market value of one of the equal parts valued annually, and to pay *B* the same amount from the other equal part. The government disallowed a charitable deduction for this unitrust, reasoning that:

the division of the trust assets into two equal parts and the provisions of the trust instrument directing the separate operation of these parts may cause the trustee, in some taxable years, not to distribute the amounts required to be paid from the entire trust under §664(d)(3) and Treas. Reg. §1.664-3(a)(1)(i)(*b*)(*1*). For example, in some taxable years of the trust, it is possible that one part of the total trust assets will earn little or no income while the other part of the total trust assets will earn income exceeding 5% of the net fair market value of its assets. Thus, under the income exception form of payment and in accordance with the provisions of the trust instrument that directs the separate operation of the two equal parts, the total payments in some taxable years, which consist of the trust income of one part limited by the amount of income earned plus the trust income of the other part limited by the amount that is not more than the designated fixed percentage of the net fair market value of that part's assets, could be less than the total of all trust income earned by the entire trust assets and required to be distributed by the trustee under §664(d)(3) and Treas. Reg. §1.664-3(a)(1)(i)(*b*)(*1*).

8. *Charitable Lead Trusts.* Charitable lead trusts are the converse of charitable remainder trusts because the noncharitable beneficiaries receive the remainder at the end of a term during which the charitable beneficiary receives annuity payments. To qualify for a deduction the charity's term interest must be a guaranteed annuity or unitrust interest as described for charitable remainder trust purposes. §2055(e)(2)(B). Differences between the two forms include the fact that a charitable lead interest cannot be defined by the life of the charity; thus, it must be for a specified term. And neither the minimum percentage nor maximum term limitations of remainder trust annuities is imposed. See Rev. Ruls. 77-233 and 78-183.

There can be significant transfer tax advantages to employing a charitable lead trust if a trust's actual investment performance will exceed the assumptions utilized in the valuation computations under §7520 to value split interests. The interest rate assumption under §7520 is 120% of the "applicable federal rate," which is keyed to a monthly fluctuating standard that cannot be below market rates. But the government's valuation assumptions ignore the possibility that the trust property could change in value. Thus, if income earned *plus* growth exceed the government's income yield assumption, the lead trust is advantageous if the taxpayer's ultimate beneficiary can do without enjoyment of the property during the term. The reason a charitable lead trust can be beneficial is illustrated below.

O creates a trust providing an annuity to a qualified charity for a term of years, with the remainder to *O*'s children. The trust assets produce aggregate income and appreciation of 20% annually and the trust is created at a time when the §7520 valuation rules use a 9% annual income assumption. If the charitable annuity is set at 12%, the valuation regime assumes that no income will be accumulated because it all must be paid out to the charity, and also assumes that principal is being invaded annually to satisfy the annuity, which means that the remainder is valued at a much lower amount than is realistic, because the trust actually is growing at 8% annually rather than shrinking at 3% as assumed. Because the charitable deduction equals the value of the charity's interest in the trust, which is overstated relative to the remainder, the amount of trust principal that will pass to O's children on termination of the trust is substantially greater than the amount determined under §7520, which assumed that a portion of the principal will be distributed to the charity as part of each annuity payment. Notwithstanding these disparities, however, the split interest trust valuation rules are thought to be such an improvement over other available alternatives that they were cloned in drafting the qualified interest requirements of §2702(b), as discussed in Chapter 15.

9.   *Complexity and Reformation.* A different form of issue is implicit in the following contingent bequest: D devised Blackacre to D's hometown "so long as the premises are used for school purposes"; Blackacre reverts to D's heirs upon cessation of the designated use. Is the value of this devise deductible under §2055? If it were, how would you know its value?

As a policy matter, should the stringent conditions imposed by the 1969 Act on qualifying for a charitable deduction be included in the estate and gift tax provisions, or should they be limited to the income tax? Their primary disadvantage is complexity, as revealed by the following excerpt from the American Bankers Association's comments on the 1973 proposals for transfer tax revision:

> Based upon our knowledge, the "manipulating" of split-interest trusts . . . to the detriment of the charitable beneficiary was extremely rare and occurred only when the trustee violated his duty of impartiality as between income beneficiaries and remaindermen. When present, it was usually found with a charitable income interest rather than a remainder interest. . . .
>
> Our experience since the passage of the Act has been that the restrictions inserted in §§2055(e)(2) and 2522(c)(2) have resulted in a significant reduction of charitable giving through split-interest trusts. We concur with a statement made by an experienced attorney that "The sheer complexity of the new rules on 'split-interest' trusts has caused some taxpayers to throw up their hands. Where a guy might have said, all the income to my wife, remainder to Harvard, today he's liable to say, oh, the hell with it. He leaves it all

to his wife and gives Harvard $5,000 and Harvard never knows what it has missed." Wall Street Journal, December 29, 1971, page 1, column 5.

The frequent and usually inadvertent failure to comply with the §664 split interest rules eventually led to amendments to §§2055(e)(3) and 2522(c)(4) to permit reformations after the fact to comply with the technical rules.

Unfortunately, the government takes a relatively rigid stance regarding the reformation of trusts that do not comply with the §2055(e)(2) charitable split interest gift rules, including the requirement under §2055(e)(3)(C)(iii) that reformation must be commenced within 90 days after an estate tax return would be due. In addition, not all interests will qualify for reformation. For example, §2055(e)(3)(C)(i) restricts reformation to transfers that would have qualified for the deduction were it not for a failure to comply with the technical split interest requirements, and §2055(e)(3)(C)(ii) requires noncharitable interests to be expressed in terms of a specified dollar amount or percentage of fair market value if the document was executed after 1978. Further, §2055(e)(3)(E) caps the available reformed deduction to the amount that would be available if the split interest rules did not exist, and §2055(e)(3)(B)(i) provides that reformation is effective only if the reformed and the unreformed interests do not differ in value by more than 5%. Finally, in a qualified charitable remainder trust, §2055(e)(3)(B)(ii)(I) requires that any reformed lead interest terminate at the same time as before reformation, with an exception allowing reduction of a greater than 20 year term to the maximum 20 year permissible period.

Sometimes it takes some ingenuity to meet all of these requirements. Informative about the reformation in PLR 9221014 was its treatment of the §664(d)(1)(A) requirement that the annual annuity must equal at least 5% of the initial value of the trust property. Because the nonqualifying annuity was a fixed amount well below the 5% minimum figure, the reformation divided the trust into two portions, one of just less than 20 times the size of the annual annuity, to be held for the term of the annuity and then distributed to the charitable remainder beneficiary, and the second to be distributed to that charity immediately. In this manner the reformation did not enlarge the original entitlement of the noncharitable annuitant but caused the first portion to satisfy the 5% annuity requisite. The Ruling allowed a charitable deduction for the full value of the second portion and for the value of the remainder interest in the first portion. PLRs 9341003 and 9326056 were similar. And in PLR 9123023, using disclaimers followed by reformation of the remaining trust interests, the estate was distributed in part outright to charity and the balance to a trust that complied with the §2055(e)(3)(B) requirements. The Ruling held that, because the disclaimers were qualified under §2518, the outright distributions were deductible under §2055(a) and reformation permitted deduction of the value of the charitable remainder under §2055(e)(2).

Reformation is only one of two options available for postmortem salvage of the charitable deduction and, as you can see, it may be difficult or impossible to accomplish in some cases. If a bona fide will contest results in a bona fide settlement by which outright distributions are made to charity, compliance with §2055(e)(3) is not necessary. Flanagan v. United States, 810 F.2d 930 (10th Cir. 1987), Estate of Strock v. United States, 655 F. Supp. 1334 (W.D. Pa. 1987), and Rev. Rul. 89-31. Both *Estate of Strock* and *Flanagan* rejected the government's denial of the charitable deduction, stating that §2055 indicates that Congress wants to encourage gifts to charity and that neither case involved any of the abuses to which the split interest rules were directed. Consequently, each court saw no reason to deny a deduction for the actual benefit passing outright to the respective charities. Moreover, because the charities were taking their bequests outright, the courts saw no need to comply with §2055(e)(3) for reformation of a nonqualified split interest trust.

In each case the government argued that a postmortem amendment of the governing instrument's dispositive provisions is not effective unless it complies with §2055(e)(3), citing Estate of Edgar v. Commissioner, 74 T.C. 983 (1980), *aff'd*, 676 F.2d 685 (3d Cir. 1982). The court in *Estate of Strock* responded that the taxpayer in *Edgar* purchased annuities for the life beneficiaries in violation of Temp. Treas. Reg. §24.1(h)(1) and that the deduction properly was denied because the estate was concerned *solely* with gaining a deduction. It regarded the situation in *Estate of Strock* as distinguishable because the contest and settlement were based in part on concerns for fiduciary duty and spousal elections against a will, which meant that it was not *just* an attempt by the estate to circumvent compliance with §2055(e); some other bona fide justification for the contest and settlement must exist.

Estate of LaMeres v. Commissioner, 98 T.C. 294 (1992), denied a deduction for a modified charitable bequest that otherwise would not have qualified, distinguishing cases[5] in which nontax considerations provided part of the explanation for the postmortem modification. In situations involving settlement of a *bona fide* will contest Rev. Rul. 89-31 stated that the government no longer will challenge the deductibility of immediate payments to charity solely on the ground that they were made in lieu of a split interest that would not constitute an allowable deduction under §2055(e)(2). The Ruling nevertheless cautioned that the government will examine these cases closely to assure that a settlement is not an attempt to circumvent §2055(e)(2) by instituting and settling a collusive contest.

---

5. *Flanagan, Strock,* First National Bank of Fayetteville v. United States, 727 F.2d 741 (8th Cir. 1984); Oetting v. United States, 712 F.2d 358 (8th Cir. 1983), *rev'g* 544 F. Supp. 20 (E.D. Mo. 1980); Estate of Thomas v. Commissioner, 55 T.C.M. (CCH) 1241 (1988); Northern Trust Co. v. United States, 78-1 U.S. Tax Cas. (CCH) ¶13,229 (N.D. Ill. 1977), and Rev. Ruls. 89-31, 83-20, and 78-152.

Thus, *LaMeres* held that the charitable deduction will not be allowed even for a direct distribution to qualified charities if the only apparent reason for termination or modification of an otherwise nonqualifying split-interest charitable bequest is to circumvent the §2055(e)(2)(A) requirements. The court specifically rejected the estate's argument that an adequate nontax reason for the modification was the fiduciary duty to conserve assets, because generating the estate tax savings attributable to the deduction was the only justification for the fiduciary's action. And the fact that a state court approved the reformation was deemed ineffective to alter the result.

Finally, Terre Haute First National Bank v. United States, 91-1 U.S. Tax Cas. (CCH) ¶60,070 (S.D. Ind. 1991), embraced the rationale in *Flanagan* and *Estate of Strock* that the trust reformation requirements of §2055(e)(3) need not be met if a will contest settlement results in property passing directly to charity, but determined that the amount passing to the charity pursuant to the settlement agreement exceeded the value that a good faith determination would assign to the charity's rights in the decedent's estate. Had the will contest been prosecuted successfully, the charity would have benefited under a prior will only if a relatively unlikely event occurred. Thus, the value of its interest in the estate under that result was de minimis, and the court concluded that the parties could not either disregard or misapply state law to generate a favorable estate tax deduction for amounts paid that bore no relation to the rights of the various parties.

These cases also show that, without first instituting a will contest, the parties cannot just commute and immediately pay the charitable remainder under a nonqualified will provision in hopes of generating a charitable deduction. In Estate of Burdick v. Commissioner, 96 T.C. 168 (1991), *aff'd*, 92-2 U.S. Tax Cas. (CCH) ¶60,122 (9th Cir. 1992), the Tax Court agreed with the government's disallowance of the charitable deduction, stating that an estate cannot rectify a defective estate plan *without litigation* unless it complies with the §2055(e)(3) reformation procedure. Is this sensible? If Congress wants to encourage private philanthropy, why should it matter how or why a distribution is made to charity, if the value and other elements essential to ascertainability are clear?

Chapter 13

COMPUTATION AND PAYMENT: UNIFIED RATES, CREDITS, AND APPORTIONMENT

Part A.   The Unified Rate Structure: Marginal Tax Rates and the Unified Credit
Part B.   The Other Estate Tax Credits
Part C.   Payment and Apportionment of Estate Taxes

PART A.   THE UNIFIED RATE STRUCTURE: MARGINAL TAX RATES AND THE UNIFIED CREDIT

Code References: *Estate Tax: §§2001, 2010, 2051*
Gift Tax: §§2502(a), 2505

1.   Once the value of the taxable estate has been determined under §2051 (the gross estate less any allowable §§2053 through 2056 deductions), the next step in computing the estate tax is to determine the tentative tax, as defined in §2001(b)(1), which is determined by applying the estate tax rates to an "estate tax base." The "estate tax base" is determined by adding the decedent's adjusted taxable gifts to the taxable estate.

It was not always the case that inter vivos gifts were included in the estate tax base. Prior to 1977, some properties that were transferred during a decedent's life were valued and included in the decedent's gross estate at death, and that continues to be so. But, prior to 1977, inter vivos transfers that were not included in a decedent's gross estate were not considered in determining the decedent's estate tax rate. The Tax Reform Act of 1976 "unified" the estate and the gift tax rate schedules, which means that cumulative transfers are subject to a single rate schedule, and inter vivos gifts that are not includible in the decedent's gross estate push the taxable estate into a higher rate bracket. The reasons for unification were described in the following Ways and Means Committee report:

House of Representatives Report No. 1380
94th Cong., 2d Sess. 11-12 (1976)

Under [prior] law, there [was] a substantial disparity of treatment between the taxation of transfers during life and transfers at death. In general, there [were] three factors which provide[d] a decided preference for lifetime transfers. First, the gift tax rates [were] set at three-fourths of the estate tax rates at each corresponding rate bracket. Second, lifetime transfers [were] not taken into account for estate tax purposes and the estate remaining at death [was] subject to a tax under a separate rate schedule starting at the lowest rates. Thus, even if the rates [had been] identical, separate rate schedules [provided] a preference for making both lifetime and deathtime transfers rather than having the total transfer subject to one tax. Third, the gift taxes paid [were] not generally taken into account for either transfer tax base. In the case of a gift, the tax base [did] not include the gift tax but the payment of the tax [resulted] in a decrease in the value of the estate retained by the donor. However, if the property were retained until death, the tax base [included] the full value of the property, even though a portion [was] likely to be required to satisfy estate taxes. Thus, even if the applicable transfer tax rates [had been] the same, the net amount transferred to a beneficiary from a given pre-tax amount of property would [have been] greater for a lifetime transfer solely because of the difference in the tax bases.

As a matter of equity, your committee believes the tax burden imposed on transfers of the same amount of wealth should be substantially the same whether the transfers are made both during life and at death or made only upon death. As a practical matter, the preferences for lifetime transfers [were] available only for wealthier individuals who [were] able to afford lifetime transfers. The preferences for lifetime transfers [were] not generally available for those of small and moderate wealth since they generally [wanted] to retain their property until death to assure financial security during lifetime. Therefore, your committee believes that the preferences for lifetime transfers principally benefit the wealthy and result in eroding the transfer tax base.

Your committee believes that it is desirable to reduce the disparity of treatment between lifetime and deathtime transfers through the adoption of a single unified estate and gift tax rate schedule providing progressive rates based on cumulative lifetime and deathtime transfers. However, your committee is retaining part of the incentives for lifetime transfers. Thus, the provisions of [prior] law under which the amount of gift tax is not included or "grossed up" in the transfer tax base are continued, except in the case of gifts made within three years of date of death. In addition, the annual gift tax exclusion . . . is continued. The advantage of avoiding a transfer tax on the appreciation which might accrue between the time of a gift and the donor's death represents a further incentive for lifetime transfers.

The mechanics by which gifts that are not includible in the gross estate at death push the taxable estate into a higher estate tax rate bracket are established in §2001(b). The tentative tax is computed by applying the unified rate schedule to the sum of the decedent's taxable estate and adjusted taxable gifts, which is the aggregate amount of the decedent's taxable gifts made *after 1976* that are not included in the decedent's gross estate.[1] The sum of the taxable estate and the adjusted taxable gifts is something referred to in this text as the "estate tax base." Those post-1976 taxable gifts that are not included in the decedent's gross estate are determined by applying whatever annual exclusion (see §2503(b)) and deductions (e.g., marital or charitable deduction) were applicable at the date that each gift was made.

The tentative tax is then reduced by the aggregate gift tax "payable" on post-1976 gifts (this amount often is identical to the amount of gift tax that actually was paid). The reduction for gift taxes refers to the taxes payable on *all* taxable gifts made after 1976, regardless of whether such gifts are included in the decedent's gross estate.

Note that §2001(b)(2) refers to the gift tax that would have been "payable" with respect to the post-1976 gifts that are included in the gift tax base, determined as if the §2001(c) rate schedule in effect at the decedent's death had applied at the time of each gift. The rationale for this is to avoid a disparity in computation if the rates have changed between the time of the gift and the estate tax computation. The term "payable" is used rather than "paid" because, as of a decedent's death, the gift tax on inter vivos transfers still might not have been remitted by the decedent.

The gift tax payable is the amount owing after applying the unified credit available to the donor when the gift was made. The current amount of the unified credit is in flux due to changes made by Congress since its adoption. The first calendar year in which the unified credit became applicable was 1977, and the amount of the unified credit for that year was $30,000. The amount of unified credit was increased over the years and it likely will continue to fluctuate. For gift tax purposes, the amount of unified credit that was available to a donor in the calendar year in which a taxable gift was made is the amount of unified credit set by the statute for that year less any amount of unified credit that was applicable to gifts made by that donor in prior calendar years. So, although the current rate schedule is used

---

1. The Revenue Act of 1978 added §2204(d) to protect the decedent's personal representative from personal liability for any deficiency in the estate tax if the personal representative "in good faith relies on gift tax returns furnished under §6103(c)(3) for determining the decedent's adjusted taxable gifts" that were made more than three years before the decedent's death and were not shown on any return. According to the committee report accompanying the introduction of §2204(d), it was added because often it is difficult to determine to whom the decedent made taxable transfers during life. S. Rep. No. 745, 95th Cong., 2d Sess. 102 (1978).

to determine the amount of gift tax that was payable for prior gifts, the actual amount of unified credit that was available to the donor at that time is used.

Note that the offset against the gross estate tax for the amount of gift tax payable on post-1976 gifts applies to *all* taxable gifts made by the donor after 1976. Unlike the determination of adjusted taxable gifts, the offset for gift taxes is not limited to gifts that are not included in the decedent's gross estate. Thus, the gift tax payable on a taxable gift made after 1976 reduces the estate tax that is payable, and it does not matter whether the post-1976 gift is subsequently (1) included in the decedent's gross estate or (2) excluded from the decedent's gross estate but included in the estate tax base as a consequence of being an adjusted taxable gift.

The unified rate schedule in §2001(c) is a table of progressively higher marginal tax rates that begin at 18% on the first $10,000 of taxable transfers. The product of the §2001(c) computation is the gross estate tax. Treas. Reg. §20.0-2(b)(4). Once that is determined, the final step is to compute the *net estate tax payable* — the amount actually payable to the government — which is the gross estate tax reduced by a number of credits. The most important credit in most estates is the *§2010 unified credit*, adopted by the Tax Reform Act of 1976. Prior to that time, the policy of exempting small estates and a certain portion of large estates from estate taxation was effected by the allowance of separate "specific exemptions" under each tax. The rationale for shifting from separate exemptions to the unified credit was explained by the House Ways and Means Committee as follows:

> . . . [S]ince the present estate tax exemption is a deduction in determining the taxable estate, it reduces each estate's tax at the highest estate tax brackets. However, a credit in lieu of an exemption will have the effect of reducing the estate tax at the lower estate tax brackets since a tax credit is applied as a dollar-for-dollar reduction of the amount otherwise due. Thus, at a given level of revenue cost, a tax credit tends to confer more tax savings on small- and medium-sized estates, whereas a deduction or exemption tends to confer more tax savings on larger estates. Your committee believes it would be more equitable if the exemption were replaced with a credit.
>
> As a practical matter, the gift tax exemption is not available to individuals who cannot afford to make lifetime transfers. Thus, the overall transfer tax exemption is effectively greater for individuals who are financially able to utilize the gift tax exemption through lifetime transfers. Your committee believes that it would be more equitable if a unified credit in lieu of an exemption were available on an equal basis without regard to whether the transfers are made only at death or are made both during lifetime and at death.

H.R. Rep. No. 1380, 94th Cong., 2d Sess. 15-16 (1976).

The Report of the Ways and Means Committee quoted above asserts that granting a deductible exemption will reduce the progressivity of transfer taxation, but the grant of a tax credit does not have that effect. Can you articulate an example showing why a deductible exemption that is made universally available (as an estate or gift tax exemption would be) is different from employing a credit? Was the Ways and Means Committee correct in believing that a credit gives rise to different consequences from those attending a deductible exemption?

Congress substituted a credit for the previously existing exemption and substantially increased the amount of estate tax base that is not taxed. The amount that is not taxed is sometimes referred to as the applicable exclusion amount or "exemption equivalent" of the unified credit (this is a shorthand way of describing the tax base needed to generate a tax equal to the credit). Because the unified credit also is applicable against gift taxes incurred for inter vivos transfers, it replaced both of the separate estate and gift tax exemptions. See §2505. We will come to understand why Congress made the full unified credit available in computing the decedent's net estate tax even if the decedent used some or all of the unified credit against gift taxes incurred on inter vivos gifts. We also will learn why it is today a mistake of history that the government continues to require, as it did in Rev. Rul. 79-398, that the unified credit must be used on the first transfers made, prohibiting the taxpayer from paying tax during life to "stockpile" the credit for later use.

PART B.   THE OTHER ESTATE TAX CREDITS

Code References: *Estate Tax §§2011-2016; 2053(d)*

2.   The *net estate tax* that actually must be paid reflects four other tax credits available to reduce the gross estate tax. In the order in which they appear in the Code, these are the credit for (1) state death taxes, (2) federal gift taxes paid on pre-1977 gifts, (3) federal estate taxes paid by reason of the death of persons who transferred certain property to the decedent, and (4) foreign death taxes paid. All four of the credits are restricted to property included in the decedent's gross estate. These credits provide some relief against double or excessively frequent taxation. The four credits must be computed in the proper sequence, because the amount of each is affected by any preceding credit. Predictably, they are not applied in the numerical order in which they are listed in the Code; instead, the correct order of application is the same as the organization of this chapter: §2010, then §§2011, 2012, 2014, and finally §2013 (although any foreign death tax credit computed under a death tax convention rather than under §2014 is computed last). These credits are a significant entitlement: historically, one

or more of them (in addition to the unified credit) was likely to apply in every estate, especially because every state imposes a death tax that is equal to the §2011 credit. See note 1 at page 1 in Chapter 1 and the accompanying text. This may change due to legislation adopted in 2001 that phases out the §2011 state death tax credit over a four year period and replaces it with a §2058 deduction for state death tax paid. The uncertainty is whether or how most states will continue to impose their death taxes after the §2011 credit has been replaced. Because of the budget impact on some states the trend has been for states to freeze their death tax at whatever it was just before the 2001 federal changes were enacted.

3.   *The Credit for State Death Taxes.*   First to be applied after the unified credit is the §2011 credit for any estate, inheritance, legacy, or succession tax imposed on property included in the decedent's gross estate and paid to any state or territory of the United States or to the District of Columbia. Death taxes paid to a city (such as the New York City death tax) or a possession of the United States (not a state or territory) do not qualify (although possessions' taxes qualify under Treas. Reg. §20.2011-1(a) for the §2014(g) foreign death tax credit). Nor do state gift taxes qualify, even if unpaid at death (although they are allowed as a §2053(a)(3) deduction from the gross estate. Treas. Reg. §20.2053-6(d); Estate of Lang v. Commissioner, 613 F.2d 770 (9th Cir. 1980); Rev. Rul. 81-302).

The maximum allowable credit is the lesser of (1) the net tax (after subtracting any discount for early payment and before adding any interest or penalties) paid to the state, (2) the ceiling imposed by the table in §2011(b) and the phase out, or (3) the federal gross estate taxes reduced by the unified credit. These limitations are rooted in the historical development of the credit.

Considerable debate in the mid-1920s questioned whether the federal estate tax improperly impinged on an area traditionally untouched by the federal government.[2] An increase in the federal estate tax rates accompanied enactment in 1924 of the first provision granting a credit for state death taxes; the maximum allowable credit was fixed at 25% of the federal estate tax. But by 1926 Congress concluded that the federal estate tax was "excessive" and that the states should "be enabled to make use of the inheritance tax without additional cost to its citizens." H.R. Rep. No. 1, 69th Cong., 1st Sess. 13-14 (1925), in 1939-1 C.B. (pt. 2) 315, 324-325. Accordingly, in 1926 the federal estate tax specific exemption was increased, the marginal tax rates were reduced, and the maximum state death tax credit was increased to 80% of the federal estate tax. In 2001 the unified credit was increased, and the marginal tax rates were reduced, but the §2011 credit was slashed, which may indicate a shift in policy or (to be cynical) a budget ploy to "pay for" the other

---

2.   A similar debate arose following World War II. See Groves, *Retention of Estate and Gift Taxes by the Federal Government*, 38 CALIF. L. REV. 28 (1950).

changes Congress made — the net effect of reducing the §2011 credit was that more of the federal tax actually goes to the federal government.

There was precedent for those moves, as seen in 1932, when the country was in the midst of the Depression and the federal government was in need of greater revenue. In 1931 the United States incurred a deficit for the first time in a decade and its need for greater revenue was met, in part, by a reduction of the federal estate tax specific exemption and an increase in the tax rates. Those changes would have generated little additional revenue if up to 80% of the higher estate tax could have been credited by state death taxes, so Congress neutralized the state death tax credit in 1932 by enacting two exemptions and two rate schedules. It was not until the 1954 Code that Congress eliminated this complex dual scheme, leaving a limitation on the state death tax credit that was preserved through the table incorporated in §2011(b).

As of 2001 every state imposed a death tax equal to the maximum credit allowable under §2011(b) and most states imposed no other wealth transfer tax. With the legislation in 2001 there has been a good bit of state death tax revision, yielding a balkanized patchwork of rules, impossible to summarize today.

The recipient of any refund of state death tax for which a §2011 credit was allowed must report to the district director, who may bill the recipient for any additional federal estate tax due. §2016. Because there is no way of knowing how long a state death tax controversy may last, there is no statute of limitation with respect to this duty to report a refund and pay any additional tax. A related timing issue is illustrated by the following Ruling:

Revenue Ruling 86-38

. . . *A*, a resident of State *S*, died in 1984 leaving a gross estate composed of stock of *X* Corporation and miscellaneous personal property. . . . *A*'s interest in *X* qualified as an interest in a closely held business as defined in §6166(b)(1) of the Code. The estate could, therefore, elect to pay in ten annual installments that portion of the federal estate tax attributable to the interest in a closely held business.

A similar provision under the law of *S* permitted *A*'s estate to elect to pay in ten annual installments that portion of the state death tax attributable to an interest in a closely held business. Deferred payments and installment payments plus interest are required to be made under state law in the manner provided in §6166 as in effect on *A*'s death.

Situation 1. In Situation 1, the representative of *A*'s estate made a timely election under §6166 to pay part of the federal estate tax in ten equal annual installments and made a similar election under state law to pay part of the state death tax in a ten annual installments. When the federal estate tax return was filed, the estate claimed as a credit under §2011 the total amount of the state death tax liability, including the state death tax paid and the state death tax the estate expected to pay in installments over the next nine years.

Situation 2. In Situation 2, the representative of the estate made a timely election under state law to pay part of the state death tax in ten annual installments. A similar election with respect to the federal estate tax was not made by the estate because the federal estate tax liability was substantially lower than the state death tax. Thus, the estate paid the federal estate tax in full.

When it filed the federal estate tax return, however, the estate claimed as a credit under §2011 the total amount of the state death tax liability that the estate expected to pay.

. . . Section 2011 of the Code provides that, within the limitations of §2011(b), the tax imposed by §2001 shall be credited with the amount of any estate, inheritance, legacy or succession taxes actually paid to any state.

Section 2011(c) generally provides that the credit allowed for state taxes described above shall include "only such taxes as were *actually* paid *and* credit therefor claimed within 4 years" after the filing of the estate tax return. (Emphasis added.)

Sections 2011(c)(1) through (3) contain exceptions to the four-year limitation on the period within which an estate may claim a credit for state taxes actually paid: . . . (2) before the date of the expiration of the period of an extension granted under §6161 or 6166 for payment of the tax shown on the return . . . . According to §2011(c), a refund based on the state death tax credit may (despite the provisions of §§6511 and 6512) be made if the claim for the credit is filed within the prescribed period.

Section 6511(a) provides that a claim for credit or refund of an overpayment of any tax for which the taxpayer is required to file a return must be filed by the taxpayer within 3 years from the time the return was filed or 2 years from the time the tax was paid, whichever period expired later. The provisions of §2011(c) provide a special 4-year period, or other extended period, as an alternative to the 2-year and 3-year periods described in §6511(a) for credits and refunds. . . .

In Situation 1, the estate elected to pay the federal estate tax in ten annual installments. Accordingly, the exception described in §2011(c)(2) is applicable, and the estate may qualify for the §2011 credit for state death taxes paid for the period ending before the date of the expiration of the 10-year period elected for paying the federal estate tax. However, when the estate tax return is filed, only the state death taxes actually paid qualify for the §2011 credit on the estate tax return. A recomputation procedure . . . may be used to recompute the total remaining estate tax liability whenever the estate submits certification of payment of additional state death tax. The recomputation would take into account the §2011 credit that may be allowed for any state death tax installment paid by the estate. After all state death taxes have been paid, a claim for refund may be made, if necessary, for an overpayment of tax but only after the federal estate tax liability has been paid in full.

In Situation 2, because the estate did not elect to extend the time to pay the federal estate tax, the extension of time within which to claim a refund based on the credit for state death taxes actually paid, described in §2011(c)(2), is not applicable. Because none of the other extensions described in §2011(c) apply, only installments paid to the state for death taxes within four years of the filing of the estate tax return can qualify for the credit described in §2011. Accordingly, when the estate files the estate tax return, only the state death taxes paid as of that time may be taken into account for a credit under §2011. Certification of additional payments or installments made relating to the state death taxes during the four year period may be submitted for recomputation of the federal estate tax liability. A subsequent claim for a refund upon payment of each state installment may be made within the four-year period.

Any death tax installments paid to State *S* in Situation 2 after expiration of the four-year period described in §2011(c) of the Code cannot be allowed as a credit against the federal estate tax liability of the estate. Because the tax was paid when the federal estate tax return was filed and none of the exceptions described in §2011(c) are applicable, only state death taxes paid within four years of the filing of the federal estate tax return can qualify for the credit described in §2011.

See also Estate of Spillar v. Commissioner, 50 T.C.M. (CCH) 1285 (1985); TAM 8947005. Any subsequent federal refund based on a state death tax credit claimed after the deferred state tax is paid does not carry interest from the federal government, because the credit is not retroactive to the decedent's date of death. As a consequence, the estate must consider the economics of deferred payment of state death tax by including the cost of paying more federal tax than necessary, followed by a refund without interest when the state tax ultimately is paid and the §2011 credit thereafter is allowed.

4.   *The Credit for Federal Gift Taxes*.   In certain cases, a transfer subject to the gift tax may be includible in the donor's gross estate at death for federal estate tax purposes. See Chapters 4 and 5. If the gift was made after 1976, the transfer tax offset (hereafter sometimes referred to as the "purge and credit mechanism") in §2001(b)(2) operates to preclude double taxation. For gifts made before 1977, §2012 performs essentially the same function. It grants a credit against the gross estate tax for any federal gift tax paid on the same property that is required to be included in the gross estate. Like the purge and credit mechanism in §2001(b)(2), however, the §2012 credit does not provide complete relief if, for example, the doubly taxed property declines in value between the date of the gift and the date of death or if the decedent transferred such a substantial amount of property during life that the effective gift tax rate under the old gift tax schedule on the doubly taxed property was higher than the effective estate tax rate on that property under the new unified schedule. And in neither event is interest allowed on the gift taxes "prepaid" during life.

The §2012 credit is available only for gift taxes attributable to gifts made by the decedent. Treas. Reg. §20.2012-1(a). However, the donor need not have paid the gift tax to get the credit: the decedent's estate is allowed a credit for gift taxes paid by the donee of a net gift ("[i]f a tax on a gift has been paid under chapter 12 . . . and thereafter on the death of the donor any amount in respect of such gift is required to be included in the value of the gross estate of the decedent"), and for gift taxes paid after death by the decedent's estate on a gift made in contemplation of death. Rev. Rul. 74-363. And like §2001(d), the credit is allowed in the estate of the decedent for the entire gift tax attributable to both halves of a gift of property owned solely by the decedent but treated under §2513 as a "split" gift by the decedent's spouse. §2012(c); Treas. Reg. §20.2012-1(e).

The §2012 credit is available only if the doubly taxed property is included in the decedent's gross estate because of the form of the transfer. For example, if D made a gift to a child, C, by transferring property to the joint names of D and C, and if C were to die first, on D's subsequent death D's estate would not be entitled to a §2012 credit, because the property would be included in D's estate as property owned by D at death and not because of the form of the prior gift to C. If, however, D were to predecease C and the full value of the property were includible in D's gross estate under the percentage of consideration rule of §2040(a), then D's estate would be entitled to the §2012 credit because the property would be includible in D's gross estate by reason of the form of the gift (creation of a joint interest for which D furnished the entire consideration).

The §2012 credit is allowed even for a gift tax that is unpaid on the date of the decedent's death and thus is deductible from the gross estate under §2053(a)(3) as a debt of the decedent; the deduction and credit are both allowed in the same manner as would apply if the decedent had timely paid the gift tax long before death. Treas. Reg. §20.2012-1(a). Given that this all is relevant only if the gift predated 1977 it is quite unlikely that any of it is going to be applicable in your practice. Still, it would be good for learning purposes to appreciate why allowance of both a deduction and a credit is appropriate. To do so, just think of the deduction as permitting estate tax treatment as if the tax had been timely paid years ago and those dollars were out of the estate at death.

Section 2012(a) limits the amount of the gift tax credit to the lesser of the gift tax or the estate tax attributable to the doubly taxed property. Treas. Reg. §20.2012 contains a detailed explanation and examples of the computations.

5.   *The Credit for Foreign Death Taxes.*   The gross estate of a decedent who was a citizen or a resident of the United States includes the decedent's property located anywhere in the world. All or a portion of that property may be subject to foreign death taxes as well, because it is located in a foreign country or because the decedent, a United States citizen, was a resident of a foreign country.

The §2014 credit for foreign death taxes was enacted in 1951 because the Senate Finance Committee became aware of cases in which "estates with foreign investments have been taxed much more heavily than similar estates subject only to domestic tax." S. Rep. No. 781, 82d Cong., 1st Sess. 89 (1951), in 1951-2 C.B. 458, 521. As revealed only obliquely by §2102(a), the credit is available only to the estate of a United States citizen residing anywhere or a resident of the United States who is not a United States citizen (a resident alien). It is not available to a nonresident who was not a citizen (a nonresident alien) whose property is subject to United States and foreign tax. The credit is allowed for estate, inheritance, legacy, or succession taxes paid to a foreign country, or to a political subdivision or possession of a foreign country, or to a possession of the United States on property that is included in the gross estate but "situated" in the jurisdiction imposing the tax. §2014(a); Treas. Reg. §20.2014-1(a)(1). Situs is determined under the rules for determining whether property of a nonresident alien is situated in the United States. §§2014(a), 2104, and 2105.

The United States has entered into a number of bilateral death tax conventions with the countries listed in the instructions to Schedule O of the estate tax return. Each convention provides for a foreign death tax credit that is similar but not identical to the §2014 credit. The situs concepts under a convention may be more favorable to the estate than the statutory situs concepts; the convention credit might not include death taxes imposed by a political subdivision or possession of the foreign country; the period for claiming the credit may be longer under the convention than the four-year period permitted by §2014. An estate may elect, on a per-country basis, whichever is most beneficial (i.e., the convention credit or the §2014 credit) for the combined death taxes paid to the foreign country and (to the extent available under the convention) its political subdivisions and possessions.[3]

The §2014 credit is the lesser of the foreign death tax or the federal estate tax attributable to "qualifying property" included in the gross estate but situated in the jurisdiction imposing the death tax. §2014(b). The regulations contain a detailed explanation and examples of these two limitations. The former is simply a proportionate share of the decedent's property subject to foreign death tax, computed by multiplying the foreign death tax (excluding interest and penalties) by a fraction of which (1) the numerator is the value of the qualifying property and (2) the denominator is the value of all qualifying and nonqualifying property subject to the foreign death tax. The federal estate tax attributable to the qualifying property is computed by multiplying the federal estate tax otherwise payable after applying the unified credit and the credits for state death taxes and federal gift taxes by a fraction of which (1) the numerator is the federal estate tax value of the qualifying property (reduced by any charitable or marital deduction attributable to the qualifying property) and (2) the denominator is the value of the entire gross estate (reduced by total charitable and marital deductions). As a consequence of the manner in which the computation of the federal estate tax attributable to qualifying property is made, the foreign death tax credit may be maximized by including a provision in the decedent's will directing that qualifying property be used to satisfy bequests that qualify for the charitable and marital deductions only to the extent that other permissible properties are not available.

The recipient of any refund of foreign death tax for which a §2014 credit was allowed must report to the district director, who may bill the recipient for any additional federal estate tax due. §2016. Because there is no way of knowing how long a foreign death tax controversy may last, there is no statute of limitation with respect to this duty to report a refund and pay any additional tax.

6.   *The Credit for Federal Estate Taxes on Prior Transfers.*   All of the foregoing credits relate to taxes imposed with respect to transfers made by the decedent to someone else. The §2013 credit for previously taxed property (sometimes referred to as the PTP credit, but there are other variations on this theme — like the TPT tax on prior transfers, or the TTP tax on transferred property) relates to federal estate taxes imposed with respect to transfers *to* the decedent. This previously taxed property credit is available if the two decedents die within a 12 year period ending two years after the decedent's death. As even this one concept illustrates, §2013 is not

---

3.   Indeed, the estate may elect the convention credit for the combined death taxes paid to the foreign country and (to the extent available under the convention) its political subdivisions and possessions *plus* the §2014 credit for political subdivision and possession death taxes not creditable under the convention. Treas. Reg. §20.2014-4(b).

altogether easy to understand and, to keep the parties straight, we will utilize the terminology employed by §2013: The person in whose estate the credit is available is referred to as the *decedent* and the person whose property was transferred to "the decedent" and who incurred a death tax that generates the credit is referred to as "the *transferor*."

Prior Law. In 1918, Congress embraced the view that relief should be granted against imposition of successive estate taxes on the same property within a short time. As explained by the Ways and Means Committee report accompanying the Revenue Act of 1918:

> An additional subdivision . . . will grant a deduction of amounts which have been received by the decedent as a share in the estate of [a transferor] who died within five years prior to the death of the decedent. It has come to the attention of the committee that persons closely related have died within such a short space of time that the same estate passing within a short period of time has been subjected to the estate tax and thereby diminished unreasonably because of the short period within which the two levies have been made. For example, a husband dies leaving a large amount of property to his wife, an elderly woman, who died within a few weeks after her husband's death. Under existing law the entire estate is taxed on the transfer from husband to wife and on the transfer from wife to other beneficiaries. The proposed amendment grants an interval of five years within which the deduction may be taken.

H.R. Rep. No. 767, 65th Cong., 2d Sess. 42-43 (1918), in 1939-1 C.B. (pt. 2) 86, 102. Note that there was no marital deduction in 1918, and none was added to the estate tax law for another 30 years. The relief measure introduced in 1918 was not a credit against the decedent's estate tax in the amount of the estate tax paid by the transferor. Rather, it was a deduction of the value of the property received by the decedent from the transferor within five years preceding the decedent's death. In effect the deduction excluded the property from the decedent's gross estate, and made the benefit of the deduction equal to the rate of tax applicable to the decedent's estate, independent of the amount of tax paid by the transferor. The deduction was available only for the value of property still in the decedent's possession at death or that could be traced to other property that was acquired in exchange for that property. Without explaining its rationale, Congress subsequently eliminated the deduction for property received from the decedent's spouse when it enacted the marital deduction in 1948. See S. Rep. No. 1013 (pt. 2), 80th Cong., 2d Sess. 21-23 (1948), in 1948-1 C.B. 331, 346-347.

In 1954 Congress changed the deduction to a credit in the amount of the tax paid by the transferor, explaining the shift as follows:

[Section 2013] provides more equitable results and removes the difficult task of tracing the property. A credit is allowed for the tax paid on the property in the estate of the [transferor] but it can never be larger than if the decedent had not received the property. To eliminate the tracing the credit is based upon the value of the property at the time of the death of the [transferor]. Moreover, property transferred between spouses, to the extent no marital deduction was available, is eligible for this credit.

The credit is to be allowed in full for 2 years following the death of the [transferor] and then decreases by 20% every 2 years thereafter until no credit is allowed after the 10th year.

H.R. Rep. No. 1337, 83d Cong., 2d Sess. 89-90 (1954); see also S. Rep. No. 1622, 83d Cong., 2d Sess. 121-122 (1954).

Current Law. Subject to limitations described beginning at page 769, the §2013(a) credit equals the federal estate tax imposed on a "transfer" of "property" by the transferor to the decedent. As defined in §2013(e), *property* includes any legal or equitable beneficial interest in property, including a general power of appointment or a life estate held by the decedent. See, e.g., Rev. Rul. 79-211; Memorandum for Associate Area Counsel 200218003.

The term *transfer* includes any passing of property from the transferor to the decedent if the property was includible in the transferor's gross estate. Hence, property may be transferred by bequest, devise, intestacy, disclaimer, election against a will, dower or curtesy (or statutory equivalents); as a surviving spouse's support allowance paid from principal to the extent not qualifying for the marital deduction (Rev. Rul. 58-167); by gift; as joint property passing by right of survivorship; as the survivor's benefit under a joint and survivor annuity; as life insurance proceeds; by the transferor designating the decedent as the donee of a general power of appointment; and by the transferor's exercise or nonexercise of a general power of appointment. Treas. Reg. §20.2013-5(b). The entitlement to the credit does *not* require that the transferred property be identified in the decedent's estate; indeed, there is no requirement that the transferred property be in existence when the decedent dies. Treas. Reg. §20.2013-1(a). Consequently, if a decedent held a life income interest in a trust at the time of death, and if the trust had been created by the will of a transferor who died a short time before, the decedent's estate can qualify for a PTP credit in an amount equal to the estate tax paid by the transferor's estate with respect to the value of that life income interest.

The credit is available only if the transferor died within (1) ten years preceding or (2) two years after the decedent's death. This means that it can apply, for example, to a life insurance policy that the transferor gave to the decedent, who died first but within two years of the transferor's subsequent death. We learned in Chapter 4 that certain gifts (e.g., life insurance) made within *three* years of the transferor's death are included in the transferor's gross estate under the authority of §2035(a). So if the transferor made such a gift and died within three years, the decedent's death could generate a §2013 credit if the decedent and the transferor die within the §2013 period of each other. The §2013 credit is limited to transferors who die within two years after the decedent, rather than three years to coincide with the §2035(a) period. S. Rep. No. 1622, 83d Cong., 2d Sess. 122 (1954), states that inclusion is not necessarily generated by §2035 and cited "administrative ease" as the rationale for the different time limit.

The amount of the credit is a percentage determined in §2013(a) of the *lesser* of: (1) the federal estate tax attributable to the transferred property in the transferor's estate, or (2) the federal estate tax in the decedent's estate attributable to a deemed inclusion[4] of the transferred property in the decedent's gross estate. The credit is 100% of this amount if the transferor and the decedent died within two years of each other (regardless of the order of their deaths), and then declines for every two years that elapsed between the decedent's death and the transferor's prior death as follows:

Period Elapsed Exceeding	But Not Exceeding	Allowable Percentage
0 years	2 years	100
2 years	4 years	80
4 years	6 years	60
6 years	8 years	40
8 years	10 years	20
10 years		0

The regulations under §2013 contain a detailed explanation and examples of the computation.

The alternative estate tax figures (known as the two "limitations") — the lesser of which is multiplied by the allowable percentage to determine

---

4. The transferred property need not actually be included in the decedent's gross estate. The amount of the decedent's estate tax attributable to the transferred property is calculated by determining the amount of the decedent's estate tax that is attributable to the *value* of the transferred property (valued at its estate tax value in the estate of the *transferor*).

the credit — are defined in §§2013(b) and (c) and effectively cause taxation at whichever is the higher tax rate between the two estates.

Under §2013(b), the federal estate tax attributable to the transferred property in the *transferor's* estate is computed by multiplying the transferor's "adjusted federal estate tax" (i.e., the federal estate tax paid by the transferor's estate increased by any gift tax credit and by any §2013 credit available to the transferor with respect to property the transferor received from yet a third decedent)[5] by a fraction of which (1) the numerator is the "value of the property transferred" (see below) and (2) the denominator is the transferor's "adjusted taxable estate" — i.e., the transferor's taxable estate reduced by the net death taxes (federal, state, and foreign) incurred by the transferor's estate. Essentially, this produces a pro rata tax attributable to the transferred property in the transferor's estate.

The federal estate tax attributable to the transferred property in the *decedent's* estate is computed on a different — incremental — basis. Under §2013(c), it is deemed to be the excess of (1) the decedent's net estate tax[6] over (2) the amount that the decedent's net estate tax[7] would be if the "value of the property transferred" (described next below) was excluded from the decedent's gross estate.[8]

The "value of the property transferred" factor in computing both limitations is the federal estate tax value of the transferred property in the *transferor's* gross estate. Any death taxes, obligations, or liens chargeable to the transferred property in the transferor's estate and that therefore reduced its value to the decedent must be deducted in determining this value. §2013(d); Rev. Rul. 78-58. Further, if the decedent was the transferor's surviving spouse, the value of the transferred property must be reduced by the amount of the total marital deduction allowed in the transferor's estate; this reduction is required to avoid allowing a credit for a tax on property that qualified for the marital deduction and, thus, was not taxed in the transferor's estate. §2013(d)(3) This has the effect of presuming that the transferred property qualified for the marital deduction regardless of whether that was the case. Moreover, if the transferor's estate

---

5.   Adding these credits to determine the "adjusted federal estate tax" may result indirectly in the decedent's receiving a credit for the transferor's gift taxes or for federal estate tax on a transfer by a third party to the transferor. See Rev. Rul. 59-73; United States v. Denison, 318 F.2d 819 (5th Cir. 1963).

6.   The figure used is the net estate tax payable (see Treas. Reg. §20.0-2(b)(5)) without, however, taking a reduction for any §2013 credit to which the decedent's estate is entitled because of the receipt of prior transfers or for foreign death taxes allowed under a death tax convention. In other words, the credits taken for the receipt of prior transfers and for foreign death taxes allowed under a death tax convention are added back to the actual amount of estate tax that is payable, and the sum is the figure used as the net estate tax for this purpose. Treas. Reg. §20.2013-3(a)(1).

7.   Treas. Reg. §20.2013-3(a)(2).

8.   In computing this hypothetical net estate tax, any charitable deduction is reduced by a proportionate part of the transferred property. §2013(c)(1).

qualified for a marital deduction, the transferor's estate may not fail to claim the marital deduction in an attempt to increase the credit in the decedent's estate. Estate of La Sala v. Commissioner, 71 T.C. 752, 762-765 (1979); Rev. Rul. 59-123. This does not, however, require the transferor's estate to qualify property for the marital deduction if it does not qualify automatically; for example, the transferor's personal representative may withhold a QTIP election for QTIPable property to intentionally incur estate tax that will produce a §2013 credit in the subsequent estate of the surviving spouse.

In *La Sala* the decedent and the transferor were spouses who both survived their daughter, all three of them having died within 26 months of each other. The transferor's estate claimed a §2013 credit with respect to property received from the daughter; but, because of the allowable marital deduction, the transferor's estate incurred a relatively small amount of estate tax against which the PTP credit was utilized to reduce the estate tax to zero. Thus, a large amount of the estate tax paid by the daughter's estate on the transferred property was not utilizable by the decedent's estate. Do you see why zero §2013 credit is available to the decedent's estate with respect to the daughter's property that subsequently was includible in the decedent's estate by virtue of the transferor's marital deduction bequest to the decedent? See United States v. Denison, 318 F.2d 819 (5th Cir. 1963).

Assume that *T* (transferor) died in Year One leaving a gross estate of $4 million. After a few relatively small pecuniary bequests, and a $1 million pecuniary bequest to a bypass trust, *T* left the residue of *T*'s estate to a Residuary Trust, which was established in *T*'s will. *T*'s personal representative did not elect the alternate valuation date. The Residuary Trust requires that all of its income be distributed quarterly to *D* (*T*'s surviving spouse) for so long as *D* shall live. Upon *D*'s death, the trust corpus is to be distributed equally among *T*'s children. *D* died 8 months after *T*'s death, leaving a gross estate of $2 million. *T*'s personal representative did not make a QTIP election, so no marital deduction was allowed to *T*'s estate. *D*'s estate is allowed a previously taxed property credit because of *D*'s life income interest in the Residuary Trust. This itself may seem counterintuitive because the life estate ends at *D*'s death. Can you explain why it is right? To do so, think about what is includible in *D*'s gross estate by virtue of having received that income interest. More important, can you say how the credit should be calculated? See §2013(e); Treas. Reg. §20.2013-5(a); Rev. Rul. 85-111.

7.   *Limitations.* In computing the second limitation (incremental taxes in the decedent's estate), any marital deduction allowed to the decedent's estate must be considered. Notice that this is a different issue from that in *La Sala* and Rev. Rul. 59-123, which involved the effect of a marital deduction in the *transferor's* estate. Guidance on how the post-1981 unlimited marital deduction in the decedent's gross estate is to be reflected in the second computation is given in Rev. Rul. 90-2. To illustrate that guidance, assume that the decedent's gross estate is worth $3.25 million, the decedent's marital deduction is $2 million, and the previously taxed property is valued at $500,000. The second limitation would be the difference in tax between the estate tax computed with and without inclusion of the $500,000 of previously taxed property. With a gross estate of $3.25 million and a marital deduction of $2 million, assume that the decedent's estate tax before the unified credit would be $458,300. With a gross estate of only $2.75 million and a marital deduction of $2 million, assume that the decedent's estate tax before the unified credit would be $258,300. Thus, the second limitation on the §2013 credit in the decedent's estate would be $200,000. The Ruling is generous in not limiting the marital deduction for purposes of computing the second limitation under post-1981 law. It effectively treats previously taxed property as allocated to nonmarital deduction bequests under the decedent's will, because its absence from the gross estate in computing the second limitation does not reduce the marital deduction.

The following Ruling reveals even more favor from the government:

Revenue Ruling 79-211

Does a decedent's noncumulative annual right, created in a prior decedent's will, to withdraw the greater of $5,000 or 5% of the value of trust corpus qualify for the credit for tax on prior transfers provided for in §2013(a)?

[Transferor], *T*, died in 1977. *T*'s will provided that *T*'s residuary estate be held in trust.

Under the terms of the trust, *D*, the decedent, had the right to withdraw the greater of $5,000 or 5% of the value of the trust corpus during each calendar year. The right was noncumulative. *A* was to receive the trust income during *D*'s lifetime. Upon the death of *D*, the remaining trust corpus was to be distributed to *B*.

On the basis of recognized valuation principles, the value of *D*'s right of withdrawal was determined to be 20x dollars on the date of *T*'s death. *D* died in 1979. *D*'s right of withdrawal had lapsed with respect to the calendar years 1977 and 1978. However, *D*'s right of withdrawal during 1979 had neither been exercised nor lapsed at the time of *D*'s death.

Section 2013(a) provides that the tax imposed by §2001 shall be credited with all or part of the amount of the federal estate tax paid with respect to the transfer of an interest in property to the decedent (designated as a transferee) from a person (designated as a transferor) who died within ten years before, or within two years after, the decedent's death. The amount of the credit for tax paid on prior transfers is based upon the value of the transferred property as used in the transferor's estate for the purpose of determining the transferor's federal estate tax liability.

Section 2013(c) defines the term "property" to include any beneficial interest in property, including a general power of appointment (as defined in §2041). See Rev. Rul. 66-38. . . .

Under §2041(b)(2) property subject to an annual non-cumulative lapsed general power to appoint the greater of $5,000 or 5% of the value of trust corpus is not includible in the gross estate of the transferee of the power. Treas. Reg. §20.2041-3(d)(3).

A right to withdraw trust corpus is regarded as a general power of appointment. See Treas. Reg. §20.2041-1(c)(1). Consequently, a noncumulative right to withdraw, each year, the greater of $5,000 or 5% of the value of trust corpus is a general power of appointment within the meaning of §2041(b)(1) notwithstanding that only the $5,000 or 5% of the value of the trust corpus (whichever is greater) that is not subject to a right of withdrawal that has lapsed at the transferee's death is included in the transferee's gross estate. See, for example, Rev. Rul. 59-9. Therefore, the right of withdrawal is a beneficial interest in property as defined by §2013(e), that qualifies for the credit for tax on prior transfers provided for in §2013(a).

Under Treas. Reg. §20.2013-1(a) there is no requirement that the transferred property be identified in the estate of the present decedent or that the property be in existence at the time of the decedent's death.

In the present situation, D's noncumulative annual right to withdraw the greater of $5,000 or 5% of the value of trust corpus was a beneficial interest in property within the meaning of §2013(e). Since the right of withdrawal was transferred to D upon the death of T, who died within ten years before D's death, it qualifies for the credit for tax on prior transfers because the right was a general power of appointment for purposes of §2041.

D's noncumulative annual right to withdraw the greater of $5,000 or 5% of the value of trust corpus is a general power of appointment that qualifies as property for purposes of the credit for tax on prior transfers under §2013(a) of the Code. The value of the interest, for purposes of determining the allowable credit, is 20x dollars, the value of the interest on the date of the transferor's death.

Extrapolate from the facts of Rev. Rul. 79-211. Determine how the credit available to D's estate would be computed if by the terms of T's will D (not A) had been given the right to the income from the trust for D's life, in addition to the noncumulative annual right to withdraw the greater of $5,000 or 5% of the value of the trust corpus.

Would D's estate be entitled to a credit under §2013 if D were T's surviving spouse and had been given both the right to the income from the trust for life plus the noncumulative annual right to withdraw the greater of $5,000 or 5% of the value of the trust corpus (and was given no other interest in T's estate)? Consider Estate of Hollingshead v. Commissioner, 70 T.C. 578 (1979), as discussed at page 630, and recall that §2056(b)(5) is an automatic entitlement.

Assume that in 1993 T gave D a remainder interest in Blackacre following T's retained life estate therein and paid a gift tax of $45,000 on that gift. D died one year later with a sizeable taxable estate. T died within two years after D and Blackacre is includible in T's gross estate under §2036(a)(1). T and D are not spouses or former spouses.

(a) D's estate is allowed a PTP credit for a portion of the estate tax paid by T's estate? Can you explain why?

(b) C and D are not spouses or former spouses. Suppose that D devised the remainder interest in Blackacre to C, that C died within 10 years after D's death, and that C's estate is allowed a §2013 credit for part of the estate tax paid on D's estate. In computing that credit, it is necessary to determine the amount of estate tax paid by D's estate. For that purpose, the "adjusted federal estate tax" paid by D's estate must reflect the credit (if any) to which D's estate is entitled on account of estate taxes paid by T's estate. Try to ascertain the statutory authority for this result.

(c) Would it affect the calculation in **(b)** if T died more than 10 years before D? Would it matter if C sold the property before C's subsequent death, or if C also predeceased T?

Let's try another: T bequeathed $1 million in trust to pay the income to D for life, remainder to X if X survived D, otherwise to Y. None of the parties are spouses or former spouses.

(d) X died one year after T, and Y died the following year, in each case while D was still alive. Is either estate entitled to a §2013 credit for any part of the estate tax paid by T's estate? Consider first whether anything is includible, especially in X's gross estate.

(e) D died at age 53, three years after T. Is D's estate entitled to a credit for any estate tax paid by T's estate? Notice that the value of T's trust is not includible in D's gross estate under §2033 or any other section. In computing the "value of the property transferred" (D's life estate), the age at T's death should be used. See Estate of Edmonds v. Commissioner, 72 T.C. 970, 990-993 (1979). Cf. Rev. Rul. 75-293. D's estate probably would not be entitled to a credit if the trustee was given discretion to either pay the trust income to D or to accumulate it and add it to corpus, although there are a few cases that provide otherwise. In this regard it should not matter that the trustee in fact paid all of the net income to *D*. See Rev. Rul. 67-53; Estate of Pollock v. Commissioner, 77 T.C. 1296 (1981); Holbrook v. United States, 575 F.2d 1288 (9th Cir. 1978).[9] Nevertheless, consider the following material:

In TAM 8608002, *D* was the surviving spouse of *T*, who by will created a family trust for the benefit of *D*, for a child, and for grand-children, authorizing the trustee to distribute income to any of these beneficiaries "as the Trustee in its absolute and sole discretion shall determine." Moreover, the Trustee could distribute principal to any of these beneficiaries "as it may deem necessary" to "generously support and maintain" *D* "and suitably to provide for" the child and grandchildren. Focusing on a specific provision stating *T*'s intent "that the income from the Family Trust shall be expended primarily for the benefit of [*D*] unless in the sole judgment and opinion of the Trustee, [child] . . . or Settlor's grandchildren have real need for any portion of said income," the government held that the income interest granted to *D* qualified for the §2013 credit in *D*'s estate. That the income interest could be diminished by distributions to others did not preclude the credit because (1) "the dispositive provisions of the trust instrument clearly evidence an intention on the part of the transferor to favor [*D*] over [the child] and grandchildren with respect to the payment of trust income," (2) "the trustee here has only a limited power to invade trust principal for others," and (3) that limited power "constitutes an ascertainable standard which renders [*D*'s] life interest susceptible of valuation." No indication was given as to how that income interest was valued, nor does it seem clear from the facts given that an ascertainable standard in fact was used. Still, the government in Memorandum for Associate Area Counsel 200218003 granted a similar credit and made it all the more attractive by giving credit for the value of a corpus invasion authority governed by an ascertainable standard, depending on factors such as the beneficiary's needs, likelihood of invasion, and the extent to which the beneficiary's income and other resources would be considered. See Rev. Rul. 75-550, 1975-2 C.B. 357.

The government has held that a credit under §2013 is allowable if the trustee's power was subject to an ascertainable standard, such that *D*'s

---

9. *Holbrook* held that the decedent's life estate in trust was incapable of valuation as of the transferor's death, and therefore ineligible for a credit under §2013, because of the trustee's discretionary power to invest trust assets in non-income-producing property. Apparently the trustee had not in fact invested in non-income-producing property, although the opinion did not make this clear. The court did, however, say that "[t]his result seems unfair and is certainly at odds with the modern trend toward vesting trustees with broad discretion in managing trust assets. Designing an accommodation between this desirable administrative flexibility and the goal of avoiding double taxation of the same property within a brief period is, however, a legislative, not a judicial problem." 575 F.2d at 1292 n.5.

interest could be valued. See Rev. Rul. 75-550 for the method of computing the credit. In Estate of Lloyd v. United States, 650 F.2d 1196 (Ct. Cl. 1981), the court held that the decedent's life estate in a trust could be valued actuarially despite the trustee's "sole and uncontrolled discretion" to invade trust corpus in favor of the decedent or issue of the transferor; the theory was that local law and the transferor's will read as a whole imposed an ascertainable standard on the trustee's discretionary power.

In Estate of Weinstein v. United States, 820 F.2d 201 (6th Cir. 1987), a §2013 credit was allowed to the estate of D who, as T's surviving spouse, was granted a nonmarital trust discretionary income interest. The standard governing the trustee's exercise of discretion to distribute income to D provided that D should "be adequately provided for . . . to continue to maintain [D] . . . [in] the manner to which . . . [T and D were] accustomed throughout their married life." The trustee was authorized to consider D's other income in deciding whether to make distributions (but not other property available to D, notwithstanding that the bypass trust also contained a standard provision directing exhaustion of the corpus of a marital deduction trust created for D before invading corpus of the bypass trust for D). D's estate produced a report of an actuary determining the value of D's income interest as of T's death, based on factors such as the expected yield of the trust (based in part on the broad investment discretion given the trustee), D's expected needs, the other income and resources available to D, and so forth, which the government did not attempt to refute. Instead, the government contended that, as a matter of law, §2013 simply could not apply in such a situation. Relying on Treas. Reg. §20.2013-4(a) and *Estate of Lloyd*, the court rejected the government's contention. The court stated that the interest will qualify for the §2013 credit if there is an ascertainable standard sufficient to permit a determination of value. The court found that such a standard did exist, notwithstanding the fact that the trustee could either accumulate or distribute income (not distributed to D) to T's children, stating that the interests of those children should be ignored because they were only secondary in import.

In sharp contrast to *Weinstein* is TAM 8717006, in which a §2013 credit was *not* allowed for the income interest in a nonmarital trust because D's estate refused to provide information regarding D's other income and assets, which were relevant in evaluating the standard used in the trust. On this basis, the government held that it was unable to ascertain the value of the income interest and therefore denied the §2013 credit.

TAM 8944005 denied the §2013 credit for S's discretionary income interest when S was merely one of several permissible income beneficiaries and there was no ascertainable standard to restrict the trustee's discretion. The TAM cited Rev. Rul. 67-53 with approval and distinguished *Lloyd* and *Weinstein* because S was neither the sole income beneficiary of the trust nor was S even treated by the terms of the trust as the primary beneficiary.

TAM 9145004 denied a §2013 credit for a surviving spouse's income interest in a discretionary income nonmarital trust, but allowed the credit with respect to the surviving spouse's mandatory income entitlement in QTIPable property as to which no QTIP election was made. Because that property was held separately from the nonmarital portion of the decedent's estate, the government allowed a credit for the "taxes attributable to the marital deduction trust," but it did not explain the proper computation of the amount of the credit. For example, if the nonmarital trust was $1 million in value and the partial QTIP election left another $250,000 taxable in the decedent's estate, the taxable estate would be $1.25 million, of which the property in question would constitute 20%. Would the tax attributable to that QTIP trust be the full increment in tax caused by the partial QTIP election or just 20% of the total tax paid by the estate? The issue is relevant because only the tax attributable to the partial QTIP elected trust, and no tax generated by the nonmarital trust, would be available for §2013 purposes at the death of the surviving spouse. Does §2013(b) indicate that the credit should be a proportionate share of the total tax paid by the decedent's estate?

(f) Suppose that *D* was in poor health at *T*'s death and not expected to live to an actuarially determined life expectancy. In computing the "value of the property transferred" in **(a)**, the state of *D*'s health would be relevant if the actuarial tables in the regulations could not be used. See Treas. Reg. §20.7520-3(b)(3) and the following discussion.

It is important to recognize that, for purposes of §2013, the value of transferred property generally equals the value that it had on the date of the *transferor's* death. If the transferred property is a temporal interest (such as a life income interest), the value of which is dependent upon the life expectancy of some person, the question arises whether the valuation should be made by using actuarial tables or whether the health of the individual who is the measuring life should be taken into account. In applying §2013, the government has long taken the position that, subject to one significant exception, the actuarial tables are to be used without regard to the actual health of the individual who is the measuring life. Rev. Rul. 66-307. The one exception is "if it is known on the valuation date that a life tenant is afflicted with a fatal and incurable disease in its advanced states, and that he cannot survive for more than a brief period of time, the value of the life or remainder interest should be determined by reference to such known facts." Id. This exception is not applicable in determining an individual's life expectancy for purposes of §§2037(b) and 2042(2); in making a valuation for the purpose of those two statutory provisions, actuarial tables are employed regardless of the poor health of the life income beneficiary. Treas. Reg. §20.7520-3(b)(3)(ii).

The meaning of the term "brief" in Rev. Rul. 66-307 (the actuarial tables must be used unless the life tenant is known to have a disease from which the individual "cannot survive for more than a *brief* period of time") was given a very narrow construction in Continental Illinois National Bank & Trust Co. v. United States, 504 F.2d 586 (7th Cir. 1974). The transferor in that case left a life estate in certain properties to D. When the transferor died D was suffering from cancer of the colon with metastasis to the liver, and D died less than one month after the transferor's death. Although two doctors testified that, at the transferor's death, they would have expected D to die within six months, one of those doctors admitted that D could have lived for more than one year. A third doctor testified that D could have lived for 18 months and that you can't "place a time span on her expected length of life." The district court found that D could have lived for longer than one year after the transferor died, and the appellate court did not overturn that finding, holding that the mortality tables must be used unless there are exceptional circumstances present that make the use of the tables "unrealistic and unreasonable." It is not sufficient for the government to show that D had an incurable and fatal disease. The government also has the burden of showing that it was known at the transferor's death that D's actual life expectancy was so brief as to justify a departure from the tables; in general, this meant showing that D had no more than one year to live. Because the government's evidence did not meet that burden, the taxpayers were allowed to use the actuarial tables (providing a life expectancy of six years for D) in calculating D's PTP credit.

Today the government promulgates tables for valuing income, annuity, remainder, and reversionary interests under the standards and direction of §7520. The cases and rulings discussed above have been supplanted by final regulations that are effective for the estates of decedents who die after December 13, 1995. Treas. Reg. §20.7520-3(b)(3). Under the current regulations, the mortality tables are not used if the individual who is the measuring life is "terminally ill" at the date on which the valuation is to be made (i.e., for §2013 purposes, the date of the transferor's death). Treas. Reg. §20.7520-3(b)(3)(i). The regulation further provides:

an individual who is known to have an incurable illness or other deteriorating physical condition is considered terminally ill if there is at least a 50% probability that the individual will die within 1 year. However, if the individual survives for eighteen months or longer after the [valuation] date, that individual shall be presumed to have not been terminally ill at [such] date . . . unless the contrary is established by clear and convincing evidence.

The terminal illness exception is not applicable for applying §§2037(b) and 2042(2), but it is for most §2013 purposes. Treas. Reg. §20.7520-

3(b)(3)(ii). However, the terminal illness exception does not apply to §2013 in certain circumstances. Treas. Reg. §20.7520-3(b)(3)(ii) states in part:

In the case of the allowance of the credit for tax on a prior transfer under §2013, if a final determination of the federal estate tax liability of the transferor's estate has been made under circumstances that required valuation of the life interest received by the transferee, the value of the property transferred, for purposes of the credit allowable to the transferee's estate, shall be the value determined previously in the transferor's estate. Otherwise, for purposes of §2013, the provisions of paragraph (b)(3)(i) of this section[10] shall govern in valuing the property transferred. . . .

What is the meaning of this paragraph? Imagine that a joint life estate in T and D is all that the transferor owned and left to the decedent.

Insofar as illness is concerned, the regulations make clear that the mortality tables must be used unless the terminal illness exception is applicable. But must the tables be used to value a life income interest when the transferor and the decedent die simultaneously in a common accident or under such circumstances that the order of their deaths cannot be determined? There usually will be no illness in such circumstances, but the events make the use of mortality tables unreasonable. The Tax Court (in a reviewed decision) and two Circuit Courts of Appeals have held that mortality tables are not used in such circumstance and that the value of the decedent's income interest is zero. Estate of Carter v. United States, 921 F.2d 63 (5th Cir. 1991); Estate of Lion v. Commissioner, 438 F.2d 56 (4th Cir. 1971); Estate of Marks v. Commissioner, 94 T.C. 720 (1990) (reviewed by the court). The regulations have adopted that approach and provide that the mortality tables cannot be used when the transferor and "the individual who is the measuring life die as the result of a common accident or other occurrence." Treas. Reg. §20.7520-3(b)(3)(iii).

Assume that T and T's child D were injured in an accident when they were passengers in the same automobile. T was killed immediately but D died two months after the accident occurred, as a consequence of injuries suffered in the accident. T left $6 million in trust to pay a life income interest to D, and bequeathed the remainder to X. D had a taxable estate of $4 million. Is D's estate allowed a PTP credit under §2013 for the life income interest that D received from T? Note that it is not necessarily to the benefit of a taxpayer for the measuring life to be valued at a lower figure. For example, if it had been X who died after having acquired the remainder interest in T's trust, the lower value of D's income interest would increase the value of the remainder and the amount of PTP credit available to X's estate.

---

10.   See the paragraph of Treas. Reg. §20.7520-3(b)(3)(i) quoted at page 776 in text.

8. *No Credit For or Against the Gift Tax.* Imagine that T and D are not spouses. T gave $100,000 to D and paid a federal gift tax for the privilege of doing so. D died four years later. Assuming that the value of this gift will not be includible in T's gross estate for any reason, why does §2013 not provide a credit against D's federal estate tax for the federal gift tax paid by T? Prior to 1954 the estate tax predecessor to §2013 was available for property taxed under either the estate or gift tax. When Congress adopted §2013 the credit was eliminated with respect to property previously taxed under the gift tax. The only explanation contained in the committee reports accompanying this change was a puzzling statement: "Since the purpose of this provision is to prevent the diminution of an estate by the imposition of successive taxes on the same property within a brief period, the credit for gift tax paid on a prior transfer has been omitted." H.R. Rep. No. 1337, 83d Cong., 2d Sess. 89-90 (1954); S. Rep. No. 1622, 83d Cong., 2d Sess. 121-122 (1954).

Suppose that T's gift had been a testamentary transfer on which an estate tax was paid and that one year after T's death D gave the $100,000 to D's child, C. The gift tax makes no provision for a credit against D's gift tax for any estate tax paid by T's estate with respect to this property. Should there be such a credit?

PART C. PAYMENT AND APPORTIONMENT OF ESTATE TAXES

Code References: *Estate Tax §§2002, 2203, 2205-2207B, 6018, 6075, 6161, 6163, 6166, 6324, 6901*

9. *Filing the Estate Tax Return and Paying the Tax.* Under §6018(a)(1), a return must be filed if a citizen or resident decedent's gross estate plus taxable gifts made after 1976 exceeds the applicable exclusion amount, irrespective of whether any tax will be due. The initial obligation to file the return and pay the entire federal estate tax imposed on a decedent's gross estate (whether probate or nonprobate property) rests on the decedent's personal representative, regardless of the fact that certain assets constituting the gross estate for federal estate tax purposes may not be in the possession or control of that fiduciary. Under §2002, "[t]he tax imposed by this chapter shall be paid by the executor," and §2203 defines "executor" to mean "the executor or administrator of the decedent . . . ." So primary is this obligation that, if any portion of the tax is paid by the recipient of nonprobate property included in the gross estate, §2205 provides that the payor is entitled to reimbursement from the personal representative.

Under §6075(a) the estate tax return is due nine months after the decedent's death. Civil penalties will be imposed for late filing unless it is shown that the late filing is due to reasonable cause and not to willful neglect. §6651(a)(1). Also, a late filing will cause a forfeiture of the right to elect the alternate valuation date. §2032(d) and Treas. Reg. §20.2032-1(b)(2). The tax must be paid when the return is required to be filed, unless an extension of the time for payment is secured. An extension of the time for filing the return does not constitute an extension of the time for payment of the tax. Treas. Reg. §20.6151-1(a). If the personal representative does not pay the tax when due, §2002 imposes personal liability on that fiduciary for the amount of the tax, effected through a lien under §6321, based on 31 U.S.C. §192, which imposes personal liability on anyone who distributes estate property prior to satisfaction of all indebtedness to the United States. Moreover, if the tax is not paid when due, liability for payment of the tax may extend to each transferee or holder of property included in the gross estate, with personal transferee liability attaching to the extent of the lesser of the total tax that is due or the value of the property received or held by the transferee. §§6324(a)(2) (lien), 6901(a)(1) and (h) (transferee liability). In addition, the lien attaches to any proceeds from the sale of assets included in the estate, under §6324(a)(2) and Treas. Reg. §301.6324-1(a)(2)(iii). Thus, transferee liability is *in addition to* the liability that normally attaches to the personal representative. In either case, personal liability is discharged once the tax is paid (or payment is adequately secured).

Several provisions authorize extensions of time that defer the obligation to pay estate taxes. Under §6161(a)(2), an extension of up to 10 years may be granted in the discretion of the Secretary for "reasonable cause." Extensions of up to 14 years are authorized by §6166 for taxes attributable to an "interest in a closely held business" if the value of that interest exceeds 35% of the value of the adjusted gross estate. Under §6166, no payment (other than interest) need be made until 5 years after the due date, and then principal payments can be made in installments over a 10-year period. Any installment due under §6166 may be extended for up to 12 months under §6161(a)(2) if reasonable cause is shown. Qualifying as "reasonable cause" for deferral would be an inability to marshal liquid assets because they are located in other jurisdictions or because litigation is required to collect them, an inability to borrow on better than disfavorable terms (in relation to returns otherwise available to the estate on its investments), or an insufficiency of funds to maintain the decedent's family while paying claims against the estate and the estate tax, coupled with an inability to borrow at prevailing market rates. Treas. Reg. §1.6161-1(a)(1) *Examples (1)* through *(4)*.

In addition, §6163 permits deferral of payment of that portion of the estate tax attributable to inclusion in a decedent's gross estate of either a reversion or a remainder. Under this provision, the tax need not be paid until six months after termination of all preceding interests in the property and, for reasonable cause, this too may be further extended for an additional three years.[11]

The taxpayer must pay interest on the deferred taxes. In general, interest is computed under §§6601 and 6621 at the same rate as that charged on any underpayment. But see §6601(j). In addition, although the personal liability of the fiduciary for payment of the deferred tax that otherwise is mandated under §6321 may be supplanted by posting a bond under §§2204 and 6165, the requirements for the bond are so onerous that this alternative often is unattractive. See Treas. Reg. §§20.2204-1(b) and 20.6165-1(a), calling for bonds not in excess of twice the deferred tax, and §§2204(c) and 6324A, which provide for a lien with respect to taxes payable in installments under §6166. Thus, the personal representative may have continuing significant liabilities if deferral is elected, making this election a troubling prospect for many estates.

10.   *Apportionment of the Estate Tax Burden.* Once the amount of the federal estate tax has been calculated, the personal representative must determine how the estate tax burden is to be apportioned among the beneficiaries of the decedent's bounty. Congressional policy is that the estate tax should be a burden on the estate as a whole, rather than on the individual beneficiaries of the estate as is the case with most inheritance taxes. §2205. Nevertheless, the Supreme Court early established in Riggs v. Del Drago, 317 U.S. 95 (1942), that this federal tax burden may be altered by state law or by the terms of the decedent's estate plan.[12] Thus, the tax payment obligation·may be apportioned. Moreover, as we soon shall see, there are several Code provisions that are aimed at facilitating apportionment by authorizing enforcement of contribution from recipients of nonprobate assets. As a consequence of this freedom to apportion, up to six major apportionment decisions must be made, several with additional subissues that usually are addressed under state law.

Apportionment Options.

Inside Apportionment

The first form of apportionment commonly is referred to as "inside apportionment" and deals with the apportionment of taxes among all dispositions within — inside — a probate estate. Like the federal presumption,

---

11.   Presumably the same standards would be applied as are utilized for extensions for reasonable cause under §6161. See Joint Comm. on Taxation, General Explanation of the Tax Reform Act of 1976, H.R. Rep. No. 1380, 94th Cong., 2d Sess. 546, 1976-2 C.B. 558.

12.   Typically a decedent may waive or alter the dictates of state law only by a provision in the decedent's will and not by any other document. See, e.g., Uniform Estate Tax Apportionment Act §2.

the common law rule is that taxes generated by the probate estate are a burden on the residue, meaning that all taxes are paid out of the residuary estate before any taxes are allocated to or payable from other dispositions, such as general, demonstrative, or specific bequests or devises under a will. If applicable, inside apportionment instead specifies that every taker under a will bears a proportionate share of the taxes payable, regardless of the priority or class of disposition involved. Although this is equitable, inside apportionment is not free of disadvantages, especially with respect to specific bequests. For example, a decedent who bequeaths an illiquid asset, such as a diamond ring, the grand piano, or even the decedent's personal residence, may not want to force the beneficiary to generate the liquidity to pay the tax attributable to that asset as a condition to receiving the bequest. As a result it is not uncommon in well-planned estates to find that apportionment within the probate estate is waived and the burden of all taxes on probate property is imposed on the residuary estate, as under the common law.

Outside Apportionment

Within testate and intestate estates alike, "outside apportionment" stands in juxtaposition to "inside apportionment," apportioning taxes generated by the total taxable estate for federal estate tax purposes among the takers of probate assets (either with or without inside apportionment) and the recipients of includible nonprobate assets. Thus, outside apportionment dictates that the recipient of nonprobate property includible in the gross estate of a decedent pay that portion of the taxes imposed on the total estate attributable to that inclusion. It is not at all uncommon to find outside apportionment dictated by an estate plan with respect to the nonprobate property notwithstanding that inside apportionment is not adopted.

Equitable Apportionment

This third form of apportionment provides that dispositions that generate a tax benefit (such as a deduction or reduced valuation) are entitled to the benefit. Thus, property qualifying for the marital deduction would be exempted from contribution toward payment of the total taxes imposed on the estate; the deductible disposition therefore benefits from the deduction, rather than the deduction benefiting all beneficiaries of the estate. Difficult apportionment questions may arise if the estate plan calls for a larger bequest to a spouse than qualifies for a deduction, as can be the case under some state laws that do not match the federal unlimited marital deduction entitlement.

Also uncertain is the treatment of distributions in satisfaction of a contractual entitlement, such as under a prenuptial agreement. If deductible under §2053(a)(3) as a claim against the estate, these dispositions should be treated in the same fashion as a charitable or marital disposition. In this respect, §2043 is relevant because it makes certain property settlements at death deductible under §2053 if incident to a divorce and otherwise meeting the requirements of §2516. See Chapter 6. Otherwise, obligations incurred incident to divorce that are satisfied out of an estate at death but that are not deductible (along with pretermitted heir shares, which are not deductible) normally are ineligible for equitable apportionment. In a limited number of cases, however, claims satisfied at death that arise from a prenuptial agreement are treated as claims against the estate similar to claims of other creditors. Notwithstanding that (unlike most creditors' claims) they are not deductible under §2053, the recipient of property under the agreement is entitled to priority in payment along with other creditors. Because creditors are unaffected by the amount of taxes (except to the extent the estate is bankrupt, so that not all otherwise entitled claimants are satisfied) the claimant in these cases effectively is granted equitable apportionment.

Apportionment of Rate Differentials

Closely related to equitable apportionment is the apportionment of state estate or inheritance tax rate differentials based on each beneficiary's share of the estate. For example, some states impose a tax that favors more closely related beneficiaries over strangers or distant relatives. In such a state, the issue is whether apportionment should reflect those rate differentials. Even in states that embrace full inside, outside, and equitable apportionment of estate taxes, state inheritance taxes usually are imposed directly on individual recipients of the decedent's wealth. In those states, any rate differential automatically is apportioned unless the decedent's estate plan directs the estate to pay those inheritance taxes and, by virtue of this direction, causes the taxes to become an item that must be apportioned against each beneficiary's respective share.

Apportionment of Credits

Similarly related is apportionment of the benefit of credits available to the estate that are connected with separate identifiable properties passing to designated individuals. For example, if some property incurs more state death tax than others, the apportionment issue is whether the beneficiaries thereof should receive the benefit of any §2011 credit or §2058 deduction attributable to the tax incurred on their bequests. Similarly, should the credit for foreign death taxes under §2014 be apportioned, or should the §2015 credit for deferred taxes attributable to future interests be apportioned to the takers of those interests? State law in most states fails to address this issue.

Apportionment to Temporal (Split) Interests

A final apportionment alternative relates to the proper method for apportioning taxes attributable to property that is split into temporal interests, such as a life estate, a term of years, or an annuity given to one individual and the remainder given to another. The law is relatively clear regarding apportionment of taxes allocable to life estates and terms of years but significant variations exist relative to taxes attributable to an annuity. Section 6 of both the Uniform Estate Tax Apportionment Act and the Revised Uniform Estate Tax Apportionment Act[13] is representative of the law in most states, specifying that taxes attributable to a life estate or term of years are to be paid out of corpus, not charged against the temporal interest. Although superficially this rule appears inequitable, it actually is sensible, given the fact that reduction of corpus by the payment of taxes correspondingly reduces income to be earned thereon and effectively amortizes the tax allocable to the income interest. The rule also is administratively attractive because the present interest income beneficiary need not contribute toward payment of taxes that might exceed any income received at the time that the tax must be paid.

With respect to annuities, however, a different situation is presented because the annuity may be a specified dollar amount, payable from corpus to the extent annual income is insufficient. Thus, a reduction of corpus to pay taxes allocable to the annuity may not cause a reduction in the amount of the annuity. Moreover, if the lead interest is nondeductible but the remainder qualifies for either the marital or charitable deduction, the consequence of this apportionment rule is to reduce the size of the deduction, incur more tax as a direct consequence, thereby further reducing the deductible amount, again increasing the taxes incurred, ad infinitum. In such cases, the result is a conflict in states that embrace both equitable apportionment and the apportionment rule allocating taxes attributable to a lead interest to the remainder. Usually that conflict is resolved in favor of forcing corpus to pay, with unfavorable results for deduction purposes. See, e.g., Estate of Leach v. Commissioner, 82 T.C. 952 (1984).

Notwithstanding reasons suggesting that annuities deserve different treatment than other term interests, the law in most states follows the Uniform Act approach for term interests in general, causing all taxes to be paid

---

13. As of 2002, 20 states had adopted either the original (1958) or revised (1964) Uniform Estate Tax Apportionment Act (most with some local modifications), or Uniform Probate Code §3-916, which contains the same provisions as the Uniform Act. They were Alaska, Colorado, Hawaii, Idaho, Maine, Maryland, Minnesota, Mississippi, Montana, New Hampshire, New Mexico, North Carolina, North Dakota, Rhode Island, South Carolina, Texas, Utah, Vermont, Washington, and Wyoming. Also as of 2002 the Uniform Act was undergoing a revision drafting project that likely will introduce added variations, but not on this particular issue. Consult Pennell & Danforth, TRANSFER TAX PAYMENT AND APPORTIONMENT, 834 Estates, Gifts, and Trusts Portfolio (Tax Mgmt. 2001), and American College of Trust & Estate Counsel (ACTEC) Study 12 (2003).

from corpus. The comments to §6 of both Uniform Acts state that this result is mandated by the fact that no other practical solution exists. There is some reason to question the view that no other treatment is practical. For example, taxes could be allocated to corpus but the annuity amount adjusted by an amortization assessment against the annuitant over the term of the annuity. This approach is justifiable on the grounds that the risk of an early termination of the annuity, prior to full amortization of the taxes allocable thereto, is matched by the benefit to the remainder beneficiaries if the annuity terminates early. See Scoles & Stephens, *The Proposed Uniform Estate Tax Apportionment Act*, 43 MINN. L. REV. 907 (1959).

Other Apportionable Items.   Outside apportionment of fees and expenses of administration has been dictated in several cases. See Roe v. Farrell, 372 N.E.2d 662 (Ill. 1978); cited in Estate of Fender v. Fender, 422 N.E.2d 107 (Ill. App. Ct. 1981); Cloutier v. Lavoie, 177 N.E.2d 584 (Mass. 1961); In re Estate of McKitrick, 172 N.E.2d 197 (Ohio Prob. Ct. 1960); 1 Casner & Pennell, ESTATE PLANNING §3.3.12.3 (6th ed. 1995). In addition, many state statutes, including both Uniform Acts, dictate apportionment of interest and penalties assessed along with the underlying taxes imposed on an estate. See §§2207A(d), 2207B(d), and Rev. Rul. 80-159. This is not a universal rule, however, and in some states these added items are not chargeable in the same manner as the underlying tax. See, e.g., Estate of Richardson v. Commissioner, 89 T.C. 1193 (1987); Annot., Construction and Application of Statutes Apportioning or Prorating Estate Taxes, 71 A.L.R.3d 247 (1976). As illustrated by Estate of Whittle v. Commissioner, 97 T.C. 362 (1991), *aff'd*, 994 F.2d 379 (7th Cir. 1993), interest on estate tax is not the same as the tax itself and may be chargeable in a different manner unless the document or applicable state or federal law specifically provide for it.

11. *Federal Apportionment Rules.* Several provisions of the Internal Revenue Code relate to apportionment of the federal estate tax burden. The first of these, §2205 (Reimbursement out of Estate), was interpreted by the Supreme Court in *Riggs* as having been intended by Congress to leave the authority to apportion the burden of the federal estate tax at the state level. Section 2205 was held not to be an apportionment provision so much as merely to provide that "if the tax must be collected after distribution, the final impact of the tax shall be the same as though it had first been taken out of the estate before distribution, thus leaving to state law the determination of where the final impact shall be." 317 U.S. at 101. Nevertheless, four federal statutory rules permit reimbursement for federal (but not any state) estate tax imposed on specific types of non-probate property, all notwithstanding state law.

For example, §2206 establishes a right of reimbursement exercisable against each beneficiary of life insurance proceeds for their proportionate share of the total estate taxes paid by the estate that is attributable to includible insurance proceeds. This is an important entitlement and great care must be exercised to avoid inappropriate waiver of it, as authorized under the introductory clause of §2206. For example, if (as has been threatened) Congress were to amend §2042 to include the proceeds of insurance not owned by the insured-decedent and over which the decedent possessed neither incidents of ownership nor control, §2206 might be the only way to reimburse the estate for the taxes caused by that inclusion.

Employing virtually identical language to §2206 is §2207, which grants an identical right of reimbursement for taxes attributable to property included in the gross estate under §2041, permitting the personal representative to recover from "the person receiving such property by reason of the exercise, nonexercise or release of a [general] power of appointment."

The third federal provision, §2207A, grants a significantly different right of reimbursement. Applicable to property includible in the gross estate by reason of §2044 (relating to the QTIP marital deduction), this right of reimbursement differs because it is an "incremental" rather than a proportionate entitlement. That is, §§2206 and 2207 apply to bottom line taxes imposed on the estate with respect to those portions causing inclusion under §§2042 and 2041, respectively (and after considering the marital deduction), effectively prorating all deductions and credits *proportionately* among all takers. Section 2207A permits recovery of the amount by which taxes were *increased* by inclusion of §2044 property, meaning the incremental taxes *without* sharing the benefit of deductions or credits available to the estate as a whole.

The §2207A right of reimbursement also extends to gift taxes generated under §2519 upon relinquishment of any portion of a qualified terminable interest. No similar right exists under either of the §2206 or §2207 reimbursement provisions if gift taxes are incurred on insurance proceeds or general power of appointment property. Section 2207A does not, however, allow recovery of gift taxes incurred under §2511 as, for example, if the beneficiary of a QTIP trust assigned a portion of the right to receive income and incurred gift tax on both the §2511 gift of income and the §2519 imputed transfer of the remainder interest in the entire QTIP trust.

Section 2207A(d) also specifies that interest and penalties attributable to QTIP property are subject to the incremental right of reimbursement. Again, this has no counterpart in §§2206 and 2207. Perhaps the most important difference about §2207A is that the failure to assert this right of reimbursement constitutes a gift from the spouse's estate to the beneficiaries of the qualified terminable interest property who benefit from that failure, although this liability can be avoided if the surviving spouse's will expressly waives the right of reimbursement. Treas. Reg. §§20.2207A-1(a)(2) and -1(a)(3).

The fourth federal provision is §2207B, applicable with respect to taxes caused by inclusion of property under §2036. Section 2207B calls for a pro rata right of reimbursement, like §§2206 and 2207, but applies with respect to penalties and interest attributable to the tax in the amount subject to reimbursement, like §2207A. The entitlement created by §2207B may be waived by the decedent, including (as in §2207A but unlike §§2206 and 2207) by a provision in the decedent's revocable trust as well as in the decedent's will. Again like §2207A there is a requirement that any waiver must make a specific reference to §2207B to be effective.

For reasons that probably are more historical than substantive, there is no other comparable federal provision for recovery of taxes attributable to nonprobate assets includible under §§2035 or 2037 through 2040.

12. _Apportionment to Nonprobate Assets._ It is not universally established that a decedent's will may apportion taxes to nonprobate assets in the absence of, or contrary to, state law. If state law calls for apportionment of taxes, clearly a decedent's will may negate that local apportionment rule by calling for payment of all taxes out of the probate estate (assuming the decedent's intent is clear). If state law contains no apportionment authority, or if state law expressly directs against apportionment, the issue is whether a decedent may affirmatively direct, by a provision in a will, that taxes will be allocated to nonprobate assets.

This is a particularly acute issue if the nonprobate disposition is an irrevocable transfer as to which the decedent relinquished all rights of control and in which the decedent included no special tax payment directive. Nevertheless, if a decedent's transfer is incomplete for federal tax purposes (or otherwise was subject to inclusion), the issue is whether there is a sufficient nexus to permit the decedent to exert control by means of a testamentary apportionment provision.

A similar but perhaps less severe issue is whether a decedent may direct a different form of apportionment than that permitted or directed under state law, again in situations in which a will otherwise would be ineffective to alter or amend an irrevocable nonprobate transfer. For example, if Congress were to follow through on threats to amend §2042 to cause inclusion of insurance owned by and payable to an irrevocable insurance trust, §2206 would allow reimbursement of the pro rata share of taxes attributable thereto. The issue here is whether a decedent's will could call for an incremental reimbursement or direct the trust to pay those taxes directly. Although the authorities in this respect are not uniform, the better supported position appears to be that a sufficient nexus to require inclusion for federal estate tax purposes is a sufficient nexus to permit the decedent to require apportionment or to direct a different form of apportionment than that specified under state law. See, e.g., United States v. Goodson, 253 F.2d 900 (8th Cir. 1958), and In re King, 239 N.E.2d 875 (N.Y. 1968); but see

Warfield v. Merchants National Bank, 147 N.E.2d 809 (Mass. 1958) (citing but refusing to follow *Goodson*). It might be argued that the maximum amount of tax that could be collected from such property under the transferee liability rules in §6324(a)(2) (an amount equal to the asset's federal estate tax value) should be the only limitation on the decedent's power to alter state or federal apportionment rules.

A particularly difficult issue with respect to nonprobate property concerns employee benefits, includible in the decedent's gross estate under §2039 but typically passing by virtue of the beneficiary designation, outside probate. No serious tax apportionment problem is raised with respect to employee benefit payments made in a lump sum because the recipient has the funds to make immediate payment. Thus, taxes attributable to §2039 easily can be apportioned to the beneficiary. However, because most employee benefits are designated for an installment or annuity payout, and because federal law does not grant a right of reimbursement with respect to these assets, apportionment can then be a significant issue because the amount of wealth tied up in the employee benefit plan is likely to generate a significant portion of the tax bill. There has been talk about adding a clone of §2207A or §2207B to apply with respect to §2039, or extending the tax deferral authority of §6163 with respect to installment payments. Until such action is taken, however, clients must be mindful of tax payment provisions when selecting employee death benefit payout options, to insure liquidity will exist if needed to pay any taxes due, including the income tax that usually also burdens these amounts.

Chapter 14

INTER VIVOS TRANSFERS
SUBJECT TO GIFT TAXATION

Part A. Computation of the Gift Tax
Part B. Transactions Subject to Gift Taxation
Part C. Gift Tax Deductions
Part D. Split Gifts

1.   *Overview.*   Some property transferred inter vivos is subject only to gift taxation, some is subject only to estate taxation, and some is subject to both taxes. The latter two categories are the topic of Chapters 4 through 9. The first category is addressed in this Chapter. As explained in Chapter 13, the computation of a decedent's estate tax reflects gifts made after 1976, even if the donated property is not includible in the decedent's gross estate at death. At first glance you might conclude that the unified transfer tax system is designed to make the total tax cost of making donative transfers essentially the same regardless of whether transfers are made during life, at death, or partly each. We will see in the first segment of this Chapter that the unified system does not provide complete equality of tax burden and was not designed to do so, notwithstanding lip service to the notion that it should not matter when a taxpayer transfers wealth. The system intentionally provides a lower overall tax cost for inter vivos gifts than is imposed on testamentary transfers, although often the message sent is that this also is not true. There are two essential differences in the treatment of inter vivos and testamentary transfers that make this reality so, and they are discussed below. Other factors that also can benefit taxpayers who make inter vivos gifts are the lax enforcement of the gift tax in actual practice, and the government's less than diligent and effective determination of values for gift tax purposes. Overall, we will soon see that making inter vivos gifts is the cheapest way to transfer wealth, and the reality is that only the very wealthy can afford to make gifts and even they seldom take advantage of the many benefits of inter vivos transfers.

It may be helpful at this point to review Chapter 1, where a brief overview of the gift tax appears.

PART A.   COMPUTATION OF THE GIFT TAX

Code References: *Gift Tax: §§2502(a), 2503(b), 2504(a), 2505(a),
6075(b)*

**2.   *The Gift Tax Rate Structure (Marginal Rates, the Unified
Credit, and the Annual Exclusion).***   The gift tax is an excise on the
gratuitous transfer of property during life. The tax was computed and
collected annually from 1932 (when the modern gift tax was enacted) until
the beginning of 1971. The gift tax was computed and collected quarterly
from 1971 through 1981 (with certain exceptions). Since 1982 the gift tax
is reported and collected annually, on a calendar year basis, with the return
due on April 15 following the calendar year in which a gift was made. If the
date for the donor to file an income tax return for that calendar year is
extended, the date for filing the gift tax return automatically is extended for
the same period. §§6019(a), 6075(b)(1) and (b)(2). An extension of the time
to file is not, however, an extension of the time within which to pay the tax.
§6151(a). Thus, a separate request to delay the time for payment is necessary to avoid imposition of additional charges for a late payment accompanying a timely filing of an extended return.

The gift tax is not an annual tax on gifts in the same way that the
income tax is an annual tax on income. The gift tax is a cumulative tax imposed on gifts made during the donor's entire life, meaning that the progressive gift tax rates do not start anew each year beginning at the bottom rate
(as is the case for income tax rates). See §2502(a). This lifetime progressivity reflects the fact that, unlike testamentary transfers, inter vivos gifts
typically are not made all at once.

The original gift tax (enacted in 1924 and repealed in 1926) was an
annual tax on gifts, imposed on a given year's gifts without regard to gifts
made in prior years. Thus, although the gift tax rates were graduated, each
year the donor started with a clean slate at the bottom rates in the progressive tables and the maximum rate of tax depended only upon the value
of the donor's gifts in that year. Coupled with a $50,000 annual exemption,
this made the 1924 gift tax ineffectual.

Congress did not make the same mistake in 1932 when the gift tax was
reinstated. As the committee reports stated:

[T]he design is to impose a tax which measurably approaches the
estate tax which would have been payable on the donor's death
had the gifts not been made. . . . The theory . . . is that the rate of
tax is measured by all gifts made after the enactment of the bill.
This scheme is adopted in order to tax gifts made over a period of
years at the same rate as if they had all been made within one
year.

H.R. Rep. No. 708, 72d Cong., 1st Sess. 28-29 (1932), in 1939-1 C.B. (pt. 2) 457, 477; S. Rep. No. 665, 72d Cong., 1st Sess. 40-41 (1932), in 1939-1 C.B. (pt. 2) 496, 525. It was not until the unified rate structure was adopted in 1976, however, that a cumulative tax on both inter vivos and testamentary transfers was effected. The 1932 gift tax granted a lifetime exemption (repealed in 1976), an annual exclusion (to permit modest gifts to be made without filing a return or incurring a tax), and a schedule of graduated marginal rates that were only three-fourths of the estate tax rates on testamentary transfers of like amounts. This system provided strong incentives to make inter vivos transfers rather than waiting until death to incur the wealth transfer tax.

When the estate and gift tax rate structures were unified in 1976, the gift tax rate imposed on gifts made after 1976 became the same as the estate tax rate schedule in §2001, and the specific exemption previously applicable to gifts was replaced with the unified credit that we studied in Chapter 13. Continuing the approach adopted in 1932, the tax rate applied to gifts depends upon the aggregate amount of taxable gifts made by the donor since 1932.[1]

In lieu of the specific exemption allowed for pre-1977 gifts, the tax otherwise payable on gifts made after 1976 is reduced by the unified credit granted by §2505. This credit, which was introduced in 1976 and greatly increased in steps to the present applicable exclusion amount, is the same credit allowed at death under §2010. The unified credit available to a donor for gifts made in any calendar year is reduced by the aggregate amount of unified credit "allowable" to the donor for gifts made in prior calendar periods.

The unified credit available against the tax imposed on subsequent gifts is reduced even if, for some reason, a donor deliberately does not utilize the unified credit to offset the gift tax for a prior calendar period. In Rev. Rul. 79-398 the Commissioner ruled that the unified credit must be used when available — it cannot be "saved" for a later transfer — and that any credit allowable to offset a gift tax is deemed exhausted regardless of whether the

---

1. Although no specific exemption is allowed for gifts made after 1976, the amount of taxable gifts made before 1977 is reduced by up to $30,000 of specific exemption allowed for any prior taxable period, which effectively reduces the rate at which post-1976 gifts are taxed. For example, if D made $40,000 of taxable gifts prior to 1977 and now makes a taxable gift of another $10,000, the total inter vivos transfers of $50,000 would be reduced by as much as $30,000 of specific exemption claimed and allowed on the pre-1977 gifts, causing the present gift to incur tax at the rates for transfers between $10,000 and $20,000 (the 20% bracket) rather than the rate for transfers between $40,000 and $50,000 (the 24% bracket). Notice, however, that if the $40,000 of prior gifts only utilized a portion of the $30,000 specific exemption, only that portion allowed would be reflected now. For example, if D made pre-1977 taxable gifts of only $10,000 and another $30,000 of taxable gifts were made in prior years but after 1976, the same total of $50,000 would be the starting figure in the tax computation but it would be reduced only by the $10,000 of exemption allowed pre-1977, leaving the $10,000 current gift to be taxed at the rates that apply to gifts of amounts between $30,000 and $40,000 (the 22% bracket).

donor actually utilized the credit to reduce the tax paid. The real reason for this "use it or lose it" regime was the then applicable gift tax statute of limitation on the government's ability to challenge the value assigned to gifted property. Before amendments made in 1997 the statute of limitation would run on the government's ability to challenge the taxpayer's valuation of the donated property if the donor could make a gift of property in kind and pay a gift tax by choosing not to claim the available unified credit. This no longer is true, but the Rev. Rul. 79-398 dictate remains applicable.

Although computation of the gift tax on transfers made after 1976 is no more complicated than was the computation of the tax on pre-1977 gifts, complexity may arise at the donor's death because of the unified tax computation regime in §2001(b). As noted in Chapter 13, a decedent's "tentative" estate tax is computed by applying the estate tax rates to the sum of the decedent's taxable estate and all "adjusted taxable gifts" (all post-1976 taxable gifts that are not includible in the decedent's gross estate under §§2035-2042). This tentative tax on the decedent's aggregate unified transfers then is reduced under §2001(b)(2) by any gift tax already incurred (actually, by the amount of gift tax that would have been payable on transfers made by the decedent after 1976 if the gift tax rate schedule that is in effect at the decedent's death had been applicable at the date of that transfer; do you see the two reasons why this refinement might be important?),[2] which leaves the donor's estate to pay only the increase in tax attributable to the property that is taxable at death.

The resulting estate tax (the tentative tax reduced by the gift tax already incurred) then is reduced by all allowable credits, including the unified credit. Although it may appear that the unified credit thus is allowed twice to decedents who made gifts (once against the gift tax and a second time against the estate tax), the benefit derived from the unified credit is not duplicated by making inter vivos gifts. This is because the reduction for gift taxes previously incurred includes only the amount of gift taxes that were payable;[3] the amount of gift tax on inter vivos transfers that was not payable because of the availability of the unified credit does not reduce the amount of the decedent's estate tax liability. The total amount of the decedent's "adjusted taxable gifts," including those gifts as to which no gift tax was payable because of the unified credit, increases the amount on which the decedent's tentative estate tax is computed, and no gift tax offset is allowed with respect to those effectively "tax-free" prior gifts. The effect is the same as if those "tax-free" gifts had never been made and had instead

---

2. One reason is to protect the government by denying a credit based on higher tax rates when the gift was made if the rates declined before the decedent's death. The other reason is to protect the taxpayer if the tax increases, which may occur if Congress raises the rates or if the government revalues a gift. See Estate of Smith v. Commissioner, 94 T.C. 872 (1990), reproduced at page 869.

3. One reason that the term "payable" (rather than "paid") is used in §2001(b)(2) is that the tax may not actually have been paid at the time of the decedent's death.

passed at death as part of the decedent's testamentary transfers. Thus, allowing the full unified credit in determining the estate tax liability for the decedent's estate does not constitute a double allowance of the same credit and is quite proper. The absence of a gift tax offset against the tentative estate tax eliminates any perceived benefit from the inter vivos use of the unified credit.[4]

3.   *Mechanics of the Computation.*   Consider the manner in which §§2502, 2504, and 2505 operate to provide graduated rates for gifts made periodically during a donor's life. Also note the changes that have occurred over the years in the amount of the specific exemption (which was repealed in 1976) and the annual exclusion (both as recorded in Treas. Reg. §§25.2504-1(a) and -1(b)).

To illustrate, let's assume that *A* made no gifts prior to 1975, in which year *A* gave $4,000 to each of four children and six grandchildren (a total of $40,000 in gifts). In March, 1978, *A* gave $2,000 to each of the four children and in September, 1978, *A* gave $3,000 to each of those four children and to each of the six grandchildren (a total of $5,000 that year to each child and $38,000 in total gifts for that year). The annual exclusion in each of these years was $3,000 per donee per year. In July of 1982, *A* gave stocks valued at $210,000 to child *S* and, in October of that same year, *A* deeded real estate having a fair market value of $130,000 to child *D*. The annual exclusion had grown to $10,000 per donee per year by this time. Earlier this current year, *A* forgave a $150,000 bona fide debt represented by a note from *A*'s sibling. If *A* made no further gifts and died in the current year, you can compute *A*'s "adjusted taxable gifts" for purposes of computing the estate tax under §2001. Try to do that now, remembering in each case to exclude the amount of the allowable annual exclusions in each year for each donee. If you did not come up with $8,000, $320,000, and $140,000, you probably overlooked the specific exemption that was applicable in 1975. See §2504(a)(3).

---

4.   To illustrate, suppose that, after 1976, *D* made taxable gifts of $80,000. Suppose further that *D* died leaving a taxable estate of $920,000 (not counting the $80,000 of gifts made by *D*). The gift tax on the gifts was $18,200, but *D* paid no gift tax because *D* used that much of the unified credit. At *D*'s death, the tentative estate tax is computed on the sum of $920,000 (the taxable estate) and $80,000 (the adjusted taxable gifts), resulting in a tax on $1 million of $345,800. Because no gift tax was paid on the gifts, the gross estate tax also will equal $345,800, the same as if *D* had made no inter vivos gifts, had retained the donated property until death, and had used none of the unified credit. At death, the unified credit will reduce *D*'s estate tax payable. If *D* had not made the taxable gifts and therefore had died with a taxable estate of $1 million (assuming that the value of the retained property still was $80,000), the gross estate tax would be $345,800 and, after using the unified credit, the net estate tax payable again would be the same. Thus, *D* did not double the benefit from using the unified credit during life.

4.   *Tax Incentives for Inter Vivos Gifts.*

Purposes of the Gift Tax.   As Explained in H.R. Rep. No. 708, 72d Cong., 1st Sess. 8, 28 (1932), in 1939-1 C.B. (pt. 2) 457, 462, 477:

To assist in the collection of the income and estate taxes, and prevent their avoidance through the splitting up of estates during the lifetime of a taxpayer, your committee recommends a gift tax. . . . The gift tax will supplement both the estate tax and the income tax. It will tend to reduce the incentive to make gifts in order that distribution of future income from the donated property may be to a number of persons with the result that the taxes imposed by the higher brackets of the income tax law are avoided. It will also tend to discourage transfers for the purpose of avoiding the estate tax.

S. Rep. No. 665, 72d Cong., 1st Sess. 11 (1932), in 1939-1 C.B. (pt. 2) 496, 504, also provided: "As a protection to both estate and income taxes, a gift tax is imposed. The rates are approximately three-quarters of the estate tax rates."

Notwithstanding adoption of the gift tax, when a person had sizeable wealth prior to 1976, there were significant tax reduction incentives for making inter vivos gifts rather than testamentary transfers. See H.R. Rep. No. 1380, 94th Cong., 2d Sess. 15-16 (1976), quoted at pages 753-754 for a list of those incentives.

Unification of the estate and gift tax rates in 1976 eliminated the reduced rate incentive for making inter vivos gifts; much of the tax savings that previously could be obtained no longer is available. Nevertheless, important tax benefits still can be derived from making inter vivos gifts in a manner that avoids inclusion of the property in the donor's gross estate at death. One modest benefit in the current income tax bracket environment is a reduction of the income tax imposed on income from donated property. This reduction is available only to the extent the donee is taxed on the income in a lower marginal income tax bracket than the donor. A more significant advantage is avoiding estate tax on the income that remains after payment of income tax; this element is shifted out of the donor's gross estate at death.

A larger potential benefit is that post-transfer appreciation in donated property escapes the transfer tax. This can be advantageous even if other growth property must be sold by the donor to pay the tax on the gift, but only if the tax rate system retains any progressivity; once it becomes a flat tax rate system this benefit disappears.[5] Another benefit is the estate tax

---

5.   To illustrate, if *D* owned nothing that could be gifted (or used to pay the gift tax) currently except stock in the *X* Corporation, which will double in value before *D*'s death,

savings attributable to inter vivos transfers that qualify for the gift tax annual exclusion. For example, for electing spouses, qualifying transfers of up to $22,000 (the current §2503(b) figure, indexed for inflation) per donee per year are not subject to either gift or estate tax, and there is no comparable exclusion if a donor waits until death to transfer property.

Finally, perhaps the most important advantage from making inter vivos gifts, as explicitly acknowledged by Congress when adopting the 1976 Act, is that the gift tax computation is tax exclusive while the estate tax is tax inclusive. That is, although gift taxes offset the subsequent estate tax, the gift tax payment itself is not subject to the estate tax (unless §2035(b) is triggered). This amounts to granting an estate tax exclusion for the gift tax that was paid. To illustrate, if D were willing to part with $100x currently and is in a 30% tax bracket, D could make a gift of $76.92x and use the remaining $23.08x to pay the 30% gift tax on that $76.92x gift. If, however, D waited until death to transfer the $100x, a tax of 30% on that $100x would leave only $70x for D's beneficiary. The difference in result to D's beneficiary is that the gift tax is not imposed on the $23.08x used to pay the gift tax (a "tax exclusive" computation) while the estate tax is imposed on the full $100x, both the $70x that reaches the beneficiary and the $30x used to pay the estate tax (a "tax inclusive" computation).

The fact that gift tax payments are excluded from transfer taxation whereas estate tax payments are not raises the question: which is the more appropriate treatment? The wealth transfer (estate or gift) taxes are imposed on the privilege of disposing of property. They are a *transfer* tax on the gratuitous transmission of wealth. The estate or gift tax paid on a transfer of property is a cost of disposing of the transferred property and not a gratuitous transfer itself. The tax exclusive gift tax computation is consistent with the notion of a transfer tax, and the tax inclusive estate tax computation might seem out of sync. To grant a comparable estate tax exclusion, however, would require an interrelated computation (to exclude the tax requires that you know the amount of tax on the amount that remains after you exclude the tax, which you can't compute until you determine the amount to be excluded). Although an algebraic formula exists to solve the equation, it is complicated if more than one rate bracket is

---

two options are available. D could hold the stock until death, letting its value double and paying estate tax on double the present value, or D could pay gift tax on its current value and lose the appreciation on the stock that must be sold to generate the cash to pay the tax. For example, if the donated stock is worth $10 today and D's marginal tax bracket is 30%, a gift today would incur $3 of gift tax; the transferred stock will be worth $20 at D's death. Alternatively, D could keep the full $13 of stock ($10 worth that otherwise would have been gifted and $3 worth that would have been sold to pay the gift tax), which would double in value to $26 before D dies. An estate tax at a 30% rate on $26 would be $7.80, leaving only $18.20 to pass to the donee. The gift provides the donee with an additional $1.80. That saving is *not* attributable to shifting the appreciation on the X stock. To what *is* it attributable? Consider §2035(b) and why, even if it is applicable, it still does not eliminate all the benefit allowed here.

involved; and the same result can be generated more easily merely by reducing the estate tax rates.[6] This may not be viable because of political considerations.

Indeed, the Treasury Department occasionally suggests that, to complete the purported unification of estate and gift tax rates begun in 1976, the gift tax computation should be changed to match the estate tax (also not an easy chore, because it requires that a gift tax be computed on the gift tax paid, and then a gift tax on that tax payment would be computed and paid, and then a tax on the tax on the tax, ad nauseam — again subject to an algebraic short-cut). At present, it is conceded implicitly that the rates of the two taxes are not unified and never were intended to be. Although the nominal rates are identical, the exclusion of gift tax payments from the gift tax base effectively produces a lower tax rate than is applied to testamentary transfers. This is thought by some to be desirable because it encourages inter vivos transfers that fragment wealth holdings and generate tax payments sooner.

In 1984 the Treasury Department promulgated proposals for wealth transfer tax reform that included a proposed abandonment of the unified estate and gift tax rate table in favor of a separate gift tax rate table that contained higher rates of tax on the amount actually given to a donee. Under that table the tax computed on the actual transfer made by gift would translate into a rate of tax (on a "grossed-up" basis) equal to what the gift tax would be on the aggregate amount of the transfer and the tax combined. Although that proposal would have produced effective unification, it was deemed politically unacceptable because the tax rates required to produce the desired effect were too high — in some cases over 100%!

The Treasury opined that its proposal would raise revenue in two ways. One was by collecting more tax on increased gifting prior to the effective date of the tax inclusive proposal, and the other was by collecting higher taxes on those (fewer?) gifts made after the effective date of the proposal. Do you think that the adoption of the Treasury proposal would reduce gifting because of the elimination of one of the principal tax benefits from gifting? If so, does that make the proposal unwise?

---

6.   The first modern federal income tax law, which was passed after the adoption of the Sixteenth Amendment, provided that federal income tax payments themselves were deductible in determining taxable income. Revenue Act of 1913, ch. 16, §II(B). The deduction for federal income tax payments was repealed by the Revenue Act of 1917 and was never reinstated. Revenue Act of 1917, ch. 63, §1200. In discussing this deduction, it has been noted that, "if a tax is deductible in computing the tax itself, one rate is a function of the other. It is therefore possible to design a rate schedule for a 'nondeductible' tax that will produce the same revenue as a seemingly higher rate schedule would produce if the tax were deductible from the base." Turnier, *Evaluating Personal Deductions in an Income Tax — The Ideal*, 66 CORNELL L. REV. 262, 267 (1981). See also 55 Cong. Rec. 6322 (1917) (remarks of Sen. Smoot). The same principle applies to the estate tax.

Policy Considerations.   Is it clear that sound tax policy requires that the tax cost of inter vivos and testamentary transfers be approximately the same? Consider the following excerpts, written before the 1976 unification of those taxes.

From C. Shoup, FEDERAL ESTATE AND GIFT TAXES 17-18 (1966):

Not only is the yield of the gift tax very small relative to that of the estate tax . . . but the number of returns and the dollar value of gifts each year are likewise very small. And we know from special statistical studies made by the Treasury Department that there are few individuals who transfer enough during their lifetimes to even approach the dividing line between inter vivos gifts and transfers at death that would minimize the combined gift tax and estate tax.

From L. Thurow, GENERATING INEQUALITY 139-142 (1975):

The mystery of large fortunes at time of death is further compounded by the U.S. tax law. Under our laws a substantial amount of money can be given to the next generation tax-free if it is given before death, and all of it can be given at much lower tax rates than if wealth is transferred at death and subject to estate taxation. If a person were really interested in the future consumption of his children, the tax laws provide a strong incentive to transfer the desired wealth before death. Yet very little use is made of this loophole. Parents do not give their money away before death even though their children would have much more wealth if they did so. Such actions hardly square with the view of parents sacrificing themselves and accumulating wealth to raise the consumption standards of their children. When given a tax-free or low-tax method to take care of their children, they do not use it. As a result, some other motivation must be found to explain large fortunes at death and the absence of deaccumulation.

Sometimes uncertainties about the precise time of death are used to explain the pattern of wealth accumulation. . . .

Although this explanation focuses on a valid problem, it once again does not explain what needs to be explained. The great fortunes exceed anything that would be needed as insurance against the uncertainties of death, and as long as an individual can trust his own children it still pays to give away all of his wealth before death. It also ignores the existence of annuities. Annuities allow an individual to insure himself some desired level of consumption for the rest of his life regardless of the uncertainties about future longevity.

The motive that has been left out of neoclassical economics is that of economic power — within either the family or the community. . . .

The role of economic power helps us understand why more individuals do not use the tax loophole of transferring their assets before death. The problem is that to do so is to give up economic power. Parents typically fear that their children will not give the assets back if they need them (unexpected medical bills, etc.), or they fear that they will not have "respect" or "filial" devotion if the family assets are transferred before death. To give up economic power within the family is to give up one's status and station. Few individuals are willing to give up their economic power even vis-á-vis their own children.

For a similar reason individuals do not buy annuities even though they would guarantee consumption expenditures over an uncertain future. To buy an annuity is to give up exactly what the individual wants — economic power. Your assets are given to some institution in exchange for a guaranteed lifetime stream of income. You lose control.

. . . The holder of wealth has some leverage to redesign his family, private charities, the economy, and the political structure in his own image. . . . The net result of a desire for economic power is an accumulation of wealth and a transmittal of wealth that is irrational from the point of view of simple consumption economics.

There are notable exceptions to this theory, such as Sam Walton, founder of Wal-Mart Inc., who divided his estate among his children during life, effectively saving hundreds of millions of dollars in tax when he died in 1992. Given these observations, was Congress correct in 2001 when it retained the gift tax while, at the same time, it repealed the estate and generation-skipping transfer taxes (effective in 2010, for just one year, under the sunset budget gimmick also adopted in 2001)? What was *that* about? Hint: think about which taxes remain.

PART B.   TRANSACTIONS SUBJECT TO GIFT TAXATION

References: *Gift Tax: §§2501(a)(1), 2501(a)(5), 2503, 2511(a), 2512, 2514, 2516, 2518, 7872*
State Law: Uniform Transfers to Minors Act

5.   House of Representatives Report No. 708, 72d Cong., 1st Sess. 27 (1932), reprinted in 1939-1 C.B. (pt. 2) 457, 476:

The tax applies only to gifts made by individuals. . . .

The terms "property," "transfer," "gift," and "indirectly" are used in the broadest and most comprehensive sense; the term "property" reaching every species of right or interest protected by law and having an exchangeable value.

The words "transfer . . . by gift" and "whether . . . direct or indirect" are designed to cover and comprehend all transactions (subject to certain express conditions and limitations) whereby, and to the extent [under §2512(b)] that, property or a property right is donatively passed to or conferred upon another, regardless of the means or the device employed in its accomplishment.

The Senate Finance Committee report contains essentially the same statement. S. Rep. No. 665, 72d Cong., 1st Sess. 39 (1932), reprinted in 1939-1 C.B. (pt. 2) 496, 524.

A gift made by an incompetent's lawfully appointed guardian, if authorized, is attributed to the incompetent and taxed accordingly. Rev. Rul. 67-280; Commissioner v. Greene, 119 F.2d 383 (9th Cir. 1941).

6.   *What Is a "Gift" of "Property"?* Section 2501 imposes a tax on the "transfer of property by gift." The term "gift" is not expressly defined in the Code, in the Treasury Regulations, or in the excerpt above from the committee reports that accompanied enactment of the modern gift tax in 1932. Section 2512(b), dealing with the valuation of gifts, states that "where property is transferred for less than an adequate and full consideration in money or money's worth," the difference between the value of the property transferred and the consideration received constitutes a gift. (Generally speaking, the valuation of property subject to gift taxation is governed by the same principles that govern estate tax valuation, as discussed in Part B of Chapter 2. See §2512 and the regulations thereto.) Thus, for gift tax purposes, with only a couple of exceptions, the transferor's subjective intent is irrelevant; a gift is made if property is transferred without full and adequate consideration in money or money's worth. Treas. Reg. §25.2511-1(g)(1). One exception is the Business Transaction Exception, which applies to transfers made "in the ordinary course of business," regardless of whether full and adequate consideration was received. Treas. Reg. §25.2512-8 defines a transaction in the ordinary course of business as one that is "bona fide, at arm's length, and free from any donative intent." Thus, the gift tax is not imposed on the sale of property for less than its market value if the seller made a business judgment error. Weller v. Commissioner, 38 T.C. 790 (1962), *acq.* The business transaction exception is not, however, restricted to strictly business activities. Rather, it is applicable to any transfer of property that is made for profit motives or for the purpose of making a bona fide economic settlement of a claim against the transferor. See Beveridge v. Commissioner, 10 T.C. 915 (1948), *acq.*; Friedman v. Commissioner, 40 T.C. 714 (1963), *acq.*

Let's take an example. Picture *E* as a valued employee of Symington, Inc. *E* has no significant shareholder interest in the corporation and is not related to any of the shareholders. In appreciation of *E*'s services, the company sold to *E* for $10,000 a plot of land valued at $50,000. What are the gift tax consequences of the sale, and who would be the donor? See Estate of Anderson v. Commissioner, 8 T.C. 706 (1947). Would it make a difference if *E* worked for *D*, an individual, rather than for a corporation, and it was *D* who sold the land to *E*? How would your answer differ if *D* and *E* are related? Consider the following on the issue of the business transaction exception:

Revenue Ruling 80-196

. . . In 1979, *A* and *B*, individual founders of corporation *X*, each owned 50% of the 30,000 shares outstanding of the common stock of *X*. *X* employed 200 individuals. On December 31, 1979, *A* and *B* each transferred 100 shares of *X* to *N*, *O*, and *P* as a bonus in consideration of past services to *X*. *N*, *O*, and *P* were key employees of *X*, had provided exceptional duties to *X* for more than 5 years, and were considered valuable to the continued success of *X*. . . . Neither *A* nor *B* was related to *N*, *O*, or *P*, nor did any special personal relationship exist with *N*, *O*, or *P*. . . .

Treas. Reg. §25.2511-1(g)(1) provides that donative intent on the part of a transferor is not an essential element in the application of the gift tax to a transfer. Whether the gift tax is applicable is based upon the objective facts of the transfer and the circumstances under which it is made, rather than on the subjective motives of the donor. The tax, however, is not applicable to transfers for full and adequate consideration in money or money's worth or to ordinary business transactions. Under Treas. Reg. §25.2512-8 a transfer of property made in the ordinary course of business (a transaction that is bona fide, at arm's length, and free of donative intent) will be considered as made for adequate and full consideration. Estate of Anderson v. Commissioner, 8 T.C. 706 (1947); Bryan v. Commissioner, 16 T.C. 972 (1951); Weller v. Commissioner, 38 T.C. 790 (1962).

In *Weller* the court noted that donative intent is not a requisite for a gift for tax purposes. However, the absence of donative intent is relevant under the regulations in determining whether a transfer is made in the ordinary course of business.

Section 2512(b) of the Code provides that where property is transferred for less than an adequate and full consideration in money or money's worth, then the amount by which the value of the property exceeded the value of the consideration shall be deemed a gift and shall be included in computing the amount of gifts during the calendar [year]. However, under Treas. Reg. §25.2512-8, a transfer of property made in the ordinary course of business (a transaction which is bona fide, at arm's length, and free from donative intent) will be considered as made for an adequate and full consideration in money or money's worth.

The transfer of 100 shares by each of *A* and *B* to each of *N, O,* and *P* were in the ordinary course of business, since they were motivated by a valid business reason, that is, retaining valuable personnel in the employment of *X.* Thus, the transfers are considered as made for adequate and full consideration for gift tax purposes. Therefore, the transfers by *A* and *B* are not subject to the gift tax.

What would be the gift tax consequence in a case like Rev. Rul. 80-196 if *A* transferred 200 shares of *X* stock to three employees but *B* made no matching transfer? Would there be a gift from *A* to *B*; if so, of what amount? Should the annual exclusion be allowed for such a gift? The taxpayer in PLR 9114023 proposed what was deemed to be transfers of shares of the taxpayer's stock in a corporation to unrelated key employees as a bonus for their contributions to the growth and success of the corporation. The stock transfers in Rev. Rul. 80-196 were made proportionately by the shareholders, so there was no gift between the shareholders. But in PLR 9114023, only one of the shareholders was going to make the stock transfer. Because the other shareholders of the corporation were not going to make matching contributions, the PLR held that the stock transfers would benefit the corporation and constitute a capital contribution to the corporation that amounts to indirect gifts to the noncontributing shareholders. Furthermore, the government held that those gifts would not qualify as present interests for annual exclusion purposes because the noncontributing shareholders would not have an immediate right to possession or enjoyment of the capital increase represented by those transfers. See Treas. Reg. §25.2511-1(h)(1). The annual exclusion is discussed beginning at page 876.

Although the gift tax applies only to transfers by individuals, a transfer of property by an entity (such as a corporation) may be attributed to individuals (e.g., the corporation's shareholders). See Treas. Reg. §25.2511-1(h)(1); H.R. Rep. No. 708, 72d Cong., 1st Sess. 28 *Example (1)* (1932), in 1939-1 C.B. (pt. 2) 457, 476-477.

Political Contributions.   *B,* who owns substantial interests in oil and gas leases, contributed $15,000 to the campaign fund of a candidate for the United States Senate from *B*'s state. *B* backs candidates who advocate maintaining tax preferences for owners of hydrocarbon interests. Because Congress felt that "the tax system should not be used to reduce or restrict political contributions," §2501(a)(5) was enacted in 1975. S. Rep. No. 1357, 93d Cong., 2d Sess. (1975), in 1975-1 C.B. 517, 535. Thus, *B* did not make a taxable gift. Prior to the adoption of §2501(a)(5), Stern v. United States, 436 F.2d 1327 (5th Cir. 1971), had applied the business transaction exception to a transfer of this kind but the government had announced its intention to litigate the issue further. Rev. Rul. 72-583; Rev. Rul. 72-355. Now §2501(a)(5) appears to resolve cases of this type.

7.   *Will Contest Settlements.*   Property received by an heir of a decedent (or a legatee of a prior will) pursuant to a bona fide settlement of a claim that the decedent's last will was invalid is treated as property inherited directly from the decedent (or bequeathed from the decedent). Lyeth v. Hoey, 305 U.S. 188 (1938). For example, *D* executed a will bequeathing $100,000 to *A*, residue to *B*. Later, *D* executed a second will, expressly revoking the first will and excluding *A* as a beneficiary. After *D*'s death, *A* claimed that the second will was invalid because of undue influence, and *B* agreed to settle *A*'s claim by consenting to *A* receiving $50,000 from *D*'s estate. If the settlement was bona fide, *A* will be deemed for tax purposes to have received the $50,000 as a bequest from *D*. Thus, *A* will have no adverse income tax consequences, and *B* will have no gift tax consequences. The tax laws would create a disincentive to settle disputes if bona fide settlements were not so treated. A court judgment that *A* was to receive property as legatee clearly would not impose adverse tax consequences. See also Farley v. United States, 581 F.2d 821 (Cl. Ct. 1978).

If, however, the claim of an heir or legatee to a share of a decedent's estate is insubstantial and the "settlement" is not bona fide, then the transaction is treated as a voluntary rearrangement of the decedent's property, which can cause adverse income, estate, and gift tax consequences. See Hardenberg v. Commissioner, 198 F.2d 63 (8th Cir. 1952); Commissioner v. Estate of Vease, 314 F.2d 79 (9th Cir. 1963). See Kemp, *How to Achieve Optimum Income, Gift, and Estate Tax Benefits in a Will Contest*, 38 J. TAX'N 285 (1973).

It is noteworthy that the Internal Revenue Service instructs its revenue agents to be alert to possible gift tax consequences if heirs agree to distribute property in some way other than that provided by the decedent's will or by state statute. Internal Revenue Service, Audit Technique Handbook for Estate Tax Examiners (26)92(2). The most prevalent area in which settlements are challenged is if they affect transfers to a surviving spouse or to charity, in which case the government may seek to disallow a claimed deduction based thereon.

To set the stage, imagine that *A* is an attorney who performed legal services for the spouse of *A*'s cousin, at no charge. The fair market value of the services was $12,000. Is there any gift tax consequence? Commissioner v. Hogle, 165 F.2d 352 (10th Cir. 1948). Compare Rev. Rul. 66-167, next below. According to §107(2) of the RESTATEMENT OF RESTITUTION (1937), "in the absence of circumstances indicating otherwise, it is inferred that a person who requests another to perform services for him . . . thereby bargains to pay therefor." How does this principle bear on the solution to the problem?

Revenue Ruling 66-167

The Internal Revenue Service has given further consideration to Rev. Rul. 56-472, 1956-2 C.B. 21, and Rev. Rul. 64-225, 1964-2 C.B. 15, which relate to the waiver of commissions by executors and similar fiduciaries.

In the instant case, the taxpayer served as the sole executor of his deceased wife's estate pursuant to the terms of a will under which he and his adult son were each given a half interest in the net proceeds thereof. The laws of the state in which the will was executed and probated impose no limitation on the use of either principal or income for the payment of compensation to an executor and do not purport to deal with whether a failure to withdraw any particular fee or commission may properly be considered as a waiver thereof.

The taxpayer's administration of his wife's estate continued for a period of approximately three full years during which time he filed two annual accountings as well as the usual final accounting with the probate court, all of which reported the collection and disposition of a substantial amount of estate assets.

At some point within a reasonable time after first entering upon the performance of his duties as executor, the taxpayer decided to make no charge for serving in such capacity, and each of the aforesaid accountings accordingly omitted any claim for statutory commissions and was so filed with the intention to waive the same. The taxpayer-executor likewise took no other action which was inconsistent with a fixed and continuing intention to serve on a gratuitous basis.

The specific questions presented are whether the amounts which the taxpayer-executor could have received as fees or commissions are includible in his gross income for Federal income tax purposes and whether his waiver of the right to receive these amounts results in a gift for Federal gift tax purposes.

In Rev. Rul. 56-472, the executor of an estate entered into an agreement to serve in such capacity for substantially less than all of the statutory commissions otherwise allowable to him and also formally waived his right to receive the remaining portion thereof. The basic agreement with respect to his acceptance of a reduced amount of compensation antedated the performance of any services and the related waiver of the disclaimed commissions was signed before he would otherwise have become entitled to receive them. Under these circumstances, the ruling held that the difference between the commissions which such executor could have otherwise acquired an unrestricted right to obtain and the lesser amount which he actually received was not includible in his income and that his disclaimer did not effect any gift thereof.

In Rev. Rul. 64-225, the trustees of a testamentary trust in the State of New York waived their rights to receive one particular class of statutory commissions. This waiver was effected by means of certain formal instruments that were not executed until long after the close of most of the years to which such commissions related. This circumstance, along with all the other facts described therein, indicated that such trustees had not intended to render their services on a gratuitous basis. The Revenue Ruling accordingly held that such commissions were includible in the trustees' gross income for the taxable year when so waived and that their execution of the waivers also effected a taxable gift of these commissions.

The crucial test of whether the executor of an estate or any other fiduciary in a similar situation may waive his right to receive statutory commissions without thereby incurring any income or gift tax liability is whether the waiver involved will at least primarily constitute evidence of an intent to render a gratuitous service. If the timing, purpose, and effect of the waiver make it serve any other important objective, it may then be proper to conclude that the fiduciary has thereby enjoyed a realization of income by means of controlling the disposition thereof, and at the same time, has also effected a taxable gift by means of any resulting transfer to a third party of his contingent beneficial interest in a part of the assets under his fiduciary control. See the above cited Revenue Rulings and the authorities therein cited, as well as Treas. Reg. §25.2511-1(c).

The requisite intention to serve on a gratuitous basis will ordinarily be deemed to have been adequately manifested if the executor or administrator of an estate supplies one or more of the decedent's principal legatees or devisees, or of those principally entitled to distribution of decedent's intestate estate, within six months after his initial appointment as such fiduciary, with a formal waiver of any right to compensation for his services. Such an intention to serve on a gratuitous basis may also be adequately manifested through an implied waiver, if the fiduciary fails to claim fees or commissions at the time of filing the usual accountings and if all the other attendant facts and circumstances are consistent with a fixed and continuing intention to serve gratuitously. If the executor or administrator of an estate claims his statutory fees or commissions as a deduction on one or more of the estate, inheritance, or income tax returns which are filed on behalf of the estate, such action will ordinarily be considered inconsistent with any fixed or definite intention to serve on a gratuitous basis. No such claim was made in the instant case.

Accordingly, the amounts which the present taxpayer-executor would have otherwise become entitled to receive as fees or commissions are not includible in his gross income for Federal income tax purposes, and are not gifts for Federal gift tax purposes.

Rev. Rul. 56-472 is clarified to remove any implication that although an executor effectively waives his right to receive commissions, such commissions are includible in his gross income unless the waiver is executed prior to performance of any service.

Rev. Rul. 64-225 is distinguished.

See also Rev. Rul. 70-237, in which the Commissioner reached a similar conclusion with respect to a trustee's formal waiver of an increase in statutory fees executed by the trustee "shortly after" the increase was enacted.

8.   *Below Market Interest Loans.*   In Crown v. Commissioner, 67 T.C. 1060 (1977), *aff'd*, 585 F.2d 234 (7th Cir. 1978), the taxpayer loaned substantial amounts (close to $20 million) to children and other close family members interest free, repayable on demand, which loans the government alleged constituted a gift equal to the value of the foregone interest (roughly $1 million per year) on the indebtedness. The government argued that a loan at less than the true economic rate of interest bestows an economic benefit on the recipient in violation of the purpose of the gift tax, which is to backstop the estate tax. According to the government, the lender avoids estate tax on the interest the lender could have charged, the receipt of which would have increased the value of the lender's estate at death. The taxpayer's successful response was that "our income tax system does not recognize unrealized earnings or accumulations of wealth and no taxpayer is under any obligation to continuously invest his money for a profit. The opportunity cost of either letting one's money remain idle or suffering a loss from an unwise investment is not taxable merely because a profit *could have been made* from a wise investment." 67 T.C. 1060, 1067 (1977) (emphasis in the original). Both the Tax Court and the Court of Appeals for the Seventh Circuit sustained the taxpayer's position.

Crown led to extensive use of interest-free demand notes, which came to be known as Crown loans, and set the stage for the following developments, which eliminated virtually all the benefit temporarily made available by *Crown*.

Dickman v. Commissioner
465 U.S. 330 (1984)

BURGER, C.J.: We granted certiorari to resolve a conflict among the Circuits as to whether intrafamily, interest-free demand loans result in taxable gifts of the value of the use of the money lent.

[Paul and Esther Dickman, spouses, made substantial interest-free demand loans to their son, Lyle, and to their closely held business. The Commissioner asserted that these loans constituted taxable gifts to the extent of the value of the use of the loaned funds, determined by multiplying the loan balances outstanding at the end of each taxable quarter by the §6621 interest rates applicable to underpayments of tax. Reaffirming its decision in *Crown*, the Tax Court concluded that intrafamily interest-free demand loans do not result in taxable gifts. The Court of Appeals for the Eleventh Circuit reversed, holding that such loans give rise to gift tax liability, and concluding] that Congress intended the gift tax to have the broadest and most comprehensive coverage possible. The court reasoned that the making of an interest-free demand loan constitutes a "transfer of property by gift" within the meaning of 26 U.S.C. §2501(a)(1), and accordingly is subject to the gift tax provisions of the Code. In so holding, the Court of Appeals squarely rejected the contrary position adopted by the United States Court of Appeals for the Seventh Circuit in *Crown v. Commissioner* . . . . We granted certiorari to resolve this conflict . . . ; we affirm.

. . . The Committee Reports accompanying the Revenue Act of 1932, which established the present scheme of federal gift taxation, make plain that Congress intended the gift tax statute to reach all gratuitous transfers of any valuable interest in property. Among other things, these Reports state:

> "The terms 'property,' 'transfer,' 'gift,' and 'indirectly' are used in the broadest and most comprehensive sense; the term 'property' reaching every species of right or interest protected by law and having an exchangeable value.
>
> "The words 'transfer . . . by gift' and 'whether . . . direct or indirect' are designed to cover and comprehend all transactions . . . whereby, and to the extent . . . that, property or a property right is donatively passed to or conferred upon another, regardless of the means or the device employed in its accomplishment." H. R. Rep. No. 708, 72d Cong., 1st Sess. 27-28 (1932); S. Rep. No. 665, 72d Cong., 1st Sess. 39 (1932).

The plain language of the statute reflects this legislative history; the gift tax was designed to encompass all transfers of property and property rights having significant value.

. . . In asserting that interest-free demand loans give rise to taxable gifts, the Commissioner does not seek to impose the gift tax upon the principal amount of the loan, but only upon the reasonable value of the use of the money lent. The taxable gift that assertedly results from an interest-free demand loan is the value of receiving and using the money without incurring a corresponding obligation to pay interest along with the loan's repayment.[7] Is such a gratuitous transfer of the right to use money a "transfer of property" within the intendment of §2501(a)(1)?

We have little difficulty accepting the theory that the use of valuable property — in this case money — is itself a legally protectible property interest. Of the aggregate rights associated with any property interest, the right of use of property is perhaps of the highest order. . . .

What was transferred here was the use of a substantial amount of cash for an indefinite period of time. An analogous interest in real property, the use under a tenancy at will, has long been recognized as a property right. E.g., RESTATEMENT (SECOND) OF PROPERTY §1.6 (1977). For example, a parent who grants to a child the rent-free, indefinite use of commercial property having a reasonable rental value of $8,000 a month has clearly transferred a valuable property right. The transfer of $100,000 in cash, interest-free and repayable on demand, is similarly a grant of the use of valuable property. Its uncertain tenure may reduce its value, but it does not undermine its status as property. In either instance, when the property owner transfers to another the right to use the object, an identifiable property interest has clearly changed hands. . . .

. . . [T]he gift tax statutes clearly encompass within their broad sweep the gratuitous transfer of the use of money. Just as a tenancy at will in real property is an estate or interest in land, so also is the right to use money a cognizable interest in personal property . . . readily measurable by reference to current interest rates . . . . Accordingly, we conclude that the interest-free loan of funds is a "transfer of property by gift" within the contemplation of the federal gift tax statutes.[8]

---

7. The Commissioner's tax treatment of interest-free demand loans may perhaps be best understood as a two-step approach to such transactions. Under this theory, such a loan has two basic economic components: an arm's-length loan from the lender to the borrower, on which the borrower pays the lender a fair rate of interest, followed by a gift from the lender to the borrower in the amount of that interest. See Crown v. Commissioner, 585 F.2d 234, 240 (7th Cir. 1978).

8. Petitioners argue that no gift tax consequences should attach to interest-free demand loans because no "transfer" of property occurs at the time the loan is made. . . .

In order to make a taxable gift, a transferor must relinquish dominion and control over the transferred property. Treas. Reg. §25.2511-2(b). At the moment an interest-free demand loan is made, the transferor has not given up all dominion and control; he could terminate the transferee's use of the funds by calling the loan. As time passes without a demand for repayment, however, the transferor allows the use of the principal to pass to the transferee, and the gift becomes complete. As the Court of Appeals realized, 690 F.2d at 819, the fact

Our holding that an interest-free demand loan results in a taxable gift of the use of the transferred funds is fully consistent with one of the major purposes of the federal gift tax statute: protection of the estate tax and the income tax. The legislative history of the gift tax provisions reflects that Congress enacted a tax on gifts to supplement existing estate and income tax laws. H.R. Rep. No. 708 at 28; S. Rep. No. 665 at 40. Failure to impose the gift tax on interest-free loans would seriously undermine this estate and income tax protection goal.

A substantial no-interest loan from parent to child creates significant tax benefits for the lender quite apart from the economic advantages to the borrower. This is especially so when an individual in a high income tax bracket transfers income-producing property to an individual in a lower income tax bracket, thereby reducing the taxable income of the high-bracket taxpayer at the expense, ultimately, of all other taxpayers and the Government. Subjecting interest-free loans to gift taxation minimizes the potential loss to the federal fisc generated by the use of such loans as an income tax avoidance mechanism for the transferor. Gift taxation of interest-free loans also effectuates Congress' desire to supplement the estate tax provisions. A gratuitous transfer of income-producing property may enable the transferor to avoid the future estate tax liability that would result if the earnings generated by the property — rent, interest, or dividends — became a part of the transferor's estate. Imposing the gift tax upon interest-free loans bolsters the estate tax by preventing the diminution of the transferor's estate in this fashion.

Petitioners contend that administrative and equitable considerations require a holding that no gift tax consequences result from the making of interest-free demand loans. In support of this position, petitioners advance several policy arguments; none withstands studied analysis.

Petitioners first advance an argument accepted by the Tax Court in *Crown v. Commissioner.*

> "[Our] income tax system does not recognize unrealized earnings or accumulations of wealth and no taxpayer is under any obligation to continuously invest his money for a profit. The opportunity cost of either letting one's money

---

that the transferor's dominion and control over the use of the principal are relinquished over time will become especially relevant in connection with the valuation of the gifts that result from such loans; it does not, however, alter the fact that the lender has made a gratuitous transfer of property subject to the federal gift tax.

remain idle or suffering a loss from an unwise investment is not taxable merely because a profit could have been made from a wise investment." 67 T.C. at 1063-1064.

Thus, petitioners argue, an interest-free loan should not be made subject to the gift tax simply because of the possibility that the money lent might have enhanced the transferor's taxable income or gross estate had the loan never been made.

This contention misses the mark. It is certainly true that no law requires an individual to invest his property in an income-producing fashion, just as no law demands that a transferor charge interest or rent for the use of money or other property. An individual may, without incurring the gift tax, squander money, conceal it under a mattress, or otherwise waste its use value by failing to invest it. Such acts of consumption have nothing to do with lending money at no interest. The gift tax is an excise tax on transfers of property; allowing dollars to lie idle involves no transfer. If the taxpayer chooses not to waste the use value of money, however, but instead transfers the use to someone else, a taxable event has occurred. That the transferor himself could have consumed or wasted the use value of the money without incurring the gift tax does not change this result. Contrary to petitioners' assertion, a holding in favor of the taxability of interest-free loans does not impose upon the transferor a duty profitably to invest; rather, it merely recognizes that certain tax consequences inevitably flow from a decision to make a "transfer of property by gift."

Petitioners next attack the breadth of the Commissioner's view that interest-free demand loans give rise to taxable gifts. Carried to its logical extreme, petitioners argue, the Commissioner's rationale would elevate to the status of taxable gifts such commonplace transactions as a loan of the proverbial cup of sugar to a neighbor or a loan of lunch money to a colleague. Petitioners urge that such a result is an untenable intrusion by the Government into cherished zones of privacy, particularly where intrafamily transactions are involved.

Our laws require parents to provide their minor offspring with the necessities and conveniences of life; questions under the tax law often arise, however, when parents provide more than the necessities, and in quantities significant enough to attract the attention of the taxing authorities. Generally, the legal obligation of support terminates when the offspring reach majority. Nonetheless, it is not uncommon for parents to provide their adult children with such things as the use of cars or vacation cottages, simply on the basis of the family relationship. We assume that the focus of the Internal Revenue Service is not on such traditional familial matters.

When the Government levies a gift tax on routine neighborly or familial gifts, there will be time enough to deal with such a case.

Moreover, the tax law provides liberally for gifts to both family members and others; within the limits of the prescribed statutory exemptions, even substantial gifts may be entirely tax free. First, under §2503(e) of the Code, amounts paid on behalf of an individual for tuition at a qualified educational institution or for medical care are not considered "[transfers] of property by gift" for purposes of the gift tax statutes. More significantly, §2503(b) of the Code provides an annual exclusion from the computation of taxable gifts of $10,000 per year, per donee; this provision allows a taxpayer to give up to $10,000 annually to each of any number of persons, without incurring any gift tax liability. The "split gift" provision of Code §2513(a), which effectively enables a husband and wife to give each object of their bounty $20,000 per year without liability for gift tax, further enhances the ability to transfer significant amounts of money and property free of gift tax consequences. Finally, should a taxpayer make gifts during one year that exceed the §2503(b) annual gift tax exclusion, no gift tax liability will result until the unified credit of Code §2505 has been exhausted. These generous exclusions, exceptions, and credits clearly absorb the sorts of de minimis gifts petitioners envision and render illusory the administrative problems that petitioners perceive in their "parade of horribles."

Finally, petitioners urge that the Commissioner should not be allowed to assert the gift taxability of interest-free demand loans because such a position represents a departure from prior Internal Revenue Service practice. This contention rests on the fact that, prior to 1966, the Commissioner had not construed the gift tax statutes and regulations to authorize the levying of a gift tax on the value of the use of money or property. See Crown v. Commissioner, 585 F.2d at 241; Johnson v. United States, 254 F. Supp. 73 (N.D. Tex. 1966). From this they argue that it is manifestly unfair to permit the Commissioner to impose the gift tax on the transactions challenged here.

Even accepting the notion that the Commissioner's present position represents a departure from prior administrative practice, which is by no means certain,[9] it is well established that the

---

9. The Treasury Regulations implementing the gift tax provisions have always reflected the broad scope of the statutory language. See Treas. Regs. 79, Art. 2 (1933); Treas. Regs. 79, Art. 2 (1936); Treas. Regs. 108, §86.2(a) (1943). The regulation presently in force is virtually identical to those in effect during the preceding five decades. . . . The longstanding interpretation of the statute embodied in these regulations indicates that the Commissioner's allegedly novel

Commissioner may change an earlier interpretation of the law, even if such a change is made retroactive in effect. This rule applies even though a taxpayer may have relied to his detriment upon the Commissioner's prior position. Dixon v. United States, 381 U.S. 68, 73 (1965). The Commissioner is under no duty to assert a particular position as soon as the statute authorizes such an interpretation.[10] Accordingly, petitioners' "taxpayer reliance" argument is unavailing.

As we have noted, Congress has provided generous exclusions and credits designed to reduce the gift tax liability of the great majority of taxpayers. Congress clearly has the power to provide a similar exclusion for the gifts that result from interest-free demand loans. Any change in the gift tax consequences of such loans, however, is a legislative responsibility, not a judicial one. Until such a change occurs, we are bound to effectuate Congress' intent to protect the estate and income tax systems with a broad and comprehensive tax upon all "[transfers] of property by gift."

We hold, therefore, that the interest-free demand loans shown by this record resulted in taxable gifts of the reasonable value of the use of the money lent.[11] Accordingly, the judgment of the United States Court of Appeals for the Eleventh Circuit is Affirmed.

BRENNAN, WHITE, MARSHALL, BLACKMUN, STEVENS, and O'CONNOR concur.

[The dissent of Justice POWELL with whom Justice REHNQUIST joined is omitted.]

The tax treatment (both gift and income tax) of below-market interest rate loans was finally resolved by Congress when it enacted §7872. Does enactment of §7872 imply that other forms of imputed transfer are not meant to be taxed, such as the use of a car or a room in a home?

Section 7872 addresses several different types of below-market interest rate loans, including gift loans, corporation to shareholder loans, and em-

---

assertion in 1966 regarding the gift taxability of interest-free demand loans was not without a reasonable and well-established foundation.

10.   Indeed, the explanation for the dearth of pre-1966 cases presenting this precise issue is probably economic; the low interest rates that prevailed until recent years diminished the attractiveness of the interest-free demand loan as a tax-planning device and reduced the likelihood that the value of such loans would exceed the annual gift tax exclusion.

11.   . . . The valuation issue is . . . not presented on the record before us. We note, however, that to support a gift tax on the transfer of the use of $100,000 for one year, the Commissioner need not establish that the funds lent did in fact produce a particular amount of revenue; it is sufficient for the Commissioner to establish that a certain yield could readily be secured and that the reasonable value of the use of the funds can be reliably ascertained. . . .

ployer to employee loans. The Code provision adopts the general approach of the *Dickman* case, but modifies and expands the tax treatment. Term loans are treated differently than demand loans; do you see why they can be subjected to tax immediately but demand loans require that a determination of the gift element be made on an annual basis until repaid? Loans made before the adoption of §7872 and exempted from its application are subject to *Dickman*, as detailed in Rev. Proc. 85-46.

The following outline of the basic elements of §7872 is drawn from Kahn, FEDERAL INCOME TAX (4th ed. 1999) at 133-135.

Section 7872 covers only the following types of "below-market loans": gift loans, compensation-related loans (i.e., a loan between an employer and an employee or between an independent contractor and a person for whom he provides services), corporate-shareholder loans, tax avoidance loans, loans to a qualified continuing care facility, and any other below-market loan in which the interest arrangement has a significant effect on the federal tax liability of the lender or the borrower. §7872(c). A "below-market loan" is either: a demand loan bearing interest at a rate that is less than the "applicable Federal rate," or a term loan in which the amount loaned exceeds the present value of all payments to be made under the loan. §7872(e)(1). For purposes of §7872, the word "loan" is broadly defined. Prop. Reg. §1.7872-2.

In general, §7872 treats the lender of a below-market loan as making a constructive payment to the borrower of an amount equal to the foregone interest, and this constructive payment will be treated as: a gift (in the case of a gratuitous transaction), a dividend (in the case of a loan from a corporation to its shareholder), paid compensation (in the case of a loan to a person providing services), or as some other payment characterization in accordance with the substance of the transaction. The constructive payment will be included in the borrower's gross income unless it is a gift or falls within some other exclusion from income. If an actual payment of the same character would have been deductible or amortizable by the lender (e.g., a payment for services rendered in connection with the lender's business), the amount of the constructive payment similarly will be deductible or amortizable by the lender. For most tax purposes, the parties will be treated as if the constructive payment had actually been made. For example, if a constructive payment to a borrower is treated as a gift, it may cause gift tax consequences.

The same amount that the borrower is deemed to have received from the lender is deemed to have been repaid simultaneously by the borrower to the lender. Note that in certain circumstances concerning a gift loan between individuals, the amount of repayment to the lender may be less than the payment to the borrower. See §7872(d)(1). This constructive repayment is treated as an actual payment of interest by the borrower to the lender. The constructive interest payment is included in the lender's gross income. The constructive interest payment may be deductible or amortizable by the borrower if an actual payment would qualify as an interest deduction. Note that as a consequence of amendments made by the Tax Reform Act of 1986, many types of interest payments are nondeductible. See, e.g., §163(d) and (h). If the constructive interest payment on a term loan can be deducted, the aggregate amount of the deduction will be allocated among the years of the loan's term as if the interest were "original issue discount" — i.e., the constructive interest will be compounded rather than simple interest . . . .

For the purposes of §7872, a "gift loan" is a loan bearing below-market interest where the foregone interest qualifies as a gift. §7872(f)(3). A "gift loan" may be either a demand loan or a term loan. A "demand loan" is a loan which is payable in full at any time on the demand of the lender. §7872(f)(5). A "term loan" is any loan which is not a demand loan. §7872(f)(6). The market interest rate is set at the "applicable Federal rate." A different applicable Federal rate is used for demand loans than is used for term loans. §7872(f)(2). The Federal short-term rate is used for demand loans, and the Federal rate for term loans depends upon the length of the term of the loan.

If a gift or demand loan is a below-market loan, the foregone interest will be treated as having been transferred from the lender to the borrower and retransferred from the borrower to the lender as an interest payment on the last day of the calendar year to which such foregone interest is attributable. §7872(a).

9.   *Forgiveness of Indebtedness.*   (a) *D* made a bona fide loan to a child, *C*, of $12,000, repayable in five years with interest at an adequate rate for purposes of §7872. *D* forgave the unpaid debt two years later, when *C* was in poor financial straits. All of the accrued interest on the debt had been paid by C. The gift is measured by the amount *D* reasonably could be expected to recover or, more accurately, what a willing buyer would pay a willing seller for *C*'s note, considering the stated terms and *C*'s financial condition.

(b) *D* made an interest-free but bona fide loan of $25,000 to child *C*. The loan was not evidenced by a written instrument and was payable on demand. *D* made no effort to collect the debt and the statute of limitation for suing on the debt expired three years later. Were there any gift tax consequences to the expiration of the statute of limitation? See Estate of Lang v. Commissioner, 613 F.2d 770 (9th Cir. 1980), holding in similar circumstances that a gift was made on the date the statute ran. If so, what was the amount of the gift? In *Lang*, the Tax Court held (64 T.C. at 413) that *D* made a gift of the face amount of the note, and the Court of Appeals for the Ninth Circuit affirmed that part of the Tax Court's decision. Do you agree? Compare Commissioner v. Kellogg, 119 F.2d 115 (9th Cir. 1941). Will the running of the statute of limitation on a debt always constitute a gift, or does it depend upon the creditor's purpose in allowing the statute to run? See *Lang*, 64 T.C. at 413. If the running of the statute constitutes a gift, must *D* file a gift tax return? See §§6019, 2503(b), 2503(e).

In *Lang*, the Tax Court imposed a penalty on *D* under §6651(a) for failing to file a gift tax return, but was reversed on appeal because no case prior to that date had determined that expiration of the statute of limitation triggered gift tax consequences. Thus, there was reasonable cause for the taxpayer to fail to file a return. Now that *Lang* held that expiration of the statute of limitation constitutes a gift, will a failure to file a return in such circumstances subject the taxpayer to a penalty?

Typically, the statute of limitation is held to begin running on a demand note from the date of execution of the note, not from the date of a demand for repayment. See Annot., When Statute of Limitations Begins to Run Against Note Payable on Demand, 71 A.L.R.2d 284 (1960).

(c) In **(b)**, What if *C* repaid the loan after the statute of limitation had run. Are there any gift tax consequences? Cf. Rev. Rul. 77-372. Quaere: why is there no previously taxed property credit like §2013 for gift tax purposes?

(d) In Rev. Rul. 81-264, *D* loaned child *A* $500,000 and received a promissory note, payable on demand, bearing interest at the market rate. Under local law, the statute of limitation for recovering the principal and accrued interest of the demand note expired three years after the loan was made, and *D* allowed the statute to run without making a demand for principal or interest. *A* had some financial resources when the statute ran. The Commissioner stated in part:

> If an individual makes a loan and as part of a prearranged plan intends to forgive or not collect on the note, the note will not be considered valuable consideration and the promisee will have made a gift at the time of the loan to the full extent of the loan. Rev. Rul. 77-299, 1977-2 C.B. 343. If there was no such prearranged plan, but the promisee later forgives the debt, the promisee will have made a gift at the time of the forgiveness. The amount of the gift will equal the principal amount forgiven and the interest accrued to the date of the forgiveness. Section 25.2511-1 of the Gift Tax Regulations and Republic Petroleum Corp. v. United States, 397 F. Supp. 900 (E.D. La. 1975).

Here, as in all such familial transactions, there is a presumption that the transfer of wealth from D to A without consideration is not entirely free of donative intent. Estate of Lang v. Commissioner, 64 T.C. 404 (1975), aff'd, 613 F.2d 770 (9th Cir. 1980). A had the resources to pay the debt, and, as D's child, was the natural object of D's bounty. On these facts, D's failing to enforce the debt obligation and permitting it to be barred by the statute has not yet been shown to be free of donative intent, and thus is not a transaction in the ordinary course of business within the meaning of Treas. Reg. §25.2512-8.

It does not matter that the running of the statute of limitations does not extinguish the debt but merely creates an affirmative defense in a collection suit. Control of the debt passes to the debtor when the statute of limitations runs. Thereafter, it is the debtor rather than the creditor who decides whether and under what terms loaned funds will be repaid. The essence of a gift is such relinquishment of control by the donor over the property. Estate of Lang v. Commissioner.

Rev. Rul. 81-264 indicates that A's financial resources were adequate to satisfy the debt. If they had not been adequate, would that have affected the gift tax consequence of D's permitting the statute of limitation to expire?

Haygood v. Commissioner
42 T.C. 936 (1964), nonacq.

[The petitioner (taxpayer) transferred realty to her two sons, who gave her deeds of trust and vendor lien notes in payment, in an aggregate face amount equal to the value of the realty. Each note was payable in annual installments equal to the gift tax annual exclusion ($3,000 at that time) and bore no interest. The petitioner intended to forgive each installment when due, and for several years she did so — thereby making a gift of $3,000 each year to each son.]

SCOTT, J. . . . It is respondent's position that petitioner transferred all of her interest in the property and in return therefor received nothing of value. Respondent does not consider there to be any substance to the notes and deeds of trust signed by petitioner's sons. . . . Respondent contends that it is immaterial whether petitioner intended to give the entire value of the property in 1961 since she in that year actually did part with dominion and control over the property without receiving any valuable consideration in return therefor, relying on his regulations which he contends so state.

Respondent cites in support of his position the case of [Deal v. Commissioner, 29 T.C. 730 (1958), which] involved a conveyance by the taxpayer there involved of real property to a trust for the benefit of her four daughters. The property was conveyed to the trust unencumbered. On the same date . . . each of her four daughters gave her a non-interest-bearing note which they would have been, with one exception, financially able to pay. The tax-payer forgave a $3,000 portion of each note to each daughter in the year of the transfer of the property, and a similar portion of each note in the 2 subsequent years, and the remaining balance of the note in the following year. . . . [W]e stated at page 736: "After carefully considering the record, we think that the notes executed by the daughters were not intended to be enforced and were not intended as consideration for the transfer by the petitioner, and that, in substance, the transfer of the property was by gift. . . ." . . .

[*Deal*] is clearly distinguishable on its facts from the instant case. Here the notes were vendor's lien notes given for the property. Clearly as a matter of law, they would have been enforce-able and respondent does not contend otherwise. Respondent's position is, and the record shows, that it was not petitioner's intention to enforce payment of the notes. . . . There is a stipulated fact that the sons were not financially able to make the $3,000 payments due on December 31, 1961. . . . However, the ability of the sons to pay $3,000 on December 31, 1961, is academic since it was petitioner's intention to and she did forgive the payment due on that day. . . .

Respondent argues that since it is not petitioner's intent to collect the notes from her sons, there existed no debt and that without a debt there can be no lien. . . .

If the notes of petitioner's sons were as a matter of law unen-forceable, there might be validity to respondent's argument that there was no debt secured by the vendor's liens and deeds of trust which would be collectible. However, under the facts in this case where the very deeds conveying the properties recited that vendor's lien notes were being given in consideration therefor, the evidence certainly supports the fact that the notes did create en-forceable indebtednesses even though petitioner had no intention of collecting the debts but did intend to forgive each payment as it became due.

In the instant case if donative intent were the criterion [for determining whether a taxable gift was made] our question would be easily solved for the record is amply clear that petitioner in-tended to donate only $3,000 per year of the property here involved to each of her sons until such time as the full value had been given to them. However, since this [was] not the criterion, it is necessary to look to the property that passed to petitioner in return for the real property transferred to see if the amount of petitioner's gifts to her sons in 1961 of the city property exceeded the $6,000 she reported. . . . [T]he gift of the land, insofar as its value exceeded the consideration received by petitioner therefor, was completed in the year 1961. The existence of the vendor's lien notes and deeds of trust would not cause the transfer to be so incomplete as not to be a consummated gift at the time of the transfer to the extent the value of the property exceeded the value of the consideration received therefor.

We hold that the value of the property transferred by petitioner did not exceed the value of the vendor's lien notes and deeds of trust received in return therefor by more than the $3,000 in the case of each son, which amounts petitioner has reported as gifts in the year 1961.

Respondent makes some point of the fact that petitioner did not report any gain or loss from sales of the properties transferred to her sons in either her 1961 or 1962 income tax return. Petitioner's income tax for neither of these years is before us, and therefore we express no opinion as to the correctness of petitioner's action in this regard. We do hold under the facts of this case that petitioner correctly reported the total gifts made by her to her sons in the year 1961.

Decision will be entered for petitioner.

(e) Is the *Deal* decision discussed in *Haygood* distinguishable from *Haygood*, as the court suggested? Is the collectibility of a note received in exchange for property significant if the transferor of the property never intends to collect on the note? Consider the material in Chapter 5 on transfers made incomplete because of the transferor's retained power to revoke, and see Treas. Reg. §§25.2511-2(b), -2(c). See also Burnet v. Guggenheim, 288 U.S. 280 (1933).

(f) The income tax consequences to the taxpayer in *Haygood* from a sale may have been greater than if she had merely given each son a fractional interest in the realty each year. In any such case the wise practitioner must compare the income tax to the tax disadvantages of making annual gifts of a fractional share of the realty.

(g) Rev. Rul. 77-299 announced that the government will not follow *Haygood*. In that Ruling the circumstances were stated as:

G had given A and B, G's grandchildren, $3,000 per year at Christmas since each grandchild was 10 years old. When A and B were, respectively, 21 and 22 years old and enrolled in graduate school, G proposed to give Blackacre, with a fair market value of $27,000, to A and Whiteacre, with a fair market value of $24,000, to B. Both Blackacre and Whiteacre were unimproved tracts of non-income-producing real property. A and B had spent the money previously given them by G, did not have any other funds, and did not have an independent source of income. When informed of G's intent, G's attorney, in order to minimize G's Federal gift tax on the transfer, suggested a sale of the property to each grandchild in return for installment notes that would be payable in yearly amounts equal to the annual gift tax exclusion.

The plan was implemented in July 1972, at which time A and B each received a package of instruments in the mail from G's attorney. A's package contained a check from G for $50, a deed to Blackacre, a mortgage on the property, one note with a face amount of $2,950 and eight notes each in the amount of $3,000. B's package contained a check from G for $50, a deed to White-acre, a mortgage on the property, one note with a face amount of $2,950 and seven notes each in the amount of $3,000. A letter also accompanied each package explaining the transaction to A and B and indicating that G did not intend to collect on the notes, but intended to forgive each payment as it became due. A and B did not have prior knowledge of the transaction. There were no negotiations concerning the transaction, and G's attorney represented all of the parties to the transaction.

The notes were noninterest-bearing and nonnegotiable. . . . Each of the deeds recited that it was given in consideration of a cash payment of $50 and the notes. Additionally, each deed described the notes and recited that the mortgages on the property were taken to secure the payment of the notes. . . . [T]he deeds (but not the mortgages) were recorded with the proper county authorities.

On December 25, 1972, G forgave the $2,950 due from A and B on January 1, 1973. On December 25 of 1973 and 1974, G forgave the $3,000 due from A and B on January 1 of the following years.

The government ruled that for federal gift tax purposes G made a transfer by gift to A in 1972 in the amount of $27,000 and a transfer to B in 1972 in the amount of $24,000, citing *Deal*, Estate of Reynolds v. Commissioner, 55 T.C. 172, 202 (1970), and De Goldschmidt-Rothschild v. Commissioner, 9 T.C. 325 (1947), *aff'd*, 168 F.2d 975 (2d. Cir. 1948), and stating:

[I]n the instant case, whether the transfer of property was a sale or a gift depends upon whether, as part of a prearranged plan

G intended to forgive the notes that were received when *G* transferred the property.

It should be noted that the intent to forgive notes is to be distinguished from donative intent, which, as indicated by Treas. Reg. §25.2511-1(g)(1), is not relevant. A finding of an intent to forgive the note relates to whether valuable consideration was received and, thus, to whether the transaction was in reality a bona fide sale or a disguised gift. Therefore, such an inquiry is necessary in situations such as the one described here. See 5 Mertens, LAW OF FEDERAL GIFT AND ESTATE TAXATION, §34.03 (1959). "Nothing can be treated as consideration that is not intended as such by the parties." Fire Insurance Association v. Wickham, 141 U.S. 579 (1891). Donative intent, on the other hand, rather than relating to whether a transaction was actually a sale or a gift, relates to whether the donor *intended* the transaction to be a sale or a gift. Although the same facts would be used in determining either type of intent, they relate to two entirely different inquiries.

In the instant case, the facts clearly indicate that *G*, as part of a prearranged plan, intended to forgive the notes that were received in return for the transfer of *G*'s land. Therefore, the transaction was merely a disguised gift rather than a bona fide sale.

10.   *Federal Disclaimer Provisions.*   Gift and estate tax §§2518 and 2046, respectively, adopt a federal disclaimer regime that is meant to rectify the lack of uniformity in state laws, which vary as to the manner in which a disclaimer must be made and the consequences on ownership of the disclaimed property following the disclaimer. As revealed in the House Ways and Means Committee Report accompanying the Tax Reform Act of 1976, which enacted these rules, the real impetus for enactment of federal rules was the decision in *Keinath v. Commissioner*,[12] in which a trust beneficiary was considered to have made a qualified disclaimer of a remainder interest within the "reasonable" time for gift tax purposes notwithstanding that no action was taken until the preceding life estate terminated some 19 years after the trust was created and the disclaimant became aware of the interest. Sections 2518 and 2046 were enacted to establish a basic nine month period as the requisite reasonable time within which a qualified disclaimer must be made to be recognized for wealth transfer tax purposes.[13] Otherwise the

---

12.   480 F.2d 57 (8th Cir. 1973), *rev'g* 58 T.C. 352 (1972). The Supreme Court repudiated *Keinath* in Jewett v. Commissioner, 455 U.S. 305 (1982), long after the disclaimer rules of §2518 were on the books, as discussed in *Kennedy*, reproduced at page 824.

13.   As stated in the House Report:

many professional study groups have recommended that definitive rules be provided with respect to the treatment of disclaimers for estate and gift tax disclaimant's renunciation of property is regarded as an acceptance followed by a taxable gift.

Section 2518 establishes requirements relating to renunciations of property that, if satisfied, cause the renunciation to be effective for federal wealth transfer tax purposes even if the applicable local law does not characterize the refusal as a disclaimer and even if the disclaimant was regarded by state law to have accepted legal title to the property before refusing its acceptance. A qualified disclaimer is treated for wealth transfer tax purposes as if the interest was not transferred to the disclaimant, meaning that there is no gift to the person to whom the interest passes by reason of the disclaimer, and that the property is deemed to pass directly from the transferor to the person entitled to receive it by virtue of the disclaimer. Thus, a qualified disclaimer is effective for charitable and marital deduction purposes, and the renunciation of a general power of appointment is not treated as a taxable release of the power.

Section 2518(b) and Treas. Reg. §25.2518-2 state the formal requirements for a qualified disclaimer. Among the issues that may need analysis in any situation are: when was the transfer to the disclaimant complete for purposes of triggering the nine-month disclaimer period, was the disclaimer an "irrevocable and unqualified" refusal of an interest in property, and did the disclaimant accept the benefits of the interest transferred or exercise any prohibited control over the interest. The following cases illustrate several of these issues.

Acceptance of Benefits.   One of the issues in the following case is whether documents executed by 29 legatees of the decedent's will constituted qualified disclaimers under §2518. Decedent (*D*) died in 1989 survived by her 92-year old husband (*H*), who was the residuary beneficiary of her will and was named as the executor of her estate. *D* made a sizeable number of specific bequests in her will to relatives, friends, and household employees. *H* received tax advice that the estate would achieve a large reduction in the substantial amount of wealth transfer taxes that the estate would bear if the legatees of many of those specific bequests would renounce their bequests. *H* was advised that a disclaimer by the legatees did not preclude *H* from making gifts to those persons. *H* was aware of the requirement that the disclaimers would not accomplish their purpose if the legatees received or were promised any benefit for renouncing. Some of the legatees were contacted by *H* personally and some were contacted by *H*'s

---

purposes. See American Bar Association recommendation number 1974-2, 27 Tax Lawyer 818 (1974); American Law Institute recommendations 21 and 22, "Federal Estate and Gift Taxation: Recommendations Adopted by the American Law Institute," pp. 39-41 (1968); "Tax Reform Studies and Proposals: U.S. Treasury Department," p. 387 (1969); American Bankers Association, "Commentary on Proposed Tax Reform Affecting Estates and Trusts," p. 166 of appendix A (1973).

nephew. After being rehearsed as to what to say, *H* (or his nephew) told the legatees that *H* was upset by the high rate of the transfer taxes, which would significantly reduce the legatees' bequests, and that *H* would like each legatee to disclaim that person's bequest. The legatees were told that, by disclaiming, they would be giving up a right and that their disclaimer had to be totally voluntary and without consideration. All 29 of the legatees executed timely disclaimers of their bequests, and the aggregate amount disclaimed was a little less than $893,000. All 29 disclaimants received a check from *H*, bearing the notation "gift," in the approximate amount that each had disclaimed. These "gifts" were all sent within one month after the disclaimers were made. The disclaimed amounts passed to *H* through the residuary clause of *D*'s will, and the estate claimed a marital deduction for those amounts. The government concluded that all but one of the disclaimers did not qualify under §2518, and accordingly denied the claim for a marital deduction for the disclaimed amounts. Other tax adjustments also were made. Please note that, although the following opinion was reversed on appeal, it remains the prescient decision, as well as a better learning tool.

Estate of Monroe v. Commissioner
104 T.C. 352 (1995), *rev'd*, 124 F.2d 699 (5th Cir. 1997)

COHEN, Judge . . . There was no single motive that prompted all of the legatees to disclaim their bequests. Some of the disclaimants were told by the nephew that [*H*] had always taken care of them and had never cheated them or that [*H*] was a generous man. Many of the disclaimants anticipated that [*H*] would continue to care for them financially or was likely to make a bequest to them in his will. Some disclaimants believed that executing the disclaimer would be in their best long-term interest, because they did not wish to upset [*H*] by refusing to renounce.

. . . In order for the amounts that were disclaimed by 29 of decedent's legatees to be treated as passing directly to [*H*] and, thus, qualifying for the marital deduction from decedent's gross estate, the disclaimers must be "qualified disclaimers" as defined in §2518. Although §2518 is a gift tax provision, §2046 makes it applicable for estate tax purposes as well. . . .

According to respondent, the disclaimers were not "irrevocable and unqualified" as required by §2518(b), because the legatees accepted consideration in return for executing the disclaimers when they received the cash gifts from [*H*] shortly after disclaiming. Petitioner contends that the disclaimers did constitute qualified disclaimers under §2518 and, specifically, that the legatees did not accept consideration in return for making such disclaimers. In petitioner's view, the disclaimers and the subsequent gifts that were received by the disclaimants from [*H*] were independent, unrelated transactions, because there was no agreement or promise between any legatee and [H] or the nephew to exchange a disclaimer for consideration.

... Petitioner maintains that Treas. Reg. §25.2518-2(d)(1) sets forth two independent tests for determining when a legatee has accepted an interest in the property to be disclaimed. The first involves the actual acceptance of an interest in property to be disclaimed, prior to making the disclaimer. Petitioner concedes that such acceptance may be express or implied. The second test, according to petitioner, involves the exchange of a disclaimer for consideration. In petitioner's view, consideration cannot be implied. It must be something identifiable, and it must have been agreed upon at the time the disclaimer was made.

Respondent disagrees with petitioner's characterization of the execution of the disclaimers and the receipt of the gifts as two separate, unrelated sets of transactions. Rather, respondent maintains that there was a single transaction: decedent left 29 legatees money, and the legatees claimed that they renounced the money, but, in substance, they accepted it. In respondent's view, if the Court were to accept petitioner's construction of §2518(b)(3), the words "irrevocable and unqualified," as used in §2518, would be rendered superfluous and nonexistent.

For a disclaimer to be "irrevocable and unqualified," as required by the language of §2518, it must have substance. A disclaimer is not "irrevocable" if a legatee or heir formally disclaims but, in substance, receives his or her bequest. A disclaimer is not "unqualified" if a legatee or heir is induced or coerced into disclaiming his or her bequest as happened in this case. Here, the evidence suggests that, with [one exception] the disclaimants expected, for one reason or another, that they would receive their renounced bequests in the form of a gift or legacy from [H]. Furthermore, the testimony of many of the disclaimants suggests that they feared what would happen if they refused to renounce their bequests.

... The nephew's testimony demonstrates that he intended to inform the disclaimants that the probability that they would receive something from [H] in the future was good. Conversely, if the legatees refused to disclaim, they were unlikely to receive anything from [H] subsequently, because their refusal would be against [H's] wishes.

... Petitioner argues that the use of the term "in exchange" in the regulations suggests that, for purposes of §2518(b)(3), the term "consideration" is meant in its traditional sense and requires a bargained-for exchange. In other words, there must have been an explicit promise or agreement existing at the time the disclaimers were entered into for the disclaimers to be disqualified under §2518(b)(3).

. . . We disagree with petitioner's application of §2518(b)(3) and the regulations thereunder to the facts here. [*H*] and the nephew's statements to the disclaimants that [*H*] would take care of "it" or take care of them if they agreed to renounce their bequests conveyed a clear message. All would be "taken care of" by [*H*] if the legatees agreed to do as he wished; conversely, [*H*] would be upset if a legatee refused to disclaim, and his care and generosity would no longer be forthcoming.

The plain language of §2518 requires a disclaimer to be "irrevocable and unqualified." See Caminetti v. United States, 242 U.S. 470, 485 (1917) (stating that a court must accord first priority in statutory interpretation to the plain meaning of the provision in question). This language is not insignificant, and petitioner has not persuaded us that the facts justify the marital deduction. See Commissioner v. Jacobson, 336 U.S. 28, 48-49 (1949) (exemptions from tax are narrowly construed); United States v. Stewart, 311 U.S. 60, 71 (1940) ("those who seek an exemption from a tax must rest it on more than a doubt or ambiguity"). The disclaimants may not have explicitly negotiated with or bargained with [*H*] or the nephew for consideration in return for executing their disclaimers. Each of the disclaimants other than [one], however, was induced or, in some instances, coerced, into executing a disclaimer. Under these circumstances, the consideration for their disclaimers was the implied promise that they would be better off if they did what [*H*] wanted them to do than if they refused to do so. Their disclaimers thus were not "unqualified" as required by §2518.

. . . In addition, petitioner has failed to persuade us that [*H's*] cash gifts to the 29 disclaimants were merely part of a pattern of generosity that [*H*] had engaged in throughout his life. These "gifts" were all cash payments of specific and substantial amounts made to the disclaimants shortly after they executed their disclaimers. The inference drawn from this targeted gift-giving is that [*H*] made them "in return" for the disclaimants' renouncing their bequests and not from a "detached and disinterested generosity." Cf. Commissioner v. Duberstein, 363 U.S. 278, 285 (1960). Even if [*H*] had no legal obligation to compensate the disclaimants, they anticipated, and received, payments from him that left them in the same economic position as if they had accepted the legacies in the first place. Cf. United States v. Estate of Grace, 395 U.S. 316, 324 (1969).

In sum, we hold that, with [one] exception . . . , none of the renunciations constituted effective disclaimers under §2518(b).

Timing. The following decision addresses an important issue for marital deduction planning especially, and one on which the government eventually capitulated in regulations amended in 1998. See Treas. Reg. §25.2518-2(c)(4).

Kennedy v. Commissioner
804 F.2d 1332 (7th Cir. 1986)

EASTERBROOK, Circuit Judge. Pearl Kennedy acquired the family farm in two steps. She received a gift of a joint tenancy in 1953 when she and her husband Frank Kennedy acquired the farm. She received the remainder when Frank died in 1978, taking Frank's share by virtue of the survivorship feature that is part of joint tenancy in Illinois. In 1979 Pearl disclaimed the interest she had acquired by surviving Frank. Under the law of Illinois, Frank's former interest passed to the Kennedys' daughter Marsha. The IRS believes that the disclaimer is a taxable gift from Pearl to Marsha. See 26 U.S.C. §§2501, 2511. The Tax Court agreed, holding that Pearl's time to make a "qualified" disclaimer (one that avoids the imposition of tax) had been running since 1953 and therefore had expired long before Frank died. It relied on Jewett v. Commissioner, 455 U.S. 305 (1982).

Frank's gift to Pearl in 1953 was taxable under the law then in effect. Pearl received one-half of the value of the farm, reflecting the nature of the joint tenancy: an immediate, irrevocable one-half undivided interest, plus a right of survivorship in the other one-half. Although Pearl's life expectancy may have been longer than Frank's, making her the more likely beneficiary of the survivorship feature, each also had an unfettered right under the law of Illinois to partition the property. Partition by either spouse, or as part of divorce, would have ended the right of survivorship. Until one spouse died, it was not possible to say who (if either) would receive the survivor's share.

Pearl relies on this uncertainty in arguing that she did not acquire an interest in Frank's share of the property until Frank's death. On her reasoning the disclaimer therefore is governed by 26 U.S.C. §2518, a provision added to the Code in 1976 and applicable to disclaimers properly made after December 31, 1976. The Tax Court held, however, that the transfer in 1953 started the time to disclaim under Treas. Reg. §25.2511-1(c) (1958), which applies to pre-1977 events and was at stake in Jewett. Treas. Reg. §25.2511-1(c) provides that only disclaimers "made within a reasonable time after knowledge of the existence of the transfer" are sufficient to avoid gift taxation, and the Tax Court believed that "the transfer" to Pearl took place in 1953. We are the first court of appeals to consider the appropriate treatment of disclaimed interests in real estate held through joint tenancies.

The IRS treats this as a replay of *Jewett*. That case involved four generations of Jewetts, which we designate by Roman numerals. Margaret Weyerhauser Jewett (Jewett I) died, creating a trust in which her spouse and children (Jewett II) had a life estate. On the death of the last life tenant, the corpus of the trust would go to surviving members of generation III. If the last life tenant survived any particular member of generation III, then that member's share of the corpus would go to generation IV, the children of the deceased member of generation III — if necessary, to the descendants of generation IV per stirpes. The trust was created in 1939, when George Jewett, one of two members of generation III, was 11 years old. In 1972, while one member of generation II was still alive, George disclaimed any interest in the corpus of the trust. Under state law the trustee treated George as if deceased, making his children (Jewett IV) the direct beneficiaries of his half share of the corpus, then worth more than $8 million. The IRS proposed to levy a gift tax on the actuarial value of George's interest in the corpus — roughly $4 million multiplied by the probability that he would survive the last life tenant. George replied that until the last life tenant died, it was not possible to know who would receive the corpus, and therefore he could not be treated as owning, and giving to his children, such an uncertain interest. The Supreme Court held, to the contrary, that George's "interest" in the corpus was created in 1939, and unless disclaimed within a "reasonable" time thereafter would be treated as received by him and given to his children. The Court both sustained the regulation and accepted the Commissioner's interpretation of the regulation.

The rationale for both the regulation and the Court's disposition of *Jewett* is straightforward. A future interest is an element of current wealth. If in 1972 George Jewett had been the remainderman of a trust, with the corpus to be paid to him in 1992, the chance that he might die earlier would decrease the value of the interest but not make the interest worthless. If he had given the interest to his children he would have transferred real wealth. A situation in which a person's interest depends on the relative longevity of several people is not fundamentally different from one in which only his own life span matters. In either case the future interest has a present value that can be computed from actuarial tables. In deciding whether to transfer the interest by disclaimer, the person will consider whether he wants to give that amount of wealth to the beneficiary of the disclaimer. George Jewett waited more than 20 years after reaching the age of majority to see whether it would be prudent to pass an interest worth millions directly to his children; this is a substitute for giving wealth to his children from his other assets. He had the option to retain his interest in the wealth or to pass it on; he waited to see which was preferable in light of his income and wealth outside the trust. One who possesses such an option has the equivalent of a power of appointment. The exercise of a power of appointment by a person able to appoint assets to himself (that is, a general power) is a taxable gift by the person holding the power. 26 U.S.C. §2514(b). The disclaimer in 1972 would have allowed George to assure his access to the wealth for an extended period and then to bypass a generation of transfer taxation, had it not been taxed as a gift.

Treas. Reg. §25.2511-1(c) and the 1976 statute treat a prompt disclaimer as collapsing the transaction into a single gift from the original owner to the ultimate recipient. A donee may refuse a gift without tax. A prompt disclaimer is a form of refusal that directs the gift to the donor's second choice. If George Jewett had disclaimed immediately on learning of his potential interest, it would be as if Jewett I's will had specified a transfer directly to generation IV on generation II's death. Whatever tax generations I, II, and IV should pay on this transfer, see 26 U.S.C. §§2601-2622, a tax on generation III plays no logical role.

Jewett shows that a belated disclaimer may be a taxable gift even though the person disclaiming has no current access to the money and may never receive it. [See Treas. Reg. §25.2518-2(c)(3) — ED.] The IRS believes that this compels a conclusion that Pearl Kennedy had only a "reasonable" time after 1953 to disclaim and to have the transaction treated as a gift from Frank Kennedy to their daughter. The problem with this position is that the interest of the different generations of Jewetts were fixed in 1939. One could get out the actuarial tables in 1939 or 1972 and determine how much each person's share was worth. Frank's gift to Pearl in 1953 did not fix the rules for succession, however, because of the right to partition the property.

To see the difficulty, suppose the Jewett trust had given the last surviving member of generation II a general power of appointment and had provided that if she died without exercising the power, the corpus would be distributed exactly as the actual trust specified. Then it would have been impossible to value the interest in the trust in 1939 or at any time before the death of the holder of the power. The general power of appointment also would cause the value of the trust to be included in the holder's estate, see 26 U.S.C. §2041(a)(2). In such a case the effective transfer occurs when the holder of the general power exercises it or lets it lapse, and the time to disclaim begins then.

This is how the regulations under the 1976 statute treat the situation. See Treas. Reg. §25.2518-2(c)(3): "A person to whom any interest in property passes by reason of the exercise or lapse of a general power [of appointment] may disclaim such interest within a 9-month period after the exercise or lapse." The regulations treat other interests similarly. Suppose A and B create a joint checking account with right of survivorship, into which A places a sum of money. B may draw any or all of the money immediately, but so may A. The account by itself therefore gives B nothing; A's placement of money at B's disposal is revocable. The Commissioner treats a joint account as a transfer to B only when it becomes irrevocable — when B draws the money or A dies. If B does not withdraw the funds during A's life, B has nine months after A's death to disclaim any interest in the account. Treas. Reg. §25.2518-2(c)(5) *Example (9)*.

The [pre-1998] regulations treat a survivorship interest in land as a completed, irrevocable gift on the date the tenancy itself was created, see Treas. Reg. §25.2518-2(c)(4)(i). [These were the regulations that changed effective January 1, 1998 — ED.] This is inconsistent with the Commissioner's treatment of general powers of appointment and joint bank accounts when, as is true in Illinois, either spouse may terminate the right of survivorship by partitioning the property. The regulations do not discuss the effects of a power to partition. Yet the prospect of partition means that only the one-half undivided interest has been transferred irrevocably; the survivorship interest may be withdrawn at will, just as funds in a joint account may be. Pearl had no greater interest in Frank's half of the farm than she did in any funds Frank deposited in a joint checking account. In either case Pearl would get the interest if she survived Frank, but only if Frank refrained from exercising his unfettered power to withdraw (or partition). There was no way to value the interest until Frank died. So Pearl's survivorship interest would have been treated as "worthless" in 1953 in valuing Frank's gift to her. See Gift Tax Regulations 108, §§86.2, 86.19(h) (1943). If the survivorship component of a joint tenancy were treated as a valuable gift in 1953, that would imply that Frank's retained interest was then worth less than half of the total value of the farm. After all, Pearl's share plus Frank's share must add to 100%. But Frank, too, had a right of survivorship, plus the half share that he could retain with certainty by partition. The Commissioner's treatment of the transfer in 1953 implies that Pearl got more than half of the value of the farm and that Frank kept more than half — which suggests that something is seriously wrong with the position.

Frank's power of partition was equivalent to a general power of appointment over Pearl's survivorship interest, because by partitioning the property Frank could direct his half to his creditors and legatees of his choice rather than Pearl. And joint tenancies cannot readily be used to skip a generation of taxes, because 26 U.S.C. §2040(a) pulls the value of the property into the estate of a deceased joint tenant, just as a general power of appointment pulls the value of the trust into the estate of the person who dies while holding the power. (Section 2040(b)(1) excludes certain "qualified" marital joint interests, but this exclusion should not influence the determination of the date of "transfer" for purposes of disclaiming, because the date selected will apply to joint tenancies other than marital ones.)

We therefore conclude that the gift of a joint tenancy with right of survivorship should be treated as more than one transfer in states that allow any tenant to partition the property at will. One transfer is an undivided interest, given on the date the tenancy is created. Additional transfers occur on the death of other joint tenants. This case, with two tenants, is simple. The time within which Pearl could disclaim the half of the property she received because of Frank's death started to run in 1978 and is therefore governed by the 1976 statute.

Reversed and Remanded.

See also Estate of Dancy v. Commissioner, 872 F.2d 84 (4th Cir. 1989), and McDonald v. Commissioner, 853 F.2d 1494 (8th Cir. 1988), adopting the position taken on appeal in *Kennedy*.

The government acquiesced to *Kennedy* in AOD 1990-06 and indicated that it would not enforce Treas. Reg. §25.2518-2(c)(4) to the extent it stated that the nine-month period begins when joint tenancy property is acquired. It then took eight years before final changes to the regulations were adopted. To understand the current treatment on this issue requires a suspension of the legal fiction that each joint tenant is 100% owner of the underlying property. That property law bromide is not how taxpayers think about concurrent ownership, nor is it how the disclaimer rules now operate in this arena. Instead, you will understand the issues in this context by considering the property as if it had been partitioned — each concurrent owner being regarded as "owning" an undivided equal share as if they were tenants in common — with disclaimer being relevant only with respect to the survivorship interest, described here as the "accretive" share increase in ownership attributable to surviving another concurrent owner's death. In those terms, the disclaimer concept relates only to a taxpayer's disclaimer of just the increase in ownership caused by a concurrent owner's death, not the portion the disclaimant would have received upon a partition while that other concurrent owner still was alive.

The government's original position that a disclaimer more than nine months after original creation of the joint tenancy was too late to be qualified under §2518 continues to apply with respect to the portion the disclaimant could receive on a partition while all concurrent owners are alive, but it no longer is the government's position with respect to the accretive share. As to that, Treas. Reg. §25.2518-2(c)(4) now provides a new nine month period within which to disclaim, beginning with the concurrent owner's death. Acceptance of enjoyment prior to that owner's death will not preclude a qualified disclaimer of the accretive share and it may not disqualify an otherwise valid disclaimer,[14] even if enjoyment continues after the disclaimer, if state law regards occupancy of the concurrently owned property as a right of undivided concurrent ownership.

One aspect of the final regulation is surreal: "The Service will . . . no longer contend that a joint tenant cannot make a qualified disclaimer of any portion of the joint interest attributable to consideration furnished by that joint tenant."[15] According to the regulation,[16] the source of the consideration is irrelevant in most concurrent ownership disclaimers — a surviving concurrent owner *may* disclaim the accretive share *even if* it originated with the disclaimant's own consideration.

The situation differs only with respect to a disclaimer of a revocable joint tenancy such as a joint bank, brokerage, or other investment account, and only to the extent the legal effect of creating the account is different from other concurrent ownership interests under state law. In most jurisdictions there is no completed gift on creation of a revocable joint tenancy like a joint bank, brokerage, or other investment account until a nondepositing concurrent owner makes a withdrawal. As to these accounts a disclaimer is not possible earlier because there has not been a completed transfer. And, until there is a completed taxable gift, there has not been an event that triggers the running of the disclaimer period.[17]

In the context of the requirement that the disclaimant not have accepted the interest or any of its benefits before making the disclaimer, or any consideration in exchange for making the disclaimer, consider the case presented in Rev. Rul. 90-45 and PLR 8817061, in which a surviving spouse elected against the decedent's will to take the statutory forced heir share entitlement guaranteed to surviving spouses, and then disclaimed that portion of this entitlement in excess of the amount of marital deduction needed in the decedent's estate to produce zero estate tax. This was a qualified disclaimer if it was timely made within nine months after the decedent's death

---

14. Continued enjoyment is completely noncontroversial if the disclaimant is a surviving spouse, as to whom an exception in §2518(b)(4)(A) is applicable. See Treas. Reg. §25.2518-2(e)(2).

15. AOD 1990-06.

16. Treas. Reg. §§25.2518-2(c)(4)(i) (penultimate sentence); 25.2518-2(c)(5) *Examples (7)* and *(8)*.

17. Treas. Reg. §25.2518-2(c)(4)(iii) (penultimate sentence).

Treas. Reg. §25.2518-3 allows partial disclaimers involving interests in trust, including separate identifiable interests, powers of appointment, and fractional or pecuniary amounts, making it easier to tailor a trust to the postmortem desires of the disclaimant without requiring an all-or-nothing renunciation.

Effective Under State Law. Notwithstanding Congress' avowed purpose in adopting §2518 to subject disclaimers to a uniform standard, the government's position was that a disclaimer was not qualified unless it was effective under local law. For example, now-discarded Prop. Treas. Reg. §25.2518-1(c)(1) stated: "If a disclaimer is not effective under applicable local law to divest ownership of the disclaimed property in the disclaimant and to vest it in another, the disclaimer is not a qualified disclaimer under §2518." To address this issue, Congress enacted §2518(c)(3), as explained by S. Rep. No. 144, 97th Cong., 1st Sess. 142 (1981):

When Congress enacted §2518, it intended to create a uniform Federal standard so that a disclaimer would be effective for Federal estate and gift tax purposes whether or not valid under local law.

Under §2518, however, because the disclaimer must be effective to divest the disclaimant of ownership, and pass the interest without direction on the part of the person making the disclaimer, the disclaimer must still satisfy local law. Because applicable law varies from State to State, there is still no uniformity.

The committee believes that a disclaimant should be able to perfect an otherwise valid disclaimer by directing that the interest pass to the person who would have received the property had the refusal been effective under local law.

EXPLANATION OF PROVISION

Under the committee bill, for purposes of the estate and gift tax, a refusal to accept any property interest that is not effective to pass title under local law will be considered to pass the property without any direction on the part of the disclaimant if the refusal otherwise satisfies the Federal requirements and the disclaimant timely transfers the property interest to the person who would have received the property had the refusal been an effective disclaimer under local law. Although the State disclaimer rules will be used to determine the transferee, the refusal need not be a valid disclaimer under local law.

Disclaimers as a Marital Deduction Planning Device. Disclaimers often are used as a postmortem device to obtain various tax and other objectives for estates that were not well planned. Section 2518(b)(4)(A) presents the opportunity to deliberately plan for a surviving spouse's disclaimer. This provision was added in 1978 to allow a surviving spouse to make a qualified disclaimer of an interest in property passing from the decedent even though, "as a result of that refusal the property passes to . . . the spouse," provided the alternative disposition to (or for the benefit of) the spouse does not result from any direction by the surviving spouse.

This provision permits the use of unlimited transfers to a decedent's surviving spouse with a proviso that any portion of the bequest disclaimed by the surviving spouse passes to a nonmarital trust that provides an income interest for the surviving spouse. Within nine months after the decedent's death the surviving spouse merely determines the optimal amount of marital deduction and disclaims the rest, based on the facts and circumstances as they exist after the decedent's death rather than by a formula written into the decedent's will, possibly many years before death.

Despite the superficial attractiveness of this device, however, there are disadvantages associated with it. To name a few: the surviving spouse's disclaimer may be disqualified if the nonmarital trust confers a power of appointment on the surviving spouse (see Treas. Reg. §§25.2518-2(e)(2), -2(e)(5) *Example (5)*); state law may not authorize the decedent to direct the disposition of disclaimed property or interests therein; state law may preclude the disclaimer if the surviving spouse is incompetent; and disclaimer may be impossible if the surviving spouse also dies (such as in a common accident) before the disclaimer can be made and if the spouse's personal representative is not permitted to make the disclaimer on behalf of the surviving spouse.

If qualifying only a portion of the decedent's estate is desirable, an alternative approach more frequently utilized is to employ the partial QTIP election permitted by §2056(b)(7), which we studied in Chapter 11. In most cases the appropriate division can be planned in a testator's will and no postmortem examination and redivision is necessary.

11. *Net Gifts.* A donor who makes a taxable gift has primary liability to pay the gift tax.[18] The donor may condition the gift on the donee's promise to pay the gift tax, in which case the promise constitutes consideration to the donor and reduces the amount of the gift. Such a gift, conditioned upon the donee's payment of the gift tax, is referred to as a "net gift." Because the amount of the gift tax and the size of the gift are interdependent, the gift tax liability is determined under an algebraic formula specified in Rev. Rul. 75-72. If the gift also is subject to state gift taxes, the formula must account for those taxes as well, as illustrated in a series of

---

18. See §2502(c). To the extent the donor does not pay, §6901(a)(1) imposes transferee liability on the donee and §6324(b) imposes a lien for enforcement.

rulings that demonstrate by example the application of this formula to net gifts that are subject to the state gift taxes of California (Rev. Rul. 76-104), New York (Rev. Rul 76-49), North Carolina (Rev. Rul. 76-57), and Virginia (Rev. Rul. 76-105). Rev. Rul. 81-223 specifies that a net gift cannot be made (that is, the donee may not pay the donor's gift tax) until the donor's unified credit has been exhausted. So this device is available only in cases in which large inter vivos transfers have consumed the credit, making this value-depressing opportunity of limited utility to the average donor.

Making a net gift may cause recognition of gain by the donor for income tax purposes if the amount of the gift tax imposed on the donee exceeds the donor's basis in the transferred property. Because the gift tax paid by the donee is consideration for the transfer, the effect is a part-sale, part-gift transaction for income tax purposes and, if the amount realized (the gift tax obligation) exceeds the donor's adjusted basis, then gain will be recognized under Diedrich v. Commissioner, 457 U.S. 191 (1982). The donee's basis in any event is the greater of either the donee's cost (the gift tax obligation assumed) or a carryover of the donor's basis. Treas. Reg. §1.1015-4. That figure, however, is increased under §1015(d)(6) by all or a portion of the donor's gift tax liability (notwithstanding that it was paid by the donee). The sum constitutes the donee's basis in the transferred property. The result is similar to the treatment of a gift of property subject to an encumbrance,[19] which is a topic to which we now turn.

12.   *Transfers in Satisfaction of Obligations.*   *P* gave $250,000 to one daughter, *A*, in exchange for *A*'s promise to pay *P*'s 32-year-old invalid daughter, *B*, $28,000 per year for the rest of *B*'s life. Assume the value of *B*'s annuity of $28,000 per year is $250,000. Are there any gift tax consequences, and to whom? See Treas. Reg. §25.2511-1(h)(2) and assume that the following statute is applicable:

Uniform Civil Liability for Support Act (1954)

Section 1. [Definitions.] As used in this act: . . .

(d) "Child" means a son or daughter under the age of [ ] years and a son or daughter of whatever age who is incapacitated from earning a living and without sufficient means.

Section 2. [Man's Duty of Support.] Every man shall support his wife, and his child [; and his parent when in need].

Section 3. [Woman's Duty of Support.] Every woman shall support her child; and her husband [and her parent] when in need. . . .

---

19.   Encumbered property given to a charity is subject to a different computation under the bargain sale to charity rules of §1011(b).

Section 6. [Amount of Support.] When determining the amount due for support the court shall consider all relevant factors including but not limited to:

(a) the standard of living and situation of the parties;

(b) the relative wealth and income of the parties;

(c) the ability of the obligor to earn;

(d) the ability of the obligee to earn;

(e) the need of the obligee;

(f) the age of the parties;

(g) the responsibility of the obligor for the support of others.

Legal duties are hard to pin down, and transfers relative to those obligations are troublesome, as shown next.

Commissioner v. Greene
119 F.2d 383 (9th Cir. 1941)

HANEY, J.: . . . Alice H. Lester and W.E. Lester were married more than forty years ago. As a result of the marriage two daughters, Carolyn and Beatrice, were born. The former is now about 47 years old, and the latter about 43. More than 30 years ago Alice H. Lester became incompetent and ever since has been and is now confined in an institution for insane persons. Prior thereto, the husband, wife and two daughters lived together as a family unit in luxury and in the manner of people of wealth. After the incompetency of the wife, the husband and two daughters lived together as a family unit until the marriage of Carolyn, and thereafter, the husband and Beatrice continued to live as a family unit until the marriage of Beatrice. Carolyn first married one Hamilton, and in 1930 married Thomas J. Loan who is now her husband. Beatrice in 1932 married one Pauli from whom she was divorced in 1938 and has since been unmarried.

The husband of Alice H. Lester died on May 29, 1933, and left an estate appraised at about $38,000 which was distributed in equal shares to the two daughters and the estate of the incompetent.

The incompetent has always been a person of large financial means. For example, the income from the principal of her estate which is in excess of $2,000,000 was: for 1932 — $121,931; for 1933 — $91,473.85; for 1934 — $88,385.74; for 1935 — $68,468.91; for 1936 — $109,673.53; and for 1937 — $142,614.13.

Loan has never contributed to the support of Carolyn, and Pauli has never contributed to the support of Beatrice. Both daughters were from birth accustomed to a life of ease and luxury, and neither of them was trained for any gainful occupation and neither of them was during any of said times able to engage in any gainful occupation. Since the incompetency of their mother, the only means of support available to them has been the incompetent's estate. Except to the extent of their interest, if any, in the incompetent's estate, the payments received therefrom, and the distributions received from their father's estate, both daughters have been at all times since prior to June 6, 1932, poor persons unable to maintain themselves by work.

From time to time since the inception of the incompetency of the mother, the proper state court has made orders directing the payment of money from the estate to the husband and the two daughters. Prior to the calendar year 1937, such court refused to direct payments except for the maintenance and support of the father and daughters. The amounts ordered to be paid were liberal. Such payments were apparently made pursuant to the following provisions of the California Civil Code and Probate Code, respectively:

§206. . . . It is the duty of the father, the mother, and the children of any poor person who is unable to maintain himself by work, to maintain such person to the extent of their ability. . . .

§1052. . . . Every guardian of an estate must manage it frugally and without waste, and apply the income, as far as may be necessary, to the comfortable and suitable support, maintenance and education of the ward and his family, if any. . . .

On October 19, 1937, the state court ordered that additional payments be made to the two daughters pursuant to Calif. Probate Code, §1558, as follows:

. . . On the application of the guardian of next of kin of an insane or incompetent person, the court may direct the guardian to pay and distribute surplus income, not used for the support and maintenance of the ward, or any part of such surplus income, to the next of kin whom the ward would, in the judgment of the court, have aided, if said ward had been of sound mind. The granting of such allowance and the amounts and proportions thereof shall be discretionary with the court, but the court shall give consideration to the amount of surplus income available after due provision has been made for the proper support and maintenance of the ward, to the circumstances and condition of life to which the ward and said next of kin have been accustomed and to the amount which the ward would, in the judgment of the court have allowed said next of kin, had said ward been of sound mind. . . .

In the order the court directed that $7,500 be paid to each daughter and found: "That in the judgment of the court, due consideration being given to the amount of said surplus income, the circumstances and condition of life to which said ward and her said children have been accustomed, said ward, if she were of sound mind, would aid said children and would pay and distribute to her said children the portion of [t]he said surplus income which is hereinafter directed to be so distributed."

The $7,500 was in addition to the amounts ordered to be paid for maintenance of the daughters.

The orders of the state court contained findings that the daughters were unable to maintain themselves by work; that the payments were necessary for the comfortable and suitable support and maintenance of the daughters as members of the ward's family; and that in the court's judgment, the incompetent would, had she been of sound mind, have aided the daughters by the payments in question. The amounts paid to the daughters were as follows:

Year	To Carolyn	To Beatrice
1932	$7,392.83	$5,000.00
1933	9,816.49	9,607.70
1934	11,000.00	11,000.00
1935	16,844.91	14,362.91
1936	21,000.00	21,000.00
1937	20,000.00	20,000.00

All such amounts were surplus income not used for the support and maintenance of the incompetent.

The Commissioner determined that the payments were gifts and assessed deficiencies in the gift taxes for 1936 and 1937. Respondent petitioned the Board [of Tax Appeals] for a redetermination of the deficiencies. The Board entered decisions that there were no deficiencies, and the Commissioner seeks review of those decisions. . . .

A majority of the Board held that all payments made to the daughters for maintenance and support were in satisfaction of an obligation imposed by law (Calif. Civil Code §206; Calif. Probate Code §1502) and were therefore not to be classed as gifts; that the $7,500 payments in 1937 were taxable as gifts. One member of the Board dissented without opinion. Three members dissented on the ground that under §[2512(b)], all payments were gifts. Two members dissented on the ground that §206, Calif. Civil Code only required the parent to supply reasonable necessities, and that the maintenance supplied was "beyond ordinary necessities."

Respondent's argument is that Calif. Probate Code, §1502, and Calif. Civil Code, §206, impose obligations upon the incompetent's estate to support the daughters; that the state court's orders were binding on that question; and that the payments were made without donative intent and were not, therefore, gifts. Respondent's argument is based on the theory that state law is applicable. The first question to be decided is whether the state law is applicable.

The rule is that "State law may control only when the federal taxing act, by express language or necessary implication, makes its own operation dependent upon state law." Burnet v. Harmel, 287 U.S. 103, 110; see, also, Thomas v. Perkins, 301 U.S. 655, 659; Biddle v. Commissioner, 302 U.S. 573, 578; Lyeth v. Hoey, 305 U.S. 188, 194; Morgan v. Commissioner, 309 U.S. 78, 81.

Since the argument of this case, United States v. Pelzer, [312 U.S. 399] (1941), was decided. That case considered §[2503(b)] which provides for an exclusion . . . in "the case of gifts [other than of future interests in property]." In the last cited case the taxpayer argued that since the statute did not define "future interests" they must be taken to be future interests as defined by the local law. The court said: " . . . But as we have often had occasion to point out, the revenue laws are to be construed in the light of their general purpose to establish a nation-wide scheme of taxation uniform in its application. Hence their provisions are not to be taken as subject to state control or limitation unless the language or necessary implication of the section involved makes its application dependent on state law. . . ."

Here, property, i.e., money, was transferred, and pursuant to §[2512(b)], the amount of the gift is "the amount by which the value of the property exceeded the value of the consideration." The only thing in question here is the "consideration." Nothing in the act expressly states that the existence of consideration is to be determined by state law. There is no more reason for saying here that Congress meant consideration as defined by state law, than there was for saying the Congress meant "future interest" as defined by state law.

The committee reports state that the tax imposed by the act "is designed to reach all transfers to the extent that they are donative, and to exclude any consideration not reducible to money or money's worth. . . . See Committee Reports on the Revenue Acts, 1939-1 C.B. (Part 2) 478, 526. . . . [Treas. Reg. §25.2512-8] provides in part:

> Transfers reached by the statute are not confined to those only which, being without a valuable consideration, accord with the common law concept of gifts. . . . A consideration not reducible to a money value, as love and affection, promise of marriage, etc., is to be wholly disregarded, and the entire value of the property transferred constitutes the amount of the gift.

It is thus apparent that there is nothing to indicate that local law was to determine what might be consideration, but, on the contrary, the taxing act considered certain transfers as gifts, whether local law so considered them or not. Since local law is not controlling, it is immaterial what local statutes said, or local courts held. . . .

Respondent's contention that there was no donative intention is immaterial because §[2512(b)] of the act in question does not require it.

The Board's decisions are reversed and the case is remanded to the Board for further proceedings in accordance with the views herein expressed.

STEPHENS, J.: I dissent.

The majority opinion holds that all moneys paid out of the incompetent's estate for the support of her adult married daughters are "gifts" and taxable as such, and holds as immaterial the legal fact that the California Code imposed a legal duty upon her to support her indigent children. This is based upon the theory that "State law may control only when the federal taxing act, by express language or necessary implication, makes its own operation dependent upon state law," citing the recent case of United States v. Pelzer, [312 U.S. 399] (1941).

I do not read the *Pelzer* case as authority for the proposition that we are not bound by the State law in the instant case. There the question involved was whether or not the gift under consideration was a gift of a "future interest." It was argued by the taxpayer that the Federal courts were bound by the State law defining what constituted a "future interest." The Supreme Court looked to the committee reports and determined that the purpose of the statute was to make taxable gifts "whether vested or contingent, limited to commence in possession or enjoyment at a future date," and that this was what was meant by the words "future interest" in the taxing statute. The Regulations had defined "future interest" in the same terms. The Court merely held that the provisions of the taxing statute were not subject to state control in this respect.

In the instant case the committee reports state that the tax imposed by the Act "is designed to reach all transfers to the extent that they are donative, and to exclude any consideration not reducible to money or money's worth. . . ." The Regulations promulgated under the Act provide that the tax shall apply to transfers without consideration, and that "a consideration not reducible to a money value, as love and affection, promise of marriage, etc., is to be wholly disregarded."

But this is not to say that a transfer in discharge of a legal obligation imposed by local law is a transfer without consideration under the taxing act. It is my opinion that the discharge of a legal obligation is clearly "consideration" without the meaning of the tax act, and that the statute by necessary implication makes its own operation in that respect dependent upon State law.

It seems clear that under California Civil Code, Section 206, and the cases construing that section, the incompetent at all times material to this controversy was subject to a legally enforceable obligation to support and maintain her daughters, who were, as pointed out by the majority, "poor persons unable to maintain themselves by work" within the meaning of the California law. Section 206 fixes the obligation as "to the extent of [her] ability." Section 1502 of the California Probate Code provides for the support of the family of an incompetent by the application of the income "as far as may be necessary, to the comfortable and suitable support, maintenance and education" of the family. The measure of the support and maintenance allowance was a matter for the discretion of the California Superior Court, sitting in probate, and its determination that the amounts distributed to the incompetent's daughters were necessary for their comfortable and suitable maintenance is binding upon us.

The decision of the Board should be affirmed.

13. Consideration. The concept of "consideration" also has a specific legal meaning for wealth transfer tax purposes, as revealed by the next case:

Commissioner v. Wemyss
324 U.S. 303 (1945)

Mr. Justice FRANKFURTER delivered the opinion of the Court.

In 1939 taxpayer proposed marriage to Mrs. More, a widow with one child. Her deceased husband had set up two trusts, one half the income of which was for the benefit of Mrs. More and the other half for that of the child with provision that, in the event of Mrs. More's remarriage, her part of the income ceased and went to the child. The corpus of the two trusts consisted of stock which brought to Mrs. More from the death of her first husband to her remarriage, about five years later, an average income of $5,484 a year. On Mrs. More's unwillingness to suffer loss of her trust income through remarriage the parties on May 24, 1939, entered upon an agreement whereby taxpayer transferred to Mrs. More a block of shares of stock. Within a month they married. The Commissioner ruled that the transfer of this stock, the value of which, $149,456.13, taxpayer does not controvert, was subject to [gift taxation under §§2501(a) and 2512(b)]. Accordingly, he assessed a deficiency which the Tax Court upheld, 2 T.C. 876, but the Circuit Court of Appeals reversed the Tax Court, 144 F.2d 78. We granted certiorari to settle uncertainties in tax administration engendered by seemingly conflicting decisions.

In view of the major role which the Tax Court plays in Federal tax litigation, it becomes important to consider how that court dealt with this problem. Fusing, as it were, §§[2501(a)] and [2512(b)], the Tax Court read them as not being limited by any common law technical notions about "consideration." And so, while recognizing that marriage was of course a valuable consideration to support a contract, the Tax Court did not deem marriage to satisfy the requirement of §[2501(a)] in that it was not a consideration reducible to money value. Accordingly, the Court found the whole value of the stock transferred to Mrs. More taxable under the statute and the relevant Treas. Reg. [§25.2512-8]. In the alternative, the Tax Court was of the view that if Mrs. More's loss of her trust income rather than the marriage was consideration for the taxpayer's transfer of his stock to her, he is not relieved from the tax because he did not receive any money's worth from Mrs. More's relinquishment of her trust income, and, in any event, the actual value of her interest in the trust, subject to fluctuations of its stock earnings, was not proved. One member of the Tax Court dissented, deeming that the gift tax legislation invoked ordinary contract conceptions of "consideration."

The Circuit Court of Appeals rejected this line of reasoning. It found in the marriage agreement an arm's-length bargain and an absence of "donative intent" which it deemed essential; "A donative intent followed by a donative act is essential to constitute a gift; and no strained and artificial constructions of a supplementary statute should be indulged to tax as a gift a transfer actually lacking donative intent." 144 F.2d 78, 82.

Sections [2501(a)] and [2512(b)] are not disparate provisions. Congress directed them to the same purpose, and they should not be separated in application. Had Congress taxed "gifts" *simpliciter*, it would be appropriate to assume that the term was used in its colloquial sense, and a search for "donative intent" would be indicated. But Congress intended to use the term "gifts" in its broadest and most comprehensive sense. H. Rep. No. 708, 72d Cong., 1st Sess. 27; S. Rep. No. 665, 72d Cong., 1st Sess. 39; cf. Smith v. Shaughnessy, 318 U.S. 176; Robinette v. Helvering, 318 U.S. 184. Congress chose not to require an ascertainment of what too often is an elusive state of mind. For purposes of the gift tax it not only dispensed with the test of "donative intent." It formulated a much more workable external test, that where "property is transferred for less than an adequate and full consideration in money or money's worth," the excess in such money value "shall, for the purpose of the tax imposed by this title, be deemed a gift. . . ." And Treasury Regulations have emphasized that common law considerations were not embodied in the gift tax.

To reinforce the evident desire of Congress to hit all the protean arrangements which the wit of man can devise that are not business transactions within the meaning of ordinary speech, the Treasury Regulations make clear that no genuine business transaction comes within the purport of the gift tax by excluding "a sale, exchange, or other transfer of property made in the ordinary course of business (a transaction which is bona fide, at arm's length, and free from any donative intent)." Treas. Reg. [§25.2512-8]. Thus on finding that a transfer in the circumstances of a particular case is not made in the ordinary course of business, the transfer becomes subject to the gift tax to the extent that it is not made "for an adequate and full consideration in money or money's worth." See 2 Paul, FEDERAL ESTATE AND GIFT TAXATION 1113 (1942).

The Tax Court in effect found the transfer of the stock to Mrs. More was not made at arm's length in the ordinary course of business. It noted that the inducement was marriage, took account of the discrepancy between what she got and what she gave up, and also of the benefit that her marriage settlement brought to her son. These were considerations the Tax Court could justifiably heed, and heeding, decide as it did. . . .

If we are to isolate as an independently reviewable question of law the view of the Tax Court that money consideration must benefit the donor to relieve a transfer by him from being a gift, we think the Tax Court was correct. . . .

The section taxing as gifts transfers that are not made for "adequate and full [money] consideration" aims to reach those transfers which are withdrawn from the donor's estate. To allow detriment to the donee to satisfy the requirement of "adequate and full consideration" would violate the purpose of the statute and open wide the door for evasion of the gift tax. . . .

Reversed.

Justice ROBERTS dissents, and would affirm the judgment for the reasons given in the opinion of the Circuit Court of Appeals.

In Merrill v. Fahs, 324 U.S. 308 (1945) (5 to 4 decision), a companion case to *Wemyss*, the Court held that a husband's transfer of property in trust for his wife pursuant to a premarital agreement constituted a gift for gift tax purposes. In return for this transfer, which was made in 1939, the wife released her marital rights (except for her right to maintenance and support), but the Court held that the wife's release did not constitute "adequate and full consideration in money or money's worth" as required by the predecessor of §2512(b). The court noted that the release of marital rights does not constitute money's worth consideration for estate tax purposes (see the current §2043(b), which was first adopted in 1932), and the Court stated that, because the estate and gift taxes are complimentary, they are "in *pari materia* and must be construed together." Although the Court noted that the estate and gift tax laws are not always correlated, it felt that the phrase "adequate and full consideration in money or money's worth" should be given the same construction in both tax systems.

See Treas. Reg. §25.2512-8.

Harris is an addition to the consideration rule — another way to avoid gift taxation:

Harris v. Commissioner
340 U.S. 106 (1950)

Mr. Justice DOUGLAS delivered the opinion of the Court.

The federal estate tax and the federal gift tax, as held in a line of cases ending with Commissioner v. Wemyss, 324 U.S. 303, and Merrill v. Fahs, 324 U.S. 308, are construed in pari materia, since the purpose of the gift tax is to complement the estate tax by preventing tax-free depletion of the transferor's estate during his lifetime. Both the gift tax and the estate tax exclude transfers made for "an adequate and full consideration in money or money's worth." In the estate tax this requirement is limited to deductions for claims based upon "a promise or agreement"; but the consideration for the "promise or agreement" may not be the release of marital rights in the decedent's property. In the *Wemyss* and *Merrill* cases the question was whether the gift tax was applicable to premarital property settlements. If the standards of the estate tax were to be applied ex proprio vigore in gift tax cases, those transfers would be taxable because there was a "promise or agreement" touching marital rights in property. We sustained the tax, thus giving "adequate and full consideration in money or money's worth" the same meaning under both statutes insofar as premarital property settlements or agreements are concerned.

The present case raises the question whether *Wemyss* and *Merrill* require the imposition of the gift tax in the type of postnuptial settlement of property rights involved here.

Petitioner divorced her husband, Reginald Wright, in Nevada in 1943. Both she and her husband had substantial property interests. They reached an understanding as respects the unscrambling of those interests, the settlement of all litigated claims to the separate properties, the assumption of obligations, and the transfer of properties.

. . . It was found that the value of the property transferred to Wright exceeded that received by petitioner by $107,150. The Commissioner assessed a gift tax on the theory that any rights which Wright might have given up by entering into the agreement could not be adequate and full consideration.

If the parties had without more gone ahead and voluntarily unravelled their business interests on the basis of this compromise, there would be no question that the gift tax would be payable. For there would have been a "promise or agreement" that effected a relinquishment of marital rights in property. It therefore would fall under the ban of the provision of the estate tax which by judicial construction has been incorporated into the gift tax statute.

But the parties did not simply undertake a voluntary contractual division of their property interests. They were faced with the fact that Nevada law not only authorized but instructed the divorce court to decree a just and equitable disposition of both the community and the separate property of the parties. The agreement recited that it was executed in order to effect a settlement of the respective property rights of the parties "in the event a divorce should be decreed"; and it provided that the agreement should be submitted to the divorce court "for its approval." It went on to say,

It is of the essence of this agreement that the settlement herein provided for shall not become operative in any manner nor shall any of the Recitals or covenants herein become binding upon either party unless a decree of absolute divorce between the parties shall be entered in the pending Nevada action.

If the agreement had stopped there and were in fact submitted to the court, it is clear that the gift tax would not be applicable. That arrangement would not be a "promise or agreement" in the statutory sense. It would be wholly conditional upon the entry of the decree; the divorce court might or might not accept the provisions of the arrangement as the measure of the respective obligations; it might indeed add to or subtract from them. The decree, not the arrangement submitted to the court, would fix the rights and obligations of the parties. That was the theory of Commissioner v. Maresi, 156 F.2d 929, and we think it sound.

Even the Commissioner concedes that the result would be correct in case the property settlement was litigated in the divorce action. That was what happened in Commissioner v. Converse, 163 F.2d 131, where the divorce court decreed a lump-sum award in lieu of monthly payments provided by the separation agreement. Yet without the decree there would be no enforceable, existing agreement whether the settlement was litigated or unlitigated. Both require the approval of the court before an obligation arises. The happenstance that the divorce court might approve the entire settlement, or modify it in unsubstantial details, or work out material changes seems to us unimportant. In each case it is the decree that creates the rights and the duties; and a decree is not a "promise or agreement" in any sense — popular or statutory.

But the present case is distinguished by reason of a further provision in the undertaking and in the decree. The former provided that "the covenants in this agreement shall survive any decree of divorce which may be entered." And the decree stated "it is ordered that said agreement and said trust agreements forming a part thereof shall survive this decree." The Court of Appeals turned the case on those provisions. It concluded that since there were two sanctions for the payments and transfers — contempt under the divorce decree and execution under the contract — they were founded not only on the decree but upon both the decree and a "promise or agreement." It therefore held the excess of the value of the property which petitioner gave her husband over what he gave her to be taxable as a gift. 178 F.2d 861.

We, however, think that the gift tax statute is concerned with the source of rights, not with the manner in which rights at some distant time may be enforced. Remedies for enforcement will vary from state to state. It is "the transfer" of the property with which the gift tax statute is concerned, not the sanctions which the law supplies to enforce transfers. If "the transfer" of marital rights in property is effected by the parties, it is pursuant to a " promise or agreement" in the meaning of the statute. If "the transfer" is effected by court decree, no "promise or agreement" of the parties is the operative fact. In no realistic sense is a court decree a "promise or agreement" between the parties to a litigation. If finer, more legalistic lines are to be drawn, Congress must do it.

If, as we hold, the case is free from any "promise or agreement" concerning marital rights in property, it presents no remaining problems of difficulty. The Treasury Regulations recognize as tax free "a sale, exchange, or other transfer of property made in the ordinary course of business (a transaction which is bona fide, at arm's length, and free from any donative intent)." This transaction is not "in the ordinary course of business" in any conventional sense. Few transactions between husband and wife ever would be; and those under the aegis of a divorce court are not. But if two partners on dissolution of the firm entered into a transaction of this character or if chancery did it for them, there would seem to be no doubt that the unscrambling of the business interests would satisfy the spirit of the Regulations. No reason is apparent why husband and wife should be under a heavier handicap absent a statute which brings all marital property settlements under the gift tax. . . . Reversed.

[The dissenting opinion of Mr. Justice FRANKFURTER, in which Justices BLACK, BURTON, and MINTON joined, is omitted].

Revenue Ruling 60-160

Advice has been requested whether an indebtedness arising from a property settlement agreement incorporated in a divorce decree is deductible from the gross estate of a decedent.

The decedent, in the instant case, has entered into an agreement with his then wife, settling their property rights and providing for alimony payments. A decree of divorce was later granted by the court and the whole agreement was incorporated in the court's decree. The terms of the agreement provided that the decedent was to pay her a specified amount of alimony, and to create a trust of 20x dollars, the income of which was to be paid to himself for life and the corpus to vest in his divorced wife upon his death. The agreement also provided that he was to execute his will and leave his divorced wife one-third of his net estate, the trust corpus to be a part of the one-third interest.

The decedent complied with all provisions except those relating to the terms of his will. However, upon his death, the court awarded his divorced wife one-third of the net estate pursuant to the divorce decree.

Section 2053(c)(1) of the Internal Revenue Code of 1954 states, in part, that the deductions allowed in case of any indebtedness, when founded on a promise or agreement, shall be limited to the extent that it was contracted bona fide and for an adequate and full consideration in money or money's worth.

Section 2043(b) of the Code states that a relinquishment or promised relinquishment of dower or curtesy, or of a statutory estate created in lieu of dower or curtesy, or of other marital rights in the decedent's property or estate, shall not be considered to any extent a consideration "in money or money's worth."

With respect to transfers made pursuant to legal separation agreements or divorce decrees, E.T. 19, 1946-2 C.B. 166, holds that only a release of support rights may constitute a consideration in money or money's worth for both estate and gift tax purposes. A release of property rights is not considered made "to any extent" for an adequate and full consideration in money or money's worth.

However, in Harris v. Commissioner, 340 U.S. 106, the court said, " . . . if 'the transfer' of marital rights in property is effected by the parties, it is pursuant to a 'promise or agreement' in the meaning of the statute. If 'the transfer' is effected by court decree, no 'promise or agreement' of the parties is the operative fact. In no realistic sense is a court decree a 'promise or agreement' between the parties to a litigation."

In McMurtry v. Commissioner, 203 F.2d 659, the court read *Harris*, supra, ". . . more broadly as supporting the proposition that . . . all transfers agreed upon in contemplation of divorce and executed after approval by a divorce court having jurisdiction to give such sanction or in its discretion to prescribe some different property settlement, should be exempt from the gift tax."

While both *Harris* and *McMurtry* were gift tax cases, their rationale was considered applicable to estate tax in accordance with the decision in Merrill v. Fahs, 324 U.S. 308, holding that the same phrases in the two tax laws should be given the same reading unless obvious reasons compel divergent treatment.

In Commissioner v. Estate of Watson, 216 F.2d 941, *aff'g* 20 T.C. 386 (1953), *acq.*, 1958-1 C.B. 6, where a separation agreement was incorporated in a divorce decree, the court held that the divorced wife's claim for her share of the decedent's estate under the agreement was founded on the divorce decree rather than on the agreement and, therefore, it was deductible from the gross estate if the decree was one within the powers of the court to make irrespective of the consent of the parties.

On the other hand, Estate of Bowers v. Commissioner, 23 T.C. 911, *acq.*, 1955-2 C.B. 4, held that where the court had no power under local law to decree a settlement of marital property rights which would vary the terms of a settlement agreement, without the consent of the parties, the obligation or "indebtedness" arising out of such settlement is founded on a promise or agreement.

Accordingly, in view of the foregoing, it is held that in a case in which the divorce court has power to decree a settlement of all property rights or to vary the terms of a prior settlement agreement, and does approve the agreement, any indebtedness arising out of such settlement is not considered to be founded upon a promise or agreement but, rather, it is considered to be founded upon such court decree and is, therefore, an allowable deduction from the gross estate in the amount of such indebtedness. If the court does not have the power to disregard the provisions of a previously existing property settlement agreement, a deduction is allowable only to the extent that the transfer does not exceed the reasonable value of the support rights of the wife.

E.T. 19 is hereby modified.

There is authority supporting the position asserted in Rev. Rul. 60-160 that the *Harris* doctrine is limited to the circumstance in which the divorce court has the power to alter the terms of the parties' agreement. Estate of Satz v. Commissioner, 78 T.C. 1172 (1982). Note also that a release of support rights, as contrasted to other marital rights, is treated as money's worth consideration. Rev. Rul. 77-314; Estate of Hundley v. Commissioner, 52 T.C. 495 (1969), *aff'd per curiam*, 435 F.2d 1311 (4th Cir. 1971).

Senate Report No. 1622
83d Cong., 2d Sess. 48 (1954)

SECTION 2516. CERTAIN PROPERTY SETTLEMENTS

Under present law there is substantial uncertainty as to whether a gift may result from transfers to the wife under a property settlement incident to a divorce. The House bill provides that where transfers are made pursuant to a separation agreement and divorce occurs within a reasonable time thereafter, such transfers as are made to a spouse in settlement of his or her marital or property rights or to provide a reasonable allowance for the support of issue of the marriage during minority will be deemed to be transfers made for a full and adequate consideration in money or money's worth.

Your committee believes that the term "reasonable time" appearing in the House bill is too indefinite and will create uncertainty as to the application of the section. Accordingly, this section has been revised to indicate that transfers of property by husband and wife pursuant to a written agreement relative to their marital and property rights or to provide a reasonable allowance for the support of the issue of the spouses during minority will be exempt from gift tax provided that divorce occurs within two years after entering into the agreement.

Impact of Unlimited Marital Deduction.   The significance of §2516 was reduced by the adoption in 1981 of an unlimited marital deduction for gifts made between spouses. §2523(a). Gifts made by one spouse to the other prior to a divorce have no transfer tax consequences regardless of whether §2516 covers the transfer. But the unlimited marital deduction does not eliminate entirely the need for §2516. Even though a written separation agreement must be made prior to a divorce for §2516 to insulate from the gift tax transfers made pursuant to that agreement, the transfers themselves can be made after the divorce. So if §2516 is operative, even transfers made after the divorce will not cause any gift tax consequences. And see §1041, making such transfers income tax free as well.

In the context of transfers incident to marriage or divorce, let's consider a few hypotheticals that bookend the existence of the marital relation:

(a) M gave F a $15,000 engagement ring when M and F became engaged. What are the gift tax consequences of M's transfer if state law provides that the gift is contingent on consummation by marriage? Think about when the gift is complete.

(b) A few months later M broke the engagement without justification. What would be the gift tax consequences if under local law F was permitted to keep the engagement ring, but voluntarily returned it to M? Notice that this fact hypothesis is the exact converse of that in **(a)**.

(c) A year later M became engaged to G. M and G executed a prenuptial agreement under which M agreed to transfer stocks valued at $700,000 to a trust on behalf of G in exchange for G's promise of marriage and release of all marital rights, except for the right of support. Shortly thereafter M transferred the $700,000 of stocks to the trust. A few months later M and G were married. Are there any gift tax consequences and, if so, what would it inform in terms of the drafting of such agreements? Pay special attention to the fact regarding support rights.

(d) *H* and *W* were divorced on June 2 of Year Four. The court awarded *W* a $300,000 property settlement, which *H* duly paid. *H* and *W* had no prior agreement as to the terms of the divorce. Any gift tax consequences?

(e) Same facts as (d) except that *H* and *W* agreed to a $300,000 property settlement on September 5 of Year Two and that agreement was incorporated in the divorce decree. As part of the agreement *W* released all marital rights including any right to support. Are there any gift tax consequences? What if the agreement was not incorporated in the divorce decree? See Treas. Reg. §25.6019-3(b) with respect to *H*'s duty regarding the filing of a gift tax return, and §6651 with respect to the consequence of *H*'s failing to file a return.

(f) Same facts as in (e) except that the agreement between *H* and *W* was executed on a bit earlier — on May 15 of Year Two. Now are there any gift tax consequences? Compare Rosenthal v. Commissioner, 205 F.2d 505, 509-510 (2d Cir. 1953), with Estate of Hundley v. Commissioner, 52 T.C. 495, 511-514 (1969), *aff'd per curiam*, 435 F.2d 1311 (4th Cir. 1971).

14. *When Was the Gift Made?* For a number of disparate reasons timing is important for gift tax purposes. One is annual exclusion entitlement. A second is the potential application of the gross up rule in §2035(b). A third is death bed gifts made literally at the eleventh hour. Fourth, gift splitting is an all-or-nothing endeavor on a year-by-year basis, which implicates timing. Similarly, generation-skipping exemption allocation is a year-by-year activity on the gift tax return, which also makes it important to know when a gift was made. And timing could impact a disclaimer by the donee or inclusion in the estate of a donee who dies shortly before or after a gift is deemed to be complete. The list could go on. The group of materials below all relate to this important and pervasive set of timing issues.

Revenue Ruling 69-347

. . . In 1965, a taxpayer and his intended wife entered into a written antenuptial agreement which provided that, in consideration of the marriage and the wife's relinquishment of her marital rights in her husband's property, the husband would pay her a fixed amount per year beginning one year after the date of their marriage and continuing for twenty years thereafter or until the wife's death, whichever event occurred first. The taxpayer and his wife were married in 1966 and the husband made the first payment in 1967. . . .

Section 2501 of the Code imposes a tax on the transfer of property by gift by any individual. The gift tax is not imposed upon the receipt of property by the donee, nor is it necessarily determined by the measure of enrichment resulting to the donee at the time of the transfer. The tax is a primary and personal liability of the donor, is an excise upon his act of making the transfer, is measured by the value of the property passing from the donor, and attaches at the time such property passes, regardless of the fact that the identity of the donee may not then be known or ascertainable. Treas. Reg. §25.2511-2(a). See also Robinette v. Helvering, 318 U.S. 184 (1943).

The gift tax is aimed at every kind and type of transfer by way of gift, whether the gift is direct or indirect, and whether the property is real or personal, tangible or intangible. Section 25.2511-1(a) of the regulations. Generally, a gift is complete when the donor has so parted with dominion or control as to leave in him no power to change its disposition, whether for his own benefit or for the benefit of another. Treas. Reg. §25.2511-2(b).

In Archbold v. Commissioner, 42 B.T.A. 453 (1940) (acq. in result only), the taxpayer and his intended wife entered into an antenuptial agreement in 1936. Under the terms of the agreement, the taxpayer agreed to transfer 10x dollars to a trust for the benefit of his wife in each of the next nine years. The agreement did not become legally enforceable until the marriage, which took place in 1937. The Service asserted a gift tax deficiency for 1936, rather than for 1937, when the promise to make the payments became legally enforceable.

The Board of Tax Appeals held that the taxpayer's promise to make future transfers of stated amounts did not constitute a taxable gift in 1936 (the taxable year in litigation), stating that the Commissioner had not rebutted the contention of the taxpayer that "a promise to make a gift in the future is not a present gift, even though the promise may be an enforceable one . . ." 42 B.T.A. 453, 455. Based on this statement the Service assumed that the Board considered that the promise before it was in fact an enforceable one in 1936.

In Estate of Copley v. Commissioner, 15 T.C. 17 (1950), *aff'd*, 194 F.2d 364 (1952), *acq.*, 1965-2 C.B. 4, the petitioner and his intended wife entered into an antenuptial agreement in 1931. Under the terms of the agreement, the petitioner promised to give his future wife a specified sum of money in consideration of the marriage and in lieu of all of her marital rights in his property. No date was specified for the transfer of such sum. The agreement became legally enforceable under state law on the date of the petitioner's marriage, which was also in 1931. The petitioner transferred part of the sum in 1936 and the remainder in 1944.

The Service relied on the *Archbold* opinion in contending that the 1936 and 1944 transfers were subject to a gift tax in such years. However, the Tax Court concluded that the petitioner's transfers were not subject to Federal gift taxes in 1936 and 1944, but that a gift tax would have been due in 1931 if there had been a gift tax law in effect at that time. The court stated: "Once the antenuptial contract became binding by the marriage, Copley became bound to make all of the payments and did not make a new gift each time he made a payment." 15 T.C. at 20.

Having stated that the transfer took place when the contract became binding, the Tax Court accordingly rejected the Commissioner's reliance upon the *Archbold* case, in which, as noted above, the Board was not faced with a binding contract in the taxable year in litigation. . . .

In the instant case, the taxpayer became legally obligated to perform according to the terms of the agreement at the time of his marriage in 1966. Since the instant gift is payable over a term of years, subject only to the wife's death, the value of the taxpayer's gift is determinable on the basis of recognized actuarial principles. See §25.2512-5 of the regulations. It follows, therefore, that the effective date of his gift for Federal gift tax purposes is in 1966.

See also Rev. Rul. 67-396. Also recall that the transfer made to the wife in Rev. Rul 69-347 would have no transfer tax consequence today because of the unlimited gift tax marital deduction. See §2523(a).

Gifts Subject to a Contingency. Rev. Rul. 69-347 suggests that the date that a gift is made for gift tax purposes is the date that the donor has no power to change the disposition, provided that a transfer subject to contingencies constitutes a completed gift on that date only if the contingencies are of such nature that the value of the gift is ascertainable. The genesis of this ascertainable value requirement apparently is the following language in Rosenthal v. Commissioner, 205 F.2d 505, 509 (2d Cir. 1953):

In Harris v. Commissioner, 178 F.2d 861 (2d Cir. 1949), *rev'd on other grounds*, 340 U.S. 106 (1950), we hold that a binding promise to make a gift becomes subject to gift taxation in the year the obligation is undertaken and not when the discharging payments are made. The Seventh Circuit followed our decision on this point in Estate of Copley v. Commissioner, 194 F.2d 364 (7th Cir. 1952). This view of the law was likewise adopted by the Commissioner and the Tax Court in the instant case in determining that a gift tax was due in 1946 on the then value of the future annual payments to be made to the taxpayer's daughters under the 1946 revised agreement. The Commissioner refused, however, to accord similar treatment to the promises made in 1944 — and hence to view their surrender as consideration for the 1946 undertakings — because part of the taxpayer's 1944 commitment was contingent on the death of his mother during his lifetime. With this we cannot agree. The obligation undertaken by the taxpayer in the 1944 agreement, which was irrevocable without consent of the wife and the daughter affected once she became of age, at all times had an ascertainable value, since the stipulated contingency was susceptible to actuarial appraisal, even though it might conceivably never have come about. Robinette v. Helvering, 318 U.S. 184; see also Commissioner v. Maresi, 156 F.2d 929 (2d Cir.). . . . The possibility of valuation by actuarial tables distinguishes the present case from City Bank Farmers Trust Co. v. Hoey, 101 F.2d 9 (2d Cir.), holding that payments made pursuant to court orders were taxable when made, since the court's orders were subject to modification at any time.

The Commissioner relied on this ascertainable value requirement in Rev. Rul. 81-31, holding that an employee's inter vivos transfer to his wife of a death benefit was not complete until the employee died. The validity of the assertion that an ascertainable value is a condition precedent for the completion of a gift is addressed in DiMarco, reproduced at page 857. In describing incomplete transfers, Treas. Reg. §25.2511-2 refers only to transfers over which the donor has retained some meaningful control. There is no mention in the regulations that the value of the gift must be ascertainable for the gift to be complete. Perhaps the proper analysis is that contingencies should speak to the value of the gift instead of precluding completion of a gift. Under normal valuation methods, significant contingencies should mean that a willing buyer would pay little for the right to the donee's interest, reducing the gift tax value of the transfer. Notice, however, that valuation from a willing buyer's perspective deviates from the notion expressed in Rev. Rul. 69-347 that gift taxation is not determined by what the donee receives but on what the donor relinquishes. Are these the same concept? That issue is addressed beginning at page 863.

As to the Commissioner's view that a gift is complete on the date it is removed from the donor's control, see Rev. Rul. 79-384 (*A* promised a child, then 16 years old, $10,000 if the child would graduate from college. The child subsequently graduated from college, but *A* refused to make the payment. The child sued, and a judgment was issued against *A* in the amount of $10,000, which *A* promptly paid. *Held,* *A* made a gift to the child of $10,000 on the day the child graduated from college, which is the date the promise became enforceable and determinable in value, notwithstanding the fact that *A* did not actually make the payment until a later date when the judgment was rendered). Rev. Rul. 84-110; Rev. Rul. 79-238; Rev. Rul 75-71; Rev. Rul. 69-346. In regard to that position, consider the following case.

Estate of Dillingham v. Commissioner
88 T.C. 1569 (1987), *aff'd*, 903 F.2d 760 (10th Cir. 1990)

WELLS, J.: Respondent determined a deficiency in petitioner's Federal gift tax for . . . 1980 . . . and an addition to tax pursuant to §6651(a) . . . . Respondent also determined a deficiency in petitioner's Federal estate tax . . . .

After concessions, the sole issue to be decided is whether a noncharitable gift made by check is complete for Federal gift and estate tax purposes when the check is delivered to the donee. . . .

On or about December 24, 1980, the decedent delivered six checks [to six individuals, each in the amount of the annual exclusion ($3,000 at that time). The six checks are hereinafter collectively referred to as "the checks," and the six individuals are hereinafter collectively referred to as the "donees."] On or about January 28, 1981, the donees presented the checks to the drawee bank for payment and the checks were paid.

On or about January 28, 1981, the decedent delivered an additional check in the amount of $3,000 to each of the donees (these six additional checks are hereinafter collectively referred to as "the additional checks"). On or about January 28, 1981, the donees presented the additional checks to the drawee bank for payment and the additional checks were paid.

With respect to the gift tax deficiency, the parties have agreed that if the delivery of the checks constituted gifts in 1980, the gifts qualify for the annual exclusion in the amount of $3,000 per donee pursuant to §2503(b). Conversely, if the delivery of the checks constituted gifts in 1981, the gifts do not qualify for the annual exclusion.

. . . Respondent contends that the gifts were not complete in 1980 because there is no relation back of the payment of the checks to the date the checks were delivered, and that the decedent did not part with dominion and control over the checks in 1980 since she retained the power to stop payment on the checks.

. . . The relation back doctrine was first applied by this Court to gifts in Estate of Spiegel v. Commissioner, 12 T.C. 524 (1942). In *Spiegel* we allowed a charitable deduction for Federal income tax purposes in calendar year 1942 where the donor delivered two checks to a charitable donee in 1942, but the checks were not cashed until 1943 (one of the checks was cashed before the donor's death and the other check was not cashed until after the donor's death). We held that payment of the checks by the drawee bank related back to the time when the checks were delivered.

The relation back doctrine was then extended to charitable contributions for Federal estate tax purposes in Estate of Belcher v. Commissioner, 83 T.C. 227 (1984), where the donor delivered checks to charities and the checks were not cashed until after the donor's death. We held that payment of the checks by the drawee bank related back to the date of delivery so as to exclude the amount from the donor's gross estate. However, we concluded with the following note of caution:

> One final word. In *Spiegel*, we observed that "Charitable contributions may be gifts in the broad sense but for tax purposes they fall into a special class and there is special legislation dealing with them. What we say here is intended to apply to charitable contributions and not necessarily to all categories of gifts." Similarly, we intend our holding in this case to apply only to charitable contributions for estate tax purposes. Sufficient unto another day the question of includability of noncharitable gifts under similar circumstances. [Estate of Belcher v. Commissioner, 83 T.C. at 238-239.]

Since our decision in *Belcher*, Federal courts in three circuits have considered the issue whether the relation back doctrine applies to noncharitable gifts by check. McCarthy v. United States, 806 F.2d 129 (7th Cir. 1986), *rev'g* 624 F. Supp. 763 (N.D. Ill. 1985); Bacchus v. United States, 86-1 U.S. Tax Cas. (CCH) ¶13,669 (D.N.J. 1985); Cullis v. United States, 85-2 U.S. Tax Cas. (CCH) ¶13,645 (N.D. Ohio 1985). The circuit court in *McCarthy* and the district court in *Cullis* refused to extend the relation back doctrine to noncharitable gifts by check, while the district court in *Bacchus* did extend the doctrine to noncharitable gifts by check.

The circuit court in *McCarthy* voiced the following concern over extending the relation back doctrine to noncharitable gifts by check:

> By issuing a check to a noncharitable donee with the understanding that it not be cashed until after his death, a decedent may effectively beque[ath] up to $10,000 per donee, thus avoiding the estate tax consequences normally attending such transactions. Clearly, §2035(b)(2) was never intended to operate in such a manner. Only after a donee has parted with complete dominion and control of funds does §2035(b)(2) exempt them from the general rule that all gifts made within 3 years of death are to be included in the

donor's gross estate. I.R.C. §2035(a) (1985). [*McCarthy v. United States*, supra at 132.]

This Court expressed a similar concern in *Estate of Belcher v. Commissioner*, supra at 232.

Because the checks in the present cases were cashed before the decedent's death, the concern of this Court in *Belcher* and the Circuit Court in *McCarthy* that the donees might have a secret agreement with the donor that the checks would not be cashed until after the donor's death is not present. To that extent these cases are distinguishable from *McCarthy* and *Belcher*.

However, a similar concern is present in these cases since the checks were not cashed until 35 days after the delivery of the checks to the donees. There is no evidence explaining the reason for the delay. The delay, connected with the failure of the donees to cash the checks until the additional checks were delivered to the donees on January 28, 1981, casts doubt as to whether the checks were unconditionally delivered. Furthermore, we do not know whether the decedent's checking account had sufficient funds to cover the checks at the time the checks were delivered. We do not even know whether the decedent intended to make a gift by delivering the checks, an essential element in proving a gift (although this might be presumed from the conclusive manner in which the parties refer to the checks as gifts). . . . In the context of the instant case, petitioner was required to prove unconditional delivery of the checks, which petitioner has failed to do. Simply put, Petitioner's wholesale reliance on the fact of delivery of the checks, alone, does not warrant the extension of the relation back doctrine to these cases.

We emphasize that because petitioner has failed to prove unconditional delivery of the checks in the present cases, we do not here decide under what circumstances, if any, the relation back doctrine applies to a gift by way of check to a noncharitable donee when the check is unconditionally delivered to the donee. We only hold that petitioner has failed to prove unconditional delivery of the checks to the donees in the present cases, and that the relation back doctrine will therefore not be extended to these cases.

Because the relation back doctrine does not apply to the present cases, we must look to the relevant state law to determine when the decedent parted with "dominion and control" over the funds in her checking account for purposes of Treas. Reg. §25.2511-2(b). See Burnet v. Harmel, 287 U.S. 103, 110 (1932) (stating that state law creates legal interests, and Federal law determines how and when those interests should be taxed).

The Oklahoma Supreme Court has not directly addressed the issue of when the delivery of a check becomes a completed gift (i.e, when a donor parts with dominion and control over the funds that a check purports to transfer). Therefore, we must decide what the law in Oklahoma would be on that issue. Commissioner v. Estate of Bosch, 387 U.S. 456 (1967).

Courts in jurisdictions with laws similar to, or the same as, those codified in Oklahoma have determined that "the gift of [a] donor's own check is but [a] promise of a gift and does not amount to a completed gift until payment or acceptance by the drawee [bank]." In fact, we have found no state court that holds that a completed gift occurs upon delivery of a donor's personal check. We therefore conclude that the highest court of the State of Oklahoma would hold that a gift by way of a donor's personal check is not complete upon delivery of the check because the donor did not part with dominion and control over the property represented by the check.

Based upon the above analysis, we hold that the decedent parted with dominion and control over the property represented by the checks for purposes of Treas. Reg. §25.2511-2(b), upon payment of the checks by decedent's bank during 1981, and that the transfer of property by gift was complete at that time.

How could the donor in *Dillingham* have made completed gifts in 1980 through the "unconditional" delivery of checks? Read on.

The position adopted by the Tax Court and the Tenth Circuit in *Dillingham* was explained in Estate of Metzger v. Commissioner, 100 T.C. 204 (1993), *aff'd by a divided court*, 38 F.3d 118 (4th Cir. 1994), which elaborated on that view. *Metzger* involved gifts of checks that were delivered to the donees late in 1985, and were deposited by the donees in a savings account (in a bank that was not the drawee) on December 31, 1985. The checks did not clear and were not paid by the drawee bank until January 2, 1986. At all times there were sufficient funds in the donor's bank account to pay the checks. The donor made additional gifts to the donees in 1986. The question was whether the checks delivered to and deposited by the donees in 1985 were completed gifts in that year rather than in the subsequent taxable year when they were paid by the drawee bank. If the gifts were made in 1986, they would cumulate with other gifts made by the donor in that year; then the aggregate gifts made by the donor in 1986 would exceed the annual exclusion.

The regulations declare that a gift is complete when the donor no longer has dominion and control over the transferred property so that the donor no longer can change the disposition of the property. Treas. Reg. §25.2511-2(b). The Tax Court and the Fourth Circuit held that the question of when a

transferor has parted with dominion and control so that a gift is complete
turns on state law, which was Maryland law in *Metzger*. The courts
determined that, under Maryland law, the transfer of the 1985 checks was
not a completed gift until the checks were presented and accepted by the
drawee, because prior to the drawee's acceptance the donor could stop
payment on the check, or withdraw the funds from the account at the
drawee bank, and either event would revoke the gift. The courts therefore
concluded that the gifts of the 1985 checks were not complete until January
2, 1986, when they were accepted by the drawee bank.

The Tax Court nevertheless held that the gifts of the 1985 checks were
made when the checks were deposited by the donees on December 31, 1985,
and the gifts were excluded by the annual exclusion. The court treated the
relation-back doctrine as an exception to the gift tax requirement that a
donor must part with dominion and control. The court distinguished
Dillingham on the ground that the facts in that case suggested that there
"may have been 'a mutual understanding between donor and donee that
gifted checks not be cashed until some future date *after* the end of the
year.'" For example, in *Dillingham*, the checks were not cashed until 35
days after delivery, and there was no evidence as to whether the donor had
sufficient funds in his account at the time of delivery. The *Metzger* court
further said:

> We see no reason for refusing to apply the relation-back doc-
> trine to noncharitable gifts where the taxpayer is able to establish:
> (1) The donor's intent to make a gift, (2) unconditional delivery of
> the check, and (3) presentment of the check within the year for
> which favorable tax treatment is sought and within a reasonable
> time of issuance. Assuming these elements are present, the prac-
> tical realities of everyday commerce . . . require a limited extension
> of the relation-back rule.
>
>   . . . [W]e hold that the acceptance of the checks by the drawee
> bank in January 1986 relates back to the time the checks were
> *deposited* in December 1985, It follows that the gifts by check
> qualify as valid annual exclusion gifts. . . .[20]

With one judge dissenting, the Fourth Circuit affirmed. Judge Luttig
dissented on the ground that there should be no exception to the "dominion
and control" standard that the regulations adopt. Judge Luttig rejected the
adoption of a judicially created "relation-back" doctrine.

In the wake of its defeat the government issued Rev. Rul. 96-56 by
which gifts by check now are regarded by the government as complete on
the *earlier* of the date on which the donor relinquishes all power to change

---

20.   100 T.C. at 215 [Emphasis added.]

the disposition (e.g., by giving a cashier's check or a form of check that cannot be the subject of a stop payment order) or the date when the donee cashes the check, deposits it, presents it for payment, or otherwise negotiates it. Negotiation, not payment, completes the gift, *if* (1) the check is paid when first presented, (2) the donor is still alive when the check is paid, (3) the donor intended to make a gift, (4) delivery of the check was unconditional, and (5) the check was cashed, deposited, presented for payment, or otherwise negotiated in the same calendar year in which completed gift treatment is sought and within a reasonable time of issuance of the check.[21]

Recall that *DiMarco* received a brief mention just before the *Levin* case at page 54 in Chapter 2, there in the context of §2033 and with the notation that the real gist of the matter is a gift tax timing issue. The taxpayer's argument in the alternative, summarized in the second full paragraph of the opinion at age 859, is a very nice job of lawyering, worthy of your special attention. Before you begin reading the opinion, it may help you to re-read §2001 to remind yourself why there is an adjusted taxable gifts issue for estate tax purposes. This decision shows why gift tax statute of limitation protection can be important for *estate* tax purposes.

Estate of DiMarco v. Commissioner
87 T.C. 653 (1986), *acq. in result*

STERRETT, Chief Judge: . . . [T]he only issue presented in this case is whether the present value of a survivors income benefit payable with respect to the decedent by decedent's employer is an adjusted taxable gift within the meaning of §2001. . . .

Anthony F. DiMarco (hereinafter referred to as the decedent) was . . . employed continuously by the International Business Machines Corporation (IBM) as an active, regular, full-time, permanent employee from January 9, 1950, until his death. . . . He was not an officer of the corporation and did not have a written employment contract.

. . . IBM maintained a non-contributory Group Life Insurance and Survivors Income Benefit Plan (hereinafter referred to as the Plan) for the benefit of its regular employees. IBM established the Plan in September of 1934, and while the Plan has been amended

---

21. Articulating slightly different standards from *Metzger* the Ruling nevertheless is essentially a total capitulation on this issue. Now see Rosano v. United States, 245 F.3d 212 (2d Cir. 2001) (gifts by checks written before death but not presented for payment until after death were ineffective); Estate of Newman v. Commissioner, 111 T.C. 81 (1998), *aff'd per curiam*, 99-2 U.S. Tax Cas. (CCH) ¶60,358 (D.C. Cir. 1999) (gifts made by a child under a power of attorney that may not have been durable, or as joint owner of the checking account, failed to remove the gifted property from the decedent's estate because the decedent died before payment of the checks).

on many occasions since that time, it has, since January of 1935, provided two basic benefits: (i) group term life insurance, and (ii) an uninsured and unfunded survivors income benefit. . . .

The Plan . . . provided a survivors income benefit on an uninsured and unfunded basis; that is, all survivors income benefits were paid out of IBM's general assets. With the exception of fewer than 30 top executives, all regular IBM employees, including decedent, were covered automatically by the survivors income benefit portion of the Plan. . . . Under the terms of the Plan, the benefit was payable only to an employee's surviving spouse, certain minor and dependent children, and dependent parents. Payment was made . . . only so long as there remained at least one eligible survivor, and if the employee left no eligible survivor at death, no benefit was payable.

Decedent never had any power to alter, amend, revoke, or terminate the Plan in whole or in part. He had no power to select or change the beneficiaries of the survivors income benefit; no power to change the amount, form, or timing of the survivors income benefit payments; no power to substitute other benefits for the survivors income benefit; and, other than by resigning his employment with IBM, no power to terminate his coverage under the Plan. However, IBM expressly reserved the right, in its discretion, to modify the Plan if it determined that it was advisable to do so.

Joan M. DiMarco, as decedent's surviving spouse, was entitled under the Plan to receive a survivors income benefit. . . . Decedent did not report the survivors income benefit as a gift on a gift tax return, and petitioner did not report it either as part of the gross estate or as an adjusted taxable gift on decedent's Federal estate tax return. However, the existence of the survivors income benefit was reported by petitioner on . . . decedent's Federal estate tax return.

In his notice of deficiency, respondent "determined that an adjusted taxable gift of the present value of the IBM Survivor Annuity was made by the decedent on the date of death as it was not susceptible of valuation until the date of death." Respondent then determined . . . the present value of the survivors income benefit . . . and he added this amount, as an adjusted taxable gift, to the taxable estate of decedent in computing the amount of the deficiency.

The only issue for decision in this case is whether the present value of the survivors income benefit that is payable by IBM to Joan M. DiMarco is an adjusted taxable gift within the meaning of §2001. The survivors income benefit that is payable by IBM to Joan M. DiMarco is an adjusted taxable gift within the meaning of

§2001 only if it is also a taxable gift within the meaning of §2503 that was made by decedent after December 31, 1976. . . .

After reviewing carefully respondent's briefs, the statutory notice of deficiency, and the stipulation of facts, it appears to us that respondent is making two arguments in this case. First, it appears that respondent argues that decedent made a completed transfer of a property interest in the survivors income benefit for gift tax purposes on January 9, 1950, but that because the interest could not be valued at that time, it was necessary to treat the transfer as an open transaction and to value the transferred property and impose the gift tax on the date of decedent's death, when the property interest finally became subject to valuation. In the alternative, respondent appears to argue that decedent made an incomplete transfer of a property interest in the survivors income benefit for gift tax purposes on January 9, 1950, because the property interest could not be valued at that time, but that the transfer became complete on November 16, 1979, when decedent died, because the transferred property could then and for the first time be valued.

Petitioner argues, for a variety of reasons, that decedent never made a taxable gift of the survivors income benefit. Petitioner argues that decedent never owned a property interest in the survivors income benefit that he was capable of transferring. Petitioner further contends that, even if decedent owned such an interest, he never transferred it, and if he did transfer it, he never did so voluntarily. Petitioner also asserts that transfers of property cannot become complete for gift tax purposes upon the death of the donor, and that decedent never made a completed transfer of any property interest he may have owned in the survivors income benefit before his death because he always had the power to revoke the transfer, if any was made, simply by resigning his employment with IBM. Petitioner finally argues that, if the decedent made a taxable gift of the survivors income benefit, he did so before December 31, 1976, and that such a gift does not qualify as an adjusted taxable gift within the meaning of §2001. For the reasons set forth below, we find for petitioner.

Section 2501(a)(1) imposes a tax on the "transfer of property by gift." Section 2511(a) provides that the tax "shall apply whether the transfer is in trust or otherwise, whether the gift is direct or indirect, and whether the property is real or personal, tangible or intangible . . . ." However, a transfer of property qualifies as a taxable gift only if the transfer is complete, and a transfer is complete for gift tax purposes only when the transferor relinquishes dominion and control over the transferred property. Treas. Reg.

§25.2511-2(b); Estate of Sanford v. Commissioner, 308 U.S. 39, 42-43 (1939). At the time the transfer is complete, the transferred property must be valued. §2512(a). This value is then used in determining the gift tax that is due. §2502.

Respondent argues that decedent transferred a property interest in the survivors income benefit for gift tax purposes on January 9, 1950. This transfer was either complete or incomplete for gift tax purposes. If the transfer was complete, we have little difficulty in disposing of this case because a completed transfer would have been a taxable gift that was made by decedent before December 31, 1976, and §2001 expressly defines an adjusted taxable gift as a taxable gift that was made after December 31, 1976. On the other hand, if the transfer was incomplete for gift tax purposes, we do not believe that it became complete or that we can deem that it became complete at the time of decedent's death. Treas. Reg. §25.2511-2(f), provides that —

> The relinquishment or termination of a power to change the beneficiaries of transferred property, *occurring otherwise than by the death of the donor (the statute being confined to transfers by living donors)*, is regarded as the event that completes the gift and causes the tax to apply. . . . [Emphasis added.]

We believe that this regulation precludes our finding in this case that the alleged transfer of property by decedent on January 9, 1950, became complete for gift tax purposes by reason of decedent's death. . . .

[W]e believe that respondent has confused the issues of completion and valuation in this case. Respondent appears to argue that, because the value of the survivors income benefit could not be determined on January 9, 1950, when the alleged transfer occurred, the transfer should be treated as incomplete for gift tax purposes until the survivors income benefit became susceptible of valuation, when decedent died, at which time the transfer became complete and subject to the gift tax. For the reasons stated above, we have already held that transfers of property do not become complete for gift tax purposes by reason of the death of the donor. We also question, however, whether the fact that the value of transferred property cannot be readily determined at the time of transfer is relevant in determining whether the transfer is complete for gift tax purposes. We have noted above that transfers of property are complete and subject to the gift tax at the time the donor relinquishes dominion and control over the transferred property. Nothing in the statute or the regulations suggests that, even if a donor relinquishes dominion and control over transferred property, the transfer is or can be considered to be incomplete for gift tax purposes if the value of the property is uncertain. To the contrary, in Smith v. Shaughnessy, 318 U.S. 176, 180 (1943), the Supreme Court appears to have considered and expressly rejected this argument in the following language:

> The government argues that for gift tax purposes the taxpayer has abandoned control of the remainder and that it is therefore taxable, while the taxpayer contends that no realistic value can be placed on the contingent remainder and that it therefore should not be classed as a gift.
>
> We cannot accept any suggestion that the complexity of a property interest . . . can serve to defeat a tax. . . . Even though these concepts of property and value may be slippery and elusive they can not escape taxation so long as they are used in the world of business. The language of the gift tax statute, "property . . . real or personal, tangible or intangible," is broad enough to include property, however conceptual or contingent. . . .

Accordingly, we reject any suggestion by respondent either that transfers of property are incomplete for gift tax purposes simply because "no realistic value can be placed" on the property at the time the transfer occurs, or that transfers of property become complete for gift tax purposes only when the value of the transferred property can be easily ascertained.

Respondent also argues that completed transfers of property for gift tax purposes can and should be treated as open transactions in those [cases in which] the transferred property is difficult to value, and that valuation of the transferred property and the imposition of the gift tax should be postponed until the value of the property can be readily determined. We reject this contention. The clear language of the statute and the regulations requires that transferred property be valued for gift tax purposes at the time the transfer becomes complete. Section 2512(a) provides that, in the case of a gift, "the value thereof at the date of the gift shall be considered the amount of the gift." (Emphasis added.) In addition, Treas. Reg. §25.2511-2(a), states as follows:

> The gift tax is not imposed upon the receipt of the property by the donee, nor is it necessarily determined by the measure of enrichment resulting to the donee from the transfer . . . . On the contrary, the tax is a primary and personal liability of the donor, is an excise upon his *act of*

making the transfer, [and] *is measured by the value of the property passing from the donor* . . . . [Emphasis added.]

As a result, property must be valued and the gift tax imposed at the time a completed transfer of the property occurs.[22]

We also agree with petitioner that decedent never made a taxable gift of any property interest in the survivors income benefit because we find no act by decedent that qualifies as an act of "transfer" of an interest in property. His participation in the Plan was involuntary, he had no power to select or change the beneficiaries of the survivors income benefit, no power to alter the amount or timing of the payment of the benefit, and no power to substitute other benefits for those prescribed by the Plan. . . .

Respondent argues, however, that decedent's simple act of going to work for IBM on January 9, 1950, constituted an act of transfer by decedent for gift tax purposes. We disagree. None of the cases cited by respondent hold that, without more, the simple act of going to work for an employer that has an automatic, non-elective, company-wide survivors income benefit plan similar to the one at issue in this case constitutes a "transfer" of an interest in the benefit for either estate or gift tax purposes. Moreover, we doubt that it can be maintained seriously that decedent began his employment with IBM on January 9, 1950 (when he was 24, unmarried, and without dependents), for the purpose or with any intention of transferring property rights in the survivors income benefit. While we agree with respondent that a taxable event may occur without a volitional act by the donor, as in a case where an incomplete transfer of property becomes complete because of the occurrence of an event outside the donor's control, we do not believe that a taxable event can occur for gift tax purposes unless there is first and in fact an act of transfer by the donor; and there can be no act of transfer unless the act is voluntary and the transferor has some awareness that he is in fact making a transfer of property, that is, he must intend to do so. See Harris v. Commissioner, 340 U.S. 106, 109 (1950) . . . .[23] It is apparent to us

---

22.   Respondent relies heavily on Rev. Rul. 81-31, 1981-1 C.B. 475, and argues here that we should adopt its reasoning and holding. To the extent that this ruling can be read as holding either that a transfer of property can become complete for gift tax purposes by reason of the death of the donor, or that it is permissible to treat a completed transfer of property as an open transaction and to value the transferred property and impose the gift tax at some time other than when the completed transfer occurs, we regard the ruling as being inconsistent with the gift tax statute and the regulations. [The government revoked Rev. Rul. 81-31 in Rev. Rul. 92-68. — Ed.]

23.   The fact that there can be no taxable gift unless there is a voluntary act of transfer does not mean that the donor also must have donative intent when he makes the transfer. Treas. Reg. §25.2511-1(g)(1); Commissioner v. Wemyss,

that decedent never intended and never voluntarily acted to transfer any interest that he may have owned in the survivors income benefit. There being no act of transfer by decedent, there can be no transfer of property by gift.

Moreover, we question whether decedent ever owned a property interest in the survivors income benefit that he was capable of transferring during his lifetime. He had no voice in selecting the beneficiaries of the survivors income benefit and no ability to affect or determine the benefits payable to them. The categories of beneficiaries, the determination whether a claimant is an eligible beneficiary, and the amounts payable to the bene-ficiaries all were controlled directly by the provisions of the Plan and indirectly by IBM, and payments were made directly to the beneficiaries by IBM. Furthermore, the benefits were payable out of the general assets of IBM, not out of any fund in which decedent had a vested interest, and the benefits did not accrue until decedent's death. Most importantly, IBM had the power and the right to modify the Plan and the survivors income benefit at any time and in its sole discretion. Under these circumstances, we have little difficulty in concluding that decedent never acquired fixed and enforceable property rights in the survivors income benefit that he was capable of transferring during his lifetime. . . .

In our opinion, decedent never made a taxable gift of any interest in the survivors income benefit to his wife. It follows that the present value of the survivors income benefit is not an adjusted taxable gift within the meaning of §2001.

In *Estate of Levin*, which we reviewed in Chapter 2, death benefit proceeds like those in *DiMarco* were deemed includible in the estate of a deceased employee who, through stock ownership, controlled the corporation. Although *DiMarco* was distinguished on the element of control, the court followed *DiMarco* in again rejecting the government's incomplete gift theory. Because the designated beneficiary in *Levin* was the decedent's surviving spouse, the estate tax marital deduction ought to match the amount includible, making inclusion of no great significance.

15. *Valuation.*

In Whose Hands Is Value Determined?   TAM 8907002 involved a family that owned all of the stock in a closely held corporation. The

---

324 U.S. 303, 306 (1945). Any completed transfer of a beneficial interest in property for less than an adequate and full consideration in money or money's worth, unless made in the ordinary course of business, will be subject to the gift tax. Treas. Reg. §25.2512-8.

taxpayer, who owned the controlling interest, relinquished that control through a redemption of shares. The government determined that the taxpayer made a gift to the other shareholders because the proceeds distributed to the taxpayer in redemption of shares of stock was inadequate to compensate the taxpayer for the control premium allocable to that interest. The taxpayer made several arguments. One contention was that, because the family together had control, the control premium should be allocated among the shares held by all the family members. The government rejected that contention and held that, if a single member of the family has control, all of the control premium is allocated to the shares of that person. The taxpayer also contended that, because no single family member acquired control as a result of the redemption, the value of the indirect gifts made to each shareholder should reflect a minority discount. The government's first response was that the taxpayer's gift should be valued as a single transfer to the other shareholders of an increased equity interest in the corporation (as contrasted to separate gifts of additional shares of stock to each shareholder). By making a bargain sale to the corporation, the taxpayer made an indirect gift to the other shareholders of an equity interest. The government further held that, even if the bargain redemption were deemed to be several separate gifts of additional shares of stock to each shareholder, the gifts would nevertheless be valued by including a control premium. The government cited authorities for the principle that the value of a gift is the value of the property relinquished by the donor rather than the value of what the donee received.

In Rev. Rul. 81-253, the government said that no minority discount is allowed for gifts between family members if control of a corporation was held by a family (even though no one member had control). That view is contrary to several court of appeal decisions. See, e.g., Estate of Bright v. United States, 650 F.2d 999 (5th Cir. 1981). Rev. Rul. 81-253 was criticized in TAM 8907002 and was revoked by Rev. Rul. 93-12.

To put some of this in perspective, imagine that *G* owned 51% of the stock of a closely held corporation and two of *G*'s children, *M* and *N*, owned equal amounts of the remaining stock. *G* gave 2% of the corporation's stock to another child, *S*. Is the value of that gift: (1) 2% of the total value of the corporation, (2) a discount from that amount because *S* received a minority interest, (3) an amount equal to 2/51 of the value of the taxpayer's 51% controlling interest, (4) an even greater premium amount because, by virtue of *S*'s ability to combine forces with *M* and *N*, *S* has the swing vote power, or (5) a greater premium amount because, by making the gift, the taxpayer relinquished the control element represented by the 51% interest? TAM 8907002 indicates that the entire control premium should be taxed as part of the gift that eliminated the taxpayer's controlling interest. Does the government's position conform with tax policy — the issue being the constitutional mandate that there be a transfer as to which the tax may apply.

In Shepherd v. Commissioner, 115 T.C. 376 (2000), *aff'd*, 283 F.3d 1258 (11th Cir. 2002), a valuation case involving steep discounts for interests involving a family limited partnership, here is what Tax Court Judge Beghe wrote in a dissenting opinion:

With all the woofing these days about using family partnerships to generate big discounts, the majority opinion provides salutary reminders that the "gift is measured by the value of the property passing from the donor, rather than by the property received by the donee or upon the measure of enrichment of the donee" and that "How [taxpayer's] transfers may have enhanced the [donees'] partnership interests is immaterial, for the gift tax is imposed on the value of what the donor transfers, not what the donee receives" . . . .

This is the "estate depletion" theory of the gift tax . . . .

The logic and the sense of the estate depletion theory require that a donor's simultaneous or contemporaneous gifts to or for the objects of his bounty be unitized for the purpose of valuing the transfers . . . . After all, the gift tax was enacted to protect the estate tax . . . . The estate and gift taxes are different from an inheritance tax, which focuses on what the individual donee-beneficiaries receive; the estate and gift taxes are taxes whose base is measured by the value of what passes from the transferor.

In a footnote, Judge Beghe then articulated the following notion about Rev. Rul. 93-12:

Contrary also to the Commissioner's concession, in Rev. Rul. 93-12, that a donor's simultaneous equal gifts aggregating 100 percent of the stock of his wholly owned corporation to his five children are to be valued for gift tax purposes without regard to the donor's control and the family relationship of the donees. The ruling is wrong because it focuses on what was received by the individual donees; what is important is that the donor has divested himself of control.

Not mentioned in this provision is the notion that, for annual exclusion purposes (to which we turn at page 886), the gift tax *does* properly look to what the donees received to test the present interest qualification, but for gift tax valuation purposes the gift tax looks to what the donor relinquished. That fine distinction has not been addressed or even hardly recognized by case law to date.

Mooneyham v. Commissioner, 61 T.C.M. (CCH) 2445 (1991), involved the gift tax valuation of a half interest in development real estate transferred to the donor's sibling. The court allowed a 15% discount. The court applied a hypothetical unrelated willing-buyer, willing-seller approach and concluded that no one would pay 50% of the fair market value of the undivided property to acquire the gifted interest. Apparently, the government did not contend that the transfer constituted a relinquishment of the donor's prior 100% ownership, and therefore constituted a gift of the donor's control. Although the opinion did not expressly discuss this issue, it lurks in the facts and the holding therefore is contrary to TAM 8907002. Reflecting on its losses in *Mooneyham* and later in Estate of Pillsbury v. Commissioner, 64 T.C.M. (CCH) 284 (1992), which also allowed a 15% fractional interest discount, the government issued TAM 9336002, in which it did not challenge the discount itself but sought to limit it to "the petitioner's *share* of the estimated cost of a partition of the property," based on the theory that partition would be the best means to generate optimum economic benefit from property owned by multiple parties. That limitation was rejected by Estate of Cervin v. Commissioner, 68 T.C.M. (CCH) 1115 (1984), which allowed a 20% fractional interest discount to an undivided half interest in agricultural property. See also Estate of Baird v. Commissioner, 82 T.C.M. (CCH) 666 (2001), which entailed undivided fractional interests in 16 different parcels of Louisiana timberland that were transferred into a trust so that family members could avoid a repeat of a prior "difficult experience" involving similar timberland ownership. The taxpayer produced an expert who was in the business of buying and selling fractional interests in Louisiana timber and the court bought this expert's suggested "average" discount of 55% and then sweetened it to 60% based on special family circumstances.

One of the issues involved in PLR 9113009 was the gift tax consequences of a parent's gratuitous guarantee of loans made for the benefit of children. According to the government:

> The agreements . . . to guarantee payment of debts are valuable economic benefits conferred upon [the children] . . . . Consequently, when [the taxpayer] guaranteed payment of the loans, [the taxpayer] transferred a valuable property interest to [the children]. The promisor of a legally enforceable promise for less than adequate and full consideration makes a completed gift on the date the promise is binding and determinable in value rather than when the promised payment is actually made.

According to the PLR, this gift was taxable immediately in the amount of "the economic benefit conferred" by the guarantee, but the PLR gave no indication of the gift value of the economic benefit bestowed. PLR 9113009 was widely criticized, and the government withdrew it in PLR 9409018. The government has not commented since on this issue, but isn't it correct to say that the benefit given to the children is equal to what they did not have to pay for similar guarantees? In that regard, are the interest free loan cases distinguishable?

Statute of Limitation for Revaluation.   At one time, long before unification of the estate and gift taxes in 1976, the amount of gifts made in a prior year was subject to adjustment for the purpose of computing the gift tax for a current year, even though the statutory period within which an additional gift tax might be assessed for the prior year had expired. See S. Rep. No. 1622, 83d Cong., 2d Sess. 479 (1954). The result was that it was impossible to be certain what amount of gift tax would be payable on gifts in the current year if the subject of gifts made in prior years was property that might be revalued at a greater amount than reported in the prior gift tax return. This uncertainty made it unwise in some cases to proceed with what otherwise would have been desirable inter vivos transfers.

Congress corrected this gift tax revaluation problem in 1954 by enacting §2504(c), which eliminated in some cases the significance of a change in the value placed on prior gifts in calculating the tax on current gifts made after 1954. The value of a gift made in a prior year was not subject to adjustment if a tax was assessed or paid for the prior year and the time had expired within which an additional gift tax could be assessed on the transfer.[24] But §2504(c) did not prevent an adjustment if no tax was assessed or paid for the prior year.[25]

Furthermore, after unification of the estate and gift taxes in 1976, a problem arose because adjusted taxable gifts made after 1976 are reflected

---

24. As noted below, the requirement that a gift tax was assessed or paid for the preceding calendar period no longer exists. Thus, the significance of Rev. Rul. 79-398 that use of the unified credit with respect to taxable gifts made after 1976 is mandatory before a gift tax may be paid largely is eliminated. See, e.g., Rev. Rul. 84-11 (use of the unified credit to eliminate the actual payment of a gift tax did not mean that a tax was assessed or paid for purposes of §2504(c), leaving those gifts open to revaluation, a result that was perverse because it permitted revaluation of the gifts for which most taxpayers would not be inclined to keep records).

25. Now Treas. Reg. §§20.2001-1(b) and 25.2504-2(a) preclude reconsideration of any issues that may impact the taxation of prior gifts: once the limitation period has expired the government will not challenge any aspect of the adequately disclosed gift except to the extent that a completed gift otherwise may be subject to estate tax inclusion (such as under the string rules of §§2036-2038). Compare the results under prior law, such as Estate of Robinson v. Commissioner, 101 T.C. 499 (1993) (the government was not precluded from challenging the number of annual exclusions claimed to offset lifetime gifts in a barred year when calculating the gift tax liability of the transferor on a later gift, or the estate tax liability at the transferor's death); Clark v. Commissioner, 65 T.C. 126 (1975) (in a closed year the donor improperly calculated gift tax liability as though §2513 gift splitting was proper; the gift tax returns for open years were subject to recalculation based on what should have been reflected in the closed years); Berzon v. Commissioner, 63 T.C. 601 (1975), *aff'd*, 534 F.2d 528 (2d Cir. 1976) (gift tax annual exclusions for prior years were erroneously claimed; although those years were closed under the statute of limitation, the court disregarded those exclusions in determining the aggregate taxable gifts made by the donor for computation of the gift tax due in open years).

in the estate tax computation and §2504(c) only provided closure for future gift tax calculations. As a result, the government successfully revalued adjusted taxable gifts in estate tax proceedings even after those gifts were protected from revaluation by §2504(c) for future gift tax purposes.

In 1997 Congress finally cured this disparity by enacting §2001(f) to extend the §2504(c) gift tax statute of limitation to the estate tax.[26] Now, reflecting technical changes made in 1998[27] and Treas. Reg. §301.6501(c)-1(f)(2), which describes adequate disclosure "to apprise the Service of the nature of the gift and the basis for the value reported," under §6501(c)(9) the value of the gift for both gift and estate tax calculation purposes is the value as finally determined for gift tax purposes. Thus, if the time within which to assess gift tax expires under the §6501(c)(9) gift tax statute of limitation, the government is bound by the value of the asset and cannot revalue it for either tax calculation purpose. Notable is that this closure is not limited just to valuation questions; if the adequate disclosure standard is met, there is statute of limitation protection that precludes investigation and litigation of any issue of qualification for the marital deduction, charitable deduction, or annual exclusion in the future.

On the other hand, the §6501(c)(9) statute of limitation *never* prevents a gift tax assessment based on a revaluation if the taxpayer failed to properly disclose the gift, although an amended return may be filed to begin the adequate disclosure statute of limitation running. The resulting lack of §2504(c) or §2001(f) protection for gifts not properly reported (or for transfers made under prior law) permits the government to redetermine the value or taxability of a prior gift, the proper gift tax thereon, the amount of unified credit exhausted thereby, and the effect on the determination of the donor's subsequent gift and estate taxes, all at any time in the future, regardless of how old and cold the facts and basis for determination of these questions may have become in the interim.

For example, §2001(f) does not preclude the kind of revaluation results in *Estate of Smith*, next below, if the taxpayer fails to properly report a taxable gift made during life. Note as you read that the effect of higher valuation was only to begin taxing the estate at a higher level in the estate tax rate tables, which will be less important as the maximum tax bracket

---

26. The 1997 legislation also amended §6501(c)(9) to provide that the government may assess a gift tax at any time, if a gift should have been returned but it was not, or if the transfer was not disclosed in a manner adequate to apprise the government of the nature of the transfer.

27. §2001(f) was amended to specifically require closure under §6501, which applies if a "return" is required to be filed "(without regard to section 2503(b))." This means that a return filed for an annual exclusion gift can start the gift tax statute of limitation, even though no return is required if the gift qualifies for annual exclusion purposes. The upshot is that returns filed to generate closure for estate tax calculation purposes are effective for both gift and estate tax purposes, even with respect to gifts covered by the gift tax annual exclusion and therefore not required to be reported in the first instance.

declines and the applicable exclusion amount increases to the point of a flat tax.

Estate of Smith v. Commissioner
94 T.C. 872 (1990)

TANNENWALD, Judge: This case is before the Court on respondent's motion for partial summary judgment in respect of the basis for determining the value of certain gifts for purposes of the estate tax. . . .

[The decedent made a gift of stock in 1982 that was reported on a timely-filed gift tax return at a value of $284,871. Gift tax was paid with that return, and the decedent lived another two years. On the federal estate tax return for the decedent's estate, the gift was included in the decedent's adjusted taxable gifts at the same value as reported for gift tax purposes. Seven months later, the gift tax statute of limitation expired. Over two years later, the Service determined an estate tax deficiency based in part on its revaluation of the 1982 gift to be $668,495.] In computing the estate tax pursuant to §2001(b), respondent increased the "adjusted taxable gifts" added to the taxable estate under §2001(b)(1)(B), but did not make a corresponding increase in the amount of gift tax payable on those gifts which was subtracted from the total of the taxable estate and adjusted taxable gifts pursuant to §2001(b)(2). . . .

The issue to be decided is the correctness of respondent's computation, particularly with respect to whether respondent may increase the value of gifts made in years which are closed to such an increase for gift tax purposes under §§2504(c) and 6501 when calculating "adjusted taxable gifts" for estate tax purposes under §2001(b)(1)(B). . . .

Respondent concedes that, under §2504(c), gifts made in prior taxable periods cannot be revalued for gift tax purposes after a gift tax has been assessed or paid and the statute of limitations for assessment of gift tax has expired. Respondent argues, however, that §2504(c), by its terms, prohibits revaluation of prior taxable gifts solely for gift tax purposes. We agree with respondent.

. . .

At the time Congress enacted §2504(c) . . . the estate and gift taxes were separate taxes, and the estate tax rate did not involve cumulative lifetime gifts. Subsequently, the Tax Reform Act of 1976 unified the estate and gift tax rate schedules, providing progressive rates based on cumulative lifetime and deathtime transfers and a unified credit. By this action, Congress meant to "reduce the disparity of treatment between lifetime and deathtime transfers." The 1976 Act did not by its terms extend the limitation of §2504(c) to valuation of prior taxable gifts for estate tax purposes. Moreover, both the statutory language and the legislative history reveal that Congress did not place any restriction in §2001 on valuing lifetime transfers. . . .

. . .

We are aware that taxpayers may face practical problems in attempting to prove value for estate tax purposes many years after a gift was given. . . . In this connection, we note that, even in the context of §2504(c), such practical problems still remain, albeit in a narrow frame of reference, [if] that section is not operative . . . . We hold that, in computing "adjustable taxable gifts" under §2001(b)(1)(B), respondent may re-examine and adjust prior taxable gifts to reflect the value of such gifts as of the date of the gifts.

Our task is not yet completed, however. There remains the question whether, in computing the amount of the gift tax subtraction under §2001(b)(2), petitioner is entitled to have the gift tax adjusted in conformity with the increase in value, if any, which may ultimately be determined in this case. Neither party has directly confronted this question. However, respondent suggests that the fact that the language "which would have been payable under Chapter 12" as used in §2001(b)(2) as opposed to the language "assessed or paid" in §2504(c) indicates that Congress contemplated a reconsideration of the value of prior gifts in computing "adjustable taxable gifts" under §2001(b)(1)(B). Such argument, although perhaps not rising to the level of a concession, impliedly recognizes that the calculation of the subtraction for gift taxes under §2001(b)(2) is not limited to the amount of gift taxes actually paid. In any event, we are persuaded that the correct disposition of the matter requires that the subtraction for gift taxes be adjusted to take into account any increase in the values of the previous gifts.

Neither the statute nor the legislative history limit the taxes payable to the amount of gift tax previously paid. The language of §2001(b)(2), the "aggregate amount which would have been payable," and the legislative history reveal Congress' intention that the taxes payable could be increased. . . .

We hold that the subtraction for gift taxes under §2001(b)(2) should be computed on the basis of the gift taxes payable under the applicable rate schedules in respect of the "adjusted taxable gifts" as subsequently determined in this proceeding. A contrary holding would permit respondent to collect the barred gift taxes through the imposition of a higher estate tax without an offsetting adjustment.

Our disposition of the issues discussed herein not only conforms to the statutory provisions but produces an appropriate result. Respondent is shielded from the use of §2504(c) to permit petitioner to avoid the payment of the estate tax which is otherwise payable under §2001(b)(1)(B); by the same token, petitioner is shielded from an indirect claim for a time-barred gift tax by virtue of a reduced offset under §2001(b)(2). . . .

It is important to note that the §2001(b)(2) credit is not for the tax actually paid on the value originally reported but, instead, the tax that would have been paid on the amount of the gift as revalued by the government at the decedent's death. The effect for estate tax purposes is to eliminate all but one problem posed by the government's attempts at revaluation: Revaluation does not generate an increase in tax on the prior gift because a larger credit would be generated at the same time; instead, revaluation only has the potential to push the estate into a higher marginal bracket for computing the estate tax. If the gift tax statute of limitation is still open the government may assess an added impost. Otherwise, if only estate tax liability is involved but the §6501(c)(9) statute of limitation does not bar the government's inquiry, then §2001(b)(2) determines the credit against estate tax for the amount of gift tax that would have been payable based on the government's assessment, not just for the gift tax actually paid.

As illustrated by a dissent in *Smith*, however, the application of §2001(b)(2) does not solve an inequity, shown by the following example: If the decedent's estate is $600,000 and a prior gift is revalued from $300,000 to $600,000, the decedent's estate tax (before applicable credits) will increase $121,000; if the decedent's estate is $2 million and a prior gift is revalued from $1 million to $1.5 million, the decedent's estate tax would increase only $65,000. The difference between these two examples is that the second estate already was taxable in the highest marginal bracket before revaluation of the prior gift. Revaluation of the prior gift generated a higher gift tax credit under §2001(b)(2) in both cases but only the first gift boosted the marginal bracket in which the estate was taxed. If the highest marginal bracket already were reached by taxable inter vivos gifts made by the taxpayer, any revaluation at death would make no difference at all, because the increase in tax would be matched by the same increase in the §2001(b)(2) credit. So smaller taxable estates are hurt by revaluation and nontaxable ones or large estates are not.

Another impropriety is illustrated by Estate of Prince v. Commissioner, 61 T.C.M. (CCH) 2594 (1991), *aff'd sub nom.*, Levin v. Commissioner, 986 F.2d 91 (4th Cir. 1993), which denied a §2001(b)(2) adjustment for the amount of gift tax that would have been payable if the gifts involved had been taxed inter vivos. This was because no gift tax would have been payable — the taxpayer's unified credit would have covered that liability. The effect of the court's holding was to consume the estate's unified credit at death as if the gift tax assessment was not time barred. In that respect the court's conclusion was improper; a §2001(b)(2) adjustment should be available even if the taxpayer did not exhaust the unified credit during life and regardless of whether gift tax actually was paid — or should have been paid — on the transfer.

To better illustrate this principle, consider an inter vivos transfer that was valued at $500,000 for gift tax purposes. The tax was $155,800 and, because the full unified credit was available, no payment actually was made. Assume this taxpayer then died with an estate of $1 million. Computing the estate tax with the adjusted taxable gift valued at $500,000 would produce a payment obligation at death of $555,800 before applying any credits. Now assume the government at death successfully revalued the gift at $600,000 so that the estate tax computation was on a tentative tax base of $1.6 million and the taxpayer owed $600,800 before applying the available credits. Allowing the unified credit, but not the §2001(b)(2) adjustment, the taxpayer would pay $45,000 more tax due to revaluation of the lifetime gift (reflecting the additional $100,000 assessed at a 45% marginal estate tax bracket).

Changing the facts, assume the lifetime transfer was reported at $3 million and was revalued at death at $3.1 million. Lifetime taxes would have consumed the unified credit and at death the §2001(b)(2) credit for gift tax that *would have* been payable on the gift produces a larger credit to match the larger value and no more tax actually will be paid at death. The difference between this and the first example is that §2001(b)(2) applied in this example because, during life, the taxpayer exhausted the unified credit.

The two illustrations should not produce the same increase in tax unless the added $100,000 would be taxed in the same marginal bracket in both cases. But that modest difference in the respective tax increases is overshadowed by the *Prince* court's denial of the §2001(b)(2) adjustment in the first example. That disparity is improper; the §2001(b)(2) adjustment to reflect the tax that would be payable on the revalued gift should be available in either case. The proper computation would ignore the unified credit in determining the increase in tax attributable to revaluation of the inter vivos transfer, whether the gift tax on the originally valued gift or the revalued gift, on both or on neither, was greater than the unified credit available with respect thereto.

One consequence of these holdings and legislation is that taxpayers must be *more* vigilant in maintaining adequate records upon which they may rely in future challenges, especially for future gift tax purposes with respect to gifts they otherwise would not think they needed to disclose, due to the annual exclusion, the marital deduction or charitable deduction, or the unified credit, than with respect to gifts as to which a gift tax actually is assessed and paid. This problem is the exact converse to most taxpayers' expectations. Nevertheless, the 1997 legislation reflects a policy that the limitation period ought to run to protect the taxpayer from stale challenges, in cases in which a gift tax return is filed, putting the government on notice and providing it with an opportunity to challenge the facts revealed therein.

Lastly, regarding valuation issues, Chapter 14 of the Code, entitled Special Valuation Rules but commonly known as the "anti-freeze" provisions, addresses perceived abuses in gift tax valuation involving transactions during life that are designed to "freeze" the value of property to preclude subsequent estate tax on future appreciation. These rules seek to preclude taxpayer efforts to minimize taxes by imposing an "easy-to-complete" regime for gift tax valuation, and are discussed in detail in Chapter 15.

16. *Savings Clauses.* Taxpayers sometimes include a "savings clause" in a transaction in an attempt to avoid gift taxation. The typical approach is to specify that consideration will be refunded or increased if the government successfully challenges the values assigned to property transferred in the transaction. The government routinely asserts that these provisions are invalid as against public policy, relying on Commissioner v. Procter, 142 F.2d 824 (4th Cir. 1944), which invalidated a condition subsequent that would cancel a transaction if the government successfully asserted that it constituted a gift. The court's principal rationale was that otherwise the government would have no incentive to expend the effort and expense needed to establish that a taxable transfer occurred, only to have the transaction rewritten to avoid that result.[28] See, e.g., Ward v. Commissioner, 87 T.C. 78 (1986); Harwood v. Commissioner, 83 T.C. 692 (1984); Rev. Rul. 86-41; TAMs 8549005 and 8531003. King v. United States, 545 F.2d 700 (7th Cir. 1976), held that a price adjustment provision is not invalid because it differs from the cancellation provision in *Procter* — it merely establishes that the parties to the transaction intend to make no gift and will make necessary modifications to adopt whatever value the government establishes to insure that intent. Estate of McLendon v. Commissioner, 66 T.C.M. (CCH) 946 (1993), suggested in dicta that *King* may not be followed by the Tax Court because of doubts about the fundamental finding in that case that the parties acted at arm's length. In TAMs 9309001 and 9133001 the government rejected the validity of *King* type price adjustment provisions, partly because those provisions indicate that the transactions were not bona fide arm's-length business arrangements, because the parties were willing to pay whatever the government was able to establish as the proper value of the assets involved in their transaction. Is that logic sound?

---

28. The court gave several other grounds for its decision. For example, the effect of the condition would obstruct the administration of justice by causing the court to pass on a moot case. Also, the condition would neutralize a final judgment of the court.

A variation on this theme that some have advocated involves the gift of an interest in a partnership. The donor can transfer to the donee "that percentage interest in the X partnership that has a value of Y." Will that arrangement successfully avoid the imposition of a gift tax? What about the planning involved in FSA 200122011 (which involves a Tax Court case that will be decided under the name McCord, which was argued in mid-2001 but the opinion still was not available in February 2003). The taxpayer's gimmick was designed to dissuade the government from challenging the valuation of an inter vivos transfer. Basically it provided that any increase in the value of difficult to value assets will constitute a gift to charity, such that any increase in value will be matched with a charitable contribution deduction, producing a wash to the government and preventing it from benefiting from the valuation challenge in the first instance. For just that reason the government regards the price adjustment provision as invalid because it contravenes public policy, as pronounced originally in *Procter*. Stay tuned.

17. *The Donee.*   Gifts can be made only by individuals because only individuals are subject to estate tax and the gift tax exists to backstop the estate tax. How then should the gift tax treat a transfer made by an entity, such as a family-controlled corporation or partnership? Interesting issues also arise when a transfer is made in the opposite direction.

To illustrate, assume that X, Y, and Z (siblings) were equal shareholders of the *XYZ* Corporation. X transferred real estate valued at $20,000 to the corporation and received nothing in exchange. What are the gift tax consequences of the transfer? See Chanin v. United States, 393 F.2d 972 (Cl. Ct. 1968); Heringer v. Commissioner, 235 F.2d 149 (9th Cir. 1956); Rev. Rul. 71-443; Treas. Reg. §25.2511-1(h)(1). The Commissioner's successful position is that X made a gift of a future interest to Y and to Z of a value equal to one-third of the value of the transferred real estate (i.e., a gift of a $6,667 future interest to each of the other two shareholders). See, e.g., Shepherd v. Commissioner, 115 T.C. 376 (2000), *aff'd*, 283 F.3d 1258 (11th Cir. 2002), a valuation case also mentioned at page 865. The characterization as a future interest is important because it precludes qualification for the annual exclusion, a topic to which we turn shortly.

Imagine that D owned all the outstanding shares of Class A preferred stock of X corporation, which was convertible at the option of the owner into an equal number of shares of Class B preferred stock of X. Both Class A and Class B preferred stock provided for the same amount of annual dividend, but the Class B dividend right was cumulative, and the Class A right was not.[29] There were no other differences between the two classes of

---

29. A corporation is not required to declare and pay dividends on its stock. The dividend rights of preferred stock are a preference to be paid first if any dividends are declared by the corporation; they do not give the shareholder a right to have dividends declared. If a

stock. *X* had no shares of Class B stock outstanding in the years in question. Both classes of stock provided the owner a right to require *X* to redeem the shares at par value plus accumulated unpaid dividends. *X* did not declare the full amount of dividend called for on the Class A preferred stock in each of a number of years. *X* was a closely held corporation. There is a gift represented by these facts: to whom? See Snyder v. Commissioner, 93 T.C. 529 (1989).

Next assume that siblings *A* and *B* own all the stock in a corporation and each has a right of first refusal to purchase the stock of the other for a striking price of $150,000. They created an employee stock ownership plan (ESOP), which is slated to purchase *A*'s shares for a negotiated fair market value of $600,000. *B* will not exercise the right of first refusal, even though *B* has the financial wherewithal to do so. In this case also a gift has been made: from which donor to which donee(s)? See PLR 9117035. Would your answer differ if *B* was not financially able to exercise the first refusal right?

Gifts can be made to any donee, whether an individual or a legal entity. A gift to a fiduciary entity (such as a trust) is treated as a gift to the beneficiaries of the entity. Helvering v. Hutchings, 312 U.S. 393 (1941); Treas. Reg. §25.2503-2(a). Similarly, a gift to a closely-held corporation or partnership may be treated as a gift to the shareholders or partners. Treas. Reg. §25.2511-1(h)(1); Shepherd v. Commissioner, 115 T.C. 376 (2000), *aff'd*, 283 F.3d 1258 (11th Cir. 2002); Heringer v. Commissioner, 235 F.2d 149 (9th Cir. 1956); Wooley v. United States, 736 F. Supp. 1506 (S.D. Ind. 1990); Chanin v. United States, 393 F.2d 972 (Cl. Ct. 1968). In *Wooley* the court held that a gift to a partnership qualified for the annual exclusion as a present interest, notwithstanding that gifts to a corporation do not qualify for the annual exclusion because they are deemed to be future interests. Why would a gift to a partnership differ from a gift to a corporation for purposes of the annual exclusion present interest requirement? We are going to discover in *Hackl*, discussed at page 902, that in some cases it does not. A gift to a charitable, public, or similar corporation or organization may be treated as a gift to the entity, depending upon the facts and circumstances. Treas. Reg. §25.2511-1(h)(1).

The significance of treating a gift to an entity as having been made to its constituents principally lies in the effect of that determination on qualification of the gift for the annual exclusion to which we now turn.

---

preferred stock dividend right is noncumulative, once a year has expired in which the full amount of dividend preference was not paid, the corporation has no obligation to distribute the unpaid amount at some future date when dividends are declared. But, if the preferred stock dividend right is cumulative, the corporation continues to be obligated to distribute the unpaid amount when dividends are declared. The redemption payment for cumulative preferred will include prior years' unpaid dividends if the holder of the preferred stock has a right to require the corporation to redeem it for par value plus unpaid accrued dividends, but the redemption payment for noncumulative preferred will not.

18. *Qualifying for the Annual Exclusion.*

House of Representatives Report No. 708
72d Cong., 1st Sess. 29 (1932), reprinted
in 1939-1 C.B. (pt. 2) 457, 478

By [§2503(b)] a gift or gifts to any one person during the calendar year, if in the amount or of the value of $3,000 or less, is not to be accounted for in determining the total amount of gifts of that or any subsequent calendar year. Likewise, the first $3,000 of a gift to any one person exceeding that amount is not to be accounted for. Such exemption, on the one hand, is to obviate the necessity of keeping an account of and reporting numerous small gifts, and, on the other, to fix the amount sufficiently large to cover in most cases wedding and Christmas gifts and occasional gifts of relatively small amounts. The exemption does not apply with respect to a gift to any donee to whom is given a future interest. The term "future interests in property" refers to any interest or estate, whether vested or contingent, limited to commence in possession or enjoyment at a future date. The exemption being available only in so far as the donees are ascertainable, the denial of the exemption in the case of gifts of future interests is dictated by the apprehended difficulty, in many instances, of determining the number of eventual donees and the values of their respective gifts.

For transfers made after 1981 the exclusion is $10,000 per donee per year, indexed for inflation in $1,000 increments. For the first time in 2002 the exclusion rose, to $11,000. References to the $10,000 amount in prior authority should be understood to include the inflation index increase.

In addition, §2503(e) provides that the direct payment of an individual's medical care expenses and the direct payment of tuition for the education or training of an individual are excluded from gift tax consequences.

House of Representatives Report No. 201
97th Cong., 1st Sess. 193-194 (1981)

. . . The [prior] annual gift tax exclusion of $3,000 per donee was set by the Revenue Act of 1942. The exclusion was intended to be a matter of administrative convenience ". . . to obviate the necessity of keeping an account of and reporting numerous small gifts. . . ." In view of the substantial increases in price levels since that date, the committee believes that the annual gift tax exclusion should be increased to $10,000.

In addition, the committee is concerned that certain payments of tuition made on behalf of children who have attained their majority, and medical expenses on behalf of elderly relatives are technically considered gifts under present law. The committee believes such payments should be exempt from gift taxes without regard to the amount paid for such purposes.

EXPLANATION OF PROVISION

In general, the [1981 Act] increases the gift tax annual exclusion to $10,000 per donee. With gift-splitting, spouses will be able to transfer a total of $20,000 per donee per year without gift tax.

In addition, the [Act] provides that any amounts paid on behalf of any individual (1) as tuition to certain educational organizations for the education or training of such individual, or (2) as payment for medical care to any person who provides medical care (as defined in §213(e)) with respect to such individual will not be considered as transfers by gift. This exclusion for medical expenses and tuition would be in addition to the $10,000 annual gift tax exclusion and would be permitted without regard to the relationship between the donor and the donee.

The exclusion for medical expenses (including medical insurance) applies only with respect to direct payments made by the donor to the individual or organization providing medical services (i.e., no reimbursement to the donee, as intermediary, will be excludible). Qualifying medical expenses are limited to those defined in §213 (i.e., those incurred essentially for the diagnosis, cure, mitigation, treatment, or prevention of disease, or for the purpose of affecting any structure or function of the body). However, medical expenses are excludible from gift tax without regard to the percentage limitation contained in §213.

However, the unlimited exclusion is not permitted for amounts that are reimbursed by insurance. Thus, if a donor pays a qualifying medical expense and the donee also receives insurance reimbursement, the donor's payment, to the extent of the reimbursement, is not eligible for the unlimited exclusion whether or not such reimbursement is paid in the same or subsequent taxable year.

With respect to educational expenses, an unlimited exclusion is permitted with respect to any tuition paid on behalf of an individual directly to the qualifying educational institution providing such service. A qualifying organization is an educational organization described in §170(b)(1)(A)(ii), i.e., an institution which normally maintains a regular faculty and curriculum and normally has a regularly enrolled body of pupils or students in attendance at the place where its educational activities are regularly carried on. The exclusion is permitted with respect to both full- and part-time students, but is limited to direct tuition costs (i.e., no exclusion is provided for books, supplies, dormitory fees, etc.).

In providing an unlimited exclusion for certain medical expenses and tuition, the committee does not intend to change the law that there is no gift if the person paying the medical expenses or tuition is under an obligation under local law to provide such items to the recipient. In addition, the [Act] does not change the income tax consequences otherwise applicable to such payments. . . .

To illustrate the mechanics of approving the exclusion, suppose that A made a gift of $2,500 in 1982 to X and of $12,000 to Y. The amount subject to the gift tax would be $2,000. The fact that A gave less than $10,000 to X has no effect on the gift to Y for purposes of the $10,000 annual exclusion.

Despite restrictions such as the dollar limitation and the present interest requirement, the annual exclusion is utilized by some taxpayers (those with multiple objects of their beneficence) to give away large amounts of property year after year without gift taxation. Should a limit be imposed on the number of exclusions that may be used in any year? That topic arises from time to time but Congress never has embraced such a change.

Adjusted Taxable Gifts. Gifts are ignored for gift tax purposes to the extent they qualify for the §2503(b) annual exclusion or the §2503(e) ed/med exclusion. These "exclusions" mean that these gifts are not included in the donor's gift or estate tax base as an adjusted taxable gift. See §§2001(b) and 2503(a). Although §2503(e) excludes direct payments of tuition and medical care costs from gift tax treatment only for purposes of chapter 12 (relating to gift taxes), the definition of adjusted taxable gifts in §2001(b) adopts the gift tax definition of taxable gifts as stated in §2503, making the exclusion complete.

Filing Gift Tax Returns. The donor is not required to file a gift tax return if all gifts made by a donor in a calendar year are excluded by §§2503(b) or 2503(e) or are deductible under the §2523 gift tax marital deduction. §6019. Note, however, that a gift to a charitable donee that is not excluded from taxable gifts by the annual exclusion does require the donor to file a gift tax return, even if the gift is deductible under §2522. See Treas. Reg. §§25.6019, 25.2513-1, and 25.2513-2, and Part D of this chapter for the filing requirements of spouses who elect split gift treatment under §2513.

Future Interests. Because the annual exclusion applies to each donee separately, there is a tax advantage of splitting gifts of present interests among a number of donees. Gift splitting by spouses is acceptable under §2513 but a different form of "split" is not. The legislative history refers to the difficulty of ascertaining the number of eventual donees of future interests and the value of their gifts as the reason for the present interest requirement. A major consequence of the discrimination against future interests is that it also prevents a donor from dividing property interests on temporal lines to multiply the number of available exclusions and thereby reduce the gift tax without reducing the enjoyment given to primary beneficiaries of the immediate present interests. This present interest requirement creates major planning issues and responses.

For gift tax purposes, Treas. Reg. §25.2503-3(a) defines a "future interest" to include reversions, remainders, and all other interests and estates (vested or contingent) that will commence in possession or enjoyment at a future date. A present right to trust income for a specific period — e.g., a life estate or a term of years — is a present interest for annual exclusion purposes only if there is a reasonable assurance that the trust beneficiary actually will enjoy use or possession of the trust property or its income. Treas. Reg. §25.2503-4(c). These and other aspects of the present interest requirement have spawned a significant amount of controversy and responsive planning.

If a donor creates both present and future interests in transferred assets, the present interest must be valued separately to determine the available annual exclusion, which normally requires the use of the §7520 valuation tables. The following illustrations give some flavor to the kinds of temporal interest issues that can arise.

(a)   *R* transferred to *E* an indefeasibly vested remainder in Blackacre that becomes possessory in ten years. The annual exclusion is not allowable for this gift. It might make a difference if *E* owned the term interest preceding the remainder. See *Clark* at page 881.

(b)   *R* transferred Whiteacre to *E*, reserving a life estate therein. This does not differ from **(a)** and the annual exclusion is not allowable for this gift either.

(c)   *R* also transferred to *E* a corporate bond that matures in ten years; principal and interest are payable only upon maturity. The annual exclusion *is* allowable for this gift. Treas. Reg. §25.2503-3(a). How would you distinguish this case?

(d)   *R* transferred cash to a trustee with instructions to invest only in interest-bearing obligations, to collect and accumulate the income, and to distribute the corpus and accumulated interest to *E* at the end of 10 years. Does this transfer differ from that in **(c)**? The annual exclusion is not allowable for this gift. Again, what is the difference?

(e)   *R* assigned to *E* all incidents of ownership in a permanent life policy insuring *R*'s life. The annual exclusion is allowable for this gift. Treas. Reg. §25.2503-3(a); Rev. Rul. 55-408.

(f) The following year, *R* paid directly to the insurance company the annual premium on the policy assigned to *E*. The annual exclusion is allowable for this payment also. Treas. Reg. §25.2503-3(c) *Example (6)*.

(g) The next year, *R* assigned a second life insurance policy to an irrevocable trust of which *E* is the sole beneficiary. Without more (which we'll learn about shortly), the annual exclusion is *not* allowable for this assignment, nor for *R*'s subsequent payment of insurance premiums. We need to ascertain why, and learn to surmount these limitations.

In Fondren v. Commissioner, 324 U.S. 18, 20-21 (1945), gifts were made in trust for the benefit of the donor's minor grandchildren. A separate trust was created for each grandchild, and the trustee of each trust was granted discretion to use income and corpus of the grandchild's trust for the grandchild's maintenance, education, and support. Any income not distributed (and it was contemplated that none would be required) would be accumulated and added to corpus. Distributions were *required* only when a beneficiary attained the ages of 25 and 35. The Court denied the annual exclusion for the gifts to each trust because the beneficiaries' interests were future interests for gift tax purposes. The Court said:

> [I]t is not enough to bring the exclusion into force that the donee has vested rights. In addition he must have the right presently to use, possess or enjoy the property. These terms are not words of art, like "fee" in the law of seizin. . . but connote the right to substantial economic benefit. The question is of time, not when title vests, but when enjoyment begins. Whatever puts the barrier of a substantial period between the will of the beneficiary or donee now to enjoy what has been given him and that enjoyment makes the gift one of a future interest within the meaning of the regulation.
>
> Accordingly, it has been held that if the income of a trust is required to be distributed periodically, as annually, but distribution of the corpus is deferred, the gift of the income is one of a present interest, that of the corpus one *in futuro*. *A fortiori*, if income is to be accumulated and paid over with the corpus at a later time, the entire gift is of a future interest, although upon [a] specified contingency some portion or all of the fund may be paid over earlier. The contingency may be the exercise of the trustee's discretion, either absolute or contingent. It may also be the need of the beneficiary, not existing when the trust or gift takes effect legally, but arising later upon anticipated though unexpected conditions, either to create a duty in the trustee to pay over or to permit him to do so in his discretion.

See also Commissioner v. Disston, 325 U.S. 442 (1945) (authority to distribute trust corpus to a minor beneficiary without regard to other assets of the beneficiary does not save the beneficiary's interest from being a future interest for annual exclusion purposes).

Clark v. Commissioner, 65 T.C. 126 (1975), *acq.*, involved a taxpayer, *D*, who created a ten-year inter vivos trust, the income from which was payable to a child. In each of the last five years of that trust *D* transferred a portion of the reversion to the child, with each transfer valued at $3,000 or less. In holding that these gifts qualified for the §2503(b) annual exclusion, the Tax Court said:

> [The Commissioner] argues that, as a matter of substance over form, [*D*] should not be allowed to invoke the doctrine of merger to convert what admittedly were, under the gift tax laws, future interests in the hands of [*D*] to present interests in the income beneficiar[y's] hands. We disagree, as "the interest upon which the gift tax is based is not that which the donor parted with, but that which the donee receives. Helvering v. Hutchings, 312 U.S. 393." Wisotzkey v. Commissioner, 144 F.2d 632, 636 (3d Cir. 1944), *aff'g* a Memorandum of this Court.

After *Clark* was decided, and after acquiescing to it, the Commissioner issued two Revenue Rulings stating the view that the transfer of a remainder or a reversion (or a fraction of either) to the income beneficiary of a trust qualifies for the annual exclusion as a gift of a present interest if, under local law, the two interests "merge" to give the beneficiary an immediate right to corpus (or the fractional part corresponding to the portion of the remainder or reversion that was transferred). Rev. Rul. 78-168. But the government will disallow the annual exclusion if the interests do not merge to give the beneficiary that right to corpus because the interest is a future one. Rev. Rul. 78-272.

It frequently is said that, in determining whether a gift qualifies for the annual exclusion, "it is the interest which the donee receives rather than the interest with which the donor parts that must be examined" See, e. g., Blasdel v. Commissioner, 58 T.C. 1014, 1018 (1972), *aff'd*, 478 F.2d 226 (5th Cir. 1973). If this idea is sound (and the Commissioner's acquiescence in *Clark* and the two Revenue Rulings seem to accept it), then the proper issue is whether the income beneficiary's receipt of a portion of the remainder or reversion generated an immediate right to absolute ownership of a corresponding portion of the trust corpus. If so, then a present interest was received; if not, it was a future interest. In other respects, however, the Commissioner's rulings are misleading. First, the two rulings taken together implicitly suggest that there is a wide split of authority among the states on the ultimate question. The fact is, however, that there is little disagreement among the states on the legal principles involved. Second, as discussed beginning at page 863, the government contends that, the value of a gift should be determined by what the donor parted with, rather than what the donee received. These positions are not compatible, nor is there reason to suggest that only one is correct. Still, the difference between them creates confusion. Third, characterizing the ultimate issue as dependent on whether the beneficiary's interests "merge" is misdirected in the case of equitable interests in a trust, as noted next.

Interests in a Trust. The well-accepted principle of American law on the ultimate question of trust interest merger is embodied in the "Claflin" doctrine. Claflin v. Claflin, 20 N.E. 454 (Mass. 1889). Under it, the premature termination of a trust (in whole or in part) can be compelled if (1) all of the beneficiaries consent, and (2) premature termination would not defeat a "material purpose" of the settlor in establishing the trust. RESTATEMENT (SECOND) OF TRUSTS §337 (1959); A. Scott & W. Fratcher, THE LAW OF TRUSTS §337 (4th ed. 1989). Because the income beneficiary (upon receipt of a fractional interest in the reversion) becomes the sole beneficiary of the trust as to that fractional portion, the first requirement of the Claflin doctrine is met — regardless of whether the two equitable interests merge to become one.

Whether the second requirement is met — that is, that a material purpose of the settlor would not be defeated if the trust is terminated prematurely — depends on the terms of the particular trust. Although an exhaustive listing of all features that constitute a material purpose is not possible, and the impending publication of the RESTATEMENT (THIRD) OF TRUSTS ultimately may alter some of these hoary old notions, the state of the law currently shows that the following routinely are held to be material purposes that prevent beneficiaries from being entitled to terminate a trust prematurely: (1) the existence of a spendthrift restraint; (2) the existence of distribution discretion in the trustee (even if not governed by an ascertainable standard); and (3) the fact that *at its inception* the trust had at least one beneficiary whose enjoyment of the corpus was directed to be postponed.[30] Even if a trust contains a material purpose, however, there is a further well-accepted principle that is of importance in a case like *Clark*: The settlor's consent to a premature termination waives the second requirement of the Claflin doctrine. RESTATEMENT (SECOND) OF TRUSTS §338 (1959); A. Scott & W. Fratcher, THE LAW OF TRUSTS §338 (4th ed. 1989). Accordingly, it is within the settlor's power in a trust like that in *Clark* to assure that the gift to the income beneficiary of a fractional interest in the reversion qualifies for the annual exclusion by accompanying the gift with a formal consent to premature termination of the corresponding portion of the trust.

---

30. A trust that was not of this type when it was created and that later became a trust with a single beneficiary by virtue of a transfer of the remainder or reversion to the income beneficiary does not fall into this category. RESTATEMENT (SECOND) OF TRUSTS §337, comment (f) and illustration 4 (1959).

Legal Interests. Assume that legal interests — not equitable interests in a trust — are involved. The doctrine of merger might be relevant because there is no Claflin doctrine to contend with. Thus, interests may merge if they are vested and successive. L. Simes and A. Smith, The Law of Future Interests §197 (2d ed. 1956); 1 American Law of Property §4.60 (A. Casner ed. 1952). For example, if real property is held by *A* for life, remainder to *B*, and *B* conveys the remainder to *A*, the life estate and indefeasibly vested remainder would merge, causing *A* to have a fee simple absolute. The Commissioner's current position on trusts presumably means that *B*'s gift to *A* of the remainder interest qualifies for the annual exclusion, even though it does not confer on *A* a right of possession of the property (for the simple reason that *A*, as the life tenant, already had that right before the gift was made).

With the foregoing in mind, consider whether the following illustrations make sense: **(a)** *R*, an unmarried individual, created an irrevocable trust and funded it with $20,000 cash. *R* made no other gifts that year. The trust provides that income is to be paid currently to *E* for 15 years, then corpus to *E*. For purposes of these questions, assume that the value of a 15-year income interest in the trust is $11,000, and the value of the remainder interest is $9,000. An annual exclusion of $11,000 is allowed. See Quatman v. Commissioner, 54 T.C. 339 (1970); Hutchinson v. Commissioner, 47 T.C. 680 (1967); Charles v. Hassett, 43 F. Supp. 432, 434-435 (D. Mass. 1942).

(b) What amount of annual exclusion would be allowed to *R* if the trust income were payable to *E* for 5 years and then corpus was to be distributed to *E*? For purposes of this question, assume that the value of a 5-year income interest in the trust is $5,500, and the value of the remainder interest is $14,500. Should the Tax Court's decision in *Clark* affect your answer to this question?

(c) Would it change your answers to **(a)** or **(b)** if the trustee were authorized to invade corpus on behalf of *E*?

Right to Demand Distribution of Income or Corpus. In Rev. Rul. 73-405 the Commissioner said:

As was stated by the Supreme Court of the United States in Fondren v. Commissioner, 324 U.S. 18 (1945), "the crucial thing" in determining whether a gift is one of a future interest in property "is postponement of enjoyment." However, it is not the actual use, possession, or enjoyment by the donee which marks the dividing line between a present and a future interest, but rather the right conferred upon the donee by the trust instrument to such use, possession, or enjoyment. A gift in trust to a minor is not a "future interest" if the donee has a present right to the use, possession, or enjoyment, although such use, possession, or enjoyment may require the appointment of a legal guardian. Crummey v. Commissioner, 397 F.2d 82 (9th Cir. 1968); Gilmore v. Commissioner, 213 F.2d 520 (6th Cir. 1954); United States v. Baker 236 F.2d 317 (4th Cir. 1956); Kieckhefer v. Commissioner, 189 F.2d 118 (7th Cir. 1951).

In view of the foregoing decisions, it is now concluded that a gift in trust for the benefit of a minor should not be classified as a future interest merely because no guardian was in fact appointed. Accordingly, if there is no impediment under the trust or local law to the appointment of a guardian and the minor donee has a right to demand distribution, the transfer is a gift of a present interest that qualifies for the annual exclusion allowable under §2503(b) of the Code.

Crummey Trusts. In Crummey v. Commissioner, 397 F.2d 82 (9th Cir. 1968) (probably the most notable annual exclusion present interest case in history), the donor created an irrevocable trust for the benefit of four children, some of whom were minors. The trustee was *authorized* to distribute trust income to the beneficiaries and was directed to accumulate any income not distributed and add it to corpus. The trustee was *required* to distribute a proportionate share of the trust to each beneficiary upon the first to occur of a beneficiary's twenty-fifth birthday or death. The donor's initial contribution was $50, but additional contributions could be made and each beneficiary had the power to demand from the trustee the lesser of $4,000 or one fourth of the amount of each additional contribution. To be valid a demand had to be made in writing no later than December 31 of the year in which the additional contribution was made and the trustee was required to distribute any amount properly demanded no later than the end of the year in which the demand was made. The trust permitted a guardian to make the demand on a minor's behalf during a beneficiary's minority. In the three years following creation of the trust the donor contributed $14,000 on June 20 of Year One, $50,000 on December 15 of Year Two, and $43,000 on December 19 of Year Three.

While holding that each contribution qualified for four annual exclusions, the court acknowledged and deemed not disqualifying the following points:

No guardian had been appointed and, except for the tax difficulties, probably never would be appointed. As a practical matter, it is likely that some, if not all, of the beneficiaries did not even know that they had any right to demand funds from the trust. They probably did not know when contributions were made to the trust or in what amounts. Even had they known, the substantial contributions were made toward the end of the year so that the time to make a demand was severely limited. Nobody had made a demand under the provision, and no distributions had been made. We think it unlikely that any demand ever would have been made.

In Rev. Rul. 81-7, the donor created and funded an irrevocable trust on December 29. Created for the benefit of *A*, a legally competent adult, for *A*'s life, the trust gave the trustee absolute discretion to distribute trust income and principal to *A* and directed that income not distributed be accumulated and added to corpus. At *A*'s death the corpus and accumulated income was payable to *B*. The trust provided:

> The beneficiary may demand immediate distribution at any time (up to December 31 of the year in which an addition, including the original corpus, is made to the trust) of the sum of $3,000 per donor or the amount of the addition from each donor, whichever is less. The demand right is not cumulative.

Neither the donor nor the trustee informed *A* of the demand right with regard to the initial contribution before the demand right lapsed. In ruling that no part of the initial contribution qualified for the annual exclusion, the Commissioner said:

> The courts have recognized that if a trust instrument gives a beneficiary the power to demand immediate possession and enjoyment of corpus or income, the beneficiary has a present interest. Crummey v. Commissioner, 397 F.2d 82 (9th Cir. 1954). See also Rev. Rul. 73-405, 1973-2 C.B. 321. However, it is necessary to consider not only the terms of the trust, but also the circumstances in which the gift was made in order to determine whether the gift is a present or future interest. When the delivery of property to a trust is accompanied by limitations upon the donee's present enjoyment of the property in the form of conditions, contingencies, or the will of another, either under the terms of the trust or other circumstances, the interest is a future interest even if the enjoyment is deferred only for a short time. The question is not when title vests, but when enjoyment begins. . . .
>
> Treas. Reg. §25.2511-1(g)(1) provides that donative intent is not an essential element of a gift. The gift tax is applied on the basis of objective facts and circumstances and not on the subjective motive of the donor. Although donative intent is not relevant to whether a transfer is subject to the gift tax, the donor's intent, as gleaned from the circumstances of the transfer, is a relevant consideration in determining when the rights actually conferred are meant to be enjoyed. . . . Where the facts and circumstances of a

particular case show that the donor did not intend to give the donee a present interest, no annual exclusion under §2503(b) of the Code is allowable.

In this case, *G* [the donor] created the trust shortly before the end of the year, at which time the supposed right would lapse. *G* did not inform *A* of the existence of the demand right before it lapsed. In failing to communicate the existence of the demand right and in narrowly restricting the time for its exercise, *G* did not give *A* a reasonable opportunity to learn of and to exercise the demand right before it lapsed. *G*'s conduct made the demand right illusory and effectively deprived *A* of the power. . . .

A trust provision giving a legally competent adult beneficiary the power to demand corpus does not qualify a transfer to the trust as a present interest eligible for the gift tax annual exclusion under §2503(b), if the donor's conduct makes the demand right illusory and effectively deprives the donee of the power.

PLR 8004172 answered a taxpayer's inquiry about the gift tax consequences of a proposed inter vivos trust. The taxpayer intended to establish an irrevocable trust for the benefit of minor grandchildren, to pay income and principal to the grandchildren in the trustee's discretion. When the oldest living grandchild reached the age of 21 the trust would divide into separate trusts for each grandchild, with income and principal still payable in the trustee's discretion. The principal was distributable as each grandchild reached the age of 35. The proposed trust provided in part:

ITEM IV

Dispositive Provisions

Section 1: Withdrawal Rights. Within seven (7) days of receipt of any and all property placed in this trust as a gift, the trustee shall notify each of the . . . [settlor's grandchildren] of the nature and value of the property received. From the time of the transfer to the trust, each such grandchild shall have the unrestricted right until thirty (30) days after the date of notification to demand and immediately receive from the trust a share of the additional contribution equal to one (1) divided by the number of such grandchildren living at the time of the transfer to the trust. The maximum value of property that may be received by a grandchild at any time shall be an amount which when added to all other amounts received by such grandchild during the calendar year pursuant to this provision shall not exceed the greater of Five Thousand Dollars ($5,000.00) or five percent (5%) of the value of the additional contribution. Should any of the settlor's grandchildren be a minor, this power of withdrawal may be exercised by his or her natural or legal guardian. . . .

The Commissioner responded:

> Item IV, section 1, of the trust agreement provides that the grandchild has 30 days from the date of notification to demand the additional contributions to the trust (subject to the $5,000 or 5% limit). The grandchild can compel immediate distribution of those additional contributions. Accordingly, provided that there is no impediment under the trust or local law to the appointment of a guardian, annual exclusions under §2503(b) of the Code will be allowable for additional contributions to the original trust. Crummey v. Commissioner, 397 F.2d 82 (9th Cir. 1968). Such annual exclusions are available to the grantor or to any other donor who makes a completed gift in accordance with the terms of the trust agreement.
>
> In future years, when a grandchild fails to exercise his power of appointment over annual contributions, there will be a lapse of that power under §2514(e) of the Code.[31] Item IV, §1, of the trust agreement limits the contribution that can be transferred to an amount which, when added to all other amounts received by such grandchild during the year, will not exceed the greater of $5,000 or 5% of the value of the additional contribution. Thus, any annual lapse in future years cannot exceed the greater of $5,000 or 5% of the value of the assets out of which the exercise of the lapsed powers could be satisfied. Under §2514(e) of the Code, this will not result in a taxable lapse for the year or years in which the demand right is unexercised.

Rev. Rul. 83-108 held that a withdrawal power may be granted in one year and lapse in the next if, for example, contributions to the trust are made late in the year and a reasonable time to exercise the withdrawal right runs over to the new year. Do you see the §2514(e) hazard this creates for the powerholder?

19.   *Crummey* withdrawal powers are the most common way that drafters qualify contributions to trusts for the gift tax annual exclusion. They are

---

31. Note that Treas. Reg. §25.2514-3(c)(4) provides: "In any case where the possessor of a general power of appointment is incapable of validly exercising or releasing a power, by reason of minority, or otherwise, and the power may not be validly exercised or released on his behalf, the failure to exercise or release the power is not a lapse of the power." Since a guardian could be appointed for a minor grandchild and could then exercise the power on behalf of the minor, this regulation likely did not apply to the circumstance to which the PLR was addressed. — Ed.

especially common in irrevocable life insurance trusts (i.e., an irrevocable trust that holds a life insurance policy) to which annual exclusion contributions are made for premium payment purposes. The government has ruled annually since Rev. Proc. 81-37 that it will not rule on whether transfers to an insurance trust qualify for the annual exclusion until the government resolves what position it wishes to take on that issue. This is a critical issue because sometimes the premium contribution to an irrevocable life insurance trust is so large that many annual exclusions are needed to zero out the gift. This has spawned planning that ingloriously involves "dummy Crummey" powers, to which the government takes exception, as it did in the following case. Note that a reviewed decision is not common — they comprise about 1% of all Tax Court cases. A unanimous reviewed opinion like this is extraordinary.

Estate of Cristofani v. Commissioner
97 T.C. 74 (1991), *acq. in result*

RUWE, Judge: . . . The sole issue for decision is whether transfers of property to a trust, where the beneficiaries possessed the right to withdraw an amount not in excess of the §2503(b) exclusion within 15 days of such transfers, constitute gifts of a present interest in property within the meaning of §2503(b).

FINDINGS OF FACT

Petitioner is the Estate of Maria Cristofani, deceased. . . .

On June 12, 1984, decedent executed an irrevocable trust entitled the Maria Cristofani Children's Trust I (Children's Trust). [The decedent's two children were the primary beneficiaries of the trust, and the decedent's five grandchildren had contingent remainder interests. Each of the seven beneficiaries had the unrestricted right to withdraw each contribution made by decedent to the trust within 15 days after the contribution was made, provided that a beneficiary could withdraw no more than the annual exclusion amount ($10,000). The trustees were required to notify the beneficiaries of each contribution.] . . .

Decedent intended to fund the corpus of the Children's Trust with 100% ownership of improved real property, on which a warehouse was located, identified as the . . . Spring Street property. Decedent intended that a one-third undivided interest in the Spring Street property be transferred to the Children's Trust during each of the 3 taxable years 1984, 1985, and 1986.

Consistent with her intent, decedent transferred, on December 17, 1984, an undivided 33% interest in the Spring Street property to the Children's Trust by a quitclaim deed. Similarly, in 1985, decedent transferred a second undivided 33% interest in the

Spring Street property to the Children's Trust by a quitclaim deed which was recorded on November 27, 1985. Decedent intended to transfer her remaining undivided interest in the Spring Street property to the Children's Trust in 1986. However, decedent died prior to making the transfer, and her remaining interest in the Spring Street property remained in her estate.

The value of the 33% undivided interest in the Spring Street property that decedent transferred in 1984 was $70,000. The value of the 33% undivided interest in the Spring Street property that decedent transferred in 1985 also was $70,000.

Decedent did not report the two $70,000 transfers on Federal gift tax returns. Rather, decedent claimed seven annual exclusions of $10,000 each under §2503(b) for each year 1984 and 1985. These annual exclusions were claimed with respect to decedent's two children and decedent's five grandchildren.

There was no agreement or understanding between decedent, the trustees, and the beneficiaries that decedent's grandchildren would not exercise their withdrawal rights following a contribution to the Children's Trust. None of decedent's five grandchildren exercised their rights to withdraw under Article Twelfth of the Children's Trust during either 1984 or 1985. None of decedent's five grandchildren received a distribution from the Children's Trust during either 1984 or 1985.

Respondent allowed petitioner to claim the annual exclusions with respect to decedent's two children. However, respondent disallowed the $10,000 annual exclusions claimed with respect to each of decedent's grandchildren claimed for the years 1984 and 1985. Respondent determined that the annual exclusions that decedent claimed with respect to her five grandchildren for the 1984 and 1985 transfers, of the Spring Street property, were not transfers of present interests in property. Accordingly, respondent increased petitioner's adjusted taxable gifts in the amount of $100,000.

OPINION

. . . In the instant case, petitioner argues that the right of decedent's grandchildren to withdraw an amount equal to the annual exclusion within 15 days after decedent's contribution of property to the Children's Trust constitutes a gift of a present interest in property, thus qualifying for a $10,000 annual exclusion for each grandchild for the years 1984 and 1985. Petitioner relies upon Crummey v. Commissioner, 397 F.2d 82 (9th Cir. 1968), *rev'g on this issue* T.C. Memo. 1966-144. . . .

Subsequent to the opinion in *Crummey*, respondent's revenue rulings have recognized that when a trust instrument gives a beneficiary the legal power to demand immediate possession of corpus, that power qualifies as a present interest in property. . . . While we recognize that revenue rulings do not constitute authority for deciding a case in this Court, we mention them to show respondent's recognition that a trust beneficiary's legal right to demand immediate possession and enjoyment of trust corpus or income constitutes a present interest in property for purposes of the annual exclusion under §2503(b). We also note that respondent allowed the annual exclusions with respect to decedent's two children who possessed the same right of withdrawal as decedent's grandchildren.

In the instant case, respondent has not argued that decedent's grandchildren did not possess a legal right to withdraw corpus from the Children's Trust within 15 days following any contribution, or that such demand could have been legally resisted by the trustees. In fact, the parties have stipulated that "following a contribution to the Children's Trust, each of the grandchildren possessed the *same right of withdrawal* as . . . the withdrawal rights of Frank Cristofani and Lillian Dawson." (Emphasis added.) The legal right of decedent's grandchildren to withdraw specified amounts from the trust corpus within 15 days following any contribution of property constitutes a gift of a present interest. *Crummey v. Commissioner*, supra.

On brief, respondent attempts to distinguish *Crummey* from the instant case. Respondent argues that in *Crummey* the trust beneficiaries not only possessed an immediate right of withdrawal, but also possessed "substantial, future economic benefits" in the trust corpus and income. Respondent emphasizes that the Children's Trust identified decedent's children as "primary beneficiaries," and that decedent's grandchildren were to be considered as "beneficiaries of secondary importance." . . .

In the instant case, the primary beneficiaries of the Children's Trust were decedent's children. Decedent's grandchildren held contingent remainder interests in the Children's Trust. Decedent's grandchildren's interests vested only in the event that their respective parent (decedent's child) predeceased decedent or failed to survive decedent by more than 120 days. We do not believe, however, that *Crummey* requires that the beneficiaries of a trust must have a vested present interest or vested remainder interest in the trust corpus or income, in order to qualify for the §2503(b) exclusion.

As discussed in *Crummey*, the likelihood that the beneficiary will actually receive present enjoyment of the property is not the test for determining whether a present interest was received.

Rather, we must examine the ability of the beneficiaries, in a legal sense, to exercise their right to withdraw trust corpus, and the trustee's right to legally resist a beneficiary's demand for payment. Crummey v. Commissioner, 397 F.2d at 88. Based upon the language of the trust instrument and stipulations of the parties, we believe that each grandchild possessed the legal right to withdraw trust corpus and that the trustees would be unable to legally resist a grandchild's withdrawal demand. We note that there was no agreement or understanding between decedent, the trustees, and the beneficiaries that the grandchildren would not exercise their withdrawal rights following a contribution to the Children's Trust.

Respondent also argues that since the grandchildren possessed only a contingent remainder interest in the Children's Trust, decedent never intended to benefit her grandchildren. Respondent contends that the only reason decedent gave her grandchildren the right to withdraw trust corpus was to obtain the benefit of the annual exclusion.

We disagree. Based upon the provisions of the Children's Trust, we believe that decedent intended to benefit her grandchildren. Their benefits, as remaindermen, were contingent upon a child of decedent's dying before decedent or failing to survive decedent by more than 120 days. We recognize that at the time decedent executed the Children's Trust, decedent's children were in good health, but this does not remove the possibility that decedent's children could have predeceased decedent.

In addition, decedent's grandchildren possessed the power to withdraw up to an amount equal to the amount allowable for the 2503(b) exclusion. Although decedent's grandchildren never exercised their respective withdrawal rights, this does not vitiate the fact that they had the legal right to do so, within 15 days following a contribution to the Children's Trust. Events might have occurred to prompt decedent's children and grandchildren (through their guardians) to exercise their withdrawal rights. For example, either or both of decedent's children and their respective families might have suddenly and unexpectedly been faced with economic hardship; or, in the event of the insolvency of one of decedent's children, the rights of the grandchildren might have been exercised to safeguard their interest in the trust assets from their parents' creditors. In light of the provisions in decedent's trust, we fail to see how respondent can argue that decedent did not intend to benefit her grandchildren.

Finally, the fact that the trust provisions were intended to obtain the benefit of the annual gift tax exclusion does not change the result. . . .

Based upon the foregoing, we find that the grandchildren's right to withdraw an amount not to exceed the §2503(b) exclusion, represents a present interest for purposes of §2503(b). Accordingly, petitioner is entitled to claim annual exclusions with respect to decedent's grandchildren as a result of decedent's transfers of property to the Children's Trust in 1984 and 1985.

Reviewed by the Court. NIMS, CHABOT, PARKER, KORNER, HAMBLEN, COHEN, CLAPP, SWIFT, GERBER, WRIGHT, PARR, WHALEN, COLVIN, HALPERN, and BEGHE, JJ., agree with the majority.

A sixteenth judge recused himself, stating once outside the court that he formerly was an estate planner and had drafted many trusts with Crummey powers. Similar cases also showing the government the back of the court's hand are Estate of Kohlsaat v. Commissioner, 73 T.C.M. (CCH) 2732 (1997), and Estate of Holland v. Commissioner, 73 T.C.M. (CCH) 3236 (1997). Although for the present time it appears to have ceased litigating such cases, the government only acquiesced in the result in *Cristofani*, which indicates a fundamental disagreement with the notion that motive is irrelevant and that on-going trust interests in Crummey powerholders is not a legitimate factor in determining the bona fides of the claimed annual exclusions. In TAM 8727003 the government indicated its ongoing intent to challenge dummy Crummey withdrawal rights — in individuals with no "legitimate" interest in the trust (such as spouses of grandchildren whose only benefit in the trust is the withdrawal right). For example, in TAM 9141008 a total of 35 annual exclusions were claimed in a trust primarily created to benefit three children. The government denied the exclusions claimed for 32 grandchildren who had only remote interests in the trust, other than their right of withdrawal. The government reasoned that the failure of any of the grandchildren to exercise a right of withdrawal when the grandchild had such a remote interest in the trust suggested that there was a preexisting agreement that they would not exercise that right, which the government therefore disregarded. The government analogized to Deal v. Commissioner, 29 T.C. 730 (1958), for its determination that the withdrawal rights of the grandchildren are to be disregarded. The government also questioned whether the 20-day period allowed for a withdrawal in that case is realistic.

The government has rejected several attempts by taxpayers to gain additional exclusions for gifts to trusts by granting withdrawal rights to persons having no other interest or merely a remote interest in the trust. See, e.g., TAM 9045002. The ground on which the government rests is an inference that there was an understanding that the withdrawal rights of such remote beneficiaries would never be exercised. To date, no court has sustained the government on this contention.

The view of the government on this issue is succinctly expressed in the following paragraph from TAM 9628004:

The Service generally does not contest annual gift tax exclusions for Crummey powers held by current income beneficiaries and persons with vested remainder interests. These individuals have current or long term economic interests in the trust and in the value of the corpus. It is understandable that in weighing these interests, they decide not to exercise their withdrawal rights. However, where nominal beneficiaries enjoy only discretionary income interests, remote contingent rights to the remainder, or no rights whatsoever in the income or remainder, their non-exercise indicates that there was some kind of prearranged understanding with the donor that these rights were not meant to be exercised or that their exercise would result in undesirable consequences, or both.

The government stated in an AOD 1996-10 that it "disagrees with the Tax Court's sweeping interpretation of *Crummey*" and will continue to litigate cases in which the facts indicate that the granting of Crummey powers was not bona fide. No appeal was filed in *Cristofani*, which actually was a pretty timid example of a dummy Crummey case.

Significant Restrictions on Enjoyment. Quite a lot different from a Crummey withdrawal power are other conditions that restrict a donee's access to funds. To make a demand is not a significant impediment to current enjoyment and will not prevent present interest qualification. But consider what might be in the context of the following Ruling.

Revenue Ruling 75-415

. . . *T* is directed to pay the net income from the trust to *G*'s children *A* and *B* in equal shares until the earlier of the expiration of three years from the date of the execution of the governing instrument or until *G*'s child *C* is no longer a full-time student in an institution of higher learning. Upon the happening of the stated event, *T* is directed to pay the net income from the trust property to *A*, *B* and *C* in equal shares. The trust is to terminate 10 years and 3 months from the date of transfer, and, upon termination, the principal of the trust is to be paid to *G*, if living, or to *G*'s estate if *G* is not then alive. . . .

A donee's interest does not qualify as a present interest if the property is subject to restrictions that postpone the present use, possession, or enjoyment thereof. Thus, if under the provisions of the instrument of transfer the donee's present enjoyment of the transferred property or income therefrom is deferred for a period of time, subject to some contingency or subject to the will of some other person, the interest is not a present interest. . . .

The fact that the payment of income or principal is not required to commence immediately but is subject to the demand of the income beneficiary does not constitute the barrier to present enjoyment of the transferred interest contemplated by the Supreme Court. Thus, the mere fact that the beneficiary must first make that demand, which must be complied with, does not preclude the classification of the interest as a present interest. . . .

This same proposition holds true if the beneficiary were required to perform an act, rather than make a demand, in order to commence enjoyment of the income interest. The act, however, must be performed with the direct effect of commencing the income payments. It cannot be an act of independent significance, the collateral consequence of which is commencement of income payments. Cf. Rev. Rul. 72-307, 1972-1 C.B. 307, which holds that the power of an insured to cancel insurance coverage by terminating employment does not constitute an incident of ownership within the meaning of §2042 of the Code.

The only way C can immediately obtain the use, possession, or enjoyment of a proportionate share of the income interest is to terminate enrollment as a full-time student in an institution of higher learning. Although C's action will result in the enjoyment of the income interest, such action is merely a collateral consequence of a power that every student has to drop out of school. C's termination of enrollment does not directly affect the trust and, therefore, is a barrier to the present enjoyment of the income interest.

Accordingly, the gift tax exclusion authorized by §2503(b) of the Code for gifts of present interests is not allowable with respect to a donee's right to receive one-third of the income from property for a term of years if enjoyment is to commence at the earlier of the expiration of three years from the date of gift or termination of enrollment as a full-time student in an institution of higher learning.

A's and B's interests are presently ascertainable only if it is assumed that C will terminate enrollment in school immediately after the transfer in trust. Since such a volitional act, however, is not mathematically predictable, it is further held that G may claim annual exclusions based on the minimum rights of A and B to receive at least one-third of the income from the transferred property for 10 years and 3 months or [$10,000], whichever is the lesser. See Rev. Rul. 55-678, 1955-2 C.B. 389, which holds that if it can be shown that a present interest has some ascertainable value, the exclusion is allowable to the extent of the minimum value of such interest, or [$10,000], whichever is the lesser.

Valuation.   Another critical element for present interest status is that the interest be susceptible of valuation, as several illustrations and then some actual cases will reveal.

(a) *P*, a widower, created a 15-year trust of securities worth $100,000 for the benefit of his three children, all of whom were minors. The trustee is required to distribute income equally among *P*'s living children no less frequently than quarterly. The annual exclusion is allowable with respect to *P*'s transfers to this trust. In what amount?

(b) Assume the same facts as **(a)** except the trustee has discretion to sprinkle the income among the three children (although all income *must* be distributed quarterly, the trustee may allocate it as it chooses; in a *spray* trust the trustee is given discretion whether and in what amounts to distribute income). In what respect, if any, must your answer to **(a)** differ? See Treas. Reg. §25.2503-3(c) *Example (3)*; Prejean v. Commissioner, 354 F.2d 995 (5th Cir. 1976).

(c) Now assume that *R* created a trust for the benefit of grandchildren, the class to remain open until *R*'s death. The income is to be distributed annually in equal shares among the class of grandchildren living at the time of each distribution. When *R* created the trust there were four living grandchildren. The government will allow the annual exclusion for transfers to the trust — how would you determine the right amount? See Rev. Rul. 55-678; Rev. Rul. 55-679.

Rosen v. Commissioner
397 F.2d 245 (4th Cir. 1968)

[Two siblings each created a trust for the benefit of their respective children. Each funded the trust with common stock in Gulf American, a publicly held corporation that the settlors controlled. The children of each settlor were the income and remainder beneficiaries of their respective trusts, with gifts over if a child failed to reach certain specified ages. The trustees were members of the settlors' family and other persons associated with the corporation. Because Gulf American had never paid a dividend on its common stock, the issue was whether the gifts could qualify for the annual exclusion.]

CRAVEN, J.: . . . The claimed exclusions relate only to the "income interests" of the donated shares. It is conceded that the corpus of each of the Rosen trusts is to be treated as a future interest, "limited to commence in use, possession, or enjoyment at some future date or time," . . . for which the Section 2503(b) exclusion is expressly not available. Since the Gulf American shares do not have, and have never had, a specific yield (no dividends have been paid), valuation of the "income interests" was made by the taxpayers by applying [Treas. Reg. §25.2512-9(f), which assumes a certain income yield[32]] intended to reflect, for tax

---

32. The current tables apply the §7520 fluctuating rates of return. — ED.

purposes, the present worth of a life estate and a remainder interest. Resort to the [valuation] tables is justified in cases where valuation necessarily presents an element of speculation and where use of the tables is actuarially sound. The factors "seldom accurately predict the value in a particular situation but prove to be accurate when used in a great number of cases." Use of the tables is prohibited to the taxpayer only in cases where such usage would result in an "unrealistic and unreasonable" valuation. Contrary to the government's contention we think it unreasonably unrealistic to deny value to the present interest concededly possessed by the donees. Only the most unsophisticated investor, certainly not the purchaser of growth stocks, looks to currently established dividend yield to value his *present* interest. Although it is hope for the future that accounts for the investment irony of *present* value inversely proportioned to yield, such hopes are not always long postponed in an era of conglomerate merger. To deny to the taxpayers here the use of the tables is to treat, for tax purposes, the donated income interests as having no value at all.

Moreover, the trust instruments vested the trustees with the power to sell the donated shares and to reinvest the proceeds in income producing property. The Tax Court, erroneously we think, considered that the power was "illusory" because the trustees were possessed of a present intention not to exercise it. True, the tax-payers have stipulated that: "In the view of the Trustees the probability of future dividends in substantial amounts was sufficient to warrant retention of stock, notwithstanding the absence of a current income. . . . It was the specific belief of the Trustees that retention of Gulf American stock would furnish greater overall benefits to the beneficiaries than would an immediate sale and investment of the proceeds in then currently income-producing property." It does not seem to us that a business decision not presently to change an investment voids the power to do so. . . .

In Estate of Green v. Commissioner, 22 T.C. 728 (1954), the specific yield of the income interest was ignored by the Commissioner in favor of an application of an actuarial table producing less income than actually realized. It is a difference without a distinction that in *Green* use of the tables benefited the government and here their use benefits the taxpayers.

There is, of course, no justification for a double standard. Neutral principles forbid that the Commissioner be allowed to apply the tables where to do so produces greater revenue and to refuse application where it does not. It is conceded that a valuable right to receive income has been donated. The right is incapable of precise valuation by reference to a specific yield. Absent extraordinary circumstances, and without regard to the amount of revenue produced, we think the taxpayers are entitled to resort to the actuary tables promulgated by the Commissioner . . . . "The United States is in business with enough different taxpayers so that the law of averages has ample opportunity to work." Gelb v. Commissioner, 298 F.2d 544, 552 (2d Cir. 1962).

Reversed.

In *Rosen*, what would have happened if the two siblings each had created a trust for their own children and for the children of their sibling? In TAM 8717003 two siblings engaged in annual gifting to their own children and to their respective nieces and nephews. Thus, sibling *A* gave property to *A*'s two children and to the three children of sibling *B*, and sibling *B* gave property to *B*'s three children and to the two children of sibling *A*. Each sibling claimed five annual exclusions for gifts to the five children of both siblings (and these gifts were split by the spouses of the siblings, meaning that $20,000 was transferred to each child by each sibling). Predictably, the government ruled that the reciprocal trust doctrine could be extended to apply to a transaction such as this to regard each sibling as making gifts only to his own children (which would exceed the annual exclusion limits), saying that the doctrine

does not require that the transferred amounts be exactly equal. In the present case, although the transfers are not exactly equal, they were interrelated and there has been a general matching or equality of transfers over the . . . years during which the transfers were made.

In fact, historically the reciprocal trust doctrine would require an uncrossing of these interrelated transfers to the extent of mutual value (that is, to the extent of two children of each sibling). With respect to the fifth child, sibling *A* has made a gift either to sibling *B* or to the "excess" child of sibling *B*, unmatched by gifts by sibling *B*, and that "excess" amount should not be subject to the doctrine and therefore should not be uncrossed. Still, the underlying principle of the ruling is clearly correct. See Schultz v. United States, 493 F.2d 1225 (4th Cir. 1974); Furst v. Commissioner, 21 T.C.M. (CCH) 1169 (1962) (both involving siblings and equal gifts). In Estate of Schuler v. Commissioner, 80 T.C.M. (CCH) 934 (2000), *aff'd* (8th Cir. 2002), *following* Sather v. Commissioner, 251 F.3d 1168 (8th Cir. 2001), the respective taxpayers were denied the annual exclusion for amounts exceeding $20,000 per child of each donor (reflecting that the siblings' spouses split all the gifts). Only a single *Sather* sibling who was childless was allowed annual exclusions for gifts to all that sibling's nieces and nephews. See page 209 for more on this topic.

In Rev. Rul. 69-344, the terms of a trust included a provision that declared:

The Grantor hereby authorizes the Trustees to invest . . . in such [securities], . . . productive or non-productive, as may, in their opinion, result in a future increase in the value or yield of any trust, notwithstanding the fact that any or all of the investments made or retained are of a character or size which but for this express authority would not be considered proper for Trustees. The Trustees are hereby authorized . . . to take out and/or continue in force and to pay the premiums on any life insurance . . . which they may deem desirable to purchase upon the life of any beneficiary. . . .

The Commissioner held that "the gift in trust on the terms and conditions stated does not qualify as a gift of a present interest under §2503(b)," adding that "the Internal Revenue Service will not follow the decision in Rosen v. Commissioner, 397 F.2d 245 (1968), in the disposition of similar cases."

In the course of its opinion in Berzon v. Commissioner, 534 F.2d 528, 531-532 (2d Cir. 1976), the court said:

The burden is on the taxpayer to show that he qualified for the gift tax exclusion under §2503(b). Specifically, where one claims a [$10,000] exclusion on that portion of a gift which is a present interest, he must show that the interest is worth at least [$10,000]. Treas. Reg. §25.2503-3(b). Of course, a donor cannot ordinarily prove *exactly* how much an income interest will yield during the term of its existence, and the tables prescribed in Treas. Reg. §25.2512-5 are an appropriate means of fixing a value for gift tax purposes in cases where they may reasonably be expected to provide a fair approximation of the typical yield generated. But the tables are not appropriate in the case of a *non*-income-yielding investment for in such a case one can predict with assurance that the income generated will be *zero*, and, therefore, that the actuarial tables would produce an obviously erroneous result. With respect to the trusts in question here, the history and business undertakings of the Simons Company, whose shares formed the only trust assets, provided ample evidentiary support for the Tax Court's conclusion that the settlor of these trusts did not intend, nor was his closely-held corporation financially able, to pay any dividends in the foreseeable future as of the time each gift of stock was made. Moreover, the restrictions imposed by the stockholders' agreement made it impossible for the trustees freely to dispose of the stock and replace it at will with income-producing assets. In these circumstances, the use of actuarial tables was not permissible, and appellants failed to show that the income interests in question had any positive value.

In Maryland National Bank v. United States, 609 F.2d 1078 (4th Cir. 1979), the court held that the income interest in an inter vivos trust created by the settlor did not qualify for the annual exclusion. The property transferred to the trust was the settlor's half interest in a partnership that had shown net losses in the several years before the transfer. In holding that its prior decision in *Rosen* was distinguishable, the court said:

The executor has failed to prove that the partnership has produced any income for distribution to the beneficiaries, that steps have been taken to eliminate the losses it has sustained annually, or that there will be any income in the foreseeable future. Moreover, the trust authorizes the trustees to hold this unproductive property, and it bars them from converting the proceeds from the sale of partnership real estate, which is the trust's only significant asset, into stocks, bonds, or other real estate to generate income. In sum, neither the circumstances of the case nor the provisions of the trust realistically establish that the beneficiaries actually will receive a steady flow of income.

Calder v. Commissioner
85 T.C. 713 (1985)

KORNER, Judge: . . . Petitioner is the widow of Alexander Calder, a well-known artist, who died on November 11, 1976. The Estate of Alexander Calder distributed approximately 1,226 gouaches [a form of original painting executed with opaque water colors] to petitioner. . . .

On December 21, 1976, petitioner created four irrevocable trusts, [and transferred the gouaches to them]. . . .

On her gift tax return, petitioner claimed the annual donee exclusion pursuant to §2503 of $3,000 for each income beneficiary of each of the four trusts, viz six persons, for an aggregate of $18,000 of total annual donee exclusions. Respondent determined that such exclusions were not allowable.

. . . Section 2503(b), as in effect at the time of transfer, provided for the exclusion of the first $3,000 of gifts to any person during a calendar year. The exclusion, however, is only available to gifts "other than gifts of future interests in property," or in other words to present interests. Accordingly, the determination of this issue requires the inquiry whether, at the date of each gift, the interest received by a beneficiary was a present or future interest. . . .

[I]n Commissioner v. Disston, [325 U.S. 442 (1945), *rev'g* 144 F.2d 115 (3d Cir. 1944), *rev'g* a Memorandum Opinion of this Court,] the Supreme Court concluded that a future interest was created when the trust had income but limitations were placed on its disbursement. In that context the Court explained:

> In the absence of some indication from the face of the trust or surrounding circumstances that a steady flow of some ascertainable portion of income to the [beneficiary] would be required, there is no basis for a conclusion that there is a gift of anything other than for the future. The taxpayer claiming the exclusion must assume the burden of showing that the value of what he claims is other than a future interest. . . . [325 U.S. at 449.]

Disston thus requires the taxpayer to prove three things: (1) that the trust will receive income, (2) that some portion of that income will flow steadily to the beneficiary, and (3) that the portion of income flowing out to the beneficiary can be ascertained. See also Maryland National Bank v. United States, 609 F.2d 1078, 1080 (4th Cir. 1979).

Application of these principles to the facts of this case does not present a problem. Petitioner has failed to meet even the first prong of the *Disston* test. At the date of transfer, although the beneficiaries had the right to periodic distributions of income, the corpora of the trusts in question merely consisted of the gouaches. There has been no showing that the trust assets will generate income for distribution to the beneficiaries. Petitioner has not, for example, shown that the gouaches will generate rental income or for that matter any other type of income. In *Maryland National Bank v. United States*, supra, the Fourth Circuit was faced with determining whether the gift of an unqualified right to receive profits from the operation of a partnership's business was a present interest. In holding that a future interest was created the court stated "The executor has failed to prove that the partnership has produced any income for distribution to the beneficiaries, that steps have been taken to eliminate the losses it has sustained annually, or that there will be any income in the foreseeable future." 609 F.2d at 1080.[33] Similarly, here the record does not establish that the

---

33. Petitioner contends that Maryland National Bank v. United States, 609 F.2d 1078, 1080 (4th Cir. 1979), is distinguishable from the present case because there, unlike here, the trustees were prohibited from converting the non-income producing assets into income-producing assets. The court in *Maryland National Bank* relied on two points in reaching its conclusion: that neither the circumstances of the case nor the provisions of the trust established that the beneficiaries received a steady flow of income. Here we are only concerned with whether

beneficiaries will actually receive a steady flow of income or any income whatsoever.[34]

Petitioner, on the other hand, contends that a present interest exists because the trustees have the discretionary power under the terms of the trusts to convert non-income-producing assets (i.e., the gouaches) into income-producing property. Moreover, petitioner argues that pursuant to the state law governing the terms of the trusts, a fiduciary duty is imposed on the trustees to liquidate the gouaches and convert them into income-producing property. In support of this proposition petitioner cites Rosen v. Commissioner, 397 F.2d 245 (4th Cir. 1968), rev'g 48 T.C. 384 (1967). In Rosen, the Fourth Circuit held that the donee exclusion was allowable, relying partially on the fact that the trustees had the power to sell non-income-producing assets (i.e., stock which had no dividend history) and to reinvest the proceeds in income-producing property.

Rosen is inapposite to the facts herein for several reasons. First, Rosen was actually addressing the third prong of the Disston test, that is, whether the income interest was subject to valuation. There the government had conceded that "a valuable right to receive income has been donated" (379 F.2d at 248) and that "a present income interest . . . was in fact donated." 397 F.2d at 245 (emphasis in original). Here no such concessions have been made. Second, in Berzon v. Commissioner, 63 T.C. 601 (1975), aff'd, 534 F.2d 528 (2d Cir. 1976), we refused to follow Rosen. There we disagreed with the Fourth Circuit's reliance in Rosen on the power of the trustees to sell gifted shares and reinvest the proceeds in income-producing property where there was no direction in the trust indenture or inclination shown by the trustees to do so. We stated "In such cases the possibility itself that the trustees would sell the gifted stock and reinvest in income-producing property is so uncertain as to be incapable of being valued." 63 T.C. at 618-619. Thus, even assuming, arguendo, that a present interest was created, it is not capable of valuation because

---

the circumstances of the case provide a basis for determining that the beneficiaries would receive a steady flow of income. The provisions of the trust will be examined infra.

34. Nor can it be said that at the date of gift a right to a "substantial present economic interest" was conferred on the donees. Although petitioner could contend that the beneficiaries have received a substantial present economic interest in that they have apparently received the proceeds from the sales of the gouaches (though this is far from made clear in the record), the distribution of the proceeds (i.e., trust corpus) is at the discretion of the trustees, and thus, not a right of the beneficiaries. It is well settled that where, as in the instant case, there is a gift of income coupled with a power in the trustee to encroach upon principal at such times and in such amounts as it deems proper, the interest of the beneficiaries in such possible advancement is a future interest. . . .

it is impossible to predict with certainty whether and to what extent the trustees would sell the gouaches and invest in income-producing property. This proposition is further supported by the Second Circuit[35] which, in affirming *Berzon*, stated "the [actuarial] tables are not appropriate in the case of a non-income yielding investment, for in such a case one can predict with assurance that the income generated will be zero and, therefore, that the actuarial tables would produce an obviously erroneous result." 534 F.2d at 532 (emphasis in original.)[36]

Finally, although the trust indentures in the present case authorize the trustees to sell the gouaches and reinvest the proceeds in income-producing property (as well as non-income producing property), there is no indication in the record that they intended to reinvest in such a manner. In fact, the record merely indicates that when a gouache was sold a check was issued to the trustee. No mention is made as to whether the proceeds were actually invested in any type of property.

In sum, neither the circumstances of the case nor the provisions of the trust indentures realistically establish that the beneficiaries will receive a steady flow of income. We therefore conclude that petitioner's gifts did not create a present interest that qualified for exclusion from the gift tax.

Straddling the fence between restrictions and valuation issues, Hackl v. Commissioner, 118 T.C. 279 (2002), held that transferred interests in a limited liability company did not afford a substantial current economic benefit. The operating agreement foreclosed the donees' ability to presently access any substantial economic or financial benefit, and the underlying property was a timber plantation that would be in a negative cash flow posture in the initial years due to large reforestation expenses. In addition, the agreement purported to foreclose any transfer of the gifted units to third parties and therefore barred alienation as a means of reaching any present economic value. On the basis of the court's factual findings — and probably both elements were necessary — the decision properly[37] disallowed

---

35. In the instant case any appeal lies to the Court of Appeals for the Second Circuit and thus we must consider that court's interpretation of the law in this area. . . .

36. Petitioner contends that *Berzon* is distinguishable from *Rosen* because in *Berzon* unlike *Rosen*, there was a shareholders' agreement restricting the transfer of the stock and because the trustee manifested no intention to generate income from its investments. Without deciding the validity of these distinctions we feel that *Rosen* is not applicable to the facts here because of the reasons enumerated in the text.

37. In addition to cases in the text, there is plenty of law on this issue, much of it inconsistent or quite fact specific. See, e.g., Phillips v. Commissioner, 12 T.C. 216 (1949) (gift of the right to income from a life insurance policy held in trust is a gift of a future

annual exclusions for transfers to the taxpayers' eight children, the children's spouses, and 25 grandchildren. Having created an entity with restrictions designed to generate significant wealth transfer tax valuation discounts, the taxpayers precluded the more immediate benefit of gift tax free annual exclusion transfer of the operating entity units.

Valuation of an Income Interest for Gift Tax Purposes.   The question in many of the cases above was directly or indirectly whether an income interest qualified for the annual exclusion. So many cases have dealt with the value of an income interest for purposes of determining the amount subject to gift taxation that Treas. Reg. §25.7520-3(b)(2)(ii) now addresses that issue. Should the standards for these endeavors vary?

20.   *Section 2503(c) Qualified Minor's Trusts.*   Section 2503(c) was adopted as part of the 1954 Code. The Senate Finance Committee report explained the purpose of this provision:

> Gifts to minors are often hindered by the fact that it is not clear how such a gift can be made in trust or through a guardian for a minor's benefit other than as a future interest, and for future interests the [annual] exclusion is not available. Doubt arises as to whether a gift in trust for a minor can be a present interest since the child does not presently have complete control over the property. Where a child's guardian who has control over gifts to a child, is personally responsible for the support of a child, since he must provide for the current needs of the child, it would appear that a valid gift could only be for a child's future benefit.

> [Section 2503(c)] provides that gifts to minors will not be considered gifts of future interests if the income and property can be spent by or for the child prior to his attaining age 21 and if not so spent passes to the child when he reaches age 21 (or to his

---

interest); McManus v. Commissioner, 40 T.C.M. (CCH) 866, 868 (1980) (transfer in trust of unproductive woodland; the trust was terminable when all the property was sold but until then the beneficiaries had only future interests: "At the time of making the gifts, any sale and subsequent distribution of the proceeds to the donees was a mere future possibility"); Rev. Rul. 76-360, 1976-2 C.B. 298 (stock transferred was subject to a restriction preventing any retransfer for two years and no dividends had been or were likely to be declared); Rev. Rul. 69-344, 1969-1 C.B. 225 (trustee investment powers authorized retention of nonproductive property and acquisition of life insurance and payment of premiums); TAM 8320007 (annual exclusion denied for transfers in trust of nonproductive nonvoting common stock).

But see TAM 9346003 (outright gifts of stock in a family farming operation that had no history of paying dividends; the government nevertheless allowed the annual exclusion because there were no restrictions on conversion of the stock); and TAM 8121003 (voting stock subject to a right of first refusal in the event of any proposed sale did not preclude present interest treatment because it did not prevent a shareholder from transferring shares; it did, however, affect the value of the gifts).

estate if he dies prior to age 21). [S. Rep. No. 1622, 83d Cong., 2d Sess. 127 (1954)]

Notwithstanding some facial appeal of this provision, it is not used often in real life, primarily because the age of 21 usually is too young to give control and the present interest requirement can be met in more cases with a Crummey withdrawal power that exposes the wealth to the beneficiary's folly for only the withdrawal period, and only in the amount of each annual addition to a trust and not the full, usually appreciated, amount available when the beneficiary reaches the age of 21. Nevertheless, a substantial body of law envelops these trusts and the following material helps to illustrate some of the more significant issues with respect to them.

(a)   *P* created a trust for the benefit of a 10-year old child, *C*. The corpus and any accumulated income is distributable to *C* or *C*'s estate on the first to occur of *C*'s death or reaching the age of 25. During the existence of the trust, the trustee is authorized to distribute income and corpus to *C* in the trustee's discretion. Because of the age used no part of the gift qualifies for the gift tax annual exclusion. If that age specified for distribution were reduced to 21 (or *C*'s earlier death) the gift would qualify.

(b)   If distribution were to *C*'s "heirs at law" rather than to *C*'s "estate" if *C* dies before reaching the age of 21 the gift would fail. See Ross v. Commissioner, 652 F.2d 1365 (9th Cir. 1981). It is good to remember that those are not the same thing.

(c)   Assume the same facts as in **(a)** except that, if *C* dies before reaching the age of 21, the trust estate (including accumulated income) is payable to such persons as *C* by will appoints and, in default of such appointment, is payable to *C*'s siblings. This will qualify even if local law precludes a person under the age of 18 from making a valid will. Recall *Alperstein* at page 116 and the conclusion that it is the existence of the power that matters. On the other hand, the trust would fail if the trust instrument provides that *C*'s power is exercisable only if *C* dies after attaining the age of 18. See Gall v. United States, 521 F.2d 878 (5th Cir. 1975), which held that the gift in trust did not qualify for the exclusion because of the age limitation stated in the trust instrument. The court reasoned that the trust provision was more restrictive than state law because state law permitted an underage donee to exercise a power if the donee is married. That ruling implicates Treas. Reg. §25.2503-4(b), which precludes the trust from imposing any substantial restriction on the beneficiary's exercise of the power. A similar concern is at work in the following case:

Ross v. United States
348 F.2d 577 (5th Cir. 1965)

WISDOM, J.: The question this gift tax exclusion case presents is whether a gift in trust to a minor, under a trust agreement authorizing the trustee to exercise all the powers of a guardian, must be "considered" a gift of a future interest for purposes of §2503(c) of the Internal Revenue Code of 1954. The district court granted a summary judgment in favor of the United States, dismissing the taxpayers' claim for a gift tax refund. 226 F. Supp. 333. We reverse.

The facts are stipulated. November 15, 1956, the taxpayers, Nell K. Ross and her husband James H. Ross, now dead, set up three trusts, one for each of their minor grandchildren. The trusts are identical, except for the names of the beneficiaries. Article III of each trust gives the trustees complete discretion to use all or part of the trust income for the "support, maintenance, and education" of the beneficiary. It also authorizes the trustees to hold and dispose of the income "to the same extent as if [the trustees] were the guardian of the beneficiary's person and estate and as if payments and distribution for his use and benefit were being made by him in that capacity as well as Trustee." Article IV directs the trustees to pay the trust principal to the beneficiary on his attaining the age of twenty-one, or to his estate if he dies before he is twenty-one. Article V sets forth the administrative powers of the trustees. Paragraph two of that article empowers the trustees

> To exercise all powers which guardians of the persons or estates of minors may, by order of Court or otherwise, be authorized to exercise from time to time under the laws of the domicile of the beneficiary of this Trust. . . .

The trust instruments, in spirit and in letter, give the trustees, at the very least, all the powers of a guardian under Texas law. (In a sense, paragraph two of article V gives the trustees even greater power than a guardian would have, because the trustees may do without a court order whatever a guardian may do only with a court order.) As to this power, the district court reached the same conclusion as this Court, but held that Texas law so restricts the powers of a guardian over the corpus of his ward's estate that the gifts failed to meet the requirements of §2503(c). We disagree.

It is true that under Texas law, a guardian may spend the corpus of his ward's estate (1) only for the maintenance and education of the ward, (2) only where the parents of the ward cannot provide adequate support, and, (3) except in cases of emergency, only after obtaining a court order. But these restrictions, in themselves, do not require that a gift through a Texas guardian be treated as a future interest for purposes of §2503. An outright gift by a donor to the guardian of a minor is considered a gift of a present and not a future interest under §2503(b); and limitations imposed by state law on the guardian's use of the property do not make the gift one of a future interest. Briggs v. Commissioner, 34 T.C. 1132 (1960). A gift in trust for a minor "as if the trustee herein were holding the property as guardian" for the donee has been held to be a gift of a present interest under §2503(b) of the Code and is, therefore, entitled to the [$10,000] exclusion from taxable gifts permitted by that section. That state laws pertaining to guardianships might pose barriers to the immediate enjoyment of a gift in trust will not cause the gift to be denied present-interest status. United States v. Baker, 236 F.2d 317 (4th Cir. 1956). The district court in Arizona has held that a gift to minors in trust qualified for the annual exclusion even though "resort to a court of equity might be necessary" in order for the trustee to invade the trust principal. DeConcini v. Wood, 60-1 U.S. Tax Cas. (CCH) ¶11,938 (D. Ariz. 1960). In light of the authorities — such as they are — we read the words *"may be expended"* in §2503(c) to mean *"may be expended within the limitations imposed on guardians by state law."*

Legislative history supports this reading of §2503(c). This section, enacted in 1954, had no antecedent. It was enacted as a result of the courts' having given unexpectedly broad scope to the future interest exception to the annual exclusion. The future interest exception, adopted in 1932, was a legislative response to the specific administrative difficulty, in some cases, "of determining the number of eventual donees and the values of their respective gifts." H.R. Rep. No. 708, 72d Cong., 1st Sess. 29 (1932); S. Rep. No. 665, 72d Cong., 1st Sess. 41 (1932). The courts, perhaps because the language of the statute was so broad, extended the future interest concept beyond the limits to which Congress, later, was willing to go. . . .

The language of [S. Rep. No. 1622, 83d Cong., 2d Sess. 478 (1954)], read in the context of the entire legislative history of §2503(c), describes the legislators' objective: to liberalize the law by removing from the future interest restriction of subsection (b) gifts for the benefit of a minor made through the garden variety guardianship. All states restrict the powers of a guardian, especially over corpus. Texas is no exception. But, when it is necessary, and with a court order, the income and property of a Texas ward, in the language of the Senate committee, "can be spent by or for the child prior to his attaining age 21." If we read the statute as the Government suggests, interpreting it to mean that a gift through a guardian can qualify for the exclusion only if the guardian has unlimited power to invade corpus for the benefit of the donee, whether or not for his maintenance or education, we would disqualify from exclusion virtually all gifts made through the ordinary type of guardianship. "An outright gift to a minor through his legal or natural guardian should clearly qualify for the annual exclusion." . . .

We find that the existence of reasonable, prudent, and ordinary restrictions imposed by state law on the powers of a guardian do not, in themselves, disqualify a gift to a minor represented by a guardian. Here the trustees had all the powers of a guardian, and more. We hold, therefore, that the taxpayers were entitled to the annual exclusion for the gifts in question. . . .

Reversed.

Accord, Williams v. United States, 378 F.2d 693 (Cl. Ct. 1967).

(d) This all raises an even more interesting and expansive topic, implicating the substantial restriction prohibition. In Rev. Rul. 69-345, a trustee's discretion to use trust property during the beneficiary's minority was subject to a limitation:

The trustee shall distribute to or for the benefit of the beneficiary, until he attains the age of twenty-one years, so much of the income and principal of the trust estate as may be necessary in the sole discretion of the trustee for the care, support, education, and welfare of the beneficiary. In determining whether such need exists, the trustee shall take into consideration other resources available to the beneficiary and other payments made to him or for his benefit.

In ruling that the transfer did not qualify for the annual exclusion, the government said:

The restrictions placed on the trustee's power to expend trust property for the benefit of the minor beneficiary are greater than those restrictions placed on a guardian under state law.

The beneficiary's parents owned considerable property and had other sources of income more than sufficient to meet their legal obligation for his support. In addition, the beneficiary held substantial property in his own name (previously acquired by gift and inheritance). . . .

Treas. Reg. §25.2503-4(b) provides that a transfer does not fail to satisfy the conditions of §2503(c) of the Code by reason of the mere fact that there is left to the discretion of a trustee the determination of the amounts, if any, of the income or property to be expended for the benefit of the minor and the purpose for which the expenditure is to be made, provided there are no substantial restrictions under the terms of the trust instrument on the exercise of such discretion.

Under the terms of the subject trust, the trust property may be used for the minor's benefit only in the event that his needs are not adequately provided for by his parents and only after his separate property has been expended. It is evident from the trust instrument and the surrounding circumstances that, at the time of the transfer, the trustee was not authorized to expend any portion of the trust for the care, support, or education of the minor beneficiary.

In view of the foregoing, it is concluded that the above trust provision imposes an effective condition precedent that is not satisfied and, hence, imposes a substantial restriction on the trustee's power to use the property for the minor's benefit that a court of equity would apply to compel compliance by the trustees. See Jennings v. Smith, 161 F.2d 74 (1947). Accordingly, it is held that the trustee's powers do not meet the requirements of §2503(c) of the Code. For this reason the annual exclusion provided by §2503(b) is not allowable with respect to transfers to the trust.

The Uniform Probate Code provides that a guardian of a minor "may . . . institute proceedings . . . to compel the performance by any person of a duty to support the ward" before using the ward's own assets for the ward's current needs for support, care, and education. Uniform Probate Code §5-209(c)(3). It also appears to provide that a conservator of the estate of a minor is under a duty to look to "any personal duty of support" before expending the minor's own assets for such purposes. Uniform Probate Code §5-424(a)(1). Neither provision, however, makes the mistake in Rev. Rul. 69-345.

In Upjohn v. United States, 72-2 U.S. Tax Cas. (CCH) ¶12,888 (W.D. Mich. 1972), the settlors created identical separate trusts for each of their five children, paragraph (1) of Article Two of which provided:

(1) Until such time as the Primary Beneficiary shall arrive at the age of twenty-one (21) years, the Trustee shall pay to or for the benefit of said Beneficiary so much of the annual net income and so much of the principal of said Beneficiary's trust as the Trustee, in its sole, absolute, uncontrolled judgment and discretion may deem desirable; Provided, However, that no income or principal shall be paid, distributed or applied for support or maintenance which the Settlors or either of them are legally obligated to provide a Beneficiary, nor to defray any legal obligation of the Settlors or either of them.

The trusts provided that a child would receive all undistributed income and corpus upon attaining the age of 21 years. If a child died before receiving distribution, all remaining assets were to be distributed pursuant to a power of appointment or, in default of exercise, to the child's estate. The government disallowed annual exclusions for property transferred to these trusts. In holding for the taxpayers, the court stated:

The parties have stipulated that the sole point of controversy is whether the proviso language of paragraph (1) of Article Two of each of the trusts herein involved contravenes the provisions of Code §2503(c).

As illuminated by Treas. Reg. §25.2503-4, this question distills to whether the referenced trust language imposes a "substantial restriction," within the meaning of the regulation, on the Trustee's discretion to distribute income and/or principal to the minor beneficiaries. This Court believes not. . . .

The proviso language of Article Two, paragraph (1) of these trusts, read in the entire context of paragraph (1), clearly operates to make any gift to said trusts more complete and available for the minor's exclusive use, free from fear of invasion or use for parental obligations.

The dominant and overriding theme of the trust language is that trust income and principal may be distributed to the respective children "as the Trustee, in its sole, absolute, uncontrolled judgment and discretion may deem desirable."

In light of this language, this Court finds it difficult to see how the crucial requirement of Code §2503(c)(1) is not met. Rather than limiting the minors' rights to benefit from untrammeled present use and enjoyment, the proviso merely assures that those rights will supplement and not duplicate rights already held by the minors as a matter of law. It thereby merely bars any possibility of plaintiffs regaining what they have purported to give away, which is a commendable objective.

The sense of that portion of Treas. Reg. §25.2503-4 quoted above is that if the trustee's discretion is so limited as to materially force deferment of the minor beneficiary's total right to benefit from the funds in issue, that beneficiary has merely received a future interest.

The proviso language in this case carries no such effect. By it the minors are not compelled to await any benefit. They are entitled to maintenance and support by law, and they are entitled to trust income and principal in whatever amounts and for whatever purposes the trustee may allocate.

The mere fact that the trustee may not duplicate or supplant the parental benefits already afforded the minors by the law of the State of Michigan does not result in the kind of "substantial restriction" which renders the trust contributions gifts of future interests.

Where the minor beneficiaries are deprived of no potential benefit from use of trust funds, there exists no "substantial restriction," within the meaning of the Code and regulations, which interferes with such beneficiaries' complete present interest.

In fact, under present Michigan law, the trust funds in this case may be totally consumed by the trustee while the beneficiaries are between the ages of 18 and 21, since parental obligations cease at age 18.

And when I say "consumed by the trustee," I mean for the benefit of the beneficiaries of the trust.

Defendant argues, quite simply, that the trust proviso prevents the trustee from paying for support and maintenance, that support and maintenance are substantial areas of possible disbursement and that, therefore, the proviso imposes a substantial restriction which defeats the effort to comply with Code §2503(c)(1). This argument, however, applies the language of Treas. Reg. §25.2503-4 too mechanically, too artificially, too unrealistically.

Treasury regulations should be read in conjunction with the Code provisions they refine and not in a conceptual vacuum, just as the trust language must be interpreted with reference to the totality of applicable state and federal law.

The "restriction" advanced in this case does not in any way impair, but, rather, insulates the minor beneficiaries' present interest in the trust contributions. The trustee is empowered to distribute all or any part of these funds for any purpose and toward any end not already provided by law.

If the trustee in Rev. Rul. 69-345 had been authorized rather than required to consider other assets and income available to the beneficiary, would the trust qualify? Consider Rev. Rul. 59-357 (reproduced at page 916), which held that gifts to minors under the Uniform Gifts to Minors Act qualify for the annual exclusion. Section 4(b) of that Act was comparable to §14(a) of the Uniform Transfers to Minors Act, which provides that distributions for the minor may be made "without regard to (i) the duty or ability of . . . any . . . person to support the minor, or (ii) any other income or property of the minor which may be applicable or available for that purpose."

(e) **Continuing a §2053(c) Trust Beyond Age 21.** One requirement to qualify a gift in trust under §2503(c) is that the trustee be required to distribute the property to the beneficiary no later than when the beneficiary reaches the age of 21. Under Treas. Reg. §25.2503-4(b)(2), however, the beneficiary may be given the right, upon reaching that age, to extend the term of the trust. The question arose whether a trust would qualify under §2503(c) if it provided for continuation past the beneficiary's age 21 but granted an unrestricted right at age 21 to withdraw the trust assets. The government initially ruled in Rev. Rul. 60-218 that such a power was not sufficient to comply with the statutory language that the property "pass" to the beneficiary at the age of 21. The government reasoned that the beneficiary's entitlement cannot be made dependent on an affirmative act (withdrawal). After unsuccessfully litigating this position, however, the government revoked Rev. Rul. 60-218 and ruled that granting the beneficiary either a continuing right or a right exercisable for a limited period beginning at age 21 to compel immediate distribution of the property is sufficient to comply with the passing-at-age-21 requirement. Rev. Rul. 74-43. In this regard, compare Rev. Rul. 81-7.

(f) The following material is about a different lack of entitlement — can just a *portion* of a trust qualify under §2503(c)?

Revenue Ruling 68-670

Advice has been requested whether a gift of trust income to a minor meets the requirements of §2503(c) of the Internal Revenue Code of 1954, so as to qualify for the annual exclusion provided for gifts of present interests in property by §2503(b), where the beneficiary has no interest in the trust corpus.

A transferred certain property in trust, the trustee being directed to pay, at his discretion, the net income of the trust to or for the benefit of B, aged 17. Upon the beneficiary's reaching 21 years of age, all undistributed income will be distributed to him. Thereafter, for the duration of the trust, all of the net income will be paid to B.

The trust will terminate at the expiration of ten years and 30 days or at the earlier death of B. At termination, the trust corpus will revert to A or to his estate, if he is not then living. In the event of B's death prior to his reaching the age of 21, income accumulated to the date of his death will be distributed as B may appoint by will or, upon his failure to exercise this power, to B's estate. . . .

The courts have held that the term "property" in §2503(c) includes a right to receive trust income alone, without an accompanying interest in the corpus. The requirements of §2503(c) of the Code are therefore satisfied because (1) the income may be used for B's benefit during his minority, (2) accumulated income will be distributed to him at the age of 21, and (3) if B should die before reaching 21, the accumulated income is payable to his estate or as he may appoint by will.

Accordingly, it is held that the right to receive trust income until B reaches majority or until his earlier death meets the requirements of §2503(c) of the Code and is not treated as a future interest for the purposes of §2503(b), even though the beneficiary has no interest in the trust corpus.

The Tax Court's decision in Herr v. Commissioner, 35 T.C. 732 (1961), *aff'd*, 303 F.2d 780 (3d Cir. 1962), ultimately led to the Commissioner's promulgation of Rev. Rul. 68-670. In *Herr*, income was to be distributed currently to a beneficiary, but the trust authorized the trustee to withhold income during the beneficiary's minority; withheld income was distributable to the beneficiary at the age of 21 (or to the beneficiary's estate if the beneficiary died at a younger age). Trust corpus was distributable no later than the beneficiary's age of 30. The Tax Court stated:

A superficial reading of [§2503(c)] would appear to exclude the present gifts from its coverage, for it requires that "the property and income therefrom" may be expended by or for the benefit of the minor prior to majority and to the extent not so expended will pass to the minor at 21 or to his estate or his appointee in the event of death before 21. And since the corpus of each trust which generates the income here in issue is payable to the beneficiary pursuant to paragraph First, only upon attaining the age of 30 (with provision for other disposition in the event of prior death), it may be argued, as is done by the Government, that subsection (c) is in-applicable. That argument would be sound if the term "property" were treated as the equivalent of the trust corpus in this case. If one were to consider only the naked words of the statute, that interpretation would be a reasonable one. However, we are satisfied, upon examining the gift tax provisions generally as they have been judicially interpreted, that such is not in accord with the intention of Congress.

As noted above, the Supreme Court has expressly recognized that a gift may be separated into component parts one of which may qualify as a present interest under the statute. Fondren v. Commissioner, 324 U.S. 18, 21 (1945); Commissioner v. Disston, 325 U.S. 442, 447 (1945). We think it highly unlikely that the draftsmen of the pertinent provisions of the 1954 Code were unaware of these decisions which loomed so large in so limited a field. Certainly, if the donor had made a gift of income only to each grandchild . . . it would comply fully with subsection (c), and the Government does not contend otherwise. . . . The word "property" as related to that situation would refer to the entire subject of the gift. And it is difficult to see why such a gift should not similarly qualify as a present interest merely because it is coupled together with two other components (income from 21 to 30 and corpus at 30) which are future interests. For both the *Fondren* and *Disston* cases have made it clear that one component may satisfy the conditions for a present interest while another fails to do so. Accordingly, it is our opinion that when considered in this context Congress intended the word "property" to mean, not the corpus of a trust, but rather the totality of elements that go to make up the entire gift that is being considered for classification as a present interest. In this case the totality of those elements consists of all the income up to majority. In the aggregate all such payments constitute the "property" in question, and since this "property" and the accretions thereto must be expended for the benefit of the donee prior to majority or paid over to the donee at 21 or to the donee's estate or appointee in the event of death prior to 21, the requirements of subsection (c) are fully met. Otherwise, Congress would have intended the incongruous result of classifying such income payments up to majority as a present interest when not accompanied by a gift of corpus but as a future interest when the gift thereof is made in conjunction with a gift of corpus that fails to qualify. We cannot believe that it intended any such strange distinction, and we hold that the gifts of income up to majority satisfy the requirements of subsection (c).

Estate of Levine v. Commissioner
526 F.2d 717 (2d Cir. 1975)

KAUFMAN, C.J.: One suspects that because the Internal Revenue Code of 1954 piles exceptions upon exclusions, it invites efforts to outwit the tax collector. The case before us is an example of adroit taxpayers seizing upon words in the Code which, if interpreted as they urge, would distort congressional intent and violate well-established rules of statutory construction. We therefore reverse the decision of the Tax Court favoring the taxpayers, 63 T.C. 136 (1974).

. . . David H. Levine . . . established identical irrevocable trusts for five grandchildren . . . . Unless a designated "Independent Trustee" saw fit in his discretion to direct otherwise, the trustees were to retain all income generated until the grandchild-beneficiary reached age 21. At that time, the accumulated income would be distributed in toto. Thereafter, the beneficiary would receive payments at least annually of all income earned by the trust. If the grandchild died before his or her twenty-first birthday, all accumulated income would go to the estate of the grandchild.

During the lifetime of the beneficiary, control over the trust corpus was vested exclusively in the "absolute and uncontrolled discretion" of the Independent Trustee. He could permit the principal to stand untouched or he could pay out any portion directly to, or for the benefit of, the beneficiary. In addition, the trustee could terminate the trust at any time by distributing the entire corpus. The trust also provided the beneficiary with a limited power of appointment in the event that any of the principal remained in the trust upon his or her death. The corpus, or any part of it, could be designated to pass to some or all of David H.

Levine's lineal descendants. The original beneficiary could not elect to leave corpus to his or her own estate, his or her creditors, or the creditors of the original beneficiary's estate. . . .

At first blush, it might seem that the Levine trusts clearly fail to satisfy the requirements of §2503(c)(2). The "property" — if defined as the corpus — would not pass to the donee when the beneficiary turned 21. Nor would it be payable to the donee's estate if death occurred before the age of 21 years. The power of appointment established by each trust over the corpus also fails the tests set forth in §2514(c).

The problem, however, is somewhat more complex. The Supreme Court . . . has recognized that a gift may be divided into component parts for tax purposes. One or more of those elements may qualify as present interests even if others do not. The Tax Court applied these principles in a 1961 decision involving a trust similar to Levine's. Herr v. Commissioner, 35 T.C. 732 (1961). Treating the income to be accumulated to age 21 (the "pre-21 income interest") as a separate element of "property," the Tax Court held that this segment satisfied the requirements of §2503(c) and the taxpayer could therefore benefit from the §2503(b) exclusion. The Third Circuit affirmed the Tax Court, 303 F.2d 780 (3d Cir. 1962). The Commissioner has acquiesced in the Herr decision, 1968-2 C.B. 2, and accordingly concedes in the present case that the pre-21 income interest is eligible for the gift tax exclusion.

The pre-21 income interests in the Levine trusts do not, however, exhaust the . . . per donee annual exclusion. Knowing that the remainder interests cannot qualify as present interests under either §2503(b) or §2503(c), the Levines have concentrated their attention on the post-21 income interests. Although the taxpayer in Herr did not suggest that the post-21 segment could properly be considered a present interest, the Tax Court explicitly spoke to the issue: "[I]ncome [after] 21 . . . [is a] future interest." 35 T.C. at 736. And the Court of Appeals commented similarly: "[T]he right[s] to income and principal after minority are future interests." 303 F.2d at 782. The taxpayers ask us to disregard these views and to extend the holding of Herr so that the post-21 income interests will be treated as present interests. We decline to do so.

If the post-21 income interests are looked upon as separate gifts, they cannot be considered present interests under §2503(b). As in the case of the remainder interests, initial enjoyment is delayed until a time in the future. Moreover, the requirements of §2503(c)(2) are not satisfied.

The taxpayers urge that we are required to treat the post-21 income interests as one with the pre-21 income interests, but that the remainder interests should be considered a separate gift. The taxpayers recognize that the combined pre- and post-21 income interests do not qualify as a present interest when viewed solely in the light of §2503(b). This is so because the accumulation of income before age 21 works as a postponement of immediate enjoyment. In addition, the combined income interests fail to meet the criteria of §2503(c)(2).

The Levines seek to overcome these obstacles by means of an ingenious argument. The combination of pre-21 and post-21 income interests resembles a unitary life estate, they argue. The only reason it cannot qualify as a §2503(b) present interest, they urge, is the accumulation provision that permits enjoyment to be delayed until age 21. But, they say, §2503(c) as interpreted by *Herr* permits the future interest characteristic of the pre-21 income interests to be disregarded for the purpose of receiving the §2503(b) exclusion. In other words, they assert that *Herr* and §2503(c) in effect transform the pre-21 income interests into present interests. Then, by a giant leap, the taxpayers conclude that a single, lifetime present interest is produced by linking the pre-21 *constructive* present interests with the post-21 income interests.

A study of the statutory language, however, convinces us that Congress did not contemplate such an "off-again, on-again" elusive treatment of the pre-21 segment of the transfers in trust. Moreover, we cannot be unmindful of the rule of construction that Congress permits exclusions only as a matter of grace, and the exclusions sections are to be strictly construed against the taxpayer. . . . Nor does the legislative history prove more helpful to the taxpayers. The House Report, H.R. Rep. No. 1337, 83d Cong., 2d Sess. (1954), explained that §2503(c) "*partially* relaxes the 'future interest' restriction contained in [§2503(b)], in the case of gifts to minors, by providing a *specific type of gift* for which the exclusion will be allowed. If *the gift* may be expended by, or for the benefit of, the minor donee prior to his attaining the age of 21 years, and, to the extent not so expended, will pass to the donee at that time, but if the donee dies prior to that time, will pass to the donee's estate or as he may appoint by will under a general power of appointment, *the gift* will not be treated as a future interest (emphasis added)." . . . The special treatment of pre-21 income interests in *Herr* could be justified as not *penalizing* the taxpayer for linking pre-21 income interests with other interests. But, the Levines would have us *reward* such a combination, since the post-21 income interest clearly could not, by itself, qualify for the annual exclusion.[38]

---

38.   In his opinion below on behalf of four dissenting judges, Judge Raum, the author of the unanimous *Herr* opinion, characterized *Herr* as "an extreme case." He viewed

There is one additional factor that we cannot ignore. The *Herr* opinions rejecting the contention that a post-21 income interest can be a §2503 present interest were rendered more than a decade ago. Extensive attention has been paid by the treatises, commentators, and tax services to the *Herr* decisions, and "no other field of legislation receives as much continuous, sustained and detailed attention" from Congress as does tax law. 3 Sutherland on Statutory Construction §66.02 at 184 (4th ed. 1974). Congress has had ample opportunity to amend the Code if it disagreed with the interpretation of §§2503(b) and (c) set forth in *Herr*.

Accordingly, we reverse the decision of the Tax Court and remand.

Do you agree with Judge Kaufman's assessment that the adoption of the taxpayer's position in *Levine* "would distort congressional intent and violate well-established rules of statutory construction"? The final paragraph of Judge Kaufman's opinion suggests that the failure of Congress to amend §2503 since the Tax Court stated in *Herr* that post-21 income was not covered by that provision constitutes a congressional acceptance of the Tax Court's earlier construction. But was the post-21 income significant in *Herr*? The pre-21 income was sufficient to provide the maximum exclusion then allowable.

(g) A common but often unsatisfactory vehicle for gifts to young beneficiaries is the UGMA or UTMA account that is the subject of the following Ruling. Many planners eschew this planning because of the tender age for distribution:

Revenue Ruling 59-357

. . . Uniform laws have been adopted in many states to facilitate gifts to minors. Generally, these laws eliminate the usual requirement that a guardian be appointed or a trust set up when a minor is to be the donee of a gift. Under the Model Gifts of Securities to Minors Act, a donor may appoint either himself or a member of the minor's family as custodian to manage a gift of securities. The Uniform Gifts to Minors Act provides that money as well as securities may be the subject of a gift to a minor and that a bank, trust company, or any adult may act as custodian. When a gift is made pursuant to the model or uniform act the property vests absolutely in the minor. The custodian is authorized to apply as much of the income or principal held by him for the benefit of the minor as he may deem advisable in his sole discretion. Income and

---

the Tax Court majority in *Levine* as "impermissibl[y] exten[ding]" *Herr* and "stretch[ing] the statute beyond the breaking point." 63 T.C. at 146.

principal not so applied are to be delivered to the donee when he reaches the age of 21 or, in event of his prior death, to his estate.

Rev. Rul. 56-86, 1956-1 C.B. 449, holds that a transfer of securities to a minor donee, pursuant to a statute similar to the Model Gifts of Securities to Minors Act, constitutes a completed gift for Federal gift tax purposes at the time the transfer was made. Such a gift qualifies for the annual gift tax exclusion authorized by §2503(b) of the Internal Revenue Code of 1954.

Rev. Rul. 56-484, 1956-2 C.B. 23, holds that income, which is derived from property transferred under the Model Gifts of Securities to Minors Act and which is used in the discharge or satisfaction, in whole or in part, of a legal obligation of any person to support or maintain a minor, is taxable to such person to the extent so used, but is otherwise taxable to the minor donee.

Rev. Rul. 57-366, 1957-2 C.B. 618, holds that the value of property transferred to a minor donee under the Model Gifts of Securities to Minors Act is includible in the gross estate of the donor for Federal estate tax purposes if the donor appoints himself custodian and dies while serving in that capacity and before the donee attains the age of 21 years.

The provision of the Uniform Gifts to Minors Act regarding the powers of the custodian as to distributions differs from the comparable provision of the Model Gifts of Securities to Minors Act in only three respects. First, the "model" act authorizes the custodian to apply so much of the income from the securities

> as he may deem advisable for the support, maintenance, general use and benefit of the minor in such manner, at such time or times, and to such extent as the custodian in his absolute discretion may deem suitable and proper, without court order, without regard to the duty of any person to support the minor and without regard to any funds which may be applicable or available for the purposes.

The "uniform" act does not use the term "absolute discretion," but this provision is otherwise virtually identical.

Second, the "uniform" act differs from the "model" act in that, in lieu of the latter part of the language quoted above, it provides that the income can be applied by the custodian for the minor's support without regard to the duty of himself or of any other person to support the minor or his ability to do so. Thus, the custodian, who may be legally obligated to support the minor, has power to use custodianship income for such support even though he may have adequate funds for this purpose.

Third, the "uniform" act contains a provision not found in the "model" act which gives a parent or guardian of the minor, or the minor himself after he reaches the age of 14, the right to petition the court to order the custodian to spend custodial property for the minor's support, maintenance or education. This provision, coupled with the "uniform" act's omission of the term "absolute" with reference to the discretion vested in the custodian, suggests the existence of a limitation on the custodian's otherwise uncontrolled power to withhold enjoyment of the custodial property from the minor, at least as to a portion of such property. Nevertheless, the custodian's power to withhold enjoyment is not substantially affected by such limitation.

In view of the foregoing, it is the opinion of the Internal Revenue Service that neither these nor other variations between the "model" act and the "uniform" act warrant any departure from the position previously published in Rev. Rul. 56-86, Rev. Rul. 56-184, and Rev. Rul. 57-366, in regard to gifts made under the "model" act.

Therefore, any transfer of property to a minor under statutes patterned after either the Model Gifts of Securities to Minors Act or the Uniform Gifts to Minors Act constitutes a completed gift for Federal gift tax purposes to the extent of the full fair market value of the property transferred. Such a gift qualifies for the annual gift tax exclusion authorized by §2503(b) of the Code. See Rev. Rul. 56-86, 1956-1 C.B. 449; and Treas. Reg. §25.2511-2(d). No taxable gift occurs for Federal gift tax purposes by reason of a subsequent resignation of the custodian or termination of the custodianship. . . .

Many states reduced the age of majority to 18 years (or even 17 in a few states) and amended their version of the Uniform Gifts to Minors Act accordingly. The government ruled that reducing the age does not affect qualification for the annual exclusion. Rev. Rul. 73-287. The Uniform Act was revised and restated as the Uniform Transfers to Minors Act promulgated in 1983: this new legislation, which has been adopted in the vast majority of states, provides in §22 that all pre-existing Uniform Gifts to Minors Act accounts are subject to the new Uniform Transfers to Minors Act to the fullest extent possible. The government has not ruled on whether the new version also qualifies for the annual exclusion but it is not significantly different from the Act it replaces in ways that should call qualification into question.

As to the nature of a custodianship arrangement under the Uniform Act, the following statement from Liberty National Life Ins. Co. v. First National Bank, 151 So. 2d 225, 227-228 (Ala. 1963), is instructive:

We do not view the "custodian" under the Act as a trustee in the strict sense of that term. Legal title to the money or securities is indefeasibly vested in the minor, not in the custodian. . . . This is entirely inconsistent with the rights surrounding a technical trust, where legal title to the trust property is generally conceded to be vested in the trustee for the benefit of the cestui que trust. . . . [W]e think it manifest that a gift under the Uniform Act is not to be construed as a "trust fund" . . . , as legal title to the trust res is vested in the minor.

See also 1 A. Scott & W. Fratcher, THE LAW OF TRUSTS §16A (4th ed. 1987); Annot., Construction and Effect of Uniform Gifts to Minors Act, 50 A.L.R.3d 528 (1973); Rev. Rul. 76-326.

21. *Lapse, Release, or Exercise of a Power of Appointment.*

General Powers of Appointment. The gift tax definition of a general power of appointment is the same as the estate tax definition. §§2514(c), 2041(b). Under §2514(b), an inter vivos *release* of a general power of appointment created after October 21, 1942 (a "post-42" general power) constitutes a gift by the holder of the power (the donee of the *power*, not of the *gift*) of the property subject to the power. Regardless of when it was created, an inter vivos *exercise* of a general power of appointment constitutes a gift for gift tax purposes. §§2514(a) and (b). The *lapse* of a general power of appointment is treated as a release of the power that is subject to tax, but only to the extent the value of the property subject to the power exceeds the greater of $5,000 or 5% of the value of the assets out of which the lapsed power could be exercised. §2514(e).

In Rev. Rul. 85-88 the government considered application of the 5 or 5 exception to the general power of appointment provisions of §2514(e), all as applied to withdrawal rights in multiple trusts or multiple withdrawal rights in a single trust. In each case the beneficiary allowed withdrawal rights to lapse during the year, raising the question whether lapse was a taxable gift to those who benefited by the beneficiary's failure to exercise the power. The government ruled that multiple withdrawal rights in a single trust do not permit multiple tax free lapses. The government was prepared to rule favorably to the taxpayer with respect to withdrawal rights in multiple trusts but effectively was reversed by the Department of the Treasury (see G.C.M 39371) and ultimately ruled that multiple withdrawal rights in multiple trusts also do not generate multiple tax free lapse opportunities. In each case, the Ruling effectively limits to one the number of $5,000 withdrawal rights that can be made available but does not restrict application of the 5% test under §2514(e). Thus, the Ruling noted that the 5% test properly is based on the value of total trust assets subject to the withdrawal right at the time of lapse, meaning that, if the donee has multiple withdrawal rights in a single trust, the 5% test is based on "the maximum amount subject to the donee's withdrawal power *on the date of lapse of any such power* during the calendar year" (emphasis added).

As regards multiple withdrawal rights in multiple trusts (regardless of their grantor(s)), the 5% test is applied by *aggregating* the amount subject to the power in each trust, determined in the same fashion. In giving examples, the Ruling first assumed a trust worth $300,000 at the time of one lapse during the year and worth $400,000 at the time of a later lapse, concluding that the 5% test would be applied against $400,000. Presumably the same result would apply even if the trust were worth $400,000 earlier in the year and only $300,000 at the time of the later lapse (but this was not stated). As a second example the Ruling assumed withdrawal powers in each of two trusts, one of $300,000 and one of $400,000, and determined that the 5% test would be applied against the aggregate value of $700,000, stating that the 5% exemption under §2514(e) would be $35,000 for the year. Quaere whether multiple trusts could be drafted to permit satisfaction of such a withdrawal right all from one trust rather than pro rata from each. If so, the Ruling may permit a greater degree of flexibility in granting Crummey withdrawal rights.

A qualified *disclaimer* of a general power of appointment that is made in compliance with §2518 is not treated as a release of the power and does not cause gift tax consequences to the disclaimant. To illustrate, assume that R transferred $100,000 to a trust, income to A for life, remainder to B. The trust instrument grants E a power to direct the trustee to pay any part of the trust corpus to anyone E selects. Immediately after R's transfer, E appointed $30,000 of trust corpus to C and executed a release of the power over the balance of the trust. E made a gift of $30,000 to C and a gift of $70,000 to A and to B — with A receiving a life estate in the $70,000 and B the remainder. Only the gifts to A and C qualify for the annual exclusion. There would be no tax consequence if E had disclaimed the power and not exercised or released it — and if the other requirements of §2518 were met.

Nongeneral Powers of Appointment.   The lapse, release, or exercise of a nongeneral power of appointment normally does not generate gift tax consequences. Thus, if A were the income beneficiary of a trust and B were the remainder beneficiary, a power granted to the trustee, T, to distribute trust corpus to A or to a third party, C, is a nongeneral power of appointment and T's exercise of it by distributing some trust assets to A and some to C is not subject to gift taxation.

There are several exceptions to the general rule that nongeneral powers cause no transfer tax consequences. One exception is the potential generation-skipping transfer tax that may be triggered by exercise of a nongeneral power of appointment. See Chapter 16.

A second exception is created by Treas. Reg. §25.2514-1(b)(2), which may apply if the donee of a presently exercisable nongeneral power of appointment also enjoys a beneficial interest in the trust or a general testamentary power to appoint the trust assets. To the extent the donee's exercise of the nongeneral power divests the beneficial interest or extinguishes the power of appointment, the donee is deemed to have made a gift of the value of the interest in the property appointed away[39] or as having released the general testamentary power of appointment.

A final limited exception to the exclusion of nongeneral powers from gift tax treatment is the Delaware tax trap of §2514(d), as discussed in the context of §2041(a)(3) at page 145.

PART C.   GIFT TAX DEDUCTIONS

Code References: *§§2207A, 251,; 2522-2524*

22.   Like the estate tax, the gift tax provides for a charitable deduction (§2522) and a marital deduction (§2523). The rules to qualify for the gift tax charitable deduction essentially are the same as those to qualify for the estate tax charitable deduction, discussed in Chapter 12.

The gift tax marital deduction for qualified gifts from a resident or citizen donor to the donor's spouse also is similar to the corresponding estate tax deduction, discussed in Chapter 11, but there are some differ-

---

39.   Treas. Reg. §25.2514-1(b)(2); Regester v. Commissioner, 83 T.C. 1 (1984). Contra, Self v. United States, 142 F. Supp. 939 (Cl. Ct. 1956); Commissioner v. Walston, 168 F.2d 211 (4th Cir. 1948). The government announced in Rev. Rul. 79-327 that it will not follow these contrary decisions. The government's position ought to be upheld because it is supported both by good tax policy and by property law principles. RESTATEMENT OF PROPERTY §325(1) (1940) states that "to whatever extent an instrument purports to create a power to divest a beneficial interest transferred by such instrument to the purported donee, . . . it is ineffective." For example, an income beneficiary's nongeneral power — to the extent it purports to permit transfer of the income from the trust's assets — is an invalid power appendant. RESTATEMENT §325 comment *f* further declares that, "if a person named as the donee of a purported power appendant executes an instrument purporting to exercise such power it is construed as a transfer of the interest described." Thus, property law regards the beneficiary's "appointment" of trust assets as a gift of the beneficiary's interest therein and should be taxable as such. Moreover, because the beneficiary's interest is an asset like any other the beneficiary owns that, if retained until death, would cause an increase in the beneficiary's net worth, its divestment through exercise of the nongeneral power of appointment ought to attract gift taxation.

The property law principle that identifies powers to divest the powerholder's beneficial interest as powers appendant and renders those powers invalid was not mentioned by the courts in *Regester*, *Self*, or *Walston*, nor by the government in Rev. Rul. 79-327.

ences. For example, under §2523(b), an inter vivos gift of a terminable interest to the donor's spouse may not qualify for the gift tax marital deduction if the donor retains a reversion or a power of appointment; there is no need for an estate tax counterpart of this provision because the donor is deceased. By §2523(d), a donor's retention of survivorship rights in property held in joint tenancy or in tenancy by the entirety does not constitute a reversion for purposes of this rule. Thus, §2523(d) permits a donor to obtain a marital deduction for the share of property given to a donee-spouse in the form of a joint tenancy or a tenancy by the entirety. Section 2523(i) denies the inter vivos marital deduction entirely if the donee-spouse is not a citizen; there is no QDOT counterpart to §2056A for gift tax purposes, although the annual exclusion for gifts to a noncitizen spouse is ten times the regular annual exclusion.

Terminable Interests. Terminable interests can qualify for the estate tax marital deduction only in certain limited circumstances, and the gift tax treatment of terminable interests generally tracks the estate tax rules. If an interest in transferred property is retained by the donor or given to a third party for less than full and adequate consideration in money or money's worth, the transfer to the spouse will not qualify for the gift tax marital deduction unless one of several exceptions is applicable. §2523(b). One exception is for transfers that meet the §2056(b)(5) all income, general power of appointment requirements. See §2523(e).

Qualified Terminable Interest Election. The more important exception tracks the §2056(b)(7) QTIP rules. See §2523(f). One difference from the estate tax treatment of QTIP marital trusts relates to the fact that Congress contemplated that the §2523(f)(4) QTIP election will be made by the donor. H.R. Rep. No. 201, 97th Cong., 1st Sess. 161 (1981). Treas. Reg. §25.2523(f)-1(b)(3)(ii) appears to permit the donor's personal representative to make the election if the donor dies before the gift tax return is due.

Related to the donor's gift tax marital deduction qualification is a gift tax rule that affects the donee-spouse, applicable whether the QTIP trust was created during the donor's life or at death. Under §2519, to the extent a QTIP election was made under §§2056(b)(7)(B)(v) or 2523(f)(4), the donee-spouse's subsequent disposition by gift, sale, or otherwise of *any part* of the spouse's qualifying income interest is treated as a taxable transfer of *the entire remainder interest* in the QTIP trust. This constructive gift is in addition to any §2511 gift taxable transfer of the income interest of the donee-spouse. It is a deemed gift of the remainder interest in the *entire* QTIP trust, not just the remainder interest in that portion of the QTIP trust that corresponds to the portion of the income interest that was transferred. And it is a gift of a future interest that does not qualify for the gift tax annual exclusion, even though the transfer of the qualifying income interest that triggered §2519 is eligible for that exclusion. H.R. Rep. No. 201, 97th Cong., 1st Sess. 161-162 (1981). Any part of the QTIP trust not subjected to §2519 during the donee-spouse's life is includible in the donee-spouse's gross estate at death under §2044. Unless the donee spouse directs otherwise by will, §2044 inclusion generates a §2207A(a) right to recoup from the recipient(s) of the QTIP property the amount by which the donee-spouse's estate tax was increased by virtue of that inclusion. Similarly, any gift taxes imposed on the donee-spouse under §2519 are subject to the same right of reimbursement from the QTIP property under §2207A(b); but this provision does not apply to any §2511 gift tax incurred with respect to a disposition of the income interest; it applies only to the §2519 gift tax on the value of the remainder interest that is deemed transferred.

The right to recover estate or gift taxes also includes a right to recover any interest or penalties thereon. §2207A(d). But the §2207A right of recovery does not permit compensation for the use of any part of the donee-spouse's unified credit consumed by virtue of §2519 constructive gifts or §2044 inclusion. H.R. Rep. No. 201 at 162. Furthermore, the amount of the donee-spouse's constructive taxable gifts deemed to have been made under §2519 constitutes an adjusted taxable gift that is reflected in computing the donee-spouse's estate tax at death.

Finally, Treas. Reg. §20.2207A-1(a)(2) specifies that the beneficiaries of the spouse's estate make a taxable gift to the extent that the estate fails to exercise the §2207A right to recover estate taxes. Reflecting the obligation and its effect on the recipients of the QTIP property, Prop. Treas. Reg. §§25.2207A-1(b) and 25.2519-1(a)(4) provide that net gift treatment applies. See page 831. This treatment reduces the gift by the tax imposed on the recipient.

Adjusted Taxable Gifts. Gifts that qualify for the charitable or marital deduction are not included in the donor's adjusted taxable gifts for estate or gift tax computation on subsequent transfers. §§2001(b), 2503(a).

Filing of a Gift Tax Return. A gift tax return must be filed for gifts made to a qualified charity unless all gifts to charity in the calendar year are excluded by the §2503(b) annual exclusion. §6019. The fact that the gifts are deductible under §2522 does not relieve the donor of the obligation to file a return. In this respect, charitable gifts are treated quite differently from gifts made to a spouse that qualify for a marital deduction, because §6019(a)(2) exempts the donor from having to file a form at all.

Inter Vivos QTIP Trusts. It is not uncommon for spouses to have substantial wealth owned mostly by one of them. In that circumstance it makes good sense to recommend that the spouse with the wealth (the donor-spouse) make a transfer to the other spouse (the donee-spouse) to hedge against the possibility that the donee-spouse will die first, in which case one unified credit, one generation-skipping transfer tax exemption, and one run through the less than maximum marginal rates all would be lost. The problem is that the donor-spouse may not be willing to make such a transfer, for all sorts of reasons that may relate to concerns about control, loss of income from the transferred property, donee-spouse creditor problems, and fear of divorce. A solution to these types of concerns often is an inter vivos QTIP trust that gives the donee-spouse little or no control over the QTIP trust property.

Frequently, however, the donor-spouse raises the question: "if I do survive (which is why we're doing this planning), can I continue to receive the income for the balance of my life?" Section 2523(f)(5) speaks to this issue and provides that a retained secondary life estate of this nature is permissible and will cause no estate tax liability under §2036(a)(1) (transfer with retained life estate), but only if the donor-spouse dies first. That doesn't address the planning scenario contemplated. But, in a string of rulings, followed by Treas. Reg. §§25.2523(f)-1(d) and 25.2523(f)-1(f) *Examples 10* and *11*, the government allows taxpayers to engage in this planning without being subjected to estate tax inclusion when the surviving donor-spouse later dies. Section 2044(a) inclusion to the donee-spouse is deemed to cause the QTIP property to be treated as passing to the donor from the donee-spouse, and is not treated as a retained interest of the original donor.

PART D.   SPLIT GIFTS

Code Reference: *§2513*

23.   *Election.*   For gift tax (Chapter 12) purposes only), spouses may elect under §2513 to treat gifts made by one of them to a third party as made half by each. The election is made on the gift tax return (or returns) for the calendar year in which the gift was made and must be made with respect to *all* gifts made by both spouses during that calendar year. Because the election is made on an annual basis, making it for one calendar year does not require the spouses to split gifts in any other year. Thus, if some gifts should be split and others not, they should be made in different years. The spouses are jointly and severally liable for all gift taxes incurred on any gifts made by either spouse in the calendar year for which a split gift election was made. §2513(d). But either spouse may pay all the tax without added gift tax liability because of the unlimited gift tax marital deduction.

A gift tax return filed without electing gift splitting cannot later be amended to make the election. Once made, the election is irrevocable after April 15 of the year after the gift was made, regardless of when the gift tax return is filed. See Treas. Reg. §§25.2513-2(b)(1), -3(a)(1); McLean v. United States, 79-1 U.S. Tax Cas. (CCH) ¶13,293 (N.D. Cal. 1979); Thompson v. United States, 79-1 U.S. Tax Cas. (CCH) ¶12,394 (C.D. Cal. 1979); Thorrez v. Commissioner, 31 T.C. 655 (1958), *aff'd per curiam*, 272 F.2d 945 (6th Cir. 1959); Rev. Rul. 80-224; Rev. Rul. 78-27.

24.   *Effect of Election.*   Split gifts are taxed for gift tax purposes as if each spouse made a gift of half, meaning each may take advantage of the annual exclusion, the unified credit, and each spouse's progressive tax brackets. To illustrate:

(a) D gave \$53,000 to X and \$8,000 to Y. Meanwhile, D's spouse, S, gave \$14,000 to Y. If D and S elect to split their gifts for the year they each are deemed to have given \$26,500 to X and \$11,000 to Y — the latter of which may be totally tax free under the annual exclusion.

(b) D transferred property to an inter vivos trust for the life of D's spouse, S. The income from the trust is payable quarterly to S. On S's death, the remainder is payable to the descendants of D and S. Assuming a timely election under §2513 and assuming that no election was made under §2523(f)(4), the gift made by D can be split by D and S under §2513 only with respect to interests *not* passing to S. So: if no part of the trust corpus can be distributed to S the split can be made with respect to the remainder but not if the trustee is authorized to distribute corpus to S to the extent necessary for S's support unless that interest is susceptible to valuation, in which case the excess will qualify. Treas. Reg. §25.2513-1(b)(4); Wang v. Commissioner, 31 T.C.M. (CCH) 719 (1972).

Chapter 15

SPECIAL VALUATION RULES TO PREVENT ESTATE FREEZING

Congress responded to perceived abuses in the form of what sometimes are called "estate freeze" transactions by enacting Chapter 14 of Subtitle B of the Code (§§2701–2704). These "freeze" transactions all have in common taxpayer efforts to reduce the value of transferred property, sometimes by merely taxing it before it appreciates in value and in more sophisticated cases by employing tactics that artificially depress values. Although Chapter 14 is an important set of provisions, their value wanes as the desirability of shifting appreciation declines (as it does when the progressive tax rate system approaches a flat tax, which occurs when the applicable exclusion amount increases and the threshold for the maximum marginal tax rate drops). In addition to the subject of this Chapter becoming less commanding in terms of its significance, time constraints may preclude an in-depth examination of these rules in your course. To accommodate the need for brevity, therefore, this Chapter begins with a discussion of the concerns that were prompted by various types of estate freezes that were employed before Chapter 14 was adopted, followed by a brief summary of the four statutory provisions that comprise Chapter 14. That summary may serve as a map to aid in exploring the more detailed discussion in the latter parts of the chapter, if you are able to engage in that detailed study.

1.   *Congressional Concerns Raised by Estate Freezes.* The Staff of the Joint Committee on Taxation issued a pamphlet on "Present Law and Proposals Relating to Federal Transfer Tax Consequences of Estate Freezes" in anticipation of a joint hearing before the Senate Finance Subcommittees on Energy and Agricultural Taxation and Taxation and Debt Management on June 27, 1990, which was reproduced in Tax Management, Primary Sources, Series V, 101st Cong. at B-18:022 (1990). There were three fundamental government objections to estate freezing techniques, as described in the following extract from the pamphlet:

First, because frozen interests are inherently difficult to value, they can be used as a means of undervaluing gifts. Second, such interests entail the creation of rights that, if not exercised in an arm's-length manner, may subsequently be used to transfer wealth free of transfer tax. Third, "frozen" interests may be used to retain substantial ownership of the entire property while nominally transferring an interest in the property to another person.

A. Undervaluation of Initial Transfer

Estate freezes provide an opportunity for undervaluation of the initial gift. Because gift tax adjustments do not generally result in additional tax (due to the unified credit) and because the Internal Revenue Service has limited audit resources, such undervaluation may go unchallenged.

Undervaluation may occur because the transferor claims a value for the transferred property lower than the amount a willing buyer would pay for the interest.[1] This undervaluation is difficult to detect because of the inherent difficulty in valuing interests created in a freeze.

The discounted cash flow method depends upon proper valuation of the preferred interest. Such interests pose substantial valuation difficulties. Even if the features of the closely held preferred interest are identical to those found in public markets, differences between the two types of securities make comparison difficult. Much publicly traded preferred stock is held by corporations, which, because of the dividend received deduction (§243), are willing to accept a dividend yield lower than individual investors. Also, the need of publicly traded companies to have continued access to the capital markets creates an incentive to pay dividends on preferred stock that may be absent for the closely held company. Further, publicly traded preferred stock is inherently more liquid than is comparable stock of a closely held company. Finally, publicly traded companies are more likely to be in more than one line of business, which may affect the variability of the firm's earnings (or cash flows).

Moreover, the features of a preferred stock issued in a freeze often vary substantially from features contained in publicly traded stocks. Stock issued in a freeze may lack features common to publicly traded comparables (such as a cumulative right to

---

1. Indeed, the very application of the willing buyer, willing seller standard to certain property rights held by related parties may be problematic. In most families, family relationships rather than contractual rights determine how and when property will pass.

dividends) or contain features missing from such comparables (such as discretionary capital call rights).

These valuation difficulties create the possibility that inconsistent valuation assumptions will be used to value a preferred interest. Taxpayers may use favorable assumptions in valuing the retained preferred stock at the time of the freeze and unfavorable assumptions in valuing such stock at death.

Undervaluation also may result from the failure to value correctly restrictions or options to buy property. Fixed price and book formula options may be used without considering the likely appreciation in the property. Options granted in exchange for services may be valued on a mistaken assumption that the parties are dealing at arm's length. Bilateral options exercisable at death may be valued without regard to the different life expectancies of the parties.

Further, undervaluation may result from the use of Treasury tables valuing annuities, life estates, terms for years, remainders and reversions. Those tables are based on assumptions regarding rates of return and life expectancy that are seldom accurate in a particular case and, therefore, may be the subject of adverse selection. Because the taxpayer decides what property to give and when to give it, use of tables, in the aggregate, more often results in undervaluation than in overvaluation.

B. Subsequent Transfers

Creation of a frozen interest in property also permits the transfer of wealth free of transfer tax through the subsequent exercise or nonexercise of rights with respect to the enterprise. Even if the transferred property is properly valued at the time of the initial transfer under the willing buyer, willing seller standard, wealth may be transferred thereafter if the rights are not exercised in an arm's-length manner. This may occur if, after the transfer, either transferor or transferee acts or fails to act or causes the enterprise to act or fail to act. It is unclear under present law whether such exercise or nonexercise results in a gift. Even if it does, it is virtually impossible for the IRS to monitor all post-transfer action or inaction with respect to such rights.

Closely held businesses provide many opportunities for subsequent transfers of wealth. Such transfers may occur through legal rights created at the time of the freeze transaction. For example, wealth may pass from a preferred shareholder to a common shareholder if the corporation fails to pay dividends to the preferred shareholder. Even if the preferred stock is cumulative, such failure results in a transfer equal to the value of the use of the money until the dividend is paid. Or, by exercising conversion, liquidation, put or voting rights in other than an arm's-length fashion (or by not exercising such rights before they lapse), the transferor may transfer part or all of the value of such rights.

Subsequent action or inaction may transfer wealth even in the absence of a preferred interest in a closely held company. For example, failure to revise a dated sales price contained in a buy-sell agreement can transfer wealth from the party who would benefit from such revision. Similarly, the failure of a life tenant to exercise rights to use the property can have the effect of transferring wealth to the remainder beneficiary. Conversely, improvements by a life tenant can enrich the remainder beneficiary.

C. Disguised Testamentary Transfers

Third, the retention of a frozen interest may be used in order to retain enjoyment of the entire property. Enjoyment may be retained through a voting right, a preferred interest in a partnership or corporation, an income interest in a trust, a life estate in property, or a right to use property. In such cases, the transfer is, in reality, incomplete at the time of the initial transfer and, if the frozen interest is retained until death, the transfer is testamentary in nature.

Failure to treat a testamentary transfer as such gives the donor the advantage of favorable rules applicable only to gifts — such as the annual exclusion and tax-exclusive gift tax base. In addition, early utilization of the unified credit increases its present value. These benefits are appropriate only when the transferor has parted with substantial ownership of the transferred property.

Prior to adoption of anti-freeze legislation, the government made numerous (but often unsuccessful) attempts to combat what it perceived to be the abuse represented by freeze transactions. These led to adoption of the first legislative salvo, in the form of estate tax §2036(c). Having enjoyed less than overwhelming success in addressing freeze transactions under existing authority, the government turned to Congress for relief and was rewarded in 1987 by the adoption of that provision. Revenue Act of 1987, Pub. L. No. 100-203, 101 Stat. 1330 (1987), as amended by the Technical and Miscellaneous Revenue Act of 1988, Pub. L. No. 100-647, 102 Stat. 3342.

This initial effort to combat estate freezes was based on a hard-to-complete model and required that certain inter vivos transfers be treated as if the transferor retained a life estate until death, causing estate tax inclusion of the transferred property under §2036(a)(1). For example, if the statutory requisites were met, common stock transferred subsequent to a preferred stock recapitalization would be included in the decedent's gross estate. Unfortunately, §2036(c) was badly drafted. The legislation and the government's administrative efforts to make the provision workable were severely criticized. In 1990, Congress succumbed to that criticism and repealed §2036(c), retroactive to the date of its enactment. In its place, as part of the Revenue Reconciliation Act of 1990, Congress adopted Chapter 14, titled "Special Valuation Rules." This is the law with which we deal today.

Before delving into more detail, it bears noting that, in large part, all Chapter 14 has done is put an end to prior planning. That was it's objective. But estate planners are an ingenious group, typically paid by rich folks to help them play keep away from the government, and Chapter 14 has largely fueled a cottage industry that constantly seeks to develop new planning that avoids or — in some cases — takes advantage of the rules in Chapter 14. In large part, this simply proves how hard it is to create a tax system without flaws that smart planners use (or sometimes abuse or exploit, depending on your perspective). The tax game often is about finding "opportunities" (or "loopholes," again the label may depend on who pays your fee), taking advantage to a point that Congress may perceive a new abuse, which eventually may generate another legislative response, that sparks another round of analysis, then invention, and finally yet another round of changes. It is a constantly evolving landscape, populated by players essentially engaged in the same dance, played round and around, over and over again.

2.   *Overview of Chapter 14.*   Congress settled on Chapter 14 as a congregation of provisions that operates in an umbrella over the estate and gift taxes (and some, but not all, for generation-skipping transfer tax purposes as well). These rules respond to the historic reality that much traditional estate planning has sought to minimize the wealth transfer tax bite by minimizing the value of property subject to the tax. The most effective way to do this in a progressive tax system has been to shift the potential for appreciation to someone else, usually taxing the property at a lower value before growth is generated. A classic example is a parent who identifies a surefire business opportunity: rather than develop that idea and then transfer the successful enterprise to a child at a future date, the wise parent informs the child about the opportunity and makes it possible for the child to develop the business as the child's own successful endeavor. The gift tax does not reach this transfer of knowledge; the wealth transfer tax only taxes the transfer of property (although the dividing line between knowledge and property may blur, as in the case of intellectual property). This form of transfer is not very common, notwithstanding that it most effectively avoids wealth transfer taxation on the growth in value attributable to successful exploitation of an idea. A second more common example is a donor who, believing that an asset (e.g., stock, undeveloped realty, or an invention) is about to balloon in value, transfers it at its current value rather than waiting to make a taxable transfer at its appreciated future value.

Techniques such as these and many others are known as estate freezing because they shift the future appreciation before it takes place. The tax is incurred at the frozen current (low) value (at least that is the hope, but don't lose sight of the fact that even in good economic times, sometimes taxpayers incur transfer taxation at the high end of the valuation spectrum and the property loses value after the transfer, sometimes known as a "negative" freeze — usually not a good thing). Neither Chapter 14 nor any other Code provision prevents the type of estate freezing in which an entire asset is conveyed, the donor relinquishing all enjoyment and control over it. Instead, the principal planning devices that have attracted Congressional ire are those in which the growth potential of a business is separated from its current value by a donor who wants to remain in control. The transferor made a gift of the growth potential, typically to a younger generation of beneficiaries, but retained the current value and usually control over the enterprise, usually in the hands of the donor and other relatives, typically in higher family generations.

Many intricate techniques are designed to obtain estate freezing for businesses that already have a substantial value. Cooper, *A Voluntary Tax? New Perspectives on Sophisticated Estate Tax Avoidance*, 77 COLUM. L. REV. 161 (1977), provides a catalog of many successful freezing devices used in prior generations, of which four general varieties attracted Congressional attention as early as 1987. To appreciate why Congress finally settled on the provisions that exist today, we need to take a brief excursion through several more sophisticated forms of asset value freezes and how they now are precluded by the provisions of Chapter 14. This will help set the stage for a more detailed explanation of these rules.

Preferred Stock Recapitalizations. The most popular form of estate freeze in the past by a business owner was the "preferred stock recapitalization" (also available in a partnership context using general and limited partnership interests, rather than stock). The entity would be structured with two classes of ownership interest, one senior and one junior, with the senior interest structured so that it would not appreciate in value. For example, a transferor might cause a closely held corporation to recapitalize in a tax free reorganization, resulting in preferred stock with voting control and common stock. The senior equity interest (the preferred stock) would carry a preference on liquidation of the entity, if that should occur, and also might be granted certain rights that were designed to inflate its value above the control value it already possessed. Examples of these additional rights ("bells and whistles") were a noncumulative preference to dividends, a right to convert to other forms of debt or equity interest, and an option (called a put) forcing the entity to purchase (redeem) the stock on the stockholder's demand. It was hoped that these rights would add value to the preferred stock, even if they were not likely to be exercised. As an added form of tax-free value shifting, many of these rights would lapse at the death of the senior equity owner, so that the estate tax value of the senior interest would be reduced when the estate tax applied.

There would be a ceiling on the amount of liquidation proceeds that could be distributed on the preferred stock, and a ceiling on the amount that could be paid as an annual dividend on the preferred. As a consequence, any appreciation in the income and value of the corporation would inure to the common stock and would not increase the value of the preferred.

The junior equity interest (the common stock) would be given to objects of the transferor's bounty, valued at what remains of the total value of the entity after assigning value to the retained senior equity interest. If the recapitalization was structured properly, the value of the junior interest would be so small at the time of transfer that it might be covered by the gift tax annual exclusion. Or the transferor's beneficiaries might just purchase that interest for its full fair market value, thereby avoiding a taxable gift entirely. The overall concept was that, if the entity did well, the junior equity interest would grow in value while the senior interest would remain constant or actually decline in value. The junior interest could be wiped out if the entity fared badly. But it might explode in value if the anticipated growth occurs. That growth would have been transferred at little or no tax cost.

To preclude this abuse §2701 operates when a person transfers a junior equity interest to a family member (the transferor's spouse, a lineal descendant of the transferor or of the transferor's spouse, or a spouse of any such descendant). If the transferor or higher generation family members ("applicable family members") retain senior interests in the entity, the donated junior equity interest is valued by a "subtraction method" that disregards most senior equity interests and treats the junior equity as having all the value of the entity. Only the value of certain "qualified payment rights" (to distributions of income or capital) are not ignored when valuing the taxable gift of the junior interests. Thus, in the paradigm example of a donor giving common stock and retaining the preferred, the value of the preferred stock likely will be zero and the gift taxable value of the common stock will equal the full value of the enterprise.

Manipulation of the Valuation Tables. The valuation tables also provided estate planners with a variety of opportunities for estate freezing. Examples are: transfers in exchange for a private annuity or a self canceling installment note (a SCIN), a grantor retained interest trust (a GRIT), or a split interest purchase. The valuation tables assume two variables, either or both of which could be wrong in any given case and at a given time. One variable is income yield. The current tables under §7520 are based on a monthly fluctuating income assumption that is related to an "applicable federal rate" (see §1274(d)). The other variable relates to life expectancy (mortality).

To illustrate how the tables produce an opportunity for freezing estate values, assume that a transferor wants to minimize the transfer tax cost of owning Blackacre. The applicable valuation approach assumes that the property will generate an income return to the present owner and that the owner will live for a predicted period. If, for example, those assumptions were a 5% annual return over a 20-year life expectancy, a retained life estate would be worth 61.341% of the total value of the property and the remainder would be worth 38.659% of the value of the property. If the transferor conveyed the remainder and retained a life estate, the gift tax would be based on the value of the future interest conveyed, notwithstanding that the full value of the property would belong to the remainder beneficiary when the transferor's retained life estate terminated.

The valuation tables ignore the potential for appreciation.[2] This offers a potential for valuation shift if the underlying property does appreciate in value. The illustrated transaction would not achieve a freeze because §2036(a)(1) would cause estate tax inclusion in the transferor's gross estate of the full appreciated value of Blackacre when the transferor dies. So the GRIT was developed to avoid §2036 inclusion. In a GRIT the taxpayer transfers a remainder following a retained *term* interest, structured such that the transferor is expected to outlive the term. The expected growth escapes wealth transfer tax if the transferor does survive the term and §2036(a)(1) therefore does not apply. This transaction becomes even more attractive if, for example, Blackacre produces less income than the tables assume, in which case the retained income interest is not worth the assumed 61%, and the transferred remainder is worth more than the 39% on which the gift tax was based.

An alternative to a GRIT is a SCIN. To create a SCIN, Blackacre is sold in exchange for a private annuity, payable for the life of the transferor. The value of the SCIN will equal the fair market value of Blackacre based on a normal life expectancy. But if the transferor actually dies earlier than the assumed life expectancy, then the payments received would be less than the value of the annuity or SCIN when the exchange took place. The buyer would have obtained the entire property at a bargain price. Although payments received by the transferor and retained at death would be subject to estate tax, they would not equal the full value of the transferred property.

---

2. During the two decades at the end of the last century when all this planning enjoyed its heyday, many investors needed to be reminded that, despite the optimism that all property only appreciates in value, properties sometimes *decline* in value too. It is the balance of the risk of depreciation against the opportunity for appreciation that explains why the valuation regime ignores changes in the value of the underlying property when establishing the value of a temporal interest such as a life estate, term or years, or remainder.

A third alternative is a split interest purchase by which the tables are manipulated in a transaction that does not trigger application of §2036(a)(1) because the transferor never owns more than a life estate and never makes a transfer that causes a string provision to apply. The transferor and the object of the transferor's bounty would jointly purchase property, but not as tenants in common or as joint tenants. Instead, the transferor would acquire a life estate or other term interest and the object would purchase the remainder, each paying full and adequate consideration for the interest acquired, based on the assumptions in the tables. To the extent those assumptions are wrong (in the right direction) the tables undervalue the remainder (it would be worth more than the object paid for it) and overvalue the term interest (it would be worth less than the transferor paid for it) and the differential would be an effective transfer between the two that does not attract wealth transfer tax. Although any unexpended amounts that the transferor received from the term interest before death would be includible in the transferor's gross estate, this is a freeze transaction to the extent of the untaxed valuation shift attributable to misvaluation by the tables.

To preclude these forms of abuse, the §2702 value of a transferred interest is determined by using another form of subtraction method in which only "qualified interests" owned by the transferor (or higher generation "applicable family members") are deemed to have value — all other higher retained interests are deemed to be worth zero. Thus, if a retained interest is not qualified the gift taxable value of the transferred interest is treated as equal to the full value of the entire asset. A qualified interest is one that essentially guarantees payment of the full amount the tables assume, either as an annuity or a unitrust interest. An exception to §2702 that has attracted much attention is sometimes referred to as a "house GRIT" or a QPRT (qualified personal residence trust) by which a transferor retains a term interest (a period of years that the transferor hopes to outlive) in a residence (which can include a vacation home). Excepting these, most temporal interest planning has ceased.

Buy-Sell Agreements. A third technique for accomplishing a valuation freeze was by way of a buy-sell agreement under which the transferor's estate would be obliged to sell property to an object of the transferor's bounty at a designated striking price. That price established the estate tax value of the property subject to the agreement (typically stock in a closely held corporation). A freeze was accomplished to the extent the actual value exceeded the striking price. Similar agreements imposed restrictions or granted options or rights that had a similar effect.

The basic operation of §2703 is to ignore most agreements, options, rights to acquire property for less than full and adequate consideration, or restrictions on the right to sell or use property when valuing property for wealth transfer tax purposes. An exception ("safe harbor") applies under

§2703(b) if three conditions are satisfied, in which case the value of the property can be affected or even established by qualifying agreements, options, or other rights or restrictions. This safe harbor exception is not new, however; even before §2703 was adopted a buy-sell agreement or similar right or restriction had to satisfy certain conditions (established by court precedent and regulations) to be effective in valuing the property. See page 73. We will see that most of those conditions are retained in §2703(b).

Lapsing Rights or Restrictions. This form of freeze entailed valuation during life on the basis of rights or restrictions that add value to retained property or decrease the value of transferred property. The retained property loses value or the transferred property increases in value tax free to the extent these rights or restrictions subsequently lapse without attracting transfer taxation. For example, stock transferred to a donee might be nonvoting for a period of years, after which it becomes voting stock, and stock retained by a transferor might be granted participation rights (above the stock preference rights) that lapse after the transfer is made.

Congress reacted to these perceived abuses with §2704, which targets very specifically two court decisions (both reproduced below). One application of §2704 causes certain lapses of voting or liquidation rights in a corporation or partnership to be treated as a transfer subject to gift or estate taxation. The deemed transferor is the individual who held the right immediately prior to its lapse, and the value of the constructive transfer is the difference in value caused by the lapse. A second prong of §2704 applies if an interest in a corporation or partnership is transferred to a member of the transferor's family; it simply requires that certain restrictions on the right to liquidate the entity ("applicable restrictions" that limit the right to liquidate the entity and that are more restrictive than state law) be ignored in valuing the transferred property.

That's It. Really: that's all there is to Chapter 14. The first two sections (§§2701 and 2702) respond to the classic form of estate freeze by applying an easy-to-complete gift tax inclusion rule that values a transferred interest at a figure that exceeds the actual value of that interest. In general, the approach adopted in those two sections is to tax a transferor on the entire value of property even though only a partial interest in the property was transferred. As we will see, that statement overly simplifies the operation of those provisions (and somewhat overstates them), but it is a useful generalization from which to begin our more detailed study. Note that §§2701 and 2702 can cause the gift tax value of a transferred item to exceed its actual value, and a transfer can cause gift tax consequences even if the transferor receives money's worth consideration equal to the actual value of the transferred item.

The last two sections of Chapter 14 (§§2703 and 2704) differ from the first two because they target specific valuation abuses, §2703 by restricting the valuation effect of buy-sell agreements and other postmortem limitations on the salability of corporate or partnership interests and §2704 by negating the effect of lapsing rights or certain restrictions on the ability of a corporation or partnership to liquidate. It is important to note that §§2703 and 2704 apply for estate, gift, *and* generation-skipping transfer tax purposes, but §§2701 and 2702 do not apply for generation-skipping transfer tax purposes and have only a limited effect on estate taxes — they operate principally through the gift tax valuation of inter vivos transfers.

PART A. SECTION 2701: TRANSFERS OF JUNIOR EQUITY INTERESTS

Code Reference: *Chapter 14: §2701*

The §2701(a)(1) special valuation regime is applied to determine whether a gift of a corporate or partnership equity interest has been made, and its value. In general, the statutory scheme is to treat the value of a transferred interest as equal to the difference between the value of all family-held interests in a corporation or partnership and the value of all senior equity interests that are retained by the transferor and applicable family members, the latter of which is specially valued, often at zero. This is referred to as the "subtraction" method of valuation. Treas. Reg. §25.2701-3(a). Thus, liquidation, put, call, and conversion rights, and noncumulative dividend rights with respect to certain retained interests are ignored under §2701 in determining the value of any corporate or partnership interests that are retained by the transferor.

Technically, the rule specifies that, in the context of transfers between family members,[3] the value of an "applicable retained interest" that is not a "qualified payment" is zero for purposes of determining the gift tax consequences of a transfer. §2701(a)(3). If this provision applies, other interests in the corporation or partnership are deemed to represent all of the value of the entity for wealth transfer tax purposes. Thus, if a taxpayer transfers a junior equity interest in the entity, the gift is subject to tax as if the transferor did not retain the applicable retained interest.

To illustrate, if *P* owned all the noncumulative preferred and common stock in Family Corp. and transferred all the common stock to a child, *C,* the value of the gift would be computed as if the preferred stock owned by

---

3. This provision employs two separate terms for related parties, and they have different definitions. One term is a "member of the family" defined in §2701(e)(1). It tends to look down the family tree, at younger generation members. The second term is "applicable family member" defined in §2701(e)(2). It tends to look up the family tree, at older members.

P (which is an applicable retained interest) had no value.[4] In effect, *P* would be taxed on a gift of 100% of the value of Family Corp. to *C*, notwithstanding *P*'s retention of the preferred stock.

To make this example a little more interesting, consider §2701(a)(1)(B), which specifies that interests retained by an "applicable family member" of a transferor also are subject to §2701 in valuing a gift. Thus, if *C* later gives the common stock received from *P* to *C*'s child, *GC*, and if at that time *P* still holds the preferred stock, *C* also would be deemed to make a gift of 100% of the value of Family Corp. to *GC*, notwithstanding that *C* owned no other interest in the corporation and engaged in no estate freeze activities.

To address the fact that there is double taxation here (*P* and *C* both incur gift tax on the value of an interest that *P* still owns and that probably will be subject to tax a third time when *P* ultimately transfers the preferred stock — during life or at death), §2701(e)(6) directs the Secretary of the Treasury to promulgate regulations that make adjustments "to reflect the increase in the amount of any prior taxable gift made by the transferor" pursuant to these rules. For example, if *P* subsequently were to give the retained preferred stock to either *C* or *GC* in this example, one possible implementation of this mandate would be to presume the preferred stock to be worthless for future wealth transfer tax purposes — the full value of what *P* owned originally already having been taxed, twice!

A second possible application of §2701(e)(6) would treat *P*'s subsequent gift of the preferred stock as a taxable gift and, to avoid double taxation (because the value of the preferred stock was subject to tax when *P* earlier transferred the common stock), to reduce *P*'s prior taxable gifts to reflect the true fair market value of the common stock that *P* had gifted. With a proper purge of the deemed gift of *P*'s preferred stock and a credit for any gift tax paid by *P* on that deemed gift, subsequent taxation of *P*'s actual gift of the preferred stock would not be unfair. But that solution provides no relief for the fact that, when *C* gave the common stock to *GC*, *C* paid tax on the value of *P*'s preferred stock as well. Moreover, if *C* should later acquire the preferred stock (for example, by legacy from *P*) and then make a gift of it, no relief would be provided for the tax *C* incurred on making the earlier gift of the common stock. The proper end result would be

---

4.   This statement is oversimplified because, as defined, any value attributable to voting power of the preferred stock would not be ignored even if all other rights of the stock fell within the §2701(b)(1) definition of an applicable retained interest. See Treas. Reg. §25.2701-1(e) *Example (2)*, in which preferred stock is deemed to have a zero value. Although no indication is given whether the stock in that example was voting preferred stock, the regulation states that only the preferred dividend right is valued at zero and all "other rights in the preferred stock are valued as if [the] dividend right does not exist but otherwise without regard to §2701." Because the stock in this illustration is noncumulative it would not be a qualified payment as defined in §2701(c)(3) unless an election were made under §2701(c)(3)(C) to treat it as a qualified payment.

to subject no more than 100% of the value of the entity to transfer tax. This is not what the mandated regulation, Treas. Reg. §25.2701-5, achieves (it comes close with respect to P, but not with respect to C),[5] as we will see beginning at page 950.

For now it is enough that you perceive the general pattern: By imposing a gift tax as if P retained no interest, the government is assured that no part of the value of the corporation will escape tax. Overvaluation of the retained preferred stock interest and undervaluation of the transferred common stock interest is no longer available. Subsequent adjustments to avoid unfairness do not work perfectly, but the government's attitude is that this is the price a taxpayer must pay for engaging in such a transaction. Knowledgeable taxpayers therefore almost never engage in these transactions unless an exception to the general rule is applicable. In that respect, although Congress may not have meant to preclude entirely legitimate use of this type of corporate or partnership capital formation, §2701 effectively has put the two-tier capital structure out of business for tax minimization purposes (unless the junior and senior interests are transferred at the same time, or family members are not involved).

In the example above, if P had owned only 60% of the preferred and common stock in Family Corp and transferred to C all of the common stock that P owned, §2701 would treat P as making a gift of the full value of what P owned — a 60% controlling interest in the corporation — and a control stock premium would be applied in valuing that 60% interest. If, however, P transferred only one-sixth of P's common stock (10% of the total common stock in the corporation) to C, how would P's preferred stock be valued in determining the amount of P's gift; and is a minority discount available for the gift of this sliver of the common stock? See Treas. Reg. §25.2701-3(b)(4)(ii), which calls for a reduction of the value of the transferred interest "if the value of the transferred interest (determined without regard to §2701) would be determined after application of a minority or similar discount with respect to the transferred interest." The reduction of the value of the gift is designed to reflect a minority discount.

---

5. In this case, the prior taxable gift that is inconsistent with 100% taxation was made by P, not by C. Treas. Reg. §25.2701-5 does not reflect that both P and C have been assessed a gift tax on an amount that includes the value of P's retained preferred stock. The explanation offered for this deficiency when these regulations originally were proposed was "[b]ecause the transferor [C] will often acquire an applicable retained interest initially held by an applicable family member and because of the administrative complexity inherent in allowing assignability. . . ." The final regulations left that treatment intact. The original statement was not persuasive; P should pay tax on the value of the preferred stock when P transfers it, and C and P should *each* receive an adjustment, not share one between them. The only issue of complexity is when and by how much C's prior taxable gifts should be adjusted to reflect this ultimate taxation to P. Nevertheless, the preamble to the final regulation stated that, after careful consideration "the IRS and the Treasury have determined that . . . the administrative complexity involved in tracking the adjustment would far outweigh the additional benefit that would be gained therefrom."

Application to the Generation-Skipping Transfer Tax. The general explanation that accompanied the proposed Chapter 14 regulations specifically stated that "§§2701 and 2702 determine gift tax consequences at the time a transfer is made [but] they do not change the value of the transferred property for other tax purposes. Thus, in general, [they] do not apply for purposes of the generation-skipping transfer tax." The preamble to the final Chapter 14 regulations confirmed this position. Thus, in the examples above, a §2701 zero valuation of P's preferred stock presumably would not apply for generation-skipping transfer tax purposes if P made a direct skip transfer of the common stock to GC, or placed it in a trust for the benefit of C for life, remainder to GC. Although §2642(b) relies on gift or estate tax values for purposes of allocating the GST exemption, the "taxable amount" and "valuation" rules in §§2622 through 2624 establish no such linkage[6] and §2701 does not dictate universal application for all wealth transfer tax purposes. Thus, the government was not obliged to regard the deemed valuation rule of §2701 as applicable for generation-skipping transfer tax purposes.

If P gives common stock to GC and retains preferred stock, it appears that P will incur gift tax on 100% of the value of the entity due to §2701 but will incur generation-skipping transfer tax only on the actual fair market value of the common stock transferred to GC. A subsequent transfer of the preferred stock should trigger the §2701(e)(6) adjustment rules to avoid gift or estate tax on that same value again. On the other hand, if the subsequent transfer is subject to generation-skipping transfer tax, that tax will be applied without regard to §2701 or to the prior gift tax incurred. If this is correct, estate freezing through the junior and senior equity interest approach remains available for generation-skipping transfer tax purposes even though it is not for gift or estate taxation.

If §2701 does not apply for generation-skipping transfer tax purposes, will a special adjustment be needed for generation-skipping transfer tax purposes? If not, why does §2701(e)(6) refer to Chapter 13? Nothing in the regulations addresses this quandary, and questions about the ultimate operation of a §2701(e)(6) adjustment and the interplay with the generation-skipping transfer tax cannot be answered on the basis of information now available.

Technical Requirements. Section 2701(a) applies only if there is a transfer of a *nonmarketable junior equity* interest in a corporation or partnership to or for the benefit of a *family* member. It does *not* apply if the

---

6. Under §2623 the taxable amount in a direct skip is the "value of the property received by the transferee," but this is designed to produce the tax exclusive character of the direct skip tax and not to establish a valuation rule for generation-skipping transfer tax purposes, so it does not speak to whether §2701 is applicable.

transferor holds and transfers any part of *only one class* of interest (ignoring nonlapsing differences in voting power or partnership management rights and limits on liability), if the transferor retains only *marketable* interests, or if the transferor retains only distribution rights that constitute *"qualified payments."* These requirements and exceptions are the heart of the statute's application.

A nonmarketable interest is one for which quotations are not readily available on an established securities market. §2701(a)(2). The terms "corporation" and "partnership" are defined in §§7701(a)(2) and (a)(3). The term "transfer" includes recapitalizations, redemptions, capital contributions, and similar transactions if the taxpayer or an "applicable family member" receives or otherwise holds thereafter an applicable retained interest. There is no transfer if the pre- and post-transaction interests of the taxpayer, the applicable family members, and the members of the transferor's family are substantially identical. §2701(e)(5). Transfers by a partnership, corporation, trust, or a similar entity (and the holdings of such entities) are attributed to the partners, shareholders, beneficiaries, settlors, or other appropriate individuals who are deemed to hold the entity's interests. §2701(e)(3)(A). The manner in which the attribution rules apply is described in Treas. Reg. §25.2701-6(a). Those rules can cause attribution to more than one person. Ordering rules are imposed by Treas. Reg. §25.2701-6(a)(5), and interests attributed to an individual in more than one capacity are treated as held only once — in the capacity that results in the largest amount being attributed. Treas. Reg. §25.2701-6(a)(1).

"Family" is used in several contexts in Chapter 14 and is defined differently in several places. For purposes of §2701(a)(1), which deals with transferees, §2701(e)(1) defines a family "member" as: the transferor's spouse, lineal descendants of the transferor or of the transferor's spouse, and spouses of those lineal descendants. For purposes of determining who retains an interest that will trigger §2701, §2701(e)(2) defines an *"applicable* family member" as: the taxpayer's spouse, ancestors of the taxpayer or of the taxpayer's spouse, and spouses of those ancestors. So, transfers look down the family tree and retention looks up it.

Treas. Reg. §25.2701-1(b)(1) specifies that "§2701 applies to a transfer that would not otherwise be a gift under chapter 12." For example, it could apply to a transfer for full and adequate consideration. The regulations list a number of transactions that are treated as "transfers" for this purpose. Treas. Reg. §25.2701-1(b)(2). The specifically listed items include certain redemptions and recapitalizations, and contributions to the capital of an entity. Treas. Reg. §25.2701-1(b)(2)(i)(A). Specifically excluded are several items not targeted by the statute, including execution of a qualified §2518 disclaimer and the release, exercise, or lapse of a nongeneral power of appointment. Treas. Reg. §25.2701-1(b)(3).

Assuming that it is correct, PLR 9321046 reveals how convoluted these rules may become. The Ruling dealt with the multiple attribution rules in Treas. Reg. §25.2701-6(a)(5) that are applicable to stock held in a trust. The situation involved a family held corporation, whose stock was owned 47% by the taxpayer, 50% by a nonmarital trust created by the taxpayer's predeceased spouse, and 3% by their descendants. The Letter Ruling addressed the consequences of a recapitalization of the corporation so that its existing common stock would be replaced with both common and preferred stock. Under Treas. Reg. §25.2701-1(b)(3)(i), a recapitalization is not a transfer for §2701 purposes if all stockholders in the transferor's family hold substantially the same interest after the transaction as before. In the case in question, each stockholder would end up with the same percentages of both common and preferred stock as they previously held of common stock alone. As a result, at first blush it appeared that the recapitalization would not trigger §2701. Then the question arose about how to regard the stock held in the trust, which the attribution rules require to be treated as held by its beneficiaries. That alone would not be a problem, because the relative interests of the beneficiaries would not change.

Upon closer inspection, however, the Ruling stated that different attribution applies with respect to the trust's preferred stock (an applicable retained interest) than with respect to its common stock (a subordinate equity interest) under the disparate rules of Treas. Reg. §§25.2701-6(a)(5)(i) and -6(a)(5)(ii). Because of this disparity, the Ruling concluded that the taxpayer and the descendants would not be deemed to hold substantially the same interest before and after the recapitalization. Therefore, the recapitalization alone would trigger §2701, even though nothing occurred other than issuance of new stock certificates to represent the same percentage ownership of the corporation.

Because of this deemed transfer, the Ruling held that the §2701 valuation rules must be employed to determine the value of what the taxpayer and the descendants were deemed to own before and after the recapitalization, taking into account deemed ownership under the attribution rules. This could cause a substantial gift tax liability. Could this possibly be Congress' intent? For example, would §2701 apply to a postmortem recapitalization by an estate in anticipation of using preferred and common stock to fund, respectively, a marital and a bypass trust to accomplish a freeze during the surviving spouse's overlife? If so, would the same liability apply if the estate made the same allocations of preferred and common stock that was held by the decedent at death?

Applicable Retained Interests. As previously noted, §2701 excludes the value of certain "applicable retained interests" in determining the value of transferred interests. Most liquidation, put, call, and conversion rights are applicable retained interests under §2701(b)(1)(B) to the extent not excepted under §§2701(c)(2)(B) or (c)(2)(C).[7] But §2701(b)(1)(A) specifies that distribution rights[8] are applicable retained interests only if, immediately before the transfer, the transferor and applicable family members hold control[9] of the entity.[10] The control requirement applies only with respect to distribution rights; no such requirement is imposed with respect to liquidation, put, call, and conversion rights.

The terms "distribution rights" and "qualified payment rights" are defined in Treas. Reg. §§25.2701-2(b)(3) and -2(b)(6). Treas. Reg. §25.2701-2(b)(2) defines an "extraordinary payment right" to include any retained "put, call, or conversion right, any right to compel liquidation, or any similar right, the exercise or nonexercise of which affects the value of the transferred interest."

Certain rights described in the regulations are neither distribution rights nor extraordinary payment rights. See Treas. Reg. §25.2701-2(b)(4). A "mandatory payment right" is a right to receive payments that are fixed as to time and amount (for example, a preferred stock redemption right), including a right to receive a specific amount on death. Id. "Liquidation participation rights" (just what the name implies) are valued specially if the transferor, members of the transferor's family, or applicable family members have the ability to compel liquidation; generally, the power to compel liquidation is ignored in valuing the liquidation participation right. Id. A "nonlapsing conversion right" entitles the owner to convert an equity interest into a fixed number or percentage of shares of the same class as the transferred interest. Id. All of these are declared to be neither extraordinary payment rights nor distribution rights.

---

7. Excepted are rights that must be exercised at a specified time and amount (§2701(c)(2)(B)) and rights to convert into a fixed number or percentage of the same class of interest transferred, if the right is nonlapsing and is adjusted to reflect stock splits, accumulated unpaid dividends, and similar changes to the capital structure that should not affect the shareholders' relative ownership interests.

8. "Distribution rights" refer to *certain* rights to a distribution from a corporation with respect to its stock or from a partnership with respect to a partnership interest. §2701(c). It does not refer to rights to distributions from a junior equity interest. Id.

9. Defined to mean (1) 50% (by vote or value) of a corporation's stock, (2) 50% of the capital or profit interests in any partnership or, (3) if the partnership is a limited partnership, any general partnership interest. §2701(b)(2); Treas. Reg. §25.2701-2(b)(5)(ii)(A). For this purpose, Treas. Reg. §25.2701-2(b)(5)(ii)(B) provides that "[e]quity interests that carry no right to vote other than on liquidation, merger, or a similar event are not considered to have voting rights," and contingent rights are ignored unless the holder has control over the contingency. An attribution rule imputes ownership from entities such as corporations, partnerships, and trusts to shareholders, partners, beneficiaries, and settlors. §2701(e)(3)(A). For the purpose of determining control, in addition to combining the holdings of an individual's "applicable family members," an individual is attributed the interests held by lineal descendants of any parent of the individual or the individual's spouse. §2701(b)(2)(C); Treas. Reg. §25.2701-2(b)(5)(i).

10. Id. §2701(b)(1)(A), with attribution under §2701(e)(3).

Two very important exceptions are relevant here. A "distribution right" is defined as a right to receive corporate or partnership distributions with respect to stock or partnership interests that are not "junior equity." This exception conforms with the policy of Chapter 14 because the special valuation rule is not necessary if junior equity is retained rather than transferred.[11] In addition, §2701 does not apply if the applicable retained interest is of the same class as the transferred interest, or is proportionally the same as the transferred interest when differences in nonlapsing[12] voting rights (or in a partnership, in management rights and limited liability) are ignored. §§2701(a)(2)(B) and (a)(2)(C). Thus, §2701 does not apply to distribution rights (1) in a corporation with only one class of stock, (2) to a one tier partnership, or (3) to a multiclass corporation or multitiered partnership if the transferor and applicable family members held only one class of stock or tier of partnership interest.[13] Because most family business entities these days are S Corporations (which can have only one class of stock), limited liability companies, or family limited partnerships, these exceptions eliminate most family businesses from the sphere of §2701.

Because §2701(a)(2)(B) excepts retained interests that are of the same class as the transferred interest, and §2701(a)(2)(C) excepts retained interests that are "proportionally the same as the transferred interest," either

---

11.   See §2701(c)(1). "Junior equity" is defined in §2701(a)(4)(B)(i) as any common stock and the most junior partnership interest. Treas. Reg. §25.2701-2(b)(3)(i) provides that "any right to receive distributions with respect to an interest that is of the same class as, or a class that is subordinate to, the transferred interest" is not a distribution right. That appears to be the regulatory embodiment of the §2701(c)(1)(B)(i) rule that "a right to distributions with respect to any junior equity interest" is not a distribution right.

    Liquidation, put, call, and conversion rights are not distribution rights. Treas. Reg. §25.2701-2(b)(3)(ii). They are separately defined as applicable retained interests and are specially valued in their own right under §2701(b)(1)(B).

12.   According to the Conference Committee Report at 151:

Except as provided in Treasury regulations, a right that lapses by reason of Federal or State law generally would be treated as nonlapsing under this exception. The conferees intend, however, that Treasury regulations may give zero value to rights which lapse by reason of Federal or State law that effectively transfer wealth that would not pass in the absence of a specific agreement. Such regulations could, for example, give zero value to a management right that lapses by reason of the death of a partner under the Uniform Partnership Act as adopted in a State if the decedent had waived in the partnership agreement the right to be redeemed at fair market value under that Act.

And see §2704.

13.   See, e.g., PLRs 9414013, 9414012, and 9229028. The exception for proportional partnership interests is denied if the transferor, or an applicable family member, can alter the transferee's liability as a partner. Id. §2701(a)(2) (flush language). PLR 9415007 held that the Treas. Reg. §25.2701-1(c)(3) same class requirement was deemed met in a limited partnership setting in which the transferor was a general partner who transferred limited partnership interests, because rights in the retained and the transferred interests were the same except for nonlapsing differences in management and liability limitations, which do not affect the application of the same class of interest exception.

provision might apply with respect to a multiclass entity in which the transferor owns interests in several classes and transfers the same proportionate share of each holding. For example, §2701 should not apply if the transferor owned 80% of the preferred stock of X Corp. and 50% of the common stock of X Corp. and transferred to a family member one-fifth of each holding (16% of the total preferred stock and 10% of the total common stock in X Corp.). In this respect, the regulations refer to transfers of a "vertical slice" of interests in an entity that effect "a proportionate reduction in each class of interest held by the transferor *and all applicable family members in the aggregate.*" This carries this concept to another level of sophistication. For example, Treas. Reg. §25.2701-1(c)(4) provides:

[S]ection 2701 does not apply if *P* owns 50% of each class of equity interest in a corporation and transfers a portion of each class to *P*'s child in a manner that reduces each interest held by *P* and any applicable family members, *in the aggregate*, by 10% *even if the transfer does not proportionately reduce P's interest in each class*.

(Emphasis added.) Apparently this means that, of *P*'s 50% ownership of each class, something other than 10% of some classes could be transferred and the proportionate transfer exception could apply.

For example, *P* owned 50% of Class A common, 50% of Class B common, and 50% of the preferred stock, and applicable family members owned another 10% of Class A common, 20% of Class B common, and 40% of the preferred stock. The proportionate transfer exception will apply if *P* transfers an amount of Class A common that reduces this aggregate 60% ownership interest by 10%, and transfers an amount of Class B common that reduces that aggregate 70% ownership interest by 10%, and transfers an amount of preferred stock that reduces that aggregate 90% ownership by 10%, even though *P*'s transfers are not proportionately the same slice of the stock interests owned solely by *P*.

On the other hand, the converse may be true as well. So, the exception likely will not apply if *P* transferred stock that reduced each of *P*'s holdings by 10%, but did not reduce the aggregate ownership proportionately.[14]

Qualified Payments Exception.   If all the threshold requirements for §2701 are met, there is yet another way to avoid its application to a gift of a junior equity interest. Under §2701(a)(3)(A), the zero valuation of retained interests does not apply to a retained distribution right that "consists of a right to receive a qualified payment," meaning a periodic *cumulative* preferred dividend (or similar partnership distribution) payable

---

14.   Pssst: just as an aside, do you think that your elected representatives who voted for this mess understood any part of it?

at a *fixed* rate or tied to a *specific* market interest rate. §2701(c)(3). As illustrated in Treas. Reg. §25.2701-2(d) *Example 5*, valuation of the retained interest reflects the rate of return specified in the qualified payment and gives "due regard to the corporation's net worth, prospective earning power, and dividend-paying capacity." As to these interests, the Code reflects a degree of assurance that the payments will be made and therefore that the assumptions underlying the usual valuation approach are reasonable. Even if not paid, the right to the payment cannot escape transfer taxation because the right to payment will persist. See §2701(d). Therefore, the Code permits a portion of the value of the entity to be assigned to a qualified payment with respect to applicable retained interests.[15]

Unpaid Distributions

Fundamental to ascertaining the proper gift tax value of a qualified payment is that the specified payments must be made. If they are not, §2701(d) dictates that the value of the applicable retained interest is deemed to include the value of unpaid qualified payments on future taxable events.[16] Subject to one limitation, the amount added to the value of the retained interest is determined by assuming that the qualified payment was distributed when due and then invested at an annually compounding yield equal to the discount rate originally used to value the applicable retained interest. §2701(d)(2). The increase in value dictated by §2701(d) is sometimes referred to as a "suspense account" increase. Consistent with the estate freeze origins of this legislation, however, the suspense account increase in value under this unpaid dividend rule cannot exceed the transferor's share of the increase in value of all equity interests that are junior to the applicable retained interest, accruing since the subject transfer. §2701(d)(2)(B). This is because it is only to the extent of appreciation in the value of junior interests that any freeze has occurred, so no more than that amount should be subject to wealth transfer tax recapture under this unpaid dividend rule. In addition, the Code provides a four-year grace

---

15. However, a qualified payment that can be reduced or eliminated because it is subject to a liquidation, put, call, or conversion right will be valued as if each such right were exercised in the manner that produces the lowest value for the entire bundle of rights held by the transferor. §2701(a)(3). See also Treas. Reg. §25.2701-2(a)(3). The operation of this provision is illustrated by an example in Treas. Reg. §25.2701-2(a)(5). In that example, the transferor had an immediate right to put retained preferred stock to the corporation for $900,000, and the transferor also had a qualified payment right valued at $1 million. Utilizing the principle described above, the regulation valued the preferred stock at the lesser figure, reflecting a valuation assumption that the put right will be exercised immediately.

16. It is not clear whether this deemed increase in value will apply for generation-skipping transfer tax purposes other than for the exemption allocation under §2642(b).

period within which to make cumulative preferred dividend payments before invoking the unpaid dividend rule. §2701(d)(2)(C).

Taxable events that will trigger this suspense account value addition include death of the transferor, disposition of the applicable retained interest,[17] or an election by the taxpayer. Who should pay the tax on the occurrence of any of these taxable events? There is no federal reimbursement provision dealing with this question, so presumably applicable state law will control. Should the recipient of the retained qualified payment interest pay the tax? Or should the entity that is holding the unpaid dividends generating this suspense account value pay the tax?

Although there are no basis provisions anywhere in Chapter 14, a §1015(d) basis adjustment should be permitted for the gift tax attributable to the suspense account value. Would it increase the basis of the holder of the transferred interest, because it is that person who is deemed to have received added value attributable to the overdue dividends? Furthermore, will §1014 apply with respect to that value if a deemed transfer occurs at the transferor's death? In this respect, should §1014(c) apply when the taxable event is the death of the transferor, because the right to the overdue dividends constitutes income in respect of a decedent for income tax purposes? None of these questions can yet be answered.

Qualified Payment Elections

Section 2701(c)(3)(C) provides two irrevocable elections, one to waive qualified payment treatment (which might be made to preclude application of the suspense account compounding rule), and the other to treat any distribution right as a qualified payment to the extent not inconsistent with the underlying legal instrument generating that right. Of the two options, election out of the qualified payment rule is the more desirable, for a number of reasons. One is to avoid the complexity of the suspense account rules in §2701(d). A related reason is that the compounding rule of §2701(d)(2)(A) is likely to subject far more value to tax than if qualified payment treatment did not apply and the gift tax were incurred on the original transfer. Not only is the gift tax computed tax exclusive, but it would be without any suspense account value. Also, the value of the applicable retained interest at the time of the initial gift is likely to be smaller than when the applicable retained interest is transferred.

Electing into qualified payment treatment has the advantage of deferring gift tax on the value of that distribution right until its subsequent transfer.

---

17. Treas. Reg. §25.2701-4(b)(2) addresses a transfer that is made during the transferor's life to a trust that would be includible at death in the transferor's gross estate for federal estate tax purposes. The added value rule is deferred until either (1) the date on which the property no longer is subject to inclusion in the transferor's gross estate, or (2) the transferor's death.

Minimum Capitalization Requirement

One final qualified payment requirement for transfer valuation purposes is that the aggregate junior equity interests in the entity (common stock or comparable partnership interests) must represent at least 10% of the total value of the entity, and a transferred junior equity interest must be worth at least a pro rata share of that total value. §2701(a)(4). In other words, the valuation of a retained interest, including its qualified payment entitlement, cannot exceed 90% of the value of the entity.

Computation of Value. The §2701 "subtraction" method of determining value is described in Treas. Reg. §25.2701-3(b) as a four-step computation. The following is a simplified description.

First, the regulation requires a determination of "the fair market value of all family-held equity interests in the entity immediately after the transfer . . . determined by assuming that the interests are held by one individual, using a consistent set of assumptions." "Family-held" means held (directly or indirectly) by an individual who is an applicable family member or a lineal descendant of the parents of the transferor or of the transferor's spouse. Treas. Reg. §§25.2701-2(b)(5)(i), -3(a)(2)(i).

Under Treas. Reg. §25.2701-3(b)(2), which describes the second computation step, the full value of the family-held equity interests in the entity is reduced by the sum of: (1) the fair market value of all family-held senior equity interests that are not applicable retained interests, and (2) the fair market value of equity interests (a) that are held by siblings of the transferor and the transferor's spouse and by those siblings' descendants, and (b) that are of the same class or a subordinate class to the interest transferred. In addition, if an interest retained by the transferor or an applicable family member is a qualified payment, its value is subtracted in this step. Finally, the resulting figure is reduced by the special §2701 valuation of applicable retained interests, which typically will be valued at zero. If "the percentage of any class of applicable retained interest held by the transferor and by applicable family members . . . exceeds . . . the highest ownership percentage (determined on the basis of relative fair market values) of family-held interests" in all subordinate equity interests (or in any class of subordinate equity interest), a "family interest percentage" adjustment is made. Treas. Reg. §25.2701-3(b)(5). For example, if a transferor owned 100% of the preferred stock in a corporation and only 40% of the common stock, with the remaining 60% of the common stock owned by nonfamily members, the failure to pay dividends on nonqualified payment preferred stock would inure only 40% to the benefit of any family member donees of the common stock owned by the transferor. Thus, the family-interest-percentage adjustment permits valuation of the remaining 60% of the preferred stock as if it were held by a nonfamily member. Under Treas. Reg.

§25.2701-3(b)(2)(i)(A), its actual fair market value (rather than its §2701 deemed zero value) would be reflected in the second step reductions.[18]

Under the third computation step, described in Treas. Reg. §25.2701-3(b)(3), the remaining value is allocated (generally pro rata) among the transferred interests and the subordinate equity interests held by the transferor, applicable family members, and members of the transferor's family. A "subordinate equity interest" is an equity interest in the entity to which an applicable retained interest is a senior interest. Treas. Reg. §25.2701-3(a)(2)(iii).

Finally, in the last step under Treas. Reg. §25.2701-3(b)(4), the amount allocated to the transferred interest in the third step is reduced by minority or "similar" discounts, by any §2702 retained-term-interest valuation adjustment that might be relevant if the gift triggers that provision, and by any consideration received by the transferor. This final figure constitutes the gift tax value under §2701 of the transferred interest.

Subsequent Transfers of §2701 Interests. The cumulative effect of §2701 in a typical preferred stock recapitalization and donation of common stock (and its counterpart partnership transaction) is to assign a value to any preferred interest retained by senior family members only if it complies with the qualified payment requirements or if another exception to §2701 applies.[19] Otherwise, the value of any applicable retained interest is deemed to be zero in determining the value of common stock (or comparable partnership interests) transferred to family members. In many cases, these transferred interests will be deemed for gift tax purposes to carry 100% of the value of the entity. Thus, the transferor effectively is taxed on the interests that the transferor (and applicable family members) retained as well as on the transferred interests. This easy-to-complete valuation and taxation rule accelerates the wealth transfer tax liability attributable to the transferor's interest and guarantees that no portion of the entity's value slips into a crack between gift and estate taxation. Under this regime, divisions into several classes of interests are respected, but taxpayers are put to a choice whether to incur tax at the time of the transfer or to guarantee through the qualified payment regime that the applicable retained interest will have an ascertainable value that is subject to tax at a later taxable event.

---

18.   Technically, the Treas. Reg. §25.2701-3(b)(5) adjustment specifies that the interest held in excess of the family interest percentage is "treated as a family-held interest that is not held by the transferor or an applicable family member," which qualifies as a reduction in step two as the "fair market value of all family-held senior equity interests (other than applicable retained interests held by the transferor or applicable family members)."

19.   The zero value rule, however, applies only to those rights that are listed in §§2701(b)(1)(A) and (b)(1)(B) — e.g. distribution rights in a controlled entity and liquidation, put, call, or conversion rights. In the case of a controlled entity, that typically will encompass all of the rights except for qualified payment rights. But, if any other rights do exist, they will be valued at fair market value. Treas. Reg. §25.2701-1(a)(2)(iii).

When the special valuation rules of §2701 are applied, the transferor is taxed on all or much of the value of the interests that the transferor (and applicable family members) retained. For convenience those retained interests that were specially valued are referred to as "section 2701 interests." Treas. Reg. §25.2701-5(a)(4). Unless prevented by Congress, the section 2701 interests will be subjected to another wealth transfer tax when transferred. It would be unfair to tax those interests a second time, at least to the extent that the same amount was previously taxed. The Code and regulations provide a number of adjustments that are intended to prevent the same amount from being taxed twice. These adjustments can apply when a subsequent gift is made of a section 2701 interest or when the initial transferor dies. Through the use of illustrations accompanied by commentary, let's examine how those adjustment provisions operate.

In each of the following illustrations, unless stated otherwise, the transferor made a gift of common stock that was subject to §2701 valuation, and the transferor retained an applicable retained interest (preferred stock) that was not a qualified payment (and was not elected to be treated as such). Prior to making the gift, the transferor owned all of the corporation's outstanding stock. For gift tax purposes, the transfer of the common stock constituted a gift of 100% of the value of the corporation's outstanding stock (common and preferred) because the applicable retained interest (preferred stock) was treated by the statute as having a zero value. The problem that the illustrations and discussion below address is the wealth transfer tax treatment of subsequent transfers of the preferred stock (the section 2701 interest) and of the initial transferor's death.

(a) *G* made a gift to *S*, a child of *G*, of common stock (a junior equity interest).[20] *S* is a member of *G*'s family, but *S* is not an applicable family member. §§2701(e)(1), (e)(2). After applying §2701, the value of the gift to *S* for gift tax purposes equals the value of all of the corporation's outstanding stock. In applying the subtraction method of valuation, the preferred stock that *G* retained is valued at zero. The actual market value of the preferred stock at that time was $1 million. In effect, *G* was taxed on the value of both the preferred and common stock, although only the common stock was transferred.

Several years later, *G* made a gift of the preferred stock to *N*, who is not an applicable family member. The actual value of the preferred stock at that later date was $900,000. For gift tax purposes, the amount of *G*'s gifts for that year that are subject to tax is reduced by $900,000 — the lesser of (1) the amount by which the actual market value of the initial transfer (of common stock) was increased because of §2701 (i.e., $1 million in this case), or (2) the amount (referred to as the "duplicated amount") of the gift of the section 2701 interest (the preferred stock) that duplicates the value of

---

20. A "junior equity interest" is defined in §2701(a)(4)(B) to include common stock.

such interest that was included in the value of the common stock when the common was previously gifted — i.e., in this case, $900,000. Treas. Reg. §§25.2701-5(a)(2), -5(b). The lesser of those two calculations is referred to as the "amount of the reduction." Id. The "duplicated amount" — which is the second of the two items, the lesser of which constitutes "the amount of the reduction" — is the difference between the transfer tax value of the section 2701 interest at the time of the subsequent transfer ($900,000 in this case) and the value given to that interest by §2701 when the initial transfer of the common stock occurred (i.e., zero). Treas. Reg. §25.2701-5(c). In other words, the gift tax valuation of the initial gift of the common stock included the $1 million value of the preferred stock at that time. When the preferred is subsequently gifted, only the value that exceeds $1 million should be subjected to another gift tax. In this example, the value of the gifted preferred stock was only $900,000, so that is the limit on the amount that can be excluded from the gift tax. If a reduction were allowed for the entire $1 million that was added to the value of the common stock at the time of the initial transfer, the excess $100,000 would offset other gifts made by G that had nothing to do with the initial transaction.

One possibility is that no annual exclusion will be allowed for the amount of the gift of the preferred stock that is reduced. Alternatively, and more likely, the annual exclusion will be allowed, and the "duplicated amount" (and therefore the "amount of the reduction") will be reduced by that amount ($889,000 if the annual exclusion is still $11,000).

If the amount of the reduction to be applied to a transferor's gift tax return exceeds the amount of the transferor's taxable gifts for that year, the unused reduction is carried over and applied to subsequent years until exhausted. Treas. Reg. §25.2701-5(a)(2). Any unused carryover reduction remaining at the death of the transferor will reduce the amount to which the estate tax applies. Treas. Reg. §§25.2701-5(a)(2), -5(a)(3). An example of a circumstance in which the reduction can exceed the transferor's gifts for that year is set forth in **(d)**.

(b) The same facts as those stated in **(a)** except that the fair market value of the preferred stock when it was gifted was $1,150,000. In that case, the amount of the reduction from the gift tax base will be $1 million. The amount of the gift that is attributable to the $150,000 of appreciation in the value of the preferred stock is subject to gift taxation. An annual exclusion may be allowable for that gift.

(c) The same facts as those stated in **(a)** except that, instead of donating the preferred stock to N, G sold the preferred stock for $800,000 to a person who was not an applicable family member. In that case, upon G's death, the amount on which G is subject to estate taxation is reduced by the $800,000 consideration that G received from the sale of the section 2701 interest. Treas. Reg. §25.2701-5(c)(3). That reduction is appropriate because the consideration received for the section 2701 interest is reflected in G's gross estate in some way, and G was effectively taxed on that interest when the common stock was transferred.

(d) The same facts as those stated in **(a)** except that, when G made the gift of the common stock, G did not own any preferred stock. Instead, the $1 million of outstanding preferred stock was held by M, the step-mother of G's spouse (i.e., G's step-mother-in-law). M is an applicable family member of G. §2701(e)(2)(B).

The tax consequences of the initial transfer by G of the common stock are the same as those described in **(a)**. That is, the $1 million value of the preferred stock will be added to the value of the donated common stock. Four years later, M made a gift of the preferred stock to her nephew, when it had a value of $950,000. M will be treated as having made a taxable gift of $939,000, after taking an $11,000 annual exclusion. But G previously incurred gift tax consequences because the value of the preferred stock was added to the value of the common stock that G gave to S. It would be harsh to tax the preferred stock a second time, and an adjustment should therefore be made under §2701(e)(6). The regulations provide that the adjustment is effected by reducing the amount of gifts made by G in the year of M's gift to her nephew. The amount of the reduction is $939,000 (the duplicated amount, because that is the lesser figure). If G made no gifts in that year (or if the amount of G's taxable gifts are less than $939,000), the unused reduction is carried over to G's subsequent taxable years. Any unused reduction remaining on G's death will reduce the amount subject to G's estate tax. Because G was the person who incurred gift tax consequence because of M holding the preferred stock, it is proper that the reduction be given to G to negate the gift tax treatment previously incurred.

Subsequent Death of Transferor

Upon the transferor's death, an adjustment will be made for section 2701 interests that either are included in the transferor's gross estate or are held by an applicable family member. Treas. Reg. §25.2701-5(c)(3)(ii). The transferor's executor will reduce the amount subject to the estate tax by the "amount of the reduction" (defined above), including any unused reduction carry over. However, the reduction is limited to the amount needed to reduce the transferor's estate tax to zero. Treas. Reg. §§25.2701-5(a)(3), -5(c)(3)(ii). If the section 2701 interest is held by an applicable family member, the value of that interest is deemed to be the value it would have for gift tax purposes if the section 2701 interest had been gifted immediately prior to the transferor's death. Id.

An adjustment will be made on the transferor's death if, during the transferor's life, the applicable family member who holds the section 2701 interest sells that interest for money or money's worth to someone other than the transferor or an applicable family member. The amount that is subject to estate taxation to the transferor will be reduced by the amount of consideration in money or money's worth received for the sale of the section 2701 interest. Treas. Reg. §25.2701-5(c)(3)(i).

Gift to Transferor's Spouse of §2701 Interest with Qualified Payment Arrearages

Under §2701(d) the suspense account value of qualified payment arrearages will cause gift tax consequences if a transferor who retained a section 2701 interest, for which there are qualified payment arrearages, makes a gift of that interest. §2701(d)(3)(A)(ii). But there will not be a gift tax consequence if the gift is made to the transferor's spouse in a manner that qualifies for the marital deduction. §2701(d)(3)(B). In that case, the spouse steps into the shoes of the transferor and is thereafter treated as if the initial transfer had been made by the spouse. §2701(d)(3)(B)(iii). A similar rule applies if, at death, the initial transferor bequeaths a §2701 interest with qualified payment arrearages to the transferor's spouse and the bequest qualifies for the marital deduction. Id.

Sale of Junior Equity

If, after a preferred stock recapitalization, the common stock is sold to a family member rather than given away, the only difference in result would be part-sale, part-gift treatment with respect to the consideration paid. The applicable retained interest still would be deemed to have zero value if no exception to §2701 were applicable, and the transferred interest still would be deemed to carry 100% of the value of the transferor's interest in the entity. Because the transfer tax value of the common stock will greatly exceed its actual value, it is virtually certain that the consideration paid for the common stock will not be sufficient to prevent gift tax liability to the transferor for the transaction. See Treas. Reg. §25.2701-3(b)(4)(iv).

Split Gift Freeze Transaction

How does Chapter 14 deal with a split gift election under §2513 for a donor's gift of a junior equity interest to which §2701 applies? For convenience, let's refer to the "donor spouse" (the one who actually made the transfer) and the "consenting spouse" (the one who consented to the split gift treatment). The treatment accorded to a split gift transaction to which §2701 applies is specified in Treas. Reg. §§25.2701-5(e) and -5(f).

If, during the joint lives of the donor and consenting spouses, the donor spouse subsequently makes a gift of the section 2701 interest, the donor spouse is treated as the transferor of half of the donated junior equity interest, the consenting spouse is treated as the transferor of the other half, and the rules of §2701 are applied as if each was the actual transferor of that half. Treas. Reg. §§25.2701-5(e)(2), -5(f) *Example 1*. This provides another example of how a carryover of the §2701(e)(6) reduction can occur. The consenting spouse's unused reduction will be carried over to future years if the consenting spouse did not make sufficient gifts that year to match the reduction.

The tax treatment is more complex if the transfer of the section 2701 interest occurs on or after the death of either spouse. In that case, except for any reduction carryover to which the consenting spouse was already entitled, the amount of any remaining allowable reduction is available only to the donor spouse. Treas. Reg. §25.2701-5(e)(3).

If the donor spouse dies first, the donor spouse will be treated as the transferor of the entire amount of the donated junior interest, including the half that was treated as having been donated by the consenting spouse. So the entire amount of the remaining §2701(e)(6) reduction (other than any carryover reduction to which the consenting spouse was then entitled) is allowed to the estate of the donor spouse. Id. and Treas. Reg. §25.2701-5(e)(3)(ii)(B). However, the reduction allowable to the donor spouse's estate for the gift deemed made by the consenting spouse cannot exceed the amount of gift tax incurred by the consenting spouse on the initial gift of the junior equity interest. Treas. Reg. §25.2701-5(f) *Example 3*.

At the death of the donor spouse with the consenting spouse surviving, the consenting spouse's prior taxable gifts for preceding periods (§2502(a)) and adjusted taxable gifts (§2001(b)(1)(B)) are reduced to eliminate the remaining effect of the §2701 interest. Treas. Reg. §25.2701-5(e)(3)(ii)(A). Any adjustments provided by §2701(e)(6) will be available only to the estate of the donor spouse. However, the consenting spouse will retain any carryover reductions to which the consenting spouse was entitled at the time of the donor's death. See Treas. Reg. §§25.2701-5(e)(3)(ii)(B), -5(e)(3)(iii). On the consenting spouse's later death, the consenting spouse's estate will not be allowed an offset for any gift tax attributable to the junior equity interest that was a deemed gift by the spouse's consent. Treas. Reg. §25.2701-5(e)(3)(ii)(A). This latter treatment is consistent with §2001(d), which provides that the donor spouse is allowed an offset for any gift tax incurred by a consenting spouse on a split gift.

If the consenting spouse dies first, except for carryover reductions to which the consenting spouse was entitled at the time of death, the consenting spouse's estate will not be permitted to reduce the amount subject to estate tax by the section 2701 interest, even if that interest is included in the consenting spouse's gross estate. Treas. Reg. §25.2701-5(e)(3)(iii). Instead, the §2701(e)(6) adjustment will be available only to the donor spouse or the donor spouse's estate. Treas. Reg. §25.2701-5(e)(3)(ii). Except for any carryover reductions to which the consenting spouse was entitled, the consenting spouse's estate will *not* be allowed to reduce the spouse's adjusted taxable gifts, and no reduction will be allowed for the gift tax previously incurred by the consenting spouse on account of the split gift. Treas. Reg. §25.2701-5(e)(3)(iii).

Negative Freeze

A negative freeze occurs when the value of the transferred interest declines rather than appreciates after the original transfer. Pursuant to Treas. Reg. §25.2701-5(b), the §2701(e)(6) double taxation adjustment is limited to the lesser of (1) the value of the deemed gift when the original transfer occurred and (2) the value of the applicable retained interest when a subsequent taxable transfer triggers the adjustment. This precludes a refund of tax paid on the basis of a higher value assigned to the transferred interest when the transaction occurred.

If the applicable retained interest declined in value, it is a virtual certainty that the transferred interest and the underlying business entity declined in value as well, meaning that the freeze did not accomplish anything useful. The government has chosen to tax the transferor on no less than the value of the section 2701 interest when the initial transfer of the junior equity interest occurred. By not excusing the tax on the amount of decline in value, the government imposes a cost on the transferor for attempting to split appreciation from current value. As to the propriety of that decision, note that §2701 permits a transferor to enjoy the benefit of the income from the entity without incurring tax on subsequent appreciation of the junior interest. Is it therefore inappropriate to deny the transferor a tax reduction for a subsequent decline in value?

Disposition of the Entity

In a "short freeze," both the donee of a junior equity interest and the holder of an applicable retained interest sell the business, or their interests in it, to a third party. Section 2701 dictates that the applicable retained interest has zero value for gift tax purposes, but that characterization does not apply for income tax purposes. The transferor would recognize a gain to the extent that the amount realized by the transferor on the sale exceeds the transferor's basis in the applicable retained interest. The fact that the transferor had previously incurred a gift tax on the value of the applicable retained interest is mitigated by allowing a §2701(e)(6) adjustment on the transferor's death. Treas. Reg. §25.2701-5(c)(3). The amount subject to estate tax is reduced by the amount of consideration received by the transferor on the sale of the applicable retained interest. Id. The failure to revalue the consideration received at the time of the transferor's death is consistent with the treatment of consideration by §2043, which we studied in Chapter 6.

Reverse Freeze

The §2701(c)(1)(B)(i) exception from the definition of applicable retained interest for retained junior equity interests should preclude application of §2701 to a transaction in which the transferor retains the growth interest and transfers the frozen interest. With sufficiently large dividend payments on the gifted preferred interest, it may be possible to prevent growth in the retained junior equity and shift value to the frozen interest holder without triggering §2701.

Preferred Debt Recapitalization

Section 2701 does not apply to the retention of a debt of the entity. Thus, debt issued in a recapitalization in lieu of preferred frozen interests will be reflected in valuing the entity for purposes of determining the value of transferred growth interests. But the receipt of debt instruments in a corporate reorganization typically will cause the recipient to recognize income. §§354(a)(2), 356(a), 356(d). Also, an excessive amount of debt may be recharacterized as an equity interest, especially if there is a high debt-capital ratio.

Sale of an interest in an entity for a note, and perhaps also for an annuity, should not be subject to the valuation rules of §2701 for the same reasons. See PLR 9436006. Nor should retained interests in the form of reasonable compensation (salary or deferred payments) or reasonable lease payments be subject to §2701, even if each entitles the payee to a percentage of the profits of the entity as part of the negotiated payments. Treas. Reg. §25.2701-3(c)(3) specifies what counts as debt for purposes of the rule providing minimum value for junior equity interests, and deferred compensation and lease payments not in arrears are specifically excluded. That regulation is unlikely to be given much weight in cases dealing with the debt versus equity issue.

Pro Rata Gift

A transaction in which the transferor makes a gift or sells a portion of the only ownership interest held will qualify under Treas. Reg. §25.2701-1(c)(3) for the §2701(a)(2)(B) exception for one class of equity. This transfer of a portion of all future appreciation is an easy and effective way to freeze a portion of the value of the entity without dealing with the complexities of §2701. The same should be true with respect to a transfer of nonvoting stock or a partnership interest that qualifies for the §2701(a)(2)(C) exception if the transferor retains nonlapsing voting interests of the same class or tier. In either case, discounts for lack of marketability and for minority interests are not affected by §2701. Similarly, as illustrated by PLR 9309018, any transaction (in that case a reverse stock split) that does not alter the ownership percentages of the existing owners of the entity will not trigger §2701 due to the exception found in Treas. Reg. §25.2701-1(b)(3)(i).

In the same vein, a gift of a proportionate share of several classes of an enterprise (if, for example, the transferor owns both common and preferred interests and gives the same percentage of the transferor's holding of each) is permissible under Treas. Reg. §25.2701-1(c)(4) because there is no freeze abuse in such a transaction. See, e.g., PLR 9226063, replaced by PLR 9248026. However, if applicable family members hold interests in the entity, the proportionate share exception will be applied by looking to the aggregate interests held by the transferor and the applicable family members.

No Retained Interest Generation-Skipping Freeze

In a transaction in which the transferor gives all frozen interests to children and all growth interests to grandchildren, §2701 should not apply because neither the transferor nor an applicable family member retains an interest in the entity. This generation-skipping freeze should continue to work under §2701. However, §2701 will apply if a grandchild subsequently transfers a growth interest to a family member while a lineal ancestor (the child) continues to hold the frozen interest. §2701(a)(1)(B).

PART B.   SECTION 2702: GARDEN VARIETY GRITs

Code Reference: *Chapter 14: §2702*

Like §2701, §2702 is another special valuation rule that is applicable to determine whether a gift has been made and its value. It involves retained and transferred interests in trusts (or trust equivalents) for the benefit of a member of the transferor's family. For purposes of §2702, the definition of the term "a member of the transferor's family" is broader than the meaning of that term in §2701 and includes: (1) an ancestor or lineal descendant of either the transferor or the transferor's spouse, (2) a sibling of the transferor, (3) a spouse of any of the above, and (4) the transferor's own spouse. §§2702(e), 2704(c)(2).

The interests that are subject to special valuation under §2702 are interests *retained* by the transferor and by "applicable family members," which term has the same meaning in §2702 as it has in §2701 — i.e., it refers to the transferor's spouse, ancestors of either the transferor or the transferor's spouse, and spouses of such ancestors. §§2702(a)(1) and 2701(e)(2). With one exception, an interest is "retained" by an individual if it is held by the individual both before and after the transfer. Treas. Reg. §25.2702-2(a)(3). The one exception is that a term interest created as part of the transaction and held by the transferor immediately after the transfer is treated as having been retained by the transferor. Id.

Any "retained" interest[21] that does not satisfy specified requirements to be a "qualified interest" is valued at zero. The value of the interest that was

---

21.   Surprisingly, §2702 does not require that the retained interest be a term interest.

transferred to a member of the transferor's family is then determined by utilizing the subtraction method of valuation.[22]

The underlying reason for adopting §2702 was a concern that the valuation tables will not reflect the true value of temporal interests when the parties involved are members of the same family. The type of transaction at which these rules are principally aimed is the grantor retained interest trust, otherwise referred to as a "GRIT."

Although the principal object of §2702 concerned transfers to a trust, Congress acted to prevent the use of comparable non-trust arrangements (such as a legal life estate) to avoid this rule. Section 2702(c)(1) therefore applies these rules to trust equivalents — i.e., to the transfer of an interest in property with respect to which there are one or more term interests. A "term interest" is an interest in property either for life or for a term of years. §2702(c)(3). The types of trust equivalents to which §2702 applies are described in Treas. Reg. §25.2702-4. For example, concurrent interests in property generally are not trust equivalents, and a leasehold interest for which a fair rental is payable generally will not be treated as a term interest, but a term of years or a legal life estate, certain insurance settlements, and similar horizontal or temporal slices of a property interest would be. Id.

3.   *Sales of Remainders and Joint Purchases.* Further, §2702(c)(2) makes the special valuation rule applicable to joint purchase transactions (a "split interest purchase") involving family members. A joint purchase may be a single transaction or a series of related transactions by which one or more persons acquire a term interest and family members acquire the balance of the fee. For example, if *P* purchased a term interest in property and, either in the same transaction or a related transaction, *P*'s child, *C*, purchased a remainder interest in the same property, *P* will be deemed to have acquired the full fee and transferred the remainder interest to *C* in exchange for the amount *C* paid to acquire the remainder. Normally the result is a gift of the full fair market value less the value of the consideration furnished by *C*. However, Treas. Reg. §25.2702-4(c) states that the value of *P*'s constructive gifts cannot exceed the consideration that *P* actually paid. As illustrated by Treas. Reg. §25.2702-4(d) *Example 4*, if *P* acquired the term interest for less than its fair market value, the deemed gift to *C* cannot exceed the total amount paid by *P* for the interests actually purchased by *P*. Curiously, the regulations do not address the possibility that *C*'s consideration may have been acquired from *P*, although that often will be the case. See, e.g., TAM 9206006.

---

22.   The value of the interest transferred to the family member is determined by subtracting the value of the interests retained by the transferor and applicable family members (as determined under §2702) from the value of the property that was transferred. Treas. Reg. §25.2702-1(b).

Section 2702 will apply if a person owning a fee sells a remainder interest to a family member. Treas. Reg. §25.2702-4(d) *Example 2*. Thus, even if the remainder is transferred for consideration equal to its fair market value, the transfer will be treated as a gift for gift tax purposes.

Similarly, §2702 will apply if the holder of a term interest transfers a portion of that interest (such as half the income, all income in excess of a certain amount, or all income after a term of years carved out of a life estate). See §2702(d). Moreover, §2702 will apply to creation of a short-term trust in which income is transferred to a third party by a transferor who retains a reversion, unless the retained reversionary interest is noncontingent and follows a qualified annuity or unitrust interest. §§2702(a)(1) and (b)(3), Treas. Reg. §25.2702-3(f)(3). A remainder interest that otherwise satisfies the §2702(b) requirements of a qualified interest will not be a qualified interest if it is stated as a dollar figure (as contrasted to all or a fraction of the trust). Treas. Reg. §25.2702-3(f)(3) *Example 3*.

Qualified Interests. The §2702 zero valuation rule does not apply if the retained interest is a "qualified interest" as defined in §2702(b) and valued under §7520. §2702(a)(2)(B). The logic behind this exception is that defects in the term interest valuation regime, which §2702 effectively negates, do not occur when qualified interests are used.

Normally a term interest is valued under §7520, which dictates interest rate and mortality assumptions that typically overvalue straight income interests and undervalue the remainder interests that follow them. One reason for this discrepancy is that the interest rate assumption under §7520 is 120% of the §1274 applicable federal rate, which seldom (if ever) is attainable by a trust because of prudent fiduciary investment confines. Moreover, most §7520 valuations rely on mortality assumptions that are based on the general population and these transactions typically are engaged in by taxpayers who are "self-selected." For example, they may know (by actual diagnosis) or at least suspect (by a general feeling regarding physical well-being or family history) that they have a shorter life expectancy than the tables predict. Because it is the remainder interest that is transferred in a GRIT and related transactions, straight §7520 valuation can produce disadvantageous results to the government. The qualified interest exception imposes requirements that minimize the risk of a misvaluation.

Qualified interests are defined in §2702(b) as (1) annuity interests that guarantee distribution of a fixed amount annually, (2) unitrust interests that guarantee distribution of a fixed percentage of the annually determined fair market value of the trust, payable annually, or (3) a noncontingent remainder interest following either. Within these restraints, the valuation provided by §7520 is more reliable because these requirements preclude manipulation of the income yield. The annuity or unitrust amount is required to be paid[23] regardless of the actual yield in the entity. Although the qualified interest requirement does not prevent application of questionable mortality assumptions, inaccuracies in those mortality assumptions are not a source of abuse because §2036(a)(1) is applicable if a life income interest is retained (making the transferor's premature death irrelevant because no value escapes wealth transfer taxation)[24] and because life expectancy plays no part in the valuation of a term of years.

Other, more subtle, consequences are generated by the qualified interest requirements that typically favor the government. For example, the §7520 interest rate assumption usually is far greater than the typical trust can produce. If the assumed rate is greater than the retained annuity payout rate in a qualified interest annuity trust (a grantor retained annuity trust, or GRAT), §7520 assumes that the excess trust income is accumulated and added to principal. This increases the value of the remainder interest, which is transferred subject to gift tax, and overvalues that interest.[25] Moreover, if the trust produces less income than the specified annuity or unitrust amount, principal will be invaded to make the requisite payment, and the valuation tables ignore principal valuation fluctuations (due to appreciation or depreciation or due to invasions). The tables assume the trust principal is frozen in value (or that it grows due to accumulations), notwithstanding that it actually may decline in value due to invasions. Thus, for gift tax purposes, the actual value of a transferred remainder interest may be less than the valuation rules assume; more gift tax may be imposed on creation of the trust than is appropriate. As a consequences, GRATs and GRUTs provide attractive planning opportunities only if income will exceed *both* the annuity payment and the §7520 rate, or if significant growth is expected and annuity or unitrust payments can be made without a net decline in the value of trust principal.

Exceptions. Not all retained interests are subject to the §2702 special valuation rule. For example, "incomplete transfers," as to which §§2036(a)(2) and 2038(a)(1) would apply at the transferor's death, are ex-

---

23. Unlike the qualified payment rules of §2701(d), no special provision is made for delayed payments, and no regime is established for payments that are not made. Unlike corporate dividends or partnership distributions, these payments *must* be made.

24. The extent to which §2036(a)(1) will operate when a transferor retains an annuity or unitrust interest is explained in Rev. Rul. 76-273 and Rev. Rul. 82-105.

25. This overvaluation of the remainder does not apply in a grantor retained unitrust (a GRUT) because interest rate assumptions are irrelevant for unitrust valuation. In recognition of this, and notwithstanding the clear rule in §2702(a)(2)(B) that "[t]he value of any . . . qualified interest shall be determined under §7520," Treas. Reg. §25.2702-2(b)(2) specifies that the value of a qualified unitrust interest is determined as if it was a §664 charitable remainder unitrust interest and specifically limits valuation of qualified interests under §7520 to the qualified annuity and remainder interests. This deviation reflects the fact that the unitrust tables under §664 do not rely directly on the §7520 interest rate valuation approach that is utilized for qualified annuity and remainder trusts.

cepted under §2702(a)(3)(A)(i). A transfer is "incomplete" if it is not treated as a gift for gift tax purposes regardless of whether consideration was received for the transfer. §2702(a)(3)(B). The rationale for this rule is *not* because estate tax inclusion precludes a tax free shift of future appreciation and makes inter vivos valuation irrelevant (if that were true all grantor retained interest trusts would be exempt until the term expired); rather, this exception simply recognizes that a gift tax valuation rule cannot apply before the gift tax applies, which requires a completed and therefore taxable gift.

As it did for §2701, the government provided in Treas. Reg. §25.2702-2(a)(2)(ii) that: although "an assignment of an interest in an existing trust" can be subject to §2702, a qualified §2518 disclaimer is not. In addition, the exercise, release, or lapse of a nongeneral power of appointment is not a transfer in trust, which means that §2702 cannot apply.

Treas. Reg. §25.2702-2(d)(1) *Example 3* provides that the creation of a trust for the benefit of a spouse for life, remainder to a child, in which the settlor retains no interest, also is not subject to §2702 (notwithstanding that the spouse is an applicable family member), because the spouse did not hold an interest in the trust both before and after its creation, as required by Treas. Reg. §25.2702-2(a)(3). According to the regulation, election of QTIP treatment will not alter this result because, (1) if the settlor did not elect the marital deduction, a gift tax would be incurred on the full value of the property transferred to the trust at its creation (meaning no valuation abuse occurs), and (2) if the settlor does elect marital deduction treatment a tax on the full value of the trust principal will be incurred when the spouse's interest in the trust terminates, again meaning there is no valuation abuse. An intriguing issue that this raises is whether a division of split interests between marital and bypass trusts (for example, a gift of a life estate to a QTIP marital deduction trust and the remainder to a bypass trust) is permissible without triggering §2702 because there is no transfer or retention by the spouse that meets the requisites for application of that section. It appears that §2702 will not apply. See Treas. Reg. §25.2702-2(d)(1) *Example 3*.

A retained term interest in tangible property[26] that is neither depreciable nor depletable[27] is excluded from the zero valuation treatment of §2702(a)(2)(A) if the failure to exercise rights under the term interest would not have a substantial effect on the value of a remainder interest in that property. §2702(c)(4). If the tangible property exception is met, the value of a retained term interest in the tangible property is *not* based on the Treasury

---

26. The tangible property can be realty or personalty. Treas. Reg. §25.2702-2(c)(2)(i)(A). A de minimis exception permits there to be appurtenant depreciable property (such as a fence) that has a fair market value not exceeding 5% of the fair market value of the entire property (such as a farm or ranch). Treas. Reg. §25.2702-2(c)(2)(ii).

27. The property must be of a type that no deduction for depreciation or depletion would be allowable if the property were used in a trade or business.

tables but, instead, is determined as the amount an unrelated third party would pay to purchase the term interest, presumably considering the illiquidity and, typically, non-income-producing nature of the interest. §2702(c)(4)(B). Treas. Reg. §25.2702-2(c)(1) adopts the traditional approach that the value of the term interest is what a willing buyer would pay a willing seller, each having reasonable knowledge of the relevant facts and neither being under any compulsion to buy or sell. Treas. Reg. §25.2702-2(c)(3) indicates that this value is best established by comparable sales or rentals of similar property held for a similar duration. In the absence of such evidence, the regulation states that "little weight" will be accorded to appraisals. Unfortunately, comparables may be impossible to garner for many types of term interests in tangible property, and Treas. Reg. §25.2702-2(c)(3) specifically denies the use of the §7520 tables to value such an interest. This will prevent the type of result reached in TAM 9313005, in which the §7520 tables were used to value the retained three-year term interest in non-income-producing artworks and reduced the value of a gift of the remainder to almost half the fair market value of the art.

QPRTs or House GRITs. A final exception, authorized by §2702(a)(3)(A)(i), has spawned a great amount of interest. As you read the description of it, however, ask yourself whether it is the kind of planning that your own family would embrace. Section 2702(a)(3)(A)(ii) excludes from §2702 the transfer of interests in a trust, all the property of which consists of a residence to be used as a personal residence by those holding term interests in the trust. This is a "house GRIT." As interpreted in Treas. Reg. §25.2702-5, both a "personal residence trust" and a "qualified personal residence trust" (QPRT) may be established, although for a number of reasons not relevant here it is the latter that most estate planners recommend.

Various requirements are specified, including what is to happen if the residence is sold, destroyed, or no longer used for residential purposes (for example, because the term interest holder moved to a nursing home). A personal residence is either the term interest holder's principal residence or one other that the term interest holder uses a certain number of days in the year. See §280A(d)(1). This may make this device attractive to families who own vacation property that the older generation is not likely to want to continue using for longer than a retained term, or who expect to move from one residence to another upon retirement in a specified number of years. But if neither of those situations exist, what will the term holder do when a retained interest expires in their principal personal residence? PLRs 9433016 and 9425028 state that a QPRT may be accompanied by a separate agreement obligating the remainder beneficiaries to sell or rent the property to the term interest holder at fair market rental value. Treas. Reg. §25.2702-5(b)(1) denies qualified trust treatment if a sale to the donor or the donor's spouse (or a controlled entity) is not prohibited. Consider the consequence: would you expect your relatives to willingly pay rent when their retained term expires and they are told to pay up or move out? As a tax matter it allows them to move more wealth tax free to the remainder beneficiaries, but many homeowners faced with paying rent for their own house will not see this as an advantage! And memories being what they are, they also may forget that the estate planner told them about it at the beginning of the term.

The regulations treat as part of a personal residence "appurtenant structures used for residential purposes and adjacent land not in excess of that which is reasonably appropriate for residential purposes" but preclude the transfer of personal property (such as furnishings). Treas. Reg. §25.2702-5(b)(2)(ii). In Treas. Reg. §25.2702-5(d) *Example 3*, the donor transferred to a trust a farm with various structures used for farming, and the donor retained a 20-year term interest. The trust did not qualify as a personal residence trust because of the inclusion of structures such as a barn and a silo. Although the farm did not qualify as a personal residence, presumably the farmhouse alone, and a bit of land around it, could have qualified if the transfer in trust had been so limited. PLR 9328040 ruled that, for purposes of the definition of appurtenant structures in a QPRT, a guest house adjoining the main home on a 1.65 acre parcel used as a vacation property qualified as part of the personal residence. So, there is some flexibility in these rules.

Valuation of the gifted remainder interest in a QPRT should be based on the normal tables used to value temporal interests and, because the property is valued for its personal use, the failure to produce income equal to the assumed rate of return employed by §7520 is not relevant. The prospect for tax saving through this device is fairly good if the property is expected to appreciate in value, particularly following a period in which the value of residential real estate has been depressed. In any event, it is difficult to justify this exception on policy grounds and occasional rumblings suggest that it might be repealed when Congress looks for revenue gains to pay for some other tax benefit it wants to bestow.

Application to Reversions.   Why should retention of a reversion trigger §2702 treatment? For example, if a transferor creates a trust to pay for the support of an elderly relative for life, reversion to the transferor, there is no freeze potential even if the trust principal appreciates and the term interest is not in qualified interest format. It might seem that guaranteed inclusion of the reversion in the transferor's gross estate should preclude application of §2702. Nevertheless, the gift of the term interest is undervalued if the income produced and paid on the term interest exceeds the amount assumed by the §7520 tables. Section 2702 was inspired by concerns over estate freezes, but it also deals with other transfer tax problems such as this, caused by the ability to manipulate the value of transferred property interests.

Adjustment to Avoid Double Taxation. In a situation in which §2702 requires 100% of the value of trust property to be taxed at creation of the trust (because the qualified interest rules were not met and the transfer was complete), subsequent inclusion in the transferor's gross estate will constitute double taxation to the extent the adjustment provided in Treas. Reg. §25.2702-6 does not work properly. Moreover, if creation of the trust was by a split gift, the failure of §2001(e) to apply means that the consenting spouse's prior taxable gifts will not be purged, which also will result in inappropriate double taxation. In each of these cases, it is clear that an adjustment is needed. It is curious that, unlike §2701(e)(6), Congress did not mandate that Treasury provide such an adjustment. Perhaps even more curiously, however, Treasury did so anyway.

Similar to the analogous provision for §2701 in Treas. Reg. 25.2701-5, Treas. Reg. §25.2702-6 provides a reduction of the amount to which wealth transfer tax applies in certain circumstances in which §2702 previously imposed a special valuation for a retained interest (which likely was valued at zero) and thereby caused its actual value to be included in the amount gifted to a family member. This regulatory provision provides a reduction if a subsequent gift is made by the initial transferor[28] who held the retained interest when §2702 imposed a special valuation. Treas. Reg. §25.2702-6(a)(1). Similarly, the reduction applies if the retained interest is included in the gross estate of the initial transferor. Treas. Reg. §25.2702-6(a)(2).

The adjustment applies only if the initial transferor subsequently makes a gift of that interest or dies having that interest included in the initial transferor's gross estate. The adjustment will not apply if the retained interest terminated by its terms (for example, if the person retained an interest for a term of years that expired before the person died). In such a case, double taxation will result if the prior gift valued under §2702 is not adjusted and the earnings generated and paid to the owner of the retained interest are taxed at the owner's death. To illustrate, assume the transferor retained an income interest in trust for 10 years and that it was not a qualified interest under §2702. The value of the transferred property was $100x when the trust was created and it was still worth $100x at expiration of the term. During the 10 year term $40x of income was paid to the transferor, who dies years later with all of that wealth intact. Without an adjustment, the transferor's adjusted taxable gifts base will be $100x, reflecting the gift upon creation, and the $40x of income received will be

---

28. Treas. Reg. §25.2702-6(b)(1)(i) limits the amount of reduction permitted to an individual or an individual's estate to the amount of value that §2702 added to the prior gift that the individual made because of the special valuation of the interest retained by the individual. That makes it clear that the reduction is available only to the initial transferor or to that person's estate. Another limitation on the amount of permissible reduction is that it cannot exceed the amount added to the individual's taxable gifts or gross estate because of the transfer of the retained interest as a consequence of a subsequent gift or the individual's death.

includible under §2033. Double taxation results because the retained value of the $40x income interest was ignored in valuing the transferred interest for gift tax purposes.

Also notice that, if an adjustment is specified in Treas. Reg. §25.2702-6(b)(1) because the retained term interest subsequently is transferred, the adjustment is restricted to the lesser of "(i) [t]he increase in the individual's taxable gifts resulting from the interest being valued [under §2702] at the time of the initial transfer," and "(ii) [t]he increase in the individual's taxable gifts (or gross estate) resulting from the subsequent transfer of the interest." That is, the adjustment is the smaller of the value of the retained interest when the original transfer triggered §2702 and when the retained interest is transferred.

Gift Splitting

If the transferor subsequently makes a split gift of the retained interest under §2513, Treas. Reg. §25.2702-6(a)(3) permits the adjustment that reduces the amount of the gift to be split equally between the transferor and the consenting spouse, if the transferor so elects. For example, *T* created a trust and retained the income interest for 10 years. In a later year, *T* gifted the balance of that term interest, and *T*'s spouse consented to split that second gift. Because the adjustment reduces the amount of the second gift, *T* has the option to split the reduction between *T* and *T*'s spouse for purposes of computing the tax on their respective shares of the second gift. Regardless of how that subsequent transfer of the retained interest occurs, Treas. Reg. §25.2702-6(a)(3) requires that the adjustment splitting decision be signified by an attachment to the consenting spouse's Form 709 gift tax return reporting the spouse's share of the split gift. Notice that whether the original transfer was a split gift is irrelevant under this provision, and no provision addresses the subsequent adjustment mechanism if the original transfer was a split gift. See, e.g., Treas. Reg. §25.2702-6(c) *Example 5*.

Retained Nonbeneficial Power Over Income

According to the regulations, a transferor's retention of a nonbeneficial power over an income interest that causes the transfer of the income interest to be incomplete for gift tax purposes (for example, the power to sprinkle income among the income beneficiaries) constitutes a retained interest that triggers §2702. Treas. Reg. §25.2702-6(c) *Example 6* addresses a case in which *T* transferred property in trust and retained the power for 10 years to distribute each year's trust income among *T*'s descendants in such shares as *T* should determine. On the expiration of the 10-year period, the trust corpus is to be distributed among *T*'s children. The regulation does not discuss the possibility that *T* had a contingent reversionary interest if *T* had no living children at the expiration of the 10-year period, so let's also ignore that possibility in discussing the wealth transfer tax consequences of the transfer.

On those facts, *T* made a completed gift of the remainder interest to *T*'s children. No annual exclusion is allowed because that gift is a future interest. *T*'s transfer of the income interest to *T*'s descendants was incomplete for gift tax purposes because of *T*'s nonbeneficial power to distribute each year's income among the descendants. Treas. Reg. §25.2511-2(c). Therefore, the transfer of the income interest was not subject to gift tax when property was transferred to the trust. As trust income distributions are made each year, the amount distributed is removed from *T*'s power of allocation. So, there is a completed gift of each distribution when made, and that gift qualifies for the annual exclusion.

The next issue is to determine the value of the gifted remainder interest. The remainder interest would be valued under §7520, using the assumed interest rates if §2702 were not applicable. However, Treas. Reg. §25.2702-6(c) *Example 6* states that *T*'s nonbeneficial power to allocate income distributions constitutes a retained interest in the trust that does not constitute a qualified interest. It is not absolutely clear whether the regulation treats the retained nonbeneficial power as the retained interest or whether, because that power made the transfer of the income interest incomplete, it is the income interest itself that is deemed to have been retained. The analysis in this example and in an earlier example in the regulations (discussed below) indicates that it is the income interest that is treated as having been retained by *T*. In any event, the regulation treats the value of *T*'s retained interest as zero, and the regulation states that the value of the remainder interest that was gifted to the children is equal to the entire value of the property transferred to the trust. In effect, the value of the income interest is taxed as a gift to the children by adding that value to the remainder interest. Again, no annual exclusion is allowable because the remainder is a future interest.

As previously noted, each distribution is subject to the gift tax when income is distributed from the trust during the 10-year term period. The regulatory example states that each such gift does not constitute a transfer of *T*'s retained interest in the trust, so no adjustment is permitted. Treas. Reg. §25.2702-6(c) *Example 6*. This means that the wealth transfer tax on the gift of the income interest is accelerated and is denied an annual exclusion, *and* double taxation results to the extent the distribution of current income exceeds the annual exclusion. If *T* were to commit all of the subsequently earned trust income to one of the children during the 10-year term (or presumably if *T* otherwise could renounce the power to allocate trust income), this would constitute a transfer of a retained interest in the trust and the adjustment provision would apply. Treas. Reg. §25.2702-6(c) *Example 7*.

These examples in the regulations are an extremely harsh application of §2702. The income interest will be subjected to wealth transfer taxation in that: (1) the income earned by the trust during the 10-year period will incur gift tax, and (2) if *T* dies during the 10-year period, the entire value of the trust will be included in *T*'s gross estate under §2036(a)(2). The only leakage is that there will be annual exclusions applied each year. It is questionable whether there are tax "abuses" of such magnitude to warrant this application of §2702, and it is punitive to withhold adjustment relief for the double taxation that attends the annual distribution of trust income.

T's power to sprinkle the annuity or unitrust payments likely would not invoke §2702 if the trust in the example above were drafted to provide a qualified annuity interest or a qualified unitrust interest to *T*'s descendants for the 10-year term. In Treas. Reg. §25.2702-2(d)(1) *Example 6*, *A* made a transfer to a trust, retained a 10-year income interest, gave *S* (*A*'s spouse) an income interest for the next 10-year period, and then gave the remainder to *C*, *A*'s child. *A* retained the power to revoke *S*'s secondary income interest. Because of *A*'s power to revoke, the transfer of *S*'s secondary income interest was incomplete. The regulation applied §2702 and treated *A* as having retained both the income interest payable to *A* and the income interest payable to *S*. Because neither of the income interests constituted a qualified interest, the value of the remainder interest (the only completed gift) was equal to the fair market value of the entirety of the property transferred in trust. However, the regulations further state that the amount of the gift would be the fair market value of the property transferred in trust reduced by the value of both *A*'s 10-year interest and *S*'s 10-year interest if those 10-year term interests were qualified annuity or unitrust interests. Treas. Reg. §25.2702-2(d) *Example 7*. In other words, only the actual value of the remainder interest would be subjected to gift tax.

The result reached in the regulatory example is consistent with Treas. Reg. §25.2702-2(a)(5), which states that the "retention of a power to revoke a qualified annuity interest (or unitrust interest) of the transferor's spouse is treated as the retention of a qualified annuity interest (or unitrust interest)." The reference to "the tranferor's spouse" raises a question whether the regulatory provision applies only to an interest held by the transferor's spouse and whether it applies only to a power to revoke. The regulations do not state that this treatment is so restricted, and there is no apparent reason why it should.

As a consequence of these regulatory interpretations of §2702, it would be wise for a grantor who wishes to retain an income interest in a transfer in trust to, instead, retain a qualified annuity or unitrust interest. Similarly, if a grantor wishes to retain control over the distribution of an income interest in property transferred in trust, it would be preferable to create a qualified annuity or unitrust interest instead. One question, however, is whether an annuity or unitrust interest that can be sprinkled among several beneficiaries can constitute a qualified interest. There is no explicit provision dealing with that issue, but there is no reason to limit qualified interests to those in which beneficial interests are predetermined. The requirement of an annuity or unitrust payment solves the problem at which §2702 was aimed (imprecise valuations under the §7520 tables), and it should not matter to whom those payments are made.

Applicable Family Member.   The §2702(a)(1) special valuation rule applies to a trust interest retained by "any applicable family member" of a transferor who created or transferred an interest. Thus, §2702 would apply if a transferor and an applicable family member owned property and the transferor alone transferred an interest in the transferor's portion, meaning that the applicable family member's interest would be valued at zero unless it was a qualified interest. If the interest retained by the applicable family member is subsequently gifted to another, the parenthetical in Treas. Reg. §25.2702-6(a)(1) appears to deny an adjustment for the double taxation of that interest.

The following illustration may give some dimension to the scope of §2702. *D* created a testamentary trust to pay the income quarterly to *S*, *D*'s surviving spouse. At *S*'s death, the principal of the trust is to be distributed equally among *D*'s children living at *S*'s death. A valid QTIP election was made for the trust under §2056(b)(7), and *D*'s estate was allowed a marital deduction for the value of the trust.

Three years later, *S* made a gift to *G*, a sibling of *S*, of the right to 40% of trust income for the rest of *S*'s life. *S*'s gift of 40% of the life income interest is subject to gift taxation. It is a present interest, so an annual exclusion is allowed. The amount of that §2511 gift is equal to 40% of the value of the life income interest, less the annual exclusion. In addition, §2519 treats *S* as having made a gift to the children of the *entire* remainder interest in the trust, and that constitutes a gift of a future interest for which no annual exclusion is allowable. The actuarial value of the remainder interest is determined under §7520. However, §§2702(e) and 2704(c)(2) include a sibling as a member of *S*'s family; therefore, §2702 applies to the constructive gift of the remainder interest. Under §2702, the value of the remainder is increased by the value of 60% of the life income interest, which is the interest that *S* retained in the trust. Using the subtraction method of valuation, the value of the retained life income interest is deemed by §2702 to be zero. The value of 40% of the life income interest that was gifted to *G* is not subject to §2702 because, among other reasons, that interest was not *retained* by *G*. So the amount of the constructive gift from *S* to the children equals the entire value of the trust less the value of the right to 40% of trust income for the rest of *S*'s life. No annual exclusion is allowed for that constructive gift.

S died 8 years later, still holding at death the right to 60% of the trust income. The right to that income terminated upon *S*'s death. Section 2044(b)(2) prevents the application of that section because §2519 had previously been applied to the trust. However, because *S* was deemed by §2519 to have made a gift of the remainder interest in the trust, and because *S* retained a life income interest in 60% of the trust, 60% of the value of the trust is included in *S*'s gross estate under §2036(a)(1). See Treas. Reg. §§25.2519-1(g) *Example 4* and 20.2044-1(e) *Example 5*.

S's adjusted taxable gifts, which constitute part of *S*'s estate tax base, is purged of the gift tax value of the 60% of the trust that was part of the constructive gift that was made to the children, because that portion of the trust is included in *S*'s gross estate. §2001(b)(last sentence). The gift of the remaining 40% of the value of the trust (less any annual exclusion that was allowed) is included in *S*'s adjusted taxable gifts because that portion is not includible in *S*'s gross estate.

Finally, under Treas. Reg. §25.2702-6, no adjustment is allowable for the 60% life income interest in the trust that §2702 caused to be valued at zero in determining the value of the constructive gift of the remainder interest to the children that took place 8 years earlier, because the life income interest terminated on *S*'s death. Thus, no amount is deemed to be included in *S*'s gross estate because of that interest, even though the income received increased *S*'s net worth. As you can see, a less than 100% §2519 assignment, or use of anything except a GRAT, a GRUT, or a QPRT can be a real disaster.

PART C.   SECTION 2703: BUY-SELL AGREEMENTS

Code Reference: *Chapter 14: §2703*

Added in 1990 to address the estate freeze valuation effect of options, rights to acquire or use property, and restrictions on the sale or use of property of any kind, §2703 should be considered as an umbrella that overlays all of the pre-existing authority dealing with buy-sell agreements. See page 73. The primary thrust of §2703 is to prevent buy-sell agreements from reducing the estate, gift, or generation-skipping transfer tax value of property subject to the agreement to a figure that is less than if there were no such agreement. It also negates the effect of restrictions on the sale or use of property on the determination of value for transfer tax purposes. It might apply to partnership agreements that restrict the ability to convey a partnership interest, to corporate or partnership limitations on liquidation of the entity, to leases with option provisions,[29] and to certain easements,[30] but

---

29. See Treas. Reg. §25.2703-1(d) *Example 1*, stating that a lease, the terms of which were not comparable to leases of similar property entered into among unrelated parties, would be regarded as a restriction that would be ignored for valuation purposes.

these applications have not yet been established. Section 2703 probably does not apply to a self-canceling installment note, notwithstanding that mandated cancellation of an installment note is the quintessential restriction on the sale or use of the installment note. Even if §2703 does apply, the bona fide business arrangement exception ought to be applicable if the self-canceling note is supported by an appropriate premium that justifies noninclusion of the notes under §2033.

Exception. An exception is provided if the option, agreement, right, or restriction meets the three safe harbor requirements in §2703(b): (1) it is "a bona fide business arrangement," (2) its terms are comparable to those of "similar arrangements entered into by persons in an arm's-length transaction," and (3) it is "not a device to transfer . . . property to members of the decedent's family[31] for less than full and adequate consideration." If those three requirements are met, §2703(a) will not apply.

Treas. Reg. §25.2703-1(b)(3) provides an added safe harbor, the satisfaction of which constitutes compliance with §2703(b): If more than 50% (by value) of the property subject to an agreement or other provision is owned by individuals who are neither related to the transferor nor objects of the transferor's bounty.

Because a buy-sell agreement or restriction may avoid the "device" aspect (for example, because family members are not involved) but fail to meet the "bona fide" or "comparable" arrangements tests, the §2703(b) exception should not be viewed as merely a family transactions provision. Each of the three §2703(b) requirements must be satisfied independently. For example, according to Treas. Reg. §25.2703-1(b)(2), "the mere showing that a right or restriction is a bona fide business arrangement is not sufficient to establish that the right or restriction is not a device to transfer property for less than full and adequate consideration." Moreover, all the pre-1990 rules regarding the validity of buy-sell agreements to peg values (such as the need to impose inter vivos restrictions on transfer) are unaffected by

---

30. Easements running to family members may be covered, but not easements granted to charities, conservation organizations, or otherwise in a deductible format, because Treas. Reg. §25.2703-1(a)(4) provides that §2703 does not apply to easements for which a charitable deduction was allowable under either §2055(f) or §2522(d); presumably this means that any other easement is subject to §2703.

31. The term "family" is not defined in §2703. Treas. Reg. §25.2703-1(b)(1)(ii) substitutes the term "natural object of the transferor's bounty." Thus, it is not clear whether "family" was meant to incorporate the §2701(e)(1) definition (decedent's spouse, lineal descendants of the decedent or of the decedent's spouse, and spouses of those descendants), the §2704(c)(2) definition (which adds ancestors of the decedent or of the decedent's spouse, siblings of the decedent, and spouses of any of them), or a totally unrelated definition of family. PLR 9222043 held that §2703 was applicable to the grant of set price purchase options to employed nieces and nephews because they met the definition of "family members" under Treas. Reg. §25.2701-2(b)(5), which is incorporated into Treas. Reg. §25.2703-1(b)(3).

§2703, meaning that even if the §2703(b) exception otherwise is applicable, the buy-sell agreement still may fail to limit value for wealth transfer tax purposes because of one or more of those pre-1990 requirements.

It is not clear whether an agreement could meet the "bona fide business arrangement" requirement if its terms are *not* "comparable to similar arrangements entered into by persons in an arm's-length transaction." The latter requirement is deemed satisfied if the agreement "could have been obtained in a fair bargain between unrelated parties in the same business," considering "such factors as the expected term of the agreement, the current fair market value of the property, anticipated changes in value during the term of the arrangement, and the adequacy of any consideration given in exchange for the rights granted" by the agreement. But "fair bargain" is not defined, nor is "comparability." Although we are told by Treas. Reg. §25.2703-1(b)(4) that, "[i]f comparables are difficult to find because the business is unique, comparables from similar businesses may be used," the regulation fails to indicate how far a unique business may stretch to show comparable sales from "similar" businesses.

It would not be likely that Congress would state three separate requirements to meet the §2703(b) exception and not mean for them to be different, but can you articulate *how* they differ?

Chronologically Exempt Agreements. Section 2703 is applicable to agreements entered into before October 9, 1990, only if the agreement is substantially modified thereafter. Treas. Reg. §25.2703-1(c) defines a modification as substantial if it results in "other than a de minimis change in the quality, value, or timing" of the rights or restrictions imposed on any party, and specifies that failure to update an agreement as required by its terms may constitute a substantial modification.

PART D.   SECTION 2704: IMPOSITION OR LAPSE OF RIGHTS AND RESTRICTIONS

Code Reference: *Chapter 14: §2704*

Section 2704 was added specifically to override *Estate of Harrison* and *Estate of Watts*, which follow:

Estate of Harrison v. Commissioner
52 T.C.M. (CCH) 1306 (1987)

SHIELDS, J.: . . . Petitioner is the estate of Daniel J. Harrison, Jr. ("decedent") who died at the age of 60 on January 14, 1980 . . . .

The independent co-executors of the estate are Daniel J. Harrison III ("Dan") and Bruce F. Harrison ("Bruce"), the sons of decedent. . . . .

Limited Partnership Interest. On June 10, 1975, decedent, whose health was declining, executed a power of attorney generally authorizing Dan to manage his assets which included extensive ranching properties and other real estate as well as oil and gas interests in both developed and undeveloped properties. Decedent's health continued to decline and Dan continued to manage his father's properties under the power of attorney until August 1, 1979. On that date Bruce and Dan, acting individually and under the power of attorney for the decedent, organized Harrison Interests, Ltd., a Texas limited partnership, with the principal purpose of consolidating and preserving decedent's assets. On the same date, Dan, under the power of attorney for decedent, contributed assets of the decedent to the partnership in return for a 1% general partnership interest and a 77.8% limited partnership interest. At the same time, Dan and Bruce also contributed assets to the partnership in return for separate 10.6% general partnership interests. The assets contributed by each of the partners consisted primarily of real estate, oil and gas interests, and marketable securities that the decedent and his sons had accumulated. None of the properties contributed to the partnership by either Dan or Bruce had been given to them by decedent.

The combined value of decedent's general partnership interest and his limited partnership interest at the time of the creation of the partnership was $59,476,523, which was the value of the properties contributed by decedent to the partnership. Dan's general partnership interest and Bruce's general partnership interest each had a value at the creation of the partnership of $7,981,351, which was the value of the assets they each contributed to the partnership.

Under the partnership agreement, the general partners had absolute control over the management of the partnership. Each general partner also had the right during life to dissolve the partnership, but neither a limited partner nor a successor to a general partner had such a right. The partnership agreement provided that the partnership was to be automatically dissolved upon the death of a general partner, or upon an election to dissolve by a living general partner, unless within 90 days of such death, or such election, all of the other general partners agreed to continue the partnership. In such case, the partnership was to continue, but the estate of the deceased general partner, or the living general partner electing to dissolve the partnership, was entitled to a payment equal to the amount he would have received had the partnership been dissolved.

Under the partnership agreement, both general partners and limited partners had the right to sell or assign their partnership interests after first giving the other general partners an option to buy such interests. Similarly, the agreement also provided that, upon the death of a general partner, his legal representative was required to give the remaining general partners an option to buy the deceased partner's general partnership interest.

On January 14, 1980, decedent died of another stroke. On February 4, 1980, Dan and Bruce exercised their option to purchase decedent's general partnership interest for $757,116. . . . Pursuant to the partnership agreement, Dan and Bruce also agreed within ninety days after decedent's death to continue the partnership.

In this case, respondent and petitioner agree that $757,116 is the value of decedent's general partnership interest. They disagree, however, as to the value of his limited partnership interest. Respondent claims that the value of the limited partnership interest is $59,555,020, which is the agreed value of the proportionate share of the partnership assets that decedent would have received for his limited partnership interest if the partnership had been dissolved or if decedent's limited partnership interest had been terminated immediately before his death pursuant to the partnership agreement. Petitioner contends that the value of the limited partnership interest is $33,000,000, which we find from the stipulation of the parties was the value of the limited partnership interest the moment after it passed from the decedent to his estate. The difference between the two values is attributable entirely to the right which decedent had as a general partner up until his death to force a dissolution of the partnership.[32] The parties agree that under the partnership agreement and applicable Texas law this right did not pass to the estate.

Respondent relies on §§2033, 2035, 2036, 2037, 2038, and 2041 in support of his argument that the value of decedent's limited partnership interest for estate tax purposes is $59,555,020, the amount at which he could have forced its liquidation immediately before his death.

Respondent's reliance upon §2033 is inapposite, however, as is well illustrated by the reasoning in United States v. Land, 303 F.2d 170, 171–173 (5th Cir. 1962), where it was stated:

---

32. In other words, decedent's right, as a general partner, to dissolve and liquidate the partnership increased the value of the limited partnership interest by the difference of $26,555,020.

The statute applicable here is . . . Section 2033 of the Internal Revenue Code . . . . This provides that "the gross estate shall include the value of all property . . . to the extent of the interest therein of the decedent at the time of his death." The Regulations reiterate the truism that the tax is "an excise tax on the transfer of property at death and is not a tax on the property transferred." Treas. Reg. §20.2033-1(a). It is of course imperative that the tax be imposed on the *transfer* of the property in order to avoid the constitutional prohibition against unapportioned direct taxes. From this . . . it follows that the valuation of the estate should be made at the time of the transfer. The time of transfer is the time of death. Treas. Reg. §20.2031-1(b). In Knowlton v. Moore, 178 U.S. 41 (1900), the Supreme Court said, "tax laws of this nature in all countries rest in their essence upon the principle that death is the generating source from which the particular taxing power takes its being and that it is the power to transmit, or the transmission from the dead to the living, on which such taxes are more immediately rested." [Emphasis supplied; citations omitted.]

Brief as is the instant of death, the court must pinpoint its valuation at this instant — the moment of truth, when the ownership of the decedent ends and the ownership of the successor begins. It is a fallacy, therefore, to argue value before — or — after death on the notion that valuation must be determined by the value either of the interest that ceases or of the interest that begins. *Instead, the valuation is determined by the interest that passes, and the value of the interest before or after death is pertinent only as it serves to indicate the value at death.* In the usual case death brings no change in the value of property. It is only in the few cases where death alters value, as well as ownership, that it is necessary to determine whether the value at the time of death reflects the change caused by death, for example, loss of services of a valuable partner to a small business. [Emphasis added.]

. . .

Underlying the determination in these instances that the valuation of property passing at death reflects the changes wrought by death is a basic economic fact: value looks ahead. *To find the fair market value of a property interest at the decedent's death we put ourselves in the position of a potential purchaser of the interest at that time. Such a person would not be influenced in his calculations by past risks that had failed to materialize or by restrictions that had ended. Death tolls the bell for risks, contingencies, or restrictions which exist only during the life of the decedent. A potential buyer focuses on the value the property has in the present or will have in the future. He attributes full value to any right that vests or matures at death, and he reduces his valuation to account for any risk or deprivation that death brings into effect, such as the effect of the death on the brains of a small, close corporation.* These are factors that would affect his enjoyment of the property should he purchase it, and on which he bases his valuation. The sense of the situation suggests that we follow suit. [Emphasis added.]

When the foregoing reasoning is applied to this case, it is apparent that the property transferred at the moment of decedent's death was the limited partnership interest that passed to decedent's estate, which did not include the right to dissolve the partnership. Nevertheless, respondent claims that when decedent's right to dissolve the partnership terminated at his death something of value passed to Dan and Bruce. However, we are unable to agree because this contention is contrary to respondent's stipulation that the value of the interests of Dan and Bruce were the same at the moment before decedent's death, at the moment of decedent's death, and at the moment after decedent's death.

Respondent also contends that we should ignore the effect the partnership agreement has upon decedent's limited partnership interest because the partnership agreement was an attempt to artificially depress the value of decedent's property for estate tax purposes. Such an agreement will be ignored only if there is no business purpose for the creation of the partnership or if the agreement is merely a substitute for testamentary disposition. See Estate of Bischoff v. Commissioner, 69 T.C. 32, 39–41 (1977).

With respect to business purpose, petitioner presented convincing proof that the partnership was created as a means of providing necessary and proper management of decedent's properties and that the partnership was advantageous to and in the best interests of decedent. Respondent presented no proof to rebut petitioner's showing.

With respect to the issue of whether the agreement was a substitute for testamentary disposition, we find in petitioner's favor for three reasons. First, the agreement applied to all the partners, and no partner's assignee or estate could liquidate the partnership without the remaining partners' consent. See Estate of Bischoff, 69

T.C. at 41; Estate of Littick v. Commissioner, 31 T.C. 181, 186–188 (1958). Furthermore, decedent received adequate consideration for his transfer to the partnership. See Estate of Bischoff, 69 T.C. at 41 n.9. Finally, although the creation of the partnership eventually resulted in a substantial decrease in estate taxes, there is no proof in the record that the partnership was created other than for business purposes.

Having determined that the property interest to be valued is that which passed to the decedent's estate, we must now decide how to value it. As stated in *United States v. Land*, we must pinpoint our valuation at the instant of death, "the moment of truth, when the ownership of the decedent ends and the ownership of the successor begins." 303 F.2d at 172. The value thus pinpointed is to be determined by reference to the classical fair market value, the amount at which the limited partnership interest would have changed hands between a willing seller and a willing buyer with neither being under any compulsion and both having reasonable knowledge of the relevant circumstances. As also noted in *Land*, a potential buyer of the partnership interest would focus on the value of such interest in the present or the future, not the past. Thus, decedent's right during life to liquidate the partnership would no longer be available to enhance the value of the partnership interest after his death. Put simply, the only purchase available to such a potential buyer in this case would be the limited partnership interest without any right to liquidate the partnership. As previously indicated, the parties have stipulated that the value of such interest is $33,000,000.

Respondent next contends that under §2035 the gross estate includes the right to liquidate the partnership as property transferred by the decedent without adequate and full consideration during the three-year period ending on his death. In this connection, respondent argues that when the decedent originally transferred his assets to the partnership he failed to retain for his estate the right to liquidate the partnership while the other partners retained such right for their estates. Thus, according to respondent, decedent transferred without adequate consideration and in contemplation of death something of value to the other partners when the partnership was created. We disagree because we find that Dan and Bruce did not retain a liquidation right for their estates since, in this respect, the partnership agreement treats all three partners equally. Furthermore, as stipulated to by respondent, the decedent received partnership interests equal in value to the assets he contributed to the partnership; thus, there was adequate and full consideration for his transfer. Moreover, no transfer was made by decedent to Dan and Bruce since they received partnership interests having stipulated values equal to the assets they contributed to the partnership.

Respondent also contends that under §2036 the gross estate includes the right to liquidate the partnership as property transferred by the decedent without adequate consideration and over which he retained for his life the right to possession, enjoyment, or the income therefrom. As noted above, decedent's transfer to the partnership was for a full and adequate consideration. In addition, he retained no rights in the transferred property, but instead acquired partnership interests having equal value. . . .

Section 2038 is equally inapplicable because there was no gratuitous transfer by the decedent and he retained no right to alter or terminate the transfer to the partnership. . . .

[The court's summary rejection of the government's §2037 and 2041 arguments has been omitted.]

In conclusion, given the facts stipulated to by respondent and the absence of any proof putting into question the purpose of the partnership, we hold that for estate tax purposes the value of the decedent's limited partnership interest was $33,000,000. . . .

Estate of Watts v. Commissioner
823 F.2d 483 (11th Cir. 1987),
aff'g 51 T.C.M. (CCH) 60 (1985)

HILL, J.: . . . Martha B. Watts, the decedent in this case, died on December 7, 1978. At the time of her death, she owned a 15% interest in Rosboro Lumber Company (Rosboro), an Oregon general partnership. . . . The partnership agreement provided in relevant part as follows: . . .

¶9. This partnership shall continue until dissolved by the voluntary action of one or more of the partners. The death of a partner shall not cause the dissolution or termination of this partnership . . . .

On taxpayer's estate tax return, decedent's 15% interest in Rosboro was valued at $2,550,000. After an audit, the Commissioner of Internal Revenue determined that the fair market value of decedent's interest in the partnership was $20,006,000. . . . This figure was based on Rosboro's liquidation value, i.e., the market value of its underlying assets should the company be liquidated. . . .

The Tax Court concluded that the value of decedent's partnership interest in Rosboro Lumber Company was $2,550,000. In reaching this conclusion, the Tax Court rejected the Commissioner's contention that the decedent's interest should be valued in terms of what Rosboro would receive for its assets upon liquidation of the company. . . .

In this case, the Commissioner does not challenge the sufficiency of the evidence or dispute the basic factual data relating to the intrinsic asset value or the earning power of the Rosboro partnership. Rather, the Commissioner contends that the Tax Court's decision to value decedent's interest as part of a going concern was erroneous . . . .

[T]he Tax Court's decision to value decedent's interest as part of a going concern is amply supported by the law governing Oregon partnerships, and the contractual restrictions placed upon Ms. Watts' partnership interest by the partnership agreement governing Rosboro Lumber Company.

First, we note that, "because the estate tax is a tax on the privilege of transferring property upon one's death, the property to be valued for estate tax purposes is that which the decedent actually transfers at his death, rather than the interest held by the decedent before death, or that held by the legatee after death." Propstra v. United States, 680 F.2d 1248, 1250 (11th Cir. 1982). The Commissioner's argument rests entirely on the notion that the interest transferred at the time of Martha Watt's death was an interest which entitled its holder to dissolve the partnership, and liquidate the company. This is not the case.

The government is correct in suggesting that normally, when a partner passes away, the partnership is automatically dissolved. However, dissolution is not the same thing as liquidation. Dissolution is the point at which the partners cease doing business together. Upon dissolution, the partnership is not terminated, but continues until the winding up of partnership affairs. The government is also correct in noting that the withdrawing partner, *unless otherwise agreed*, has the right, upon dissolution, to compel the "winding up" or liquidation of the company, and receive the value of his interest in the partnership.

But that is not the end of our analysis. This rule imposes an obvious hardship upon those partners who may wish to continue the business. In order to circumvent the problem posed by a partner's liquidation right, the Uniform Partnership Act, as adopted in Oregon, allows the partners to incorporate a continuation provision in the partnership agreement. The most common type of continuation agreements are created to avoid the exact contingency present here, i.e., automatic dissolution by virtue of a partner's death.

. . . The Rosboro Partnership Agreement clearly provided that the death of a partner would not cause dissolution, and that the business would continue upon the death of a partner. Thus, while in the absence of such an agreement the partnership would have dissolved upon Ms. Watts' death, here the interest that passed to her estate was, by terms of the partnership agreement, an interest in an undissolved partnership.

This point is crucial, because the liquidation right, which forms the basis of the Commissioner's claim, is granted only to outgoing partners upon dissolution. No dissolution occurred here. We therefore conclude that the Tax Court was correct, as a matter of law, in determining that the value of Ms. Watts interest in Rosboro could not be ascertained by reference to the value of that interest upon the lumber company's liquidation. This is true not because of the partner's current intent, but because of the legal restrictions placed upon the partner's interest by contract, fully commensurate with Oregon law. . . .

Given that the Tax Court's decision adequately reflected a correct application of state and federal law in defining and valuing the property interest at stake, we do not have any reason to disturb the court's conclusion. Accordingly, the decision of the Tax Court is affirmed.

Section 2704 causes a constructive transfer when voting or liquidation right restrictions applicable to corporations or partnerships lapse in certain circumstances. It may require a transfer to be valued by ignoring restrictions that have "the effect of reducing the value of the transferred interest [for wealth transfer tax purposes] but [do] not ultimately reduce the value of such interest to the transferee." §2704(b)(4).

Applicable only to corporations and partnerships in which the transferor and family members[33] hold control under the §2701(b)(2) 50% test,[34] §2704(a) essentially regards the lapse of a restriction as a transfer of the value differential before and after the lapse. Further, §2704(b) requires that restrictions on liquidation rights be disregarded in valuing a transferred interest in the entity if the restriction will lapse or can be removed by the transferor or by family members after the transfer.

Excepted from §2704(b) (disregard of liquidation restriction) — but not §2704(a) (lapse of voting or liquidation rights) — is "[a]ny commercially reasonable restriction" imposed as part of a financing arrangement with

---

33. Defined by §2704(c)(2) to include ancestors and lineal descendants of the transferor or of the transferor's spouse, siblings of the transferor, spouses of any of these relatives, and the transferor's spouse, and the §2701(e)(3)(A) entity attribution rule also is imposed under §2704(c)(3) for all purposes of determining ownership or transfers of interests.

34. Dealing with liquidation rights, §2704(b) requires control only before the transfer. Although this difference from §2704(a), which requires control both before and after the transfer, was intentional, no indication is given why these provisions should differ.

anyone who is not related to the transferor, to the transferee, or to any member of the family of either, and any restriction imposed by law.[35] However, the Code authorizes promulgation of regulations that will disregard other restrictions for §2704(a) or §2704(b) purposes if consistent with the intent of §2704, which constitutes an open invitation to the Treasury Department to go after unspecified abuses in the future.[36] Treas. Reg. §25.2704-1(e) is reserved for promulgation of such rules under §2704(a)(3). No provision was reserved for the same purpose under §2704(b)(4).

Section 2704(a) "deems" a transfer to occur when a right or a restriction lapses and subjects that deemed transfer to tax. As so viewed, does this rule violate the constitutional mandate that the wealth transfer tax constitute a tax on the *transfer* of property and not be a direct tax on property itself? That is, would a tax on the imputed transfer of value that disappears, rather than a tax on property that passes to another, be a prohibited tax on one of the incidents of the property itself as opposed to a tax on the transfer of the property?[37] To answer this metaphysical question, ask yourself: where did the $26,555,020 of value "go" when Harrison died — was it destroyed, did it go to the two sons, was it still in the decedent's partnership interest, or . . . what? Was there a constitutionally taxable transfer of that value?

---

35. I.R.C. §2704(b)(3). Treas. Reg. §25.2704-2(b) defines "related" as found in §267(b), with an exception for any trustee that is a bank.

36. §§2704(a)(3) and 2704(b)(4). For example, if a decedent sold an interest in a corporation or partnership in exchange for a self-canceling installment note, the government might take the position that cancellation of the note at the death of the seller is a §2704(b)(4) "other restriction" that "has the effect of reducing the value of the transferred interest for purposes of [the wealth transfer taxes] but does not ultimately reduce the value of such interest to the transferee."

37. See Eastland, *The Legacy of I.R.C. Section 2036(c): Saving The Closely Held Business After Congress Made "Enterprise" a Dirty Word*, 24 REAL PROP., PROB. & TRUST J. 259 (1989).

Chapter 16

GENERATION-SKIPPING TRANSFER TAX[1]

Part A.   Introduction
Part B.   The Current Generation-Skipping Transfer Tax

PART A.   INTRODUCTION: THE FIRST GENERATION-SKIPPING TRANSFER TAX

1.   *Pre-1976 Tax Avoidance.* Before 1976, §§2033 and 2041 made it possible, and among more wealthy individuals popular, to preserve family fortunes by passing them from generation to generation without incurring federal wealth transfer taxation. The key to this "generation-skipping" technique was to create a trust that provided for a succession of life estates. For example, a trust could "pay the income in equal shares to such of my children as are living from time to time, and after the death of my last living child, to such of my grandchildren as are living from time to time, and after the death of my last living grandchild, to such of my great grandchildren as are living from time to time," and so on, until expiration of the permissible period of the Rule Against Perpetuities. Such a trust would avoid the estate tax at the death of each younger generation. So would a trust that permitted the trustee to "distribute so much or all of the trust income and principal to any one or more of my descendants as may be living from time to time as the trustee deems appropriate in its sole discretion for the health, education (including postgraduate), maintenance and support in reasonable comfort . . ." of those descendants.

In addition to granting income interests and the right to receive principal in the discretion of an independent trustee, the trust could give the beneficiaries in each generation powers to withdraw up to $5,000 or 5% of the trust principal each year, powers to withdraw principal pursuant to an ascertainable standard, or both. The trust also could give the beneficiaries nongeneral inter vivos or testamentary powers to appoint the trust assets

---

1.   The "generation-skipping transfer tax" is sometimes referred to in this book and elsewhere as the "generation-skipping tax," the "GST," or the "GSTT."

outright or in further trust, permitting them to redirect the trust property within a designated class of appointees that, as we saw in Chapter 3, could include anyone in the world except the powerholder, his or her estate, or creditors of either. Beneficiaries could even serve as trustee of the trust, if their powers properly were limited to avoid characterization as a general power of appointment. In sum, such a generation-skipping trust could give beneficiaries in each generation considerable rights and powers, without causing any change in the tax minimization or tax avoidance possibilities of the trust.

As each beneficiary (child, grandchild, great grandchild and so forth) died, no part of the trust property would be includible in the beneficiary's estate for federal estate tax purposes because no beneficiary possessed more than a life income interest that terminated at death and nontaxable powers of appointment. Thus, after the transferor's[2] payment of gift or estate tax when the trust was created, no additional wealth transfer tax would be imposed on the successive economic enjoyment of the trust property by one generation after another. Instead, the transfer tax would be avoided or "skipped" by successive generations of beneficiaries who nevertheless enjoyed substantial benefits from the property.

In the ever increasing number of states that have modified their laws to permit various forms of perpetual trusts,[3] generation-skipping trusts may be created for successive generations to last forever. In more traditional states, it still is possible for a generation-skipping trust to continue for a century or longer through the use of a carefully drafted perpetuities saving clause.[4] In effect then, before enactment of the generation-skipping transfer tax, trust property, having been taxed at the time the trust was established, could be removed from the transfer tax rolls until it passed into the outright ownership of beneficiaries when the trust terminated. Indeed, the property would not actually be taxed until those beneficiaries died or made inter vivos gifts.

Because a principal purpose of the wealth transfer tax system is to impose a cost on intergenerational transfers (albeit the tax is not limited to just those transfers), the use of these devices to avoid the tax for entire generations (i.e., to skip a generation) was especially distasteful to critics of the system. See, e.g., Bittker, *Recommendations for Revision of Federal*

---

2.   Because the generation-skipping transfer tax refers to the "transferor" who creates a generation-skipping trust, this chapter uses that term, which is synonymous with "grantor" or "settlor."

3.   See Bloom, *The GST Tax Tail Is Killing The Rule Against Perpetuities*, 87 TAX NOTES 569, 572 n.24 (2000); 2 Casner & Pennell, ESTATE PLANNING §11.2 n.3 (2002), which lists at last count 16 states that have modified their version of the Rule.

4.   For example: "This trust shall terminate 21 years after the death of the last to die of all of the descendants of my parents who were alive on the date this trust was established. Upon termination, the trust principal shall be distributed per stirpes to my then living descendants."

Estate and Gift Taxes, in Joint Committee on the Economic Report, 84th Cong., 1st Sess., Federal Tax Policy for Economic Growth and Stability 864, 870 (Joint Committee Print 1955). By one estimate, prior to 1976 the duPont family, through the use of dynastic trusts and other sophisticated planning arrangements, lost only 5% of its aggregate wealth to the transfer tax system since its inception. G. Cooper, *A Voluntary Tax? New Perspectives on Sophisticated Estate Tax Avoidance*, 77 COLUM. L. REV. 161 (1977). All of this finally prompted Professor A. James Casner to testify in 1976 regarding the proposed generation-skipping transfer tax: "We haven't got an estate tax; what we have, you pay an estate tax if you want to; if you don't want to, you don't have to." Estate and Gift Taxes: Hearings Before the House Ways and Means Committee, 94th Cong., 2d Sess., part 2, 1335 (1976).

In 1976, Congress decided to halt this abuse. It concluded that such dispositions frustrated the policies and purposes of the wealth transfer tax system because the estate tax fell on most families every generation while wealthier families, who received proper advice and had enough property to employ the requisite devices, incurred wealth transfer taxes only after several generations of beneficiaries had enjoyed and controlled the family wealth. According to Congress, this perceived gap in the coverage of the transfer taxes had to be plugged to make the system work properly.

2.   *The 1976 Generation-Skipping Transfer Tax.* The first generation-skipping transfer tax was enacted as part of the Tax Reform Act of 1976. The objective of the tax was to assess dispositions that provided economic benefits to several generations of beneficiaries. See H.R. Rep. No. 1380, 94th Cong., 2d Sess. 46-48 (1976). Thus, the 1976 tax applied only to generation-skipping trusts (and "trust equivalents" such as legal life estates, annuities, or insurance settlement options):[5] trusts (or comparable transfers) that had younger generation beneficiaries assigned to more than one generation below the transferor. The classic example would be a trust for the benefit of the transferor's child for life, remainder to the child's descendants. The 1976 Act did not, however, tax so-called "direct skips": gifts or trusts that entirely omitted or skipped a generation. For example, a bequest to or in trust for the benefit of a grandchild, entirely omitting the grandchild's parents, was not subject to the 1976 tax because the omitted generation had not enjoyed the property. In addition, the 1976 tax allowed a "grandchild exclusion" of $250,000 per child of the transferor; this provision allowed tax-free generation-skips ultimately benefiting the transferor's grandchildren.

---

5. For convenience throughout this chapter, only generation-skipping trusts are mentioned, with the understanding that the term also includes trust equivalents. See page 992.

The 1976 tax was imposed only when and if a generation-skipping transfer occurred and was designed to approximate the gift or estate tax that would have been imposed if the property had been given to the first level of younger generation beneficiaries (called the "deemed transferors") and then transferred by them to more remote generation beneficiaries. Thus, the marginal estate or gift tax bracket of each deemed transferor was used to determine the amount of tax.

The tax itself was imposed only on "taxable distributions" and "taxable terminations." A *taxable distribution* was any distribution out of the principal of a generation-skipping trust to a beneficiary assigned to a generation lower than that of some other younger generation beneficiary of the trust. Thus, in a discretionary trust for the settlor's descendants, a distribution of trust principal to a grandchild or more remote descendant would be a taxable distribution. Distributions of income were not taxed. A *taxable termination* was the termination of an interest or power of a younger generation beneficiary who was assigned to a generation higher than the generation assignment of any other younger generation beneficiary. Thus, in a trust for the transferor's descendants, a taxable termination would occur on the death of the last child to die, again on the death of the last grandchild to die, and so forth, the notion being that at each event enjoyment of the property at a given generation had finally ceased and the property had "moved down" another step on the generational ladder.

Finally (and this, like the rest of this overview, is only a very brief explanation of a far more complex tax), a "beneficiary" was any person with a present or future right to receive distributions from the trust, either absolutely or in the trustee's discretion. Contrary to property law, even a remote possibility of receiving a distribution was treated as an interest. Subject to some complicated exceptions, the term "beneficiary" also included any person who held a "power" to control beneficial enjoyment. Thus, a trustee who held a discretionary distribution power could be a beneficiary for generation-skipping transfer tax purposes, as could the holder of a nongeneral power of appointment. The rules governing who had an interest or a power, whether it was a present or future interest or power, and when the interest or power terminated in a manner that triggered the generation-skipping transfer tax were so complicated that they made the Rule Against Perpetuities look like child's play.

Eventually everyone — tax professionals, the Treasury Department, and Congress — agreed that the 1976 version of the generation-skipping transfer tax was a failure, for a number of reasons. The statutory scheme was extremely complicated, making it difficult to understand and causing additional planning costs that were borne by taxpayers and the government alike. Collection of the tax was postponed by Congress in a series of steps over several years to enable professionals and taxpayers to become familiar with its provisions and the government never trained its personnel to enforce this tax. After the last of those extensions expired, the tax was technically applicable for a period of time but compliance was virtually nonexistent and there was zero enforcement. The only final regulations that were promulgated dealt with the effective date provisions and tax return filing requirements but other regulations, proposed in 1981, were extensively criticized and never became final. Eventually the 1976 tax was repealed retroactively. Graphically underscoring how ineffective the 1976 tax had been, all taxes due thereunder were abated and any tax that had been paid was refundable, even if the statute of limitation had run out in the government's favor.

The 1976 tax taught Congress many valuable lessons. For example, the scope of the 1976 tax was overbroad because of the expansive definition of interests subject to the tax. This made the 1976 version applicable to transfers (including custodial accounts under the Uniform Gifts to Minors Act) regardless of size. Thus, every trust, no matter how small, that had beneficiaries in two or more generations below the transferor was subject to Chapter 13. Trusts of this variety are often found in even the most simple wills. Moreover, because the tax could be imposed if a person held a "power" over property, injudicious selection of a trustee or custodian or the grant of overly broad fiduciary powers could inadvertently invoke the tax. The tax also proved to be administratively unworkable because determination of the amount of tax was based on the marginal estate or gift tax bracket of the "deemed transferor." With the increased unified credit introduced in 1981 many "deemed transferors" did not file estate or gift tax returns, but taxpayers and the government were still required to ascertain estate and gift tax information for these individuals.

More importantly, the 1976 tax could be avoided, minimized, or deferred through sophisticated planning techniques that, as a practical matter, were available only to the truly wealthy who had sufficient wealth and expert advice to implement certain schemes.[6] Thus, the tax fell disproportionately on middle and upper-middle class taxpayers. Further, the tax was severely cost-ineffective. Projected revenues from the tax were modest, far out of line with compliance and enforcement costs to both taxpayers and the government.

---

6. For example, rather than creating a trust to pay the income to the transferor's children for life, remainder in corpus to the transferor's grandchildren (which would cause a taxable termination to occur on the death of the last child), a transferor could transfer an amount equal to the actuarial value of the income interest to the children (or buy a straight life annuity for the children in that amount) and transfer an amount equal to the actuarial value of the remainder interest to the grandchildren (or put that amount into an accumulation trust — a trust that would accumulate the income during the children's lives and pay the corpus plus accumulated income to the grandchildren on the death of the last living child).

PART B.   THE CURRENT GENERATION-SKIPPING TRANSFER TAX

Code References: *Generation-Skipping Transfer Tax: §§2601-2663. Really, read the Code, Chapter 13, "cover to cover." Indeed, if you can spare the time, do it twice: it will make much better sense the second time.*

3.   *Overview.* In 1986 Congress attempted to correct major deficiencies in the 1976 tax while simplifying the law through several fundamental changes. First and foremost, every taxpayer is granted an exemption (the "GST exemption") from the tax that can be applied to transfers during life or at death. This began at $1 million, was indexed for inflation and went to $1.1 million in 2002, and is linked with the applicable exclusion amount for years after 2003. A married couple may transfer community property or can elect to treat one spouse's transfer as made half by each spouse (along the lines of the consent to split gifts under §2513), in effect giving married couples double the amount of GST exemption. In addition to being more generous in most cases than the grandchild exclusion that it replaced, the GST exemption is far easier to understand and to apply. This exemption alone insulates most estate plans from Chapter 13, the way the applicable exclusion amount insulates most estates from estate tax. However, as we will learn, it does so in a very different manner.

As a result, a caution is in order. At first blush this GST exemption might suggest that only the truly wealthy and their counselors must be concerned about the generation-skipping transfer tax. Unfortunately even smaller estates (as to which the estate and gift taxes are not a problem and as to which the generation-skipping transfer tax *should* be no problem), will require competent planning properly to allocate and utilize the exemption. Planners must guarantee that generation-skipping transfers that could be protected by the exemption are made exempt under the not-always-simple allocation rules. Moreover, generation-skipping promises to become more popular than ever, now that attention has been drawn to the subject and now that the tax excepts smaller estates from its reach. Ironically, the GST exemption may encourage the creation of more trusts designed to run for the full period of the Rule Against Perpetuities or to move assets to one of the states having no Rule Against Perpetuities. Thus, *all* estate planners, not just those who represent clients with estates of more than the GST exemption amount (or married couples with more than double that amount), must at least understand the basics of the generation-skipping transfer tax.

Adding to the list of beneficial changes made in 1986, Congress also provided that certain transfers qualifying for the gift tax annual exclusion are excluded for generation-skipping transfer tax purposes. See §2642(c). For married couples, this can amount to an annual generation-skipping transfer tax exclusion for transfers of up to double the annual exclusion amount per donee if the gifts are split or if community property is involved. Thus, if properly planned, a §2503(c) qualified minor's trust for a grandchild, funded exclusively by annual exclusion gifts, can be made wholly exempt from the generation-skipping transfer tax, regardless of how many annual exclusion gifts are made into that trust. However, the operation of this provision to transfers made in trust is subject to several restrictions that are discussed at page 1008. The annual exclusion is discussed in detail in Chapter 14.

A third change makes the tax far more simple than the 1976 version, although it made the impact of the tax more onerous when the tax first was adopted. Instead of tying the tax rate to the marginal tax bracket of the deemed transferor as was employed by the 1976 tax, a flat tax rate equal to the maximum federal estate tax rate in effect at the time of the transfer was imposed on nonexempt transfers. Thus, the generation-skipping transfer tax rate was a flat 55% when adopted, which impressed many commentators and clients as too high. That rate is slated to drop to 45% according to the 2001 legislation, still applicable at the time of this writing, and the estate tax is slated to become a flat tax in 2006 when the applicable exclusion amount and maximum tax rate threshold reach equilibrium at the 45% bracket. Thus, a prior draconian impact of the GST on any transfer that is subject to the tax will become the norm. Meanwhile, the flat tax eliminates administrative problems raised by the deemed transferor concept of the prior law.

A fourth change applies the generation-skipping transfer tax to direct skip transfers (such as an outright gift or bequest to a grandchild or a trust for the benefit of the transferor's grandchildren). The tax on direct skips is subject to the annual exclusion and GST exemption exceptions discussed above.[7] The direct skip tax reflects a very different philosophy about the objectives of a generation-skipping transfer tax. The purpose of the 1976 tax was to prevent transfer tax avoidance through the creation of successive life estates over several generations. The objective in 1976 was to impose a tax at any generation that enjoyed economic benefits. The decision in 1986 to tax direct skips represented a fundamental theoretical shift. Congress believed that it was improper to permit direct skipping transfers to avoid the generation-skipping transfer tax,

that the purpose of the three transfer taxes (gift, estate, and generation-skipping) is not only to raise revenue, but also to do so in a manner that has as nearly as possible a uniform effect. This

---

7. Prior to 1990, qualified direct skip transfers also were entitled to a $2 million-per-grandchild exclusion. TRA'86 §1433(b)(3). If spouses were involved, this was a $4 million-per-grandchild exclusion. This remarkable benefit for direct skips, known as the "Gallo amendment," was severely restricted by technical qualification requirements and does not apply to transfers made after 1989.

policy is best served when transfer tax consequences do not vary widely depending on whether property is transferred outright to immediately succeeding generations or is transferred in ways that skip generations.

H.R. Rep. No. 426, 99th Cong., 1st Sess. 824 (1985). As expressed by one commentator, avoidance of tax on direct skipping gifts was available only to the wealthy because only their children could afford not to receive the transferor's wealth, and "[t]his discrimination in favor of the wealthy should not be perpetuated under an enlightened transfer tax system." Bloom, *The Generation-skipping Loophole: Narrowed, But Not Closed, By The Tax Reform Act of 1976*, 53 WASH. L. REV. 31, 34-35 (1977).

The 1986 revision also deleted the income exclusion of the 1976 tax. Now distributions of both income and principal can trigger the tax. But the definition of "beneficiary" was narrowed to exclude persons with only future interests or persons who hold only powers over the beneficial enjoyment of trust property. The current version of Chapter 13 does not use the term "beneficiary." Instead, the statute refers to "interests" in trust property or in a trust. See, e.g., §§2612(a), 2613(a)(2), 2652(c). Presumably, Congress chose to use the term "interest" to avoid the confusion that using "beneficiary" would cause, because the usual meaning of "beneficiary" is broader than the restricted concept employed for generation-skipping transfer tax purposes. Under the current version of the tax, only persons with present interests in income or principal or persons with presently exercisable general powers of appointment meet the "interest" definition. Consequently, most trustees and holders of only nongeneral powers of appointment (including discretionary powers to distribute income or principal to others) do not have an "interest" for generation-skipping transfer tax purposes.

On balance, the 1986 changes simplified the operation and administration of the generation-skipping transfer tax and the GST exemption has the potential to take most individuals outside the system entirely.

4. *Operation of the Tax.* The key to understanding the generation-skipping transfer tax is to keep in mind the object of the tax and the abuses it is meant to prevent: enjoyment of property followed by its movement down the generational "ladder," or a direct skip, in either case without incurring estate or gift tax. All of Chapter 13 of the Code is related in some way to these objectives. Thus, for example, to invoke the tax, there must be either: (1) a nonexempt "direct skip" or (2) a trust with a so-called "skip person" as beneficiary. Under §2612(c), a direct skip is defined as any transfer of an interest in property to a "skip person" that is also subject to estate or gift tax. As defined in §2613(a)(1), a "skip person" is any natural person who is assigned to a generation more than one below the transferor's generation. A "skip person" also can be a trust if either: (1) all interests in the trust are held by skip persons (i.e. natural persons more than one generation below the transferor's generation and trusts meeting this definition), or (2) no person has an interest in the trust and no distribution can ever be made from the trust to a non-skip person. To understand these simple rules, two concepts must be discussed: what is an "interest" and how are generations assigned? Looking at the latter first will help.

Generation Assignments. A skip person is defined in §2613(a) as a natural person assigned to a generation more than one below the transferor. By §2613(a)(2), a trust (as a legal entity) also can be a skip person, if either (1) all present interests in the trust are held by skip persons, or (2) no present interest is held by *any* person and no distribution may be made to a "non-skip" person at any future time. For these purposes, a charity is defined by §2651(e)(3) as a non-skip person. Otherwise, an individual is defined as a non-skip person if he or she is — guess what? — "any person who is not a skip person." §2613(b).

Individuals are assigned to generations under §2651 in one of three ways, depending on the individual's relation to the transferor. First, all lineal descendants of the transferor's grandparents ("relatives" of the transferor) are assigned to generations on the basis of consanguinity. For purposes of this rule, relatives by adoption or by the half blood are treated as natural relatives by the whole blood. For example, a child is in the first generation below the transferor, an adopted grandchild is in the second generation below the transferor, the transferor's siblings are in the transferor's own generation, a nephew or niece by the half blood (a half sibling's child) is in the first generation, and a cousin twice removed is in the second generation, all as illustrated in the chart at page 990.

Second, any person who was at any time married to any lineal descendant of the transferor's grandparents (including the transferor's own spouse or any former spouse) automatically is assigned to the lineal descendant's generation, regardless of the spouse's age. Thus, for example, a child's spouse is assigned to the first generation below the transferor, even if young enough to be the transferor's grandchild, and even if subsequently divorced from the child. Moreover, the consanguinity rules apply to relatives of the transferor's spouse (or any former spouse) as if the transferor and the spouse were one person. Thus, for example, a spouse's child by a former marriage would be in the first generation below the transferor, even if the transferor never adopted that child. That child's spouse also would be assigned to the first generation below the transferor. All of the persons included in this second group also are referred to as "relatives" of the transferor.

All other beneficiaries ("non-relatives," being persons who are not related by blood, adoption, or marriage) are assigned on the basis of age. This means that married non-relatives are *not* automatically assigned to the same generation as each other. Beware this trap for the unwary: many students of Chapter 13 improperly assume that spouses always are assigned to the same generation, which is not true if neither spouse is a descendant of either the transferor's grandparents or the grandparents of a spouse or former spouse of the transferor. In assigning generations on the basis of age, the fundamental assumption is that each generation is 25 years in length, and that the transferor is exactly in the middle of his or her generation. Thus, someone within 12½ years above or below the transferor in age is deemed to be in the same generation as the transferor; thereafter, every 25 years is a new generation. So, someone more than 12½ years but not more than 37½ years younger than the transferor is in the first generation below the transferor, while someone more than 37½ years but not more than 62½ years younger than the transferor is in the second generation below the transferor, and so on.

ILLUSTRATION OF GENERATION ASSIGNMENTS
(excludes spouses and relatives of spouses)

Second Level	Grandparent	Grandparent	And So On	Another 25 years
First Level Above: Non-Skip Persons	Parent	Aunt/Uncle	First Cousin Once Removed	Non-Relative 12.5 to 37.5 years older
Transferor's Own Generation	*Transferor and Spouse*	Sibling	Cousin	Non-Relative within 12.5 years older or younger
First Level Below: Non-Skip Persons	Child	Niece or Nephew	First Cousin Once Removed	Non-Relative 12.5 to 37.5 years younger
Second Level Below: *Skip Persons*	Grandchild	Grandniece or Grandnephew	First Cousin Twice Removed	Non-Relative 37.5 to 62.5 years younger
More Skips	Great Grand	Great Grand	And So On	Another 25 years

If a person is assigned to two different generations by virtue of these rules (for example, if the transferor adopts a grandchild as a child, if the transferor's daughter-in-law divorces the transferor's son and marries a grandson of the transferor's second spouse or, in a state that allows it, if the transferor's son marries the transferor's cousin twice removed), the general rule under §2651(f)(1) is that the younger generation assignment governs (making the adopted grandchild, the daughter-in-law, and the son all skip persons and preventing efforts to move up a generation to avoid the tax).

What Constitutes an "Interest." Section 2652(c)(l) provides that a person has an "interest" in a trust if, at the time of the determination, the person has a present right to receive (or is a permissible recipient of) income or principal from the trust, either in the trustee's discretion, as an absolute entitlement, or pursuant to a power of withdrawal.

It does not matter how small an interest is. If the interest exists, the holder will be treated as a skip person (if assigned to an appropriate generation) as to the entire trust or that degradable portion from which the interest may be satisfied. Note, however, that if the interest was "created primarily to postpone or avoid application of the tax," it will be ignored under the abuse avoidance provisions of §2652(c)(2). Although Prop. Treas. Reg. §26.2613-4(c)(3) under the repealed 1976 tax provided that a person also had an interest if distributions to some other beneficiary served to discharge the person's legal obligation to support the distributee, the addition of §2652(c)(3) in 1988 it clear that this is *not* the intent of Congress *unless* the trust was created with the specific objective of making mandatory distributions that would discharge or supplant a person's support obligation. Distributions in a fiduciary's discretion (including the discretion held by a custodian under the Uniform Gift or Transfers to Minors Act) pursuant to a "support" or "maintenance" standard do not rise to the required level of this objective intent. Treas. Reg. §§26.2612-1(e)(2)(i) and -1(f) *Example 15*. This provision is consistent with state law in many jurisdictions, to the effect that distributions from a trust do not normally discharge another person's legal obligation to support the distributee. Moreover, concerns about the scope of this rule can be obviated by including an "Upjohn" clause in generation-skipping trusts, prohibiting distributions that otherwise might be deemed to discharge an obligation to support the distributee. See Pennell, *Estate Planning: Drafting and Tax Considerations In Employing Individual Trustees*, 60 N.C. L. REV. 799, 810-813 (1982), abridged and reprinted in 9 EST. PLAN. 264 (1982), and 2 Casner & Pennell, ESTATE PLANNING §7.1.1.10.1 (1999).

Also unlike prior law, powers to affect beneficial enjoyment no longer constitute "interests." Thus, the identity of the trustee is irrelevant, provided the trustee does not have a general power of appointment that would be regarded as an "interest" due to the extent of the trustee's powers. Also, it is possible to create nongeneral powers of appointment in nonbeneficiaries if desirable for flexibility, again provided the powers are not so broad that they would be treated as general powers of appointment that would be regarded as "interests" under §2652(c). The donee of a nongeneral power does not have an interest, but the objects of the power will have an interest if the power is presently exercisable.

The government has not resolved to answer the question whether a permissible appointee of trust assets under a power of appointment (i.e., an object of the power) is a person with an interest in trust property for generation-skipping trust purposes, nor whether it matters if the power is presently exercisable or testamentary, general or nongeneral. Cf. the now defunct Prop. Treas. Reg. §§26.2613-4(c)(3) and -4(d), promulgated under the 1976 version of the generation-skipping tax. It appears that a general inter vivos power of appointment is an interest in the powerholder for generation-skipping trust purposes. See TRA'86 Bluebook at 1264. The practical import of this treatment relates to deferral of the tax, under rules discussed at page 995.

The current version of Chapter 13 does not use the term "generation-skipping trust," but the term is useful for discussion purposes and as used here means a trust (or trust equivalent) in which a possibility exists that the trust assets will be subject to a generation-skipping tax. Which of the following is *not* a generation-skipping trust?

(1) *T* creates a trust to pay income to *T*'s child for life, remainder to the child's descendants per stirpes.

(2) *T* creates a trust to pay income to *T*'s spouse for life, remainder in equal shares to *T*'s children who survive the spouse.

(3) *T* creates a trust to pay income to *T*'s spouse for life, remainder to *T*'s child, with the trustee having discretion to distribute principal to *T*'s descendants during the spouse's life.

(4) *T* creates a trust to pay income to *T*'s grandchildren until no living grandchild is under the age of 21, at which time principal is to be distributed to the then living grandchildren in equal shares.

The first trust clearly benefits more than one generation below the transferor, the third might benefit a second generation (or lower) in the trustee's discretion, and the fourth begins with skip persons, meaning that a "direct skip" occurs on creation (more about this at page 993). Only the second is not a generation-skipping trust and even it might become subject to the tax if a state law antilapse statute were to apply if a child predeceased the spouse. The survivorship provision ought to prevent that result but state law in some jurisdictions may apply nevertheless.

Trust Equivalents.   Section 2652(b)(1) provides that any reference in Chapter 13 to a "trust" includes generation-skipping "trust equivalents." These are legal arrangements (other than estates) that have the same effect as a trust. Obvious examples may include a legal life estate to child, remainder to grandchild, or a life insurance policy settlement option or an annuity arrangement that benefits a child for life with a refund or secondary annuity to a grandchild.

5.   *Taxable Transfers.*   Having met these initial requisites does not mean a generation-skipping transfer tax will be incurred; it just opens the door to potential application of the tax. To incur a generation-skipping transfer tax, there must be a §2611(a) "generation-skipping transfer," of which there are three types: direct skips, taxable distributions, and taxable terminations.

Direct Skips.   A direct skip is defined in §2612(c) as a transfer that is subject to the estate or gift tax, made directly to or in trust for the benefit of a skip person. All deductions, exclusions (including the gift tax annual exclusion),[8] and credits are ignored in determining whether a transfer is "subject to" the estate or gift tax. Thus, a gift can be a direct skip regardless of whether a gift tax is imposed. Treas. Reg. §26.2652-1(a)(2). See S. Rep. No. 45, 100th Cong, 1st Sess. 376 (1988). A transfer in trust is a direct skip if (1) only skip persons have an "interest" in the trust, or (2) no person has an "interest" in the trust and no distribution can ever be made to a non-skip person. You will recall that the term "interest" has a limited meaning for purposes of the generation-skipping tax provisions. Because of this definition of "direct skips," do you see why some drafters might be tempted to give a charity or other non-skip person an insignificant interest in a trust, and why Congress felt that §2652(c)(2) was necessary to preclude that gaming?

Applying a vision of property moving down the generations, the direct skip tax is imposed even when no interest exists at the first level below the transferor. In essence, the direct skip rule is Congress' way of saying that enjoyment at the non-skip level is not necessary; instead, Congress wants the tax to apply as the property moves past every available generation. Thus, a generation-skipping transfer tax should be paid immediately if the property passes immediately to the second or a more remote generation.[9] A direct skip will incur an estate or gift tax and then an immediate generation-skipping transfer tax as well. It is the functional equivalent of the donor paying the tax and then the donor's child paying tax as the property drops to the grandchild or more remote level.

---

8.   If §2642(c) (discussed at page 1008) also applies there will be no generation-skipping tax if a direct skip is excluded in its entirety from gift tax consequence by the gift tax annual exclusion or the medical and education expense exclusion of §2503(e). If a direct skip only partially is excluded from gift tax by the gift tax annual exclusion, the "inclusion ratio" for the transferred property may reflect that exclusion. Treas. Reg. §26.2642-1(d) *Examples 3, 4.*

9.   Do you see why this analysis, and Congress' rationale, are an uneasy fit if the property is left to a more remote generation, such as the great grandchild level? Skipping both the child and grandchild levels, a true once-per-generation tax would impose the direct skip tax twice, in addition to the estate or gift tax. Probably because such triple taxation would rarely be incurred and, if imposed, would virtually wipe out the subject wealth, Congress chose not to extend the direct skip treatment in this additional respect. See Treas. Reg. §§26.2612-1(a)(1), -1(f) *Example 2.* We will see other examples of "leapfrog" transfers that avoid the once-per-generation appearance of the generation-skipping transfer tax.

By providing a *predeceased ancestor exception*, Congress granted relief from direct skip treatment in one specific type of circumstance in which it is highly unlikely that abusive tax planning was involved in a transferor's decision to skip a generation. For example, assume that a transfer is made to or in trust for the benefit of a grandchild whose parent (the one who was the child of the transferor or of the transferor's spouse) is deceased. The "predeceased ancestor" exception of §2612(c)(2) was changed to §2651(e)(1) in 1997 but in either iteration precludes application of the direct skip tax because it provides that the grandchild is treated as a child (and all lineal descendants of the grandchild similarly are "moved up" a generation). To illustrate, assume the transferor, T, died leaving a will that bequeaths T's residuary estate "to my descendants, by representation." T is survived by two children, A and B, and by grandchild X, the child of T's deceased child C. One third of the residuary estate passes to grandchild X and is not taxed as a direct skip because C was not alive to be "skipped." As the flush language of §2651(e)(1) states, the same exception would apply if the bequest were for a great-grandchild whose two lineal ancestors who are lineal descendants of T are deceased. See also Treas. Reg. §26.2612-1(a)(2).

In the illustration above, if C had survived T but disclaimed all interests under the will, the interest passing to X by reason of the disclaimer would be taxable as a direct skip transfer. C must be deceased in fact and not just under a state law presumption such as Uniform Probate Code §2-801(d) ("the disclaimed interest devolves as if the disclaimant had predeceased the decedent").[10]

Taxable Distributions. A taxable distribution is any distribution from a trust (or from a trust equivalent) to a skip person unless the distribution also qualifies as either a direct skip or a taxable termination. See §2612(b). For example, in a trust for the transferor's descendants, a distribution to a child would not be a taxable distribution because the child is not a skip person. In the same trust, however, a distribution of either income or principal to a grandchild would be a taxable distribution because grandchildren are skip persons. It is just that simple. A wealth transfer tax may be incurred when the trust is created, and again when the property passes to a skip person. The §2651(e)(1) predeceased ancestor exception also applies here but only if the ancestor of the distributee was deceased when the taxable transfer creating the trust was made.

Taxable Terminations. A taxable termination is the termination (by death, passage of time, release or lapse of a general power, or other-

---

10.   Note that §2654(c) refers to §2518 to determine the effect of a qualified disclaimer. Section 2518 does not treat the person making a qualified disclaimer as deceased. Instead, §2518 treats that person as never having received the disclaimed interest.

wise) of any *present* interest in a generation-skipping trust. See §2612(a). In addition to the §2651(e)(1) predeceased ancestor exception, there are three other exceptions to this definition.

"Postponed Termination" Exception

No taxable termination occurs under this exception if "immediately after such termination, a non-skip person has an interest in such property." §2612(a)(1)(A). This "postponed termination" exception serves to defer imposition of the generation-skipping transfer tax until termination of the present interests of all beneficiaries who are non-skip persons. To illustrate, assume T creates a trust to pay income to children for life, remainder (on the death of the last surviving child) to grandchildren in equal shares. T has two children, A and B. A dies first. Although A's death constitutes the termination of A's present interest, this is not a taxable termination because B is a non-skip person and has an interest in the trust. The taxable termination will occur on B's death (unless another non-skip person acquires an interest in the trust, such as by B's exercise of a nongeneral power of appointment). Similarly, in this example, if grandchild X were to die while either A or B were alive, X's death would not be a taxable termination for two reasons: (1) a non-skip person (A or B) still has an interest in the trust, and (2) X's interest was a future interest, not a present interest, making the definition of a taxable termination inapplicable.

"Stopped Moving Down" Exception

Termination of a present interest is not taxable under this exception if "at no time after such termination may a distribution (including distributions on termination) be made from such trust to a skip person." §2612(a)(1)(B). This "no possible distribution to a skip person" exception is consistent with the purpose of the statute, which is to impose a tax only if a generation-skipping transfer actually occurs. No generation-skipping transfer can occur if the property does not move down the generational ladder by passing to a more remote generation. For example, assume in the prior illustration that the trust specifies that the trust property passes to a charity if no grandchild is living when the last child dies. In this event, if the last surviving child outlives all the grandchildren, that child's death — although constituting the termination of a present interest — would not be a taxable event because the property passes to charity, which by definition is a non-skip person. This result illustrates that the primary focus of the generation-skipping transfer tax is not on the child's enjoyment but, instead, on the trust property moving down a generation after the child's interest terminates. This aspect of the tax may make understanding Chapter 13 easier.

Imagine in this last case that the last surviving child and grandchild die together under such circumstances that the order of their deaths cannot be proven (for example, in a car crash). Under the original Uniform Simultaneous Death Act or the terms of the document, the grandchild might be deemed to have predeceased the child and the property would pass to the charity, and no taxable termination would occur. If, however, the child died and the grandchild died shortly thereafter, the generation-skipping transfer tax would be imposed by reason of the child's death and the trust property would be taxed again under the estate tax in the grandchild's estate. For this reason, it is appropriate to insert a provision requiring that remainder beneficiaries survive the income beneficiaries by a specified period (such as 60 days) as a condition to taking.[11] Note also that state law may provide that a person who fails to survive another by a specified time (such as 120 hours) is deemed to have predeceased. See, e.g., Uniform Simultaneous Death Act (Revised 1993). Alternatively, if state law permits a personal representative of a decedent to disclaim an interest that otherwise passes to the decedent, a qualified disclaimer under §2518 would prevent imposition of a tax. See §2654(c).

"Override" Exception

No taxable termination takes place under this exception to the extent that a transfer is subject to estate or gift tax with respect to the trust property at the same time as the termination occurs. Treas. Reg. §26.2612-1(b)(1)(i). To illustrate, T transfers property in trust to pay the income to T for life, remainder to grandchild (GC). On T's death, the trust property will be included in T's gross estate and subjected to estate tax by §2036(a)(1). T's death also will terminate T's interest in the trust but it is not a taxable termination because this event is subject to estate taxation. However, the distribution of the trust property to GC will constitute a direct skip if T's child who is the parent of GC is then living. If T's child is not then living the §2651(e)(1) predeceased ancestor exception is applicable.

Note that the same consequence as above would occur upon the death of S (the spouse of T) if the trust that T created had provided S with income for life and with a general testamentary power of appointment at death, if S exercised that power by a will appointing the trust property to grandchild, GC. The property would then be included in S's gross estate (because of the general power of appointment) and S's death would not constitute a taxable termination. However, distribution of the trust assets to GC could constitute a direct skip, if the child of S who was GC's parent was then living. Note

---

11. Although Treas. Reg. §26.2612-1(f) *Example 10* speaks of a simultaneous termination of interests, it is not helpful in this context and no other provision is on point. Chapter 13 contains no counterpart to the §2013 estate tax credit for previously taxed property. Do you see why, if it did, simultaneous or near-simultaneous deaths would not be a problem?

that *S* will be treated as the transferor of the direct skip, because the property was subjected to estate tax in *S*'s estate. See Treas. Reg. §§26.2652-1(a)(1), -1(a)(2), -1(a)(5) *Example 5.*

Overlaps

No distribution or transfer of property can satisfy the definitions of both a taxable termination and a direct skip. One of the requirements of a direct skip is that the transfer be subject to estate or gift taxation. But a transfer subject to estate or gift taxation cannot be a taxable termination because of the override exception. Consequently, a distribution or transfer that constitutes a direct skip cannot cause a taxable termination, even if the interest of a higher generation beneficiary is terminated thereby.

Either a taxable termination or a direct skip can, however, also satisfy the definition of a taxable distribution, in which case §2612(b) provides that the direct skip or taxable termination classification governs. For example, assume *T* created a trust to pay income to child for life, remainder to grandchildren and, during child's life, the trustee has a discretionary power to distribute income or principal to grandchildren. A distribution of principal to a grandchild during the child's life would be a taxable distribution. It also would extinguish the child's income interest in that portion of the trust. Under Treas. Reg. §26.2612-1(f) *Example 9*, the classification as a taxable termination would prevail if the distribution causes a complete termination of the child's interest because the entire corpus is distributed. By contrast, a distribution of trust income or of less than all the corpus to a grandchild would not extinguish all of the child's interest in the trust and would not be a taxable termination. Treas. Reg. §26.2612-1(f) *Example 12*. Thus, the taxable distribution rule would apply in the latter circumstance.

By these collective rules, the Code (as embellished by the regulations) establishes a priority for treatment of transfers that meet more than one of the taxable event definitions: first direct skips, then taxable terminations, and finally taxable distributions. These ordering rules can have consequences relating to who pays the tax, deferral consequences of a taxable termination as compared to a taxable distribution, and as to the method of computing the tax on direct skips as compared to the method employed for taxable terminations and taxable distributions. These differences are revealed next below.

6.   *Amount and Payment of the Tax.*

Flat Tax Rate.   Antithetical although it is to the historical method of imposing wealth transfer taxes, the generation-skipping transfer tax is based on a flat rate of tax equal to the maximum stated estate tax rate. See §2641(a)(1). Abandonment of a progressive tax represents a significant departure from the preferred method of taxation that typically is employed throughout the federal tax system. The flat-rate mechanism is designed to make the tax administratively workable, and it simplifies operation of the tax. At the rate imposed, however, the generation-skipping transfer tax reaches nearly confiscatory levels if it is incurred when the same property is subjected to gift or estate taxation (as in the case of a direct skip) or to income taxation (as in the case of a taxable distribution of trust income).

Congress' policy in adopting the flat rate was that the generation-skipping transfer tax should approximate the tax that would be paid if the property were left outright to beneficiaries in the first generation below the transferor, who then left the property outright to beneficiaries in the next generation, and so on. An additional premise of this statutory scheme is that the last dollar in the estates of the beneficiaries in each intervening generation would have been taxable at the highest marginal estate tax bracket. This is not necessarily true, but with the estate tax effectively becoming a flat tax through reduction in the highest marginal rate and increase in the applicable exclusion amount, today the historical legitimacy of the 1986 GST and these assumptions is of little significance. Note, however, that generation-skipping planning may not have been employed, as Congress assumed, for tax minimization or avoidance purposes. For example, a generation-skipping trust might have been used because a beneficiary is a profligate and would squander any money received outright, or because that beneficiary has special needs.

Planning.   A clear planning alternative must be considered in all cases. Always keeping in mind that the non-tax objectives of the client are paramount, it may be less costly to expose property to estate or gift tax at a lower generation level than it is to skip that generation. Because of the Treas. Reg. §26.2612-1(b)(1)(i) estate or gift tax override to the taxable termination rule, it is worth considering whether sheltering a beneficiary's generation-skipping exemption or exposing enough property to estate or gift tax to utilize the beneficiary's unified credit would be more appropriate than incurring the flat-rate generation-skipping transfer tax.

Opting for estate or gift taxation rather than for generation-skipping transfer taxation is not always desirable, however. For example, combined federal *and state* estate or gift taxes may exceed the generation-skipping transfer tax if the applicable state does not impose a generation-skipping transfer tax in excess of the allowable §2604 credit but does impose a gift tax or estate tax.

Moreover, some planning is available for generation-skipping transfer tax purposes that is not possible under either the estate or gift taxes. One example of this is the ability to defer the generation-skipping transfer tax under the provisions of §2612(a)(1). Thus, in a trust for child for life, remainder to grandchild, child could appoint the property to child's sibling or surviving spouse for life, deferring the generation-skipping transfer tax until the death of the sibling or spouse. Another illustration is the opportunity of a younger generation beneficiary to "layer" property to a more remote generation beneficiary through exercise of a nongeneral power of appointment. If the trust property were includible in the beneficiary's estate, such layering would be subject to the direct skip tax, yielding a double tax. This form of planning can escape the second tax if made within the generation-skipping transfer tax system. For example, in a trust for child for life, remainder to child's descendants as the child shall appoint by a nongeneral testamentary power of appointment, child could appoint the trust property to child's grandchild (transferor's great-grandchild) without incurring an additional tax at the intervening generation and still avoid the direct skip tax. Thus, only the generation-skipping transfer tax at child's death would apply, rather than an estate tax and then an immediate direct skip tax. Neither the deferral nor layering planning opportunities would be available if the trust property were subject to estate or gift tax in the child's hands.

Also working against a plan that subjects trust property to estate or gift tax to avoid generation-skipping transfer tax is the fact that some property may escape both systems of taxation under proper circumstances. For example, assume a trust for child for life, remainder to child's descendants, if any, otherwise to child's siblings if child dies without descendants. If the property passes to the siblings, it will pass to them free of generation-skipping transfer tax because they are non-skip persons, and will pass free of estate tax if the child was given no inclusion-causing interest or power. In this situation, it would be foolish to cause the trust property to incur estate or gift tax as the child's property. Thus, estate plans must be drafted to provide sufficient flexibility to determine which system of tax will be most favorable, by providing an opportunity to subject trust property to either the generation-skipping transfer tax or the estate or gift tax, as appears best when the choice must be made.

Amount Subject to the Tax.   Under §2621, the amount subject to tax in the case of a taxable distribution is the amount received by the distributee.[12] Because the tax on a taxable distribution is imposed by §2603 on the distributee, this system of tax (like the estate tax) is known as a "tax-inclusive" system because dollars that the distributee uses to pay the tax are themselves subject to the tax: they are included in the tax base. For example, if the transfer were $1 million and no exemption were applicable, at a tax rate of, say, 50% the tax would be $500,000 and the distributee would pay the tax out of the distribution, leaving only $500,000. Moreover, if the trust making the distribution pays the tax on behalf of the distributee out of other trust funds, that payment is regarded as an additional taxable

---

12. This amount may be reduced by any §212(3)-type expenses attributable to compliance with any tax laws triggered by the transfer.

distribution that also is subject to the generation-skipping transfer tax, under §2621(b). Under Treas. Reg. §26.2612-1(c), that added distribution is regarded as made in the same year as the underlying distribution that generated the tax that the trust paid. Do you see why Treasury made this assumption and the computational and procedural problems it avoids? The approach adopted by Treasury creates its own computational problem, but simple application of algebra solves that problem. The algebraic formula to determine the total amount deemed to have been distributed is:

$$\text{Total distribution} = \frac{\text{actual distribution}}{1 - \text{rate of tax}}$$

In a taxable termination, §2622 provides that the full amount with respect to which an interest terminated is the amount subject to tax.[13] Because the tax is paid out of this fund by the trustee (§2603), the result is another tax-inclusive system, with the dollars used to pay the tax again being subject to the tax.

Direct skips receive a different treatment. The GST on a direct skip is paid by the transferor. See §2603(a)(3). Under §2623, the amount subject to tax in a direct skip is the value of the property actually received by the beneficiary. Because the beneficiary does not pay the tax, the tax on a direct skip is cheaper because no rule treats the tax payment (by the transferor in most cases, under §2603(a)(3)) as an additional generation-skipping taxable transfer. Thus, the direct skip (like the gift tax) is a "tax-exclusive" computation. For example, if a transferor left $1 million of property in a direct skipping transfer at death and directed that the direct skip tax be paid out of the residue of the transferor's estate, the direct skip subject to tax would be the $1 million actually received by the beneficiary. If the tax rate is 50%, for example, and if the transferor's estate was obliged by the transferor's tax clause to come up with the additional $500,000 of tax on that $1 million direct skip transfer, that added $500,000 would not be subject to the generation-skipping transfer tax.

In the last example, if the transferor had specified that the legatee should pay the tax on the $1 million bequest (or had allowed §2603(b) to operate, with the same effect), then the direct skip transfer would first be reduced under §2642(a)(2)(B)(ii) by any federal or state estate or other death tax that is paid out of the bequest, and then the generation-skipping transfer tax would be determined on the fair market value of the bequest remaining after payment of the generation-skipping transfer tax. To determine the tax on the amount left after the tax requires the use of the following algebraic formula:

---

13.   This amount may be reduced by any §2053-type expenses of administration.

$$\text{Generation-Skipping Tax } = \text{ rate } \times \frac{\text{fair market value}}{1+ \text{ rate of tax}}$$

For example, if a legatee received a direct skip bequest of $1 million (after payment of any state and federal estate tax), with the generation-skipping transfer tax to be paid from that amount, the generation-skipping transfer tax (assuming a 50% rate) would be $333,333 and the transfer would be $166,666, determined as follows:[14]

$$\text{Generation-Skipping Tax } = .50 \times \frac{\$1,000,000}{1.50}$$

Thus, the amount of the direct skip transfer is the net amount passing to the beneficiary, after payment of all wealth transfer taxes.

The effect of the direct skip tax-exclusive rule is to avoid paying generation-skipping transfer tax on the dollars used to pay the generation-skipping tax, and that is a valuable benefit. Congress chose not to be even more generous than this when it adopted §2515, which provides that, if the donor is alive and, therefore, incurs and must pay the direct skip generation-skipping transfer tax, then the generation-skipping transfer tax imposed on the direct skipping transfer is taxed as an added gift for gift tax purposes if the transferor uses added monies to pay that tax. Thus, the dollars used to pay the GST escape the generation-skipping transfer tax but not the gift tax. In the prior example, if the $1 million direct skip transfer were made during the transferor's life and the transferor came up with the generation-skipping transfer tax rather than paying it from the $1 million gift, the generation-skipping taxable amount would be $1 million and the generation-skipping transfer tax on that amount would be $500,000. The taxable gift would be the aggregate of the $1 million transferred and the $500,000 GST payment (ignoring the annual exclusion and gift splitting, if applicable). Total gift tax would depend on the transferor's marginal gift tax bracket.

No similar rule applies (or is needed) if the donor makes the direct skip transfer at death and the donor's estate pays the generation-skipping tax. Section 2515 essentially is a gift tax "gross-up" rule (subjecting to gift tax the amount of generation-skipping transfer tax that was paid). No similar rule is needed at death because the estate tax is a tax-inclusive method of computation, which effectively imposes a gross-up result without the need for a special provision. That is, the full $1,500,000 in the prior example would be subject to estate tax.

---

14.   An alternative method to determine the tax (if the flat rate is 50%) is to divide fair market value by 3.0. The divisor can be determined under any other rate of tax as:

$$\frac{1+ \text{ rate of tax}}{\text{rate of tax}}$$

Note that requiring the donee to pay the generation-skipping transfer tax on a direct skip gift (a sort of "net gift" generation-skipping transfer) probably will not avoid the gross-up rule of §2515, which applies to generation-skipping taxes "imposed on" the transferor, not just to taxes actually paid by the transferor. What would be the tax consequences of requiring the donee to pay the generation-skipping transfer tax?

To illustrate the relative costs of the various forms of generation-skipping transfer, both inter vivos and at death, consider the following examples, all of which assume that the transferor wishes to accomplish a transfer that will net $1 million to a grandchild after all taxes have been paid. Also assumed is that no exemptions or exclusions are available, that the property will not change in value over the time periods involved, and that the transfer is taxed at a maximum wealth transfer tax rate of 50% for estate and gift tax as well as for generation-skipping transfer tax purposes. Although all these assumptions are unrealistic, they allow a fair comparison of the aggregate effective tax rates imposed on the generation-skipping alternatives illustrated and thereby permit an accurate comparison of alternative methods of making generation-skipping transfers.

First, let's examine the easiest situation: during life the transferor gives $1 million to grandchild as an outright direct skip. The gift tax on the $1 million transfer is $500,000. If the generation-skipping transfer tax is paid by the transferor using other assets, the generation-skipping transfer tax on the same $1 million direct skipping transfer would be an additional $500,000. The $500,000 of generation-skipping transfer tax paid by the transferor then would be subjected to an added gift tax under §2515 in the amount of $250,000. Total taxes incurred on this $1 million outright transfer to the grandchild would be $1,250,000,[15] which is 125% of the amount that the grandchild actually received. The total out of pocket cost would be the $1 million passing to the grandchild, plus the tax for a total of $2,250,000, making this a very expensive transfer.

Second, assume the transferor wishes to create an inter vivos generation-skipping trust to benefit child for life and then distribute $1 million to grandchild after all taxes have been paid. To accomplish this planning would require an inter vivos transfer into the trust of $2 million. The gift tax on the $2 million transferred would be $1 million, which the transferor would pay from other funds. Because a generation-skipping transfer tax would be imposed if income were earned and paid to grandchild, such income will be ignored, again to make these comparisons more nearly identical. On termination of the child's interest the generation-skipping transfer tax would be $1 million (assuming that the trust still is worth $2 million). This tax would be paid from the trust assets, leaving $1

---

15.   The same taxes would apply if the transfer were made in trust for the grandchild.

million to be distributed to grandchild. Total taxes incurred to move this $1 million to the grandchild would be $2 million, $750,000 more than if the direct skip transfer were used, and constituting 200% of the amount actually reaching the grandchild. The total out of pocket cost is the $2 million placed in the trust plus $1 million of gift tax for a total outlay of $3 million.[16] And, although $250,000 less tax was paid during the transferor's life, the overall tax increase is $750,000 over the first option.

The *third* alternative assumes the transferor is unwilling to incur *any* tax during life, waiting instead until death to make a direct skipping testamentary bequest of $1 million to grandchild. Here the result is that it will again cost $3 million out of pocket to make this $1 million bequest. Starting with that amount, the estate tax on $3 million would be $1,500,000, leaving $1,500,000. One million dollars of that $1,500,000 could then be transferred to the grandchild, incurring a generation-skipping transfer tax of $500,000, which would exhaust the undistributed funds. Here the total tax cost is the same $2 million as in the second example and the total $3 million out of pocket outlay is the same as in that inter vivos transfer.[17] The advantage over the second alternative, however, is deferral: the same transfer is made without incurring any of the $1 million of gift tax during life, although the opportunity to defer some tax until the child's later death is sacrificed. As between this and the inter vivos direct skip in the first example, however, the question is whether using $1,250,000 during the balance of the transferor's life is worth an added tax of $750,000.

The *fourth* and final alternative is what *most* taxpayers will do: they wait until death and create a trust for child for life, remainder to grandchild, as in the second alternative. If created at the transferor's death, the out of pocket cost would be $4 million to move $1 million to the grandchild level. The estate tax on this $4 million would be $2 million, leaving $2 million in trust for child for life, remainder to grandchild. On the taxable termination represented by child's death, the $2 million trust would incur $1 million of generation-skipping transfer tax, leaving $1 million for grandchild. Here the total tax cost is $3 million, 300% of the amount passing to the grandchild, to work the most "normal" form of disposition

16.   The difference in result here is attributable to the tax-exclusive computation of the generation-skipping transfer tax in the direct skip transfer as contrasted with the tax-inclusive computation of the generation-skipping transfer tax on the taxable termination of the child's interest.

17.   The reason this alternative and the second alternative produce the same tax is that (1) we assumed all taxes were imposed at a 50% rate for estate, gift, and generation-skipping tax purposes, and (2) one tax (here the estate tax) is imposed tax-inclusive while one is imposed tax-exclusive (the direct skip generation-skipping transfer tax). In the second alternative, one tax (the gift tax) was imposed tax-exclusive and one tax (the generation-skipping transfer tax) was imposed tax-inclusive, producing the same net result.

known to estate planners before adoption of the generation-skipping transfer tax.[18]

To summarize these alternatives and their tax cost in chart form:

	Out-of-Pocket Outlay	Gift Tax	§2515 Tax	Estate Tax	Generation-Skipping Tax	Total Tax
First	$2,250,000	$500,000	$250,000	—	$500,000	$1,250,000
Second	3,000,000	1,000,000	—	—	1,000,000	2,000,000
Third	3,000,000	—	—	1,500,000	500,000	2,000,000
Fourth	4,000,000	—	—	2,000,000	1,000,000	3,000,000

As these alternatives illustrate, the decision whether to incur tax at a later time involves a question not only of the time-use value of the taxes deferred but, more importantly, of the different manner of computation involved. The differences in consequences are dramatic. Moreover, use of the deferred tax must be discounted by the generation-skipping transfer tax on income earned in the trust (if it is made subject to the generation-skipping transfer tax by a distribution to the grandchild level as earned, or accumulated and then distributed at the child's death) in addition to normal income taxes on that income earned. Because the results are so dramatic, the choice for planning purposes ought to be relatively clear, but experience shows that the fourth alternative will remain the most common because most clients do not want to incur tax during life and are unwilling to cut children out of the wealth involved by using direct skip transfers.

Valuation. Property is valued at the time of the generation-skipping transfer unless alternate valuation is allowed. In valuing property for purposes of the generation-skipping transfer tax, §2624 adopts general estate and gift tax principles, including an alternate valuation date election if the taxable transfer occurs at and as a result of an individual's death. In addition, if the transfer is a direct skip at the transferor's death, and if the transferor's estate elects either special use valuation or the alternate valuation date or both, that election also applies to the generation-skipping tax valuation.[19]

---

18. Total taxes were highest here because each imposition of tax (both estate tax and generation-skipping transfer tax) was computed tax-inclusive.

19. Although there is no direct generation-skipping transfer tax counterpart to the estate tax three-year rule involving some death-bed transfers, §2624(b) will have the same effect as §2035(d)(3)(B) does on special use valuation in the case of some direct skipping transfers because, "in the case of any direct skip of property which is included in the transferor's gross estate, the value of such property for purposes of this chapter shall be the same as its value for purposes of chapter 11." In addition, §2642(f) creates an "Estate

Source of Payment of the Tax.   Under §2603(a), the tax is paid (and refund claims may be filed) by the distributee in the case of a taxable distribution,[20] the trustee in the case of a taxable termination or a direct skip from a trust, and the transferor in the case of a direct skip not from a trust. Further, §2603(b) provides that, "unless otherwise directed pursuant to the governing instrument *by specific reference to the tax imposed by this chapter*, the tax imposed by this chapter on a generation-skipping transfer shall be charged to the property constituting such transfer."[21] Collectively, these provisions establish an apparently easy rule that the person with the generation-skipping property pays the tax, using that property.

Like most simplifications, however, this statement is not entirely accurate in cases involving direct skips. For example, because the transferor (or the transferor's estate) pays the tax in the case of most direct skips, the picture is drawn of a transfer that triggers the tax, with the transferor withholding enough dollars to pay the tax thereon. Because the tax is computed tax exclusive, however, the transferor effectively makes the direct skip transfer and then comes up with additional monies to pay the tax. So §2603(b) is essentially a fiction in the case of a direct skip because the tax is not actually paid from the taxable property that constituted the transfer.[22]

There are probably two reasons why §2603(b) is drafted as it is. First, if the transferor does not produce the added dollars to pay the direct skip tax, then transferee liability and lien provisions allow the government to proceed against the transferee who received the direct skip property. See §2661. This would produce a result similar to what the statute appears to provide under §2603. Second, the transferor is protected in the case of an inadvertent or unexpected direct skip. For example, assume the transferor gives property to a child who disclaims, causing a direct skip to the child's descendants. If the transferor did not anticipate the generation-skipping transfer tax on this event, §2603(b) would protect the transferor by imposing the tax on the transferred and then disclaimed property. Indeed, in recognition of this disclaimer possibility, some estate planners provide in

---

Tax Inclusion Period" rule that essentially says that property transferred to a trust will be valued for GST exemption allocation purposes when the transferor's exposure to estate tax inclusion under §§2036-2044 ceases. Although this will not directly change the valuation of property for generation-skipping transfer tax purposes, it effectively will prevent the kind of gaming (known as "leveraging" the exemption) that most likely would lead to death bed transfers.

20.   Presumably distributees of undivided interests will have joint and several liability. See Prop. Treas. Reg. §26.2621-1(b)(4), promulgated under prior law, with no counterpart under the current regulations.

21.   Emphasis added. By virtue of the emphasized language, a general tax clause directing payment of "all taxes caused by reason of my death" will not overcome this provision.

22.   This reality is reflected by §2515, which imposes a gift tax on the dollars used by the transferor to pay the direct skip tax, thereby insuring that those dollars do not also escape gift tax liability.

their tax payment provisions that generation-skipping transfer taxes caused by the decedent's death shall be paid from the residue of the decedent's estate, *except* taxes "caused by" such a disclaimer.[23]

In non-direct skip cases, however, §2603(b) merely states what should seem obvious: the trustee who holds the property following a taxable termination, or the distributee who just received a taxable distribution, should use the property to pay the tax imposed under §2603(a). This rule should operate with relatively few problems, although a number of interpretative questions may arise. Consider the following.

(a) What constitutes a sufficiently "specific reference to the tax imposed" by Chapter 13 to overcome §2603(b)? If a general waiver of reimbursement rights will not suffice, what type of provision is likely to be appropriate? Where might you find a suitable analog to answer this question? Consider §§2270A and 2207B.

(b) *D*'s will leaves $2 million to grandchild as a direct skip transfer. *D*'s will provides that the estate and inheritance taxes imposed at *D*'s death are to be paid out of *D*'s residuary estate (so the bequest to the grandchild will not bear any of those taxes). Assume a tax rate of 50% to make matters easy: How much will the grandchild receive, and how much generation-skipping transfer tax will be incurred, if no exemption or exclusion is applicable? Although this math is not so difficult, you may want to apply the algebraic formula found at page 1001 so that it will be familiar to you when the rates are not so easy to apply.

(c) As the income beneficiary of a trust, *T* assigns that income interest to *T*'s grandchild. The assignment of the income interest constitutes both a taxable gift and a direct skip. Is this one of the rare cases in which §2603(a)(2) should apply ("a direct skip from a trust," in which case the trust pays the tax) or should §2603(a)(3) apply (the transferor pays the tax)? Further, does it matter that §2603(b) says, in either case, that the direct skip tax should be paid from "the property constituting such transfer"? How would that be done in a case such as this?

(d) *D* named Grandchild as beneficiary of an insurance policy on *D*'s life. On *D*'s death, the proceeds are included in *D*'s gross estate and are paid to Grandchild, whose parents are living. Is the direct skip represented thereby at *D*'s death "from a trust" for purposes of §2603(a)(2), meaning that the insurer would be treated like a trustee and be primarily liable to pay the generation-skipping transfer tax? And must the tax be paid from the

---

23. This exception would not apply if a bequest were made to a grandchild who disclaimed in favor of a great-grandchild. In that case, the generation-skipping transfer tax would not be caused by the disclaimer: it would have been incurred even if the grandchild had not disclaimed — and presumably the transferor already anticipated and planned for the payment of that tax. An unartfully drafted exception might not properly reflect this distinction.

insurance proceeds due to §2603(b)? See Treas. Reg. §§26.2662-1(c)(2)(iii), -1(c)(2)(v), and Schedule R-1 of Form 706. See also §2652(b)(2).

(e)   Imagine a trust with several beneficiaries and staggered ("peel-off") distributions when each beneficiary reaches a specified age (or dies prior thereto). A generation-skipping transfer taxable termination of each beneficiary's interest in the trust will occur if distribution is due to the death of a lineal descendant of the transferor. How is the tax to be charged to the trust? See §2612(a)(2) and Treas. Reg. §26.2612-1(f) *Example 11*.

7.   *Exceptions to the Tax.*

Estate and Gift Tax Override.   To prevent double taxation when a taxable transfer (other than a direct skip) is also subject to either estate or gift taxation, the generation-skipping transfer tax as originally enacted contained a provision (in §2611(b)(1), which was repealed in 1988) providing that Chapter 13 was superseded by Chapters 11 and 12. Thus, if a beneficiary of a generation-skipping trust were to have a power to withdraw principal in an amount not to exceed 5% of the corpus during any year, the amount subject to withdrawal on death would be includible in the beneficiary's estate under §2041(a)(2) and the balance of the trust would be subject to Chapter 13. Congress repealed this provision only because it thought that codifying this priority was unnecessary, because Congress thought it existed notwithstanding the statutory provision. See Treas. Reg. §26.2612-1(b)(1)(i) and PLR 9123052. The beneficiary becomes the "transferor" to the extent that the property is includible in that person's wealth transfer tax base, but not to the extent the five or five exception protects the beneficiary from estate and gift tax exposure. See Treas. Reg. §26.2652-1(a)(5) *Example 5*.

Second-Time Around.   A similar exception under §2611(b)(2) provides that, if property has been taxed once under the generation-skipping transfer tax at a given generation (or at a lower generation), it will not be taxed at that level again. As an example, imagine a trust for child for life (at death there being a taxable termination), then for grandchild's education and, if child's spouse is still alive after the grandchild's education is complete, then back up to the spouse for life, finally distributing on the spouse's death to the child's descendants. Having been taxed once at the child level, this exception insures against taxing the trust at that level a second time at the death of child's spouse.[24] Section 2612(a)(1)(A) also insures that, when the grandchild's formal education is completed and the

---

24.   As written — "any transfer *to the extent* (A) the property transferred was subject to a prior tax . . ." (emphasis added) — §2611(b)(2) might be construed to protect only the value of the trust as of the prior taxable event, allowing taxation of any appreciation since that time. The regulations do not clarify this issue.

grandchild's interest terminates (at least until death of the spouse), no taxable termination is deemed to occur because the spouse's interest (the spouse is the "non-skip person" referred to in that section) prevents the property from moving down a generation.

Nontaxable Gifts. There are two similar yet quite distinct sections granting relief for nontaxable gifts. Section 2611(b)(1) grants an overall exemption for any transfer *from* a trust that would, if made by an individual, qualify as a gift tax free payment of medical expenses or tuition under §2503(e). Section 2642(c) provides a zero inclusion ratio with respect to *certain* direct skip transfers made outright or *into* a trust that are nontaxable gifts.

Section 2642(c) does not guarantee that nontaxable additions to a qualifying trust will be exempt for *subsequent* generation-skipping transfers of the trust property. For example, assume a transfer is made that is nontaxable because it qualifies for the gift tax annual exclusion and constitutes an addition to a generation-skipping trust that is only one-third exempt (i.e., there is a 2/3 inclusion ratio on generation-skipping transfers of trust assets). If the trust were valued at $100,000, adding $10,000 as a nonreportable gift under §2503(b) would not alter the exempt portion of the trust. Thus, of the now $110,000 held in the trust, only one-third would still be exempt; two-thirds of the $10,000 transfer effectively becomes subject to the generation-skipping transfer tax when a subsequent generation-skipping transfer takes place. That might not be what Congress intended (or what the transferor expected).

In addition, §2642(c) is not very generous. It provides a zero inclusion ratio only for direct skipping transfers and only if the transfer either is outright to a natural person or is into a trust in which a sole beneficiary has exclusive enjoyment of the trust *and* the trust will be includible in the estate of that beneficiary if the beneficiary dies before trust termination.[25] If more than one individual enjoys current benefits in the trust, or if estate tax inclusion of the trust in the beneficiary's estate is not guaranteed, these nontaxable direct skipping additions to the trust will not generate a zero inclusion ratio. In most cases, neither requisite will be met, which reduces the value of this exception for day to day planning.

Assume now that Insured created an irrevocable insurance trust in which skip and non-skip persons are each granted powers to withdraw $5,000 by the end of the year. You may remember from Chapter 14 that

---

25. If the beneficiary dies while the trust still exists, the beneficiary's death itself will not trigger a generation-skipping transfer tax. This is because the value of the trust will be included in the beneficiary's gross estate. If the trust assets are to be distributed after the beneficiary's death to a person more than one generation below the beneficiary, the distribution will be a generation-skipping transfer of which the beneficiary is the transferor.

these powers of withdrawal often are called "Crummey powers," named for the case, Crummey v. Commissioner, 397 F.2d 82 (9th Cir. 1968), which held that they qualified contributions to a trust for the gift tax annual exclusion. Crummey powers typically lapse if they are not exercised within a fairly short period of time, such as 30 or 60 days. Lapse of those powers is not a taxable event for gift tax purposes by virtue of §2514(e), but the exception under §2642(c) applies only to transfers that are nontaxable under §2503. What are the generation-skipping transfer tax consequences of contributions to the trust that are nontaxable for gift tax purposes because of the gift tax annual exclusion made applicable by the existence of the Crummey powers, and as to which the lapse of a Crummey power of withdrawal is nontaxable for gift tax purposes? See TAM 8901004 and Treas. Reg. §§26.2612-1(f) *Example 3*, 26.2652-1(a)(5) *Example 5*. The bottom line is that there is no new transferor to the extent of the five or five exception, but it will be good for you to wrestle with the authority and be sure you appreciate where this result "comes from." Would your answer differ if the trust had only a single beneficiary? See §§2642(c)(2) and 2653(a).

Stopped Moving Down.   The exceptions under §§2612(a)(1)(A) and (a)(1)(B) should be considered again here. They preclude taxable termination treatment if the property has stopped moving down the generational ladder (either permanently or just temporarily) if "(A) immediately after such termination, a non-skip person has an interest in such property or (B) at no time after such termination may a distribution (including distributions on termination) be made from such trust to a skip person." To illustrate, consider a trust for a child *C* and a grandchild *G*, with present interests at both generations. If *G* dies, no generation-skipping transfer tax will be incurred because *C*, a non-skip person, has a continuing interest. See §2612(a)(1)(A). If, when *C* later dies, the property does not move down the generational ladder (for example, if the trust goes to *C*'s sibling in this event), §2612(a)(1)(B) would prevent application of the generation-skipping transfer tax. Thus, the only generation-skipping transfer tax incurred in this trust would be on actual distributions made to *G* before death, as to which no exception would apply. This is the right result because only those distributed amounts in fact skipped a generation. The possibility that facts like these might develop illustrates why it would be foolish to draft this trust to be includible in *C*'s estate for estate tax purposes in the thought that this would be a wise way to avoid generation-skipping transfer tax. Here, with respect to property left in the trust at *C*'s death, both estate and generation-skipping transfer taxes could be avoided.

As a second example of these exceptions, consider a "pot" or "group" trust for children for life, with distribution to grandchildren only when the last child dies. Here the death of any but the last child is not a taxable event because every child is a non-skip person and, while any child has an interest in the trust, the exception in §2612(a)(1)(A) will apply. Suppose that, after the last child's death, the trust continued as a group trust for grandchildren until the last grandchild reached a specified age. If a grandchild died before the trust was distributed, the existence of any other living grandchild as a beneficiary would similarly prevent termination of the dying grandchild's interest from being a taxable event.

It is easy to see how the Code provides for this result at the child level, but less easy to see how it provides for the same result at more remote generation levels. The answer is found in §2653(a). Under this provision, the generation assignment of all remaining beneficiaries of a trust is adjusted once a taxable termination occurs. The rule provides that the transferor is deemed to "move down" to "the first generation above the highest generation" assignment of any beneficiary remaining in the trust after the prior termination. It might have been easier to visualize this result had the Code provided that the generation assignment of the highest remaining beneficiaries is moved up to the first level below the transferor, but the result is the same. To illustrate, suppose a trust were to be held for child for life, then for the child's descendants until a certain future event. The child's death will trigger a taxable termination. Immediately following the child's death, the transferor of the trust would be deemed to be at the child generation. By virtue of that change, each grandchild would be deemed to be in the first generation below the transferor. By virtue of being in the first generation below the transferor, the grandchildren would become non-skip persons, meaning that the existence of a present interest in any grandchild would work deferral under §2612(a)(1)(A) upon an otherwise taxable termination (for example, death of another grandchild).

By virtue of the same rules, if a grandchild died while the child in the foregoing example still was alive and still had an interest in the trust, the grandchild's death would not be a taxable termination because a non-skip person (the child) would have a present interest in the trust immediately after termination of the grandchild's interest. Also looking at the foregoing example, there would not be a generation-skipping transfer if the child died but, by virtue of exercising a nongeneral power of appointment, created a following life estate in child's surviving spouse. The spouse's present interest in the trust would generate deferral because the spouse is assigned to the child's generation and is a non-skip person.

Assume that *T* created and funded a trust giving the trustee discretion to make distributions among a child *C*, a grandchild *G*, and a great-grandchild *GG*. This type of trust is often called a "spray trust." *G* died before *C*. Then *C* died. Thereafter, distributions are made to *GG*. Map out the generation-skipping transfer tax consequences of these events, including the estate and gift tax results that may change the transferor, and the respective generation-skipping transfer tax results that flow from those changes. If this property had been given outright to *C* or otherwise was includible in *C*'s estate, how would the tax consequences have differed if, after *C*'s death, the property were to have been held in trust for *GG*? Would it matter whether *GG* is a grandchild of *C*?

You may wish to make a note of the following unresolved question: In applying the §2653(a) new generation assignment rule, what happens if the beneficiaries are assigned to generations on the basis of age? For example, assume the transferor is dead when a trust that was created for friends and their descendants encounters a taxable termination. The surviving beneficiaries are children and grandchildren of the friends, now aged 50, 47, 43, 22, 20, 18, 16, 13 and 9. What is the "new" transferor's age for purposes of determining the "new" generation assignment of these beneficiaries? An early version of GST technical corrections would have amended §2653(a) to assume that the new deemed transferor is 25 years older than the oldest beneficiary. But the final Act did not include this provision. Had it been adopted, the change would have meant that individuals who may have been in the same generation prior to application of this rule (for example, because they were all between 37½ and 62½ years younger than the original transferor) could find themselves in two different generations after application of this rule (for example, the oldest might be 25 years younger than — and therefore be in the first generation below — the new deemed transferor, but another might be 38 years younger and thus in the second generation below the new deemed transferor); thus, some of these originally same-generation beneficiaries might fail to become non-skip persons and would not acquire the benefits that would flow therefrom. This inappropriate result may explain why the provision was dropped from the technical corrections bill, but some rule still is needed.

Think about the advantages and disadvantages of deferral. Consider not only the obvious consequences but also study §§2654(a)(2), 2604(a), and 2624(c).

Finally, put on your tax policy antenna and see how you would react to the following. Assume that you have been asked to comment on the effects of a trust providing that income shall be accumulated for two years, after which (at the trustee's discretion) income and principal may be paid to grandchildren and more remote descendants. In addition, the trust gives at least one grandchild a presently exercisable nongeneral power to appoint to non-skip persons during the two-year accumulation period, but does not allow trust property to be distributed to an appointee until after the two-year accumulation period has expired. The drafter believes that the trust is a non-skip person as defined in §2613(a)(2)(B) during the two-year accumulation period because there is (1) no person with a present interest in the trust and (2) property may be distributed to a non-skip person by virtue of the grandchild's nongeneral power of appointment. Consequently, the drafter believes that the transfer to the trust cannot constitute a direct skip and, therefore, that any generation-skipping transfer tax will be deferred until the trust makes taxable distributions or suffers a taxable termination. Given what you understand about the tax, read the following references and give an opinion on whether this is correct. See §§2654(b)(2) and 2652(c)(2), Treas. Reg. §§26.2612-1(e)(1) and 26.2612-1(e)(2)(ii), and PLR 9109032. Even if the drafter is correct that the original contribution to the trust will not trigger a generation-skipping transfer tax, note that the GST on a subsequent taxable distribution or taxable termination will be greater because the tax on those types of generation-skipping transfers is computed on a tax-inclusive basis while a tax on a direct skip is tax exclusive. This planning requires a balancing of a greater overall tax against the benefits of deferral.

8.   *GST Exemption.*   The final, and most important, exception to the generation-skipping transfer tax is the §2631(a) exemption. Often referred to as the $1 million exemption because it began life at that amount, it indexed for inflation to $1.1 million in 2002 and it further increases in lock stem with future increases to the applicable exclusion amount (for example, it is $1.5 million after 2003, $2.0 million after 2005, etc.) Available to all transferors, the exemption is not as simple — or as direct — as it might be, because it is granted in the form of an "inclusion ratio" that is then tied, under §2641, to the rate of tax for computation purposes. The probable rationale for this approach is that keeping track of a portion of a trust as to which the exemption has been allocated would pose administrative and valuation problems. The "inclusion ratio" approach anticipates those problems by specifying that, once determined, the exempt portion does not change with fluctuations in values or distributions that subsequently occur.[26] By incorporating the exemption into the rate for computing the tax with respect to that particular trust, the exempt portion, once determined, can be "retained" in a manner that allows it to be ignored for all other purposes.

For reasons that shortly will become clear, astute planners avoid this "reduced rate" use of the exemption by crafting trusts that either are fully taxable or fully exempt — with inclusion ratios of either 1 or 0. As a simple example of the operation of the §2642 "inclusion ratio" approach, assume that a transferor wishes to place $3 million in trust, of which the transferor wishes to exempt $1 million. One way to accomplish this would be to have the transferor contribute $3 million to the trust and allocate $1 million of GST exemption to the trust. Note that it is not $1 million that is exempted thereby, but rather a percentage of the trust, the value of which can change over time. If that approach were adopted, the trust can be referred to as a "1/3 exempt trust."

---

26.   It is, however, adjusted under §2653(b)(1) for any subsequent generation-skipping transfer tax that is paid from the trust because of a generation-skipping transfer in which the property is held in trust immediately after the transfer takes place.

Instead, a different way to accomplish the transferor's goal would be to create two trusts, one of $1 million — to be totally exempt — and one of $2 million — to be totally taxable. Section 2654(b) states that "nothing in [Chapter 13] shall be construed as authorizing a single trust to be treated as 2 or more trusts." This means that the trust instrument or state law must grant the authority to divide an existing trust into two funds or must create two trusts initially to accomplish such an allocation. Treas. Reg. §§26.2654-1(a)(3), 26.2654-1(b)(1). Statutes in several states and the RESTATEMENT (THIRD) — PROPERTY (WILLS AND OTHER DONATIVE TRANSFERS) §12.2 (Tent. Draft No. 1, approved by the American Law Institute, May 16, 1995) now authorize the division of a trust into separate trusts. For purposes of this illustration, however, assume that no authority permits division into two funds, and that the transferor initially created a single $3 million trust.

As a consequence, the inclusion ratio would be determined by subtracting an "applicable fraction" from the number 1. The applicable fraction here would be 1/3, determined by taking the exemption amount allocated to the trust ($1 million) as the numerator and the value of the trust[27] ($3 million) as the denominator. The "inclusion ratio" would thus be 2/3 (1 minus 1/3). This fraction would then be multiplied by the rate of tax to determine the applicable rate of tax on all subsequent taxable transfers with respect to trust property. Thus, in this example, if the maximum federal estate tax rate were 50%, the applicable rate for this 1/3 exempt trust would be 33.33% (2/3 times 50%). The result of incorporating the GST exemption into the tax rate is that a subsequent generation-skipping transfer of trust property will not be free of the generation-skipping transfer tax. Instead, a subsequent generation-skipping transfer will incur a tax equal to 2/3 of the maximum federal estate tax rate. In contrast, when the full amount of a trust is covered by the exemption, the applicable fraction is 1/1, producing an inclusion ratio of 0 for multiplication by the applicable federal estate tax rate. There would then be a zero rate of tax on subsequent generation-skipping transfers of trust property.

For a number of reasons, it is advisable to avoid creating trusts that are partially exempt. One advantage of separate trusts is that the GST exemption protects appreciation in value. The totally exempt trust can be invested to maximize growth under the umbrella of the exemption and the totally nonexempt trust can be invested to maximize income for non-skip beneficiaries. A second advantage of separate trusts is flexibility. The fiduciary can be authorized to choose whether to make distributions from the exempt or from the taxable trust, based on the generation assignment of the beneficiary, the time of distribution, the applicable tax rate at that time,

---

27.   After reduction by any taxes recovered at any time from the trust, either on creation, following any transfer of property to the trust, or under §2653(b)(1) following a taxable generation-skipping transfer.

the possibility of further growth in the respective trusts, and so forth. This flexibility is lost if every distribution will be taxable, albeit at a reduced rate. A final advantage of separate trusts is that, under §2654(a)(2), the basis increase provided for generation-skipping taxable transfers will not totally eliminate gain in a partially taxable trust but would if the trust were a separate, totally taxable entity and the transfer occurred at the death of a beneficiary. These reasons are so powerful (and so many planners failed to provide for division of trusts) that Congress in 2001 added §2642(a)(3) to respect retroactive severance of trusts to cure a partially exempt trust exemption allocation. The document or state law still must provide the authority to sever, but the federal rule means it need not be done before exemption is allocated and can be performed to clean up a flawed prior allocation.

Also note that the GST exemption is wasted to the extent an otherwise taxable transfer qualifies for any other exclusion or exception. When the GST exemption allocation must be made, it may be possible but not certain that a generation-skipping transfer will occur at a later date. If so, a decision must be made whether to gamble on the generation-skipping transfer never taking place, or to play it "safe" and allocate a part of the GST exemption and thereby risk wasting that allocation if no generation-skipping transfer does occur. The GST exemption allocation need not always be made when a transferor contributes property to a trust (§2632), and the longer the allocation can be delayed, the more information that will be available to help make that decision.

Some planners have decided that, if either an estate tax or a generation-skipping transfer tax is going to apply, it would be easier to give every younger generation beneficiary a general power of appointment so that the estate tax will apply, and no one need worry about learning or dealing with Chapter 13. This approach could waste the tax-free generation-skip available under the GST exemption and could unnecessarily expose property to estate tax. Although an estate tax is preferable to a generation-skipping transfer tax in some cases, *both* can be avoided with a totally exempt generation-skipping trust.

Allocating the GST Exemption. It is important for planning purposes to recognize that inequities may arise by virtue of allocating the GST exemption. Under §§2631 and 2632, the GST exemption is elective, in the sense that a transferor or the transferor's personal representative may decide how to allocate it (or whether to allocate it at all) among any generation-skipping trusts created. Unfortunately, the procedure for allocating the exemption may result in inequities, as illustrated by the following exemption allocation conundrums.

(a) Assume your client has several children and creates generation-skipping trusts for the benefit of grandchildren and more remote descendants. If one of the transferor's children already is deceased, should the GST exemption be allocated to the other children's shares? What inequity might arise in making such an allocation? Think about the predeceased ancestor exception, and the possibility of multiple future taxable events in the deceased child's share.

(b) Assume that separate trusts are created for children, with one child's trust to continue past that child's death but the others to distribute to the respective child-beneficiary at a certain age. Should the GST exemption be allocated to the one ongoing trust? If so, do you see the potential inequity if another child dies before receiving distribution from that child's share?

(c) How should you anticipate inequalities and provide for the issue in drafting wills and trust instruments for trusts in which a GST might subsequently be incurred? No offense intended, but do you feel smart enough today to provide instructions on this issue? Will that likely change as you mature in the estate planning endeavor? How do you draft for the reality that sometimes it is impossible to be smart enough today to know what the best result might be in the future?

Automatic Allocation. Failure to make an express allocation of the GST exemption results in an allocation being automatically made under §§2632(b), (c), and (e). In each case, the automatic allocation rules consume enough exemption to cause the inclusion ratio to be zero, if possible, with allocation first seriatim to lifetime direct skips, then seriatim to lifetime GST transfers that are *not* direct skips, then pro rata to direct skips at the transferor's death, and finally pro rata among all other generation-skipping transfers.

The automatic allocation rules have two important features. First, some generation-skipping transfers occurring during a transferor's life do not qualify for automatic allocation until the transferor's death and then only if not all of the GST exemption has been previously allocated. Thus, it is not wise to rely on the automatic allocation rules to make desired allocations. Second, in each case, an automatic allocation can be prevented if a better method can be identified (which easily could be true, as the problems above regarding inequities in allocation illustrated). If a transferor makes a direct skip during life that qualifies for an automatic allocation at that time, the allocation will be made unless the transferor elects to prevent it on a timely filed gift tax (and generation-skipping transfer tax) return (Form 709). See Treas. Reg. §26.2632-1(b)(1)(i). Important about all of this is that the GST exemption does not make it possible to ignore the generation-skipping transfer tax in smaller estates unless the estate planner is confident that the automatic allocation rules will produce appropriate results.

Consider also the summary chart at page 1004 that illustrated the consequences of various alternative forms of transfer. If the automatic allocation rules are allowed to apply, the exemption will be wasted on the cheapest transfers a transferor can make, going in order from the top down in that chart. This may be appropriate in some cases, because lifetime direct skips, to which automatic allocation is first made, are the earliest transfers to incur the tax. The choice that must be made is between deferral of tax by allowing the exemption to be used on direct skips during life versus maximizing the exemption by allocation against the more expensive forms of transfer or allocation to those dispositions that will occur the farthest into the future. In this respect, consider that allocation of the exemption against any outright transfer usually is the least beneficial use of it, while allocation to trusts that will last for a long time, to prevent application of the generation-skipping transfer tax on multiple taxable transfers in the future, usually is the most expeditious use of the exemption (all other factors being equal).

Misappropriation of the exemption also can occur in other situations. For example, automatic allocation to a §2056(b)(5) trust that will be includible in the surviving spouse's gross estate at death (meaning that the transferor will change, under the rule in §2652(a)(1)) means that use of the settlor's exemption would be a waste. Similarly, in a bypass trust that grants the surviving spouse a withdrawal power, allocation of exemption could be a waste to the extent lapse of the withdrawal power constitutes a constructive addition as to which the surviving spouse is the transferor. In these respects, Treas. Reg. §26.2632-1(d)(2) contains a curious rule that prevents automatic allocation to any trust that will have a new transferor with respect to the *entire* trust before any generation-skipping transfer occurs. Although this is a generous means of preserving a transferor's exemption from useless allocation, the safety net apparently does not apply at all if any part of the trust will not have a new transferor (for example, by virtue of estate tax inclusion) before any generation-skipping taxable transfer occurs with respect to the trust. In addition, anticipating that a disclaimer may alter the generation-skipping landscape and make an automatic allocation useless, the last sentence of Treas. Reg. §26.2632-1(d)(2) provides that no automatic allocation will be made to a trust during the first nine months after the transferor's death if no generation-skipping transfer occurs during that time and, at the end of the nine-month disclaimer period, no future generation-skipping transfers can occur with respect to the trust. Unfortunately, neither rule applies if the exemption is allocated affirmatively (and badly) rather than by the automatic allocation rules.

Time of Allocation. Treas. Reg. §§26.2632-1(a) through -1(c) establish the procedure for allocating or for precluding automatic allocation of the exemption during a transferor's life. Section 26.2632-1(d)(2) relates to automatic allocations at death. In either case, *preventing* the automatic allocation rules from applying may be more important than making an affirmative allocation. Under Treas. Reg. §26.2632-1(b)(1)(i), automatic allocation can be prevented by timely filing a gift tax return stating the extent to which the automatic allocation rule should not apply, or by making payment of generation-skipping tax on the inter vivos transfer, which thereby gives notice of an election out of automatic allocation. Preventing automatic allocation at death requires a timely filed estate tax return.

If the intent is to allocate exemption to an inter vivos transfer, Treas. Reg. §26.2632-1(b)(2) specifies that exemption may be allocated during life by filing a gift tax return at any time (although valuation will be different for an allocation on a late-filed return). Now two returns may be required: one to prevent automatic allocation and another if subsequently it is desired to make an affirmative allocation. What is the logic of requiring a return *preventing* an automatic allocation to be timely-filed (or, if no return is required for a particular transfer, to be filed within the time a return would have been timely if it were required)? See Treas. Reg. §26.2632-1(b)(1)(ii).

Valuation Rules.   Valuation rules for exemption allocation are provided in Treas. Reg. §26.2642-2. Gift tax values control on an automatic inter vivos allocation or on a timely-filed gift tax return that affirmatively allocates exemption. A late allocation to a trust requires use of values on the date of allocation, although the regulation allows the transferor to determine the value of the trust assets as of the first day of the month in which the late allocation is made. This permits use of that value to avoid the administrative inconvenience of having to determine value on the same day the return making the allocation is filed. Notably, this late allocation rule applies only to transfers in trust; no rule appears to address an allocation to outright transfers, perhaps because those would be direct skips as to which the automatic allocation rules are applicable and the regulations did not anticipate the issue.

Particularly interesting is that the deemed first-of-the-month allocation is denied "with respect to life insurance" if the insured has died, to preclude a late allocation in the month in which an insured dies and thereby to preclude allocation at the value of the insurance before death. Ignoring any insurance policy value change from the first day of a month to the date of actual allocation suggests that allocation looks to the value of the trust and not the value of the assets actually contributed to the trust (because the insurance policy would mature at death and trigger the receipt of the proceeds under the scenario sought to be prevented). Does this indicate that this exception "with respect to life insurance" is applicable only to a policy of life insurance and not with respect to property contributed to a trust to be used to pay life insurance premiums? In that regard, compare Treas. Reg. §26.2642-2(c) *Examples 1* and *2*, which refer to the value of the property contributed to the trust, with Treas. Reg. §26.2642-2(c) *Example 3*, which describes the late allocation with reference only to "the value of the trust."

Allocation to Life Insurance.   Allocating the GST exemption to life insurance appears particularly attractive because life insurance is the one asset most people own that is certain to appreciate in value. Because an exempt trust is protected regardless of how large it grows, the issue is whether to use the exemption with respect to a trust that skips generations and holds life insurance. This issue is made all the more significant if the insurance is term coverage that lapses at the end of each year, because it is wasteful to allocate exemption to a policy that will not mature. Because it is seldom possible to predict accurately when an insured will die (at least not in most legal contexts), the question that tantalizes estate planners is whether it is possible to allocate the exemption on a timely filed gift tax return (by April 15 of the year following the premium payment, or August 15 if an extension to file the taxpayer's income tax return is applicable) — when the insured dies during the term — and generate an inclusion ratio of zero with an amount of exemption equal to the amount of the premium paid rather than an amount equal to the proceeds of the policy.

In theory, should this kind of "cheap" allocation be permitted, or does this represent some form of abuse? Along the same line, can exemption be allocated to permanent insurance on a late filed gift tax return so that the value of the trust at that time, rather than the value of the premium payment, will control (the difference being those amounts that are paid in the form of the agent's commission and the company's administrative costs, which reduce the amount of any increase in policy value)? The notion is that, if the insurance matures during the year, exemption would be allocated on a timely-filed gift tax return in an amount equal to the premiums paid for that year, but if the insurance does not mature, allocation of the exemption would be on a late return in an amount equal to any cash surrender value increase attributable to premium payments, thus producing an inclusion ratio of zero with a smaller amount of exemption in most cases.

The unanswered question is whether allocation of the exemption under §2642(b)(3) looks to the dollar amount of the actual premium paid or to the value of that premium payment at the time of the exemption allocation. The Code is not clear on this point and the government might be expected to argue that an abuse is involved if an allocation can be made after seeing that the insurance has already matured.

A curious feature of the Treas. Reg. §26.2642-2 late-allocation valuation rule is that it does not specifically require that the actual property transferred be valued. Instead, it appears that reinvestments between the transfer date and the late allocation date will be reflected in determining the amount of exemption that must be allocated. This is not entirely clear, however, as revealed by a comparison of Treas. Reg. §26.2642-2(c) *Example 1* (which states that "the value of the property transferred to the trust is determined on the date the allocation is filed") with *Example 3* (which refers to "the value of the trust" rather than to the value of the actual property transferred to the trust).

Assuming for the moment that the allocation can be done in a manner that leverages the exemption, is "selective" allocation (other than when the policy has already matured) of the exemption to life insurance as desirable as many people would suggest? "Selective" allocation means an allocation to life insurance when the insured's health suggests that the risk of death is greater than the price payable for the premium compensates. This could occur when the insured is seriously ill, but the insurer is precluded from raising the premium because the policy provides an automatic right of renewal.

Estate Tax Inclusion Period.   The estate tax inclusion period (ETIP) rule of §2642(f) prevents allocating the exemption until the time when estate tax inclusion of transferred property in the transferor's gross estate is no longer possible under §§2036 through 2042 (i.e., at death in most cases).[28] See Treas. Reg. §26.2632-1(c)(2). Do you see why such a rule was thought to be necessary? Under §2642(f)(4), a transferor's spouse is treated as the transferor for purposes of this exemption allocation preclusion "except as provided in regulations." Treas. Reg. §26.2632-1(c)(2)(i)(B) provides that the ETIP rule is applicable if death would cause inclusion of the transferred property in the estate of the spouse.

Funding Exempt Trusts.   A will or trust often contains a "funding" provision. Such a provision specifies how money and assets are to be allocated in satisfaction of a bequest or gift: to a surviving spouse or a marital trust, to a credit shelter bypass trust, to a trust that will be made exempt for generation-skipping transfer tax purposes, or outright to a grandchild or other skip person. For example, if the decedent's will made a bequest to a separate trust of the maximum amount that can be made totally exempt for generation-skipping transfer tax purposes, an amount ultimately will be determined under this formula bequest. At the appropriate time, that amount of money (or that value of property) will be transferred into the trust. The element that is addressed by a funding provision is how that transfer will be made, there being two basic options: a pecuniary bequest (meaning a dollar amount) or a fractional bequest (meaning a portion of the available assets).

In this context, it is necessary briefly to examine a statutory requirement the meaning of which is unsettled. It is clear (and it has been admitted by the government) that the regulations on this issue are imperfect and that they will be revised. Reluctance to delve into this issue in depth is due to it being far more complex than it ought to be. Consequently, let's briefly consider the problem, without discussing the treatment accorded by the regulations, which are ponderous and somewhat impenetrable.

---

28.   Sections 2036 through 2042 require the inclusion in a decedent's gross estate of the value of property (at the estate tax valuation date) that the decedent had transferred during life but in which (or over which) the decedent had retained some prohibited interest or power.

Selection among the available funding alternatives requires consideration of the dictates of §2642(b)(2)(A):

If property is transferred as a result of the death of the transferor, the value of such property [for exemption allocation purposes] shall be its value for purposes of chapter 11; *except that, if the requirements prescribed by the Secretary respecting allocation of post-death changes in value are not met, the value of such property shall be determined as of the time of the distribution concerned.* **[Emphasis added.]**

As explained by its terse legislative history, "[i]t is expected that in appropriate circumstances the Secretary of the Treasury will require that property distributed from the estate be fairly representative of the appreciation or depreciation in the value of all property available for distribution. *Cf.* Rev. Proc. 64-19, 1964-1 C.B. 682." H.R. Rep. No. 795, 100th Cong., 2d Sess. 349 n.87 (1988). It is this "fairly representative" requirement to which we now turn our attention. We saw it previously in the context of marital deduction planning at pages 702-705.

The problem at which this requirement is addressed can arise when the assets of an estate appreciate substantially in value between the time of the decedent's death and the time when the assets are distributed by the decedent's personal representative. If there is a bequest to a generation-skipping trust, it will be desirable to allocate a sufficient amount of GST exemption to that bequest to provide a zero inclusion ratio for the trust and thus to make it fully exempt from the generation-skipping transfer tax. The smaller the amount of GST exemption that needs to be allocated to the trust to accomplish that purpose, the more exemption that is available for other generation-skipping transfers. The estate can simultaneously maximize the amount of its tax-exempt generation-skipping and minimize the amount of GST exemption allocation that exempts the generation-skipping from the tax if a major part or all of the economic benefit of the post-death appreciation of the estate's assets can be allocated to the generation-skipping trust (thereby increasing the dollar value of that trust and therefore the amount that passes to lower generation beneficiaries free of the GST), and if the amount of allocated GST exemption that is needed to have a zero inclusion ratio is based on the value of the bequest at the date of the decedent's death rather than based on its value at the date of distribution.

In determining the applicable fraction for the bequest to the trust, the denominator of the fraction will equal the value of the properties transferred to the trust. See Treas. Reg. §26.2642-1(c)(1). If the value of appreciating properties were the value they had at the time of the decedent's death, the denominator would be smaller than it would be if the value at the time of distribution were used. The smaller the denominator, the less the numerator must be to make an applicable fraction of 1 (so that the inclusion ratio will be zero). The numerator is the amount of GST exemption that has been allocated to the bequest, so valuing the properties at the time of the decedent's death will minimize the amount of GST exemption that must be allocated.

Treas. Reg. §26.2642-2(b)(1) sets forth the general rule that, in determining the denominator of the applicable fraction, the value of property bequeathed to a trust is the estate tax value of that property. If that general rule had no exceptions, then the appreciated properties transferred to an exempt generation-skipping trust in satisfaction of a bequest would be valued at the date of death in determining the denominator of the applicable fraction. The complex regulations seek to avoid abuse of this rule by creating exceptions to it. Several illustrations of how this abuse could arise (absent special regulatory prevention) are noted next below.

Easily the most confused, and confusing, aspect of the regulations is the special valuation rules for exemption allocation in Treas. Reg. §26.2642-2(b) and the related valuation element in the separate trust rules of Treas. Reg. §§26.2654-1(a)(1)(ii) and -1(b)(1). All of these regulations relate to Congress' desire to prevent leveraging of the GST exemption by funding an exempt trust with more than its pro rata share of post-death appreciation of the assets included in the decedent's gross estate and using date of death values to determine the denominator of the applicable fraction. The classic example arises when there is a pecuniary marital deduction bequest, with the residue of the transferor's estate passing into a generation-skipping exempt bypass trust. The economic benefit of any postmortem appreciation of the estate's assets will flow to the residue if the marital bequest requires using date of distribution values and if the personal representative uses highly appreciated property to satisfy the marital bequest.

To illustrate, assume the transferor's estate was valued at $2 million for federal estate tax purposes and contains a pecuniary bequest of $1 million to a marital deduction trust, with the remaining assets of the estate (having a date of death value of the other $1 million) passing to a generation-skipping bypass trust. Further assume that the $2 million grows to $3 million during the several years it takes to administer the estate. If the decedent's will permits the pecuniary bequest to be satisfied by distributing cash, or property "in kind" valued at the date of distribution, or a combination of the two, the amount distributed to the marital trust will be frozen at the $1 million pecuniary figure that was set at the decedent's death. The residue of the estate, now worth $2 million, will pass into the generation-skipping bypass trust. The issue is how much exemption is needed to make the bypass trust totally exempt for generation-skipping transfer tax purposes: $1 million, $2 million, or something in between? The general rule for valuing the denominator of the applicable fraction would use the estate tax value of the property transferred to the trust (probably its date of death value of $1 million). If that amount were the denominator, only $1 million of GST exemption need be allocated to the bequest to exempt the generation-skipping of a $2 million trust. The complex regulatory provisions are aimed at preventing that perceived abuse.

Instead of making a pecuniary bequest to the surviving spouse and leaving the residue to a bypass trust, the arrangement can be reversed. A pecuniary bequest can be made to the generation-skipping bypass trust, and the residue left to a QTIP marital trust. Using the facts employed in the example above, the decedent could leave a $1 million pecuniary bequest to the bypass trust, and leave the residue (having a value of $1 million at the decedent's death) to the QTIP marital trust. If the $1 million pecuniary credit shelter bequest is satisfied at distribution date values and if the marital deduction residue were valued at $2 million at the date of distribution, the issue arises as to how to divide the QTIP marital trust to permit a reverse QTIP election that will exempt the maximum amount. Should the division of the marital trust into separate shares (or trusts) be based on the $1 million estate tax value, the $2 million date of distribution value, or some other amount? Planning strategy for the marital deduction is discussed in Chapter 11.

Caution in Making GST Allocations. There are pitfalls in making a GST exemption allocation. To illustrate, assume an unmarried transferor makes what is thought to be a nontaxable direct skipping annual exclusion transfer into a generation-skipping trust, to be held exclusively for a grandchild, G. The assets of the trust will be included in G's gross estate if G should die before the trust terminates. If the transfer qualifies for the gift tax annual exclusion, the zero inclusion ratio granted by §2642(c) will apply. But if the transfer does not qualify entirely for the gift tax annual exclusion, it will be partially taxable as a gift and, therefore, the inclusion ratio for the trust would not automatically be zero under §2642(c). This might occur because a portion of the annual exclusion might be allocable to another gift made during the same year to G, or because the value of the transferred property may subsequently be determined to be greater than the annual exclusion resulting in an inadvertent gift slightly in excess of the available annual exclusion. According to Treas. Reg. §26.2642-1(d) *Examples 3* and *4*, solely for the purpose of determining the GST on the direct skip (i.e., the transfer to the trust), the transfer is divided into two parts. One part is made up of the amount that qualifies for the gift tax annual exclusion. That part has a zero inclusion ratio. The second part is made up of the balance of the transfer. The inclusion ratio for the second part must be calculated separately after taking into account the amount (if any) of GST exemption that is allocated to the transfer.

For example, if the value of the inadvertent gift were very small — say $10 — and if the donor allocated $10 of the GST exemption to the trust, the applicable fraction for the second part of the transfer would be 10/10 and the inclusion ratio would be 1 minus that fraction, or zero. If, however, the modest gift were overlooked and no allocation were made, the applicable fraction would be 0/10 and the inclusion ratio would be 1 minus that fraction. Because a fraction of 0 over anything (except 0) is 0, the inclusion ratio would be 1 minus 0 or 1, meaning that the second part of the transfer would be subject to the generation-skipping transfer tax.

In most cases, the default allocation rules of §2632 will apply to protect against such a result. But allowing default allocation of the GST exemption to this type of transfer will not always be wise, because §2642(c)(2) requires the trust to be includible in the grandchild's estate to qualify for the zero inclusion ratio. Such a trust does not make maximum use of the exemption, meaning that it might be better to save the exemption for trusts that skip multiple generations over the full permissible period of the Rule Against Perpetuities. In some cases, it will be important to *prevent* allocation of the exemption to the trust under §2632 by filing a Form 709 electing against an automatic allocation of the GST exemption.

The point to be made here is simply that allocating or preventing automatic allocation of the GST exemption can be tricky and will require a good deal of thought, especially in terms of the optimum use of the exemption and whether the default allocation rules of §2632 should be negated. Few planners will want to rely on the default rules if it is possible in advance to determine how best to allocate. And drafters may want to make formula allocations of the GST exemption in the amount needed to zero out the inclusion ratio in appropriate situations. That can be tricky business, however, even with the limited guidance provided by the regulations. Indeed, this formula approach may require the filing of a protective return, to make a protective GST allocation, even if it is thought that §§2503(b) and 2642(c) operate to produce zero taxable results. Perhaps most importantly, it should be clear that estate planners cannot simply ignore the generation-skipping transfer tax in smaller estates with "simple" dispositive patterns.

Inclusion Ratio Statute of Limitation. The inclusion ratio of most generation-skipping trusts is not relevant until there is a taxable transfer. As a result, Treas. Reg. §26.2642-5 provides that the inclusion ratio may be redetermined until the later of (1) the limitation period for assessing the transferor's estate tax and (2) the first generation-skipping transfer tax computed with that inclusion ratio. The valuations used in calculating the inclusion ratio thus may not become final until many decades after a transfer to the trust is made. The government regards this rule as legitimate because it does not want to mess with controversies until they become real and in many trusts that may invoke the GST tax the reality is that no taxable transfer actually will occur, ever. Taxpayers and their advisors regard the delay as harsh because they would prefer to resolve controversies when facts that inform things like valuation and exemption allocation are fresh.

Reverse QTIP Allocation. Section 2652(a)(3) makes it possible to treat a decedent or a donor as the transferor of property to a generation-skipping trust notwithstanding that the decedent or donor's spouse will be regarded for other tax purposes as the owner of the trust property. Recall from Chapter 11 that the favored method of transferring property to a spouse prior to 1982 other than by outright gift was by a trust paying all income annually to the spouse and granting the spouse a general power of appointment. When Congress made the marital deduction an unlimited entitlement in 1981, it also decided that forcing transferors to give their spouses control over most or all of their entire estates was asking too much, so it enacted the QTIP provisions of §2056(b)(7). The marital deduction is allowed to the settlor of a QTIP trust who makes an appropriate election with respect to a trust granting the spouse only an income interest. To preserve the symmetry of marital deduction trust planning, §§2044 and 2519 treat the QTIP trust as if the spouse had been granted a general power of appointment. Thus, by virtue of the deduction and subsequent inclusion, QTIP trust property is regarded for most tax purposes as property of the spouse. This is true for generation-skipping transfer tax purposes as well, by virtue of the "new transferor" rule in §2652(a)(1). Under that rule, the transferor's spouse becomes the "transferor" of the QTIP trust upon the spouse's death.

The problem with this treatment can be illustrated best in the context of an average decedent's estate. The typical marital deduction estate plan qualifies any property in a decedent's estate for the marital deduction that cannot pass tax free under the unified credit, which usually means the entire estate in excess of a credit shelter bequest of the applicable exclusion amount. Often the credit shelter bequest is made to a bypass trust that will skip generations after the spouse's death. A portion of the settlor's GST exemption is allocated to that trust, but this use may not consume the entire exemption. Thus, a portion of the exemption normally would be wasted, and cannot really be utilized by allocation to a QTIP trust because that property will be regarded as the spouse's by virtue of §§2044, 2519, and 2652(a)(1). Indeed, if the QTIP trust will skip generations after the spouse's death, this tax treatment would mean that the spouse's exemption must be allocated to the QTIP to make it exempt from generation-skipping transfer tax. It was to prevent wasting part of the settlor's exemption that §2652(a)(3) was enacted. This "reverse QTIP" provision permits allocating any part of a transferor's exemption to a QTIP trust by exercise of an election, with the effect explained in Treas. Reg. §26.2652-1(a)(3): to the extent this reverse QTIP election is made, the original settlor of the QTIP trust remains the transferor for generation-skipping transfer tax purposes, notwithstanding taxation of the trust as if it were the property of the transferor's spouse.

Alluded to by the flush language in §2652(a)(3) and stated directly by Treas. Reg. §26.2652-2(a) is the requirement that a reverse QTIP election must relate to *all* of the property in a trust for which a QTIP election is made. The gist of this rule is to preclude an inclusion ratio of zero through allocating the transferor's exemption to a portion of a single trust and treating that portion as if it were a separate trust. Instead, this rule effectively requires a split of the QTIP trust into multiple portions before allocating the exemption to only one of them. That severance is subject to Treas. Reg. §26.2654-1(b), which applies because the QTIP trust has only one beneficiary (the spouse), not different beneficiaries of the separated portions. According to the regulations, "severance of a single trust into separate trusts is not recognized" for generation-skipping transfer tax purposes unless Treas. Reg. §26.2654-1(b) is applicable. Under it, severance is allowed only if the governing instrument or state law authorizes the division and if the division occurs in a timely manner under one of the approaches discussed in the regulation.

Another possibility is for the transferor to create several marital trusts, divide the marital bequests or gifts between them, make a QTIP election for both, and make a reverse QTIP election for one of the trusts.

These requirements for proper exemption allocation effectively cause a multiplicity of trusts in typical marital deduction planning for estates of more than the GST exemption amount. Indeed, estate plans for larger situations typically create at least three trusts: a generation-skipping exempt bypass trust, a QTIP trust with the §2653(a)(3) election making it a generation-skipping exempt reverse QTIP trust, and a marital deduction trust as to which no §2653(a)(3) election is made. In some larger estates, there may be a fourth trust if a partial QTIP election is made to create a non-QTIP-elected marital trust. Another alternative is to create a reverse QTIP trust that has generation-skipping provisions and is the right size to soak up the decedent's full GST exemption. This approach might be used if the bypass trust will be invaded for the benefit of children, thereby diminishing its value for generation-skipping exemption allocation purposes, or if there is no bypass trust because, for example, lifetime giving, nonprobate transfers, or debts, expenses, and other taxes have exhausted the unified credit shelter amount.

A valid QTIP trust requires that all income be paid to the surviving spouse annually. Because of this, allocating a portion of the exemption to a reverse QTIP trust fails to maximize the exemption to the extent accumulations of income otherwise might be possible were the exemption allocated elsewhere. Similarly, to maximize the benefit of the exemption, invasions of principal for the spouse should not be made from that portion of a QTIP trust that is exempt from generation-skipping transfer tax by virtue of the §2652(a)(3) reverse QTIP election. Given these negatives of reverse QTIP allocation, other alternatives for preserving the transferor's full exemption should be considered. The most promising alternative is creating a bypass trust as to which no QTIP election will be made and as to which, after payment of federal estate tax, the remaining corpus will be made generation-skipping exempt without marital deduction complications. Notwithstanding payment of estate tax at the death of the first spouse to die, this is a wise economic approach for large estates with substantial generation-skipping transfer tax problems because it maximizes the exemption. Indeed, this approach may work even better if done during life, because the tax cost of creating the exempt trust may drop under the tax exclusive gift tax computation. The uncertainty here is a function of the possibility of there being different unified credits for gift and estate tax purposes.

9.   *Effective Dates.* The generation-skipping transfer tax excepts from its application trusts that were irrevocable on 25 September 1985.[29] Amendments made to these chronologically exempt trusts after that date or transfers made from principal that was added to them after that date are taxable. Thus, for example, if a trust was worth $85x when, post-1985, an added $15x was contributed thereto (and no exemption was allocated to the trust to cover that contribution), and thereafter the $100x trust doubled in value to $200x, 15% of a later taxable distribution would be subject to the tax. See Treas. Reg. §§26.2601-1(b)(1)(iv)(A) and 26.2601-1(b)(1)(iv)(C) (defining two separate portions, one exempt, one not, but then regarding all subsequent events as occurring pro rata from each). Administratively, to determine the requisite percentage, this rule requires revaluation of the entire trust when a tainting addition is made, which speaks in favor of avoiding tainting additions to chronologically exempt trusts.

For purposes of this tainting addition rule, Treas. Reg. §26.2601-1(b)(1)(v) adopts a special interpretation applicable with respect to taxable powers of appointment: property subject to inclusion in a donee's gross estate for estate tax purposes is treated as an addition to the trust if the power lapses, is exercised, or is released, with the donee being treated as the transferor with respect thereto. This rule is applicable regardless of when the power or the trust was created. For this reason, it is important to pay careful attention to older trusts that grant powers of appointment that might attract estate tax inclusion to the donee.

In addition, it is imperative that no changes be made to chronologically exempt trusts that might, by inadvertence, destroy their protection from tax by successive generations of beneficiaries. A substantial jurisprudence has developed with respect to the type of modifications that may be made to exempt trusts without destroying the chronological exemption. For our purposes here, it is sufficient to state simply that nothing should be done to a chronologically exempt trust before making a thorough analysis of whether the modification will destroy this favorable tax benefit.

---

29.   Also protected are trusts created under wills or trusts executed before enactment of Chapter 13, if death of the transferor occurred before 1987 and the trust was not amended or increased after enactment. In addition, exempted are trusts created under the will or trust of an individual who was incompetent as of enactment and remained incompetent until death. See Treas. Reg. §26.2601-1(b)(3)(i).

Unless otherwise noted or apparent, all case names are Taxpayer [v. Comm'r]

The page citation for material that is an extract appears in *italic*. Major extracts are indicated with the page reference also in **bold**.

Cases

Federal Authorities

United States Constitution

Article I §2   3
Article I §9   3

United States Code

15 U.S.C. §80a-1   85
15 U.S.C. §80a-1(b)   87
15 U.S.C. §80a-2(a)(32)   86
15 U.S.C. §80a-2(a)(35)   86
15 U.S.C. §80a-2(b)   87
15 U.S.C. §80a-22(e)   86, 87
31 U.S.C. §203   82

Code of Federal Regulations

31 C.F.R. §315.5   395
31 C.F.R. §315.7   395
31 C.F.R. §315.15   395
31 C.F.R. §315.22(b)   395
31 C.F.R. §315.37   395
31 C.F.R. §315.47   396
31 C.F.R. §315.49   395
31 C.F.R. §315.51   396
31 C.F.R. §315.70   395

House Reports

1, 69th Cong., 1st Sess. (1925)
     41, 154, 758
179, 68th Cong., 1st Sess. (1924)
     270, 299
201, 97th Cong., 1st Sess. (1981)
     180, 657, 661, 662, 675, *876*,
     922, 923

215, 97th Cong., 1st Sess. (1981)
     172, 181
247, 101st Cong., 1st Sess.
     (1989)   12
327, 82d Cong., 1st Sess. (1951)
     134, 137, 147
413, 91st Cong., 1st Sess. (pt. 1)
     (1969)   741
426, 99th Cong., 1st Sess. (1985)
     988
704, 73d Cong., 2d Sess. (1934)
     269
708, 72d Cong., 1st Sess. (1931)
     10, 191, 269, 275, 600, 791,
     794, *798*, 801, 806, 808, 840,
     876, 906
767, 65th Cong., 2d Sess. (1918)
     58, 442, 506, 765
795, 100th Cong., 2d Sess.
     (1988)   1020
894, 83d Cong, 1st Sess. (1953)
     191
920, 81st Cong., 1st Sess. (1949)
     198
922, 64th Cong., 1st Sess. (1916)
     10
1274, 80th Cong., 2d Sess. (1948)
     603
1337, 83d Cong., 2d Sess. (1954)
     258, 259, 264, 444, 493, 525,
     528, 532, 534, 554, 628, 634,
     766, 778, 915
1380, 94th Cong., 2d Sess.
     (1976)   155, 156, 162, 163,
     170, 276, 405, *753*, 757, 780,
     794, 983
1412, 81st Cong., 1st Sess.
     (1949)   193, 257, 259
1681, 74th Cong., 1st Sess.
     (1935)   3
2333, 77th Cong., 1st Sess. (1942)
     115, 137, 454

Treasury Authorities

Actions on Decision

1996-10	893
1999-06	70, 828, 829
2001-06	405

General Counsel Memoranda

38593	528
39371	919

Internal Revenue Service Audit Technique Handbook

(10)33	410
(10)40	410
(10)41	410
(10)42	411
(10)43	411
(10)44	412
(10)50	413
(11)00	42
(26)92(2)	802
620(2)	*77*

Internal Revenue Service Statistics of Income — 1997 Estate Tax Returns

102	396
107	396

Informal Advice

TAM	7744005	733

TAM	7744007	733
TAM	7836008	145
TAM	7916006	649
TAM	7923001	728
PLR	8004172	886
PLR	8006013	549
PLR	8006109	477
PLR	8021058	477
TAM	8029001	208
PLR	8037116	230
PLR	8049011	131
PLR	8103074	477
TAM	8121003	903
TAM	8121010	144
TAM	8213004	230
TAM	8308001	84
TAM	8314001	708
TAM	8314005	708
TAM	8320007	903
TAM	8330004	148
TAM	8339004	37, 144
PLR	8351098	663
PLR	8351141	663
PLR	8352062	663
PLR	8422011	709
TAM	8432012	83
PLR	8450018	692
PLR	8508022	692
TAM	8512004	717
PLR	8517036	692
PLR	8523071	143
TAM	8526003	362
TAM	8526009	661
TAM	8531003	873
TAM	8549005	873
TAM	8551001	132
TAM	8611004	344
PLR	8622022	692
TAM	8701004	661
TAM	8706008	642
TAM	8717003	209, 897
TAM	8717006	774
PLR	8724014	502
TAM	8727003	892

76-165	742	78-27	925
76-166	618	78-58	768
76-178	257, *258*	78-74	210
76-225	746	78-101	735
76-234	*100*	78-105	728
76-235	174	78-137	506
76-261	466	78-152	735, 750
76-273	960	78-168	881
76-274	476	78-183	747
76-275	252	78-214	398
76-291	*745*, 746	78-215	401
76-303	*430*	78-242	580
76-304	257	78-255	*744*
76-309	280	78-271	590
76-310	746	78-272	881
76-326	919	78-323	567
76-348	429	78-362	399
76-357	742	78-378	98
76-358	728	78-379	593, 600
76-360	903	78-398	151
76-368	145, 230	78-409	222
76-369	565	79-7	72, 174
76-380	546	79-14	691, 692
76-472	*45*	79-46	464
76-490	477	79-62	265
76-501	51	79-63	136
76-543	742	79-94	244, 247
76-544	742	79-109	223
76-547	145	79-117	265
77-30	636	79-154	151, 440
77-99	*252*	79-177	*308*
77-181	513	79-211	*770*, 771
77-182	310, 313	79-224	616
77-183	546, 547	79-231	486
77-232	733	79-238	851
77-233	747	79-302	423, 426
77-299	227, 229, 814, 817	79-327	921
77-314	*378*, 846	79-353	27, 145, 310, 313
77-357	381	79-372	418, 419
77-372	814	79-373	151
77-378	230, 315	79-384	377, 851
77-460	324	79-397	51
77-461	578	79-398	757, 791, 792, 867
78-15	*256*	79-399	27

80-80	75, *262*, 263, 717	84-130	480
80-142	180, ***415***, 421	84-179	466, 468, 472
80-159	784	85-24	209
80-196	***800***, 801	85-35	642
80-224	925	85-88	919
80-250	579	85-111	769
80-255	131	86-38	***759***
80-289	***485***	86-39	148
80-346	345	86-41	873
81-7	885, 911	88-90	627
81-15	342	89-31	735, 750
81-20	707	90-2	770
81-31	56, 307, 851, 862	90-3	706
81-51	145, 310	90-21	***503***
81-63	44	90-45	829
81-85	169	90-110	615
81-118	719	92-22	534
81-128	476	92-68	56, 862
81-164	243	93-12	71, 864, 865
81-166	*472*	95-58	145, 283, ***310***
81-182	51	96-56	856
81-183	426	2002-2	673
81-184	426	2002-20	27
81-221	214		
81-223	832		
81-227	429		

Technical Directives

81-229	192		
81-253	71, 864	3648	191
81-264	814, 815	4729	193
81-302	156, 758	4868	193
82-23	712, 713	5834	195
82-85	474	6296	129
82-105	247, 529, 960	8630	75
82-141	504		
82-145	476		

Treasury Regulations

82-156	136		
82-198	169		
83-20	750	67, art. 1	191
83-44	451	67, art. 7(7)	191
83-108	887	79, art. 2	810
83-158	742	80, art. 24	114
84-11	867	105, §81.18	195
84-110	851	105, §81.25	448

State Statutes

Restatements

Uniform Acts

Uniform Civil Liability for Support Act

§1	832
§2	832
§3	832
§6	833

Uniform Estate Tax Apportionment Act

generally	691, 783
§2	780

Uniform Gifts to Minors Act

§4(b)	910

Uniform Probate Code

§2-201	149
§2-202	149
§2-203	149, 155
§2-204	149, 155
§2-205	149, 155
§2-205(1)(ii)	392
§2-205(2)(i)	189, 267
§2-206	149, 155
§2-207	149, 155
§2-208	149
§2-209	149
§2-210	149
§2-211	149
§2-212	149
§2-213	149
§2-214	149
§2-402	617

§2-403	617
§2-404	*617*
§2-405	394
§2-514	632
§2-710	255
§2-801(a)	149
§3-916	691, 783
§5-209(c)(3)	908
§5-424(a)(1)	908

Uniform Simultaneous Death Act

generally	996
§4	432

Uniform Statutory Rule Against Perpetuities

§1	147
§2	147

Uniform Transfers to Minors Act

§14(a)	910
§14(c)	148
§22	918

Uniform Trustees' Powers Act

§3(b)	*645*

Ethics Authorities

Secondary Authorities

ISBN 0–314–14453–6

90000

9 780314 144539